# CRIMINAL PROCEDURE

## *ARREST AND INVESTIGATION*

ANDERSON'S
*Law School Publications*

ADMINISTRATIVE LAW ANTHOLOGY
by Thomas O. Sargentich

ADMINISTRATIVE LAW: CASES AND MATERIALS
by Daniel J. Gifford

ADMIRALTY LAW ANTHOLOGY
by Robert M. Jarvis

ANALYTIC JURISPRUDENCE ANTHOLOGY
by Anthony D'Amato

AN ANTITRUST ANTHOLOGY
by Andrew I. Gavil

APPELLATE ADVOCACY: PRINCIPLES AND PRACTICE (Second Edition)
Cases and Materials
by Ursula Bentele and Eve Cary

A CAPITAL PUNISHMENT ANTHOLOGY
by Victor L. Streib

CASES AND PROBLEMS IN CRIMINAL LAW (Third Edition)
by Myron Moskovitz

THE CITATION WORKBOOK
by Maria L. Ciampi, Rivka Widerman and Vicki Lutz

CIVIL PROCEDURE: CASES, MATERIALS AND PROBLEMS
by Richard D. Freer and Wendy C. Perdue

COMMERCIAL TRANSACTIONS: PROBLEMS AND MATERIALS
Vol. 1: Secured Transactions Under the UCC
Vol. 2: Sales Under the UCC and the CISG
Vol. 3: Negotiable Instruments Under the UCC and the CIBN
by Louis F. Del Duca, Egon Guttman and Alphonse M. Squillante

A CONSTITUTIONAL LAW ANTHOLOGY
by Michael J. Glennon

CONSTITUTIONAL LAW COURSEBOOK
by Phoebe A. Haddon, Donald E. Lively, Dorothy E. Roberts and Russell L. Weaver

CONSTITUTIONAL TORTS
by Sheldon H. Nahmod, Michael L. Wells, and Thomas A. Eaton

CONTRACTS
Contemporary Cases, Comments, and Problems
by Michael L. Closen, Richard M. Perlmutter and Jeffrey D. Wittenberg

A CONTRACTS ANTHOLOGY (Second Edition)
by Peter Linzer

CORPORATE AND WHITE COLLAR CRIME: AN ANTHOLOGY
by Leonard Orland

A CRIMINAL LAW ANTHOLOGY
by Arnold H. Loewy

CRIMINAL LAW: CASES AND MATERIALS
by Arnold H. Loewy

A CRIMINAL PROCEDURE ANTHOLOGY
by Silas Wasserstrom and Christie L. Snyder

CRIMINAL PROCEDURE: ARREST AND INVESTIGATION
by Arnold H. Loewy and Arthur B. LaFrance

CRIMINAL PROCEDURE: TRIAL AND SENTENCING
by Arthur B. LaFrance and Arnold H. Loewy

ECONOMIC REGULATION: CASES AND MATERIALS
by Richard J. Pierce, Jr.

ELEMENTS OF LAW
by Eva H. Hanks, Michael E. Herz and Steven S. Nemerson

ENDING IT: DISPUTE RESOLUTION IN AMERICA
Descriptions, Examples, Cases and Questions
by Susan M. Leeson and Bryan M. Johnston

AN EVIDENCE ANTHOLOGY
by Edward J. Imwinkelreid and Glen Weissenberger

ENVIRONMENTAL LAW (Second Edition)
Vol. 1: Environmental Decisionmaking: NEPA and the Endangered Species Act
Vol. 2: Water Pollution; Vol. 3: Air Pollution; Vol. 4: Hazardous Wastes
by Jackson B. Battle, Mark Squillace, Maxine I. Lipeles and Robert L. Fischman

ENVIRONMENTAL PROTECTION AND JUSTICE
Readings and Commentary on Environmental Law and Practice
by Kenneth A. Manaster

FEDERAL EVIDENCE COURTROOM MANUAL
by Glen Weissenberger

FEDERAL INCOME TAXATION OF PARTNERSHIPS AND OTHER PASS-THRU ENTITIES
by Howard E. Abrams

FEDERAL RULES OF EVIDENCE (Second Edition)
Rules, Legislative History, Commentary and Authority
by Glen Weissenberger

FIRST AMENDMENT ANTHOLOGY
by Donald E. Lively, Dorothy E. Roberts and Russell L. Weaver

INTERNATIONAL ENVIRONMENTAL LAW ANTHOLOGY
by Anthony D'Amato and Kirsten Engel

INTERNATIONAL HUMAN RIGHTS: LAW, POLICY AND PROCESS
Problems and Materials
by Frank Newman and David Weissbrodt

INTERNATIONAL LAW ANTHOLOGY
by Anthony D'Amato

INTERNATIONAL LAW COURSEBOOK
by Anthony D'Amato

INTRODUCTION TO THE STUDY OF LAW: CASES AND MATERIALS
by John Makdisi

JUDICIAL EXTERNSHIPS: THE CLINIC INSIDE THE COURTHOUSE
by Rebecca A. Cochran

JUSTICE AND THE LEGAL SYSTEM
A Coursebook
by Anthony D'Amato and Arthur J. Jacobson

THE LAW OF DISABILITY DISCRIMINATION
by Ruth Colker

THE LAW OF MODERN PAYMENT SYSTEMS AND NOTES
by Fred H. Miller and Alvin C. Harrell

LAWYERS AND FUNDAMENTAL MORAL RESPONSIBILITY
by Daniel R. Coquillette

PATIENTS, PSYCHIATRISTS AND LAWYERS
Law and the Mental Health System
by Raymond L. Spring, Roy B. Lacoursiere, M.D., and Glen Weissenberger

PROBLEMS AND SIMULATIONS IN EVIDENCE (Second Edition)
by Thomas F. Guernsey

A PRODUCTS LIABILITY ANTHOLOGY
by Anita Bernstein

PROFESSIONAL RESPONSIBILITY ANTHOLOGY
by Thomas B. Metzloff

A PROPERTY ANTHOLOGY
by Richard H. Chused

*Continued*

THE REGULATION OF BANKING
Cases and Materials on Depository Institutions and Their Regulators
by Michael P. Malloy

A SECTION 1983 CIVIL RIGHTS ANTHOLOGY
by Sheldon H. Nahmod

SPORTS LAW: CASES AND MATERIALS (Second Edition)
by Raymond L. Yasser, James R. McCurdy and C. Peter Goplerud

A TORTS ANTHOLOGY
by Lawrence C. Levine, Julie A. Davies and Edward J. Kionka

TRIAL PRACTICE
Text by Lawrence A. Dubin and Thomas F. Guernsey
Problems and Case Files with *Video* Presentation
by Edward R. Stein and Lawrence A. Dubin

# CRIMINAL PROCEDURE

*ARREST AND INVESTIGATION*

Arnold H. Loewy

Graham Kenan Professor of Law
University of North Carolina School of Law
Chapel Hill, North Carolina

Arthur B. LaFrance

Professor of Law
Lewis and Clark School of Law
Portland, Oregon

CINCINNATI
ANDERSON PUBLISHING CO.

Loewy & LaFrance, Criminal Procedure: Arrest and Investigation

©1996 by Anderson Publishing Co.
2035 Reading Road / Cincinnati, Ohio 45202
800 582-7295 / E-mail: andpubco@aol.com / FAX 513 562-8110

Library of Congress Cataloging-in-Publication Data

Loewy, Arnold H.
     Criminal procedure : arrest and investigation / Arnold H. Loewy,
  Arthur B. LaFrance.
        p.   cm.
     Includes bibliographical references.
     ISBN 0-87084-183-1 (alk. paper)
     1. Criminal investigation--United States--Cases. 2. Police-
-United States--Cases. 3. Arrest--United States--Cases.
4. Searches and seizures--United States--Cases. I. LaFrance,
Arthur B. II. Title.
KF9625.A7L64 1995
345.73'052--dc20
[347.30552]                       95-45301
                                 CIP

# DEDICATION

To
LAURA GARDNER WEBSTER
(The Best)

# CONTENTS

# TABLE OF CASES

# PREFACE

This volume (the first of a two-volume set) is about police practices. Besides being essential to the criminal practitioner, understanding the constitutional limitations on police practices should be a part of any citizen-lawyer's legal repertoire. Consequently, this course should not be deemed for "future practitioners of criminal law only."

The presentation of the materials is focused, rather than scatter-gun. That is, each case is presented, lightly edited (deletions not usually noted in the material), with a series of focused questions and notes (mostly questions) following it. It is contemplated that the student will read the case, focus on the question, reread the case, and be prepared to discuss some of all of the questions in class. If your professor covers the entire book in a three hour course, the material may seem unusually long. Although the average class will cover between three and four fairly long cases and between fifteen and twenty pages, the precise focus of the material should render it manageable.

As a matter of editing style, law review articles and other collateral material are usually not cited in the questions and notes. This is not because of the authors' belief that they are unimportant. To the contrary, we believe that they are extremely important, and towards the end of your reading them, we have included a glossary of suggested law review articles at the end of the book. (Obviously, this glossary is intended to be illustrative and not exhaustive.) Our rationale for generally not including collateral sources is our concern about directing focus away from the narrow question before the student.

This project was supported by the University of North Carolina Law Foundation and by Judith Wegner the Dean of the Law School who provided funds for hiring highly competent research assistants: Michael Kolb, Robert Pleasant, Keith Kadlec, Roland McReynolds, and David Teeples. I would also like to thank my soulmate, Professor Laura Webster of the Mercer law school, who, in the early stages of this book, assisted by discussing my thoughts for inclusion and exclusion of material. Sadly, on October 6, 1993, she was involved in a serious automobile accident, leaving her unable to move her limbs or to speak (except on rare occasions to say "I love you.") My caring for her undoubtedly delayed the completion of this book, but her spirit, which continues to move me, contributed positively to the quality of the final product.

Arnold H. Loewy
Graham Kenan Professor of Law
Chapel Hill, North Carolina
August 1, 1995

# 1.

# THE PROTECTIONS OF AND RATIONALE FOR THE FOURTH AMENDMENT

*The right of the people to be secure in their persons, houses, papers, and effects, against unreasonable searches and seizures, shall not be violated, and no Warrants shall issue, but upon probable cause, supported by Oath or affirmation, and particularly describing the place to be searched, and the persons or things to be seized.*

The Fourth Amendment offers two major protections — one substantive, and the other procedural. The primary substantive protection is probable cause. The primary procedural protection is the requirement that a warrant be issued by an independent magistrate prior to the search or seizure. Before assessing the wisdom of these, or other ancillary, protections of the Fourth Amendment, it is helpful to ask why we should limit searches and seizures at all. Any limit on a policeman's power to conduct searches and seizures would ordinarily impact adversely on police efficiency.[1] Although some might argue that a limitation on police efficiency is desirable for its own sake, it is probably more realistic to think of it as an incidental detriment in order to ensure the security of us all.

How, you might ask, does rendering the police more inefficient ensure our security? One possible answer is that the Fourth Amendment strikes a balance between our need to be secure from criminals and our need to be secure from the police. To the extent that police are free to conduct unlimited searches and seizures, more criminals are likely to be caught, but at the same time, more innocent citizens are likely to be subjected to the embarrassment and/or offense of a search or seizure. On the other hand, if police are totally precluded from conducting searches or seizures (as we have heard anecdotally was suggested for the new Russian Republic), an

---

[1] Arguably there could be instances when a search is so unlikely to turn up evidence of crime that it would be inefficient for the police to invest the time necessary to conduct it. Presumably, internal police procedures would eliminate most such searches. In any event, the Fourth Amendment is hardly necessary for that purpose.

unacceptably high amount of crime would go undetected, and perhaps undeterred. Under the Fourth Amendment compromise, police are free to conduct a search and/or seizure, but only if they have been approved in advance by an independent magistrate, who has determined that the police have probable cause to conduct the search (unless the particular search or seizure is one that is an exception to the warrant and/or probable cause requirement).

There are possible alternative rules that a government might set up. In the extreme, it could provide that all searches conducted by policemen in the line of duty (perhaps limited by a good faith belief that evidence would be found) are valid. Alternatively, a government could uphold all searches that in fact yielded evidence.

If you were in a position to enact any rules that you thought desirable for your society, what rules would you enact? Do you think that you would want to increase or decrease the number of searches permitted? Is it such a bad thing to be searched, relative to the good that can come from finding evidence or dispelling suspicion? What is the point of the warrant requirement? As you think about these questions, consider the following excerpts:

## Brinegar v. United States
### 338 U.S. 160 (1949)

Mr. Justice JACKSON, dissenting.

When this Court recently has promulgated a philosophy that some rights derived from the Constitution are entitled to "a preferred position," I have not agreed. We cannot give some constitutional rights a preferred position without relegating others to a deferred position; we can establish no firsts without thereby establishing seconds. Indications are not wanting that Fourth Amendment freedoms are tacitly marked as secondary rights, to be relegated to a deferred position. The Fourth Amendment states: "The right of the people to be secure in their persons, houses, papers, and effects, against unreasonable searches and seizures, shall not be violated, and no Warrants shall issue, but upon probable cause, supported by Oath or affirmation, and particularly describing the place to be searched, and the persons or things to be seized." These, I protest, are not mere second-class rights but belong in the catalog of indispensable freedoms. Among deprivations of rights, none is so effective in cowing a population, crushing the spirit of the individual and putting terror in every heart. Uncontrolled search and seizure is one of the first and most effective weapons in the arsenal of every arbitrary government. And one need only briefly to have dwelt and worked among a people possessed of many admirable qualities but deprived of these rights to know that the human personality deteriorates and dignity and self-reliance disappear where homes, persons and possessions are subject at any hour to unheralded search and seizure by the police.

But the right to be secure against searches and seizures is one of the most difficult to protect. Since the officers are themselves the chief invaders, there is no enforcement outside of court.

Only occasional and more flagrant abuses come to the attention of the courts, and then only those where the search and seizure yields incriminating evidence and the defendant is at least sufficiently compromised to be indicted. If the officers raid a home, an office, or stop and search an automobile but find nothing incriminating, this invasion of the personal liberty of the innocent too often finds no practical redress. There may be, and I am convinced that there are, many unlawful searches of homes and automobiles of innocent people which turn up nothing incriminating, in which no arrest is made, about which courts do nothing, and about which we never hear.

Courts can protect the innocent against such invasions indirectly and through the medium of excluding evidence obtained against those who frequently are guilty. Federal courts have used this method of enforcement of the Amendment, in spite of its unfortunate consequences on law enforcement, although many state courts do not. This inconsistency does not disturb me, for local excesses or invasions of liberty are more amenable to political correction, the Amendment was directed only against the new and centralized government, and any really dangerous threat to the general liberties of the people can come only from this source. We must therefore look upon the exclusion of evidence in federal prosecutions if obtained in violation of the Amendment as a means of extending protection against the central government's agencies. So a search against Brinegar's car must be regarded as a search of the car of every man.

We must remember that the extent of any privilege of search and seizure without warrant which we sustain, the officers interpret and apply themselves and will push to the limit. We must remember, too, that freedom from unreasonable search differs from some of the other rights of the Constitution in that there is no way the innocent citizen can invoke advance protection. For example, any effective interference with freedom of the press, or free speech, or religion, usually requires a course of suppressions against which the citizen can and often does go to the court and obtain an injunction. Other rights, such as that to an impartial jury or the aid of counsel, are within the supervisory power of the courts themselves. Such a right as just compensation for the taking of private property may be vindicated after the act in terms of money.

But an illegal search and seizure usually is a single incident, perpetrated by surprise, conducted in haste, kept purposely beyond the court's supervision and limited only by the judgment and moderation of officers whose own interests and records are often at stake in the search. There is no opportunity for injunction or appeal to disinterested intervention. The citizen's choice is quietly to submit to whatever the officers undertake or to resist at risk of arrest or immediate violence.

And we must remember that the authority which we concede to conduct searches and seizures without warrant may be exercised by the most unfit and ruthless officers as well as by the fit and responsible, and resorted to in case of petty misdemeanors as well as in the case of the gravest felonies.

One reason for the Fourth Amendment's being taken less seriously than other Amendments is suggested by Justice Douglas' dissenting opinion in *Draper*.

## Draper v. United States
### 358 U.S. 307 (1959)

MR. JUSTICE DOUGLAS, dissenting.

Decisions under the Fourth Amendment, taken in the long view, have not given the protection to the citizen which the letter and spirit of the Amendment would seem to require. One reason, I think, is that wherever a culprit is caught red-handed, as in leading Fourth Amendment cases, it is difficult to adopt and enforce a rule that would turn him loose. A rule protective of law-abiding citizens is not apt to flourish where its advocates are usually criminals. Yet the rule we fashion is for the innocent and guilty alike. If the word of the informer on which the present arrest was made is sufficient to make the arrest legal, his word would also protect the police who, acting on it, hauled the innocent citizen off to jail.

Of course, the education we receive from mystery stories and television shows teaches that what happened in this case is efficient police work. The police are tipped off that a man carrying narcotics will step off the morning train. A man meeting the precise description does alight from the train. No warrant for his arrest has been—or, as I see it, could then be—obtained. Yet he is arrested; and narcotics are found in his pocket and a syringe in the bag he carried. This is the familiar pattern of crime detection which has been dinned into public consciousness as the correct and efficient one. It is, however, a distorted reflection of the constitutional system under which we are supposed to live.

Has anything that you have read thus far affected your answers to the questions preceding them? We will examine both *Brinegar* and *Draper* in greater depth in the next chapter which explores probable cause.

# 2.

# PROBABLE CAUSE

Probable cause, the substantive heart of the Fourth Amendment, is the standard by which the legality of most searches is measured. In assessing what the term means, the relevant inquiry is whether the police ought to be allowed to search on the basis of the information they had *before* the search occurred. Consider how well the Court evaluated probable cause in the following cases in light of that purpose.

## Brinegar v. United States
### 338 U.S. 160 (1949)

Mr. Justice RUTLEDGE delivered the opinion of the Court.

Brinegar was convicted of importing intoxicating liquor into Oklahoma from Missouri in violation of the federal statute which forbids such importation contrary to the laws of any state. His conviction was based in part on the use in evidence against him of liquor seized from his automobile in the course of the alleged unlawful importation.

The facts are substantially undisputed. At about six o'clock on the evening of March 3, 1947, Malsed, an investigator of the Alcohol Tax Unit, and Creehan, a special investigator, were parked in a car beside a highway near the Quapaw Bridge in northeastern Oklahoma. The point was about five miles west of the Missouri-Oklahoma line. Brinegar drove past headed west in his Ford coupe. Malsed had arrested him about five months earlier for illegally transporting liquor; had seen him loading liquor into a car or truck in Joplin, Missouri, on at

least two occasions during the preceding six months; and knew him to have a reputation for hauling liquor. As Brinegar passed, Malsed recognized both him and the Ford. He told Creehan, who was driving the officers' car, that Brinegar was the driver of the passing car. Both agents later testified that the car, but not especially its rear end, appeared to be 'heavily loaded' and 'weighted down with something.' Brinegar increased his speed as he passed the officers. They gave chase. After pursuing him for about a mile at top speed, they gained on him as his car skidded on a curve, sounded their siren, overtook him, and crowded his car to the side of the road by pulling across in front of it. The highway was one leading from Joplin, Missouri, toward Vinita, Oklahoma, Brinegar's home.

As the agents got out of their car and walked back toward petitioner, Malsed said, 'Hello, Brinegar, how much liquor have you got in the car?' or 'How much liquor have you got in the car this time?' Petitioner replied, 'Not too much,' or 'Not so much.' After further questioning he admitted that he had twelve cases in the car. Malsed testified that one case, which was on the front seat, was visible from outside the car, but petitioner testified that it was covered by a lap robe. Twelve more cases were found under and behind the front seat. The agents then placed Brinegar under arrest and seized the liquor. The district judge, after a hearing on the motion to suppress at which the facts stated above appeared in evidence, was of the opinion that "the mere fact that the agents knew that this defendant was engaged in hauling whiskey, even coupled with the statement that the car appeared to be weighted, would not be probable cause for the search of this car." Therefore, he thought, there was no probable cause when the agents began the chase. He held, however, that the voluntary admission made by petitioner after his car had been stopped constituted probable cause for a search, regardless of the legality of the arrest and detention, and that therefore the evidence was admissible. At the trial, as has been said, the court overruled petitioner's renewal of the objection.

The crucial question is whether there was probable cause for Brinegar's arrest, in the light of prior adjudications on this problem, more particularly Carroll v. United States, 267 U.S. 132, which on its face most closely approximates the situation presented here.

In this case, the record shows that Brinegar had used Joplin, Missouri, to Malsed's personal knowledge derived from direct observation, not merely from hearsay as seems to be suggested, as a source of supply on other occasions within the preceding six months. It also discloses that Brinegar's home was in Vinita, Oklahoma, and that Brinegar when apprehended was traveling in a direction leading from Joplin to Vinita, at a point about four or five miles west of the Missouri-Oklahoma line.

Joplin, like Detroit in the Carroll case, was a ready source of supply. But unlike Detroit it was not an illegal source. So far as appears, Brinegar's purchases there were entirely legal. And so, we may assume for present purposes, was his transportation of the liquor in Missouri, until he reached and crossed the state line into Oklahoma.

This difference, however, is insubstantial. For the important thing here is not whether Joplin was an illegal source of a supply; it is rather that Joplin was a ready, convenient and probable one for persons disposed to violate the Oklahoma and federal statutes. That fact was demonstrated fully, not only by the geographic facts, but by Malsed's direct and undisputed testimony of his personal observation of Brinegar's use of liquor dispensing establishments in Joplin for procuring his whiskey.

The situation relating to the probable place of market, as bearing on the probability of unlawful importation, is somewhat different. Broadly on the

facts this may well have been taken to be the State of Oklahoma as a whole or its populous northeastern region. From the facts of record we know, as the agents knew, that Oklahoma was a 'dry' state. At the time of the search, its law forbade the importation of intoxicating liquors from other states, except under a permit not generally procurable and which there is no pretense Brinegar had secured or attempted to secure. This fact, taken in connection with the known 'wet' status of Missouri and the location of Joplin close to the Oklahoma line, affords a very natural situation for persons inclined to violate the Oklahoma and federal statutes to ply their trade. The proof therefore concerning the source of supply, the place of probable destination and illegal market, and hence the probability that Brinegar was using the highway for the forbidden transportation, was certainly no less strong than the showing in these respects in the Carroll case.[9]

Finally, as for the most important potential distinction, namely, that concerning the primary and ultimate fact that the petitioner was engaging in liquor running, Malsed's personal observation of Brinegar's recent activities established that he was so engaged quite as effectively as did the agent's prior bargaining with the defendants in the Carroll case.[*] He saw Brinegar loading liquor, in larger quantities than would be normal for personal consumption, into a car or a truck in Joplin on other occasions during the six months prior to the search. He saw the car Brinegar was using in this case in use by him at least once in Joplin within that period and followed it. And several months prior to the search he had arrested Brinegar for unlawful transportation of liquor and this arrest had resulted in an indictment which was pending at the time of this trial. Moreover Malsed instantly recognized Brinegar's Ford coupe and Brinegar as the driver when he passed the parked police car. And at that time Brinegar was moving in a direction from Joplin toward Vinita only a short distance inside Oklahoma from the state line.

All these facts are undisputed. Wholly apart from Malsed's knowledge that Brinegar bore the general reputation of being engaged in liquor running, they

---

[9] On the present record judicial notice is hardly needed to give us cognizance of the differing laws of Missouri and Oklahoma, or of Joplin's proximity to the state line, and its ready convenience to one living as near by as Vinita who might be disposed to use it as a base of supply for importing liquor into Oklahoma in violation of the state and federal statutes.

[*] [Ed.] In *Carroll*, the agents knew that Carroll was in the business of selling illegal liquor because he had previously offered to sell some to them.

constitute positive and convincing evidence that Brinegar was engaged in that activity, no less convincing than the evidence in *Carroll* that the defendants had offered to sell liquor to the officers. The evidence here is undisputed, is admissible on the issue of probable cause, and clearly establishes that the agent had good ground for believing that Brinegar was engaged regularly throughout the period in illicit liquor running and dealing.

In dealing with probable cause, however, as the very name implies, we deal with probabilities. These are not technical; they are the factual and practical considerations of everyday life on which reasonable and prudent men, not legal technicians, act. The standard of proof is accordingly correlative to what must be proved.

"The substance of all the definitions" of probable cause "is a reasonable ground for belief of guilt." And this "means less than evidence which would justify condemnation" or conviction, as Marshall, C.J., said for the Court more than a century ago in *Locke v. United States,* 7 Cranch 339, 348, 3 L.Ed. 364. Since Marshall's time, at any rate,[14] it has come to mean more than bare suspicion: Probable cause exists where the facts and circumstances within their [the officers'] knowledge and of which they had reasonably trustworthy information [are] sufficient in themselves to warrant a man of reasonable caution in the belief that" an offense has been or is being committed.

These long-prevailing standards seek to safeguard citizens from rash and unreasonable interferences with privacy and from unfounded charges of crime. They also seek to give fair leeway for enforcing the law in the community's protection. Because many situations which confront officers in the course of executing their duties are more or less ambiguous, room must be allowed for some mistakes on their part. But the mistakes must be those of reasonable men, acting on facts leading sensibly to their conclusions of probability. The rule of probable cause is a practical, nontechnical conception affording the best compromise that has been found for accommodating these often opposing interests. Requiring more would unduly hamper law enforcement. To allow less would be to leave law-abiding citizens at the mercy of the officers' whim or caprice.

The troublesome line posed by the facts in the *Carroll* case and this case is one between mere suspicion and probable cause. That line necessarily must be drawn by an act of judgment formed in the light of the particular situation and with account taken of all the circumstances. No problem of searching the home or any other place of privacy was presented either in *Carroll* or here. Both cases involve freedom to use public highways in swiftly moving vehicles for dealing in contraband, and to be unmolested by investigation and search in those movements. In such a case the citizen who has given no good cause for believing he is engaged in that sort of activity is entitled to proceed on his way without interference. But one who recently and repeatedly has given substantial ground for believing that he is engaging in the forbidden transportation in the area of his usual operations has no such immunity, if the officer who intercepts him in that region knows that fact at the time he makes the interception and the circumstances under which it is made are not such as to indicate the suspect going about legitimate affairs.

This does not mean, as seems to be assumed, that every traveler along the public highways may be stopped and searched at the officers' whim, caprice or mere suspicion.[17] The question presented in the *Carroll* case lay on the border between suspicion and probable cause. But the Court carefully considered that problem and resolved it by concluding that the facts within the officers' knowledge when they intercepted the *Carroll* defendants amounted to more than mere suspicion and constituted probable cause for their action. We cannot say this conclusion was wrong, or was so lacking in reason and consistency with the Fourth Amendment's purposes that it should now be overridden.

Accordingly the judgment is affirmed.

---

[14] Marshall's full statement in Locke v. United States was: "It may be added, that the term 'probable cause,' according to its usual acceptation, means less than evidence which would justify condemnation; and, in all cases of seizure, has a fixed, and well known meaning. It imports a seizure made under circumstances which warrant suspicion."

[17] "It would be intolerable and unreasonable if a prohibition agent were authorized to stop every automobile on the chance of finding liquor, and thus subject all persons lawfully using the highways to the inconvenience and indignity of such a search. Travelers may be so stopped in crossing an international boundary because of national self-protection reasonably requiring one entering the country to identify himself as entitled to come in, and his belongings as effects which may be lawfully brought in. But those lawfully within the country, entitled to use the public highways, have a right to free passage without interruption or search unless there is known to a competent official, authorized to search, probable cause for believing that their vehicles are carrying contraband or illegal merchandise." *Carroll v. United States,* 267 U.S. 132, 153, 154.

Mr. Justice BURTON, concurring.

Whether or not the necessary probable cause for a search of the petitioner's car existed before the government agents caught up with him and said to him, "How much liquor have you got in the car this time?" and he replied, "Not too much," it is clear, and each of the lower courts found, that, under all of the circumstances of this case, the necessary probable cause for the search of the petitioner's car then existed. If probable cause for the search existed at that point, the search which then was begun was lawful without a search warrant as is demonstrated in the opinion of the Court. That search disclosed that a crime was in the course of its commission in the presence of the arresting officers, precisely as those officers had good reason to believe was the fact. The ensuing arrest of the petitioner was lawful and the subsequent denial of his motion to suppress the evidence obtained by the search was properly sustained.

It is my view that it is not necessary, for the purposes of this case, to establish probable cause for the search at any point earlier than that of the above colloquy. The earlier events, recited in the opinion of the Court, disclose at least ample grounds to justify the chase and official interrogation of the petitioner by the government agents in the manner adopted. This interrogation quickly disclosed indisputable probable cause for the search and for the arrest. In my view, these earlier events not only justified the steps taken by the government agents but those events imposed upon the government agents a positive duty to investigate further, in some such manner as they adopted. It is only by alertness to proper occasions for prompt inquiries and investigations that effective prevention of crime and enforcement of law is possible. Government agents are commissioned to represent the interests of the public in the enforcement of the law and this requires affirmative action not only when there is reasonable ground for an arrest or probable cause for a search but when there is reasonable ground for an investigation. This is increasingly true when the facts point directly to a crime in the course of commission in the presence of the agent. Prompt investigation may then not only discover but, what is still more important may interrupt the crime and prevent some or all of its damaging consequences. In the present case, from the moment that the agents saw this petitioner driving his heavily laden car in Oklahoma, evidently en route from Missouri, the events justifying and calling for an interrogation of him rapidly gained cumulative force. Nothing occurred that even tended to lessen the reasonableness of the original basis for the suspicion of the agents that a crime within their particular line of duty was being committed in their presence.

Nothing occurred to make it unlawful for them, in line of duty, to make the interrogation which suggested itself to them. When their interrogation of the petitioner to his voluntary response as quoted above, that response demonstrated ample probable cause for an immediate search of the petitioner's car for the contraband liquor which he had indicated might be found there. The interrogation of the petitioner, thus made by the agents in their justifiable investigation of a crime reasonably suspected by them to be in the course of commission in their presence, cannot now be resorted to by the petitioner in support of a motion to suppress the evidence of that crime. Government agents have duties of crime prevention and crime detection as well as the duty of arresting offenders caught in the commission of a crime or later identified as having committed a crime. The performance of the first duties is as important as the performance of the last. In this case the performance of the first halted the commission of the crime and also resulted in the arrest of the offender.

Mr. Justice JACKSON, dissenting.

With this prologue [referring to the portion of his opinion reproduced in chapter 1] I come to the case of Brinegar. His automobile was one of his 'effects' and hence within the express protection of the Fourth Amendment. Undoubtedly the automobile presents peculiar problems for enforcement agencies, is frequently a facility for the perpetration of crime and an aid in the escape of criminals. But if we are to make judicial exceptions to the Fourth Amendment for these reasons, it seems to me they should depend somewhat upon the gravity of the offense. If we assume, for example, that a child is kidnaped and the officers throw a roadblock about the neighborhood and search every outgoing car, it would be a drastic and undiscriminating use of the search. The officers might be unable to show probable cause for searching any particular car. However, I should candidly strive hard to sustain such an action, executed fairly and in good faith, because it might be reasonable to subject travelers to that indignity if it was the only way to save a threatened life and detect a vicious crime. But I should not strain to sustain such a roadblock and universal search to salvage a few bottles of bourbon and catch a bootlegger.

The Court sustains this search as an application of *Carroll*. I dissent because I regard it as an extension of the *Carroll* case, which already has been too much taken by enforcement officers as blanket authority to stop and search cars on suspicion.

While the Court sustained the search without warrant in the Carroll case, it emphatically declined to dispense with the necessity for evidence of probable cause for making such a search. It said: "It would be intolerable and unreasonable if a prohibition agent were authorized to stop every automobile on the chance of finding liquor, and thus subject all persons lawfully using the highways to the inconvenience and indignity of such a search. Travelers may be so stopped in crossing an international boundary because of national self-protection reasonably requiring one entering the country to identify himself as entitled to come in, and his belongings as effects which may be lawfully brought in. But those lawfully within the country, entitled to use the public highways, have a right to free passage without interruption or search unless there is known to a competent official, authorized to search, probable cause for believing that their vehicles are carrying contraband or illegal merchandise."

Analysis of the *Carroll* facts shows that while several facts are common to the two cases, the setting from which those facts take color and meaning differ in essential respects.

In the *Carroll* case the primary and the ultimate fact that the accused was engaged in liquor running was not surmise or hearsay, as it is here. Carroll and his companion, some time before their arrest, had come to meet the two arresting officers, not then known as officials, upon the understanding that they were customers wanting liquor. Carroll promised to sell and deliver them three cases at $130 a case. For some reason there was a failure to deliver, but when the officers arrested them they had this positive and personal knowledge that these men were trafficking in liquor. Also, it is to be noted that the officers, when bargaining for liquor, saw and learned the number of the car these bootleggers were using in the business and, at the time of the arrest, recognized it as the same car.

Then this Court took judicial notice that the place whence Carroll, when stopped, was coming, on the international boundary, "is one of the most active centers for introducing illegally into this country spirituous liquors for distribution into the interior." These facts provided the very foundation of the opinion of this Court on the subject of probable cause, which it summed up as follows: "The partners in the original combination to sell liquor in Grand Rapids were together in the same automobile they had been in the night when they tried to furnish the whiskey to the officers, which was thus identified as part of the firm equipment. They were coming from the direction of the great source of supply for their stock to Grand Rapids, where they plied their trade. That the officers, when they saw the defendants, believed that they were carrying liquor, we can have no doubt, and we think it is equally clear that they had reasonable cause for thinking so."

Not only did the Court rely almost exclusively on information gained in personal negotiations of the officers to buy liquor from defendants to show probable cause, but the dissenting members asserted it to be the only circumstance which could have subjected the accused to any reasonable suspicion. And that is the sort of direct evidence on personal knowledge that is lacking here.

In contrast, the proof that Brinegar was trafficking in illegal liquor rests on inferences from two circumstances, neither one of which would be allowed to be proved at a trial: One, it appears that the same officers previously had arrested Brinegar on the same charge. But there had been no conviction and it does not appear whether the circumstances of the former arrest indicated any strong probability of it. In any event, this evidence of a prior arrest of the accused would not even be admissible in a trial to prove his guilt on this occasion.

As a second basis for inference, the officers also say that Brinegar had the reputation of being a liquor runner. The weakness of this hearsay evidence is revealed by contrasting it with the personal negotiations which proved that Carroll was one. The officers' testimony of reputation would not be admissible in a trial of defendant unless he was unwise enough to open the subject himself by offering character testimony.

I do not say that no evidence which would be inadmissible to prove guilt at a trial may be considered in weighing probable cause, but I am surprised that the Court is ready to rule that inadmissible evidence alone, as to vital facts without which other facts give little indication of guilt, establish probable cause as matter of law. The only other fact is that officer Malsed stated that twice, on September 23 and on September 30, about six months before this arrest, he saw Brinegar in a Missouri town where liquor is lawful, loading liquor into a truck, not the car in this case. That is all. The Court from that draws the inference which the courts below, familiar we presume with the local conditions, refused to draw, viz., that to be seen loading liquor into a truck where it is lawful is proof that defendant is unlawfully trafficking in liquor some distance away. There is not, as in the *Carroll* case, evidence that he was offering liquor for sale to anybody at any time. In the *Carroll* case, the offer to sell liquor to the officers would itself have been a law violation. It seems rather foggy reasoning to say that the courts are obliged to draw the same conclusion from legal conduct as from illegal conduct. I think we cannot say the lower courts were wrong as matter of law in holding that there was no probable cause up to the time the car was put off the road and stopped, and that we cannot say it was proper to consider the deficiency supplied by what followed. When these officers engaged in a chase at speeds dangerous to those who participated, and to other lawful wayfarers, and ditched the defendant's car, they were either taking the initial steps in arrest, search and seizure, or they were committing a completely lawless and unjustifiable act. That they intended to set out on a search is unquestioned, and there seems no reason to doubt that in their own minds they thought there was cause and right to search. They have done exactly what they would have done, and done rightfully, if they had been executing a warrant. At all events, whatever it may have lacked technically of arrest, search and seizure, it was a form of coercion and duress under color of official authority-and a very formidable type of duress at that.

I do not, of course, contend that officials may never stop a car on the highway without the halting being considered an arrest or a search. Regulations of traffic, identifications where proper, traffic census, quarantine regulations, and many other causes give occasion to stop cars in circumstances which do not imply arrest or charge of crime. And to trail or pursue a suspected car to its destination, to observe it and keep it under surveillance, is not in itself an arrest nor a search. But when a car is forced off the road, summoned to stop by a siren, and brought to a halt under such circumstances as are here disclosed, we think the officers are then in the position of one who has entered a home: the search at its commencement must be valid and cannot be saved by what it turns up.

The findings of the two courts below make it clear that this search began and proceeded through critical and coercive phases without the justification of probable cause. What it yielded cannot save it. I would reverse the judgment.

Mr. Justice FRANKFURTER and Mr. Justice MURPHY join in this opinion.

## QUESTIONS AND NOTES

**1.** Do you believe that the police had probable cause to stop Brinegar? On what basis?

**2.** According to *Brinegar,* what does probable cause mean? More likely than not? Reasonable suspicion? Substantial probability? Some probability? Remote probability?

**3.** At the time that Brinegar was stopped, did the police have any reason to believe that he was not returning from an ordinary shopping trip? Presumably even bootleggers (if you believe that the evidence showed that he was regularly in that business) travel a short distance to a "source city" for things other than contraband.

**4.** Doesn't the fact that Brinegar was close to home support the "shopping trip" theory rather than the "bootlegger" theory? Why didn't the Court see it that way? Does one incident of bootlegging make one a perpetual outlaw on the highways?

**5.** Should probable cause vary according to the severity of the crime as Justice Jackson seems to suggest? Why? Isn't the constitutional standard the same?

**6.** Should probable cause be less stringent in regard to automobiles than to homes (compare *Spinelli, infra*)? Why? Why not?

**7.** Justice Burton's suggestion that reasonable suspicion (short of probable cause) may justify a brief stop, and that if probable cause develops from the stop, a search may be undertaken is a concept of some currency (Chapter 7, *infra*). Even on that theory, however, one would have to establish reasonable suspicion.

**8.** As you read *Draper,* consider whether the Court was applying a tougher, more lenient, or identical standard of probable cause as compared to *Brinegar.*

## Draper v. United States
### 358 U.S. 307 (1959)

MR. JUSTICE WHITTAKER delivered the opinion of the Court.

Petitioner was convicted of knowingly concealing and transporting narcotic drugs in Denver, Colorado, in violation of 35 Stat. 614. His conviction was based in part on the use in evidence against him of two "envelopes containing [865 grains of] heroin" and a hypodermic syringe that had been taken from his person, following his arrest, by the arresting officer.

The evidence offered at the hearing on the motion to suppress was not substantially disputed. It established that one Marsh, a federal narcotic agent with 29 years' experience, was stationed at Denver; that one Hereford had been engaged as a "special employee" of the Bureau of Narcotics at Denver for about six months, and from time to time gave information to Marsh regarding violations of the narcotic laws, for which Hereford was paid small sums of money, and that Marsh had always found the information given by Hereford to be accurate and reliable. On September 3, 1956, Hereford told Marsh that James Draper (petitioner) recently had taken up abode at a stated address in Denver and "was peddling narcotics to several addicts" in that city. Four days later, on September 7, Hereford told Marsh "that Draper had gone to Chicago the day before [September 6] by train [and] that he was going to bring back three ounces of heroin [and] that he would return to Denver either on the morning of the 8th of September or the morning of the 9th of September also by train." Hereford also gave Marsh a detailed physical description of Draper and of the clothing he was wearing,[2] and said that he would be carrying "a tan zipper bag," and that he habitually "walked real fast."

On the morning of September 8, Marsh and a Denver police officer went to the Denver Union Station and kept watch over all incoming trains from Chicago, but they did not see anyone fitting the description that Hereford had given. Repeating the process on the morning of September 9, they saw a person, having the exact physical attributes and wearing the precise clothing described by Hereford, alight from an incoming Chicago train and start walking "fast" toward the exit. He was carrying a

---

[2] Hereford told Marsh that Draper was a Negro of light brown complexion, 27 years of age, 5 feet 8 inches tall, weighed about 160 pounds, and that he was wearing a light colored raincoat, brown slacks and black shoes.

tan zipper bag in his right hand and the left was thrust in his raincoat pocket. Marsh, accompanied by the police officer, overtook, stopped and arrested him. They then searched him and found the two "envelopes containing heroin" clutched in his left hand in his raincoat pocket, and found the syringe in the tan zipper bag. Marsh then took him (petitioner) into custody. Hereford died four days after the arrest and therefore did not testify at the hearing on the motion. The crucial question for us then is whether knowledge of the related facts and circumstances gave Marsh "probable cause" within the meaning of the Fourth Amendment to believe that petitioner had committed or was committing a violation of the narcotic laws. If it did, the arrest, though without a warrant, was lawful and the subsequent search of petitioner's person and the seizure of the found heroin were validly made incident to a lawful arrest, and therefore the motion to suppress was properly overruled and the heroin was competently received in evidence at the trial.

Petitioner does not dispute this analysis of the question for decision. Rather, he contends (1) that the information given by Hereford to Marsh was "hearsay" and, because hearsay is not legally competent evidence in a criminal trial, could not legally have been considered, but should have been put out of mind, by Marsh in assessing whether he had "probable cause" and "reasonable grounds" to arrest petitioner without a warrant, and (2) that, even if hearsay could lawfully have been considered, Marsh's information should be held insufficient to show "probable cause" and "reasonable grounds" to believe that petitioner had violated or was violating the narcotic laws and to justify his arrest without a warrant.

Considering the first contention, we find petitioner entirely in error. *Brinegar* has settled the question the other way. There, in a similar situation, the convict contended "that the factors relating to inadmissibility of the evidence [for] *purposes of proving guilt at the trial*, deprive[d] the evidence as a whole of sufficiency to show probable cause for the search." (Emphasis added.) But this Court, rejecting that contention, said: "The so-called distinction places a wholly unwarranted emphasis upon the criterion of admissibility in evidence, to prove the accused's guilt, of the facts relied upon to show probable cause. That emphasis, we think, goes much too far in confusing and disregarding the difference between what is required to prove guilt in a criminal case and what is required to show probable cause for arrest or search. It approaches requiring (if it does not in practical effect require) proof sufficient to establish guilt in order to substantiate the existence of probable cause. There is a large difference between the two things to be proved [guilt and probable cause], as well as between the tribunals which determine them, and therefore a like difference in the *quanta* and modes of proof required to establish them."

Nor can we agree with petitioner's second contention that Marsh's information was insufficient to show probable cause and reasonable grounds to believe that petitioner had violated or was violating the narcotic laws and to justify his arrest without a warrant. The information given to narcotic agent Marsh by "special employee" Hereford may have been hearsay to Marsh, but coming from one employed for that purpose and whose information had always been found accurate and reliable, it is clear that Marsh would have been derelict in his duties had he not pursued it. And when, in pursuing that information, he saw a man, having the exact physical attributes and wearing the precise clothing and carrying the tan zipper bag that Hereford had described, alight from one of the very trains from the very place stated by Hereford and start to walk at a "fast" pace toward the station exit, Marsh had personally verified every facet of the information given him by Hereford except whether petitioner had accomplished his mission and had the three ounces of heroin on his person or in his bag. And surely, with every other bit of Hereford's information being thus personally verified, Marsh had "reasonable grounds" to believe that the remaining unverified bit of Hereford's information—that Draper would have the heroin with him—was likewise true.

"In dealing with probable cause, . . . as the very name implies, we deal with probabilities. These are not technical; they are the factual and practical considerations of everyday life on which reasonable and prudent men, not legal technicians, act." *Brinegar*. Probable cause exists where "the facts and circumstances within [the arresting officers'] knowledge and of which they had reasonably trustworthy information [are] sufficient in themselves to warrant a man of reasonable caution in the belief that" an offense has been or is being committed.

We believe that, under the facts and circumstances here, Marsh had probable cause to believe that petitioner was committing a violation of the laws of the United States relating to narcotic drugs at the time he arrested him. The arrest was therefore lawful, and the subsequent search and seizure, having been made incident to that lawful arrest, were likewise valid. It follows that petitioner's motion to suppress was properly denied and that the seized heroin was competent evidence lawfully received at the trial.

Affirmed.

MR. JUSTICE DOUGLAS, dissenting. [After beginning with the excerpt quoted in chapter 1.]

With all due deference, the arrest made here on the mere word of an informer violated the spirit of the Fourth Amendment. If an arrest is made without a warrant, the offense must be committed in the presence of the officer or the officer must have "reasonable grounds to believe that the person to be arrested has committed or is committing" a violation of the narcotics law. The arresting officers did not have a bit of evidence, known to them and as to which they could take an oath had they gone to a magistrate for a warrant, that petitioner had committed any crime. The arresting officers did not know the grounds on which the informer based his conclusion; nor did they seek to find out what they were. They acted solely on the informer's word. In my view that was not enough.

The Virginia Declaration of Rights, adopted June 12, 1776, included the forerunner of the Fourth Amendment:

"That general warrants, whereby an officer or messenger may be commanded to search suspected places without evidence of a fact committed, or to seize any person or persons not named, or whose offence is not particularly described and *supported by evidence*, are grievous and oppressive, and ought not to be granted." (Italics added.)

The requirement that a warrant of arrest be "supported by evidence" was by then deeply rooted in history. And it is inconceivable that in those days, when the right of privacy was so greatly cherished, the mere word of an informer—such as we have in the present case—would be enough. For whispered charges and accusations, used in lieu of evidence of unlawful acts, were the main complaint of the age. *Frisbie v. Butler,* Kirby's Rep. (Conn.) 1785-1788, p. 213, decided in 1787, illustrates, I think, the mood of the day in the matter of arrests on suspicion. A warrant of arrest and search was issued by a justice of the peace on the oath of a citizen who had lost some pork from a cellar, the warrant stating, "said Butler suspects one Benjamin Frisbie, of Harwinton, to be the person that hath taken said pork." The court on appeal reversed the judgment of conviction, holding inter alia that the complaint "contained no direct charge of the theft, but only an averment that the defendant was suspected to be guilty." Nothing but suspicion is shown in the instant case—suspicion of an informer, not that of the arresting officers. Nor did they seek to obtain from the informer any information on which he based his belief. The arresting officers did not have a bit of evidence that the petitioner had committed or was committing a crime before the arrest. The only evidence of guilt was provided by the arrest itself.

The determination that arrests and searches on mere suspicion would find no place in American law enforcement did not abate following the adoption of a Bill of Rights applicable to the Federal Government. In *Conner v. Commonwealth,* 3 Binn. (Pa.) 38, an arrest warrant issued by a magistrate stating his "strong reason to suspect" that the accused had committed a crime because of "common rumor and report" was held illegal under a constitutional provision identical in relevant part to the Fourth Amendment. "It is true, that by insisting on an oath, felons may sometimes escape. This must have been very well known to the framers of our constitution; but they thought it better that the guilty should sometimes escape, than that every individual should be subject to vexation and oppression." It was against this long background that Professors Hogan and Snee of Georgetown University recently wrote:

". . . it must be borne in mind that any arrest based on suspicion alone is illegal. This indisputable rule of law has grave implications for a number of traditional police investigative practices. The round-up or dragnet arrest, the arrest on suspicion, for questioning, for investigation or on an open charge all are prohibited by the law. It is undeniable that if those arrests were sanctioned by law, the police would be in a position to investigate a crime and to detect the real culprit much more easily, much more efficiently, much more economically, and with much more dispatch. It is equally true, however, that society cannot confer such power on the police without ripping away much of the fabric of a way of life which seeks to give the maximum of liberty to the individual citizen. The finger of suspicion is a long one. In an individual case it may point to all of a certain race, age group or locale. Commonly it extends to any who have committed similar crimes in the past. Arrest on mere suspicion collides violently with the basic human right of liberty. It can be tolerated only in a society which is willing to concede to its government powers which history and experience teach are the inevitable accoutrements of tyranny." 47 Geo. L. J. 1, 22.

Down to this day our decisions have closely heeded that warning. So far as I can ascertain the mere word of an informer, not bolstered by some evidence a crime had been or was being committed, has never been approved by this Court as "reasonable grounds" for making an arrest without a warrant. Whether the act complained of be seizure of goods, search of premises, or the arrest of the citizen, the judicial inquiry has been directed toward the reasonableness of inferences to be drawn from suspicious circumstances attending the action thought to be unlawful. Evidence required to prove guilt is not necessary. But the attendant circumstances must be sufficient to give rise in the mind of the arresting officer at least to inferences of guilt.

The Court is quite correct in saying that proof of "reasonable grounds" for believing a crime was being committed need not be proof admissible at the trial. It could be inferences from suspicious acts, *e.g.,* consort with known peddlers, the surreptitious passing of a package, an intercepted message suggesting criminal activities, or any number of such events coming to the knowledge of the officer. But, if he takes the law into his own hands and does not seek the protection of a warrant, he must act on some evidence known to him. The law goes far to protect the citizen. Even suspicious acts observed by the officers may be as consistent with innocence as with guilt. That is not enough, for even the guilty may not be implicated on suspicion alone. The reason is, as I have said, that the standard set by the Constitution and by the statute is one that will protect both the officer and the citizen. For if the officer acts with "probable cause" or on "reasonable grounds," he is protected even though the citizen is innocent. This important requirement should be strictly enforced, lest the whole process of arrest revert once more to whispered accusations by people. When we lower the guards as we do today, we risk making the role of the informer – odious in our history – once more supreme.

Here the officers had no evidence – apart from the mere word of an informer – that petitioner was committing a crime. The fact that petitioner walked fast and carried a tan zipper bag was not evidence of any crime. The officers knew nothing except what they had been told by the informer. If they went to a magistrate to get a warrant of arrest and relied solely on the report of the informer, it is not conceivable to me that one would be granted. For they could not present to the magistrate any of the facts which the informer may have had. They could swear only to the fact that the informer had made the accusation. They could swear to no evidence that lay in their own knowledge. They could present, on information and belief, no facts which the informer disclosed. No magistrate could issue a warrant on the mere word of an officer, without more. We are not justified in lowering the standard when an arrest is made without a warrant and allowing the officers more leeway than we grant the magistrate.

With all deference I think we break with tradition when we sustain this arrest. "[A] search is not to be made legal by what it turns up. In law it is good or bad when it starts and does not change character from its success." In this case it was only after the arrest and search were made that there was a shred of evidence known to the officers that a crime was in the process of being committed.

## QUESTIONS AND NOTES

**1.** At what point in this case was there probable cause? When Hereford provided the information, or when the officers corroborated the information by spotting Draper?

**2.** If your answer to question I was when the officers spotted Draper, is Justice Douglas correct in saying that at the time that the information was received, no warrant could issue?

**3.** Justice Douglas (who concurred in *Brinegar*) seems particularly repulsed by the informer (whom he describes as "odious."). Do you share that distrust? Given the informant's information, wasn't Draper far more likely than Brinegar to have been engaged in criminal activity?

**4.** Should the fact that Hereford was revealed by name be relevant? Frequently informants, even when known by the police, do not have their names revealed. Because of the danger to informants in releasing their names (one can speculate about the cause of Hereford's death), coupled with the value that at least some Justices believe they serve, the practice of not naming informants was upheld in *McCray v. Illinois,* 386 U.S. 300 (1967).

**5.** Are there any special dangers in allowing arrests of this type without a warrant? Assuming that there was no probable cause to believe that Draper was carrying drugs until he alighted from the train, is there any way that a warrant could have been obtained?

**6.** As you read *Spinelli* consider whether there was more or less probable cause there than in *Draper*.

## Spinelli v. United States
### 393 U.S. 410 (1969)

MR. JUSTICE HARLAN delivered the opinion of the Court.

William Spinelli was convicted of traveling to St. Louis, Missouri, from a nearby Illinois suburb with the intention of conducting gambling activities proscribed by Missouri law. At every appropriate stage in the proceedings in the lower courts, the petitioner challenged the constitutionality of the warrant which authorized the FBI search that uncovered the evidence necessary for his conviction.

In *Aguilar v. Texas,* 378 U.S. 1 (1964), a search warrant had issued upon an affidavit of police officers who swore only that they had "received reliable information from a credible person and do believe" that narcotics were being illegally stored on the described premises. While recognizing that the constitutional requirement of probable cause can be satisfied by hearsay information, this Court held the affidavit inadequate for two reasons. First, the application failed to set forth any of the "underlying circumstances" necessary to enable the magistrate independently to judge of the validity of the informant's conclusion that the narcotics were where he said they were. Second, the affiant-officers did not attempt to support their claim that their informant was " 'credible' or his information 'reliable.' " The Government is, however, quite right in saying that the FBI affidavit in the present case is more ample than that in Aguilar. Not only does it contain a report from an anonymous informant, but it also contains a report of an independent FBI investigation which is said to corroborate the informant's tip. We are, then, required to delineate the manner in which Aguilar's two-pronged test should be applied in these circumstances.

In essence, the affidavit contained the following allegations:

1. The FBI had kept track of Spinelli's movements on five days during the month of August 1965. On four of these occasions, Spinelli was seen crossing one of two bridges leading from Illinois into St. Louis, Missouri, between 11 a.m. and 12:15 p.m. On four of the five days, Spinelli was also seen parking his car in a lot used by residents of an apartment house at 1108 Indian Circle Drive in St. Louis, between 3:30 p.m. and 4:45 p.m.[4] On one day, Spinelli was followed further and seen to enter a particular apartment in the building.

---

[4] No report was made as to Spinelli's movements during the period between his arrival in St. Louis at noon and his arrival at the parking lot in the late afternoon. In fact, the evidence at trial indicated that Spinelli frequented the offices of his stockbroker during this period.

2. An FBI check with the telephone company revealed that this apartment contained two telephones listed under the name of Grace P. Hagen, and carrying the numbers WYdown 4-0029 and WYdown 4-0136.

3. The application stated that "William Spinelli is known to this affiant and to federal law enforcement agents and local law enforcement agents as a bookmaker, an associate of bookmakers, a gambler, and an associate of gamblers."

4. Finally, it was stated that the FBI "has been informed by a confidential reliable informant that William Spinelli is operating a handbook and accepting wagers and disseminating wagering information by means of the telephones which have been assigned the numbers WYdown 4-0029 and WYdown 4-0136."

There can be no question that the last item mentioned, detailing the informant's tip, has a fundamental place in this warrant application. Without it, probable cause could not be established. The first two items reflect only innocent-seeming activity and data. Spinelli's travels to and from the apartment building and his entry into a particular apartment on one occasion could hardly be taken as bespeaking gambling activity; and there is surely nothing unusual about an apartment containing two separate telephones. Many a householder indulges himself in this petty luxury. Finally, the allegation that Spinelli was "known" to the affiant and to other federal and local law enforcement officers as a gambler and an associate of gamblers is but a bald and unilluminating assertion of suspicion that is entitled to no weight in appraising the magistrate's decision.

So much indeed the Government does not deny. Rather, following the reasoning of the Court of Appeals, the Government claims that the informant's tip gives a suspicious color to the FBI's reports detailing Spinelli's innocent-seeming conduct and that, conversely, the FBI's surveillance corroborates the informant's tip, thereby entitling it to more weight. It is true, of course, that the magistrate is obligated to render a judgment based upon a common-sense reading of the entire affidavit. We believe, however, that the "totality of circumstances" approach taken by the Court of Appeals paints with too broad a brush. Where, as here, the informer's tip is a necessary element in a finding of probable cause, its proper weight must be determined by a more precise analysis.

The informer's report must first be measured against Aguilar's standards so that its probative value can be assessed. If the tip is found inadequate under Aguilar, the other allegations which corroborate the information contained in the hearsay report should then be considered. At this stage as well, however, the standards enunciated in Aguilar must inform the magistrate's decision. He must ask: Can it fairly be said that the tip, even when certain parts of it have been corroborated by independent sources, is as trustworthy as a tip which would pass Aguilar's tests without independent corroboration?

Applying these principles to the present case, we first consider the weight to be given the informer's tip when it is considered apart from the rest of the affidavit. It is clear that a Commissioner could not credit it without abdicating his constitutional function. Though the affiant swore that his confidant was "reliable," he offered the magistrate no reason in support of this conclusion. Perhaps even more important is the fact that Aguilar's other test has not been satisfied. The tip does not contain a sufficient statement of the underlying circumstances from which the informer concluded that Spinelli was running a bookmaking operation. We are not told how the FBI's source received his information—it is not alleged that the informant personally observed Spinelli at work or that he had ever placed a bet with him. Moreover, if the informant came by the information indirectly, he did not explain why his sources were reliable. In the absence of a statement detailing the manner in which the information was gathered, it is especially important that the tip describe the accused's criminal activity in sufficient detail that the magistrate may know that he is relying on something more substantial than a casual rumor circulating in the underworld or an accusation based merely on an individual's general reputation.

The detail provided by the informant in *Draper,* provides a suitable benchmark. While Hereford, the Government's informer in that case, did not state the way in which he had obtained his information, he reported that Draper had gone to Chicago the day before by train and that he would return to Denver by train with three ounces of heroin on one of two specified mornings. Moreover, Hereford went on to describe, with minute particularity, the clothes that Draper would be wearing upon his arrival at the Denver station. A magistrate, when confronted with such detail, could reasonably infer that the informant had gained his information in a reliable way.[5] Such an inference cannot be made in the present case. Here, the only facts supplied were that Spinelli was using two specified telephones and that these phones were being used in gambling operations. This meager report could easily have been obtained from an

---

[5] While Draper involved the question whether the police had probable cause for an arrest without a warrant, the analysis required for an answer to this question is basically similar to that demanded of a magistrate when he considers whether a search warrant should issue.

offhand remark heard at a neighborhood bar.

Nor do we believe that the patent doubts Aguilar raises as to the report's reliability are adequately resolved by a consideration of the allegations detailing the FBI's independent investigative efforts. At most, these allegations indicated that Spinelli could have used the telephones specified by the informant for some purpose. This cannot by itself be said to support both the inference that the informer was generally trustworthy and that he had made his charge against Spinelli on the basis of information obtained in a reliable way. Once again, *Draper* provides a relevant comparison. Independent police work in that case corroborated much more than one small detail that had been provided by the informant. There, the police, upon meeting the inbound Denver train on the second morning specified by informer Hereford, saw a man whose dress corresponded precisely to Hereford's detailed description. It was then apparent that the informant had not been fabricating his report out of whole cloth; since the report was of the sort which in common experience may be recognized as having been obtained in a reliable way, it was perfectly clear that probable cause had been established.

We conclude, then, that in the present case the informant's tip – even when corroborated to the extent indicated – was not sufficient to provide the basis for a finding of probable cause. This is not to say that the tip was so insubstantial that it could not properly have counted in the magistrate's determination. Rather, it needed some further support. When we look to the other parts of the application, however, we find nothing alleged which would permit the suspicions engendered by the informant's report to ripen into a judgment that a crime was probably being committed. As we have already seen, the allegations detailing the FBI's surveillance of Spinelli and its investigation of the telephone company records contain no suggestion of criminal conduct when taken by themselves – and they are not endowed with an aura of suspicion by virtue of the informer's tip. Nor do we find that the FBI's reports take on a sinister color when read in light of common knowledge that bookmaking is often carried on over the telephone and from premises ostensibly used by others for perfectly normal purposes. Such an argument would carry weight in a situation in which the premises contain an unusual number of telephones or abnormal activity is observed, but it does not fit this case where neither of these factors is present.[6]

All that remains to be considered is the flat statement that Spinelli was "known" to the FBI and others as a gambler. But just as a simple assertion of police suspicion is not itself a sufficient basis for a magistrate's finding of probable cause, we do not believe it may be used to give additional weight to allegations that would otherwise be insufficient.

The affidavit, then, falls short of the standards set forth in *Aguilar, Draper,* and our other decisions that give content to the notion of probable cause. In holding as we have done, we do not retreat from the established propositions that only the probability, and not a prima facie showing, of criminal activity is the standard of probable cause, that affidavits of probable cause are tested by much less rigorous standards than those governing the admissibility of evidence at trial, that in judging probable cause issuing magistrates are not to be confined by niggardly limitations or by restrictions on the use of their common sense, and that their determination of probable cause should be paid great deference by reviewing courts. But we cannot sustain this warrant without diluting important safeguards that assure that the judgment of a disinterested judicial officer will interpose itself between the police and the citizenry.

MR. JUSTICE WHITE, concurring.

An investigator's affidavit that he has seen gambling equipment being moved into a house at a specified address will support the issuance of a search warrant. The oath affirms the honesty of the statement and negatives the lie or imagination. Personal observation attests to the facts asserted – that there is gambling equipment on the premises at the named address.

But if the officer simply avers, without more, that there is gambling paraphernalia on certain premises, the warrant should not issue, even though the belief of the officer is an honest one, as evidenced by his oath, and even though the magistrate knows him to be an experienced, intelligent officer who has been reliable in the past.

Neither should the warrant issue if the officer states that there is gambling equipment in a particular apartment and that his information comes from an informant, named or unnamed, since the honesty of the informant and the basis for his report are unknown. Nor would the missing elements be completely supplied by the officer's oath that the informant has often furnished reliable information in the past. This attests to the honesty of the informant, but *Aguilar* requires something more – did the information come from observation, or did the informant in turn receive it from another? Absent additional facts for believing the informant's report, his assertion stands no better than the oath of the officer to the same effect. Indeed, if the affidavit of an officer,

---

[6] A box containing three uninstalled telephones was found in the apartment, but only after execution of the search warrant.

known by the magistrate to be honest and experienced, stating that gambling equipment is located in a certain building is unacceptable, it would be quixotic if a similar statement from an honest informant were found to furnish probable cause. A strong argument can be made that both should be acceptable under the Fourth Amendment, but under our cases neither is. The past reliability of the informant can no more furnish probable cause for believing his current report than can previous experience with the officer himself.

If the affidavit rests on hearsay—an informant's report—what is necessary under Aguilar is one of two things: the informant must declare either (1) that he has himself seen or perceived the fact or facts asserted; or (2) that his information is hearsay, but there is good reason for believing it—perhaps one of the usual grounds for crediting hearsay information. The first presents few problems: since the report, although hearsay, purports to be first-hand observation, remaining doubt centers on the honesty of the informant, and that worry is dissipated by the officer's previous experience with the informant. The other basis for accepting the informant's report is more complicated. But if, for example, the informer's hearsay comes from one of the actors in the crime in the nature of admission against interest, the affidavit giving this information should be held sufficient.

I am inclined to agree with the majority that there are limited special circumstances in which an "honest" informant's report, if sufficiently detailed, will in effect verify itself—that is, the magistrate when confronted with such detail could reasonably infer that the informant had gained his information in a reliable way. Detailed information may sometimes imply that the informant himself has observed the facts. Suppose an informant with whom an officer has had satisfactory experience states that there is gambling equipment in the living room of a specified apartment and describes in detail not only the equipment itself but also the appointments and furnishings in the apartment. Detail like this, if true at all, must rest on personal observation either of the informant or of someone else. If the latter, we know nothing of the third person's honesty or sources; he may be making a wholly false report. But it is arguable that on these facts it was the informant himself who has perceived the facts, for the information reported is not usually the subject of casual, day-to-day conversation. Because the informant is honest and it is probable that he has viewed the facts, there is probable cause for the issuance of a warrant.

So too in the special circumstances of *Draper*, the kind of information related by the informant is not generally sent ahead of a person's arrival in a city except to those who are intimately connected with making careful arrangements for meeting him.

The informant, posited as honest, somehow had the reported facts, very likely from one of the actors in the plan, or as one of them himself. The majority's suggestion is that a warrant could have been obtained based only on the informer's report. I am inclined to agree, although it seems quite plain that if it may be so easily inferred from the affidavit that the informant has himself observed the facts or has them from an actor in the event, no possible harm could come from requiring a statement to that effect, thereby removing the difficult and recurring questions which arise in such situations.

Of course, *Draper* itself did not proceed on this basis. Instead, the Court pointed out that when the officer saw a person getting off the train at the specified time, dressed and conducting himself precisely as the informant had predicted, all but the critical fact with respect to possessing narcotics had then been verified and for that reason the officer had "reasonable grounds" to believe also that Draper was carrying narcotics. Unquestionably, verification of arrival time, dress, and gait reinforced the honesty of the informant—he had not reported a made-up story. But if what *Draper* stands for is that the existence of the tenth and critical fact is made sufficiently probable to justify the issuance of a warrant by verifying nine other facts coming from the same source, I have my doubts about that case.

In the first place, the proposition is not that the tenth fact may be logically inferred from the other nine or that the tenth fact is usually found in conjunction with the other nine. No one would suggest that just anyone getting off the 10:30 train dressed as Draper was, with a brisk walk and carrying a zipper bag, should be arrested for carrying narcotics. The thrust of Draper is not that the verified facts have independent significance with respect to proof of the tenth. The argument instead relates to the reliability of the source: because an informant is right about some things, he is more probably right about other facts, usually the critical, unverified facts.

But the Court's cases have already rejected for Fourth Amendment purposes the notion that the past reliability of an officer is sufficient reason for believing his current assertions. Nor would it suffice, I suppose, if a reliable informant states there is gambling equipment in Apartment 607 and then proceeds to describe in detail Apartment 201, a description which is verified before applying for the warrant. He was right about 201, but that hardly makes him more believable about the equipment in 607. But what if he states that there are narcotics locked in a safe in Apartment 300, which is described in detail, and the apartment manager verifies everything but the contents of the safe? I doubt that the report about the narcotics is made appreciably more believable by the verification.

The informant could still have gotten his information concerning the safe from others about whom nothing is known or could have inferred the presence of narcotics from circumstances which a magistrate would find unacceptable.

The tension between *Draper* and the *Aguilar* line of cases is evident from the course followed by the majority opinion. First, it is held that the report from a reliable informant that Spinelli is using two telephones with specified numbers to conduct a gambling business plus Spinelli's reputation in police circles as a gambler does not add up to probable cause. This is wholly consistent with *Aguilar*: the informant did not reveal whether he had personally observed the facts or heard them from another and, if the latter, no basis for crediting the hearsay was presented. Nor were the facts, as MR. JUSTICE HARLAN says, of such a nature that they normally would be obtainable only by the personal observation of the informant himself. The police, however, did not stop with the informant's report. Independently, they established the existence of two phones having the given numbers and located them in an apartment house which Spinelli was regularly frequenting away from his home. There remained little question but that Spinelli was using the phones, and it was a fair inference that the use was not for domestic but for business purposes. The informant had claimed the business involved gambling. Since his specific information about Spinelli using two phones with particular numbers had been verified, did not his allegation about gambling thereby become sufficiently more believable if the *Draper* principle is to be given any scope at all? I would think so, particularly since the information from the informant which was verified was not neutral, irrelevant information but was material to proving the gambling allegation: two phones with different numbers in an apartment used away from home indicates a business use in an operation, like bookmaking, where multiple phones are needed. The *Draper* approach would reasonably justify the issuance of a warrant in this case, particularly since the police had some awareness of Spinelli's past activities. The majority, however, while seemingly embracing *Draper*, confines that case to its own facts. Pending full-scale reconsideration of that case, on the one hand, or of *Aguilar* on the other, I join the opinion of the Court and the judgment of reversal, especially since a vote to affirm would produce an equally divided Court.

MR. JUSTICE BLACK, dissenting.

In my view, this Court's decision in *Aguilar* was bad enough. That decision went very far toward elevating the magistrate's hearing for issuance of a search warrant to a full-fledged trial, where witnesses must be brought forward to attest personally to all the facts alleged. But not content with this, the Court today expands *Aguilar* to almost unbelievable proportions. Of course, it would strengthen the probable-cause presentation if eyewitnesses could testify that they saw the defendant commit the crime. It would be stronger still if these witnesses could explain in detail the nature of the sensual perceptions on which they based their "conclusion" that the person they had seen was the defendant and that he was responsible for the events they observed. Nothing in our Constitution, however, requires that the facts be established with that degree of certainty and with such elaborate specificity before a policeman can be authorized by a disinterested magistrate to conduct a carefully limited search.

The Fourth Amendment provides that "no Warrants shall issue, but upon probable cause, supported by Oath or affirmation, and particularly describing the place to be searched, and the persons or things to be seized." In this case a search warrant was issued supported by an oath and particularly describing the place to be searched and the things to be seized. The supporting oath was three printed pages and the full text of it is included in an Appendix to the Court's opinion. The magistrate, I think properly, held the information set forth sufficient facts to show "probable cause" that the defendant was violating the law. Six members of the Court of Appeals also agreed that the affidavit was sufficient to show probable cause. A majority of this Court today holds, however, that the magistrate and all of these judges were wrong. In doing so, they substitute their own opinion for that of the local magistrate and the circuit judges, and reject the *en banc* factual conclusion of the Eighth Circuit and reverse the judgment based upon that factual conclusion. I cannot join in any such disposition of an issue so vital to the administration of justice, and dissent as vigorously as I can.

I repeat my belief that the affidavit given the magistrate was more than ample to show probable cause of the petitioner's guilt. The affidavit meticulously set out facts sufficient to show the following:

1. The petitioner had been shown going to and coming from a room in an apartment which contained two telephones listed under the name of another person. Nothing in the record indicates that the apartment was of that large and luxurious type which could only be occupied by a person to whom it would be a "petty luxury" to have two separate telephones, with different numbers, both listed under the name of a person who did not live there.

2. The petitioner's car had been observed parked in the apartment's parking lot. This fact was, of course, highly relevant in showing that the petitioner

was extremely interested in some enterprise which was located in the apartment.

3. The FBI had been informed by a reliable informant that the petitioner was accepting wagering information by telephones – the particular telephones located in the apartment the defendant had been repeatedly visiting. Unless the Court, going beyond the requirements of the Fourth Amendment, wishes to require magistrates to hold trials before issuing warrants, it is not necessary – as the Court holds – to have the affiant explain "the underlying circumstances from which the informer concluded that Spinelli was running a bookmaking operation."

4. The petitioner was known by federal and local law enforcement agents as a bookmaker and an associate of gamblers. I cannot agree with the Court that this knowledge was only a "bald and unilluminating assertion of suspicion that is entitled to no weight in appraising the magistrate's decision." Although the statement is hearsay that might not be admissible in a regular trial, everyone knows, unless he shuts his eyes to the realities of life, that this is a relevant fact which, together with other circumstances, might indicate a factual probability that gambling is taking place.

The foregoing facts should be enough to constitute probable cause for anyone who does not believe that the only way to obtain a search warrant is to prove beyond a reasonable doubt that a defendant is guilty.

Notwithstanding the Court's belief to the contrary, I think that in holding as it does, the Court does: "retreat from the established propositions that only the probability, and not a prima facie showing, of criminal activity is the standard of probable cause, that affidavits of probable cause are tested by much less rigorous standards than those governing the admissibility of evidence at trial, that in judging probable cause issuing magistrates are not to be confined by niggardly limitations or by restrictions on the use of their common sense, and that their determination of probable cause should be paid great deference by reviewing courts."

In fact, I believe the Court is moving rapidly, through complex analyses and obfuscatory language, toward the holding that no magistrate can issue a warrant unless according to some unknown standard of proof he can be persuaded that the suspect defendant is actually guilty of a crime. I would affirm this conviction.

MR. JUSTICE FORTAS, dissenting.

While I do not subscribe to the criticism of the majority expressed by my Brother BLACK in dissent, I believe – with all respect – that the majority is in error in holding that the affidavit supporting the warrant in this case is constitutionally inadequate.

The affidavit is unusually long and detailed. In fact, it recites so many minute and detailed facts developed in the course of the investigation of Spinelli that its substance is somewhat obscured. It is paradoxical that this very fullness of the affidavit may be the source of the constitutional infirmity that the majority finds. Stated in language more direct and less circumstantial than that used by the FBI agent who executed the affidavit, it sets forth that the FBI has been informed that Spinelli is accepting wagers by means of telephones numbered WY 4-0029 and WY 4-0136; that Spinelli is known to the affiant agent and to law enforcement agencies as a bookmaker; that telephones numbered WY 4-0029 and WY 4-0136 are located in a certain apartment; that Spinelli was placed under surveillance and his observed movements were such as to show his use of that apartment and to indicate that he frequented the apartment on a regular basis.

*Aguilar* holds that the reference in an affidavit to information described only as received from "a confidential reliable informant," standing alone, is not an adequate basis for issuance of a search warrant. The majority agrees that the "FBI affidavit in the present case is more ample than that in *Aguilar*," but concludes that it is nevertheless constitutionally inadequate. The majority states that the present affidavit fails to meet the "two-pronged test" of *Aguilar* because (a) it does not set forth the basis for the assertion that the informer is "reliable" and (b) it fails to state the "underlying circumstances" upon which the informant based his conclusion that Spinelli was engaged in bookmaking.

The majority acknowledges, however, that its reference to a "two-pronged test" should not be understood as meaning that an affidavit deficient in these respects is necessarily inadequate to support a search warrant. Other facts and circumstances may be attested which will supply the evidence of probable cause needed to support the search warrant. On this general statement we are agreed. Our difference is that I believe such facts and circumstances are present in this case, and the majority arrives at the opposite conclusion.

*Aguilar* expressly recognized that if, in that case, the affidavit's conclusory report of the informant's story had been supplemented by "the fact and results of . . . a surveillance . . . this would, of course, present an entirely different case." In the present case, as I view it, the affidavit showed not only relevant surveillance, entitled to some probative weight for purposes of the issuance of a search warrant, but also additional, specific facts of significance and adequate reliability: that Spinelli was using two telephone numbers, identified by an "informant" as being used for bookmaking, in his illegal operations; that these telephones were in an identified apartment; and that Spinelli, a known bookmaker,[5] frequented the apartment. Certainly, this is enough.

A policeman's affidavit should not be judged as

---

[5] Although Spinelli's reputation standing alone would not, of course, justify the search, this Court has held that such a reputation may make the informer's report "much less subject to scepticism than would be

an entry in an essay contest. As the majority recognizes, a policeman's affidavit is entitled to commonsense evaluation. So viewed, I conclude that the judgment of the Court of Appeals for the Eighth Circuit should be affirmed.

MR. JUSTICE STEWART also dissented.

---

such a charge against one without such a history." *Jones v. United States*, 362 U.S. 257, 271 (1960).

## QUESTIONS AND NOTES

**1.** Do you agree with Harlan, White, Black, or Fortas? Why?

**2.** Of the cases that we have read so far, *Brinegar, Draper,* and *Spinelli,* the Court failed to find probable cause only in *Spinelli.* Do you think that *Spinelli* was the weakest of the three cases for finding probable cause? Do you think it was the strongest?

**3.** Did (should) it matter that *Spinelli* was the only case of the three in which a warrant was obtained?

**4.** Did (should) it matter that *Spinelli* involved a search whereas *Draper* involved an arrest?

**5.** Did (should) it matter that *Spinelli* involved a home whereas *Brinegar* involved a car, and *Draper* involved a public area?

**6.** Do you see the two telephones as a petty luxury or an indicator of criminal activity?

**7.** Should we assume (as Justice Black suggests) that Grace Hagen is a nonexistent person, or should we assume that she was a friend of Spinelli's whom he frequently visited? Does the answer to that question affect on your assessment of probable cause?

**8.** As a police attorney with the benefit of hindsight, what additional information would you have put in the warrant?

**9.** In *Gates,* we will see that some of the specificity required by *Spinelli* has not survived. As you read *Gates,* see if you can ascertain why this is so.

## Illinois v. Gates
### 462 U.S. 213 (1983)

Justice REHNQUIST delivered the opinion of the Court.

Respondents Lance and Susan Gates were indicted for violation of state drug laws after police officers, executing a search warrant, discovered marijuana and other contraband in their automobile and home. Prior to trial the Gates' moved to suppress evidence seized during this search. The Illinois Supreme Court affirmed the decisions of lower state courts granting the motion. It held that the affidavit submitted in support of the State's application for a

warrant to search the Gateses' property was inadequate under this Court's decisions in *Aguilar* and *Spinelli.* A chronological statement of events usefully introduces the issues at stake. Bloomingdale, Ill., is a suburb of Chicago located in DuPage County. On May 3, 1978, the Bloomingdale Police Department received by mail an anonymous handwritten letter which read as follows:

"This letter is to inform you that you have a couple in your town who strictly make their living on selling drugs. They are Sue and Lance Gates, they live on Greenway, off Bloomingdale Rd. in the condominiums. Most of their buys are done in Florida. Sue his wife drives their car to Florida, where she leaves it to be loaded up with drugs, then Lance flies down and drives it back. Sue flies back after she drops the car off in Florida. May 3 she is driving down there again and Lance will be flying down in a few days to drive it back. At the time Lance drives the car back he has the trunk loaded with over $100,000.00 in drugs. Presently they have over $100,000.00 worth of drugs in their basement.

"They brag about the fact they never have to work, and make their entire living on pushers.

"I guarantee if you watch them carefully you will make a big catch. They are friends with some big drugs dealers, who visit their house often.

"Lance & Susan Gates

"Greenway

"in Condominiums"

The letter was referred by the Chief of Police of the Bloomingdale Police Department to Detective Mader, who decided to pursue the tip. Mader learned, from the office of the Illinois Secretary of State, that an Illinois driver's license had been issued to one Lance Gates, residing at a stated address in Bloomingdale. He contacted a confidential informant, whose examination of certain financial records revealed a more recent address for the Gateses, and he also learned from a police officer assigned to O'Hare Airport that "L. Gates" had made a reservation on Eastern Airlines flight 245 to West Palm Beach, Fla., scheduled to depart from Chicago on May 5 at 4:15 p.m.

Mader then made arrangements with an agent of the Drug Enforcement Administration for surveillance of the May 5 Eastern Airlines flight. The agent later reported to Mader that Gates had boarded the flight, and that federal agents in Florida had observed him arrive in West Palm Beach and take a taxi to the nearby Holiday Inn. They also reported that Gates went to a room registered to one Susan Gates and that, at 7:00 a.m. the next morning, Gates and an unidentified woman left the motel in a Mercury bearing Illinois license plates and drove northbound on an interstate frequently used by travelers to the Chicago area. In addition, the DEA agent informed Mader that the license plate number on the Mercury was registered to a Hornet station wagon owned by Gates. The agent also advised Mader that the driving time between West Palm Beach and Bloomingdale was approximately 22 to 24 hours.

Mader signed an affidavit setting forth the foregoing facts, and submitted it to a judge of the Circuit Court of DuPage County, together with a copy of the anonymous letter. The judge of that court thereupon issued a search warrant for the Gateses' residence and for their automobile. The judge, in deciding to issue the warrant, could have determined that the

*modus operandi* of the Gateses had been substantially corroborated. As the anonymous letter predicted, Lance Gates had flown from Chicago to West Palm Beach late in the afternoon of May 5th, had checked into a hotel room registered in the name of his wife, and, at 7:00 a.m. the following morning, had headed north, accompanied by an unidentified woman, out of West Palm Beach on an interstate highway used by travelers from South Florida to Chicago in an automobile bearing a license plate issued to him.

At 5:15 a.m. on March 7th, only 36 hours after he had flown out of Chicago, Lance Gates, and his wife, returned to their home in Bloomingdale, driving the car in which they had left West Palm Beach some 22 hours earlier. The Bloomingdale police were awaiting them, searched the trunk of the Mercury, and uncovered approximately 350 pounds of marijuana. A search of the Gateses' home revealed marijuana, weapons, and other contraband.

The Illinois Supreme Court concluded—and we are inclined to agree—that, standing alone, the anonymous letter sent to the Bloomingdale Police Department would not provide the basis for a magistrate's determination that there was probable cause to believe contraband would be found in the Gateses' car and home. The letter provides virtually nothing from which one might conclude that its author is either honest or his information reliable; likewise, the letter gives absolutely no indication of the basis for the writer's predictions regarding the Gateses' criminal activities. Something more was required, then, before a magistrate could conclude that there was probable cause to believe that contraband would be found in the Gateses' home and car.

The Illinois Supreme Court also properly recognized that Detective Mader's affidavit might be capable of supplementing the anonymous letter with information sufficient to permit a determination of probable cause. In holding that the affidavit in fact did not contain sufficient additional information to sustain a determination of probable cause, the Illinois court applied a "two-pronged test," derived from our decision in *Spinelli*. The Illinois Supreme Court, like some others, apparently understood *Spinelli* as requiring that the anonymous letter satisfy each of two independent requirements before it could be relied on. According to this view, the letter, as supplemented by Mader's affidavit, first had to adequately reveal the "basis of knowledge" of the letter writer—the particular means by which he came by the information given in his report. Second, it had to provide facts sufficiently establishing either the "veracity" of the affiant's informant, or, alternatively, the "reliability" of the informant's report in this particular case.

The Illinois court, alluding to an elaborate set of legal rules that have developed among various lower courts to enforce the "two-pronged test,"[4] found that the test had not been satisfied. First, the "veracity" prong was not satisfied because, "there was simply no basis [for] . . . conclud[ing] that the anonymous person [who wrote the letter to the Bloomingdale Police Department] was credible." The court indicated that corroboration by police of details contained in the letter might never satisfy the "veracity" prong, and in any event, could not do so if, as in the present case, only "innocent" details are corroborated. In addition, the letter gave no indication of the basis of its writer's knowledge of the Gateses' activities. The Illinois court understood *Spinelli* as permitting the detail contained in a tip to be used to infer that the informant had a reliable basis for his statements, but it thought that the anonymous letter failed to provide sufficient detail to permit such an inference. Thus, it concluded that no showing of probable cause had been made.

We agree with the Illinois Supreme Court that an informant's "veracity," "reliability" and "basis of knowledge" are all highly relevant in determining the value of his report. We do not agree, however, that these elements should be understood as entirely separate and independent requirements to be rigidly

---

[4] See, *e.g., Stanley v. State*, 19 Md.App. 507, 313 A.2d 847 (Md. App.1974). In summary, these rules posit that the "veracity" prong of the *Spinelli* test has two "spurs" — the informant's "credibility" and the "reliability" of his information. Various interpretations are advanced for the meaning of the "reliability" spur of the "veracity" prong. Both the "basis of knowledge" prong and the "veracity" prong are treated as entirely separate requirements, which must be independently satisfied in every case in order to sustain a determination of probable cause. See n. 5, *infra*. Some ancillary doctrines are relied on to satisfy certain of the foregoing requirements. For example, the "self-verifying detail" of a tip may satisfy the "basis of knowledge" requirement, although not the "credibility" spur of the "veracity" prong. Conversely, corroboration would seem not capable of supporting the "basis of knowledge" prong, but only the "veracity" prong.

The decision in *Stanley*, while expressly approving and conscientiously attempting to apply the "two-pronged test" observes that "[t]he built-in subtleties [of the test] are such, however, that a slipshod application calls down upon us the fury of Murphy's Law." The decision also suggested that it is necessary "to evolve analogous guidelines [to hearsay rules employed in trial settings] for the reception of hearsay in a probable cause setting."

exacted in every case,[5] which the opinion of the Supreme Court of Illinois would imply. Rather, as detailed below, they should be understood simply as closely intertwined issues that may usefully illuminate the common sense, practical question whether there is "probable cause" to believe that contraband or evidence is located in a particular place.

### III

This totality of the circumstances approach is far more consistent with our prior treatment of probable cause than is any rigid demand that specific "tests" be satisfied by every informant's tip. Perhaps the central teaching of our decisions bearing on the probable cause standard is that it is a "practical, nontechnical conception." *Brinegar.* "In dealing with probable cause, . . . as the very name implies, we deal with probabilities. These are not technical; they are the factual and practical considerations of everyday life on which reasonable and prudent men, not legal technicians, act." Our observation in *United States v. Cortez*, 449 U.S. 411, 418 (1981), regarding "particularized suspicion," is also applicable to the probable cause standard:

"The process does not deal with hard certainties, but with probabilities. Long before the law of probabilities was articulated as such, practical people formulated certain common-sense conclusions about human behavior; jurors as fact finders are permitted to do the same — and so are law enforcement officers. Finally, the evidence thus collected must be seen and weighed not in terms of library analysis by scholars, but as understood by those versed in the field of law enforcement."

Moreover, the "two-pronged test" directs analysis into two largely independent channels — the informant's "veracity" or "reliability" and his "basis of knowledge." There are persuasive arguments against according these two elements such independent status. Instead, they are better understood as relevant considerations in the totality of circumstances analysis that traditionally has guided probable cause determinations: a deficiency in one may be compensated for, in determining the overall reliability of a tip, by a strong showing as to the other, or by some other indicia of reliability.

---

[5] The entirely independent character that the *Spinelli* prongs have assumed is indicated both by the opinion of the Illinois Supreme Court in this case, and by decisions of other courts. One frequently cited decision, *Stanley v. State*, remarks that "the dual requirements represented by the 'two-pronged test' are 'analytically severable' and an 'overkill' on one prong will not carry over to make up for a deficit on the other prong."

If, for example, a particular informant is known for the unusual reliability of his predictions of certain types of criminal activities in a locality, his failure, in a particular case, to thoroughly set forth the basis of his knowledge surely should not serve as an absolute bar to a finding of probable cause based on his tip. Likewise, if an unquestionably honest citizen comes forward with a report of criminal activity—which if fabricated would subject him to criminal liability—we have found rigorous scrutiny of the basis of his knowledge unnecessary. Conversely, even if we entertain some doubt as to an informant's motives, his explicit and detailed description of alleged wrongdoing, along with a statement that the event was observed first-hand, entitles his tip to greater weight than might otherwise be the case. Unlike a totality of circumstances analysis, which permits a balanced assessment of the relative weights of all the various indicia of reliability (and unreliability) attending an informant's tip, the "two-pronged test" has encouraged an excessively technical dissection of informants' tips,[9] with undue attention being focused on isolated issues that cannot sensibly be divorced from the other facts presented to the magistrate.

Similarly, we have repeatedly said that after-the-fact scrutiny by courts of the sufficiency of an affidavit should not take the form of *de novo* review. A magistrate's "determination of probable cause should be paid great deference by reviewing courts." "A grudging or negative attitude by reviewing courts toward warrants" is inconsistent with the Fourth Amendment's strong preference for searches conducted pursuant to a warrant; "courts should not invalidate . . . warrant[s] by interpreting affidavit[s] in a hypertechnical, rather than a common sense, manner."

If the affidavits submitted by police officers are subjected to the type of scrutiny some courts have deemed appropriate, police might well resort to warrantless searches, with the hope of relying on consent or some other exception to the warrant clause that might develop at the time of the search. In addition, the possession of a warrant by officers conducting an arrest or search greatly reduces the perception of unlawful or intrusive police conduct, by assuring "the individual whose property is searched or seized of the lawful authority of the executing officer, his need to search, and the limits of his power to search." Reflecting this preference for the warrant process, the traditional standard for review of an issuing magistrate's probable cause determination has been that so long as the magistrate had a "substantial basis for . . . conclud[ing]" that a search would uncover evidence of wrongdoing, the Fourth Amendment requires no more. We think reaffirmation of this standard better serves the purpose of encouraging recourse to the warrant procedure and is more consistent with our traditional deference to the probable cause determinations of magistrates than is the "two-pronged test."

Finally, the direction taken by decisions following *Spinelli* poorly serves "the most basic function of any government": "to provide for the security of the individual and of his property." The strictures that inevitably accompany the "two-pronged test" cannot avoid seriously impeding the task of law enforcement, see, *e.g.*, n. 9, *supra*. If, as the Illinois Supreme Court apparently thought, that test must be rigorously applied in every case, anonymous tips would be of greatly diminished value in police work. Ordinary citizens, like ordinary witnesses, generally do not provide extensive recitations of the basis of their everyday observations. Likewise, as the Illinois Supreme Court observed in this case, the veracity of persons supplying anonymous tips is by hypothesis largely unknown, and unknowable. As a result, anonymous tips seldom could survive a rigorous application of either of the *Spinelli* prongs. Yet, such tips, particularly when supplemented by independent police investigation, frequently contribute to the solution of otherwise "perfect crimes." While a conscientious assessment of the basis for crediting such tips is required by the Fourth Amendment, a standard that leaves virtually no place for anonymous citizen informants is not. For all these reasons, we conclude that it is wiser to abandon the "two-pronged test" established by our decisions in *Aguilar* and *Spinelli*.[11] In its place we reaffirm the totality

---

[9] Some lower court decisions, brought to our attention by the State, reflect a rigid application of such rules. In *Bridger v. State,* 503 S.W.2d 801 (Tex.Cr.App.1974), the affiant had received a confession of armed robbery from one of two suspects in the robbery; in addition, the suspect had given the officer $800 in cash stolen during the robbery. The suspect also told the officer that the gun used in the robbery was hidden in the other suspect's apartment. A warrant issued on the basis of this was invalidated on the ground that the affidavit did not satisfactorily describe how the accomplice had obtained his information regarding the gun.

---

[11] Whether the allegations submitted to the magistrate in *Spinelli* would, under the view we now take, have supported a finding of probable cause, we think it would not be profitable to decide. There are so many variables in the probable cause equation that

of the circumstances analysis that traditionally has informed probable cause determinations. The task of the issuing magistrate is simply to make a practical, common-sense decision whether, given all the circumstances set forth in the affidavit before him, including the "veracity" and "basis of knowledge" of persons supplying hearsay information, there is a fair probability that contraband or evidence of a crime will be found in a particular place. And the duty of a reviewing court is simply to ensure that the magistrate had a "substantial basis for . . . conclud[ing]" that probable cause existed. We are convinced that this flexible, easily applied standard will better achieve the accommodation of public and private interests that the Fourth Amendment requires than does the approach that has developed from *Aguilar* and *Spinelli.*

Our earlier cases illustrate the limits beyond which a magistrate may not venture in issuing a warrant. A sworn statement of an affiant that "he has cause to suspect and does believe that" liquor illegally brought into the United States is located on certain premises will not do. *Nathanson v. United States*, 290 U.S. 41 (1933). An affidavit must provide the magistrate with a substantial basis for determining the existence of probable cause, and the wholly conclusory statement at issue in *Nathanson* failed to meet this requirement. An officer's statement that "affiants have received reliable information from a credible person and believe" that heroin is stored in a home, is likewise inadequate. *Aguilar.* As in *Nathanson,* this is a mere conclusory statement that gives the magistrate virtually no basis at all for making a judgment regarding probable cause. Sufficient information must be presented to the magistrate to allow that official to determine probable cause; his action cannot be a mere ratification of the bare conclusions of others. In order to ensure that such an abdication of the magistrate's duty does not occur, courts must continue to conscientiously review the sufficiency of affidavits on which warrants are issued. But when we move beyond the "bare bones" affidavits present in cases such as *Nathanson* and *Aguilar,* this area simply does not lend itself to a prescribed set of rules, like that which had developed

one determination will seldom be a useful "precedent" for another. Suffice it to say that while we in no way abandon *Spinelli*'s concern for the trustworthiness of informers and for the principle that it is the magistrate who must ultimately make a finding of probable cause, we reject the rigid categorization suggested by some of its language.

from *Spinelli.* Instead, the flexible, common-sense standard articulated in *Brinegar* better serves the purposes of the Fourth Amendment's probable cause requirement. Justice Brennan's dissent suggests in several places that the approach we take today somehow downgrades the role of the neutral magistrate, because *Aguilar* and *Spinelli* "preserve the role of magistrates as independent arbiters of probable cause. . . ." Quite the contrary, we believe, is the case. Nothing in our opinion in any way lessens the authority of the magistrate to draw such reasonable inferences as he will from the material supplied to him by applicants for a warrant; indeed, he is freer than under the regime of *Aguilar* and *Spinelli* to draw such inferences, or to refuse to draw them if he is so minded.

The real gist of Justice Brennan's criticism seems to be a second argument, somewhat at odds with the first, that magistrates should be restricted in their authority to make probable cause determinations by the standards laid down in *Aguilar* and *Spinelli,* and that such findings "should not be authorized unless there is some assurance that the information on which they are based has been obtained in a reliable way by an honest or credible person." However, under our opinion magistrates remain perfectly free to exact such assurances as they deem necessary, as well as those required by this opinion, in making probable cause determinations. Justice Brennan would apparently prefer that magistrates be restricted in their findings of probable cause by the development of an elaborate body of case law dealing with the "veracity" prong of the *Spinelli* test, which in turn is broken down into two "spurs" — the informant's "credibility" and the "reliability" of his information, together with the "basis of knowledge" prong of the Spinelli test. That such a labyrinthine body of judicial refinement bears any relationship to familiar definitions of probable cause is hard to imagine. Probable cause deals "with probabilities. These are not technical; they are the factual and practical considerations of everyday life on which reasonable and prudent men, not legal technicians, act," *Brinegar.*

Justice Brennan's dissent also suggests that "words such as 'practical,' 'nontechnical,' and 'common sense,' as used in the Court's opinion, are but code words for an overly-permissive attitude towards police practices in derogation of the rights secured by the Fourth Amendment." An easy, but not a complete, answer to this rather florid statement would be that nothing we know about Justice Rutledge suggests that he would have used the words he chose in *Brinegar* in such a manner. More fundamentally, no one doubts that "under our Constitution only measures consistent with the Fourth Amendment may be employed by government to cure [the horrors of drug trafficking]," but this agreement does not advance the inquiry as to which measures are, and which measures are not, consistent with the Fourth Amendment. "Fidelity" to the commands of the Constitution suggests balanced judgment rather than exhortation. The highest "fidelity" is achieved neither by the judge who instinctively goes furthest in upholding even the most bizarre claim of individual constitutional rights, any more than it is achieved by a judge who instinctively goes furthest in accepting the most restrictive claims of governmental authorities. The task of this Court, as of other courts, is to "hold the balance true," and we think we have done that in this case.

## IV

Our decisions applying the totality of circumstances analysis outlined above have consistently recognized the value of corroboration of details of an informant's tip by independent police work. *Draper* is the classic case.[12]

The showing of probable cause in the present case was fully as compelling as that in Draper. Even standing alone, the facts obtained through the independent investigation of Mader and the DEA at least suggested that the Gates were involved in drug trafficking. In addition to being a popular vacation site, Florida is well-known as a source of narcotics and other illegal drugs. Lance Gates' flight to Palm Beach, his brief, overnight stay in a motel, and apparent immediate return north to Chicago in the family car, conveniently awaiting him in West Palm Beach, is as suggestive of a pre-arranged drug run, as it is of an ordinary vacation trip. In addition, the magistrate could rely on the anonymous letter, which

---

[12] The tip in *Draper* might well not have survived the rigid application of the "two-pronged test" that developed following *Spinelli*. The only reference to Hereford's reliability was that he had "been engaged as a 'special employee' of the Bureau of Narcotics at Denver for about six months, and from time to time gave information to [the police] for small sums of money, and that [the officer] had always found the information given by Hereford to be accurate and reliable." Likewise, the tip gave no indication of how Hereford came by his information. At most, the detailed and accurate predictions in the tip indicated that, however Hereford obtained his information, it was reliable.

had been corroborated in major part by Mader's efforts—just as had occurred in *Draper*.[13] The Supreme Court of Illinois reasoned that *Draper* involved an informant who had given reliable information on previous occasions, while the honesty and reliability of the anonymous informant in this case were unknown to the Bloomingdale police. While this distinction might be an apt one at the time the police department received the anonymous letter, it became far less significant after Mader's independent investigative work occurred. The corroboration of the letter's predictions that the Gates' car would be in Florida, that Lance Gates would fly to Florida in the next day or so, and that he would drive the car north toward Bloomingdale all indicated, albeit not with certainty, that the informant's other assertions also were true. "Because an informant is right about some things, he is more probably right about other facts," *Spinelli* (White, J., concurring)—including the claim regarding the Gateses' illegal activity. This may well not be the type of "reliability" or "veracity" necessary to satisfy some views of the "veracity prong" of Spinelli, but we think it suffices for the practical, common-sense judgment called for in making a probable cause determination. It is enough, for purposes of assessing probable cause, that "corroboration through other sources of information reduced the chances of a reckless or prevaricating tale," thus providing "a substantial basis for crediting the hearsay."

Finally, the anonymous letter contained a range of details relating not just to easily obtained facts and conditions existing at the time of the tip, but to future actions of third parties ordinarily not easily predicted. The letter writer's accurate information as to the travel plans of each of the Gateses was of a character likely obtained only from the Gateses themselves, or from someone familiar with their not entirely ordinary travel plans. If the informant had access to accurate information of this type a magistrate could properly conclude that it was not unlikely

---

[13] The Illinois Supreme Court thought that the verification of details contained in the anonymous letter in this case amounted only to "the corroboration of innocent activity," and that this was insufficient to support a finding of probable cause. We are inclined to agree, however, with the observation of Justice Moran in his dissenting opinion that "In this case, just as in *Draper*, seemingly innocent activity became suspicious in the light of the initial tip." And it bears noting that *all* of the corroborating detail established in *Draper* was of entirely innocent activity.

that he also had access to reliable information of the Gateses' alleged illegal activities.[14] Of course, the Gateses' travel plans might have been learned from a talkative neighbor or travel agent; under the "two-pronged test" developed from *Spinelli*, the character of the details in the anonymous letter might well not permit a sufficiently clear inference regarding the letter writer's "basis of knowledge." But, as discussed previously, probable cause does not demand the certainty we associate with formal trials. It is enough that there was a fair probability that the

---

[14] The dissent seizes on one inaccuracy in the anonymous informant's letter – its statement that Sue Gates would fly from Florida to Illinois, when in fact she drove – and argues that the probative value of the entire tip was undermined by this allegedly "material mistake." We have never required that informants used by the police be infallible, and can see no reason to impose such a requirement in this case. Probable cause, particularly when police have obtained a warrant, simply does not require the perfection the dissent finds necessary.

Likewise, there is no force to the dissent's argument that the Gateses' action in leaving their home unguarded undercut the informant's claim that drugs were hidden there. Indeed, the line-by-line scrutiny that the dissent applies to the anonymous letter is akin to that which we find inappropriate in reviewing magistrates' decisions. The dissent apparently attributes to the magistrate who issued the warrant in this case the rather implausible notion that persons dealing in drugs always stay at home, apparently out of fear that to leave might risk intrusion by criminals. If accurate, one could not help sympathizing with the self-imposed isolation of people so situated. In reality, however, it is scarcely likely that the magistrate ever thought that the anonymous tip "kept one spouse" at home, much less that he relied on the theory advanced by the dissent. The letter simply says that Sue would fly from Florida to Illinois, without indicating whether the Gateses made the bitter choice of leaving the drugs in their house, or those in their car, unguarded. The magistrate's determination that there might be drugs or evidence of criminal activity in the Gateses' home was well-supported by the less speculative theory, noted in text, that if the informant could predict with considerable accuracy the somewhat unusual travel plans of the Gateses, he probably also had a reliable basis for his statements that the Gateses' kept a large quantity of drugs in their home and frequently were visited by other drug traffickers there.

writer of the anonymous letter had obtained his entire story either from the Gateses or someone they trusted. And corroboration of major portions of the letter's predictions provides just this probability. It is apparent, therefore, that the judge issuing the warrant had a "substantial basis for . . . conclud[ing]" that probable cause to search the Gateses' home and car existed. The judgment of the Supreme Court of Illinois therefore must be reversed.

Justice WHITE, concurring in the judgment. Abandoning the "two-pronged test" of *Aguilar* and *Spinelli,* the Court upholds the validity of the warrant under a new "totality of the circumstances" approach. Although I agree that the warrant should be upheld, I reach this conclusion in accordance with the *Aguilar-Spinelli* framework.

In the present case, it is undisputed that the anonymous tip, by itself, did not furnish probable cause. The question is whether those portions of the affidavit describing the results of the police investigation of the respondents, when considered in light of the tip, "would permit the suspicions engendered by the informant's report to ripen into a judgment that a crime was probably being committed." The Illinois Supreme Court concluded that the corroboration was insufficient to permit such a ripening. The court reasoned as follows: "[T]he nature of the corroborating evidence in this case would satisfy neither the "basis of knowledge" nor the 'veracity' prong of *Aguilar.* Looking to the affidavit submitted as support for Detective Mader's request that a search warrant issue, we note that the corroborative evidence here was only of innocent activity. Mader's independent investigation revealed only that Lance and Sue Gates lived on Greenway Drive; that Lance Gates booked passage on a flight to Florida; that upon arriving he entered a room registered to his wife; and that he and his wife left the hotel together by car. The corroboration of innocent activity is insufficient to support a finding of probable cause."

In my view, the lower court's characterization of the Gateses' activity here as totally "innocent" is dubious. In fact, the behavior was quite suspicious. I agree with the Court that Lance Gates' flight to Palm Beach, an area known to be a source of narcotics, the brief overnight stay in a motel, and apparent immediate return North, suggest a pattern that trained law-enforcement officers have recognized as indicative of illicit drug-dealing activity.

Even, however, had the corroboration related only to completely innocuous activities, this fact alone would not preclude the issuance of a valid warrant. The critical issue is not whether the activities observed by the police are innocent or suspicious. Instead, the proper focus should be on whether the actions of the suspects, whatever their nature, give rise to an inference that the informant is credible and that he obtained his information in a reliable manner. 1nb

Thus, in *Draper*, an informant stated on Sept. 7 that Draper would be carrying narcotics when he arrived by train in Denver on the morning of Sept. 8 or Sept. 9. The informant also provided the police with a detailed physical description of the clothes Draper would be wearing when he alighted from the train. The police observed Draper leaving a train on the morning of Sept. 9, and he was wearing the precise clothing described by the informant. The Court held that the police had probable cause to arrest Draper at this point, even though the police had seen nothing more than the totally innocent act of a man getting off a train carrying a briefcase. As we later explained in *Spinelli*, the important point was that the corroboration showed both that the informant was credible, *i.e.* that he "had not been fabricating his report out of whole cloth," and that he had an adequate basis of knowledge for his allegations, "since the report was of the sort which in common experience may be recognized as having been obtained in a reliable way." The fact that the informer was able to predict, two days in advance, the exact clothing Draper would be wearing dispelled the possibility that his tip was just based on rumor or "an off-hand remark heard at a neighborhood bar." Probably Draper had planned in advance to wear these specific clothes so that an accomplice could identify him. A clear inference could therefore be drawn that the informant was either involved in the criminal scheme himself or that he otherwise had access to reliable, inside information.[22]

As in *Draper*, the police investigation in the present case satisfactorily demonstrated that the informant's tip was as trustworthy as one that would alone satisfy the *Aguilar* tests. The tip predicted that Sue Gates would drive to Florida, that Lance Gates would fly there a few days after May 3, and that Lance would then drive the car back. After the police corroborated these facts, the magistrate could reasonably have inferred, as he apparently did, that the informant, who had specific knowledge of these unusual travel plans, did not make up his story and that he obtained his information in a reliable way. It is theoretically possible, as respondents insist, that the tip could have been supplied by a "vindictive travel agent" and that the Gateses' activities, although unusual, might not have been unlawful.[24] But *Aguilar* and *Spinelli*, like our other cases, do not require that certain guilt be established before a warrant may properly be issued. "[O]nly the probability, and not a prima facie showing, of criminal activity is the standard of probable cause." I therefore conclude that the judgment of the Illinois Supreme Court invalidating the warrant must be reversed. The Court agrees that the warrant was valid, but, in the process of reaching this conclusion, it overrules the *Aguilar-Spinelli* tests and replaces them with a "totality of the circumstances" standard. As I read the majority opinion, it appears that the question whether the probable cause standard is to be diluted is left to the common-sense judgments of issuing magistrates. I am reluctant to approve any standard that does not expressly require, as a prerequisite to issuance of a warrant, some showing of facts from which an inference may be drawn that the informant is credible and that his information was obtained in a reliable way. The Court is

---

[22] Thus, as interpreted in *Spinelli*, the Court in *Draper* held that there was probable cause because "the kind of information related by the informant [was] not generally sent ahead of a person's arrival in a city except to those who are intimately connected with making careful arrangements for meeting him." *Spinelli* (White, J., concurring). As I said in Spinelli, the conclusion that Draper itself was based on this fact is far from inescapable. Prior to *Spinelli*, *Draper* was susceptible to the interpretation that it stood for the proposition that "the existence of the tenth and critical fact is made sufficiently probable to justify the issuance of a warrant by verifying nine other facts coming from the same source." But it now seems clear that the Court in Spinelli rejected this reading of *Draper*.

Justice Brennan erroneously interprets my *Spinelli* concurrence as espousing the view that "corroboration of certain details in a tip may be sufficient

to satisfy the veracity, but not the basis of knowledge, prong of *Aguilar*." Others have made the same mistake. I did not say that corroboration could *never* satisfy the basis of knowledge prong. My concern was, and still is, that the prong might be deemed satisfied on the basis of corroboration of information that does not in any way suggest that the informant had an adequate basis of knowledge for his report. If, however, as in *Draper*, the police corroborate information from which it can be inferred that the informant's tip was grounded on inside information, this corroboration is sufficient to satisfy the basis of knowledge prong. The rules would indeed be strange if, as Justice Brennan suggests, the basis of knowledge prong could be satisfied by detail in the tip alone, but not by independent police work.

[24] It is also true, as Justice Stevens points out, that the fact that respondents were last seen leaving West Palm Beach on a northbound interstate highway is far from conclusive proof that they were heading directly to Bloomingdale.

correctly concerned with the fact that some lower courts have been applying *Aguilar-Spinelli* in an unduly rigid manner. I believe, however, that with clarification of the rule of corroborating information, the lower courts are fully able to properly interpret *Aguilar-Spinelli* and avoid such unduly rigid applications. I may be wrong; it ultimately may prove to be the case that the only profitable instruction we can provide to magistrates is to rely on common sense. But the question whether a particular anonymous tip provides the basis for issuance of a warrant will often be a difficult one, and I would at least attempt to provide more precise guidance by clarifying *Aguilar-Spinelli* and the relationship of those cases with *Draper* before totally abdicating our responsibility in this area. Hence, I do not join the Court's opinion rejecting the *Aguilar-Spinelli* rules.

Justice BRENNAN, with whom Justice MARSHALL joins, dissenting.

Although I join Justice Stevens' dissenting opinion and agree with him that the warrant is invalid even under the Court's newly announced "totality of the circumstances" test, I write separately to dissent from the Court's unjustified and ill-advised rejection of the two-prong test for evaluating the validity of a warrant based on hearsay.

I

In order to emphasize the magistrate's role as an independent arbiter of probable cause and to insure that searches or seizures are not effected on less than probable cause, the Court has insisted that police officers provide magistrates with the underlying facts and circumstances that support the officers' conclusions.

Although the rules drawn from the cases are cast in procedural terms, they advance an important underlying substantive value: Findings of probable cause, and attendant intrusions, should not be authorized unless there is some assurance that the information on which they are based has been obtained in a reliable way by an honest or credible person. As applied to police officers, the rules focus on the way in which the information was acquired. As applied to informants, the rules focus both on the honesty or credibility of the informant and on the reliability of the way in which the information was acquired. Insofar as it is more complicated, an evaluation of affidavits based on hearsay involves a more difficult inquiry. This suggests a need to structure the inquiry in an effort to insure greater accuracy. The standards announced in *Aguilar*, as refined by *Spinelli*, fulfill that need. The standards inform the police of what information they have to provide and magistrates of what information they should demand. The standards also inform magistrates of the subsidiary findings they must make in order to arrive at an ultimate finding of probable cause. *Spinelli*, properly understood, directs the magistrate's attention to the possibility that the presence of self-verifying detail might satisfy *Aguilar*'s basis of knowledge prong and that corroboration of the details of a tip might satisfy *Aguilar*'s veracity prong. By requiring police to provide certain crucial information to magistrates and by structuring magistrates' probable cause inquiries, *Aguilar* and *Spinelli* assure the magistrate's role as an independent arbiter of probable cause, insure greater accuracy in probable cause determinations, and advance the substantive value identified above.

Until today the Court has never squarely addressed the application of the *Aguilar* and *Spinelli* standards to tips from anonymous informants. Both *Aguilar* and *Spinelli* dealt with tips from informants known at least to the police. And surely there is even more reason to subject anonymous informants' tips to the tests established by *Aguilar* and *Spinelli*. By definition nothing is known about an anonymous informant's identity, honesty, or reliability. One commentator has suggested that anonymous informants should be treated as presumptively unreliable. In any event, there certainly is no basis for treating anonymous informants as presumptively reliable. Nor is there any basis for assuming that the information provided by an anonymous informant has been obtained in a reliable way. If we are unwilling to accept conclusory allegations from the police, who are presumptively reliable, or from informants who are known, at least to the police, there cannot possibly be any rational basis for accepting conclusory allegations from anonymous informants.

To suggest that anonymous informants' tips are subject to the tests established by *Aguilar* and *Spinelli* is not to suggest that they can never provide a basis for a finding of probable cause. It is conceivable that police corroboration of the details of the tip might establish the reliability of the informant under *Aguilar*'s veracity prong, as refined in *Spinelli*, and that the details in the tip might be sufficient to qualify under the "self-verifying detail" test established by *Spinelli* as a means of satisfying *Aguilar*'s basis of knowledge prong. The *Aguilar* and *Spinelli* tests must be applied to anonymous informants' tips, however, if we are to continue to insure that findings of probable cause, and attendant intrusions, are based on information provided by an honest or credible person who has acquired the information in a reliable way.

II

[O]ne can concede that probable cause is a "practical, nontechnical" concept without betraying the values that *Aguilar* and *Spinelli* reflect. *Aguilar* and *Spinelli* require the police to provide magistrates with certain crucial information. They also provide structure for magistrates' probable cause inquiries. In so doing, *Aguilar* and *Spinelli* preserve the role of magistrates as independent arbiters of probable cause, insure greater accuracy in probable cause determinations, and advance the substantive value of precluding findings of probable cause, and attendant intrusions, based on anything less than information from an honest or credible person who has acquired his information in a reliable way. Neither the standards nor their effects are inconsistent with a "practical, nontechnical" conception of probable cause. Once a magistrate has determined that he has information before him that he can reasonably say has been obtained in a reliable way by a credible person, he has ample room to use his common sense and to apply a practical, nontechnical conception of probable cause.

The Court also insists that the *Aguilar-Spinelli* standards must be abandoned because they are inconsistent with the fact that non-lawyers frequently serve as magistrates. To the contrary, the standards help to structure probable cause inquiries and, properly interpreted, may actually help a non-lawyer magistrate in making a probable cause determination.

At the heart of the Court's decision to abandon *Aguilar* and *Spinelli* appears to be its belief that "the direction taken by decisions following *Spinelli* poorly serves 'the most basic function of any government: to provide for the security of the individual and of his property.'" This conclusion rests on the judgment that *Aguilar* and *Spinelli* "seriously imped[e] the task of law enforcement," and render anonymous tips valueless in police work. Surely, the Court overstates its case. But of particular concern to all Americans must be that the Court gives virtually no consideration to the value of insuring that findings of probable cause are based on information that a magistrate can reasonably say has been obtained in a reliable way by an honest or credible person. I share Justice WHITE's fear that the Court's rejection of *Aguilar* and *Spinelli* and its adoption of a new totality of the circumstances test "may foretell an evisceration of the probable cause standard. . . ."

### III

The Court's complete failure to provide any persuasive reason for rejecting *Aguilar* and *Spinelli* doubtlessly reflects impatience with what it perceives to be "overly technical" rules governing searches and seizures under the Fourth Amendment. Words such as "practical," "nontechnical," and "common sense," as used in the Court's opinion, are but code words for an overly permissive attitude towards police practices in derogation of the rights secured by the Fourth Amendment. Everyone shares the Court's concern over the horrors of drug trafficking, but under our Constitution only measures consistent with the Fourth Amendment may be employed by government to cure this evil. We must be ever mindful of Justice Stewart's

admonition in *Coolidge v. New Hampshire,* 403 U.S. 443 (1971), that "[i]n times of unrest, whether caused by crime or racial conflict or fear of internal subversion, this basic law and the values that it represents may appear unrealistic or 'extravagant' to some. But the values were those of the authors of our fundamental constitutional concepts."

Rights secured by the Fourth Amendment are particularly difficult to protect because their "advocates are usually criminals." But the rules "we fashion [are] for the innocent and guilty alike." By replacing *Aguilar* and *Spinelli* with a test that provides no assurance that magistrates, rather than the police, or informants, will make determinations of probable cause; imposes no structure on magistrates' probable cause inquiries; and invites the possibility that intrusions may be justified on less than reliable information from an honest or credible person, today's decision threatens to "obliterate one of the most fundamental distinctions between our form of government, where officers are under the law, and the police-state where they are the law."

Justice STEVENS, with whom Justice BRENNAN joins, dissenting.

The fact that Lance and Sue Gates made a 22-hour nonstop drive from West Palm Beach, Florida, to Bloomingdale, Illinois, only a few hours after Lance had flown to Florida provided persuasive evidence that they were engaged in illicit activity. That fact, however, was not known to the magistrate when he issued the warrant to search their home.

What the magistrate did know at that time was that the anonymous informant had not been completely accurate in his or her predictions. The informant had indicated that "Sue drives their car to Florida *where she leaves it to be loaded up with drugs. . . . Sue flies back after she drops the car off in Florida.*" (emphasis added). Yet Detective Mader's affidavit reported that she "left the West Palm Beach area driving the Mercury northbound."

The discrepancy between the informant's predictions and the facts known to Detective Mader is significant for three reasons. First, it cast doubt on the informant's hypothesis that the Gates already had "over $100,000 worth of drugs in their basement," The informant had predicted an itinerary that always kept one spouse in Bloomingdale, suggesting that the Gates did not want to leave their home unguarded because something valuable was hidden within. That inference obviously could not be drawn when it was known that the pair was actually together over a thousand miles from home. Second, the discrepancy made the Gates' conduct seem substantially less unusual than the informant had predicted it would be.

It would have been odd if, as predicted, Sue had driven down to Florida on Wednesday, left the car, and flown right back to Illinois. But the mere facts that Sue was in West Palm Beach with the car,[1] that she was joined by her husband at the Holiday Inn on Friday,[2] and that the couple drove north together the next morning[3] are neither unusual nor probative of criminal activity. Third, the fact that the anonymous letter contained a material mistake undermines the reasonableness of relying on it as a basis for making a forcible entry into a private home.[4]

Of course, the activities in this case did not stop when the magistrate issued the warrant. The Gates drove all night to Bloomingdale, the officers searched the car and found 400 pounds of marijuana, and then they searched the house. However, none of these subsequent events may be considered in evaluating the warrant, and the search of the house was legal only if the warrant was valid. I cannot accept the Court's casual conclusion that, *before the Gates arrived in Bloomingdale,* there was probable cause to justify a valid entry and search of a private home. No one knows who the informant in this case was, or what motivated him or her to write the note. Given that the note's predictions were faulty in one significant respect, and were corroborated by nothing except ordinary innocent activity, I must surmise that the Court's evaluation of the warrant's validity has been colored by subsequent events.[7]

Although the foregoing analysis is determinative as to the house search, the car search raises additional issues because "there is a constitutional difference between houses and cars." An officer who has probable cause to suspect that a highly movable automobile contains contraband does not need a valid warrant in order to search it. In a fact-bound inquiry of this sort, the judgment of three levels of state courts, all of whom are better able to evaluate the probable reliability of anonymous informants in Bloomingdale, Illinois, than we are, should be entitled to at least a presumption of accuracy.[8] I would simply vacate the judgment of the Illinois Supreme Court and remand the case for reconsideration in the light of our intervening decision in *United States v. Ross,* 476 U.S. 798 (1982).

---

[1] The anonymous note suggested that she was going down on Wednesday, but for all the officers knew she had been in Florida for a month.

[2] Lance does not appear to have behaved suspiciously in flying down to Florida. He made a reservation in his own name and gave an accurate home phone number to the airlines. Cf. *Florida v. Royer,* 460 U.S. 491, 493 (1983); *United States v. Mendenhall,* 446 U.S. 544, 548 (1980) (Stewart, J., announcing the judgment). And Detective Mader's affidavit does not report that he did any of the other things drug couriers are notorious for doing, such as paying for the ticket in cash, *Royer,* dressing casually, *ibid.,* looking pale and nervous, *ibid.*; *Mendenhall,* improperly filling out baggage tags, *Royer,* carrying American Tourister luggage, ibid., not carrying any luggage, *Mendenhall* (Powell, J., concurring in part and concurring in the judgment), or changing airlines en route, *ibid.*

[3] Detective Mader's affidavit hinted darkly that the couple had set out upon "that interstate highway commonly used by travelers to the Chicago area." But the same highway is also commonly used by travelers to Disney World, Sea World, and Ringling Brothers and Barnum and Bailey Circus World. It is also the road to Cocoa Beach, Cape Canaveral, and Washington, D.C. I would venture that each year dozens of perfectly innocent people fly to Florida, meet a waiting spouse, and drive off together in the family car.

[4] The Court purports to rely on the proposition that "if the [anonymous] informant could predict with *considerable accuracy the somewhat unusual travel plans* of the Gateses, he probably also had a reliable basis for his statements that the Gateses kept a large quantity of drugs in their home." (emphasis added). Even if this syllogism were sound, but see *Spinelli* (White, J., concurring), its premises are not met in this case.

---

[7] *Draper* affords no support for today's holding. That case did not involve an anonymous informant. On the contrary, as the Court twice noted, Mr. Hereford was "employed for that purpose and [his] information had always been found accurate and reliable." In this case, the police had no prior experience with the informant, and some of his or her information in this case was unreliable and inaccurate.

[8] The Court holds that what were heretofore considered two independent "prongs" — "veracity" and "basis of knowledge" — are now to be considered together as circumstances whose totality must be appraised. "A deficiency in one may be compensated for, in determining the overall reliability of a tip, by a strong showing as to the other, or by some other indicia of reliability." Yet in this case, the lower courts found neither factor present. And the supposed "other indicia" in the affidavit take the form of activity that is not particularly remarkable. I do not understand how the Court can find that the "totality" so far exceeds the sum of its "circumstances."

## QUESTIONS AND NOTES

**1.** Of the four opinions, two (Rehnquist and Stevens) would discard *Spinelli* (or at least ignore it), and two (White and Brennan) would retain it. One of each group found probable cause in *Gates* (Rehnquist and White), and one of each group found no probable cause (Brennan and Stevens). Does this breakdown suggest that whether to retain *Spinelli* is much ado about nothing?

**2.** Which of the four opinions (if any) would you have joined had you been on the Court? Why?

**3.** Do you agree with Justice Rehnquist's admonition that the most important job of a constitutional jurist is "to hold the balance true?" Which Justice do you think did the best job of that?

**4.** What does probable cause mean after *Gates*? Did it mean something different before *Gates*?

**5.** Should *Draper* control *Gates*? Why? Why not?

**6.** Should information from anonymous (in the sense of unknown) informants be entitled to much weight in the probable cause determination? Would (should) the adoption of a test that severely limited their weight be subject to criticism on that account?

**7.** If the magistrate had not found probable cause in *Gates*, what could the police have done? Does your answer suggest that a warrant should not have been issued in this case?

**8.** Are we more or less secure as a populace after *Gates* than we were before? Explain.

**9.** The breadth of the *Gates* decision is explored in *Upton*.

### Massachusetts v. Upton
### 466 U.S. 727 (1984)

PER CURIAM.

Last Term, in *Gates,* we held that the Fourth Amendment's requirement of probable cause for the issuance of a warrant is to be applied, not according to a fixed and rigid formula, but rather in the light of the "totality of the circumstances" made known to the magistrate. We also emphasized that the task of a reviewing court is not to conduct a *de novo* determination of probable cause, but only to determine whether there is substantial evidence in the record supporting the magistrate's decision to issue the warrant. In this case, the Supreme Judicial Court of Massachusetts, interpreting the probable cause requirement of the Fourth Amendment to the United States Constitution, continued to rely on the approach set forth in cases such as *Aguilar* and *Spinelli.* Since this approach was rejected in *Gates,* we grant the petition for certiorari in this case and reverse the judgment of the Supreme Judicial Court.

At noon on September 11, 1980, Lt. Beland of the Yarmouth Police Department assisted in the execution of a search warrant for a motel room reserved by one Richard Kelleher at the Snug Harbor Motel in West Yarmouth. The search produced several items of identification, including credit cards, belonging to two persons whose homes had recently been burglarized. Other items taken in the burglaries, such as jewelry, silver and gold, were not found at the motel.

At 3:20 p.m. on the same day, Lt. Beland received a call from an unidentified female who told him that there was "a motor home full of stolen stuff" parked behind 5 Jefferson Ave., the home of respondent George Upton and his mother. She stated that the stolen items included jewelry, silver and gold. As set out in Lt. Beland's affidavit in support of a search warrant:

"She further stated that George Upton was going to move the motor home any time now because of the fact that Ricky Kelleher's motel room was raided and that George Upton had purchased these stolen items from Ricky Kelleher. This unidentified female stated that she had seen the stolen items but refused to identify herself because 'he'll kill me,' referring to George Upton. I then told this unidentified female that I knew who she was, giving her the name of Lynn Alberico, who I had met on May 16, 1980, at George Upton's repair shop off Summer St., in Yarmouthport. She was identified to me by George Upton as being his girlfriend, Lynn Alberico. The unidentified female admitted that she was the girl that I had named, stating that she was surprised that I knew who she was. She then told me that she'd broken up with George Upton and wanted to burn him. She also told me that she wouldn't give me her address or phone number but that she would contact me in the future, if need be.''

Following the phone call, Lt. Beland went to Upton's house to verify that a motor home was parked on the property. Then, while other officers watched the premises, Lt. Beland prepared the application for a search warrant, setting out all the information noted above in an accompanying affidavit. He also attached the police reports on the two prior burglaries, along with lists of the stolen property. A magistrate issued the warrant, and a subsequent search of the motor home produced the items described by the caller and other incriminating evidence. The discovered evidence led to Upton's conviction on multiple counts of burglary, receiving stolen property, and related crimes. On appeal to the Supreme Judicial Court, respondent argued that the search warrant was not supported by a sufficient showing of "probable cause" under the Fourth Amendment. With respect to our *Gates* opinion, that court said:

"It is not clear that the *Gates* opinion has announced a significant change in the appropriate Fourth Amendment treatment of applications for search warrants. Looking at what the Court did on the facts before it, and rejecting an expansive view of certain general statements not essential to the decision, we conclude that the *Gates* opinion deals principally with what corroboration of an informant's tip, not adequate by itself, will be sufficient to meet probable cause standards."

Prior to *Gates*, the Fourth Amendment was understood by many courts to require strict satisfaction of a "two-pronged test" whenever an affidavit supporting the issuance of a search warrant relies on an informant's tip. The Massachusetts court apparently viewed *Gates* as merely adding a new wrinkle to this two-pronged test: where an informant's veracity and/or basis of knowledge are not sufficiently clear, substantial corroboration of the tip may save an otherwise invalid warrant.

Turning to the facts of this case, the Massachusetts court reasoned, first, that the basis of the informant's knowledge was not "forcefully apparent" in the affidavit. Although the caller stated that she had seen the stolen items and that they were in the motor home, she did not specifically state that she saw them in the motor home. Second, the court concluded that "[n]one of the common bases for determining the credibility of an informant or the reliability of her information is present here." The caller was not a "tried and true" informant, her statement was not against penal interest, and she was not an "ordinary

citizen" providing information as a witness to a crime. "She was an anonymous informant, and her unverified assent to the suggestion that she was Lynn Alberico does not take her out of that category."

Finally, the court felt that there was insufficient corroboration of the informant's tip to make up for its failure to satisfy the two-pronged test. The facts that tended to corroborate the informant's story were that the motor home was where it was supposed to be, that the caller knew of the motel raid which took place only three hours earlier, and that the caller knew the name of Upton and his girlfriend. But, much as the Supreme Court of Illinois did in the opinion we reviewed in *Gates*, the Massachusetts court reasoned that each item of corroborative evidence either related to innocent, non-suspicious conduct or related to an event that took place in public. To sustain the warrant, the court concluded, more substantial corroboration was needed. The court therefore held that the warrant violated the Fourth Amendment to the United States Constitution and reversed respondent's convictions.

We noted in *Gates* that "the 'two-pronged test' has encouraged an excessively technical dissection of informants' tips, with undue attention being focused on isolated issues that cannot sensibly be divorced from the other facts presented to the magistrate." This, we think, is the error of the Massachusetts court in this case. The court did not consider Lt. Beland's affidavit in its entirety, giving significance to each relevant piece of information and balancing the relative weights of all the various indicia of reliability (and unreliability) attending the tip. Instead, the court insisted on judging bits and pieces of information in isolation against the artificial standards provided by the two-pronged test.

The Supreme Judicial Court also erred in failing to grant any deference to the decision of the magistrate to issue a warrant. Instead of merely deciding whether the evidence viewed as a whole provided a "substantial basis" for the magistrate's finding of probable cause, the court conducted a *de novo* probable cause determination. We rejected just such after-the-fact, *de novo* scrutiny in *Gates*.

Examined in light of *Gates*, Lt. Beland's affidavit provides a substantial basis for the issuance of the warrant. No single piece of evidence in it is conclusive. But the pieces fit neatly together and, so viewed, support the magistrate's determination that there was "a fair probability that contraband or evidence of crime" would be found in Upton's motor home. The informant claimed to have seen the stolen goods and gave a description of them which tallied with the items taken in recent burglaries. She knew of the raid on the motel room—which produced evidence connected to those burglaries—and that the room had been reserved by Kelleher. She explained the connection between Kelleher's motel room and the stolen goods in Upton's motor home. And she provided a motive both for her attempt at anonymity—fear of Upton's retaliation—and for furnishing the information—her recent breakup with Upton and her desire "to burn him."

The Massachusetts court dismissed Lt. Beland's identification of the caller as a mere "unconfirmed guess." But "probable cause does not demand the certainty we associate with formal trials." Lt. Beland noted that the caller "admitted that she was the girl I had named, stating that she was surprised that I knew who she was." It is of course possible that the caller merely adopted Lt. Beland's suggestion as "a convenient cover for her true identity." But given the caller's admission, her obvious knowledge of who Alberico was and how she was connected with Upton, and her explanation of her motive in calling, Lt. Beland's inference appears stronger than a mere uninformed and unconfirmed guess. It is enough that the inference was a reasonable one and conformed with the other pieces of evidence making up the total showing of probable cause.

In concluding that there was probable cause for the issuance of this warrant, the magistrate can hardly be accused of approving a mere "hunch" or a bare recital of legal conclusions. The informant's story and the surrounding facts possessed an internal coherence that gave weight to the whole. Accordingly, we conclude that the information contained in Lt. Beland's affidavit provided a sufficient basis for the "practical, common-sense decision" of the magistrate. "Although in a particular case it may not be easy to determine when an affidavit demonstrates the existence of probable cause, the resolution of doubtful or marginal cases in this area should be largely determined by the preference to be accorded warrants."

The judgment of the Supreme Judicial Court of Massachusetts is reversed, and the case is remanded for further proceedings not inconsistent with this opinion.

Justice STEVENS, concurring in the judgment.

In my opinion the judgment of the Supreme Judicial Court of Massachusetts reflects an error of a more fundamental character than the one this Court corrects today. It rested its decision on the Fourth Amendment to the United States Constitution without telling us whether the warrant was valid as a matter of Massachusetts law.[1] It has thereby increased its own burdens as well as ours. For when the case returns to that court, it must then review the probable cause issue once again and decide whether or not a violation of the state constitutional protection against unreasonable searches and seizures has occurred. If such a violation did take place, much of that court's first opinion and all of this Court's opinion are for naught. If no such violation occurred, the second proceeding in that court could have been avoided by a ruling to that effect when the case was there a year ago.

It must be remembered that for the first century of this nation's history, the Bill of Rights of the Constitution of the United States was solely a protection for the individual in relation to federal authorities. State constitutions protected the liberties of the people of the several States from abuse by state authorities. The Bill of Rights is now largely applicable to state authorities and is the ultimate guardian of individual rights. The States in our federal system, however, remain the primary guardian of the liberty of the people. The Massachusetts court, I believe, ignored this fundamental premise of our constitutional system of government. In doing so, it made an ill-advised entry into the federal domain.

Accordingly, I concur in the Court's judgment.

Justice BRENNAN and Justice MARSHALL dissent from the summary disposition of this case and would deny the petition for certiorari.

---

[1] Indeed, that court rather pointedly refused to consider whether the search violated the provisions of Art. 14 of the Massachusetts Declaration of Rights. It stated, in part:

"If we have correctly construed the significance of *Gates*, the Fourth Amendment standards for determining probable cause to issue a search warrant have not been made so much less clear and so relaxed as to compel us to try our hand at a definition of standards under art. 14. If we have misassessed the consequences of the *Gates* opinion and in fact the *Gates* standard proves to be unacceptably shapeless and permissive, this court may have to define the protections guaranteed to the people against unreasonable searches and seizures by art. 14, and the consequences of the violation of those protections."

## QUESTIONS AND NOTES

**1.** Was *Upton* a stronger or weaker case for probable cause than *Gates*?

**2.** Was the potential mobility of the motor home a factor in finding probable cause? Should it have been?

**3.** Was the fact that the caller claimed to want to "burn" George, a point in favor of or against the finding of probable cause?

**4.** As we shall now see, *Upton* was ultimately resolved in accordance with Justice Stevens suggestion: the State Constitution. Although *Upton* presents us with our first opportunity to consider state constitutions or state laws as providing more protection than the Federal Constitution, it is a possibility that no good defense attorney should overlook and of which no good prosecutor should be unaware. Indeed as Justice Stevens suggested, perhaps it should be the first resort of state courts and defense attorneys.

### Commonwealth v. Upton
### 476 N.E. 2d 548 (Mass. 1985)

WILKINS, Justice.

We consider the defendant's State law challenges to the denial of his motions to suppress evidence seized pursuant to a search warrant. When this case was before us for the first time, we concluded that the search was unreasonable in violation of the Fourth Amendment to the Constitution of the United States because there was no demonstrated probable cause to issue the search warrant. In a per curiam opinion, the Supreme Court of the United States reversed our judgment, concluding that there was a proper showing of probable cause under the "totality of the circumstances" test articulated in *Gates*. The Supreme Court remanded the case to us for further proceedings consistent with its opinion.

We must now consider what standard art. 14 of the Declaration of Rights of the Constitution of the Commonwealth prescribes for determining the existence of probable cause.[6] We have equated the word

"cause" in art. 14 with the words "probable cause." *Commmonwealth v. Dana,* 2 Met. 329 (1841). In each case, the basic question for the magistrate is whether he has a substantial basis for concluding that any of the articles described in the warrant are probably in the place to be searched. Strong reason to suspect is not adequate.[7] Concerning search warrants for allegedly stolen property, we have said that the affidavit must "contain enough information for an issuing magistrate to determine that the items sought are related to the criminal activity under investigation, and that they reasonably may be expected to be located in the place to be searched."

The Commonwealth argues that art. 14 requires no more than is required by the Fourth Amendment as construed and implemented by the Supreme Court of the United States in *Gates* and *Upton.* By this view, the question whether probable cause exists is to be determined according to the "totality of the circumstances." The defendant, on the other hand, urges us to express a stricter standard for the determination of probable cause, specifically arguing that under art. 14 we should require a showing similar to that required by the Supreme Court of the United States before its adoption of the "flexible" standard of the *Gates* case.

This court has understandably had little occasion to

---

[6] Article 14 provides: "Every subject has a right to be secure from all unreasonable searches, and seizures, of his person, his houses, his papers, and all his possessions. All warrants, therefore, are contrary to this right, if the cause or foundation of them be not previously supported by oath or affirmation; and if the order in the warrant to a civil officer, to make search in suspected places, or to arrest one or more suspected persons, or to seize their property, be not accompanied with a special designation of the persons or objects of search, arrest, or seizure: and no warrant ought to be issued but in cases, and with the formalities prescribed by the laws."

[7] We do not know whether the Supreme Court of the United States intended a lower definition of probable cause when in *Gates,* it used words such as "fair probability" and "substantial chance."

determine what art. 14 requires be shown to a magistrate in order to constitute probable cause. When the Fourth Amendment became applicable to the States through the Fourteenth Amendment, the battle over the existence of probable cause to issue a warrant came to be fought on Federal constitutional turf. Defendants simply raised the Federal issues to the substantial exclusion of arguments based on the State law.

As a practical matter, therefore, cases involving probable cause questions did not call for consideration of any State constitutional question. Nor did our earlier opinion in this case appear to call for such a consideration. There we erroneously concluded that the Federal constitutional principles expressed in *Gates* required the exclusion of the seized evidence. We simply failed to perceive that the Supreme Court could permit a test for probable cause as "'flexible' and 'easily applied'" as the fluid *Gates* standard has turned out to be.

The Constitution of the Commonwealth preceded and is independent of the Constitution of the United States. In fact, portions of the Constitution of the United States are based on provisions in the Constitution of the Commonwealth, and this has been thought to be particularly true of the relationship between the Fourth Amendment and art. 14. In particular situations, on similar facts, we have reached different results under the State Constitution from those that were reached by the Supreme Court of the United States under the Federal Constitution. On occasion, the differences can be explained because of different language in the two Constitutions. On the other hand, in deciding similar constitutional questions, the two courts have reached contrary results based on differences of opinion concerning the application of similar constitutional principles.

Although we have never afforded more substantive protection to criminal defendants under art. 14 of the Declaration of Rights than prevails under the Constitution of the United States, on several occasions we have recognized the possibility of doing so. [W]e have had no appropriate occasion to consider what standard of probable cause is required by art. 14.

We conclude that art. 14 provides more substantive protection to criminal defendants than does the Fourth Amendment in the determination of probable cause. We reject the "totality of the circumstances" test now espoused by a majority of the United States Supreme Court. That standard is flexible, but is also "unacceptably shapeless and permissive." The Federal test lacks the precision that we believe can and should be articulated in stating a test for determining probable cause. The "totality of the circumstances" test is used in deciding several constitutional questions, but it has been applied where no more definite,

universal standard could reasonably be developed.

In the area of probable cause to issue a search warrant, specific and worthwhile standards can be articulated, as opinions of the Supreme Court prior to *Gates* have demonstrated. "Clear lines defining constitutionally permissible conduct are most desirable to guide the police, magistrates, prosecutors, defense counsel, and judges." We thus reject the "totality of the circumstances" test as the appropriate standard for determining that probable cause which must be shown under art. 14.

We conclude instead that the principles developed under *Aguilar* and *Spinelli*, if not applied hypertechnically, provide a more appropriate structure for probable cause inquiries under art. 14.

Each prong of the *Aguilar-Spinelli* test—the basis of knowledge and the veracity of the informant—presents an independently important consideration. We have said that independent police corroboration can make up for deficiencies in either or both prongs of the *Aguilar-Spinelli* test. We reiterate today, however, that each element of the test must be separately considered and satisfied or supplemented in some way.

The test we adopt has been followed successfully by the police in this Commonwealth for approximately twenty years. It is a test that aids lay people, such as the police and certain magistrates, in a way that the "totality of the circumstances" test never could. We believe it has encouraged and will continue to encourage more careful police work and thus will tend to reduce the number of unreasonable searches conducted in violation of art. 14. We reject the argument that the higher standard will cause police to avoid seeking search warrants. We have no sense, and certainly we have no factual support for the proposition, that in recent years police in this Commonwealth have risked conducting warrantless searches because of the unreasonable strictures of the *Aguilar-Spinelli* test.

We also do not believe that the *Aguilar-Spinelli* test has interfered or will interfere with the deference that a reviewing court should show to the issuing magistrate's determination. "Once a magistrate has determined that he has information before him that he can reasonably say has been obtained in a reliable way by a credible person, he has ample room to use his common sense and to apply a practical, nontechnical conception of probable cause." In this Commonwealth, we have always urged reviewing courts to "be slow to jettison" warrants which exhibit such a commonsense approach.

Finally, we note that the number of cases in which evidence has been suppressed because of a failure to follow the requirements of the *Aguilar-Spinelli* test has not been substantial in relation to the number of challenges made to the adequacy of applications for search warrants. And, of course, there is no way to document the salutary circumstance that numerous unreasonable searches were never made because of the application of the *Aguilar-Spinelli* test. We conclude, therefore, that the *Aguilar-Spinelli* test, as modified by our earlier decision in this case, is the standard for determining probable cause under art. 14.

*Probable cause in this case.*

Pursuant to the appropriate standard, we must undertake an analysis of the affidavit presented in support of the warrant to search the motor home. We apply the *Aguilar-Spinelli* standard, with the modification we thought had been made in the *Gates* opinion. We also acknowledge that our attitude is not and should not be a grudging or negative one and that we should give great deference to the magistrate's determination of probable cause. We grant that the question is a close one.

Probable cause was not shown on the affidavit in this case. In our earlier opinion we concluded that the basis of the informant's knowledge was narrowly established, even though the reason why she believed the stolen property to be in the motor home was not presented. The veracity of the informant, however, was not shown. Anyone who might conclude that the veracity of the informant was demonstrated would have to place substantial credence in the unknown informant's uncorroborated statements as self-verifying. To paraphrase our earlier opinion, "[i]f the affidavit in the case before us were to be upheld, [art. 14 of the Declaration of Rights] would be weakened to the level of permitting the search of any person's premises based on a telephone tip from an anonymous informer who told a story connecting those premises with the fact of a recent police search of a third person's room on premises to which the public had access." The probability of a link between the search of the motel room and the motor home was not shown, as it could have been if other information known to the police had been set forth in the affidavit (particularly the fact that a wallet containing identification of Upton's wife had been found in the motel room).

*Conclusion.*

In our earlier opinion, we noted that, apart from the evidence seized from the motor home, "there was other evidence to support the defendant's conviction on at least some of the charges against him." The case is, therefore, remanded to the Superior Court subject to the same orders that we previously entered.

## QUESTIONS AND NOTES

**1.** Is there anything in the language of the two constitutional provisions (Mass. & U.S.) that warrants a different result?

**2.** Is the fact that the Massachusetts Constitution predated the U.S. Constitution relevant to the resolution of the case? Suppose the Massachusetts provision had been adopted in 1900? In 1980?

**3.** Is the Massachusetts Supreme Court essentially thumbing its nose at the U.S. Supreme Court? Is that anyway for a state court to act? Explain your thinking fully.

# 3.

# THE NEED FOR A WARRANT

In chapter 1, we briefly examined the importance of having a Fourth Amendment that limits the power of the police. In chapter 2, we examined probable cause which can be conceived as the substantive heart of the Fourth Amendment. In this chapter, our focus is on the need for a warrant which procedurally is (sometimes) thought to be the heart of the Fourth Amendment.

The first question upon which we should focus is the procedural value of requiring a warrant *before* a policeman commences a search. Before considering the cases, try to think of all of the values served by requiring a warrant.

## A.   Is The Warrant Requirement The Exception Or The Rule?

It is sometimes not easy to determine whether the Court requires a warrant subject to a limited number of exceptions, or does not require a warrant unless the particular search is singled out as one subject to the warrant requirement. *Vale, Chambers,* and *Chadwick* are three substantially contemporaneous efforts to deal with the problem. Understanding the Court's thinking in these cases is a good starting point for comprehending that which follows.

### Vale v. Louisiana
### 399 U.S. 30 (1970)

Mr. Justice STEWART delivered the opinion of the Court.

The appellant, Donald Vale, was convicted in a Louisiana court on a charge of possessing heroin and was sentenced as a multiple offender to 15 years' imprisonment at hard labor. The Louisiana Supreme Court affirmed the conviction, rejecting the claim that evidence introduced at the trial was the product of an unlawful search and seizure.

The evidence adduced at the pretrial hearing on a motion to suppress showed that on April 24, 1967, officers possessing two warrants for Vale's arrest and having information that he was residing at a specified address proceeded there in an unmarked car and set up a surveillance of the house. The evidence of what then took place was summarized by the Louisiana Supreme Court as follows:

"After approximately 15 minutes the officers observed a green 1958 Chevrolet drive up and sound the horn and after backing into a parking place, again blew the horn. At this juncture Donald Vale, who was well known to Officer Brady having arrested him twice in the previous month, was seen coming out of the house and walking up to the passenger side of the Chevrolet where he had a close brief conversation with the driver; and after looking up and down the street returned inside of the house. Within a few minutes he reappeared on the porch, and again cautiously looked up and down the street before proceeding to the passenger side of the Chevrolet, leaning through the window. From this the officers were convinced a narcotics sale had taken place. They returned to their car and immediately drove toward Donald Vale, and as they reached within approximately three cars lengths from the accused, (Donald Vale) he looked up and, obviously recognizing the officers, turned around, walking quickly toward the house. At the same time the driver of the Chevrolet started to make his get away when the car was blocked by the police vehicle. The three officers promptly alighted from the car, whereupon Officers Soule and Laumann called to Donald Vale to stop as he reached the front steps of the house, telling him he was under arrest. Officer Brady at the same time, seeing the driver of the Chevrolet, Arizzio Saucier, whom the officers knew to be a narcotic addict, place something hurriedly in his mouth, immediately placed him under arrest and joined his co-officers. Because of the transaction they had just observed they, informed Donald Vale they were going to search the house, and thereupon advised him of his constitutional rights. After they all entered the front room, Officer Laumann made a cursory inspection of the house to ascertain if anyone else was present and within about three minutes Mrs. Vale and James Vale, mother and brother of Donald Vale, returned home carrying groceries and were informed of the arrest and impending search."

The search of a rear bedroom revealed a quantity of narcotics.

"Belief, however well founded, that an article sought is concealed in a dwelling house furnishes no justification for a search of that place without a warrant." That basic rule "has never been questioned in this Court."

The Louisiana Supreme Court thought the search independently supportable because it involved narcotics, which are easily removed, hidden, or destroyed. It would be unreasonable, the Louisiana court concluded, "to require the officers under the facts of the case to first secure a search warrant before searching the premises, as time is of the essence inasmuch as the officers never know whether there is anyone on the premises to be searched who could very easily destroy the evidence." Such a rationale could not apply to the present case, since by their own account the arresting officers satisfied themselves that no one else was in the house when they first entered the premises. But entirely apart from that point, our past decisions make clear that only in "a few specifically established and well-delineated" situations, may a warrantless search of a dwelling withstand constitutional scrutiny, even though the authorities have probable cause to conduct it. The burden rests on the State to show the existence of such an exceptional situation. And the record before us discloses none.

There is no suggestion that anyone consented to the search. The officers were not responding to an emergency. They were not in hot pursuit of a fleeing felon. The goods ultimately seized were not in the process of destruction. Nor were they about to be removed from the jurisdiction.

The officers were able to procure two warrants for Vale's arrest. They also had information that he was residing at the address where they found him. There is thus no reason, so far as anything before us appears, to suppose that it was impracticable for them to obtain a search warrant as well. We decline to hold that an arrest on the street can provide its own "exigent circumstance" so as to justify a warrantless search of the arrestee's house.

Accordingly, the judgment is reversed and the case is remanded to the Louisiana Supreme Court for further proceedings not inconsistent with this opinion.

Mr. Justice BLACK, with whom THE CHIEF JUSTICE joins, dissenting.

The Fourth Amendment to the United States Constitution prohibits only "unreasonable searches." A warrant has never been thought to be an absolute requirement for a constitutionally proper search. Searches, whether with or without a warrant, are to be judged by whether they are reasonable, and, as I said, speaking for the Court in *Preston v. United States,* 376 U.S. 364, 366-367 (1964), common sense dictates that reasonableness varies with the circumstances of the search. The Louisiana Supreme Court held not only that the police action here was reasonable but also that failure to conduct an immediate search would have been unreasonable. With that view I am in complete agreement, for the following reasons.

From Vale's behavior the officers were convinced that a narcotics transaction was taking place at that very moment. The police placed both Vale and Saucier under arrest.

At this point the police had probable cause to believe that Vale was engaged in a narcotics transfer, and that a supply of narcotics would be found in the house, to which Vale had returned after his first conversation, from which he had emerged furtively bearing what the police could readily deduce was a supply of narcotics, and toward which he hurried after seeing the police. But the police did not know then who else might be in the house. Vale's arrest took place near the house, and anyone observing from inside would surely have been alerted to destroy the stocks of contraband which the police believed Vale had left there. The police had already seen Saucier, the narcotics addict, apparently swallow what Vale had given him. Believing that some evidence had already been destroyed and that other evidence might well be, the police were faced with the choice of risking the immediate destruction of evidence or entering the house and conducting a search. I cannot say that their decision to search was unreasonable. Delay in order to obtain a warrant would have given an accomplice just the time he needed.

That the arresting officers did, in fact, believe that others might be in the house is attested to by their actions upon entering the door left open by Vale. The police at once checked the small house to determine if anyone else was present. Just as they discovered the house was empty, however, Vale's mother and brother arrived. Now what had been a suspicion became a certainty: Vale's relatives were in possession and knew of his arrest. To have abandoned the search at this point, and left the house with Vale, would not have been the action of reasonable police officers.

[T]he circumstances here were sufficiently exceptional to justify a search. The Court recognizes that searches to prevent the destruction or removal of evidence have long been held reasonable by this Court.

The Court, however, finds the search here unreasonable. First, the Court suggests that the contraband was not "in the process of destruction." None of the cases cited by the Court supports the proposition that "exceptional circumstances" exist only when the process of destruction has already begun. On the contrary we implied that those circumstances did exist when "evidence or contraband was threatened with removal or destruction."

Second, the Court seems to argue that the search was unreasonable because the police officers had time to obtain a warrant. I agree that the opportunity to obtain a warrant is one of the factors to be weighed in determining reasonableness. But the record conclusively shows that there was no such opportunity here. As I noted above, once the officers had observed Vale's conduct in front of the house they had probable cause to believe that a felony had been committed and that immediate action was necessary. At no time after the events in front of Mrs. Vale's house would it have been prudent for the officers to leave the house in order to secure a warrant.

The Court asserts, however, that because the police obtained two warrants for Vale's arrest there is "no reason . . . to suppose that it was impracticable for them to obtain a search warrant as well." The difficulty is that the two arrest warrants on which the Court seems to rely so heavily were not issued because of any present misconduct of Vale's; they were issued because the bond had been increased for an earlier narcotics charge then pending against Vale. When the police came to arrest Vale, they knew only that his bond had been increased. There is nothing in the record to indicate that, absent the increased bond, there would have been probable cause for an arrest, much less a search. Probable cause for the search arose for the first time when the police observed the activity of Vale and Saucier in and around the house.

I do not suggest that all arrests necessarily provide the basis for a search of the arrestee's house. In this case there is far more than a mere street arrest. The police also observed Vale's use of the house as a base of operations for his commercial business, his attempt to return hurriedly to the house on seeing the officers, and the apparent destruction of evidence by the man with whom Vale was dealing. Furthermore the police arrival and Vale's arrest were plainly visible to anyone within the house, and the police had every reason to believe that someone in the house was likely to destroy the contraband if the search were postponed.

This case raises most graphically the question how does a policeman protect evidence necessary to the State if he must leave the premises to get a warrant, allowing the evidence he seeks to be destroyed. The Court's answer to that question makes unnecessarily difficult the conviction of those who prey upon society.

## QUESTIONS AND NOTES

**1.** Is the Court saying that search warrants are (nearly) always required, or only that they are (nearly) always required when dealing with houses? If the latter, what is so special about a house?

**2.** Do you think that there were exigent circumstances in this case? As between Stewart and Black, who has the more powerful argument on this point?

**3.** What should the police have done to secure the situation? Would it have been better if they had denied Vale's relatives access to their own home pending a warrant? Why? Why not?

**4.** If it were possible to radio for a warrant (as it is in some locales), should the police have been required to do that? (note: *Vale* seems predicated on the assumption that the police would have to drive downtown to obtain a warrant.)

**5.** *Chambers,* decided the same day as *Vale*, clearly indicates that the importance of a warrant may well depend on what is being searched.

## Chambers v. Maroney
### 399 U.S. 42 (1970)

Mr. Justice WHITE delivered the opinion of the Court.

The principal question in this case concerns the admissibility of evidence seized from an automobile, in which petitioner was riding at the time of his arrest, after the automobile was taken to a police station and was there thoroughly searched without a warrant. The Court of Appeals for the Third Circuit found no violation of petitioner's Fourth Amendment rights. We affirm.

I

During the night of May 20, 1963, a Gulf service station in North Braddock, Pennsylvania, was robbed by two men, each of whom carried and displayed a gun. The robbers took the currency from the cash register; the service station attendant, one Stephen Kovacich, was directed to place the coins in his right-hand glove, which was then taken by the robbers. Two teenagers, who had earlier noticed a blue compact station wagon circling the block in the vicinity of the Gulf station, then saw the station wagon speed away from a parking lot close to the Gulf station. About the same time, they learned that the Gulf station had been robbed. They reported to police, who arrived immediately, that four men were in the station wagon and one was wearing a green sweater. Kovacich told the police that one of the men who robbed him was wearing a green sweater and the other was wearing a trench coat. A description of the car and the two robbers was broadcast over the police radio. Within an hour, a light blue compact station wagon answering the description and carrying four men was stopped by the police about two miles from the Gulf station. Petitioner was one of the men in the station wagon. He was wearing a green sweater and there was a trench coat in the car. The occupants were arrested and the car was driven to the police station. In the course of a thorough search of the car at the station, the police found concealed in a compartment under the dashboard two .38-caliber revolvers (one loaded with dumdum bullets), a right-hand glove containing small change, and certain cards bearing the name of Raymond Havicon, the attendant at a Boron service station in McKeesport, Pennsylvania, who had been robbed at gunpoint on May 13, 1963. In the course of a warrant-authorized search of petitioner's home the day after petitioner's arrest, police found and seized certain .38-caliber ammunition, including some dumdum bullets similar to those found in one of the guns taken from the station wagon.

II

In terms of the circumstances justifying a warrantless search, the Court has long distinguished between an automobile and a home or office. In *Carroll v. United States*, 267 U.S. 132 (1925), the issue was the admissibility in evidence of contraband liquor seized in a warrantless search of a car on the highway. After surveying the law from the time of the adoption of the Fourth Amendment onward, the Court held that automobiles and other conveyances may be searched without a warrant in circumstances that would not justify the search without a warrant of a house or an office, provided that there is probable cause to believe that the car contains articles that the officers are entitled to seize. The Court expressed its holding as follows:

"We have made a somewhat extended reference to these statutes to show that the guaranty of freedom from unreasonable searches and seizures by the Fourth Amendment has been construed, practically since the beginning of the government, as recognizing a necessary difference between a search of a store, dwelling house, or other structure in respect of which a proper official warrant readily may be obtained and a search of a ship, motor boat, wagon, or automobile for contraband goods, where it is not practicable to secure a warrant, because the vehicle can be quickly moved out of the locality or jurisdiction in which the warrant must be sought.

"The measure of legality of such a seizure is that the seizing officer shall have reasonable or probable cause for believing that the automobile which he stops and seizes has contraband liquor therein which is being illegally transported."

Neither *Carroll* nor other cases in this Court require or suggest that in every conceivable circumstance the search of an auto even with probable cause may be made without the extra protection for privacy that a warrant affords. But the circumstances that furnish probable cause to search a particular auto for particular articles are most often unforeseeable; moreover, the opportunity to search is fleeting since a car is readily movable. Where this is true, as in *Carroll* and the case before us now, if an effective search is to be made at any time, either the search must be made immediately without a warrant or the car itself must be seized and held without a warrant for whatever period is necessary to obtain a warrant for the search.[9]

In enforcing the Fourth Amendment's prohibition against unreasonable searches and seizures, the Court has insisted upon probable cause as a minimum requirement for a reasonable search permitted by the Constitution. As a general rule, it has also required the judgment of a magistrate on the probable-cause issue and the issuance of a warrant before a search is made. Only in exigent circumstances will the judgment of the police as to probable cause serve

as a sufficient authorization for a search. *Carroll* holds a search warrant unnecessary where there is probable cause to search an automobile stopped on the highway; the car is movable, the occupants are alerted, and the car's contents may never be found again if a warrant must be obtained. Hence an immediate search is constitutionally permissible.

Arguably, because of the preference for a magistrate's judgment, only the immobilization of the car should be permitted until a search warrant is obtained; arguably, only the "lesser" intrusion is permissible until the magistrate authorizes the "greater." But which is the "greater" and which the "lesser" intrusion is itself a debatable question and the answer may depend on a variety of circumstances. For constitutional purposes, we see no difference between on the one hand seizing and holding a car before presenting the probable cause issue to a magistrate and on the other hand carrying out an immediate search without a warrant. Given probable cause to search, either course is reasonable under the Fourth Amendment.

On the facts before us, the blue station wagon could have been searched on the spot when it was stopped since there was probable cause to search and it was a fleeting target for a search. The probable-cause factor still obtained at the station house and so did the mobility of the car unless the Fourth Amendment permits a warrantless seizure of the car and the denial of its use to anyone until a warrant is secured. In that event there is little to choose in terms of practical consequences between an immediate search without a warrant and the car's immobilization until a warrant is obtained.[10] The same consequences may not follow where there is unforeseeable cause to search a house. Compare *Vale*. But as *Carroll* held, for the purposes of the Fourth Amendment there is a constitutional difference between houses and cars.

Mr. Justice HARLAN, dissenting in part.

In sustaining the search of the automobile I believe the Court ignores the framework of our past decisions circumscribing the scope of permissible search without a warrant. The Court has long read the Fourth Amendment's proscription of "unreasonable" searches as imposing a general principle that

---

[9] Following the car until a warrant can be obtained seems an impractical alternative since, among other things, the car may be taken out of the jurisdiction. Tracing the car and searching it hours or days later would of course permit instruments or fruits of crime to be removed from the car before the search.

[10] It was not unreasonable in this case to take the car to the station house. All occupants in the car were arrested in a dark parking lot in the middle of the night. A careful search at that point was impractical and perhaps not safe for the officers, and it would serve the owner's convenience and the safety of his car to have the vehicle and the keys together at the station house.

a search without a warrant is not justified by the mere knowledge by the searching officers of facts showing probable cause. The "general requirement that a search warrant be obtained" is basic to the Amendment's protection of privacy, and "the burden is on those seeking [an] exemption . . . to show the need for it."

Where officers have probable cause to search a vehicle on a public way, a limited exception to the warrant requirement is reasonable because "the vehicle can be quickly moved out of the locality or jurisdiction in which the warrant must be sought." Because the officers might be deprived of valuable evidence if required to obtain a warrant before effecting any search or seizure, I agree with the Court that they should be permitted to take the steps necessary to preserve evidence and to make a search possible. The Court holds that those steps include making a warrantless search of the entire vehicle on the highway — a conclusion reached by the Court in *Carroll* without discussion — and indeed appears to go further and to condone the removal of the car to the police station for a warrantless search there at the convenience of the police. I cannot agree that this result is consistent with our insistence in other areas that departures from the warrant requirement strictly conform to the exigency presented.

The Court concedes that the police could prevent removal of the evidence by temporarily seizing the car for the time necessary to obtain a warrant. It does not dispute that such a course would fully protect the interests of effective law enforcement; rather it states that whether temporary seizure is a "lesser" intrusion than warrantless search "is itself a debatable question and the answer may depend on a variety of circumstances."[8] I believe it clear that a warrantless search involves the greater sacrifice of Fourth Amendment values.

The Fourth Amendment proscribes, to be sure, unreasonable "seizures" as well as "searches." However, in the circumstances in which this problem is likely to occur, the lesser intrusion will almost always be the simple seizure of the car for the period — perhaps a day — necessary to enable the officers to obtain a search warrant. In the first place, as this case shows, the very facts establishing probable cause to search will often also justify arrest of the occupants of the vehicle. Since the occupants themselves are to be taken into custody, they will suffer minimal further inconvenience from the temporary immobilization of their vehicle. Even where no arrests are made, persons who wish to avoid a search — either to protect their privacy or to conceal incriminating evidence — will almost certainly prefer a brief loss of the use of the vehicle in exchange for the opportunity to have a magistrate pass upon the justification for the search. To be sure, one can conceive of instances in which the occupant, having nothing to hide and lacking concern for the privacy of the automobile, would be more deeply offended by a temporary immobilization of his vehicle than by a prompt search of it. However, such a person always remains free to consent to an immediate search, thus avoiding any delay. Where consent is not forthcoming, the occupants of the car have an interest in privacy that is protected by the Fourth Amendment even where the circumstances justify a temporary seizure. The Court's endorsement of a warrantless invasion of that privacy where another course would suffice is simply inconsistent with our repeated stress on the Fourth Amendment's mandate of "adherence to judicial processes."[9]

---

[8] The Court, unable to decide whether search or temporary seizure is the "lesser" intrusion, in this case authorizes both. The Court concludes that it was reasonable for the police to take the car to the station, where they searched it once to no avail. The searching officers then entered the station, interrogated petitioner and the car's owner, and returned later for another search of the car — this one successful. At all times the car and its contents were secure against removal or destruction. Nevertheless the Court approves the searches without even an inquiry into the officers' ability promptly to take their case before a magistrate.

[9] Circumstances might arise in which it would be impracticable to immobilize the car for the time required to obtain a warrant — for example, where a single police officer must take arrested suspects to the station, and has no way of protecting the suspects' car during his absence. In such situations it might be wholly reasonable to perform an on-the-spot search based on probable cause. However, where nothing in the situation makes impracticable the obtaining of a warrant, I cannot join the Court in shunting aside that vital Fourth Amendment safeguard.

## QUESTIONS AND NOTES

**1.** Is the Court saying that an automobile on the highway is *per se* exigent, or is it saying that exigency is not necessary in regard to automobiles?

**2.** Assuming that there would have been an exigency had the search been undertaken on the highway, how could there have been one when the car was locked in the impound lot? Are we to take seriously the Court's concern about denying access of the car to anyone pending a warrant? To whom did the Court think access was denied?

**3.** Might the Court have had some other concern? If so, what?

**4.** Were *Vale* and *Chambers* both wrongly decided in that the Court overlooked a real exigency in *Vale* and made up a phony exigency in *Chambers*?

**5.** The question of whether *Vale* or *Chambers* was the basic rule was answered, at least temporarily, in *Chadwick*.

## United States v. Chadwick
### 433 U.S. 1 (1977)

Mr. Chief Justice BURGER delivered the opinion of the Court.

We granted certiorari in this case to decide whether a search warrant is required before federal agents may open a locked footlocker which they have lawfully seized at the time of the arrest of its owners, when there is probable cause to believe the footlocker contains contraband.

On May 8, 1973, Amtrak railroad officials in San Diego observed respondents Gregory Machado and Bridget Leary load a brown footlocker onto a train bound for Boston. Their suspicions were aroused when they noticed that the trunk was unusually heavy for its size, and that it was leaking talcum power, a substance often used to mask the odor of marihuana or hashish. Because Machado matched a profile used to spot drug traffickers, the railroad officials reported these circumstances to federal agents in San Diego, who in turn relayed the information, together with detailed descriptions of Machado and the footlocker, to their counterparts in Boston.

When the train arrived in Boston two days later, federal narcotics agents were on hand. Though the officers had not obtained an arrest or search warrant, they had with them a police dog trained to detect marihuana. The agents identified Machado and Leary and kept them under surveillance as they claimed their suitcases and the footlocker, which had been transported by baggage cart from the train to the departure area. Machado and Leary lifted the footlocker from the baggage cart, placed it on the floor and sat down on it.

The agents then released the dog near the footlocker. Without alerting respondents, the dog signaled the presence of a controlled substance inside. Respondent Chadwick then joined Machado and Leary, and they engaged an attendant to move the footlocker outside to Chadwick's waiting automobile. Machado, Chadwick, and the attendant together lifted the 200-pound footlocker into the trunk of the car, while Leary waited in the front seat. At that point, while the trunk of the car was still open and before the car engine had been started, the officers arrested all three. A search disclosed no weapons, but the keys to the footlocker were apparently taken from Machado.

Respondents were taken to the Federal Building in Boston; the agents followed with Chadwick's car and the footlocker. As the Government concedes, from the moment of respondents' arrests at about 9 p.m., the footlocker remained under the exclusive control of law enforcement officers at all times. The footlocker and luggage were placed in the Federal Building, where, as one of the agents later testified, "there was no risk that whatever was contained in the footlocker trunk would be removed by the defendants or their associates." The agents had no reason to believe that the footlocker contained explosives or other inherently dangerous items, or that it contained evidence which would lose its value unless the footlocker were opened at once. Facilities were readily available in which the footlocker could have been stored securely; it is not contended that there was any exigency calling for an immediate search.

At the Federal Building an hour and a half after

the arrests, the agents opened the footlocker and luggage. They did not obtain respondents' consent; they did not secure a search warrant. The footlocker was locked with a padlock and a regular trunk lock. It is unclear whether it was opened with the keys taken from respondent Machado, or by other means. Large amounts of marihuana were found in the footlocker.

Drawing on its reading of history, the Government argues that only homes, offices, and private communications implicate interests which lie at the core of the Fourth Amendment. Accordingly, it is only in these contexts that the determination whether a search or seizure is reasonable should turn on whether a warrant has been obtained. In all other situations, the Government contends, less significant privacy values are at stake, and the reasonableness of a government intrusion should depend solely on whether there is probable cause to believe evidence of criminal conduct is present. Where personal effects are lawfully seized outside the home on probable cause, the Government would thus regard searches without a warrant as not "unreasonable."

We do not agree that the Warrant Clause protects only dwellings and other specifically designated locales. As we have noted before, the Fourth Amendment "protects people, not places," *Katz v. United States*, 389 U.S. 347, 351 (1967); more particularly, it protects people from unreasonable government intrusions into their legitimate expectations of privacy. In this case, the Warrant Clause makes a significant contribution to that protection. The question, then, is whether a warrantless search in these circumstances was unreasonable.

It cannot be doubted that the Fourth Amendment's commands grew in large measure out of the colonists' experience with the writs of assistance and their memories of the general warrants formerly in use in England. These writs, which were issued on executive rather than judicial authority, granted sweeping power to customs officials and other agents of the King to search at large for smuggled goods. Though the authority to search granted by the writs was not limited to the home, searches conducted pursuant to them often were carried out in private residences.

Although the searches and seizures which deeply concerned the colonists, and which were foremost in the minds of the Framers, were those involving invasions of the home, it would be a mistake to conclude, as the Government contends, that the Warrant Clause was therefore intended to guard only against intrusions into the home. First, the Warrant Clause does not in terms distinguish between searches conducted in private homes and other searches. There is also a strong historical connection between the Warrant Clause and the initial clause of the Fourth Amendment, which draws no distinctions among "persons, houses, papers, and effects" in safeguarding against unreasonable searches and seizures.

Moreover, if there is little evidence that the Framers intended the Warrant Clause to operate outside the home, there is no evidence at all that they intended to exclude from protection of the Clause all searches occurring outside the home. The absence of a contemporary outcry against warrantless searches in public places was because, aside from searches incident to arrest, such warrantless searches were not a large issue in colonial America. Thus, silence in the historical record tells us little about the Framers' attitude toward application of the Warrant Clause to the search of respondents' footlocker. What we do know is that the Framers were men who focused on the wrongs of that day but who intended the Fourth Amendment to safeguard fundamental values which would far outlast the specific abuses which gave it birth.

The judicial warrant has a significant role to play in that it provides the detached scrutiny of a neutral magistrate, which is a more reliable safeguard against improper searches than the hurried judgment of a law enforcement officer "engaged in the often competitive enterprise of ferreting out crime." *Johnson v. United States,* 333 U.S. 10, 14 (1948). Once a lawful search has begun, it is also far more likely that it will not exceed proper bounds when it is done pursuant to a judicial authorization "particularly describing the place to be searched and the persons or things to be seized." Further, a warrant assures the individual whose property is searched or seized of the lawful authority of the executing officer, his need to search, and the limits of his power to search. *Camara v. Municipal Court*, 387 U.S. 523 (1967).

Just as the Fourth Amendment "protects people, not places," the protections a judicial warrant offers against erroneous governmental intrusions are effective whether applied in or out of the home. Accordingly, we have held warrantless searches unreasonable, and therefore unconstitutional, in a variety of settings; *e.g.* electronic interception of conversation in public telephone booth, automobile on private premises, automobile in custody, hotel room, office. These cases illustrate the applicability of the Warrant Clause beyond the narrow limits suggested by the Government. They also reflect the settled constitutional principle that a fundamental purpose of the

Fourth Amendment is to safeguard individuals from unreasonable government invasions of legitimate privacy interests, and not simply those interests found inside the four walls of the home.

In this case, important Fourth Amendment privacy interests were at stake. By placing personal effects inside a double-locked footlocker, respondents manifested an expectation that the contents would remain free from public examination. No less than one who locks the doors of his home against intruders, one who safeguards his personal possessions in this manner is due the protection of the Fourth Amendment Warrant Clause. There being no exigency, it was unreasonable for the Government to conduct this search without the safeguards a judicial warrant provides.

## QUESTIONS AND NOTES

**1.** Does the text of the Fourth Amendment support a heavy presumption in favor of warrants? Why? Why not?

**2.** Assuming that the text and history are ambiguous, do policy reasons support an expansive or restrictive view of the warrant requirement? What are the relevant policy reasons?

## B.   Who Can Issue A Warrant?

To some extent, the value of warrants depends on the qualifications of those who are empowered to issue them. In *Coolidge* and *Shadwick,* the Court evaluated somewhat different challenges to the competence of the warrant issuer.

### Coolidge v. New Hampshire
### 403 U.S. 443 (1971)

Mr. Justice STEWART delivered the opinion of the Court.

Pamela Mason, a 14-year-old girl, left her home in Manchester, New Hampshire, on the evening of January 13, 1964, during a heavy snowstorm, apparently in response to a man's telephone call for a babysitter. Eight days later, after a thaw, her body was found by the site of a major north-south highway several miles away. She had been murdered. The event created great alarm in the area, and the police immediately began a massive investigation.

On January 28, having learned from a neighbor that the petitioner, Edward Coolidge, had been away from home on the evening of the girl's disappearance, the police went to his house to question him. They asked him, among other things, if he owned any guns, and he produced three, two shotguns and a rifle. They also asked whether he would take a lie-detector test concerning his account of his activities on the night of the disappearance. He agreed to do so on the following Sunday, his day off. The police later described his attitude on the occasion of this visit as fully "cooperative." His wife was in the house throughout the interview.

During the ensuing two and a half weeks, the State accumulated a quantity of evidence to support the theory that it was he who had killed Pamela Mason. On February 19, the results of the investigation were presented at a meeting between the police officers working on the case and the State Attorney General, who had personally taken charge of all police activities relating to the murder, and was later to serve as chief prosecutor at the trial. At this meeting, it was decided that there was enough evidence to justify the arrest of Coolidge on the murder charge and a search of his house and two cars. At the conclusion of the meeting, the Manchester police chief made formal application, under oath, for the arrest and search warrants. The complaint supporting the warrant for a search of Coolidge's Pontiac automobile, the only warrant that concerns us here, stated that the affiant "has probable cause to suspect and believe, and does suspect and believe, and herewith offers satisfactory evidence, that there are certain objects and things used in the Commission of said offense, now kept, and concealed in or upon a certain vehicle, to wit: 1951 Pontiac two-door sedan. . . .'' The warrants were then signed and issued by the Attorney General himself, acting as a justice of the peace. Under New Hampshire law in force at that time, all justices of the peace were authorized to issue search warrants.

The police arrested Coolidge in his house on the day the warrant issued. Mrs. Coolidge asked whether she might remain in the house with her small child, but was told that she must stay elsewhere, apparently in part because the police believed that she would be harassed by reporters if she were accessible to them. When she asked whether she might take her car, she was told that both cars had been ''impounded,'' and that the police would provide transportation for her. Some time later, the police called a towing company, and about two and a half hours after Coolidge had been taken into custody the cars were towed to the police station. It appears that at the time of the arrest the cars were parked in the Coolidge driveway, and that although dark had fallen they were plainly visible both from the street and from inside the house where Coolidge was actually arrested. The 1951 Pontiac was searched and vacuumed on February 21, two days after it was seized, again a year later, in January 1965, and a third time in April 1965.

At Coolidge's subsequent jury trial on the charge of murder, vacuum sweepings, including particles of gun powder, taken from the Pontiac were introduced in evidence against him, as part of an attempt by the State to show by microscopic analysis that it was highly probable that Pamela Mason had been in Coolidge's car.

The petitioner's first claim is that the warrant authorizing the seizure and subsequent search of his 1951 Pontiac automobile was invalid because not issued by a ''neutral and detached magistrate.'' Since we agree with the petitioner that the warrant was invalid for this reason, we need not consider his further argument that the allegations under oath supporting the issuance of the warrant were so conclusory as to violate relevant constitutional standards. Cf. *Aguilar v. Texas,* 378 U.S. 108.

The classic statement of the policy underlying the warrant requirement of the Fourth Amendment is that of Mr. Justice Jackson, writing for the Court in *Johnson v. United States,* 333 U.S. 10, 13-14;

''The point of the Fourth Amendment, which often is not grasped by zealous officers, is not that it denies law enforcement the support of the usual inferences which reasonable men draw from evidence. Its protection consists in requiring that those inferences be drawn by a neutral and detached magistrate instead of being judged by the officer engaged in the often competitive enterprise of ferreting out crime. Any assumption that evidence sufficient to support a magistrate's disinterested determination to issue a search warrant will justify the officers in making a search without a warrant would reduce the Amendment to a nullity and leave the people's homes secure only in the discretion of police officers. When the right of privacy must reasonably yield to the right of search is, as a rule, to be decided by a judicial officer, not by a policeman or Government enforcement agent.''

In this case, the determination of probable cause was made by the chief ''government enforcement agent'' of the State—the Attorney General—who was actively in charge of the investigation and later was to be chief prosecutor at the trial. To be sure, the determination was formalized here by a writing bearing the title ''Search Warrant,'' whereas in *Johnson* there was no piece of paper involved, but the State has not attempted to uphold the warrant on any such artificial basis. Rather, the State argues that the Attorney General, who was unquestionably authorized as a justice of the peace to issue warrants under then existing state law, did in fact act as a ''neutral and detached magistrate.'' Further, the State claims that any magistrate, confronted with the showing of probable cause made by the Manchester chief of police, would have issued the warrant in question. To the first proposition it is enough to answer that there could hardly be a more appropriate setting than this for a *per se* rule of disqualification rather than a case-by-case evaluation of all the circumstances. Without disrespect to the state law enforcement agent here involved, the whole point of the basic rule so well expressed by Mr. Justice Jackson is that prosecutors and policemen simply cannot be asked to maintain the requisite neutrality with regard to their own investigations—the ''competitive enterprise'' that must rightly engage their single-minded attention.[3] As for the proposition that the existence of probable cause renders noncompliance with the warrant procedure an irrelevance, it is enough to cite *Agnello v. United States,* 269 U.S. 20, 33, decided in 1925:

''Belief, however well founded, that an article

---

[3] After hearing the Attorney General's testimony on the issuance of the warrants, the trial judge said: ''I found that an impartial Magistrate would have done the same as you did. I don't think, in all sincerity, that I would expect that you could wear two pairs of shoes.''

sought is concealed in a dwelling house, furnishes no justification for a search of that place without a warrant. And such searches are held unlawful notwithstanding facts unquestionably showing probable cause.'' See also *Silverthorne Lumber Co. v. United States,* 251 U.S. 385, 392. (''[T]he rights . . . against unlawful search and seizure are to be protected even if the same result might have been achieved in a lawful way.'') It is urged that the New Hampshire statutes which at the time of the searches here involved permitted a law enforcement officer himself to issue a warrant was one of those ''workable rules governing arrests, searches and seizures to meet 'the practical demands of effective criminal investigation and law enforcement' in the States.''

That such a procedure was indeed workable from the point of view of the police is evident from testimony at the trial in this case:

''The Court: You mean that another police officer issues these (search warrants)?

''The Witness: Yes. Captain Couture and Captain Shea and Captain Loveren are J.P.'s.

''The Court: Well, let me ask you, Chief, your answer is to the effect that you never go out of the department for the Justice of the Peace?

''The Witness: It hasn't been our—policy to go out of the department.

''Q. Right. Your policy and experience, is to have a fellow police officer take the warrant in the capacity of Justice of the Peace?

''A. That has been our practice.''

But it is too plain for extensive discussion that this now abandoned New Hampshire method of issuing ''search warrants'' violated a fundamental premise of both the Fourth and Fourteenth Amendments—a premise fully developed and articulated long [ago]. As Mr. Justice Frankfurter put it in *Wolf v. Colorado,* 338 U.S. 25, 27-28;

''The security of one's privacy against arbitrary intrusion by the police—which is at the core of the Fourth Amendment—is basic to a free society. It is therefore implicit in 'the concept of ordered liberty' and as such enforceable against the States through the Due Process Clause. The knock at the door, whether by day or by night, as a prelude to a search, without authority of law but solely on the authority of the police, did not need the commentary of recent history to be condemned. . . .''

We find no escape from the conclusion that the seizure and search of the Pontiac automobile cannot constitutionally rest upon the warrant issued by the state official who was the chief investigator and prosecutor in this case. Since he was not the neutral and detached magistrate required by the Constitution, the search stands on no firmer ground than if there had been no warrant at all. If the seizure and search are to be justified, they must, therefore, be justified on some other theory.

Justice BLACK, dissenting.

The majority holds that the warrant authorizing the seizure and search of petitioner's automobile was constitutionally defective and void. With respect to search warrants, the Fourth Amendment provides that ''no Warrants shall issue, but upon probable cause, supported by Oath or affirmation, and particularly describing the place to be searched, and the persons or things to be seized.'' The majority concedes that the police did show probable cause for the issuance of the warrant. The majority does not contest that the warrant particularly described the place to be searched, and the thing to be seized.

But compliance with state law and the requirements of the Fourth Amendment apparently is not enough. The majority holds that the state attorney general's connection with the investigation automatically rendered the search warrant invalid. In the first place, there is no language in the Fourth Amendment which provides any basis for the disqualification of the state attorney general to act as a magistrate. He is a state official of high office. The Fourth Amendment does not indicate that his position of authority over state law enforcement renders him ineligible to issue warrants upon a showing of probable cause supported by oath or affirmation. The majority's argument proceeds on the ''little trial'' theory that the magistrate is to sit as a judge and weigh the evidence and practically determine guilt or innocence before issuing a warrant. There is nothing in the Fourth Amendment to support such a magnified view of the magistrate's authority. The state attorney general was not barred by the Fourth Amendment or any other constitutional provision from issuing the warrant.

In the second place, the New Hampshire Supreme Court held in effect that the state attorney general's participation in the investigation of the case at the time he issued the search warrant was ''harmless error'' if it was error at all. I agree. It is difficult to imagine a clearer showing of probable cause. There was no possibility of prejudice because there was no room for discretion. Indeed, it could be said that a refusal to issue a warrant on the showing of probable cause made in this case would have been an abuse of discretion. In light of the showing made by the police, there is no reasonable possibility that the state attorney general's own knowledge of the investigation contributed to the issuance of the warrant. I see no error in the state attorney general's action. But even if there was error, it was harmless beyond reasonable doubt.

## QUESTIONS AND NOTES

**1.** Is there a good reason for disqualifying the attorney general as a magistrate, or is the Court releasing a murderer on a technicality?

**2.** If the attorney general had not been working on this case, could he have issued a warrant? Could a police officer not working on the case issue a warrant? Why? Why not?

**3.** If, as Justice Black suggests, it would have been error for a magistrate *not* to issue a warrant in this case, should the employment of the attorney general as magistrate be deemed harmless error? In general? In this case?

**4.** As *Shadwick* makes clear, a magistrate is not required to have any particular training.

## Shadwick v. Tampa
### 407 U.S. 345 (1972)

Mr. Justice POWELL delivered the opinion of the Court.

The charter of Tampa, Florida, authorizes the issuance of certain arrest warrants by clerks of the Tampa Municipal Court. The sole question in this case is whether these clerks qualify as neutral and detached magistrates for purposes of the Fourth Amendment. We hold that they do.

Appellant was arrested for impaired driving on a warrant issued by a clerk of the municipal court. He moved the court to quash the warrant on the ground that it was issued by a nonjudicial officer in violation of the Fourth and Fourteenth Amendments.

II

Past decisions of the Court have mentioned review by a "judicial officer" prior to issuance of a warrant. In some cases the term "judicial officer" appears to have been used interchangeably with that of "magistrate." In others, it was intended simply to underscore the now accepted fact that someone independent of the police and prosecution must determine probable cause. The very term "judicial officer" implies, of course, some connection with the judicial branch. But it has never been held that only a lawyer or judge could grant a warrant, regardless of the court system or the type of warrant involved. [T]he Court [has] implied that United States Commissioners, many of whom were not lawyers or judges, were nonetheless "independent judicial officers."

The substance of the Constitution's warrant requirements does not turn on the labeling of the issuing party. The warrant traditionally has represented an independent assurance that a search and arrest will not proceed without probable cause to believe that a crime has been committed and that the person or place named in the warrant is involved in the crime. Thus, an issuing magistrate must meet two tests. He must be neutral and detached, and he must be capable of determining whether probable cause exists for the requested arrest or search. This Court long has insisted that inferences of probable cause be drawn by "a neutral and detached magistrate instead of being judged by the officer engaged in the often competitive enterprise of ferreting out crime." In *Coolidge*, the Court last Term voided a search warrant issued by the state attorney general "who was actively in charge of the investigation and later was to be chief prosecutor at trial." If, on the other hand, detachment and capacity do conjoin, the magistrate has satisfied the Fourth Amendment's purpose.

III

The requisite detachment is present in the case at hand. Whatever else neutrality and detachment might entail, it is clear that they require severance and disengagement from activities of law enforcement. There has been no showing whatever here of partiality, or affiliation of these clerks with prosecutors or police. The record shows no connection with any law enforcement activity or authority which would distort the independent judgment the Fourth Amendment requires. Appellant himself expressly refused to allege anything to that effect. The municipal court clerk is assigned not to the police or prosecutor but to the municipal court judge for whom he does much of his work. In this sense, he may well be termed a "judicial officer." While a statutorily specified term of office and appointment by someone other than "an executive authority" might be desirable, the absence of such features is hardly disqualifying. Judges themselves take office under differing circumstances. Some are appointed, but many are elected by legislative bodies or by the people. Many enjoy but limited terms and are subject to re-appointment or re-election. Most depend for their salary level upon the legislative branch. We will not elevate requirements for the independence of a municipal clerk to a level higher than that prevailing with respect to many judges. The clerk's neutrality has not been impeached: he is removed from prosecutor or police and works within the judicial branch subject to the supervision of the municipal court judge.

Appellant likewise has failed to demonstrate that these clerks lack capacity to determine probable cause. The clerk's authority extends only to the issuance of arrest warrants for breach of municipal ordinances. We presume from the nature of the clerk's position that he would be able to deduce from the facts on an affidavit before him whether there was probable cause to believe a citizen guilty of impaired driving, breach of peace, drunkenness, trespass, or the multiple other common offenses covered by a municipal code. There has been no showing that this is too difficult a task for a clerk to accomplish. Our legal system has long entrusted nonlawyers to evaluate more complex and significant factual data than that in the case at hand. Grand juries daily determine probable cause prior to rendering indictments, and trial juries assess whether guilt is proved beyond a reasonable doubt. The significance and responsibility of these lay judgments betray any belief that the Tampa clerks could not determine probable cause for arrest.

Nor need we determine whether a State may lodge warrant authority in someone entirely outside the sphere of the judicial branch. Many persons may not qualify as the kind of "public civil officers" we have come to associate with the term "magistrate." Had the Tampa clerk been entirely divorced from a judicial position, this case would have presented different considerations. Here, however, the clerk is an employee of the judicial branch of the city of Tampa, disassociated from the role of law enforcement. On the record in this case, the independent status of the clerk cannot be questioned.

What we do reject today is any *per se* invalidation of a state or local warrant system on the ground that the issuing magistrate is not a lawyer or judge. Communities may have sound reasons for delegating the responsibility of issuing warrants to competent personnel other than judges or lawyers. Many municipal courts face stiff and unrelenting caseloads. A judge pressured with the docket before him may give warrant applications more brisk and summary treatment than would a clerk. All this is not to imply that a judge or lawyer would not normally provide the most desirable review of warrant requests. But our federal system warns of converting desirable practice into constitutional commandment. It recognizes in plural and diverse state activities one key to national innovation and vitality. States are entitled to some flexibility and leeway in their designation of magistrates, so long as all are neutral and detached and capable of the probable-cause determination required of them.

We affirm the judgment of the Florida Supreme Court.

## QUESTIONS AND NOTES

**1.** Would (should) it matter that these clerks are limited to issuing misdemeanor warrants? Would you expect the same result if they could issue a search warrant in felony cases?

**2.** How does (should) the educational non-requirement of these magistrates affect the *Gates* debate about the desirability of specific guidelines to constrain magistrates?

**3.** How close can the relationship be between magistrate and police officer? Suppose they are located in the same building? The same suite of offices? They regularly go to lunch together?

**4.** If the magistrate doesn't read the warrant before signing it, should it be invalid *per se*?

**5.** As we will see in *Connally*, the limits on who can serve as a magistrate remain substantial.

# Connally v. Georgia
## 429 U.S. 245 (1977)

PER CURIAM:

Appellant John Connally was indicted, tried, and convicted in the Superior Court of Walker County, Ga., for possession of marihuana in violation of the Georgia Controlled Substances Act, Ga. Code Ann. § 79A-801 et seq. (1973). On his appeal to the Supreme Court of Georgia, he asserted trial error in the constitutional impropriety of the fee system governing the issuance of search warrants by justices of the peace in Georgia.

Pursuant to a search warrant issued by a justice of the peace, appellant's house was raided and marihuana found there was seized. Connally was arrested. At his trial he moved to suppress the evidence so seized on the ground that the justice who had issued the warrant was not "a neutral and detached magistrate" because he had a pecuniary interest in issuing the warrant. The trial court denied that motion, and the Supreme Court of Georgia, in affirming, rejected the constitutional challenge.

Under Ga. Code Ann. § 24-1601 (1971), the fee for the issuance of a search warrant by a Georgia justice of the peace "shall be" $5, "and it shall be lawful for said [justice] of the peace to charge and collect the same." If the requested warrant is refused, the justice of the peace collects no fee for reviewing and denying the application. The fee so charged apparently goes into county funds and from there to the issuing justice as compensation.

At a pretrial hearing in Connally's case, the issuing justice testified on cross-examination that he was a justice primarily because he was "interested in a livelihood;" that he received no salary; that his compensation was "directly dependent on how many warrants" he issued; that since January 1, 1973, he had issued "some 10,000" warrants for arrests or searches; and that he had no legal background other than attendance at seminars and reading law.

Fifty years ago, in *Tumey v. Ohio,* 273 U.S. 510 (1927), the Court considered state statutes that permitted a charge of violating the State's prohibition laws to be tried without a jury before a village mayor. Any fine imposed was divided between the State and the village. The latter's share was used to hire attorneys and detectives to arrest offenders and prosecute them before the mayor. When the mayor convicted, he received fees and costs, and these were in addition to his salary. The Court, in an opinion by Mr. Chief Justice Taft, unanimously held that subjecting a defendant to trial before a judge having "a direct, personal, pecuniary interest in convicting the defendant," that is, in the $12 of fees and costs imposed, effected a denial of due process in violation of the Fourteenth Amendment.

This approach was reiterated in *Ward v. Village of Monroeville,* 409 U.S. 57. There, an Ohio statute authorized mayors to sit as judges of ordinance violations and certain traffic offenses. The petitioner was so convicted and fined by the mayor of Monroeville. Although the mayor had no direct personal financial stake in the outcome of cases before him, a major portion of the village's income was derived from the fines, fees, and costs imposed in the mayor's court. This Court, id., at 59-60, cited *Tumey* and repeated the test formulated in that case, namely, "whether the mayor's situation is one 'which would offer a possible temptation to the average man as a judge to forget the burden of proof required to convict the defendant, or which might lead him not to hold the balance nice, clear, and true between the State and the accused.'"

The present case, of course, is not precisely the same as *Tumey* or as *Ward,* but the principle of those cases, we conclude, is applicable to the Georgia system for the issuance of search warrants by justices of the peace. The justice is not salaried. He is paid, so far as search warrants are concerned, by receipt of the fee prescribed by statute for his *issuance* of the warrant, and he receives nothing for his *denial* of the warrant. His financial welfare, therefore is enhanced by positive action and is not enhanced by negative action. The situation, again, is one which offers "a possible temptation to the average man as a judge . . . or which might lead him not to hold the balance nice, clear and true between the State and the accused." It is, in other words, another situation where the defendant is subjected to what surely is judicial action by an officer of a court who has "a direct, personal, substantial, pecuniary interest" in his conclusion to issue or to deny the warrant.

*Shadwick* does not weigh to the contrary. The issue there centered in the qualification of municipal court clerks to issue arrest warrants for breaches of ordinances. The Court held that the clerks, although laymen, worked within the judicial branch under the supervision of judges and were qualified to determine the existence of probable cause. They were, therefore, "neutral and detached magistrates for purposes of the Fourth Amendment." There was no element of personal financial gain in the clerks' issuance or nonissuance of arrest warrants. Cf. *Coolidge.*

We disagree with the Supreme Court of Georgia's rulings, that the amount of the search warrant fee is de minimis in the present context, that the unilateral character of the justice's adjudication of probable cause distinguishes the present case from *Tumey,* and that, instead, this case equates with *Bevan v. Krieger,* 289 U.S. 459, 465-466 (1933), where a notary public's fee for taking a deposition was measured by the folios of testimony taken.

We therefore hold that the issuance of the search warrant by the justice of the peace in Connally's case effected a violation of the protections afforded him by the Fourth and Fourteenth Amendments of the United States Constitution. The judgment of the Supreme Court of Georgia is vacated, and the case is remanded for further proceedings not inconsistent with this opinion.

## QUESTIONS AND NOTES

**1.** Why was it so obvious to the Court that *Tumey* and *Ward,* rather than *Bevan* controlled this case? Do you agree?

# 4.

# ARRESTS

In this chapter, our focus is on the rules applicable to arrest. In part A, we explore the general rule that permits arrests without warrants. We follow that in part B with an examination of the right to a post-arrest probable cause hearing for those arrested without warrants. In part C, we consider the right of the state to hold an arrested, but presumptively innocent, person pending trial. Part D considers the need for a warrant for an in-the-house arrest. Part E examines the force that the Fourth Amendment permits the police to use in effectuating an arrest. Finally part F explores the items that may be seized in the course of an arrest.

## A. The Paradigm

In reading *Watson,* evaluate the reasons for not requiring an arrest warrant.

### United States v. Watson
### 423 U.S. 411 (1976)

Mr. Justice WHITE delivered the opinion of the Court.

This case presents questions under the Fourth Amendment as to the legality of a warrantless arrest and of an ensuing search of the arrestee's automobile carried out with his purported consent.

The relevant events began on August 17, 1972, when an informant, one Khoury, telephoned a postal inspector informing him that respondent Watson was in possession of a stolen credit card and had asked Khoury to cooperate in using the card to their mutual advantage. On five to 10 previous occasions Khoury had provided the inspector with reliable information on postal inspection matters, some involving Watson. Later that day Khoury delivered the card to the inspector. On learning that Watson had agreed to furnish additional cards, the inspector asked Khoury to arrange to meet with Watson. Khoury had been instructed that if Watson had additional stolen credit cards, Khoury was to give a designated signal. The signal was given, the officers closed in, and Watson was forthwith arrested. He was removed from the restaurant to the street where he was given the warnings required by *Miranda v. Arizona,* 384 U.S. 436 (1966). A search having revealed that Watson had no credit cards on his person, the inspector asked if he could look inside Watson's car, which was standing within view. Watson said, "Go ahead," and repeated these words when the inspector cautioned that "(I)f I find anything, it is going to go against you." Using keys furnished by Watson, the inspector entered the car and found under the floor mat an envelope containing two credit cards in the names of other persons. These cards were the basis for two counts of a four-count indictment charging Watson with possessing stolen mail in violation of 18 U.S.C. § 1708.

Title 18 U.S.C. § 3061(a)(3) expressly empowers the Board of Governors of the Postal Service to authorize Postal Service officers and employees "performing duties related to the inspection of postal matters" to

> "make arrests without warrant for felonies cognizable under the laws of the United States if they have reasonable grounds to believe that the person to be arrested has committed or is committing such a felony."

Section 3061 represents a judgment by Congress that it is not unreasonable under the Fourth Amendment for postal inspectors to arrest without a warrant provided they have probable cause to do so. This was not an isolated or quixotic judgment of the legislative branch. Other federal law enforcement officers have been expressly authorized by statute for many years to make felony arrests on probable cause but without a warrant.

Because there is a "strong presumption of constitutionality due to an Act of Congress, especially when it turns on what is 'reasonable,'" "[o]bviously the Court should be reluctant to decide that a search thus authorized by Congress was unreasonable and that the Act was therefore unconstitutional." Moreover, there is nothing in the Court's prior cases indicating that under the Fourth Amendment a warrant is required to make a valid arrest for a felony. Indeed, the relevant prior decisions are uniformly to the contrary.

The cases construing the Fourth Amendment thus reflect the ancient common-law rule that a peace officer was permitted to arrest without a warrant for a misdemeanor or felony committed in his presence as well as for a felony not committed in his presence if there was reasonable ground for making the arrest. This has also been the prevailing rule under state constitutions and statutes. "The rule of the common law, that a peace officer or a private citizen may arrest a felon without a warrant, has been generally held by the courts of the several States to be in force in cases of felony punishable by the civil tribunals."

Because the common-law rule authorizing arrests without a warrant generally prevailed in the States, it is important for present purposes to note that in 1792 Congress invested United States marshals and their deputies with "the same powers in executing the laws of the United States, as sheriffs and their deputies in the several states have by law, in executing the laws of their respective states." The Second Congress thus saw no inconsistency between the Fourth Amendment and legislation giving United States marshals the same power as local peace officers to arrest for a felony without a warrant. That provision, however, was supplemented in 1935 by § 504a of the Judicial Code, which expressly empowered marshals to make felony arrests without warrant and on probable cause.

The balance struck by the common law in generally authorizing felony arrests on probable cause, but without a warrant, has survived substantially intact. It appears in almost all of the States in the form of express statutory authorization.

Law enforcement officers may find it wise to seek arrest warrants where practicable to do so, and their judgments about probable cause may be more readily accepted where backed by a warrant issued by a magistrate. But we decline to transform this judicial preference into a constitutional rule when the judgment of the Nation and Congress has for so long been to authorize warrantless public arrests on probable cause rather than to encumber criminal prosecutions with endless litigation with respect to the existence of exigent circumstances, whether it was practicable to get a warrant, whether the suspect was about to flee, and the like.

Watson's arrest did not violate the Fourth Amendment, and the Court of Appeals erred in holding to the contrary.

Justice POWELL, concurring.

Respondent was arrested without a warrant in a public restaurant six days after postal inspectors learned from a reliable source that he possessed stolen credit cards in violation of 18 U.S.C. § 1708. The Government made no effort to show that circumstances precluded the obtaining of a warrant, relying instead for the validity of the arrest solely upon the showing of probable cause to believe that respondent had committed a felony. Respondent contends, and the Court of Appeals held, that the absence of any exigency justifying the failure to procure a warrant renders this arrest violative of the Fourth Amendment.

In reversing the Court of Appeals, the Court concludes that nothing in our previous cases involving warrantless arrests supports the position of respondent and the Court of Appeals. But it is fair to say, I think, that the prior decisions of the Court have assumed the validity of such arrests without addressing in a reasoned way the analysis advanced by respondent. Today's decision is the first square holding that the Fourth Amendment permits a duly authorized law enforcement officer to make a warrantless arrest in a public place even though he had adequate opportunity to procure a warrant after developing probable cause for arrest.

On its face, our decision today creates a certain anomaly. There is no more basic constitutional rule in the Fourth Amendment area than that which makes a warrantless search unreasonable except in a few "jealously and carefully drawn" exceptional circumstances. On more than one occasion this Court has rejected an argument that a law enforcement officer's own probable cause to search a private place for contraband or evidence of crime should excuse his otherwise unexplained failure to procure a warrant beforehand.

Since the Fourth Amendment speaks equally to both searches and seizures, and since an arrest, the taking hold of one's person, is quintessentially a seizure, it would seem that the constitutional provision should impose the same limitations upon arrests that it does upon searches. Indeed, as an abstract matter an argument can be made that the restrictions upon arrest perhaps should be greater. A search may cause only annoyance and temporary inconvenience to the law-abiding citizen, assuming more serious dimension only when it turns up evidence of criminality. An arrest, however, is a serious personal intrusion regardless of whether the person seized is guilty or innocent. Although an arrestee cannot be held for a significant period without some neutral determination that there are grounds to do so, no decision that he should go free can come quickly enough to erase the invasion of his privacy that already will have occurred. Logic therefore would seem to dictate that arrests be subject to the warrant requirement at least to the same extent as searches.

But logic sometimes must defer to history and experience. The Court's opinion emphasizes the historical sanction accorded warrantless felony arrests. In the early days of the common law most felony arrests were made upon personal knowledge and without warrants. So established were such arrests as the usual practice that Lord Coke seriously questioned whether a justice of the peace, receiving his information secondhand instead of from personal knowledge, even could authorize an arrest by warrant. There is no historical evidence that the Framers or proponents of the Fourth Amendment, outspokenly opposed to the infamous general warrants and writs of assistance, were at all concerned about warrantless arrests by local constables and other peace officers. As the Court today notes, the Second Congress' passage of an Act authorizing such arrests so soon after the adoption of the Fourth Amendment itself underscores the probability that the constitutional provision was intended to restrict entirely different practices.

The decision of the Court of Appeals in this case was virtually unprecedented.[3] Of course, no practice that is inconsistent with constitutional protections can be saved merely by appeal to previous uncritical acceptance. But the warrantless felony arrest, long preferred at common law and unimpeached at the passage of the Fourth Amendment, is not such a practice. Given the revolutionary implications of such a holding, a declaration at this late date that warrantless felony arrests are constitutionally infirm would have to rest upon reasons more substantial than a desire to harmonize the rules for arrest with those governing searches.

Moreover, a constitutional rule permitting felony arrests only with a warrant or in exigent circumstances could severely hamper effective law enforcement. Good police practice often requires postponing an arrest, even after probable cause has been established, in order to place the suspect under surveillance or otherwise develop further evidence necessary to prove guilt to a jury. Under the holding of the Court of Appeals such additional investigative work could imperil the entire prosecution. Should the officers fail to obtain a warrant initially, and later be required by unforeseen circumstances to arrest immediately with no chance to procure a last-minute warrant, they would risk a court decision that the subsequent exigency did not excuse their failure to get a warrant in the interim since they first developed probable cause. If the officers attempted to meet such a contingency by procuring a warrant as soon as they had probable cause and then merely held it during their subsequent investigation, they would risk a court decision that the warrant had grown stale

---

[3] Respondent has cited no other decision, state or federal, in support of the Court of Appeals' result in this case. The Government stated in its petition that the decision below was the first of which it was aware that required a warrant for an arrest in a public place.

by the time it was used.[5] Law enforcement personnel caught in this squeeze could ensure validity of their arrests only by obtaining a warrant and arresting as soon as probable cause existed, thereby foreclosing the possibility of gathering vital additional evidence from the suspect's continued actions.

In sum, the historical and policy reasons sketched above fully justify the Court's sustaining of a warrantless arrest upon probable cause, despite the resulting divergence between the constitutional rule governing searches and that now held applicable to seizures of the person.[6]

Mr. Justice MARSHALL, with whom Mr. Justice BRENNAN joins, dissenting.

By granting police broad powers to make warrantless arrests, the Court today sharply reverses the course of our modern decisions construing the Warrant Clause of the Fourth Amendment.

Before addressing what the Court does today, I note what it does not do. It does not decide this case on the narrow question that is presented. That is unfortunate for this is, fundamentally, a simple case.

On the afternoon of August 23, 1972, Awad Khoury, an informant of proved reliability, met with respondent Watson at a public restaurant under the surveillance of two postal inspectors. Khoury was under instructions to light a cigarette as a signal to the watching agents if Watson was in possession of

---

[5] The probable cause to support issuance of an arrest warrant normally would not grow stale as easily as that which supports a warrant to search a particular place for particular objects. This is true because once there is probable cause to believe that someone is a felon the passage of time often will bring new supporting evidence. But in some cases the original grounds supporting the warrant could be disproved by subsequent investigation that at the same time turns up wholly new evidence supporting probable cause on a different theory. In those cases the warrant could be stale because based upon discredited information.

[6] I do not understand today's decision to suggest any retreat from our longstanding position that such an arrest should receive careful judicial scrutiny if challenged. "An arrest without a warrant bypasses the safeguards provided by an objective predetermination of probable cause, and substitutes instead the far less reliable procedure of an after-the-event justification for the arrest . . ., too likely to be subtly influenced by the familiar shortcomings of hindsight judgment."

stolen credit cards. Khoury lit a cigarette, and the postal inspectors moved in, made the arrest, and, ultimately, discovered under the floor mat of Watson's automobile the stolen credit cards that formed the basis of Watson's conviction and this appeal.

The signal of the reliable informant that Watson was in possession of stolen credit cards gave the postal inspectors probable cause to make the arrest. This probable cause was separate and distinct from the probable cause relating to the offense six days earlier, and provided an adequate independent basis for the arrest. Whether or not a warrant ordinarily is required prior to making an arrest, no warrant is required when exigent circumstances are present. When law enforcement officers have probable cause to believe that an offense is taking place in their presence and that the suspect is at that moment in possession of the evidence, exigent circumstances exist. Delay could cause the escape of the suspect or the destruction of the evidence. Accordingly, Watson's warrantless arrest was valid under the recognized exigent-circumstances exception to the warrant requirement, and the Court has no occasion to consider whether a warrant would otherwise be necessary.

Since, for reasons it leaves unexpressed, the Court does not take this traditional course, I am constrained to express my views on the issues it unnecessarily decides.

There is no doubt that by the reference to the seizure of persons, the Fourth Amendment was intended to apply to arrests. Indeed, we have often considered whether arrests were made in conformity with the Fourth Amendment. Admittedly, as the Court observes, some of our decisions make passing reference to the common-law rule on arrests. However, none of the cases cited by the Court, nor any other warrantless arrest case in this Court, mandates the decision announced today. Frequently exigent circumstances were present, so that the warrantless arrest was proper even if a warrant ordinarily may be required. Many cases have invalidated arrests as not based on probable cause, thereby bypassing the need to reach the warrant question. Elsewhere the Court has simply assumed the propriety of the arrest and resolved the case before it on other grounds. And in other cases, the Court noted, but did not reach, the warrantless-arrest issue. In sum, as the case-by-case analysis undertaken by my Brother Powell demonstrates, the dicta relied upon by the Court in support of its decision today are just that dicta. They are no substitute for reasoned analysis of the relationship between the warrant requirement and the law of arrest.

The Court next turns to history. It relies on the

English common-law rule of arrest and the many state and federal statutes following it. There are two serious flaws in this approach. First, as a matter of factual analysis, the substance of the ancient common-law rule provides no support for the far-reaching modern rule that the Court fashions on its model. Second, as a matter of doctrine, the long-standing existence of a Government practice does not immunize the practice from scrutiny under the mandate of our Constitution.

The common-law rule was indeed as the Court states it:

> "[A] peace officer was permitted to arrest without a warrant for a misdemeanor or felony committed in his presence as well as for a felony not committed in his presence if there was reasonable grounds for making the arrest." To apply the rule blindly today, however, makes as much sense as attempting to interpret Hamlet's admonition to Ophelia, "Get thee to a nunnery, go," without understanding the meaning of Hamlet's words in the context of their age.[3] For the fact is that a felony at common law and a felony today bear only slight resemblance, with the result that the relevance of the common-law rule of arrest to the modern interpretation of our Constitution is minimal.

Both at common law and today, felonies find definition in the penal consequences of crime rather than the nature of the crime itself. At common law, as this Court has several times recognized,

> "No crime was considered a felony which did not occasion a total forfeiture of the offender's lands or goods or both."

At present, on the other hand,

> "Any offense punishable by death or imprisonment for a term exceeding one year is a felony." 18 U.S.C. § 1(1).

This difference reflects more than changing notions of penology. It reflects a substantive change in the kinds of crimes called felonies. Only the most serious crimes were felonies at common law, and many crimes now classified as felonies under federal or state law were treated as misdemeanors.

To make an arrest for any of these crimes at

---

[3] Nunnery was Elizabethan slang for house of prostitution. 7 Oxford English Dictionary 264 (1933).

common law, the police officer was required to obtain a warrant, unless the crime was committed in his presence. Since many of these same crimes are commonly classified as felonies today, however, under the Court's holding a warrant is no longer needed to make such arrests, a result in contravention of the common law.

I do not mean by this that a modern warrant requirement should apply only to arrests precisely analogous to common-law misdemeanors, and be inapplicable to analogues of common-law felonies. Rather, the point is simply that the Court's unblinking literalism cannot replace analysis of the constitutional interests involved. While we can learn from the common law, the ancient rule does not provide a simple answer directly transferable to our system. Thus, in considering the applicability of the common-law rule to our present constitutional scheme, we must consider *both* of the rule's two opposing constructs: the presumption favoring warrants, as well as the exception allowing immediate arrests of the most dangerous criminals. The Court's failure to do so, indeed its failure to recognize any tension in the common-law rule at all, drains all validity from its historical analysis.

Lastly, the Court relies on the numerous state and federal statutes codifying the common-law rule. But this, too, is no substitute for reasoned analysis. Our function in constitutional cases is weightier than the Court today suggests: where reasoned analysis shows a practice to be constitutionally deficient, our obligation is to the Constitution, not the Congress.

In sum, the Court's opinion is without foundation. It relies on precedents that are not precedents. It relies on history that offers no clear rule to impose, but only conflicting interests to balance. It relies on statutes that constitute, at best, no more than an aid to construction. The Court never grapples with the warrant requirement of the Fourth Amendment and the cases construing it. It simply announces, by *ipse dixit,* a rule squarely rejecting the warrant requirement we have favored for so long.

My Brother Powell concludes: "[L]ogic . . . would seem to dictate that arrests be subject to the warrant requirement at least to the same extent as searches." I agree.

Given "[t]he history of the use, and not infrequent abuse, of the power to arrest," and the fact that arrests are, in terms, as fully governed by the Fourth Amendment as searches, the logical presumption is that arrests and searches should be treated equally under the Fourth Amendment. Analysis of the interests involved confirms this supposition.

The Court has typically engaged in a two-part

analysis in deciding whether the presumption favoring a warrant should be given effect in situations where a warrant has not previously been clearly required. Utilizing that approach we must now consider (1) whether the privacy of our citizens will be better protected by ordinarily requiring a warrant to be issued before they may be arrested; and (2) whether a warrant requirement would unduly burden legitimate governmental interests.

The first question is easily answered. Of course, the privacy of our citizens will be better protected by a warrant requirement.

We come then to the second part of the warrant test: whether a warrant requirement would unduly burden legitimate law enforcement interests. I believe that the suggested concerns are wholly illusory. Indeed, the argument that a warrant requirement for arrests would be an onerous chore for the police seems somewhat anomalous in light of the Government's concession that ''it is the standard practice of the Federal Bureau of Investigation (FBI) to present its evidence to the United States Attorney, and to obtain a warrant, before making an arrest.'' In the past, the practice and experience of the FBI have been taken as a substantial indication that no intolerable burden would be presented by a proposed rule of procedure. *Miranda v. Arizona,* 384 U.S. 436, 483-486 (1966). There is no reason to accord less deference to the FBI practice here.[13]

The Government's assertion that a warrant requirement would impose an intolerable burden stems, in large part, from the specious supposition that procurement of an arrest warrant would be necessary as soon as probable cause ripens. There is no requirement that a search warrant be obtained the moment police have probable cause to search. The rule is only that present probable cause be shown and a warrant obtained before a search is undertaken. The same rule should obtain for arrest warrants, where it may even make more sense. Certainly, there is less need for prompt procurement of a warrant in the arrest situation. Unlike probable cause to search, probable cause to arrest, once formed will continue to exist for the indefinite future, at least if no intervening exculpatory facts come to light.

Likewise, if in the course of the continued investigation police uncover evidence tying the suspect to another crime, they may immediately arrest him for that crime if exigency demands it, and still be in full conformity with the warrant rule. This is why the arrest in this case was not improper.[15] Other than where police attempt to evade the warrant requirement, the rule would invalidate an arrest only in the obvious situation: where police, with probable cause but without exigent circumstances, set out to arrest a suspect.

In sum, the requirement that officers about to arrest a suspect ordinarily obtain a warrant before they do so does not seem unduly burdensome, at least no more burdensome than any other requirement that law enforcement officials undertake a new procedure in order to comply with the dictates of the Constitution.

---

[13] The *Miranda* Court rejected as irrelevant the argument that the FBI deals with crimes different from those dealt with by state authorities.

[15] Although the postal inspectors here anticipated the occurrence of the second crime, they could not have obtained a warrant for Watson's arrest for that crime until probable cause formed, just moments before the arrest. A warrant based on anticipated facts is premature and void. *United States v. Roberts,* 333 F. Supp. 786 (ED Tenn. 1971).

## QUESTIONS AND NOTES

**1.** Is there anything other than history and deference to Congress to support Justice White's opinion?

**2.** Are either or both of those reasons persuasive?

**3.** Is history too easily manipulated to support one's policy preferences? (Compare White and Marshall opinions)

**4.** How does Justice Powell's opinion differ? Is it more persuasive?

**5.** In general, should arrests be freer from the warrant requirement than searches? Why? Why not?

**6.** Why did Justice Marshall concur?

**7.** Should an arrest for all crimes committed in the officer's presence be exempt from the warrant requirement? Would that have covered *Draper*? *Gates*? *Spinelli*? *Vale*? Anything wrong with that?

## B.    Post-Arrest Probable Cause Hearings

To some extent the question of whether a warrant should be required for all arrests might depend on what happens to an arrestee after she is arrested. That question is explored in *Riverside*.

### Riverside v. McLaughlin
### 111 S.Ct. 1661 (1991)

Justice O'CONNOR delivered the opinion of the Court.

In *Gerstein v. Pugh,* 420 U.S. 103 (1975), this Court held that the Fourth Amendment requires a prompt judicial determination of probable cause as a prerequisite to an extended pretrial detention following a warrantless arrest. This case requires us to define what is "prompt" under *Gerstein*.

The Ninth Circuit joined the Fourth and Seventh Circuits in interpreting *Gerstein* as requiring a probable cause determination immediately following completion of the administrative procedures incident to arrest. By contrast, the Second Circuit understands *Gerstein* to "stres[s] the need for flexibility" and to permit States to combine probable cause determinations with other pretrial proceedings. We granted certiorari to resolve this conflict among the Circuits as to what constitutes a "prompt" probable cause determination under *Gerstein*.

Under *Gerstein*, warrantless arrests are permitted but persons arrested without a warrant must promptly be brought before a neutral magistrate for a judicial determination of probable cause. Significantly, the Court stopped short of holding that jurisdictions were constitutionally compelled to provide a probable cause hearing immediately upon taking a suspect into custody and completing booking procedures. We acknowledged the burden that proliferation of pretrial proceedings places on the criminal justice system and recognized that the interests of everyone involved, including those persons who are arrested, might be disserved by introducing further procedural complexity into an already intricate system. Accordingly, we left it to the individual States to integrate prompt probable cause determinations into their differing systems of pretrial procedures.

Inherent in *Gerstein*'s invitation to the States to experiment and adapt was the recognition that the Fourth Amendment does not compel an immediate determination of probable cause upon completing the administrative steps incident to arrest. Plainly, if a probable cause hearing is constitutionally compelled the moment a suspect is finished being "booked," there is no room whatsoever for "flexibility and experimentation by the States." Incorporating probable cause determinations "into the procedure for setting bail or fixing other conditions of pretrial release"—which *Gerstein* explicitly contemplated—would be impossible. Waiting even a few hours so that a bail hearing or arraignment could take place at the same time as the probable cause determination would amount to a constitutional violation. Clearly *Gerstein* is not that inflexible.

Nothwithstanding *Gerstein*'s discussion of flexibility, the Ninth Circuit Court of Appeals held that no flexibility was permitted. It construed *Gerstein* as "requiring a probable cause determination to be made *as soon as the administrative steps incident to arrest were completed*, and that such steps should require only a brief period." This same reading is advanced by the dissent. The foregoing discussion readily demonstrates the error of this approach. As we have explained, *Gerstein* struck a balance between competing interests; a proper understanding of the decision is possible only if one takes into account both sides of the equation.

Given that *Gerstein* permits jurisdictions to incorporate probable cause determinations into other pretrial procedures, some delays are inevitable. For example, where, as in Riverside County, the probable cause determination is combined with arraignment, there will be delays caused by paperwork and logistical problems. Records will have to be reviewed, charging documents drafted, appearance of counsel arranged, and appropriate bail determined. On weekends, when the number of arrests is often higher and available resources tend to be limited, arraignments may get pushed back even further. In our view, the Fourth Amendment permits a reasonable postponement of a probable cause determination while the police cope with the everyday problems of processing suspects through an overly burdened criminal justice system.

But flexibility has its limits; *Gerstein* is not a blank check. A State has no legitimate interest in detaining for extended periods individuals who have been arrested without probable cause. The Court recognized in *Gerstein* that a person arrested without a warrant is entitled to a fair and reliable determination of probable cause and that this determination must be made promptly.

Our task in this case is to articulate more clearly the boundaries of what is permissible under the Fourth Amendment. Although we hesitate to announce that the Constitution compels a specific time limit, it is important to provide some degree of certainty so that States and counties may establish procedures with confidence that they fall within constitutional bounds. Taking into account the competing interests articulated in *Gerstein,* we believe that a jurisdiction that provides judicial determinations of probable cause within 48 hours of arrest will, as a general matter, comply with the promptness requirement of *Gerstein.* For this reason, such jurisdictions will be immune from systemic challenges.

This is not to say that the probable cause determination in a particular case passes constitutional muster simply because it is provided within 48 hours. Such a hearing may nonetheless violate *Gerstein* if the arrested individual can prove that his or her probable cause determination was delayed unreasonably. Examples of unreasonable delay are delays for the purpose of gathering additional evidence to justify the arrest, a delay motivated by ill will against the arrested individual, or delay for delay's sake. In evaluating whether the delay in a particular case is unreasonable, however, courts must allow a substantial degree of flexibility. Courts cannot ignore the often unavoidable delays in transporting arrested persons from one facility to another, handling late-night bookings where no magistrate is readily available, obtaining the presence of an arresting officer who may be busy processing other suspects or securing the premises of an arrest, and other practical realities.

Where an arrested individual does not receive a probable cause determination within 48 hours, the calculus changes. In such a case, the arrested individual does not bear the burden of proving an unreasonable delay. Rather, the burden shifts to the government to demonstrate the existence of a bona fide emergency or other extraordinary circumstance. The fact that in a particular case it may take longer than 48 hours to consolidate pretrial proceedings does not qualify as an extraordinary circumstance. Nor, for that matter, do intervening weekends. A jurisdiction that chooses to offer combined proceedings must do so as soon as is reasonably feasible, but in no event later than 48 hours after arrest.

The dissent urges that 24 hours is a more appropriate outer boundary for providing probable cause determinations. In arguing that any delay in probable cause hearings beyond completing the administrative steps incident to arrest and arranging for a magistrate is unconstitutional, the dissent, in effect, adopts the view of the Court of Appeals. Yet the dissent ignores entirely the Court of Appeals' determination of the time required to complete those procedures. That court, better situated than this one, concluded that it takes 36 hours to process arrested persons in Riverside County. In advocating a 24-hour rule, the dissent would compel Riverside County—and countless others across the Nation—to speed up its criminal justice mechanisms substantially, presumably by allotting local tax dollars to hire additional police officers and magistrates. There may be times when the Constitution compels such direct interference with local control, but this is not one. As we have explained, *Gerstein* clearly contemplated a reasonable accommodation between legitimate competing concerns. We do no more than recognize that such accommodation can take place without running afoul of the Fourth Amendment.

Everyone agrees that the police should make every attempt to minimize the time a presumptively innocent individual spends in jail. One way to do so is to provide a judicial determination of probable cause immediately upon completing the administrative steps incident to arrest—i.e., as soon as the suspect has been booked, photographed, and fingerprinted. As the dissent explains, several States, laudably, have adopted this approach. The Constitution does not compel so rigid a schedule, however. Under *Gerstein,* jurisdictions may choose to combine probable cause determinations with other pretrial proceedings, so long as they do so promptly. This necessarily means that only certain proceedings are candidates for combination. Only those proceedings that arise very early in the pretrial process—such as bail hearings and arraignments—may be chosen. Even then, every effort must be made to expedite the combined proceedings.

For the reasons we have articulated, we conclude that Riverside County is entitled to combine probable cause determinations with arraignments. The record indicates, however, that the County's current policy and practice do not comport fully with the principles we have outlined. The County's current policy is to offer combined proceedings within two days, exclusive of Saturdays, Sundays, or holidays. As a result, persons arrested on Thursdays may have to wait until the following Monday before they receive a probable cause determination. The delay is even longer if there is an intervening holiday. Thus, the County's regular practice exceeds the 48-hour period we deem constitutionally permissible, meaning that the County is not immune from systemic challenges, such as this class action.

As to arrests that occur early in the week, the County's practice is that "arraignment[s] usually tak[e] place on the last day" possible. There may well be legitimate reasons for this practice; alternatively, this may constitute delay for delay's sake. We leave it to the Court of Appeals and the District Court, on remand, to make this determination.

The judgment of the Court of Appeals is vacated and the case is remanded for further proceedings consistent with this opinion.

Mr. Justice SCALIA, dissenting.

The story is told of the elderly judge who, looking back over a long career, observes with satisfaction that "when I was young, I probably let stand some convictions that should have been overturned, and when I was old I probably set aside some that should have stood; so overall, justice was done." I sometimes think that is an appropriate analog to this Court's constitutional jurisprudence, which alternately creates rights that the Constitution does not contain and denies rights that it does. Compare *Roe v. Wade,* 410 U.S. 113 (1973) (right to abortion does exist) with *Maryland v. Craig,* 497 U.S. 836, (1990) (right to be confronted with witnesses, Amdt. 6, does not). Thinking that neither the one course nor the other is correct, nor the two combined, I dissent from today's decision, which eliminates a very old right indeed.

I

The Court views the task before it as one of "balanc[ing] [the] competing concerns" of "protecting public safety," on the one hand, and avoiding "prolonged detention based on incorrect or unfounded suspicion." It purports to reaffirm the "practical compromise" between these concerns struck in *Gerstein.* There is assuredly room for such an approach in resolving novel questions of search and seizure under the "reasonableness" standard that the Fourth Amendment sets forth. But not, I think, in resolving those questions on which a clear

answer already existed in 1791 and has been generally adhered to by the traditions of our society ever since. As to those matters, the "balance" has already been struck, the "practical compromise" reached—and it is the function of the Bill of Rights to *preserve* that judgment, not only against the changing views of Presidents and Members of Congress, but also against the changing views of Justices whom Presidents appoint and Members of Congress confirm to this Court.

The issue before us today is of precisely that sort. As we have recently had occasion to explain, the Fourth Amendment's prohibition of "unreasonable seizures," insofar as it applies to seizure of the person, preserves for our citizens the traditional protections against unlawful arrest afforded by the common law. One of those—one of the most important of those—was that a person arresting a suspect without a warrant must deliver the arrestee to a magistrate "as soon as he reasonably can." It was clear, moreover, that the only element bearing upon the reasonableness of delay was, not such circumstances as the pressing need to conduct further investigation, but the arresting officer's ability, once the prisoner had been secured, to reach a magistrate who could issue the needed warrant for further detention. Any detention beyond the period within which a warrant could have been obtained rendered the officer liable for false imprisonment.

We discussed and relied upon this common-law understanding in *Gerstein,* holding that the period of warrantless detention must be limited to the time necessary to complete the arrest and obtain the magistrate's review.

Today, however, the Court discerns something quite different in *Gerstein.* It finds that the plain statements set forth above (not to mention the common-law tradition of liberty upon which they were based) were trumped by the *implication* of a later dictum in the case which, according to the Court, manifests a "recognition that the Fourth Amendment does *not* compel an immediate determination of probable cause upon completing the administrative steps incident to arrest." (emphasis added). Of course *Gerstein* did not say, nor do I contend, that an "immediate" determination is required. But what the Court today means by "not immediate" is that the delay can be attributable to something other than completing the administrative steps incident to arrest and arranging for the magistrate—namely, to the administrative convenience of combining the probable-cause determination with other state proceedings. The result, we learn later in the opinion, is that what *Gerstein* meant by "a brief period of detention to take the administrative steps incident to arrest" is two full days. I think it is clear that the case neither said nor meant any such thing.

The Court's holding today rests upon the statement that "we recognize the desirability of flexibility and experimentation." But in its context that statement plainly refers to the *nature* of the hearing and not to its *timing*.

Of course even if the implication of the dictum in *Gerstein* were what the Court says, that would be poor reason for keeping a wrongfully arrested citizen in jail contrary to the clear dictates of the Fourth Amendment. What is most revealing of the frailty of today's opinion is that it relies upon *nothing* but that implication from a dictum, plus its own (quite irrefutable because entirely value laden) "balancing" of the competing demands of the individual and the State. To expand Gerstein, however, into an authorization for 48-hour detention related neither to the obtaining of a magistrate nor the administrative "completion" of the arrest seems to me utterly unjustified. Mr. McLaughlin was entitled to have a prompt impartial determination that there was reason to deprive him of his liberty — not according to a schedule that suits the State's convenience in piggybacking various proceedings, but as soon as his arrest was completed and the magistrate could be procured.

## II

I have finished discussing what I consider the principal question in this case, which is what factors determine whether the post-arrest determination of probable cause has been (as the Fourth Amendment requires) "reasonably prompt." The Court and I both accept two of those factors, completion of the administrative steps incident to arrest and arranging for a magistrate's probable-cause determination. Since we disagree, however, upon a third factor — the Court believing, as I do not, that "combining" the determination with other proceedings justifies a delay — we necessarily disagree as well on the subsequent question, which can be described as the question of the absolute time limit. Any determinant of "reasonable promptness" that is within the control of the State (as the availability of the magistrate, the personnel and facilities for completing administrative procedures incident to arrest, and the timing of "combined procedures" all are) must be restricted by some outer time limit, or else the promptness guarantee would be worthless. If, for example, it took a full year to obtain a probable-cause determination in California because only a single magistrate had been authorized to perform that function throughout the State, the hearing would assuredly

not qualify as "reasonably prompt." At some point, legitimate reasons for delay become illegitimate.

I do not know how the Court calculated its outer limit of 48 hours. I must confess, however, that I do not know how I would do so either, if I thought that one justification for delay could be the State's "desire to combine." There are no standards for "combination," and as we acknowledged in *Gerstein* the various procedures that might be combined "vary widely" from State to State. So as far as I can discern (though I cannot pretend to be able to do better), the Court simply decided that, given the administrative convenience of "combining," it is not so bad for an utterly innocent person to wait 48 hours in jail before being released.

In my view, absent extraordinary circumstances, it is an "unreasonable seizure" within the meaning of the Fourth Amendment for the police, having arrested a suspect without a warrant, to delay a determination of probable cause for the arrest either (1) for reasons unrelated to arrangement of the probable-cause determination or completion of the steps incident to arrest, or (2) beyond 24 hours after the arrest. Like the Court, I would treat the time limit as a presumption; when the 24 hours are exceeded the burden shifts to the police to adduce unforeseeable circumstances justifying the additional delay.

A few weeks before issuance of today's opinion there appeared in the Washington Post the story of protracted litigation arising from the arrest of a student who entered a restaurant in Charlottesville, Virginia, one evening, to look for some friends. Failing to find them, he tried to leave — but refused to pay a $5 fee (required by the restaurant's posted rules) for failing to return a red tab he had been issued to keep track of his orders. According to the story, he "was taken by police to the Charlottesville jail" at the restaurant's request. "There, a magistrate refused to issue an arrest warrant," and he was released. That is how it used to be; but not, according to today's decision, how it must be in the future. If the Fourth Amendment meant then what the Court says it does now, the student could lawfully have been held for as long as it would have taken to arrange for his arraignment, up to a maximum of 48 hours.

Justice Story wrote that the Fourth Amendment "is little more than the affirmance of a great constitutional doctrine of the common law." It should not become less than that. One hears the complaint, nowadays, that the Fourth Amendment has become constitutional law for the guilty; that it benefits the career criminal (through the exclusionary rule) often and directly, but the ordinary citizen remotely if at all. By failing to protect the innocent arrestee, today's opinion reinforces that view. The common-law rule of *prompt* hearing had as its primary beneficiaries the innocent—not those whose fully justified convictions must be overturned to scold the police; nor those who avoid conviction because the evidence, while convincing, does not establish guilt beyond a reasonable doubt; but those so blameless that there was not even good reason to arrest them. While in recent years we have invented novel applications of the Fourth Amendment to release the unquestionably guilty, we today repudiate one of its core applications so that the presumptively innocent may be left in jail. Hereafter a law-abiding citizen wrongfully arrested may be compelled to await the grace of a Dickensian bureaucratic machine, as it churns its cycle for up to two days—never once given the opportunity to show a judge that there is absolutely no reason to hold him, that a mistake has been made. In my view, this is the image of a system of justice that has lost its ancient sense of priority, a system that few Americans would recognize as our own.

I respectfully dissent.

## QUESTIONS AND NOTES

**1.** How do O'Connor and Scalia differ in regard to pragmatism, federalism, and history?

**2.** How do they differ in regard to substance?

**3.** How would you have resolved *Riverside*? Why?

**4.** If the State does not grant a prompt hearing, may the defendant nevertheless be prosecuted? If not, why not? If so, on what theory?

## C.   Bail

After an arrest with a warrant, or an arrest upheld following a *Gerstein-Riverside* hearing, the arrestee can ordinarily be released pending trial, but as *Salerno* tells us, that is not uniformly true.

### United States v. Salerno
481 U.S. 739 (1987)

Chief Justice REHNQUIST delivered the opinion of the Court.

I

Responding to "the alarming problem of crimes committed by persons on release," Congress formulated the Bail Reform Act of 1984, as the solution to a bail crisis in the federal courts. The Act represents the National Legislature's considered response to numerous perceived deficiencies in the federal bail process. By providing for sweeping changes in both the way federal courts consider bail applications and the circumstances under which bail is granted, Congress hoped to "give the courts adequate authority to make release decisions that give appropriate recognition to the danger a person may pose to others if released."

To this end, § 3141(a) of the Act requires a judicial officer to determine whether an arrestee shall be detained. Section 3142(e) provides that "[i]f, after a hearing pursuant to the provisions of subsection (f), the judicial officer finds that no condition or combination of conditions will reasonably assure the appearance of the person as required and the safety of any other person and the community, he shall order the detention of the person prior to trial." Section 3142(f) provides the arrestee with a number of procedural safeguards. He may request the presence of counsel at the detention hearing, he may testify and present witnesses in his behalf, as well as proffer evidence, and he may cross-examine other witnesses appearing at the hearing. If the judicial officer finds that no conditions of pretrial release can reasonably assure the safety of other persons and the community, he must state his findings of fact in writing, § 3142(i), and support his conclusion with "clear and convincing evidence," § 3142(f).

The judicial officer is not given unbridled discretion in making the detention determination. Congress has specified the considerations relevant to that decision. These factors include the nature and seriousness of the charges, the substantiality of the Government's evidence against the arrestee, the arrestee's background and characteristics, and the nature and seriousness of the danger posed by the suspect's release. § 3142(g). Should a judicial officer order detention, the detainee is entitled to expedited appellate review of the detention order. §§ 3145(b), (c).

Respondents Anthony Salerno and Vincent Cafaro were arrested on March 21, 1986, after being charged in a 29-count indictment alleging various Racketeer Influenced and Corrupt Organizations Act (RICO) violations, mail and wire fraud offenses, extortion, and various criminal gambling violations. At respondents' arraignment, the Government moved to have Salerno and Cafaro detained pursuant to § 3142(e), on the ground that no condition of release would assure the safety of the community or any person. The District Court held a hearing at which the Government made a detailed proffer of evidence. The Government's case showed that Salerno was the "boss" of the Genovese crime family of La Cosa Nostra and that Cafaro was a "captain" in the Genovese family. According to the Government's proffer, based in large part on conversations intercepted by a court-ordered wiretap, the two respondents had participated in wide-ranging conspiracies to aid their illegitimate enterprises through violent means. The Government also offered the testimony of two of its trial witnesses, who would assert that Salerno personally participated in two murder conspiracies. Salerno opposed the motion for detention, challenging the credibility of the Government's witnesses. He offered the testimony of several character witnesses as well as a letter from his doctor stating that he was suffering from a serious medical condition. Cafaro presented no evidence at the hearing, but instead characterized the wiretap conversations as merely "tough talk."

The District Court granted the Government's detention motion, concluding that the Government had established by clear and convincing evidence that no condition or combination of conditions of release would ensure the safety of the community or any person.

Respondents appealed, contending that to the extent that the Bail Reform Act permits pretrial detention on the ground that the arrestee is likely to commit future crimes, it is unconstitutional on its face. Over a dissent, the United States Court of Appeals for the Second Circuit agreed. Although the court agreed that pretrial detention could be imposed if the defendants were likely to intimidate witnesses or otherwise jeopardize

the trial process, it found "§ 3142(e)'s authorization of pretrial detention [on the ground of future dangerousness] repugnant to the concept of substantive due process, which we believe prohibits the total deprivation of liberty simply as a means of preventing future crimes." The court concluded that the Government could not, consistent with due process, detain persons who had not been accused of any crime merely because they were thought to present a danger to the community. It reasoned that our criminal law system holds persons accountable for past actions, not anticipated future actions. Although a court could detain an arrestee who threatened to flee before trial, such detention would be permissible because it would serve the basic objective of a criminal system—bringing the accused to trial. The court distinguished our decision in *Gerstein*, in which we upheld police detention pursuant to arrest. The court construed *Gerstein* as limiting such detention to the "administrative steps incident to arrest." The dissenting judge concluded that on its face, the Bail Reform Act adequately balanced the Federal Government's compelling interests in public safety against the detainee's liberty interests.

## II

Respondents present two grounds for invalidating the Bail Reform Act's provisions permitting pretrial detention on the basis of future dangerousness. First, they rely upon the Court of Appeals' conclusion that the Act exceeds the limitations placed upon the Federal Government by the Due Process Clause of the Fifth Amendment. Second, they contend that the Act contravenes the Eighth Amendment's proscription against excessive bail. We treat these contentions in turn.

## A

Respondents first argue that the Act violates substantive due process because the pretrial detention it authorizes constitutes impermissible punishment before trial. The Government, however, has never argued that pretrial detention could be upheld if it were "punishment." The Court of Appeals assumed that pretrial detention under the Bail Reform Act is regulatory, not penal, and we agree that it is. Unless Congress expressly intended to impose punitive restrictions, the punitive/regulatory distinction turns on "whether an alternative purpose to which [the restriction] may rationally be connected is assignable for it, and whether it appears excessive in relation to the alternative purpose assigned [to it]."

The Bail Reform Act narrowly focuses on a particularly acute problem in which the Government interests are overwhelming. The Act operates only on individuals who have been arrested for a specific category of extremely serious offenses. Congress specifically found that these individuals are far more likely to be responsible for dangerous acts in the community after arrest. Nor is the Act by any means a scattershot attempt to incapacitate those who are merely suspected of these serious crimes. The Government must first of all demonstrate probable cause to believe that the charged crime has been committed by the arrestee, but that is not enough. In a full-blown adversary hearing, the Government must convince a neutral decision maker by clear and convincing evidence that no conditions of release can reasonably assure the safety of the community or any person. While the Government's general interest in preventing crime is compelling, even this interest is heightened when the Government musters convincing proof that the arrestee, already indicted or held to answer for a serious crime, presents a demonstrable danger to the community. Under these narrow circumstances, society's interest in crime prevention is at its greatest.

On the other side of the scale, of course, is the individual's strong interest in liberty. We do not minimize the importance and fundamental nature of this right. But, as our cases hold, this right may, in circumstances where the government's interest is sufficiently weighty, be subordinated to the greater needs of society. We think that Congress' careful delineation of the circumstances under which detention will be permitted satisfies this standard. When the Government proves by clear and convincing evidence that an arrestee presents an identified and articulable threat to an individual or the community, we believe that, consistent with the Due Process Clause, a court may disable the arrestee from executing that threat. Under these circumstances, we cannot categorically state that pretrial detention "offends some principle of justice so rooted in the traditions and conscience of our people as to be ranked as fundamental."

### B

Respondents also contend that the Bail Reform Act violates the Excessive Bail Clause of the Eighth Amendment. The Court of Appeals did not address this issue because it found that the Act violates the Due Process Clause. We think that the Act survives a challenge founded upon the Eighth Amendment.

The Eighth Amendment addresses pretrial release by providing merely that "[e]xcessive bail shall not be required." This Clause, of course, says nothing about whether bail shall be available at all. Respondents nevertheless contend that this Clause grants them a right to bail calculated solely upon considerations of flight. They rely on *Stack v. Boyle,* 342 U.S. 1, 5 (1951), in which the Court stated that "[b]ail set at a figure higher than an amount reasonably calculated [to ensure the defendant's presence at trial] is 'excessive' under the Eighth Amendment." In respondents' view, since the Bail Reform Act allows a court essentially to set bail at an infinite amount for reasons not related to the risk of flight, it violates the Excessive Bail Clause. Respondents concede that the right to bail they have discovered in the Eighth Amendment is not absolute. A court may, for example, refuse bail in capital cases. And, as the Court of Appeals noted and respondents admit, a court may refuse bail when the defendant presents a threat to the judicial process by intimidating witnesses. Respondents characterize these exceptions as consistent with what they claim to be the sole purpose of bail—to ensure the integrity of the judicial process.

While we agree that a primary function of bail is to safeguard the courts' role in adjudicating the guilt or innocence of defendants, we reject the proposition that the Eighth Amendment categorically prohibits the government from pursuing other admittedly compelling interests through regulation of pretrial release. The above-quoted dictum in *Stack v. Boyle* is far too slender a reed on which to rest this argument. The Court in *Stack* had no occasion to consider whether the Excessive Bail Clause requires courts to admit all defendants to bail, because the statute before the Court in that case in fact allowed the defendants to be bailed. Thus, the Court had to determine only whether bail, admittedly available in that case, was excessive if set at a sum greater than that necessary to ensure the arrestees' presence at trial.

The holding of *Stack* is illuminated by the Court's holding just four months later in *Carlson v. Landon,* 342 U.S. 524 (1952). In that case, remarkably similar to the present action, the detainees had been arrested and held without bail pending a determination of deportability. The Attorney General refused to release the individuals, "on the ground that there was reasonable cause to believe that [their] release would be prejudicial to the public interest and *would endanger the welfare and safety of the United States.*" (emphasis added). The detainees brought the same challenge that respondents bring to us today: the Eighth Amendment required them to be admitted to bail. The Court squarely rejected this proposition. We believe that when Congress has mandated detention on the basis of a compelling interest other than prevention of flight, as it has here, the Eighth Amendment does not require release on bail.

The judgment of the Court of Appeals is therefore reversed.

Justice MARSHALL, with whom Justice BRENNAN joins, dissenting.

This case brings before the Court for the first time a statute in which Congress declares that a person innocent of any crime may be jailed indefinitely, pending the trial of allegations which are legally presumed to be untrue, if the Government shows to the satisfaction of a judge that the accused is likely to commit crimes, unrelated to the pending charges, at any time in the future. Such statutes, consistent with the usages of tyranny and the excesses of what bitter experience teaches us to call the police state, have long been thought incompatible with the fundamental human rights protected by our Constitution. Today a majority of this Court holds otherwise. Its decision disregards basic principles of justice established centuries ago and enshrined beyond the reach of governmental interference in the Bill of Rights.

The majority approaches respondents' challenge to the Act by dividing the discussion into two sections, one concerned with the substantive guarantees implicit in the Due Process Clause, and the other concerned with the protection afforded by the Excessive Bail Clause of the Eighth Amendment. This is a sterile formalism, which divides a unitary argument into two independent parts and then professes to demonstrate that the parts are individually inadequate.

On the due process side of this false dichotomy appears an argument concerning the distinction between regulatory and punitive legislation. The majority concludes that the Act is a regulatory rather than a punitive measure. The ease with which the conclusion is reached suggests the worthlessness of the achievement. The major premise is that "[u]nless Congress expressly intended to impose punitive restrictions, the punitive/regulatory distinction turns on 'whether an alternative purpose to which [the restriction] may rationally be connected is assignable for it, and whether it appears excessive in relation to the alternative purpose assigned [to it].'" The majority finds that "Congress did not formulate the pretrial detention provisions as punishment for dangerous individuals," but instead was pursuing the "legitimate regulatory goal" of "preventing danger to the community." Concluding that pretrial detention is not an excessive solution to the problem of preventing danger to the community, the majority thus finds that no substantive element of the guarantee of due process invalidates the statute.

This argument does not demonstrate the conclusion it purports to justify. Let us apply the majority's reasoning to a similar, hypothetical case. After investigation, Congress determines (not unrealistically) that a large proportion of violent crime is perpetrated by persons who are unemployed. It also determines, equally reasonably, that much violent crime is committed at night. From amongst the panoply of "potential solutions," Congress chooses a statute which permits, after judicial proceedings, the imposition of a dusk-to-dawn curfew on anyone who is unemployed. Since this is not a measure enacted for the purpose of punishing the unemployed, and since the majority finds that preventing danger to the community is a legitimate regulatory goal, the curfew statute would, according to the majority's analysis, be a mere "regulatory" detention statute, entirely compatible with the substantive components of the Due Process Clause.

The absurdity of this conclusion arises, of course, from the majority's cramped concept of substantive due process. The majority proceeds as though the only substantive right protected by the Due Process Clause is a right to be free from punishment before conviction. The majority's technique for infringing this right is simple: merely redefine any measure which is claimed to be punishment as "regulation," and, magically, the Constitution no longer prohibits its imposition.

The logic of the majority's Eighth Amendment analysis is equally unsatisfactory. The Eighth Amendment, as the majority notes, states that "[e]xcessive bail shall not be required." The majority then declares, as if it were undeniable, that: "[t]his Clause, of course, says nothing about whether bail shall be available at all." If excessive bail is imposed the defendant stays in jail. The same result is achieved if bail is denied altogether. Whether the magistrate sets bail at $1 million or refuses to set bail at all, the consequences are indistinguishable. It would be mere sophistry to suggest that the Eighth Amendment protects against the former decision, and not the latter. Indeed, such a result would lead to the conclusion that there was no need for Congress to pass a preventive detention measure of any kind; every federal magistrate and district judge could simply refuse, despite the absence of any evidence of risk of flight or danger to the community, to set bail. This would be entirely constitutional, since, according to the majority, the Eighth Amendment "says nothing about whether bail shall be available at all."

The majority's attempts to deny the relevance of the Bail Clause to this case are unavailing, but the majority is nonetheless correct that the prohibition of excessive bail means that in order "to determine whether the Government's response is excessive, we must compare that response against the interest the Government seeks to protect by means of that response." The majority concedes, as it must, that "when the Government has admitted that its only interest is in preventing flight, bail must be set by a court at a sum designed to ensure that goal, and no more." But, the majority says, "when Congress has mandated detention on the basis of a compelling interest other than prevention of flight, as it has here, the Eighth Amendment does not require release on bail." This conclusion follows only if the "compelling" interest upon which Congress acted is an interest which the Constitution permits Congress to further through the denial of bail. The majority does not ask, as a result of its disingenuous division of the analysis, if there are any substantive limits contained in both the Eighth Amendment and the Due Process Clause which render this system of preventive detention unconstitutional. The majority does not ask because the answer is apparent and, to the majority, inconvenient.

"The principle that there is a presumption of innocence in favor of the accused is the undoubted law, axiomatic and elementary, and its enforcement lies at the foundation of the administration of our criminal law." Our society's belief, reinforced over the centuries, that all are innocent until the state has proved them to be guilty, like the companion principle that guilt must be proved beyond a reasonable doubt, is "implicit in the concept of ordered liberty," *Palko v. Connecticut*, 302 U.S. 319, 325 (1937), and is established beyond legislative contravention in the Due Process Clause.

The statute now before us declares that persons who have been indicted may be detained if a judicial officer finds clear and convincing evidence that they pose a danger to individuals or to the community. The statute does not authorize the Government to imprison anyone it has evidence is dangerous; indictment is necessary. But let us suppose that a defendant is indicted and the Government shows by clear and convincing evidence that he is dangerous and should be detained pending a trial, at which trial the defendant is acquitted. May the Government continue to hold the defendant in detention based upon its showing that he is dangerous? The answer cannot be yes, for that would allow the Government to imprison someone for uncommitted crimes based upon "proof" not beyond a reasonable doubt. The result must therefore be that once the indictment has failed, detention cannot continue. But our fundamental principles of justice declare that the defendant is as innocent on the day before his trial as he is on the morning after his acquittal. Under this statute an untried indictment somehow acts to permit a detention, based on other charges, which after an acquittal would be unconstitutional. The conclusion is inescapable that the indictment has been turned into evidence, if not that the defendant is guilty of the crime charged, then that left to his own devices he will soon be guilty of something else. "If it suffices to

accuse, what will become of the innocent?"

To be sure, an indictment is not without legal consequences. It establishes that there is probable cause to believe that an offense was committed, and that the defendant committed it. Upon probable cause a warrant for the defendant's arrest may issue; a period of administrative detention may occur before the evidence of probable cause is presented to a neutral magistrate. Once a defendant has been committed for trial he may be detained in custody if the magistrate finds that no conditions of release will prevent him from becoming a fugitive. But in this connection the charging instrument is evidence of nothing more than the fact that there will be a trial, and

> "release before trial is conditioned upon the accused's giving adequate assurance that he will stand trial and submit to sentence if found guilty. Like the ancient practice of securing the oaths of responsible persons to stand as sureties for the accused, the modern practice of requiring a bail bond or the deposit of a sum of money subject to forfeiture serves as additional assurance of the presence of an accused." *Stack.*[6]

The finding of probable cause conveys power to try, and the power to try imports of necessity the power to assure that the processes of justice will not be evaded or obstructed.[7] "Pretrial detention to prevent future crimes against society at large, however,

---

[6] The majority states that denial of bail in capital cases has traditionally been the rule rather than the exception. And this of course is so, for it has been the considered presumption of generations of judges that a defendant in danger of execution has an extremely strong incentive to flee. If in any particular case the presumed likelihood of flight should be made irrebuttable, it would in all probability violate the Due Process Clause. Thus what the majority perceives as an exception is nothing more than an example of the traditional operation of our system of bail.

[7] It is also true, as the majority observes, that the Government is entitled to assurance, by incarceration if necessary, that a defendant will not obstruct justice through destruction of evidence, procuring the absence or intimidation of witnesses, or subornation of perjury. But in such cases the Government benefits from no presumption that any particular defendant is likely to engage in activities inimical to the administration of justice, and the majority offers no authority for the proposition that bail has traditionally been denied prospectively, upon speculation that witnesses would be tampered with. Cf. *Carbo*

is not justified by any concern for holding a trial on the charges for which a defendant has been arrested.'' The detention purportedly authorized by this statute bears no relation to the Government's power to try charges supported by a finding of probable cause, and thus the interests it serves are outside the scope of interests which may be considered in weighing the excessiveness of bail under the Eighth Amendment.

It is not a novel proposition that the Bail Clause plays a vital role in protecting the presumption of innocence. Reviewing the application for bail pending appeal by members of the American Communist Party convicted under the Smith Act, 18 U.S.C. § 2385, Justice Jackson wrote:

> "Grave public danger is said to result from what [the defendants] may be expected to do, in addition to what they have done since their conviction. If I assume that defendants are disposed to commit every opportune disloyal act helpful to Communist countries, it is still difficult to reconcile with traditional American law the jailing of persons by the courts because of anticipated but as yet uncommitted crimes. Imprisonment to protect society from predicted but unconsummated offenses is . . . unprecedented in this country and . . . fraught with danger of excesses and injustice. . . .'' *Williamson v. United States*, 95 L. Ed. 1379, 1382 (1950) (opinion in chambers).

There is a connection between the peculiar facts of this case and the evident constitutional defects in the statute which the Court upholds today. Respondent Cafaro was originally incarcerated for an indeterminate period at the request of the Government, which believed (or professed to believe) that his release imminently threatened the safety of the community. That threat apparently vanished, from the Government's point of view, when Cafaro agreed to act as a covert agent of the Government. There could be no more eloquent demonstration of the coercive power of authority to imprison upon prediction, or of the dangers which the almost inevitable abuses pose to the cherished liberties of a free society.

"It is a fair summary of history to say that the safeguards of liberty have frequently been forged in controversies involving not very nice people.''

---

*v. United States,* 82 S.Ct. 662 (1962) (Douglas, J., in chambers) (bail pending appeal denied when more than 200 intimidating phone calls made to witness, who was also severely beaten).

*United States v. Rabinowitz,* 339 U.S. 56, 69 (1950) (Frankfurter, J., dissenting). Honoring the presumption of innocence is often difficult; sometimes we must pay substantial social costs as a result of our commitment to the values we espouse. But at the end of the day the presumption of innocence protects the innocent; the shortcuts we take with those whom we believe to be guilty injure only those wrongfully accused and, ultimately, ourselves.

Throughout the world today there are men, women, and children interned indefinitely, awaiting trials which may never come or which may be a mockery of the word, because their governments believe them to be "dangerous.'' Our Constitution, whose construction began two centuries ago, can shelter us forever from the evils of such unchecked power. Over 200 years it has slowly, through our efforts, grown more durable, more expansive, and more just. But it cannot protect us if we lack the courage, and the self-restraint, to protect ourselves. Today a majority of the Court applies itself to an ominous exercise in demolition. Theirs is truly a decision which will go forth without authority, and come back without respect.

I dissent.

Justice STEVENS, Dissenting.

There may be times when the Government's interest in protecting the safety of the community will justify the brief detention of a person who has not committed any crime.[1] To use Judge Feinberg's example, it is indeed difficult to accept the proposition that the Government is without power to detain a person when it is a virtual certainty that he or she would otherwise kill a group of innocent people in the immediate future. Similarly, I am unwilling to decide today that the police may never impose a limited curfew during a time of crisis. These questions are obviously not presented in this case, but they lurk in the background and preclude me from answering the question that is presented in as broad a manner as Justice Marshall has. Nonetheless, I firmly agree with Justice Marshall that the provision

---

[1] "If the evidence overwhelmingly establishes that a skyjacker, for example, was insane at the time of his act, and that he is virtually certain to resume his violent behavior as soon as he is set free, must we then conclude that the only way to protect society from such predictable harm is to find an innocent man guilty of a crime he did not have the capacity to commit?'' *United States v. Greene,* 497 F.2d, at 1088.

of the Bail Reform Act allowing pretrial detention on the basis of future dangerousness is unconstitutional. Whatever the answers are to the questions I have mentioned, it is clear to me that a pending indictment may not be given any weight in evaluating an individual's risk to the community or the need for immediate detention.

If the evidence of imminent danger is strong enough to warrant emergency detention, it should support that preventive measure regardless of whether the person has been charged, convicted, or acquitted of some other offense. In this case, for example, it is unrealistic to assume that the danger to the community that was present when respondents were at large did not justify their detention before they were indicted, but did require that measure the moment that the grand jury found probable cause to believe they had committed crimes in the past.[2] It is equally unrealistic to assume that the danger will vanish if a jury happens to acquit them. Justice Marshall has demonstrated that the fact of indictment cannot, consistent with the presumption of innocence and the Eighth Amendment's Excessive Bail Clause, be used to create a special class, the members of which are, alone, eligible for detention because of future dangerousness.

Accordingly, I respectfully dissent.

---

[2] The Government's proof of future dangerousness was not dependent on any prediction that, as a result of the indictment, respondents posed a threat to potential witnesses or to the judicial system.

## QUESTIONS AND NOTES

**1.** Is preventative detention inherently unfair?

**2.** Should gang leaders be able to argue that they are just as dangerous in jail as out of it, so there is no reason to hold them?

**3.** In the ordinary bail situation (*e.g. Stack v. Boyle*), should money determine freedom? Would it not be more equitable to release everybody on their own recognizance, and make it a serious offense (perhaps a felony) to fail to appear at trial? What would be the advantages and disadvantages of such a system?

**4.** Is there good reason to deny bail to a capital defendant?

**5.** What factors ought to determine the fact and amount of bail?

## D.   Arrests In The Home

Arrests in the home involve a clash of principles. *Watson* suggests that ordinarily arrests do not require a warrant. *Vale,* on the other hand, suggests that warrants are ordinarily required before entering one's home. The question of whether a warrant is required for arrests in the home, and if so, what must the warrant allege, was ultimately resolved in *Payton v. New York* and somewhat embellished in *Steagald v. United States.* Shortly, we will examine those cases. However, we will begin with *United States v. Santana,* a classic law professor's case, which involves a woman standing at the door of her home, one foot in and one foot out.

# United States v. Santana
## 427 U.S. 38 (1976)

Mr. Justice REHNQUIST delivered the opinion of the Court.

On August 16, 1974, Michael Gilletti, an undercover officer with the Philadelphia Narcotics Squad arranged a heroin "buy" with one Patricia McCafferty (from whom he had purchased narcotics before). McCafferty told him it would cost $115 "and we will go down to Mom Santana's for the dope."

Gilletti notified his superiors of the impending transaction, recorded the serial numbers of $110 [Sic] in marked bills, and went to meet McCafferty at a prearranged location. She got in his car and directed him to drive to 2311 North Fifth Street, which, as she had previously informed him, was respondent Santana's residence.

McCafferty took the money and went inside the house, stopping briefly to speak to respondent Alejandro who was sitting on the front steps. She came out shortly afterwards and got into the car. Gilletti asked for the heroin; she thereupon extracted from her bra several glassine envelopes containing a brownish-white powder and gave them to him.

Gilletti then stopped the car, displayed his badge, and placed McCafferty under arrest. He told her that the police were going back to 2311 North Fifth Street and that he wanted to know where the money was. She said, "Mom has the money." At this point Sergeant Pruitt and other officers came up to the car. Gilletti showed them the envelope and said "Mom Santana has the money." Gilletti then took McCafferty to the police station.

Pruitt and the others then drove approximately two blocks back to 2311 North Fifth Street. They saw Santana standing in the doorway of the house[1] with a brown paper bag in her hand. They pulled up to within 15 feet of Santana and got out of their van, shouting "police," and displaying their identification. As the officers approached, Santana retreated into the vestibule of her house.

The officers followed through the open door, catching her in the vestibule. As she tried to pull away, the bag tilted and "two bundles of glazed paper packets with a white powder" fell to the floor.

In *Watson,* we held that the warrantless arrest of an individual in a public place upon probable cause did not violate the Fourth Amendment. Thus the first question we must decide is whether, when the police first sought to arrest Santana, she was in a public place.

While it may be true that under the common law of property the threshold of one's dwelling is "private," as is the yard surrounding the house, it is nonetheless clear that under the cases interpreting the Fourth Amendment Santana was in a "public" place. She was not in an area where she had any expectation of privacy. "What a person knowingly exposes to the public, even in his own house or office, is not a subject of Fourth Amendment protection." She was not merely visible to the public but was as exposed to public view, speech, hearing, and touch as if she had been standing completely outside her house. Thus, when the police, who concededly had probable cause to do so, sought to arrest her, they merely intended to perform a function which we have approved in *Watson.*

The only remaining question is whether her act of retreating into her house could thwart an otherwise proper arrest. We hold that it could not. In *Warden v. Hayden,* 387 U.S. 294 (1967), we recognized the right of police, who had probable cause to believe that an armed robber had entered a house a few minutes before, to make a warrantless entry to arrest the robber and to search for weapons. This case, involving a true "hot pursuit," is clearly governed by *Warden*; the need to act quickly here is even greater than in that case while the intrusion is much less. The District Court was correct in concluding that "hot pursuit" means some sort of a chase, but it need not be an extended hue and cry "in and about (the) public streets." The fact that the pursuit here ended almost as soon as it began did not render it any the less a "hot pursuit" sufficient to justify the warrantless entry into Santana's house. Once Santana saw the police, there was likewise a realistic expectation that any delay would result in destruction of evidence. See *Vale.* Once she had been arrested the search, incident to that arrest, which produced the drugs and money was clearly justified.

We thus conclude that a suspect may not defeat an arrest which has been set in motion in a public place, and is therefore proper under *Watson,* by the expedient of escaping to a private place. The judgment of the Court of Appeals is reversed. (Concurring and Dissenting opinions omitted.)

---

[1] An Officer Strohm testified that he recognized Santana, whom he had seen before. He also indicated that she was standing directly in the doorway one step forward would have put her outside, one step backward would have put her in the vestibule of her residence.

## QUESTIONS AND NOTES

**1.** Was the Court playing fast and loose with the facts in analogizing *Santana* to *Watson*?

**2.** Would (should) the result have been different if "Mom" Santana had been totally inside the house, but visible from the street?

**3.** Does the Court's citation to *Vale,* strengthen or weaken its argument?

**4.** In *Payton,* the Court finally resolved the need for a warrant for an arrest in the home.

### Payton v. New York
### 445 U.S. 573 (1980)

Mr. Justice STEVENS delivered the opinion of the Court.

These appeals challenge the constitutionality of New York statutes that authorize police officers to enter a private residence without a warrant and with force, if necessary, to make a routine felony arrest.

The important constitutional question presented by this challenge has been expressly left open in a number of our prior opinions. In *Watson,* we upheld a warrantless "midday public arrest," expressly noting that the case did not pose "the still unsettled question . . . 'whether and under what circumstances an officer may enter a suspect's home to make a warrantless arrest.'"

#### I

On January 14, 1970, after two days of intensive investigation, New York detectives had assembled evidence sufficient to establish probable cause to believe that Theodore Payton had murdered the manager of a gas station two days earlier. At about 7:30 a. m. on January 15, six officers went to Payton's apartment in the Bronx, intending to arrest him. They had not obtained a warrant. Although light and music emanated from the apartment, there was no response to their knock on the metal door. They summoned emergency assistance and, about 30 minutes later, used crowbars to break open the door and enter the apartment. No one was there. In plain view, however, was a .30-caliber shell casing that was seized and later admitted into evidence at Payton's murder trial.

Before addressing the narrow question presented by these appeals, we put to one side other related problems that are not presented today. Although it is arguable that the warrantless entry to effect Payton's arrest might have been justified by exigent circumstances, none of the New York courts relied on any such justification. The Court of Appeals majority treated Payton's case as involving routine arrests in which there was ample time to obtain a warrant, and we will do the same. Accordingly, we have no occasion to consider the sort of emergency or dangerous situation, described in our cases as "exigent circumstances," that would justify a warrantless entry into a home for the purpose of either arrest or search.

#### II

The simple language of the Amendment applies equally to seizures of persons and to seizures of property. Our analysis in this case may therefore properly commence with rules that have been well established in Fourth Amendment litigation involving tangible items. As the Court reiterated just a few years ago, the "physical entry of the home is the chief evil against which the wording of the Fourth Amendment is directed." And we have long adhered to the view that the warrant procedure minimizes the danger of needless intrusions of that sort.

It is a "basic principle of Fourth Amendment law" that searches and seizures inside a home without a warrant are presumptively unreasonable. Yet it is also well settled that objects such as weapons or contraband found in a public place may be seized by the police without a warrant. The seizure of property in plain view involves no invasion of privacy and is presumptively reasonable, assuming that there is probable cause to associate the property with criminal activity. The distinction between a warrantless seizure in an open area and such a seizure on private premises was plainly stated in *G. M. Leasing Corp. v. United States,* 429 U.S. 338, 354.

As the late Judge Leventhal recognized, this distinction has equal force when the seizure of a person is involved. Writing on the constitutional issue now before us for the United States Court of Appeals for the District of Columbia Circuit sitting en banc, *Dorman v. United States,* 435 F.2d 385 (1970), Judge Leventhal first noted the settled rule that warrantless arrests in public places are valid. He immediately recognized, however, that "[a] greater burden is placed

. . . on officials who enter a home or dwelling without consent. Freedom from intrusion into the home or dwelling is the archetype of the privacy protection secured by the Fourth Amendment.''

His analysis of this question then focused on the long-settled premise that, absent exigent circumstances, a warrantless entry to search for weapons or contraband is unconstitutional even when a felony has been committed and there is probable cause to believe that incriminating evidence will be found within. He reasoned that the constitutional protection afforded to the individual's interest in the privacy of his own home is equally applicable to a warrantless entry for the purpose of arresting a resident of the house; for it is inherent in such an entry that a search for the suspect may be required before he can be apprehended. Judge Leventhal concluded that an entry to arrest and an entry to search for and to seize property implicate the same interest in preserving the privacy and the sanctity of the home, and justify the same level of constitutional protection.

We find this reasoning to be persuasive and in accord with this Court's Fourth Amendment decisions.

The majority of the New York Court of Appeals, however, suggested that there is a substantial difference in the relative intrusiveness of an entry to search for property and an entry to search for a person. It is true that the area that may legally be searched is broader when executing a search warrant than when executing an arrest warrant in the home. This difference may be more theoretical than real, however, because the police may need to check the entire premises for safety reasons, and sometimes they ignore the restrictions on searches incident to arrest.

But the critical point is that any differences in the intrusiveness of entries to search and entries to arrest are merely ones of degree rather than kind. The two intrusions share this fundamental characteristic: the breach of the entrance to an individual's home. The Fourth Amendment protects the individual's privacy in a variety of settings. In none is the zone of privacy more clearly defined than when bounded by the unambiguous physical dimensions of an individual's home—a zone that finds its roots in clear and specific constitutional terms: ''The right of the people to be secure in their . . . houses . . . shall not be violated.'' That language unequivocally establishes the proposition that ''[a]t the very core [of the Fourth Amendment] stands the right of a man to retreat into his own home and there be free from unreasonable governmental intrusion.'' In terms that apply equally to seizures of property and to seizures of persons, the Fourth Amendment has drawn a firm line at the entrance to the house. Absent exigent circumstances, that threshold may not reasonably be crossed without a warrant.

### III

Without contending that *Watson,* decided the question presented by these appeals, New York argues that the reasons that support the *Watson* holding require a similar result here. In *Watson* the Court relied on (a) the well-settled common-law rule that a warrantless arrest in a public place is valid if the arresting officer had probable cause to believe the suspect is a felon; (b) the clear consensus among the States adhering to that well-settled common-law rule; and (c) the expression of the judgment of Congress that such an arrest is ''reasonable.'' We consider each of these reasons as it applies to a warrantless entry into a home for the purpose of making a routine felony arrest.

### A

An examination of the common-law understanding of an officer's authority to arrest sheds light on the obviously relevant, if not entirely dispositive, consideration of what the Framers of the Amendment might have thought to be reasonable.

A study of the common law on the question whether a constable had the authority to make warrantless arrests in the home on mere suspicion of a felony—as distinguished from an officer's right to arrest for a crime committed in his presence—reveals a surprising lack of judicial decisions and a deep divergence among scholars.

The common-law commentators disagreed sharply on the subject. Three distinct views were expressed. Lord Coke, widely recognized by the American colonists ''as the greatest authority of his time on the laws of England,'' clearly viewed a warrantless entry for the purpose of arrest to be illegal. Burn, Foster, and Hawkins agreed, as did East and Russell, though the latter two qualified their opinions by stating that if an entry to arrest was made without a warrant, the officer was perhaps immune from liability for the trespass if the suspect was actually guilty. Blackstone, Chitty, and Stephen took the opposite view, that entry to arrest without a warrant was legal, though Stephen relied on Blackstone who, along with Chitty, in turn relied exclusively on Hale. But Hale's view was not quite so unequivocally expressed.[41]

---

[41] Hale writes that in the case where the constable suspects a person of a felony, ''if the supposed offender fly and take house, and the door will not be opened upon demand of the constable and notification of his business, the constable may break the

It is obvious that the common-law rule on warrantless home arrests was not as clear as the rule on arrests in public places. Indeed, particularly considering the prominence of Lord Coke, the weight of authority as it appeared to the Framers was to the effect that a warrant was required, or at the minimum that there were substantial risks in proceeding without one. The common-law sources display a sensitivity to privacy interests that could not have been lost on the Framers. The zealous and frequent repetition of the adage that a "man's house is his castle," made it abundantly clear that both in England and in the Colonies "the freedom of one's house" was one of the most vital elements of English liberty.

Thus, our study of the relevant common law does not provide the same guidance that was present in *Watson*. Whereas the rule concerning the validity of an arrest in a public place was supported by cases directly in point and by the unanimous views of the commentators, we have found no direct authority supporting forcible entries into a home to make a routine arrest and the weight of the scholarly opinion is somewhat to the contrary. Indeed, the absence of any 17th- or 18th-century English cases directly in point, together with the unequivocal endorsement of the tenet that "a man's house is his castle," strongly suggests that the prevailing practice was not to make such arrests except in hot pursuit or when authorized by a warrant. In all events, the issue is not one that can be said to have been definitively settled by the common law at the time the Fourth Amendment was adopted.

### B

A majority of the States that have taken a position on the question permit warrantless entry into the home to arrest even in the absence of exigent circumstances. At this time, 24 States permit such warrantless entries; 15 States clearly prohibit them, though 3 States do so on federal constitutional grounds alone; and 11 States have apparently taken no position on the question.

But these current figures reflect a significant decline during the last decade in the number of States permitting warrantless entries for arrest. Recent dicta in this Court raising questions about the practice, and Federal Courts of Appeals' decisions on point have led state courts to focus on the issue. Virtually all of the state courts that have had to confront the constitutional issue directly have held warrantless entries into the home to arrest to be invalid in the absence of exigent circumstances. Three state courts have relied on Fourth Amendment grounds alone, while seven have squarely placed their decisions on both federal and state constitutional grounds. A number of other state courts, though not having had to confront the issue directly, have recognized the serious nature of the constitutional question. Apparently, only the Supreme Court of Florida and the New York Court of Appeals in this case have expressly upheld warrantless entries to arrest in the face of a constitutional challenge.

A longstanding, widespread practice is not immune from constitutional scrutiny. But neither is it to be lightly brushed aside. This is particularly so when the constitutional standard is as amorphous as the word "reasonable," and when custom and contemporary norms necessarily play such a large role in the constitutional analysis. In this case, although the weight of state-law authority is clear, there is by no means the kind of virtual unanimity on this question that was present in *Watson*, with regard to warrantless arrests in public places.

### C

No congressional determination that warrantless entries into the home are "reasonable" has been called to our attention. None of the federal statutes cited in the *Watson* opinion reflects any such legislative judgment. Thus, that support for the *Watson* holding finds no counterpart in this case.

Mr. Justice Powell, concurring in *Watson*, stated: "But logic sometimes must defer to history and experience. The Court's opinion emphasizes the historical sanction accorded warrantless felony arrests [in public places]." In this case, however, neither history nor this Nation's experience requires us to disregard the overriding respect for the sanctity of the home that has been embedded in our traditions since the origins of the Republic.[54]

### IV

The parties have argued at some length about the

---

door, tho he have no warrant." Although it would appear that Hale might have meant to limit warrantless home arrests to cases of hot pursuit, the quoted passage has not typically been read that way.

[54] There can be no doubt that Pitt's address in the House of Commons in March 1763 echoed and re-echoed throughout the Colonies: "The poorest man may in his cottage bid defiance to all the forces of the Crown. It may be frail; its roof may shake; the wind may blow through it; the storm may enter; the rain may enter; but the King of England cannot enter—all his force dares not cross the threshold of the ruined tenement!" *Miller v. United States,* 357 U.S., at 307.

practical consequences of a warrant requirement as a precondition to a felony arrest in the home.[55] In the absence of any evidence that effective law enforcement has suffered in those States that already have such a requirement, we are inclined to view such arguments with skepticism. More fundamentally, however, such arguments of policy must give way to a constitutional command that we consider to be unequivocal.

Finally, we note the State's suggestion that only a search warrant based on probable cause to believe the suspect is at home at a given time can adequately protect the privacy interests at stake, and since such a warrant requirement is manifestly impractical, there need be no warrant of any kind. We find this ingenious argument unpersuasive. It is true that an arrest warrant requirement may afford less protection than a search warrant requirement, but it will suffice to interpose the magistrate's determination of probable cause between the zealous officer and the citizen. If there is sufficient evidence of a citizen's participation in a felony to persuade a judicial officer that his arrest is justified, it is constitutionally reasonable to require him to open his doors to the officers of the law. Thus, for Fourth Amendment purposes, an arrest warrant founded on probable cause implicitly carries with it the limited authority to enter a dwelling in which the suspect lives when there is reason to believe the suspect is within.

Because no arrest warrant was obtained, the judgments must be reversed and the cases remanded to the New York Court of Appeals for further proceedings not inconsistent with this opinion.

---

[55] The State of New York argues that the warrant requirement will pressure police to seek warrants and make arrests too hurriedly, thus increasing the likelihood of arresting innocent people; that it will divert scarce resources thereby interfering with the police's ability to do thorough investigations; that it will penalize the police for deliberate planning; and that it will lead to more injuries. Appellants counter that careful planning is possible and that the police need not rush to get a warrant, because if an exigency arises necessitating immediate arrest in the course of an orderly investigation, arrest without a warrant is permissible; that the warrant procedure will decrease the likelihood that an innocent person will be arrested; that the inconvenience of obtaining a warrant and the potential for diversion of resources is exaggerated by the State; and that there is no basis for the assertion that the time required to obtain a warrant would create peril.

Mr. Justice BLACKMUN, concurring.

I joined the Court's opinion in *Watson,* upholding, on probable cause, the warrantless arrest in a public place. I, of course, am still of the view that the decision in *Watson* is correct. The Court's balancing of the competing governmental and individual interests properly occasioned that result. Where, however, the warrantless arrest is in the suspect's home, that same balancing requires that, absent exigent circumstances, the result be the other way. The suspect's interest in the sanctity of his home then outweighs the governmental interests.

I therefore join the Court's opinion, firm in the conviction that the result in *Watson* and the result here, although opposite, are fully justified by history and by the Fourth Amendment

Mr. Justice WHITE, with whom THE CHIEF JUSTICE and Mr. Justice REHNQUIST join, dissenting.

The Court today holds that absent exigent circumstances officers may never enter a home during the daytime to arrest for a dangerous felony unless they have first obtained a warrant. This hard-and-fast rule, founded on erroneous assumptions concerning the intrusiveness of home arrest entries, finds little or no support in the common law or in the text and history of the Fourth Amendment. I respectfully dissent.

I

As the Court notes, the common law of searches and seizures, as evolved in England, as transported to the Colonies, and as developed among the States, is highly relevant to the present scope of the Fourth Amendment. Today's decision virtually ignores these centuries of common-law development, and distorts the historical meaning of the Fourth Amendment, by proclaiming for the first time a rigid warrant requirement for all nonexigent home arrest entries.

As the Court notes, commentators have differed as to the scope of the constable's inherent authority, when not acting under a warrant, to break doors in order to arrest. Probably the majority of commentators would permit arrest entries on probable suspicion even if the person arrested were not in fact guilty. Blackstone, Burn, Dalton, [and] Hale would have permitted the type of home arrest entries that occurred in the present cases. The inclusion of Blackstone in this list is particularly significant in light of his profound impact on the minds of the colonists at the time of the framing of the Constitution and the ratification of the Bill of Rights. And Coke is flatly contrary to the Court's rule requiring a warrant, since he believed that even a warrant would not justify an arrest entry until the suspect had been indicted.

## B

The history of the Fourth Amendment does not support the rule announced today. At the time that Amendment was adopted the constable possessed broad inherent powers to arrest. The limitations on those powers derived, not from a warrant "requirement," but from the generally ministerial nature of the constable's office at common law. Far from restricting the constable's arrest power, the institution of the warrant was used to expand that authority by giving the constable delegated powers of a superior officer such as a justice of the peace. Hence at the time of the Bill of Rights, the warrant functioned as a powerful tool of law enforcement rather than as a protection for the rights of criminal suspects.

In fact, it was the abusive use of the warrant power, rather than any excessive zeal in the discharge of peace officers' inherent authority, that precipitated the Fourth Amendment. That Amendment grew out of colonial opposition to the infamous general warrants known as writs of assistance, which empowered customs officers to search at will, and to break open receptacles or packages, wherever they suspected uncustomed goods to be.

## C

Probably because warrantless arrest entries were so firmly accepted at common law, there is apparently no recorded constitutional challenge to such entries in the 19th-century cases. Common-law authorities on both sides of the Atlantic, however, continued to endorse the validity of such arrests.

This Court apparently first questioned the reasonableness of warrantless nonexigent entries to arrest in *Jones v. United States,* 357 U.S. 493, 499-500 (1958), noting in dictum that such entries would pose a "grave constitutional question" if carried out at night. In *Coolidge v. New Hampshire,* 403 U.S. 443, (1971), the Court stated, again in dictum:

"[I]f [it] is correct that it has generally been assumed that the Fourth Amendment is not violated by the warrantless entry of a man's house for purposes of arrest, it might be wise to re-examine the assumption. Such a re-examination 'would confront us with a grave constitutional question, namely, whether the forcible nighttime entry into a dwelling to arrest a person reasonably believed within, upon probable cause that he has committed a felony, under circumstances where no reason appears why an arrest warrant could not have been sought, is consistent with the Fourth Amendment.'"

Although *Coolidge* and *Jones* both referred to the special problem of warrantless entries during the nighttime, it is not surprising that state and federal courts have tended to read those dicta as suggesting a broader infirmity applying to daytime entries also, and that the majority of recent decisions have been against the constitutionality of all types of warrantless, nonexigent home arrest entries. As the Court concedes, however, even despite *Coolidge* and *Jones* it remains the case that "[a] majority of the States that have taken a position on the question permit warrantless entry into the home to arrest even in the absence of exigent circumstances. At this time, 24 States permit such warrantless entries; 15 States clearly prohibited them, though 3 States do so on federal constitutional grounds alone; and 11 States have apparently taken no position on the question." This consensus, in the face of seemingly contrary dicta from this Court, is entitled to more deference than the Court today provides. Cf. *Watson.*

## D

In the present cases, as in *Watson,* the applicable federal statutes are relevant to the reasonableness of the type of arrest in question. Under 18 U.S.C. § 3052, specified federal agents may "make arrests without warrants for any offense against the United States committed in their presence, or for any felony cognizable under the laws of the United States, if they have reasonable grounds to believe that the person to be arrested has committed or is committing such felony." On its face this provision authorizes federal agents to make warrantless arrests anywhere, including the home. Particularly in light of the accepted rule at common law and among the States permitting warrantless home arrests, the absence of any explicit exception for the home from § 3052 is persuasive evidence that Congress intended to authorize warrantless arrests there as well as elsewhere.

Further, Congress has not been unaware of the special problems involved in police entries into the home. In 18 U.S.C. § 3109, it provided that "[t]he officer may break open any outer or inner door or window of a house, or any part of a house, or anything therein, to execute a search warrant, if, after notice of its authority and purpose, he is refused admittance. . . ." In explicitly providing authority to enter when executing a search warrant, Congress surely did not intend to derogate from the officers' power to effect an arrest entry either with or without a warrant. Rather, Congress apparently assumed that this power was so firmly established either at common law or by statute that no explicit grant of arrest authority was required in § 3109. In short, although the Court purports to find no guidance in the relevant federal statutes, I believe that fairly read they authorize the type of police conduct at issue in these cases.

## II

### A

Today's decision rests, in large measure, on the premise that warrantless arrest entries constitute a particularly severe invasion of personal privacy. I do not dispute that the home is generally a very private area or that the common law displayed a special "reverence . . . for the individual's right of privacy in his house." However, the Fourth Amendment is concerned with protecting people, not places, and no talismanic significance is given to the fact that an arrest occurs in the home rather than elsewhere. It is necessary in each case to assess realistically the actual extent of invasion of constitutionally protected privacy. Further, as Mr. Justice POWELL observed in *Watson,* all arrests involve serious intrusions into an individual's privacy and dignity. Yet we settled in *Watson* that the intrusiveness of a public arrest is not enough to mandate the obtaining of a warrant. The inquiry in the present case, therefore, is whether the incremental intrusiveness that results from an arrest's being made in the dwelling is enough to support an inflexible constitutional rule requiring warrants for such arrests whenever exigent circumstances are not present.

Today's decision ignores the carefully crafted restrictions on the common-law power of arrest entry and thereby overestimates the dangers inherent in that practice. At common law, absent exigent circumstances, entries to arrest could be made only for felony. Even in cases of felony, the officers were required to announce their presence, demand admission, and be refused entry before they were entitled to break doors. Further, it seems generally accepted that entries could be made only during daylight hours. And, in my view, the officer entering to arrest must have reasonable grounds to believe, not only that the arrestee has committed a crime, but also that the person suspected is present in the house at the time of the entry.

These four restrictions on home arrests—felony, knock and announce, daytime, and stringent probable cause—constitute powerful and complementary protections for the privacy interests associated with the home. The felony requirement guards against abusive or arbitrary enforcement and ensures that invasions of the home occur only in case of the most

serious crimes. The knock-and-announce and daytime requirements protect individuals against the fear, humiliation, and embarrassment of being aroused from their beds in states of partial or complete undress. And these requirements allow the arrestee to surrender at his front door, thereby maintaining his dignity and preventing the officers from entering other rooms of the dwelling. The stringent probable-cause requirement would help ensure against the possibility that the police would enter when the suspect was not home, and, in searching for him, frighten members of the family or ransack parts of the house, seizing items in plain view. In short, these requirements, taken together, permit an individual suspected of a serious crime to surrender at the front door of his dwelling and thereby avoid most of the humiliation and indignity that the Court seems to believe necessarily accompany a house arrest entry. Such a front-door arrest, in my view, is no more intrusive on personal privacy than the public warrantless arrests which we found to pass constitutional muster in *Watson.*[14]

### B

While exaggerating the invasion of personal privacy involved in home arrests, the Court fails to account for the danger that its rule will "severely hamper effective law enforcement." The policeman on his beat must now make subtle discriminations that perplex even judges in their chambers. As Mr. Justice POWELL noted, concurring in *Watson,* police will sometimes delay making an arrest, even after probable cause is established, in order to be sure that they have enough evidence to convict. Then, if they suddenly have to arrest, they run the risk that the subsequent exigency will not excuse their prior failure to obtain a warrant. This problem cannot effectively be cured by obtaining a warrant as soon as probable cause is established because of the chance that the warrant will go stale before the arrest is made.

Further, police officers will often face the difficult task of deciding whether the circumstances are sufficiently exigent to justify their entry to arrest without a warrant. This is a decision that must be made quickly in the most trying of circumstances. If the officers mistakenly decide that the circumstances are exigent, the arrest will be invalid and any evidence seized incident to the arrest or in plain

---

[14] If the suspect flees or hides, of course, the intrusiveness of the entry will be somewhat greater; but the policeman's hands should not be tied merely because of the possibility that the suspect will fail to cooperate with legitimate actions by law enforcement personnel.

view will be excluded at trial. On the other hand, if the officers mistakenly determine that exigent circumstances are lacking, they may refrain from making the arrest, thus creating the possibility that a dangerous criminal will escape into the community. The police could reduce the likelihood of escape by staking out all possible exits until the circumstances become clearly exigent or a warrant is obtained. But the costs of such a stakeout seem excessive in an era of rising crime and scarce police resources.

Mr. Justice REHNQUIST, dissenting.

I fully concur in and join the dissenting opinion of Mr. Justice White. There is significant historical evidence that we have over the years misread the history of the Fourth Amendment in connection with searches, elevating the warrant requirement over the necessity for probable cause in a way which the Framers of that Amendment did not intend. See T. Taylor, Two Studies in Constitutional Interpretation 38-50 (1969). But one may accept all of that as *stare decisis,* and still feel deeply troubled by the transposition of these same errors into the area of actual arrests of felons within their houses with respect to whom there is probable cause to suspect guilt of the offense in question.

## QUESTIONS AND NOTES

**1.** Do you perceive history and deference to Congress to have played the same role in *Payton* that it did in *Watson*? If not, why not?

**2.** Are the policy reasons for not requiring a warrant significantly different in *Payton* than they were in *Watson*?

**3.** To some extent, *Payton* involves a clash between flexibility and certainty (bright line). The Court's rule provides certainty. Justice White would allow more flexibility. In general, which of those values ought to predominate? Why? In the context of this case, who reached the better result? Why?

**4.** In Justice White's four-part standard, is there a difference between "stringent probable cause" and ordinary probable cause? If so, do we want judges determining what constitutes stringent probable cause as opposed to ordinary probable cause? What kind of guidance would such a standard provide the police?

**5.** Should failure to knock and announce (absent special or exigent circumstances) invalidate an arrest or search in the home even when the police *do* have a warrant and probable cause? The Supreme Court unanimously said, "yes" in *Wilson v. Arkansas*, 514 U.S. ___, 131 L.Ed.2d 976 (1995). What circumstances might justify a departure from the "knock and announce" requirement? Why?

**6.** Do you agree with the Court that an arrest warrant, as opposed to a search warrant, adequately protects the homeowners' interest? In regard thereto, contrast the *Payton* situation to *Steagald*.

### Steagald v. United States
#### 451 U.S. 204 (1980)

Justice MARSHALL delivered the opinion of the Court.

The issue in this case is whether, under the Fourth Amendment, a law enforcement officer may legally search for the subject of an arrest warrant in the home of a third party without first obtaining a search warrant. Concluding that a search warrant must be obtained absent exigent circumstances or consent, we reverse the judgment of the United States Court of Appeals for the Fifth Circuit affirming petitioner's conviction.

In early January 1978, an agent of the Drug Enforcement Administration (DEA) was contacted in Detroit, Mich., by a confidential informant who suggested that he might be able to locate Ricky Lyons, a federal fugitive wanted on drug charges. On January 14, 1978, the informant called the agent again, and gave him a telephone number in the Atlanta, Ga., area where, according to the informant, Ricky Lyons could be reached during the next 24 hours. On January 16, 1978, the agent called fellow DEA Agent Kelly Goodowens in Atlanta and relayed the information he had obtained from the informant. Goodowens contacted Southern Bell Telephone Co., and secured the address corresponding to the telephone number obtained by the informant. Goodowens also discovered that Lyons was the subject of a 6-month-old arrest warrant.

Two days later, Goodowens and 11 other officers drove to the address supplied by the telephone company to search for Lyons. The officers observed two men standing outside the house to be searched. These men were Hoyt Gaultney and petitioner Gary Steagald. The officers approached with guns drawn, frisked both men, and, after demanding identification, determined that neither man was Lyons. Several agents proceeded to the house. Gaultney's wife answered the door, and informed the agents that she was alone in the house. She was told to place her hands against the wall and was guarded in that position while one agent searched the house. Ricky Lyons was not found, but during the search of the house the agent observed what he believed to be cocaine.

The question before us is a narrow one.[6] The search at issue here took place in the absence of consent or exigent circumstances. Except in such special situations, we have consistently held that the entry into a home to conduct a search or make an arrest is unreasonable under the Fourth Amendment unless done pursuant to a warrant. Thus, as we recently observed: "[I]n terms that apply equally to seizures of property and to seizures of persons, the Fourth Amendment has drawn a firm line at the entrance to the house. Absent exigent circumstances, that threshold may not reasonably be crossed without a warrant." *Payton.* Here, of course, the agents had a warrant—one authorizing the arrest of Ricky Lyons. However, the Fourth Amendment claim here is not being raised by Ricky Lyons. Instead, the challenge to the search is asserted by a person not named in the warrant who was convicted on the basis of evidence uncovered during a search of his residence for Ricky Lyons. Thus, the narrow issue before us is whether an arrest warrant—as opposed to a search warrant—is adequate to protect the Fourth Amendment interests of persons not named

in the warrant, when their homes are searched without their consent and in the absence of exigent circumstances.

The purpose of a warrant is to allow a neutral judicial officer to assess whether the police have probable cause to make an arrest or conduct a search. As we have often explained, the placement of this checkpoint between the Government and the citizen implicitly acknowledges that an "officer engaged in the often competitive enterprise of ferreting out crime," may lack sufficient objectivity to weigh correctly the strength of the evidence supporting the contemplated action against the individual's interests in protecting his own liberty and the privacy of his home. However, while an arrest warrant and a search warrant both serve to subject the probable-cause determination of the police to judicial review, the interests protected by the two warrants differ. An arrest warrant is issued by a magistrate upon a showing that probable cause exists to believe that the subject of the warrant has committed an offense and thus the warrant primarily serves to protect an individual from an unreasonable seizure. A search warrant, in contrast is issued upon a showing of probable cause to believe that the legitimate object of a search is located in a particular place, and therefore safeguards an individual's interest in the privacy of his home and possessions against the unjustified intrusion of the police.

Thus, whether the arrest warrant issued in this case adequately safeguarded the interests protected by the Fourth Amendment depends upon what the warrant authorized the agents to do. To be sure, the warrant embodied a judicial finding that there was probable cause to believe that Ricky Lyons had committed a felony, and the warrant therefore authorized the officers to seize Lyons. However, the agents sought to do more than use the warrant to arrest Lyons in a public place or in his home; instead, they relied on the warrant as legal authority to enter the home of a third person based on their belief that Ricky Lyons might be a guest there. Regardless of how reasonable this belief might have been, it was never subjected to the detached scrutiny of a judicial officer. Thus, while the warrant in this case may have protected Lyons from an unreasonable seizure, it did absolutely nothing to protect petitioner's privacy interest in being free from an unreasonable invasion and search of his home. Instead, petitioner's only protection from an illegal entry and search was the agent's personal determination of probable cause. In the absence of exigent circumstances, we have consistently held that such judicially untested determinations are not reliable enough to justify an entry into a person's home to arrest him without a warrant, or a search of a home for objects in the absence of a search warrant. We see no reason to

---

[6] Initially, we assume without deciding that the information relayed to Agent Goodowens concerning the whereabouts of Ricky Lyons would have been sufficient to establish probable cause to believe that Lyons was at the house searched by the agents.

depart from this settled course when the search of a home is for a person rather than an object.[7]

---

[7] Indeed, the plain wording of the Fourth Amendment admits of no exemption from the warrant requirement when the search of a home is for a person rather than for a thing. As previously noted, absent exigent circumstances or consent, an entry into a private dwelling to conduct a search or effect an arrest is unreasonable without a warrant. The second clause of the Fourth Amendment, which governs the issuance of such warrants, provides that "no Warrants shall issue but upon probable cause, supported by Oath or affirmation, and particularly describing the place to be searched, and the persons or things to be seized." This language plainly suggests that the same sort of judicial determination must be made when the search of a person's home is for another person as is necessary when the search is for an object. Specifically, absent exigent circumstances the magistrate, rather than the police officer, must make the decision that probable cause exists to believe that the person or object to be seized is within a particular place.

In *Payton,* of course, we recognized that an arrest warrant alone was sufficient to authorize the entry into a person's home to effect his arrest. We reasoned: "If there is sufficient evidence of a citizen's participation in a felony to persuade a judicial officer that his arrest is justified, it is constitutionally reasonable to require him to open his doors to the officers of the law. Thus, for Fourth Amendment purposes, an arrest warrant founded on probable cause implicitly carries with it the limited authority to enter a dwelling in which the suspect lives when there is reason to believe the suspect is within." Because an arrest warrant authorizes the police to deprive a person of his liberty, it necessarily also authorizes a limited invasion of that person's privacy interest when it is necessary to arrest him in his home. This analysis, however, is plainly inapplicable when the police seek to use an arrest warrant as legal authority to enter the home of a third party to conduct a search. Such a warrant embodies no judicial determination whatsoever regarding the person whose home is to be searched. Because it does not authorize the police to deprive the third person of his liberty, it cannot embody any derivative authority to deprive this person of his interest in the privacy of his home. Such a deprivation must instead be based on an independent showing that a legitimate object of a search is located in the third party's home. We have consistently held, however, that such a determination is the province of the magistrate, and not that of the police officer.

A contrary conclusion—that the police, acting alone and in the absence of exigent circumstances, may decide when there is sufficient justification for searching the home of a third party for the subject of an arrest warrant—would create a significant potential for abuse. Armed solely with an arrest warrant for a single person, the police could search all the homes of that individual's friends and acquaintances. See, *e.g., Lankford v. Gelston,* 364 F.2d 197 (CA4 1966) (enjoining police practice under which 300 homes were searched pursuant to arrest warrants for two fugitives). Moreover, an arrest warrant may serve as the pretext for entering a home in which the police have a suspicion, but not probable cause to believe, that illegal activity is taking place.

In sum, two distinct interests were implicated by the search at issue here—Ricky Lyons' interest in being free from an unreasonable seizure and petitioner's interest in being free from an unreasonable search of his home. Because the arrest warrant for Lyons addressed only the former interest, the search of petitioner's home was no more reasonable from petitioner's perspective than it would have been if conducted in the absence of any warrant. Since warrantless searches of a home are impermissible absent consent or exigent circumstances, we conclude that the instant search violated the Fourth Amendment.

The Government concedes that this view is "apparently logical," that it furthers the general policies underlying the Fourth Amendment, and that it "has the virtue of producing symmetry between the law of entry to conduct a search for things to be seized and the law of entry to conduct a search for persons to be seized." Yet we are informed that this conclusion is "not without its flaws" in that it is contrary to common-law precedent and creates some practical problems of law enforcement. We treat these contentions in turn.

The common law may, within limits, be instructive in determining what sorts of searches the Framers of the Fourth Amendment regarded as reasonable. The Government contends that at common law an officer could forcibly enter the home of a third party to execute an arrest warrant. To be sure, several commentators do suggest that a constable could "break open doors" to effect such an arrest. As support for this proposition, these commentators all rely on a single decision, *Semayne's Case,* 5 Co.Rep. 91a, 92b-93a, 77 Eng.Rep. 194, 198 (K.B.1603). Although that case involved only the authority of a sheriff to effect civil service on a person within his own home, the court noted in dictum that a person could not "escape the ordinary process of law" by seeking refuge in the home of a third party. However, the language of the decision, while not free from ambiguity, suggests that forcible entry into a third party's house was permissible only when the person to be arrested was pursued to the house. The decision refers to a person who "flies" to another's home, and the annotation notes that "in order to justify the breaking of the outer door; after denial on request to take a person . . . in the house of a stranger, it must be understood . . . that the person upon a pursuit taketh refuge in the house of another." The common-law commentators appear to have adopted this limitation. We have long recognized that such "hot pursuit" cases fall within the exigent-circumstances exception to the warrant requirement, see *Warden v. Hayden*, 387 U.S. 294 (1967), and therefore are distinguishable from the routine search situation presented here.

While the common law thus sheds relatively little light on the narrow question before us, the history of the Fourth Amendment strongly suggests that its Framers would not have sanctioned the instant search. The Fourth Amendment was intended partly to protect against the abuses of the general warrants that had occurred in England and of the writs of assistance used in the Colonies. The general warrant specified only an offense — typically seditious libel — and left to the discretion of the executing officials the decision as to which persons should be arrested and which places should be searched. Similarly, the writs of assistance used in the Colonies noted only the object of the search — any uncustomed goods — and thus left customs officials completely free to search any place where they believed such goods might be. The central objectionable feature of both warrants was that they provided no judicial check on the determination of the executing officials that the evidence available justified an intrusion into any particular home. An arrest warrant, to the extent that it is invoked as authority to enter the homes of third parties, suffers from the same infirmity. Like a writ of assistance, it specifies only the object of a search — in this case, Ricky Lyons — and leaves to the unfettered discretion of the police the decision as to which particular homes should be searched. We do not believe that the Framers of the Fourth Amendment would have condoned such a result.

The Government also suggests that practical problems might arise if law enforcement officers are required to obtain a search warrant before entering the home of a third party to make an arrest. The basis of this concern is that persons, as opposed to objects, are inherently mobile, and thus officers seeking to effect an arrest may be forced to return to the magistrate several times as the subject of the arrest warrant moves from place to place. We are convinced, however, that a search warrant requirement will not significantly impede effective law enforcement efforts.

First, the situations in which a search warrant will be necessary are few. As noted in *Payton*, an arrest warrant alone will suffice to enter a suspect's own residence to effect his arrest. Furthermore, if probable cause exists, no warrant is required to apprehend a suspected felon in a public place. *Watson*. Thus, the subject of an arrest warrant can be readily seized before entering or after leaving the home of a third party.[14] Finally, the exigent-circumstances doctrine significantly limits the situations in which a search warrant would be needed. For example, a warrantless entry of a home would be justified if the police were in "hot pursuit" of a fugitive. Thus, to the extent that searches for persons pose special problems, we believe that the exigent-circumstances doctrine is adequate to accommodate legitimate law enforcement needs.

Moreover, in those situations in which a search warrant is necessary, the inconvenience incurred by the police is simply not that significant. First, if the police know of the location of the felon when they obtain an arrest warrant, the additional burden of obtaining a search warrant at the same time is minuscule. The inconvenience of obtaining such a warrant does not increase significantly when an outstanding arrest warrant already exists. In this case, for example, Agent Goodowens knew the address of the house to be searched two days in advance, and planned the raid from the federal courthouse in Atlanta where, we are informed, three full-time magistrates were on duty. In routine search cases such as this, the short time required to obtain a search warrant from a magistrate will seldom hinder efforts to apprehend a felon. Finally, if a magistrate is not nearby, a telephonic search warrant can usually be obtained.

Whatever practical problems remain, however, cannot outweigh the constitutional interests at stake. Any warrant requirement impedes to some extent the vigor with which the Government can seek to enforce its laws, yet the Fourth Amendment recognizes that this restraint is necessary in some cases to protect against unreasonable searches and seizures. We conclude that this is such a case. The additional burden imposed on the police by a warrant requirement is minimal. In contrast, the right protected — that of presumptively innocent people to be secure in their homes from unjustified, forcible intrusions by the Government — is weighty. Thus, in order to render the instant search reasonable under the Fourth Amendment, a search warrant was required.

---

[14] Indeed, the "inherent mobility" of persons noted by the Government suggests that in most situations the police may avoid altogether the need to obtain a search warrant simply by waiting for a suspect to leave the third person's home before attempting to arrest that suspect.

Accordingly, the judgment of the Court of Appeals is reversed, and the case is remanded to that court for further proceedings consistent with this opinion.

Justice REHNQUIST, with whom Justice WHITE joins, dissenting.

The Court's opinion reversing petitioner's conviction proceeds in a pristinely simple manner: Steagald had a Fourth Amendment privacy interest in the dwelling entered by the police, and even though the police entered the premises for the sole purpose of executing a valid arrest warrant for Lyons, a fugitive from justice, whom they had probable cause to believe was within, the arrest warrant was not sufficient absent exigent circumstances to justify invading Steagald's privacy interest in the dwelling. Petitioner Steagald's privacy interest is different from Lyons' interest in being free from an unreasonable seizure, according to the Court, and the arrest warrant only validated the invasion of the latter. In the words of the Court:

> "[T]he search of petitioner's home was no more reasonable from petitioner's perspective than it would have been if conducted in the absence of any warrant. Since warrantless searches of a home are impermissible absent consent or exigent circumstances, we conclude that the instant search violated the Fourth Amendment."

This case, therefore, cannot be resolved by the simple Aristotelian syllogism which the Court employs. Concluding as it does that the arrest warrant did not address the privacy interest affected by the search by no means ends the matter; it simply presents the issue for decision. Resolution of that issue depends upon a balancing of the "need to search against the invasion which the search entails." Here, as in all Fourth Amendment cases, "reasonableness is still the ultimate standard." In determining the reasonableness of dispensing with the requirement of a separate search warrant in this case, I believe that the existence of a valid arrest warrant is highly relevant.

The government's interests in the warrantless entry of a third-party dwelling to execute an arrest warrant are compelling. The basic problem confronting police in such situations is the inherent mobility of the fugitive. By definition, the police have probable cause to believe that the fugitive is in a dwelling which is not his home. He may stay there for a week, a day, or 10 minutes. Fugitives from justice tend to be mobile, and police officers will generally have no way of knowing whether the subject of an arrest warrant will be at the dwelling when they return from seeking a search warrant. Imposition of a search warrant requirement in such circumstances will frustrate the compelling interests of the government and indeed the public in the apprehension of those subject to outstanding arrest warrants.

The Court's ivory tower misconception of the realities of the apprehension of fugitives from justice reaches its apogee when it states: "In routine search cases such as this, the short time required to obtain a search warrant from a magistrate will seldom hinder efforts to apprehend a felon." The cases we are considering are not "routine search cases." They are cases of attempted arrest, pursuant to a warrant, when the object of the arrest may flee at any time — including the "short time" during which the police are endeavoring to obtain a search warrant.

At the same time the interference with the Fourth Amendment privacy interests of those whose homes are entered to apprehend the felon is not nearly as significant as suggested by the Court. The arrest warrant serves some of the functions a separate search warrant would. It assures the occupants that the police officer is present on official business. The arrest warrant also limits the scope of the search, specifying what the police may search for — *i.e.*, the subject of the arrest warrant. No general search is permitted, but only a search of those areas in which the object of the search might hide. Indeed there may be no intrusion on the occupant's privacy at all, since if present the suspect will have the opportunity to voluntarily surrender at the door. Even if the suspect does not surrender but secretes himself within the house, the occupant can limit the search by pointing him out to the police. It is important to remember that the contraband discovered during the entry and search for Lyons was in plain view, and was discovered during a "sweep search" for Lyons, not a probing of drawers or cabinets for contraband.

Because the burden on law enforcement officers to obtain a separate search warrant before entering the dwelling of a third party to execute a concededly valid arrest warrant is great, and carries with it a high possibility that the fugitive named in the arrest warrant will escape apprehension, I would conclude that the application of the traditional "reasonableness" standard of the Fourth Amendment does not require a separate search warrant in a case such as this.

The basic error in the Court's treatment of the common law is its reliance on the adage that "a man's home is his castle." Though there is undoubtedly early case support for this in the common law, it cannot be accepted as an uncritical statement of black letter law which answers all questions in this area. William Pitt, when he was Prime Minister of England, used it with telling effect in a speech on the floor of the House of Commons; but parliamentary speaking ability and analytical legal ability ought not to be equated with one another. It is clear that the privilege of the home did not extend when the King was a party, *i.e.*, when a warrant in a criminal case had been issued. The suggestion in the Court's opinion that "[t]he language of *Semayne's Case. . . .* suggests that although the subject of an arrest warrant could not find sanctuary in the home of the third party, the home remained a 'castle or privilege' for its residents," is thus completely unfounded in the present context.

While I cannot subscribe to the Court's decision today, I will not falsely cry "wolf" in this dissent. The decision rests on a very special set of facts, and with a change in one or more of them it is clear that no separate search warrant would be required even under the reasoning of the Court.

On the one side *Payton* makes clear that an arrest warrant is all that is needed to enter the suspect's "home" to effect the arrest. If a suspect has been living in a particular dwelling for any significant period, say a few days, it can certainly be considered his "home" for Fourth Amendment purposes, even if the premises are owned by a third party and others are living there, and even if the suspect concurrently maintains a residence elsewhere as well. In such a case the police could enter the premises with only an arrest warrant. On the other side, the more fleeting a suspect's connection with the premises, such as

when he is a mere visitor, the more likely that exigent circumstances will exist justifying immediate police action without departing to obtain a search warrant. The practical damage done to effective law enforcement by today's decision, without any basis in the Constitution, may well be minimal if courts carefully consider the various congeries of facts in the actual case before them.

The genuinely unfortunate aspect of today's ruling is not that fewer fugitives will be brought to book, or fewer criminals apprehended, though both of these consequences will undoubtedly occur; the greater misfortune is the increased uncertainty imposed on police officers in the field, committing magistrates, and trial judges, who must confront variations and permutations of this factual situation on a day-to-day basis. They will, in their various capacities, have to weigh the time during which a suspect for whom there is an outstanding arrest warrant has been in the building, whether the dwelling is the suspect's home, how long he has lived there, whether he is likely to leave immediately, and a number of related and equally imponderable questions. Certainty and repose, as Justice Holmes said, may not be the destiny of man, but one might have hoped for a higher degree of certainty in this one narrow but important area of the law than is offered by today's decision.

## QUESTIONS AND NOTES

1. Is it always easy to determine one's residence? Suppose that Lyons had been visiting for a week? A month? Suppose that the police reasonably thought that he was such a visitor?

2. In any of the question 1 hypotheticals, should it matter whether Lyons has a permanent address elsewhere?

3. In the case of a crime lord who owns several mansions, should the police be able to enter any of them to arrest him with only an arrest warrant? Should it matter whether they have probable cause to believe that he is present at the particular one being searched? Suppose that they have no idea where he is?

4. Could a smart criminal increase her chances of beating a charge by floating from friend to friend rather than staying at home?

5. What harm did the Court see in allowing an arrest without a search warrant in a home other than the arrestee's? Could that harm be ameliorated by a requirement that there be probable cause to find the arrestee there?

6. How would you advise a police department that is not sure whether the potential arrestee lives at the address at which they expect to find her? Would you advise them to get an arrest warrant? A search warrant? Or both?

7. As you read *Welsh,* consider whether the special protection given homes from warrantless entries should extend to some exigent circumstances.

## Welsh v. Wisconsin
### 466 U.S. 740 (1984)

Justice BRENNAN delivered the opinion of the Court.

Shortly before 9:00 p.m. on the rainy night of April 24, 1978, a lone witness, Randy Jablonic, observed a car being driven erratically. After changing speeds and veering from side to side, the car eventually swerved off the road and came to a stop in an open field. No damage to any person or property occurred. Concerned about the driver and fearing that the car would get back on the highway, Jablonic drove his truck up behind the car so as to block it from returning to the road. Another passerby also stopped at the scene, and Jablonic asked her to call the police. Before the police arrived, however, the driver of the car emerged from his vehicle, approached Jablonic's truck, and asked Jablonic for a ride home. Jablonic instead suggested that they wait for assistance in removing or repairing the car. Ignoring Jablonic's suggestion, the driver walked away from the scene.

A few minutes later, the police arrived and questioned Jablonic. He told one officer what he had seen, specifically noting that the driver was either very inebriated or very sick. The officer checked the motor vehicle registration of the abandoned car and learned that it was registered to the petitioner, Edward G. Welsh. In addition, the officer noted that the petitioner's residence was a short distance from the scene, and therefore easily within walking distance.

Without securing any type of warrant, the police proceeded to the petitioner's home, arriving about 9:00 p.m. When the petitioner's stepdaughter answered the door, the police gained entry into the house. Proceeding upstairs to the petitioner's bedroom, they found him lying naked in bed. At this point, the petitioner was placed under arrest for driving or operating a motor vehicle while under the influence of an intoxicant. The petitioner was taken to the police station, where he refused to submit to a breathalyzer test.

Consistently with long-recognized principles, the Court decided in *Payton,* that warrantless felony arrests in the home are prohibited by the Fourth Amendment, absent probable cause and exigent circumstances. At the same time, the Court declined to consider the scope of any exception for exigent circumstances that might justify warrantless home arrests, thereby leaving to the lower courts the initial application of the exigent-circumstances exception. Prior decisions of this Court, however, have emphasized that exceptions to the warrant requirement are "few in number and carefully delineated," and that the police bear a heavy burden when attempting to demonstrate

an urgent need that might justify warrantless searches or arrests. Indeed, the Court has recognized only a few such emergency conditions, and has actually applied only the "hot pursuit" doctrine to arrests in the home, see *Santana.*

Our hesitation in finding exigent circumstances, especially when warrantless arrests in the home are at issue, is especially appropriate when the underlying offense for which there is probable cause to arrest is relatively minor. Before agents of the government may invade the sanctity of the home, the burden is on the government to demonstrate exigent circumstances that overcome the presumption of unreasonableness that attaches to all warrantless home entries. When the government's interest is only to arrest for a minor offense,[12] that presumption of unreasonableness is difficult to rebut, and the government usually should be allowed to make such arrests only with a warrant issued upon probable cause by a neutral and detached magistrate.

Consistently with this approach, the lower courts have looked to the nature of the underlying offense as an important factor to be considered in the exigent-circumstances calculus.

We conclude that the common sense approach utilized by most lower courts is required by the Fourth Amendment prohibition on "unreasonable searches and seizures," and hold that an important factor to be considered when determining whether any exigency exists is the gravity of the underlying offense for which the arrest is being made. Moreover, although no exigency is created simply because there is probable cause to believe that a serious crime has been committed, application of the exigent-circumstances exception in the context of a home entry should rarely be sanctioned when there is probable cause to believe that only a minor offense, such as the kind at issue in this case, has been committed.

Application of this principle to the facts of the present case is relatively straightforward. The petitioner was arrested in the privacy of his own bedroom for a noncriminal, traffic offense. The State attempts to justify the arrest by relying on the hot-pursuit doctrine, on the threat to public safety, and on the need

---

[12] Even the dissenters in *Payton,* although believing that warrantless home arrests are not prohibited by the Fourth Amendment, recognized the importance of the felony limitation on such arrests.

to preserve evidence of the petitioner's blood-alcohol level. On the facts of this case, however, the claim of hot pursuit is unconvincing because there was no immediate or continuous pursuit of the petitioner from the scene of a crime. Moreover, because the petitioner had already arrived home, and had abandoned his car at the scene of the accident, there was little remaining threat to the public safety. Hence, the only potential emergency claimed by the State was the need to ascertain the petitioner's blood-alcohol level.

Even assuming, however, that the underlying facts would support a finding of this exigent circumstance, mere similarity to other cases involving the imminent destruction of evidence is not sufficient. The State of Wisconsin has chosen to classify the first offense for driving while intoxicated as a noncriminal, civil forfeiture offense for which no imprisonment is possible. This is the best indication of the state's interest in precipitating an arrest, and is one that can be easily identified both by the courts and by officers faced with a decision to arrest. Given this expression of the state's interest, a warrantless home arrest cannot be upheld simply because evidence of the petitioner's blood-alcohol level might have dissipated while the police obtained a warrant.[14] To allow a warrantless home entry on these facts would be to approve unreasonable police behavior that the principles of the Fourth Amendment will not sanction.

The Supreme Court of Wisconsin let stand a warrantless, nighttime entry into the petitioner's home to arrest him for violation of a civil traffic offense. Such an arrest, however, is clearly prohibited by the special protection afforded the individual in his home by the Fourth Amendment. The petitioner's arrest was therefore invalid, the judgment of the Supreme Court of Wisconsin is vacated, and the case is remanded for further proceedings not inconsistent with this opinion.

Justice WHITE, with whom Justice REHNQUIST joins, dissenting

It follows from *Payton,* that warrantless non-felony arrests in the home are prohibited by the Fourth

---

[14] Nor do we mean to suggest that the prevention of drunk driving is not properly of major concern to the States. The State of Wisconsin, however, along with several other States, has chosen to limit severely the penalties that may be imposed after a first conviction for driving while intoxicated. Given that the classification of state crimes differs widely among the States, the penalty that may attach to any particular offense seems to provide the clearest and most consistent indication of the state's interest in arresting individuals suspected of committing that offense.

Amendment absent probable cause and exigent circumstances. Although I continue to believe that the Court erred in *Payton* in requiring exigent circumstances to justify warrantless in-home felony arrests, I do not reject the obvious logical implication of the Court's decision. But I see little to commend an approach that looks to "the nature of the underlying offense as an important factor to be considered in the exigent-circumstances calculus."

The gravity of the underlying offense is, I concede, a factor to be considered in determining whether the delay that attends the warrant-issuance process will endanger officers or other persons. The seriousness of the offense with which a suspect may be charged also bears on the likelihood that he will flee and escape apprehension if not arrested immediately. But if, under all the circumstances of a particular case, an officer has probable cause to believe that the delay involved in procuring an arrest warrant will gravely endanger the officer or other persons or will result in the suspect's escape, I perceive no reason to disregard those exigencies on the ground that the offense for which the suspect is sought is a "minor" one.

As a practical matter, I suspect, the Court's holding is likely to have a greater impact in cases where the officer acted without a warrant to prevent the imminent destruction or removal of evidence. If the evidence the destruction or removal of which is threatened documents only the suspect's participation in a "minor" crime, the Court apparently would preclude a finding that exigent circumstances justified the warrantless arrest. I do not understand why this should be so.

A warrantless home entry to arrest is no more intrusive when the crime is "minor" than when the suspect is sought in connection with a serious felony. The variable factor, if there is one, is the governmental interest that will be served by the warrantless entry. Wisconsin's Legislature and its Supreme Court have both concluded that warrantless in-home arrests under circumstances like those present here promote valid and substantial state interests. In determining whether the challenged governmental conduct was reasonable, we are not bound by these determinations. But nothing in our previous decisions suggests that the fact that a State has defined an offense as a misdemeanor for a variety of social, cultural, and political reasons necessarily requires the conclusion that warrantless in-home arrests designed to prevent the imminent destruction or removal of evidence of that offense are always impermissible. If anything, the Court's prior decisions support the opposite conclusion.

A test under which the existence of exigent circumstances turns on the perceived gravity of the crime would significantly hamper law enforcement and burden courts with pointless litigation concerning the nature and gradation of various crimes. The decision to arrest without a warrant typically is made in the field under less-than-optimal circumstances; officers have neither the time nor the competence to determine whether a particular offense for which warrantless arrests have been authorized by statute is serious enough to justify a warrantless home entry to prevent the imminent destruction or removal of evidence.

This problem could be lessened by creating a bright-line distinction between felonies and other crimes, but the Court—wisely in my view—does not adopt such an approach. There may have been a time when the line between misdemeanors and felonies marked off those offenses involving a sufficiently serious threat to society to justify warrantless in-home arrests under exigent circumstances. But the category of misdemeanors today includes enough serious offenses to call into question the desirability of such line drawing. If I am correct in asserting that a bright-line distinction between felonies and misdemeanors is untenable and that the need to prevent the imminent destruction or removal of evidence of some non-felony crimes can constitute an exigency justifying warrantless in-home arrests under certain circumstances, the Court's approach will necessitate a case-by-case evaluation of the seriousness of particular crimes, a difficult task for which officers and courts are poorly equipped.

[T]he fact that Wisconsin has chosen to punish the first offense for driving under the influence with a fine rather than a prison term does not demand the conclusion that the State's interest in punishing first offenders is insufficiently substantial to justify warrantless in-home arrests under exigent circumstances. As the Supreme Court of Wisconsin observed, "[t]his is a model case demonstrating the urgency involved in arresting the suspect in order to preserve evidence of the statutory violation." We have previously recognized that "the percentage of alcohol in the blood begins to diminish shortly after drinking stops, as the body functions to eliminate it from the system." Moreover, a suspect could cast substantial doubt on the validity of a blood or breath test by consuming additional alcohol upon arriving at his home. In light of the promptness with which the officers reached Welsh's house, therefore, I would hold that the need to prevent the imminent and ongoing destruction of evidence of a serious violation of Wisconsin's traffic laws provided an exigent circumstance justifying the warrantless in-home arrest.

I respectfully dissent.

## QUESTIONS AND NOTES

**1.** Ought Welsh's arrest have been justified under the *Santana* "hot pursuit" principle?

**2.** Is the Court adopting a *per se* rule about warrantless arrests for misdemeanors in the home, or is it only making that a factor?

**3.** Would (should) the case have been different if Wisconsin had made drunk driving a felony?

**4.** Suppose second offense drunk driving were a felony, and the police did not know whether Welsh had previously been convicted. What result? Why?

**5.** In *Olson,* we see the Court's unwillingness to allow a warrantless in-home arrest even for a very serious felony, unless the circumstances are truly exigent.

### Minnesota v. Olson
110 S.Ct. 1684 (1990)

WHITE, J., delivered the opinion of the Court.

The police in this case made a warrantless, nonconsensual entry into a house where Olson was an overnight guest and arrested him. The issue is whether the arrest violated Olson's Fourth Amendment rights. We hold that it did.

Shortly before 6 a.m. on Saturday, July 18, 1987, a lone gunman robbed an Amoco gasoline station in Minneapolis, Minnesota, and fatally shot the station manager. A police officer heard the police dispatcher report and suspected Joseph Ecker. The officer and his partner drove immediately to Ecker's home, arriving at about the same time that an Oldsmobile arrived. The Oldsmobile took evasive action, spun out of control, and came to a stop. Two men fled the car on foot. Ecker, who was later identified as the gunman, was captured shortly thereafter inside his home. The second man escaped.

Inside the abandoned Oldsmobile, police found a sack of money and the murder weapon. They also found a title certificate with the name Rob Olson crossed out as a secured party, a letter addressed to a Roger R. Olson of 3151 Johnson Street, and a videotape rental receipt made out to Rob Olson and dated two days earlier. The police verified that a Robert Olson lived at 3151 Johnson Street.

The next morning, Sunday, July 19, a woman identifying herself as Dianna Murphy called the police and said that a man by the name of Rob drove the car in which the gas-station killer left the scene and that Rob was planning to leave town by bus. About noon, the same woman called again, gave her address and phone number, and said that a man named Rob had told a Maria and two other women, Louanne and Julie, that he was the driver in the Amoco robbery. The caller stated that Louanne was Julie's mother and that the two women lived at 2406 Fillmore Northeast. The detective-in-charge who took the second phone call sent police officers to 2406 Fillmore to check out Louanne and Julie. When police arrived they determined that the dwelling was a duplex and that Louanne Bergstrom and her daughter Julie lived in the upper unit but were not home. Police spoke to Louanne's mother, Helen Niederhoffer, who lived in the lower unit. She confirmed that a Rob Olson had been staying upstairs but was not then in the unit. She promised to call the police when Olson returned. At 2 p.m., a pickup order, or "probable cause arrest bulletin," was issued for Olson's arrest. The police were instructed to stay away from the duplex.

At approximately 2:45 p.m., Niederhoffer called police and said Olson had returned. The detective-in-charge instructed police officers to go to the house and surround it. He then telephoned Julie from headquarters and told her Rob should come out of the house. The detective heard a male voice say "tell them I left." Julie stated that Rob had left, whereupon at 3 p.m. the detective ordered the police to enter the house. Without seeking permission and with weapons drawn, the police entered the upper unit and found respondent hiding in a closet. Less than an hour after his arrest, respondent made an inculpatory statement at police headquarters.

The Hennepin County trial court held a hearing and denied respondent's motion to suppress his statement. The statement was admitted into evidence at Olson's trial, and he was convicted on one count of first degree murder, three counts of armed robbery, and three counts of second degree assault. On appeal, the Minnesota Supreme Court reversed. The

court ruled that respondent had a sufficient interest in the Bergstrom home to challenge the legality of his warrantless arrest there, that the arrest was illegal because there were no exigent circumstances to justify a warrantless entry,[1] and that respondent's statement was tainted by that illegality and should have been suppressed.

In *Payton,* the Court had no occasion to "consider the sort of emergency or dangerous situation, described in our cases as 'exigent circumstances,' that would justify a warrantless entry into a home for the purpose of either arrest or search." This case requires us to determine whether the Minnesota Supreme Court was correct in holding that there were no exigent circumstances that justified the warrantless entry into the house to make the arrest.

The Minnesota Supreme Court applied essentially the correct standard in determining whether exigent circumstances existed. The court observed that "a warrantless intrusion may be justified by hot pursuit of a fleeing felon, or imminent destruction of evidence, *Welsh,* or the need to prevent a suspect's escape, or the risk of danger to the police or to other persons inside or outside the dwelling." The court also apparently thought that in the absence of hot pursuit there must be at least probable cause to believe that one or more of the other factors justifying the entry were present and that in assessing the risk of danger, the gravity of the crime and likelihood that the suspect is armed should be considered. Applying this standard, the state court determined that exigent circumstances did not exist.

We are not inclined to disagree with this fact-specific application of the proper legal standard. The court pointed out that although a grave crime was involved, respondent "was known not to be the murderer but thought to be the driver of the getaway car," and that the police had already recovered the murder weapon. "The police knew that Louanne and Julie were with the suspect in the upstairs duplex with no suggestion of danger to them. Three or four Minneapolis police squads surrounded the house. The time was 3 p.m., Sunday. . . . It was evident the suspect was going nowhere. If he came out of the house he would have been promptly apprehended." We do not disturb the state court's judgment that these facts do not add up to exigent circumstances.

---

[1] Because the absence of a warrant made respondent's arrest illegal, the court did not review the trial court's determination that the police had probable cause for the arrest. Hence, we judge the case on the assumption that there was probable cause.

We therefore affirm the judgment of the Minnesota Supreme Court.

**Justice KENNEDY, Concurring**

I interpret the last two paragraphs of [the opinion] as deference to a State court's application of the exigent circumstances test to the facts of this case, and not as an endorsement of that particular application of the standard. With that understanding, I join in the opinion of the Court.

REHNQUIST, C.J. and BLACKMUN, J dissented.

## QUESTIONS AND NOTES

**1.** Do you agree with Justice Kennedy's reading of the majority?

**2.** If he is correct, would the result have been different if the State Supreme Court had reached the opposite conclusion?

**3.** Should constitutional principles turn on the happenstance of a particular state court opinion?

**4.** How would you have voted if you had been on the Minnesota Supreme Court? The United States Supreme Court?

## PROBLEM

About 8 a.m. on March 17, 1962, an armed robber entered the business premises of the Diamond Cab Company in Baltimore, Maryland. He took some $363 and ran. Two cab drivers in the vicinity, attracted by shouts of "Holdup," followed the man to 2111 Cocoa Lane. One driver notified the company dispatcher by radio that the man was black, about 5'8'' tall, wearing a light cap and dark jacket, and that he had entered the house on Cocoa Lane. The dispatcher relayed the information to police who were proceeding to the scene of the robbery. Within minutes, police arrived at the house in a number of patrol cars. An officer knocked and announced their presence. Mrs. Hayden answered, and the officers told her they believed that a robber had entered the house, and asked to search the house.

The officers spread out through the first and second floors and the cellar in search of the robber. Hayden was found in an upstairs bedroom feigning sleep. He was arrested when the officers on the first floor and in the cellar reported that no other man was in the house. Meanwhile an officer was attracted to an adjoining bathroom by the noise of running water, and discovered a shotgun and a pistol in a flush tank; another officer who, according to the District Court, 'was searching the cellar for a man or the money' found in a washing machine a jacket and trousers of the type the fleeing man was said to have worn. A clip of ammunition for the pistol and a cap were found under the mattress of Hayden's bed, and ammunition for the shotgun was found in a bureau drawer in Hayden's room. All these items of evidence were introduced against him at his trial.

Should Hayden's warrantless arrest have been upheld? For the Supreme Court's pre-*Payton* answer, see *Warden v. Hayden,* 387 U.S. 294 (1967).

## E. Force In Effectuating An Arrest

For most of our history, the amount of force used in effectuating an arrest was not thought to raise any Fourth Amendment concerns. That changed abruptly in 1985 when the Supreme Court decided *Tennessee v. Garner.* As you read *Garner* consider whether the Court is giving the Fourth Amendment more weight than it can properly bear.

## Tennessee v. Garner
### 471 U.S. 1 (1985)

Justice WHITE delivered the opinion of the Court.

This case requires us to determine the constitutionality of the use of deadly force to prevent the escape of an apparently unarmed suspected felon. We conclude that such force may not be used unless it is necessary to prevent the escape and the officer has probable cause to believe that the suspect poses a significant threat of death or serious physical injury to the officer or others.

### I

At about 10:45 p.m. on October 3, 1974, Memphis Police Officers Elton Hymon and Leslie Wright were dispatched to answer a "prowler inside call." Upon arriving at the scene they saw a woman standing on her porch and gesturing toward the adjacent house. She told them she had heard glass breaking and that "they" or "someone" was breaking in next door. While Wright radioed the dispatcher to say that they were on the scene, Hymon went behind the house. He heard a door slam and saw someone run across the backyard. The fleeing suspect, who was decedent, Edward Garner, stopped at a 6-feet-high chain link fence at the edge of the yard. With the aid of a flashlight, Hymon was able to see Garner's face and hands. He saw no sign of a weapon, and, though not certain, was "reasonably sure" and "figured" that Garner was unarmed. He thought Garner was 17 or 18 years old and about 5'5" or 5'7" tall.[2] While Garner was crouched at the base of the fence, Hymon called out "police, halt" and took a few steps toward him. Garner then began to climb over the fence. Convinced that if Garner made it over the fence he would elude capture, Hymon shot him. The bullet hit Garner in the back of the head. Garner was taken by ambulance to a hospital, where he died on the operating table. Ten dollars and a purse taken from the house were found on his body.[4]

### II

Whenever an officer restrains the freedom of a person to walk away, he has seized that person. While it is not always clear just when minimal police interference becomes a seizure, there can be no question that apprehension by the use of deadly force is a seizure subject to the reasonableness requirement of the Fourth Amendment.

### A

A police officer may arrest a person if he has probable cause to believe that person committed a crime. *Watson.* Petitioners and appellant argue that if this requirement is satisfied the Fourth Amendment has nothing to say about *how* that seizure is made. This submission ignores the many cases in which this Court, by balancing the extent of the intrusion against the need for it, has examined the reasonableness of the manner in which a search or seizure is conducted. To determine the constitutionality of a seizure "[w]e must balance the nature and quality of the intrusion on the individual's Fourth Amendment interests against the importance of the governmental interests alleged to justify the intrusion." We have described "the balancing of competing interests" as "the key principle of the Fourth Amendment." Because one of the factors is the extent of the intrusion, it is plain that reasonableness depends on not only when a seizure is made, but also how it is carried out.

### B

The intrusiveness of a seizure by means of deadly force is unmatched. The suspect's fundamental interest in his own life need not be elaborated upon. The use of deadly force also frustrates the interest of the individual, and of society, in judicial determination of guilt and punishment. Against these interests are ranged governmental interests in effective law enforcement.[8] It is argued that overall violence will be

---

[2] In fact, Garner, an eighth-grader, was 15. He was 5'4" tall and weighed somewhere around 100 or 110 pounds.

[4] Garner had rummaged through one room in the house, in which, in the words of the owner, "[a]ll the stuff was out on the floors, all the drawers was pulled out, and stuff was scattered all over." The owner testified that his valuables were untouched but that, in addition to the purse and the 10 dollars, one of his wife's rings was missing. The ring was not recovered.

---

[8] The dissent emphasizes that subsequent investigation cannot replace immediate apprehension. We recognize that this is so, see n. 13, *infra*; indeed, that is the reason why there is any dispute. If subsequent arrest were assured, no one would argue that use of deadly force was justified. Thus, we proceed on the assumption that subsequent arrest is not likely. Nonetheless, it should be remembered that failure to apprehend at the scene does not necessarily mean that the suspect will never be caught.

reduced by encouraging the peaceful submission of suspects who know that they may be shot if they flee. Effectiveness in making arrests requires the resort to deadly force, or at least the meaningful threat thereof. "Being able to arrest such individuals is a condition precedent to the state's entire system of law enforcement."

Without in any way disparaging the importance of these goals, we are not convinced that the use of deadly force is a sufficiently productive means of accomplishing them to justify the killing of nonviolent suspects. The use of deadly force is a self-defeating way of apprehending a suspect and so setting the criminal justice mechanism in motion. If successful, it guarantees that that mechanism will not be set in motion. And while the meaningful threat of deadly force might be thought to lead to the arrest of more live suspects by discouraging escape attempts, the presently available evidence does not support this thesis. Petitioners and appellant have not persuaded us that shooting non-dangerous fleeing suspects is so vital as to outweigh the suspect's interest in his own life.

The use of deadly force to prevent the escape of all felony suspects, whatever the circumstances, is constitutionally unreasonable. It is not better that all felony suspects die than that they escape. Where the suspect poses no immediate threat to the officer and no threat to others, the harm resulting from failing to apprehend him does not justify the use of deadly force to do so. It is no doubt unfortunate when a suspect who is in sight escapes, but the fact that the police arrive a little late or are a little slower afoot does not always justify killing the suspect. A police officer may not seize an unarmed, non-dangerous suspect by shooting him dead. The Tennessee statute is unconstitutional insofar as it authorizes the use of deadly force against such fleeing suspects.

### III

#### A

It is insisted that the Fourth Amendment must be construed in light of the common-law rule, which allowed the use of whatever force was necessary to effect the arrest of a fleeing felon, though not a misdemeanant. As stated in Hale's posthumously published Pleas of the Crown: "[I]f persons that are pursued by these officers for felony or the just suspicion thereof . . . shall not yield themselves to these officers, but shall either resist or fly before they are apprehended or being apprehended shall rescue themselves and resist or fly, so that they cannot be otherwise apprehended, and are upon necessity slain therein, because they cannot be otherwise taken, it is no felony." Most American jurisdictions also imposed a flat prohibition against

the use of deadly force to stop a fleeing misdemeanant, coupled with a general privilege to use such force to stop a fleeing felon.

The State and city argue that because this was the prevailing rule at the time of the adoption of the Fourth Amendment and for some time thereafter, and is still in force in some States, use of deadly force against a fleeing felon must be "reasonable." It is true that this Court has often looked to the common law in evaluating the reasonableness, for Fourth Amendment purposes, of police activity. On the other hand, it "has not simply frozen into constitutional law those law enforcement practices that existed at the time of the Fourth Amendment's passage." Because of sweeping change in the legal and technological context, reliance on the common-law rule in this case would be a mistaken literalism that ignores the purposes of a historical inquiry.

#### B

It has been pointed out many times that the common-law rule is best understood in light of the fact that it arose at a time when virtually all felonies were punishable by death. "Though effected without the protections and formalities of an orderly trial and conviction, the killing of a resisting or fleeing felon resulted in no greater consequences than those authorized for punishment of the felony of which the individual was charged or suspected." Courts have also justified the common-law rule by emphasizing the relative dangerousness of felons.

Neither of these justifications makes sense today. Almost all crimes formerly punishable by death no longer are or can be. And while in earlier times "the gulf between the felonies and the minor offences was broad and deep," today the distinction is minor and often arbitrary. Many crimes classified as misdemeanors, or nonexistent, at common law are now felonies. These changes have undermined the concept, which was questionable to begin with, that use of deadly force against a fleeing felon is merely a speedier execution of someone who has already forfeited his life. They have also made the assumption that a "felon" is more dangerous than a misdemeanant untenable. Indeed, numerous misdemeanors involve conduct more dangerous than many felonies.[12]

There is an additional reason why the common-law rule cannot be directly translated to the present day. The common-law rule developed at a time when

---

[12] White-collar crime, for example, poses a less significant physical threat than, say, drunken driving.

weapons were rudimentary. Deadly force could be inflicted almost solely in a hand-to-hand struggle during which, necessarily, the safety of the arresting officer was at risk. Handguns were not carried by police officers until the latter half of the last century. Only then did it become possible to use deadly force from a distance as a means of apprehension. As a practical matter, the use of deadly force under the standard articulation of the common-law rule has an altogether different meaning—and harsher consequences—now than in past centuries.[13]

One other aspect of the common-law rule bears emphasis. It forbids the use of deadly force to apprehend a misdemeanant, condemning such action as disproportionately severe.

In short, though the common-law pedigree of Tennessee's rule is pure on its face, changes in the legal and technological context mean the rule is distorted almost beyond recognition when literally applied.

### C

In evaluating the reasonableness of police procedures under the Fourth Amendment, we have also looked to prevailing rules in individual jurisdictions.

It cannot be said that there is a constant or overwhelming trend away from the common-law rule. In recent years, some States have reviewed their laws and expressly rejected abandonment of the common-law rule. Nonetheless, the long-term movement has been away from the rule that deadly force may be used against any fleeing felon, and that remains the rule in less than half the States.

This trend is more evident and impressive when viewed in light of the policies adopted by the police departments themselves. Overwhelmingly, these are

---

[13] It has been argued that sophisticated techniques of apprehension and increased communication between the police in different jurisdictions have made it more likely that an escapee will be caught than was once the case, and that this change has also reduced the "reasonableness" of the use of deadly force to prevent escape. *E.g.,* Sherman, Execution Without Trial: Police Homicide and the Constitution, 33 Vand.L.Rev. 71, 76 (1980). We are unaware of any data that would permit sensible evaluation of this claim. Current arrest rates are sufficiently low, however, that we have some doubt whether in past centuries the failure to arrest at the scene meant that the police had missed their only chance in a way that is not presently the case. In 1983, 21% of the offenses in the Federal Bureau of Investigation crime index were cleared by arrest.

more restrictive than the common-law rule. The Federal Bureau of Investigation and the New York City Police Department, for example, both forbid the use of firearms except when necessary to prevent death or grievous bodily harm. A 1974 study reported that the police department regulations in a majority of the large cities of the United States allowed the firing of a weapon only when a felon presented a threat of death or serious bodily harm. Overall, only 7.5% of departmental and municipal policies explicitly permit the use of deadly force against any felon; 86.8% explicitly do not. In light of the rules adopted by those who must actually administer them, the older and fading common-law view is a dubious indicium of the constitutionality of the Tennessee statute now before us.

### D

Actual departmental policies are important for an additional reason. We would hesitate to declare a police practice of long standing "unreasonable" if doing so would severely hamper effective law enforcement. But the indications are to the contrary. There has been no suggestion that crime has worsened in any way in jurisdictions that have adopted, by legislation or departmental policy, rules similar to that announced today. *Amici* noted that "[a]fter extensive research and consideration, [they] have concluded that laws permitting police officers to use deadly force to apprehend unarmed, nonviolent fleeing felony suspects actually do not protect citizens or law enforcement officers, do not deter crime or alleviate problems caused by crime, and do not improve the crime-fighting ability of law enforcement agencies." The submission is that the obvious state interests in apprehension are not sufficiently served to warrant the use of lethal weapons against all fleeing felons.

Nor do we agree with petitioners and appellant that the rule we have adopted requires the police to make impossible, split-second evaluations of unknowable facts. We do not deny the practical difficulties of attempting to assess the suspect's dangerousness. However, similarly difficult judgments must be made by the police in equally uncertain circumstances. Nor is there any indication that in States that allow the use of deadly force only against dangerous suspects, the standard has been difficult to apply or has led to a rash of litigation involving inappropriate second-guessing of police officers' split-second decisions. Moreover, the highly technical felony/misdemeanor distinction is equally, if not more, difficult to apply in the field. An officer is in no position to know, for example, the precise value of property stolen, or whether the crime was a first or second offense. Finally, as noted above, this claim must be viewed with suspicion in light of the similar self-imposed limitations of so many police departments.

## IV

The District Court concluded that Hymon was justified in shooting Garner because state law allows, and the Federal Constitution does not forbid, the use of deadly force to prevent the escape of a fleeing felony suspect if no alternative means of apprehension is available. This conclusion made a determination of Garner's apparent dangerousness unnecessary. The court did find, however, that Garner appeared to be unarmed, though Hymon could not be certain that was the case. Restated in Fourth Amendment terms, this means Hymon had no articulable basis to think Garner was armed.

The dissent argues that the shooting was justified by the fact that Officer Hymon had probable cause to believe that Garner had committed a nighttime burglary. While we agree that burglary is a serious crime, we cannot agree that it is so dangerous as automatically to justify the use of deadly force. The FBI classifies burglary as a "property" rather than a "violent" crime. Although the armed burglar would present a different situation, the fact that an unarmed suspect has broken into a dwelling at night does not automatically mean he is physically dangerous. This case demonstrates as much. In fact, the available statistics demonstrate that burglaries only rarely involve physical violence. During the 10-year period from 1973-1982, only 3.8% of all burglaries involved violent crime.[23] We hold that the statute is

---

[23] The dissent points out that three-fifths of all rapes in the home, three-fifths of all home robberies, and about a third of home assaults are committed by burglars. These figures mean only that if one knows that a suspect committed a rape in the home, there is a good chance that the suspect is also a burglar. That has nothing to do with the question here, which is whether the fact that someone has committed a burglary indicates that he has committed, or might commit, a violent crime. The dissent also points out that this 3.8% adds up to 2.8 million violent crimes over a 10-year period, as if to imply that today's holding will let loose 2.8 million violent burglars. The relevant universe is, of course, far smaller. At issue is only that tiny fraction of cases where violence has taken place and an officer who has no other means of apprehending the suspect is unaware of its occurrence.

invalid insofar as it purported to give Hymon the authority to act as he did.

Justice O'CONNOR, with whom the CHIEF JUSTICE and Justice REHNQUIST join, dissenting.

The Court today holds that the Fourth Amendment prohibits a police officer from using deadly force as a last resort to apprehend a criminal suspect who refuses to halt when fleeing the scene of a nighttime burglary. This conclusion rests on the majority's balancing of the interests of the suspect and the public interest in effective law enforcement. Notwithstanding the venerable common-law rule authorizing the use of deadly force if necessary to apprehend a fleeing felon, and continued acceptance of this rule by nearly half the States, the majority concludes that Tennessee's statute is unconstitutional inasmuch as it allows the use of such force to apprehend a burglary suspect who is not obviously armed or otherwise dangerous. Although the circumstances of this case are unquestionably tragic and unfortunate, our constitutional holdings must be sensitive both to the history of the Fourth Amendment and to the general implications of the Court's reasoning. By disregarding the serious and dangerous nature of residential burglaries and the longstanding practice of many States, the Court effectively creates a Fourth Amendment right allowing a burglary suspect to flee unimpeded from a police officer who has probable cause to arrest, who has ordered the suspect to halt, and who has no means short of firing his weapon to prevent escape. I do not believe that the Fourth Amendment supports such a right, and I accordingly dissent.

## I

The facts below warrant brief review because they highlight the difficult, split-second decisions police officers must make in these circumstances. Memphis Police Officers Elton Hymon and Leslie Wright responded to a late-night call that a burglary was in progress at a private residence. When the officers arrived at the scene, the caller said that "they" were breaking into the house next door. The officers found the residence had been forcibly entered through a window and saw lights on inside the house. Officer Hymon testified that when he saw the broken window he realized "that something was wrong inside," but that he could not determine whether anyone – either a burglar or a member of the household – was within the residence. As Officer Hymon walked behind the house, he heard a door slam. He saw Edward Eugene Garner run away from the house through the dark and cluttered backyard. Garner crouched next to a 6-foot-high fence. Officer Hymon thought Garner was an adult and was unsure whether Garner was armed because Hymon "had no idea what was in the hand [that he could not see] or what he might have had on his person." In fact, Garner was 15 years old and unarmed. Hymon also did not know whether accomplices remained inside the house. The officer identified himself as a police officer and ordered Garner to halt. Garner paused briefly and then sprang to the top of the fence. Believing that Garner would escape if he climbed over the fence, Hymon fired his revolver and mortally wounded the suspected burglar.

The precise issue before the Court deserves emphasis, because both the decision below and the majority obscure what must be decided in this case. The issue is not the constitutional validity of the Tennessee statute on its face or as applied to some hypothetical set of facts. Instead, the issue is whether the use of deadly force by Officer Hymon under the circumstances of this case violated Garner's constitutional rights. Thus, the majority's assertion that a police officer who has probable cause to seize a suspect "may not always do so by killing him" is unexceptionable but also of little relevance to the question presented here. The same is true of the rhetorically stirring statement that "[t]he use of deadly force to prevent the escape of all felony suspects, whatever the circumstances, is constitutionally unreasonable." The question we must address is whether the Constitution allows the use of such force to apprehend a suspect who resists arrest by attempting to flee the scene of a nighttime burglary of a residence.

## II

For purposes of Fourth Amendment analysis, I agree with the Court that Officer Hymon "seized" Garner by shooting him. Whether that seizure was reasonable and therefore permitted by the Fourth Amendment requires a careful balancing of the important public interest in crime prevention and detection and the nature and quality of the intrusion upon legitimate interests of the individual. In striking this balance here, it is crucial to acknowledge that police use of deadly force to apprehend a fleeing criminal suspect falls within the "rubric of police conduct . . . necessarily [involving] swift action predicated upon the on-the-spot observations of the officer on the beat." The clarity of hindsight cannot provide the standard for judging the reasonableness of police decisions made in uncertain and often dangerous circumstances. Moreover, I am far more reluctant than is the Court to conclude that the Fourth Amendment proscribes a police practice that was accepted at the time of the adoption of the Bill of Rights and has continued to receive the support of many state legislatures. Although the Court has recognized that the requirements

of the Fourth Amendment must respond to the reality of social and technological change, fidelity to the notion of *constitutional* — as opposed to purely judicial — limits on governmental action requires us to impose a heavy burden on those who claim that practices accepted when the Fourth Amendment was adopted are now constitutionally impermissible.

The public interest involved in the use of deadly force as a last resort to apprehend a fleeing burglary suspect relates primarily to the serious nature of the crime. Household burglaries not only represent the illegal entry into a person's home, but also "pos[e] real risk of serious harm to others." According to recent Department of Justice statistics, "[t]hree-fifths of all rapes in the home, three-fifths of all home robberies, and about a third of home aggravated and simple assaults are committed by burglars." During the period 1973-1982, 2.8 million such violent crimes were committed in the course of burglaries. Victims of a forcible intrusion into their home by a nighttime prowler will find little consolation in the majority's confident assertion that "burglaries only rarely involve physical violence." Moreover, even if a particular burglary, when viewed in retrospect, does not involve physical harm to others, the "harsh potentialities for violence" inherent in the forced entry into a home preclude characterization of the crime as "innocuous, inconsequential, minor, or 'nonviolent.'"

Because burglary is a serious and dangerous felony, the public interest in the prevention and detection of the crime is of compelling importance. Where a police officer has probable cause to arrest a suspected burglar, the use of deadly force as a last resort might well be the only means of apprehending the suspect. With respect to a particular burglary, subsequent investigation simply cannot represent a substitute for immediate apprehension of the criminal suspect at the scene. Indeed, the Captain of the Memphis Police Department testified that in his city, if apprehension is not immediate, it is likely that the suspect will not be caught. Although some law enforcement agencies may choose to assume the risk that a criminal will remain at large, the Tennessee statute reflects a legislative determination that the use of deadly force in prescribed circumstances will serve generally to protect the public. Such statutes assist the police in apprehending suspected perpetrators of serious crimes and provide notice that a lawful police order to stop and submit to arrest may not be ignored with impunity.

The Court unconvincingly dismisses the general deterrence effects by stating that "the presently available evidence does not support [the] thesis" that the threat of force discourages escape and that "there is a substantial basis for doubting that the use of such force is an essential attribute to the arrest power in all felony cases.'' There is no question that the effectiveness of police use of deadly force is arguable and that many States or individual police departments have decided not to authorize it in circumstances similar to those presented here. But it should go without saying that the effectiveness or popularity of a particular police practice does not determine its constitutionality.

Against the strong public interests justifying the conduct at issue here must be weighed the individual interests implicated in the use of deadly force by police officers. The majority declares that ''[t]he suspect's fundamental interest in his own life need not be elaborated upon.'' This blithe assertion hardly provides an adequate substitute for the majority's failure to acknowledge the distinctive manner in which the suspect's interest in his life is even exposed to risk. For purposes of this case, we must recall that the police officer, in the course of investigating a nighttime burglary, had reasonable cause to arrest the suspect and ordered him to halt. The officer's use of force resulted because the suspected burglar refused to heed this command and the officer reasonably believed that there was no means short of firing his weapon to apprehend the suspect. Without questioning the importance of a person's interest in his life, I do not think this interest encompasses a right to flee unimpeded from the scene of a burglary. Cf. *Payton* (White, J., dissenting) (''[T]he policeman's hands should not be tied merely because of the possibility that the suspect will fail to cooperate with legitimate actions by law enforcement personnel''). The legitimate interests of the suspect in these circumstances are adequately accommodated by the Tennessee statute: to avoid the use of deadly force and the consequent risk to his life, the suspect need merely obey the valid order to halt.

A proper balancing of the interests involved suggests that use of deadly force as a last resort to apprehend a criminal suspect fleeing from the scene of a nighttime burglary is not unreasonable within the meaning of the Fourth Amendment. Admittedly, the events giving rise to this case are in retrospect deeply regrettable. No one can view the death of an unarmed and apparently nonviolent 15-year-old without sorrow, much less disapproval. Nonetheless, the reasonableness of Officer Hymon's conduct for purposes of the Fourth Amendment cannot be evaluated by what later appears to have been a preferable course of police action. The officer pursued a suspect in the darkened backyard of a house that from all indications had just been burglarized. The police officer was not certain whether the suspect was alone or unarmed; nor did he know what had transpired inside the house. He ordered the suspect to halt, and when the suspect refused to obey and attempted to flee into the night, the officer fired his weapon to prevent escape. The reasonableness of this action for purposes of the Fourth Amendment is not determined by the unfortunate nature of this particular case; instead, the question is whether it is constitutionally impermissible for police officers, as a last resort, to shoot a burglary suspect fleeing the scene of the crime.

IV

I cannot accept the majority's creation of a constitutional right to flight for burglary suspects seeking to avoid capture at the scene of the crime. Whatever the constitutional limits on police use of deadly force in order to apprehend a fleeing felon, I do not believe they are exceeded in a case in which a police officer has probable cause to arrest a suspect at the scene of a residential burglary, orders the suspect to halt, and then fires his weapon as a last resort to prevent the suspect's escape into the night. I respectfully dissent.

## QUESTIONS AND NOTES

**1.** Is there a difference in approach between *Watson* and *Garner* insofar as deference to history is concerned?

**2.** Isn't there more reason to defer to tradition in *Garner* in that all *Watson* asked for was a warrant when practicable prior to arrest, whereas Garner was functionally asking for the right to escape?

**3.** Do you think that the amount of force used has much to do with Fourth Amendment values? Why?

**4.** Assuming that the Court was correct on the relationship of force and the severity of the crime, do you agree that it properly categorized nighttime burglary? Explain your answer.

**5.** Arguably *Garner* could have been limited to cases of deadly force, however, in *Graham* any such limitation was explicitly rejected.

# Graham v. Connor
## 490 U.S. 386 (1989)

REHNQUIST C.J. delivered the opinion of the Court.

This case requires us to decide what constitutional standard governs a free citizen's claim that law enforcement officials used excessive force in the course of making an arrest, investigatory stop, or other "seizure" of his person. We hold that such claims are properly analyzed under the Fourth Amendment's "objective reasonableness" standard, rather than under a substantive due process standard.

In this action under 42 U.S.C. § 1983, petitioner Dethorne Graham seeks to recover damages for injuries allegedly sustained when law enforcement officers used physical force against him during the course of an investigatory stop. Because the case comes to us from a decision of the Court of Appeals affirming the entry of a directed verdict for respondents, we take the evidence hereafter noted in the light most favorable to petitioner. On November 12, 1984, Graham, a diabetic, felt the onset of an insulin reaction. He asked a friend, William Berry, to drive him to a nearby convenience store so he could purchase some orange juice to counteract the reaction. Berry agreed, but when Graham entered the store, he saw a number of people ahead of him in the checkout line. Concerned about the delay, he hurried out of the store and asked Berry to drive him to a friend's house instead.

Respondent Connor, an officer of the Charlotte, North Carolina, Police Department, saw Graham hastily enter and leave the store. The officer became suspicious that something was amiss and followed Berry's car. About one-half mile from the store, he made an investigative stop. Although Berry told Connor that Graham was simply suffering from a "sugar reaction," the officer ordered Berry and Graham to wait while he found out what, if anything, had happened at the convenience store. When Officer Connor returned to his patrol car to call for backup assistance, Graham got out of the car, ran around it twice, and finally sat down on the curb, where he passed out briefly.

In the ensuing confusion, a number of other Charlotte police officers arrived on the scene in response to Officer Connor's request for backup. One of the officers rolled Graham over on the sidewalk and cuffed his hands tightly behind his back, ignoring Berry's pleas to get him some sugar. Another officer said: "I've seen a lot of people with sugar diabetes that never acted like this. Ain't nothing wrong with the M.F. but drunk. Lock the S.B. up." Several officers then lifted Graham up from behind, carried him over to Berry's car, and placed him face down on its hood. Regaining consciousness, Graham asked the officers to check in his wallet for a diabetic decal that he carried. In response, one of the officers told him to "shut up" and shoved his face down against the hood of the car. Four officers grabbed Graham and threw him headfirst into the police car. A friend of Graham's brought some orange juice to the car, but the officers refused to let him have it. Finally, Officer Connor received a report that Graham had done nothing wrong at the convenience store, and the officers drove him home and released him.

At some point during his encounter with the police, Graham sustained a broken foot, cuts on his wrists, a bruised forehead, and an injured shoulder; he also claims to have developed a loud ringing in his right ear that continues to this day. He commenced this action against the individual officers involved in the incident, all of whom are respondents here, alleging that they had used excessive force in making the investigatory stop, in violation of "rights secured to him under the Fourteenth Amendment to the United States Constitution."

Where, as here, the excessive force claim arises in the context of an arrest or investigatory stop of a free citizen, it is most properly characterized as one invoking the protections of the Fourth Amendment, which guarantees citizens the right "to be secure in their persons . . . against unreasonable . . . seizures" of the person. This much is clear from our decision in *Garner*. In *Garner*, we addressed a claim that the use of deadly force to apprehend a fleeing suspect who did not appear to be armed or otherwise dangerous violated the suspect's constitutional rights, notwithstanding the existence of probable cause to arrest. Though the complaint alleged violations of both the Fourth Amendment and the Due Process Clause, we analyzed the constitutionality of the challenged application of force solely by reference to the Fourth Amendment's prohibition against unreasonable seizures of the person, holding that the "reasonableness" of a particular seizure depends not only on *when* it is made, but also on *how* it is carried out. Today we make explicit what was implicit in *Garner*'s analysis, and hold that *all* claims that law enforcement officers have used excessive force—deadly or not—in the course of an arrest, investigatory stop, or other "seizure" of a free citizen should be analyzed under the Fourth Amendment and its "reasonableness" standard, rather than under a "substantive due process" approach. Because the Fourth Amendment provides an explicit textual source of constitutional protection against this sort of physically intrusive governmental conduct, that Amendment, not the more generalized notion of "substantive due process," must be the guide for analyzing these claims.

Determining whether the force used to effect a particular seizure is "reasonable" under the Fourth Amendment requires a careful balancing of "the nature and quality of the intrusion on the individual's Fourth Amendment interests" against the countervailing governmental interests at stake. Our Fourth Amendment jurisprudence has long recognized that the right to make an arrest or investigatory stop necessarily carries with it the right to use some degree of physical coercion or threat thereof to effect it. Because "[t]he test of reasonableness under the Fourth Amendment is not capable of precise definition or mechanical application," however, its proper application requires careful attention to the facts and circumstances of each particular case, including the severity of the crime at issue, whether the suspect poses an immediate threat to the safety of the officers or others, and whether he is actively resisting arrest or attempting to evade arrest by flight.

The "reasonableness" of a particular use of force must be judged from the perspective of a reasonable officer on the scene, rather than with the 20/20 vision of hindsight. The Fourth Amendment is not violated by an arrest based on probable cause, even though the wrong person is arrested, nor by the mistaken execution of a valid search warrant on the wrong premises. With respect to a claim of excessive force, the same standard of reasonableness at the moment applies: "Not every push or shove, even if it may later seem unnecessary in the peace of a judge's chambers," violates the Fourth Amendment. The calculus of reasonableness must embody allowance for the fact that police officers are often forced to make split-second judgments – in circumstances that are tense, uncertain, and rapidly evolving – about the amount of force that is necessary in a particular situation.

As in other Fourth Amendment contexts, however, the "reasonableness" inquiry in an excessive force case is an objective one: the question is whether the officers' actions are "objectively reasonable" in light of the facts and circumstances confronting them, without regard to their underlying intent or motivation. An officer's evil intentions will not make a Fourth Amendment violation out of an objectively reasonable use of force; nor will an officer's good intentions make an objectively unreasonable use of force constitutional.

Because petitioner's excessive force claim is one

arising under the Fourth Amendment, the Court of Appeals erred in analyzing it under the *Johnson v. Glick* [481 F.2d 1028 (2d. Cir. 1973)] test. That test, which requires consideration of whether the individual officers acted in "good faith" or "maliciously and sadistically for the very purpose of causing harm," is incompatible with a proper Fourth Amendment analysis. We do not agree with the Court of Appeals' suggestion that the "malicious and sadistic" inquiry is merely another way of describing conduct that is objectively unreasonable under the circumstances. Whatever the empirical correlations between "malicious and sadistic" behavior and objective unreasonableness may be, the fact remains that the "malicious and sadistic" factor puts in issue the subjective motivations of the individual officers, which our prior cases make clear has no bearing on whether a particular seizure is "unreasonable" under the Fourth Amendment. Nor do we agree with the Court of Appeals' conclusion that because the subjective motivations of the individual officers are of central importance in deciding whether force used against a convicted prisoner violates the Eighth Amendment, it cannot be reversible error to inquire into them in deciding whether force used against a suspect or arrestee violates the Fourth Amendment. Differing standards under the Fourth and Eighth Amendments are hardly surprising: the terms "cruel" and "punishment" clearly suggest some inquiry into subjective state of mind, whereas the term "unreasonable" does not. Moreover, the less protective Eighth Amendment standard applies "only after the State has complied with the constitutional guarantees traditionally associated with criminal prosecutions." The Fourth Amendment inquiry is one of "objective reasonableness" under the circumstances, and subjective concepts like "malice" and "sadism" have no proper place in that inquiry.[12]

---

[12] Of course, in assessing the credibility of an officer's account of the circumstances that prompted the use of force, a fact finder may consider, along with other factors, evidence that the officer may have harbored ill-will toward the citizen. Similarly, the officer's objective "good faith" – that is, whether he could reasonably have believed that the force used did not violate the Fourth Amendment – may be relevant to the availability of the qualified immunity defense to monetary liability under § 1983. Since no claim of qualified immunity has been raised in this case, however, we express no view on its proper application in excessive force cases that arise under the Fourth Amendment.

Because the Court of Appeals reviewed the District Court's ruling on the motion for directed verdict under an erroneous view of the governing substantive law, its judgment must be vacated and the case remanded to that court for reconsideration of that issue under the proper Fourth Amendment standard.

## QUESTIONS AND NOTES

**1.** Does *Garner* or *Graham* present a stronger Fourth Amendment claim? Explain your answer.

**2.** On retrial, do you think that Graham will prevail? Why? Why not?

**3.** Does *Graham* put an undue burden on the police? Does it put enough of a burden on them?

## F. Search Incident To Arrest

From a police perspective, perhaps the single most important factor in the rules governing arrest is the right to search incident to the arrest. Recall that in *Draper* (Chapter 2, *supra*), the legality of the arrest was significant only insofar as it allowed the government to introduce in evidence, the heroin seized from Draper's person. In the cases that follow, we will focus on the rationale for and limitations on a search incident to the arrest.

### Chimel v. California
### 395 U.S. 752 (1969)

Mr. Justice STEWART delivered the opinion of the Court.

This case raises basic questions concerning the permissible scope under the Fourth Amendment of a search incident to a lawful arrest.

The relevant facts are essentially undisputed. Late in the afternoon of September 13, 1965, three police officers arrived at the Santa Ana, California, home of the petitioner with a warrant authorizing his arrest for the burglary of a coin shop. The officers knocked on the door, identified themselves to the petitioner's wife, and asked if they might come inside. She ushered them into the house, where they waited 10 or 15 minutes until the petitioner returned home from work. When the petitioner entered the house, one of the officers handed him the arrest warrant and asked for permission to "look around." The petitioner objected, but was advised that "on the basis of the lawful arrest," the officers would nonetheless conduct a search. No search warrant had been issued.

Accompanied by the petitioner's wife, the officers then looked through the entire three-bedroom house, including the attic, the garage, and a small workshop. In some rooms the search was relatively cursory. In the master bedroom and sewing room, however, the officers directed the petitioner's wife to open drawers and "to physically move contents of the drawers from side to side so that [they] might view any items that would have come from [the] burglary." After completing the search, they seized numerous items—primarily coins, but also several medals, tokens, and a few other objects. The entire search took between 45 minutes and an hour.

Without deciding the question, we proceed on the hypothesis that the California courts were correct in holding that the arrest of the petitioner was valid under the Constitution. This brings us directly to the question whether the warrantless search of the petitioner's entire house can be constitutionally justified as incident to that arrest. The decisions of this Court bearing upon that question have been far from consistent, as even the most cursory review makes evident.

Approval of a warrantless search incident to a lawful arrest seems first to have been articulated by the Court in 1914 as dictum in *Weeks v. United States*, 232 U.S. 383. Without explanation, the principle emerged in expanded form in *Agnello v. United States*, 269 U.S. 20—although still by way of dictum:

"The right without a search warrant contemporaneously to search persons lawfully arrested while committing crime and to search the place where the arrest is made in order to find and seize things connected with the crime as its fruits or as the means by which it was committed, as well as weapons and other things to effect an escape from custody, is not to be doubted.''

And in *Marron v. United States,* 275 U.S. 192, two years later, the dictum of *Agnello* appeared to be the foundation of the Court's decision. In that case federal agents had secured a search warrant authorizing the seizure of liquor and certain articles used in its manufacture. When they arrived at the premises to be searched, they saw "that the place was used for retailing and drinking intoxicating liquors." They proceeded to arrest the person in charge and to execute the warrant. In searching a closet for the items listed in the warrant they came across an incriminating ledger, concededly not covered by the warrant, which they also seized. The Court upheld the seizure of the ledger by holding that since the agents had made a lawful arrest, "[t]hey had a right without a warrant contemporaneously to search the place in order to find and seize the things used to carry on the criminal enterprise."

That the *Marron* opinion did not mean all that it seemed to say became evident, however, a few years later in *Go-Bart Importing Co. v. United States,* 282 U.S. 344, and *United States v. Lefkowitz,* 285 U.S. 452. In each of those cases the opinion of the Court was written by Mr. Justice Butler, the author of the opinion in *Marron.* In *Go-Bart,* agents had searched the office of persons whom they had lawfully arrested, and had taken several papers from a desk, a safe, and other parts of the office. The Court noted that no crime had been committed in the agents' presence, and that although the agent in charge "had an abundance of information and time to swear out a valid (search) warrant, he failed to do so." In holding the search and seizure unlawful, the Court stated:

> "Plainly the case before us is essentially different from *Marron.* There, officers executing a valid search warrant for intoxicating liquors found and arrested one Birdsall who in pursuance of a conspiracy was actually engaged in running a saloon. As an incident to the arrest they seized a ledger in a closet where the liquor or some of it was kept and some bills beside the cash register. These things were visible and accessible and in the offender's immediate custody. There was no threat of force or general search or rummaging of the place."

This limited characterization of *Marron* was reiterated in *Lefkowitz,* a case in which the Court held unlawful a search of desk drawers and a cabinet despite the fact that the search had accompanied a lawful arrest.

The limiting views expressed in *Go-Bart* and *Lefkowitz* were thrown to the winds, however, in *Harris v. United States,* 331 U.S. 145, decided in 1947. In that case, officers had obtained a warrant for Harris' arrest on the basis of his alleged involvement with the cashing and interstate transportation of a forged check. He was arrested in the living room of his four-room apartment, and in an attempt to recover two canceled checks thought to have been used in effecting the forgery, the officers undertook a thorough search of the entire apartment. Inside a desk drawer they found a sealed envelope marked "George Harris, personal papers." The envelope, which was then torn open, was found to contain altered Selective Service documents, and those documents were used to secure Harris' conviction for violating the Selective Training and Service Act of 1940. The Court rejected Harris' Fourth Amendment claim, sustaining the search as "incident to arrest."

Only a year after *Harris,* however, the pendulum swung again. In *Trupiano v. United States,* 334 U.S. 699, agents raided the site of an illicit distillery, saw one of several conspirators operating the still, and arrested him, contemporaneously "seiz[ing] the illicit distillery." The Court held that the arrest and others made subsequently had been valid, but that the unexplained failure of the agents to procure a search warrant—in spite of the fact that they had had more than enough time before the raid to do so—rendered the search unlawful.

In 1950, two years after *Trupiano,* came *United States v. Rabinowitz,* 339 U.S. 56, the decision upon which California primarily relies in the case now before us. In *Rabinowitz,* federal authorities had been informed that the defendant was dealing in stamps bearing forged overprints. On the basis of that information they secured a warrant for his arrest, which they executed at his one-room business office. At the time of the arrest, the officers "searched the desk, safe, and file cabinets in the office for about an hour and a half," and seized 573 stamps with forged overprints. The stamps were admitted into evidence at the defendant's trial, and this Court affirmed his conviction, rejecting the contention that the warrantless search had been unlawful. The opinion rejected the rule of *Trupiano* that "in seizing goods and articles, law enforcement agents must secure and use search warrants wherever reasonably practicable." The test, said the Court, "is not whether it is reasonable to procure a search warrant, but whether the search was reasonable."

*Rabinowitz* has come to stand for the proposition, *inter alia,* that a warrantless search "incident to a lawful arrest" may generally extend to the area that is considered to be in the "possession" or under the "control" of the person arrested. And it was on the basis of that proposition that the California courts upheld the search of the petitioner's entire house in this case. That doctrine, however, at least in the broad sense in which it was applied by the California courts in this case, can withstand neither historical nor rational analysis.

"We are not dealing with formalities. The presence of a search warrant serves a high function. Absent some grave emergency, the Fourth Amendment has interposed a magistrate between the citizen and the police. This was done not to shield criminals nor to make the home a safe haven for illegal activities. It was done so that an objective mind might weigh the need to invade that privacy in order to enforce the law. The right of privacy was deemed too precious to entrust to the discretion of those whose job is the detection of crime and the arrest of criminals. * * * And so the Constitution requires a magistrate to pass on the desires of the police before they violate the privacy of the home. We cannot be true to that constitutional requirement and excuse the absence of a search warrant without a showing by those who seek exemption from the constitutional mandate that the exigencies of the situation made that course imperative."

When an arrest is made, it is reasonable for the arresting officer to search the person arrested in order to remove any weapons that the latter might seek to use in order to resist arrest or effect his escape. Otherwise, the officer's safety might well be endangered, and the arrest itself frustrated. In addition, it is entirely reasonable for the arresting officer to search for and seize any evidence on the arrestee's person in order to prevent its concealment or destruction. And the area into which an arrestee might reach in order to grab a weapon or evidentiary items must, of course, be governed by a like rule. A gun on a table or in a drawer in front of one who is arrested can be as dangerous to the arresting officer as one concealed in the clothing of the person arrested. There is ample justification, therefore, for a search of the arrestee's person and the area "within his immediate control" – construing that phrase to mean the area from within which he might gain possession of a weapon or destructible evidence. There is no comparable justification, however, for routinely searching any room other than that in which an arrest occurs – or, for that matter, for searching through all the desk drawers or other closed or concealed areas in that room itself. Such searches in the absence of well-recognized exceptions, may be made only under the authority of a search warrant. The

"adherence to the judicial process" mandated by the Fourth Amendment requires no less.

It would be possible, of course, to draw a line between *Rabinowitz* and *Harris* on the one hand, and this case on the other. For *Rabinowitz* involved a single room, and *Harris* a four-room apartment, while in the case before us an entire house was searched. But such a distinction would be highly artificial. The rationale that allowed the searches and seizures in *Rabinowitz* and *Harris* would allow the searches and seizures in this case. No consideration relevant to the Fourth Amendment suggests any point of rational limitation, once the search is allowed to go beyond the area from which the person arrested might obtain weapons or evidentiary items.[11] The only reasoned distinction is one between a search of the person arrested and the area within his reach on the one hand, and more extensive searches on the other.[12]

*Rabinowitz* and *Harris* have been the subject of

---

[11] Cf. Mr. Justice Jackson's dissenting comment in *Harris*:

"The difficulty with this problem for me is that once the search is allowed to go beyond the person arrested and the objects upon him or in his immediate physical control, I see no practical limit short of that set in the opinion of the Court – and that means to me no limit at all."

[12] It is argued in dissent that so long as there is probable cause to search the place where an arrest occurs, a search of that place should be permitted even though no search warrant has been obtained. This position seems to be based principally on two premises: first, that once an arrest has been made, the additional invasion of privacy stemming from the accompanying search is "relatively minor"; and second, that the victim of the search may "shortly thereafter" obtain a judicial determination of whether the search was justified by probable cause. With respect to the second premise, one may initially question whether all of the States in fact provide the speedy suppression procedures the dissent assumes. More fundamentally, however, we cannot accept the view that Fourth Amendment interests are vindicated so long as "the rights of the criminal" are "protect(ed) * * * against introduction of evidence seized without probable cause." The Amendment is designed to prevent, not simply to redress, unlawful police action. In any event, we cannot join in characterizing the invasion of privacy that results from a top-to-bottom search of a man's house as "minor." And we can see no reason why, simply because some interference with an individual's privacy and free-

critical commentary for many years, and have been relied upon less and less in our own decisions. It is time, for the reasons we have stated, to hold that on their own facts, and insofar as the principles they stand for are inconsistent with those that we have endorsed today, they are no longer to be followed.

Application of sound Fourth Amendment principles to the facts of this case produces a clear result. The search here went far beyond the petitioner's person and the area from within which he might have obtained either a weapon or something that could have been used as evidence against him. There was no constitutional justification, in the absence of a search warrant, for extending the search beyond that area. The scope of the search was, therefore, 'unreasonable' under the Fourth and Fourteenth Amendments and the petitioner's conviction cannot stand.

*Reversed.*

(Justice Harlan wrote a brief concurring opinion)

Mr. Justice WHITE, with whom Mr. Justice BLACK joins, dissenting.

Few areas of the law have been as subject to shifting constitutional standards over the last 50 years as that of the search "incident to an arrest." There has been a remarkable instability in this whole area, which has seen at least four major shifts in emphasis. Today's opinion makes an untimely fifth. In my view, the Court should not now abandon the old rule.

An arrest itself may often create an emergency situation making it impracticable to obtain a warrant before embarking on a related search. Assuming that there is probable cause to search premises at the spot where a suspect is arrested, it seems to me unreasonable to require the police to leave the scene in order to obtain a search warrant when they are already legally there to make a valid arrest, and when there must almost always be a strong possibility that confederates of the arrested man will in the meanwhile remove the items for which the police have probable cause to search. This must so often be the case that it seems to me as unreasonable to require a warrant for a search of the premises as to require a warrant for search of the person and his very immediate surroundings.

This case provides a good illustration of my point that it is unreasonable to require police to leave the scene of an arrest in order to obtain a search warrant

dom of movement has lawfully taken place, further intrusions should automatically be allowed despite the absence of a warrant that the Fourth Amendment would otherwise require.

when they already have probable cause to search and there is a clear danger that the items for which they may reasonably search will be removed before they return with a warrant. Petitioner was arrested in his home after an arrest whose validity will be explored below, but which I will now assume was valid. There was doubtless probable cause not only to arrest petitioner, but also to search his house. He had obliquely admitted, both to a neighbor and to the owner of the burglarized store, that he had committed the burglary. In light of this, and the fact that the neighbor had seen other admittedly stolen property in petitioner's house, there was surely probable cause on which a warrant could have issued to search the house for the stolen coins. Moreover, had the police simply arrested petitioner, taken him off to the station house, and later returned with a warrant, it seems very likely that petitioner's wife, who in view of petitioner's generally garrulous nature must have known of the robbery, would have removed the coins. For the police to search the house while the evidence they had probable cause to search out and seize was still there cannot be considered unreasonable.

The majority today proscribes searches for which there is probable cause and which may prove fruitless unless carried out immediately. This rule will have no added effect whatsoever in protecting the rights of the criminal accused at trial against introduction of evidence seized without probable cause. Such evidence could not be introduced under the old rule. Nor does the majority today give any added protection to the right of privacy of those whose houses there is probable cause to search. A warrant would still be sworn out for those houses, and the privacy of their owners invaded. The only possible justification for the majority's rule is that in some instances arresting officers may search when they have no probable cause to do so and that such unlawful searches might be prevented if the officers first sought a warrant from a magistrate. Against the possible protection of privacy in that class of cases, in which the privacy of the house has already been invaded by entry to make the arrest—an entry for which the majority does not assert that any warrant is necessary—must be weighed the risk of destruction of evidence for which there is probable cause to search, as a result of delays in obtaining a search warrant. Without more basis for radical change than the Court's opinion reveals, I would not upset the balance of these interests which has been struck by the former decisions of this Court.

In considering searches incident to arrest, it must be remembered that there will be immediate opportunity to challenge the probable cause for the search in an adversary proceeding. The suspect has been apprised of the search by his very presence at the scene, and having been arrested, he will soon be brought into contact with people who can explain his rights.

An arrested man, by definition conscious of the police interest in him, and provided almost immediately with a lawyer and a judge, is in an excellent position to dispute the reasonableness of his arrest and contemporaneous search in a full adversary proceeding. I would uphold the constitutionality of this search contemporaneous with an arrest since there were probable cause both for the search and for the arrest, exigent circumstances involving the removal or destruction of evidence, and satisfactory opportunity to dispute the issues of probable cause shortly thereafter. In this case, the search was reasonable.

## QUESTIONS AND NOTES

**1.** Ought a search incident to an arrest be permissible in every case regardless of the likelihood of a weapon being present or evidence being destroyed? Why? Why not?

**2.** Assuming that a search incident to an arrest is going to be permitted at all, are the *Chimel* limitations arbitrary?

**3.** Does (should) *Chimel* permit a search of locked containers within the arrestee's reach?

**4.** What values does *Chimel* serve?

**5.** Could *Rabinowitz* be legitimately distinguished from *Chimel*? Could *Harris*?

**6.** Given probable cause to search the Chimel home, what if anything is wrong with Justice White's suggestion that probable cause to search will be determined soon enough?

**7.** In addition to a search incident to an arrest, it is sometimes argued that the police should be able to make a "protective sweep" of the house in which an arrest is effectuated. The Supreme Court resolved that issue in *Buie*. As you read *Buie* consider whether the Court gave the police too much power, too little power, or the correct amount of power.

### Maryland v. Buie
#### 494 U.S. 325 (1990)

Justice WHITE delivered the opinion of the Court.

A "protective sweep" is a quick and limited search of a premises, incident to an arrest and conducted to protect the safety of police officers or others. It is narrowly confined to a cursory visual inspection of those places in which a person might be hiding. In this case we must decide what level of justification is required by the Fourth and Fourteenth Amendments before police officers, while effecting the arrest of a suspect in his home pursuant to an arrest warrant, may conduct a warrantless protective sweep of all or part of the premises. The Court of Appeals of Maryland held that a running suit seized in plain view during such a protective sweep should have been suppressed at respondent's armed robbery trial because the officer who conducted the sweep did not have probable cause to believe that a serious and demonstrable potentiality for danger existed. We conclude that the Fourth Amendment would permit the protective sweep undertaken here if the searching officer "possesse[d] a reasonable belief based on 'specific and articulable facts which, taken together with the rational inferences from those facts, reasonably warrant[ed]' the officer in believing," that the area swept harbored an individual posing a danger to the officer or others. We accordingly vacate the judgment below and remand for application of this standard.

I

On February 3, 1986, two men committed an armed robbery of a Godfather's Pizza restaurant in Prince George's County, Maryland. One of the robbers was wearing a red running suit. That same day, Prince George's County police obtained arrest warrants for respondent Jerome Edward Buie and his suspected accomplice in the robbery, Lloyd Allen. Buie's house was placed under police surveillance.

On February 5, the police executed the arrest warrant for Buie. They first had a police department secretary telephone Buie's house to verify that he was home. The secretary spoke to a female first, then to Buie himself. Six or seven officers proceeded to Buie's house. Once inside, the officers fanned out through the first and second floors. Corporal James Rozar announced that he would "freeze" the basement so that no one could come up and surprise the officers. With his service revolver drawn, Rozar twice shouted into the basement, ordering anyone down there to come out. When a voice asked who was calling, Rozar announced three times: "this is the police, show me your hands." Eventually, a pair of hands appeared around the bottom of the stairwell and Buie emerged from the basement. He was arrested, searched, and handcuffed by Rozar. Thereafter, Detective Joseph Frolich entered the basement "in case there was someone else" down there. He noticed a red running suit lying in plain view on a stack of clothing and seized it.

## II

Petitioner, the State of Maryland, argues that, under a general reasonableness balancing test, police should be permitted to conduct a protective sweep whenever they make an in-home arrest for a violent crime. As an alternative to this suggested bright-line rule, the State contends that protective sweeps may be conducted in conjunction with a valid in-home arrest whenever the police reasonably suspect a risk of danger to the officers or others at the arrest scene. Respondent argues that a protective sweep may not be undertaken without a warrant unless the exigencies of the situation render such warrantless search objectively reasonable. According to Buie, because the State has shown neither exigent circumstances to immediately enter Buie's house nor an unforeseen danger that arose once the officers were in the house, there is no excuse for the failure to obtain a search warrant to search for dangerous persons believed to be on the premises. Buie further contends that, even if the warrant requirement is inapplicable, there is no justification for relaxing the probable-cause standard. If something less than probable cause is sufficient, respondent argues that it is no less than individualized suspicion—specific, articulable facts supporting a reasonable belief that there are persons on the premises who are a threat to the officers. According to Buie, there were no such specific, articulable facts to justify the search of his basement.

## III

It goes without saying that the Fourth Amendment bars only unreasonable searches and seizures.

Our cases show that in determining reasonableness, we have balanced the intrusion on the individual's Fourth Amendment interests against its promotion of legitimate governmental interests. Under this test, a search of the house or office is generally not reasonable without a warrant issued on probable cause. There are other contexts, however, where the public interest is such that neither a warrant nor probable cause is required.

The *Terry* case (*Terry v. Ohio*, ch. 7 , *infra.*) is most instructive for present purposes. There we held that an on-the-street "frisk" for weapons must be tested by the Fourth Amendment's general proscription against unreasonable searches because such a frisk involves "an entire rubric of police conduct—necessarily swift action predicated upon the on-the-spot observations of the officer on the beat—which historically has not been, and as a practical matter could not be, subjected to the warrant procedure." We stated that there is "no ready test for determining reasonableness other than by balancing the need to search . . . against the invasion which the search . . . entails." Applying that balancing test, it was held that although a frisk for weapons "constitutes a severe, though brief, intrusion upon cherished personal security," such a frisk is reasonable when weighed against the "need for law enforcement officers to protect themselves and other prospective victims of violence in situations where they may lack probable cause for an arrest." We therefore authorized a limited patdown for weapons where a reasonably prudent officer would be warranted in the belief, based on "specific and articulable facts," and not on a mere "inchoate and unparticularized suspicion or 'hunch,'" "that he is dealing with an armed and dangerous individual."

In *Michigan v. Long* (Chapter 7, *infra*), the principles of Terry were applied in the context of a roadside encounter: "the search of the passenger compartment of an automobile, limited to those areas in which a weapon may be placed or hidden, is permissible if the police officer possesses a reasonable belief based on 'specific and articulable facts which, taken together with the rational inferences from those facts, reasonably warrant' the officer in believing that the suspect is dangerous and the suspect may gain immediate control of weapons." The *Long* Court expressly rejected the contention that *Terry* restricted preventative searches to the person of a detained suspect. In a sense, *Long* authorized a "frisk" of an automobile for weapons.

A *Terry* or *Long* frisk occurs before a police-citizen confrontation has escalated to the point of arrest. A protective sweep, in contrast, occurs as an adjunct to the serious step of taking a person into custody for the purpose of prosecuting him for a crime. Moreover, unlike an encounter on the street or along a highway, an in-home arrest puts the officer at the disadvantage of being on his adversary's "turf." An ambush in a confined setting of unknown configuration is more to be feared than it is in open, more familiar surroundings.

We recognized in *Terry* that "[e]ven a limited search of the outer clothing for weapons constitutes a severe, though brief, intrusion upon cherished personal security, and it must surely be an annoying, frightening, and perhaps humiliating experience." But we permitted the intrusion, which was no more than necessary to protect the officer from harm. Nor do we here suggest, as the State does, that entering rooms not examined prior to the arrest is a *de minimis* intrusion that may be disregarded. We are quite sure, however, that the arresting officers are permitted in such circumstances to take reasonable steps to ensure their safety after, and while making, the arrest. That interest is sufficient to outweigh the intrusion such procedures may entail.

We agree with the State, as did the court below, that a warrant was not required.[1] We also hold that as an incident to the arrest the officers could, as a precautionary matter and without probable cause or reasonable suspicion, look in closets and other spaces immediately adjoining the place of arrest from which an attack could be immediately launched. Beyond that, however, we hold that there must be articulable facts which, taken together with the rational inferences from those facts, would warrant a reasonably prudent officer in believing that the area to be swept harbors an individual posing a danger to those on the arrest scene. This is no more and no less than was required in *Terry* and *Long*, and as in those cases, we think this balance is the proper one.[2]

---

[1] Buie suggests that because the police could have sought a warrant to search for dangerous persons in the house, they were constitutionally required to do so. But the arrest warrant gave the police every right to enter the home to search for Buie. Once inside, the potential for danger justified a standard of less than probable cause for conducting a limited protective sweep.

[2] The State's argument that no level of objective justification should be required because of "the danger that inheres in the in-home arrest for a violent crime," is rebutted by *Terry* itself. The State argues that "[o]fficers facing the life threatening situation of arresting a violent criminal in the home should not be forced to pause and ponder the legal subtleties associated with a quantum of proof analysis." But despite the danger that inheres in on-the-street en-

We should emphasize that such a protective sweep, aimed at protecting the arresting officers, if justified by the circumstances, is nevertheless not a full search of the premises, but may extend only to a cursory inspection of those spaces where a person may be found. The sweep lasts no longer than is necessary to dispel the reasonable suspicion of danger and in any event no longer than it takes to complete the arrest and depart the premises.

IV

Affirmance is not required by *Chimel*, where it was held that in the absence of a search warrant, the justifiable search incident to an in-home arrest could not extend beyond the arrestee's person and the area from within which the arrestee might have obtained a weapon. First, *Chimel* was concerned with a full-blown search of the entire house for evidence of the crime for which the arrest was made, not the more limited intrusion contemplated by a protective sweep. Second, the justification for the search incident to arrest considered in *Chimel* was the threat posed by the arrestee, not the safety threat posed by the house, or more properly by unseen third parties in the house. To reach our conclusion today, therefore, we need not disagree with the Court's statement in *Chimel*, that "the invasion of privacy that results from a top-to-bottom search of a man's house [cannot be characterized] as 'minor,'" nor hold that "simply because some interference with an individual's privacy and freedom of movement has lawfully taken place, further intrusions should automatically be allowed despite the absence of a warrant that the Fourth Amendment would otherwise require." The type of search we authorize today is far removed from the "top-to-bottom" search involved in *Chimel*; moreover, it is decidedly not "automati[c]," but may be conducted only when justified by a reasonable, articulable suspicion that the house is harboring a person posing a danger to those on the arrest scene.

V

We conclude that by requiring a protective sweep to be justified by probable cause to believe that a

---

counters and the need for police to act quickly for their own safety, the Court in *Terry* did not adopt a bright-line rule authorizing frisks for weapons in all confrontational encounters. Even in high crime areas, where the possibility that any given individual is armed is significant, *Terry* requires reasonable, individualized suspicion before a frisk for weapons can be conducted. That approach is applied to the protective sweep of a house.

serious and demonstrable potentiality for danger existed, the Court of Appeals of Maryland applied an unnecessarily strict Fourth Amendment standard. The Fourth Amendment permits a properly limited protective sweep in conjunction with an in-home arrest when the searching officer possesses a reasonable belief based on specific and articulable facts that the area to be swept harbors an individual posing a danger to those on the arrest scene. We therefore vacate the judgment below and remand this case to the Court of Appeals of Maryland for further proceedings not inconsistent with this opinion.

Justice STEVENS, concurring.

Today the Court holds that reasonable suspicion, rather than probable cause, is necessary to support a protective sweep while an arrest is in progress. I agree with that holding and with the Court's opinion, but I believe it is important to emphasize that the standard applies only to *protective* sweeps. Officers conducting such a sweep must have a reasonable basis for believing that their search will reduce the danger of harm to themselves or of violent interference with their mission; in short, the search must be protective.

In this case, to justify Officer Frolich's entry into the basement, it is the State's burden to demonstrate that the officers had a reasonable basis for believing not only that someone in the basement might attack them or otherwise try to interfere with the arrest, but also that it would be safer to go down the stairs instead of simply guarding them from above until respondent had been removed from the house. The fact that respondent offered no resistance when he emerged from the basement is somewhat inconsistent with the hypothesis that the danger of an attack by a hidden confederate persisted after the arrest. Moreover, Officer Rozar testified that he was not worried about any possible danger when he arrested Buie.[1] Officer Frolich, who conducted the search, supplied no explanation for why he might have thought another person was in the basement. He said only that he "had no idea who lived there." This admission is made telling by Officer Frolich's participation in the three-day pre-arrest surveillance of Buie's home. The Maryland Supreme Court was under the impression that the search took place after "Buie was safely outside the house, handcuffed and unarmed." All of this suggests that no reasonable suspicion of danger justified the entry into the basement.

---

[1] Buie's attorney asked, "You weren't worried about there being any danger or anything like that?" Officer Rozar answered, "No."

Indeed, were the officers concerned about safety, one would expect them to do what Officer Rozar did before the arrest: guard the basement door to prevent surprise attacks. As the Court indicates, Officer Frolich might, at the time of the arrest, reasonably have "looked in" the already open basement door to ensure that no accomplice had followed Buie to the stairwell. But Officer Frolich did not merely "look in" the basement; he entered it.[2] That strategy is sensible if one wishes to search the basement. It is a surprising choice for an officer, worried about safety, who need not risk entering the stairwell at all.

The State may thus face a formidable task on remand. However, the Maryland courts are better equipped than are we to review the record. Moreover, the Maryland Court of Special Appeals suggested that Officer Frolich's search could survive a "reasonable suspicion" test, and the Maryland Court of Appeals has not reviewed this conclusion. I therefore agree that a remand is appropriate.

Justice KENNEDY, concurring.

The Court adopts the prudent course of explaining the general rule and permitting the state court to apply it in the first instance. The concurrence by Justice Stevens, however, makes the gratuitous observation that the State has a formidable task on remand. My view is quite to the contrary. Based on my present understanding of the record, I should think the officers' conduct here was in full accord with standard police safety procedure, and that the officers would have been remiss if they had not taken these precautions. This comment is necessary, lest by acquiescence the impression be left that Justice Stevens' views can be interpreted as authoritative guidance for application of our ruling to the facts of the case.

Justice BRENNAN, with whom Justice MARSHALL joins, dissenting.

Today the Court for the first time extends *Terry,* into the home, dispensing with the Fourth Amendment's general requirements of a warrant and probable cause and carving a "reasonable suspicion" exception for protective sweeps in private dwellings.

The Court today holds that *Terry*'s "reasonable

---

[2] What more the officers might have done to protect themselves against threats from other places is obviously a question not presented on the facts of this case, and so is not one we can answer. Indeed, the peculiarity of Officer Frolich's search is that it appears to have concentrated upon the part of the house least likely to make the departing officers vulnerable to attack.

suspicion" standard "strikes the proper balance between officer safety and citizen privacy" for protective sweeps in private dwellings. I agree with the majority that officers executing an arrest warrant within a private dwelling have an interest in protecting themselves against potential ambush by third parties, but the majority offers no support for its assumption that the danger of ambush during planned home arrests approaches the danger of unavoidable "on-the-beat" confrontations in "the myriad daily situations in which policemen and citizens confront each other on the street."[2] In any event, the Court's implicit judgment that a protective sweep constitutes a "minimally intrusive" search akin to that involved in *Terry* markedly undervalues the nature and scope of the privacy interests involved.

While the Fourth Amendment protects a person's privacy interests in a variety of settings, "physical entry of the home is the chief evil against which the wording of the Fourth Amendment is directed." The Court discounts the nature of the intrusion because it believes that the scope of the intrusion is limited. The Court explains that a protective sweep's scope is "narrowly confined to a cursory visual inspection of those places in which a person might be hiding," and confined in duration to a period "no longer than is necessary to dispel the reasonable suspicion of danger and in any event no longer than it takes to complete the arrest and depart the premises."[4] But these spatial and temporal restrictions are not particularly limiting. A protective sweep would bring within police purview virtually all personal possessions within the house not hidden from view in a small enclosed space. Police

officers searching for potential ambushers might enter every room including basements and attics; open up closets, lockers, chests, wardrobes, and cars; and peer under beds and behind furniture. The officers will view letters, documents and personal effects that are on tables or desks or are visible inside open drawers; books, records, tapes, and pictures on shelves; and clothing, medicines, toiletries and other paraphernalia not carefully stored in dresser drawers or bathroom cupboards. While perhaps not a "full-blown" or "top-to-bottom" search, a protective sweep is much closer to it than to a "limited patdown for weapons" or a " 'frisk' of an automobile."[5] Because the nature and scope of the intrusion sanctioned here are far greater than those upheld in *Terry* and *Long,* the Court's conclusion that "[t]he ingredients to apply the balance struck in *Terry* and *Long* are present in this case," is unwarranted. The "ingredient" of a minimally intrusive search is absent, and the Court's holding today therefore unpalatably deviates from *Terry* and its progeny.[6]

In light of the special sanctity of a private residence and the highly intrusive nature of a protective

---

[2] Individual police officers necessarily initiate street encounters without advance planning "for a wide variety of purposes." But officers choosing to execute an arrest warrant in the suspect's house may minimize any risk of ambush by, for example, a show of force; in this case, at least six armed officers secured the premises. And, of course, officers could select a safer venue for making their arrest.

[4] The protective sweep in this case may have exceeded the permissible temporal scope defined by the Court. The Court of Appeals of Maryland expressly noted that "at the time of the warrantless search, Buie was safely outside the house, handcuffed and unarmed." On remand, therefore, the state court need not decide whether the "reasonable suspicion" standard is satisfied in this case should it determine that the sweep of the basement took place after the police had sufficient time to "complete the arrest and depart the premises."

[5] Indeed, a protective sweep is sufficiently broad in scope that today's ruling might encourage police officers to execute arrest warrants in suspects' homes so as to take advantage of the opportunity to peruse the premises for incriminating evidence left in "plain view." This incentive runs directly counter to our central tenet that "in [no setting] is the zone of privacy more clearly defined than when bounded by the unambiguous physical dimensions of an individual's home – a zone that finds its roots in clear and specific constitutional terms."

[6] The Court's decision also to expand the "search incident to arrest" exception previously recognized in *Chimel,* allowing police officers without any requisite level of suspicion to look into "closets and other spaces immediately adjoining the place of arrest from which an attack could be immediately launched," is equally disquieting. *Chimel* established that police officers may presume as a matter of law, without need for factual support in a particular case, that arrestees might take advantage of weapons or destroy evidence in the area "within [their] immediate control"; therefore, a protective search of that area is *per se* reasonable under the Fourth Amendment. I find much less plausible the Court's implicit assumption today that arrestees are likely to sprinkle hidden allies throughout the rooms in which they might be arrested. Hence there is no comparable justification for permitting arresting officers to presume as a matter of law that they are threatened by ambush from "immediately adjoining" spaces.

sweep, I firmly believe that police officers must have probable cause to fear that their personal safety is threatened by a hidden confederate of an arrestee before they may sweep through the entire home. Given the state-court determination that the officers searching Buie's home lacked probable cause to perceive such a danger and therefore were not lawfully present in the basement, I would affirm the state court's decision to suppress the incriminating evidence. I respectfully dissent.

## QUESTIONS AND NOTES

**1.** How is the Court likely to rule on remand? How do you think that you would rule? Why?

**2.** How intrusive do you consider a "protective sweep" to be?

**3.** Would it be better to allow a "protective sweep" as a matter of routine (similar to search incident to an arrest) rather than litigate every single case?

**4.** Conversely, would a probable cause standard be more consistent with sound Fourth Amendment theory?

**5.** If the police were suspicious of cohorts couldn't they have so indicated on their warrant application? Why should we let them decide on the spot?

# 5.

# PLAIN VIEW

The concept of "plain view" is a recurring theme in Fourth Amendment jurisprudence. In *Buie,* for example, the importance of the right to make a protective sweep was not related to an abstract claim of right by the homeowner. Rather, it was to ascertain whether the red running suit, found in "plain view" during the course of the protective sweep, was admissible in evidence. In this chapter, we will focus upon the rationale for the "plain view" doctrine, along with an analysis of its scope and limitations. The first case to really develop the doctrine was *Coolidge v. New Hampshire* (Chapter 3, *supra*). *Coolidge,* you will recall, involved the search of an automobile pursuant to a warrant that was defective because it was issued by the Attorney General. The State argued, *inter alia,* that the automobile, and evidence found therein, should have been admissible because it was found in "plain view."

## Coolidge v. New Hampshire
### 403 U.S. 443 (1971)

Mr. Justice STEWART delivered the opinion of the Court. [Speaking for only four Justices, himself, DOUGLAS, BRENNAN, and MARSHALL, on the "plain view" issue]

The State's third theory in support of the warrantless seizure and search of the Pontiac car is that the car itself was an "instrumentality of the crime," and as such might be seized by the police on Coolidge's property because it was in plain view. [W]e may assume that the police had probable cause to seize the automobile.[22] But, for the reasons that fol-

---

[22] Coolidge had admitted that on the night of Pamela Mason's disappearance he had stopped his Pontiac on the side of the highway opposite the place where the body was found. He claimed the car was stuck in the snow. Two witnesses, who had stopped and asked him if he needed help, testified that his car was not stuck.

low, we hold that the "plain view" exception to the warrant requirement is inapplicable to this case.

It is well established that under certain circumstances the police may seize evidence in plain view without a warrant. But it is important to keep in mind that, in the vast majority of cases, *any* evidence seized by the police will be in plain view, at least at the moment of seizure. The problem with the "plain view" doctrine has been to identify the circumstances in which plain view has legal significance rather than being simply the normal concomitant of any search, legal or illegal.

An example of the applicability of the "plain view" doctrine is the situation in which the police have a warrant to search a given area for specified objects, and in the course of the search come across some other article of incriminating character. Where the initial intrusion that brings the police within plain view of such an article is supported, not by a warrant, but by one of the recognized exceptions to the warrant requirement, the seizure is also legitimate. Thus the police may inadvertently come across evidence while in "hot pursuit" of a fleeing suspect. And an object that comes into view during a search incident to arrest that is appropriately limited in scope under existing law may be seized without a warrant.[24]

---

[24] The "plain view" exception to the warrant requirement is not in conflict with the law of search incident to a valid arrest expressed in *Chimel*. The Court there held that "[t]here is ample justification . . . for a search of the arrestee's person and the area 'within his immediate control' — construing that phrase to mean the area from within which he might gain possession of a weapon or destructible evidence." The "plain view" doctrine would normally justify as well the seizure of other evidence that came to light during such an appropriately limited search. The Court in *Chimel* went on to hold that "[t]here is no comparable justification, however, for routinely searching any room other than that in which an arrest occurs — or, for that matter, for searching through all the desk drawers or other closed or concealed areas in that room itself. Such searches, in the absence of well-recognized exceptions, may be made only under the authority of a search warrant." Where, however, the arresting officer inadvertently comes within plain view of a piece of evidence, not concealed, although outside of the area under the immediate control of the arrestee, the officer may seize it, so long as the plain view was obtained in the course of an appropriately limited search of the arrestee.

Finally, the "plain view" doctrine has been applied where a police officer is not searching for evidence against the accused, but nonetheless inadvertently comes across an incriminating object.

What the "plain view" cases have in common is that the police officer in each of them had a prior justification for an intrusion in the course of which he came inadvertently across a piece of evidence incriminating the accused. The doctrine serves to supplement the prior justification — whether it be a warrant for another object, hot pursuit, search incident to lawful arrest, or some other legitimate reason for being present unconnected with a search directed against the accused — and permits the warrantless seizure. Of course, the extension of the original justification is legitimate only where it is immediately apparent to the police that they have evidence before them; the "plain view" doctrine may not be used to extend a general exploratory search from one object to another until something incriminating at last emerges.

The rationale for the "plain view" exception is evident if we keep in mind the two distinct constitutional protections served by the warrant requirement. First, the magistrate's scrutiny is intended to eliminate altogether searches not based on probable cause. The premise here is that *any* intrusion in the way of search or seizure is an evil, so that no intrusion at all is justified without a careful prior determination of necessity. The second, distinct objective is that those searches deemed necessary should be as limited as possible. Here, the specific evil is the "general warrant" abhorred by the colonists, and the problem is not that of intrusion *per se,* but of a general, exploratory rummaging in a person's belongings. The warrant accomplishes this second objective by requiring a "particular description" of the things to be seized.

The "plain view" doctrine is not in conflict with the first objective because plain view does not occur until a search is in progress. In each case, this initial intrusion is justified by a warrant or by an exception such as "hot pursuit" or search incident to a lawful arrest, or by an extraneous valid reason for the officer's presence. And, given the initial intrusion, the seizure of an object in plain view is consistent with the second objective, since it does not convert the search into a general or exploratory one. As against the minor peril to Fourth Amendment protections, there is a major gain in effective law enforcement. Where, once an otherwise lawful search is in progress, the police inadvertently come upon a piece of evidence, it would often be a needless inconvenience, and sometimes dangerous — to the evidence or to the police themselves — to require them to ignore it until they have obtained a warrant particularly describing it.

The limits on the doctrine are implicit in the statement of its rationale. The first of these is that plain view alone is never enough to justify the warrantless seizure of evidence. This is simply a corollary of the familiar principle discussed above, that no amount of probable cause can justify a warrantless search or seizure absent "exigent circumstances." Incontrovertible testimony of the senses that an incriminating object is on premises belonging to a criminal suspect may establish the fullest possible measure of probable cause. But even where the object is contraband, this Court has repeatedly stated and enforced the basic rule that the police may not enter and make a warrantless seizure.

The second limitation is that the discovery of evidence in plain view must be inadvertent. The rationale of the exception to the warrant requirement, as just stated, is that a plain-view seizure will not turn an initially valid (and therefore limited) search into a "general" one, while the inconvenience of procuring a warrant to cover an inadvertent discovery is great. But where the discovery is anticipated, where the police know in advance the location of the evidence and intend to seize it, the situation is altogether different. The requirement of a warrant to seize imposes no inconvenience whatever, or at least none which is constitutionally cognizable in a legal system that regards warrantless searches as "*per se* unreasonable" in the absence of "exigent circumstances."

If the initial intrusion is bottomed upon a warrant that fails to mention a particular object, though the police know its location and intend to seize it, then there is a violation of the express constitutional requirement of "Warrants . . . particularly describing . . . (the) things to be seized." The initial intrusion may, of course, be legitimated not by a warrant but by one of the exceptions to the warrant requirement, such as hot pursuit or search incident to lawful arrest. But to extend the scope of such an intrusion to the seizure of objects—not contraband nor stolen nor dangerous in themselves—which the police know in advance they will find in plain view and intend to seize, would fly in the face of the basic rule that no amount of probable cause can justify a warrantless seizure.[27]

---

[27] Mr. Justice Black laments that the Court today "abolishes seizure incident to arrest," while Mr. Justice White no less forcefully asserts that the Court's "new rule" will "accomplish nothing." In assessing these claims, it is well to keep in mind that we deal here with a *planned* warrantless seizure. This Court has never permitted the legitimation of a planned warrantless seizure on plain-view grounds,

In the light of what has been said, it is apparent that the "plain view" exception cannot justify the police seizure of the Pontiac car in this case. The police had ample opportunity to obtain a valid warrant; they knew the automobile's exact description and location well in advance; they intended to seize it when they came upon Coolidge's property. And this is not a case involving contraband or stolen goods or objects dangerous in themselves.

The seizure was therefore unconstitutional, and so was the subsequent search at the station house. Since evidence obtained in the course of the search was admitted at Coolidge's trial, the judgment must be reversed and the case remanded to the New Hampshire Supreme Court.

BLACK, J., concurring and dissenting.

### III

### C

I believe the seizure of petitioner's automobile was valid under the well-established right of the police to seize evidence in plain view at the time and place of arrest. The majority concedes that the police were rightfully at petitioner's residence to make a valid arrest at the time of the seizure. To use the majority's words, the "initial intrusion" which brought the police within plain view of the automobile was legitimate. The majority also concedes that the automobile was "plainly visible both from the

---

and to do so here would be flatly inconsistent with the existing body of Fourth Amendment law. A long line of cases make it clear beyond doubt that the mere fact that the police have legitimately obtained a plain view of a piece of incriminating evidence is not enough to justify a warrantless seizure. Although Mr. Justice Black and Mr. Justice White appear to hold contrasting views of the import of today's decision, they are in agreement that this warrant requirement should be ignored whenever the seizing officers are able to arrange to make an arrest within sight of the object they are after. "The exceptions cannot be enthroned into the rule." *Rabinowitz* (Frankfurter, J., dissenting). We recognized the dangers of allowing the extent of Fourth Amendment protections to turn on the location of the arrestee in *Chimel*, noting that under the law of search incident to arrest as enunciated prior to *Chimel*, "law enforcement officials (had) the opportunity to engage in searches not justified by probable cause, by the simple expedient of arranging to arrest suspects at home rather than elsewhere."

street and from inside the house where Coolidge was actually arrested,'' and that the automobile itself was evidence which the police had probable cause to seize. Indeed, the majority appears to concede that the seizure of petitioner's automobile was valid under the doctrine upholding seizures of evidence in plain view at the scene of arrest, at least as it stood before today.

However, even after conceding that petitioner's automobile itself was evidence of the crime, that the police had probable cause to seize it as such, and that the automobile was in plain view at the time and place of arrest, the majority holds the seizure to be a violation of the Fourth Amendment because the discovery of the automobile was not "inadvertent." The majority confidently states: "What the 'plain view' cases have in common is that the police officer in each of them had a prior justification for an intrusion in the course of which he came inadvertently across a piece of evidence incriminating the accused." But the prior holdings of this Court not only fail to support the majority statement they flatly contradict it.

The majority confuses the historically justified right of the police to seize visible evidence of the crime in open view at the scene of arrest with the "plain view" exception to the requirement of particular description in search warrants. The majority apparently reasons that unless the seizure made pursuant to authority conferred by a warrant is limited to the particularly described object of seizure, the warrant will become a general writ of assistance. Evidently, as a check on the requirement of particular description in search warrants, the majority announces a new rule that items not named in a warrant cannot be seized unless their discovery was unanticipated or "inadvertent." The majority's concern is with the scope of the intrusion authorized by a warrant. But the right to seize items properly subject to seizure because in open view at the time of arrest is quite independent of any power to search for such items pursuant to a warrant. The entry in the present case did not depend for its authority on a search warrant but was concededly authorized by probable cause to effect a valid arrest. The intrusion did not exceed that authority. The intrusion was limited in scope to the circumstances which justified the entry in the first place—the arrest of petitioner. There was no general search; indeed, there was no search at all. The automobile itself was evidence properly subject to seizure and was in open view at the time and place of arrest.

Only rarely can it be said that evidence seized incident to an arrest is truly unexpected or inadvertent. Indeed, if the police officer had no expectation of discovering weapons, contraband, or other evidence, he would make no search. It appears to me that the rule adopted by the Court today, for all practical purposes, abolishes seizure incident to arrest. The majority rejects the test of reasonableness provided in the Fourth Amendment and substitutes a *per se* rule—if the police could have obtained a warrant and did not, the seizure, no matter how reasonable, is void. But the Fourth Amendment does not require that every search be made pursuant to a warrant. It prohibits only "unreasonable searches and seizures." The relevant test is not the reasonableness of the opportunity to procure a warrant, but the reasonableness of the seizure under all the circumstances. The test of reasonableness cannot be fixed by *per se* rules; each case must be decided on its own facts.

For the reasons stated above, I believe the seizure and search of petitioner's car was reasonable and, therefore, authorized by the Fourth Amendment.

Mr. Justice WHITE, with whom THE CHIEF JUSTICE joins, concurring and dissenting.

[O]fficers may be on a suspect's premises executing a search warrant and in the course of the authorized search discover evidence of crime not covered by the warrant. *Marron v. United States,* 275 U.S. 192, flatly held that legal presence under a warrant did not itself justify the seizure of such evidence. However, seizure of the same evidence was permitted because it was found in plain sight in the course of making an arrest and an accompanying search. It is at least odd to me to permit plain-sight seizures arising in connection with warrantless arrests, as the long line of cases ending with *Chimel* has done, or arising in the course of a hot-pursuit search for a felon; and yet forbid the warrantless seizure of evidence in plain sight when officers enter a house under a search warrant that is perfectly valid but does not cover the items actually seized. I have my doubts that this aspect of *Marron* can survive later cases in this Court, particularly *Zap v. United States,* 328 U.S. 624 (1946), where federal investigators seized a canceled check evidencing a crime that had been observed during the course of an otherwise lawful search. Apparently the majority agrees, for it lumps plain-sight seizures in such circumstances along with other situations where seizures are made after a legal entry.

In all of these situations, it is apparent that seizure of evidence without a warrant is not itself an invasion either of personal privacy or of property rights beyond that already authorized by law. Only the possessory interest of a defendant in his effects is implicated. And in these various circumstances, at least where the discovery of evidence is "inadvertent," the Court would permit the seizure because, it is said, "the minor peril to Fourth Amendment protections" is overridden by the "major gain in effective law enforcement" inherent in avoiding the "needless inconvenience" of procuring a warrant. I take this to mean that both the possessory interest of the defendant and the importance of having a magistrate confirm that what the officer saw with his own eyes is in fact contraband or evidence of crime are not substantial constitutional considerations. Officers in these circumstances need neither guard nor ignore the evidence while a warrant is sought. Immediate seizure is justified and reasonable under the Fourth Amendment.

The Court would interpose in some or all of these situations, however, a condition that the discovery of the disputed evidence be "inadvertent." If it is "anticipated," that is if "the police know in advance the location of the evidence and intend to seize it," the seizure is invalid.

I have great difficulty with this approach. Let us suppose officers secure a warrant to search a house for a rifle. While staying well within the range of a rifle search, they discover two photographs of the murder victim, both in plain sight in the bedroom. Assume also that the discovery of the one photograph was inadvertent but finding the other was anticipated. The Court would permit the seizure of only one of the photographs. But in terms of the "minor" peril to Fourth Amendment values there is surely no difference between these two photographs: the interference with possession is the same in each case and the officers' appraisal of the photograph they expected to see is no less reliable than their judgment about the other. And in both situations the actual inconvenience and danger to evidence remain identical if the officers must depart and secure a warrant. The Court, however, states that the State will suffer no constitutionally cognizable inconvenience from invalidating anticipated seizures since it had probable cause to search for the items seized and could have included them in a warrant.

This seems a punitive and extravagant application of the exclusionary rule. If the police have probable cause to search for a photograph as well as a rifle and they proceed to seek a warrant, they could have no possible motive for deliberately including the rifle but omitting the photograph. Quite the contrary is true. Only oversight or careless mistake would explain the omission in the warrant application if the police were convinced they had probable cause to search for the photograph. Of course, they may misjudge the facts and not realize they have probable cause for the picture, or the magistrate may find against them and not issue a warrant for it. In either

event the officers may validly seize the photograph for which they had no probable cause to search but the other photograph is excluded from evidence when the Court subsequently determines that the officers, after all, had probable cause to search for it.

More important, the inadvertence rule is unnecessary to further any Fourth Amendment ends and will accomplish nothing. Police with a warrant for a rifle may search only places where rifles might be and must terminate the search once the rifle is found; the inadvertence rule will in no way reduce the number of places into which they may lawfully look. So, too, the areas of permissible search incident to arrest are strictly circumscribed by *Chimel*. Excluding evidence seen from within those areas can hardly be effective to operate to prevent wider, unauthorized searches. If the police stray outside the scope of an authorized *Chimel* search they are already in violation of the Fourth Amendment, and evidence so seized will be excluded; adding a second reason for excluding evidence hardly seems worth the candle. Perhaps the Court is concerned that officers, having the right to intrude upon private property to make arrests, will use that right as a pretext to obtain entry to search for objects in plain sight, but, if so, such a concern is unfounded. The reason is that under *Chimel* the police can enter only into those portions of the property into which entry is necessary to effect the arrest. Given the restrictions of *Chimel*, the police face a substantial risk that in effecting an arrest and a search incident thereto they will never enter into those portions of the property from which they can plainly see the objects for which they are searching and that, if they do not, those objects will be destroyed before they can return and conduct a search of the entire premises pursuant to a warrant. If the police in fact possess probable cause to believe that weapons, contraband, or evidence of crime is in plain view on the premises, it will be far safer to obtain a search warrant than to take a chance that in making an arrest they will come into plain view of the object they are seeking. It is only when they lack probable cause for a search—when, that is, discovery of objects in plain view from a lawful vantage point is inadvertent—that entry to make an arrest might, as a practical matter, assist the police in discovering an object for which they could not have obtained a warrant. But the majority in that circumstance would uphold their authority to seize what they see. I thus doubt that the Court's new rule will have any measurable effect on police conduct. It will merely attach undue consequences to what will most often be an unintended mistake or a misapprehension of some of this Court's probable-cause decisions, a failing which, I am afraid, we all have.

[The Court] is careful to note that Coolidge's car is not contraband, stolen, or in itself dangerous. Apparently, contraband, stolen, or dangerous materials may be seized when discovered in the course of an otherwise authorized search even if the discovery is fully anticipated and a warrant could have been obtained. The distinction the Court draws between contraband and mere evidence of crime is reminiscent of the confusing and unworkable approach that I thought *Warden v. Hayden* had firmly put aside.[•]

Neither does the Court in so many words limit *Chimel*; on the contrary, it indicates that warrantless *Chimel*-type searches will not be disturbed, even if the police "anticipate that they will find specific evidence during the course of such a search." The Court also concedes that, when an arresting officer "comes within plain view of a piece of evidence, not concealed, although outside of the area under the immediate control of the arrestee, the officer may seize it, so long as the plain view was obtained in the course of an appropriately limited search of the arrestee." Yet today's decision is a limitation

---

[•] The "mere evidence" issue will be developed further in Chapter 11, *infra*. For now, it is sufficient to understand that at one point in our Fourth Amendment jurisprudence, evidence could not be seized unless it was either the fruit of a crime, an instrumentality of a crime, or contraband. *Hayden* specifically rejected that rule, holding that evidence is not unseizable simply because it is "mere evidence."

on *Chimel,* for in the latter example, the Court would permit seizure only if the plain view was inadvertently obtained. If the police, that is, fully anticipate that, when they arrest a suspect as he is entering the front door of his home, they will find a credit card in his pocket and a picture in plain sight on the wall opposite the door, both of which will implicate him in a crime, they may under today's decision seize the credit card but not the picture. This is a distinction that I find to be without basis and which the Court makes no attempt to explain. I can therefore conclude only that *Chimel* and today's holding are squarely inconsistent and that the Court, unable to perceive any reasoned distinction, has abandoned any attempt to find one.

Aware of these inconsistencies, the Court admits that "it would be nonsense to pretend that our decision today reduces Fourth Amendment law to complete order and harmony." But it concludes that logical consistency cannot be attained in constitutional law and ultimately comes to rest upon its belief "that the result reached in this case is correct." It may be that constitutional law cannot be fully coherent and that constitutional principles ought not always be spun out to their logical limits, but this does not mean that we should cease to strive for clarity and consistency of analysis. Here the Court has a ready opportunity, one way or another, to bring clarity and certainty to a body of law that lower courts and law enforcement officials often find confusing. Instead, without apparent reason, it only increases their confusion by clinging to distinctions that are both unexplained and inexplicable.

## QUESTIONS AND NOTES

**1.** What is the root justification for the "plain view" doctrine?

**2.** Is "plain view" an exception to the law of "search" or the law of "seizure?" Does it matter?

**3.** Who among Stewart, Black, or White, has the best of the argument as a matter of policy? Who has the best argument as a matter of precedent?

**4.** In *Hicks,* the court emphasizes the need for prior justification as a condition of "plain view."

## Arizona v. Hicks
### 480 U.S. 321 (1987)

Justice SCALIA delivered the opinion of the Court.

In *Coolidge,* we said that in certain circumstances a warrantless seizure by police of an item that comes within plain view during their lawful search of a private area may be reasonable under the Fourth Amendment. We granted certiorari in the present case to decide whether this "plain view" doctrine may be invoked when the police have less than probable cause to believe that the item in question is evidence of a crime or is contraband.

### I

On April 18, 1984, a bullet was fired through the floor of respondent's apartment, striking and injuring a man in the apartment below. Police officers arrived and entered respondent's apartment to search for the shooter, for other victims, and for weapons. They found and seized three weapons, including a sawed-off rifle, and in the course of their search also discovered a stocking-cap mask.

One of the policemen, Officer Nelson, noticed two sets of expensive stereo components, which seemed out of place in the squalid and otherwise ill-appointed four-room apartment. Suspecting that they were stolen, he read and recorded their serial numbers—moving some of the components, including a Bang and Olufsen turntable, in order to do so—which he then reported by phone to his headquarters. On being advised that the turntable had been taken in an armed robbery, he seized it immediately. It was later determined that some of the other serial numbers matched those on other stereo equipment taken in the same armed robbery, and a warrant was obtained and executed to seize that equipment as well. Respondent was subsequently indicted for the robbery.

The state trial court granted respondent's motion to suppress the evidence that had been seized. The Court of Appeals of Arizona affirmed. It was conceded that the initial entry and search, although warrantless, were justified by the exigent circumstance of the shooting. The Court of Appeals viewed the obtaining of the serial numbers, however, as an additional search, unrelated to that exigency. Relying upon a statement in *Mincey v. Arizona,* 437 U.S. 385, that a "warrantless search must be 'strictly circumscribed by the exigencies which justify its initiation,'" the Court of Appeals held that the police conduct violated the Fourth Amendment, requiring the evidence derived from that conduct to be excluded. Both courts—the trial court explicitly and

the Court of Appeals by necessary implication—rejected the State's contention that Officer Nelson's actions were justified under the "plain view" doctrine of *Coolidge.* The Arizona Supreme Court denied review, and the State filed this petition.

### II

As an initial matter, the State argues that Officer Nelson's actions constituted neither a "search" nor a "seizure" within the meaning of the Fourth Amendment. We agree that the mere recording of the serial numbers did not constitute a seizure. To be sure, that was the first step in a process by which respondent was eventually deprived of the stereo equipment. In and of itself, however, it did not "meaningfully interfere" with respondent's possessory interest in either the serial numbers or the equipment, and therefore did not amount to a seizure.

Officer Nelson's moving of the equipment, however, did constitute a "search" separate and apart from the search for the shooter, victims, and weapons that was the lawful objective of his entry into the apartment. Merely inspecting those parts of the turntable that came into view during the latter search would not have constituted an independent search, because it would have produced no additional invasion of respondent's privacy interest. But taking action, unrelated to the objectives of the authorized intrusion, which exposed to view concealed portions of the apartment or its contents, did produce a new invasion of respondent's privacy unjustified by the exigent circumstance that validated the entry. This is why, contrary to Justice Powell's suggestion, the "distinction between 'looking' at a suspicious object in plain view and 'moving' it even a few inches" is much more than trivial for purposes of the Fourth Amendment. It matters not that the search uncovered nothing of any great personal value to respondent—serial numbers rather than (what might conceivably have been hidden behind or under the equipment) letters or photographs. A search is a search, even if it happens to disclose nothing but the bottom of a turntable.

### III

The remaining question is whether the search was "reasonable" under the Fourth Amendment.

On this aspect of the case we reject, at the outset, the apparent position of the Arizona Court of Appeals that because the officers' action directed to the stereo equipment was unrelated to the justification for their entry into respondent's apartment, it was *ipso facto* unreasonable. That lack of relationship *always* exists with regard to action validated under the "plain view" doctrine; where action is taken for the purpose justifying the entry, invocation of the doctrine is superfluous. *Mincey,* in saying that a warrantless search must be "strictly circumscribed by the exigencies which justify its initiation," was addressing only the scope of the primary search itself, and was not overruling by implication the many cases acknowledging that the "plain view" doctrine can legitimate action beyond that scope.

We turn, then, to application of the doctrine to the facts of this case. "It is well established that under certain circumstances the police may *seize* evidence in plain view without a warrant," *Coolidge* (plurality opinion) (emphasis added). Those circumstances include situations "[w]here the initial intrusion that brings the police within plain view of such [evidence] is supported . . . by one of the recognized exceptions to the warrant requirement," such as the exigent-circumstances intrusion here. It would be absurd to say that an object could lawfully be seized and taken from the premises, but could not be moved for closer examination. It is clear, therefore, that the search here was valid if the "plain view" doctrine would have sustained a seizure of the equipment.

There is no doubt it would have done so if Officer Nelson had probable cause to believe that the equipment was stolen. The State has conceded, however, that he had only a "reasonable suspicion," by which it means something less than probable cause. We have not ruled on the question whether probable cause is required in order to invoke the "plain view" doctrine. Dicta in *Payton,* suggested that the standard of probable cause must be met, but our later opinions in *Brown,* explicitly regarded the issue as unresolved.

We now hold that probable cause is required. To say otherwise would be to cut the "plain view" doctrine loose from its theoretical and practical moorings. The theory of that doctrine consists of extending to nonpublic places such as the home, where searches and seizures without a warrant are presumptively unreasonable, the police's longstanding authority to make warrantless seizures in public places of such objects as weapons and contraband. And the practical justification for that extension is the desirability of sparing police, whose viewing of the object in the course of a lawful search is as legitimate as it would have been in a public place, the inconvenience and the risk—to themselves or to preservation of the evidence—of going to obtain a warrant. Dispensing with the need for a warrant is worlds apart from permitting a lesser standard of *cause* for the seizure than a warrant would require,

*i.e.,* the standard of probable cause. No reason is apparent why an object should routinely be seizable on lesser grounds, during an unrelated search and seizure, than would have been needed to obtain a warrant for that same object if it had been known to be on the premises.

We do not say, of course, that a seizure can never be justified on less than probable cause. We have held that it can—where, for example, the seizure is minimally intrusive and operational necessities render it the only practicable means of detecting certain types of crime. No special operational necessities are relied on here, however—but rather the mere fact that the items in question came lawfully within the officer's plain view. That alone cannot supplant the requirement of probable cause.

The same considerations preclude us from holding that, even though probable cause would have been necessary for a *seizure,* the *search* of objects in plain view that occurred here could be sustained on lesser grounds. A dwelling-place search, no less than a dwelling-place seizure, requires probable cause, and there is no reason in theory or practicality why application of the "plain view" doctrine would supplant that requirement. Although the interest protected by the Fourth Amendment injunction against unreasonable searches is quite different from that protected by its injunction against unreasonable seizures, neither the one nor the other is of inferior worth or necessarily requires only lesser protection. We have not elsewhere drawn a categorical distinction between the two insofar as concerns the degree of justification needed to establish the reasonableness of police action, and we see no reason for a distinction in the particular circumstances before us here. Indeed, to treat searches more liberally would especially erode the plurality's warning in *Coolidge* that "the 'plain view' doctrine may not be used to extend a general exploratory search from one object to another until something incriminating at last emerges." In short, whether legal authority to move the equipment could be found only as an inevitable concomitant of the authority to seize it, or also as a consequence of some independent power to search certain objects in plain view, probable cause to believe the equipment was stolen was required.

Justice O'Connor's dissent suggests that we uphold the action here on the ground that it was a "cursory inspection" rather than a "full-blown search," and could therefore be justified by reasonable suspicion instead of probable cause. As already noted, a truly cursory inspection—one that involves merely looking at what is already exposed to view, without disturbing it—is not a "search" for Fourth

Amendment purposes, and therefore does not even require reasonable suspicion. We are unwilling to send police and judges into a new thicket of Fourth Amendment law, to seek a creature of uncertain description that is neither a "plain view" inspection nor yet a "full-blown search."

Justice Powell's dissent reasonably asks what it is we would have had Officer Nelson do in these circumstances. The answer depends, of course, upon whether he had probable cause to conduct a search, a question that was not preserved in this case. If he had, then he should have done precisely what he did. If not, then he should have followed up his suspicions, if possible, by means other than a search—just as he would have had to do if, while walking along the street, he had noticed the same suspicious stereo equipment sitting inside a house a few feet away from him, beneath an open window. It may well be that, in such circumstances, no effective means short of a search exist. But there is nothing new in the realization that the Constitution sometimes insulates the criminality of a few in order to protect the privacy of us all. Our disagreement with the dissenters pertains to where the proper balance should be struck; we choose to adhere to the textual and traditional standard of probable cause.

For the reasons stated, the judgment of the Court of Appeals of Arizona is affirmed.

Justice WHITE, concurring.

I write only to emphasize that this case does not present, and we have no occasion to address, the so-called "inadvertent discovery" prong of the plain-view exception to the Warrant Clause. This "requirement" of the plain-view doctrine has never been accepted by a judgment supported by a majority of this Court, and I therefore do not accept Justice O'Connor's dissent's assertion that evidence seized in plain view must have been inadvertently discovered in order to satisfy the dictates of the Fourth Amendment. I join the majority opinion today without regard to the inadvertence of the officers' discovery of the stereo components' serial numbers. The police officers conducted a search of respondent's stereo equipment absent probable cause that the equipment was stolen. It is for this reason that the judgment of the Court of Appeals of Arizona must be affirmed.

Justice POWELL, with whom the CHIEF JUSTICE and Justice O'CONNOR join, dissenting.

I join Justice O'Connor's dissenting opinion, and write briefly to highlight what seem to me the unfortunate consequences of the Court's decision.

Today the Court holds for the first time that the requirement of probable cause operates as a separate limitation on the application of the plain-view doctrine. The plurality opinion in *Coolidge,* required only that it be "immediately apparent to the police that they have evidence before them; the 'plain view' doctrine may not be used to extend a general exploratory search from one object to another until something incriminating at last emerges." There was no general exploratory search in this case, and I would not approve such a search. All the pertinent objects were in plain view and could be identified as objects frequently stolen. There was no looking into closets, opening of drawers or trunks, or other "rummaging around." Justice O'Connor properly emphasizes that the moving of a suspicious object in plain view results in a minimal invasion of privacy. The Court nevertheless holds that "merely looking at" an object in plain view is lawful, but "moving" or "disturbing" the object to investigate a reasonable suspicion is not. The facts of this case well illustrate the unreasonableness of this distinction.

The officers' suspicion that the stereo components at issue were stolen was both reasonable and based on specific, articulable facts. Indeed, the State was unwise to concede the absence of probable cause. The police lawfully entered respondent's apartment under exigent circumstances that arose when a bullet fired through the floor of the apartment struck a man in the apartment below. What they saw in the apartment hardly suggested that it was occupied by law-abiding citizens. A .25-caliber automatic pistol lay in plain view on the living room floor. During a concededly lawful search, the officers found a .45-caliber automatic, a .22-caliber, sawed-off rifle, and a stocking-cap mask. The apartment was littered with drug paraphernalia. The officers also observed two sets of expensive stereo components of a type that frequently was stolen.[2]

It is fair to ask what Officer Nelson should have done in these circumstances. Accepting the State's concession that he lacked probable cause, he could not have obtained a warrant to seize the stereo components. Neither could he have remained on the premises and forcibly prevented their removal. Officer Nelson's testimony indicates that he was able to read some of the serial numbers without moving the

---

[2] Responding to a question on cross-examination, Officer Nelson explained that his suspicion was "based on 12 years' worth of police experience. I have worked in different burglary crimes throughout that period of time and . . . I'm just very familiar with people converting stolen stereos and TV's into their own use."

component.[3] To read the serial number on a Bang and Olufsen turntable, however, he had to "turn it around or turn it upside down." Officer Nelson noted the serial numbers on the stereo components and telephoned the National Crime Information Center to check them against the Center's computerized listing of stolen property. The computer confirmed his suspicion that at least the Bang and Olufsen turntable had been stolen. On the basis of this information, the officers obtained a warrant to seize the turntable and other stereo components that also proved to be stolen.

The Court holds that there was an unlawful search of the turntable. It agrees that the "mere recording of the serial numbers did not constitute a seizure." Thus, if the computer had identified as stolen property a component with a visible serial number, the evidence would have been admissible. But the Court further holds that "Officer Nelson's moving of the equipment . . . did constitute a 'search'. . . ." It perceives a constitutional distinction between reading a serial number on an object and moving or picking up an identical object to see its serial number. To make its position unmistakably clear, the Court concludes that a "search is a search, even if it happens to disclose nothing but the bottom of a turntable." With all respect, this distinction between "looking" at a suspicious object in plain view and "moving" it even a few inches trivializes the Fourth Amendment.[4] The Court's new rule will

---

[3] Officer Nelson testified that there was an opening of about a foot between the back of one set of stereo equipment and the wall. Presumably this opening was large enough to permit Officer Nelson to view serial numbers on the backs of the components without moving them.

[4] Numerous articles that frequently are stolen have identifying numbers, including expensive watches and cameras, and also credit cards. Assume for example that an officer reasonably suspects that two identical watches, both in plain view, have been stolen. Under the Court's decision, if one watch is lying face up and the other lying face down, reading the serial number on one of the watches would not be a search. But turning over the other watch to read its serial number would be a search. Moreover, the officer's ability to read a serial number may depend on its location in a room and light conditions at a particular time. Would there be a constitutional difference if an officer, on the basis of a reasonable suspicion, used a pocket flashlight or turned on a light to read a number rather than moving the object to a point where a serial number was clearly visible?

cause uncertainty, and could deter conscientious police officers from lawfully obtaining evidence necessary to convict guilty persons. Apart from the importance of rationality in the interpretation of the Fourth Amendment, today's decision may handicap law enforcement without enhancing privacy interests. Accordingly, I dissent.

Justice O'CONNOR, with whom the CHIEF JUSTICE and Justice POWELL join, dissenting.

The Court today gives the right answer to the wrong question. The Court asks whether the police must have probable cause before either seizing an object in plain view or conducting a full-blown search of that object, and concludes that they must. I agree. In my view, however, this case presents a different question: whether police must have probable cause before conducting a cursory inspection of an item in plain view. Because I conclude that such an inspection is reasonable if the police are aware of facts or circumstances that justify a reasonable suspicion that the item is evidence of a crime, I would reverse the judgment of the Arizona Court of Appeals, and therefore dissent.

In *Coolidge,* Justice Stewart summarized three requirements that the plurality thought must be satisfied for a plain-view search or seizure. First, the police must lawfully make an initial intrusion or otherwise be in a position from which they can view a particular area. Second, the officer must discover incriminating evidence "inadvertently." Third, it must be "immediately apparent" to the police that the items they observe may be evidence of a crime, contraband, or otherwise subject to seizure. As another plurality observed in *Texas v. Brown,* 460 U.S. 730 (1983), these three requirements have never been expressly adopted by a majority of this Court, but "as the considered opinion of four Members of this Court [the *Coolidge* plurality] should obviously be the point of reference for further discussion of the issue." There is no dispute in this case that the first two requirements have been satisfied. The officers were lawfully in the apartment pursuant to exigent circumstances, and the discovery of the stereo was inadvertent—the officers did not "'know in advance the location of [certain] evidence and intend to seize it,' relying on the plain-view doctrine only as a pretext." Instead, the dispute in this case focuses on the application of the "immediately apparent" requirement; at issue is whether a police officer's reasonable suspicion is adequate to justify a cursory examination of an item in plain view.

The purpose of the "immediately apparent" requirement is to prevent "general, exploratory rummaging in a person's belongings." If an officer could indiscriminately search every item in plain view, a search justified by a limited purpose—such as exigent circumstances—could be used to eviscerate the protections of the Fourth Amendment. In order to prevent such a general search, therefore, we require that the relevance of the item be "immediately apparent."

Thus, I agree with the Court that even under the plain-view doctrine, probable cause is required before the police seize an item, or conduct a full-blown search of evidence in plain view. Such a requirement of probable cause will prevent the plain-view doctrine from authorizing general searches. This is not to say, however, that even a mere inspection of a suspicious item must be supported by probable cause. When a police officer makes a cursory inspection of a suspicious item in plain view in order to determine whether it is indeed evidence of a crime, there is no "exploratory rummaging." Only those items that the police officer "reasonably suspects" as evidence of a crime may be inspected, and perhaps more importantly, the scope of such an inspection is quite limited. In short, if police officers have a reasonable, articulable suspicion that an object they come across during the course of a lawful search is evidence of crime, in my view they may make a cursory examination of the object to verify their suspicion. If the officers wish to go beyond such a cursory examination of the object, however, they must have probable cause.

This distinction between a full-blown search and seizure of an item and a mere inspection of the item was first suggested by Justice Stewart. In his concurrence in *Stanley v. Georgia*, 394 U.S. 557 (1969), which is cited in *Coolidge*, Justice Stewart observed that the federal agents there had acted within the scope of a lawful warrant in opening the drawers of the defendant's desk. When they found in one of the drawers not the gambling material described in the warrant but movie films, they proceeded to exhibit the films on the defendant's projector, and thereafter arrested the defendant for possession of obscene matter. Justice Stewart agreed with the majority that the film had to be suppressed, but in doing so he suggested that a less intrusive inspection of evidence in plain view would present a different case: "This is not a case where agents in the course of a lawful search came upon contraband, criminal activity, or criminal evidence in plain view. For the record makes clear that the contents of the films could not be determined by *mere inspection*." (emphasis added).

Following Justice Stewart's suggestion, the overwhelming majority of both state and federal courts have held that probable cause is not required for a minimal inspection of an item in plain view. As Professor LaFave summarizes the view of these courts, "the minimal additional intrusion which results from an inspection or examination of an object in plain view is reasonable if the officer was first aware of some facts and circumstances which justify a reasonable suspicion (not probable cause, in the traditional sense) that the object is or contains a fruit, instrumentality, or evidence of crime." 2 W. LaFave, Search and Seizure § 6.7(b), p. 717 (2d ed. 1987); see also id., at 345 ("It is generally assumed that there is nothing improper in merely picking up an unnamed article for the purpose of noting its brand name or serial number or other identifying characteristics to be found on the surface"). Thus, while courts require probable cause for more extensive examination, cursory inspections—including picking up or moving objects for a better view—require only a reasonable suspicion.

This distinction between searches based on their relative intrusiveness—and its subsequent adoption by a consensus of American courts—is entirely consistent with our Fourth Amendment jurisprudence. We have long recognized that searches can vary in intrusiveness, and that some brief searches "may be so minimally intrusive of Fourth Amendment interests that strong countervailing governmental interests will justify a [search] based only on specific articulable facts" that the item in question is contraband or evidence of a crime.

In my view, the balance of the governmental and privacy interests strongly supports a reasonable-suspicion standard for the cursory examination of items in plain view. The additional intrusion caused by an inspection of an item in plain view for its serial number is minuscule. Weighed against this minimal additional invasion of privacy are rather major gains in law enforcement. The use of identification numbers in tracing stolen property is a powerful law enforcement tool. Serial numbers are far more helpful and accurate in detecting stolen property than simple police recollection of the evidence. Given the prevalence of mass produced goods in our national economy, a serial number is often the only sure method of detecting stolen property. The balance of governmental and private interests strongly supports the view accepted by a majority of courts that a standard of reasonable suspicion meets the requirements of the Fourth Amendment.

Unfortunately, in its desire to establish a "bright-line" test, the Court has taken a step that ignores a substantial body of precedent and that places serious roadblocks to reasonable law enforcement practices. Indeed, in this case no warrant to search the stereo equipment for its serial number could have been obtained by the officers based on reasonable suspicion alone, and in the Court's view the officers may not even move the stereo turntable to examine its serial number. The theoretical advantages of the "search is a search" approach adopted by the Court today are simply too remote to justify the tangible and severe damage it inflicts on legitimate and effective law enforcement.

Even if probable cause were the appropriate standard, I have little doubt that it was satisfied here. When police officers, during the course of a search inquiring

into grievously unlawful activity, discover the tools of a thief (a sawed-off rifle and a stocking mask) and observe in a small apartment two sets of stereo equipment that are both inordinately expensive in relation to their surroundings and known to be favored targets of larcenous activity, the "flexible, common-sense standard" of probable cause has been satisfied.

Because the Court today ignores the existence of probable cause, and in doing so upsets a widely accepted body of precedent on the standard of reasonableness for the cursory examination of evidence in plain view, I respectfully dissent.

## QUESTIONS AND NOTES

**1.** Do you think that Officer Nelson acted properly? If you were his superior, would you have praised or criticized him? What else could he have done?

**2.** Should the State have conceded the probable cause issue? Why do you suppose that it did?

**3.** Is this the type of issue that ought to be decided by flexible standards (O'Connor) or a bright-line rule (Scalia)? What are the advantages either way?

**4.** Did the Court trivialize the Fourth Amendment, or announce a significant principle? Explain your answer.

**5.** We conclude this section with *Horton,* where the Court finally confronted the question of whether "inadvertence" is a *sine qua non* of "plain view."

### Horton v. California
### 496 U.S. 128 (1990)

Justice STEVENS delivered the opinion of the Court.

In this case we revisit an issue that was considered, but not conclusively resolved, in *Coolidge*: Whether the warrantless seizure of evidence of crime in plain view is prohibited by the Fourth Amendment if the discovery of the evidence was not inadvertent. We conclude that even though inadvertence is a characteristic of most legitimate "plain view" seizures, it is not a necessary condition.

I

Petitioner was convicted of the armed robbery of Erwin Wallaker, the treasurer of the San Jose Coin Club. When Wallaker returned to his home after the Club's annual show, he entered his garage and was accosted by two masked men, one armed with a machine gun and the other with an electrical shocking device, sometimes referred to as a "stun gun." The two men shocked Wallaker, bound and handcuffed him, and robbed him of jewelry and cash.

During the encounter sufficient conversation took place to enable Wallaker subsequently to identify petitioner's distinctive voice. His identification was partially corroborated by a witness who saw the robbers leaving the scene, and by evidence that petitioner had attended the coin show.

Sergeant LaRault, an experienced police officer, investigated the crime and determined that there was probable cause to search petitioner's home for the proceeds of the robbery and for the weapons used by the robbers. His affidavit for a search warrant referred to police reports that described the weapons as well as the proceeds, but the warrant issued by the Magistrate only authorized a search for the proceeds, including three specifically described rings.

Pursuant to the warrant, LaRault searched petitioner's residence, but he did not find the stolen property. During the course of the search, however, he discovered the weapons in plain view and seized them. Specifically, he seized an Uzi machine gun, a .38 caliber revolver, two stun guns, a handcuff key, a San Jose

Coin Club advertising brochure, and a few items of clothing identified by the victim.[1] LaRault testified that while he was searching for the rings, he also was interested in finding other evidence connecting petitioner to the robbery. Thus, the seized evidence was not discovered "inadvertently."

## II

The right to security in person and property protected by the Fourth Amendment may be invaded in quite different ways by searches and seizures. A search compromises the individual interest in privacy; a seizure deprives the individual of dominion over his or her person or property. The "plain view" doctrine is often considered an exception to the general rule that warrantless searches are presumptively unreasonable, but this characterization overlooks the important difference between searches and seizures. If an article is already in plain view, neither its observation nor its seizure would involve any invasion of privacy. A seizure of the article, however, would obviously invade the owner's possessory interest. If "plain view" justifies an exception from an otherwise applicable warrant requirement, therefore, it must be an exception that is addressed to the concerns that are implicated by seizures rather than by searches.

The criteria that generally guide "plain view" seizures were set forth in *Coolidge*. The Court held that the seizure of two automobiles parked in plain view on the defendant's driveway in the course of arresting the defendant violated the Fourth Amendment. Accordingly, particles of gun powder that had been subsequently found in vacuum sweepings from one of the cars could not be introduced in evidence against the defendant. The State endeavored to justify the seizure of the automobiles, and their subsequent search at the police station, on four different grounds, including the "plain view" doctrine.[6] The scope of that doctrine as it had developed in earlier cases was fairly summarized in these three paragraphs from Justice Stewart's opinion:

"It is well established that under certain circumstances the police may seize evidence in plain view without a warrant. But it is important to keep in mind that, in the vast majority of cases, any evidence seized by the police will be in plain view, at least at the moment of seizure. The problem with the 'plain view' doctrine has been to identify the circumstances in which plain view has legal significance rather than being simply the normal concomitant of any search, legal or illegal.

"An example of the applicability of the 'plain view' doctrine is the situation in which the police have a warrant to search a given area for specified objects, and in the course of the search come across some other article of incriminating character. Where the initial intrusion that brings the police within plain view of such an article is supported, not by a warrant, but by one of the recognized exceptions to the warrant requirement, the seizure is also legitimate. Thus the police may inadvertently come across evidence while in 'hot pursuit' of a fleeing suspect. And an object that comes into view during a search incident to arrest that is appropriately limited in scope under existing law may be seized without a warrant. Finally, the 'plain view' doctrine has been applied where a police officer is not searching for evidence against the accused, but nonetheless inadvertently comes across an incriminating object.

"What the 'plain view' cases have in common is that the police officer in each of them had a prior justification for an intrusion in the course of which he came inadvertently across a piece of evidence incriminating the accused. The doctrine serves to supplement the prior justification – whether it be a warrant for another object, hot pursuit, search incident to lawful arrest, or some other legitimate reason for being present unconnected with a search directed against the accused – and permits the warrantless seizure. Of course, the extension of the original justification is legitimate only where it is immediately apparent to the police that they have evidence before them; the 'plain view' doctrine may not be used to extend a general exploratory search from one object to another until something incriminating at last emerges."

---

[1] Although the officer viewed other handguns and rifles, he did not seize them because there was no probable cause to believe they were associated with criminal activity.

[6] The State primarily contended that the seizures were authorized by a warrant issued by the Attorney General, but the Court held the warrant invalid because it had not been issued by "a neutral and detached magistrate." In addition, the State relied on three exceptions from the warrant requirement: (1) search incident to arrest; (2) the automobile exception; and (3) the "plain view" doctrine.

Justice Stewart then described the two limitations on the doctrine that he found implicit in its rationale: First, "that plain view *alone* is never enough to justify the warrantless seizure of evidence," and second, "that the discovery of evidence in plain view must be inadvertent."

Justice Stewart's analysis of the "plain view" doctrine did not command a majority and a plurality of the Court has since made clear that the discussion is "not a binding precedent." *Brown* (opinion of Rehnquist, J.). The decision nonetheless is a binding precedent. Before discussing the second limitation, which is implicated in this case, it is therefore necessary to explain why the first adequately supports the Court's judgment.

It is, of course, an essential predicate to any valid warrantless seizure of incriminating evidence that the officer did not violate the Fourth Amendment in arriving at the place from which the evidence could be plainly viewed. There are, moreover, two additional conditions that must be satisfied to justify the warrantless seizure. First, not only must the item be in plain view, its incriminating character must also be "immediately apparent." Thus, in *Coolidge,* the cars were obviously in plain view, but their probative value remained uncertain until after the interiors were swept and examined microscopically. Second, not only must the officer be lawfully located in a place from which the object can be plainly seen, but he or she must also have a lawful right of access to the object itself.[7] As the Solicitor General has suggested, Justice Harlan's vote in *Coolidge* may have rested on the fact that the seizure of the cars was accomplished by means of a warrantless trespass on the defendant's property. In all events, we are satisfied that the absence of inadvertence was not essential to the Court's rejection of the State's "plain view" argument in *Coolidge*.

### III

Justice Stewart concluded that the inadvertence requirement was necessary to avoid a violation of the express constitutional requirement that a valid warrant must particularly describe the things to be seized. He explained:

"The rationale of the exception to the warrant requirement, as just stated, is that a plain-view seizure will not turn an initially valid (and therefore limited) search into a 'general' one, while the inconvenience of procuring a warrant to cover an inadvertent discovery is great. But where the discovery is anticipated, where the police know in advance the location of the evidence and intend to seize it, the situation is altogether different. The requirement of a warrant to seize imposes no inconvenience whatever, or at least none which is constitutionally cognizable in a legal system that regards warrantless searches as '*per se* unreasonable' in the absence of 'exigent circumstances.'

"If the initial intrusion is bottomed upon a warrant that fails to mention a particular object, though the police know its location and intend to seize it, then there is a violation of the express constitutional requirement of 'Warrants . . . particularly describing . . . [the] things to be seized.'"

We find two flaws in this reasoning. First, even-handed law enforcement is best achieved by the application of objective standards of conduct, rather than standards that depend upon the subjective state of mind of the officer. The fact that an officer is interested in an item of evidence and fully expects to find it in the course of a search should not invalidate its seizure if the search is confined in area and duration by the terms of a warrant or a valid exception to the warrant requirement. If the officer has knowledge approaching certainty that the item will be found, we see no reason why he or she would deliberately omit a particular description of the item to be seized from the application for a search warrant.[8] Specification of the additional item could only

---

[7] "This is simply a corollary of the familiar principle discussed above, that no amount of probable cause can justify a warrantless search or seizure absent 'exigent circumstances.' Incontrovertible testimony of the senses that an incriminating object is on premises belonging to a criminal suspect may establish the fullest possible measure of probable cause. But even where the object is contraband, this Court has repeatedly stated and enforced the basic rule that the police may not enter and make a warrantless seizure."

[8] "If the police have probable cause to search for a photograph as well as a rifle and they proceed to seek a warrant, they could have no possible motive for deliberately including the rifle but omitting the photograph. Quite the contrary is true. Only oversight or careless mistake would explain the omission in the warrant application if the police were convinced they had probable cause to search for the photograph." *Coolidge* (White, J., dissenting).

permit the officer to expand the scope of the search. On the other hand, if he or she has a valid warrant to search for one item and merely a suspicion concerning the second, whether or not it amounts to probable cause, we fail to see why that suspicion should immunize the second item from seizure if it is found during a lawful search for the first. The hypothetical case put by Justice White in his dissenting opinion in Coolidge is instructive:

"Let us suppose officers secure a warrant to search a house for a rifle. While staying well within the range of a rifle search, they discover two photographs of the murder victim, both in plain sight in the bedroom. Assume also that the discovery of the one photograph was inadvertent but finding the other was anticipated. The Court would permit the seizure of only one of the photographs. But in terms of the 'minor' peril to Fourth Amendment values there is surely no difference between these two photographs: the interference with possession is the same in each case and the officers' appraisal of the photograph they expected to see is no less reliable than their judgment about the other. And in both situations the actual inconvenience and danger to evidence remain identical if the officers must depart and secure a warrant."

Second, the suggestion that the inadvertence requirement is necessary to prevent the police from conducting general searches, or from converting specific warrants into general warrants, is not persuasive because that interest is already served by the requirements that no warrant issue unless it "particularly describ[es] the place to be searched and the persons or things to be seized," and that a warrantless search be circumscribed by the exigencies which justify its initiation. Scrupulous adherence to these requirements serves the interests in limiting the area and duration of the search that the inadvertence requirement inadequately protects. Once those commands have been satisfied and the officer has a lawful right of access, however, no additional Fourth Amendment interest is furthered by requiring that the discovery of evidence be inadvertent. If the scope of the search exceeds that permitted by the terms of a validly issued warrant or the character of the relevant exception from the warrant requirement, the subsequent seizure is unconstitutional without more. Thus, in the case of a search incident to a lawful arrest, "[i]f the police stray outside the scope of an authorized *Chimel* search they are already in violation of the Fourth Amendment, and evidence so seized will be excluded; adding a second reason for excluding evidence hardly seems worth the candle." Similarly, the object of a warrantless search of an automobile also defines its scope:

"The scope of a warrantless search of an automobile thus is not defined by the nature of the container in which the contraband is secreted. Rather, it is defined by the object of the search and the places in which there is probable cause to believe that it may be found. Just as probable cause to believe that a stolen lawnmower may be found in a garage will not support a warrant to search an upstairs bedroom, probable cause to believe that undocumented aliens are being transported in a van will not justify a warrantless search of a suitcase. Probable cause to believe that a container placed in the trunk of a taxi contains contraband or evidence does not justify a search of the entire cab." *United States v. Ross* (Chapter 6, *infra.*)

In this case, the scope of the search was not enlarged in the slightest by the omission of any reference to the weapons in the warrant. Indeed, if the three rings and other items named in the warrant had been found at the outset—or if petitioner had them in his possession and had responded to the warrant by producing them immediately—no search for weapons could have taken place. Again, Justice White's dissenting opinion in *Coolidge* is instructive: "Police with a warrant for a rifle may search only places where rifles might be and must terminate the search once the rifle is found; the inadvertence rule will in no way reduce the number of places into which they may lawfully look."

In this case the items seized from petitioner's home were discovered during a lawful search authorized by a valid warrant. When they were discovered, it was immediately apparent to the officer that they constituted incriminating evidence. He had probable cause, not only to obtain a warrant to search for the stolen property, but also to believe that the weapons and handguns had been used in the crime he was investigating. The search was authorized by the warrant, the seizure was authorized by the "plain view" doctrine. The judgment is affirmed.

Justice BRENNAN, with whom Justice MARSHALL joins, dissenting

I remain convinced that Justice Stewart correctly articulated the plain view doctrine in *Coolidge*. The Fourth Amendment permits law enforcement officers to seize items for which they do not have a warrant when those items are found in plain view and (1) the officers are lawfully in a position to observe the items, (2) the discovery of the items is "inadvertent," and (3) it is immediately apparent to the officers that the items are evidence of a crime, contraband, or otherwise subject to seizure. In eschewing the inadvertent discovery requirement, the majority ignores the Fourth Amendment's express command that warrants particularly describe not only the places to be searched, but also the things to be seized. I respectfully dissent from this rewriting of the Fourth Amendment.

## I

The Fourth Amendment protects two distinct interests. The prohibition against unreasonable searches and the requirement that a warrant "particularly describ[e] the place to be searched" protect an interest in privacy. The prohibition against unreasonable seizures and the requirement that a warrant "particularly describ[e] . . . the . . . things to be seized" protect a possessory interest in property. The Fourth Amendment, by its terms, declares the privacy and possessory interests to be equally important. As this Court recently stated, "Although the interest protected by the Fourth Amendment injunction against unreasonable searches is quite different from that protected by its injunction against unreasonable seizures, neither the one nor the other is of inferior worth or necessarily requires only lesser protection."

The Amendment protects these equally important interests in precisely the same manner: by requiring a neutral and detached magistrate to evaluate, before the search or seizure, the government's showing of probable cause and its particular description of the place to be searched and the items to be seized. Accordingly, just as a warrantless search is *per se* unreasonable absent exigent circumstances, so too a seizure of personal property is "*per se* unreasonable within the meaning of the Fourth Amendment unless it is accomplished pursuant to a judicial warrant issued upon probable cause and particularly describing the items to be seized." "Prior review by a neutral and detached magistrate is the time-tested means of effectuating Fourth Amendment rights." A decision to invade a possessory interest in property is too important to be left to the discretion of zealous officers "engaged in the often competitive enterprise of ferreting out crime." "The requirement that warrants shall particularly describe the things to be seized makes general searches under them impossible and prevents the seizure of one thing under a warrant describing another. As to what is to be taken, nothing is left to the discretion of the officer executing the warrant."

The plain view doctrine is an exception to the general rule that a seizure of personal property must be authorized by a warrant. As Justice Stewart explained in *Coolidge,* we accept a warrantless seizure when an officer is lawfully in a location and inadvertently sees evidence of a crime because of "the inconvenience of procuring a warrant" to seize this newly discovered piece of evidence. But "where the discovery is anticipated, where the police know in advance the location of the evidence and intend to seize it," the argument that procuring a warrant would be "inconvenient" loses much, if not all, of its force. Barring an exigency, there is no reason why the police officers could not have obtained a warrant to seize this evidence before entering the premises. The rationale behind the inadvertent discovery requirement is simply that we will not excuse officers from the general requirement of a warrant to seize if the officers know the location of evidence, have probable cause to seize it, intend to seize it, and yet do not bother to obtain a warrant particularly describing that evidence. To do so would violate "the express constitutional requirement of 'Warrants . . . particularly describing . . . [the] things to be seized,'" and would "fly in the face of the basic rule that no amount of probable cause can justify a warrantless seizure."

Although joined by only three other Members of the Court, Justice Stewart's discussion of the inadvertent discovery requirement has become widely accepted. See *Brown* (Powell, J., concurring in judgment) ("Whatever my view might have been when *Coolidge* was decided, I see no reason at this late date to imply criticism of its articulation of this exception. It has been accepted generally for over a decade"). Forty-six States and the District of Columbia and twelve United States Courts of Appeals now require plain view seizures to be inadvertent. There has been no outcry from law enforcement officials that the inadvertent discovery requirement unduly burdens their efforts. Given that the requirement is inescapably rooted in the plain language of the Fourth Amendment, I cannot fathom the Court's enthusiasm for discarding this element of the plain view doctrine.

The Court posits two "flaws" in Justice Stewart's reasoning that it believes demonstrate the inappropriateness of the inadvertent discovery requirement. But these flaws are illusory. First, the majority explains that it can see no reason why an officer who "has knowledge approaching certainty" that an item will be found in a particular location "would deliberately omit a particular description of the item to be seized from the application for a search warrant." But to the individual whose possessory interest has been invaded, it matters not why the police officer decided to omit a particular item from his application for a search warrant. When an officer with probable cause to seize an item fails to mention that item in his application for a search warrant – for whatever reason – and then seizes the item anyway, his conduct is *per se* unreasonable. Suppression of the evidence so seized will encourage officers to be more precise and complete in future warrant applications.

Furthermore, there are a number of instances in which a law enforcement officer might deliberately choose to omit certain items from a warrant application even though he has probable cause to seize them, knows they are on the premises, and intends to seize them when they are discovered in plain view. For example, the warrant application process can often be time-consuming, especially when the police attempt to seize a large number of items. An officer interested in conducting a search as soon as possible might decide to save time by listing only one or two hard-to-find items, such as the stolen rings in this case, confident that he will find in plain view all of the other evidence he is looking for before he discovers the listed items. Because rings could be located almost anywhere inside or outside a house, it is unlikely that a warrant to search for and seize the rings would restrict the scope of the search. An officer might rationally find the risk of immediately discovering the items listed in the warrant—thereby forcing him to conclude the search immediately—outweighed by the time saved in the application process.

The majority also contends that, once an officer is lawfully in a house and the scope of his search is adequately circumscribed by a warrant, "no additional Fourth Amendment interest is furthered by requiring that the discovery of evidence be inadvertent." Put another way, "the inadvertence rule will in no way reduce the number of places into which [law enforcement officers] may lawfully look." The majority is correct, but it has asked the wrong question. It is true that the inadvertent discovery requirement furthers no privacy interests. The requirement in no way reduces the scope of a search or the number of places into which officers may look. But it does protect possessory interests. Cf. *Illinois v. Andreas,* 463 U.S. 765, 771 (1983) ("The plain-view doctrine is grounded on the proposition that once police are lawfully in a position to observe an item first-hand, its owner's privacy interest in that item is lost; *the owner may retain the incidents of title and possession* but not privacy") (emphasis added). The inadvertent discovery requirement is essential if we are to take seriously the Fourth Amendment's protection of possessory interests as well as privacy interests. The Court today eliminates a rule designed to further possessory interests on the ground that it fails to further privacy interests. I cannot countenance such constitutional legerdemain.

II

Fortunately, this decision should have only a limited impact, for the Court is not confronted today with what lower courts have described as a "pretextual"

search. For example, if an officer enters a house pursuant to a warrant to search for evidence of one crime when he is really interested only in seizing evidence relating to another crime, for which he does not have a warrant, his search is "pretextual" and the fruits of that search should be suppressed. See, *e.g., State v. Kelsey,* 592 S.W.2d 509 (Mo.App.1979) (evidence suppressed because officers, who had ample opportunity to obtain warrant relating to murder investigation, entered the premises instead pursuant to a warrant relating to a drug investigation, and searched only the hiding place of the murder weapon, rather than conducting a "top to bottom" search for drugs). Similarly, an officer might use an exception to the generally applicable warrant requirement, such as "hot pursuit," as a pretext to enter a home to seize items he knows he will find in plain view. Such conduct would be a deliberate attempt to circumvent the constitutional requirement of a warrant "particularly describing the place to be searched, and the persons or things to be seized," and cannot be condoned.

The discovery of evidence in pretextual searches is not "inadvertent" and should be suppressed for that reason. But even state courts that have rejected the inadvertent discovery requirement have held that the Fourth Amendment prohibits pretextual searches. The Court's opinion today does not address pretextual searches, but I have no doubt that such searches violate the Fourth Amendment.[4]

III

The Fourth Amendment demands that an individual's possessory interest in property be protected from unreasonable governmental seizures, not just by requiring a showing of probable cause, but also by requiring a neutral and detached magistrate to authorize the seizure in advance. The Court today ignores the explicit language of the Fourth Amendment, which protects possessory interests in the same manner as it protects privacy interests, in order to eliminate a

---

[4] The Court also does not dispute the unconstitutionality of a search that goes "so far astray of a search for the items mentioned in the warrant that it [becomes] a general exploratory search for any evidence of wrongdoing that might be found." Indeed, the Court reiterates that "converting specific warrants into general warrants" is unconstitutional and emphasizes the need for scrupulous adherence to the requirements that warrants particularly describe the place to be searched and the things to be seized and that a warrantless search "be circumscribed by the exigencies which justify its initiation."

generally accepted element of the plain view doctrine that has caused no apparent difficulties for law enforcement officers. I am confident, however, that when confronted with more egregious police conduct than that found in this case, such as pretextual searches, the Court's interpretation of the Constitution will be less parsimonious than it is today. I respectfully dissent.

## QUESTIONS AND NOTES

**1.** In general, do you see any Fourth Amendment values served by the inadvertence rule?

**2.** Is Justice White's *Coolidge* hypothetical about colored and black and white photographs persuasive?

**3.** Even if Justice Brennan's concerns were generally correct, would (should) they be applied to the facts of *Horton,* where the police *tried* to get a warrant for the items seized, but were turned down?

# 6.

# AUTOMOBILES

## A.  The Rule And Its Rationale

Automobile searches are governed by sufficiently different rules from other types of searches that a substantial separate study of them is warranted. You should begin this section by reviewing and refamiliarizing yourself with *Chambers v. Maroney* (Chapter 3, *supra*). We follow that with the ubiquitous *Coolidge* case. This time, *Coolidge* develops a limitation on the automobile exception to a warrant rule. When the warrant was held invalid, and the "plain view" exception failed, New Hampshire argued that it could seize the car without a warrant because of the automobile exception. We will now study the Court's response to that contention.

### Coolidge v. New Hampshire
### 403 U.S. 443 (1971)

Justice STEWART delivered the judgment of the Court.

The underlying rationale of *Carroll* and of all the cases that have followed it is that there is "a necessary difference between a search of a store, dwelling house, or other structure in respect of which a proper official warrant readily may be obtained and a search of a ship, motor boat, wagon, or automobile for contraband goods, where *it is not practicable to secure a warrant,* because the vehicle can be quickly moved out of the locality or jurisdiction in which the warrant must be sought." (Emphasis supplied.) As we said in *Chambers,* "exigent circumstances" justify the warrantless search of "an automobile *stopped on the highway,*" where there is probable cause, because the car is

"movable, the occupants are alerted, and the car's contents may never be found again if a warrant must be obtained." "[T]he opportunity to search is fleeting." (Emphasis supplied.)

In this case, the police had known for some time of the probable role of the Pontiac car in the crime. Coolidge was aware that he was a suspect in the Mason murder, but he had been extremely cooperative throughout the investigation, and there was no indication that he meant to flee. He had already had ample opportunity to destroy any evidence he thought incriminating. There is no suggestion that, on the night in question, the car was being used for any illegal purpose, and it was regularly parked in the driveway of his house. The opportunity for search was thus hardly "fleeting." The objects that the police are assumed to have had probable cause to search for in the car were neither stolen nor contraband nor dangerous.

When the police arrived at the Coolidge house to arrest him, two officers were sent to guard the back door while the main party approached from the front. Coolidge was arrested inside the house, without resistance of any kind on his part, after he had voluntarily admitted the officers at both front and back doors. There was no way in which he could conceivably have gained access to the automobile after the police arrived on his property. When Coolidge had been taken away, the police informed Mrs. Coolidge, the only other adult occupant of the house, that she and her baby had to spend the night elsewhere and that she could not use either of the Coolidge cars. Two police officers then drove her in a police car to the house of a relative in another town, and they stayed with her there until around midnight, long after the police had had the Pontiac towed to the station house. The Coolidge premises were guarded throughout the night by two policemen.[18]

---

[18] It is frequently said that occupied automobiles stopped on the open highway may be searched without a warrant because they are "mobile," or "movable." No other basis appears for Mr. Justice White's suggestion in his dissenting opinion that we should "treat searches of automobiles as we do the arrest of a person." In this case, it is, of course, true that even though Coolidge was in jail, his wife was miles away in the company of two plainclothesmen, and the Coolidge property was under the guard of two other officers, the automobile was in a literal sense "mobile." A person who had the keys and could slip by the guard could drive it away. We attach no constitutional significance to this sort of mobility.

First, a good number of the containers that the police might discover on a person's property and want to search are equally movable, *e.g.*, trunks, suitcases, boxes, briefcases, and bags. How are such objects to be distinguished from an unoccupied automobile—not then being used for any illegal purpose—sitting on the owner's property? It is true that the automobile has wheels and its own locomotive power. But given the virtually universal availability of automobiles in our society there is little difference between driving the container itself away and driving it away in a vehicle brought to the scene for that purpose. Of course, if there is a criminal suspect close enough to the automobile so that he might get a weapon from it or destroy evidence within it, the

The word "automobile" is not a talisman in whose presence the Fourth Amendment fades away and disappears. And surely there is nothing in this case to invoke the meaning and purpose of the rule of *Carroll*—no alerted criminal bent on flight, no fleeting opportunity on an open highway after a hazardous chase, no contraband or stolen goods or weapons, no confederates waiting to move the evidence, not even the inconvenience of a special police detail to guard the immobilized automobile. In short, by no possible stretch of the legal imagination can this be made into a case where "it is not practicable to secure a warrant," and the "automobile exception," despite its label, is simply irrelevant.

Since *Carroll* would not have justified a warrantless search of the Pontiac at the time Coolidge was arrested, the later search at the station house was plainly illegal, at least so far as the automobile exception is concerned. *Chambers* is of no help to the State, since that case held only that, where the police may stop and search an automobile under *Carroll*, they may also seize it and search it later at the police station. Rather, this case is controlled by *Dyke v. Taylor Implement Mfg. Co.*, 391 U.S. 216 (1968). There the police lacked probable cause to seize or search the defendant's automobile at the time of his arrest, and this was enough by itself to condemn the subsequent search at the station house. Here there was probable cause, but no exigent circumstances justified the police in proceeding without a warrant. As in *Dyke*, the later search at the station house was therefore illegal.

Justice BLACK, dissenting.

[U]nder our decision last Term in *Chambers*, the police were entitled not only to seize petitioner's car but also to search the car after it had been taken to the police station. The police had probable cause to believe that the car had been used in the commission of the murder and that it contained evidence of the crime. Under *Carroll* and *Chambers*, such belief was sufficient justification for the seizure and the search of petitioner's automobile.

The majority reasons that the *Chambers* and *Carroll* rationale, based on the mobility of automobiles,

---

police may make a search of appropriately limited scope. *Chimel*. But if *Carroll* permits a warrantless search of an unoccupied vehicle, on private property and beyond the scope of a valid search incident to an arrest, then it would permit as well a warrantless search of a suitcase or a box. We have found no case that suggests such an extension of *Carroll*.

is inapplicable here because the petitioner's car could have been placed under guard and, thereby, rendered immobile. But this Court explicitly rejected such reasoning in *Chambers*: "For constitutional purposes, we see no difference between on the one hand seizing and holding a car before presenting the probable cause issue to a magistrate and on the other hand carrying out an immediate search without a warrant. . . . The probable-cause factor still obtained at the station house and so did the mobility of the car. . . ." This Court held there that the delayed search at the station house, as well as an immediate search at the time of seizure, was reasonable under the Fourth Amendment.

As a second argument for holding that the *Chambers* decision does not apply to this case, the majority reasons that the evidence could not have been altered or the car moved because petitioner was in custody and his wife was accompanied by police, at least until the police towed the car to the station. But the majority's reasoning depends on two assumptions: first, that the police should, or even could, continue to keep petitioner's wife effectively under house arrest; and, second, that no one else had any motivation to alter or remove the car. I cannot accept the first assumption, nor do I believe that the police acted unreasonably in refusing to accept the second.

Justice WHITE, dissenting.

I find nothing in the language or the underlying rationale of the line of cases from *Carroll* to *Chambers* limiting vehicle searches as the Court now limits them in situations such as the one before us. Although each of those cases may, as the Court argues, have involved vehicles or vessels in motion prior to their being stopped and searched, each of them approved the search of a vehicle that was no longer moving and, with the occupants in custody, no more likely to move than the unattended but movable vehicle parked on the street or in the driveway of a person's house. In both situations the probability of movement at the instance of family or friends is equally real, and hence the result should be the same whether the car is at rest or in motion when it is discovered.

In *Husty v. United States,* 282 U.S. 694 (1931), the police had learned from a reliable informant that Husty had two loads of liquor in automobiles of particular make and description parked at described locations. The officers found one of the cars parked and unattended at the indicated spot. Later, as officers watched, Husty and others entered and started to drive away. The car was stopped after having moved no more than a foot or two; immediate search of the car produced contraband. Husty was then arrested. The Court, in a unanimous opinion, sustained

denial of a motion to suppress the fruits of the search, saying that "[t]he Fourth Amendment does not prohibit the search, without warrant, of an automobile, for liquor illegally transported or possessed, if the search is upon probable cause. . . ." Further, "[t]he search was not unreasonable because, as petitioners argue, sufficient time elapsed between the receipt by the officer of the information and the search of the car to have enabled him to procure a search warrant. He could not know when Husty would come to the car or how soon it would be removed. In such circumstances we do not think the officers should be required to speculate upon the chances of successfully carrying out the search, after the delay and withdrawal from the scene of one or more officers which would have been necessary to procure a warrant. The search was, therefore, on probable cause, and not unreasonable. . . ."

The Court apparently cites *Husty* with approval as involving a car in motion on the highway. But it was obviously irrelevant to the Court that the officers could have obtained a warrant before Husty attempted to drive the car away. Equally immaterial was the fact that the car had moved one or two feet at the time it was stopped. The search would have been approved even if it had occurred before Husty's arrival or after his arrival but before he had put the car in motion. The Court's attempt to distinguish *Husty* on the basis of the car's negligible movement prior to its being stopped is without force.

The Court states flatly, however, that this case is not ruled by the *Carroll-Chambers* line of cases but by *Dyke v. Taylor Implement Mfg. Co.* There the car was properly stopped and the occupants arrested for reckless driving, but the subsequent search at the station house could not be justified as incident to the arrest. Nor could the car itself be seized and later searched, as it was, absent probable cause to believe it contained evidence of crime. In *Dyke,* it was pointed out that probable cause did not exist at the time of the search, and we expressly rested our holding on this fact, noting that, "[s]ince the search was not shown to have been based upon sufficient cause," it was not necessary to reach other grounds urged for invalidating it. Given probable cause, however, we would have upheld the search in *Dyke*.

For Fourth Amendment purposes, the difference between a moving and movable vehicle is tenuous at best. It is a metaphysical distinction without roots in the common sense standard of reasonableness governing search and seizure cases. Distinguishing the case before us from the *Carroll-Chambers* line of cases further enmeshes Fourth Amendment law in litigation breeding refinements having little relation to reality. I suggest that in the interest of coherence and credibility we either overrule our prior cases and treat automobiles precisely as we do houses or apply those cases to readily movable as well as moving vehicles and thus treat searches of automobiles as we do the arrest of a person. By either course we might bring some modicum of certainty to Fourth Amendment law and give the law enforcement officers some slight guidance in how they are to conduct themselves.

## QUESTIONS AND NOTES

**1.** Which of the three opinions (Stewart, Black, White) do you think best captures the essence of *Carroll, Chambers, Dyke,* and *Husty*?

**2.** Which of the opinions reached the best result? Why?

**3.** The next case, *Cardwell v. Lewis,* was more or less of a trial balloon. The eight Justices who would have resolved the automobile search issue split 4-4. The case was ultimately resolved by Justice Powell, who voted for the Government on the ground that the issue should not have been raised on habeas corpus.

### Cardwell v. Lewis
### 417 U.S. 583 (1974)

Mr. Justice BLACKMUN announced the judgment of the Court and an opinion in which THE CHIEF JUSTICE, Mr. Justice WHITE, and Mr. Justice REHNQUIST join.

This case presents the issue of the legality, under the Fourth and Fourteenth Amendments, of a warrantless seizure of an automobile and the examination of its exterior at a police impoundment area after the car had been removed from a public parking lot.

I

In 1968 respondent Arthur Ben Lewis, Jr., was tried and convicted by a jury in an Ohio state court for the first-degree murder of Paul Radcliffe. On appeal, the Supreme Court of Ohio affirmed the judgment of conviction. This Court denied review.

Respondent Lewis complied with [a] request to appear [at the Division of Criminal Detectives Office of the Columbus police]. He drove his car to the Activities Office, placed it in a public commercial parking lot a half block away, and arrived shortly after 10 a.m. Although the police were in possession of [an] arrest warrant for the entire period that Lewis was present, he was not served with that warrant or arrested until late that afternoon, at approximately 5 p.m. Two hours earlier, Lewis had been permitted to call his lawyer, and two attorneys were present on his behalf in the office at the time of the formal arrest. Upon the arrest, Lewis' car keys and the parking lot claim check were released to the police. A tow truck was dispatched to remove the car from the parking lot to the police impoundment lot.

The impounded car was examined the next day by a technician from the Ohio Bureau of Criminal Investigation. The tread of its right rear tire was found to match the cast of a tire impression made at the scene of the crime.[4] The technician testified that, in his opinion, the foreign paint on the fender of Radcliffe's car was not different from the paint samples taken from respondent's vehicle, that is, there was no difference in color, texture, or order of laying of the paint.

II

This case is factually different from prior car search cases decided by this Court. The evidence with which we are concerned is not the product of a "search" that implicates traditional considerations of the owner's privacy interest. It consisted of paint scrapings from the exterior and an observation of the tread of a tire on an operative wheel. The issue, therefore, is whether the examination of an automobile's exterior upon probable cause invades a right to privacy which the interposition of a warrant is meant to protect. This is an issue this Court has not previously addressed.

At least since *Carroll,* the Court has recognized

---

[4] Apparently, the car's trunk was also opened and a tire in the trunk was observed. No evidence obtained from any part of the interior of the vehicle, however, was introduced.

a distinction between the warrantless search and seizure of automobiles or other movable vehicles, on the one hand, and the search of a home or office, on the other. Generally, less stringent warrant requirements have been applied to vehicles. An underlying factor in the *Carroll-Chambers* line of decisions has been the exigent circumstances that exist in connection with movable vehicles. "[T]he circumstances that furnish probable cause to search a particular auto for particular articles are most often unforeseeable; moreover, the opportunity to search is fleeting since a car is readily movable." This is strikingly true where the automobile's owner is alerted to police intentions and, as a consequence, the motivation to remove evidence from official grasp is heightened.

There is still another distinguishing factor. "The search of an automobile is far less intrusive on the rights protected by the Fourth Amendment than the search of one's person or building." One has a lesser expectation of privacy in a motor vehicle because its function is transportation and it seldom serves as one's residence or as the repository of personal effects. A car has little capacity for escaping public scrutiny. It travels public thoroughfares where both its occupants and its contents are in plain view. "What a person knowingly exposes to the public, even in his own home or office, is not a subject of Fourth Amendment protection." This is not to say that no part of the interior of an automobile has Fourth Amendment protection; the exercise of a desire to be mobile does not, of course, waive one's right to be free of unreasonable government intrusion. But insofar as Fourth Amendment protection extends to a motor vehicle, it is the right to privacy that is the touchstone of our inquiry.

In the present case, nothing from the interior of the car and no personal effects, which the Fourth Amendment traditionally has been deemed to protect, were searched or seized and introduced in evidence.[6] With the "search" limited to the examination of the tire on the wheel and the taking of paint scrapings from the exterior of the vehicle left in the public parking lot, we fail to comprehend what expectation of privacy was infringed. Stated simply, the invasion of privacy, "if it can be said to exist, is abstract and theoretical." Under circumstances such as these, where probable cause exists, a warrantless examination of the exterior of a car is not unreasonable under the Fourth and Fourteenth Amendments.

Here, it has been established and is conceded that the police had probable cause to search Lewis' car. An automobile similar in color and model to his car had been seen leaving the scene of the crime. This similarity was corroborated by comparison of the paint scrapings taken from the victim's car with the color and paint of Lewis' automobile. Lewis had had repair work done on his car immediately following the death of the victim. And he had a nexus with Radcliffe on the day of death. All this provided reason to believe that the car was used in the commission of the crime for which Lewis was arrested.

### III

Concluding, as we have, that the examination of the exterior of the vehicle upon probable cause was reasonable, we have yet to determine whether the prior impoundment of the automobile rendered that examination a violation of the Fourth and Fourteenth Amendments. We do not think that, because the police impounded the car prior to the examination, which they could have made on the spot, there is a constitutional barrier to the use of the evidence obtained thereby. Under the circumstances of this case, the seizure itself was not unreasonable.

Respondent asserts that this case is indistinguishable from *Coolidge*. We do not agree. The present case differs from *Coolidge* both in the scope of the search[9] and in the circumstances of the seizure. Since the Coolidge car was parked on the defendant's driveway, the seizure of that automobile required an entry upon private property. Here, as in *Chambers,* the automobile was seized from a public place where

---

[6] Petitioner contends that Lewis' car keys and the parking lot claim check were seized in plain view as an incident to his arrest, and that this seizure served to transfer constructive possession of the vehicle which could then be searched and seized as an instrumentality of the crime. We feel that the District Court and the Court of Appeals were correct in rejecting this argument. Irrespective of the plain-view or instrumentality analyses, the concept of constructive possession has not been found to justify the search or seizure of an item not in actual possession.

[9] *Coolidge* concerned a thorough and extensive search of the entire automobile including the interior from which, by vacuum sweepings, incriminating evidence was obtained. A search of that kind raises different and additional considerations not present in the examination of a tire on an operative wheel and in the taking of exterior paint samples from the vehicle in the present case for which there was no reasonable expectation of privacy.

access was not meaningfully restricted. This is, in fact, the ground upon which the *Coolidge* plurality opinion distinguished *Chambers*.

In considering whether the lack of a warrant to seize a vehicle invalidates the otherwise legal examination of the car, *Chambers* is highly pertinent. In *Chambers*, four men in an automobile were arrested shortly after an armed robbery. The Court concluded that there was probable cause to arrest and probable cause to search the vehicle. The car was taken from the highway to the police station where, some time later, a search producing incriminating evidence, was conducted. We stated:

> "For constitutional purposes, we see no difference between on the one hand seizing and holding a car before presenting the probable cause issue to a magistrate and on the other hand carrying out an immediate search without a warrant. Given probable cause to search, either course is reasonable under the Fourth Amendment.
>
> ". . . The probable-cause factor still obtained at the station house and so did the mobility of the car unless the Fourth Amendment permits a warrantless seizure of the car and the denial of its use to anyone until a warrant is secured. In that event there is little to choose in terms of practical consequences between an immediate search without a warrant and the car's immobilization until a warrant is obtained."

The fact that the car in *Chambers* was seized after being stopped on a highway, whereas Lewis' car was seized from a public parking lot, has little, if any, legal significance. The same arguments and considerations of exigency, immobilization on the spot, and posting a guard obtain. In fact, because the interrogation session ended with awareness that Lewis had been arrested and that his car constituted incriminating evidence, the incentive and potential for the car's removal substantially increased. There was testimony at the federal hearing that Lewis asked one of his attorneys to see that his wife and family got the car, and that the attorney relinquished the keys to the police in order to avoid a physical confrontation. In *Chambers*, all occupants of the car were in custody and there were no means of relating this fact or the location of the car (if it had not been impounded) to a friend or confederate. *Chambers* also stated that a search of the car on the spot was impractical because it was dark and the search could not be carefully

executed. Here too, the seizure facilitated the type of close examination necessary.[11]

Respondent contends that here, unlike *Chambers*, probable cause to search the car existed for some time prior to arrest and that, therefore, there were no exigent circumstances. Assuming that probable cause previously existed, we know of no case or principle that suggests that the right to search on probable cause and the reasonableness of seizing a car under exigent circumstances are foreclosed if a warrant was not obtained at the first practicable moment. Exigent circumstances with regard to vehicles are not limited to situations where probable cause is unforeseeable and arises only at the time of arrest. The exigency may arise at any time, and the fact that the police might have obtained a warrant earlier does not negate the possibility of a current situation's necessitating prompt police action.

The judgment of the Court of Appeals is reversed.

Mr. Justice STEWART, with whom Justices DOUGLAS, BRENNAN, and MARSHALL join, dissenting.

In casting about for some way to avoid the impact of our previous decisions, the plurality opinion first suggests that no "search" really took place in this case, since all that the police did was to scrape paint from the respondent's car and make observations of its tires. Whatever merit this argument might possess in the abstract, it is irrelevant in the circumstances disclosed by this record. The argument is irrelevant for the simple reason that the police before taking the paint scrapings and looking at the tires, first took possession of the car itself. The Fourth and Fourteenth Amendments protect against "unreasonable searches and *seizures*," and there most assuredly was a seizure here.

The plurality opinion next seems to suggest that the basic constitutional rule can be overlooked in this case because the subject of the seizure was an automobile. It is true, of course, that a line of decisions, beginning with *Carroll*, have recognized a so-called "automobile exception" to the constitutional requirement of a warrant. But "[t]he word 'automobile' is not a talisman in whose presence the Fourth Amendment fades away and disappears." *Coolidge*. Rather, the *Carroll*

---

[11] To make a comparison with a paint scraping required that a section of the painted exterior that had not been recently repaired be sampled. This conceivably could necessitate several scrapings if the first sample was not conclusive after laboratory analysis. Similarly, to make a cast of the tire tread on the operative wheel would require laboratory equipment.

doctrine simply recognizes the obvious—that a *moving* automobile on the open road presents a situation "where it is not practicable to secure a warrant, because the vehicle can be quickly moved out of the locality or jurisdiction in which the warrant must be sought." Where there is no reasonable likelihood that the automobile would or could be moved, the *Carroll* doctrine is simply inapplicable.

The facts of this case make clear beyond peradventure that the "automobile exception" is not available to uphold the warrantless seizure of the respondent's car. Well before the time that the automobile was seized, the respondent—and the keys to his car—were securely within police custody. There was thus absolutely no likelihood that the respondent could have either moved the car or meddled with it during the time necessary to obtain a search warrant. And there was no realistic possibility that anyone else was in a position to do so either. I am at a loss, therefore, to understand the plurality opinion's conclusion that there was a "potential for the car's removal" during the period immediately preceding the car's seizure. The facts of record can only support a diametrically opposite conclusion.

Finally, the plurality opinion suggests that other "exigent circumstances" might have excused the failure of the police to procure a warrant. The opinion nowhere states what these mystical exigencies might have been, and counsel for the petitioner has not been so inventive as to suggest any.[2] Since the

authorities had taken care to procure an arrest warrant even before the respondent arrived for questioning, it can scarcely be said that probable cause was not discovered until so late a point in time as to prevent the obtaining of a warrant for seizure of the automobile. And, with the automobile effectively immobilized during the period of the respondent's interrogation, the fear that evidence might be destroyed was hardly an exigency, particularly when it is remembered that no such fear prompted a seizure during all the preceding months while the respondent, though under investigation, had been in full control of the car.[3] This is, quite simply, a case where no exigent circumstances existed.

Until today it has been clear that "[n]either *Carroll* . . . nor other cases in this Court require or suggest that in every conceivable circumstance the search of an auto even with probable cause may be made without the extra protection for privacy that a warrant affords." I would follow the settled constitutional law established in our decisions and affirm the judgment of the Court of Appeals.

---

[2] Even the Solicitor General, who appeared as *amicus curiae* urging a reversal of the Court of Appeals' judgment in this case, has candidly admitted in his brief that "no satisfactory reason appears for the failure of the law enforcement officers to have obtained a warrant—there appears on the facts of this case to have been no real likelihood that respondent would have destroyed or concealed the evidence sought during the time required to seek and procure a warrant."

[3] It can hardly be argued that the questioning of the respondent by the police for the first time alerted him to their intentions, thus suddenly providing him a motivation to remove the car from "official grasp." Even putting to one side the question of how the respondent could have acted to destroy any evidence while he was in police custody, the fact is that he was fully aware of official suspicion during several months preceding the interrogation. He had been questioned on several occasions prior to his arrest, and he had been alerted on the day before the interrogation that the police wished to see him. Nonetheless, he voluntarily drove his car to Columbus to keep his appointment with the investigators.

## QUESTIONS AND NOTES

**1.** Does taking paint scrapings implicate the Fourth Amendment? How?

**2.** Is the plurality suggesting that the police can scrape paint from any car found in the street? Explain your answer.

**3.** Should this case be controlled by *Chambers* or *Coolidge*? Why?

**4.** In *Carney,* the Court, as an institution, resolved the permissibility of a warrantless search of a vehicle parked in public. It also determined that, ordinarily, motor homes should be treated more like cars than houses.

## California v. Carney
### 471 U.S. 386 (1985)

Chief Justice BURGER delivered the opinion of the Court.

We granted certiorari to decide whether law enforcement agents violated the Fourth Amendment when they conducted a warrantless search, based on probable cause, of a fully mobile "motor home" located in a public place.

### I

On May 31, 1979, Drug Enforcement Agency Agent Robert Williams watched respondent, Charles Carney, approach a youth in downtown San Diego. The youth accompanied Carney to a Dodge Mini Motor Home parked in a nearby lot. Carney and the youth closed the window shades in the motor home, including one across the front window. Agent Williams had previously received uncorroborated information that the same motor home was used by another person who was exchanging marihuana for sex. Williams, with assistance from other agents, kept the motor home under surveillance for the entire one and one-quarter hours that Carney and the youth remained inside. When the youth left the motor home, the agents followed and stopped him. The youth told the agents that he had received marijuana in return for allowing Carney sexual contacts.

At the agents' request, the youth returned to the motor home and knocked on its door; Carney stepped out. The agents identified themselves as law enforcement officers. Without a warrant or consent, one agent entered the motor home and observed marihuana, plastic bags, and a scale of the kind used in weighing drugs on a table. Agent Williams took Carney into custody and took possession of the motor home. A subsequent search of the motor home at the police station revealed additional marihuana in the cupboards and refrigerator.

Respondent was charged with possession of marihuana for sale. At a preliminary hearing, he moved to suppress the evidence discovered in the motor home. The Magistrate denied the motion, upholding the initial search as a justifiable search for other persons, and the subsequent search as a routine inventory search.

The California Supreme Court reversed the conviction. The Supreme Court did not disagree with the conclusion of the trial court that the agents had probable cause to arrest respondent and to believe that the vehicle contained evidence of a crime; however, the court held that the search was unreasonable because no warrant was obtained, rejecting the State's argument that the vehicle exception to the warrant requirement should apply. That court reached its decision by concluding that the mobility of a vehicle "is no longer the prime justification for the automobile exception; rather, 'the answer lies in the diminished expectation of privacy which surrounds the automobile.'" The California Supreme Court held that the expectations of privacy in a motor home are more like those in a dwelling than in an automobile because the primary function of motor homes is not to provide transportation but to "provide the occupant with living quarters."

We reverse.

### II

"[T]he guaranty of freedom from unreasonable searches and seizures by the Fourth Amendment has been construed, practically since the beginning of Government, as recognizing a necessary difference between a search of a store, dwelling house or other structure in respect of which a proper official warrant readily may be obtained, and a search of a ship, motor boat, wagon or automobile, for contraband goods, where it is not practicable to secure a warrant because the vehicle can be *quickly moved* out of the locality or jurisdiction in which the warrant must be sought." (emphasis added).

The capacity to be "quickly moved" was clearly the basis of the holding in *Carroll,* and our cases have consistently recognized ready mobility as one of the principal bases of the automobile exception. In *Chambers,* for example, commenting on the rationale for the vehicle exception, we noted that "the opportunity to search is fleeting since a car is readily movable." More recently, in *United States v. Ross* (sec. B, *infra*), we once again emphasized that "an immediate intrusion is necessary" because of "the nature of an automobile in transit. . . ." The mobility of automobiles, we have observed, "creates circumstances of such exigency that, as a practical necessity, rigorous enforcement of the warrant requirement is impossible."

However, although ready mobility alone was perhaps the original justification for the vehicle exception, our later cases have made clear that ready mobility is not the only basis for the exception. The reasons for the vehicle exception, we have said, are twofold. "Besides the element of mobility, less rigorous warrant requirements govern because the expectation of privacy with respect to one's automobile is significantly less than that relating to one's home or office.''

Even in cases where an automobile was not immediately mobile, the lesser expectation of privacy resulting from its use as a readily mobile vehicle justified application of the vehicular exception. In some cases, the configuration of the vehicle contributed to the lower expectations of privacy; for example, we held in *Cardwell* that, because the passenger compartment of a standard automobile is relatively open to plain view, there are lesser expectations of privacy. But even when enclosed ''repository'' areas have been involved, we have concluded that the lesser expectations of privacy warrant application of the exception. We have applied the exception in the context of a locked car trunk, a sealed package in a car trunk, a closed compartment under the dashboard, the interior of a vehicle's upholstery, or sealed packages inside a covered pickup truck.

These reduced expectations of privacy derive not from the fact that the area to be searched is in plain view, but from the pervasive regulation of vehicles capable of traveling on the public highways. As we explained in *South Dakota v. Opperman*, an inventory search case:

> ''Automobiles, unlike homes, are subjected to pervasive and continuing governmental regulation and controls, including periodic inspection and licensing requirements. As an everyday occurrence, police stop and examine vehicles when license plates or inspection stickers have expired, or if other violations, such as exhaust fumes or excessive noise, are noted, or if headlights or other safety equipment are not in proper working order.'' 428 U.S., at 368.

The public is fully aware that it is accorded less privacy in its automobiles because of this compelling governmental need for regulation. Historically, ''individuals always [have] been on notice that movable vessels may be stopped and searched on facts giving rise to probable cause that the vehicle contains contraband, without the protection afforded by a magistrate's prior evaluation of those facts.'' In short, the pervasive schemes of regulation, which necessarily lead to reduced expectations of privacy, and the exigencies attendant to ready mobility justify searches without prior recourse to the authority of a magistrate so long as the overriding standard of probable cause is met.

When a vehicle is being used on the highways, or if it is readily capable of such use and is found stationary in a place not regularly used for residential purposes—temporary or otherwise—the two justifications for the vehicle exception come into play. First, the vehicle is obviously readily mobile by the turn of an ignition key, if not actually moving. Second, there is a reduced expectation of privacy stemming from its use as a licensed motor vehicle subject to a range of police regulation inapplicable to a fixed dwelling. At least in these circumstances, the overriding societal interests in effective law enforcement justify an immediate search before the vehicle and its occupants become unavailable.

While it is true that respondent's vehicle possessed some, if not many of the attributes of a home, it is equally clear that the vehicle falls clearly within the scope of the exception laid down in *Carroll* and applied in succeeding cases. Like the automobile in *Carroll*, respondent's motor home was readily mobile. Absent the prompt search and seizure, it could readily have been moved beyond the reach of the police. Furthermore, the vehicle was licensed to ''operate on public streets; [was] serviced in public places; . . . and [was] subject to extensive regulation and inspection.'' And the vehicle was so situated that an objective observer would conclude that it was being used not as a residence, but as a vehicle.

Respondent urges us to distinguish his vehicle from other vehicles within the exception because it was *capable of functioning as a home*. In our increasingly mobile society, many vehicles used for transportation can be and are being used not only for transportation but for shelter, *i.e.*, as a ''home'' or ''residence.'' To distinguish between respondent's motor home and an ordinary sedan for purposes of the vehicle exception would require that we apply the exception depending upon the size of the vehicle and the quality of its appointments. Moreover, to fail to apply the exception to vehicles such as a motor home ignores the fact that a motor home lends itself easily to use as an instrument of illicit drug traffic and other illegal activity. In *Ross*, we declined to distinguish between ''worthy'' and ''unworthy'' containers, noting that ''the central purpose of the Fourth Amendment forecloses such a distinction.'' We decline today to distinguish between ''worthy'' and ''unworthy'' vehicles which are either on the public roads and highways, or situated such that it is reasonable to conclude that the vehicle is not being used as a residence.

Our application of the vehicle exception has never turned on the other uses to which a vehicle might be put. The exception has historically turned on the ready mobility of the vehicle, and on the presence of the vehicle in a setting that objectively indicates that the vehicle is being used for transportation.[3] These two requirements for application of the exception ensure that law enforcement officials are not unnecessarily hamstrung in their efforts to detect and prosecute criminal activity, and that the legitimate privacy interests of the public are protected. Applying the vehicle exception in these circumstances allows the essential purposes served by the exception to be fulfilled, while assuring that the exception will acknowledge legitimate privacy interests.

### III

The question remains whether, apart from the lack of a warrant, this search was unreasonable. Under the vehicle exception to the warrant requirement, "[o]nly the prior approval of the magistrate is waived; the search otherwise [must be such] as the magistrate could authorize."

This search was not unreasonable; it was plainly one that the magistrate could authorize if presented with these facts. The DEA agents had fresh, direct, uncontradicted evidence that the respondent was distributing a controlled substance from the vehicle, apart from evidence of other possible offenses. The agents thus had abundant probable cause to enter and search the vehicle for evidence of a crime notwithstanding its possible use as a dwelling place.

The judgment of the California Supreme Court is reversed, and the case is remanded for further proceedings not inconsistent with this opinion.

Justice STEVENS, with whom Justice BRENNAN and Justice MARSHALL join, dissenting.

The character of "the place to be searched" plays an important role in Fourth Amendment analysis. In this case, police officers searched a Dodge/Midas Mini Motor Home. The California Supreme Court correctly characterized this vehicle as a "hybrid" which combines "the mobility attribute of an automobile . . . with most of the privacy characteristics of a house."

---

[3] We need not pass on the application of the vehicle exception to a motor home that is situated in a way or place that objectively indicates that it is being used as a residence. Among the factors that might be relevant in determining whether a warrant would be required in such a circumstance is its location, whether the vehicle is readily mobile or instead, for instance, elevated on blocks, whether the vehicle is licensed, whether it is connected to utilities, and whether it has convenient access to a public road.

The hybrid character of the motor home places it at the crossroads between the privacy interests that generally forbid warrantless invasions of the home, and the law enforcement interests that support the exception for warrantless searches of automobiles based on probable cause. By choosing to follow the latter route, the Court errs in three respects: it has entered new territory prematurely, it has accorded priority to an exception rather than to the general rule, and it has abandoned the limits on the exception imposed by prior cases.

### II

"'The warrant requirement . . . is not an inconvenience to be somehow "weighed" against the claims of police efficiency. It is, or should be, an important working part of our machinery of government, operating as a matter of course to check the "well-intentioned but mistakenly overzealous executive officers" who are a part of any system of law enforcement." [*Coolidge*]

". . . By requiring that conclusions concerning probable cause and the scope of a search 'be drawn by a neutral and detached magistrate instead of being judged by the officer engaged in the often competitive enterprise of ferreting out crime', we minimize the risk of unreasonable assertions of executive authority."

If the motor home were parked in the exact middle of the intersection between the general rule and the exception for automobiles, priority should be given to the rule rather than the exception.

### III

The motor home, however, was not parked in the middle of that intersection. Our prior cases teach us that inherent mobility is not a sufficient justification for the fashioning of an exception to the warrant requirement, especially in the face of heightened expectations of privacy in the location searched. Motor homes, by their common use and construction, afford their owners a substantial and legitimate expectation of privacy when they dwell within. When a motor home is parked in a location that is removed from the public highway, I believe that society is prepared to recognize that the expectations of privacy within it are not unlike the expectations one has in a fixed dwelling. As a general rule, such places may only be searched with a warrant based upon probable cause. Warrantless searches of motor homes are only reasonable when the motor home is traveling on the public streets or highways, or when exigent circumstances otherwise require an immediate search without the expenditure of time necessary to obtain a warrant.

As we explained in *Ross,* the automobile exception is the product of a long history:

"[S]ince its earliest days Congress had recognized the impracticability of securing a warrant in cases involving the transportation of contraband goods. It is this impracticability, viewed in historical perspective, that provided the basis for the *Carroll* decision. Given the nature of an automobile in transit, the Court recognized that an immediate intrusion is necessary if police officers are to secure the illicit substance. In this class of cases, the Court held that a warrantless search of an automobile is not unreasonable."

The automobile exception has been developed to ameliorate the practical problems associated with the search of vehicles that have been stopped on the streets or public highways because there was probable cause to believe they were transporting contraband. Until today, however, the Court has never decided whether the practical justifications that apply to a vehicle that is stopped in transit on a public way apply with the same force to a vehicle parked in a lot near a court house where it could easily be detained while a warrant is issued.[15]

---

[15] In *Coolidge,* a plurality refused to apply the automobile exception to an automobile that was seized while parked in the driveway of the suspect's house, towed to a secure police compound, and later searched:

"The word 'automobile' is not a talisman in whose presence the Fourth Amendment fades away and disappears. And surely there is nothing in this case to invoke the meaning and purpose of the rule of *Carroll* – no alerted criminal bent on flight, no fleeting opportunity on an open highway after a hazardous chase, no contraband or stolen goods or weapons, no confederates waiting to move the evidence, not even the inconvenience of a special police detail to guard the immobilized automobile. In short, by no possible stretch of the legal imagination can this be made into a case where 'it is not practicable to secure a warrant.' and the 'automobile exception' despite its label, is simply irrelevant." (opinion of Stewart, J., joined by Douglas, Brennan, and Marshall, JJ.).

In *Cardwell,* a different plurality approved the seizure of an automobile from a public parking lot, and a later examination of its exterior. (opinion of Blackmun, J.). Here, of course, we are concerned with the reasonableness of the search, not the seizure. Even if the diminished expectations of privacy associated with an automobile

In this case, the motor home was parked in an off-the-street lot only a few blocks from the courthouse in downtown San Diego where dozens of magistrates were available to entertain a warrant application.[16] The officers clearly had the element of surprise with them, and with curtains covering the windshield, the motor home offered no indication of any imminent departure. The officers plainly had probable cause to arrest the respondent and search the motor home, and on this record, it is inexplicable why they eschewed the safe harbor of a warrant.[17]

In the absence of any evidence of exigency in the circumstances of this case, the Court relies on the inherent mobility of the motor home to create a conclusive presumption of exigency. This Court, however, has squarely held that mobility of the place to be searched is not a sufficient justification for abandoning the warrant requirement. In *Chadwick,* the Court held that a warrantless search of a footlocker violated the Fourth Amendment even though there was ample probable cause to believe it contained contraband. The Government had argued that the rationale of the automobile exception applied to movable containers in general, and that the warrant requirement should be limited to searches of homes and other "core" areas of privacy. We categorically rejected the Government's argument, observing that there are greater privacy interests associated with containers than with automobiles,[18] and that there are less practical problems associated with the temporary detention of a container than with the detention of an automobile.

---

justify the warrantless search of a parked automobile notwithstanding the diminished exigency, the heightened expectations of privacy in the interior of a motor home require a different result.

[16] In addition, a telephonic warrant was only 20 cents and the nearest phone booth away.

[17] This willingness to search first and later seek justification has properly been characterized as "a decision roughly comparable in prudence to determining whether an electrical wire is charged by grasping it."

[18] "The factors which diminish the privacy aspects of an automobile do not apply to respondent's footlocker. Luggage contents are not open to public view, except as a condition to a border entry or common carrier travel; nor is luggage subject to regular inspections and official scrutiny on a continuing basis. Unlike an automobile, whose primary function is transportation, luggage is intended as a repository of personal effects. In sum, a person's expectations of privacy in personal luggage are substantially greater than in an automobile."

It is perfectly obvious that the citizen has a much greater expectation of privacy concerning the interior of a mobile home than of a piece of luggage such as a footlocker. If "inherent mobility" does not justify warrantless searches of containers, it cannot rationally provide a sufficient justification for the search of a person's dwelling place.

Unlike a brick bungalow or a frame Victorian, a motor home seldom serves as a permanent lifetime abode. The motor home in this case, however, was designed to accommodate a breadth of ordinary everyday living. Photographs in the record indicate that its height, length, and beam provided substantial living space inside: stuffed chairs surround a table; cupboards provide room for storage of personal effects; bunk beds provide sleeping space; and a refrigerator provides ample space for food and beverages. Moreover, curtains and large opaque walls inhibit viewing the activities inside from the exterior of the vehicle. The interior configuration of the motor home establishes that the vehicle's size, shape, and mode of construction should have indicated to the officers that it was a vehicle containing mobile living quarters.

The State contends that officers in the field will have an impossible task determining whether or not other vehicles contain mobile living quarters. It is not necessary for the Court to resolve every unanswered question in this area in a single case, but common English usage suggests that we already distinguish between a "motor home" which is "equipped as a self-contained traveling home," a "camper" which is only equipped for "casual travel and camping," and an automobile which is "designed for passenger transportation." Surely the exteriors of these vehicles contain clues about their different functions which could alert officers in the field to the necessity of a warrant.[21]

The California Vehicle Code also refutes the State's argument that the exclusion of "motor homes" from the automobile exception would be impossible to apply in practice. In its definitional section, the Code distinguishes campers and house cars from station wagons, and suggests that they are special categories of the more general terms—motor vehicles and passenger vehicles. A "house car" is "a motor vehicle originally designed, or permanently altered, and equipped for human habitation, or to which a camper has been permanently attached." Alcoholic beverages may not be opened or consumed in motor vehicles traveling on the highways, except in the "living quarters of a housecar or camper." The same definitions might not necessarily apply in the context of the Fourth Amendment, but they do indicate that descriptive distinctions are humanly possible. They also reflect the California Legislature's judgment that "house cars" entertain different kinds of activities than the ordinary passenger vehicle.

In my opinion, searches of places that regularly accommodate a wide range of private human activity are fundamentally different from searches of automobiles which primarily serve a public transportation function. Although it may not be a castle, a motor home is usually the functional equivalent of a hotel room, a vacation and retirement home, or a hunting and fishing cabin. These places may be as spartan as a humble cottage when compared to the most majestic mansion, but the highest and most legitimate expectations of privacy associated with these temporary abodes should command the respect of this Court. In my opinion, a warrantless search of living quarters in a motor home is "presumptively unreasonable absent exigent circumstances."

I respectfully dissent.

---

[21] In refusing to extend the California Supreme Court's decision in *Carney* beyond its context, the California Courts of Appeals have had no difficulty in distinguishing the motor home involved there from a Ford van, and a cab-high camper shell on the back of a pickup truck. There is no reason to believe that trained officers could not make similar distinctions between different vehicles, especially when state vehicle laws already require them to do so.

## QUESTIONS AND NOTES

**1.** Would (should) it have mattered if the motor home was Carney's *only* residence?

**2.** In what sense wasn't the motor home being used as a home? It was parked, curtains were drawn across the front windshield, and the very reason that he was arrested was in part *because* he performed an unlawful intimate act in the motor home.

**3.** Do you agree that police would have difficulty with a "worthier vehicle" rule?

**4.** Should there be a special rule for states that designate certain vehicles as "house cars?"

**5.** If there were a special rule for motor homes, should that rule extend to (some) vans and campers? What about a used Volkswagen in which a homeless person regularly sleeps?

**6.** What could (should) the police have done in a case like this if the Stevens opinion had prevailed? Would that have been unduly burdensome?

**7.** Would it have been better to apply *Coolidge*, rather than *Chambers*, to parked vehicles? Why? Why not?

**8.** After *Carney*, is the word "automobile" "a talisman in whose presence the Fourth Amendment disappears?"

**9.** Would the automobile exception aspect of *Coolidge* be decided the same way if it arose today? Explain.

## B.  Cars and Containers

As we know from *Chambers* and *Carney*, warrantless searches of automobiles, with probable cause, will ordinarily be upheld. However, as *Chadwick* (Chapter 3, *supra*) tells us, the same deferential attitude does not extend to searches of containers, however movable they may be. This section concerns the problem of containers found within cars. The question is when do we apply *Chambers* and when do we apply *Chadwick*. The answers, with less than perfect consistency, come from *Sanders, Ross,* and *Acevedo*.

### Arkansas v. Sanders
442 U.S. 753 (1979)

Mr. Justice POWELL delivered the opinion of the Court.

This case presents the question whether, in the absence of exigent circumstances, police are required to obtain a warrant before searching luggage taken from an automobile properly stopped and searched for contraband. We took this case by writ of certiorari to the Supreme Court of Arkansas to resolve some apparent misunderstanding as to the application of our decision in *Chadwick*, to warrantless searches of luggage seized from automobiles.

I

On April 23, 1976, Officer David Isom of the Little Rock, Ark., Police Department received word from an informant that at 4:35 that afternoon respondent would arrive aboard an American Airlines flight at gate No. 1 of the Municipal Airport of Little Rock. According to the informant, respondent would be carrying a green suitcase containing marihuana. Both Isom and the informant

knew respondent well, as in January 1976 the informant had given the Little Rock Police Department information that had led to respondent's arrest and conviction for possession of marihuana. Acting on the tip, Officer Isom and two other police officers placed the airport under surveillance. As the informant had predicted, respondent duly arrived at gate No. 1. The police watched as respondent deposited some hand luggage in a waiting taxicab, returned to the baggage claim area, and met a man whom police subsequently identified as David Rambo. While Rambo waited, respondent retrieved from the airline baggage service a green suitcase matching that described by the informant. Respondent gave this suitcase to his companion and went outside, where he entered the taxi into which he had put his luggage. Rambo waited a short while in the airport and then joined respondent in the taxi, after placing the green suitcase in the trunk of the vehicle.

When respondent's taxi drove away carrying respondent, Rambo, and the suitcase, Officer Isom and one of his fellow officers gave pursuit and, with the help of a patrol car, stopped the vehicle several blocks from the airport. At the request of the police, the taxi driver opened the trunk of his vehicle, where the officers found the green suitcase. Without asking the permission of either respondent or Rambo, the police opened the unlocked suitcase and discovered what proved to be 9.3 pounds of marihuana packaged in 10 plastic bags.

## II

Only two Terms ago, we held that a locked footlocker could not lawfully be searched without a warrant, even though it had been loaded into the trunk of an automobile parked at a curb. *Chadwick.* In earlier cases, on the other hand, the Court sustained the constitutionality of warrantless searches of automobiles and their contents under what has become known as the "automobile exception" to the warrant requirement. See, *e. g., Chambers* [and] *Carroll.* We thus are presented with the task of determining whether the warrantless search of respondent's suitcase falls on the *Chadwick* or the *Chambers/Carroll* side of the Fourth Amendment line. Although in a sense this is a line-drawing process, it must be guided by established principles.

In the ordinary case, a search of private property must be both reasonable and pursuant to a properly issued search warrant. The mere reasonableness of a search, assessed in the light of the surrounding circumstances, is not a substitute for the judicial warrant required under the Fourth Amendment.

Nonetheless, there are some exceptions to the warrant requirement. These have been established where it was concluded that the public interest required some flexibility in the application of the general rule that a valid warrant is a prerequisite for a search. Thus, a few "jealously and carefully drawn" exceptions provide for those cases where the societal costs of obtaining a warrant, such as danger to law officers or the risk of loss or destruction of evidence, outweigh the reasons for prior recourse to a neutral magistrate. But because each exception to the warrant requirement invariably impinges to some extent on the protective purpose of the Fourth Amendment, the few situations in which a search may be conducted in the absence of a warrant have been carefully delineated and "the burden is on those seeking the exemption to show the need for it." Moreover, we have limited the reach of each exception to that which is necessary to accommodate the identified needs of society.

One of the circumstances in which the Constitution does not require a search warrant is when the police stop an automobile on the street or highway because they have probable cause to believe it contains contraband or evidence of a crime.[7]

There are essentially two reasons for the distinction between automobiles and other private property. First, as the Court repeatedly has recognized, the inherent mobility of automobiles often makes it impracticable to obtain a warrant. In addition, the configuration, use, and regulation of automobiles often may dilute the reasonable expectation of privacy that exists with respect to differently situated property.

## III

In the present case, the State argues that the warrantless search of respondent's suitcase was proper under *Carroll* and its progeny. The police acted properly—indeed commendably—in apprehending respondent and his luggage. They had ample probable cause to believe that respondent's green suitcase contained marihuana. A previously reliable informant had provided a detailed account of respondent's expected arrival at the Little Rock Airport, which account proved to be accurate in every detail, including the color of the suitcase in which respondent would be carrying the marihuana. Having probable cause to believe that contraband was being driven away in the taxi, the police were justified in stopping the vehicle, searching it on the spot, and seizing the suitcase they suspected contained contraband. See *Chambers.* At oral argument, respondent conceded that the stopping of the taxi and the seizure of the suitcase were constitutionally unobjectionable.

The State argues that the warrantless search of respondent's suitcase was proper, not because the property searched was luggage, but rather because it was taken from an automobile lawfully stopped and searched on the street. In effect, the State would have us extend *Carroll* to allow warrantless searches of everything found within an automobile, as well as of the vehicle itself. The Supreme Court of Arkansas found our decision in *Chadwick* virtually controlling in this case. The State contends, however, that *Chadwick* does not control because in that case the vehicle had

---

[7] The willingness of courts to excuse the absence of a warrant where spontaneous searches are required of a vehicle on the road has led to what is called the "automobile exception" to the warrant requirement, although the exception does not invariably apply whenever automobiles are searched. See, *e.g., Coolidge* ("The word 'automobile' is not a talisman in whose presence the Fourth Amendment fades away and disappears").

remained parked at the curb where the footlocker had been placed in its trunk and that therefore no argument was made that the "automobile exception" was applicable. This Court has not had occasion previously to rule on the constitutionality of a warrantless search of luggage taken from an automobile lawfully stopped. Rather, the decisions to date have involved searches of some integral part of the automobile.

We conclude that the State has failed to carry its burden of demonstrating the need for warrantless searches of luggage properly taken from automobiles. A closed suitcase in the trunk of an automobile may be as mobile as the vehicle in which it rides. But as we noted in *Chadwick,* the exigency of mobility must be assessed at the point immediately before the search – after the police have seized the object to be searched and have it securely within their control. Once police have seized a suitcase, as they did here, the extent of its mobility is in no way affected by the place from which it was taken.[11] Accordingly as a general rule there is no greater need for warrantless searches of luggage taken from automobiles than of luggage taken from other places.

Similarly, a suitcase taken from an automobile stopped on the highway is not necessarily attended by any lesser expectation of privacy than is associated with luggage taken from other locations. One is not less inclined to place private, personal possessions in a suitcase merely because the suitcase is to be carried in an automobile rather than transported by other means or temporarily checked or stored. Indeed, the very purpose of a suitcase is to serve as a repository for personal items when one wishes to transport them. Accordingly, the reasons for not requiring a warrant for the search of an automobile do not apply to searches of personal luggage taken by police from automobiles. We therefore find no

justification for the extension of *Carroll* and its progeny to the warrantless search of one's personal luggage merely because it was located in an automobile lawfully stopped by the police.[14]

In sum, we hold that the warrant requirement of the Fourth Amendment applies to personal luggage taken from an automobile to the same degree it applies to such luggage in other locations. Thus, insofar as the police are entitled to search such luggage without a warrant, their actions must be justified under some exception to the warrant requirement other than that applicable to automobiles stopped on the highway. Where – as in the present case – the police, without endangering themselves or risking loss of the evidence, lawfully have detained one suspected of criminal activity and secured his suitcase, they should delay the search thereof until after judicial approval has been obtained. In this way, constitutional rights of suspects to prior judicial review of searches will be fully protected.

The judgment of the Arkansas Supreme Court is affirmed.

Mr. Chief Justice BURGER, with whom Mr. Justice STEVENS joins, concurring in judgment.

I concur in the Court's judgment but cannot join its unnecessarily broad opinion, which seems to treat this case as if it involved the "automobile" exception to the warrant requirement. It is not such a case.

Because the police officers had probable cause to believe that respondent's green suitcase contained

---

[11] There may be cases in which the special exigencies of the situation would justify the warrantless search of a suitcase. Generally, however, such exigencies will depend upon the probable contents of the luggage and the suspect's access to those contents – not upon whether the luggage is taken from an automobile. In the present case the State has conceded that there were no special exigencies. Nor do we consider the constitutionality of searches of luggage incident to the arrest of its possessor. The State has not argued that respondent's suitcase was searched incident to his arrest, and it appears that the bag was not within his "immediate control" at the time of the search.

[14] We are not persuaded by the State's argument that, under *Chambers,* if the police were entitled to seize the suitcase, then they were entitled to search it. We view the seizure of a suitcase as quite different from the seizure of an automobile. In *Chambers,* if the Court had required seizure and holding of the vehicle, it would have imposed a constitutional requirement upon police departments of all sizes around the country to have available the people and equipment necessary to transport impounded automobiles to some central location until warrants could be secured. Moreover, once seized automobiles were taken from the highway the police would be responsible for providing some appropriate location where they could be kept, with due regard to the safety of the vehicles and their contents, until a magistrate ruled on the application for a warrant. Such a constitutional requirement therefore would have imposed severe, even impossible, burdens on many police departments. No comparable burdens are likely to exist with respect to the seizure of personal luggage.

marihuana before it was placed in the trunk of the taxicab, their duty to obtain a search warrant before opening it is clear under *Chadwick*. The essence of our holding in *Chadwick* is that there is a legitimate expectation of privacy in the contents of a trunk or suitcase accompanying or being carried by a person; that expectation of privacy is not diminished simply because the owner's arrest occurs in a public place. Whether arrested in a hotel lobby, an airport, a railroad terminal, or on a public street, as here, the owner has the right to expect that the contents of his luggage will not, without his consent, be exposed on demand of the police. If not carrying contraband, many persons arrested in such circumstances might choose to consent to a search of their luggage to obviate any delay in securing their release. But even if wholly innocent, some persons might well prefer not to have the contents of their luggage exposed in a public place. They may stand on their right to privacy and require a search warrant. The warrant requirement is not so onerous as to command suspension of Fourth Amendment guarantees once the receptacle involved is securely in the control of the police, as it was here after Sanders' arrest.

The breadth of the Court's opinion and its repeated references to the "automobile" from which respondent's suitcase was seized at the time of his arrest, however, might lead the reader to believe— as the dissenters apparently do—that this case involves the "automobile" exception to the warrant requirement. It does not. Here, as in *Chadwick*, it was the *luggage* being transported by respondent at the time of the arrest, not the automobile in which it was being carried, that was the suspected locus of the contraband. The relationship between the automobile and the contraband was purely coincidental, as in *Chadwick*. The fact that the suitcase was resting in the trunk of the automobile at the time of respondent's arrest does not turn this into an "automobile" exception case. The Court need say no more.

This case simply does not present the question of whether a warrant is required before opening luggage when the police have probable cause to believe contraband is located *somewhere* in the vehicle, but when they do *not* know whether, for example, it is inside a piece of luggage in the trunk, in the glove compartment, or concealed in some part of the car's structure. I am not sure whether that would be a stronger or weaker case for requiring a warrant to search the suitcase when a warrantless search of the automobile is otherwise permissible. But it seems to me it would be better to await a case in which the question must be decided.

The dissent complains that the Court does not adopt a "clear" rule, presumably one capable of resolving future Fourth Amendment litigation. That is not cause for lament, however desirable it might be to fashion a universal prescription governing the myriad Fourth Amendment cases that might arise. We are construing the Constitution, not writing a statute or a manual for law enforcement officers. My disagreement with the Court's opinion is very different from that of the dissenters. Our institutional practice, based on hard experience, generally has been to refrain from deciding questions not presented by the facts of a case; there are risks in formulating constitutional rules broader than required by the facts to which they are applied.

Mr. Justice BLACKMUN, with whom Mr. Justice REHNQUIST joins, dissenting.

I am unpersuaded by the Court's casual statement that *Chadwick* and this case are factually similar "in several critical respects." Even accepting *Chadwick* as good law, which I do not, this, for me, is a different case. In *Chadwick,* the defendants were arrested, and a 200-pound, double-locked footlocker was seized, as the locker was being loaded into the open trunk of a stationary automobile. The relationship between the footlocker and the vehicle was sufficiently attenuated that the Government chose not to argue in this Court that the automobile exception applied. Here, in contrast, the Little Rock police stopped a taxicab on a busy highway at the height of late afternoon traffic. They had probable cause to believe the taxi contained contraband narcotics. They opened the trunk, and briefly examined the contents of a small unlocked suitcase inside. The State has vigorously contended throughout these proceedings that the warrantless search of the trunk and the unlocked suitcase was constitutionally permissible under the automobile exception.

I fully agree. If "contraband goods concealed and illegally transported in an automobile or other vehicle may be searched for without a warrant," then, in my view, luggage and similar containers found in an automobile may be searched for contraband without a warrant. The luggage, like the automobile transporting it, is mobile. And the expectation of privacy in a suitcase found in the car is probably not significantly greater than the expectation of privacy in a locked glove compartment or trunk.

To be sure, as the dissent acknowledged in *Chadwick,* impounding the luggage without searching it would be a less intrusive alternative than searching it on the spot. But this Court has not distinguished between the "lesser" intrusion of a seizure and the "greater" intrusion of a search, either with respect to automobiles, or with respect to persons subject to custodial arrest. And I see no reason to impose such a distinction here. Given the significant encroachment on privacy interests entailed by a seizure of personal property, the additional intrusion of a search may well be regarded as incidental. Moreover, the additional protection provided by a search warrant will be minimal. Since the police, by hypothesis, have probable cause to seize the property, we can assume that a warrant will be routinely forthcoming in the overwhelming majority of cases. Finally, the carving out of a special warrant requirement for one type of personal property, but not for others, will impose untoward costs on the criminal justice systems of this country in terms of added delay and uncertainty.[3]

The impractical nature of the Court's line drawing is brought into focus if one places himself in the position of the policeman confronting an automobile that properly has been stopped. In approaching the vehicle and its occupants, the officer must divide the world of personal property into three groups. If there is probable cause to arrest the occupants, then under *Chimel*, he may search objects within the occupants'

---

[3] The opinion concurring in the judgment would distinguish between a case where there is probable cause to search the car and its contents as a whole, and a case where there is probable cause to search a particular item of luggage within the car. The opinion suggests, without deciding, that the automobile exception might apply in the former case, but not the latter. Surely, however, the intrusion on privacy, and consequently the need for the protection of the Warrant Clause, is, if anything, greater when the police search the entire interior area of the car, including possibly several suitcases, than when they confine their search to a single suitcase. Moreover, given the easy transferability of articles to and from luggage once it is placed in a vehicle, the police would be entitled to assume that if contraband was not found in the suspect suitcase, it would likely be secreted somewhere else in the car. The possibility the opinion concurring in the judgment would preserve for future decision thus contemplates the following two-step ritual: first, the police would take the targeted suitcase to the station for a search pursuant to a warrant; then, if the contraband was not discovered in the suitcase, they would return for a *warrantless* search of other luggage and compartments of the car. It does not require the adjudication of a future controversy to reject that result.

immediate control, with or without probable cause. If there is probable cause to search the automobile itself, then under *Carroll* and *Chambers* the entire interior area of the automobile may be searched, with or without a warrant. But under *Chadwick* and the present case, if any suitcase-like object is found in the car outside the immediate control area of the occupants, it cannot be searched, in the absence of exigent circumstances without a warrant.

The inherent opaqueness of these "principles" in terms of the policies underlying the Fourth and Fourteenth Amendments, and the confusion to be created for all concerned, are readily illustrated. Suppose a portable luggage-container-rack is affixed to the top of the vehicle. Is the arresting officer constitutionally able to open this on the spot, on the theory that it is like the car's trunk, or must he remove it and take it to the station for a warrant, on the theory that it is like the 200-pound footlocker in *Chadwick*? Or suppose there is probable cause to arrest persons seated in the front seat of the automobile, and a suitcase rests on the back seat. Is that suitcase within the area of immediate control, such that the *Chadwick-Sanders* rules do not apply? Or suppose the arresting officer opens the car's trunk and finds that it contains an array of containers—an orange crate, a lunch bucket, an attache case, a duffel bag, a cardboard box, a backpack, a tote bag, and a paper bag. Which of these may be searched immediately, and which are so "personal" that they must be impounded for future search only pursuant to a warrant? The problems of distinguishing between "luggage" and "some integral part of the automobile," between luggage that is within the "immediate control" of the arrestee and luggage that is not, and between "personal luggage" and other "containers and packages" such as those most curiously described will be legion. The lines that will be drawn will not make much sense in terms of the policies of the Fourth and Fourteenth Amendments. And the heightened possibilities for error will mean that many convictions will be overturned, highly relevant evidence again will be excluded, and guilty persons will be set free in return for little apparent gain in precise and clearly understood constitutional analysis.

In my view, it would be better to adopt a clear-cut rule to the effect that a warrant should not be required to seize and search any personal property found in an automobile that may in turn be seized and searched without a warrant pursuant to *Carroll* and *Chambers*. Such an approach would simplify the constitutional law of criminal procedure without seriously derogating from the values protected by the Fourth Amendment's prohibition of unreasonable searches and seizures.

## QUESTIONS AND NOTES

**1.** Which of the three opinions do you find most persuasive? Why? (The influence of the Burger opinion will appear in *Ross,* and the influence of the Blackmun opinion will appear in *Acevedo.*)

**2.** Is a bright line rule desirable in this area? Is it possible?

**3.** Should it be relevant that the police could have arrested Sanders at the airport (compare *Draper,* Chapter 2, *supra*), and searched his briefcase incident to that arrest?

**4.** Given that the police could stop the taxi in which Sanders was riding, arrest Sanders and Rambo, and seize Sanders' briefcase, how much additional intrusion was caused by searching the briefcase? Would not most innocent people prefer that the briefcase be searched so that they could establish their innocence? Is that a relevant question?

**5.** In *Ross,* the Court resolved the hypothetical posed by Burger in *Sanders.*

## United States v. Ross
### 456 U.S. 798 (1982)

Justice STEVENS delivered the opinion of the Court.

In *Carroll,* the Court held that a warrantless search of an automobile stopped by police officers who had probable cause to believe the vehicle contained contraband was not unreasonable within the meaning of the Fourth Amendment. The Court in *Carroll* did not explicitly address the scope of the search that is permissible. In this case, we consider the extent to which police officers—who have legitimately stopped an automobile and who have probable cause to believe that contraband is concealed somewhere within it—may conduct a probing search of compartments and containers within the vehicle whose contents are not in plain view. We hold that they may conduct a search of the vehicle that is as thorough as a magistrate could authorize in a warrant "particularly describing the place to be searched."

I

In the evening of November 27, 1978, an informant who had previously proved to be reliable telephoned Detective Marcum of the District of Columbia Police Department and told him that an individual known as "Bandit" was selling narcotics kept in the trunk of a car parked at 439 Ridge Street. The informant stated that he had just observed "Bandit" complete a sale and that "Bandit" had told him that additional narcotics were in the trunk. The informant gave Marcum a detailed description of "Bandit" and stated that the car was a "purplish maroon" Chevrolet Malibu with District of Columbia license plates.

Accompanied by Detective Cassidy and Sergeant Gonzales, Marcum immediately drove to the area and found a maroon Malibu parked in front of 439 Ridge Street. A license check disclosed that the car was registered to Albert Ross; a computer check on Ross revealed that he fit the informant's description and used the alias "Bandit." In two passes through the neighborhood the officers did not observe anyone matching the informant's description. To avoid alerting persons on the street, they left the area.

The officers returned five minutes later and observed the maroon Malibu turning off Ridge Street onto Fourth Street. They pulled alongside the Malibu, noticed that the driver matched the informant's description, and stopped the car. Marcum and Cassidy told the driver—later identified as Albert Ross, the respondent in this action—to get out of the vehicle. While they searched Ross, Sergeant Gonzales discovered a bullet on the car's front seat. He searched the interior of the car and found a pistol in the glove compartment. Ross then was arrested and handcuffed. Detective Cassidy took Ross' keys and opened the trunk, where he found a closed brown paper bag. He opened the bag and discovered a number of glassine bags containing a white powder. Cassidy replaced the bag, closed the trunk, and drove the car to headquarters.

At the police station Cassidy thoroughly searched the car. In addition to the "lunch-type" brown paper bag, Cassidy found in the trunk a zippered red leather pouch. He unzipped the pouch and discovered $3,200 in cash. The police laboratory later determined that the powder in the paper bag was heroin. No warrant was obtained.

Ross was charged with possession of heroin with intent to distribute. Prior to trial, he moved to suppress the heroin found in the paper bag and the currency found in the leather pouch. After an evidentiary hearing, the District Court denied the motion to suppress. The heroin and currency were introduced in evidence at trial and Ross was convicted.

A three-judge panel of the Court of Appeals reversed the conviction. It held that the police had probable cause to stop and search Ross' car and that, under *Carroll* and *Chambers,* the officers lawfully could search the automobile—including its trunk—without a warrant. The court considered separately, however, the warrantless search of the two containers found in the trunk. On the basis of *Sanders,* the court concluded that the constitutionality of a warrantless search of a container found in an automobile depends on whether the owner possesses a reasonable expectation of privacy in its contents. Applying that test, the court held that the warrantless search of the paper bag was valid but the search of the leather pouch was not. The court remanded for a new trial at which the items taken from the paper bag, but not those from the leather pouch, could be admitted.

The entire Court of Appeals then voted to rehear the case en banc. A majority of the court rejected the panel's conclusion that a distinction of constitutional significance existed between the two containers found in respondent's trunk; it held that the police should not have opened either container without first obtaining a warrant. The court reasoned: "No specific, well-delineated exception called to our attention permits the police to dispense with a warrant to open and search 'unworthy' containers. Moreover, we believe that a rule under which the validity of a warrantless search would turn on judgments about the durability of a container would impose an unreasonable and unmanageable burden on police and courts. For these reasons, and because the Fourth Amendment protects all persons, not just those with the resources or fastidiousness to place their effects in containers that decision-makers would rank in the luggage line, we hold that the Fourth Amendment warrant requirement forbids the warrantless opening of a closed, opaque paper bag to the same extent that it forbids the warrantless opening of a small unlocked suitcase or a zippered leather pouch."

There is no dispute among judges about the importance of striving for clarification in this area of the law. For countless vehicles are stopped on highways and public streets every day, and our cases demonstrate that it is not uncommon for police officers to have probable cause to believe that contraband may be found in a stopped vehicle. In every such case a conflict is presented between the individual's constitutionally protected interest in privacy and the public interest in effective law enforcement. No single rule of law can resolve every conflict, but our conviction that clarification is feasible led us to grant the Government's petition for certiorari in this case.

## II

We begin with a review of the decision in *Carroll* itself. In the fall of 1921, federal prohibition agents obtained evidence that George Carroll and John Kiro were "bootleggers" who frequently traveled between Grand Rapids and Detroit in an Oldsmobile Roadster. On December 15, 1921, the agents unexpectedly encountered Carroll and Kiro driving west on that route in that car. The officers gave pursuit, stopped the roadster on the highway, and directed Carroll and Kiro to get out of the car.

No contraband was visible in the front seat of the Oldsmobile and the rear portion of the roadster was closed. One of the agents raised the rumble seat but found no liquor. He raised the seat cushion and again found nothing. The officer then struck at the "lazyback" of the seat and noticed that it was "harder than upholstery ordinarily is in those backs." He tore open the seat cushion and discovered 68 bottles of gin and whiskey concealed inside. No warrant had been obtained for the search.

The exception to the warrant requirement established in *Carroll*—the scope of which we consider in this case—applies only to searches of vehicles that are supported by probable cause. In this class of cases, a search is not unreasonable if based on facts that would justify the issuance of a warrant, even though a warrant has not actually been obtained.

## III

The rationale justifying a warrantless search of an automobile that is believed to be transporting contraband arguably applies with equal force to any movable container that is believed to be carrying an illicit substance. That argument, however, was squarely rejected in *Chadwick* [and *Sanders*].

[T]he Chief Justice noted in his opinion concurring in the judgment [in *Sanders*]:

"Because the police officers had probable cause to believe that respondent's green suitcase contained marihuana before it was placed in the trunk of the taxicab, their duty to obtain a search warrant before opening it is clear under *Chadwick*. Here, as in *Chadwick,* it was the luggage being transported by respondent at the time of the arrest, not the automobile in which it was being carried, that was the suspected locus of the contraband. The relationship between the automobile and the contraband was purely coincidental, as in *Chadwick*. The fact that the suitcase was resting in the trunk of the automobile at the time of respondent's arrest does not turn this into an 'automobile' exception case. The Court need say no more.''

The Court in *Sanders* did not, however, rest its decision solely on the authority of *Chadwick*. In rejecting the State's argument that the warrantless search of the suitcase was justified on the ground that it had been taken from an automobile lawfully stopped on the street, the Court broadly suggested that a warrantless search of a container found in an automobile could never be sustained as part of a warrantless search of the automobile itself.[19] The Court did not suggest that it mattered whether probable cause existed to search the entire vehicle. It is clear, however, that in neither *Chadwick* nor *Sanders* did the police have probable cause to search the vehicle or anything within it except the footlocker in the former case and the green suitcase in the latter.

*Robbins v. California*, 453 U.S. 420, however, was a case in which suspicion was not directed at a specific container. In that case the Court for the first time was forced to consider whether police officers who are entitled to conduct a warrantless search of an automobile stopped on a public roadway may open a container found within the vehicle. In the early morning of January 5, 1975, police officers stopped Robbins' station wagon because he was driving erratically. Robbins got out of the car, but later returned to obtain the vehicle's registration papers. When he opened the car door, the officers smelled marihuana smoke. One of the officers searched Robbins and discovered a vial of liquid; in a search of the interior of the car the officer found marihuana. The police officers then opened the tailgate of the station wagon and raised the cover of a recessed luggage compartment. In the compartment they found two packages wrapped in green opaque plastic. The police unwrapped the packages and discovered a large amount of marihuana in each.

---

[19] The Court stated that "the extent to which the Fourth Amendment applies to containers and other parcels depends not at all upon whether they are seized from an automobile." This general rule was limited only by the observation that "[n]ot all containers and packages found by police during the course of a search will deserve the full protection of the Fourth Amendment. Thus, some containers (for example a kit of burglar tools or a gun case) by their very nature cannot support any reasonable expectation of privacy because their contents can be inferred from their outward appearance. Similarly, in some cases the contents of a package will be open to 'plain view,' thereby obviating the need for a warrant."

Writing for a plurality, Justice Stewart rejected the argument that the outward appearance of the packages precluded Robbins from having a reasonable expectation of privacy in their contents. He also squarely rejected the argument that there is a constitutional distinction between searches of luggage and searches of "less worthy" containers. Justice Stewart reasoned that all containers are equally protected by the Fourth Amendment unless their contents are in plain view. The plurality concluded that the warrantless search was impermissible because *Chadwick* and *Sanders* had established that "a closed piece of luggage found in a lawfully searched car is constitutionally protected to the same extent as are closed pieces of luggage found anywhere else."

In an opinion concurring in the judgment, Justice Powell, the author of the Court's opinion in *Sanders*, stated that "[t]he plurality's approach strains the rationales of our prior cases and imposes substantial burdens on law enforcement without vindicating any significant values of privacy."[21] He noted that possibly "the controlling question should be the scope of the automobile exception to the warrant requirement," and explained that under that view "when

---

[21] "While the plurality's blanket warrant requirement does not even purport to protect any privacy interest, it would impose substantial new burdens on law enforcement. Confronted with a cigar box or a Dixie cup in the course of a probable-cause search of an automobile for narcotics, the conscientious policeman would be required to take the object to a magistrate, fill out the appropriate forms, await the decision, and finally obtain the warrant. Suspects or vehicles normally will be detained while the warrant is sought. This process may take hours, removing the officer from his normal police duties. Expenditure of such time and effort, drawn from the public's limited resources for detecting or preventing crimes, is justified when it protects an individual's reasonable privacy interests. In my view, the plurality's requirement cannot be so justified. The aggregate burden of procuring warrants whenever an officer has probable cause to search the most trivial container may be heavy and will not be compensated by the advancement of important Fourth Amendment values." (Powell, J., concurring in judgment). The substantial burdens on law enforcement identified by Justice Powell would, of course, not be affected by the character of the container found during an automobile search. No comparable practical problems arise when the official suspicion is confined to a particular piece of luggage, as in *Chadwick* and *Sanders*.

the police have probable cause to search an automobile, rather than only to search a particular container that fortuitously is located in it, the exigencies that allow the police to search the entire automobile without a warrant support the warrantless search of every container found therein. This analysis is entirely consistent with the holdings in *Chadwick* and *Sanders*, neither of which is an 'automobile case,' because the police there had probable cause to search the double-locked footlocker and the suitcase respectively before either came near an automobile.''

The parties in *Robbins* had not pressed that argument, however, and Justice Powell concluded that institutional constraints made it inappropriate to reexamine basic doctrine without full adversary presentation. He concurred in the judgment, since it was supported – although not compelled – by the Court's opinion in *Sanders*, and stated that a future case might present a better opportunity for thorough consideration of the basic principles in this troubled area.

That case has arrived. Unlike *Chadwick* and *Sanders*, in this case police officers had probable cause to search respondent's entire vehicle. Unlike *Robbins*, in this case the parties have squarely addressed the question whether, in the course of a legitimate warrantless search of an automobile, police are entitled to open containers found within the vehicle. We now address that question. Its answer is determined by the scope of the search that is authorized by the exception to the warrant requirement set forth in *Carroll*.

### IV

In *Carroll* itself, the whiskey that the prohibition agents seized was not in plain view. It was discovered only after an officer opened the rumble seat and tore open the upholstery of the lazyback. The Court did not find the scope of the search unreasonable. Having stopped Carroll and Kiro on a public road and subjected them to the indignity of a vehicle search – which the Court found to be a reasonable intrusion on their privacy because it was based on probable cause that their vehicle was transporting contraband – prohibition agents were entitled to tear open a portion of the roadster itself. The scope of the search was no greater than a magistrate could have authorized by issuing a warrant based on the probable cause that justified the search. Since such a warrant could have authorized the agents to open the rear portion of the roadster and to rip the upholstery in their search for concealed whiskey, the search was constitutionally permissible.

In *Chambers* the police found weapons and stolen property "concealed in a compartment under the dashboard." No suggestion was made that the scope of the search was impermissible. It would be illogical to assume that the outcome of *Chambers* – or the outcome of *Carroll* itself – would have been different if the police had found the secreted contraband enclosed within a secondary container and had opened that container without a warrant. If it was reasonable for prohibition agents to rip open the upholstery in *Carroll*, it certainly would have been reasonable for them to look into a burlap sack stashed inside; if it was reasonable to open the concealed compartment in *Chambers*, it would have been equally reasonable to open a paper bag crumpled within it. A contrary rule could produce absurd results inconsistent with the decision in *Carroll* itself.

In its application of *Carroll*, this Court in fact has sustained warrantless searches of containers found during a lawful search of an automobile. In *Husty v. United States*, 282 U.S. 694, the Court upheld a warrantless seizure of whiskey found during a search of an automobile, some of which was discovered in "whiskey bags" that could have contained other goods.[23] In *Scher v. United States*, 305 U.S. 251, federal officers seized and searched packages of unstamped liquor found in the trunk of an automobile searched without a warrant. As described by a police officer who participated in the search: "I turned the handle and opened the trunk and found the trunk completely filled with packages wrapped in brown paper, and tied with twine; I think somewhere around thirty packages, each one containing six bottles."[24] In these cases it was not contended that police officers needed a warrant to open the whiskey bags or to unwrap the brown paper packages. These decisions nevertheless "have much weight, as they show that this point neither occurred to the bar or the bench." The fact that no such argument was even made illuminates the profession's understanding of the scope of the search permitted under *Carroll*. Indeed, prior to the decisions in *Chadwick* and *Sanders*, courts routinely had held that containers and packages found during a legitimate warrantless search of an automobile also could be searched without a warrant.

As we have stated, the decision in *Carroll* was

---

[23] At the suppression hearing, defense counsel asked the police officer who had conducted the search: "Isn't it possible to put other goods in a bag that has the resemblance of a whiskey bag?" The officer responded: "I suppose it is. I did not think of that at that time. I knew it was whiskey, I was sure it was."

[24] The brief of then Solicitor General Robert Jackson noted that the items searched "were wrapped in very heavy brown wrapping paper with at least two wrappings and with a heavy cord around them cross-wise so that they could readily be lifted."

based on the Court's appraisal of practical considerations viewed in the perspective of history. It is therefore significant that the practical consequences of the *Carroll* decision would be largely nullified if the permissible scope of a warrantless search of an automobile did not include containers and packages found inside the vehicle. Contraband goods rarely are strewn across the trunk or floor of a car; since by their very nature such goods must be withheld from public view, they rarely can be placed in an automobile unless they are enclosed within some form of container.[26] The Court in *Carroll* held that "contraband goods *concealed* and illegally transported in an automobile or other vehicle may be searched for without a warrant." (emphasis added). As we noted in *Henry v. United States*, 361 U.S. 98, the decision in *Carroll* "merely relaxed the requirements for a warrant on grounds of practicability." It neither broadened nor limited the scope of a lawful search based on probable cause.

A lawful search of fixed premises generally extends to the entire area in which the object of the search may be found and is not limited by the possibility that separate acts of entry or opening may be required to complete the search. Thus, a warrant that authorizes an officer to search a home for illegal weapons also provides authority to open closets, chests, drawers, and containers in which the weapon might be found. A warrant to open a footlocker to search for marihuana would also authorize the opening of packages found inside. A warrant to search a vehicle would support a search of every part of the vehicle that might contain the object of the search. When a legitimate search is under way, and

when its purpose and its limits have been precisely defined, nice distinctions between closets, drawers, and containers, in the case of a home, or between glove compartments, upholstered seats, trunks, and wrapped packages, in the case of a vehicle, must give way to the interest in the prompt and efficient completion of the task at hand.[28]

This rule applies equally to all containers, as indeed we believe it must. One point on which the Court was in virtually unanimous agreement in *Robbins* was that a constitutional distinction between "worthy" and "unworthy" containers would be improper. Even though such a distinction perhaps could evolve in a series of cases in which paper bags, locked trunks, lunch buckets, and orange crates were placed on one side of the line or the other, the central purpose of the Fourth Amendment forecloses such a distinction. For just as the most frail cottage in the kingdom is absolutely entitled to the same guarantees of privacy as the most majestic mansion,[31] so also may a traveler who carries a toothbrush and a few articles of clothing in a paper bag or knotted scarf claim an equal right to conceal his possessions from official inspection as the sophisticated executive with the locked attache case.

---

[26] It is noteworthy that the early legislation on which the Court relied in *Carroll* concerned the enforcement of laws imposing duties on imported merchandise. Presumably such merchandise was shipped then in containers of various kinds, just as it is today. Since Congress had authorized warrantless searches of vessels and beasts for imported merchandise, it is inconceivable that it intended a customs officer to obtain a warrant for every package discovered during the search; certainly Congress intended customs officers to open shipping containers when necessary and not merely to examine the exterior of cartons or boxes in which smuggled goods might be concealed. During virtually the entire history of our country—whether contraband was transported in a horse-drawn carriage, a 1921 roadster, or a modern automobile—it has been assumed that a lawful search of a vehicle would include a search of any container that might conceal the object of the search.

[28] The practical considerations that justify a warrantless search of an automobile continue to apply until the entire search of the automobile and its contents has been completed. Arguably, the entire vehicle itself (including its upholstery) could be searched without a warrant, with all wrapped articles and containers found during that search then taken to a magistrate. But prohibiting police from opening immediately a container in which the object of the search is most likely to be found and instead forcing them first to comb the entire vehicle would actually exacerbate the intrusion on privacy interests. Moreover, until the container itself was opened the police could never be certain that the contraband was not secreted in a yet undiscovered portion of the vehicle; thus in every case in which a container was found, the vehicle would need to be secured while a warrant was obtained. Such a requirement would be directly inconsistent with the rationale supporting the decisions in *Carroll* and *Chambers*.

[31] "The poorest man may in his cottage bid defiance to all the forces of the Crown. It may be frail; its roof may shake; the wind may blow through it; the storm may enter; the rain may enter; but the King of England cannot enter—all his force dares not cross the threshold of the ruined tenement!" *Miller v. United States*, 357 U.S. 301, 307 (quoting remarks attributed to William Pitt).

As Justice Stewart stated in *Robbins*, the Fourth Amendment provides protection to the owner of every container that conceals its contents from plain view. But the protection afforded by the Amendment varies in different settings. The luggage carried by a traveler entering the country may be searched at random by a customs officer; the luggage may be searched no matter how great the traveler's desire to conceal the contents may be. A container carried at the time of arrest often may be searched without a warrant and even without any specific suspicion concerning its contents. A container that may conceal the object of a search authorized by a warrant may be opened immediately; the individual's interest in privacy must give way to the magistrate's official determination of probable cause.

In the same manner, an individual's expectation of privacy in a vehicle and its contents may not survive if probable cause is given to believe that the vehicle is transporting contraband. Certainly the privacy interests in a car's trunk or glove compartment may be no less than those in a movable container. An individual undoubtedly has a significant interest that the upholstery of his automobile will not be ripped or a hidden compartment within it opened. These interests must yield to the authority of a search, however, which—in light of *Carroll* — does not itself require the prior approval of a magistrate. The scope of a warrantless search based on probable cause is no narrower—and no broader—than the scope of a search authorized by a warrant supported by probable cause. Only the prior approval of the magistrate is waived; the search otherwise is as the magistrate could authorize.

The scope of a warrantless search of an automobile thus is not defined by the nature of the container in which the contraband is secreted. Rather, it is defined by the object of the search and the places in which there is probable cause to believe that it may be found. Just as probable cause to believe that a stolen lawnmower may be found in a garage will not support a warrant to search an upstairs bedroom, probable cause to believe that undocumented aliens are being transported in a van will not justify a warrantless search of a suitcase. Probable cause to believe that a container placed in the trunk of a taxi contains contraband or evidence does not justify a search of the entire cab.

### V

Our decision today is inconsistent with the disposition in *Robbins* and with the portion of the opinion in *Sanders* on which the plurality in *Robbins* relied. Nevertheless, the doctrine of *stare decisis* does not preclude this action. Although we have rejected some of the reasoning in *Sanders*, we adhere to our holding in that case; although we reject the precise holding in *Robbins*, there was no Court opinion supporting a single rationale for its judgment, and the reasoning we adopt today was not presented by the parties in that case. Moreover, it is clear that no legitimate reliance interest can be frustrated by our decision today.[33] Of greatest importance, we are convinced that the rule we apply in this case is faithful to the interpretation of the Fourth Amendment that the Court has followed with substantial consistency throughout our history.

The judgment of the Court of Appeals is reversed. The case is remanded for further proceedings consistent with this opinion.

**Justice BLACKMUN, concurring.**

My dissents in prior cases have indicated my continuing dissatisfaction and discomfort with the Court's vacillation in what is rightly described as "this troubled area."

I adhere to the views expressed in those dissents. It is important, however, not only for the Court as an institution, but also for law enforcement officials and defendants, that the applicable legal rules be clearly established. Justice Stevens' opinion for the Court now accomplishes much in this respect, and it should clarify a good bit of the confusion that has existed. In order to have an authoritative ruling, I join the Court's opinion and judgment.

[Justice POWELL's concurring opinion and Justice WHITE's dissenting opinion are omitted.]

**Justice MARSHALL, with whom Justice BRENNAN joins, dissenting.**

### I

According to the majority, whenever police have probable cause to believe that contraband may be found within an automobile that they have stopped on the highway,[1] they may search not only the automobile but also any container found inside it, without obtaining a warrant. The scope of the search, we are told, is as broad as a magistrate could authorize in a warrant to search the automobile. The majority

---

[33] Any interest in maintaining the status quo that might be asserted by persons who may have structured their business of distributing narcotics or other illicit substances on the basis of judicial precedents clearly would not be legitimate.

[1] The Court confines its holding today to automobiles stopped on the highway which police have probable cause to believe contain contraband. I do not understand the Court to address the applicability of the automobile exception rule announced today to parked cars. Cf. *Coolidge*.

makes little attempt to justify this rule in terms of recognized Fourth Amendment values. The Court simply ignores the critical function that a magistrate serves. And although the Court purports to rely on the mobility of an automobile and the impracticability of obtaining a warrant, it never explains why these concerns permit the warrantless search of a *container*, which can easily be seized and immobilized while police are obtaining a warrant.

The new rule adopted by the Court today is completely incompatible with established Fourth Amendment principles, and takes a first step toward an unprecedented ''probable cause'' exception to the warrant requirement. In my view, under accepted standards, the warrantless search of the containers in this case clearly violates the Fourth Amendment.

### B

The majority's rule is flatly inconsistent with established Fourth Amendment principles concerning the scope of the automobile exception and the importance of the warrant requirement. Historically, the automobile exception has been limited to those situations where its application is compelled by the justifications described above. Today, the majority makes no attempt to base its decision on these justifications. This failure is not surprising, since the traditional rationales for the automobile exception plainly do not support extending it to the search of a container found inside a vehicle.

The practical mobility problem—deciding what to do with both the car and the occupants if an immediate search is not conducted—is simply not present in the case of movable containers, which can easily be seized and brought to the magistrate. The lesser-expectation-of-privacy rationale also has little force. A container, as opposed to the car itself, does not reflect diminished privacy interests. Moreover, the practical corollary that this Court has recognized—that depriving occupants of the use of a car may be a greater intrusion than an immediate search—is of doubtful relevance here, since the owner of a container will rarely suffer significant inconvenience by being deprived of its use while a warrant is being obtained.

In purported reliance on *Carroll*, the Court defines the permissible scope of a search by reference to the scope of a probable-cause search that a magistrate could authorize. Under *Carroll*, however, the mobility of an automobile is what is critical to the legality of a warrantless search. Of course, *Carroll* properly confined the search to the probable-cause limits that would also limit a magistrate, but it did not suggest that the search could be as broad as a

magistrate could authorize upon a warrant. A magistrate could authorize a search encompassing containers, even though the mobility rationale does not justify such a broad search. Indeed, the Court's reasoning might have justified the search of the entire car in *Coolidge* despite the fact that the car was not ''mobile'' at all. Thus, in blithely suggesting that *Carroll* ''neither broadened nor limited the scope of a lawful search based on probable cause,'' the majority assumes what has never been the law: that the scope of the automobile-mobility exception to the warrant requirement is as broad as the scope of a ''lawful'' probable-cause search of an automobile, *i.e.*, one authorized by a magistrate.

The majority's sleight-of-hand ignores the obvious differences between the function served by a magistrate in making a determination of probable cause and the function of the automobile exception. It is irrelevant to a magistrate's function whether the items subject to search are mobile, may be in danger of destruction, or are impractical to store, or whether an immediate search would be less intrusive than a seizure without a warrant. A magistrate's only concern is whether there is probable cause to search them. Where suspicion has focused not on a particular item but only on a vehicle, home, or office, the magistrate might reasonably authorize a search of closed containers at the location as well. But an officer on the beat who searches an automobile without a warrant is not entitled to conduct a broader search than the exigency obviating the warrant justifies. After all, what justifies the warrantless search is not probable cause alone, but *probable cause coupled with the mobility of the automobile*. Because the scope of a warrantless search should depend on the scope of the justification for dispensing with a warrant, the entire premise of the majority's opinion fails to support its conclusion.

### C

Our recent decisions in *Chadwick, Sanders,* and *Robbins* clearly affirm that movable containers are different from automobiles for Fourth Amendment purposes. In light of these considerations, I conclude that any movable container found within an automobile deserves precisely the same degree of Fourth Amendment warrant protection that it would deserve if found at a location outside the automobile. *Chadwick,* as the majority notes, ''reaffirmed the general principle that closed packages and containers may not be searched without a warrant.'' Although there is no need to describe the exact contours of that protection in this dissenting opinion, it is clear enough that closed, opaque containers—regardless of whether they are "worthy" or are always used to store personal items – are ordinarily fully protected.

## II

[T]he majority's new rule is theoretically unsound and will create anomalous and unwarranted results. These consequences are readily apparent from the Court's attempt to reconcile its new rule with the holdings of *Chadwick* and *Sanders*. The Court suggests that probable cause to search only a container does not justify a warrantless search of an automobile in which it is placed, absent reason to believe that the contents could be secreted elsewhere in the vehicle. This, the majority asserts, is an indication that the new rule is carefully limited to its justification, and is not inconsistent with *Chadwick* and *Sanders*. But why is such a container more private, less difficult for police to seize and store, or in any other relevant respect more properly subject to the warrant requirement, than a container that police discover in a probable-cause search of an entire automobile?[10] This rule plainly has peculiar and unworkable consequences: the Government "must show that the investigating officer knew enough but not too much, that he had sufficient knowledge to establish probable cause but insufficient knowledge to know exactly where the contraband was located."

Alternatively, the majority may be suggesting that *Chadwick* and *Sanders* may be explained because the connection of the container to the vehicle was incidental in these two cases. That is, because police had pre-existing probable cause to seize and search the containers, they were not entitled to wait until the item was placed in a vehicle to take advantage of the automobile exception. I wholeheartedly agree that police cannot employ a pretext to escape Fourth Amendment prohibitions and cannot rely on an exigency that they could easily have avoided. This interpretation, however, might well be an exception that swallows up the majority's rule. In neither *Chadwick* nor *Sanders* did the Court suggest that the delay of the police was a pretext for taking advantage of the automobile exception. For all that appears, the Government may have had legitimate reasons for not searching as soon as they had probable cause. In any event, asking police to rely on such an uncertain line in distinguishing between legitimate and illegitimate searches for containers in automobiles hardly indicates that the majority's approach has brought clarification to this area of the law.

## III

The Court today ignores the clear distinction that *Chadwick* established between movable containers and automobiles. It also rejects all of the relevant reasoning of *Sanders*[12] and offers a substitute rationale that appears inconsistent with the result. *Sanders* is therefore effectively overruled.

The only convincing explanation I discern for the majority's broad rule is expediency: it assists police in conducting automobile searches, ensuring that the private containers into which criminal suspects often place goods will no longer be a Fourth Amendment shield. "When a legitimate search is under way," the Court instructs us, "nice distinctions between . . . glove compartments, upholstered seats, trunks, and wrapped packages . . . must give way to the interest in the prompt and efficient completion of the task at hand." No "nice distinctions" are necessary, however, to comprehend the well-recognized differences between movable containers (which, even after today's decision, would be subject to the warrant requirement if located outside an automobile), and the automobile itself, together with its integral parts. Nor can I pass by the majority's glib assertion that the "prompt and efficient completion of the task at hand" is paramount to the Fourth Amendment interests of our

---

[10] In a footnote, the Court appears to suggest a more pragmatic rationale for distinguishing *Chadwick* and *Sanders* – that no practical problems comparable to those engendered by a general search of a vehicle would arise if the official suspicion is confined to a particular piece of luggage. n. 21. This suggestion is illogical. A general search might disclose only a single item worth searching; conversely, pre-existing suspicion might attach to a number of items later placed in a car. Surely the protection of the warrant requirement cannot depend on a numerical count of the items subject to search.

---

[12] The Court suggests that it rejects "some of the reasoning in *Sanders*." But the Court in *Sanders* unambiguously stated: "[W]e hold that the warrant requirement of the Fourth Amendment applies to personal luggage taken from an automobile to the same degree it applies to such luggage in other locations." The Court today instead adopts the reasoning of the opinion of the Chief Justice, joined by Justice Stevens, who refused to join the majority opinion because of the breadth of its rationale.

citizens. I had thought it well established that "the mere fact that law enforcement may be made more efficient can never by itself justify disregard of the Fourth Amendment."[13]

This case will have profound implications for the privacy of citizens traveling in automobiles, as the Court well understands. "For countless vehicles are stopped on highways and public streets every day and our cases demonstrate that it is not uncommon for police officers to have probable cause to believe that contraband may be found in a stopped vehicle." A closed paper bag, a toolbox, a knapsack, a suitcase, and an attache case can alike be searched without the protection of the judgment of a neutral magistrate, based only on the rarely disturbed decision of a police officer that he has probable cause to search for contraband in the vehicle.[14] The Court derives

satisfaction from the fact that its rule does not exalt the rights of the wealthy over the rights of the poor. A rule so broad that all citizens lose vital Fourth Amendment protection is no cause for celebration.

I dissent.

---

[13] Of course, efficiency and promptness can never be substituted for due process and adherence to the Constitution. Is not a dictatorship the most "efficient" form of government?

[14] The Court purports to restrict its rule to areas that the police have probable cause to search, as "defined by the object of the search and the places in which there is probable cause to believe that it may be found." I agree, of course, that the probable-cause component of the automobile exception must be strictly construed. I fear, however, that the restriction that the Court emphasizes may have little practical value. If police open a container within a car and find contraband, they may acquire probable cause to believe that other portions of the car, and other containers within it, will contain contraband. In practice, the Court's rule may amount to a wholesale authorization for police to search any car from top to bottom when they have suspicion, whether localized or general, that it contains contraband.

## QUESTIONS AND NOTES

**1.** Who better captures the essence of prior decisions, Stevens or Marshall? Explain.

**2.** Is Marshall's opinion overly apocalyptic?

**3.** If Marshall had prevailed, would the law permit a warrantless tearing open of upholstery, forcing open a car trunk, but forbidding looking inside a paper bag in either of those places?

**4.** If that were the law, could you explain it in a way that would make sense to someone like Albert "Bandit" Ross?

**5.** If the police were required to get a warrant to look in the paper bag, *could* they have done so? There was probable cause to believe that the drugs were somewhere in the car, but no apparent probable cause to believe that they were in any particular container.

**6.** Is the Court holding that containers are *less* protected in cars than any place else? Assuming that your answer was "no", does it change after *Acevedo*?

## California v. Acevedo
### 111 S.Ct. 1982 (1991)

Justice BLACKMUN delivered the opinion of the Court.

This case requires us once again to consider the so-called "automobile exception" to the warrant requirement of the Fourth Amendment and its application to the search of a closed container in the trunk of a car.

I

On October 28, 1987, Officer Coleman of the Santa Ana, Cal., Police Department received a telephone call from a federal drug enforcement agent in Hawaii. The agent informed Coleman that he had seized a package containing marijuana which was to have been delivered to the Federal Express Office in Santa Ana and which was addressed to J.R. Daza at 805 West Stevens Avenue in that city. The agent arranged to send the package to Coleman instead. Coleman then was to take the package to the Federal Express office and arrest the person who arrived to claim it.

Coleman received the package on October 29, verified its contents, and took it to the Senior Operations Manager at the Federal Express office. At about 10:30 a.m. on October 30, a man, who identified himself as Jamie Daza, arrived to claim the package. He accepted it and drove to his apartment on West Stevens. He carried the package into the apartment.

At 11:45 a.m., officers observed Daza leave the apartment and drop the box and paper that had contained the marijuana into a trash bin. Coleman at that point left the scene to get a search warrant. About 12:05 p.m., the officers saw Richard St. George leave the apartment carrying a blue knapsack which appeared to be half full. The officers stopped him as he was driving off, searched the knapsack, and found 1½ pounds of marijuana.

At 12:30 p.m., respondent Charles Steven Acevedo arrived. He entered Daza's apartment, stayed for about 10 minutes, and reappeared carrying a brown paper bag that looked full. The officers noticed that the bag was the size of one of the wrapped marijuana packages sent from Hawaii. Acevedo walked to a silver Honda in the parking lot. He placed the bag in the trunk of the car and started to drive away. Fearing the loss of evidence, officers in a marked police car stopped him. They opened the trunk and the bag, and found marijuana.[1]

## II

*Ross* endeavored to distinguish between *Carroll*, which governed the *Ross* automobile search, and *Chadwick*, which governed the *Sanders* automobile search. It held that the *Carroll* doctrine covered searches of automobiles when the police had probable cause to search an entire vehicle but that the *Chadwick* doctrine governed searches of luggage when the officers had probable cause to search only a container within the vehicle. Thus, in a *Ross* situation, the police could conduct a reasonable search under the Fourth Amendment without obtaining a warrant, whereas in a *Sanders* situation, the police had to obtain a warrant before they searched.

The dissent is correct, of course, that *Ross* involved the scope of an automobile search. *Ross* held

---

[1] When Officer Coleman returned with a warrant, the apartment was searched and bags of marijuana were found there. We are here concerned, of course, only with what was discovered in the automobile.

that closed containers encountered by the police during a warrantless search of a car pursuant to the automobile exception could also be searched. Thus, this Court in *Ross* took the critical step of saying that closed containers in cars could be searched without a warrant because of their presence within the automobile. Despite the protection that *Sanders* purported to extend to closed containers, the privacy interest in those closed containers yielded to the broad scope of an automobile search.

## III

The facts in this case closely resemble the facts in *Ross*. In *Ross*, the police had probable cause to believe that drugs were stored in the trunk of a particular car. Here, the California Court of Appeal concluded that the police had probable cause to believe that respondent was carrying marijuana in a bag in his car's trunk. Furthermore, for what it is worth, in *Ross*, as here, the drugs in the trunk were contained in a brown paper bag.

This Court in *Ross* rejected *Chadwick*'s distinction between containers and cars. It concluded that the expectation of privacy in one's vehicle is equal to one's expectation of privacy in the container, and noted that "the privacy interests in a car's trunk or glove compartment may be no less than those in a movable container." It also recognized that it was arguable that the same exigent circumstances that permit a warrantless search of an automobile would justify the warrantless search of a movable container. In deference to the rule of *Chadwick* and *Sanders*, however, the Court put that question to one side. It concluded that the time and expense of the warrant process would be misdirected if the police could search every cubic inch of an automobile until they discovered a paper sack, at which point the Fourth Amendment required them to take the sack to a magistrate for permission to look inside. We now must decide the question deferred in *Ross*: whether the Fourth Amendment requires the police to obtain a warrant to open the sack in a movable vehicle simply because they lack probable cause to search the entire car. We conclude that it does not.

## IV

Dissenters in *Ross* asked why the suitcase in *Sanders* was "more private, less difficult for police to seize and store, or in any other relevant respect more properly subject to the warrant requirement, than a container that police discover in a probable-cause search of an entire automobile?" We now agree that a container found after a general search of the automobile and a container found in a car after a limited search for the container are equally easy for the police to store and for the suspect to hide or destroy. In fact, we see no principled distinction in terms of either the privacy expectation or the exigent circumstances between the paper bag found by the police in *Ross* and the paper bag found by the police here. Furthermore, by attempting to distinguish between a container for which the police are specifically searching and a container which they come across in a car, we have provided only minimal protection for privacy and have impeded effective law enforcement.

The line between probable cause to search a vehicle and probable cause to search a package in that vehicle is not always clear, and separate rules that govern the two objects to be searched may enable the police to broaden their power to make warrantless searches and disserve privacy interests. We noted this in *Ross* in the context of a search of an entire vehicle. Recognizing that under *Carroll*, the "entire vehicle itself . . . could be searched without a warrant," we concluded that "prohibiting police from opening immediately a container in which the object of the search is most likely to be found and instead forcing them first to comb the entire vehicle would actually exacerbate the intrusion on privacy interests." At the moment when officers stop an automobile, it may be less than clear whether they suspect with a high degree of certainty that the vehicle contains drugs in a bag or simply contains drugs. If the police know that they may open a bag only if they are actually searching the entire car, they may search more extensively than they otherwise would in order to establish the general probable cause required by *Ross*.

Such a situation is not far fetched. In *United States v. Johns*, 469 U.S. 478 (1985), customs agents saw two trucks drive to a private airstrip and approach two small planes. The agents drew near the trucks, smelled marijuana, and then saw in the backs of the trucks packages wrapped in a manner that marijuana smugglers customarily employed. The agents took the trucks to headquarters and searched the packages without a warrant. Relying on *Chadwick*, the defendants argued that the search was unlawful. The defendants contended that *Ross* was inapplicable because the agents lacked probable cause to search anything but the packages themselves and supported this contention by noting that a search of the entire vehicle never occurred. We rejected that argument and found *Chadwick* and *Sanders* inapposite because the agents had probable cause to search the entire body of each truck, although they had chosen not to do so. We cannot see the benefit of a rule that requires law enforcement officers to conduct a more intrusive search in order to justify a less intrusive one.

To the extent that the *Chadwick-Sanders* rule protects privacy, its protection is minimal. Law enforcement officers may seize a container and hold it until they obtain a search warrant. "Since the police, by hypothesis, have probable cause to seize the property, we can assume that a warrant will be routinely forthcoming in the overwhelming majority of cases." *Sanders* (dissenting opinion). And the police often will be able to search containers without a warrant, despite the *Chadwick-Sanders* rule, as a search incident to a lawful arrest. In *New York v. Belton* (Sec. C. *infra*), the Court said:

> "[W]e hold that when a policeman has made a lawful custodial arrest of the occupant of an automobile, he may, as a contemporaneous incident of that arrest, search the passenger compartment of that automobile.
>
> "It follows from this conclusion that the police may also examine the contents of any containers found within the passenger compartment."

Under *Belton,* the same probable cause to believe that a container holds drugs will allow the police to arrest the person transporting the container and search it.

Finally, the search of a paper bag intrudes far less on individual privacy than does the incursion sanctioned long ago in *Carroll*. In that case, prohibition agents slashed the upholstery of the automobile. This Court nonetheless found their search to be reasonable under the Fourth Amendment. If destroying the interior of an automobile is not unreasonable, we cannot conclude that looking inside a closed container is. In light of the minimal protection to privacy afforded by the *Chadwick-Sanders* rule, and our serious doubt whether that rule substantially serves privacy interests, we now hold that the Fourth Amendment does not compel separate treatment for an automobile search that extends only to a container within the vehicle.

## V

The *Chadwick-Sanders* rule not only has failed to protect privacy but it has also confused courts and police officers and impeded effective law enforcement. The conflict between the *Carroll* doctrine cases and the *Chadwick-Sanders* line has been criticized in academic commentary. One leading authority on the Fourth Amendment, after comparing *Chadwick* and *Sanders* with *Carroll* and its progeny, observed: "These two lines of authority cannot be completely reconciled, and thus how one comes out in the container-in-the-car situation depends upon which line of authority is used as a point of departure." 3 W. LaFave, Search & Seizure 53 (2d ed. 1987).

The discrepancy between the two rules has led to confusion for law enforcement officers. For example, when an officer, who has developed probable cause to believe that a vehicle contains drugs, begins to search the vehicle and immediately discovers a closed container, which rule applies? The defendant will argue that the fact that the officer first chose to search the container indicates that his probable cause extended only to the container and that *Chadwick* and *Sanders* therefore require a warrant. On the other hand, the fact that the officer first chose to search in the most obvious location should not restrict the propriety of the search. The *Chadwick* rule, as applied in *Sanders,* has devolved into an anomaly such that the more likely the police are to discover drugs in a container, the less authority they have to search it. We have noted the virtue of providing "'clear and unequivocal' guidelines to the law enforcement profession." The *Chadwick-Sanders* rule is the antithesis of a "'clear and unequivocal' guideline."

The dissent argues that law enforcement has not been impeded because the Court has decided 29 Fourth Amendment cases since *Ross* in favor of the government. In each of these cases, the government appeared as the petitioner. The dissent fails to explain how the loss of 29 cases below, not to mention the many others which this Court did not hear, did not interfere with law enforcement. The fact that the state courts and the federal courts of appeals have been reversed in their Fourth Amendment holdings 29 times since 1982 further demonstrates the extent to which our Fourth Amendment jurisprudence has confused the courts.

The *Chadwick* dissenters predicted that the container rule would have "the perverse result of allowing fortuitous circumstances to control the outcome" of various searches. The rule also was so confusing that within two years after *Chadwick,* this Court found it necessary to expound on the meaning of that decision and explain its application to luggage in general. *Sanders.* Again, dissenters bemoaned the "inherent opaqueness" of the difference between the *Carroll* and *Chadwick* principles and noted "the confusion to be created for all concerned." Three years after *Sanders,* we returned in *Ross* to "this troubled area," in order to assert that *Sanders* had not cut back on *Carroll.*

Although we have recognized firmly that the doctrine of *stare decisis* serves profoundly important purposes in our legal system, this Court has overruled a prior case on the comparatively rare occasion when it has bred confusion or been a derelict or led to anomalous results. *Sanders* was explicitly undermined in *Ross,* and the existence of the dual regimes for automobile searches that uncover containers has proved as confusing as the *Chadwick* and *Sanders* dissenters predicted. We conclude that it is better to adopt one clear-cut rule to govern automobile searches and eliminate the warrant requirement for closed containers set forth in *Sanders.*

## VI

The interpretation of the *Carroll* doctrine set forth in *Ross* now applies to all searches of containers found in an automobile. In other words, the police may search without a warrant if their search is supported by probable cause. The Court in *Ross* put it this way: "The scope of a warrantless search of an automobile . . . is not defined by the nature of the container in which the contraband is secreted. Rather, it is defined by the object of the search and the places in which there is probable cause to believe that it may be found." It went on to note: "Probable cause to believe that a container placed in the trunk of a taxi contains contraband or evidence does not justify a search of the entire cab." We reaffirm that principle. In the case before us, the police had probable cause to believe that the paper bag in the automobile's trunk contained marijuana. That probable cause now allows a warrantless search of the paper bag. The facts in the record reveal that the police did not have probable cause to believe that contraband was hidden in any other part of the automobile and a search of the entire vehicle would have been without probable cause and unreasonable under the Fourth Amendment.

Our holding today neither extends the *Carroll* doctrine nor broadens the scope of the permissible automobile search delineated in *Carroll, Chambers,* and *Ross.* It remains a "cardinal principle that 'searches conducted outside the judicial process, without prior approval by judge or magistrate, are *per se* unreasonable under the Fourth Amendment—subject only to a few specifically established and well-delineated exceptions.'" We held in *Ross:* "The exception recognized in *Carroll* is unquestionably one that is 'specifically established and well delineated.'"

Until today, this Court has drawn a curious line between the search of an automobile that coincidentally turns up a container and the search of a container that coincidentally turns up in an automobile. The protections of the Fourth Amendment must not turn on such coincidences. We therefore interpret *Carroll* as providing one rule to govern all automobile searches. The police may search an automobile and the containers within it where they have probable cause to believe contraband or evidence is contained.

The judgment of the California Court of Appeal is reversed and the case is remanded to that court for further proceedings not inconsistent with this opinion.

Justice SCALIA, concurring in the judgment

I agree with the dissent that it is anomalous for a briefcase to be protected by the "general requirement" of a prior warrant when it is being carried along the street, but for that same briefcase to become unprotected as soon as it is carried into an automobile. On the other hand, I agree with the Court that it would be anomalous for a locked compartment in an automobile to be unprotected by the "general requirement" of a prior warrant, but for an unlocked briefcase within the automobile to be protected. I join in the judgment of the Court because I think its holding is more faithful to the text and tradition of the Fourth Amendment, and if these anomalies in our jurisprudence are ever to be eliminated that is the direction in which we should travel.

The Fourth Amendment does not by its terms require a prior warrant for searches and seizures; it merely prohibits searches and seizures that are "unreasonable." What it explicitly states regarding warrants is by way of limitation upon their issuance rather than requirement of their use. For the warrant was a means of insulating officials from personal liability assessed by colonial juries. An officer who searched or seized without a warrant did so at his own risk; he would be liable for trespass, including exemplary damages, unless the jury found that his action was "reasonable." If, however, the officer acted pursuant to a proper warrant, he would be absolutely immune. By restricting the issuance of warrants, the Framers endeavored to preserve the jury's role in regulating searches and seizures.

Although the Fourth Amendment does not explicitly impose the requirement of a warrant, it is of course textually possible to consider that implicit within the requirement of reasonableness. For some years after the (still continuing) explosion in Fourth Amendment litigation that followed our announcement of the exclusionary rule in *Weeks v. United States,* 232 U.S. 383 (1914), our jurisprudence lurched back and forth between imposing a categorical warrant requirement and looking to reasonableness alone. By the late 1960's, the preference for a warrant had won out, at least rhetorically. See *Chimel; Coolidge.*

The victory was illusory. Even before today's decision, the "warrant requirement" had become so riddled with exceptions that it was basically unrecognizable. In 1985, one commentator cataloged nearly 20 such exceptions, including "searches incident to arrest . . . automobile searches . . . border searches . . . administrative searches of regulated businesses . . . exigent circumstances . . . search[es] incident to nonarrest when there is probable cause to arrest . . . boat boarding for document checks . . . welfare searches . . . inventory searches . . . airport searches . . . school search[es]. . . ." Bradley, Two Models of the Fourth Amendment, 83 Mich.L.Rev. 1468, 1473-1474 (1985). Since then, we have added at least two more. *Carney* (searches of mobile homes); *O'Connor v. Ortega,* 480 U.S. 709 (1987) (searches of offices of government employees). Our intricate body of law regarding "reasonable expectation of privacy" has been developed largely as a means of creating these exceptions, enabling a search to be denominated not a Fourth Amendment "search" and therefore not subject to the general warrant requirement.

Unlike the dissent, therefore, I do not regard today's holding as some momentous departure, but rather as merely the continuation of an inconsistent jurisprudence that has been with us for years. Cases like *Chadwick* and *Sanders* have taken the "preference for a warrant" seriously, while cases like *Ross* and *Carroll* have not. There can be no clarity in this area unless we make up our minds, and unless the principles we express comport with the actions we take.

In my view, the path out of this confusion should be sought by returning to the first principle that the "reasonableness" requirement of the Fourth Amendment affords the protection that the common law afforded. I have no difficulty with the proposition that that includes the requirement of a warrant, where the common law required a warrant; and it may even be that changes in the surrounding legal rules (for example, elimination of the common-law rule that reasonable, good-faith belief was no defense to absolute liability for trespass) may make a warrant indispensable to reasonableness where it once was not. But the supposed "general rule" that a warrant is always required does not appear to have any basis in the common law, and confuses rather than facilitates any attempt to develop rules of reasonableness in light of changed legal circumstances, as the anomaly eliminated and the anomaly created by today's holding both demonstrate.

And there are more anomalies still. Under our precedents (as at common law), a person may be arrested outside the home on the basis of probable cause, without an arrest warrant. *Watson.* Upon arrest, the person, as well as the area within his grasp, may be searched for evidence related to the crime. *Chimel.* Under these principles, if a known drug dealer is carrying a briefcase reasonably believed to contain marijuana (the unauthorized possession of which is a crime), the police may arrest him and search his person on the basis of probable cause alone. And, under our precedents, upon arrival at the station house, the police may inventory his possessions, including the briefcase, even if there is no reason to suspect that they contain contraband. *Illinois v. Lafayette,* 462 U.S. 640 (1983). According to our current law, however, the police may not, on the basis of the same probable cause, take the less intrusive step of stopping the individual on the street and demanding to see the contents of his briefcase. That makes no sense *a priori,* and in the absence of any common-law tradition supporting such a distinction, I see no reason to continue it.

\* \* \*

I would reverse the judgment in the present case, not because a closed container carried inside a car becomes subject to the "automobile" exception to the general warrant requirement, but because the search of a closed container, outside a privately owned building, with probable cause to believe that the container contains contraband, and when it in fact does contain contraband, is not one of those searches whose Fourth Amendment reasonableness depends upon a warrant. For that reason I concur in the judgment of the Court.

Justice STEVENS, with whom Justice MARSHALL, joins; and with whom Justice WHITE substantially joins, dissenting.

At the end of its opinion, the Court pays lip service to the proposition that should provide the basis for a correct analysis of the legal question presented by this case: It is "a cardinal principle that 'searches conducted outside the judicial process, without prior approval by judge or magistrate, are *per se* unreasonable under the Fourth Amendment—subject only to a few specifically established and well-delineated exceptions.'"

Relying on arguments that conservative judges have repeatedly rejected in past cases, the Court today—despite its disclaimer to the contrary, enlarges the scope of the automobile exception to this "cardinal principle," which undergirded our Fourth Amendment jurisprudence prior to the retirement of the author of the landmark opinion in *Chadwick.* As a preface to my response to the Court's arguments,

it is appropriate to restate the basis for the warrant requirement, the significance of the *Chadwick* case, and the reasons why the limitations on the automobile exception that were articulated in *Ross,* represent a fair accommodation between the basic rule requiring prior judicial approval of searches and the automobile exception.

I

The Fourth Amendment is a restraint on Executive power. The Amendment constitutes the Framers' direct constitutional response to the unreasonable law enforcement practices employed by agents of the British Crown. Over the years—particularly in the period immediately after World War II and particularly in opinions authored by Justice Jackson after his service as a special prosecutor at the Nuremberg trials—the Court has recognized the importance of this restraint as a bulwark against police practices that prevail in totalitarian regimes.

This history is, however, only part of the explanation for the warrant requirement. The requirement also reflects the sound policy judgment that, absent exceptional circumstances, the decision to invade the privacy of an individual's personal effects should be made by a neutral magistrate rather than an agent of the Executive. In his opinion for the Court in *Johnson v. United States,* Justice Jackson explained: "The point of the Fourth Amendment, which often is not grasped by zealous officers, is not that it denies law enforcement the support of the usual inferences which reasonable men draw from evidence. Its protection consists in requiring that those inferences be drawn by a neutral and detached magistrate instead of being judged by the officer engaged in the often competitive enterprise of ferreting out crime."

Our decisions have always acknowledged that the warrant requirement imposes a burden on law enforcement. And our cases have not questioned that trained professionals normally make reliable assessments of the existence of probable cause to conduct a search. We have repeatedly held, however, that these factors are outweighed by the individual interest in privacy that is protected by advance judicial approval. The Fourth Amendment dictates that the privacy interest is paramount, no matter how marginal the risk of error might be if the legality of warrantless searches were judged only after the fact.

In the concluding paragraph of his opinion in *Chadwick,* Chief Justice Burger made the point this way: "Even though on this record the issuance of a warrant by a judicial officer was reasonably predictable, a line must be drawn. In our view, when no exigency is shown to support the need for an immediate search, the Warrant Clause places the line at the point where the property to be searched comes under the exclusive dominion of police authority. Respondents were therefore entitled to the protection of the Warrant Clause with the evaluation of a neutral magistrate, before their privacy interests in the contents of [their luggage] were invaded.''

Two Terms after *Chadwick*, we decided [*Sanders*], a case in which the relevant facts were identical to those before the Court today.

Chief Justice Burger wrote separately to identify the distinction between cases in which police have probable cause to believe contraband is located somewhere in a vehicle—the typical automobile exception case—and cases like *Chadwick* and *Sanders* in which they had probable cause to search a particular container before it was placed in the car.

Chief Justice Burger thus carefully explained that *Sanders*, which the Court overrules today, ''simply d[id] not present the question of whether a warrant is required before opening luggage when the police have probable cause to believe contraband is located somewhere in the vehicle, but when they do not know whether, for example, it is inside a piece of luggage in the trunk, in the glove compartment, or concealed in some part of the car's structure.''

We held in *Ross* that ''the scope of the warrantless search authorized by [the automobile] exception is no broader and no narrower than a magistrate could legitimately authorize by warrant.'' The inherent mobility of the vehicle justified the immediate search without a warrant, but did not affect the scope of the search. Thus, the search could encompass containers, which might or might not conceal the object of the search, as well as the remainder of the vehicle.

Our conclusion was supported not only by prior cases defining the proper scope of searches authorized by warrant, as well as cases involving the automobile exception, but also by practical considerations that apply to searches in which the police have only generalized probable cause to believe that contraband is somewhere in a vehicle. We explained that, in such instances, ''prohibiting police from opening immediately a container in which the object of the search is most likely to be found and instead forcing them first to comb the entire vehicle would actually exacerbate the intrusion on privacy interests.'' Indeed, because ''the police could never be certain that the contraband was not secreted in a yet undiscovered portion of the vehicle,'' the most likely result would be that ''the vehicle would need to be secured while a warrant was obtained.''

These concerns that justified our holding in *Ross* are not implicated in cases like *Chadwick* and *Sanders* in which the police have probable cause to search a *particular* container rather than the *entire* vehicle. Because the police can seize the container which is the object of their search, they have no need either to search or to seize the entire vehicle. Indeed, as even the Court today recognizes, they have no authority to do so.

In reaching our conclusion in *Ross,* we therefore did not retreat at all from the holding in either *Chadwick* or *Sanders*. Instead, we expressly endorsed the reasoning in Chief Justice Burger's separate opinion in *Sanders*. We explained repeatedly that *Ross* involved the scope of the warrantless search authorized by the automobile exception, and, unlike *Chadwick* and *Sanders,* did not involve the applicability of the exception to closed containers.

Thus, we recognized in *Ross* that *Chadwick* and *Sanders* had not created a special rule for container searches, but rather had merely applied the cardinal principle that warrantless searches are *per se* unreasonable unless justified by an exception to the general rule.[8] *Ross* dealt with the scope of the automobile exception; *Chadwick* and *Sanders* were cases in which the exception simply did not apply.

## II

In its opinion today, the Court recognizes that the police did not have probable cause to search respondent's vehicle and that a search of anything but the paper bag that respondent had carried from Daza's apartment and placed in the trunk of his car would have been unconstitutional. Moreover, as I read the opinion, the Court assumes that the police could not have made a warrantless inspection of the bag before it was placed in the car. Finally, the Court also does not question the fact that, under our prior cases, it would have been lawful for the police to seize the container and detain it (and respondent) until they obtained a search warrant. Thus, all of the relevant facts that governed our decisions in *Chadwick* and *Sanders* are present here whereas the relevant fact that justified the vehicle search in *Ross* is not present.

The Court does not attempt to identify any exigent circumstances that would justify its refusal to

---

[8] Although the Court today purports to acknowledge that the warrant requirement is the general rule, it nonetheless inexplicably persists in referring to *Chadwick* and *Sanders* as announcing a ''separate rule, unique to luggage and other closed packages, bags, and containers.'' Equally inexplicable is the Court's contention that, in overruling *Sanders,* it has not ''extend[ed] the *Carroll* doctrine'' that created the automobile exception.

apply the general rule against warrantless searches. Instead, it advances these three arguments: First, the rules identified in the foregoing cases are confusing and anomalous. Second, the rules do not protect any significant interest in privacy. And, third, the rules impede effective law enforcement. None of these arguments withstands scrutiny.

### The "Confusion"

In the case the Court decides today, the California Court of Appeal also had no difficulty applying the critical distinction. Relying on *Chadwick,* it explained that "the officers had probable cause to believe marijuana would be found only in a brown lunch bag and nowhere else in the car. We are compelled to hold they should have obtained a search warrant before opening it."

In the case in which the police had probable cause to search two vehicles, *Johns,* we rejected the respondent's reliance on *Chadwick* with a straightforward explanation of why that case, unlike *Ross,* did not involve an exception to the warrant requirement. We first expressed our agreement with the Court of Appeals that the Customs officers who had conducted the search had probable cause to search the vehicles. We then explained: "Under the circumstances of this case, respondents' reliance on *Chadwick* is misplaced. . . . *Chadwick* . . . did not involve the exception to the warrant requirement recognized in *Carroll* because the police had no probable cause to believe that the automobile, as contrasted to the footlocker, contained contraband. This point is underscored by our decision in *Ross,* which held that notwithstanding *Chadwick* police officers may conduct a warrantless search of containers discovered in the course of a lawful vehicle search. Given our conclusion that the Customs officers had probable cause to believe that the pickup trucks contained contraband, *Chadwick* is simply inapposite.

The decided cases thus provide no support for the Court's concern about "confusion." The Court instead relies primarily on predictions that were made by Justice Blackmun in his dissenting opinions in *Chadwick* and *Sanders.* The Court, however, cites no evidence that these predictions have in fact materialized or that anyone else has been unable to understand the "inherent opaqueness" of this uncomplicated issue. The only support offered by the Court, other than the unsubstantiated allegations of prior dissents, is three law review comments and a sentence from Professor LaFave's treatise. None of the law review pieces criticizes the holdings in *Chadwick* and *Sanders.* The sentence from Professor LaFave's treatise, at most, indicates that, as is often the case, there may be some factual situations at the margin of the relevant rules that are difficult to decide. Moreover, to the extent Professor LaFave criticizes our jurisprudence in this area, he is critical of *Ross* rather than *Chadwick* or *Sanders.* And he ultimately concludes that even *Ross* was correctly decided.

The Court summarizes the alleged "anomaly" created by the coexistence of *Ross, Chadwick,* and *Sanders* with the statement that "the more likely the police are to discover drugs in a container, the less authority they have to search it." This juxtaposition is only anomalous, however, if one accepts the flawed premise that the degree to which the police are likely to discover contraband is correlated with their authority to search *without a warrant.* Yet, even proof beyond a reasonable doubt will not justify a warrantless search that is not supported by one of the exceptions to the warrant requirement. And, even when the police have a warrant or an exception applies, once the police possess probable cause, the extent to which they are more or less certain of the contents of a container has no bearing on their authority to search it.

To the extent there was any "anomaly" in our prior jurisprudence, the Court has "cured" it at the expense of creating a more serious paradox. For, surely it is anomalous to prohibit a search of a briefcase while the owner is carrying it exposed on a public street yet to permit a search once the owner has placed the briefcase in the locked trunk of his car. One's privacy interest in one's luggage can certainly not be diminished by one's removing it from a public thoroughfare and placing it—out of sight—in a privately owned vehicle. Nor is the danger that evidence will escape increased if the luggage is in a car rather than on the street. In either location, if the police have probable cause, they are authorized to seize the luggage and to detain it until they obtain judicial approval for a search. Any line demarking an exception to the warrant requirement will appear blurred at the edges, but the Court has certainly erred if it believes that, by erasing one line and drawing another, it has drawn a clearer boundary.

### The Privacy Argument

The Court's statement that *Chadwick* and *Sanders* provide only "minimal protection to privacy" is also unpersuasive. Every citizen clearly has an interest in the privacy of the contents of his or her luggage, briefcase, handbag or any other container that conceals private papers and effects from public scrutiny. That privacy interest has been recognized repeatedly in cases spanning more than a century.

Under the Court's holding today, the privacy interest that protects the contents of a suitcase or a briefcase from a warrantless search when it is in public view simply vanishes when its owner climbs into a taxicab. Unquestionably the rejection of the *Sanders* line of cases by today's decision will result in a significant loss of individual privacy.

To support its argument that today's holding works only a minimal intrusion on privacy, the Court suggests that "[i]f the police know that they may open a bag only if they are actually searching the entire car, they may search more extensively than they otherwise would in order to establish the general probable cause required by *Ross*." [T]his fear is unexplained and inexplicable. Neither evidence uncovered in the course of a search nor the scope of the search conducted can be used to provide *post hoc* justification for a search unsupported by probable cause at its inception.

The Court also justifies its claim that its holding inflicts only minor damage by suggesting that, under *Belton,* the police could have arrested respondent and searched his bag if respondent had placed the bag in the passenger compartment of the automobile instead of the trunk. In *Belton,* however, the justification for stopping the car and arresting the driver had nothing to do with the subsequent search, which was based on the potential danger to the arresting officer.

### The Burden on Law Enforcement

The Court's suggestion that *Chadwick* and *Sanders* have created a significant burden on effective law enforcement is unsupported, inaccurate, and, in any event, an insufficient reason for creating a new exception to the warrant requirement.

Despite repeated claims that *Chadwick* and *Sanders* have "impeded effective law enforcement," the Court cites no authority for its contentions. Moreover, all evidence that does exist points to the contrary conclusion. In the years since *Ross* was decided, the Court has heard argument in 30 Fourth Amendment cases involving narcotics. In all but one, the government was the petitioner. All save two involved a search or seizure without a warrant or with a defective warrant. And, in all except three, the Court upheld the constitutionality of the search or seizure.

In the meantime, the flow of narcotics cases through the courts has steadily and dramatically increased. No impartial observer could criticize this Court for hindering the progress of the war on drugs. On the contrary, decisions like the one the Court makes today will support the conclusion that this Court has become a loyal foot soldier in the Executive's fight against crime.

Even if the warrant requirement does inconvenience the police to some extent, that fact does not distinguish this constitutional requirement from any other procedural protection secured by the Bill of Rights. It is merely a part of the price that our society must pay in order to preserve its freedom. Thus, in a unanimous opinion that relied on both *Johnson* and *Chadwick,* Justice Stewart wrote: "Moreover, the mere fact that law enforcement may be made more efficient can never by itself justify disregard of the Fourth Amendment. The investigation of crime would always be simplified if warrants were unnecessary. But the Fourth Amendment reflects the view of those who wrote the Bill of Rights that the privacy of a person's home and property may not be totally sacrificed in the name of maximum simplicity in enforcement of the criminal law." *Mincey v. Arizona* (1978).

It is too early to know how much freedom America has lost today. The magnitude of the loss is, however, not nearly as significant as the Court's willingness to inflict it without even a colorable basis for its rejection of prior law.

I respectfully dissent.

## QUESTIONS AND NOTES

**1.** Would our jurisprudence be improved if the Court forthrightly adopted the Scalia approach? What, if anything, would be lost?

**2.** Did Justice Scalia really mean to make anything turn on whether, *in fact,* evidence was found in the bag? Is Scalia suggesting that if the probable cause turned out to be wrong, and that Acevedo merely had lunch in his bag, Acevedo could sue the police officer?

**3.** If the Stevens opinion had prevailed, and the *Sanders-Ross* dichotomy had been maintained, what would (should) have been the result in a case in which a reliable informant tells a police officer that a particular individual has drugs in a suitcase, *currently* in the trunk of a particularly described car?

**4.** Does the Court's opinion bring clarity to the area? Was it all that confused to begin with?

**5.** What, if any, costs are associated with the Court's opinion?

## C.   Search Incident To Arrest In An Automobile

In addition to probable cause searches of automobiles (and containers within automobiles), a *Chimel* search incident to arrest can occur when an individual is arrested in his automobile (or presumably motor home). The permissible scope of that search is explored in *Belton,* a companion case to the ill-fated *Robbins* case that was overruled in *Ross.* One of the questions that you should think about in conjunction with *Belton* is whether it too should be overruled now that we have *Ross* and *Acevedo* which allow extensive searches based on probable cause.

### Belton v. New York
### 453 U.S. 454 (1981)

Mr. Justice STEWART delivered the opinion of the Court.

When the occupant of an automobile is subjected to a lawful custodial arrest, does the constitutionally permissible scope of a search incident to his arrest include the passenger compartment of the automobile in which he was riding? That is the question at issue in the present case.

#### I

On April 9, 1978, Trooper Douglas Nicot, a New York State policeman driving an unmarked car on the New York Thruway, was passed by another automobile traveling at an excessive rate of speed. Nicot gave chase, overtook the speeding vehicle, and ordered its driver to pull it over to the side of the road and stop. There were four men in the car, one of whom was Roger Belton, the respondent in this case. The policeman asked to see the driver's license and automobile registration, and discovered that none of the men owned the vehicle or was related to its owner. Meanwhile, the policeman had smelled burnt marihuana and had seen on the floor of the car an envelope marked "Supergold" that he associated with marihuana. He therefore directed the men to get out of the car, and placed them under arrest for the unlawful possession of marihuana. He patted down each of the men and "split them up into four separate areas of the Thruway at this time so they would not be in physical touching area of each other." He then picked up the envelope marked "Supergold" and found that it contained marihuana. After giving the arrestees the warnings required by *Miranda v. Arizona,* the state policeman searched each one of them. He then searched the passenger compartment of the car. On the back seat he found

a black leather jacket belonging to Belton. He unzipped one of the pockets of the jacket and discovered cocaine. Placing the jacket in his automobile, he drove the four arrestees to a nearby police station.

#### II

It is a first principle of Fourth Amendment jurisprudence that the police may not conduct a search unless they first convince a neutral magistrate that there is probable cause to do so. This Court has recognized, however, that "the exigencies of the situation" may sometimes make exemption from the warrant requirement "imperative." Specifically, the Court held in *Chimel* that a lawful custodial arrest creates a situation which justifies the contemporaneous search without a warrant of the person arrested and of the immediately surrounding area. Such searches have long been considered valid because of the need "to remove any weapons that [the arrestee] might seek to use in order to resist arrest or effect his escape" and the need to prevent the concealment or destruction of evidence.

The Court's opinion in *Chimel* emphasized the principle that "the scope of [a] search must be 'strictly tied to and justified by' the circumstances which rendered its initiation permissible." Thus while the Court in *Chimel* found "ample justification" for a search of "the area from within which [an arrestee] might gain possession of a weapon or destructible evidence," the Court found "no comparable justification . . . for routinely searching any room other than that in which an arrest occurs – or, for that matter, for searching through all the desk drawers or other closed or concealed areas in that room itself."

Although the principle that limits a search incident to a lawful custodial arrest may be stated clearly enough, courts have discovered the principle difficult to apply in specific cases. Yet, as one commentator has pointed out, the protection of the Fourth and Fourteenth Amendments "can only be realized if the police are acting under a set of rules which, in most instances, makes it possible to reach a correct determination beforehand as to whether an invasion of privacy is justified in the interest of law enforcement." LaFave, "Case-By-Case Adjudication" Versus "Standardized Procedures": The Robinson Dilemma, 1974 S.Ct.Rev. 127, 142. This is because

"Fourth Amendment doctrine, given force and effect by the exclusionary rule, is primarily intended to regulate the police in their day-to-day activities and thus ought to be expressed in terms that are readily applicable by the police in the context of the law enforcement activities in which they are necessarily engaged. A highly sophisticated set of rules, qualified by all sorts of ifs, ands, and buts and requiring the drawing of subtle nuances and hairline distinctions, may be the sort of heady stuff upon which the facile minds of lawyers and judges eagerly feed, but they may be 'literally impossible of application by the officer in the field.'"

In short, "[a] single, familiar standard is essential to guide police officers, who have only limited time and expertise to reflect on and balance the social and individual interests involved in the specific circumstances they confront."

So it was that, in *United States v. Robinson*, 414 U.S. 218, the Court hewed to a straightforward rule, easily applied, and predictably enforced: "[I]n the case of a lawful custodial arrest a full search of the person is not only an exception to the warrant requirement of the Fourth Amendment, but is also a 'reasonable' search under that Amendment." In so holding, the Court rejected the suggestion that "there must be litigated in each case the issue of whether or not there was present one of the reasons supporting the authority for a search of the person incident to a lawful arrest."

But no straightforward rule has emerged from the litigated cases respecting the question involved here—the question of the proper scope of a search of the interior of an automobile incident to a lawful custodial arrest of its occupants. The difficulty courts have had is reflected in the conflicting views of the New York judges who dealt with the problem in the present case, and is confirmed by a look at even a small sample drawn from the narrow class of cases in which courts have decided whether, in the course of a search incident to the lawful custodial arrest of the occupants of an automobile, police may search inside the automobile after the arrestees are no longer in it. On the one hand, decisions have

upheld such warrantless searches as incident to lawful arrests. On the other hand, such searches, in comparable factual circumstances, have been held constitutionally invalid.

When a person cannot know how a court will apply a settled principle to a recurring factual situation, that person cannot know the scope of his constitutional protection, nor can a policeman know the scope of his authority. While the *Chimel* case established that a search incident to an arrest may not stray beyond the area within the immediate control of the arrestee, courts have found no workable definition of "the area within the immediate control of the arrestee" when that area arguably includes the interior of an automobile and the arrestee is its recent occupant. Our reading of the cases suggests the generalization that articles inside the relatively narrow compass of the passenger compartment of an automobile are in fact generally, even if not inevitably, within "the area into which an arrestee might reach in order to grab a weapon or evidentiary ite[m]." In order to establish the workable rule this category of cases requires, we read *Chimel*'s definition of the limits of the area that may be searched in light of that generalization. Accordingly, we hold that when a policeman has made a lawful custodial arrest of the occupant of an automobile, he may, as a contemporaneous incident of that arrest, search the passenger compartment of that automobile.[3]

It follows from this conclusion that the police may also examine the contents of any containers found within the passenger compartment, for if the passenger compartment is within reach of the arrestee, so also will containers in it be within his reach.[4] Such a container may, of course, be searched whether it is open or closed, since the justification for the search is not that the arrestee has no privacy interest in the container, but that the lawful custodial arrest justifies the infringement of any privacy interest the arrestee may have. Thus, while the Court in

---

[3] Our holding today does no more than determine the meaning of *Chimel*'s principles in this particular and problematic content. It in no way alters the fundamental principles established in the *Chimel* case regarding the basic scope of searches incident to lawful custodial arrests.

[4] "Container" here denotes any object capable of holding another object. It thus includes closed or open glove compartments, consoles, or other receptacles located anywhere within the passenger compartment, as well as luggage, boxes, bags, clothing, and the like. Our holding encompasses only the interior of the passenger compartment of an automobile and does not encompass the trunk.

*Chimel* held that the police could not search all the drawers in an arrestee's house simply because the police had arrested him at home, the Court noted that drawers within an arrestee's reach could be searched because of the danger their contents might pose to the police.

It is true, of course, that these containers will sometimes be such that they could hold neither a weapon nor evidence of the criminal conduct for which the suspect was arrested. However, in *Robinson,* the Court rejected the argument that such a container—there a "crumpled up cigarette package"—located during a search of Robinson incident to his arrest could not be searched: "The authority to search the person incident to a lawful custodial arrest, while based upon the need to disarm and to discover evidence, does not depend on what a court may later decide was the probability in a particular arrest situation that weapons or evidence would in fact be found upon the person of the suspect. A custodial arrest of a suspect based on probable cause is a reasonable intrusion under the Fourth Amendment; that intrusion being lawful, a search incident to the arrest requires no additional justification."

The New York Court of Appeals relied upon *Chadwick,* and *Sanders,* concluding that the search and seizure in the present case were constitutionally invalid.[5] But neither of those cases involved an arguably valid search incident to a lawful custodial arrest. As the Court pointed out in the *Chadwick* case: "Here the search was conducted more than an hour after federal agents had gained exclusive control of the footlocker and long after respondents were securely in custody; the search therefore cannot be viewed as incidental to the arrest or as justified by any other exigency." And in the *Sanders* case, the Court explicitly stated that it did not "consider the constitutionality of searches of luggage incident to the arrest of its possessor. The State has not argued that respondent's suitcase was searched incident to his arrest, and it appears that the bag was not within his 'immediate control' at the time of the search."

---

[5] It seems to have been the theory of the Court of Appeals that the search and seizure in the present case could not have been incident to the respondent's arrest, because Trooper Nicot, by the very act of searching the respondent's jacket and seizing the contents of its pocket, had gained "exclusive control" of them. But under this fallacious theory no search or seizure incident to a lawful custodial arrest would ever be valid; by seizing an article even on the arrestee's person, an officer may be said to have reduced that article to his "exclusive control."

## III

It is not questioned that the respondent was the subject of a lawful custodial arrest on a charge of possessing marihuana. The search of the respondent's jacket followed immediately upon that arrest. The jacket was located inside the passenger compartment of the car in which the respondent had been a passenger just before he was arrested. The jacket was thus within the area which we have concluded was "within the arrestee's immediate control" within the meaning of *Chimel.*[6] The search of the jacket, therefore, was a search incident to a lawful custodial arrest, and it did not violate the Fourth and Fourteenth Amendments. Accordingly, the judgment is reversed.

Justice BRENNAN, with whom Justice MARSHALL joins, dissenting.

The *Chimel* exception to the warrant requirement was designed with two principal concerns in mind: the safety of the arresting officer and the preservation of easily concealed or destructible evidence. Recognizing that a suspect might have access to weapons or contraband at the time of arrest, the Court declared:

"When an arrest is made, it is reasonable for the arresting officer to search the person arrested in order to remove any weapons that the latter might seek to use in order to resist arrest or effect his escape. Otherwise, the officer's safety might well be endangered, and the arrest itself frustrated. In addition, it is entirely reasonable for the arresting officer to search for and seize any evidence on the arrestee's person in order to prevent its concealment or destruction. And the area into which an arrestee might reach in order to grab a weapon or evidentiary items must, of course, be governed by a like rule."

The *Chimel* standard was narrowly tailored to address these concerns: it permits police officers who have effected a custodial arrest to conduct a warrantless search "of the arrestee's person and the area 'within his immediate control'—construing that phrase to mean the area from within which he might

---

[6] Because of this disposition of the case, there is no need here to consider whether the search and seizure were permissible under the so-called "automobile exception."

gain possession of a weapon or destructible evidence.'' It thus places a temporal and a spatial limitation on searches incident to arrest, excusing compliance with the warrant requirement only when the search "is substantially contemporaneous with the arrest and is confined to the *immediate* vicinity of the arrest.'' When the arrest has been consummated and the arrestee safely taken into custody, the justifications underlying Chimel's limited exception to the warrant requirement cease to apply: at that point there is no possibility that the arrestee could reach weapons or contraband.

## II

As the facts of this case make clear, the Court today substantially expands the permissible scope of searches incident to arrest by permitting police officers to search areas and containers the arrestee could not possibly reach at the time of arrest. These facts demonstrate that at the time Belton and his three companions were placed under custodial arrest — which was *after* they had been removed from the car, patted down, and separated — none of them could have reached the jackets that had been left on the back seat of the car. The New York Court of Appeals described the sequence of events as follows:

"On April 9, 1978 defendant and three companions were traveling on the New York State Thruway in Ontario County when their car was stopped by a State trooper for speeding. Upon approaching the vehicle, the officer smelled the distinct odor of marijuana emanating from within and observed on the floor an envelope which he recognized as a type that is commonly used to sell the substance. At that point the officer ordered the occupants out of the vehicle, patted each down, removed the envelope from the floor and ascertained that it contained a small amount of marijuana. *After the marijuana was found, the individuals, still standing outside the car, were placed under arrest. The officer then re-entered the vehicle, searched the passenger compartment* and seized the marihuana cigarette butts lying in the ashtrays. *He also rifled through the pockets of five jackets on the back seat.* Upon opening the zippered pocket of one of them, he discovered a small amount of cocaine and defendant's identification.'' (emphasis added).

Concluding that a "warrantless search of the zippered pockets of an *unaccessible jacket* may not be

upheld as a search incident to a lawful arrest where there is *no longer any danger that the arrestee or a confederate might gain access to the article.*'' (emphasis added), the court further stated:

"One searches the record in vain for support of the dissenter's claim that at the time of the arrest — the point from which the predicate for the warrantless search is measured — 'the jackets were within reach of the four suspects and had not yet been reduced to the exclusive control of the officer.'"

By approving the constitutionality of the warrantless search in this case, the Court carves out a dangerous precedent that is not justified by the concerns underlying *Chimel*. Disregarding the principle "that the scope of a warrantless search must be commensurate with the rationale that excepts the search from the warrant requirement,'' the Court for the first time grants police officers authority to conduct a warrantless "area" search under circumstances where there is no chance that the arrestee "might gain possession of a weapon or destructible evidence.'' Under the approach taken today, the result would presumably be the same even if Officer Nicot had handcuffed Belton and his companions in the patrol car before placing them under arrest, and even if his search had extended to locked luggage or other inaccessible containers located in the back seat of the car.

This expansion of the *Chimel* exception is both analytically unsound and inconsistent with every significant search-incident-to-arrest case we have decided in which the issue was whether the police could lawfully conduct a warrantless search of the area surrounding the arrestee.

## III

The Court seeks to justify its departure from the principles underlying *Chimel* by proclaiming the need for a new "bright-line" rule to guide the officer in the field. As we pointed out in *Mincey v. Arizona*, however, "the mere fact that law enforcement may be made more efficient can never by itself justify disregard of the Fourth Amendment.'' Moreover, the Court's attempt to forge a "bright-line" rule fails on its own terms. While the "interior/trunk" distinction may provide a workable guide in certain routine cases — for example, where the officer arrests the driver of a car and then immediately searches the seats and floor — in the long run, I suspect it will create far more problems than it solves. The Court's new approach leaves open too many questions and, more important, it provides the police and the courts with too few tools with which to find the answers.

Thus, although the Court concludes that a warrantless search of a car may take place even though the suspect was arrested outside the car, it does not indicate how long after the suspect's arrest that search may validly be conducted. Would a warrantless search incident to arrest be valid if conducted five minutes after the suspect left his car? Thirty minutes? Three hours? Does it matter whether the suspect is standing in close proximity to the car when the search is conducted? Does it matter whether the police formed probable cause to arrest before or after the suspect left his car? And *why* is the rule announced today necessarily limited to searches of cars? What if a suspect is seen walking out of a house where the police, peering in from outside, had formed probable cause to believe a crime was being committed? Could the police then arrest that suspect and enter the house to conduct a search incident to arrest? Even assuming today's rule is limited to searches of the "interior" of cars – an assumption not demanded by logic – what is meant by "interior?" Does it include locked glove compartments, the interior of door panels, or the area under the floorboards? Are special rules necessary for station wagons and hatchbacks, where the luggage compartment may be reached through the interior, or taxicabs, where a glass panel might separate the driver's compartment from the rest of the car? Are the only containers that may be searched those that are large enough to be "capable of holding another object?" Or does the new rule apply to any container even if it "could hold neither a weapon nor evidence of the criminal conduct for which the suspect was arrested?"

The Court does not give the police any "bright-line" answers to these questions. More important, because the Court's new rule abandons the justifications underlying *Chimel, it offers no guidance to the police officer seeking to work out these answers for himself.* As we warned in *Chimel*: "No consideration relevant to the Fourth Amendment suggests any point of rational limitation, once the search is allowed to go beyond the area from which the person arrested might obtain weapons or evidentiary items." By failing to heed this warning, the Court has undermined rather than furthered the goal of consistent law enforcement: it has failed to offer any principles to guide the police and the courts in their application of the new rule to nonroutine situations.

Justice WHITE, with whom Justice MARSHALL joins, dissenting.

In *Robbins,* it was held that a wrapped container in the trunk of a car could not be searched without a warrant even though the trunk itself could be searched without a warrant because there was probable cause to search the car and even though there was probable cause to search the container as well. This was because of the separate interest in privacy with respect to the container. The Court now holds that as incident to the arrest of the driver or any other person in an automobile, the interior of the car and any container found therein, whether locked or not, may be not only seized but also searched even absent probable cause to believe that contraband or evidence of crime will be found. As to luggage, briefcases, or other containers this seems to me an extreme extension of *Chimel* and one to which I cannot subscribe. Even if the decision in *Robbins* had been otherwise and *Chadwick* and *Sanders* had been overruled, luggage found in the trunk of a car could not be searched without probable cause to believe it contained contraband or evidence. Here, searches of luggage, briefcases, and other containers in the interior of an auto are authorized in the absence of any suspicion whatsoever that they contain anything in which the police have a legitimate interest. This calls for more caution than the Court today exhibits, and, with respect, I dissent.

Justice STEVENS, [concurring in result (from his dissenting opinion in *Robbins,* that covered both cases)]

[I]nstead of relying on the automobile exception to uphold the search of respondent's jacket pocket, the Court takes an extraordinarily dangerous detour to reach the same result by adopting an admittedly new rationale applicable to every "lawful custodial arrest" of the occupant of an automobile.

The Court's careful and repeated use of the term "lawful custodial arrest" seems to imply that a significant distinction between custodial arrests and ordinary arrests exists. I am familiar with the distinction between a "stop," and an "arrest," but I am not familiar with any difference between custodial arrests and any other kind of arrest. It is, or course, true that persons apprehended for traffic violations are frequently not required to accompany the arresting officer to the police station before they are permitted to leave on their own recognizance or by using their driver's licenses as a form of bond. It is also possible that state law or local regulations may in some cases prohibit police officers from taking persons into custody for violation of minor traffic laws. As a matter of constitutional law, however, any person lawfully arrested for the pettiest misdemeanor may be temporarily placed in custody.[11] Indeed, as the Court has repeatedly held, every arrest is a seizure of the person within the meaning of the Fourth Amendment. The rule of constitutional law the Court fashions today therefore potentially applies to every arrest of every occupant of an automobile.

After the vehicle in which respondent was riding was stopped, the officer smelled marihuana and thereby acquired probable cause to believe that the vehicle contained contraband. A thorough search of the car was therefore reasonable. But if there were no reason to believe that anything more than a traffic violation had occurred, I should think it palpably unreasonable to require the driver of a car to open his briefcase or his luggage for inspection by the officer.[14]

---

[11] Justice Stewart apparently believes that the Fourth and Fourteenth Amendments might provide some impediment to police taking a defendant into custody for violation of a "minor traffic offense." See *Gustafson v. Florida,* 414 U.S. 260,266 (Stewart, J. concurring). Although I agree that a police officer's authority to restrain an individual's liberty should be limited in the context of stops for routine traffic violations, see *Pennsylvania v. Mimms,* 434 U.S. 106, 115 (Stevens, J. dissenting), the Court has not directly considered the question whether "there are some constitutional limits upon the use of 'custodial arrests' as the means for invoking the criminal process when relatively minor offenses are involved." See 2 W. LaFave, Search and Seizure § 5.2, p. 290 (1978). To the extent that the Court has considered the scope of an officer's authority in making routine traffic stops, the Court has not imposed constitutional restrictions on that authority. Thus the Court may be assuming that its new rule will be limited by a constitutional restriction that does not exist.

[14] It would seem equally unreasonable to require a driver to open the trunk of his car, which the Court would not permit, and to require a driver to open luggage located in the back of a station wagon, which would be permissible under the Court's rule. The

The driver so compelled, however, could make no constitutional objection to a decision by the officer to take the driver into custody and thereby obtain justification for a search of the entire interior of the vehicle. Indeed, under the Court's new rule, the arresting officer may find reason to follow that procedure whenever he sees an interesting looking briefcase or package in a vehicle that has been stopped for a traffic violation. That decision by a police officer will therefore provide the constitutional predicate for broader vehicle searches than any neutral magistrate could authorize by issuing a warrant.

The Court's reasoning, which will lead to a massive broadening of the automobile exception, is particularly unfortunate because that reasoning is not necessary to the decision. By taking the giant step of permitting searches in the absence of probable cause, the Court misses the shorter step of relying on the automobile exception to uphold the search.[15] By taking this shorter step the Court could have adhered to the fundamental distinction between a search that a magistrate could authorize because it is based on probable cause and one that is not so justified under that standard. Although I am persuaded that the Court has reached the right result, its opinion misconstrues the Fourth Amendment.

---

Court attempts to justify the search in *Belton* on the basis of the officer's safety, but Justice Brennan, dissenting, has forcefully demonstrated the inadequacy of that rationale.

[15] It is true that the State in *Belton* did not argue that the automobile exception justified the search of respondent's jacket pocket. Nevertheless, just as the admission of a piece of evidence will be affirmed if any valid reason for admission existed — even if the one relied upon by the trial judge was not valid — I would uphold the admission of this evidence if any theory justifying the search is valid. This is particularly appropriate given the State's understandable reluctance to argue an issue that many courts have considered to be foreclosed by *Sanders.*

## QUESTIONS AND NOTES

**1.** Is a bright-line rule important in this area?

**2.** How bright is this line? Does it apply to locked containers, locked glove compartments, floorboards, or the living area of a motor home? Should it?

**3.** Should it matter that at the time of the search, Belton (who was in handcuffs outside of the car) was no longer within grabbing distance of the jacket? Why?

**4.** *Belton* and *Robbins,* taken together worked something of a compromise. *Belton* allowed the passenger compartment to be searched incident to an arrest. *Robbins,* on the other hand, insisted on a warrant before the trunk could be searched. Now that *Robbins* (and *Sanders*) have been overruled, should the Court reconsider *Belton*?

**5.** Should a search *always* be permitted incident to an arrest, even if it is unlikely that the suspect is armed or that evidence will be found?

**6.** Is Justice Stevens' approach preferable to that of the Court? Why? Why not?

## D.    Suspicionless Highway Stops

In every automobile case that we have discussed thus far, the police had a particular reason to stop and search the vehicle. In none of those cases did the Government argue that the searchee was subject to a search or seizure simply because he was on the highway. In the cases that follow, that is precisely the Government's argument. It argues that because an individual is on the highway, she can be subjected to a license or sobriety check. In *Prouse* and *Sitz,* we will see how the Court dealt with this argument.

### Delaware v. Prouse
### 440 U.S. 648 (1979)

Mr. Justice WHITE delivered the opinion of the Court.

The question is whether it is an unreasonable seizure to stop an automobile, being driven on a public highway, for the purpose of checking the driving license of the operator and the registration of the car, where there is neither probable cause nor reasonable suspicion that the car is being driven contrary to the laws governing the operation of motor vehicles or that either the car or any of its occupants is subject to seizure or detention in connection with the violation of any other applicable law.

#### I

At 7:20 p.m. on November 30, 1976, a New Castle County, Del., patrolman in a police cruiser stopped an automobile occupied by respondent. The patrolman smelled marihuana smoke as he was walking toward the stopped vehicle, and he seized marihuana in plain view on the car floor. Respondent was subsequently indicted for illegal possession of a controlled substance. At a hearing on respondent's motion to suppress the marihuana seized as a result of the stop, the patrolman testified that prior to stopping the vehicle he had observed neither traffic or equipment violations nor any suspicious activity, and

that he made the stop only in order to check the driver's license and registration. The patrolman was not acting pursuant to any standards, guidelines, or procedures pertaining to document spot checks, promulgated by either his department or the State Attorney General. Characterizing the stop as "routine," the patrolman explained, "I saw the car in the area and wasn't answering any complaints, so I decided to pull them off." The trial court granted the motion to suppress, finding the stop and detention to have been wholly capricious and therefore violative of the Fourth Amendment.

#### III

The Fourth and Fourteenth Amendments are implicated in this case because stopping an automobile and detaining its occupants constitute a "seizure" within the meaning of those Amendments, even though the purpose of the stop is limited and the resulting detention quite brief. The essential purpose of the proscriptions in the Fourth Amendment is to impose a standard of "reasonableness" upon the exercise of discretion by government officials, including law enforcement agents, in order "to safeguard the privacy and security of individuals against arbitrary invasions." Thus, the permissibility of a particular law enforcement practice is judged by balancing its intrusion on the individual's Fourth Amendment interests against its promotion of legitimate governmental interests. Implemented in this manner, the reasonableness standard usually requires, at a minimum, that the facts upon which an intrusion is based be capable of measurement against "an objective standard," whether this be probable cause or a less stringent test. In those situations in which the balance of interests precludes insistence upon "some quantum of individualized suspicion," other safeguards are generally relied upon to assure that the individual's reasonable expectation of privacy is not "subject to the discretion of the official in the field."

In this case, however, the State of Delaware urges that patrol officers be subject to no constraints in deciding which automobiles shall be stopped for a license and registration check because the State's interest in discretionary spot checks as a means of ensuring the safety of its roadways outweighs the resulting intrusion on the privacy and security of the persons detained.

## V

We agree that the States have a vital interest in ensuring that only those qualified to do so are permitted to operate motor vehicles, that these vehicles are fit for safe operation, and hence that licensing, registration, and vehicle inspection requirements are being observed. Automobile licenses are issued periodically to evidence that the drivers holding them are sufficiently familiar with the rules of the road and are physically qualified to operate a motor vehicle. The registration requirement and, more pointedly, the related annual inspection requirement in Delaware are designed to keep dangerous automobiles off the road. Unquestionably, these provisions, properly administered, are essential elements in a highway safety program. Furthermore, we note that the State of Delaware requires a minimum amount of insurance coverage as a condition to automobile registration, implementing its legitimate interest in seeing to it that its citizens have protection when involved in a motor vehicle accident.

The question remains, however, whether in the service of these important ends the discretionary spot check is a sufficiently productive mechanism to justify the intrusion upon Fourth Amendment interests which such stops entail. On the record before us, that question must be answered in the negative. Given the alternative mechanisms available, both those in use and those that might be adopted, we are unconvinced that the incremental contribution to highway safety of the random spot check justifies the practice under the Fourth Amendment.

The foremost method of enforcing traffic and vehicle safety regulations, it must be recalled, is acting upon observed violations. Vehicle stops for traffic violations occur countless times each day; and on these occasions, licenses and registration papers are subject to inspection and drivers without them will be ascertained. Furthermore, drivers without licenses are presumably the less safe drivers whose propensities may well exhibit themselves. Absent some empirical data to the contrary, it must be assumed that finding an unlicensed driver among those who commit traffic violations is a much more likely event than finding an unlicensed driver by choosing randomly from the entire universe of drivers. If this were not so, licensing of drivers would hardly be an effective means of promoting roadway safety. It seems common sense that the percentage of all drivers on the road who are driving without a license is very small and that the number of licensed drivers who will be stopped in order to find one unlicensed operator will be large indeed. The contribution to highway safety made by discretionary stops selected from among drivers generally will therefore be marginal at best. Furthermore, and again absent something more than mere assertion to the contrary, we find it difficult to believe that the unlicensed driver would not be deterred by the possibility of being involved in a traffic violation or having some other experience calling for proof of his entitlement to drive but that he would be deterred by the possibility that he would be one of those chosen for a spot check. In terms of actually discovering unlicensed drivers or deterring them from driving, the spot check does not appear sufficiently productive to qualify as a reasonable law enforcement practice under the Fourth Amendment.

The marginal contribution to roadway safety possibly resulting from a system of spot checks cannot justify subjecting every occupant of every vehicle on the roads to a seizure — limited in magnitude compared to other intrusions but nonetheless constitutionally cognizable — at the unbridled discretion of law enforcement officials. To insist neither upon an appropriate factual basis for suspicion directed at a particular automobile nor upon some other substantial and objective standard or rule to govern the exercise of discretion "would invite intrusions upon constitutionally guaranteed rights based on nothing more substantial than inarticulate hunches." By hypothesis, stopping apparently safe drivers is necessary only because the danger presented by some drivers is not observable at the time of the stop. When there is not probable cause to believe that a driver is violating any one of the multitude of applicable traffic and equipment regulations – or other articulable basis amounting to reasonable suspicion that the driver is unlicensed or his vehicle unregistered – we cannot conceive of any legitimate basis upon which a patrolman could decide that stopping a particular driver for a spot check would be more productive than stopping any other driver. This kind of standardless and unconstrained discretion is the evil the Court has discerned when in previous cases it has insisted that the discretion of the official in the field be circumscribed, at least to some extent.

## VI

An individual operating or traveling in an automobile does not lose all reasonable expectation of privacy simply because the automobile and its use are subject to government regulation. Automobile travel is a basic, pervasive, and often necessary mode of transportation to and from one's home, workplace, and leisure activities. Many people spend more hours each day traveling in cars than walking on the streets. Undoubtedly, many find a greater sense of security and privacy in traveling in an automobile than they do in exposing themselves by pedestrian or other modes of travel. Were the individual subject to unfettered governmental intrusion every time he entered an automobile, the security guaranteed by the Fourth Amendment would be seriously circumscribed. [P]eople are not shorn of all Fourth Amendment protection when they step from their homes onto the public sidewalks. Nor are they shorn of those interests when they step from the sidewalks into their automobiles.

## VII

Accordingly, we hold that except in those situations in which there is at least articulable and reasonable suspicion that a motorist is unlicensed or that an automobile is not registered, or that either the vehicle or an occupant is otherwise subject to seizure for violation of law, stopping an automobile and detaining the driver in order to check his driver's license and the registration of the automobile are unreasonable under the Fourth Amendment. This holding does not preclude the State of Delaware or other States from developing methods for spot checks that involve less intrusion or that do not involve the unconstrained exercise of discretion.[26]

---

[26] Nor does our holding today cast doubt on the permissibility of roadside truck weigh-stations and inspection checkpoints, at which some vehicles may be subject to further detention for safety and regulatory inspection than are others.

Questioning of all oncoming traffic at roadblock-type stops is one possible alternative. We hold only that persons in automobiles on public roadways may not for that reason alone have their travel and privacy interfered with at the unbridled discretion of police officers. The judgment below is affirmed.

Justice BLACKMUN, with whom Justice POWELL joins, concurring.

The Court carefully protects from the reach of its decision other less intrusive spot checks "that do not involve the unconstrained exercise of discretion." The roadblock stop for all traffic is given as an example. I necessarily assume that the Court's reservation also includes other not purely random stops (such as every 10th car to pass a given point) that equate with, but are less intrusive than, a 100% roadblock stop. And I would not regard the present case as a precedent that throws any constitutional shadow upon the necessarily somewhat individualized and perhaps largely random examinations by game wardens in the performance of their duties. In a situation of that type, it seems to me, the Court's balancing process, and the value factors under consideration, would be quite different.

With this understanding, I join the Court's opinion and its judgment.

Mr. Justice REHNQUIST, dissenting.

The Court holds, in successive sentences, that absent an articulable, reasonable suspicion of unlawful conduct, a motorist may not be subjected to a random license check, but that the States are free to develop "methods for spot checks that . . . do not involve the unconstrained exercise of discretion," such as "[q]uestioning . . . all oncoming traffic at roadblock-type stops. . . ." Because motorists, apparently like sheep, are much less likely to be "frightened" or "annoyed" when stopped en masse, a highway patrolman needs neither probable cause nor articulable suspicion to stop all motorists on a particular thoroughfare, but he cannot without articulable suspicion stop *less* than all motorists. The Court thus elevates the adage "misery loves company" to a novel role in Fourth Amendment jurisprudence. The rule becomes "curiouser and curiouser" as one attempts to follow the Court's explanation for it.

In executing this balancing process, the Court concludes that given the alternative mechanisms available, discretionary spot checks are not a "sufficiently productive mechanism" to safeguard the State's admittedly "vital interest in ensuring that only those qualified to do so are permitted to operate motor vehicles, that these vehicles are fit for safe operation, and hence that licensing, registration, and vehicle inspection requirements are being observed.'' Foremost among the alternative methods of enforcing traffic and vehicle safety regulations, according to the Court, is acting upon observed violations, for ''drivers without licenses are presumably the less safe drivers whose propensities may well exhibit themselves.'' Noting that ''finding an unlicensed driver among those who commit traffic violations is a much more likely event than finding an unlicensed driver by choosing randomly from the entire universe of drivers,'' the Court concludes that the contribution to highway safety made by random stops would be marginal at best. The State's primary interest, however, is in traffic safety, not in apprehending unlicensed motorists for the sake of apprehending unlicensed motorists. The whole point of enforcing motor vehicle safety regulations is to remove from the road the unlicensed driver before he demonstrates why he is unlicensed. The Court would apparently prefer that the State check licenses and vehicle registrations as the wreckage is being towed away.

Nor is the Court impressed with the deterrence rationale, finding it inconceivable that an unlicensed driver who is not deterred by the prospect of being involved in a traffic violation or other incident requiring him to produce a license would be deterred by the possibility of being subjected to a spot check. The Court arrives at its conclusion without the benefit of a shred of empirical data in this record suggesting that a system of random spot checks would fail to deter violators. In the absence of such evidence, the State's determination that random stops would serve a deterrence function should stand.

On the other side of the balance, the Court advances only the most diaphanous of citizen interests. Indeed, the Court does not say that these interests can never be infringed by the State, just that the State must infringe them en masse rather than citizen by citizen. To comply with the Fourth Amendment, the State need only subject *all* citizens to the same ''anxiety'' and ''inconvenien[ce]'' to which it now subjects only a few.

For constitutional purposes, the action of an individual law enforcement officer is the action of the State itself, and state acts are accompanied by a presumption of validity until shown otherwise. Although a system of discretionary stops could conceivably be abused, the record before us contains no showing that such abuse is probable or even likely. Nor is there evidence in the record that a system of random license checks would fail adequately to further the State's interest in deterring and apprehending violators. Nevertheless, the Court concludes ''[o]n the record before us'' that the random spot check is not ''a sufficiently productive mechanism to justify the intrusion upon Fourth Amendment interests which such stops entail.'' I think that the Court's approach reverses the presumption of constitutionality accorded acts of the States. The burden is not upon the State to demonstrate that its procedures are consistent with the Fourth Amendment, but upon respondent to demonstrate that they are not. ''On this record'' respondent has failed to make such a demonstration.

Neither the Court's opinion, nor the opinion of the Supreme Court of Delaware, suggests that the random stop made in this case was carried out in a manner inconsistent with the Equal Protection Clause of the Fourteenth Amendment. Absent an equal protection violation, the fact that random stops may entail ''a possibly unsettling show of authority,'' and ''may create substantial anxiety,'' seems an insufficient basis to distinguish for Fourth Amendment purposes between a roadblock stopping all cars and the random stop at issue here. Accordingly, I would reverse the judgment of the Supreme Court of Delaware.

## QUESTIONS AND NOTES

**1.** Do you agree with Justice White that the balance of individual inconvenience to societal gain militates against allowing license checks?

**2.** If so, how would that be changed by inconveniencing everybody? Does misery really love company, and is that a constitutional principle?

**3.** Although *Prouse* explicitly refrained from deciding the constitutionality of general license check roadblocks, later cases [(*e.g.*, *Texas v. Brown*, 460 U.S. 730 (1983))] have assumed that *Prouse* decided the issue in favor of their constitutionality.

The next step, sobriety roadblocks, was at issue in *Sitz*.

## Michigan Department of State Police v. Sitz
### 496 U.S. 444 (1990)

Chief Justice REHNQUIST delivered the opinion of the Court.

This case poses the question whether a State's use of highway sobriety checkpoints violates the Fourth and Fourteenth Amendments to the United States Constitution. We hold that it does not and therefore reverse the contrary holding of the Court of Appeals of Michigan.

Petitioners, the Michigan Department of State Police and its Director, established a sobriety checkpoint pilot program in early 1986. The Director appointed a Sobriety Checkpoint Advisory Committee comprising representatives of the State Police force, local police forces, state prosecutors, and the University of Michigan Transportation Research Institute. Pursuant to its charge, the Advisory Committee created guidelines setting forth procedures governing checkpoint operations, site selection, and publicity.

Under the guidelines, checkpoints would be set up at selected sites along state roads. All vehicles passing through a checkpoint would be stopped and their drivers briefly examined for signs of intoxication. In cases where a checkpoint officer detected signs of intoxication, the motorist would be directed to a location out of the traffic flow where an officer would check the motorist's driver's license and car registration and, if warranted, conduct further sobriety tests. Should the field tests and the officer's observations suggest that the driver was intoxicated, an arrest would be made. All other drivers would be permitted to resume their journey immediately.

The first—and to date the only—sobriety checkpoint operated under the program was conducted in Saginaw County with the assistance of the Saginaw County Sheriff's Department. During the hour-and-fifteen-minute duration of the checkpoint's operation, 126 vehicles passed through the checkpoint. The average delay for each vehicle was approximately 25 seconds. Two drivers were detained for field sobriety testing, and one of the two was arrested for driving under the influence of alcohol. A third driver who drove through without stopping was pulled over by an officer in an observation vehicle and arrested for driving under the influence.

On the day before the operation of the Saginaw County checkpoint, respondents filed a complaint in the Circuit Court of Wayne County seeking declaratory and injunctive relief from potential subjection to the checkpoints. Each of the respondents "is a licensed driver in the State of Michigan . . . who regularly travels throughout the State in his automobile." During pretrial proceedings, petitioners agreed to delay further implementation of the checkpoint program pending the outcome of this litigation.

After the trial, at which the court heard extensive testimony concerning the "effectiveness" of highway sobriety checkpoint programs, the court ruled that the Michigan program violated the Fourth Amendment and Art. 1, § 11, of the Michigan Constitution. On appeal, the Michigan Court of Appeals affirmed the holding that the program violated the Fourth Amendment and, for that reason, did not consider whether the program violated the Michigan Constitution. After the Michigan Supreme Court denied petitioners' application for leave to appeal, we granted certiorari.

To decide this case the trial court performed a balancing test derived from our opinion in *Brown v. Texas,* 443 U.S. 47. As described by the Court of Appeals, the test involved "balancing the state's interest in preventing accidents caused by drunk drivers, the effectiveness of sobriety checkpoints in achieving that goal, and the level of intrusion on an individual's privacy caused by the checkpoints."

As characterized by the Court of Appeals, the trial court's findings with respect to the balancing factors were that the State has "a grave and legitimate" interest in curbing drunken driving; that sobriety checkpoint programs are generally "ineffective" and, therefore, do not significantly further that interest; and that the checkpoints' "subjective intrusion" on individual liberties is substantial. According to the court, the record disclosed no basis for disturbing the trial court's findings, which were made within the context of an analytical framework prescribed by this Court for determining the constitutionality of seizures less intrusive than traditional arrests.

Petitioners concede, correctly in our view, that a Fourth Amendment "seizure" occurs when a vehicle is stopped at a checkpoint. The question thus becomes whether such seizures are "reasonable" under the Fourth Amendment.

No one can seriously dispute the magnitude of the drunken driving problem or the States' interest in eradicating it. Media reports of alcohol-related death and mutilation on the Nation's roads are legion. The anecdotal is confirmed by the statistical. "Drunk drivers cause an annual death toll of over 25,000 and in the same time span cause nearly one million personal injuries and more than five billion dollars in property damage."

Conversely, the weight bearing on the other

scale—the measure of the intrusion on motorists stopped briefly at sobriety checkpoints—is slight. We reached a similar conclusion as to the intrusion on motorists subjected to a brief stop at a highway checkpoint for detecting illegal aliens. See *United States v. Martinez-Fuerte,* 428 U.S. 543 (1976). We see virtually no difference between the levels of intrusion on law-abiding motorists from the brief stops necessary to the effectuation of these two types of checkpoints, which to the average motorist would seem identical save for the nature of the questions the checkpoint officers might ask. The trial court and the Court of Appeals, thus, accurately gauged the "objective" intrusion, measured by the duration of the seizure and the intensity of the investigation, as minimal.

With respect to what it perceived to be the "subjective" intrusion on motorists, however, the Court of Appeals found such intrusion substantial. The court first affirmed the trial court's finding that the guidelines governing checkpoint operation minimize the discretion of the officers on the scene. But the court also agreed with the trial court's conclusion that the checkpoints have the potential to generate fear and surprise in motorists. This was so because the record failed to demonstrate that approaching motorists would be aware of their option to make U-turns or turnoffs to avoid the checkpoints. On that basis, the court deemed the subjective intrusion from the checkpoints unreasonable.

We believe the Michigan courts misread our cases concerning the degree of "subjective intrusion" and the potential for generating fear and surprise. The "fear and surprise" to be considered are not the natural fear of one who has been drinking over the prospect of being stopped at a sobriety checkpoint but, rather, the fear and surprise engendered in law abiding motorists by the nature of the stop. This was made clear in *Martinez-Fuerte.* Comparing checkpoint stops to roving patrol stops considered in prior cases, we said,

> "we view checkpoint stops in a different light because the subjective intrusion—the generating of concern or even fright on the part of lawful travelers—is appreciably less in the case of a checkpoint stop. "[T]he circumstances surrounding a checkpoint stop and search are far less intrusive than those attending a roving-patrol stop. Roving patrols often operate at night on seldom-traveled roads, and their approach may frighten motorists. At traffic checkpoints the motorist can see that other vehicles are being stopped, he can see visible signs of the officers' authority,

and he is much less likely to be frightened or annoyed by the intrusion."

Here, checkpoints are selected pursuant to the guidelines, and uniformed police officers stop every approaching vehicle. The intrusion resulting from the brief stop at the sobriety checkpoint is for constitutional purposes indistinguishable from the checkpoint stops we upheld in *Martinez-Fuerte.*

The Court of Appeals went on to consider as part of the balancing analysis the "effectiveness" of the proposed checkpoint program. Based on extensive testimony in the trial record, the court concluded that the checkpoint program failed the "effectiveness" part of the test, and that this failure materially discounted petitioners' strong interest in implementing the program. We think the Court of Appeals was wrong on this point as well.

The actual language from *Brown v. Texas,* upon which the Michigan courts based their evaluation of "effectiveness," describes the balancing factor as "the degree to which the seizure advances the public interest." This passage from *Brown* was not meant to transfer from politically accountable officials to the courts the decision as to which among reasonable alternative law enforcement techniques should be employed to deal with a serious public danger. Experts in police science might disagree over which of several methods of apprehending drunken drivers is preferable as an ideal. But for purposes of Fourth Amendment analysis, the choice among such reasonable alternatives remains with the governmental officials who have a unique understanding of, and a responsibility for, limited public resources, including a finite number of police officers.

In *Prouse,* we disapproved random stops made by Delaware Highway Patrol officers in an effort to apprehend unlicensed drivers and unsafe vehicles. We observed that *no* empirical evidence indicated that such stops would be an effective means of promoting roadway safety and said that "[i]t seems common sense that the percentage of all drivers on the road who are driving without a license is very small and that the number of licensed drivers who will be stopped in order to find one unlicensed operator will be large indeed." We observed that the random stops involved the "kind of standardless and unconstrained discretion [which] is the evil the Court has discerned when in previous cases it has insisted that the discretion of the official in the field be circumscribed, at least to some extent." We went on to state that our holding did not "cast doubt on the permissibility of roadside truck weigh-stations and inspection checkpoints, at which some vehicles may be subject to further detention for safety and regulatory inspection than are others.''

Unlike *Prouse,* this case involves neither a complete absence of empirical data nor a challenge to random highway stops. During the operation of the Saginaw County checkpoint, the detention of each of the 126 vehicles that entered the checkpoint resulted in the arrest of two drunken drivers. Stated as a percentage, approximately 1.5 percent of the drivers passing through the checkpoint were arrested for alcohol impairment. In addition, an expert witness testified at the trial that experience in other States demonstrated that, on the whole, sobriety checkpoints resulted in drunken driving arrests of around 1 percent of all motorists stopped. By way of comparison, the record from one of the consolidated cases in *Martinez-Fuerte,* showed that in the associated checkpoint, illegal aliens were found in only 0.12 percent of the vehicles passing through the checkpoint. The ratio of illegal aliens detected to vehicles stopped (considering that on occasion two or more illegal aliens were found in a single vehicle) was approximately 0.5 percent. We concluded that this ''record . . . provides a rather complete picture of the effectiveness of the San Clemente checkpoint'', and we sustained its constitutionality. We see no justification for a different conclusion here.

In sum, the balance of the State's interest in preventing drunken driving, the extent to which this system can reasonably be said to advance that interest, and the degree of intrusion upon individual motorists who are briefly stopped, weighs in favor of the state program. We therefore hold that it is consistent with the Fourth Amendment. The judgment of the Michigan Court of Appeals is accordingly reversed, and the cause is remanded for further proceedings not inconsistent with this opinion.

Reversed.

Justice BRENNAN, with whom Justice MARSHALL joins, dissenting.

The majority opinion creates the impression that the Court generally engages in a balancing test in order to determine the constitutionality of all seizures, or at least those ''dealing with police stops of motorists on public highways.'' This is not the case. In most cases, the police must possess probable cause for a seizure to be judged reasonable. Only when a seizure is ''substantially less intrusive,'' than a typical arrest is the general rule replaced by a balancing test. I agree with the Court that the initial stop of a car at a roadblock under the Michigan State Police sobriety checkpoint policy is sufficiently less intrusive than an arrest so that the reasonableness of

the seizure may be judged, not by the presence of probable cause, but by balancing ''the gravity of the public concerns served by the seizure, the degree to which the seizure advances the public interest, and the severity of the interference with individual liberty.'' But one searches the majority opinion in vain for any acknowledgment that the *reason* for employing the balancing test is that the seizure is minimally intrusive.

Indeed, the opinion reads as if the minimal nature of the seizure *ends* rather than begins the inquiry into reasonableness. Once the Court establishes that the seizure is ''slight,'' it asserts without explanation that the balance ''weighs in favor of the state program.'' The Court ignores the fact that in this class of minimally intrusive searches, we have generally required the Government to prove that it had reasonable suspicion for a minimally intrusive seizure to be considered reasonable. By holding that no level of suspicion is necessary before the police may stop a car for the purpose of preventing drunken driving, the Court potentially subjects the general public to arbitrary or harassing conduct by the police. I would have hoped that before taking such a step, the Court would carefully explain how such a plan fits within our constitutional framework.

I do not dispute the immense social cost caused by drunken drivers, nor do I slight the government's efforts to prevent such tragic losses. Indeed, I would hazard a guess that today's opinion will be received favorably by a majority of our society, who would willingly suffer the minimal intrusion of a sobriety checkpoint stop in order to prevent drunken driving. But consensus that a particular law enforcement technique serves a laudable purpose has never been the touchstone of constitutional analysis.

''The Fourth Amendment was designed not merely to protect against official intrusions whose social utility was less as measured by some 'balancing test' than its intrusion on individual privacy; it was designed in addition to grant the individual a zone of privacy whose protections could be breached only where the 'reasonable' requirements of the probable cause standard were met. Moved by whatever momentary evil has aroused their fears, officials — perhaps even supported by a majority of citizens — may be tempted to conduct searches that sacrifice the liberty of each citizen to assuage the perceived evil. But the Fourth Amendment rests on the principle that a true balance between the individual and society depends on the recognition of 'the right to be let alone — the most comprehensive of rights and the right most valued by civilized men.' ''

In the face of the ''momentary evil'' of drunken

driving, the Court today abdicates its role as the protector of that fundamental right. I respectfully dissent.

Justice STEVENS, with whom Justice MARSHALL join as to parts I and II, dissenting.

A sobriety checkpoint is usually operated at night at an unannounced location. Surprise is crucial to its method. The test operation conducted by the Michigan State Police and the Saginaw County Sheriff's Department began shortly after midnight and lasted until about 1 a.m. During that period, the 19 officers participating in the operation made two arrests and stopped and questioned 125 other unsuspecting and innocent drivers.[1] It is, of course, not known how many arrests would have been made during that period if those officers had been engaged in normal patrol activities. However, the findings of the trial court, based on an extensive record and affirmed by the Michigan Court of Appeals, indicate that the net effect of sobriety checkpoints on traffic safety is infinitesimal and possibly negative.

Indeed, the record in this case makes clear that a decision holding these suspicionless seizures unconstitutional would not impede the law enforcement community's remarkable progress in reducing the death toll on our highways.[2] Because the Michigan program was patterned after an older program in Maryland, the trial judge gave special attention to that State's experience. Over a period of several years, Maryland operated 125 checkpoints; of the 41,000 motorists passing through those checkpoints, only 143 persons (0.3%) were arrested.[3] The number of man-hours devoted to these operations is not in the record, but it seems inconceivable that a higher arrest rate could not have been achieved by more conventional means.[4] Yet, even if the 143 checkpoint

---

[1] The 19 officers present at the sole Michigan checkpoint were not the standard detail; a few were observers. Nevertheless, the standard plan calls for having at least 8 and as many as 12 officers on hand.

[2] The fatality rate per 100 million miles traveled has steadily declined from 5.2 in 1968 to 2.3 in 1988.

[3] The figures for other States are roughly comparable.

[4] "The then sheriffs of Macomb County, Kalamazoo County, and Wayne County all testified as to other means used in their counties to combat drunk driving and as to their respective opinions that other methods currently in use, *e.g.,* patrol cars, were more effective means of combating drunk driving and utilizing law enforcement resources than sobriety checkpoints."

arrests were assumed to involve a net increase in the number of drunk driving arrests per year, the figure would still be insignificant by comparison to the 71,000 such arrests made by Michigan State Police without checkpoints in 1984 alone.

Any relationship between sobriety checkpoints and an actual reduction in highway fatalities is even less substantial than the minimal impact on arrest rates. As the Michigan Court of Appeals pointed out, "Maryland had conducted a study comparing traffic statistics between a county using checkpoints and a control county. The results of the study showed that alcohol-related accidents in the checkpoint county decreased by ten percent, whereas the control county saw an eleven percent decrease; and while fatal accidents in the control county fell from sixteen to three, fatal accidents in the checkpoint county actually doubled from the prior year."

In light of these considerations, it seems evident that the Court today misapplies the balancing test announced in *Brown v. Texas.* The Court overvalues the law enforcement interest in using sobriety checkpoints, undervalues the citizen's interest in freedom from random, unannounced investigatory seizures, and mistakenly assumes that there is "virtually no difference" between a routine stop at a permanent, fixed checkpoint and a surprise stop at a sobriety checkpoint. I believe this case is controlled by our several precedents condemning suspicionless random stops of motorists for investigatory purposes. [*E.g.*] *Prouse.*

I

There is a critical difference between a seizure that is preceded by fair notice and one that is effected by surprise. That is one reason why a border search, or indeed any search at a permanent and fixed checkpoint, is much less intrusive than a random stop. A motorist with advance notice of the location of a permanent checkpoint has an opportunity to avoid the search entirely, or at least to prepare for, and limit, the intrusion on her privacy.

No such opportunity is available in the case of a random stop or a temporary checkpoint, which both depend for their effectiveness on the element of surprise. A driver who discovers an unexpected checkpoint on a familiar local road will be startled and distressed. She may infer, correctly, that the checkpoint is not simply "business as usual," and may likewise infer, again correctly, that the police have made a discretionary decision to focus their law enforcement efforts upon her and others who pass the chosen point.

This element of surprise is the most obvious distinction between the sobriety checkpoints permitted by today's majority and the interior border checkpoints approved by this Court in *Martinez-Fuerte*. The distinction casts immediate doubt upon the majority's argument, for *Martinez-Fuerte* is the only case in which we have upheld suspicionless seizures of motorists. But the difference between notice and surprise is only one of the important reasons for distinguishing between permanent and mobile checkpoints. With respect to the former, there is no room for discretion in either the timing or the location of the stop – it is a permanent part of the landscape. In the latter case, however, although the checkpoint is most frequently employed during the hours of darkness on weekends (because that is when drivers with alcohol in their blood are most apt to be found on the road), the police have extremely broad discretion in determining the exact timing and placement of the roadblock.

There is also a significant difference between the kind of discretion that the officer exercises after the stop is made. A check for a driver's license, or for identification papers at an immigration checkpoint, is far more easily standardized than is a search for evidence of intoxication. A Michigan officer who questions a motorist at a sobriety checkpoint has virtually unlimited discretion to detain the driver on the basis of the slightest suspicion. A ruddy complexion, an unbuttoned shirt, bloodshot eyes or a speech impediment may suffice to prolong the detention. Any driver who had just consumed a glass of beer, or even a sip of wine, would almost certainly have the burden of demonstrating to the officer that her driving ability was not impaired.

Finally, it is significant that many of the stops at permanent checkpoints occur during daylight hours, whereas the sobriety checkpoints are almost invariably operated at night. A seizure followed by interrogation and even a cursory search at night is surely more offensive than a daytime stop that is almost as routine as going through a toll gate. Thus we thought it important to point out that the random stops at issue in *Ortiz* [v. *United States*] frequently occurred at night. 422 U.S., at 894.

These fears are not, as the Court would have it, solely the lot of the guilty. To be law abiding is not necessarily to be spotless, and even the most virtuous can be unlucky. Unwanted attention from the local police need not be less discomforting simply because one's secrets are not the stuff of criminal prosecutions. Moreover, those who have found – by reason of prejudice or misfortune – that encounters with the police may become adversarial or unpleasant without good cause will have grounds for worrying at any

stop designed to elicit signs of suspicious behavior. Being stopped by the police is distressing even when it should not be terrifying, and what begins mildly may by happenstance turn severe.

For all these reasons, I do not believe that this case is analogous to *Martinez-Fuerte*. In my opinion, the sobriety checkpoints are instead similar to – and in some respects more intrusive than – the random investigative stops that the Court held unconstitutional in *Prouse*. In [that] case the Court held that the State must produce evidence comparing the challenged seizure to other means of law enforcement, so as to show that the seizure "is a sufficiently productive mechanism to justify the intrusion upon Fourth Amendment interests which such stops entail. On the record before us, that question must be answered in the negative. Given the alternative mechanisms available, both those in use and those that might be adopted, we are unconvinced that the incremental contribution to highway safety of the random spot check justifies the practice under the Fourth Amendment."

II

The Court, unable to draw any persuasive analogy to *Martinez-Fuerte,* rests its decision today on application of a more general balancing test taken from *Brown v. Texas*. In that case the appellant, a pedestrian, had been stopped for questioning in an area of El Paso, Texas, that had "a high incidence of drug traffic" because he "looked suspicious." He was then arrested and convicted for refusing to identify himself to police officers. We set aside his conviction because the officers stopped him when they lacked any reasonable suspicion that he was engaged in criminal activity. In our opinion, we stated:

> "Consideration of the constitutionality of such seizures involves a weighing of the gravity of the public concerns served by the seizure, the degree to which the seizure advances the public interest, and the severity of the interference with individual liberty."

The gravity of the public concern with highway safety that is implicated by this case is, of course, undisputed.[7] Yet, that same grave concern was implicated in *Prouse*. Moreover, I do not understand the Court to have placed any lesser value on the importance of the drug problem implicated in *Brown,* or on the need to control the illegal border crossings that

---

[7] It is, however, inappropriate for the Court to exaggerate that concern.

were at stake in *Almeida-Sanchez* and its progeny.[8] A different result in this case must be justified by the other two factors in the *Brown* formulation.

As I have already explained, I believe the Court is quite wrong in blithely asserting that a sobriety checkpoint is no more intrusive than a permanent checkpoint. In my opinion, unannounced investigatory seizures are, particularly when they take place at night, the hallmark of regimes far different from ours;[9] the surprise intrusion upon individual liberty is not minimal. On that issue, my difference with the Court may amount to nothing less than a difference in our respective evaluations of the importance of individual liberty, a serious albeit inevitable source of constitutional disagreement. On the degree to which the sobriety checkpoint seizures advance the public interest, however, the Court's position is wholly indefensible.

The Court's analysis of this issue resembles a business decision that measures profits by counting gross receipts and ignoring expenses. The evidence in this case indicates that sobriety checkpoints result in the arrest of a fraction of one percent of the drivers who are stopped,[11] but there is absolutely no evidence that this figure represents an increase over the number of arrests that would have been made by using the same law enforcement resources in conventional patrols.[12] Thus, although the *gross* number of arrests is more than zero, there is a complete failure of proof on the question whether the wholesale seizures have produced any *net* advance in the public interest in arresting intoxicated drivers.

Indeed, the position adopted today by the Court is not one endorsed by any of the law enforcement authorities to whom the Court purports to defer. The Michigan police do not rely, as the Court does, on the *arrest rate* at sobriety checkpoints to justify the stops made there. Colonel Hough, the commander of the Michigan State Police and a leading proponent of the checkpoints, admitted at trial that the arrest rate at the checkpoints was "very low." Instead, Colonel Hough and the State have maintained that the mere *threat* of such arrests is sufficient to deter drunk driving and so to reduce the accident rate. The Maryland police officer who testified at trial took the same position with respect to his State's program. There is, obviously, nothing wrong with a law enforcement technique that reduces crime by pure deterrence without punishing anybody; on the contrary, such an approach is highly commendable. One cannot, however, prove its efficacy by counting the arrests that were made. One must instead measure the number of crimes that were avoided. Perhaps because the record is wanting, the Court simply ignores this point.

The Court's sparse analysis of this issue differs markedly from Justice Powell's opinion for the Court in *Martinez-Fuerte*. He did not merely count the 17,000 arrests made at the San Clemente checkpoint in 1973; he also carefully explained why those

---

[8] The dissents in those cases touted the relevant state interests in detail. In *Almeida-Sanchez,* Justice White, joined by the author of today's majority opinion, wrote:

"The fact is that illegal crossings at other than the legal ports of entry are numerous and recurring. If there is to be any hope of intercepting illegal entrants and of maintaining any kind of credible deterrent, it is essential that permanent or temporary checkpoints be maintained away from the borders, and roving patrols be conducted to discover and intercept illegal entrants as they filter to the established roads and highways and attempt to move away from the border area. It is for this purpose that the Border Patrol maintained the roving patrol involved in this case and conducted random, spot checks of automobiles and other vehicular traffic." *Almeida-Sanchez v. United States,* 413 U.S. 266, 293 (1973).

Justice Rehnquist argued in a similar vein in his dissent in *Prouse,* in which he observed that: "The whole point of enforcing motor vehicle safety regulations is to remove from the road the unlicensed driver before he demonstrates why he is unlicensed."

[9] "It is well to recall the words of Mr. Justice Jackson, soon after his return from the Nuremberg Trials:

"'These [Fourth Amendment rights], I protest, are not mere second-class rights but belong in the catalog of indispensable freedoms. Among deprivations of rights, none is so effective in cowing a population, crushing the spirit of the individual and putting terror in every heart. Uncontrolled search and seizure is one of the first and most effective weapons in the arsenal of every arbitrary government.' *Brinegar* (Jackson, J., dissenting)."

[11] The Court refers to the expert testimony that the arrest rate is "around 1 percent," but a fair reading of the entire testimony of that witness, together with the other statistical evidence in the record, points to a significantly lower percentage.

[12] Indeed, a single officer in a patrol car parked at the same place as the sobriety checkpoint would no doubt have been able to make some of the arrests based on the officer's observation of the way the intoxicated driver was operating his vehicle.

arrests represented a net benefit to the law enforcement interest at stake.[15] Common sense, moreover, suggests that immigration checkpoints are more necessary than sobriety checkpoints: there is no reason why smuggling illegal aliens should impair a motorist's driving ability, but if intoxication did not noticeably affect driving ability it would not be unlawful. Drunk driving, unlike smuggling, may thus be detected absent any checkpoints. A program that produces thousands of otherwise impossible arrests is not a relevant precedent for a program that produces only a handful of arrests which would be more easily obtained without resort to suspicionless seizures of hundreds of innocent citizens.

### III

The most disturbing aspect of the Court's decision today is that it appears to give no weight to the citizen's interest in freedom from suspicionless unannounced investigatory seizures. Although the author of the opinion does not reiterate his description of that interest as "diaphanous," see *Prouse* (REHNQUIST, J., dissenting), the Court's opinion implicitly adopts that characterization. On the other hand, the Court places a heavy thumb on the law enforcement interest by looking only at gross receipts instead of net benefits. Perhaps this tampering with the scales of justice can be explained by the Court's obvious concern about the slaughter on our highways, and a resultant tolerance for policies designed to alleviate the problem by "setting an example" of a few motorists. This possibility prompts two observations.

---

[15] "These checkpoints are located on important highways; in their absence such highways would offer illegal aliens a quick and safe route into the interior. Routine checkpoint inquiries apprehend many smugglers and illegal aliens who succumb to the lure of such highways. And the prospect of such inquiries forces others onto less efficient roads that are less heavily traveled, slowing their movement and making them more vulnerable to detection by roving patrols.

A requirement that stops on major routes inland always be based on reasonable suspicion would be impractical because the flow of traffic tends to be too heavy to allow the particularized study of a given car that would enable it to be identified as a possible carrier of illegal aliens. In particular, such a requirement would largely eliminate any deterrent to the conduct of well-disguised smuggling operations, even though smugglers are known to use these highways regularly."

First, my objections to random seizures or temporary checkpoints do not apply to a host of other investigatory procedures that do not depend upon surprise and are unquestionably permissible. These procedures have been used to address other threats to human life no less pressing than the threat posed by drunken drivers. It is, for example, common practice to require every prospective airline passenger, or every visitor to a public building, to pass through a metal detector that will reveal the presence of a firearm or an explosive. Permanent, nondiscretionary checkpoints could be used to control serious dangers at other publicly operated facilities. Because concealed weapons obviously represent one such substantial threat to public safety, I would suppose that all subway passengers could be required to pass through metal detectors, so long as the detectors were permanent and every passenger was subjected to the same search.[18] Likewise, I would suppose that a State could condition access to its toll roads upon not only paying the toll but also taking a uniformly administered breathalyzer test. That requirement might well keep all drunken drivers off the highways that serve the fastest and most dangerous traffic. This procedure would not be subject to the constitutional objections that control this case: the checkpoints would be permanently fixed, the stopping procedure would apply to all users of the toll road in precisely the same way, and police officers would not be free to make arbitrary choices about which neighborhoods should be targeted or about which individuals should be more thoroughly searched. Random, suspicionless seizures designed to search for evidence of firearms, drugs, or intoxication belong, however, in a fundamentally different category. These seizures play upon the detained individual's reasonable expectations of privacy, injecting a suspicionless search into a context where none would normally occur. The imposition that seems diaphanous today may be intolerable tomorrow.

Second, sobriety checkpoints are elaborate, and disquieting, publicity stunts. The possibility that anybody, no matter how innocent, may be stopped for police inspection is nothing if not attention-getting. The shock value of the checkpoint program may be its most effective feature: Lieutenant Cotton of the Maryland State Police, a defense witness, testified that "the media coverage . . . has been absolutely overwhelming. . . . Quite frankly we got benefits just from the controversy of the sobriety checkpoints."

---

[18] Permanent, nondiscretionary checkpoints are already a common practice at public libraries, which now often require every patron to submit to a brief search for books, or to leave by passing through a special detector.

This is a case that is driven by nothing more than symbolic state action – an insufficient justification for an otherwise unreasonable program of random seizures. Unfortunately, the Court is transfixed by the wrong symbol – the illusory prospect of punishing countless intoxicated motorists – when it should keep its eyes on the road plainly marked by the Constitution.

I respectfully dissent.

## QUESTIONS AND NOTES

**1.** Would you categorize the plaintiff's interest in *Sitz* as "diaphanous?" Why? Why not?

**2.** What exactly is the plaintiff's interest? Is it different from or greater than that alleged in *Martinez-Fuerte*?

**3.** Is the *Brown* balancing test (which balances the importance of the State's interest, the effectiveness of the seizure in implementing the State's interest, and the importance of the defendant's interest) a good way to decide cases like *Sitz*?

**4.** In deferring completely to the police in regard to effectiveness, did the Court shirk its Fourth Amendment responsibilities?

**5.** Under *Sitz*, could the police set up a walker's roadblock in a drug-infested neighborhood and check all walkers who come by for drugs? If not, why not? Are drugs not at least as great of a problem as drunk driving?

## E.   Inventory Searches

When the police impound a towed car, or impound the car of an arrestee, it is sometimes argued that the police should be permitted to inventory the contents of that car. In a couple of closely divided cases in the seventies, the Supreme Court upheld inventory searches under the special facts of each case. In *Bertine,* the State argued that inventory searches were always permitted, at least if conducted according to guidelines.

### Colorado v. Bertine
### 479 U.S. 367 (1987)

Chief Justice REHNQUIST delivered the opinion of the Court.

On February 10, 1984, a police officer in Boulder, Colorado, arrested respondent Steven Lee Bertine for driving while under the influence of alcohol. After Bertine was taken into custody and before the arrival of a tow truck to take Bertine's van to an impoundment lot,[1] a backup officer inventoried the contents of the van. The officer opened a closed backpack in which he found controlled substances, cocaine paraphernalia, and a large amount of cash. Bertine was subsequently charged with driving while under the influence of alcohol, unlawful possession of cocaine with intent to dispense, sell, and distribute, and unlawful possession of methaqualone. We are asked to decide whether the Fourth Amendment prohibits the State from proving these charges with the evidence discovered during the inventory of Bertine's van. We hold that it does not.

* * *

[1] Section 7-7-2(a)(4) of the Boulder Revised Code authorizes police officers to impound vehicles when drivers are taken into custody. Section 7-7-2(a)(4) provides:

"A peace officer is authorized to remove or cause to be removed a vehicle from any street, parking lot, or driveway when:

(4) The driver of a vehicle is taken into custody by the police department." Boulder Rev.Code § 7-7-2(a)(4) (1981).

The backup officer inventoried the van in accordance with local police procedures, which require a detailed inspection and inventory of impounded vehicles. He found the backpack directly behind the front seat of the van. Inside the pack, the officer observed a nylon bag containing metal canisters. Opening the canisters, the officer discovered that they contained cocaine, methaqualone tablets, cocaine paraphernalia, and $700 in cash. In an outside zippered pouch of the backpack, he also found $210 in cash in a sealed envelope. After completing the inventory of the van, the officer had the van towed to an impound lot and brought the backpack, money, and contraband to the police station.

> "The standard of probable cause is peculiarly related to criminal investigations, not routine, noncriminal procedures. . . . The probable-cause approach is unhelpful when analysis centers upon the reasonableness of routine administrative caretaking functions,

After Bertine was charged with the offenses described above, he moved to suppress the evidence found during the inventory search on the ground, *inter alia,* that the search of the closed backpack and containers exceeded the permissible scope of such a search under the Fourth Amendment. The Colorado trial court ruled that probable cause supported Bertine's arrest and that the police officers had made the decisions to impound the vehicle and to conduct a thorough inventory search in good faith. Although noting that the inventory of the vehicle was performed in a "somewhat slipshod" manner, the District Court concluded that "the search of the backpack was done for the purpose of protecting the owner's property, protection of the police from subsequent claims of loss or stolen property, and the protection of the police from dangerous instrumentalities."

[T]he Supreme Court of Colorado recognized that in *South Dakota v. Opperman,* 428 U.S. 364 (1976), we had held inventory searches of automobiles to be consistent with the Fourth Amendment, and that in *Illinois v. Lafayette,* 462 U.S. 640 (1983), we had held that the inventory search of personal effects of an arrestee at a police station was also permissible under that Amendment. The Supreme Court of Colorado felt, however, that our decisions in *Sanders* and *Chadwick,* holding searches of closed trunks and suitcases to violate the Fourth Amendment, meant that *Opperman* and *Lafayette* did not govern this case.

We granted certiorari to consider the important and recurring question of federal law decided by the Colorado Supreme Court. As that court recognized, inventory searches are now a well-defined exception to the warrant requirement of the Fourth Amendment. The policies behind the warrant requirement are not implicated in an inventory search, nor is the related concept of probable cause: "particularly when no claim is made that the protective procedures are a subterfuge for criminal investigations." *Opperman. South Dakota v. Opperman,* 428 U.S. 364 (1976).

For these reasons, the Colorado Supreme Court's reliance on *Sanders* and *Chadwick* was incorrect. Both of these cases concerned searches solely for the purpose of investigating criminal conduct, with the validity of the searches therefore dependent on the application of the probable-cause and warrant requirements of the Fourth Amendment.

By contrast, an inventory search may be "reasonable" under the Fourth Amendment even though it is not conducted pursuant to a warrant based upon probable cause. In *Opperman,* this Court assessed the reasonableness of an inventory search of the glove compartment in an abandoned automobile impounded by the police. We found that inventory procedures serve to protect an owner's property while it is in the custody of the police, to insure against claims of lost, stolen, or vandalized property, and to guard the police from danger. In light of these strong governmental interests and the diminished expectation of privacy in an automobile, we upheld the search. In reaching this decision, we observed that our cases accorded deference to police caretaking procedures designed to secure and protect vehicles and their contents within police custody.[4]

In our more recent decision, *Illinois v. Lafayette,* 462 U.S. 640 (1988), a police officer conducted an inventory search of the contents of a shoulder bag in the possession of an individual being taken into custody. In deciding whether this search was reasonable, we recognized that the search served legitimate governmental interests similar to those identified in *Opperman.* We determined that those interests outweighed the individual's Fourth Amendment interests and upheld the search.

The Supreme Court of Colorado expressed the view that the search in this case was unreasonable because Bertine's van was towed to a secure, lighted

---

[4] The Colorado Supreme Court correctly stated that *Opperman* did not address the question whether the scope of an inventory search may extend to closed containers located in the interior of an impounded vehicle. We did note, however, that "when the police take custody of any sort of container [such as] an automobile . . . it is reasonable to search the container to itemize the property to be held by the police."

facility and because Bertine himself could have been offered the opportunity to make other arrangements for the safekeeping of his property. But the security of the storage facility does not completely eliminate the need for inventorying; the police may still wish to protect themselves or the owners of the lot against false claims of theft or dangerous instrumentalities. And while giving Bertine an opportunity to make alternative arrangements would undoubtedly have been possible, we said in *Lafayette*: "[T]he real question is not what 'could have been achieved,' but whether the Fourth Amendment *requires* such steps. . . ." "The reasonableness of any particular governmental activity does not necessarily or invariably turn on the existence of alternative 'less intrusive' means." (emphasis in original). We conclude that here, as in *Lafayette*, reasonable police regulations relating to inventory procedures administered in good faith satisfy the Fourth Amendment, even though courts might as a matter of hindsight be able to devise equally reasonable rules requiring a different procedure.[6]

The Supreme Court of Colorado also thought it necessary to require that police, before inventorying a container, weigh the strength of the individual's privacy interest in the container against the possibility that the container might serve as a repository for dangerous or valuable items. We think that such a requirement is contrary to our decisions in *Opperman* and *Lafayette*, and by analogy to our decision in *Ross*:

> "When a legitimate search is under way, and when its purpose and its limits have been precisely defined, nice distinctions between closets, drawers, and containers, in the case of a home, or between glove compartments, upholstered seats, trunks, and wrapped packages, in the case of a vehicle, must give way

to the interest in the prompt and efficient completion of the task at hand." *Ross*.

We reaffirm these principles here: "[a] single familiar standard is essential to guide police officers, who have only limited time and expertise to reflect on and balance the social and individual interests involved in the specific circumstances they confront."

Bertine finally argues that the inventory search of his van was unconstitutional because departmental regulations gave the police officers discretion to choose between impounding his van and parking and locking it in a public parking place. The Supreme Court of Colorado did not rely on this argument in reaching its conclusion, and we reject it. Nothing in *Opperman* or *Lafayette* prohibits the exercise of police discretion so long as that discretion is exercised according to standard criteria and on the basis of something other than suspicion of evidence of criminal activity. Here, the discretion afforded the Boulder police was exercised in light of standardized criteria, related to the feasibility and appropriateness of parking and locking a vehicle rather than impounding it.[7] There was no showing that the police chose to impound Bertine's van in order to investigate suspected criminal activity.

While both *Opperman* and *Lafayette* are distinguishable from the present case on their facts, we think that the principles enunciated in those cases govern the present one. The judgment of the Supreme Court of Colorado is therefore reversed.

Justice BLACKMUN, with whom Justice POWELL and Justice O'CONNOR join, concurring.

The Court today holds that police officers may open closed containers while conducting a routine inventory search of an impounded vehicle. I join the

---

[6] We emphasize that, in this case, the trial court found that the Police Department's procedures mandated the opening of closed containers and the listing of their contents. Our decisions have always adhered to the requirement that inventories be conducted according to standardized criteria. See *Lafayette, Opperman*.

By quoting a portion of the Colorado Supreme Court's decision out of context, the dissent suggests that the inventory here was not authorized by the standard procedures of the Boulder Police Department. Yet that court specifically stated that the procedure followed here was "officially authorized." In addition, the court did not disturb the trial court's finding that the police procedures for impounding vehicles required a detailed inventory of Bertine's van.

[7] In arguing that the Boulder Police Department procedures set forth no standardized criteria guiding an officer's decision to impound a vehicle, the dissent selectively quotes from the police directive concerning the care and security of vehicles taken into police custody. The dissent fails to mention that the directive establishes several conditions that must be met before an officer may pursue the park-and-lock alternative. For example, police may not park and lock the vehicle where there is reasonable risk of damage or vandalism to the vehicle or where the approval of the arrestee cannot be obtained. Not only do such conditions circumscribe the discretion of individual officers, but they also protect the vehicle and its contents and minimize claims of property loss.

Court's opinion, but write separately to underscore the importance of having such inventories conducted only pursuant to standardized police procedures. The underlying rationale for allowing an inventory exception to the Fourth Amendment warrant rule is that police officers are not vested with discretion to determine the scope of the inventory search. This absence of discretion ensures that inventory searches will not be used as a purposeful and general means of discovering evidence of crime. Thus, it is permissible for police officers to open closed containers in an inventory search only if they are following standard police procedures that mandate the opening of such containers in every impounded vehicle. As the Court emphasizes, the trial court in this case found that the Police Department's standard procedures did mandate the opening of closed containers and the listing of their contents.

Justice MARSHALL, with whom Justice BRENNAN joins, dissenting.

Recognizing that "both *Opperman* and *Lafayette* are distinguishable from the present case on their facts," the majority applies the balancing test enunciated in those cases to uphold as reasonable the inventory of a closed container in a car impounded when its driver was placed under arrest. However, the distinctive facts of this case require a different result. This search — it cannot legitimately be labeled an inventory — was unreasonable and violated the Fourth Amendment. Unlike the inventories in *Opperman* and *Lafayette*, it was not conducted according to standardized procedures. Furthermore, the governmental interests justifying the intrusion are significantly weaker than the interests identified in either *Opperman* or *Lafayette* and the expectation of privacy is considerably stronger.

### I

As the Court acknowledges, inventory searches are reasonable only if conducted according to standardized procedures. In both *Opperman* and *Lafayette*, the Court relied on the absence of police discretion in determining that the inventory searches in question were reasonable. Chief Justice Burger's opinion in *Opperman* repeatedly referred to this standardized nature of inventory procedures. Justice Powell's concurring opinion in that case also stressed that "no significant discretion is placed in the hands of the individual officer: he usually has no choice as to the subject of the search or its scope." Similarly, the Court in *Lafayette* emphasized the

standardized procedure under which the stationhouse inventory was conducted. In assessing the reasonableness of searches conducted in limited situations such as these, where we do not require probable cause or a warrant, we have consistently emphasized the need for such set procedures: "standardless and unconstrained discretion is the evil the Court has discerned when in previous cases it has insisted that the discretion of the official in the field be circumscribed, at least to some extent." *E.g. Prouse.*

The Court today attempts to evade [the] clear prohibitions on unfettered police discretion by declaring that "the discretion afforded the Boulder police was exercised in light of standardized criteria, related to the feasibility and appropriateness of parking and locking a vehicle rather than impounding it." This vital assertion is flatly contradicted by the record in this case. The officer who conducted the inventory, Officer Reichenbach, testified at the suppression hearing that the decision not to "park and lock" respondent's vehicle was his "own individual discretionary decision." Indeed, application of these supposedly standardized "criteria" upon which the Court so heavily relies would have yielded a different result in this case. Since there was ample public parking adjacent to the intersection where respondent was stopped, consideration of "feasibility" would certainly have militated in favor of the "park and lock" option, not against it. I do not comprehend how consideration of "appropriateness" serves to channel a field officer's discretion; nonetheless, the "park and lock" option would seem particularly appropriate in this case, where respondent was stopped for a traffic offense and was not likely to be in custody for a significant length of time.

Indeed, the record indicates that *no* standardized criteria limit a Boulder police officer's discretion. According to a departmental directive, after placing a driver under arrest, an officer has three options for disposing of the vehicle. First, he can allow a third party to take custody. Second, the officer or the driver (depending on the nature of the arrest) may take the car to the nearest public parking facility, lock it, and take the keys. Finally, the officer can do what was done in this case: impound the vehicle, and search and inventory its contents, including closed containers.

Under the first option, the police have no occasion to search the automobile. Under the "park and lock" option, "[c]losed containers that give no indication of containing either valuables or a weapon *may not be opened and the contents searched* (i.e., inventoried)." (emphasis added). Only if the police choose the third option are they entitled to search closed containers in the vehicle. Where the vehicle is not itself evidence of a crime,[5] as in this case, the police apparently have totally unbridled discretion as to which procedure to use. ("[T]he Boulder Police Department's regulations and rules do not require that an automobile be inventoried and searched in accordance with the procedures followed in this case"). Consistent with this conclusion, Officer Reichenbach testified that such decisions were left to the discretion of the officer on the scene.

Once a Boulder police officer has made this initial completely discretionary decision to impound a vehicle, he is given little guidance as to which areas to search and what sort of items to inventory. The arresting officer, Officer Toporek, testified at the suppression hearing as to what items would be inventoried: "That would I think be very individualistic as far as what an officer may or may not go into. I think whatever arouses his suspicious [sic] as far as what may be contained in any type of article in the car." In application, these so-called procedures left the breadth of the "inventory" to the whim of the individual officer. Clearly, "[t]he practical effect of this system is to leave the [owner] subject to the discretion of the official in the field."

## II

Officer Reichenbach's inventory in this case would not have protected the police against claims lodged by respondent, false or otherwise. Indeed, the trial court's characterization of the inventory as "slip-shod" is the height of understatement. For example, Officer Reichenbach failed to list $150 in cash found in respondent's wallet or the contents of a sealed envelope marked "rent," $210, in the relevant section of the property form. His reports make no reference to other items of value, including respondent's credit cards, and a converter, a hydraulic jack, and a set of tire chains, worth a total of $125. The $700 in cash found in respondent's backpack,

---

[5] Respondent's van was not evidence of a crime within the meaning of the departmental directive; Officer Reichenbach testified that it was not his practice to impound all cars following an arrest for driving while under the influence of alcohol. The Memorandum also requires the "approval of the arrestee" before the police can "park and lock" his car. In this case, however, respondent was never advised of this option and had no opportunity to consent. At the suppression hearing, he indicated that he would have consented to such a procedure.

along with the contraband, appeared only on a property form completed later by someone other than Officer Reichenbach. The interior of the vehicle was left in disarray, and the officer "inadvertently" retained respondent's keys—including his house keys—for two days following his arrest.

Protecting the police from potential danger— failed to receive the endorsement of a majority of the Court in *Opperman*. After noting that "there is little danger associated with impounding unsearched vehicles," Justice POWELL recognized that "there does not appear to be any effective way of identifying in advance those circumstances or classes of automobile impoundments which represent a greater risk." As with the charge of overtime parking in *Opperman*, there is nothing in the nature of the offense for which respondent was arrested that suggests he was likely to be carrying weapons, explosives, or other dangerous items. Cf. *Cady v. Dombrowski* (police reasonably believed that the defendant's service revolver was in the car). Not only is protecting the police from dangerous instrumentalities an attenuated justification for most automobile inventory searches, but opening closed containers to inventory the contents can only increase the risk. In the words of the District Court in *United States v. Cooper*, 428 F.Supp. 652, 654-655 (SD Ohio 1977): "The argument that the search was necessary to avoid a possible booby-trap is . . . easily refuted. No sane individual inspects for booby-traps by simply opening the container."

Thus, only the government's interest in protecting the owner's property actually justifies an inventory search of an impounded vehicle. While I continue to believe that preservation of property does not outweigh the privacy and security interests protected by the Fourth Amendment, I fail to see how preservation can even be asserted as a justification for the search in this case. In *Opperman*, the owner of the impounded car was not available to safeguard his possessions, and it could plausibly be argued that, in his absence, the police were entitled to act for his presumed benefit. See also *Cady* (comatose defendant). When the police conducted the inventory in *Opperman*, they could not predict how long the car would be left in their possession. ("[M]any owners might leave valuables in their automobiles temporarily that they would not leave there unattended for the several days that police custody may last"). In this case, however, the owner was "present to make other arrangements for the safekeeping of his belongings," yet the police made no attempt to ascertain whether in fact he wanted them to "safeguard" his property. Furthermore, since respondent was charged with a traffic offense, he was unlikely to remain in custody for more than a few hours. He might well have been willing to leave his valuables unattended in the locked van for such a short period of time. (had he been given the choice, respondent indicated at the suppression hearing that he "would have parked [the van] in the lot across the street [and] [h]ad somebody come and get it").

Thus, the government's interests in this case are weaker than in *Opperman,* but the search here is much more intrusive. *Opperman* did not involve a search of closed containers or other items that "touch upon intimate areas of an individual's personal affairs." To expand the *Opperman* rationale to include containers in which the owner clearly has a reasonable expectation of privacy, the Court relies on *Lafayette.* Such reliance is fundamentally misplaced, however; the inventory in *Lafayette* was justified by considerations which are totally absent in this context.

In *Lafayette,* we upheld a station-house inventory search of an arrestee's shoulder bag. Notwithstanding the Court's assertions to the contrary, the inventory in that case *was* justified primarily by compelling governmental interests unique to the station house, preincarceration context. There is a powerful interest in preventing the introduction of contraband or weapons into a jail.[7] "Arrested persons have also

been known to injure themselves – or others – with belts, knives, drugs, or other items on their person while being detained. Dangerous instrumentalities – such as razor blades, bombs, or weapons – can be concealed in innocent-looking articles taken from the arrestee's possession." Removing such items from persons about to be incarcerated is necessary to reasonable jail security; once these items have been identified and removed, "inventorying them is an entirely reasonable administrative procedure." Although *Lafayette* also involved the property justifications relied on in *Opperman,* I do not believe it can fairly be read to expand the scope of inventory searches where the pressing security concerns of the station house are absent.

### III

In *Coolidge,* a plurality of this Court stated: "The word 'automobile' is not a talisman in whose presence the Fourth Amendment fades away and disappears." By upholding the search in this case, the Court not only ignores that principle, but creates another talisman to overcome the requirements of the Fourth Amendment – the term "inventory." Accordingly, I dissent.

---

[7] The importance of this justification to the outcome in *Lafayette,* is amply demonstrated by the Court's direction on remand: "The record is unclear as to whether respondent was to have been incarcerated after being booked for disturbing the peace. That is an appropriate inquiry on remand."

## QUESTIONS AND NOTES

**1.** What, if anything, can justify a routine inventory search?

**2.** Were any of those justifications present in *Bertine*?

**3.** Justice Rehnquist refers to the *Ross* statement about not allowing "nice distinctions" to determine the scope of the search. In view of the rationale for the search in *Ross* (finding evidence for which there is probable cause to look) as opposed to the *Bertine* rationale (protecting property and protecting the police from false claims), is Rehnquist's quotation an unjustifiable out-of-context lifting of a phrase?

**4.** Should the "slipshod" nature of the search have been relevant? Does it establish the insubstantiality of the inventory justification (excuse?)?

**5.** Is there a difference between an *authorized* inventory, and a *mandated* inventory? If so, what is the difference? Did the Court essentially establish that the inventory was "authorized" and treat it as if it were "mandatory?"

**6.** In reading these opinions, do you come away with the sense that Officer Reichenbach would have been in trouble with his department if he had *not* conducted an inventory search of the van?

**7.** Did the police treat this inventory search as if the Fourth Amendment were no big deal? Is there anything in the court's language that invites such a view?

**8.** Is *Bertine* explicable because of the trial court's determination that the search was mandated? (See particularly Justice Blackmun's concurring opinion.)

**9.** Any thought that *Bertine* allowed *carte blanche* automobile inventory searches was squelched in *Wells*.

## Florida v. Wells
### 495 U.S. 1 (1990)

Chief Justice REHNQUIST delivered the opinion of the Court.

A Florida Highway Patrol trooper stopped respondent Wells for speeding. After smelling alcohol on Wells' breath, the trooper arrested Wells for driving under the influence. Wells then agreed to accompany the trooper to the station to take a breathalyzer test. The trooper informed Wells that the car would be impounded and obtained Wells' permission to open the trunk. At the impoundment facility, an inventory search of the car turned up two marijuana cigarette butts in an ashtray and a locked suitcase in the trunk. Under the trooper's direction, employees of the facility forced open the suitcase and discovered a garbage bag containing a considerable amount of marijuana.

The Supreme Court of Florida relied on the opinions in *Bertine* (Blackmun, J., concurring). Referring to language in the *Bertine* concurrence and a footnote in the majority opinion, the court held that

> "[i]n the absence of a policy specifically requiring the opening of closed containers found during a legitimate inventory search, *Bertine* prohibits us from countenancing the procedure followed in this instance."

According to the court, the record contained no evidence of any Highway Patrol policy on the opening of closed containers found during inventory searches. The court added, however:

> "The police under *Bertine* must mandate either that all containers will be opened during an inventory search, or that no containers will be opened. There can be no room for discretion."

While this latter statement of the Supreme Court of Florida derived support from a sentence in the *Bertine* concurrence taken in isolation, we think it is at odds with the thrust of both the concurrence and the opinion of the Court in that case. We said in *Bertine*:

> "Nothing in *Opperman* or *Lafayette* prohibits the exercise of police discretion so long as that discretion is exercised according to standard criteria and on the basis of something other than suspicion of evidence of criminal activity."

Our view that standardized criteria, or established routine, must regulate the opening of containers found during inventory searches is based on the principle that an inventory search must not be a ruse for a general rummaging in order to discover incriminating evidence. The policy or practice governing inventory searches should be designed to produce an inventory. The individual police officer must not be allowed so much latitude that inventory searches are turned into "a purposeful and general means of discovering evidence of crime."

But in forbidding uncanalized discretion to police officers conducting inventory searches, there is no reason to insist that they be conducted in a totally mechanical "all or nothing" fashion. "[I]nventory procedures serve to protect an owner's property while it is in the custody of the police, to insure against claims of lost, stolen, or vandalized property, and to guard the police from danger." A police officer may be allowed sufficient latitude to determine whether a particular container should or should not be opened in light of the nature of the search and characteristics of the container itself. Thus, while policies of opening all containers or of opening no containers are unquestionably permissible, it would be equally permissible, for example, to allow the opening of closed containers whose contents officers determine they are unable to ascertain from examining the containers' exteriors. The allowance of the exercise of judgment based on concerns related to the purposes of an inventory search does not violate the Fourth Amendment.

In the present case, the Supreme Court of Florida found that the Florida Highway Patrol had no policy whatever with respect to the opening of closed containers encountered during an inventory search. We hold that absent such a policy, the instant search was not sufficiently regulated to satisfy the Fourth Amendment and that the marijuana which was found in the suitcase, therefore, was properly suppressed by the Supreme Court of Florida. Its judgment is therefore affirmed.

[BRENNAN, MARSHALL, BLACKMUN, and STEVENS, JJ, concurred only in result.]

## QUESTIONS AND NOTES

**1.** Would one who was worried about excessive police discretion after *Bertine* be more or less worried after *Wells* ?

**2.** Do you see any difference between *Wells* and *Bertine*?

# 7.

# LIMITED SEARCHES ON LESS THAN PROBABLE CAUSE

## A. Protection Of The Officer

During the sixties, it was frequently argued that a policeman ought to be able to frisk a suspect for weapons before talking to the suspect, in order to protect himself. In the leading case of *Terry v. Ohio,* the Supreme Court adopted that viewpoint. In *Terry* and its progeny, we will examine the scope and limitation of this power.

### Terry v. Ohio
### 392 U.S. 1 (1968)

Mr. Chief Justice WARREN delivered the opinion of the Court.

This case presents serious questions concerning the role of the Fourth Amendment in the confrontation on the street between the citizen and the policeman investigating suspicious circumstances. Petitioner Terry was convicted of carrying a concealed weapon and sentenced to the statutorily prescribed term of one to three years in the penitentiary. Following the denial of a pretrial motion to suppress, the prosecution introduced in evidence two revolvers and a number of bullets seized from Terry and a codefendant, Richard Chilton, by Cleveland Police Detective Martin McFadden. At the hearing on the motion to suppress this evidence, Officer McFadden testified that while he was patrolling in plain clothes in downtown Cleveland at approximately 2:30 in the afternoon of October 31, 1963, his attention was attracted by two men, Chilton and Terry, standing on the corner of Huron Road and Euclid Avenue. He had never seen the two men before, and he was unable to say precisely what first drew his eye to them. However, he testified that he had been a policeman for 39 years and a detective for 35 and that he had been assigned to patrol this vicinity of downtown Cleveland for shoplifters and pickpockets for 30 years. He explained that he had developed routine habits of observation over the years and that he would "stand and watch people or walk and watch people at many intervals of the day." He added: "Now, in this case when I looked over they didn't look right to me at the time."

His interest aroused, Officer McFadden took up a post of observation in the entrance to a store 300 to 400 feet away from the two men. "I get more purpose to watch them when I seen their movements," he testified. He saw one of the men leave the other one and walk southwest on Huron Road, past some stores. The man paused for a moment and looked in a store window, then walked on a short distance, turned around and walked back toward the corner, pausing once again to look in the same store window. He rejoined his companion at the corner, and the two conferred briefly. Then the second man went through the same series of motions, strolling down Huron Road, looking in the same window, walking on a short distance, turning back, peering in the store window again, and returning to confer with the first man at the corner. The two men repeated this ritual alternately between five and six times apiece—in all, roughly a dozen trips. At one point, while the two were standing together on the corner, a third man approached them and engaged them briefly in conversation. This man then left the two others and walked west on Euclid Avenue. Chilton and Terry resumed their measured pacing, peering and conferring. After this had gone on for 10 to 12 minutes, the two men walked off together, heading west on Euclid Avenue, following the path taken earlier by the third man.

By this time Officer McFadden had become thoroughly suspicious. He testified that after observing their elaborately casual and oft-repeated reconnaissance of the store window on Huron Road, he suspected the two men of "casing a job, a stick-up," and that he considered it his duty as a police officer to investigate further. He added that he feared "they may have a gun." Thus, Officer McFadden followed Chilton and Terry and saw them stop in front of Zucker's store to talk to the same man who had conferred with them earlier on the street corner. Deciding that the situation was ripe for direct action, Officer McFadden approached the three men, identified himself as a police officer and asked for their names. At this point his knowledge was confined to what he had observed. He was not acquainted with any of the three men by name or by sight, and he had received no information concerning them from any other source. When the men "mumbled something" in response to his inquiries, Officer McFadden grabbed petitioner Terry, spun him around so that they were facing the other two, with Terry between McFadden and the others, and patted down the outside of his clothing. In the left breast pocket of Terry's overcoat Officer McFadden felt a pistol. He reached inside the overcoat pocket, but was unable to remove the gun. At this point, keeping Terry

between himself and the others, the officer ordered all three men to enter Zucker's store. As they went in, he removed Terry's overcoat completely, removed a .38-caliber revolver from the pocket and ordered all three men to face the wall with their hands raised. Officer McFadden proceeded to pat down the outer clothing of Chilton and the third man, Katz. He discovered another revolver in the outer pocket of Chilton's overcoat, but no weapons were found on Katz. The officer testified that he only patted the men down to see whether they had weapons, and that he did not put his hands beneath the outer garments of either Terry or Chilton until he felt their guns. So far as appears from the record, he never placed his hands beneath Katz' outer garments. Officer McFadden seized Chilton's gun, asked the proprietor of the store to call a police wagon, and took all three men to the station, where Chilton and Terry were formally charged with carrying concealed weapons.

On the motion to suppress the guns the prosecution took the position that they had been seized following a search incident to a lawful arrest. The trial court rejected this theory, stating that it "would be stretching the facts beyond reasonable comprehension" to find that Officer McFadden had had probable cause to arrest the men before he patted them down for weapons. However, the court denied the defendants' motion on the ground that Officer McFadden, on the basis of his experience, "had reasonable cause to believe * * * that the defendants were conducting themselves suspiciously, and some interrogation should be made of their action." Purely for his own protection, the court held, the officer had the right to pat down the outer clothing of these men, who he had reasonable cause to believe might be armed. The court distinguished between an investigatory "stop" and an arrest, and between a "frisk" of the outer clothing for weapons and a full-blown search for evidence of crime. The frisk, it held, was essential to the proper performance of the officer's investigatory duties, for without it "the answer to the police officer may be a bullet, and a loaded pistol discovered during the frisk is admissible."

I

We would be less than candid if we did not acknowledge that this question thrusts to the fore difficult and troublesome issues regarding a sensitive area of police activity—issues which have never before been squarely presented to this Court. Reflective of the tensions involved are the practical and constitutional arguments pressed with great vigor on both sides of the public debate over the power of the police to "stop and frisk"—as it is sometimes euphemistically termed – suspicious persons.

On the one hand, it is frequently argued that in dealing with the rapidly unfolding and often dangerous situations on city streets the police are in need of an escalating set of flexible responses, graduated in relation to the amount of information they possess. For this purpose it is urged that distinctions should be made between a "stop" and an "arrest" (or a "seizure" of a person), and between a "frisk" and a "search." Thus, it is argued, the police should be allowed to "stop" a person and detain him briefly for questioning upon suspicion that he may be connected with criminal activity. Upon suspicion that the person may be armed, the police should have the power to "frisk" him for weapons. If the "stop" and the "frisk" give rise to probable cause to believe that the suspect has committed a crime, then the police should be empowered to make a formal "arrest," and a full incident "search" of the person. This scheme is justified in part upon the notion that a "stop" and a "frisk" amount to a mere "minor inconvenience and petty indignity," which can properly be imposed upon the citizen in the interest of effective law enforcement on the basis of a police officer's suspicion.

On the other side the argument is made that the authority of the police must be strictly circumscribed by the law of arrest and search as it has developed to date in the traditional jurisprudence of the Fourth Amendment. It is contended with some force that there is not – and cannot be – a variety of police activity which does not depend solely upon the voluntary cooperation of the citizen and yet which stops short of an arrest based upon probable cause to make such an arrest. The heart of the Fourth Amendment, the argument runs, is a severe requirement of specific justification for any intrusion upon protected personal security, coupled with a highly developed system of judicial controls to enforce upon the agents of the State the commands of the Constitution. Acquiescence by the courts in the compulsion inherent in the field interrogation practices at issue here, it is urged, would constitute an abdication of judicial control over, and indeed an encouragement of, substantial interference with liberty and personal security by police officers whose judgment is necessarily colored by their primary involvement in "the often competitive enterprise of ferreting out crime." This, it is argued, can only serve to exacerbate police-community tensions in the crowded centers of our Nation's cities.

In this context we approach the issues in this case mindful of the limitations of the judicial function in controlling the myriad daily situations in which policemen and citizens confront each other on the street. The State has characterized the issue here as "the right of a police officer * * * to make an on-the-street stop, interrogate and pat down for weapons (known in street vernacular as 'stop and frisk')." But this is only partly accurate. For the issue is not the abstract propriety of the police conduct, but the admissibility against petitioner of the evidence uncovered by the search and seizure. Ever since its inception, the rule excluding evidence seized in violation of the Fourth Amendment has been recognized as a principal mode of discouraging lawless police conduct. Thus in our system evidentiary rulings provide the context in which the judicial process of inclusion and exclusion approves some conduct as comporting with constitutional guarantees and disapproves other actions by state agents. A ruling admitting evidence in a criminal trial, we recognize, has the necessary effect of legitimizing the conduct which produced the evidence, while an application of the exclusionary rule withholds the constitutional imprimatur.

The exclusionary rule has its limitations, however, as a tool of judicial control. It cannot properly be invoked to exclude the products of legitimate police investigative techniques on the ground that much conduct which is closely similar involves unwarranted intrusions upon constitutional protections. Moreover, in some contexts the rule is ineffective as a deterrent. Street encounters between citizens and police officers are incredibly rich in diversity. They range from wholly friendly exchanges of pleasantries or mutually useful information to hostile confrontations of armed men involving arrests, or injuries, or loss of life. Moreover, hostile confrontations are not all of a piece. Some of them begin in a friendly enough manner, only to take a different turn upon the injection of some unexpected element into the conversation. Encounters are initiated by the police for a wide variety of purposes, some of which are wholly unrelated to a desire to prosecute for crime. Doubtless some police "field interrogation" conduct violates the Fourth Amendment. But a stern refusal by this Court to condone such activity does not necessarily render it responsive to the exclusionary rule. Regardless of how effective the rule may be where obtaining convictions is an important objective of the police, it is powerless to deter invasions of constitutionally guaranteed rights where the police either have no interest in prosecuting or are willing to forgo successful prosecution in the interest of serving some other goal.

Proper adjudication of cases in which the exclusionary rule is invoked demands a constant awareness of these limitations. The wholesale harassment by certain elements of the police community, of which minority groups, particularly Negroes, frequently complain, will not be stopped by the exclusion of any evidence from any criminal trial. Yet a rigid and unthinking application of the exclusionary rule, in futile protest against practices which it can never be used effectively to control, may exact a high toll in human injury and frustration of efforts to prevent crime. No judicial opinion can comprehend the protean variety of the street encounter, and we can only judge the facts of the case before us. Nothing we say today is to be taken as indicating approval of police conduct outside the legitimate investigative sphere. Under our decision, courts still retain their traditional responsibility to guard against police conduct which is over-bearing or harassing, or which trenches upon personal security without the objective evidentiary justification which the Constitution requires. When such conduct is identified, it must be condemned by the judiciary and its fruits must be excluded from evidence in criminal trials. And, of course, our approval of legitimate and restrained investigative conduct undertaken on the basis of ample factual justification should in no way discourage the employment of other remedies than the exclusionary rule to curtail abuses for which that sanction may prove inappropriate.

## II

Our first task is to establish at what point in this encounter the Fourth Amendment becomes relevant. That is, we must decide whether and when Officer McFadden "seized" Terry and whether and when he conducted a "search." There is some suggestion in the use of such terms as "stop" and "frisk" that such police conduct is outside the purview of the Fourth Amendment because neither action rises to the level of a "search" or "seizure" within the meaning of the Constitution.[12] We emphatically reject this notion. It is quite plain that the Fourth Amendment governs "seizures" of the person which do not eventuate in a trip to the station house and prosecution for crime — "arrests" in traditional terminology. It must be recognized

that whenever a police office accosts an individual and restrains his freedom to walk away, he has "seized" that person. And it is nothing less than sheer torture of the English language to suggest that a careful exploration of the outer surfaces of a person's clothing all over his or her body in an attempt to find weapons is not a "search." Moreover, it is simply fantastic to urge that such a procedure performed in public by a policeman while the citizen stands helpless, perhaps facing a wall with his hands raised, is a "petty indignity."[13] It is a serious intrusion upon the sanctity of the person, which may inflict great indignity and arouse strong resentment, and it is not to be undertaken lightly.[14]

In this case there can be no question, then, that Officer McFadden "seized" petitioner and subjected him to a "search" when he took hold of him and patted down the outer surfaces of his clothing. We must decide whether at that point it was reasonable for Officer McFadden to have interfered with petitioner's personal security as he did.[16] And in determining whether the seizure and search were "unreasonable"

---

[12] In this case, for example, the Ohio Court of Appeals stated that "we must be careful to distinguish that the 'frisk' authorized herein includes only a 'frisk' for a dangerous weapon. It by no means authorizes a search for contraband, evidentiary material, or anything else in the absence of reasonable grounds to arrest. Such a search is controlled by the requirements of the Fourth Amendment, and probable cause is essential."

[13] Consider the following apt description: "[T]he officer must feel with sensitive fingers every portion of the prisoner's body. A thorough search must be made of the prisoner's arms and armpits, waistline and back, the groin and area about the testicles, and entire surface of the legs down to the feet." Priar & Martin, Searching and Disarming Criminals, 45 J.Crim.L.C. & P.S. 481 (1954).

[14] We have noted that the abusive practices which play a major, though by no means exclusive, role in creating this friction are not susceptible of control by means of the exclusionary rule, and cannot properly dictate our decision with respect to the powers of the police in genuine investigative and preventive situations. However, the degree of community resentment aroused by particular practices is clearly relevant to an assessment of the quality of the intrusion upon reasonable expectations of personal security caused by those practices.

[16] We thus decide nothing today concerning the constitutional propriety of an investigative "seizure" upon less than probable cause for purposes of "detention" and/or interrogation. Obviously, not all personal intercourse between policemen and citizens involves "seizures" of persons. Only when the officer, by means of physical force or show of authority, has in some way restrained the liberty of a citizen may we conclude that a "seizure" has occurred. We cannot tell with any certainty upon this record whether any such "seizure" took place here

our inquiry is a dual one—whether the officer's action was justified at its inception, and whether it was reasonably related in scope to the circumstances which justified the interference in the first place.

### III

If this case involved police conduct subject to the Warrant Clause of the Fourth Amendment, we would have to ascertain whether "probable cause" existed to justify the search and seizure which took place. However, that is not the case. We do not retreat from our holdings that the police must, whenever practicable, obtain advance judicial approval of searches and seizures through the warrant procedure, or that in most instances failure to comply with the warrant requirement can only be excused by exigent circumstances. But we deal here with an entire rubric of police conduct—necessarily swift action predicated upon the on-the-spot observations of the officer on the beat—which historically has not been, and as a practical matter could not be, subjected to the warrant procedure. Instead, the conduct involved in this case must be tested by the Fourth Amendment's general proscription against unreasonable searches and seizures.

Nonetheless, the notions which underlie both the warrant procedure and the requirement of probable cause remain fully relevant in this context. In order to assess the reasonableness of Officer McFadden's conduct as a general proposition, it is necessary "first to focus upon the governmental interest which allegedly justifies official intrusion upon the constitutionally protected interests of the private citizen," for there is "no ready test for determining reasonableness other than by balancing the need to search [or seize] against the invasion which the search [or seizure] entails." And in justifying the particular intrusion the police officer must be able to point to specific and articulable facts which, taken together with rational inferences from those facts, reasonably warrant that intrusion.[18] The scheme of the Fourth Amendment becomes meaningful only when it is assured that at some point the conduct of those charged with

enforcing the laws can be subjected to the more detached, neutral scrutiny of a judge who must evaluate the reasonableness of a particular search or seizure in light of the particular circumstances. And in making that assessment it is imperative that the facts be judged against an objective standard: would the facts available to the officer at the moment of the seizure or the search "warrant a man of reasonable caution in the belief" that the action taken was appropriate? Anything less would invite intrusions upon constitutionally guaranteed rights based on nothing more substantial than inarticulate hunches, a result this Court has consistently refused to sanction.

### IV

We must now examine the conduct of Officer McFadden in this case to determine whether his search and seizure of petitioner were reasonable, both at their inception and as conducted. He had observed Terry, together with Chilton and another man, acting in a manner he took to be preface to a "stick-up." We think on the facts and circumstances Officer McFadden detailed before the trial judge a reasonably prudent man would have been warranted in believing petitioner was armed and thus presented a threat to the officer's safety while he was investigating his suspicious behavior. The actions of Terry and Chilton were consistent with McFadden's hypothesis that these men were contemplating a daylight robbery—which, it is reasonable to assume, would be likely to involve the use of weapons—and nothing in their conduct from the time he first noticed them until the time he confronted them and identified himself as a police officer gave him sufficient reason to negate that hypothesis. Although the trio had departed the original scene, there was nothing to indicate abandonment of an intent to commit a robbery at some point. Thus, when Officer McFadden approached the three men gathered before the display window at Zucker's store he had observed enough to make it quite reasonable to fear that they were armed; and nothing in their response to his hailing them, identifying himself as a police officer, and asking their names served to dispel that reasonable belief. We cannot say his decision at that point to seize Terry and pat his clothing for weapons was the product of a volatile or inventive imagination, or was undertaken simply as an act of harassment; the record evidences the tempered act of a policeman who in the course of an investigation had to make a quick decision as to how to protect himself and others from possible danger, and took limited steps to do so.

---

prior to Officer McFadden's initiation of physical contact for purposes of searching Terry for weapons, and we may assume that up to that point no intrusion upon constitutionally protected rights had occurred.

[18] This demand for specificity in the information upon which this police action is predicated is the central teaching of this Court's Fourth Amendment jurisprudence.

The manner in which the seizure and search were conducted is, of course, as vital a part of the inquiry as whether they were warranted at all. We need not develop at length in this case, however, the limitations which the Fourth Amendment places upon a protective seizure and search for weapons. These limitations will have to be developed in the concrete factual circumstances of individual cases. See *Sibron, infra,* decided today. Suffice it to note that such a search, unlike a search without a warrant incident to a lawful arrest, is not justified by any need to prevent the disappearance or destruction of evidence of crime. The sole justification of the search in the present situation is the protection of the police officer and others nearby, and it must therefore be confined in scope to an intrusion reasonably designed to discover guns, knives, clubs, or other hidden instruments for the assault of the police officer.

The scope of the search in this case presents no serious problem in light of these standards. Officer McFadden patted down the outer clothing of petitioner and his two companions. He did not place his hands in their pockets or under the outer surface of their garments until he had felt weapons, and then he merely reached for and removed the guns. He never did invade Katz' person beyond the outer surfaces of his clothes, since he discovered nothing in his patdown which might have been a weapon. Officer McFadden confined his search strictly to what was minimally necessary to learn whether the men were armed and to disarm them once he discovered the weapons. He did not conduct a general exploratory search for whatever evidence of criminal activity he might find.

Affirmed.

Mr. Justice BLACK concurs in the judgment.

Mr. Justice HARLAN, concurring.

While I unreservedly agree with the Court's ultimate holding in this case, I am constrained to fill in a few gaps, as I see them, in its opinion. I do this because what is said by this Court today will serve as initial guidelines for law enforcement authorities and courts throughout the land as this important new field of law develops.

In the first place, if the frisk is justified in order to protect the officer during an encounter with a citizen, the officer must first have constitutional grounds to insist on an encounter, to make a *forcible* stop. Any person, including a policeman, is at liberty to avoid a person he considers dangerous. If and when a policeman has a right instead to disarm such a person for his own protection, he must first have

a right not to avoid him but to be in his presence. That right must be more than the liberty (again, possessed by every citizen) to address questions to other persons, for ordinarily the person addressed has an equal right to ignore his interrogator and walk away; he certainly need not submit to a frisk for the questioner's protection. I would make it perfectly clear that the right to frisk in this case depends upon the reasonableness of a forcible stop to investigate a suspected crime.

Where such a stop is reasonable, however, the right to frisk must be immediate and automatic if the reason for the stop is, as here, an articulable suspicion of a crime of violence. Just as a full search incident to a lawful arrest requires no additional justification, a limited frisk incident to a lawful stop must often be rapid and routine. There is no reason why an officer, rightfully but forcibly confronting a person suspected of a serious crime, should have to ask one question and take the risk that the answer might be a bullet.

The facts of this case are illustrative of a proper stop and an incident frisk. Officer McFadden had no probable cause to arrest Terry for anything, but he had observed circumstances that would reasonably lead an experienced, prudent policeman to suspect that Terry was about to engage in burglary or robbery. His justifiable suspicion afforded a proper constitutional basis for accosting Terry, restraining his liberty of movement briefly, and addressing questions to him, and Officer McFadden did so. When he did, he had no reason whatever to suppose that Terry might be armed, apart from the fact that he suspected him of planning a violent crime. McFadden asked Terry his name, to which Terry "mumbled something." Whereupon McFadden, without asking Terry to speak louder and without giving him any chance to explain his presence or his actions, forcibly frisked him.

I would affirm this conviction for what I believe to be the same reasons the Court relies on. I would, however, make explicit what I think is implicit in affirmance on the present facts. Officer McFadden's right to interrupt Terry's freedom of movement and invade his privacy arose only because circumstances warranted forcing an encounter with Terry in an effort to prevent or investigate a crime. Once that forced encounter was justified, however, the officer's right to take suitable measures for his own safely followed automatically.

Upon the foregoing premises, I join the opinion of the Court.

[Justice WHITE's concurring opinion is omitted.]

Mr. Justice DOUGLAS, dissenting.

I agree that petitioner was "seized" within the meaning of the Fourth Amendment. I also agree that frisking petitioner and his companions for guns was a "search." But it is a mystery how that "search" and that "seizure" can be constitutional by Fourth Amendment standards, unless there was "probable cause"[1] to believe that (1) a crime had been committed or (2) a crime was in the process of being committed or (3) a crime was about to be committed.

The opinion of the Court disclaims the existence of "probable cause." If loitering were in issue and that was the offense charged, there would be "probable cause" shown. But the crime here is carrying concealed weapons; and there is no basis for concluding that the officer had "probable cause" for believing that that crime was being committed. Had a warrant been sought, a magistrate would, therefore, have been unauthorized to issue one, for he can act only if there is a showing of "probable cause." We hold today that the police have greater authority to make a "seizure" and conduct a "search" than a judge has to authorize such action. We have said precisely the opposite over and over again.

In other words, police officers up to today have been permitted to effect arrests or searches without

---

[1] The meaning of "probable cause" has been developed in cases where an officer has reasonable grounds to believe that a crime has been or is being committed. In such cases, of course, the officer may make an "arrest" which results in charging the individual with commission of a crime. But while arresting persons who have already committed crimes is an important task of law enforcement, an equally if not more important function is crime prevention and deterrence of would-be criminals. "[T]here is no war between the Constitution and common sense." Police officers need not wait until they see a person actually commit a crime before they are able to "seize" that person. Respect for our constitutional system and personal liberty demands in return, however, that such a "seizure" be made only upon "probable cause."

warrants only when the facts within their personal knowledge would satisfy the constitutional standard of *probable cause*. At the time of their "seizure" without a warrant they must possess facts concerning the person arrested that would have satisfied a magistrate that "probable cause" was indeed present. The term "probable cause" rings a bell of certainty that is not sounded by phrases such as "reasonable suspicion." Moreover, the meaning of "probable cause" is deeply imbedded in our constitutional history.

The infringement on personal liberty of any "seizure" of a person can only be "reasonable" under the Fourth Amendment if we require the police to possess "probable cause" before they seize him. Only that line draws a meaningful distinction between an officer's mere inkling and the presence of facts within the officer's personal knowledge which would convince a reasonable man that the person seized has committed, is committing, or is about to commit a particular crime. "In dealing with probable cause, * * * as the very name implies, we deal with probabilities. These are not technical; they are the factual and practical considerations of everyday life on which reasonable and prudent men, not legal technicians, act."

To give the police greater power than a magistrate is to take a long step down the totalitarian path. Perhaps such a step is desirable to cope with modern forms of lawlessness. But if it is taken, it should be the deliberate choice of the people through a constitutional amendment. Until the Fourth Amendment is rewritten, the person and the effects of the individual are beyond the reach of all government agencies until there are reasonable grounds to believe (probable cause) that a criminal venture has been launched or is about to be launched.

There have been powerful hydraulic pressures throughout our history that bear heavily on the Court to water down constitutional guarantees and give the police the upper hand. That hydraulic pressure has probably never been greater than it is today.

Yet if the individual is no longer to be sovereign, if the police can pick him up whenever they do not like the cut of his jib, if they can "seize" and "search" him in their discretion, we enter a new regime. The decision to enter it should be made only after a full debate by the people of this country.

## QUESTIONS AND NOTES

**1.** Do you think that there was probable cause for the frisk?

**2.** If your answer to question 1 was "no" and probable cause means (as *Gates* later said it meant) "fair probability," would you be concluding that McFadden's belief did not amount to a fair probability?

**3.** If McFadden lacked a fair probability, how can we say that his suspicion was reasonable?

**4.** Do you perceive a meaningful difference between reasonable suspicion and probable cause?

**5.** Do you see any good reason for dispensing with the probable cause requirement?

**6.** To what extent did Terry's "number" contribute to reasonable suspicion?

**7.** Is the Court analyzing this case as an "exclusionary rule" case? That is, is the Court saying that the exclusionary rule will not work when the police are concerned with protecting themselves so why bother to apply it? Put differently, would (should) the case have been decided differently if it were a lawsuit by Katz against McFadden for violating his Fourth Amendment rights?

**8.** Conversely, would it be reasonable to allow a protective frisk for the policeman's benefit, but disallow the evidence to be admitted?

**9.** The scope and limitation of *Terry* was fairly well fleshed out in the companion case of *Sibron v. New York.*

## Sibron v. New York
### 392 U.S. 40 (1968)

Mr. Chief Justice WARREN delivered the opinion of the Court.

Sibron was convicted of the unlawful possession of heroin. He moved before trial to suppress the heroin seized from his person by the arresting officer, Brooklyn Patrolman Anthony Martin. After the trial court denied his motion, Sibron pleaded guilty to the charge, preserving his right to appeal the evidentiary ruling. At the hearing on the motion to suppress, Officer Martin testified that while he was patrolling his beat in uniform on March 9, 1965, he observed Sibron "continually from the hours of 4:00 P.M. to 12:00, midnight * * * in the vicinity of 742 Broadway." He stated that during this period of time he saw Sibron in conversation with six or eight persons whom he (Patrolman Martin) knew from past experience to be narcotics addicts. The officer testified that he did not overhear any of these conversations, and that he did not see anything pass between Sibron and any of the others. Late in the evening Sibron entered a restaurant. Patrolman Martin saw Sibron speak with three more known addicts inside the restaurant. Once again, nothing was overheard and nothing was seen to pass between Sibron and the addicts. Sibron sat down and ordered pie and coffee, and, as he was eating Patrolman Martin approached him and told him to come outside. Once outside, the officer said to Sibron, "You know what I am after." According to the officer, Sibron "mumbled something and reached into his pocket." Simultaneously, Patrolman Martin thrust his hand into the same pocket, discovering several glassine envelopes, which, it turned out, contained heroin.

Turning to the facts of Sibron's case, it is clear that the heroin was inadmissible in evidence against him. The prosecution has quite properly abandoned the notion that there was probable cause to arrest Sibron for any crime at the time Patrolman Martin accosted him in the restaurant, took him outside and searched him. The officer was not acquainted with Sibron and had no information concerning him. He merely saw Sibron talking to a number of known narcotics addicts over a period of eight hours. It must be emphasized that Patrolman Martin was completely ignorant regarding the content of these conversations, and that he saw nothing pass between Sibron and the addicts. So far as he knew, they might "have been talking about the World Series." The inference that persons who talk to narcotics addicts are engaged in the criminal traffic in narcotics is simply not the sort of reasonable inference required to support an intrusion by the police upon an individual's personal security. Nothing resembling probable cause existed until after the search had turned up the envelopes of heroin. It is axiomatic that an incident search may not precede an arrest and serve as part of its justification. Thus the search cannot be justified as incident to a lawful arrest.

The police officer is not entitled to seize and search every person whom he sees on the street or of whom he makes inquiries. Before he places a hand on the person of a citizen in search of anything, he must have constitutionally adequate, reasonable grounds for doing so. In the case of the self-protective search for weapons, he must be able to point to particular facts from which he reasonably inferred that the individual was armed and dangerous. Patrolman Martin's testimony reveals no such facts. The suspect's mere act of talking with a number of known narcotics addicts over an eight-hour period no more gives rise to reasonable fear of life or limb on the part of the police officer than it justifies an arrest for committing a crime. Nor did Patrolman Martin urge that when Sibron put his hand in his pocket, he feared that he was going for a weapon and acted in self-defense. His opening statement to Sibron – "You know what I am after" – made it abundantly clear that he sought narcotics, and his testimony at the hearing left no doubt that he thought there were narcotics in Sibron's pocket.

Even assuming *arguendo* that there were adequate grounds to search Sibron for weapons, the nature and scope of the search conducted by Patrolman Martin were so clearly unrelated to that justification as to render the heroin inadmissible. The search for weapons approved in *Terry* consisted solely of a limited patting of the outer clothing of the suspect for concealed objects which might be used as instruments of assault. Only when he discovered such objects did the officer in *Terry* place his hands in the pockets of the men he searched. In this case, with no attempt at an initial limited exploration for arms, Patrolman Martin thrust his hand into Sibron's pocket and took from him envelopes of heroin. His testimony shows that he was looking for narcotics, and he found them. The search was not reasonably limited in scope to the accomplishment of the only goal which might conceivably have justified its inception – the protection of the officer by disarming a potentially dangerous man. Such a search violates the guarantee of the Fourth Amendment, which protects the sanctity of the person against unreasonable intrusions on the part of all government agents.

[Concurring and dissenting opinions omitted.]

## QUESTIONS AND NOTES

**1.** Was Officer Martin's search unjustified (a) because his search was not limited to a frisk for weapons, (b) because he lacked reasonable suspicion to believe that Sibron was armed, or (c) both?

**2.** Is a person who repeatedly converses with known drug users less likely to be armed than one who, as in *Terry*, "cases a joint"? Would your answer be different in 1993 than it was in 1968?

**3.** Was Sibron's behavior less suspicious than Terry's?

**4.** What lesson do you take from a composite of *Terry* and *Sibron*?

## PROBLEM

On the evening of November 9, 1989, two Minneapolis police officers were patrolling an area on the city's north side in a marked squad car. At about 8:15 p.m., one of the officers observed respondent leaving a 12-unit apartment building on Morgan Avenue North. The officer, having previously responded to complaints of drug sales in the building's hallways and having executed several search warrants on the premises, considered the building to be a notorious "crack house." According to testimony credited by the trial court, respondent began walking toward the police but, upon spotting the squad car and making eye contact with one of the officers, abruptly halted and began walking in the opposite direction. His suspicion aroused, this officer watched as respondent turned and entered an alley on the other side of the apartment building. Based upon respondent's seemingly evasive actions and the fact that he had just left a building known for cocaine traffic, the officers decided to stop respondent and investigate further.

The officers pulled their squad car into the alley and ordered respondent to stop and submit to a patdown search. The search revealed no weapons, but the officer conducting the search did take an interest in a small lump in respondent's nylon jacket. The officer later testified: "[A]s I pat-searched the front of his body, I felt a lump, a small lump, in the front pocket. I examined it with my fingers and it slid and it felt to be a lump of crack cocaine in cellophane.'' The officer then reached into respondent's pocket and retrieved a small plastic bag containing one fifth of one gram of crack cocaine. Respondent was arrested and charged in Hennepin County District Court with possession of a controlled substance.

Assuming that all parties concede that the stop was lawful and that a frisk for weapons was appropriate, should the crack cocaine be suppressed at respondent's trial. For the Supreme Court's resolution of this question, *see Minnesota v. Dickerson* 508 U.S. __, 113 S. Ct. 2130, 124 L.Ed.2d 334 (1993).

Fifteen years after *Terry* and *Sibron,* in *Long,* a Court with different Justices expanded the potential scope of a ''frisk.''

## Michigan v. Long
### 463 U.S. 1032 (1983)

Justice O'CONNOR delivered the opinion of the Court.

In *Terry,* we upheld the validity of a protective search for weapons in the absence of probable cause to arrest because it is unreasonable to deny a police officer the right ''to neutralize the threat of physical harm,'' when he possesses an articulable suspicion that an individual is armed and dangerous. We did not, however, expressly address whether such a protective search for weapons could extend to an area beyond the person in the absence of probable cause to arrest. In the present case, respondent David Long was convicted for possession of marijuana found by police in the passenger compartment and trunk of the automobile that he was driving. The police searched the passenger compartment because they had reason to believe that the vehicle contained weapons potentially dangerous to the officers. We hold that the protective search of the passenger compartment was reasonable under the principles articulated in *Terry* and other decisions of this Court.

### I

Deputies Howell and Lewis were on patrol in a rural area one evening when, shortly after midnight, they observed a car traveling erratically and at excessive speed.[1] The officers observed the car turning

down a side road, where it swerved off into a shallow ditch. The officers stopped to investigate. Long, the only occupant of the automobile, met the deputies at the rear of the car, which was protruding from the ditch onto the road. The door on the driver's side of the vehicle was left open.

Deputy Howell requested Long to produce his operator's license, but he did not respond. After the request was repeated, Long produced his license. Long again failed to respond when Howell requested him to produce the vehicle registration. After another repeated request, Long, whom Howell thought ''appeared to be under the influence of something,'' turned from the officers and began walking toward the open

---

Long could have been arrested for a speeding violation under Michigan law, he was *not* arrested because ''[a]s a matter of practice,'' police in Michigan do not arrest for speeding violations unless ''more'' is involved. The officers did issue Long an appearance ticket. The petitioner also confirmed that the officers could have arrested Long for driving while intoxicated but they ''would have to go through a process to make a determination as to whether the party is intoxicated and then go from that point.'' The court below treated this case as involving a protective search, and not a search justified by probable cause to arrest for speeding, driving while intoxicated, or any other offense. Further, the petitioner does not argue that if probable cause to arrest exists, but the officers do not actually effect the arrest, *that* the police may nevertheless conduct a search as broad as those authorized by *Belton* and *Ross.* Accordingly, we do not address that issue.

---

[1] It is clear, and the respondent concedes, that if the officers had arrested Long for speeding or for driving while intoxicated, they could have searched the passenger compartment under *Belton,* and the trunk under *Ross,* if they had probable cause to believe that the trunk contained contraband. However, at oral argument, the State informed us that while

door of the vehicle. The officers followed Long and both observed a large hunting knife on the floorboard of the driver's side of the car. The officers then stopped Long's progress and subjected him to a *Terry* protective pat down, which revealed no weapons.

Long and Deputy Lewis then stood by the rear of the vehicle while Deputy Howell shined his flashlight into the interior of the vehicle, but did not actually enter it. The purpose of Howell's action was "to search for other weapons." The officer noticed that something was protruding from under the armrest on the front seat. He knelt in the vehicle and lifted the armrest. He saw an open pouch on the front seat, and upon flashing his light on the pouch, determined that it contained what appeared to be marijuana. After Deputy Howell showed the pouch and its contents to Deputy Lewis, Long was arrested for possession of marijuana. A further search of the interior of the vehicle, including the glove box, revealed neither more contraband nor the vehicle registration. The officers decided to impound the vehicle. Deputy Howell opened the trunk, which did not have a lock, and discovered inside it approximately 75 pounds of marijuana.

### III

The court below held, and respondent Long contends, that Deputy Howell's entry into the vehicle cannot be justified under the principles set forth in *Terry* because "*Terry* authorized only a limited pat down search of a *person* suspected of criminal activity" rather than a search of an area. Although *Terry* did involve the protective frisk of a person, we believe that the police action in this case is justified by the principles that we have already established in *Terry* and other cases.

Examining the reasonableness of the officer's conduct in *Terry,* we held that there is "no ready test for determining reasonableness other than by balancing the need to search [or seize] against the invasion which the search [or seizure] entails." Although the conduct of the officer in *Terry* involved a "severe, though brief, intrusion upon cherished personal security," we found that the conduct was reasonable when we weighed the interest of the individual against the legitimate interest in "crime prevention and detection," and the "need for law enforcement officers to protect themselves and other prospective victims of violence in situations where they lack probable cause for an arrest." When the officer has a reasonable belief "that the individual whose suspicious behavior he is investigating at close range is armed and presently dangerous to the officer or to others, it would appear to be clearly unreasonable to deny the officer the power to take necessary measures to determine whether the person is in fact carrying a weapon and to neutralize the threat of physical harm."

Although *Terry* itself involved the stop and subsequent pat down search of a person, we were careful to note that "[w]e need not develop at length in this case, however, the limitations which the Fourth Amendment places upon a protective search and seizure for weapons. These limitations will have to be developed in the concrete factual circumstances of individual cases." Contrary to Long's view, *Terry* need not be read as restricting the preventative search to the person of the detained suspect.[12]

In two cases in which we applied *Terry* to specific factual situations, we recognized that investigative detentions involving suspects in vehicles are especially fraught with danger to police officers. In *Pennsylvania v. Mimms*, 434 U.S. 106 (1977), we held that police may order persons out of an automobile during a stop for a traffic violation, and may frisk those persons for weapons if there is a reasonable belief that they are armed and dangerous. Our decision rested in part on the "inordinate risk confronting an officer as he approaches a person seated in an automobile." In *Adams v. Williams*, 407 U.S. 143 (1972), we held that the police, acting on an informant's tip, may reach into the passenger compartment of an automobile to remove a gun from a driver's waistband even where the gun was not apparent to police from outside the car and the police knew of its existence only because of the tip. Again, our decision rested in part on our view of the danger presented to police officers in "traffic stop" and automobile situations.[13]

Finally, we have also expressly recognized that suspects may injure police officers and others by virtue of their access to weapons, even though they may not themselves be armed. In the Term following

---

[12] As Chief Justice Coleman noted in her dissenting opinion in the present case: "The opinion in *Terry* authorized the frisking of an overcoat worn by defendant because that was the issue presented by the facts. One could reasonably conclude that a different result would not have been constitutionally required if the overcoat had been carried, folded over the forearm, rather than worn. The constitutional principles stated in *Terry* would still control."

[13] According to one study, "approximately 30% of police shootings occurred when a police officer approached a suspect seated in an automobile."

*Terry*, we decided *Chimel*, which involved the limitations imposed on police authority to conduct a search incident to a valid arrest. Relying explicitly on *Terry*, we held that when an arrest is made, it is reasonable for the arresting officer to search "the arrestee's person and the area 'within his immediate control' – construing that phrase to mean the area from within which he might gain possession of a weapon or destructible evidence." We reasoned that "[a] gun on a table or in a drawer in front of one who is arrested can be as dangerous to the arresting officer as one concealed in the clothing of the person arrested." In *Belton*, we determined that the lower courts "have found no workable definition of 'the area within the immediate control of the arrestee' when that area arguably includes the interior of an automobile and the arrestee is its recent occupant." In order to provide a "workable rule," we held that "articles inside the relatively narrow compass of the passenger compartment of an automobile are in fact generally, even if not inevitably, within 'the area into which an arrestee might reach in order to grab a weapon'. . . ." We also held that the police may examine the contents of any open or closed container found within the passenger compartment, "for if the passenger compartment is within the reach of the arrestee, so will containers in it be within his reach."

Our past cases indicate then that protection of police and others can justify protective searches when police have a reasonable belief that the suspect poses a danger, that roadside encounters between police and suspects are especially hazardous, and that danger may arise from the possible presence of weapons in the area surrounding a suspect. These principles compel our conclusion that the search of the passenger compartment of an automobile, limited to those areas in which a weapon may be placed or hidden, is permissible if the police officer possesses a reasonable belief based on "specific and articulable facts which, taken together with the rational inferences from those facts, reasonably warrant" the officers in believing that the suspect is dangerous and the suspect may gain immediate control of weapons.[14]

---

[14] We stress that our decision does not mean that the police may conduct automobile searches *whenever* they conduct an investigative stop, although the "bright line" that we drew in *Belton* clearly authorizes such a search whenever officers effect a custodial arrest. An additional interest exists in the arrest context, *i.e.*, preservation of evidence, and this justifies an "automatic" search. However, that additional interest does not exist in the *Terry* context. A *Terry* search, "unlike a search without a warrant

The circumstances of this case clearly justified Deputies Howell and Lewis in their reasonable belief that Long posed a danger if he were permitted to reenter his vehicle. The hour was late and the area rural. Long was driving his automobile at excessive speed, and his car swerved into a ditch. The officers had to repeat their questions to Long, who appeared to be "under the influence" of some intoxicant. Long was not frisked until the officers observed that there was a large knife in the interior of the car into which Long was about to reenter. The subsequent search of the car was restricted to those areas to which Long would generally have immediate control, and that could contain a weapon. The trial court determined that the leather pouch containing marijuana could have contained a weapon.[15] It is clear that the intrusion was "strictly circumscribed by the exigencies which justifi[ed] its initiation."

The Michigan Supreme Court appeared to believe that it was not reasonable for the officers to fear that Long could injure them, because he was effectively under their control during the investigative stop and could not get access to any weapons that might have been located in the automobile. This reasoning is mistaken in several respects. During any investigative detention, the suspect is "in the control" of the officers in the sense that he "may be briefly detained against his will. . . ." Just as a *Terry* suspect on the street may, despite being under the brief control of a police officer, reach into his clothing and retrieve a weapon, so might a *Terry* suspect in Long's position break away from police control and retrieve a

---

incident to a lawful arrest, is not justified by any need to prevent the disappearance or destruction of evidence of crime. . . . The sole justification of the search . . . is the protection of police officers and others nearby. . . ." What we borrow now from *Chimel* and *Belton* is merely the recognition that part of the reason to allow area searches incident to an arrest is that the arrestee, who may not himself be armed, may be able to gain access to weapons to injure officers or others nearby, or otherwise to hinder legitimate police activity. This recognition applies as well in the *Terry* context. However, because the interest in collecting and preserving evidence is not present in the *Terry* context, we require that officers who conduct area searches during investigative detentions must do so only when they have the level of suspicion identified in *Terry*.

[15] Of course, our analysis would apply to justify the search of Long's person that was conducted by the officers after the discovery of the knife.

weapon from his automobile. In addition, if the suspect is not placed under arrest, he will be permitted to reenter his automobile, and he will then have access to any weapons inside. Or, as here, the suspect may be permitted to reenter the vehicle before the Terry investigation is over, and again, may have access to weapons. In any event, we stress that a Terry investigation, such as the one that occurred here, involves a police investigation "at close range," when the officer remains particularly vulnerable in part because a full custodial arrest has not been effected, and the officer must make a "quick decision as to how to protect himself and others from possible danger. . . ." In such circumstances, we have not required that officers adopt alternate means to ensure their safety in order to avoid the intrusion involved in a *Terry* encounter.[16]

The judgment of the Michigan Supreme Court is reversed, and the case is remanded for further proceedings not inconsistent with this opinion.

Justice BRENNAN, with whom Justice MARSHALL joins, dissenting.

The Court today holds that "the protective search of the passenger compartment" of the automobile involved in this case "was reasonable under the principles articulated in *Terry* and other decisions of this Court." I disagree. *Terry* does not support the

---

[16] Contrary to Justice Brennan's suggestion in dissent, the reasoning of *Terry, Chimel,* and *Belton* point clearly to the direction that we have taken today. Although *Chimel* involved a full custodial arrest, the rationale for *Chimel* rested on the recognition in *Terry* that it is unreasonable to prevent the police from taking reasonable steps to protect their safety. Justice Brennan suggests that we are expanding the scope of a *Terry*-type search to include a search incident to a valid arrest. However, our opinion clearly indicates that the area search that we approve is limited to a search for weapons in circumstances where the officers have a reasonable belief that the suspect is potentially dangerous to them.

Justice Brennan concedes that "police should not be exposed to unnecessary danger in the performance of their duties," but then would require that police officers, faced with having to make quick determinations about self-protection and the defense of innocent citizens in the area, must also decide instantaneously what "less intrusive" alternative exists to ensure that any threat presented by the suspect will be neutralized. For the practical reasons explained in *Terry,* we have not in the past, and do not now, require police to adopt alternate measures to avoid a legitimate *Terry*-type intrusion.

Court's conclusion and the reliance on "other decisions" is patently misplaced. Plainly, the Court is simply continuing the process of distorting *Terry* beyond recognition and forcing it into service as an unlikely weapon against the Fourth Amendment's fundamental requirement that searches and seizures be based on probable cause. I, therefore, dissent.

It is clear that *Terry* authorized only limited searches of the person for weapons. In light of what *Terry* said, relevant portions of which the Court neglects to quote, the Court's suggestion that "*Terry* need not be read as restricting the preventive search to the person of the detained suspect," can only be described as disingenuous. Nothing in *Terry* authorized police officers to search a suspect's car based on reasonable suspicion.

The Court's reliance on *Chimel* and *Belton* as support for its new "area search" rule within the context of a *Terry* stop is misplaced. The critical distinction between this case and *Terry* on the one hand, and *Chimel* and *Belton* on the other, is that the latter two cases arose within the context of lawful custodial arrests supported by probable cause. The Court in *Terry* expressly recognized the difference between a search incident to arrest and the "limited search for weapons," involved in that case. The Court stated: ". . . An arrest is a wholly different kind of intrusion upon individual freedom from a limited search for weapons, and the interests each is designed to serve are likewise quite different. An arrest is the initial stage of a criminal prosecution. It is intended to vindicate society's interest in having its laws obeyed, and it is inevitably accompanied by future interference with the individual's freedom of movement, whether or not trial or conviction ultimately follows. The protective search for weapons, on the other hand, constitutes a brief, though far from inconsiderable, intrusion upon the sanctity of the person."

In *United States v. Robinson,* 414 U.S. 218 (1973), the Court relied on the differences between searches incident to lawful custodial arrests and *Terry* "stop-and-frisk" searches to reject an argument that the limitations established in *Terry* should be applied to a search incident to arrest. The Court noted that "*Terry* clearly recognized the distinction between the two types of searches, and that a different rule governed one than governed the other," and described *Terry* as involving "stricter . . . standards," than those governing searches incident to arrest. The Court went on to state: "A custodial arrest of a suspect based on probable cause is a reasonable intrusion under the Fourth Amendment; that intrusion being lawful, a search incident to the arrest requires no additional justification. It is the fact of the lawful arrest which establishes the authority to search, and we hold that in the case of a lawful custodial arrest a full search of the person is not only an exception to the warrant requirement of the Fourth Amendment, but is also a 'reasonable' search under that Amendment.''

As these cases recognize, there is a vital difference between searches incident to lawful custodial arrests and *Terry* protective searches. The Court deliberately ignores that difference in relying on principles developed within the context of intrusions supported by probable cause to arrest to construct an "area search" rule within the context of a *Terry* stop.

The Court suggests no limit on the "area search" it now authorizes. The Court states that a "search of the passenger compartment of an automobile, limited to those areas in which a weapon may be placed or hidden, is permissible if the police officer possesses a reasonable belief based on 'specific and articulable facts which, taken together with the rational inferences from those facts, reasonably warrant' the officers in believing that the suspect is dangerous and the suspect may gain immediate control of weapons.'' Presumably a weapon "may be placed or hidden" anywhere in a car. A weapon also might be hidden in a container in the car. In this case, the Court upholds the officer's search of a leather pouch because it "could have contained a weapon." In addition, the Court's requirement that an officer have a reasonable suspicion that a suspect is armed and dangerous does little to check the initiation of an area search. In this case, the officers saw a hunting knife in the car, but the Court does not base its holding that the subsequent search was permissible on the ground that possession of the knife may have been illegal under state law. An individual can lawfully possess many things that can be used as weapons. A hammer, or a baseball bat, can be used as a very effective weapon. Finally, the Court relies on the following facts to conclude that the officers had a reasonable suspicion that respondent was presently dangerous: the hour was late; the area was rural; respondent had been driving at an excessive speed; he had been involved in an accident; he was not immediately responsive to the officers' questions; and he appeared to be under the influence of some intoxicant. Based on these facts, one might reasonably conclude that respondent was drunk. A drunk driver is indeed dangerous while driving, but not while stopped on the roadside by the police. Even when an intoxicated person lawfully has in his car an object that could be used as a weapon, it requires imagination to conclude that he is presently dangerous. Even assuming that the facts in this case justified the officers' initial "frisk" of respondent, they hardly provide adequate justification for a search of a suspect's car and the containers within it. This represents an intrusion not just different in degree, but in kind, from the intrusion sanctioned by *Terry*. In short, the implications of the Court's decision are frightening.

The Court also rejects the Michigan Supreme Court's view that it "was not reasonable for the officers to fear that [respondent] could injure them, because he was effectively under their control during the investigative stop and could not get access to any weapons that might have been located in the automobile." In this regard, the Court states: "[W]e stress that a *Terry* investigation, such as the one that occurred here, involves a police investigation 'at close range,' . . . when the officer remains particularly vulnerable in part *because* a full custodial arrest has not been effected, and the officer must make a 'quick decision as to how to protect himself and others from possible danger.' . . . In such circumstances, we have not required that officers adopt alternate means to ensure their safety in order to avoid the intrusion involved in a *Terry* encounter." (emphasis in original). Putting aside the fact that the search at issue here involved a far more serious intrusion than that "involved in a *Terry* encounter," and as such might suggest the need for resort to "alternate means," the Court's reasoning is perverse. The Court's argument in essence is that the *absence* of probable cause to arrest compels the conclusion that a broad search, traditionally associated in scope with a search incident to arrest, must be permitted based on reasonable suspicion. But *United States v. Robinson* stated: "It is scarcely open to doubt that the danger to an officer is far greater in the case of the extended exposure which follows the taking of a suspect into custody and transporting him to the police station than in the case of the relatively fleeting contact resulting from the typical *Terry*-type stop." In light of *Robinson*'s observation, today's holding leaves in grave doubt the question of whether the Court's assessment of the relative dangers posed by given confrontations is based on any principled standard.

Hornbook law has been that "the police may not conduct a search unless they first convince a neutral magistrate that there is probable cause to do so." While under some circumstances the police may search a car without a warrant, "the exception to the warrant requirement established in *Carroll* . . . applies only to searches of vehicles that are supported by probable cause." *Ross*. Today the Court discards these basic principles and employs the very narrow exception established by *Terry* "to swallow the general rule that Fourth Amendment [searches of cars] are 'reasonable' only if based on probable cause.''[6]

---

[6] Of course, the Court's decision also swallows the general rule that searches of containers must be based on probable cause. Without probable cause to search the car, *Ross* does not apply. Moreover, in the absence of a lawful custodial arrest, *Belton* does not apply.

"The needs of law enforcement stand in constant tension with the Constitution's protections of the individual against certain exercises of official power. It is precisely the predictability of these pressures that counsels a resolute loyalty to constitutional safeguards." Of course, police should not be exposed to unnecessary danger in the performance of their duties. But a search of a car and the containers within it based on nothing more than reasonable suspicion, even under the circumstances present here, cannot be sustained without doing violence to the requirements of the Fourth Amendment. There is no reason in this case why the officers could not have pursued less intrusive, but equally effective, means of insuring their safety.[7] The Court takes a long step today toward "balancing" into oblivion the protections the Fourth Amendment affords. I dissent, for as Justice Jackson said in *Brinegar*:

> "[Fourth Amendment rights] are not mere second-class rights but belong in the catalog of indispensable freedoms. Among deprivations of rights, none is so effective in cowing a population, crushing the spirit of the individual and putting terror in every heart. Uncontrolled search and seizure is one of the first and most effective weapons in the arsenal of every arbitrary government." (dissenting opinion).

[Justice STEVENS dissenting opinion is omitted.]

---

[7] The police, for example, could have continued to detain respondent outside the car and asked him to tell them where his registration was. The police then could have retrieved the registration themselves. This would have resulted in an intrusion substantially less severe than the one at issue here.

## QUESTIONS AND NOTES

**1.** Accepting the Court's contention that it is not approving generic "car frisks" simply because a car was stopped, what is there about *Long* that warrants the frisk?

**2.** Did (should) the hunting knife influence (have influenced) the Court? Why? Why not?

**3.** Would (should) the *Long* reasoning permit the police to look inside a knapsack in a *Terry* situation?

**4.** Do you think that the *Brinegar* quote at the end of the Brennan opinion was overly apocalyptic?

**5.** Would *Long* have seemed less threatening to libertarians if it were accompanied by a decision, like *Sibron*, disallowing an automobile frisk when the evidence for it was less persuasive than it was in *Long*?

**6.** We close this section with *Ybarra*, a case clearly establishing that *Terry* "is not a talisman in whose presence the Fourth Amendment disappears."

### Ybarra v. Illinois
444 U.S. 85 (1979)

Mr. Justice STEWART delivered the opinion of the Court.

An Illinois statute authorizes law enforcement officers to detain and search any person found on premises being searched pursuant to a search warrant, to protect themselves from attack or to prevent the disposal or concealment of anything described in the warrant. The question before us is whether the application of this statute to the facts of the present case violated the Fourth and Fourteenth Amendments.

I

On March 1, 1976, a special agent of the Illinois Bureau of Investigation presented a "Complaint for Search Warrant" to a judge of an Illinois Circuit Court. The complaint recited that the agent had spoken with an informant known to the police to be reliable and:

"3. The informant related . . . that over the weekend of 28 and 29 February he was in the [Aurora Tap Tavern, located in the city of Aurora, Ill.] and observed fifteen to twenty-five tin-foil packets on the person of the bartender 'Greg' and behind the bar. He also has been in the tavern on at least ten other occasions and has observed tin-foil packets on 'Greg' and in a drawer behind the bar. The informant has used heroin in the past and knows that tin-foil packets are a common method of packaging heroin.

"4. The informant advised . . . that over the weekend of 28 and 29 February he had a conversation with 'Greg' and was advised that 'Greg' would have heroin for sale on Monday, March 1, 1976. This conversation took place in the tavern described."

On the strength of this complaint, the judge issued a warrant.

In the late afternoon of that day, seven or eight officers proceeded to the tavern. Upon entering it, the officers announced their purpose and advised all those present that they were going to conduct a "cursory search for weapons." One of the officers then proceeded to patdown each of the 9 to 13 customers present in the tavern, while the remaining officers engaged in an extensive search of the premises.

The police officer who frisked the patrons found the appellant, Ventura Ybarra, in front of the bar standing by a pinball machine. In his first patdown of Ybarra, the officer felt what he described as "a cigarette pack with objects in it." He did not remove this pack from Ybarra's pocket. Instead, he moved on and proceeded to patdown other customers. After completing this process the officer returned to Ybarra and frisked him once again. This second search of Ybarra took place approximately 2 to 10 minutes after the first. The officer relocated and retrieved the cigarette pack from Ybarra's pants pocket. Inside the pack he found six tinfoil packets containing a brown powdery substance which later turned out to be heroin.

## II

There is no reason to suppose that, when the search warrant was issued on March 1, 1976, the authorities had probable cause to believe that any person found on the premises of the Aurora Tap Tavern, aside from "Greg," would be violating the law.[2] The search warrant complaint did not allege

that the bar was frequented by persons illegally purchasing drugs. It did not state that the informant had ever seen a patron of the tavern purchase drugs from "Greg" or from any other person. Nowhere, in fact, did the complaint even mention the patrons of the Aurora Tap Tavern.

It is true that the police possessed a warrant based on probable cause to search the tavern in which Ybarra happened to be at the time the warrant was executed. But, a person's mere propinquity to others independently suspected of criminal activity does not, without more, give rise to probable cause to search that person. *Sibron.* Where the standard is probable cause, a search or seizure of a person must be supported by probable cause particularized with respect to that person. This requirement cannot be undercut or avoided by simply pointing to the fact that coincidentally there exists probable cause to search or seize another or to search the premises where the person may happen to be. The Fourth and Fourteenth Amendments protect the "legitimate expectations of privacy" of persons, not places.

Each patron who walked into the Aurora Tap Tavern on March 1, 1976, was clothed with constitutional protection against an unreasonable search or an unreasonable seizure. That individualized protection was separate and distinct from the Fourth and Fourteenth Amendment protection possessed by the proprietor of the tavern or by "Greg." Although the search warrant, issued upon probable cause, gave the officers authority to search the premises and to search "Greg," it gave them no authority whatever to invade the constitutional protections possessed individually by the tavern's customers.[4]

---

2 The warrant issued on March 1, 1976, did not itself authorize the search of Ybarra or of any other patron found on the premises of the Aurora Tap Tavern. It directed the police to search "the follow-

ing person or place: . . . the Aurora Tap Tavern. . . . Also the person of 'Greg'. . . ." Had the issuing judge intended that the warrant would or could authorize a search of every person found within the tavern, he would hardly have specifically authorized the search of "Greg" alone. "Greg" was an employee of the tavern, and the complaint upon which the search warrant was issued gave every indication that he would be present at the tavern on March 1.

4 The Fourth Amendment directs that "no Warrants shall issue, but upon probable cause . . . and particularly describing the place to be searched, and the persons or things to be seized." Thus, "open-ended" or "general" warrants are constitutionally prohibited. It follows that a warrant to search a place cannot normally be construed to authorize a search of each individual in that place. The warrant for the Aurora Tap Tavern provided no basis for departing from this general rule. Consequently, we need not

Notwithstanding the absence of probable cause to search Ybarra, the State argues that the action of the police in searching him and seizing what was found in his pocket was nonetheless constitutionally permissible. We are asked to find that the first patdown search of Ybarra constituted a reasonable frisk for weapons under the doctrine of *Terry*. If this finding is made, it is then possible to conclude, the State argues, that the second search of Ybarra was constitutionally justified. The argument is that the patdown yielded probable cause to believe that Ybarra was carrying narcotics, and that this probable cause constitutionally supported the second search, no warrant being required in light of the exigencies of the situation coupled with the ease with which Ybarra could have disposed of the illegal substance.

We are unable to take even the first step required by this argument. The initial frisk of Ybarra was simply not supported by a reasonable belief that he was armed and presently dangerous, a belief which this Court has invariably held must form the predicate to a patdown of a person for weapons.[5] When the police entered the Aurora Tap Tavern on March 1, 1976, the lighting was sufficient for them to observe the customers. Upon seeing Ybarra, they neither recognized him as a person with a criminal history nor had any particular reason to believe that he might be inclined to assault them. Moreover, as Police Agent Johnson later testified, Ybarra, whose hands were empty, gave no indication of possessing a weapon, made no gestures or other actions indicative of an intent to commit an assault, and acted generally in a manner that was not threatening. At the suppression hearing, the most Agent Johnson could point to was that Ybarra was wearing a ¾-length lumber jacket, clothing which the State admits could be expected on almost any tavern patron in Illinois in early March. In short, the State is unable to articulate any specific fact that would have justified a police officer at the scene in even suspecting that Ybarra was armed and dangerous.

---

consider situations where the warrant itself authorizes the search of unnamed persons in a place and is supported by probable cause to believe that persons who will be in the place at the time of the search will be in possession of illegal drugs.

[5] Since we conclude that the initial patdown of Ybarra was not justified under the Fourth and Fourteenth Amendments, we need not decide whether or not the presence on Ybarra's person of "a cigarette pack with objects in it" yielded probable cause to believe that Ybarra was carrying any illegal substance.

*Terry* created an exception to the requirement of probable cause, an exception whose "narrow scope" this Court "has been careful to maintain." Under that doctrine a law enforcement officer, for his own protection and safety, may conduct a patdown to find weapons that he reasonably believes or suspects are then in the possession of the person he has accosted. Nothing in *Terry* can be understood to allow a generalized "cursory search for weapons" or indeed, any search whatever for anything but weapons. The "narrow scope" of the *Terry* exception does not permit a frisk for weapons on less than reasonable belief or suspicion directed at the person to be frisked, even though that person happens to be on premises where an authorized narcotics search is taking place.

[The Court then held that the State's interest in controlling narcotics did not justify an evidence search of everybody who happened to be at the place that was searched.]

For these reasons, we conclude that the searches of Ybarra and the seizure of what was in his pocket contravened the Fourth and Fourteenth Amendments.

Mr. Chief Justice BURGER, with whom Mr. Justice BLACKMUN and Mr. Justice REHNQUIST join, dissenting.

I join Mr. Justice Rehnquist's dissent since I cannot subscribe to the Court's unjustifiable narrowing of the rule of *Terry*. The Court would require a particularized and individualized suspicion that a person is armed and dangerous as a condition to a *Terry* search. This goes beyond the rationale of *Terry* and overlooks the practicalities of a situation which no doubt often confronts officers executing a valid search warrant.

These officers had validly obtained a warrant to search a named person and a rather small, one-room tavern for narcotics. Upon arrival, they found the room occupied by 12 persons. Were they to ignore these individuals and assume that all were unarmed and uninvolved? Given the setting and the reputation of those who trade in narcotics, it does not go too far to suggest that they might pay for such an easy assumption with their lives. The law does not require that those executing a search warrant must be so foolhardy. That is precisely what Mr. Chief Justice Warren's opinion in *Terry* stands for. Indeed, the *Terry* Court recognized that a balance must be struck between the privacy interest of individuals and the safety of police officers in performing their duty. I would hold that when police execute a search warrant for narcotics in a place of known narcotics activity they may protect themselves by conducting a *Terry* search. They are not required to assume that they will not be harmed by patrons of the kind of establishment shown here, something quite different from a ballroom at the Waldorf. "The officer need not be absolutely certain that the individual is armed; the issue is whether a reasonably prudent man in the circumstances would be warranted in the belief that his safety or that of others was in danger."

I do not find it controlling that the heroin was not actually retrieved from appellant until the officer returned after completing the first search. The "cigarette pack with objects in it" was noticed in the first search. In the "second search," the officer did no more than return to the appellant and retrieve the pack he had already discovered. That there was a delay of minutes between the search and the seizure is not dispositive in this context, where the searching officer made the on-the-spot judgment that he need not seize the suspicious package immediately. He could first reasonably make sure that none of the patrons was armed before returning to appellant. Thus I would treat the second search and its fruits just as I would had the officer taken the pack immediately upon noticing it, which plainly would have been permissible.

Mr. Justice REHNQUIST, with whom the CHIEF JUSTICE and Mr. Justice BLACKMUN join, dissenting.

When police arrived at the Aurora Tap, a drab, dimly lit tavern, they found about a dozen or so persons standing or sitting at the bar. The police announced their purpose and told everyone at the bar to stand for a patdown search. Agent Jerome Johnson, the only officer to testify in the proceedings below, explained that the initial search was a frisk for weapons to protect the officers executing the warrant. Johnson frisked several patrons, including appellant Ybarra. During this patdown, Johnson felt "a cigarette pack with objects in it" in Ybarra's front pants pocket. He finished frisking the other patrons and then returned to Ybarra. At that time, he frisked Ybarra once again, reached into Ybarra's pocket, and removed the cigarette package that he had felt previously. The package, upon inspection, confirmed the officer's previously aroused suspicion that it contained not cigarettes but packets of heroin.

Confronted with these facts, the Court concludes that the police were without authority under the warrant to search any of the patrons in the tavern and that, absent probable cause to believe that Ybarra possessed contraband, the search of his person violated the Fourth and Fourteenth Amendments. Because I believe that this analysis is faulty, I dissent.

[Justice Rehnquist then concluded that the search of Ybarra was justified because a warrant to search the bar included all persons found therein.]

Viewed sequentially, the actions of the police in this case satisfy the scope/justification test of reasonableness established by the first clause of the Fourth Amendment as interpreted in *Terry*. The police entered the Aurora Tap pursuant to the warrant and found themselves confronting a dozen people, all standing or sitting at the bar, the suspected location of the contraband. Because the police were aware that heroin was being offered for sale in the tavern, it was quite reasonable to assume that any one or more of the persons at the bar could have been involved in drug trafficking. This assumption, by itself, might not have justified a full-scale search of all the individuals in the tavern. Nevertheless, the police also were quite conscious of the possibility that one or more of the patrons could be armed in preparation for just such an intrusion. In the narcotics business, "firearms are as much 'tools of the trade' as are most commonly recognized articles of narcotics paraphernalia." The potential danger to the police executing the warrant and to innocent individuals in this dimly lit tavern cannot be minimized. By conducting an immediate frisk of those persons at the bar, the police eliminated this danger and "froze" the area in preparation for the search of the premises.

Ybarra contends that *Terry* requires an "individualized" suspicion that a particular person is armed and dangerous. While this factor may be important in the case of an on-the-street stop, where the officer must articulate some reason for singling the person out of the general population, there are at least two reasons why it has less significance in the present situation, where execution of a valid warrant had thrust the police into a confrontation with a small but potentially dangerous, group of people. First, in place of the requirement of "individualized suspicion" as a guard against arbitrary exercise of authority, we have here the determination of a neutral and detached magistrate that a search was necessary. The question then becomes whether, given the initial decision to intrude, the scope of the intrusion is reasonable.

In addition, the task performed by the officers executing a search warrant is inherently more perilous than is a momentary encounter on the street. The danger is greater "not only because the suspect and officer will be in close proximity for a longer period of time, but also . . . because the officer's investigative responsibilities under the warrant require him to direct his attention to the premises rather than the person." To hold a police officer in such a situation to the same standard of "individualized suspicion" as might be required in the case of an on-the-street stop would defeat the purpose of gauging reasonableness in terms of all the circumstances surrounding an encounter.

Measured against the purpose for the initial search is the scope of that search. I do not doubt that a patdown for weapons is a substantial intrusion into one's privacy. Nevertheless, such an intrusion was more than justified, under the circumstances here, by the potential threat to the lives of the searching officers and innocent bystanders. In the rubric of *Terry* itself, a "man of reasonable caution" would have been warranted in the belief that it was appropriate to frisk the 12 or so persons in the vicinity of the bar for weapons.

I would conclude that Officer Johnson, acting under the authority of a valid search warrant, did not exceed the reasonable scope of that warrant in locating and retrieving the heroin secreted in Ybarra's pocket. This is not a case where Ybarra's Fourth Amendment rights were at the mercy of overly zealous officers "engaged in the often competitive enterprise of ferreting out crime." On the contrary, the need for a search was determined, as contemplated by the second clause of the Fourth Amendment, by a neutral and detached magistrate, and the officers performed their duties pursuant to their warrant in an appropriate fashion. The Fourth Amendment requires nothing more.

## QUESTIONS AND NOTES

**1.** Did the Court show insufficient sensitivity to the fact that the Aurora Tap was not like "a ballroom at the Waldorf?" Or is the point of the Fourth Amendment that a person should not be subject to a search because he frequents establishments that fail to meet a threshold standard of elegance?

**2.** Is the danger of a weapon being found on Ybarra more like the danger of a weapon being found on Terry, on Sibron, or in Long's car, or none of the above? Explain.

**3.** What can the police now do to protect themselves in an *Ybarra*-type situation? Could they order all of the patrons to leave? Could they give the patrons an option to leave or be frisked? Could they order all of the patrons to stay?

## B.   What Is Reasonable Suspicion? How Is It Different From Probable Cause?

In the questions following *Terry,* we saw the difficulty inherent in trying to distinguish reasonable suspicion from probable cause. While the Court's opinions have been less than perfectly clear, there is a series of opinions that have tried to define reasonable suspicion, sometimes, but not always, distinguishing it from probable cause. In this section, we examine those cases.

### Adams v. Williams
### 407 U.S. 143 (1972)

Mr. Justice REHNQUIST delivered the opinion of the Court.

Police Sgt. John Connolly was alone early in the morning on car patrol duty in a high-crime area of Bridgeport, Connecticut. At approximately 2:15 a.m. a person known to Sgt. Connolly approached his cruiser and informed him that an individual seated in a nearby vehicle was carrying narcotics and had a gun at his waist.

After calling for assistance on his car radio, Sgt. Connolly approached the vehicle to investigate the informant's report. Connolly tapped on the car window and asked the occupant, Robert Williams, to open the door. When Williams rolled down the window instead, the sergeant reached into the car and removed a fully loaded revolver from Williams' waistband. The gun had not been visible to Connolly from outside the car, but it was in precisely the place indicated by the informant. Williams was then arrested by Connolly for unlawful possession of the pistol. A search incident to that arrest was conducted after other officers arrived. They found substantial quantities of heroin on Williams' person and in the car, and they found a machete and a second revolver hidden in the automobile.

Respondent contends that the initial seizure of his pistol, upon which rested the later search and seizure of other weapons and narcotics, was not justified by the informant's tip to Sgt. Connolly. He claims that absent a more reliable informant, or some corroboration of the tip, the policeman's actions were unreasonable under the standards set forth in *Terry*.

The Court recognized in *Terry* that the policeman making a reasonable investigatory stop should not be denied the opportunity to protect himself from attack by a hostile suspect. "When an officer is justified in believing that the individual whose suspicious behavior he is investigating at close range is armed and presently dangerous to the officer or to others," he may conduct a limited protective search for concealed weapons. The purpose of this limited search is not to discover evidence of crime, but to allow the officer to pursue his investigation without fear of violence, and thus the frisk for weapons might be equally necessary and reasonable, whether or not carrying a concealed weapon violated any applicable state law. So long as the officer is entitled to make a forcible stop, and has reason to believe that the suspect is armed and dangerous, he may conduct a weapons search limited in scope to this protective purpose.

Applying these principles to the present case, we believe that Sgt. Connolly acted justifiably in responding to his informant's tip. The informant was known to him personally and had provided him with information in the past. This is a stronger case than obtains in the case of an anonymous telephone tip. The informant here came forward personally to give information that was immediately verifiable at the scene. Indeed, under Connecticut law, the informant

might have been subject to immediate arrest for making a false complaint had Sgt. Connolly's investigation proved the tip incorrect.[2] Thus, while the Court's decisions indicate that this informant's unverified tip may have been insufficient for a narcotics arrest or search warrant, see, *e.g.*, *Spinelli*, the information carried enough indicia of reliability to justify the officer's forcible stop of Williams.

In reaching this conclusion, we reject respondent's argument that reasonable cause for a stop and frisk can only be based on the officer's personal observation, rather than on information supplied by another person. Informants' tips, like all other clues and evidence coming to a policeman on the scene, may vary greatly in their value and reliability. One simple rule will not cover every situation. Some tips, completely lacking in indicia of reliability, would either warrant no police response or require further investigation before a forcible stop of a suspect would be authorized. But in some situations—for example, when the victim of a street crime seeks immediate police aid and gives a description of his assailant, or when a credible informant warns of a specific impending crime—the subtleties of the hearsay rule should not thwart an appropriate police response.

While properly investigating the activity of a person who was reported to be carrying narcotics and a concealed weapon and who was sitting alone in a car in a high-crime area at 2:15 in the morning, Sgt. Connolly had ample reason to fear for his safety. When Williams rolled down his window, rather than complying with the policeman's request to step out of the car so that his movements could more easily be seen, the revolver allegedly at Williams' waist became an even greater threat. Under these circumstances the policeman's action in reaching to the spot where the gun was thought to be hidden constituted a limited intrusion designed to insure his safety, and we conclude that it was reasonable. The loaded gun seized as a result of this intrusion was therefore admissible at Williams' trial.

Under the circumstances surrounding Williams' possession of the gun seized by Sgt. Connolly, the arrest on the weapons charge was supported by probable cause, and the search of his person and of the

---

[2] Section 53–168 of the Connecticut General Statutes, in force at the time of these events, provided that a "person who knowingly makes to any police officer * * * a false report or a false complaint alleging that a crime or crimes have been committed" is guilty of a misdemeanor.

car incident to that arrest was lawful. The fruits of the search were therefore properly admitted at Williams' trial, and the Court of Appeals erred in reaching a contrary conclusion.

Justice BRENNAN, dissenting.

The crucial question on which this case turns, as the Court concedes, is whether, there being no contention that Williams acted voluntarily in rolling down the window of his car, the State had shown sufficient cause to justify Sgt. Connolly's "forcible" stop. I would affirm, believing, for the following reasons stated by Judge, now Chief Judge, Friendly, dissenting, 436 F.2d 30, 38–39, that the State did not make that showing:

"To begin, I have the gravest hesitancy in extending [*Terry*] to crimes like the possession of narcotics. . . . There is too much danger that, instead of the stop being the object and the protective frisk an incident thereto, the reverse will be true. Against that we have here the added fact of the report that Williams had a gun on his person. . . . [But] Connecticut allows its citizens to carry weapons, concealed or otherwise, at will, provided only they have a permit, Conn.Gen.Stat. §§ 29–35 and 29–38, and gives its police officers no special authority to stop for the purpose of determining whether the citizen has one. . . .

"If I am wrong in thinking that *Terry* should not be applied at all to mere possessory offenses, . . . I would not find the combination of Officer Connolly's almost meaningless observation and the tip in this case to be sufficient justification for the intrusion. The tip suffered from a threefold defect, with each fold compounding the others. The informer was unnamed, he was not shown to have been reliable with respect to guns or narcotics, and he gave no information which demonstrated personal knowledge or—what is worse—could not readily have been manufactured by the officer after the event. To my mind, it has not been sufficiently recognized that the difference between this sort of tip and the accurate prediction of an unusual event is as important on the latter score as on the former. [In *Draper*] Narcotics Agent Marsh would hardly have been at the Denver Station at the exact moment of the arrival of the train Draper had taken from Chicago unless *someone* had told him *something* important, although the agent might later have embroidered the details to fit the observed facts. . . . There

is no such guarantee of a patrolling officer's veracity when he testifies to a 'tip' from an unnamed informer saying no more than that the officer will find a gun and narcotics on a man across the street, as he later does. If the state wishes to rely on a tip of that nature to validate a stop and frisk, revelation of the name of the informer or demonstration that his name is unknown and could not reasonably have been ascertained should be the price.

"*Terry* was intended to free a police officer from the rigidity of a rule that would prevent his doing anything to a man reasonably suspected of being about to commit or having just committed a crime of violence, no matter how grave the problem or impelling the need for swift action, unless the officer had what a court would later determine to be probable cause for arrest. It was meant for the serious cases of imminent danger or of harm recently perpetrated to persons or property, not the conventional ones of possessory offenses. If it is to be extended to the latter at all, this should be only where observation by the officer himself or well authenticated information shows 'that criminal activity may be afoot.' I greatly fear that if the [contrary view] should be followed, *Terry* will have opened the sluice gates for serious and unintended erosion of the protection of the Fourth Amendment."

Mr. Justice MARSHALL, with whom Mr. Justice DOUGLAS joins, dissenting.

In today's decision the Court ignores the fact that *Terry* begrudgingly accepted the necessity for creating an exception from the warrant requirement of the Fourth Amendment and treats this case as if warrantless searches were the rule rather than the "narrowly drawn" exception. This decision betrays the careful balance that *Terry* sought to strike between a citizen's right to privacy and his government's responsibility for effective law enforcement and expands the concept of warrantless searches far beyond anything heretofore recognized as legitimate. I dissent.

The only information that the informant had previously given the officer involved homosexual conduct in the local railroad station. The following colloquy took place between respondent's counsel and the officer at the hearing on respondent's motion to suppress the evidence that had been seized from him.

"Q. Now, with respect to the information that was given you about homosexuals in the Bridgeport Police Station [*sic*], did that lead to an arrest? A. No.

"Q. An arrest was not made. A. No. There was no substantiating evidence.

"Q. There was no substantiating evidence? A. No.

"Q. And what do you mean by that? A. I didn't have occasion to witness these individuals committing any crime of any nature.

"Q. In other words, after this person gave you the information, you checked for corroboration before you made an arrest. Is that right? A. Well, I checked to determine the possibility of homosexual activity.

"Q. And since an arrest was made, I take it you didn't find any substantiating information. A. I'm sorry counselor, you say since an arrest was made."

Q. Was not made. Since an arrest was not made, I presume you didn't find any substantiating information. A. No.

"Q. So that, you don't recall any other specific information given you about the commission of crimes by this informant. A. No.

"Q. And you still thought this person was reliable. A. Yes."

*Terry* did not hold that whenever a policeman has a hunch that a citizen is engaging in criminal activity, he may engage in a stop and frisk. It held that if police officers want to stop and frisk, they must have specific facts from which they can reasonably infer that an individual is engaged in criminal activity and is armed and dangerous. It was central to our decision in *Terry* that the police officer acted on the basis of his own personal observations and that he carefully scrutinized the conduct of his suspects before interfering with them in any way. When we legitimated the conduct of the officer in *Terry* we did so because of the substantial *reliability* of the information on which the officer based his decision to act.

If the Court does not ignore the care with which we examined the knowledge possessed by the officer in *Terry* when he acted, then I cannot see how the actions of the officer in this case can be upheld. The Court explains what the officer knew about respondent before accosting him. But what is more significant is what he did not know. With respect to the scene generally, the officer had no idea how long respondent had been in the car, how long the car had been parked, or to whom the car belonged. With respect to the gun,[5]

the officer did not know if or when the informant had ever seen the gun, or whether the gun was carried legally, as Connecticut law permitted, or illegally. And with respect to the narcotics, the officer did not know what kind of narcotics respondent allegedly had, whether they were legally or illegally possessed, what the basis of the informant's knowledge was, or even whether the informant was capable of distinguishing narcotics from other substances.

Unable to answer any of these questions, the officer nevertheless determined that it was necessary to intrude on respondent's liberty. I believe that his determination was totally unreasonable. As I read *Terry*, an officer may act on the basis of *reliable* information short of probable cause to make a stop, and ultimately a frisk, if necessary; but the officer may not use unreliable, unsubstantiated, conclusory hearsay to justify an invasion of liberty. *Terry* never meant to approve the kind of knee-jerk police reaction that we have before us in this case.

Even assuming that the officer had some legitimate reason for relying on the informant, *Terry* requires, before any stop and frisk is made, that the reliable information in the officer's possession demonstrate that the suspect is both armed and *dangerous*. The fact remains that Connecticut specifically authorizes persons to carry guns so long as they have a permit. Thus, there was no reason for the officer to infer from anything that the informant said that the respondent was dangerous. His frisk was, therefore, illegal under *Terry*.

Mr. Justice Douglas was the sole dissenter in *Terry*. He warned of the "powerful hydraulic pressures throughout our history that bear heavily on the Court to water down constitutional guarantees. . . ." While I took the position then that we were not watering down rights, but were hesitantly and cautiously striking a necessary balance between the rights of American citizens to be free from government intrusion into their privacy and their government's urgent need for a narrow exception to the warrant requirement of the Fourth Amendment, today's decision demonstrates just how prescient Mr. Justice Douglas was.

It seems that the delicate balance that *Terry* struck was simply too delicate, too susceptible to the "hydraulic pressures" of the day. As a result of today's decision, the balance struck in *Terry* is now heavily weighted in favor of the government. And the Fourth Amendment, which was included in the Bill of Rights to prevent the kind of arbitrary and oppressive police action involved herein, is dealt a serious blow. Today's decision invokes the specter of a society in which innocent citizens may be stopped, searched, and arrested at the whim of police officers who have only the slightest suspicion of improper conduct.

---

[5] The fact that the respondent carried his gun in a high-crime area is irrelevant. In such areas it is more probable than not that citizens would be more likely to carry weapons authorized by the State to protect themselves.

## QUESTIONS AND NOTES

**1.** If you had been Officer Connolly, would you have been suspicious of Williams? If so, would you have considered your suspicions reasonable? Why? Why not?

**2.** Do we want police officers to do what Connolly did in this case?

**3.** Is the Brennan/Friendly opinion insensitive to the need to combat drugs?

**4.** How important is it that the informant was known? Suppose that Connolly had been told by an anonymous phone call earlier in the day that at 2 a.m. someone meeting Williams' description would be sitting in a car like the one in which Williams sat, and that he would have a gun in his waistband and narcotics in his glove compartment?

**5.** How, if at all, does *Adams* expand *Terry*? Wasn't it *more* likely that Williams was armed than that Terry, Chilton, and Katz were armed?

**6.** In *Cortez,* we see significantly more police affirmation prior to the stop.

### United States v. Cortez
### 449 U.S. 411 (1981)

Chief Justice BURGER delivered the opinion of the Court.

We granted certiorari to consider whether objective facts and circumstantial evidence suggesting that a particular vehicle is involved in criminal activity may provide a sufficient basis to justify an investigative stop of that vehicle.

I

Late in 1976, Border Patrol officers patrolling a sparsely populated section of southern central Arizona found human footprints in the desert. In time, other sets of similar footprints were discovered in the same area. From these sets of footprints, it was deduced that, on a number of occasions, groups of from 8 to 20 persons had walked north from the Mexican border, across 30 miles of desert and mountains, over a fairly well-defined path, to an isolated point on Highway 86, an east-west road running roughly parallel to the Mexican border.

Officers observed that one recurring shoe print bore a distinctive and repetitive V-shaped or chevron design. Because the officers knew from recorded experience that the area through which the groups passed was heavily trafficked by aliens illegally entering the country from Mexico, they surmised that a person, to whom they gave the case-name "Chevron," was guiding aliens illegally into the United States over the path marked by the tracks to a point where they could be picked up by a vehicle.

The tracks led into or over obstacles that would have been avoided in daylight. From this, the officers deduced that "Chevron" probably led his groups across the border and to the pickup point at night. Moreover, based upon the times when they had discovered the distinctive sets of tracks, they concluded that "Chevron" generally traveled during or near weekends and on nights when the weather was clear.

Their tracking disclosed that when "Chevron's" groups came within 50 to 75 yards of Highway 86, they turned right and walked eastward, parallel to the road. Then, approximately at highway milepost 122, the tracks would turn north and disappear at the road. From this pattern, the officers concluded that the aliens very likely were picked up by a vehicle—probably one approaching from the east, for after a long overland march the group was most likely to walk parallel to the highway *toward* the approaching vehicle. The officers also concluded that, after the pickup, the vehicle probably returned to the east, because it was unlikely that the group would be walking away from its ultimate destination.

On the Sunday night of January 30-31, 1977, Officers Gray and Evans, two Border Patrolmen who had been pursuing the investigation of "Chevron," were on duty in the Casa Grande area. The latest set of observed "Chevron" tracks had been made on Saturday night, January 15-16. January 30-31 was the first clear night after three days of rain. For these reasons, Gray and Evans decided there was a strong possibility that "Chevron" would lead aliens from the border to the highway that night.

The officers assumed that, if "Chevron" did conduct a group that night, he would not leave Mexico until after dark, that is, about 6 p.m. They knew from their experience that groups of this sort, traveling on foot, cover about two and a half to three miles an hour. Thus, the 30-mile journey would take from 8 to 12 hours. From this, the officers calculated that "Chevron" and his group would arrive at Highway 86 somewhere between 2 a.m. and 6 a.m. on January 31.

About 1 a.m., Gray and Evans parked their patrol car on an elevated location about 100 feet off Highway 86 at milepost 149, a point some 27 miles east of milepost 122. From their vantage point, the officers could observe the Altar Valley, an adjoining territory they had been assigned to watch that night, and they also could see vehicles passing on Highway 86. They estimated that it would take approximately one hour and a half for a vehicle to make a round trip from their vantage point to milepost 122. Working on the hypothesis that the pickup vehicle approached milepost 122 from the east and thereafter returned to its starting point, they focused upon vehicles that passed them from the east and, after about one hour and a half, passed them returning to the east.

Because "Chevron" appeared to lead groups of between 8 and 20 aliens at a time, the officers deduced that the pickup vehicle would be one that was capable of carrying that large a group without arousing suspicion. For this reason, and because they knew that certain types of vehicles were commonly used for smuggling sizable groups of aliens, they decided to limit their attention to vans, pickup trucks, other small trucks, campers, motor homes, and similar vehicles.

Traffic on Highway 86 at milepost 149 was normal on the night of the officers' surveillance. In the 5-hour period between 1 a.m. and 6 a.m., 15 to 20 vehicles passed the officers heading west, toward milepost 122. Only two of them—both pickup trucks with camper shells—were of the kind that the officers had concluded "Chevron" would likely use if he was to carry aliens that night. One, a distinctively colored pickup truck with a camper shell, passed for the first time at 4:30 a.m. Officer Gray was able to see and record only a partial license number, "GN 88-."[1] At 6:12 a.m., almost exactly the estimated one hour and a half later, a vehicle looking like this same pickup passed them again, this time heading east.

The officers followed the pickup and were satisfied from its license plate, "GN 8804" that it was the same vehicle that had passed at 4:30 a.m. At that point, they flashed their police lights and intercepted the vehicle. Respondent Jesus Cortez was the driver and owner of the pickup; respondent Pedro

Hernandez-Loera was sitting in the passenger's seat. Hernandez-Loera was wearing shoes with soles matching the distinctive "chevron" shoeprint.

The officers identified themselves and told Cortez they were conducting an immigration check. They asked if he was carrying any passengers in the camper. Cortez told them he had picked up some hitchhikers, and he proceeded to open the back of the camper. In the camper, there were six illegal aliens. The officers then arrested the respondents.

Cortez and Hernandez-Loera were charged with six counts of transporting illegal aliens. By pretrial motion, they sought to suppress the evidence obtained by Officers Gray and Evans as a result of stopping their vehicle. They argued that the officers did not have adequate cause to make the investigative stop. The District Court denied the motion. A jury found the respondents guilty as charged. They were sentenced to concurrent prison terms of five years on each of six counts. In addition, Hernandez-Loera was fined $12,000.

A divided panel of the Court of Appeals for the Ninth Circuit reversed, holding that the officers lacked a sufficient basis to justify the stop of the pickup. That court recognized that *United States v. Brignoni-Ponce*, 422 U.S. 873 (1975), provides a standard governing investigative stops of the kind involved in this case, stating:

> "The quantum of cause necessary in . . . cases [like this one] was established . . . in *Brignoni-Ponce* . . . '[O]fficers on roving patrol may stop vehicles only if they are aware of specific articulable facts, together with rational inferences from those facts, that reasonably warrant suspicion that the vehicles contain aliens who may be illegally in the country.'"

The court also recognized that "the ultimate question on appeal is whether the trial judge's finding that founded suspicion was present here was clearly erroneous." Here, because, in the view of the facts of the two judges constituting the majority, "[t]he officers did not have a valid basis for singling out the Cortez vehicle," and because the circumstances admitted "far too many innocent inferences to make the officers' suspicions reasonably warranted," the panel concluded that the stop of Cortez' vehicle was a violation of the respondents' rights under the Fourth Amendment. In dissent, Judge Chambers was persuaded that *Brignoni-Ponce* recognized the validity of permitting an officer to assess the facts in light of his past experience.

## II

### A

The Fourth Amendment applies to seizures of the

---

[1] The second camper passed them 15 or 20 minutes later. As far as the record shows, it did not return.

person, including brief investigatory stops such as the stop of the vehicle here. An investigatory stop must be justified by some objective manifestation that the person stopped is, or is about to be, engaged in criminal activity.[2]

Courts have used a variety of terms to capture the elusive concept of what cause is sufficient to authorize police to stop a person. Terms like "articulable reasons" and "founded suspicion" are not self-defining; they fall short of providing clear guidance dispositive of the myriad factual situations that arise. But the essence of all that has been written is that the totality of the circumstances—the whole picture—must be taken into account. Based upon that whole picture the detaining officers must have a particularized and objective basis for suspecting the particular person stopped of criminal activity.

The idea that an assessment of the whole picture must yield a particularized suspicion contains two elements, each of which must be present before a stop is permissible. First, the assessment must be based upon all the circumstances. The analysis proceeds with various objective observations, information from police reports, if such are available, and consideration of the modes or patterns of operation of certain kinds of lawbreakers. From these data, a trained officer draws inferences and makes deductions—inferences and deductions that might well elude an untrained person.

The process does not deal with hard certainties, but with probabilities. Long before the law of probabilities was articulated as such, practical people formulated certain common sense conclusions about human behavior; jurors as fact finders are permitted to do the same—and so are law enforcement officers. Finally, the evidence thus collected must be seen and weighed not in terms of library analysis by scholars, but as understood by those versed in the field of law enforcement.

The second element contained in the idea that an assessment of the whole picture must yield a particularized suspicion is the concept that the process just described must raise a suspicion that the particular individual being stopped is engaged in wrongdoing. Chief Justice Warren, speaking for the Court in *Terry,* said that, "[t]his demand for specificity in the information upon which police action is predicated is *the central teaching of this Court's Fourth Amendment jurisprudence.*" (emphasis added).

---

[2] Of course, an officer may stop and question a person if there are reasonable grounds to believe that person is wanted for past criminal conduct.

## B

This case portrays at once both the enormous difficulties of patrolling a 2,000-mile open border and the patient skills needed by those charged with halting illegal entry into this country. It implicates all of the principles just discussed—especially the imperative of recognizing that, when used by trained law enforcement officers, objective facts, meaningless to the untrained, can be combined with permissible deductions from such facts to form a legitimate basis for suspicion of a particular person and for action on that suspicion. We see here the kind of police work often suggested by judges and scholars as examples of appropriate and reasonable means of law enforcement. Here, fact on fact and clue on clue afforded a basis for the deductions and inferences that brought the officers to focus on "Chevron."

Of critical importance, the officers knew that the area was a crossing point for illegal aliens. They knew that it was common practice for persons to lead aliens through the desert from the border to Highway 86, where they could—by prearrangement—be picked up by a vehicle. Moreover, based upon clues they had discovered in the 2-month period prior to the events at issue here, they believed that one such guide, whom they designated "Chevron," had a particular pattern of operations.

By piecing together the information at their disposal, the officers tentatively concluded that there was a reasonable likelihood that "Chevron" would attempt to lead a group of aliens on the night of Sunday, January 30-31. Someone with chevron-soled shoes had led several groups of aliens in the previous two months, yet it had been two weeks since the latest crossing. "Chevron," they deduced, was therefore due reasonably soon. "Chevron" tended to travel on clear weekend nights. Because it had rained on the Friday and Saturday nights of the weekend involved here, Sunday was the only clear night of that weekend; the officers surmised it was therefore a likely night for a trip.

Once they had focused on that night, the officers drew upon other objective facts known to them to deduce a time frame within which "Chevron" and the aliens were likely to arrive. From what they knew of the practice of those who smuggle aliens, including what they knew of "Chevron's" previous activities, they deduced that the border crossing and journey through the desert would probably be at night. They knew the time when sunset would occur at the point of the border crossing; they knew about how long the trip would take. They were thus able to deduce that "Chevron" would likely arrive at the pickup point on Highway 86 in the time frame between 2 a.m. and 6 a.m.

From objective facts, the officers also deduced the probable point on the highway – milepost 122 – at which "Chevron" would likely rendezvous with a pickup vehicle. They deduced from the direction taken by the sets of "Chevron" footprints they had earlier discovered that the pickup vehicle would approach the aliens from, and return with them to, a point east of milepost 122. They therefore staked out a position east of milepost 122 (at milepost 149) and watched for vehicles that passed them going west and then, approximately one and a half hours later, passed them again, this time going east.

From what they had observed about the previous groups guided by the person with "chevron" shoes, they deduced that "Chevron" would lead a group of 8 to 20 aliens. They therefore focused their attention on enclosed vehicles of that passenger capacity.

The analysis produced by Officers Gray and Evans can be summarized as follows: if, on the night upon which they believed "Chevron" was likely to travel, sometime between 2 a.m. and 6 a.m., a large enclosed vehicle was seen to make an east-west-east round trip to and from a deserted point (milepost 122) on a deserted road (Highway 86), the officers would stop the vehicle on the return trip. In a 4-hour period the officers observed only one vehicle meeting that description. And it is not surprising that when they stopped the vehicle on its return trip it contained "Chevron" and several illegal aliens.

C

The limited purpose of the stop in this case was to question the occupants of the vehicle about their citizenship and immigration status and the reasons for the round trip in a short timespan in a virtually deserted area. No search of the camper or any of its occupants occurred until after respondent Cortez voluntarily opened the back door of the camper; thus, only the stop, not the search is at issue here. The intrusion upon privacy associated with this stop was limited and was "reasonably related in scope to the justification for [its] initiation."

We have recently held that stops by the Border Patrol may be justified under circumstances less than those constituting probable cause for arrest or search. *Brignoni-Ponce.* Thus, the test is not whether Officers Gray and Evans had probable cause to conclude that the vehicle they stopped would contain "Chevron" and a group of illegal aliens. Rather the question is whether, based upon the whole picture, they, as experienced Border Patrol officers, could reasonably surmise that the particular vehicle they stopped was engaged in criminal activity. On this record, they could so conclude.

Reversed.

Justice STEWART, concurring the result.

The Border Patrol officers in this case knew, or had rationally deduced, that "Chevron" had repeatedly shepherded illegal aliens up from the border; that his treks had commonly ended early in the morning around milepost 122 on Highway 86; that he usually worked on weekends; that he probably had made no trips for two weeks; and that trips were most likely when the weather was good. Knowing of this pattern, the officers could reasonably anticipate, even if they could not guarantee, the arrival of another group of aliens, led by Chevron, at milepost 122 on the first clear weekend night in late January 1977. Route 86 leads through almost uninhabited country, so little traveled in the hours of darkness that only 15 to 20 westbound vehicles passed the police during the five hours they watched that Sunday night. Only two vehicles capacious enough to carry a sizable group of illegal aliens went by. One of those two vehicles not only drove past them, but returned in the opposite direction after just enough time had elapsed for a journey to milepost 122 and back. This nocturnal round trip into "desolate desert terrain" would in any event have been puzzling. Coming when and as it did, surely the most likely explanation for it was that Chevron was again shepherding aliens.

In sum, the Border Patrol officers had discovered an abundance of "specific articulable facts" which, "together with rational inferences from [them]," entirely warranted a "suspicion that the vehicl[e] contain[ed] aliens who [might] be illegally in the country." Because the information possessed by the officers thus met the requirements established by the *Brignoni-Ponce* case for the kind of stop made here, I concur in the reversal of the judgment of the Court of Appeals

[Justice MARSHALL also concurred in the result, only.]

## QUESTIONS AND NOTES

**1.** If it were necessary, could the Court have found probable cause? Is *Cortez* a stronger or weaker case for probable cause than *Gates*?

**2.** Is there any reason that the Court might *not* have wanted to find probable cause here?

**3.** Does Justice Stewart's concurrence say something different from the majority? Why do you suppose that he only concurred in result?

**4.** Distinctions between probable cause and reasonable suspicion were never more important than they were in *Royer*.

### Florida v. Royer
### 460 U.S. 491 (1983)

Justice WHITE announced the judgment of the Court and delivered an opinion in which Justices MARSHALL, POWELL and STEVENS joined.

We are required in this case to determine whether the Court of Appeal of Florida, Third District, properly applied the precepts of the Fourth Amendment in holding that respondent Royer was being illegally detained at the time of his purported consent to a search of his luggage.

I

On January 3, 1978, Royer was observed at Miami International Airport by two plain-clothes detectives of the Dade County, Florida, Public Safety Department assigned to the County's Organized Crime Bureau, Narcotics Investigation Section. Detectives Johnson and Magdalena believed that Royer's appearance, mannerisms, luggage, and actions fit the so-called "drug courier profile."[2] Royer, apparently unaware of the attention he had attracted,

---

[2] The "drug courier profile" is an abstract of characteristics found to be typical of persons transporting illegal drugs. In Royer's case, the detectives' attention was attracted by the following facts which were considered to be within the profile: a) Royer was carrying American Tourister luggage, which appeared to be heavy, b) he was young, apparently between 25-35, c) he was casually dressed, d) Royer appeared pale and nervous, looking around at other people, e) Royer paid for his ticket in cash with a large number of bills, and f) rather than completing the airline identification tag to be attached to checked baggage, which had space for a name, address, and telephone number, Royer wrote only a name and the destination.

purchased a one-way ticket to New York City and checked his two suitcases, placing on each suitcase an identification tag bearing the name "Holt" and the destination, "LaGuardia". As Royer made his way to the concourse which led to the airline boarding area, the two detectives approached him, identified themselves as policemen working out of the sheriff's office, and asked if Royer had a "moment" to speak with them; Royer said "Yes."

Upon request, but without oral consent, Royer produced for the detectives his airline ticket and his driver's license. The airline ticket, like the baggage identification tags, bore the name "Holt," while the driver's license carried respondent's correct name, "Royer." When the detectives asked about the discrepancy, Royer explained that a friend had made the reservation in the name of "Holt." Royer became noticeably more nervous during this conversation, whereupon the detectives informed Royer that they were in fact narcotics investigators and that they had reason to suspect him of transporting narcotics.

The detectives did not return his airline ticket and identification but asked Royer to accompany them to a room, approximately forty feet away, adjacent to the concourse. Royer said nothing in response but went with the officers as he had been asked to do. The room was later described by Detective Johnson as a "large storage closet," located in the stewardesses' lounge and containing a small desk and two chairs. Without Royer's consent or agreement, Detective Johnson, using Royer's baggage check stubs, retrieved the "Holt" luggage from the airline and brought it to the room where respondent and Detective Magdalena were waiting. Royer was asked if he would consent to a search of the suitcases. Without orally responding to this request, Royer produced a key and unlocked one of the suitcases, which the detective then opened without seeking further assent from Royer. Drugs were found in that suitcase. According to Detective Johnson, Royer stated that he did not know the combination to the lock on the second suitcase. When asked if he objected to the detective opening the second suitcase, Royer said "no, go ahead," and did not object when the detective explained that the suitcase might have to be broken open. The suitcase was pried open by the officers and more marihuana was found. Royer was then told that he was under arrest. Approximately fifteen minutes had elapsed from the time the detectives initially approached respondent until his arrest upon the discovery of the contraband.

Prior to his trial for felony possession of marihuana, Royer made a motion to suppress the evidence obtained in the search of the suitcases. The trial court found that Royer's consent to the search was "freely and voluntarily given," and that, regardless of the consent, the warrantless search was reasonable because "the officer doesn't have the time to run out and get a search warrant because the plane is going to take off." Following the denial of the motion to suppress, Royer changed his plea from "not guilty" to "*nolo contendere*," specifically reserving the right to appeal the denial of the motion to suppress. Royer was convicted.

The District Court of Appeal reversed Royer's conviction. The court held that Royer had been involuntarily confined in a small room without probable cause; that the involuntary detention had exceeded the limited restraint permitted by *Terry*, at the time his consent to the search was obtained; and that the consent to search was therefor invalid because tainted by the unlawful confinement.[7]

Several factors led the court to conclude that respondent's confinement was tantamount to arrest. Royer had "found himself in a small enclosed area being confronted by two police officers — a situation which presents an almost classic definition of imprisonment." The detectives' statement to Royer that he

---

[7] The Florida court was also of the opinion that "a mere similarity with the contents of the drug courier profile is insufficient even to constitute the articulable suspicion required to justify" the stop authorized by *Terry*. It went on to hold that even if it followed a contrary rule, or even if articulable suspicion occurred at some point prior to Royer's consent to search, the facts did not amount to probable cause that would justify the restraint imposed on Royer. As will become clear, we disagree on the reasonable-suspicion issue but do concur that probable cause to arrest was lacking.

was suspected of transporting narcotics also bolstered the finding that Royer was "in custody" at the time the consent to search was given. In addition, the detectives' possession of Royer's airline ticket and their retrieval and possession of his luggage made it clear, in the District Court of Appeal's view, that Royer was not free to leave.

At the suppression hearing Royer testified that he was under the impression that he was not free to leave the officers' presence. The Florida Court of Appeal found that this apprehension "was much more than a well-justified subjective belief," for the State had conceded at oral argument before that court that "the officers would not have permitted Royer to leave the room even if [Royer] had erroneously thought he could." The nomenclature used to describe Royer's confinement, the court found, was unimportant because under *Dunaway v. New York*, 442 U.S. 200 (1979), "[a] police confinement which . . . goes beyond the limited restraint of a *Terry* investigatory stop may be constitutionally justified only by probable cause." Detective Johnson, who conducted the search, had specifically stated at the suppression hearing that he did not have probable cause to arrest Royer until the suitcases were opened and their contents revealed.

## II

Some preliminary observations are in order. First, it is unquestioned that without a warrant to search Royer's luggage and in the absence of probable cause and exigent circumstances, the validity of the search depended on Royer's purported consent. Neither is it disputed that where the validity of a search rests on consent, the State has the burden of proving that the necessary consent was obtained and that it was freely and voluntarily given, a burden that is not satisfied by showing a mere submission to a claim of lawful authority.

[I]t is also clear that not all seizures of the person must be justified by probable cause to arrest for a crime. Prior to *Terry*, any restraint on the person amounting to a seizure for the purposes of the Fourth Amendment was invalid unless justified by probable cause. *Terry* created a limited exception to this general rule: certain seizures are justifiable under the Fourth Amendment if there is articulable suspicion that a person has committed or is about to commit a crime. In that case, a stop and a frisk for weapons were found unexceptionable. *Adams* applied the same approach in the context of an informant's report that an unnamed individual in a nearby vehicle was carrying narcotics and a gun. Although not expressly authorized in *Terry*, *Brignoni-Ponce* was unequivocal in saying that reasonable suspicion of criminal activity warrants a temporary seizure for the purpose of questioning limited to the purpose of the stop. Royer does not suggest, nor do we, that a similar rationale would not warrant temporary detention for questioning on less than probable cause where the public interest involved is the suppression of illegal transactions in drugs or of any other serious crime.

### III

[T]he State submits that if Royer was seized, there existed reasonable, articulable suspicion to justify a temporary detention and that the limits of a *Terry*-type stop were never exceeded. We agree with the State that when the officers discovered that Royer was traveling under an assumed name, this fact, and the facts already known to the officers—paying cash for a one-way ticket, the mode of checking the two bags, and Royer's appearance and conduct in general—were adequate grounds for suspecting Royer of carrying drugs and for temporarily detaining him and his luggage while they attempted to verify or dispel their suspicions in a manner that did not exceed the limits of an investigative detention. We also agree that had Royer voluntarily consented to the search of his luggage while he was justifiably being detained on reasonable suspicion, the products of the search would be admissible against him. We have concluded, however, that at the time Royer produced the key to his suitcase, the detention to which he was then subjected was a more serious intrusion on his personal liberty than is allowable on mere suspicion of criminal activity.

### IV

The State's final argument is that Royer was not being illegally held when he gave his consent because there was probable cause to arrest him at that time. Officer Johnson testified at the suppression hearing and the Florida Court of Appeal held that there was no probable cause to arrest until Royer's bags were opened, but the fact that the officers did not believe there was probable cause and proceeded on a consensual or *Terry*-stop rationale would not foreclose the State from justifying Royer's custody by proving probable cause and hence removing any barrier to relying on Royer's consent to search. We agree with the Florida Court of Appeal, however, that probable cause to arrest Royer did not exist at the time he consented to the search of his luggage. The facts are that a nervous young man with two American Tourister bags paid cash for an airline ticket to a "target city". These facts led to inquiry, which in turn revealed that the ticket had been bought under an assumed name. The proffered explanation did not satisfy the officers. We cannot agree with the State, if this is its position, that every nervous young man paying cash for a ticket to New York City under an assumed name and carrying two heavy American Tourister bags may be arrested and held to answer for a serious felony charge.

### V

Because we affirm the Florida Court of Appeal's conclusion that Royer was being illegally detained when he consented to the search of his luggage, we agree that the consent was tainted by the illegality and was ineffective to justify the search. The judgment of the Florida Court of Appeal is accordingly affirmed.

Justice BRENNAN, concurring in result.

I dissent from the plurality's view that the initial stop of Royer was legal. Before *Terry*, only "seizures" of persons based on probable cause were held to satisfy the Fourth Amendment. As we stated in *Brignoni-Ponce*, however, *Terry* and *Adams* "establish that in appropriate circumstances the Fourth Amendment allows a properly limited 'search' or 'seizure' on facts that do not constitute probable cause to arrest or to search for contraband or evidence of crime." But to justify such a seizure an officer must have a reasonable suspicion of criminal activity based on "specific and articulable facts . . . [and] rational inferences from those facts. . . ." In this case, the officers decided to approach Royer because he was carrying American Tourister luggage, which appeared to be heavy; he was young; he was casually dressed; he appeared to be pale and nervous and was looking around at other people; he paid for his airline ticket in cash with a large number of bills; and he did not completely fill out the identification tags for his luggage, which was checked to New York. These facts clearly are not sufficient to provide the reasonable suspicion of criminal activity necessary to justify the officers' subsequent seizure of Royer. Indeed, considered individually or collectively, they are perfectly consistent with innocent behavior and cannot possibly give rise to any inference supporting a reasonable suspicion of criminal activity. The officers' seizure of Royer, therefore, was illegal.

Although I recognize that the traffic in illicit drugs is a matter of pressing national concern, that cannot excuse this Court from exercising its unflagging duty to strike down official activity that exceeds the confines of the Constitution. In discussing the Fourth Amendment in *Coolidge*, Justice Stewart stated: "In times of unrest, whether caused by crime or racial conflict or fear of internal subversion, this basic law and the values that it represents may appear unrealistic or 'extravagant' to some. But the values were those of the authors of our fundamental constitutional concepts.'' We must not allow our zeal for effective law enforcement to blind us to the peril to our free society that lies in this Court's disregard of the protections afforded by the Fourth Amendment.

Justice BLACKMUN, dissenting.

[Justice Blackmun agreed with the plurality's holding that there was reasonable suspicion, but that there was not probable cause. For reasons that will appear, *section C, infra*, he concluded that Royer was not unlawfully detained at the time that he consented to the opening of his suitcase.]

Justice REHNQUIST, dissenting.

The plurality's meandering opinion contains in it a little something for everyone, and although it affirms the reversal of a judgment of conviction, it can scarcely be said to bespeak a total indifference to the legitimate needs of law enforcement agents seeking to curb trafficking in dangerous drugs. Indeed, in both manner and tone, the opinion brings to mind the old nursery rhyme:

"The King of France
With forty thousand men
Marched up the hill
And then marched back again."

The opinion nonetheless, in my view, betrays a mind-set more useful to those who officiate at shuffleboard games, primarily concerned with which particular square the disc has landed on, than to those who are seeking to administer a system of justice whose twin purposes are the conviction of the guilty and the vindication of the innocent. The plurality loses sight of the very language of the Amendment which it purports to interpret:

"The right of the people to be secure in their persons, houses, papers, and effects, against *unreasonable* searches and seizures, shall not be violated. . . .'' (Emphasis added).

Analyzed simply in terms of its "reasonableness'' as that term is used in the Fourth Amendment, the conduct of the investigating officers toward Royer would pass muster with virtually all thoughtful, civilized persons not overly steeped in the mysteries of this Court's Fourth Amendment jurisprudence. Analyzed even in terms of the most meticulous regard for our often conflicting cases, it seems to me to pass muster equally well.

The plurality concedes that after their initial conversation with Royer, the officers had "grounds for suspecting Royer of carrying drugs and for temporarily detaining him and his luggage while they attempted to verify or dispel their suspicions. . . .'' I agree that their information reached at least this level. The detectives had learned, among other things, that (1) Royer was carrying two heavy suitcases; (2) he was visibly nervous, exhibiting the behavior of a person trying to identify and evade police officers; (3) at a ticket counter in a major import center for illicit drugs, he had purchased a ticket for a city that is a major distribution center for such drugs; (4) he paid for his ticket from a large roll of small denomination bills, avoiding the need to show identification; (5) in filling out his baggage tags, Royer listed only a last name and the airport of destination, failing to give his full name, address, and phone number in the provided spaces, and (6) he was traveling under an assumed name.

The Florida court felt that even these facts did not amount to articulable suspicion, reasoning that this behavior was "at least equally, and usually far more frequently, consistent with complete innocence.''[5] This evaluation of the evidence seems to me singularly akin to observing that because a stranger who was loitering near a building shortly before an arsonist set fire to the building could not be detained against his will for questioning solely on the basis of that fact, the same conclusion would be reached even though the same stranger had been found loitering in the presence of four other buildings shortly before arsonists had likewise set them on fire. Any one of these factors relied upon by the Miami police may have been as consistent with innocence as with guilt; but the combination of several of these factors is the essence of both "articulable suspicion'' and "probable cause.''[6]

---

[5] The Florida District Court of Appeal took specific exception to the officers' conclusion that Royer appeared to be nervously attempting to evade police contact. The lower court said that since police officers are not psychiatrists, this conclusion "must be completely disregarded.'' This Court, however, has repeatedly emphasized that a trained police officer may draw inferences and make deductions that could elude any untrained person observing the same conduct. See, *e.g. Cortez.* We have noted as an example the behavior of a suspect who appears to the officer to be evading police contact.

[6] While the plurality does not address the use of "drug courier profiles'' in narcotics investigations, it affirms a decision where the Florida District Court of Appeal took the liberty to fashion a bright-line rule with regard to the use of these profiles. The state court concluded that conformity with a "drug courier profile,''

"without more," is insufficient to establish even reasonable suspicion that criminal activity is afoot.

In 1974 the Department of Justice Drug Enforcement Administration instituted training programs for its narcotics officers wherein instruction was given on a "drug courier profile." A "profile" is, in effect, the collective or distilled experience of narcotics officers concerning characteristics repeatedly seen in drug smugglers. As one DEA agent explained:

"Basically it's a number of characteristics which we attribute or which we believe can be used to pick out drug couriers. And these characteristics are basically things that normal travelers do not do. . . .

"Essentially, when we started this detail at the airport, we didn't really know what we were looking for. The majority of our cases, when we first started, involved cases we made based on information from law enforcement agencies or from airline personnel. And as these cases were made, certain characteristics were noted among the defendants.

"At a later time we began to see a pattern in these characteristics and began using them to pick out individuals we suspected as narcotic couriers without any prior information."

Few statistics have been kept on the effectiveness of "profile" usage, but the data available suggests it has been a success. In the first few months of a "profile" program at the Detroit Metropolitan Airport, 141 persons were searched in 96 different encounters; drugs were discovered in 77 of the searches. A DEA agent working at the La Guardia Airport in New York City estimated that some 60% percent of the persons identified as having "profile" characteristics are found to be carrying drugs.

Because of this success, state and local law enforcement agencies also have instructed narcotics officers according to "drug courier profiles." It was partly on the basis of "profile" characteristics that Detectives Johnson and Magdalena initially began surveillance of Royer. Certainly in this case the use of the "profile" proved effective.

Use of "drug courier profiles" has played an important part in a number of lower court decisions. In fact, the function of the "profile" has been somewhat overplayed. Certainly, a law enforcement officer can rely on his own experience in detection and prevention of crime. Likewise, in training police officers, instruction focuses on what has been learned through the collective experience of law enforcers. The "drug courier profile" is an example of such instruction. It is not intended to provide a mathematical formula that automatically establishes grounds for a belief that criminal activity is afoot. By the same reasoning, however, simply because these characteristics are accumulated in a "profile," they are not to be given less weight in assessing whether a suspicion is well founded. While each case will turn on its own facts, sheer logic dictates that where certain characteristics repeatedly are found among drug smugglers, the existence of those characteristics in a particular case is to be considered accordingly in determining whether there are grounds to believe that further investigation is appropriate. Cf. *Cortez*.

The "drug courier profile" is not unfamiliar to this Court. We have held that conformity with certain aspects of the "profile" does not automatically create a particularized suspicion which will justify an investigatory stop. *Reid v. Georgia*, 448 U.S. 438 (1980) (*per curiam*). Yet our decision in *United States v. Mendenhall*, 446 U.S. 544 (1980), made it clear that a police officer is entitled to assess the totality of the circumstances in the light of his own training and experience and that instruction on a "drug courier profile" would be a part of his accumulated knowledge. This process is not amenable to bright-line rules such as the Florida court tried to establish. We are not dealing "with hard certainties, but with probabilities. Long before the law of probabilities was articulated as such, practical people formulated certain common-sense conclusions about human behavior; jurors as fact finders are permitted to do the same—and so are law enforcement officers. Finally, the evidence thus collected must be seen and weighed not in terms of library analysis by scholars, but as understood by those versed in the field of law enforcement." *Cortez*.

# QUESTIONS AND NOTES

**1.** Why did a majority of the Court fail to find probable cause? As between Mark Royer and Lance Gates (See *Gates*, Chapter 2, *supra*), who did more objective things to manifest guilt? If your answer is "Royer," why does the plurality wax so eloquently about not allowing every young, casually-dressed man with heavy luggage who pays for his ticket in cash and uses an alias to answer for a serious crime?

**2.** If you were on the Court, would you have found reasonable suspicion (like White), probable cause (like Rehnquist), or neither (like Brennan)?

**3.** The extent to which the "drug courier profile" can (should) play a part in reasonable suspicion is explored by both the majority and dissent in *Sokolow*. We will return to *Royer* (section C, *infra* and Chapter 9, *infra*).

## United States v. Sokolow
### 490 U.S. 1 (1989)

Chief Justice REHNQUIST delivered the opinion of the Court.

Respondent Andrew Sokolow was stopped by Drug Enforcement Administration (DEA) agents upon his arrival at Honolulu International Airport. The agents found 1,063 grams of cocaine in his carry-on luggage. When respondent was stopped, the agents knew, *inter alia*, that (1) he paid $2,100 for two airplane tickets from a roll of $20 bills; (2) he traveled under a name that did not match the name under which his telephone number was listed; (3) his original destination was Miami, a source city for illicit drugs; (4) he stayed in Miami for only 48 hours, even though a round-trip flight from Honolulu to Miami takes 20 hours; (5) he appeared nervous during his trip; and (6) he checked none of his luggage. A divided panel of the United States Court of Appeals for the Ninth Circuit held that the DEA agents did not have a reasonable suspicion to stop respondent, as required by the Fourth Amendment. We take the contrary view.

This case involves a typical attempt to smuggle drugs through one of the Nation's airports. On a Sunday in July 1984, respondent went to the United Airlines ticket counter at Honolulu Airport, where he purchased two round-trip tickets for a flight to Miami leaving later that day. The tickets were purchased in the names of "Andrew Kray" and "Janet Norian" and had open return dates. Respondent paid $2,100 for the tickets from a large roll of $20 bills, which appeared to contain a total of $4,000. He also gave the ticket agent his home telephone number. The ticket agent noticed that respondent seemed nervous; he was about 25 years old; he was dressed in a black jumpsuit and wore gold jewelry; and he was accompanied by a woman, who turned out to be Janet Norian. Neither respondent nor his companion checked any of their four pieces of luggage.

After the couple left for their flight, the ticket agent informed Officer John McCarthy of the Honolulu Police Department of respondent's cash purchase of tickets to Miami. Officer McCarthy determined that the telephone number respondent gave to the ticket agent was subscribed to a "Karl Herman," who resided at 348-A Royal Hawaiian Avenue in Honolulu. Unbeknownst to McCarthy (and later to the DEA agents), respondent was Herman's roommate. The ticket agent identified respondent's voice on the answering machine at Herman's number. Officer McCarthy was unable to find any listing under the name "Andrew Kray" in Hawaii. McCarthy subsequently learned that return reservations from Miami to Honolulu had been made in the names of Kray and Norian, with their arrival scheduled for July 25, three days after respondent and his companion had left. He also learned that Kray and Norian were scheduled to make stopovers in Denver and Los Angeles.

On July 25, during the stopover in Los Angeles, DEA agents identified respondent. He "appeared to be very nervous and was looking all around the waiting area." Later that day, at 6:30 p.m., respondent and Norian arrived in Honolulu. As before, they had not checked their luggage. Respondent was still wearing a black jumpsuit and gold jewelry. The couple proceeded directly to the street and tried to hail a cab, where Agent Richard Kempshall and three other DEA agents approached them. Kempshall displayed his credentials, grabbed respondent by the arm, and moved him back onto the sidewalk. Kemp-shall asked respondent for his airline ticket and identification; respondent said that he had neither. He told the agents that his name was "Sokolow," but that he was traveling under his mother's maiden name, "Kray."

Respondent and Norian were escorted to the DEA office at the airport. There, the couple's luggage was examined by "Donker," a narcotics detector dog, which alerted on respondent's brown shoulder bag. The agents arrested respondent. He was advised of his constitutional rights and declined to make any statements. The agents obtained a warrant to search the shoulder bag. They found no illicit drugs, but the bag did contain several suspicious documents indicating respondent's involvement in drug trafficking. The agents had Donker reexamine the remaining luggage, and this time the dog alerted on a medium sized Louis Vuitton bag. By now, it was 9:30 p.m., too late for the agents to obtain a second warrant. They allowed respondent to leave for the night, but kept his luggage. The next morning, after a second dog confirmed Donker's alert, the agents obtained a warrant and found 1,063 grams of cocaine inside the bag.

The officer, of course, must be able to articulate something more than an "inchoate and unparticularized suspicion or 'hunch.'" The Fourth Amendment requires "some minimal level of objective justification" for making the stop. That level of suspicion is considerably less than proof of wrongdoing by a preponderance of the evidence. We have held that probable cause means "a fair probability that contraband or evidence of a crime will be found," and the level of suspicion required for a *Terry* stop is obviously less demanding than that for probable cause.

The concept of reasonable suspicion, like probable cause, is not "readily, or even usefully, reduced to a neat set of legal rules." We think the Court of Appeals' effort to refine and elaborate the requirements of "reasonable suspicion" in this case creates unnecessary difficulty in dealing with one of the relatively simple concepts embodied in the Fourth Amendment. In evaluating the validity of a stop such as this, we must consider "the totality of the circumstances—the whole picture." As we said in *Cortez*:

> "The process does not deal with hard certainties, but with probabilities. Long before the law of probabilities was articulated as such, practical people formulated certain common-sense conclusions about human behavior; jurors as fact-finders are permitted to do the same—and so are law enforcement officers."

The rule enunciated by the Court of Appeals, in which evidence available to an officer is divided into evidence of "ongoing criminal behavior," on the one hand, and "probabilistic" evidence, on the other, is not in keeping with the quoted statements from our decisions. It also seems to us to draw a sharp line between types of evidence, the probative value of which varies only in degree. The Court of Appeals classified evidence of traveling under an alias, or evidence that the suspect took an evasive or erratic path through an airport, as meeting the test for showing "ongoing criminal activity." But certainly instances are conceivable in which traveling under an alias would not reflect ongoing criminal activity: for example, a person who wished to travel to a hospital or clinic for an operation and wished to conceal that fact. One taking an evasive path through an airport might be seeking to avoid a confrontation with an angry acquaintance or with a creditor. This is not to say that each of these types of evidence is not highly probative, but they do not have the sort of ironclad significance attributed to them by the Court of Appeals.

On the other hand, the factors in this case that the Court of Appeals treated as merely "probabilistic" also have probative significance. Paying $2,100 in cash for two airplane tickets is out of the ordinary, and it is even more out of the ordinary to pay that sum from a roll of $20 bills containing nearly twice that amount of cash. Most business travelers, we feel confident, purchase airline tickets by credit card or check so as to have a record for tax or business purposes, and few vacationers carry with them thousands of dollars in $20 bills. We also think the agents had a reasonable ground to believe that respondent was traveling under an alias; the evidence was by no means conclusive, but it was sufficient to warrant consideration.[3] While a trip from Honolulu to Miami, standing alone, is not a cause for any sort of suspicion, here there was more: surely few residents of Honolulu travel from that city for 20 hours to spend 48 hours in Miami during the month of July.

---

[3] Respondent also claims that the agents should have conducted a further inquiry to resolve the inconsistency between the name he gave the airline and the name, "Karl Herman," under which his telephone number was listed. Brief for Respondent 26. This argument avails respondent nothing; had the agents done further checking, they would have discovered not only that respondent was Herman's roommate but also that his name was "Sokolow" and not "Kray," the name listed on his ticket.

Any one of these factors is not by itself proof of any illegal conduct and is quite consistent with innocent travel. But we think taken together they amount to reasonable suspicion. See *Royer*. We said in *Reid v. Georgia*, 448 U.S. 438 (1980) (*per curiam*), "there could, of course, be circumstances in which wholly lawful conduct might justify the suspicion that criminal activity was afoot."[5] Indeed, *Terry* itself involved "a series of acts, each of them perhaps innocent" if viewed separately, "but which taken together warranted further investigation." We noted in *Gates* that "innocent behavior will frequently provide the basis for a showing of probable cause," and that "[i]n making a determination of probable cause the relevant inquiry is not whether particular conduct is 'innocent' or 'guilty,' but the degree of suspicion that attaches to particular types of non-criminal acts." That principle applies equally well to the reasonable suspicion inquiry.

We do not agree with respondent that our analysis is somehow changed by the agents' belief that his behavior was consistent with one of the DEA's "drug courier profiles."[6] A court sitting to determine the existence of reasonable suspicion must require the agent to articulate the factors leading to that conclusion, but the fact that these factors may be set forth in a "profile" does not somehow detract from their evidentiary significance as seen by a trained agent.

We hold that the agents had a reasonable basis to suspect that respondent was transporting illegal drugs on these facts. The judgment of the Court of Appeals is therefore reversed, and the case is remanded for

---

[5] In *Reid*, the Court held that a DEA agent stopped the defendant without reasonable suspicion. At the time of the stop, the agent knew that (1) the defendant flew into Atlanta from Fort Lauderdale, a source city for cocaine; (2) he arrived early in the morning, when police activity was believed to be at a low ebb; (3) he did not check his luggage; and (4) the defendant and his companion appeared to be attempting to hide the fact that they were together. The Court held that the first three of these facts were not sufficient to supply reasonable suspicion, because they "describe a very large category of presumably innocent travelers," while the last fact was insufficient on the facts of that case to establish reasonable suspicion.

[6] Agent Kempshall testified that respondent's behavior "had all the classic aspects of a drug courier." Since 1974, the DEA has trained narcotics officers to identify drug smugglers on the basis of the sort of circumstantial evidence at issue here.

further proceedings consistent with our decision.

Justice MARSHALL, with whom Justice BRENNAN joins, dissenting.

Because the strongest advocates of Fourth Amendment rights are frequently criminals, it is easy to forget that our interpretations of such rights apply to the innocent and the guilty alike. In the present case, the chain of events set in motion when respondent, Andrew Sokolow, was stopped by Drug Enforcement Administration (DEA) agents at Honolulu International Airport led to the discovery of cocaine and, ultimately, to Sokolow's conviction for drug trafficking. But in sustaining this conviction on the ground that the agents reasonably suspected Sokolow of ongoing criminal activity, the Court diminishes the rights of *all* citizens "to be secure in their persons," as they traverse the Nation's airports. Finding this result constitutionally impermissible, I dissent.

The Fourth Amendment cabins government's authority to intrude on personal privacy and security by requiring that searches and seizures usually be supported by a showing of probable cause. The reasonable suspicion standard is a derivation of the probable-cause command, applicable only to those brief detentions which fall short of being full-scale searches and seizures and which are necessitated by law enforcement exigencies such as the need to stop ongoing crimes, to prevent imminent crimes, and to protect law enforcement officers in highly charged situations. By requiring reasonable suspicion as a prerequisite to such seizures, the Fourth Amendment protects innocent persons from being subjected to "overbearing or harassing" police conduct carried out solely on the basis of imprecise stereotypes of what criminals look like, or on the basis of irrelevant personal characteristics such as race.

To deter such egregious police behavior, we have held that a suspicion is not reasonable unless officers have based it on "specific and articulable facts." It is not enough to suspect that an individual has committed crimes in the past, harbors unconsummated criminal designs, or has the propensity to commit crimes. On the contrary, before detaining an individual, law enforcement officers must reasonably suspect that he is engaged in, or poised to commit, a criminal act *at that moment*. The rationale for permitting brief, warrantless seizures is, after all, that it is impractical to demand strict compliance with the Fourth Amendment's ordinary probable-cause requirement in the face of ongoing or imminent criminal activity demanding "swift action predicated upon the on-the-spot observations of the officer on the beat." *Terry*. Observations raising suspicions of past criminality demand no such immediate action, but instead should appropriately trigger routine police investigation, which may ultimately generate sufficient information to blossom into probable cause.

Evaluated against this standard, the facts about Andrew Sokolow known to the DEA agents at the time they stopped him fall short of reasonably indicating that he was engaged at the time in criminal activity. It is highly significant that the DEA agents stopped Sokolow because he matched one of the DEA's "profiles" of a paradigmatic drug courier. In my view, a law enforcement officer's mechanistic application of a formula of personal and behavioral traits in deciding whom to detain can only dull the officer's ability and determination to make sensitive and fact-specific inferences "in light of his experience," *Terry*, particularly in ambiguous or borderline cases. Reflexive reliance on a profile of drug courier characteristics runs a far greater risk than does ordinary, case-by-case police work of subjecting innocent individuals to unwarranted police harassment and detention. This risk is enhanced by the profile's "chameleon-like way of adapting to any particular set of observations." Compare [the following different and sometimes contradictory standards: (suspect was first to deplane), (last to deplane), (deplaned from middle); (one-way tickets), (round-trip tickets), (nonstop flight), (changed planes); (no luggage), (gym bag), (new suitcases); (traveling alone), (traveling with companion); (acted nervously), (acted too calmly). In asserting that it is not "somehow" relevant that the agents who stopped Sokolow did so in reliance on a prefabricated profile of criminal characteristics, the majority thus ducks serious issues relating to a questionable law enforcement practice, to address the validity of which we granted certiorari in this case.[1]

That the factors comprising the drug courier profile relied on in this case are especially dubious indices of ongoing criminal activity is underscored by *Reid v. Georgia*, a strikingly similar case. There, four facts, encoded in a drug courier profile, were alleged in support of the DEA's detention of a suspect at the Atlanta Airport. First, Reid had arrived from Fort Lauderdale, Florida, a source city for cocaine. Second, he arrived in the early morning, when law enforcement activity is diminished. Third, he and his companion appeared to have no luggage other than their shoulder bags. And fourth, he and his companion appeared to be trying to conceal the fact that they were traveling together.

This collection of facts, we held, was inadequate to support a finding of reasonable suspicion. All but the last of these facts, we observed, "describe a very large category of presumably innocent travelers, who would be subject to virtually random seizures were the Court to conclude that as little foundation as there was in this case could justify a seizure." The sole fact that suggested criminal activity was that Reid "preceded another person and occasionally looked backward at him as they proceeded through the concourse." This observation did not of itself provide a reasonable basis for suspecting wrongdoing, for inferring criminal activity from such evidence reflected no more than an "inchoate and unparticularized suspicion or 'hunch.'"[2]

The facts known to the DEA agents at the time they detained the traveler in this case are scarcely more suggestive of ongoing criminal activity than those in *Reid*. Unlike traveler Reid, who sought to conceal the fact that he was traveling with a companion, and who even attempted to run away after being approached by a DEA agent, traveler Sokolow gave no indications of evasive activity. On the contrary, the sole behavioral detail about Sokolow noted by the DEA agents was that he was nervous. With news accounts proliferating of plane crashes, near collisions, and air terrorism, there are manifold and good reasons for being agitated while awaiting a flight, reasons that have nothing to do with one's involvement in a criminal endeavor.

The remaining circumstantial facts known about Sokolow, considered either singly or together, are scarcely indicative of criminal activity. Like the information disavowed in *Reid* as nonprobative, the fact that Sokolow took a brief trip to a resort city for which he brought only carry-on luggage also "describe[s] a very large category of presumably innocent travelers." That Sokolow embarked from Miami, "a source city for illicit drugs," is no more suggestive of illegality; thousands of innocent persons travel from "source

---

[1] Even if such profiles had reliable predictive value, their utility would be short lived, for drug couriers will adapt their behavior to sidestep detection from profile-focused officers.

[2] Nor was *Reid* a close case: eight Members of the Court found the challenged detention insupportable, five of whom saw fit to dispose of the case by reversing the court below in a *per curiam* opinion. In a separate concurrence, Justice Powell, joined by Chief Justice Burger and Justice Blackmun, agreed that "the fragmentary facts apparently relied on by the DEA agents" provided "no justification" for Reid's detention. Only then-Justice Rehnquist, the author of today's majority opinion, dissented, on the ground that the police conduct involved did not implicate Reid's constitutional rights.

cities'' every day and, judging from the DEA's testimony in past cases, nearly every major city in the country may be characterized as a source or distribution city. That Sokolow had his phone listed in another person's name also does not support the majority's assertion that the DEA agents reasonably believed Sokolow was using an alias; it is commonplace to have one's phone registered in the name of a roommate, which, it later turned out, was precisely what Sokolow had done.[3] That Sokolow was dressed in a black jumpsuit and wore gold jewelry also provides no grounds for suspecting wrongdoing, the majority's repeated and unexplained allusions to Sokolow's style of dress notwithstanding. For law enforcement officers to base a search, even in part, on a pop guess that persons dressed in a particular fashion are likely to commit crimes not only stretches the concept of reasonable suspicion beyond recognition, but also is inimical to the self-expression which the choice of wardrobe may provide.

Finally, that Sokolow paid for his tickets in cash indicates no imminent or ongoing criminal activity. The majority "feel[s] confident" that "[m]ost business travelers . . . purchase airline tickets by credit card or check.'' Why the majority confines its focus only to "business travelers" I do not know, but I would not so lightly infer ongoing crime from the use of legal tender. Making major cash purchases, while surely less common today, may simply reflect the traveler's aversion to, or inability to obtain, plastic money. Conceivably, a person who spends large amounts of cash may be trying to launder his proceeds from past criminal enterprises by converting them into goods and services. But, as I have noted, investigating completed episodes of crime goes beyond the appropriately limited purview of the brief, *Terry*-style seizure. Moreover, it is unreasonable to suggest that, had Sokolow left the airport, he would have been gone forever and thus immune from subsequent investigation. Sokolow, after all, had given the airline his phone number, and the DEA, having ascertained that it was indeed Sokolow's voice on the answering machine at that number, could have learned from that information where Sokolow resided.

The fact is that, unlike the taking of patently evasive action, *Florida v. Rodriguez*, 469 U.S. 1 (1984), the use of an alias, *Royer*, the casing of a store, *Terry*, or the provision of a reliable report from an informant that wrongdoing is imminent, *Gates*, nothing about the characteristics shown by airport traveler Sokolow reasonably suggests that criminal activity is afoot. The majority's hasty conclusion to the contrary serves only to indicate its willingness, when drug crimes or antidrug policies are at issue, to give short shrift to constitutional rights. In requiring that seizures be based on at least some evidence of criminal conduct, the Court of Appeals was faithful to the Fourth Amendment principle that law enforcement officers must reasonably suspect a person of criminal activity before they can detain him. Because today's decision, though limited to its facts, disobeys this important constitutional command, I dissent.

---

[3] That Sokolow was, in fact, using an alias was not known to the DEA agents until after they detained him. Thus, it cannot legitimately be considered as a basis for the seizure in this case.

## QUESTIONS AND NOTES

**1.** Do you see the "drug courier profile" as a good thing or a bad thing?

**2.** Does Justice Marshall's rejection of the profile encourage the sort of unbridled discretion that he and Justice Brennan have abhorred in other areas of the Fourth Amendment? Doesn't the profile, compiled by somebody other than the "officer on the beat," at least channel discretion? Or is this profile just too amorphous?

**3.** Is Justice Marshall requiring too much probative value from each point? Might not the whole tell you more than the sum of its parts?

**4.** For an example of reasonable suspicion as little more than watered-down probable cause, we conclude with *Alabama v. White*.

## Alabama v. White
### 496 U.S. 325 (1990)

Justice WHITE delivered the opinion of the Court.

Based on an anonymous telephone tip, police stopped respondent's vehicle. A consensual search of the car revealed drugs. The issue is whether the tip, as corroborated by independent police work, exhibited sufficient indicia of reliability to provide reasonable suspicion to make the investigatory stop. We hold that it did.

On April 22, 1987, at approximately 3 p.m., Corporal B.H. Davis of the Montgomery Police Department received a telephone call from an anonymous person, stating that Vanessa White would be leaving 235-C Lynwood Terrace Apartments at a particular time in a brown Plymouth station wagon with the right taillight lens broken, that she would be going to Dobey's Motel, and that she would be in possession of about an ounce of cocaine inside a brown attache case. Corporal Davis and his partner, Corporal P. A. Reynolds, proceeded to the Lynwood Terrace Apartments. The officers saw a brown Plymouth station wagon with a broken right taillight in the parking lot in front of the 235 building. The officers observed respondent leave the 235 building, carrying nothing in her hands, and enter the station wagon. They followed the vehicle as it drove the most direct route to Dobey's Motel. When the vehicle reached the Mobile Highway, on which Dobey's Motel is located, Corporal Reynolds requested a patrol unit to stop the vehicle. The vehicle was stopped at approximately 4:18 p.m., just short of Dobey's Motel. Corporal Davis asked respondent to step to the rear of her car, where he informed her that she had been stopped because she was suspected of carrying cocaine in the vehicle. He asked if they could look for cocaine and respondent said they could look. The officers found a locked brown attache case in the car and, upon request, respondent provided the combination to the lock. The officers found marijuana in the attache case and placed respondent under arrest. During processing at the station, the officers found three milligrams of cocaine in respondent's purse.

*Adams* sustained a *Terry* stop and frisk undertaken on the basis of a tip given in person by a known informant who had provided information in the past. We concluded that, while the unverified tip may have been insufficient to support an arrest or search warrant, the information carried sufficient "indicia of reliability" to justify a forcible stop. We did not address the issue of anonymous tips in *Adams*, except to say that

"[t]his is a stronger case than obtains in the case of an anonymous telephone tip."

*Gates* dealt with an anonymous tip in the probable cause context. The Court there abandoned the "two-pronged test" of *Aguilar* and *Spinelli*, in favor of a "totality of the circumstances" approach to determining whether an informant's tip establishes probable cause. *Gates* made clear, however, that those factors that had been considered critical under *Aguilar* and *Spinelli* — an informant's "veracity," "reliability," and "basis of knowledge" — remain "highly relevant in determining the value of his report." These factors are also relevant in the reasonable suspicion context, although allowance must be made in applying them for the lesser showing required to meet that standard.

The opinion in *Gates* recognized that an anonymous tip alone seldom demonstrates the informant's basis of knowledge or veracity inasmuch as ordinary citizens generally do not provide extensive recitations of the basis of their everyday observations and given that the veracity of persons supplying anonymous tips is "by hypothesis largely unknown, and unknowable." This is not to say that an anonymous caller could never provide the reasonable suspicion necessary for a *Terry* stop. But the tip in *Gates* was not an exception to the general rule, and the anonymous tip in this case is like the one in *Gates*: "[It] provides virtually nothing from which one might conclude that [the caller] is either honest or his information reliable; likewise, the [tip] gives absolutely no indication of the basis for the [caller's] predictions regarding [Vanessa White's] criminal activities." By requiring "[s]omething more," as *Gates* did, we merely apply what we said in *Adams*: "Some tips, completely lacking in indicia of reliability, would either warrant no police response or require further investigation before a forcible stop of a suspect would be authorized." Simply put, a tip such as this one, standing alone, would not "'warrant a man of reasonable caution in the belief' that [a stop] was appropriate."

As there was in *Gates*, however, in this case there is more than the tip itself. The tip was not as detailed, and the corroboration was not as complete, as in *Gates*, but the required degree of suspicion was likewise not as high. We discussed the difference in the two standards last Term in *Sokolow*:

"The officer [making a *Terry* stop] . . . must be able to articulate something more than an 'inchoate and unparticularized suspicion or "hunch."' The Fourth Amendment requires 'some minimal level of objective justification' for making the stop. That level of suspicion is considerably less than proof of wrongdoing by a preponderance of the evidence. We have held that probable cause means 'a fair probability that contraband or evidence of a crime will be found,' and the level of suspicion required for a *Terry* stop is obviously less demanding than for probable cause."

Reasonable suspicion is a less demanding standard than probable cause not only in the sense that reasonable suspicion can be established with information that is different in quantity or content than that required to establish probable cause, but also in the sense that reasonable suspicion can arise from information that is less reliable than that required to show probable cause. *Adams* demonstrates as much. We there assumed that the unverified tip from the known informant might not have been reliable enough to establish probable cause, but nevertheless found it sufficiently reliable to justify a *Terry* stop. Reasonable suspicion, like probable cause, is dependent upon both the content of information possessed by police and its degree of reliability. Both factors — quantity and quality — are considered in the "totality of the circumstances — the whole picture," that must be taken into account when evaluating whether there is reasonable suspicion. Thus, if a tip has a relatively low degree of reliability, more information will be required to establish the requisite quantum of suspicion than would be required if the tip were more reliable. The *Gates* Court applied its totality of the circumstances approach in this manner, taking into account the facts known to the officers from personal observation, and giving the anonymous tip the weight it deserved in light of its indicia of reliability as established through independent police work. The same approach applies in the reasonable suspicion context, the only difference being the level of suspicion that must be established. Contrary to the court below, we conclude that when the officers stopped respondent, the anonymous tip had been sufficiently corroborated to furnish reasonable suspicion that respondent was engaged in criminal activity and that the investigative stop therefore did not violate the Fourth Amendment.

It is true that not every detail mentioned by the tipster was verified, such as the name of the woman leaving the building or the precise apartment from which she left; but the officers did corroborate that a woman left the 235 building and got into the particular vehicle that was described by the caller. With respect to the time of departure predicted by the informant, Corporal Davis testified that the caller gave a particular time when the woman would be leaving, but he did not state what that time was. He did testify that, after the call, he and his partner proceeded to the Lynwood Terrace Apartments to put the 235 building under surveillance. Given the fact that the officers proceeded to the indicated address immediately after the call and that respondent emerged not too long thereafter, it appears from the record before us that respondent's departure from the building was within the time frame predicted by the caller. As for the caller's prediction of respondent's destination, it is true that the officers stopped her just short of Dobey's Motel and did not know whether she would have pulled in or continued on past it. But given that the four-mile route driven by respondent was the most direct route possible to Dobey's Motel, but nevertheless involved several turns, we think respondent's destination was significantly corroborated.

The Court's opinion in *Gates* gave credit to the proposition that because an informant is shown to be right about some things, he is probably right about other facts that he has alleged, including the claim that the object of the tip is engaged in criminal activity. Thus, it is not unreasonable to conclude in this case that the independent corroboration by the police of significant aspects of the informer's predictions imparted some degree of reliability to the other allegations made by the caller.

We think it also important that, as in *Gates*, "the anonymous [tip] contained a range of details relating not just to easily obtained facts and conditions existing at the time of the tip, but to future actions of third parties ordinarily not easily predicted." The fact that the officers found a car precisely matching the caller's description in front of the 235 building is an example of the former. Anyone could have "predicted" that fact because it was a condition presumably existing at the time of the call. What was important was the caller's ability to predict respondent's *future behavior*, because it demonstrated inside information — a special familiarity with respondent's affairs. The general public would have had no way of knowing that respondent would shortly leave the building, get in the described car, and drive the most direct route to Dobey's Motel. Because only a small number of people are generally privy to an individual's itinerary, it is reasonable for police to believe that a person with access to such information is likely to also have access to reliable information about that individual's illegal activities. When significant aspects of the caller's predictions were verified, there was reason to believe not only that the caller was honest but also that he was well informed, at least well enough to justify the stop.

Although it is a close case, we conclude that under the totality of the circumstances the anonymous tip, as corroborated, exhibited sufficient indicia of reliability to justify the investigatory stop of respondent's car. We therefore reverse the judgment of the Court of Criminal Appeals of Alabama and remand for further proceedings not inconsistent with this opinion.

Justice STEVENS, with whom Justice BRENNAN and Justice MARSHALL join, dissenting.

Millions of people leave their apartments at about the same time every day carrying an attache case and heading for a destination known to their neighbors. Usually, however, the neighbors do not know what the briefcase contains. An anonymous neighbor's prediction about somebody's time of departure and probable destination is anything but a reliable basis for assuming that the commuter is in possession of an illegal substance — particularly when the person is not even carrying the attache case described by the tipster.

The record in this case does not tell us how often respondent drove from the Lynwood Terrace Apartments to Dobey's Motel; for all we know, she may have been a room clerk or telephone operator working the evening shift. It does not tell us whether Officer Davis made any effort to ascertain the informer's identity, his reason for calling, or the basis of his prediction about respondent's destination. Indeed, for all that this record tells us, the tipster may well have been another police officer who had a "hunch" that respondent might have cocaine in her attache case.

Anybody with enough knowledge about a given person to make her the target of a prank, or to harbor a grudge against her, will certainly be able to formulate a tip about her like the one predicting Vanessa White's excursion. In addition, under the Court's holding, every citizen is subject to being seized and questioned by any officer who is prepared to testify that the warrantless stop was based on an anonymous tip predicting whatever conduct the officer just observed. Fortunately, the vast majority of those in our law enforcement community would not adopt such a practice. But the Fourth Amendment was intended to protect the citizen from the overzealous and unscrupulous officer as well as from those who are conscientious and truthful. This decision makes a mockery of that protection.

I respectfully dissent.

## QUESTIONS AND NOTES

**1.** Do you think that the police had reasonable suspicion in this case?

**2.** If your answer to question 1 was "no," what would you have expected the police to do under these circumstances?

**3.** If your answer to question 1 was "yes," how do you deal with the problem of nonexistent informants manufactured by the police out of whole cloth after the fact?

**4.** Does *White* undervalue the importance of a known informant risking criminal charges for lying (see *Adams*, section B, *supra*) by according this much significance to an unknown informant?

**5.** Given *Gates* and *Sokolow*, was *White* almost inevitable?

## C.   Limits on *Terry*-type Stops

Having explored the distinction between probable cause and reasonable suspicion, we will now examine the limitations on stops based on reasonable suspicion. The case most clearly developing those limitations is our old friend from section B, *Royer*. Following *Royer*, we will consider *Place* and *Sharpe*, two cases that, when taken together, put some flesh on the *Royer* skeletal framework. We conclude with *Summers*, a case upholding the detention of a resident of a to be searched home pursuant to a search warrant for that home.

## Florida v. Royer
### 460 U.S. 491 (1983)

Justice WHITE announced the judgment of the Court and delivered an opinion in which Justices MARSHALL, POWELL and STEVENS joined.

[For a statement of the facts, see section B, *supra*.]

*Terry* and its progeny created only limited exceptions to the general rule that seizures of the person require probable cause to arrest. Detentions may be "investigative" yet violative of the Fourth Amendment absent probable cause. In the name of investigating a person who is no more than suspected of criminal activity, the police may not carry out a full search of the person or of his automobile or other effects. Nor may the police seek to verify their suspicions by means that approach the conditions of arrest. *Dunaway v. New York* made this clear. There, the suspect was taken to the police station from his home and, without being formally arrested, interrogated for an hour. The resulting incriminating statements were held inadmissible: reasonable suspicion of crime is insufficient to justify custodial interrogation even though the interrogation is investigative.

The Fourth Amendment's prohibition against unreasonable searches and seizures has always been interpreted to prevent a search that is not limited to the particularly described "place to be searched, and the persons or things to be seized," even if the search is made pursuant to a warrant and based upon probable cause. The Amendment's protection is not diluted in those situations where it has been determined that legitimate law enforcement interests justify a warrantless search: the search must be limited in scope to that which is justified by the particular purposes served by the exception. For example, a warrantless search is permissible incident to a lawful arrest because of legitimate concerns for the safety of the officer and to prevent the destruction of evidence by the arrestee. Nevertheless, such a search is limited to the person of the arrestee and the area immediately within his control. *Terry* also embodies this principle: "The scope of the search must be 'strictly tied to and justified by' the circumstances which rendered its initiation permissible."

The predicate permitting seizures on suspicion short of probable cause is that law enforcement interests warrant a limited intrusion on the personal security of the suspect. The scope of the intrusion permitted will vary to some extent with the particular facts and circumstances of each case. This much, however, is clear: an investigative detention must be temporary and last no longer than is necessary to effectuate the purpose of the stop. Similarly, the investigative methods employed should be the least intrusive means reasonably available to verify or dispel the officer's suspicion in a short period of time. It is the State's burden to demonstrate that the seizure it seeks to justify on the basis of a reasonable suspicion was sufficiently limited in scope and duration to satisfy the conditions of an investigative seizure.

The Florida Court of Appeal in the case before us, however, concluded not only that Royer had been seized when he gave his consent to search his luggage but also that the bounds of an investigative stop had been exceeded. In its view the "confinement" in this case went beyond the limited restraint of a *Terry* investigative stop, and Royer's consent was thus tainted by the illegality, a conclusion that required reversal in the absence of probable cause to arrest. The question before us is whether the record warrants that conclusion. We think that it does.

We also think that the officers' conduct was more intrusive than necessary to effectuate an investigative detention otherwise authorized by the *Terry* line of cases. First, by returning his ticket and driver's license, and informing him that he was free to go if he so desired, the officers may have obviated any claim that the encounter was anything but a consensual matter from start to finish.[a] Second, there are undoubtedly reasons of safety and security that would justify moving a suspect from one location to another during an investigatory detention, such as from an airport concourse to a more private area. There is no indication in this case that such reasons prompted the officers to transfer the site of the encounter from the concourse to the interrogation room. It appears, rather, that the primary interest of the officers was not in having an extended conversation with Royer but in the contents of his luggage, a matter which the officers did not pursue orally with Royer until after the encounter was relocated to the police room. The record does not reflect any facts which would support a finding that the legitimate law enforcement purposes which justified the detention in the first instance were furthered by removing Royer to the police room prior to the officers' attempt to gain his consent to a search of his luggage. As we have noted, had Royer consented to a search on the spot, the search could have been conducted with Royer present in the area where the

---

[a] A point dealt with more clearly in chapter 9, *infra*.

bags were retrieved by Officer Johnson and any evidence recovered would have been admissible against him. If the search proved negative, Royer would have been free to go much earlier and with less likelihood of missing his flight, which in itself can be a very serious matter in a variety of circumstances.

[T]he State has not touched on the question whether it would have been feasible to investigate the contents of Royer's bags in a more expeditious way. The courts are not strangers to the use of trained dogs to detect the presence of controlled substances in luggage.[10] There is no indication here that this means was not feasible and available. If it had been used, Royer and his luggage could have been momentarily detained while this investigative procedure was carried out. Indeed, it may be that no detention at all would have been necessary. A negative result would have freed Royer in short order; a positive result would have resulted in his justifiable arrest on probable cause.

We do not suggest that there is a litmus-paper test for distinguishing a consensual encounter from a seizure or for determining when a seizure exceeds the bounds of an investigative stop. Even in the discrete category of airport encounters, there will be endless variations in the facts and circumstances, so much variation that it is unlikely that the courts can reduce to a sentence or a paragraph a rule that will provide unarguable answers to the question whether there has been an unreasonable search or seizure in violation of the Fourth Amendment. Nevertheless, we must render judgment, and we think that the Florida Court of Appeal cannot be faulted in concluding that the limits of a *Terry*-stop had been exceeded.

---

[10] Courts of Appeals are in disagreement as to whether using a dog to detect drugs in luggage is a search, but no Court of Appeals has held that more than an articulable suspicion is necessary to justify this kind of a warrantless search if indeed it is a search. [A point discussed in chapter 10, *infra* – ed.] Furthermore, the law of the circuit from which this case comes was and is that "use of [drug-detecting canines] constitute[s] neither a search nor a seizure under the Fourth Amendment."

In any event, we hold here that the officers had reasonable suspicion to believe that Royer's luggage contained drugs, and we assume that the use of dogs in the investigation would not have entailed any prolonged detention of either Royer or his luggage which may involve other Fourth Amendment concerns. In the case before us, the officers, with founded suspicion, could have detained Royer for the brief period during which Florida authorities at busy airports seem able to carry out the dog-sniffing procedure.

Justice BRENNAN, concurring in result.

[E]ven assuming the legality of the initial stop, the plurality correctly holds, and I agree, that the officers' subsequent actions clearly exceeded the permissible bounds of a *Terry* "investigative" stop. "[A]ny 'exception' that could cover a seizure as intrusive as that in this case would threaten to swallow the general rule that Fourth Amendment seizures are 'reasonable' only if based on probable cause." *Dunaway*. Thus, most of the plurality's discussion of the permissible scope of *Terry* investigative stops is also unnecessary to the decision.

I emphasize that *Terry* was a very limited decision that expressly declined to address the "constitutional propriety of an investigative 'seizure' upon less than probable cause for purposes of 'detention' and/or interrogation." *Terry* simply held that under certain carefully defined circumstances a police officer "is entitled for the protection of himself and others in the area to conduct a carefully limited search of the outer clothing . . . in an attempt to discover weapons which might be used to assault him." *Adams* endorsed "brief" investigative stops based on reasonable suspicion, but the search for weapons upheld in that case was very limited and was based on *Terry*'s safety rationale. In *Adams*, we stated that the purpose of the "limited" weapons search was "not to discover evidence of crime, but to allow the officer to pursue his investigation without fear of violence. . . ." In *Brignoni-Ponce*, we held that "when an officer's observations lead him reasonably to suspect that a particular vehicle may contain aliens who are illegally in the country, he may stop the car briefly and investigate the circumstances that provoke suspicion." We based this holding on the importance of the governmental interest in stemming the flow of illegal aliens, on the minimal intrusion of a brief stop, and on the absence of practical alternatives for policing the border. We noted the limited holdings of *Terry* and *Adams* and while authorizing the police to "question the driver and passengers about their citizenship and immigration status, and . . . ask them to explain suspicious circumstances," we expressly stated that "any further detention or search must be based on consent or probable cause."

The scope of a *Terry*-type "investigative" stop and any attendant search must be extremely limited or the *Terry* exception would "swallow the general rule that Fourth Amendment seizures [and searches] are 'reasonable' only if based on probable cause." In my view, any suggestion that the *Terry* reasonable-suspicion standard justifies anything but the briefest of detentions or the most limited of searches finds no support in the *Terry* line of cases.*

Justice BLACKMUN, dissenting.

In my view, the police conduct in this case was minimally intrusive. Given the strength of society's interest in overcoming the extraordinary obstacles to the detection of drug traffickers, such conduct should not be subjected to a requirement of probable cause. Because the Court holds otherwise, I dissent.

I

The dispositive issue is whether the officers needed probable cause to arrest before they could take the actions that led to Royer's consent and the subsequent discovery of the contraband. I conclude that they did not.

A

"[T]he key principle of the Fourth Amendment is reasonableness – the balancing of competing interests." Previous cases suggest a two-step analysis to distinguish seizures requiring probable cause from those requiring reasonable suspicion. On the one hand, any formal arrest, and any seizure "having the essential attributes of a formal arrest, is unreasonable unless it is supported by probable cause." On the other hand, a more limited intrusion, if supported by a special law enforcement need for greater

flexibility, may be justifiable under the lesser "reasonable suspicion" standard. These lesser seizures are "not confined to the momentary, on-the-street detention accompanied by a frisk for weapons." In the case of a seizure less intrusive than a formal arrest, determining whether the less demanding reasonable suspicion standard will be applied requires balancing the amount of intrusion upon individual privacy against the special law enforcement interests that would be served by permitting such an intrusion on less than probable cause.

B

At the suppression hearing in this case, Royer agreed that he was not formally arrested until after his suitcases were opened. In my view, it cannot fairly be said that, prior to the formal arrest, the functional equivalent of an arrest had taken place. The encounter had far more in common with automobile stops justifiable on reasonable suspicion than with the detention deemed the functional equivalent of a formal arrest in *Dunaway*. In *Dunaway*, the suspect was taken from his neighbor's home and involuntarily transported to the police station in a squad car. At the precinct house, he was placed in an interrogation room and subjected to extended custodial interrogation. Here, Royer was not taken from a private residence, where reasonable expectations of privacy perhaps are at their greatest. Instead, he was approached in a major international airport where, due in part to extensive anti-hijacking surveillance and equipment, reasonable privacy expectations are of significantly lesser magnitude, certainly no greater than the reasonable privacy expectations of travelers in automobiles. As in the automobile stop cases, and indeed as in every case in which the Court has upheld seizures upon reasonable suspicion, Royer was questioned where he was found, and all questions were directly related to the purpose of the stop. Thus, the officers asked about Royer's identity, the purposes of his travel, and the suspicious circumstances they had noted. As the plurality appears to concede, probable cause was certainly not required at this point, and the officers' conduct was fully supported by reasonable suspicion.

What followed was within the scope of the lesser intrusions approved on less than probable cause in our prior cases, and was far removed from the circumstances of *Dunaway*. In the context of automobile stops, the Court has held that an officer "may question the driver and passengers about their citizenship and immigration status, and he may ask them to explain suspicious circumstances, but any further detention or search must be based on consent or probable cause."

---

* I interpret the plurality's requirement that the investigative methods employed pursuant to a *Terry* stop be "the least intrusive means reasonably available to verify or dispel the officer's suspicion in a short period of time" to mean that the availability of a less intrusive means may make an otherwise reasonable stop unreasonable. I do not interpret it to mean that the absence of a less intrusive means can make an otherwise unreasonable stop reasonable.

In addition, contrary to the plurality's apparent suggestion, I am not at all certain that the use of trained narcotics dogs constitutes a less intrusive means of conducting a lawful *Terry* investigative stop. Such a suggestion finds no support in our cases and any question concerning the use of trained dogs to detect the presence of controlled substances in luggage is clearly not before us.

In any event, the relevance of a least intrusive means requirement within the context of a *Terry* investigative stop is not clear to me. As I have discussed, a lawful stop must be so strictly limited that it is difficult to conceive of a less intrusive means that would be effective to accomplish the purpose of the stop.

Here, Royer was not subjected to custodial interrogation, for which probable cause is required.

## II

The officers in this case began their encounter with Royer with reasonable suspicion. They continued their questioning and requested further cooperation only as more facts, heightening their suspicion, came to their attention. Certainly, as any such detention continues or escalates, a greater degree of reasonable suspicion is necessary to sustain it, and at some point probable cause will be required. But here, the intrusion was short-lived and minimal. Only 15 minutes transpired from the initial approach to the opening of the suitcases. The officers were polite, and sought and immediately obtained Royer's consent at each significant step of the process.[3] Royer knew that if the search of the suitcases did not turn up contraband, he would be free to go on his way.[4] Thus, it seems clear to me that "the police [were] diligently pursuing a means of investigation which [was] likely to resolve the matter one way or another very soon. . . ."[5]

The special need for flexibility in uncovering illicit drug couriers is hardly debatable. Surely the problem is as serious, and as intractable, as the problem of illegal immigration. In light of the extraordinary and well-documented difficulty of identifying drug couriers, the minimal intrusion in this case, based on particularized suspicion, was eminently reasonable.

I dissent.

Justice REHNQUIST, with whom the CHIEF JUSTICE and Justice O'CONNOR join, dissenting.

The point at which I part company with the plurality's opinion is in the assessment of the reasonableness of the officers' conduct following their initial conversation with Royer. The plurality focuses on the transfer of the place of the interview from the main concourse of the airport to the room off the concourse and observes that Royer "found himself in a small room—a large closet—equipped with a desk and two chairs. He was alone with two police officers who again told him that they thought he was carrying narcotics. He also found that the officers, without his consent, had retrieved his checked luggage from the airlines."

Obviously, this quoted language is intended to convey stern disapproval of the described conduct of the officers. To my mind, it merits no such disapproval and was eminently reasonable. Would it have been preferable for the officers to have detained Royer for further questioning, as they concededly had a right to do, without paying any attention to the fact that his luggage had already been checked on the flight to New York, and might be put aboard the flight even though Royer himself was not on the plane? Would it have been more "reasonable" to interrogate Royer about the contents of his suitcases, and to seek his permission to open the suitcases when they were retrieved, in the busy main concourse of the Miami Airport, rather than to find a room off the concourse where the confrontation would surely be less embarrassing to Royer? If the room had been large and spacious, rather than small, if it had possessed three chairs rather than two, would the officers' conduct have been made reasonable by these facts?

The plurality's answers to these questions, to the extent that it attempts any, are scarcely satisfying. It commences with the observation that "the officers conduct was more intrusive than necessary to effectuate an investigative detention otherwise authorized by the *Terry* line of cases." Earlier in its opinion, the plurality set the stage for this standard when the familiar "least intrusive means" principle of First Amendment law is suddenly carried over into Fourth Amendment law by the citation of two cases, *Brignoni-Ponce* and *Adams*, neither one of which lends any support to the principle as a part of Fourth Amendment law. The plurality goes on to say that had the officers returned Royer's ticket and driver's

---

[3] The officers acted reasonably in taking Royer's baggage stubs and bringing his luggage to the police room without his consent. Royer had already surrendered the suitcases to a third party, the airline. The officers brought the suitcases to him immediately, and their contents were not revealed until Royer gave his consent. Thus, Royer's privacy was not substantially invaded. At that time, moreover, Royer himself was validly detained, the object of the encounter had become the securing of Royer's consent to search his luggage, and the luggage would otherwise have been loaded onto the airplane.

[4] The fact that Royer knew the search was likely to turn up contraband is of course irrelevant; the potential intrusiveness of the officers' conduct must be judged from the viewpoint of an innocent person in Royer's position.

[5] Like Justice Rehnquist, I cannot accept the "least intrusive" alternative analysis the plurality would impose on the law of the Fourth Amendment. Prior cases do establish that "an investigative detention must be temporary and last no longer than is necessary to effectuate the purpose of the stop." The detention at issue fully met that standard.

license, the encounter clearly would have been consensual. The plurality also states that while there were good reasons to justify moving Royer from one location to another, the officers' motives in seeking to examine his luggage renders these reasons unavailing—a conclusion the reason for which wholly escapes me. Finally, the plurality suggests that the officers might have examined Royer's bags in a more expeditious way, such as the use of trained dogs.

All of this to my mind adds up to little more than saying that if my aunt were a man, she would be my uncle. The officers might have taken different steps than they did to investigate Royer, but the same may be said of virtually every investigative encounter that has more than one step to it. The question we must decide is what was *unreasonable* about the steps which *these officers* took with respect to *this* suspect in the Miami Airport on this particular day. On this point, the plurality stutters, fudges, and hedges:

> "What had begun as a consensual inquiry in a public place had escalated into an investigatory procedure in a police interrogation room, where the police, unsatisfied with previous explanations, sought to confirm their suspicions."

But since even the plurality concedes that there was articulable suspicion warranting an investigatory detention, the fact that the inquiry had become an "investigatory procedure in a police interrogation room" would seem to have little bearing on the proper disposition of a claim that the officers violated the Fourth Amendment. The plurality goes on to say:

> "At least as of that moment, any consensual aspects of the encounter had evaporated, and we cannot fault the Florida Court of Appeal in concluding that *Terry* and the cases following it did not justify the restraint to which Royer was then subjected. As a practical matter, Royer was under arrest."

Does the plurality intimate that if the Florida Court of Appeal had reached the opposite conclusion with respect to the holdings of *Terry* and the cases which follow it, it would affirm that holding? Does it mean that the 15-minute duration of the total encounter, and the even lesser amount of elapsed time during which Royer was in the "interrogation room," was more than a *Terry* investigative stop can ever consume? These possible conclusions are adumbrated, but not stated; if the plurality's opinion were to be judged by standards appropriate to Impressionist paintings, it would perhaps receive a high grade, but the same cannot be said if it is to be judged by the standards of a judicial opinion.

Since the plurality concedes the existence of "articulable suspicion" at least after the initial conversation with Royer, the only remaining question is whether the detention of Royer during that period of time was permissible under the rule enunciated in *Terry*. Although *Terry* itself involved only a protective pat down for weapons, subsequent cases have expanded the permissible scope of such a "seizure." In *Adams*, we upheld both a search and seizure of a pistol being carried by a suspect seated in a parked automobile. In *Martinez-Fuerte*, we allowed government officials to stop, and divert for visual inspection and questioning, automobiles which were suspected of harboring illegal aliens. These stops, including waiting time, could clearly have approximated in length the time which Royer was detained, and yet *Martinez-Fuerte* allowed them to be made "in the absence of *any individualized suspicion* at reasonably located checkpoints." 428 U.S., at 562 (emphasis supplied). Unless we are to say that commercial drug trafficking is somehow quantitatively less weighty on the Fourth Amendment scale than trafficking in the illegal aliens, I think the articulable suspicion which concededly focused upon Royer justified the length and nature of his detention.

## QUESTIONS AND NOTES

**1.** The Court split 5-4 in favor of the least intrusive means test. This is contrary to the position that it has taken in other areas, notably "inventory searches." Is there something about *Terry*-stops that warrants such a stringent standard?

**2.** As a practical matter, does the "least intrusive means" test practically insure defeat for the government in that a reasonably competent attorney can ordinarily think of something "less intrusive" than what the police actually did? (We will consider this point further in conjunction with *Sharpe*.)

**3.** Would (should) the result have been different if the Florida Court of Appeal had found the detention to be constitutional?

**4.** In regard to Justice Rehnquist's questions, what exactly did the DEA agents do wrong? Is fifteen minutes too long *per se*? Were they insufficiently expeditious? Did they interview Royer in the wrong place?

**5.** These questions are somewhat clarified in *Place*.

## United States v. Place
### 462 U.S. 696 (1983)

Justice O'CONNOR delivered the opinion of the Court.

This case presents the issue whether the Fourth Amendment prohibits law enforcement authorities from temporarily detaining personal luggage for exposure to a trained narcotics detection dog on the basis of reasonable suspicion that the luggage contains narcotics. Given the enforcement problems associated with the detection of narcotics trafficking and the minimal intrusion that a properly limited detention would entail, we conclude that the Fourth Amendment does not prohibit such a detention. On the facts of this case, however, we hold that the police conduct exceeded the bounds of a permissible investigative detention of the luggage.

I

Respondent Raymond J. Place's behavior aroused the suspicions of law enforcement officers as he waited in line at the Miami International Airport to purchase a ticket to New York's LaGuardia Airport. As Place proceeded to the gate for his flight, the agents approached him and requested his airline ticket and some identification. Place complied with the request and consented to a search of the two suitcases he had checked. Because his flight was about to depart, however, the agents decided not to search the luggage.

Prompted by Place's parting remark that he had recognized that they were police, the agents inspected the address tags on the checked luggage and noted discrepancies in the two street addresses. Further investigation revealed that neither address existed and that the telephone number Place had given the airline belonged to a third address on the same street. On the basis of their encounter with Place and this information, the Miami agents called Drug Enforcement Administration (DEA) authorities in New York to relay their information about Place.

Two DEA agents waited for Place at the arrival gate at LaGuardia Airport in New York. There again, his behavior aroused the suspicion of the agents. After he had claimed his two bags and called a limousine, the agents decided to approach him.

They identified themselves as federal narcotics agents, to which Place responded that he knew they were "cops" and had spotted them as soon as he had deplaned. One of the agents informed Place that, based on their own observations and information obtained from the Miami authorities, they believed that he might be carrying narcotics. After identifying the bags as belonging to him, Place stated that a number of police at the Miami Airport had surrounded him and searched his baggage. The agents responded that their information was to the contrary. The agents requested and received identification from Place – a New Jersey driver's license, on which the agents later ran a computer check that disclosed no offenses, and his airline ticket receipt. When Place refused to consent to a search of his luggage, one of the agents told him that they were going to take the luggage to a federal judge to try to obtain a search warrant and that Place was free to accompany them. Place declined, but obtained from one of the agents telephone numbers at which the agents could be reached.

The agents then took the bags to Kennedy Airport, where they subjected the bags to a "sniff test" by a trained narcotics detection dog. The dog reacted positively to the smaller of the two bags but ambiguously to the larger bag. Approximately 90 minutes had elapsed since the seizure of respondent's luggage. Because it was late on a Friday afternoon, the agents retained the luggage until Monday morning, when they secured a search warrant from a magistrate for the smaller bag. Upon opening that bag, the agents discovered 1,125 grams of cocaine.

II

In this case, the Government asks us to recognize the reasonableness under the Fourth Amendment of warrantless seizures of personal luggage from the custody of the owner on the basis of less than probable cause, for the purpose of pursuing a limited course of investigation, short of opening the luggage, that would quickly confirm or dispel the authorities' suspicion. Specifically, we are asked to apply the principles of *Terry* to permit such seizures on the basis of reasonable, articulable suspicion, premised on objective facts, that the luggage contains contraband or evidence of a crime. In our view, such application is appropriate.

The exception to the probable-cause requirement for limited seizures of the person recognized in *Terry* and its progeny rests on a balancing of the competing interests to determine the reasonableness of the type of seizure involved within the meaning of "the Fourth Amendment's general proscription against unreasonable searches and seizures." We must balance the nature and quality of the intrusion on the individual's Fourth Amendment interests against the importance of the governmental interests alleged to justify the intrusion. When the nature and extent of the detention are minimally intrusive of the individual's Fourth Amendment interests, the opposing law enforcement interests can support a seizure based on less than probable cause.

We examine first the governmental interest offered as a justification for a brief seizure of luggage from the suspect's custody for the purpose of pursuing a limited course of investigation. The Government contends that, where the authorities possess specific and articulable facts warranting a reasonable belief that a traveler's luggage contains narcotics, the governmental interest in seizing the luggage briefly to pursue further investigation is substantial. We agree. As observed in *United States v. Mendenhall*, (chapter 9, *infra*.) "[t]he public has a compelling interest in detecting those who would traffic in deadly drugs for personal profit."

Respondent suggests that, absent some special law enforcement interest such as officer safety, a generalized interest in law enforcement cannot justify an intrusion on an individual's Fourth Amendment interests in the absence of probable cause. Our prior cases, however, do not support this proposition. In *Terry*, we described the governmental interests supporting the initial seizure of the person as "effective crime prevention and detection; it is this interest which underlies the recognition that a police officer may in appropriate circumstances and in an appropriate manner approach a person for purposes of investigating possibly criminal behavior even though there is no probable cause to make an arrest." Similarly, in *Michigan v. Summers* (*infra*), we identified three law enforcement interests that justified limited detention of the occupants of the premises during execution of a valid search warrant: "preventing flight in the event that incriminating evidence is found," "minimizing the risk of harm" both to the officers and the occupants, and "orderly completion of the search." Cf. *Royer*. The test is

whether those interests are sufficiently "substantial," not whether they are independent of the interest in investigating crimes effectively and apprehending suspects. The context of a particular law enforcement practice, of course, may affect the determination whether a brief intrusion on Fourth Amendment interests on less than probable cause is essential to effective criminal investigation. Because of the inherently transient nature of drug courier activity at airports, allowing police to make brief investigative stops of persons at airports on reasonable suspicion of drug-trafficking substantially enhances the likelihood that police will be able to prevent the flow of narcotics into distribution channels.[5]

Against this strong governmental interest, we must weigh the nature and extent of the intrusion upon the individual's Fourth Amendment rights when the police briefly detain luggage for limited investigative purposes. On this point, respondent Place urges that the rationale for a *Terry* stop of the person is wholly inapplicable to investigative detentions of personalty. Specifically, the *Terry* exception to the probable-cause requirement is premised on the notion that a *Terry*-type stop of the person is substantially less intrusive of a person's liberty interests than a formal arrest. In the property context, however, Place urges, there are no degrees of intrusion. Once the owner's property is seized, the dispossession is absolute.

We disagree. The intrusion on possessory interests occasioned by a seizure of one's personal effects can vary both in its nature and extent. The seizure may be made after the owner has relinquished control of the property to a third party or, as here, from the immediate custody and control of the owner. Moreover, the police may confine their investigation to an on-the-spot inquiry – for example, immediate

---

[5] Referring to the problem of intercepting drug couriers in the nation's airports, Justice Powell has observed:

"Much of the drug traffic is highly organized and conducted by sophisticated criminal syndicates. The profits are enormous. And many drugs . . . may be easily concealed. As a result, the obstacles to detection of illegal conduct may be unmatched in any other area of law enforcement." *United States v. Mendenhall*, 446 U.S., at 561-562 (opinion of Powell, J.). (chapter 9, *infra*).

See *Royer* (Blackmun, J., dissenting) ("The special need for flexibility in uncovering illicit drug couriers is hardly debatable") (airport context).

exposure of the luggage to a trained narcotics detection dog – or transport the property to another location. Given the fact that seizures of property can vary in intrusiveness, some brief detentions of personal effects may be so minimally intrusive of Fourth Amendment interests that strong countervailing governmental interests will justify a seizure based only on specific articulable facts that the property contains contraband or evidence of a crime.

### III

There is no doubt that the agents made a "seizure" of Place's luggage for purposes of the Fourth Amendment when, following his refusal to consent to a search, the agent told Place that he was going to take the luggage to a federal judge to secure issuance of a warrant. As we observed in *Terry*, "[t]he manner in which the seizure . . . [was] conducted is, of course, as vital a part of the inquiry as whether [it was] warranted at all."

At the outset, we must reject the Government's suggestion that the point at which probable cause for seizure of luggage from the person's presence becomes necessary is more distant than in the case of a *Terry* stop of the person himself. The premise of the Government's argument is that seizures of property are generally less intrusive than seizures of the person. While true in some circumstances, that premise is faulty on the facts we address in this case. The precise type of detention we confront here is seizure of personal luggage from the immediate possession of the suspect for the purpose of arranging exposure to a narcotics detection dog. Particularly in the case of detention of luggage within the traveler's immediate possession, the police conduct intrudes on both the suspect's possessory interest in his luggage as well as his liberty interest in proceeding with his itinerary. The person whose luggage is detained is technically still free to continue his travels or carry out other personal activities pending release of the luggage. Moreover, he is not subjected to the coercive atmosphere of a custodial confinement or to the public indignity of being personally detained. Nevertheless, such a seizure can effectively restrain the person since he is subjected to the possible disruption of his travel plans in order to remain with his luggage or to arrange for its return.[8] Therefore, when

---

[8] "At least when the authorities do not make it absolutely clear how they plan to reunite the suspect and his possessions at some future time and place, seizure of the object is tantamount to seizure of the person. This is because that person must either remain on the scene or else seemingly surrender his effects permanently to the police."

the police seize luggage from the suspect's custody, we think the limitations applicable to investigative detentions of the person should define the permissible scope of an investigative detention of the person's luggage on less than probable cause. Under this standard, it is clear that the police conduct here exceeded the permissible limits of a *Terry*-type investigative stop.

The length of the detention of respondent's luggage alone precludes the conclusion that the seizure was reasonable in the absence of probable cause. Although we have recognized the reasonableness of seizures longer than the momentary ones involved in *Terry, Adams*, and *Brignoni-Ponce*, the brevity of the invasion of the individual's Fourth Amendment interests is an important factor in determining whether the seizure is so minimally intrusive as to be justifiable on reasonable suspicion. Moreover, in assessing the effect of the length of the detention, we take into account whether the police diligently pursue their investigation. We note that here the New York agents knew the time of Place's scheduled arrival at LaGuardia, had ample time to arrange for their additional investigation at that location, and thereby could have minimized the intrusion on respondent's Fourth Amendment interests.[9] Thus, although we decline to adopt any outside time limitation for a permissible *Terry* stop,[10] we have never approved a seizure of the person for the prolonged 90-minute period involved here and cannot do so on the facts presented by this case. See *Dunaway*.

Although the 90-minute detention of respondent's luggage is sufficient to render the seizure unreasonable, the violation was exacerbated by the failure of the agents to accurately inform respondent of the

---

[9] Cf. *Royer* (plurality opinion) ("If [trained narcotics detection dogs] had been used, Royer and his luggage could have been momentarily detained while this investigative procedure was carried out"). This course of conduct also would have avoided the further substantial intrusion on respondent's possessory interests caused by the removal of his luggage to another location.

[10] Cf. ALI, Model Code of Pre-Arraignment Procedure § 110.2(1) (1975) (recommending a maximum of 20 minutes for a *Terry* stop). We understand the desirability of providing law enforcement authorities with a clear rule to guide their conduct. Nevertheless, we question the wisdom of a rigid time limitation. Such a limit would undermine the equally important need to allow authorities to graduate their responses to the demands of any particular situation.

place to which they were transporting his luggage, of the length of time he might be dispossessed, and of what arrangements would be made for return of the luggage if the investigation dispelled the suspicion. In short, we hold that the detention of respondent's luggage in this case went beyond the narrow authority possessed by police to detain briefly luggage reasonably suspected to contain narcotics.

### IV

We conclude that, under all of the circumstances of this case, the seizure of respondent's luggage was unreasonable under the Fourth Amendment. Consequently, the evidence obtained from the subsequent search of his luggage was inadmissible, and Place's conviction must be reversed. The judgment of the Court of Appeals, accordingly, is affirmed.

Justice BRENNAN, with whom Justice MARSHALL joins, concurring in result.

In some respects the Court's opinion in this case can be seen as the logical successor of the plurality opinion in *Royer*. The plurality opinion in *Royer* contained considerable language, which was unnecessary to the judgment regarding the permissible scope of *Terry* investigative stops. Even assuming, however, that the Court finds some support in *Royer* for its discussion of the scope of *Terry* stops, the Court today goes well beyond *Royer* in endorsing the notion that the principles of *Terry* permit "warrantless seizures of personal luggage from the custody of the owner on the basis of less than probable cause, for the purpose of pursuing a limited course of investigation, short of opening the luggage, that would quickly confirm or dispel the authorities' suspicion." In addition to being unnecessary to the Court's judgment, this suggestion finds no support in *Terry* or its progeny and significantly dilutes the Fourth Amendment's protections against government interference with personal property. In short, it represents a radical departure from settled Fourth Amendment principles.

As noted, *Terry* and the cases that followed it authorize a brief "investigative" stop of an individual based on reasonable suspicion and a limited search for weapons if the officer reasonably suspects that the individual is armed and presently dangerous. The purpose of this brief stop is "to determine [the individual's] identity or to maintain the status quo momentarily while obtaining more information. . . ." *Adams*. Anything more than a brief stop "must be based on consent or probable cause." *Brignoni-Ponce*. During the course of this stop, "the suspect must not be moved or asked to move more than a short distance; physical searches are permitted only to the extent necessary to protect

the police officers involved during the encounter; and, most importantly, the suspect must be free to leave after a short time and to decline to answer the questions put to him." It is true that *Terry* stops may involve seizures of personal effects incidental to the seizure of the person involved. Obviously, an officer cannot seize a person without also seizing the personal effects that the individual has in his possession at the time. But there is a difference between incidental seizures of personal effects and seizures of property independent of the seizure of the person.

The officers did not develop probable cause to arrest respondent during their encounter with him. Therefore, they had to let him go. But despite the absence of probable cause to arrest respondent, the officers seized his luggage and deprived him of possession. Respondent, therefore, was subjected not only to an invasion of his personal security and privacy, but also to an independent dispossession of his personal effects based simply on reasonable suspicion. It is difficult to understand how this intrusion is not more severe than a brief stop for questioning or even a limited, on-the-spot patdown search for weapons.

In my view, as soon as the officers seized respondent's luggage, independent of their seizure of him, they exceeded the scope of a permissible *Terry* stop and violated respondent's Fourth Amendment rights. In addition, the officers' seizure of respondent's luggage violated the established rule that seizures of personal effects must be based on probable cause. Their actions, therefore, should not be upheld.

The Court acknowledges that seizures of personal property must be based on probable cause. Despite this recognition, the Court employs a balancing test drawn from *Terry* to conclude that personal effects may be seized based on reasonable suspicion. In *Dunaway*, the Court stated that "[t]he narrow intrusions involved in [*Terry* and its progeny] were judged by a balancing test rather than by the general principle that Fourth Amendment seizures must be supported by the 'long-prevailing standards' of probable cause . . . only because these intrusions fell far short of the kind of intrusion associated with an arrest." As *Dunaway* suggests, the use of a balancing test in this case is inappropriate. First, the intrusion involved in this case is no longer the "narrow" one contemplated by the *Terry* line of cases. In addition, the intrusion involved in this case involves not only the seizure of a person, but also the seizure of property. *Terry* and its progeny did not address seizures of property. Those cases left unchanged the rule that seizures of property must be based on probable cause. The *Terry* balancing test should not be wrenched from its factual and conceptual moorings.

Justice Douglas was the only dissenter in *Terry*. He stated that "[t]here have been powerful hydraulic pressures throughout our history that bear heavily on the Court to water down constitutional guarantees and give the police the upper hand." Today, the Court uses *Terry* as a justification for submitting to these pressures. Their strength is apparent, for even when the Court finds that an individual's Fourth Amendment rights have been violated it cannot resist the temptation to weaken the protections the Amendment affords.

Justice BLACKMUN, with whom Justice MARSHALL joins, concurring in result.

In providing guidance to other courts, we often include in our opinions material that, technically, constitutes dictum. I cannot fault the Court's desire to set guidelines for *Terry* seizures of luggage based on reasonable suspicion. I am concerned, however, with what appears to me to be an emerging tendency on the part of the Court to convert the *Terry* decision into a general statement that the Fourth Amendment requires only that any seizure be reasonable.[1]

I pointed out in dissent in *Royer*, that our prior cases suggest a two-step evaluation of seizures under the Fourth Amendment. The Amendment generally prohibits a seizure unless it is pursuant to a judicial

---

[1] The Court states that the applicability of the *Terry* exception "rests on a balancing of the competing interests to determine the reasonableness of the type of seizure involved within the meaning of 'the Fourth Amendment's general proscription against unreasonable searches and seizures.'" As the context of the quotation from *Terry* makes clear, however, this balancing to determine reasonableness occurs only under the exceptional circumstances that justify the *Terry* exception:

> "But we deal here with an entire rubric of police conduct—necessarily swift action predicated upon the on-the-spot observations of the officer on the beat—which historically has not been, and as a practical matter could not be, subjected to the warrant procedure. Instead, the conduct involved in this case must be tested by the Fourth Amendment's general proscription against unreasonable searches and seizures."

warrant issued upon probable cause and particularly describing the items to be seized. The Court correctly observes that a warrant may be dispensed with if the officer has probable cause and if some exception to the warrant requirement, such as exigent circumstances, is applicable. While the Fourth Amendment speaks in terms of freedom from unreasonable seizures, the Amendment does not leave the reasonableness of most seizures to the judgment of courts or government officers: the Framers of the Amendment balanced the interests involved and decided that a seizure is reasonable only if supported by a judicial warrant based on probable cause.

*Terry*, however, teaches that in some circumstances a limited seizure that is less restrictive than a formal arrest may constitutionally occur upon mere reasonable suspicion, if "supported by a special law enforcement need for greater flexibility." When this exception to the Fourth Amendment's warrant and probable cause requirements is applicable, a reviewing court must balance the individual's interest in privacy against the Government's law enforcement interest and determine whether the seizure was reasonable under the circumstances. Only in this limited context is a court entitled to engage in any balancing of interests in determining the validity of a seizure.

Because I agree with the Court that there is a significant law enforcement interest in interdicting illegal drug traffic in the Nation's airports, a limited intrusion caused by a temporary seizure of luggage for investigative purposes could fall within the *Terry* exception. The critical threshold issue is the intrusiveness of the seizure.[2] In this case, the seizure went well beyond a minimal intrusion and therefore cannot fall within the *Terry* exception.

---

[2] I cannot agree with the Court's assertion that the diligence of the police in acting on their suspicion is relevant to the extent of the intrusion on Fourth Amendment interests. It makes little difference to a traveler whose luggage is seized whether the police conscientiously followed a lead or bungled the investigation. The duration and intrusiveness of the seizure is not altered by the diligence the police exercise. Of course, diligence may be relevant to a court's determination of the reasonableness of the seizure once it is determined that the seizure is sufficiently nonintrusive as to be eligible for the *Terry* exception.

## QUESTIONS AND NOTES

**1.** Is the Court holding that 90 minutes is *per se* too long? Isn't the Court trying to avoid *per se* time limits?

**2.** If you had been on the Court would you have allowed luggage to have been detained at all? Why? Why not?

**3.** Assuming that your answer to question 2 is "yes," should it be subject to detention for less time, more time, or the same time that a person is subject to detention?

**4.** Did all nine Justices adopt the "least intrusive means" test?

**5.** A fairly extreme version of the "least intrusive means" test was rejected in *Sharpe*. As you read the case, see if you can ascertain the reason for that rejection.

### United States v. Sharpe
### 470 U.S. 675 (1984)

Chief Justice BURGER delivered the opinion of the Court.

We granted certiorari to decide whether an individual reasonably suspected of engaging in criminal activity may be detained for a period of 20 minutes, when the detention is necessary for law enforcement officers to conduct a limited investigation of the suspected criminal activity.

#### I

On the morning of June 9, 1978, Agent Cooke of the Drug Enforcement Administration (DEA) was on patrol in an unmarked vehicle on a coastal road near Sunset Beach, North Carolina, an area under surveillance for suspected drug trafficking. At approximately 6:30 a.m., Cooke noticed a blue pickup truck with an attached camper shell traveling on the highway in tandem with a blue Pontiac Bonneville. Respondent Savage was driving the pickup, and respondent Sharpe was driving the Pontiac. The Pontiac also carried a passenger, Davis, the charges against whom were later dropped. Observing that the truck was riding low in the rear and that the camper did not bounce or sway appreciably when the truck drove over bumps or around curves, Agent Cooke concluded that it was heavily loaded. A quilted material covered the rear and side windows of the camper.

Cooke's suspicions were sufficiently aroused to follow the two vehicles for approximately 20 miles as they proceeded south into South Carolina. He then decided to make an "investigative stop" and radioed the State Highway Patrol for assistance. Officer Thrasher, driving a marked patrol car, responded to the call. Almost immediately after Thrasher caught up with the procession, the Pontiac and the pickup turned off the highway and onto a campground road.[1] Cooke and Thrasher followed the two vehicles as the latter drove along the road at 55 to 60 miles an hour, exceeding the speed limit of 35 miles an hour. The road eventually looped back to the highway, onto which Savage and Sharpe turned and continued to drive south.

At this point, all four vehicles were in the middle lane of the three right-hand lanes of the highway. Agent Cooke asked Officer Thrasher to signal both vehicles to stop. Thrasher pulled alongside the Pontiac, which was in the lead, turned on his flashing light, and motioned for the driver of the Pontiac to stop. As Sharpe moved the Pontiac into the right lane, the pickup truck cut between the Pontiac and Thrasher's patrol car, nearly hitting the patrol car, and continued down the highway. Thrasher pursued the truck while Cooke pulled up behind the Pontiac.

Cooke approached the Pontiac and identified himself. He requested identification, and Sharpe produced a Georgia driver's license bearing the name of Raymond J. Pavlovich. Cooke then attempted to radio Thrasher to determine whether he had been successful in stopping the pickup truck, but he was unable to make contact for several minutes, apparently because Thrasher was not in his patrol car. Cooke radioed the local police for assistance, and two officers from the Myrtle Beach Police Department arrived about 10 minutes later. Asking the two officers to "maintain the situation," Cooke left to join Thrasher.

---

[1] Officer Thrasher testified that the respondents' vehicles turned off the highway "[a]bout one minute" after he joined the procession.

In the meantime, Thrasher had stopped the pickup truck about one-half mile down the road. After stopping the truck, Thrasher had approached it with his revolver drawn, ordered the driver, Savage, to get out and assume a ''spread eagled'' position against the side of the truck, and patted him down. Thrasher then holstered his gun and asked Savage for his driver's license and the truck's vehicle registration. Savage produced his own Florida driver's license and a bill of sale for the truck bearing the name of Pavlovich. In response to questions from Thrasher concerning the ownership of the truck, Savage said that the truck belonged to a friend and that he was taking it to have its shock absorbers repaired. When Thrasher told Savage that he would be held until the arrival of Cooke, whom Thrasher identified as a DEA agent, Savage became nervous, said that he wanted to leave, and requested the return of his driver's license. Thrasher replied that Savage was not free to leave at that time.

Agent Cooke arrived at the scene approximately 15 minutes after the truck had been stopped. Thrasher handed Cooke Savage's license and the bill of sale for the truck; Cooke noted that the bill of sale bore the same name as Sharpe's license. Cooke identified himself to Savage as a DEA agent and said that he thought the truck was loaded with marihuana. Cooke twice sought permission to search the camper, but Savage declined to give it, explaining that he was not the owner of the truck. Cooke then stepped on the rear of the truck and, observing that it did not sink any lower, confirmed his suspicion that it was probably overloaded. He put his nose against the rear window, which was covered from the inside, and reported that he could smell marihuana. Without seeking Savage's permission, Cooke removed the keys from the ignition, opened the rear of the camper, and observed a large number of burlap-wrapped bales resembling bales of marihuana that Cooke had seen in previous investigations. Agent Cooke then placed Savage under arrest and left him with Thrasher.

Cooke returned to the Pontiac and arrested Sharpe and Davis. Approximately 30 to 40 minutes had elapsed between the time Cooke stopped the Pontiac and the time he returned to arrest Sharpe and Davis. Cooke assembled the various parties and vehicles and led them to the Myrtle Beach police station. That evening, DEA agents took the truck to the Federal Building in Charleston, South Carolina. Several days later, Cooke supervised the unloading of the truck, which contained 43 bales weighing a total of 2,629 pounds. Acting without a search warrant, Cooke had eight randomly selected bales opened and sampled. Chemical tests showed that the samples were marihuana.

## II

### A

The Fourth Amendment is not, of course, a guarantee against *all* searches and seizures, but only against *unreasonable* searches and seizures. The authority and limits of the Amendment apply to investigative stops of vehicles such as occurred here. In *Terry*, we adopted a dual inquiry for evaluating the reasonableness of an investigative stop. Under this approach, we examine

> ''whether the officer's action was justified at its inception, and whether it was reasonably related in scope to the circumstances which justified the interference in the first place.''

As to the first part of this inquiry, the Court of Appeals assumed that the police had an articulable and reasonable suspicion that Sharpe and Savage were engaged in marihuana trafficking, given the setting and all the circumstances when the police attempted to stop the Pontiac and the pickup. That assumption is abundantly supported by the record.[3] As to the second part of the inquiry, however, the court concluded that the 30- to 40-minute detention of Sharpe and the 20-minute detention of Savage ''failed to meet the [Fourth Amendment's] requirement of brevity.''

It is not necessary for us to decide whether the length of Sharpe's detention was unreasonable, because that detention bears no causal relation to Agent Cooke's discovery of the marihuana. The marihuana was in Savage's pickup, not in Sharpe's Pontiac; the contraband introduced at respondents' trial cannot logically be considered the ''fruit'' of Sharpe's detention. The only issue in this case, then, is whether it was reasonable under the circumstances facing Agent Cooke and Officer Thrasher to detain Savage,

---

[3] Agent Cooke had observed the vehicles traveling in tandem for 20 miles in an area near the coast known to be frequented by drug traffickers. Cooke testified that pickup trucks with camper shells were often used to transport large quantities of marihuana. Savage's pickup truck appeared to be heavily loaded, and the windows of the camper were covered with a quilted bed-sheet material rather than curtains. Finally, both vehicles took evasive actions and started speeding as soon as Officer Thrasher began following them in his marked car. Perhaps none of these facts, standing alone, would give rise to a reasonable suspicion; but taken together as appraised by an experienced law enforcement officer, they provided clear justification to stop the vehicles and pursue a limited investigation.

whose vehicle contained the challenged evidence, for approximately 20 minutes. We conclude that the detention of Savage clearly meets the Fourth Amendment's standard of reasonableness.

In *Royer*, government agents stopped the defendant in an airport, seized his luggage, and took him to a small room used for questioning, where a search of the luggage revealed narcotics. The Court held that the defendant's detention constituted an arrest. As in *Dunaway*, though, the focus was primarily on facts other than the duration of the defendant's detention—particularly the fact that the police confined the defendant in a small airport room for questioning.

The plurality in *Royer* did note that "an investigative detention must be temporary and last no longer than is necessary to effectuate the purpose of the stop." The Court followed a similar approach in *Place*. In that case, law enforcement agents stopped the defendant after his arrival in an airport and seized his luggage for 90 minutes to take it to a narcotics detection dog for a "sniff test." We decided that an investigative seizure of personal property could be justified under the *Terry* doctrine, but that "[t]he length of the detention of respondent's luggage alone precludes the conclusion that the seizure was reasonable in the absence of probable cause." However, the rationale underlying that conclusion was premised on the fact that the police knew of respondent's arrival time for several hours beforehand, and the Court assumed that the police could have arranged for a trained narcotics dog in advance and thus avoided the necessity of holding respondent's luggage for 90 minutes. "[I]n assessing the effect of the length of the detention, we take into account whether the police diligently pursue their investigation."

Here, the Court of Appeals did not conclude that the police acted less than diligently, or that they *unnecessarily* prolonged Savage's detention. *Place* and *Royer* thus provide no support for the Court of Appeals' analysis.

Admittedly, *Terry*, *Dunaway*, *Royer*, and *Place*, considered together, may in some instances create difficult line-drawing problems in distinguishing an investigative stop from a *de facto* arrest. Obviously, if an investigative stop continues indefinitely, at some point it can no longer be justified as an investigative stop. But our cases impose no rigid time limitation on *Terry* stops. While it is clear that "the brevity of the invasion of the individual's Fourth Amendment interests is an important factor in determining whether the seizure is so minimally intrusive as to be justifiable on reasonable suspicion," we have emphasized the need to consider the law enforcement purposes to be served by the stop as well as the time reasonably needed to effectuate those purposes. Much as a "bright line" rule would be desirable, in evaluating whether an investigative detention is unreasonable, common

sense and ordinary human experience must govern over rigid criteria.

The Court of Appeals' decision would effectively establish a *per se* rule that a 20-minute detention is too long to be justified under the *Terry* doctrine. Such a result is clearly and fundamentally at odds with our approach in this area.

### B

In assessing whether a detention is too long in duration to be justified as an investigative stop, we consider it appropriate to examine whether the police diligently pursued a means of investigation that was likely to confirm or dispel their suspicions quickly, during which time it was necessary to detain the defendant. A court making this assessment should take care to consider whether the police are acting in a swiftly developing situation, and in such cases the court should not indulge in unrealistic second-guessing. A creative judge engaged in *post hoc* evaluation of police conduct can almost always imagine some alternative means by which the objectives of the police might have been accomplished. But "[t]he fact that the protection of the public might, in the abstract, have been accomplished by 'less intrusive' means does not, itself, render the search unreasonable." *Cady v. Dombrowski*, 413 U.S. 433, 447 (1973); see also *United States v. Martinez-Fuerte*, 428 U.S. 543, 557, n.12 (1976). The question is not simply whether some other alternative was available, but whether the police acted unreasonably in failing to recognize or to pursue it.

We readily conclude that, given the circumstances facing him, Agent Cooke pursued his investigation in a diligent and reasonable manner. During most of Savage's 20-minute detention, Cooke was attempting to contact Thrasher and enlisting the help of the local police who remained with Sharpe while Cooke left to pursue Officer Thrasher and the pickup. Once Cooke reached Officer Thrasher and Savage,[5] he proceeded expeditiously: within the space of a few minutes, he examined Savage's driver's license and the truck's bill

---

[5] It was appropriate for Officer Thrasher to hold Savage for the brief period pending Cooke's arrival. Thrasher could not be certain that he was aware of all of the facts that had aroused Cooke's suspicions; and, as a highway patrolman, he lacked Cooke's training and experience in dealing with narcotics investigations. In this situation, it cannot realistically be said that Thrasher, a state patrolman called in to assist a federal agent in making a stop, acted unreasonably because he did not release Savage based solely on his own limited investigation of the situation and without the consent of Agent Cooke.

of sale, requested (and was denied) permission to search the truck, stepped on the rear bumper and noted that the truck did not move, confirming his suspicion that it was probably overloaded. He then detected the odor of marihuana.

Clearly this case does not involve any delay unnecessary to the legitimate investigation of the law enforcement officers. Respondents presented no evidence that the officers were dilatory in their investigation. The delay in this case was attributable almost entirely to the evasive actions of Savage, who sought to elude the police as Sharpe moved his Pontiac to the side of the road.[6] Except for Savage's maneuvers, only a short and certainly permissible pre-arrest detention would likely have taken place. The somewhat longer detention was simply the result of a "graduate[d] . . . respons[e] to the demands of [the] particular situation."

We reject the contention that a 20-minute stop is unreasonable when the police have acted diligently and a suspect's actions contribute to the added delay about which he complains. The judgment of the Court of Appeals is reversed, and the case is remanded for further proceedings consistent with this opinion.

Justice MARSHALL, concurring in the judgment.

I join the result in this case because only the evasive actions of the defendants here turned what otherwise would have been a permissibly brief *Terry* stop into the prolonged encounter now at issue. I write separately, however, because in my view the Court understates the importance of *Terry*'s brevity requirement to the constitutionality of *Terry* stops.

I

*Terry* recognized a "narrowly drawn" exception to the probable-cause requirement of the Fourth Amendment for certain seizures of the person that do not rise to the level of full arrests. Two justifications supported this "major development in Fourth

Amendment jurisprudence." First, a legitimate *Terry* stop—brief and narrowly circumscribed—was said to involve a "wholly different kind of intrusion upon individual freedom" than a traditional arrest. Second, under some circumstances, the government's interest in preventing imminent criminal activity could be substantial enough to outweigh the still-serious privacy interests implicated by a limited *Terry* stop. Thus, when the intrusion on the individual is minimal, and when law enforcement interests outweigh the privacy interests infringed in a *Terry* encounter, a stop based on objectively reasonable and articulable suspicions, rather than upon probable cause, is consistent with the Fourth Amendment.

To those who rank zealous law enforcement above all other values, it may be tempting to divorce *Terry* from its rationales and merge the two prongs of *Terry* into the single requirement that the police act reasonably under all the circumstances when they stop and investigate on less than probable cause. As long as the police are acting diligently to complete their investigation, it is difficult to maintain that law enforcement goals would better be served by releasing an individual after a brief stop than by continuing to detain him for as long as necessary to discover whether probable cause can be established. But while the preservation of order is important to any society, the "needs of law enforcement stand in constant tension with the Constitution's protections of the individual against certain exercises of official power. It is precisely the predictability of these pressures that counsels a resolute loyalty to constitutional safeguards." *Terry* must be justified, not because it makes law enforcement easier, but because a *Terry* stop does not constitute the sort of arrest that the Constitution requires be made only upon probable cause.

For this reason, in reviewing any *Terry* stop, the "critical threshold issue is the intrusiveness of the seizure." *Place* (Blackmun, J., concurring in judgment). Regardless how efficient it may be for law enforcement officials to engage in prolonged questioning to investigate a crime, or how reasonable in light of law enforcement objectives it may be to detain a suspect until various inquiries can be made and answered, a seizure that in duration, scope, or means goes beyond the bounds of *Terry* cannot be reconciled with the Fourth Amendment in the absence of probable cause. Legitimate law enforcement interests that do not rise to the level of probable cause simply cannot turn an overly intrusive seizure into a constitutionally permissible one.

In my view, the length of the stop in and of

---

[6] Even if it could be inferred that Savage was not attempting to elude the police when he drove his car *between* Thrasher's patrol car and Sharpe's Pontiac—in the process nearly hitting the patrol car—such an assumption would not alter our analysis or our conclusion. The significance of Savage's actions is that, whether innocent or purposeful, they made it necessary for Thrasher and Cooke to split up, placed Thrasher and Cooke out of contact with each other, and required Cooke to enlist the assistance of local police before he could join Thrasher and Savage.

itself may make the stop sufficiently intrusive to be unjustifiable in the absence of probable cause to arrest.[2] *Terry* "stops" are justified, in part, because they are stops, rather than prolonged seizures. "[A] stopping differs from an arrest not in the incompleteness of the seizure but in the brevity of it."

Consistent with the rationales that make *Terry* stops legitimate, we have recognized several times that the requirement that *Terry* stops be brief imposes an independent and *per se* limitation on the extent to which officials may seize an individual on less than probable cause. The Court explicitly so held in *Place*, where we invalidated a search that was the product of a lengthy detention; as the Court said: "The length of the detention . . . alone precludes the conclusion that the seizure was reasonable in the absence of probable cause. . . . [T]he 90-minute detention . . . is sufficient to render the seizure unreasonable. . . ."[3] A *Terry* stop valid in its inception may become unduly intrusive on personal liberty and privacy simply by lasting too long. That remains true even if valid law enforcement objectives account for the length of the seizure.

The requirement that *Terry* stops be brief no matter what the needs of law enforcement in the particular case is buttressed by several sound pragmatic considerations. First, if the police know they must structure their *Terry* encounters so as to confirm or dispel the officer's reasonable suspicion in a brief time, police practices will adapt to minimize the intrusions worked by these encounters. Cf. *Place* (to assure brevity of *Terry* airport stops, narcotic detection dogs must, under some circumstances, be kept in same airport to which suspect is arriving). Firm adherence to the requirement that stops be brief forces law enforcement officials to take into account from the start the serious and constitutionally protected liberty and privacy interests implicated in *Terry* stops, and to alter official conduct accordingly.

Second, a *per se* ban on stops that are not brief yields the sort of objective standards mandated by our Fourth Amendment precedents, standards that would avoid placing courts in the awkward position of second-guessing police as to what constitutes reasonable police practice. We have recognized that the methods employed in a *Terry* stop "should be the least intrusive means reasonably available to verify or dispel the officer's suspicion in a short period of time." *Royer*.[6] Yet in the absence of a *per se* requirement that stops be brief, defining what means are "least intrusive" is a virtually unmanageable and unbounded task. Whether the police have acted with due diligence is a function not just of how quickly they completed their investigation, but of an almost limitless set of alternative ways in which the investigation *might* have been completed. For example, in this case the Court posits that the officers acted with due diligence, but they might have acted with more diligence had Cooke summoned two rather than one highway patrolman to assist him, or had Cooke, who had the requisite "training and experience," stopped the pickup truck—the vehicle thought to be carrying the marihuana. And if due diligence takes as fixed the amount of resources a community is willing to devote to law enforcement, officials in one community may act with due diligence in holding an individual at an airport for 35 minutes while waiting for the sole narcotics detection dog they possess, while officials who have several dogs readily available may be dilatory in prolonging an airport stop to even 10 minutes.

Constitutional rights should not vary in this manner. Yet in the absence of a brevity standard that is independent of the actions or needs of the

---

[2] A stop can also be unduly intrusive if the individual is moved or asked to move more than a short distance, if a search is more extensive than necessary to protect the police from an objective fear of danger, or if tactics amounting to custodial interrogation are used.

[3] The majority suggests that the 90-minute detention in *Place* was held too long only because the police had not acted diligently enough. In my view, the statements quoted in text adequately demonstrate that the length of the detention "alone" was "sufficient" to invalidate the seizure.

[6] At least we have until today. The language from *Cady v. Dombrowski*, quoted to the effect that full-scale Fourth Amendment searches may be reasonable even if not accomplished in the least intrusive means is of course wholly inconsistent with the holding of *Royer*. *Cady*, quite obviously, has nothing to do with the *Terry* stop issue here; there the question was whether a search that the Court found legitimate had to be accomplished in any particular way, while here the issue is whether the police have intruded on an individual so substantially as to need probable cause. I assume *Royer*'s holding remains the law on this point, and that the Court's mere quotation out of context of *Cady*, unsupported by any argument or reasoned discussion, is not meant to overrule *Royer*. Legal reasoning hardly consists of finding isolated sentences in wholly different contexts and using them to overrule *sub silentio* prior holdings.

police, that variance is one of two inescapable results. The other is that the Court will have to take seriously its requirement that the police act with due diligence, which will require the Court to inject itself into such issues as whether this or that alternative investigative method ought to have been employed.[7] The better and judicially more manageable rule would be a *per se* requirement that *Terry* stops be brief, for that rule would avoid the Court's measuring police conduct according to a virtually standardless yardstick.

Finally, dissolving the brevity requirement into the general standard that the seizure simply be reasonable will "inevitably produce friction and resentment [among the police], for there are bound to be inconsistent and confusing decisions." The police themselves may have done nothing unreasonable in holding a motorist for one hour while waiting for a registration computer to come back on line, but surely such a prolonged detention would be unlawful. Indeed, in my view, as soon as a patrolman called in and learned that the computer was down, the suspect would have to be released. That is so not because waiting for information in this circumstance is unreasonable, but simply because the stop must be brief if it is to be constitutional on less than probable cause. A "balancing" test suggests that a stop is invalid only if officials have crossed over some line they should have avoided; the finding that such a "balance" has been struck improperly casts a certain moral opprobrium on official conduct. A brevity requirement makes clear that the Constitution imposes certain limitations on police powers no matter how reasonably those powers have been exercised. "[H]air-splitting distinctions that currently plague our Fourth Amendment jurisprudence" serve nobody's interest, but measuring the legitimacy of a *Terry* stop by the reasonableness and diligence of the official's actions, rather than by the intrusiveness of the stop, would proliferate such distinctions. Maintaining the clarity of *Terry*'s brevity requirement will instead breed respect for the law among both police and citizens.

For these reasons, fidelity to the rationales that

---

[7] It is clear from the Court's distaste for the task of "second-guessing" the police, and from Justice Brennan's critique of the cursory way in which the Court analyzes the investigative methods employed in this case, that the Court has little intention of choosing this option and taking seriously the requirement that the police act with "due diligence." That demonstrated lack of will makes a strict brevity requirement all the more important.

justify *Terry* stops requires that the intrusiveness of the stop be measured independently of law enforcement needs. A stop must first be found not unduly intrusive, particularly in its length, before it is proper to consider whether law enforcement aims warrant limited investigation.

In my view, the record demonstrates that the lengthy stop at issue in this case would have been permissibly brief but for the respondents' efforts to evade law enforcement officials. Accordingly, I agree with the Court's judgment. But because there is no way to fathom the extent to which the majority's holding rests on this basis, and because the majority acts with unseemly haste to decide other issues not presented [particularly referring to the Court's footnote 3, where it concluded that there was clearly reasonable suspicion to justify this stop. Justice Marshall thought that this resolution should only be assumed, and not resolved.], I join only its judgment.

Justice BRENNAN, dissenting.

The respondent William Sharpe and his passenger were pulled over to the side of the highway, concededly without probable cause, and held for more than 30 minutes, much of that time in the back seat of a police cruiser, before they ultimately were arrested and informed of the charges against them. In the meantime, the respondent Donald Savage was stopped one-half mile down the road, also according to the Court without probable cause. He was ordered out of his pickup truck at gunpoint, spread-eagled and frisked, and questioned by the detaining patrolman, Kenneth Thrasher, about a suspected shipment of marihuana in his vehicle. Although Savage repeatedly asked to be released, Thrasher held him for almost 15 minutes until DEA Agent Luther Cooke, the officer who had stopped Sharpe back up the road, could arrive and sniff the vehicle's windows to determine whether he could smell the suspected marihuana. As Thrasher later conceded, Savage "was under custodial arrest" the entire time.

The Court today concludes that these lengthy detentions constituted reasonable investigative stops within the meaning of *Terry*. It explains that, although the length of an investigative stop made without probable cause may at some point become so excessive as to violate the Fourth Amendment, the primary inquiry must nevertheless be whether the investigating officers acted "diligently" in pursuing a stop that was no longer than "necessary" to the "legitimate investigation of the law enforcement officers." The Court reasons that *Terry*'s brevity requirement is in fact an accordion-like concept that may be expanded outward depending on "the law enforcement purposes to be served by the stop." Applying this analysis to the instant case, the Court concludes that the lengthy detentions of Sharpe and Savage were reasonable because the delay was the fault of Savage, whom the Court contends "sought to elude the police" by speeding away when signaled to stop; had Savage not taken these "evasive actions," Agent Cooke could have questioned Sharpe and Savage together and "only a short and certainly permissible pre-arrest detention would likely have taken place."

I dissent. [T]he Court in criminal cases increasingly has evaded the plain requirements of our precedents where they would stand in the way of a judgment for the government. For a *Terry* stop to be upheld, for example, the government must show at a minimum that the "least intrusive means reasonably available" were used in carrying out the stop. *Royer* (opinion of White, J.).[1] The Government has made no such showing here, and the Court's bald assertion that "[c]learly this case does not involve any delay unnecessary" to "legitimate" law enforcement is completely undermined by the record before us.

The Court's discussion of Savage's purported attempt "to elude the police" amounts to nothing more than a *de novo* factual finding made on a record that is, at best, hopelessly ambiguous. Neither the District Court nor the Court of Appeals ever found that Savage's actions constituted evasion or flight. If we are nevertheless to engage in *de novo* fact finding, I submit the Court has taken insufficient account of several factors.

First, Savage's actions in continuing to drive down the highway could well have been entirely consistent with those of any driver who sees the police hail someone in front of him over to the side of the road. Sharpe's Pontiac was at least several car lengths in front of Savage's pickup truck; Thrasher thought there was a separation of "a car length or two," while

---

[1] Concurring in the plurality's result in *Royer*, I argued that the Fourth Amendment requires an even more stringent standard: "a lawful stop must be so strictly limited that it is difficult to conceive of a less intrusive means that would be effective to accomplish the purpose of the stop."

Cooke testified that the distance was anywhere from between 30-50 and 100-150 feet. Approaching in the far-left lane, Thrasher pulled even with Sharpe's lead vehicle, "turned the blue light on," "blew the siren," and "motioned for *him* to pull over." (emphasis added). Savage moved into the right lane so as to avoid hitting Thrasher, who was slowing along with Sharpe, and continued on his way. Neither Cooke nor Thrasher ever testified that Savage "sought to elude" them, and there is nothing here that is necessarily inconsistent with the actions of any motorist who happens to be behind a vehicle that is being pulled over to the side of the road.

Because it has not been shown that Savage "sought to elude" the police, I agree with the Court that the constitutional propriety of these detentions is governed by *Terry* and its progeny. These precedents lead inexorably to the conclusion that the investigative actions at issue here violated the Fourth Amendment.

If the officers believed that the suspected marihuana was in Savage's pickup truck, and if only Cooke was capable of investigating for the presence of marihuana, I am at a loss why Cooke did not follow the truck and leave Thrasher with the Pontiac, rather than vice versa.

The Government has offered no plausible explanation why Thrasher, a trained South Carolina highway patrolman, could not have carried out the limited *Terry* investigation of Savage and the pickup truck. Once he had stopped Savage, Thrasher not only "held" him, but carried out his own investigation of the situation. He pointed out that the truck had been riding low and asked Savage what was inside. He inspected the exterior and even jumped up on the bumper to test how loaded down the camper might be. Moreover, although Cooke certainly had more drug enforcement experience than Thrasher, there is no reason why Thrasher could not have conducted the simple sniffing investigation that Cooke later did: Thrasher, like all South Carolina highway patrolmen, had received basic narcotics detection training and knew exactly what marihuana smells like. He did not even attempt to smell the windows of the camper shell for two reasons: first, that was not his assigned "job"; and second, "[m]y sinuses were stopped up that morning." Thrasher's sinuses apparently cleared up several hours later, however, because once the pickup was at the police station he decided, "[j]ust as a matter of curiosity," to "get right up on the window" of the vehicle, and reported decisively that "I smelled some marijuana up around the windows." I would have thought that,

before the Court chose to uphold a lengthy detention of a citizen without probable cause based on the "reasonable" ignorance of the detaining officer, it would have taken the time to get its facts straight.[19]

Finally, the record strongly suggests that the delay may have been attributable in large measure to the poor investigative coordination and botched communications on the part of the DEA. Drug enforcement agents were swarming throughout the immediate area on the morning that Savage and Sharpe were detained, conducting numerous roadblocks and "profile stops" of campers and recreational vehicles similar to Savage's. Even accepting the Court's dubious premise that a highway patrolman is somehow incapable of carrying out a simple investigative stop, it is clear that Cooke had followed Sharpe and Savage for over 30 minutes and, knowing that a multiple-vehicle stop was in the offing, should have obtained assistance from other DEA agents. This was, in fact, precisely what he attempted to do. He repeatedly tried to contact the area DEA headquarters but complained over his police radio that "I can't raise anybody else right now." He asked the local police dispatcher to telephone the DEA office to "ask them if anybody there has any contact with me on my DEA frequency." The dispatcher reported that the line was busy; local police units had to be sent out to headquarters "to tell these people to get off the telephone." Once the units arrived, it was learned that "[t]here's no one there. They're all down at the Mar Vista Motel." Additional units had to be sent to the motel to "get those people out of the sack." Agents apparently were eventually located at the motel and at Don's Pancake House, for by the time that Cooke returned to the Pontiac to complete the arrests there were several other DEA agents waiting to assist him. In the meantime, of course, Cooke had had to request Thrasher as a local backup.

---

[19] The Court has responded by insisting that Thrasher "could not be certain that he was aware" of all the facts and therefore was justified in detaining Savage indefinitely. The Court has not pointed to anything that would support this bald *de novo* finding, which is squarely contradicted by the record. In addition, the Court's reasoning flies directly in the face of the Fourth Amendment, which requires the authorities to ground their conduct on what is known at the time of their actions rather than on what might subsequently turn up.

Far from demonstrating that these investigative stops were carried out in the most "expeditious way" using all "reasonably available" investigative methods, the record in this case therefore strongly suggests custodial detentions more accurately characterized as resulting from hopelessly bungled communications and from Thrasher's unwillingness to tread on Cooke's investigative turf. I do not mean to suggest that Cooke and Thrasher bore the entire blame for these delays; it was not Cooke's fault that his DEA backups apparently were sleeping or eating breakfast rather than monitoring their radios for his calls, and Thrasher might well have felt that it was not his place to carry out an investigation he apparently was fully capable of conducting. But constitutional rights should not so easily be balanced away simply because the individual officers may have subjectively been acting in good faith, especially where an objective evaluation of the facts suggests an unnecessarily intrusive exercise of police power.[20]

---

[20] In response to this dissent, the Court offers several justifications for its failure to consult the record in making its *de novo* factual determinations. First, the Court asserts that judges "should not indulge in unrealistic second-guessing" of police conduct. There is nothing "unrealistic" about requiring police officers to pursue the "least intrusive means reasonably available" when detaining citizens on less than probable cause, and it is the *duty* of courts in every Fourth Amendment case to determine whether police conduct satisfied constitutional standards. Moreover, the public will understandably be perplexed why the Court ignores the record and refuses to engage in "second-guessing" where police conduct is challenged while it simultaneously engages in second-guessing of a defendant's conduct where necessary to ensure a verdict for the Government. In addition, the Court attempts to slip into a footnote the astonishing assertion that *even if its textual discussion of Savage's actions is completely untrue*, this "would not alter our analysis or our conclusion." n.6 (emphasis added). The Court contends that, "*whether innocent* or purposeful," *Savage's* conduct "made . . . necessary" the length of these detentions. Ibid. (emphasis added). If the authorities did not reasonably carry out the stops, however, and if Savage's continued driving was "innocent" conduct, it is logically and constitutionally intolerable to hold that Savage waived important Fourth Amendment rights because the events were his "innocent" fault.

## QUESTIONS AND NOTES

**1.** What is the status of the "least intrusive means" test in regard to *Terry* stops after *Sharpe*? What should it be?

**2.** After *Royer, Place*, and *Sharpe* is there an outside limit on *Terry* stops? Should there be? Why? Why not?

**3.** Do you think that Savage was evasive? Should that matter?

**4.** If the issue were before the Court, should the Court have found reasonable suspicion on this record?

**5.** We conclude with *Summers*, a case that arguably strips *Terry* from its moorings, although only where a search warrant has previously been obtained.

### Michigan v. Summers
### 452 U.S. 692 (1981)

Justice STEVENS delivered the opinion of the Court.

As Detroit police officers were about to execute a warrant to search a house for narcotics, they encountered respondent descending the front steps. They requested his assistance in gaining entry and detained him while they searched the premises. After finding narcotics in the basement and ascertaining that respondent owned the house, the police arrested him, searched his person, and found in his coat pocket an envelope containing 8.5 grams of heroin.[1]

---

[1] The execution of the warrant is described in greater detail in Justice Moody's opinion for the Michigan Supreme Court:

"Upon arriving at the named address, Officer Roger Lehman saw the defendant go out the front door of the house and proceed across the porch and down the steps. When defendant was asked to open the door he replied that he could not because he left his keys inside, but he could ring someone over the intercom. Dwight Calhoun came to the door, but did not admit the police officers. As a result, the officers obtained entrance to the premises by forcing open the front door. Once admittance had been gained Officer Lehman instructed Officer Conant, previously stationed along the side of the house, to bring the defendant, still on the porch, into the house.

"After the eight occupants of the house were detained, a search of the premises revealed two plastic bags of suspected narcotics under the bar in the basement. After finding the suspected

I

The dispositive question in this case is whether the initial detention of respondent violated his constitutional right to be secure against an unreasonable seizure of his person. The State attempts to justify the eventual search of respondent's person by arguing that the authority to search premises granted by the warrant implicitly included the authority to search persons on those premises, just as that authority included an authorization to search furniture and containers in which the particular things described might be concealed. But as the Michigan Court of Appeals correctly noted, even if otherwise acceptable, this argument could not justify the initial detention of respondent outside the premises described in the warrant. If that detention was permissible, there is no need to reach the question whether a search warrant for premises includes the right to search persons found there, because when the police searched respondent, they had probable cause to arrest him and had done so.[3] Our appraisal of the validity of the search of respondent's person therefore depends

---

narcotics in the basement and upon determining that the defendant was the owner of the house, Officer Conant formally arrested the defendant for violation of the Controlled Substances Act of 1971. A custodial search conducted by Officer Conant revealed a plastic bag containing suspected heroin in the defendant's jacket pocket. It is this heroin, discovered on the person of the defendant, that forms the basis of the instant possession charge."

[3] Because there were several other occupants of the house, under Michigan law the evidence that narcotics had been found in the basement of respon-

upon a determination whether the officers had the authority to require him to re-enter the house and to remain there while they conducted their search.[4]

### III

Of prime importance in assessing the intrusion is the fact that the police had obtained a warrant to search respondent's house for contraband. A neutral and detached magistrate had found probable cause to believe that the law was being violated in that house and had authorized a substantial invasion of the privacy of the persons who resided there. The detention of one of the residents while the premises were searched, although admittedly a significant restraint on his liberty, was surely less intrusive than the search itself. Indeed, we may safely assume that most citizens — unless they intend flight to avoid arrest — would elect to remain in order to observe the search of their possessions. Furthermore, the type of detention imposed here is not likely to be exploited by the officer or unduly prolonged in order to gain more information, because the information the officers seek normally will be obtained through the search and not through the detention.[14] Moreover, because the detention in this case was in respondent's own residence, it could add only minimally to the public stigma associated with the search itself and would involve neither the inconvenience nor the indignity associated with a compelled visit to the police station. In sharp contrast to the custodial interrogation in *Dunaway*, the detention of this respondent was "substantially less intrusive" than an arrest.[16]

In assessing the justification for the detention of an occupant of premises being searched for contraband pursuant to a valid warrant, both the law enforcement interest and the nature of the "articulable facts" supporting the detention are relevant. Most obvious is the legitimate law enforcement interest in preventing flight in the event that incriminating evidence is found. Less obvious, but sometimes of greater importance, is the interest in minimizing the risk of harm to the officers. Although no special danger to the police is suggested by the evidence in this record, the execution of a warrant to search for narcotics is the kind of transaction that may give rise to sudden violence or frantic efforts to conceal or destroy evidence. The risk of harm to both the police and the occupants is minimized if the officers routinely exercise unquestioned command of the situation. Finally, the orderly completion of the search may be facilitated if the occupants of the premises are present. Their self-interest may induce them to open locked doors or locked containers to avoid the use of force that is not only damaging to property but may also delay the completion of the task at hand.

It is also appropriate to consider the nature of the articulable and individualized suspicion on which the police base the detention of the occupant of a home subject to a search warrant. We have already noted that the detention represents only an incremental intrusion on personal liberty when the search of a home has been authorized by a valid warrant. The existence of a search warrant, however, also provides an objective justification for the detention. A judicial officer has determined that police have probable cause to believe that someone in the home is committing a crime. Thus a neutral magistrate rather than an officer in the field has made the critical determination that the police should be given a special authorization to thrust themselves into the privacy of a home. The connection of an occupant to that home gives the police officer an easily identifiable and certain basis for determining that suspicion of criminal activity justifies a detention of that occupant.

In *Payton*, we held that police officers may not

---

dent's house would apparently be insufficient to support a conviction. Respondent does not challenge the conclusion that the evidence found in his home established probable cause to arrest him.

[4] The "seizure" issue in this case should not be confused with the "search" issue presented in *Ybarra*. In *Ybarra* the police executing a search warrant for a public tavern detained and searched all of the customers who happened to be present. No question concerning the legitimacy of the detention was raised. Rather, the Court concluded that the search of Ybarra was invalid because the police had no reason to believe he had any special connection with the premises, and the police had no other basis for suspecting that he was armed or in possession of contraband. In this case, only the detention is at issue. The police knew respondent lived in the house, and they did not search him until after they had probable cause to arrest and had done so.

[14] Professor LaFave has noted that the reasonableness of a detention may be determined in part by "whether the police are diligently pursuing a means of investigation which is likely to resolve the matter one way or another very soon. . . ."

---

[16] We do not view the fact that respondent was leaving his house when the officers arrived to be of constitutional significance. The seizure of respondent on the sidewalk outside was no more intrusive than the detention of those residents of the house whom the police found inside.

enter a private residence to make a routine felony arrest without first obtaining a warrant. In that case we rejected the suggestion that only a search warrant could adequately protect the privacy interests at stake, noting that the distinction between a search warrant and an arrest warrant was far less significant than the interposition of the magistrate's determination of probable cause between the zealous officer and the citizen:

> "It is true that an arrest warrant requirement may afford less protection than a search warrant requirement, but it will suffice to interpose the magistrate's determination of probable cause between the zealous officer and the citizen. If there is sufficient evidence of a citizen's participation in a felony to persuade a judicial officer that his arrest is justified, it is constitutionally reasonable to require him to open his doors to the officers of the law. Thus, for Fourth Amendment purposes, an arrest warrant founded on probable cause implicitly carries with it the limited authority to enter a dwelling in which the suspect lives when there is reason to believe the suspect is within."

That holding is relevant today. If the evidence that a citizen's residence is harboring contraband is sufficient to persuade a judicial officer that an invasion of the citizen's privacy is justified, it is constitutionally reasonable to require that citizen to remain while officers of the law execute a valid warrant to search his home. Thus, for Fourth Amendment purposes, we hold that a warrant to search for contraband[20] founded on probable cause implicitly carries with it the limited authority to detain the occupants of the premises while a proper search is conducted.[21]

Because it was lawful to require respondent to re-enter and to remain in the house until evidence establishing probable cause to arrest him was found, his arrest and the search incident thereto were constitutionally permissible. The judgment of the Supreme Court of Michigan must therefore be reversed.

---

[20] We do not decide whether the same result would be justified if the search warrant merely authorized a search for evidence.

[21] Although special circumstances, or possibly a prolonged detention, might lead to a different conclusion in an unusual case, we are persuaded that this routine detention of residents of a house while it was being searched for contraband pursuant to a valid warrant is not such a case.

Justice STEWART, with whom Justice BRENNAN and Justice MARSHALL join, dissenting.

It seems clear that before a court can uphold a detention on less than probable cause on the ground that it is "reasonable" in the light of the competing interests, the government must demonstrate an important purpose beyond the normal goals of criminal investigation, or must demonstrate an extraordinary obstacle to such investigation.

## II

What the Court approves today is justified by no such special governmental interest or law enforcement need. There were only two governmental purposes supporting the detention of the respondent.[1] One was "the legitimate law enforcement interest in preventing flight in the event that incriminating evidence is found." The other was that "the orderly completion of the search may be facilitated if the occupants of the premises are present." Unlike the law enforcement objectives that justified the police conduct in *Terry* and the border stop cases, these objectives represented nothing more than the ordinary police interest in discovering evidence of crime and apprehending wrongdoers. And the Fourth and Fourteenth Amendments impose significant restraints upon these traditional police activities, even though the police and the courts may find those restraints unreasonably inconvenient.

If the police, acting without probable cause, can seize a person to make him available for arrest in case probable cause is later developed to arrest him, the requirement of probable cause for arrest has been turned upside down. And if the police may seize a person without probable cause in order to "facilitate" the execution of a warrant that did not authorize his arrest, the fundamental principle that the scope of a search and seizure can be justified only by the scope of the underlying warrant has suffered

---

[1] As the Court acknowledges, the record in this case presents no evidence whatsoever that the police feared any threat to their safety or that of others from the conduct of the respondent, or that they could reasonably have so feared. The Court says that this nevertheless was the "kind of transaction that may give rise to sudden violence. . . ." But where the police cannot demonstrate, on the basis of specific and articulable facts, a reasonable belief that a person threatens physical harm to them or others, the speculation that other persons in that circumstance might pose such a threat cannot justify a search or seizure. *Ybarra.*

serious damage. There is no authority in this Court for the principle that the police can engage in searches and seizures without probable cause simply because to do so enhances their ability to conduct investigations which may eventually lead to probable cause.[2]

Beyond the issue of the governmental interest justifying the detention, I question the Court's view that the detention here is of the limited, unintrusive sort that permits the Court to engage in a "reasonableness" balancing test. As the Court said in *Dunaway, Terry* "defined a special category of Fourth Amendment 'seizures' *so substantially less intrusive* than arrests that the general rule requiring probable cause to make Fourth Amendment 'seizures' reasonable could be replaced by a balancing test." (Emphasis added.) As we then noted in *Dunaway*, the patdown searches in *Terry* [and] *Adams* were declared legal because they were extremely limited in time and in the degree of personal intrusion. The Court also noted that in the border cases, the stops normally consumed less than a minute and involved no more than brief interrogation. Thus, in the rare cases in which the Court has permitted an independent balancing of interests, the police intrusion has been extremely narrow. Moreover, the Court has required that the stop and inquiry or search be "reasonably related in scope to the justification for their initiation," and, under that requirement, the unusual governmental or law enforcement interests justifying the patdown stops and border stops have provided a limiting principle ensuring the narrowness of the police action. The detention approved by the Court today, however, is of a very different order.[o]

The explicit holding of the Court is that "a warrant to search for contraband founded on probable cause implicitly carries with it the limited authority to detain the occupants of the premises while a

proper search is conducted." Though on superficial reading, this language may suggest a minor intrusion of brief duration, a detention "while a proper search is being conducted" can mean a detention of several hours.[3] The police thereby make the person a prisoner in his own home for a potentially very long period of time.[4] Moreover, because of the questionable nature of the governmental interest asserted by the State and acknowledged by the Court in this case, the requirement that the scope of the intrusion be reasonably related to its justification does not provide a limiting principle for circumscribing the detention. If the purpose of the detention is to help the police make the search, the detention can be as long

---

[2] In perplexing citation, the Court notes our holding in *Payton*, that an arrest warrant based on probable cause justifies entering a person's home to carry out the arrest, and declares that *Payton* "is relevant today." But I had thought that the very point of the passage of the Court quotes from *Payton*, is that the police would be justified in arresting a person in his own home because they had a warrant for his arrest based upon probable cause to believe that he had violated the criminal law. Since it is the absence of such probable cause that lies at the heart of this case, I fail to understand *Payton*'s "relevance."

[o] This case preceded *Royer, Place,* and *Sharpe.*

[3] The record does not clearly reveal the length of the search in this case. In *Harris v. United States,* 331 U.S. 145, a Federal Bureau of Investigation search of a one-bedroom apartment for burglar tools and a pair of checks consumed five hours.

[4] I also question the Court's confident assertions about the inoffensive nature of the detention in this case. First, the Court says the detention was innocuous because it was less intrusive than the search that was mandated by the warrant. This reasoning is, of course, circular, since the very question of the severity of the detention arises only because it was not based on a warrant or probable cause.

Second, the Court says that the intrusion was not a serious one because a reasonable-minded citizen would in fact want to be present at a search of his house unless he was fleeing to avoid arrest. But I must infer that the respondent here did not want to be present in his house during the search, else he would not have brought this claim, and the law cannot penalize him for "fleeing arrest" when the police did not have probable cause to arrest him. This second reason amounts to the view that a person cannot assert his rights under the exclusionary rule if he stands to benefit from the exclusion.

Finally, the Court observes that this sort of detention is not likely to be exploited or unduly prolonged by the police, since the officers are more likely to find the information they seek through the search than through the detention. I confess I do not understand this reason. It seems no more than a restatement of the view that the police may detain the person to have him available for arrest when they complete the search, but that view merely begs the question whether the potential duration of the search threatens the person with a lengthy detention.

as the police find it necessary to protract the search.[5]

---

[5] The Court adverts to this problem only by suggesting that "special circumstances, or possibly a prolonged detention, might lead to a different conclusion in an unusual case." But the Court provides no criteria for identifying "special circumstances" or for determining when a detention is "prolonged"; in particular, it fails to tell law enforcement officers whether a detention will always be permissible, however protracted, so long as it does not exceed the length of the search of the house. This ambiguity casts doubt on the Court's assertion, that its holding

In *Dunaway*, the Court reaffirmed that the " 'long-prevailing standards' of probable cause embodied 'the best compromise that has been found for accommodating [the] often opposing interests' in 'safeguard[ing] citizens from rash and unreasonable interferences with privacy' and in 'seek[ing] to give fair leeway for enforcing the law in the community's protection.' " Because the present case presents no occasion for departing from this principle, I respectfully dissent.

---

will not require individual police officers to engage in the sort of on-the-scene, ad hoc legal judgments which pose a serious threat to Fourth and Fourteenth Amendment protections.

## QUESTIONS AND NOTES

**1.** How extensive of a detention did the Court authorize?

**2.** In regard to question 1, how long do you think that a search would last if the home owners were innocent, and there were in fact *no* drugs on the premises?

**3.** What reasons does the Court give to justify this detention? How persuasive are they?

**4.** Would the Court's reasoning justify detaining a non-owner/resident of the house? How about a patron in a bar, such as in *Ybarra* (section A, *supra*.)?

# 8.

# UNUSUAL SITUATIONS

## A. Administrative Searches

When a building inspector seeks to determine whether or not a home or business is in violation of a safety code, the question of whether or not that inspection should be treated as a search within the meaning of the Fourth Amendment arises. If that question is answered "yes," the further question of the appropriate standard to apply is presented. Both of those questions were presented and resolved in *Camara*.

### Camara v. Municipal Court
387 U.S. 523 (1967)

Mr. Justice WHITE delivered the opinion of the Court.

On November 6, 1963, an inspector of the Division of Housing Inspection of the San Francisco Department of Public Health entered an apartment building to make a routine annual inspection for possible violations of the city's Housing Code. The building's manager informed the inspector that appellant, lessee of the ground floor, was using the rear of his leasehold as a personal residence. Claiming that the building's occupancy permit did not allow residential use of the ground floor, the inspector confronted appellant and demanded that he permit an inspection of the premises. Appellant refused to allow the inspection because the inspector lacked a search warrant.

The inspector returned on November 8, again without a warrant, and appellant again refused to allow an inspection. A citation was then mailed ordering appellant to appear at the district attorney's office. When appellant failed to appear, two inspectors returned to his apartment on November 22. They informed appellant that he was required by law to permit an inspection under § 503 of the Housing Code:

"Sec. 503 RIGHT TO ENTER BUILD-ING. Authorized employees of the City departments or City agencies, so far as may be necessary for the performance of their duties, shall, upon presentation of proper credentials, have the right to enter, at reasonable times, any building, structure, or premises in the City to perform any duty imposed upon them by the Municipal Code."

Appellant nevertheless refused the inspectors access to his apartment without a search warrant. Thereafter, a complaint was filed charging him with refusing to permit a lawful inspection in violation of the Code.

## I.

Under the present system, when the inspector demands entry, the occupant has no way of knowing whether enforcement of the municipal code involved requires inspection of his premises, no way of knowing the lawful limits of the inspector's power to search, and no way of knowing whether the inspector himself is acting under proper authorization. These are questions which may be reviewed by a neutral magistrate without any reassessment of the basic agency decision to canvass an area. Yet, only by refusing entry and risking a criminal conviction can the occupant at present challenge the inspector's decision to search. And even if the occupant possesses sufficient fortitude to take this risk, as appellant did here, he may never learn any more about the reason for the inspection than that the law generally allows housing inspectors to gain entry. The practical effect of this system is to leave the occupant subject to the discretion of the official in the field. This is precisely the discretion to invade private property which we have consistently circumscribed by a requirement that a disinterested party warrant the need to search. We simply cannot say that the protections provided by the warrant procedure are not needed in this context; broad statutory safeguards are no substitute for individualized review, particularly when those safeguards may only be invoked at the risk of a criminal penalty.

## II.

The Fourth Amendment provides that, "no Warrants shall issue, but upon probable cause." Borrowing from more typical Fourth Amendment cases, appellant argues not only that code enforcement inspection programs must be circumscribed by a warrant procedure, but also that warrants should issue only when the inspector possesses probable cause to believe that a particular dwelling contains violations of the minimum standards prescribed by the code being enforced. We disagree.

In cases in which the Fourth Amendment requires that a warrant to search be obtained, "probable cause" is the standard by which a particular decision to search is tested against the constitutional mandate of reasonableness. To apply this standard, it is obviously necessary first to focus upon the governmental interest which allegedly justifies official intrusion upon the constitutionally protected interests of the private citizen. For example, in a criminal investigation, the police may undertake to recover specific stolen or contraband goods. But that public interest would hardly justify a sweeping search of an entire city conducted in the hope that these goods might be found. Consequently, a search for these goods, even with a warrant, is "reasonable" only when there is "probable cause" to believe that they will be uncovered in a particular dwelling.

Unlike the search pursuant to a criminal investigation, the inspection programs at issue here are aimed at securing city-wide compliance with minimum physical standards for private property. The primary governmental interest at stake is to prevent even the unintentional development of conditions which are hazardous to public health and safety. Because fires and epidemics may ravage large urban areas, because unsightly conditions adversely affect the economic values of neighboring structures, numerous courts have upheld the police power of municipalities to impose and enforce such minimum standards even upon existing structures. In determining whether a particular inspection is reasonable – and thus in determining whether there is probable cause to issue a warrant for that inspection – the need for the inspection must be weighed in terms of these reasonable goals of code enforcement.

There is unanimous agreement among those most familiar with this field that the only effective way to seek universal compliance with the minimum standards required by municipal codes is through routine periodic inspections of all structures. It is here that the probable cause debate is focused, for the agency's decision to conduct an area inspection is unavoidably based on its appraisal of conditions in the area as a whole, not on its knowledge of conditions in each particular building. Appellee contends that, if the probable cause standard urged by appellant is adopted, the area inspection will be eliminated as a means of seeking compliance with code standards and the reasonable goals of code enforcement will be dealt a crushing blow.

In meeting this contention, appellant argues first, that his probable cause standard would not jeopardize area inspection programs because only a minute portion of the population will refuse to consent to such inspections, and second, that individual privacy in any event should be given preference to the public interest in conducting such inspections. The first argument, even if true, is irrelevant to the question whether the area inspection is reasonable within the meaning of the Fourth Amendment. The second argument is in effect an assertion that the area inspection is an unreasonable search. Unfortunately, there can be no ready test for determining reasonableness other than by balancing the need to search against the invasion which the search entails. But we think that a number of persuasive factors combine to support the reasonableness of area code-enforcement inspections. First, such programs have a long history of judicial and public acceptance. Second, the public interest demands that all dangerous conditions be prevented or abated, yet it is doubtful that any other canvassing technique would achieve acceptable results. Many such conditions—faulty wiring is an obvious example—are not observable from outside the building and indeed may not be apparent to the inexpert occupant himself. Finally, because the inspections are neither personal in nature nor aimed at the discovery of evidence of crime, they involve a relatively limited invasion of the urban citizen's privacy.

Having concluded that the area inspection is a "reasonable" search of private property within the meaning of the Fourth Amendment, it is obvious that "probable cause" to issue a warrant to inspect must exist if reasonable legislative or administrative standards for conducting an area inspection are satisfied with respect to a particular dwelling. Such standards, which will vary with the municipal program being enforced, may be based upon the passage of time, the nature of the building (*e.g.*, a multifamily apartment house), or the condition of the entire area, but they will not necessarily depend upon specific knowledge of the condition of the particular dwelling. It has been suggested that so to vary the probable cause test from the standard applied in criminal cases would be to authorize a "synthetic search warrant" and thereby to lessen the overall protections of the Fourth Amendment. But we do not agree. The warrant procedure is designed to guarantee that a decision to search private property is justified by a reasonable governmental interest. But reasonableness is still the ultimate standard. If a valid public interest justifies the intrusion contemplated, then there is probable cause to issue a suitably restricted search warrant. Such an approach neither endangers time-honored doctrines applicable to criminal investigations nor makes a nullity of the probable cause requirement in this area. It merely gives full recognition to the competing public and private interests here at stake and, in so doing, best fulfills the historic purpose behind the constitutional right to be free from unreasonable government invasions of privacy.

### III.

Since our holding emphasizes the controlling standard of reasonableness, nothing we say today is intended to foreclose prompt inspections, even without a warrant, that the law has traditionally upheld in emergency situations. On the other hand, in the case of most routine area inspections, there is no compelling urgency to inspect at a particular time or on a particular day. Moreover, most citizens allow inspections of their property without a warrant. Thus, as a practical matter and in light of the Fourth Amendment's requirement that a warrant specify the property to be searched, it seems likely that warrants should normally be sought only after entry is refused unless there has been a citizen complaint or there is other satisfactory reason for securing immediate entry. Similarly, the requirement of a warrant procedure does not suggest any change in what seems to be the prevailing local policy, in most situations, of authorizing entry, but not entry by force, to inspect.

### IV.

In this case, appellant has been charged with a crime for his refusal to permit housing inspectors to enter his leasehold without a warrant. There was no emergency demanding immediate access; in fact, the inspectors made three trips to the building in an attempt to obtain appellant's consent to search. Yet no warrant was obtained and thus appellant was unable to verify either the need for or the appropriate limits of the inspection. No doubt, the inspectors entered the public portion of the building with the consent of the landlord, through the building's manager, but appellee does not contend that such consent was sufficient to authorize inspection of appellant's premises. Assuming the facts to be as the parties have alleged, we therefore conclude that appellant had a constitutional right to insist that the inspectors obtain a warrant to search and that appellant may not constitutionally be convicted for refusing to consent to the inspection.

Mr. Justice CLARK, with whom Mr. Justice HARLAN and Mr. Justice STEWART join, dissenting.

### II.

The majority say that under the present system the occupant has no way of knowing the necessity for the inspection, the limits of the inspector's power, or whether the inspector is himself authorized to perform the search. [A]ll of these doubts raised by the Court could be resolved very quickly. Indeed, the inspectors all have identification cards which they show the occupant and the latter could easily resolve the remaining questions by a call to the inspector's superior or, upon demand, receive a written answer thereto. The record here shows these challenges could have been easily interposed. The inspectors called on several occasions, but still no such questions were raised.[3]

---

[3] Indeed, appellant Camara was summoned to the office of the district attorney—but failed to appear—where he certainly could have raised these questions.

### III.

The great need for health and safety inspection is emphasized by the experience of San Francisco, a metropolitan area known for its cleanliness and safety ever since it suffered earthquake and fire back in 1906. For the fiscal year ending June 30, 1965, over 16,000 dwelling structures were inspected, of which over 5,600 required some type of compliance action in order to meet code requirements. And in 1965–1966 over 62,000 apartments, hotels, and dwellings were inspected with similar results. During the same period the Public Works Department conducted over 52,000 building inspections, over 43,000 electrical ones and over 33,000 plumbing inspections. During the entire year 1965–1966 inspectors were refused entry on less than 10 occasions where the ordinance required the householder to so permit.

### IV.

The majority propose two answers to this admittedly pressing problem of need for constant inspection of premises for fire, health, and safety infractions of municipal codes. First, they say that there will be few refusals of entry to inspect. Unlike the attitude of householders as to codes requiring entry for inspection, we have few empirical statistics on attitudes where consent must be obtained. It is true that in the required entry-to-inspect situations most occupants welcome the periodic visits of municipal inspectors. In my view this will not be true when consent is necessary. The City of Portland, Oregon, has a voluntary home inspection program. The 1966 record shows that out of 16,171 calls where the occupant was at home, entry was refused in 2,540 cases – approximately one out of six. This is a large percentage and would place an intolerable burden on the inspection service when required to secure warrants. What is more important is that out of the houses inspected 4,515 hazardous conditions were found! Hence, on the same percentage, there would be approximately 840 hazardous situations in the 2,540 in which inspection was refused in Portland.

Human nature being what it is, we must face up to the fact that thousands of inspections are going to be denied. The economics of the situation alone will force this result. Homeowners generally try to minimize maintenance costs, and some landlords make needed repairs only when required to do so. Immediate prospects for costly repairs to correct possible defects are going to keep many a door closed to the inspector.

The Court then addresses itself to the propriety of warrantless area inspections.[4] The basis of "probable cause" for area inspection warrants the Court says, begins with the Fourth Amendment's reasonableness requirement; in determining whether an inspection is reasonable "the need for the inspection must be weighed in terms of these reasonable goals of code enforcement." Upon this reasoning, the Court concludes that probable cause exists "if reasonable legislative or administrative standards for conducting an area inspection are satisfied with respect to a particular dwelling." These standards will vary, it says, according to the code program and the condition of the area with reference thereto rather than the condition of a particular dwelling. The majority seem to hold that warrants may be obtained after a refusal of initial entry; I can find no such constitutional distinction or command. These boxcar warrants will be identical as to every dwelling in the area, save the street number itself. I daresay they will be printed up in pads of a thousand or more – with space for the street number to be inserted – and issued by magistrates in broadcast fashion as a matter of course.

I ask: Why go through such an exercise, such a pretense? As the same essentials are being followed under the present procedures, I ask: Why the ceremony, the delay, the expense, the abuse of the search warrant? In my view this will not only destroy its integrity but will degrade the magistrate issuing them and soon bring disrepute not only upon the practice but upon the judicial process. It will be very costly to the city in paperwork incident to the issuance of the paper warrants, in loss of time of inspectors and waste of the time of magistrates and will result in more annoyance to the public. It will also be more burdensome to the occupant of the premises to be inspected. Under a search warrant the inspector can enter any time he chooses. Under the existing procedures he can enter only at reasonable times and invariably the convenience of the occupant is considered. In the Court's anxiety to limit its own holding as to mass searches it hopes to divert attention from the fact that it destroys the health and safety codes as they apply to individual inspections of specific problems as contrasted to area ones. While the latter

---

[4] It is interesting to note that in each of the cases here the authorities were making periodic area inspections when the refusals to allow entry occurred. Under the holding of the Court today, "probable cause" would therefore be present in each case and a "paper warrant" would issue as a matter of course. This but emphasizes the absurdity of the holding.

are important, the individual inspection is often more so. Frankly, I cannot understand how the Court can authorize warrants in wholesale fashion in the case of an area inspection, but hold the hand of the inspector when a specific dwelling is hazardous to the health and safety of its neighbors.

## QUESTIONS AND NOTES

**1.** Do you think that the majority or dissenting opinion better captures the spirit of the Fourth Amendment? Why?

**2.** Does probable cause mean the same thing after *Camara* that it meant before? If your answer is "no," how does it differ?

**3.** If probable cause means what *Camara* says it means, should all of the *Terry* cases have been found to have been based on probable cause?

**4.** What are the arguments for and against requiring a warrant in the inspection context? Which side is more persuasive? Why?

**5.** The Court has carved an exception to the warrant requirement for closely regulated industries. Under that exception, establishments that deal in alcohol, firearms, or mining operations are subject to unwarranted searches. In a fairly extreme example of this exception, the Court held that junk yards are not only subject to an unwarranted request for administrative records, but that the cars in the junkyard can be searched to determine whether or not they have been stolen. *New York v. Burger*, 482 U.S. 691 (1987).

## B.   School Searches

The question of whether, and to what extent, the Fourth Amendment applies to searches of students conducted by school personnel was addressed and partially resolved in *T.L.O.*

### New Jersey v. T.L.O.
### 469 U.S. 325 (1985)

Justice WHITE delivered the opinion of the Court.

#### I

On March 7, 1980, a teacher at Piscataway High School in Middlesex County, N.J., discovered two girls smoking in a lavatory. One of the two girls was the respondent T.L.O., who at that time was a 14-year-old high school freshman. Because smoking in the lavatory was a violation of a school rule, the teacher took the two girls to the Principal's office, where they met with Assistant Vice Principal Theodore Choplick. In response to questioning by Mr. Choplick, T.L.O.'s companion admitted that she had violated the rule. T.L.O., however, denied that she had been smoking in the lavatory and claimed that she did not smoke at all.

Mr. Choplick asked T.L.O. to come into his private office and demanded to see her purse. Opening the purse, he found a pack of cigarettes, which he removed from the purse and held before T.L.O. as he accused her of having lied to him. As he reached into the purse for the cigarettes, Mr. Choplick also noticed a package of cigarette rolling papers. In his experience, possession of rolling papers by high school students was closely associated with the use of marihuana. Suspecting that a closer examination of the purse might yield further evidence of drug use, Mr. Choplick proceeded to search the purse thoroughly. The search revealed a small amount of marihuana, a pipe, a number of empty plastic bags, a substantial quantity of money in one-dollar bills, an index card that appeared to be a list of students who owed T.L.O. money, and two letters that implicated T.L.O. in marihuana dealing.

Mr. Choplick notified T.L.O.'s mother and the police, and turned the evidence of drug dealing over to the police. At the request of the police, T.L.O.'s mother took her daughter to police headquarters, where T.L.O. confessed that she had been selling marihuana at the high school. On the basis of the confession and the evidence seized by Mr. Choplick, the State brought delinquency charges against T.L.O. in the Juvenile and Domestic Relations Court of Middlesex County. Contending that Mr. Choplick's search of her purse violated the Fourth Amendment, T.L.O. moved to suppress the evidence found in her purse as well as her confession, which, she argued, was tainted by the allegedly unlawful search.

## II

In determining whether the search at issue in this case violated the Fourth Amendment, we are faced initially with the question whether that Amendment's prohibition on unreasonable searches and seizures applies to searches conducted by public school officials. We hold that it does.

[T]wo propositions—that the Fourth Amendment applies to the States through the Fourteenth Amendment, and that the actions of public school officials are subject to the limits placed on state action by the Fourteenth Amendment—might appear sufficient to answer the suggestion that the Fourth Amendment does not proscribe unreasonable searches by school officials. On reargument, however, the State of New Jersey has argued that the history of the Fourth Amendment indicates that the Amendment was intended to regulate only searches and seizures carried out by law enforcement officers; accordingly, although public school officials are concededly state agents for purposes of the Fourteenth Amendment, the Fourth Amendment creates no rights enforceable against them.

It may well be true that the evil toward which the Fourth Amendment was primarily directed was the resurrection of the pre-Revolutionary practice of using general warrants or "writs of assistance" to authorize searches for contraband by officers of the Crown. But this Court has never limited the Amendment's prohibition on unreasonable searches and seizures to operations conducted by the police. Rather, the Court has long spoken of the Fourth Amendment's strictures as restraints imposed upon "governmental action"—that is, "upon the activities of sovereign authority." Accordingly, we have held the Fourth Amendment applicable to the activities of civil as well as criminal authorities: building inspectors, see *Camara*, Occupational Safety and Health Act inspectors, and even firemen entering privately owned premises to battle a fire, are all subject to the restraints imposed by the Fourth Amendment. As we observed in *Camara*, "[t]he basic purpose of this Amendment, as recognized in countless decisions of this Court, is to safeguard the privacy and security of individuals against arbitrary invasions by governmental officials." Because the individual's interest in privacy and personal security "suffers whether the government's motivation is to investigate violations of criminal laws or breaches of other statutory or regulatory standards," it would be "anomalous to say that the individual and his private property are fully protected by the Fourth Amendment only when the individual is suspected of criminal behavior."

Notwithstanding the general applicability of the Fourth Amendment to the activities of civil authorities, a few courts have concluded that school officials are exempt from the dictates of the Fourth Amendment by virtue of the special nature of their authority over schoolchildren. Teachers and school administrators, it is said, act *in loco parentis* in their dealings with students: their authority is that of the parent, not the State, and is therefore not subject to the limits of the Fourth Amendment.

Such reasoning is in tension with contemporary reality and the teachings of this Court. We have held school officials subject to the commands of the First Amendment and the Due Process Clause. If school authorities are state actors for purposes of the constitutional guarantees of freedom of expression and due process, it is difficult to understand why they should be deemed to be exercising parental rather than public authority when conducting searches of their students. More generally, the Court has recognized that "the concept of parental delegation" as a source of school authority is not entirely "consonant with compulsory education laws." Today's public school officials do not merely exercise authority voluntarily conferred on them by individual parents; rather, they act in furtherance of publicly mandated educational and disciplinary policies. In carrying out searches and other disciplinary functions pursuant to such policies, school officials act as representatives of the State, not merely as surrogates for the parents, and they cannot claim the parents' immunity from the strictures of the Fourth Amendment.

## III

To hold that the Fourth Amendment applies to searches conducted by school authorities is only to begin the inquiry into the standards governing such searches. Although the underlying command of the Fourth Amendment is always that searches and seizures be reasonable, what is reasonable depends on the context within which a search takes place. The determination of the standard of reasonableness governing any specific class of searches requires "balancing the need to search against the invasion which the search entails." On one side of the balance are arrayed the individual's legitimate expectations of privacy and personal security; on the other, the government's need for effective methods to deal with breaches of public order.

We have recognized that even a limited search of the person is a substantial invasion of privacy. *Terry.* We have also recognized that searches of closed items of personal luggage are intrusions on protected privacy interests, for "the Fourth Amendment provides protection to the owner of every container that conceals its contents from plain view." *Ross.* A search of a child's person or of a closed purse or other bag carried on her person,[5] no less than a similar search carried out on an adult, is undoubtedly a severe violation of subjective expectations of privacy.

Of course, the Fourth Amendment does not protect subjective expectations of privacy that are unreasonable or otherwise "illegitimate." To receive the protection of the Fourth Amendment, an expectation of privacy must be one that society is "prepared to recognize as legitimate." The State of New Jersey has argued that because of the pervasive supervision to which children in the schools are necessarily subject, a child has virtually no legitimate expectation of privacy in articles of personal property "unnecessarily" carried into a school. This argument has two factual premises: (1) the fundamental incompatibility of expectations of privacy with the maintenance of a sound educational environment; and (2) the minimal interest of the child in bringing any items of personal property into the school. Both premises are severely flawed.

Although this Court may take notice of the difficulty of maintaining discipline in the public schools today, the situation is not so dire that students in

----

[5] We do not address the question, not presented by this case, whether a schoolchild has a legitimate expectation of privacy in lockers, desks, or other school property provided for the storage of school supplies. Nor do we express any opinion on the standards (if any) governing searches of such areas by school officials or by other public authorities acting at the request of school officials.

the schools may claim no legitimate expectations of privacy. We have recently recognized that the need to maintain order in a prison is such that prisoners retain no legitimate expectations of privacy in their cells, but it goes almost without saying that "[t]he prisoner and the schoolchild stand in wholly different circumstances, separated by the harsh facts of criminal conviction and incarceration." We are not yet ready to hold that the schools and the prisons need be equated for purposes of the Fourth Amendment.

Nor does the State's suggestion that children have no legitimate need to bring personal property into the schools seem well anchored in reality. Students at a minimum must bring to school not only the supplies needed for their studies, but also keys, money, and the necessaries of personal hygiene and grooming. In addition, students may carry on their persons or in purses or wallets such nondisruptive yet highly personal items as photographs, letters, and diaries. Finally, students may have perfectly legitimate reasons to carry with them articles of property needed in connection with extracurricular or recreational activities. In short, schoolchildren may find it necessary to carry with them a variety of legitimate, noncontraband items, and there is no reason to conclude that they have necessarily waived all rights to privacy in such items merely by bringing them onto school grounds.

Against the child's interest in privacy must be set the substantial interest of teachers and administrators in maintaining discipline in the classroom and on school grounds. Maintaining order in the classroom has never been easy, but in recent years, school disorder has often taken particularly ugly forms: drug use and violent crime in the schools have become major social problems. Even in schools that have been spared the most severe disciplinary problems, the preservation of order and a proper educational environment requires close supervision of schoolchildren, as well as the enforcement of rules against conduct that would be perfectly permissible if undertaken by an adult. "Events calling for discipline are frequent occurrences and sometimes require immediate, effective action." Accordingly, we have recognized that maintaining security and order in the schools requires a certain degree of flexibility in school disciplinary procedures, and we have respected the value of preserving the informality of the student-teacher relationship.

How, then, should we strike the balance between the schoolchild's legitimate expectations of privacy and the school's equally legitimate need to maintain an environment in which learning can take place? It is evident that the school setting requires some easing of the restrictions to which searches by public authorities are ordinarily subject. The warrant requirement, in particular, is unsuited to the school environment: requiring a teacher to obtain a warrant before searching a child suspected of an infraction of school rules (or of the criminal law) would unduly interfere with the maintenance of the swift and informal disciplinary procedures needed in the schools. Just as we have in other cases dispensed with the warrant requirement when "the burden of obtaining a warrant is likely to frustrate the governmental purpose behind the search," we hold today that school officials need not obtain a warrant before searching a student who is under their authority.

The school setting also requires some modification of the level of suspicion of illicit activity needed to justify a search. Ordinarily, a search—even one that may permissibly be carried out without a warrant—must be based upon "probable cause" to believe that a violation of the law has occurred. However, "probable cause" is not an irreducible requirement of a valid search. The fundamental command of the Fourth Amendment is that searches and seizures be reasonable, and although "both the concept of probable cause and the requirement of a warrant bear on the reasonableness of a search, . . . in certain limited circumstances neither is required." Thus, we have in a number of cases recognized the legality of searches and seizures based on suspicions that, although "reasonable," do not rise to the level of probable cause. See, *e.g.*, *Terry, Brignoni-Ponce, Prouse, Martinez-Fuerte*; cf. *Camara*. Where a careful balancing of governmental and private interests suggests that the public interest is best served by a Fourth Amendment standard of reasonableness that stops short of probable cause, we have not hesitated to adopt such a standard.

We join the majority of courts that have examined this issue in concluding that the accommodation of the privacy interests of schoolchildren with the substantial need of teachers and administrators for freedom to maintain order in the schools does not require strict adherence to the requirement that searches be based on probable cause to believe that the subject of the search has violated or is violating the law. Rather, the legality of a search of a student should depend simply on the reasonableness, under all the circumstances, of the search. Determining the reasonableness of any search involves a twofold inquiry: first, one must consider "whether the . . . action was justified at its inception," *Terry*; second, one must determine whether the search as actually conducted "was reasonably related in scope to the circumstances which justified the interference in the first place," *ibid*. Under ordinary circumstances, a search of a student by a teacher or other school official[7] will be "justified at its inception" when there are reasonable grounds for suspecting that the search will turn up evidence that the student has violated or is violating either the law or the rules of the school.[8] Such a search will be permissible in its scope when the measures adopted are reasonably related to the objectives of the search and not excessively intrusive in light of the age and sex of the student and the nature of the infraction.

This standard will, we trust, neither unduly burden the efforts of school authorities to maintain order in their schools nor authorize unrestrained intrusions upon the privacy of schoolchildren. By focusing attention on the question of reasonableness, the standard will spare teachers and school administrators the necessity of schooling themselves in the niceties of probable cause and permit them to regulate their conduct according to the dictates of reason and common sense. At the same time, the reasonableness standard should ensure that the interests of students will be invaded no more than is necessary to achieve the legitimate end of preserving order in the schools.

IV

There remains the question of the legality of the search in this case. We recognize that the "reasonable grounds" standard applied by the New Jersey

---

[7] We here consider only searches carried out by school authorities acting alone and on their own authority. This case does not present the question of the appropriate standard for assessing the legality of searches conducted by school officials in conjunction with or at the behest of law enforcement agencies, and we express no opinion on that question.

[8] We do not decide whether individualized suspicion is an essential element of the reasonableness standard we adopt for searches by school authorities. In other contexts, however, we have held that although "some quantum of individualized suspicion is usually a prerequisite to a constitutional search or seizure[,] . . . the Fourth Amendment imposes no irreducible requirement of such suspicion." *Martinez-Fuerte*. See also *Camara*. Exceptions to the requirement of individualized suspicion are generally appropriate only where the privacy interests implicated by a search are minimal and where "other safeguards" are available "to assure that the individual's reasonable expectation of privacy is not 'subject to the discretion of the official in the field.'" *Prouse*. Because the search of T.L.O.'s purse was based upon an individualized suspicion that she had violated school rules, we need not consider the circumstances that might justify school authorities in conducting searches unsupported by individualized suspicion.

Supreme Court in its consideration of this question is not substantially different from the standard that we have adopted today. Nonetheless, we believe that the New Jersey court's application of that standard to strike down the search of T.L.O.'s purse reflects a somewhat crabbed notion of reasonableness. Our review of the facts surrounding the search leads us to conclude that the search was in no sense unreasonable for Fourth Amendment purposes.[10]

The incident that gave rise to this case actually involved two separate searches, with the first – the search for cigarettes – providing the suspicion that gave rise to the second search for marihuana. Although it is the fruits of the second search that are at issue here, the validity of the search for marihuana must depend on the reasonableness of the initial search for cigarettes, as there would have been no reason to suspect that T.L.O. possessed marihuana had the first search not taken place. Accordingly, it is to the search for cigarettes that we first turn our attention.

The New Jersey Supreme Court pointed to two grounds for its holding that the search for cigarettes was unreasonable. First, the court observed that possession of cigarettes was not in itself illegal or a violation of school rules. Because the contents of T.L.O.'s purse would therefore have "no direct bearing on the infraction" of which she was accused (smoking in a lavatory where smoking was prohibited), there was no reason to search her purse. Second, even assuming that a search of T.L.O.'s purse might under some circumstances be reasonable in light of the accusation made against T.L.O., the New Jersey court concluded that Mr. Choplick in this particular case had no reasonable grounds to suspect that T.L.O. had cigarettes in her purse. At best, according to the court, Mr. Choplick had "a good hunch."

Both these conclusions are implausible. T.L.O. had been accused of smoking, and had denied the accusation in the strongest possible terms when she stated that she did not smoke at all. Surely it cannot be said that under these circumstances, T.L.O.'s possession of cigarettes would be irrelevant to the charges against her or to her response to those charges. T.L.O.'s possession of cigarettes, once it

was discovered, would both corroborate the report that she had been smoking and undermine the credibility of her defense to the charge of smoking. To be sure, the discovery of the cigarettes would not prove that T.L.O. had been smoking in the lavatory; nor would it, strictly speaking, necessarily be inconsistent with her claim that she did not smoke at all. But it is universally recognized that evidence, to be relevant to an inquiry, need not conclusively prove the ultimate fact in issue, but only have "any tendency to make the existence of any fact that is of consequence to the determination of the action more probable or less probable than it would be without the evidence." The relevance of T.L.O.'s possession of cigarettes to the question whether she had been smoking and to the credibility of her denial that she smoked supplied the necessary "nexus" between the item searched for and the infraction under investigation. Thus, if Mr. Choplick in fact had a reasonable suspicion that T.L.O. had cigarettes in her purse, the search was justified despite the fact that the cigarettes, if found, would constitute "mere evidence" of a violation.

Of course, the New Jersey Supreme Court also held that Mr. Choplick had no reasonable suspicion that the purse would contain cigarettes. This conclusion is puzzling. A teacher had reported that T.L.O. was smoking in the lavatory. Certainly this report gave Mr. Choplick reason to suspect that T.L.O. was carrying cigarettes with her; and if she did have cigarettes, her purse was the obvious place in which to find them. Mr. Choplick's suspicion that there were cigarettes in the purse was not an "inchoate and unparticularized suspicion or 'hunch,'" rather, it was the sort of "common-sense conclusio[n] about human behavior" upon which "practical people" – including government officials – are entitled to rely. *Cortez*. Of course, even if the teacher's report were true, T.L.O. *might* not have had a pack of cigarettes with her; she might have borrowed a cigarette from someone else or have been sharing a cigarette with another student. But the requirement of reasonable suspicion is not a requirement of absolute certainty: "sufficient probability, not certainty, is the touchstone of reasonableness under the Fourth Amendment. . . ." Because the hypothesis that T.L.O. was carrying cigarettes in her purse was itself not unreasonable, it is irrelevant that other hypotheses were also consistent with the teacher's accusation. Accordingly, it cannot be said that Mr. Choplick acted

---

[10] Of course, New Jersey may insist on a more demanding standard under its own Constitution or statutes. In that case, its courts would not purport to be applying the Fourth Amendment when they invalidate a search.

unreasonably when he examined T.L.O.'s purse to see if it contained cigarettes.[12]

Our conclusion that Mr. Choplick's decision to open T.L.O.'s purse was reasonable brings us to the question of the further search for marihuana once the pack of cigarettes was located. The suspicion upon which the search for marihuana was founded was provided when Mr. Choplick observed a package of rolling papers in the purse as he removed the pack of cigarettes. Although T.L.O. does not dispute the reasonableness of Mr. Choplick's belief that the rolling papers indicated the presence of marihuana, she does contend that the scope of the search Mr. Choplick conducted exceeded permissible bounds when he seized and read certain letters that implicated T.L.O. in drug dealing. This argument, too, is unpersuasive. The discovery of the rolling papers concededly gave rise to a reasonable suspicion that T.L.O. was carrying marihuana as well as cigarettes in her purse. This suspicion justified further exploration of T.L.O.'s purse, which turned up more evidence of drug-related activities: a pipe, a number of plastic bags of the type commonly used to store marihuana, a small quantity of marihuana, and a fairly substantial amount of money. Under these circumstances, it was not unreasonable to extend the search to a separate zippered compartment of the

---

[12] T.L.O. contends that even if it was reasonable for Mr. Choplick to open her purse to look for cigarettes, it was not reasonable for him to reach in and take the cigarettes out of her purse once he found them. Had he not removed the cigarettes from the purse, she asserts, he would not have observed the rolling papers that suggested the presence of marihuana, and the search for marihuana could not have taken place. T.L.O.'s argument is based on the fact that the cigarettes were not "contraband," as no school rule forbade her to have them. Thus, according to T.L.O., the cigarettes were not subject to seizure or confiscation by school authorities, and Mr. Choplick was not entitled to take them out of T.L.O.'s purse regardless of whether he was entitled to peer into the purse to see if they were there. Such hairsplitting argumentation has no place in an inquiry addressed to the issue of reasonableness. If Mr. Choplick could permissibly search T.L.O.'s purse for cigarettes, it hardly seems reasonable to suggest that his natural reaction to finding them — picking them up — could be a constitutional violation. We find that neither in opening the purse nor in reaching into it to remove the cigarettes did Mr. Choplick violate the Fourth Amendment.

purse; and when a search of that compartment revealed an index card containing a list of "people who owe me money" as well as two letters, the inference that T.L.O. was involved in marihuana trafficking was substantial enough to justify Mr. Choplick in examining the letters to determine whether they contained any further evidence. In short, we cannot conclude that the search for marihuana was unreasonable in any respect.

Because the search resulting in the discovery of the evidence of marihuana dealing by T.L.O. was reasonable, the New Jersey Supreme Court's decision to exclude that evidence from T.L.O.'s juvenile delinquency proceedings on Fourth Amendment grounds was erroneous. Accordingly, the judgment of the Supreme Court of New Jersey is reversed.

Justice BLACKMUN, concurring in judgment.

I join the judgment of the Court and agree with much that is said in its opinion. I write separately, however, because I believe the Court omits a crucial step in its analysis of whether a school search must be based upon probable-cause. The Court correctly states that we have recognized limited exceptions to the probable-cause requirement "[w]here a careful balancing of governmental and private interests suggests that the public interest is best served" by a lesser standard. I believe that we have used such a balancing test, rather than strictly applying the Fourth Amendment's Warrant and Probable-Cause Clause, only when we were confronted with "a special law enforcement need for greater flexibility." I pointed out in *Place*:

> "While the Fourth Amendment speaks in terms of freedom from unreasonable [searches], the Amendment does not leave the reasonableness of most [searches] to the judgment of courts or government officers; the Framers of the Amendment balanced the interests involved and decided that a [search] is reasonable only if supported by a judicial warrant based on probable cause."

Only in those exceptional circumstances in which special needs, beyond the normal need for law enforcement, make the warrant and probable-cause requirement impracticable, is a court entitled to substitute its balancing of interests for that of the Framers.

The Court's implication that the balancing test is the rule rather than the exception is troubling for me because it is unnecessary in this case. The elementary and secondary school setting presents a special need for flexibility justifying a departure from the balance struck by the Framers. Maintaining order in the classroom can be a difficult task. A single teacher often must watch over a large number of students, and, as any parent knows, children at certain ages are inclined to test the outer boundaries of acceptable conduct and to imitate the misbehavior of a peer if that misbehavior is not dealt with quickly. Every adult remembers from his own schooldays the havoc a water pistol or peashooter can wreak until it is taken away. Thus, the Court has recognized that "[e]vents calling for discipline are frequent occurrences and sometimes require immediate, effective action." Indeed, because drug use and possession of weapons have become increasingly common among young people, an immediate response frequently is required not just to maintain an environment conducive to learning, but to protect the very safety of students and school personnel.

Such immediate action obviously would not be possible if a teacher were required to secure a warrant before searching a student. Nor would it be possible if a teacher could not conduct a necessary search until the teacher thought there was probable cause for the search. A teacher has neither the training nor the day-to-day experience in the complexities of probable cause that a law enforcement officer possesses, and is ill-equipped to make a quick judgment about the existence of probable cause. The time required for a teacher to ask the questions or make the observations that are necessary to turn reasonable grounds into probable cause is time during which the teacher, and other students, are diverted from the essential task of education. A teacher's focus is, and should be, on teaching and helping students, rather than on developing evidence against a particular troublemaker.

Education "is perhaps the most important function" of government, *Brown v. Board of Education*, 347 U.S. 483, 493 (1954), and government has a heightened obligation to safeguard students whom it compels to attend school. The special need for an immediate response to behavior that threatens either the safety of schoolchildren and teachers or the educational process itself justifies the Court in excepting school searches from the warrant and probable-cause requirement, and in applying a standard determined by balancing the relevant interests. I agree with the standard the Court has announced, and with its application of the standard to the facts of this case. I therefore concur in its judgment.

Justice BRENNAN, with whom Justice MARSHALL joins, concurring in part and dissenting in part.

I fully agree with Part II of the Court's opinion. Teachers, like all other government officials, must conform their conduct to the Fourth Amendment's protections of personal privacy and personal security.

I do not, however, otherwise join the Court's opinion. Today's decision sanctions school officials to conduct full-scale searches on a "reasonableness" standard whose only definite content is that it is *not* the same test as the "probable cause" standard found in the text of the Fourth Amendment. In adopting this unclear, unprecedented, and unnecessary departure from generally applicable Fourth Amendment standards, the Court carves out a broad exception to standards that this Court has developed over years of considering Fourth Amendment problems. Its decision is supported neither by precedent nor even by a fair application of the "balancing test" it proclaims in this very opinion.

I

Three basic principles underlie this Court's Fourth Amendment jurisprudence. First, warrantless searches are *per se* unreasonable, subject only to a few specifically delineated and well-recognized exceptions. Second, full-scale searches—whether conducted in accordance with the warrant requirement or pursuant to one of its exceptions—are "reasonable" in Fourth Amendment terms only on a showing of probable cause to believe that a crime has been committed and that evidence of the crime will be found in the place to be searched. Third, categories of intrusions that are substantially less intrusive than full-scale searches or seizures may be justifiable in accordance with a balancing test even absent a warrant or probable cause, provided that the balancing test used gives sufficient weight to the privacy interests that will be infringed.

Assistant Vice Principal Choplick's thorough excavation of T.L.O.'s purse was undoubtedly a serious intrusion on her privacy. Unlike the searches in *Terry* or *Adams*, the search at issue here encompassed a detailed and minute examination of respondent's pocketbook, in which the contents of private papers and letters were thoroughly scrutinized.[1] Wisely, neither petitioner nor the Court today attempts to justify the search of T.L.O.'s pocketbook as a minimally intrusive search in the *Terry* line. To

---

[1] A purse typically contains items of highly personal nature. Especially for shy or sensitive adolescents, it could prove extremely embarrassing for a teacher or principal to rummage through its contents, which could include notes from friends, fragments of love poems, caricatures of school authorities, and items of personal hygiene.

be faithful to the Court's settled doctrine, the inquiry therefore must focus on the warrant and probable-cause requirements.

## A

I agree that schoolteachers or principals, when not acting as agents of law enforcement authorities, generally may conduct a search of their students' belongings without first obtaining a warrant. To agree with the Court on this point is to say that school searches may justifiably be held to that extent to constitute an exception to the Fourth Amendment's warrant requirement. Such an exception, however, is not to be justified, as the Court apparently holds, by assessing net social value through application of an unguided "balancing test" in which "the individual's legitimate expectations of privacy and personal security" are weighed against "the government's need for effective methods to deal with breaches of public order." The Warrant Clause is something more than an exhortation to this Court to maximize social welfare as *we* see fit. It requires that the authorities must obtain a warrant before conducting a full-scale search. The undifferentiated governmental interest in law enforcement is insufficient to justify an exception to the warrant requirement. Rather, some *special* governmental interest beyond the need merely to apprehend lawbreakers is necessary to justify a categorical exception to the warrant requirement. For the most part, special governmental needs sufficient to override the warrant requirement flow from "exigency" – that is, from the press of time that makes obtaining a warrant either impossible or hopelessly infeasible. Only after finding an extraordinary governmental interest of this kind do we – or ought we – engage in a balancing test to determine if a warrant should nonetheless be required.

To require a showing of some extraordinary governmental interest before dispensing with the warrant requirement is not to undervalue society's need to apprehend violators of the criminal law. To be sure, forcing law enforcement personnel to obtain a warrant before engaging in a search will predictably deter the police from conducting some searches that they would otherwise like to conduct. But this is not an unintended *result* of the Fourth Amendment's protection of privacy; rather, it is the very *purpose* for which the Amendment was thought necessary. Only where the governmental interests at stake exceed those implicated in any ordinary law enforcement context – that is, only where there is some extraordinary governmental interest involved – is it legitimate to engage in a balancing test to determine whether a warrant is indeed necessary.

In this case, such extraordinary governmental interests do exist and are sufficient to justify an exception to the warrant requirement. Students are necessarily confined for most of the schoolday in close proximity to each other and to the school staff. I agree with the Court that we can take judicial notice of the serious problems of drugs and violence that plague our schools. As Justice Blackmun notes, teachers must not merely "maintain an environment conducive to learning" among children who "are inclined to test the outer boundaries of acceptable conduct," but must also "protect the very safety of students and school personnel." A teacher or principal could neither carry out essential teaching functions nor adequately protect students' safety if required to wait for a warrant before conducting a necessary search.

## B

I emphatically disagree with the Court's decision to cast aside the constitutional probable-cause standard when assessing the constitutional validity of a schoolhouse search. The Court's decision jettisons the probable-cause standard – the only standard that finds support in the text of the Fourth Amendment – on the basis of its Rohrschach-like "balancing test." Use of such a "balancing test" to determine the standard for evaluating the validity of a full-scale search represents a sizable innovation in Fourth Amendment analysis. This innovation finds support neither in precedent nor policy and portends a dangerous weakening of the purpose of the Fourth Amendment to protect the privacy and security of our citizens. Moreover, even if this Court's historic understanding of the Fourth Amendment were mistaken and a balancing test of some kind were appropriate, any such test that gave adequate weight to the privacy and security interests protected by the Fourth Amendment would not reach the preordained result the Court's conclusory analysis reaches today. Therefore, because I believe that the balancing test used by the Court today is flawed both in its inception and in its execution, I respectfully dissent.

### 1

I fully agree with the Court that "the underlying command of the Fourth Amendment is always that searches and seizures be reasonable." But this "underlying command" is not directly interpreted in each category of cases by some amorphous "balancing test." Rather, the provisions of the Warrant Clause – a warrant and probable cause – provide the yardstick against which official searches and seizures are to be measured. The Fourth Amendment neither requires nor authorizes the conceptual free-for-all that ensues when an unguided balancing test is used to assess specific categories of searches. If the search in question is more than a minimally intrusive *Terry* stop, the constitutional probable-cause standard determines its validity.

2

I thus do not accept the majority's premise that "[t]o hold that the Fourth Amendment applies to searches conducted by school authorities is only to begin the inquiry into the standards governing such searches." For me, the finding that the Fourth Amendment applies, coupled with the observation that what is at issue is a full-scale search, is the end of the inquiry. But even if I believed that a "balancing test" appropriately replaces the judgment of the Framers of the Fourth Amendment, I would nonetheless object to the cursory and shortsighted "test" that the Court employs to justify its predictable weakening of Fourth Amendment protections. In particular, the test employed by the Court vastly overstates the social costs that a probable-cause standard entails and, though it plausibly articulates the serious privacy interests at stake, inexplicably fails to accord them adequate weight in striking the balance.

In order to tote up the costs of applying the probable-cause standard, it is necessary first to take into account the nature and content of that standard, and the likelihood that it would hamper achievement of the goal – vital not just to "teachers and administrators" – of maintaining an effective educational setting in the public schools.

Two Terms ago, in *Gates*, this Court expounded at some length its view of the probable-cause standard. Among the adjectives used to describe the standard were "practical," "fluid," "flexible," "easily applied," and "nontechnical." The probable-cause standard was to be seen as a "common sense" test whose application depended on an evaluation of the "totality of the circumstances."

Ignoring what *Gates* took such great pains to emphasize, the Court today holds that a new "reasonableness" standard is appropriate because it "will spare teachers and school administrators the necessity of schooling themselves in the niceties of probable cause and permit them to regulate their conduct according to the dictates of reason and common-sense." I had never thought that our pre-*Gates* understanding of probable cause defied either reason or common sense. But after *Gates*, I would have thought that there could be no doubt that this "non-technical," "practical," and "easily applied" concept was eminently serviceable in a context like a school, where teachers require the flexibility to respond quickly and decisively to emergencies.

A consideration of the likely operation of the probable-cause standard reinforces this conclusion. Discussing the issue of school searches, Professor LaFave has noted that the cases that have reached the appellate courts "strongly suggest that in most instances the evidence of wrongdoing prompting teachers or principals to conduct searches is sufficiently detailed and specific to meet the traditional probable cause test."[2] The problems that have caused this Court difficulty in interpreting the probable-cause standard have largely involved informants. However, three factors make it likely that problems involving informants will not make it difficult for teachers and school administrators to make probable-cause decisions. This Court's decision in *Gates* applying a "totality of the circumstances" test to determine whether an informant's tip can constitute probable cause renders the test easy for teachers to apply. The fact that students and teachers interact daily in the school building makes it more likely that teachers will get to know students who supply information; the problem of informants who remain anonymous even to the teachers – and who are therefore unavailable for verification or further questioning – is unlikely to arise. Finally, teachers can observe the behavior of students under suspicion to corroborate any doubtful tips they do receive.

As compared with the relative ease with which teachers can apply the probable-cause standard, the amorphous "reasonableness under all the circumstances" standard freshly coined by the Court today will likely spawn increased litigation and greater uncertainty among teachers and administrators. Of course, as this Court should know, an essential purpose of developing and articulating legal norms is to enable individuals to conform their conduct to those norms. A school system conscientiously attempting to obey the Fourth Amendment's dictates under a probable-cause standard could, for example, consult decisions and other legal materials and prepare a booklet expounding the rough outlines of the concept. Such a booklet could be distributed to teachers to provide them with guidance as to when a search may be lawfully conducted. I cannot but believe that the same school system faced with interpreting what is permitted under the Court's new "reasonableness" standard would be hopelessly adrift as to when a search may be permissible. The

---

[2] It should be noted that Professor LaFave reached this conclusion in 1978, *before* this Court's decision in *Gates* made clear the "flexibility" of the probable-cause concept.

sad result of this uncertainty may well be that some teachers will be reluctant to conduct searches that are fully permissible and even necessary under the constitutional probable-cause standard, while others may intrude arbitrarily and unjustifiably on the privacy of students.[3]

A legitimate balancing test whose function was something more substantial than reaching a predetermined conclusion acceptable to this Court's impressions of what authority teachers need would therefore reach rather a different result than that reached by the Court today. On one side of the balance would be the costs of applying traditional Fourth Amendment standards—the "practical" and "flexible" probable-cause standard where a full-scale intrusion is sought, a lesser standard in situations where the intrusion is much less severe and the need for greater authority compelling. Whatever costs were toted up on this side would have to be discounted by the costs of applying an unprecedented and ill-defined "reasonableness under all the circumstances" test that will leave teachers and administrators uncertain as to their authority and will encourage excessive fact-based litigation.

## II

Applying the constitutional probable-cause standard to the facts of this case, I would find that Mr. Choplick's search violated T.L.O.'s Fourth Amendment rights. After escorting T.L.O. into his private

---

[3] A comparison of the language of the standard ("reasonableness under all the circumstances") with the traditional language of probable cause ("facts sufficient to warrant a person of reasonable caution in believing that a crime had been committed and the evidence would be found in the designated place") suggests that the Court's new standard may turn out to be probable cause under a new guise. If so, the additional uncertainty caused by this Court's innovation is surely unjustifiable; it would be naive to expect that the addition of this extra dose of uncertainty would do anything other than "burden the efforts of school authorities to maintain order in their schools." If, on the other hand, the new standard permits searches of students in instances when probable cause is absent—instances, according to this Court's consistent formulations, when a person of reasonable caution would not think it likely that a violation existed or that evidence of that violation would be found—the new standard is genuinely objectionable and impossible to square with the premise that our citizens have the right to be free from arbitrary intrusions on their privacy.

office, Mr. Choplick demanded to see her purse. He then opened the purse to find evidence of whether she had been smoking in the bathroom. When he opened the purse, he discovered the pack of cigarettes. At this point, his search for evidence of the smoking violation was complete.

Mr. Choplick then noticed, below the cigarettes, a pack of cigarette rolling papers. Believing that such papers were "associated" with the use of marihuana, he proceeded to conduct a detailed examination of the contents of her purse, in which he found some marihuana, a pipe, some money, an index card, and some private letters indicating that T.L.O. had sold marihuana to other students. The State sought to introduce this latter material in evidence at a criminal proceeding, and the issue before the Court is whether it should have been suppressed.

On my view of the case, we need not decide whether the initial search conducted by Mr. Choplick—the search for evidence of the smoking violation that was completed when Mr. Choplick found the pack of cigarettes—was valid. For Mr. Choplick at that point did not have probable cause to continue to rummage through T.L.O.'s purse. Mr. Choplick's suspicion of marihuana possession at this time was based solely on the presence of the package of cigarette papers. The mere presence without more of such a staple item of commerce is insufficient to warrant a person of reasonable caution in inferring both that T.L.O. had violated the law by possessing marihuana and that evidence of that violation would be found in her purse. Just as a police officer could not obtain a warrant to search a home based solely on his claim that he had seen a package of cigarette papers in that home, Mr. Choplick was not entitled to search possibly the most private possessions of T.L.O. based on the mere presence of a package of cigarette papers. Therefore, the fruits of this illegal search must be excluded and the judgment of the New Jersey Supreme Court affirmed.

Justice STEVENS, with whom Justice MARSHALL joins, concurring in part and dissenting in part.

The Court embraces the standard applied by the New Jersey Supreme Court as equivalent to its own, and then deprecates the state court's application of the standard as reflecting "a somewhat crabbed notion of reasonableness." There is no mystery, however, in the state court's finding that the search in this case was unconstitutional; the decision below was not based on a manipulation of reasonable suspicion, but on the trivial character of the activity that promoted the official search. The New Jersey Supreme Court wrote:

"We are satisfied that when a school official has reasonable grounds to believe that a student possesses evidence of *illegal activity or activity that would interfere with school discipline and order*, the school official has the right to conduct a reasonable search for such evidence.

"In determining whether the school official has reasonable grounds, courts should consider 'the child's age, history, and school record, *the prevalence and seriousness of the problem in the school to which the search was directed*, the exigency to make the search without delay, and the probative value and reliability of the information used as a justification for the search.'" (emphasis added)

The emphasized language in the state court's opinion focuses on the character of the rule infraction that is to be the object of the search.

In the view of the state court, there is a quite obvious and material difference between a search for evidence relating to violent or disruptive activity, and a search for evidence of a smoking rule violation. This distinction does not imply that a no-smoking rule is a matter of minor importance. Rather, like a rule that prohibits a student from being tardy, its occasional violation in a context that poses no threat of disrupting school order and discipline offers no reason to believe that an immediate search is necessary to avoid unlawful conduct, violence, or a serious impairment of the educational process.

A correct understanding of the New Jersey court's standard explains why that court concluded in T.L.O.'s case that "the assistant principal did not have reasonable grounds to believe that the student was concealing in her purse evidence of criminal activity or evidence of activity that *would seriously interfere with school discipline or order*." The importance of the nature of the rule infraction to the New Jersey Supreme Court's holding is evident from its brief explanation of the principal basis for its decision:

"A student has an expectation of privacy in the contents of her purse. Mere possession of cigarettes did not violate school rule or policy, since the school allowed smoking in designated areas. The contents of the handbag had no direct bearing on the infraction.

"The assistant principal's desire, legal in itself, to gather evidence to impeach the student's credibility at a hearing on the disciplinary infraction does not validate the search."[28]

Like the New Jersey Supreme Court, I would view this case differently if the Assistant Vice Principal had reason to believe T.L.O.'s purse contained evidence of criminal activity, or of an activity that would seriously disrupt school discipline. There was, however, absolutely no basis for any such assumption—not even a "hunch."

In this case, Mr. Choplick overreacted to what appeared to be nothing more than a minor infraction—a rule prohibiting smoking in the bathroom of the freshmen's and sophomores' building. It is, of course, true that he actually found evidence of serious wrongdoing by T.L.O., but no one claims that the prior search may be justified by his unexpected discovery. As far as the smoking infraction is concerned, the search for cigarettes merely tended to corroborate a teacher's eyewitness account of T.L.O.'s violation of a minor regulation designed to channel student smoking behavior into designated locations. Because this conduct was neither unlawful nor significantly disruptive of school order or the educational process, the invasion of privacy associated with the forcible opening of T.L.O.'s purse was entirely unjustified at its inception.

A review of the sampling of school search cases relied on by the Court demonstrates how different this case is from those in which there was indeed a valid justification for intruding on a student's privacy. In most of them the student was suspected of a criminal violation; in the remainder either violence or substantial disruption of school order or the integrity of the academic process was at stake. Few involved matters as trivial as the no-smoking rule violated by T.L.O. The rule the Court adopts today is so open-ended that it may make the Fourth Amendment virtually meaningless in the school context. Although I agree that school administrators must have broad latitude to maintain order and discipline in our classrooms, that authority is not unlimited.

The schoolroom is the first opportunity most citizens have to experience the power of government. Through it passes every citizen and public official,

---

[28] The court added:

"Moreover, there were not reasonable grounds to believe that the purse contained cigarettes, if they were the object of the search. No

---

one had furnished information to that effect to the school official. He had, at best, a good hunch. No doubt good hunches would unearth much more evidence of crime on the persons of students and citizens as a whole. But more is required to sustain a search."

It is this portion of the New Jersey Supreme Court's reasoning—a portion that was not necessary to its holding—to which this Court makes its principal response.

from schoolteachers to policemen and prison guards. The values they learn there, they take with them in life. One of our most cherished ideals is the one contained in the Fourth Amendment: that the government may not intrude on the personal privacy of its citizens without a warrant or compelling circumstance. The Court's decision today is a curious moral for the Nation's youth. Although the search of T.L.O.'s purse does not trouble today's majority, I submit that we are not dealing with "matters relatively trivial to the welfare of the Nation. There are village tyrants as well as village Hampdens, but none who acts under color of law is beyond reach of the Constitution." *West Virginia State Board of Education v. Barnette*, 319 U.S. 624, 638 (1943).

I respectfully dissent.

## QUESTIONS AND NOTES

**1.** The entire Court agrees with the concept of not requiring a warrant. Do you? Why? Why not?

**2.** Do you believe that the probable cause standard should have been jettisoned also? Why? Why not?

**3.** Did Mr. Choplick have probable cause to believe that he would find cigarettes in T.L.O.'s purse? Why? Why not?

**4.** If Mr. Choplick knew that he could not look in T.L.O.'s purse, how would he have likely resolved the matter? Does your answer affect your judgment as to whether he should have been permitted to look?

**5.** If T.L.O. had prevailed, would the students have learned that the criminal justice system is not to be taken seriously, but is rife with technicalities that prevail over justice?

**6.** Does (should) *T.L.O.* apply to searches of desks, lockers, and cars (in the school parking lot)? How might those cases be different?

## C. Probationers

Arguably probationers' right to be free from searches is at a different level from that of the rest of us. That question was explored in *Griffin*.

### Griffin v. Wisconsin
### 483 U.S. 868 (1987)

Justice SCALIA delivered the opinion of the Court.

Petitioner Joseph Griffin, who was on probation, had his home searched by probation officers acting without a warrant. The officers found a gun that later served as the basis of Griffin's conviction of a state-law weapons offense. We granted certiorari to consider whether this search violated the Fourth Amendment.

I

On September 4, 1980, Griffin, who had previously been convicted of a felony, was convicted in Wisconsin state court of resisting arrest, disorderly conduct, and obstructing an officer. He was placed on probation.

Wisconsin law puts probationers in the legal custody of the State Department of Health and Social Services and renders them "subject . . . to . . . conditions set by the court and rules and regulations established by the department." One of the Department's regulations permits any probation officer to search a probationer's home without a warrant as long as his supervisor approves and as long as there are "reasonable grounds" to believe the presence of contraband—including any item that the probationer cannot possess under the probation conditions. The rule provides that an officer should consider a variety of factors in determining whether "reasonable grounds" exist, among which are information provided by an informant, the reliability and specificity of that information, the reliability of the informant (including whether the informant has any incentive to supply inaccurate information), the officer's own experience with the probationer, and the "need to verify compliance with rules of supervision and state and federal law." Another regulation makes it a violation of the terms of probation to refuse to consent to a home search. And still another forbids a probationer to possess a firearm without advance approval from a probation officer.

On April 5, 1983, while Griffin was still on probation, Michael Lew, the supervisor of Griffin's probation officer, received information from a detective on the Beloit Police Department that there were or might be guns in Griffin's apartment. Unable to secure the assistance of Griffin's own probation officer, Lew, accompanied by another probation officer and three plainclothes policemen, went to the apartment. When Griffin answered the door, Lew told him who they were and informed him that they were going to search his home. During the subsequent search—carried out entirely by the probation officers under the authority of Wisconsin's probation regulation—they found a handgun.

Griffin was charged with possession of a firearm by a convicted felon, which is itself a felony. He moved to suppress the evidence seized during the search. The trial court denied the motion, concluding that no warrant was necessary and that the search was reasonable. A jury convicted Griffin of the firearms violation, and he was sentenced to two years' imprisonment. The conviction was affirmed by the Wisconsin Court of Appeals. On further appeal, the Wisconsin Supreme Court also affirmed.

## II

We think the Wisconsin Supreme Court correctly concluded that this warrantless search did not violate the Fourth Amendment. To reach that result, however, we find it unnecessary to embrace a new principle of law, as the Wisconsin court evidently did, that any search of a probationer's home by a probation officer satisfies the Fourth Amendment as long as the information possessed by the officer satisfies a federal "reasonable grounds" standard. As his sentence for the commission of a crime, Griffin was committed to the legal custody of the Wisconsin State Department of Health and Social Services, and thereby made subject to that Department's rules and

regulations. The search of Griffin's home satisfied the demands of the Fourth Amendment because it was carried out pursuant to a regulation that itself satisfies the Fourth Amendment's reasonableness requirement under well-established principles.

### A

A probationer's home, like anyone else's, is protected by the Fourth Amendment's requirement that searches be "reasonable." Although we usually require that a search be undertaken only pursuant to a warrant (and thus supported by probable cause, as the Constitution says warrants must be), we have permitted exceptions when "special needs, beyond the normal need for law enforcement, make the warrant and probable-cause requirement impracticable." Thus, we have held that government employers and supervisors may conduct warrantless, work-related searches of employees' desks and offices without probable cause, *O'Connor v. Ortega*, 480 U.S. 709 (1987), and that school officials may conduct warrantless searches of some student property, also without probable cause, *T.L.O.* We have also held, for similar reasons, that in certain circumstances government investigators conducting searches pursuant to a regulatory scheme need not adhere to the usual warrant or probable-cause requirements as long as their searches meet "reasonable legislative or administrative standards."

### B

In determining whether the "special needs" of its probation system justify Wisconsin's search regulation, we must take that regulation as it has been interpreted by state corrections officials and state courts. As already noted, the Wisconsin Supreme Court—the ultimate authority on issues of Wisconsin law—has held that a tip from a police detective that Griffin "had" or "may have had" an illegal weapon at his home constituted the requisite "reasonable grounds." Whether or not we would choose to interpret a similarly worded federal regulation in that fashion, we are bound by the state court's interpretation, which is relevant to our constitutional analysis only insofar as it fixes the meaning of the regulation. We think it clear that the special needs of Wisconsin's probation system make the warrant requirement impracticable and justify replacement of the standard of probable cause by "reasonable grounds," as defined by the Wisconsin Supreme Court.

A warrant requirement would interfere to an appreciable degree with the probation system, setting up a magistrate rather than the probation officer as the judge of how close a supervision the probationer requires. Moreover, the delay inherent in obtaining a warrant would make it more difficult for probation officials to respond quickly to evidence of misconduct, see *T.L.O.*, and would reduce the deterrent effect that the possibility of expeditious searches would otherwise create. By way of analogy, one might contemplate how parental custodial authority would be impaired by requiring judicial approval for search of a minor child's room. And on the other side of the equation—the effect of dispensing with a warrant upon the probationer: Although a probation officer is not an impartial magistrate, neither is he the police officer who normally conducts searches against the ordinary citizen. He is an employee of the State Department of Health and Social Services who, while assuredly charged with protecting the public interest, is also supposed to have in mind the welfare of the probationer (who in the regulations is called a "client." The applicable regulations require him, for example, to "[p]rovid[e] individualized counseling designed to foster growth and development of the client as necessary," and "[m]onito[r] the client's progress where services are provided by another agency and evaluat[e] the need for continuation of the services." In such a setting, we think it reasonable to dispense with the warrant requirement.

Justice Blackmun's dissent would retain a judicial warrant requirement, though agreeing with our subsequent conclusion that reasonableness of the search does not require probable cause. This, however, is a combination that neither the text of the Constitution nor any of our prior decisions permits. While it is possible to say that Fourth Amendment reasonableness demands probable cause without a judicial warrant, the reverse runs up against the constitutional provision that "no Warrants shall issue, but upon probable cause." The Constitution prescribes, in other words, that where the matter is of such a nature as to require a judicial warrant, it is also of such a nature as to require probable cause. Although we have arguably come to permit an exception to that prescription for administrative search warrants,[4] which may but do not necessarily have to be issued

by courts,[5] we have never done so for constitutionally mandated judicial warrants. There it remains true that "[i]f a search warrant be constitutionally required, the requirement cannot be flexibly interpreted to dispense with the rigorous constitutional restrictions for its issue." *Frank v. Maryland*, 359 U.S. 360 (1959). Justice Blackmun neither gives a justification for departure from that principle nor considers its implications for the body of Fourth Amendment law.

We think that the probation regime would also be unduly disrupted by a requirement of probable cause. To take the facts of the present case, it is most unlikely that the unauthenticated tip of a police officer—bearing, as far as the record shows, no indication whether its basis was firsthand knowledge or, if not, whether the firsthand source was reliable, and merely stating that Griffin "had or might have" guns in his residence, not that he certainly had them—would meet the ordinary requirement of probable cause. But this is different from the ordinary case in two related respects: First, even more than the requirement of a warrant, a probable-cause requirement would reduce the deterrent effect of the supervisory arrangement. The probationer would be assured that so long as his illegal (and perhaps socially dangerous) activities were sufficiently concealed as to give rise to no more than reasonable suspicion, they would go undetected and uncorrected. The second difference is well reflected in the regulation specifying what is to be considered "[i]n deciding whether there are reasonable grounds to believe . . . a client's living quarters or property contain contraband." The factors include not only the usual elements that a police officer or magistrate would consider, such as the detail and consistency of the information suggesting the presence of contraband and the reliability and motivation to dissemble of the informant, but also "[i]nformation provided by the client which is relevant to whether the client possesses contraband," and "[t]he experience of a staff member with that client or in a similar circumstance." As was true, then, in *T.L.O.*, we deal with a situation in which there is an ongoing supervisory relationship—and one that is not, or at least not entirely, adversarial—between the object of the search and the decisionmaker.

In such circumstances it is both unrealistic and destructive of the whole object of the continuing

---

[4] In the administrative search context, we formally require that administrative warrants be supported by "probable cause," because in that context we use that term as referring not to a quantum of evidence, but merely to a requirement of reasonableness. In other contexts, however, we use "probable cause" to refer to a quantum of evidence for the belief justifying the search, to be distinguished from a lesser quantum such as "reasonable suspicion." It is plainly in this sense that the dissent uses the term. See, *e.g.* (less than probable cause means "a reduced level of suspicion").

---

[5] The "neutral magistrate," *Camara*, envisioned by our administrative search cases is not necessarily the "neutral judge" envisioned by the dissent.

probation relationship to insist upon the same degree of demonstrable reliability of particular items of supporting data, and upon the same degree of certainty of violation, as is required in other contexts. In some cases – especially those involving drugs or illegal weapons – the probation agency must be able to act based upon a lesser degree of certainty than the Fourth Amendment would otherwise require in order to intervene before a probationer does damage to himself or society. The agency, moreover, must be able to proceed on the basis of its entire experience with the probationer, and to assess probabilities in the light of its knowledge of his life, character, and circumstances.

To allow adequate play for such factors, we think it reasonable to permit information provided by a police officer,[6] whether or not on the basis of firsthand knowledge, to support a probationer search. The same conclusion is suggested by the fact that the police may be unwilling to disclose their confidential sources to probation personnel. For the same reason, and also because it is the very assumption of the institution of probation that the probationer is in need of rehabilitation and is more likely than the ordinary citizen to violate the law, we think it enough if the information provided indicates, as it did here, only the likelihood (''had or might have guns'') of facts justifying the search.[7]

---

[6] The dissenters speculate that the information might not have come from the police at all, ''but from someone impersonating an officer.'' The trial court, however, found as a matter of fact that Lew received the tip on which he relied from a police officer. The Wisconsin Supreme Court affirmed that finding, and neither the petitioner nor the dissenters assert that it is clearly erroneous.

[7] The dissenters assert that the search did not comport with all the governing Wisconsin regulations. There are reasonable grounds on which the Wisconsin court could find that it did. But we need not belabor those here, since the only regulation upon which we rely for our constitutional decision is that which permits a warrantless search on ''reasonable grounds.'' The Wisconsin Supreme Court found the requirement of ''reasonable grounds'' to have been met on the facts of this case and, we hold that such a requirement, so interpreted, meets constitutional minimum standards as well. That the procedures followed, although establishing ''reasonable grounds'' under Wisconsin law, and adequate under federal constitutional standards, may have violated Wisconsin state regulations, is irrelevant to the case before us.

The search of Griffin's residence was ''reasonable'' within the meaning of the Fourth Amendment because it was conducted pursuant to a valid regulation governing probationers. This conclusion makes it unnecessary to consider whether, as the court below held and the State urges, any search of a probationer's home by a probation officer is lawful when there are ''reasonable grounds'' to believe contraband is present. For the foregoing reasons, the judgment of the Wisconsin Supreme Court is affirmed.

Justice BLACKMUN, with whom Justice MARSHALL joins and, as to Parts I-B and I-C, Justice BRENNAN joins and, as to Part I-C, Justice STEVENS joins, dissenting.

In ruling that the home of a probationer may be searched by a probation officer without a warrant, the Court today takes another step that diminishes the protection given by the Fourth Amendment to the ''right of the people to be secure in their persons, houses, papers, and effects, against unreasonable searches and seizures.'' In my view, petitioner's probationary status provides no reason to abandon the warrant requirement. The probation system's special law enforcement needs may justify a search by a probation officer on the basis of ''reasonable suspicion,'' but even that standard was not met in this case.

I

The need for supervision in probation presents one of the ''exceptional circumstances in which special needs, beyond the normal need for law enforcement,'' *T.L.O.* (opinion concurring in judgment), justify an application of the Court's balancing test and an examination of the practicality of the warrant and probable-cause requirements.

My application of the balancing test leads me to conclude that special law enforcement needs justify a search by a probation agent of the home of a probationer on the basis of a reduced level of suspicion. The acknowledged need for supervision, however, does not also justify an exception to the warrant requirement, and I would retain this means of protecting a probationer's privacy.[1] Moreover, the necessity for the neutral check provided by the warrant

---

[1] There is no need to deny the protection by the warrant requirement simply because a search can be justified by less than probable cause. The Court recognizes that administrative warrants are issued on less than probable cause, but it concludes that this has never been the case for ''judicial warrants.'' This conclusion overlooks the fact that administrative warrants *are* issued by the judiciary.

requirement is demonstrated by this case, in which the search was conducted on the basis of information that did not begin to approach the level of "reasonable grounds."

### A

The probation officer is not dealing with an average citizen, but with a person who has been convicted of a crime. This presence of an offender in the community creates the need for special supervision. I therefore agree that a probation agent must have latitude in observing a probationer if the agent is to carry out his supervisory responsibilities effectively. Recidivism among probationers is a major problem, and supervision is one means of combating that threat. Supervision also provides a crucial means of advancing rehabilitation by allowing a probation agent to intervene at the first sign of trouble.

One important aspect of supervision is the monitoring of a probationer's compliance with the conditions of his probation. In order to ensure compliance with those conditions, a probation agent may need to search a probationer's home to check for violations. While extensive inquiry may be required to gather the information necessary to establish probable cause that a violation has occurred, a "reasonable grounds" standard allows a probation agent to avoid this delay and to intervene at an earlier stage of suspicion. This standard is thus consistent with the level of supervision necessary to protect the public and to aid rehabilitation. At the same time, if properly applied, the standard of reasonable suspicion will protect a probationer from unwarranted intrusions into his privacy.

### B

I do not think, however, that special law enforcement needs justify a modification of the protection afforded a probationer's privacy by the warrant requirement. The search in this case was conducted in petitioner's *home*, the place that traditionally has been regarded as the center of a person's private life, the bastion in which one has a legitimate expectation of privacy protected by the Fourth Amendment.

A probationer usually lives at home, and often, as in this case, with a family. He retains a legitimate privacy interest in the home that must be respected to the degree that it is not incompatible with substantial governmental needs. The Court in *T.L.O.* acknowledged that the Fourth Amendment issue needs to be resolved in such a way as to "ensure that the [privacy] interests of students will be invaded no more than is necessary to achieve the legitimate end of preserving order in the schools." The privacy interests of probationers should be protected by a similar standard, and

invaded no more than is necessary to satisfy probation's dual goals of protecting the public safety and encouraging the rehabilitation of the probationer.

The search in this case was not the result of an ordinary home visit by petitioner's probation agent for which no warrant is required. It was a search pursuant to a tip, ostensibly from the police, for the purpose of uncovering evidence of a criminal violation. There is nothing about the status of probation that justifies a special exception to the warrant requirement under these circumstances. If in a particular case there is a compelling need to search the home of a probationer without delay, then it is possible for a search to be conducted immediately under the established exception for exigent circumstances. There is no need to create a separate warrant exception for probationers. The existing exception provides a probation agent with all the flexibility the agent needs.

The circumstances of this case illustrate the fact that the warrant requirement does not create any special impediment to the achievement of the goals of probation. The probation supervisor, Michael T. Lew, waited "[t]wo or three hours" after receiving the telephone tip before he proceeded to petitioner's home to conduct the search. He testified that he was waiting for the return of petitioner's official agent who was attending a legal proceeding, and that eventually he requested another probation agent to initiate the search. Mr. Lew thus had plenty of time to obtain a search warrant. If the police themselves had investigated the report of a gun at petitioner's residence, they would have been required to obtain a warrant. There simply was no compelling reason to abandon the safeguards provided by neutral review.

The Court notes that a probation officer does not normally conduct searches, as does a police officer, and, moreover, the officer is "supposed to have in mind the welfare of the probationer." The implication is that a probation agent will be less likely to initiate an inappropriate search than a law-enforcement officer, and is thus less in need of neutral review. Even if there were data to support this notion, a *reduced* need for review does not justify a complete removal of the warrant requirement. Furthermore, the benefit that a probationer is supposed to gain from probation is rehabilitation. I fail to see how the role of the probation agent in "foster[ing] growth and development of the client" is enhanced the slightest bit by the ability to conduct a search without the checks provided by prior neutral review. If anything, the power to decide to search will prove a barrier to establishing any degree of trust between agent and "client."

The Court's justification for the conclusion that the

warrant requirement would interfere with the probation system by way of an analogy to the authority possessed by parents over their children is completely unfounded. The difference between the two situations is too obvious to belabor. Unlike the private nature of a parent's interaction with his or her child, the probation system is a governmental operation, with explicit standards. Experience has shown that a neutral judge can best determine if those standards are met and a search is justified. This case provides an excellent illustration of the need for neutral review of a probation officer's decision to conduct a search, for it is obvious that the search was not justified even by a reduced standard of reasonable suspicion.

### C

The Court concludes that the search of petitioner's home satisfied the requirements of the Fourth Amendment "because it was carried out pursuant to a regulation that itself satisfies the Fourth Amendment's reasonableness requirement under well-established principles." In the Court's view, it seems that only the single regulation requiring "reasonable grounds" for a search is relevant to its decision. When faced with the patent failure of the probation agents to comply with the Wisconsin regulations, the Court concludes that it "is irrelevant to the case before us" that the probation agents "may have violated Wisconsin state regulations." All of these other regulations, which happen to define the steps necessary to ensure that reasonable grounds are present, can be ignored. This conclusion that the existence of a facial requirement for "reasonable grounds" automatically satisfies the constitutional protection that a search be reasonable can only be termed tautological. The content of a standard is found in its application and, in this case, I cannot discern the application of any standard whatsoever.

The suspicion in this case was based on an unverified tip from an unknown source. With or without the Wisconsin regulation, such information cannot constitutionally justify a search. Mr. Lew testified that he could not recall which police officer called him with the information about the gun, although he thought it "probably" was Officer Pittner. Officer Pittner, however, did not remember making any such telephone call. From all that the record reveals, the call could have been placed by anyone. It is even plausible that the information did not come from the police at all, but from someone impersonating an officer.

Even assuming that a police officer spoke to Mr. Lew, there was little to demonstrate the reliability of the information he received from that unknown officer. The record does not reveal even the precise content

of the tip. The unknown officer actually may have reported that petitioner "had" contraband in his possession, or he merely may have suggested that petitioner "may have had guns in his apartment." Mr. Lew testified to both at different stages of the proceedings. Nor do we know anything about the ultimate source of the information. The unknown officer's belief may have been founded on a hunch, a rumor, or an informant's tip. Without knowing more about the basis of the tip, it is impossible to form a conclusion, let alone a reasonable conclusion, that there were "reasonable grounds" to justify a search.

Mr. Lew failed completely to make the most rudimentary effort to confirm the information he had received or to evaluate whether reasonable suspicion justified a search. Conspicuously absent was any attempt to comply with the Wisconsin regulations that governed the content of the "reasonable grounds" standard.[2] No observations of a staff member could

---

[2] The version of the regulations cited by the Court provided:

"(7) In deciding whether there are reasonable grounds to believe a client possesses contraband, or a client's living quarters or property contain contraband, a staff member should consider:

"(a) The observations of a staff member;

"(b) Information provided by an informant;

"(c) The reliability of the information relied on; in evaluating reliability, attention should be given to whether the information is detailed and consistent and whether it is corroborated;

"(d) The reliability of an informant; in evaluating reliability, attention should be given to whether the informant has supplied reliable information in the past, and whether the informant has reason to supply inaccurate information;

"(e) The activity of the client that relates to whether the client might possess contraband;

"(f) Information provided by the client which is relevant to whether the client possesses contraband;

"(g) The experience of a staff member with that client or in a similar circumstance;

"(h) Prior seizures of contraband from the client; and

"(I) The need to verify compliance with rules of supervision and state and federal law." Wis. Admin. Code HSS § 328.21(7) (1981). The regulations governing the administration of Wisconsin's probation system have been amended recently. See ante, at 3166, n. 1. Under the new rule the word "should" has been changed to "shall" throughout this subsection. See Wis. Admin. Code HSS § 328.21(6) (1986).

have been considered, as required by subsection (7)(a), for Mr. Lew did not consult the agent who had personal knowledge of petitioner's case. When information was provided by an informant, subsections (7)(c) and (d) required evaluation of the reliability of the information relied upon and the reliability of the informant. Mr. Lew proceeded in violation of these basic requirements. Subsection (7)(f) referred to "information provided by the client" and the explanatory notes stated that "the client should be talked to before the search. Sometimes, this will elicit information helpful in determining whether a search should be made." This requirement, too, was ignored. Nor do any of the other considerations support a finding of reasonable grounds to conduct the search. There is no indication that there had been prior seizures of contraband from petitioner, or that his case presented any special need to verify compliance with the law. See §§ (7)(h) and (I).

The majority acknowledges that it is "most unlikely" that the suspicion in this case would have met the normal "probable cause" standard. It concludes, however, that this is not an "ordinary" case because of the need for supervision and the continuing relationship between the probationer and the probation agency. In view of this continuing relationship, the regulations mandated consideration of factors that go beyond those normally considered in determining probable cause to include information provided by the probationer and the experience of the staff member with the probationer. But unless the agency adheres to the regulations, it is sophistic to rely on them as a justification for conducting a search on a lesser degree of suspicion. Mr. Lew drew on no special knowledge of petitioner in deciding to search his house. He had no contact with the agent familiar with petitioner's case before commencing the search. Nor, as discussed above, was there the slightest attempt to obtain information from petitioner. In this case, the continuing relationship between petitioner and the agency did not supply support for any suspicion, reasonable or otherwise, that would justify a search of petitioner's home.

### II

There are many probationers in this country, and they have committed crimes that range widely in seriousness. The Court has determined that all of them may be subjected to such searches in the absence of a warrant. Moreover, in authorizing these searches on the basis of a reduced level of suspicion, the Court overlooks the feeble justification for the search in this case.

I respectfully dissent.

Justice STEVENS, with whom Justice MARSHALL joins, dissenting.

Mere speculation by a police officer that a probationer "may have had" contraband in his possession is not a constitutionally sufficient basis for a warrantless, nonconsensual search of a private home. I simply do not understand how five Members of this Court can reach a contrary conclusion. Accordingly, I respectfully dissent.

## QUESTIONS AND NOTES

**1.** Is *Griffin* a stronger or weaker case than *T.L.O.* for dispensing with a warrant? Why?

**2.** Is *Griffin* a stronger or weaker case than *T.L.O.* for dispensing with probable cause? Why?

**3.** How relevant should it be that innocent housemates or family members will have *their* privacy invaded whenever the probation department searches the probationer's home?

**4.** Would the Court's opinion allow a systematic weekly search (unannounced, but at reasonable daylight hours) to be undertaken of probationers? Should such a search be permitted? Why? Why not?

## D.  Especially Intrusive Searches

Some of the searches that we have considered heretofore have dispensed with the requirement of a warrant and/or probable cause, at least in part, because of the minor nature of the intrusion. In *Winston v. Lee*, the Court was compelled to determine whether a *more* than ordinarily intrusive search could be denied *even with* a warrant and probable cause.

## Winston v. Lee
### 470 U.S. 753 (1985)

Justice BRENNAN delivered the opinion of the Court.

*Schmerber v. California* (1966), held, *inter alia*, that a State may, over the suspect's protest, have a physician extract blood from a person suspected of drunken driving without violation of the suspect's right secured by the Fourth Amendment not to be subjected to unreasonable searches and seizures. However, *Schmerber* cautioned: "That we today hold that the Constitution does not forbid the States['] minor intrusions into an individual's body under stringently limited conditions in no way indicates that it permits more substantial intrusions, or intrusions under other conditions." In this case, the Commonwealth of Virginia seeks to compel the respondent Rudolph Lee, who is suspected of attempting to commit armed robbery, to undergo a surgical procedure under a general anesthetic for removal of a bullet lodged in his chest. Petitioners allege that the bullet will provide evidence of respondent's guilt or innocence. We conclude that the procedure sought here is an example of the "more substantial intrusion" cautioned against in *Schmerber*, and hold that to permit the procedure would violate respondent's right to be secure in his person guaranteed by the Fourth Amendment.

### I

### A

At approximately 1 a.m. on July 18, 1982, Ralph E. Watkinson was closing his shop for the night. As he was locking the door, he observed someone armed with a gun coming toward him from across the street. Watkinson was also armed and when he drew his gun, the other person told him to freeze. Watkinson then fired at the other person, who returned his fire. Watkinson was hit in the legs, while the other individual, who appeared to be wounded in his left side, ran from the scene. The police arrived on the scene shortly thereafter, and Watkinson was taken by ambulance to the emergency room of the Medical College of Virginia (MCV) Hospital.

Approximately 20 minutes later, police officers responding to another call found respondent eight blocks from where the earlier shooting occurred. Respondent was suffering from a gunshot wound to his left chest area and told the police that he had been shot when two individuals attempted to rob him. An ambulance took respondent to the MCV Hospital. Watkinson was still in the MCV emergency room and, when respondent entered that room, said "[t]hat's the man that shot me." After an investigation, the police decided that respondent's story of having been himself the victim of a robbery was untrue and charged respondent with attempted robbery, malicious wounding, and two counts of using a firearm in the commission of a felony.

### B

The Commonwealth shortly thereafter moved in state court for an order directing respondent to undergo surgery to remove an object thought to be a bullet lodged under his left collarbone. The court conducted several evidentiary hearings on the motion. At the first hearing, the Commonwealth's expert testified that the surgical procedure would take 45 minutes and would involve a three to four percent chance of temporary nerve damage, a one percent chance of permanent nerve damage, and a one-tenth of one percent chance of death. At the second hearing, the expert testified that on reexamination of respondent, he discovered that the bullet was not "back inside close to the nerves and arteries," as he originally had thought. Instead, he now believed the bullet to be located "just beneath the skin." He testified that the surgery would require an incision of only one and one-half centimeters (slightly more than one-half inch), could be performed under local anesthesia, and would result in "no danger on the basis that there's no general anesthesia employed."

The state trial judge granted the motion to compel surgery. Respondent petitioned the Virginia Supreme Court for a writ of prohibition and/or a writ of habeas corpus, both of which were denied. Respondent then brought an action in the United States District Court for the Eastern District of Virginia to enjoin the pending operation on Fourth Amendment grounds. The court refused to issue a preliminary injunction, holding that respondent's cause had little likelihood of success on the merits.

On October 18, 1982, just before the surgery was scheduled, the surgeon ordered that X rays be taken of respondent's chest. The X rays revealed that the bullet was in fact lodged two and one-half to three centimeters (approximately one inch) deep in muscular tissue in respondent's chest, substantially deeper than had been thought when the state court granted the motion to compel surgery. The surgeon now believed that a general anesthetic would be desirable for medical reasons.

Respondent moved the state trial court for a re-hearing based on the new evidence. After holding an evidentiary hearing, the state trial court denied the rehearing, and the Virginia Supreme Court affirmed. Respondent then returned to federal court, where he moved to alter or amend the judgment previously entered against him. After an evidentiary hearing, the District Court enjoined the threatened surgery. A divided panel of the Court of Appeals for the Fourth Circuit affirmed. We granted certiorari to consider whether a State may consistently with the Fourth Amendment compel a suspect to undergo surgery of this kind in a search for evidence of a crime.

## II

A compelled surgical intrusion into an individual's body for evidence implicates expectations of privacy and security of such magnitude that the intrusion may be "unreasonable" even if likely to produce evidence of a crime. In *Schmerber*, we addressed a claim that the State had breached the Fourth Amendment's protection of the "right of the people to be secure in their *persons* . . . against unreasonable searches and seizures" (emphasis added) when it compelled an individual suspected of drunken driving to undergo a blood test. Schmerber had been arrested at a hospital while receiving treatment for injuries suffered when the automobile he was driving struck a tree. Despite Schmerber's objection, a police officer at the hospital had directed a physician to take a blood sample from him. Schmerber subsequently objected to the introduction at trial of evidence obtained as a result of the blood test.

The authorities in *Schmerber* clearly had probable cause to believe that he had been driving while intoxicated, and to believe that a blood test would provide evidence that was exceptionally probative in confirming this belief. Because the case fell within the exigent-circumstances exception to the warrant requirement, no warrant was necessary. The search was not more intrusive than reasonably necessary to accomplish its goals. Nonetheless, Schmerber argued that the Fourth Amendment prohibited the authorities from intruding into his body to extract the blood that was needed as evidence.

The reasonableness of surgical intrusions beneath the skin depends on a case-by-case approach, in which the individual's interests in privacy and security are weighed against society's interests in conducting the procedure. In a given case, the question whether the community's need for evidence outweighs the substantial privacy interests at stake is a delicate one admitting of few categorical answers. We believe that *Schmerber*, however, provides the appropriate framework of analysis for such cases.

*Schmerber* recognized that the ordinary requirements of the Fourth Amendment would be the threshold requirements for conducting this kind of surgical search and seizure. We noted the importance of probable cause. And we pointed out: "Search warrants are ordinarily required for searches of dwellings, and, absent an emergency, no less could be required where intrusions into the human body are concerned. . . . The importance of informed, detached and deliberate determinations of the issue whether or not to invade another's body in search of evidence of guilt is indisputable and great."

Beyond these standards, *Schmerber*'s inquiry considered a number of other factors in determining the "reasonableness" of the blood test. A crucial factor in analyzing the magnitude of the intrusion in *Schmerber* is the extent to which the procedure may threaten the safety or health of the individual. "[F]or most people [a blood test] involves virtually no risk, trauma, or pain." Moreover, all reasonable medical precautions were taken and no unusual or untested procedures were employed in *Schmerber*; the procedure was performed "by a physician in a hospital environment according to accepted medical practices." Notwithstanding the existence of probable cause, a search for evidence of a crime may be unjustifiable if it endangers the life or health of the suspect.

Another factor is the extent of intrusion upon the individual's dignitary interests in personal privacy and bodily integrity. Intruding into an individual's living room, eavesdropping upon an individual's telephone conversations, or forcing an individual to accompany police officers to the police station, typically do not injure the physical person of the individual. Such intrusions do, however, damage the individual's sense of personal privacy and security and are thus subject to the Fourth Amendment's dictates. In noting that a blood test was "a commonplace in these days of periodic physical examinations," *Schmerber* recognized society's judgment that blood tests do not constitute an unduly extensive imposition on an individual's personal privacy and bodily integrity.

Weighed against these individual interests is the community's interest in fairly and accurately determining guilt or innocence. This interest is of course of great importance. We noted in *Schmerber* that a blood test is "a highly effective means of determining the degree to which a person is under the influence of alcohol." Moreover, there was "a clear indication that in fact [desired] evidence [would] be found" if the blood test were undertaken. Especially given the difficulty of proving drunkenness by other means, these considerations showed that results of the blood test were of vital importance if the State were to enforce its drunken driving laws. In *Schmerber*, we concluded that this state interest was sufficient to justify the intrusion, and the compelled blood test was thus "reasonable" for Fourth Amendment purposes.

### III

Applying the *Schmerber* balancing test in this case, we believe that the Court of Appeals reached the correct result. The Commonwealth plainly had probable cause to conduct the search. In addition, all parties apparently agree that respondent has had a full measure of procedural protections and has been able fully to litigate the difficult medical and legal questions necessarily involved in analyzing the reasonableness of a surgical incision of this magnitude.[6] Our inquiry therefore must focus on the extent of the intrusion on respondent's privacy interests and on the State's need for the evidence.

The threats to the health or safety of respondent posed by the surgery are the subject of sharp dispute between the parties. Before the new revelations of October 18, the District Court found that the procedure could be carried out "with virtually no risk to [respondent]." On rehearing, however, with new evidence before it, the District Court held that "the risks previously involved have increased in magnitude even as new risks are being added."

The Court of Appeals examined the medical evidence in the record and found that respondent would suffer some risks associated with the surgical procedure.[7] One surgeon had testified that the difficulty of discovering the exact location of the bullet "could require extensive probing and retracting of the muscle tissue," carrying with it "the concomitant risks of injury to the muscle as well as injury to the nerves, blood vessels and other tissue in the chest and pleural

cavity." The court further noted that "the greater intrusion and the larger incisions increase the risks of infection." Moreover, there was conflict in the testimony concerning the nature and the scope of the operation. One surgeon stated that it would take 15-20 minutes, while another predicted the procedure could take up to two and one-half hours. The court properly took the resulting uncertainty about the medical risks into account.[8]

Both lower courts in this case believed that the proposed surgery, which for purely medical reasons required the use of a general anesthetic,[9] would be an "extensive" intrusion on respondent's personal privacy and bodily integrity. When conducted with the consent of the patient, surgery requiring general anesthesia is not necessarily demeaning or intrusive. In such a case, the surgeon is carrying out the patient's own will concerning the patient's body and the patient's right to privacy is therefore preserved. In this case, however, the Court of Appeals noted that the Commonwealth proposes to take control of respondent's body, to "drug this citizen--not yet convicted of a criminal offense—with narcotics and barbiturates into a state of unconsciousness," and then to search beneath his skin for evidence of a crime. This kind of surgery involves a virtually total divestment of respondent's ordinary control over surgical probing beneath his skin.

The other part of the balance concerns the Commonwealth's need to intrude into respondent's body to retrieve the bullet. The Commonwealth claims to need the bullet to demonstrate that it was fired from Watkinson's gun, which in turn would show that respondent was the robber who confronted Watkinson. However, although we recognize the difficulty of making determinations in advance as to the strength of the case against respondent, petitioners'

---

[6] Because the State has afforded respondent the benefit of a full adversary presentation and appellate review, we do not reach the question whether the State may compel a suspect to undergo a surgical search of this magnitude for evidence absent such special procedural protections.

[7] The Court of Appeals concluded, however, that "the specific physical risks from putting [respondent] under general anesthesia may therefore be considered minimal." Testimony had shown that "the general risks of harm or death from general anesthesia are quite low, and that [respondent] was in the statistical group of persons with the lowest risk of injury from general anesthesia."

[8] One expert testified that this would be "minor" surgery. The question whether the surgery is to be characterized in medical terms as "major" or "minor" is not controlling. We agree with the Court of Appeals and the District Court in this case that "there is no reason to suppose that the definition of a medical term of art should coincide with the parameters of a constitutional standard." This does not mean that the application of medical concepts in such cases is to be ignored. However, no specific medical categorization can control the multifaceted legal inquiry that the court must undertake.

[9] Somewhat different issues would be raised if the use of a general anesthetic became necessary because of the patient's refusal to cooperate.

assertions of a compelling need for the bullet are hardly persuasive. The very circumstances relied on in this case to demonstrate probable cause to believe that evidence will be found tend to vitiate the Commonwealth's need to compel respondent to undergo surgery. The Commonwealth has available substantial additional evidence that respondent was the individual who accosted Watkinson on the night of the robbery. No party in this case suggests that Watkinson's entirely spontaneous identification of respondent at the hospital would be inadmissible. In addition, petitioners can no doubt prove that Watkinson [ed. Was "Lee" intended?] was found a few blocks from Watkinson's store shortly after the incident took place. And petitioners can certainly show that the location of the bullet (under respondent's left collarbone) seems to correlate with Watkinson's report that the robber "jerked" to the left. The fact that the Commonwealth has available such substantial evidence of the origin of the bullet restricts the need for the Commonwealth to compel respondent to undergo the contemplated surgery.[10]

---

[10] There are also some questions concerning the probative value of the bullet, even if it could be retrieved. The evidentiary value of the bullet depends on a comparison between markings, if any, on the bullet in respondent's shoulder and markings, if any, found on a test bullet that the police could fire from Watkinson's gun. However, the record supports some doubt whether this kind of comparison is possible. This is because the bullet's markings may have been corroded in the time that the bullet has been in respondent's shoulder, thus making it useless for comparison purposes. In addition, respondent argues that any given gun may be incapable of firing bullets that have a consistent set of markings. The record is devoid of any evidence that the police have attempted to test-fire Watkinson's gun, and there thus remains the additional possibility that a comparison of bullets is impossible because Watkinson's gun does not consistently fire bullets with the same markings. However, because the courts below made no findings on this point, we hesitate to give it significant weight in our analysis.

In weighing the various factors in this case, we therefore reach the same conclusion as the courts below. The operation sought will intrude substantially on respondent's protected interests. The medical risks of the operation, although apparently not extremely severe, are a subject of considerable dispute; the very uncertainty militates against finding the operation to be "reasonable." In addition, the intrusion on respondent's privacy interests entailed by the operation can only be characterized as severe. On the other hand, although the bullet may turn out to be useful to the Commonwealth in prosecuting respondent, the Commonwealth has failed to demonstrate a compelling need for it. We believe that in these circumstances the Commonwealth has failed to demonstrate that it would be "reasonable" under the terms of the Fourth Amendment to search for evidence of this crime by means of the contemplated surgery.

IV

The Fourth Amendment is a vital safeguard of the right of the citizen to be free from unreasonable governmental intrusions into any area in which he has a reasonable expectation of privacy. Where the Court has found a lesser expectation of privacy, or where the search involves a minimal intrusion on privacy interests, the Court has held that the Fourth Amendment's protections are correspondingly less stringent. Conversely, however, the Fourth Amendment's command that searches be "reasonable" requires that when the State seeks to intrude upon an area in which our society recognizes a significantly heightened privacy interest, a more substantial justification is required to make the search "reasonable." Applying these principles, we hold that the proposed search in this case would be "unreasonable" under the Fourth Amendment.

[Justice BLACKMUN and Justice REHNQUIST concurred in the judgment.]

Chief Justice BURGER, concurring. I join because I read the Court's opinion as not preventing detention of an individual if there are reasonable grounds to believe that natural bodily functions will disclose the presence of contraband materials secreted internally.

## QUESTIONS AND NOTES

**1.** Does the State lose because it has *too much probable cause*? If the State's case against Lee were weaker, would its need to retrieve the bullet be stronger, and perhaps successful? If so, doesn't the case turn the concept of probable cause on its head?

**2.** Should Lee's claim be discounted by the harm of *not* removing the bullet? Presumably leaving a bullet in a person carries its own risks?

**3.** Is the Court manufacturing an exception to the Fourth Amendment? Given a warrant (indeed an adversary hearing with multiple appeals) and probable cause, how can the Court conclude that Fourth Amendment standards were not met?

## E.  Border Searches

As *Montoya de Hernandez* makes clear, border searches of considerable intensity (*e.g.* thorough search of luggage) are routinely permitted simply because an individual has crossed the border. *Montoya de Hernandez* raises the further question of the extent to which searches of the *Schmerber* and *Winston* type are permissible, and the criteria for conducting them. Think of Chief Justice Burger's *Winston* concurrence as you read *Montoya de Hernandez,* decided later that same term.

### United States v. Montoya de Hernandez
473 U.S. 531 (1985)

Justice REHNQUIST delivered the opinion of the Court.

Respondent Rosa Elvira Montoya de Hernandez was detained by customs officials upon her arrival at the Los Angeles Airport on a flight from Bogota, Colombia. She was found to be smuggling 88 cocaine-filled balloons in her alimentary canal, and was convicted after a bench trial of various federal narcotics offenses. A divided panel of the United States Court of Appeals for the Ninth Circuit reversed her convictions, holding that her detention violated the Fourth Amendment to the United States Constitution because the customs inspectors did not have a "clear indication" of alimentary canal smuggling at the time she was detained. Because of a conflict in the decisions of the Courts of Appeals on this question and the importance of its resolution to the enforcement of customs laws, we granted certiorari. We now reverse. Respondent arrived at Los Angeles International Airport shortly after midnight, March 5, 1983, on Avianca Flight 080, a direct 10-hour flight from Bogota, Colombia. Her visa was in order so she was passed through Immigration and proceeded to the customs desk. At the customs desk she encountered Customs Inspector Talamantes, who reviewed her documents and noticed from her passport that she had made at least eight recent trips to either Miami or Los Angeles. Talamantes referred respondent to a secondary customs desk for further questioning. At this desk Talamantes and another

inspector asked respondent general questions concerning herself and the purpose of her trip. Respondent revealed that she spoke no English and had no family or friends in the United States. She explained in Spanish that she had come to the United States to purchase goods for her husband's store in Bogota. The customs inspectors recognized Bogota as a "source city" for narcotics. Respondent possessed $5,000 in cash, mostly $50 bills, but had no billfold. She indicated to the inspectors that she had no appointments with merchandise vendors, but planned to ride around Los Angeles in taxicabs visiting retail stores such as J.C. Penney and K-Mart in order to buy goods for her husband's store with the $5,000.

Respondent admitted that she had no hotel reservations, but stated that she planned to stay at a Holiday Inn. Respondent could not recall how her airline ticket was purchased. When the inspectors opened respondent's one small valise they found about four changes of "cold weather" clothing. Respondent had no shoes other than the high-heeled pair she was wearing. Although respondent possessed no checks, waybills, credit cards, or letters of credit, she did produce a Colombian business card and a number of old receipts, waybills, and fabric swatches displayed in a photo album. At this point Talamantes and the other inspector suspected that respondent was a "balloon swallower," one who attempts to smuggle narcotics into this country hidden in her alimentary canal. Over the years Inspector Talamantes had apprehended dozens of alimentary canal smugglers arriving on Avianca Flight 080.

The inspectors requested a female customs inspector to take respondent to a private area and conduct a patdown and strip search. During the search the female inspector felt respondent's abdomen area and noticed a firm fullness, as if respondent were wearing a girdle. The search revealed no contraband, but the inspector noticed that respondent was wearing two pairs of elastic underpants with a paper towel lining the crotch area.

When respondent returned to the customs area and the female inspector reported her discoveries, the inspector in charge told respondent that he suspected she was smuggling drugs in her alimentary canal. Respondent agreed to the inspector's request that she be x-rayed at a hospital but in answer to the inspector's query stated that she was pregnant. She agreed to a pregnancy test before the x ray. Respondent withdrew the consent for an x ray when she learned that she would have to be handcuffed en route to the hospital. The inspector then gave respondent the option of returning to Colombia on the next available flight, agreeing to an x ray, or remaining in detention until she produced a monitored bowel movement that would confirm or rebut the inspectors' suspicions. Respondent chose the first option and was placed in a customs office under observation. She was told that if she went to the toilet she would have to use a wastebasket in the women's restroom, in order that female customs inspectors could inspect her stool for balloons or capsules carrying narcotics. The inspectors refused respondent's request to place a telephone call.

Respondent sat in the customs office, under observation, for the remainder of the night. During the night customs officials attempted to place respondent on a Mexican airline that was flying to Bogota via Mexico City in the morning. The airline refused to transport respondent because she lacked a Mexican visa necessary to land in Mexico City. Respondent was not permitted to leave, and was informed that she would be detained until she agreed to an x ray or her bowels moved. She remained detained in the customs office under observation, for most of the time curled up in a chair leaning to one side. She refused all offers of food and drink, and refused to use the toilet facilities. The Court of Appeals noted that she exhibited symptoms of discomfort consistent with "heroic efforts to resist the usual calls of nature."

At the shift change at 4 o'clock the next afternoon, almost 16 hours after her flight had landed, respondent still had not defecated or urinated or partaken of food or drink. At that time customs officials sought a court order authorizing a pregnancy test, an x ray, and a rectal examination. The Federal Magistrate issued an order just before midnight that evening, which authorized a rectal examination and involuntary x ray, provided that the physician in charge considered respondent's claim of pregnancy. Respondent was taken to a hospital and given a pregnancy test, which later turned out to be negative. Before the results of the pregnancy test were known, a physician conducted a rectal examination and removed from respondent's rectum a balloon containing a foreign substance. Respondent was then placed formally under arrest. By 4:10 a.m. respondent had passed 6 similar balloons; over the next four days she passed 88 balloons containing a total of 528 grams of 80% pure cocaine hydrochloride.

The Fourth Amendment commands that searches and seizures be reasonable. What is reasonable depends upon all of the circumstances surrounding the search or seizure and the nature of the search or seizure itself. *T.L.O.*. The permissibility of a particular law enforcement practice is judged by "balancing its intrusion on the individual's Fourth Amendment interests against its promotion of legitimate governmental interests."

Here the seizure of respondent took place at the international border. Since the founding of our Republic, Congress has granted the Executive plenary authority to conduct routine searches and seizures at the border, without probable cause or a warrant, in order to regulate the collection of duties and to prevent the introduction of contraband into this country.

Consistently, therefore, with Congress' power to protect the Nation by stopping and examining persons entering this country, the Fourth Amendment's balance of reasonableness is qualitatively different at the international border than in the interior. Routine searches of the persons and effects of entrants are not subject to any requirement of reasonable suspicion, probable cause, or warrant,[1] and first-class mail may be opened without a warrant on less than probable cause. Automotive travelers may be stopped at fixed checkpoints near the border without individualized suspicion even if the stop is based largely on ethnicity, *Martinez-Fuerte*, and boats on inland waters with ready access to the sea may be hailed and

---

[1] As the Court stated in *Carroll*:

"Travelers may be so stopped in crossing an international boundary because of national self protection reasonably requiring one entering the country to identify himself as entitled to come in and his belongings as effects which may be lawfully brought in."

boarded with no suspicion whatever. *United States v. Villamonte-Marquez*, 462 U.S. 579 (1983).

These cases reflect longstanding concern for the protection of the integrity of the border. This concern is, if anything, heightened by the veritable national crisis in law enforcement caused by smuggling of illicit narcotics, and in particular by the increasing utilization of alimentary canal smuggling. This desperate practice appears to be a relatively recent addition to the smugglers' repertoire of deceptive practices, and it also appears to be exceedingly difficult to detect.

Balanced against the sovereign's interests at the border are the Fourth Amendment rights of respondent. Having presented herself at the border for admission, and having subjected herself to the criminal enforcement powers of the Federal Government, respondent was entitled to be free from unreasonable search and seizure. But not only is the expectation of privacy less at the border than in the interior, the Fourth Amendment balance between the interests of the Government and the privacy right of the individual is also struck much more favorably to the Government at the border.

We hold that the detention of a traveler at the border, beyond the scope of a routine customs search and inspection, is justified at its inception if customs agents, considering all the facts surrounding the traveler and her trip, reasonably suspect that the traveler is smuggling contraband in her alimentary canal.[4]

The "reasonable suspicion" standard has been applied in a number of contexts and effects a needed balance between private and public interests when law enforcement officials must make a limited intrusion on less than probable cause. It thus fits well into the situations involving alimentary canal smuggling at the border: this type of smuggling gives no external signs and inspectors will rarely possess probable cause to arrest or search, yet governmental interests in stopping smuggling at the border are high indeed. Under this standard officials at the border must have a "particularized and objective basis for

suspecting the particular person" of alimentary canal smuggling. *Cortez.*

The facts, and their rational inferences, known to customs inspectors in this case clearly supported a reasonable suspicion that respondent was an alimentary canal smuggler. We need not belabor the facts, including respondent's implausible story, that supported this suspicion. The trained customs inspectors had encountered many alimentary canal smugglers and certainly had more than an "inchoate and unparticularized suspicion or 'hunch,'" that respondent was smuggling narcotics in her alimentary canal. The inspectors' suspicion was a "'commonsense conclusio[n] about human behavior' upon which 'practical people,' – including government officials, are entitled to rely."

The final issue in this case is whether the detention of respondent was reasonably related in scope to the circumstances which justified it initially. In this regard we have cautioned that courts should not indulge in "unrealistic second-guessing," *Sharpe*, and we have noted that "creative judge[s], engaged in *post hoc* evaluations of police conduct can almost always imagine some alternative means by which the objectives of the police might have been accomplished." But "[t]he fact that the protection of the public might, in the abstract, have been accomplished by 'less intrusive' means does not, in itself, render the search unreasonable." Authorities must be allowed "to graduate their response to the demands of any particular situation." Here, respondent was detained incommunicado for almost 16 hours before inspectors sought a warrant; the warrant then took a number of hours to procure, through no apparent fault of the inspectors. This length of time undoubtedly exceeds any other detention we have approved under reasonable suspicion. But we have also consistently rejected hard-and-fast time limits, *Sharpe, Place.* Instead, "common sense and ordinary human experience must govern over rigid criteria."

The rudimentary knowledge of the human body which judges possess in common with the rest of humankind tells us that alimentary canal smuggling cannot be detected in the amount of time in which other illegal activity may be investigated through brief *Terry*-type stops. It presents few, if any external signs; a quick frisk will not do, nor will even a strip search. In the case of respondent the inspectors had available, as an alternative to simply awaiting her bowel movement, an x ray. They offered her the alternative of submitting herself to that procedure. But when she refused that alternative, the customs inspectors were left with only two practical alternatives: detain her for such time as necessary to confirm their suspicions, a detention which would

---

[4] It is also important to note what we do *not* hold. Because the issues are not presented today we suggest no view on what level of suspicion, if any, is required for nonroutine border searches such as strip, body cavity, or involuntary x-ray searches. Both parties would have us decide the issue of whether aliens possess lesser Fourth Amendment rights at the border; that question was not raised in either court below and we do not consider it today.

last much longer than the typical *Terry* stop, or turn her loose into the interior carrying the reasonably suspected contraband drugs.

The inspectors in this case followed this former procedure. They no doubt expected that respondent, having recently disembarked from a 10-hour direct flight with a full and stiff abdomen, would produce a bowel movement without extended delay. But her visible efforts to resist the call of nature, which the court below labeled "heroic," disappointed this expectation and in turn caused her humiliation and discomfort. Our prior cases have refused to charge police with delays in investigatory detention attributable to the suspect's evasive actions, see *Sharpe* (Marshall, J., concurring in judgment), and that principle applies here as well. Respondent alone was responsible for much of the duration and discomfort of the seizure.

Under these circumstances, we conclude that the detention in this case was not unreasonably long. It occurred at the international border, where the Fourth Amendment balance of interests leans heavily to the Government. At the border, customs officials have more than merely an investigative law enforcement role. They are also charged, along with immigration officials, with protecting this Nation from entrants who may bring anything harmful into this country, whether that be communicable diseases, narcotics, or explosives. In this regard the detention of a suspected alimentary canal smuggler at the border is analogous to the detention of a suspected tuberculosis carrier at the border: both are detained until their bodily processes dispel the suspicion that they will introduce a harmful agent into this country.

Respondent's detention was long, uncomfortable, indeed, humiliating; but both its length and its discomfort resulted solely from the method by which she chose to smuggle illicit drugs into this country. In *Adams*, we said that "[t]he Fourth Amendment does not require a policeman who lacks the precise level of information necessary for probable cause to arrest to simply shrug his shoulders and allow a crime to occur or a criminal to escape." Here, by analogy, in the presence of articulable suspicion of smuggling in her alimentary canal, the customs officers were not required by the Fourth Amendment to pass respondent and her 88 cocaine-filled balloons into the interior. Her detention for the period of time necessary to either verify or dispel the suspicion was not unreasonable. The judgment of the Court of Appeals is therefore reversed.

Justice STEVENS, concurring in judgment.

If a seizure and a search of the person of the kind disclosed by this record may be made on the basis of reasonable suspicion, we must assume that a significant number of innocent persons will be required to undergo similar procedures. The rule announced in this case cannot, therefore, be supported on the ground that respondent's prolonged and humiliating detention "resulted solely from the method by which she chose to smuggle illicit drugs into this country."

The prolonged detention of respondent was, however, justified by a different choice that respondent made; she withdrew her consent to an x-ray examination that would have easily determined whether the reasonable suspicion that she was concealing contraband was justified. I believe that customs agents may require that a nonpregnant person reasonably suspected of this kind of smuggling submit to an x-ray examination as an incident to a border search. I therefore concur in the judgment.

Justice BRENNAN, with whom Justice MARSHALL joins, dissenting.

We confront a "disgusting and saddening episode" at our Nation's border. Shortly after midnight on March 5, 1983, the respondent Rosa Elvira Montoya De Hernandez was detained by customs officers because she fit the profile of an "alimentary canal smuggler." This profile did not of course give the officers probable cause to believe that De Hernandez was smuggling drugs into the country, but at most a "reasonable suspicion" that she might be engaged in such an attempt. After a thorough strip search failed to uncover any contraband, De Hernandez agreed to go to a local hospital for an abdominal x ray to resolve the matter. When the officers approached with handcuffs ready to lead her away, however, "she crossed her arms by her chest and began stepping backwards shaking her head negatively," protesting: "You are not going to put those on me. That is an insult to my character."

Stymied in their efforts, the officers decided on an alternative course: they would simply lock De Hernandez away in an adjacent manifest room "until her peristaltic functions produced a monitored bowel movement." The officers explained to De Hernandez that she could not leave until she had excreted by squatting over a wastebasket pursuant to the watchful eyes of two attending matrons. De Hernandez responded: "I will not submit to your degradation and I'd rather die." She was locked away with the matrons.

De Hernandez remained locked up in the room for almost *24 hours*. Three shifts of matrons came and went during this time. The room had no bed or couch on which she could lie, but only hard chairs and a table. The matrons told her that if she wished to sleep she could lie down on the hard, uncarpeted floor. De Hernandez instead "sat in her chair clutching her purse," "occasionally putting her head down on the table to nap." Most of the time she simply wept and pleaded "to go home." She repeatedly begged for permission "to call my husband and tell him what you are doing to me." Permission was denied. Sobbing, she insisted that she had to "make a phone call home so that she could talk to her children and to let them know that everything was all right." Permission again was denied. In fact, the matrons considered it highly "unusual" that "each time someone entered the search room, she would take out two small pictures of her children and show them to the person." De Hernandez also demanded that her attorney be contacted. Once again, permission was denied. As far as the outside world knew, Rosa de Hernandez had simply vanished. And although she already had been stripped and searched and probed, the customs officers decided about halfway through her ordeal to repeat that process—"to ensure the safety of the surveilling officers. The result was again negative." After almost 24 hours had passed, someone finally had the presence of mind to consult a Magistrate and to obtain a court order for an x ray and a body-cavity search.[13] De Hernandez, "very agitated," was handcuffed and led away to

---

[13] A customs inspector had initially suggested that a court order for an x-ray examination be obtained, but his supervisor vetoed the idea on the grounds that (1) it was not Government policy to seek judicial authorization in such circumstances, and (2) "they did not have sufficient facts to support the issuance of the order." The inspector called several hours later and reiterated his suggestion; again it was denied. Not until 16 hours had elapsed did the supervisor begin to consider obtaining a court order. Another eight hours passed before the supervisor got around to contacting a Federal Magistrate, who after putting the supervisor under oath and listening to the available evidence promptly issued a telephonic order to proceed with the x-ray examination.

The Magistrate's order was based largely on the observations by customs officials of De Hernandez' behavior during her detention. As the Ninth Circuit concluded, because the unlawful detention produced the "additional evidence" that was used to obtain the order, the contraband discovered in implementing the order was tainted and therefore improperly introduced at De Hernandez' trial.

the hospital. A rectal examination disclosed the presence of a cocaine-filled balloon. At approximately 3:15 on the morning of March 6, *almost 27 hours after her initial detention*, De Hernandez was formally placed under arrest and advised of her *Miranda* rights. Over the course of the next four days she excreted a total of 88 balloons.

"[T]hat the [respondent] so degraded herself as to offend the sensibilities of any decent citizen is not questioned." That is not the issue we face. For "[i]t is a fair summary of history to say that the safeguards of liberty have frequently been forged in controversies involving not very nice people." The standards we fashion to govern the ferreting out of the guilty apply equally to the detention of the innocent, and "may be exercised by the most unfit and ruthless officers as well as by the fit and responsible." Nor is the issue whether there is a "veritable national crisis in law enforcement caused by smuggling of illicit narcotics." There is, and "[s]tern enforcement of the criminal law is the hallmark of a healthy and self-confident society." "But in our democracy such enforcement presupposes a moral atmosphere and a reliance upon intelligence whereby the effective administration of justice can be achieved with due regard for those civilized standards in the use of the criminal law which are formulated in our Bill of Rights."

The issue, instead, is simply this: Does the Fourth Amendment permit an international traveler, citizen or alien, to be subjected to the sort of treatment that occurred in this case without the sanction of a judicial officer and based on nothing more than the "reasonable suspicion" of low-ranking investigative officers that something might be amiss? The Court today concludes that the Fourth Amendment grants such sweeping and unmonitored authority to customs officials. It reasons that "[t]he permissibility of a particular law enforcement practice is judged by 'balancing its intrusion on the individual's Fourth Amendment interests against its promotion of legitimate governmental interests.'" The Court goes on to assert that the "balance of reasonableness is qualitatively different at the international border," and that searches and seizures in these circumstances may therefore be conducted without probable cause or a warrant. Thus a traveler at the Nation's border may be detained for criminal investigation merely if the authorities "reasonably suspect that the traveler is smuggling contraband." There are no "hard-and-fast time limits" for such investigative detentions, because "'common sense and ordinary human experience must govern over rigid criteria.'" Applying this "reasonableness" test to the instant case, the Court concludes that the "[r]espondent alone was responsible for much of the duration and discomfort of the seizure.''

Justice Stevens takes a somewhat different tack. Apparently convinced that the health effects of x-irradiation on human beings stand established as so minimal as to be little cause for concern, he believes that low-ranking customs officials on their own initiative may require nonpregnant international travelers to submit to warrantless x rays on nothing more than suspicion if such travelers wish to avoid indeterminate warrantless detentions. Because De Hernandez withdrew her consent to proceed in handcuffs to such an examination, ''[t]he prolonged detention of respondent was . . . justified.''

I dissent. Indefinite involuntary incommunicado detentions ''for investigation'' are the hallmark of a police state, not a free society. In my opinion, Government officials may no more confine a person at the border under such circumstances for purposes of criminal investigation than they may within the interior of the country. The nature and duration of the detention here may well have been tolerable for spoiled meat or diseased animals, but not for human beings held on simple suspicion of criminal activity. I believe such indefinite detentions can be ''reasonable'' under the Fourth Amendment only with the approval of a magistrate. I also believe that such approval can be given only upon a showing of probable cause. Finally, I believe that the warrant and probable-cause safeguards equally govern Justice Stevens' proffered alternative of exposure to x-irradiation for criminal-investigative purposes.

## I

Travelers at the national border are routinely subjected to questioning, patdowns, and thorough searches of their belongings. These measures, which involve relatively limited invasions of privacy and which typically are conducted on all incoming travelers, do not violate the Fourth Amendment given the interests of ''national self protection reasonably requiring one entering the country to identify himself as entitled to come in, and his belongings as effects which may be lawfully brought in.'' Individual travelers also may be singled out on ''reasonable suspicion'' and briefly held for further investigation. At some point, however, further investigation involves such severe intrusions on the values the Fourth Amendment protects that more stringent safeguards are required. For example, the length and nature of a detention may, at least when conducted for criminal-investigative purposes, ripen into something approximating a full-scale custodial arrest—indeed, the arrestee, unlike the detainee in cases such as this,

is at least given such basic rights as a telephone call, *Miranda* warnings, a bed, a prompt hearing before the nearest federal magistrate, an appointed attorney, and consideration of bail. In addition, border detentions may involve the use of such highly intrusive investigative techniques as body-cavity searches, x-ray searches, and stomach-pumping.

Something has gone fundamentally awry in our constitutional jurisprudence when a neutral and detached magistrate's authorization is required before the authorities may inspect ''the plumbing, heating, ventilation, gas, and electrical systems'' in a person's home, investigate the back rooms of his workplace, or poke through the charred remains of his gutted garage, but not before they may hold him in indefinite involuntary isolation at the Nation's border to investigate whether he might be engaged in criminal wrongdoing. No less than those who conduct administrative searches, those charged with investigative duties at the border ''should not be the sole judges of when to utilize constitutionally sensitive means in pursuing their tasks,'' because ''unreviewed executive discretion may yield too readily to pressures to obtain incriminating evidence and overlook potential invasions of privacy.'' And unlike administrative searches, which typically involve ''relatively limited invasion[s]'' of individual privacy interests, many border searches carry grave potential for ''arbitrary and oppressive interference by enforcement officials with the privacy and personal security of individuals.'' The conditions of De Hernandez' detention in this case—indefinite confinement in a squalid back room cut off from the outside world, the absence of basic amenities that would have been provided to even the vilest of hardened criminals, repeated strip searches—in many ways surpassed the conditions of a full custodial arrest. Although the Court previously has declined to require a warrant for border searches involving ''minor interference with privacy resulting from the mere stop for questioning,'' surely there is no parallel between such ''minor'' intrusions and the extreme invasion of personal privacy and dignity that occurs in detentions and searches such as that before us today.

Moreover, the available evidence suggests that the number of highly intrusive border searches of suspicious-looking but ultimately innocent travelers may be very high. One physician who at the request of customs officials conducted many ''internal searches''—rectal and vaginal examinations and stomach pumping—estimated that he had found contraband in only 15 to 20 percent of the persons he had examined. It has similarly been estimated that only 16 percent of women subjected to body-cavity searches at the border were in fact found to be carrying contraband. It is precisely to minimize the risk of harassing so many innocent people that the Fourth Amendment requires the intervention of a judicial officer.

The Court supports its evasion of the warrant requirement, however, by analogizing to the *Terry* line of cases authorizing brief detentions based on reasonable suspicion. It argues that no "hard-and-fast time limits" can apply in this context because "alimentary canal smuggling cannot be detected in the amount of time in which other illegal activity may be investigated through brief *Terry*-type stops." I have previously set forth my views on the proper scope and duration of *Terry* stops, and need not repeat those views in detail today. It is enough for present purposes to note that today's opinion is the most extraordinary example to date of the Court's studied effort to employ the *Terry* decision as a means of converting the Fourth Amendment into a general "reasonableness" balancing process — a process "in which the judicial thumb apparently will be planted firmly on the law enforcement side of the scales." We previously have emphasized that *Terry* allows the authorities *briefly* to detain an individual for investigation and questioning, but that "any *further detention* or search must be based on consent or probable cause." *Brignoni-Ponce* (emphasis added). Allowing such warrantless detentions under *Terry* suggests that the authorities might hold a person on suspicion for "however long it takes" to get him to cooperate, or to transport him to the station where the "legitimate" state interests more fully can be pursued, or simply to lock him away while deciding what the State's "legitimate" interests require. But the Fourth Amendment flatly prohibits such "wholesale intrusions upon the personal security" of individuals, and any application of *Terry* even by analogy to permit such indefinite detentions "would threaten to swallow" the basic probable-cause and warrant safeguards. *Dunaway*. It is simply staggering that the Court suggests that *Terry* would even begin to sanction a *27-hour criminal-investigative detention*, even one occurring at the border.

The Court argues, however, that the length and "discomfort" of De Hernandez' detention "resulted *solely* from the method by which she chose to smuggle illicit drugs into this country," and it speculates that only her "heroic" efforts prevented the detention from being brief and to the point. (emphasis added). Although we now know that De Hernandez was indeed guilty of smuggling drugs internally, such *post hoc* rationalizations have no place in our Fourth Amendment jurisprudence, which demands that we "prevent hindsight from coloring the evaluation of the reasonableness of a search or seizure."

At the time the authorities simply had, at most, a reasonable suspicion that De Hernandez might be engaged in such smuggling. Neither the law of the land nor the law of nature supports the notion that petty government officials can require people to excrete on command; indeed, the Court relies elsewhere on "[t]he rudimentary knowledge of the human body" in sanctioning the "much longer than . . . typical" duration of detentions such as this. And, with all respect to the Court, it is not "unrealistic second-guessing," to predict that an innocent traveler, locked away in incommunicado detention in unfamiliar surroundings in a foreign land, might well be so frightened and exhausted as to be unable so to "cooperate" with the authorities.[30]

The Court further appears to believe that such investigative practices are "reasonable," however, on the premise that a traveler's "expectation of privacy [is] less at the border than in the interior." This may well be so with respect to routine border inspections, but I do not imagine that decent and law-abiding international travelers have yet reached the point where they "expect" to be thrown into locked rooms and ordered to excrete into wastebaskets, held incommunicado until they cooperate, or led away in handcuffs to the nearest hospital for exposure to various medical procedures — all on nothing more than the "reasonable" suspicions of low-ranking enforcement agents. In fact, many people from around the world travel to our borders precisely to escape such unchecked executive investigatory discretion. What a curious first lesson in American liberty awaits them on their arrival.

## II

Contrary to the Court's reasoning the Government in carrying out immigration and customs functions does not simply have the two stark alternatives

---

[30] As De Hernandez' counsel observed at argument: "What if an innocent traveler just because they have had a long flight was unable to excrete and found themselves in a position where a border agent said well, we wish you to excrete [on] command so that we will be sure that you're not carrying anything internally. An innocent person might be unable to do that on command, and it wouldn't be heroic efforts in that case. . . . It's certainly possible that a person who is nervous or afraid anyway because they are being confined would be unable to excrete for a lengthy period of time, but that wouldn't necessarily mean evidence of guilt."

of either forcing a traveler to submit to such procedures or allowing him to "pass . . . into the interior." There is a third alternative: to instruct the traveler who refuses to submit to burdensome conditions of entry that he is free to turn around and leave the country. In fact, I believe that the "reasonableness" of any burdensome requirement for entry is necessarily conditioned on the potential entrant's freedom to leave the country if he objects to that requirement. Surely the Government's manifest interest in preventing potentially excludable individuals carrying potential contraband from crossing our borders is fully vindicated if those individuals voluntarily decided not to cross the borders.

This does not, of course, mean that such individuals are not fully subject to the criminal laws while on American soil. If there is probable cause to believe they have violated the law, they may be arrested just like any other person within our borders. And if there is "reasonable suspicion" to believe they may be engaged in such violations, they may briefly be detained pursuant to *Terry* for further investigation, subject to the same limitations and conditions governing *Terry* stops anywhere else in the country. But if such *Terry* suspicion does not promptly ripen into probable cause, such travelers must be given a meaningful choice: either agree to further detention as a condition of eventual entry, or leave the country.

The Government disagrees. We were advised at oral argument that it "definitely" is the policy of customs authorities "not to allow such people, if they're reasonably suspected of drug smuggling, to return before that suspicion can be checked out" and that, whether citizen, resident alien, or alien, "[w]e would not simply let them go back." The result is to sanction an authoritarian twilight zone on the border. The suspicious-looking traveler may not enter the country. Nor may he leave. Instead, he is trapped on the border. Because he is on American soil, he is fully subject "to the criminal enforcement powers of the Federal Government." But notwithstanding that he is on American soil, he is not fully protected by the guarantees of the Bill of Rights applicable everywhere else in the country. To be sure, a watered-down "reasonableness" requirement will technically govern such detentions, but it will accommodate itself to assaults on privacy and personal autonomy that would not for one moment pass constitutional muster anywhere else in the country and that would surely provide grounds for an open-and-shut damages action for violations of basic civil rights if conducted anywhere but on the border.

Nothing in the underlying premises of the "border exception" supports such a ring of unbridled

authoritarianism surrounding freedom's soil. If the traveler does not wish to consent to prolonged detentions or intrusive examinations, the Nation's customs and immigration interests are fully served by sending the traveler on his way elsewhere. If the authorities nevertheless propose to detain the traveler for purposes of subjecting him to criminal investigation and possible arrest and punishment, they may do so only pursuant to constitutional safeguards applicable to everyone else in the country.[37] Chief among those safeguards is the requirement that, except in limited circumstances not present here, custodial detentions occur only on probable cause. The probable-cause standard rests on "a practical, nontechnical conception affording the best compromise that has been found for accommodating" the "often opposing" interests of law enforcement and individual liberty. That standard obviously is not met, and was not met here, simply by courier profiles, "common rumor or report, suspicion, or even 'strong reason to suspect.'" Because the contraband in this case was the fruit of the authorities' indefinite detention of Rosa de Hernandez without probable cause or a warrant, I would affirm the judgment of the Court of Appeals for the Ninth Circuit reversing her conviction.

### III

In my opinion, allowing the Government to hold someone in indefinite, involuntary, incommunicado isolation without probable cause and a judicial warrant violates our constitutional charter whether the purpose is to extract ransom or to investigate suspected criminal activity. Nothing in the Fourth Amendment permits an exception for such actions at the Nation's border. It is tempting, of course,

---

[37] The Government argues that giving a traveler the option of leaving the country rather than being forced to undergo lengthy custodial criminal investigations based on mere suspicion "is an unsatisfactory alternative because it would allow the suspect to escape apprehension and return to repeat his smuggling efforts another day. In addition, this approach would remove a disincentive to smuggling activity by materially reducing the risk of apprehension and prosecution." This is exactly the same argument made whenever courts enforce the safeguards of the Fourth Amendment, and we have consistently stressed that if constitutionally permissible investigative stops do not promptly uncover sufficient evidence to support an arrest, the detainee must be released as a necessary consequence of constitutional liberty.

to look the other way in a case that so graphically illustrates the "veritable national crisis" caused by narcotics trafficking. But if there is one enduring lesson in the long struggle to balance individual rights against society's need to defend itself against lawlessness, it is that "[i]t is easy to make light of insistence on scrupulous regard for the safeguards of civil liberties when invoked on behalf of the unworthy. It is too easy. History bears testimony that by such disregard are the rights of liberty extinguished, heedlessly at first, then stealthily, and brazenly in the end."

## QUESTIONS AND NOTES

**1.** Was the procedure in *Montoya de Hernandez* more or less invasive than the procedure in *Winston*? Explain.

**2.** Should the unnecessary humiliation, *e.g.,* no phone calls, handcuffs to go to the hospital, etc., have been a factor in assessing the reasonableness of the seizure?

**3.** Is the Court really sustaining a 24 hour seizure on the basis of *Terry*? If so, are *Royer* and *Place* truly reconcilable?

**4.** Would (should) the result have been different if Montoya de Hernandez were a United States citizen? Why? Why not?

**5.** Should Montoya de Hernandez be deemed responsible for her own humiliation because of the manner in which she chose to degrade herself?

**6.** If the Brennan position had prevailed, would the "war on drugs" have been compromised significantly? Explain.

## F.   The Fourth Amendment Beyond Our Borders

We conclude this chapter with a look at the Fourth Amendment as applied to searches of an alien's home in the alien's country. *Verdugo-Urquidez* presents five different opinions. Which one best captures the spirit of the Fourth Amendment?

### United States v. Verdugo-Urquidez
#### 494 U.S. 259 (1990)

Chief Justice REHNQUIST delivered the opinion of the Court.

The question presented by this case is whether the Fourth Amendment applies to the search and seizure by United States agents of property that is owned by a nonresident alien and located in a foreign country. We hold that it does not.

Respondent Rene Martin Verdugo-Urquidez is a citizen and resident of Mexico. He is believed by the United States Drug Enforcement Agency (DEA) to be one of the leaders of a large and violent organization in Mexico that smuggles narcotics into the United States. Based on a complaint charging respondent with various narcotics-related offenses, the

Government obtained a warrant for his arrest on August 3, 1985. In January 1986, Mexican police officers, after discussions with United States Marshals, apprehended Verdugo-Urquidez in Mexico and transported him to the United States Border Patrol station in Calexico, California. There, United States Marshals arrested respondent and eventually moved him to a correctional center in San Diego, California, where he remains incarcerated pending trial.

Following respondent's arrest, Terry Bowen, a DEA agent assigned to the Calexico DEA office, decided to arrange for searches of Verdugo-Urquidez's Mexican residences located in Mexicali and San Felipe. Bowen believed that the searches would reveal evidence related to respondent's alleged narcotics trafficking activities and his involvement in the kidnaping and torture-murder of DEA Special Agent Enrique Camarena Salazar (for which respondent subsequently has been convicted in a separate prosecution). Bowen telephoned Walter White, the Assistant Special Agent in charge of the DEA office in Mexico City, and asked him to seek authorization for the search from the Director General of the Mexican Federal Judicial Police (MFJP). After several attempts to reach high ranking Mexican officials, White eventually contacted the Director General, who authorized the searches and promised the cooperation of Mexican authorities. Thereafter, DEA agents working in concert with officers of the MFJP searched respondent's properties in Mexicali and San Felipe and seized certain documents. In particular, the search of the Mexicali residence uncovered a tally sheet, which the government believes reflects the quantities of marijuana smuggled by Verdugo-Urquidez into the United States.

Before analyzing the scope of the Fourth Amendment, we think it significant to note that it operates in a different manner than the Fifth Amendment, which is not at issue in this case. The privilege against self-incrimination guaranteed by the Fifth Amendment is a fundamental trial right of criminal defendants. Although conduct by law enforcement officials prior to trial may ultimately impair that right, a constitutional violation occurs only at trial. The Fourth Amendment functions differently. It prohibits "unreasonable searches and seizures" whether or not the evidence is sought to be used in a criminal trial, and a violation of the Amendment is "fully accomplished" at the time of an unreasonable governmental intrusion. For purposes of this case, therefore, if there were a constitutional violation, it occurred solely in Mexico. Whether evidence obtained from respondent's Mexican residences should be excluded at trial in the United States is a remedial question separate from the existence *vel non* of the constitutional violation.

The Fourth Amendment provides that:

> "[t]he right of the people to be secure in their persons, houses, papers, and effects, against unreasonable searches and seizures, shall not be violated, and no Warrants shall issue, but upon probable cause, supported by Oath or affirmation, and particularly describing the place to be searched, and the persons or things to be seized."

That text, by contrast with the Fifth and Sixth Amendments, extends its reach only to "the people." Contrary to the suggestion of *amici curiae* that the Framers used this phrase "simply to avoid [an] awkward rhetorical redundancy," "the people" seems to have been a term of art employed in select parts of the Constitution. The Preamble declares that the Constitution is ordained and established by "the People of the United States." The Second Amendment protects "the right of the people to keep and bear Arms," and the Ninth and Tenth Amendments provide that certain rights and powers are retained by and reserved to "the people." See also U.S. Const., Amdt. 1, ("Congress shall make no law . . . abridging . . . *the right of the people* peaceably to assemble"); Art. I, § 2, cl. 1 ("The House of Representatives shall be composed of Members chosen every second Year *by the People of the several States*") (emphasis added). While this textual exegesis is by no means conclusive, it suggests that "the people" protected by the Fourth Amendment, and by the First and Second Amendments, and to whom rights and powers are reserved in the Ninth and Tenth Amendments, refers to a class of persons who are part of a national community or who have otherwise developed sufficient connection with this country to be considered part of that community. The language of these Amendments contrasts with the words "person" and "accused" used in the Fifth and Sixth Amendments regulating procedure in criminal cases.

What we know of the history of the drafting of the Fourth Amendment also suggests that its purpose was to restrict searches and seizures which might be conducted by the United States in domestic matters. The Framers originally decided not to include a provision like the Fourth Amendment, because they believed the National Government lacked power to conduct searches and seizures. Many disputed the original view that the Federal Government possessed only narrow delegated powers over domestic affairs, however, and ultimately felt an Amendment prohibiting unreasonable searches and seizures was necessary. Madison, for example, argued that "there is a clause granting to Congress the power to make all laws which shall be necessary and proper for carrying into execution all of the powers vested in the Government of the United States," and that general warrants might be considered "necessary" for the purpose of collecting revenue. The driving force behind the adoption of the Amendment, as suggested by Madison's advocacy, was widespread hostility among the former Colonists to the issuance of writs of assistance empowering revenue officers to search suspected places for smuggled goods, and general search warrants permitting the search of private houses, often to uncover papers that might be used to convict persons of libel. The available historical data show, therefore, that the purpose of the Fourth Amendment was to protect the people of the United States against arbitrary action by their own Government; it was never suggested that the provision was intended to restrain the actions of the Federal Government against aliens outside of the United States territory.

Verdugo-Urquidez relies on a series of cases in which we have held that aliens enjoy certain constitutional rights. These cases, however, establish only that aliens receive constitutional protections when they have come within the territory of the United States and developed substantial connections with this country. Respondent is an alien who has had no previous significant voluntary connection with the United States, so these cases avail him not.

Justice Stevens' concurrence in the judgment takes the view that even though the search took place in Mexico, it is nonetheless governed by the requirements of the Fourth Amendment because respondent was "lawfully present in the United States . . . even though he was brought and held here against his will." But this sort of presence—lawful but involuntary—is not of the sort to indicate any substantial connection with our country. The extent to which respondent might claim the protection of the Fourth Amendment if the duration of his stay in the United States were to be prolonged—by a prison sentence, for example—we need not decide. When the search of his house in Mexico took place, he had been present in the United States for only a matter of days. We do not think the applicability of the Fourth Amendment to the search of premises in Mexico should turn on the fortuitous circumstance of whether the custodian of its nonresident alien owner had or had not transported him to the United States at the time the search was made.

The Court of Appeals found some support for its holding in our decision in *INS v. Lopez-Mendoza*, where a majority of Justices assumed that the Fourth Amendment applied to illegal aliens in the United States. We cannot fault the Court of Appeals for placing some reliance on the case, but our decision did not expressly address the proposition gleaned by the court below. Even assuming such aliens would be entitled to Fourth Amendment protections, their situation is different from respondent's. The illegal aliens in *Lopez-Mendoza* were in the United States voluntarily and presumably had accepted some societal obligations; but respondent had no voluntary connection with this country that might place him among "the people" of the United States.

Were respondent to prevail, aliens with no attachment to this country might well bring actions for damages to remedy claimed violations of the Fourth Amendment in foreign countries or in international waters. The Members of the Executive and Legislative Branches are sworn to uphold the Constitution, and they presumably desire to follow its commands. But the Court of Appeals' global view of its applicability would plunge them into a sea of uncertainty as to what might be reasonable in the way of searches and seizures conducted abroad. Indeed, the Court of Appeals held that absent exigent circumstances, United States agents could not effect a "search or seizure" for law enforcement purposes in a foreign country without first obtaining a warrant—which would be a dead letter outside the United States—from a magistrate in this country. Even if no warrant were required, American agents would have to articulate specific facts giving them probable cause to undertake a search or seizure if they wished to comply with the Fourth Amendment as conceived by the Court of Appeals.

We think that the text of the Fourth Amendment, its history, and our cases discussing the application of the Constitution to aliens and extraterritorially require rejection of respondent's claim. At the time of the search, he was a citizen and resident of Mexico with no voluntary attachment to the United States, and the place searched was located in Mexico. Under these circumstances, the Fourth Amendment has no application.

For better or for worse, we live in a world of nation-states in which our Government must be able to "functio[n] effectively in the company of sovereign nations." Some who violate our laws may live outside our borders under a regime quite different from that which obtains in this country. Situations threatening to important American interests may arise half-way around the globe, situations which in the view of the political branches of our Government require an American response with armed force. If there are to be restrictions on searches and seizures which occur incident to such American action, they must be imposed by the political branches through diplomatic understanding, treaty, or legislation.

The judgment of the Court of Appeals is accordingly reversed.

Justice KENNEDY, concurring.

I agree that no violation of the Fourth Amendment has occurred and that we must reverse the judgment of the Court of Appeals. Although some explanation of my views is appropriate given the difficulties of this case, I do not believe they depart in fundamental respects from the opinion of the Court, which I join.

I cannot place any weight on the reference to "the people" in the Fourth Amendment as a source of restricting its protections. With respect, I submit these words do not detract from its force or its reach. Given the history of our Nation's concern over warrantless and unreasonable searches, explicit recognition of "the right of the people" to Fourth Amendment protection may be interpreted to underscore the importance of the right, rather than to restrict the category of persons who may assert it. The restrictions that the United States must observe with reference to aliens beyond its territory or jurisdiction depend, as a consequence, on general principles of interpretation, not on an inquiry as to who formed the Constitution or a construction that some rights are mentioned as being those of "the people."

The conditions and considerations of this case would make adherence to the Fourth Amendment's warrant requirement impracticable and anomalous. Just as the Constitution in the *Insular Cases* did not require Congress to implement all constitutional guarantees in its territories because of their "wholly dissimilar traditions and institutions," the Constitution does not require United States agents to obtain a warrant when searching the foreign home of a nonresident alien. If the search had occurred in a residence within the United States, I have little doubt that the full protections of the Fourth Amendment would apply. But that is not this case. The absence of local judges or magistrates available to issue warrants, the differing and perhaps unascertainable conceptions of reasonableness and privacy that prevail abroad, and the need to cooperate with foreign officials all indicate that the Fourth Amendment's warrant requirement should not apply in Mexico as it does in this country. For this reason, in addition to the other persuasive justifications stated by the Court, I agree that no violation of the Fourth Amendment has occurred in the case before us. The rights of a citizen, as to whom the United States has continuing obligations, are not presented by this case.

I do not mean to imply, and the Court has not decided, that persons in the position of the respondent have no constitutional protection. The United States is prosecuting a foreign national in a court established under Article III, and all of the trial proceedings are governed by the Constitution. All would agree, for instance, that the dictates of the Due Process Clause of the Fifth Amendment protect the defendant. Indeed, as Justice Harlan put it, "the question of which specific safeguards . . . are appropriately to be applied in a particular context . . . can be reduced to the issue of what process is 'due' a defendant in the particular circumstances of a particular case." Nothing approaching a violation of due process has occurred in this case.

Justice STEVENS, concurring in judgment.

In my opinion aliens who are lawfully present in the United States are among those "people" who are entitled to the protection of the Bill of Rights, including the Fourth Amendment. Respondent is surely such a person even though he was brought and held here against his will. I therefore cannot join the Court's sweeping opinion.* I do agree, however, with the Government's submission that the search conducted by the United States agents with the approval and cooperation of the Mexican authorities was not "unreasonable" as that term is used in the first clause of the Amendment. I do not believe the Warrant Clause has any application to searches of noncitizens' homes in foreign jurisdictions because American magistrates have no power to authorize such searches. I therefore concur in the Court's judgment.

Justice BRENNAN, with whom Justice MARSHALL join, dissenting.

Today the Court holds that although foreign nationals must abide by our laws even when in their own countries, our Government need not abide by the Fourth Amendment when it investigates them for violations of our laws. I respectfully dissent.

I

Particularly in the past decade, our Government has sought, successfully, to hold foreign nationals criminally liable under federal laws for conduct committed entirely beyond the territorial limits of the United States that nevertheless has effects in this country. Foreign nationals must now take care not to violate our drug laws, our antitrust laws, our securities laws, and a host of other federal criminal statutes. The enormous expansion of federal criminal jurisdiction outside our Nation's boundaries has led one commentator to suggest that our country's three largest exports are now "rock music, blue jeans, and United States law."

A

The Fourth Amendment guarantees the right of "the people" to be free from unreasonable searches

---

* The Court's interesting historical discussion is simply irrelevant to the question whether an alien lawfully within the sovereign territory of the United States is entitled to the protection of our laws. Nor is comment on illegal aliens' entitlement to the protections of the Fourth Amendment necessary to resolve this case.

and seizures and provides that a warrant shall issue only upon presentation of an oath or affirmation demonstrating probable cause and particularly describing the place to be searched and the persons or things to be seized. According to the majority, the term "the people" refers to "a class of persons who are part of a national community or who have otherwise developed sufficient connection with this country to be considered part of that community." The Court admits that "the people" extends beyond the citizenry, but leaves the precise contours of its "sufficient connection" test unclear. At one point the majority hints that aliens are protected by the Fourth Amendment only when they come within the United States and develop "substantial connections" with our country. At other junctures, the Court suggests that an alien's presence in the United States must be voluntary and that the alien must have "accepted some societal obligations." At yet other points, the majority implies that respondent would be protected by the Fourth Amendment if the place searched were in the United States.[7]

What the majority ignores, however, is the most obvious connection between Verdugo-Urquidez and the United States: he was investigated and is being prosecuted for violations of United States law and may well spend the rest of his life in a United States prison. The "sufficient connection" is supplied not by Verdugo-Urquidez, but by the Government. Respondent is entitled to the protections of the Fourth Amendment because our Government, by investigating him and attempting to hold him accountable under United States criminal laws, has treated him as a member of our community for purposes of enforcing our laws. He has become, quite literally, one of the governed. Fundamental fairness and the ideals underlying our Bill of Rights compel the conclusion that when we impose "societal obligations," such as the obligation to comply with our criminal laws, on foreign nationals, we in turn are obliged to respect certain correlative rights, among them the Fourth Amendment.

By concluding that respondent is not one of "the people" protected by the Fourth Amendment, the majority disregards basic notions of mutuality. If we expect aliens to obey our laws, aliens should be able to expect that we will obey our Constitution when we investigate, prosecute, and punish them. We have recognized this fundamental principle of mutuality since the time of the Framers. James Madison, universally recognized as the primary architect of the Bill of Rights, emphasized the importance of mutuality when he spoke out against the Alien and Sedition Acts less than a decade after the adoption of the Fourth Amendment:

> "[I]t does not follow, because aliens are not parties to the Constitution, as citizens are parties to it, that, whilst they actually conform to it, they have no right to its protection. Aliens are no more parties to the laws than they are parties to the Constitution; yet it will not be disputed that, as they owe, on one hand, a temporary obedience, they are entitled, in return, to their protection and advantage." Madison's Report on the Virginia Resolutions (1800), reprinted in 4 Elliot's Debates 556 (2d ed. 1836).

Mutuality serves to inculcate the values of law and order. By respecting the rights of foreign nationals, we encourage other nations to respect the rights of our citizens. Moreover, as our Nation becomes increasingly concerned about the domestic effects of international crime, we cannot forget that the behavior of our law enforcement agents abroad sends a powerful message about the rule of law to individuals everywhere. As Justice Brandeis warned in *Olmstead v. United States*, 277 U.S. 438 (1928):

> "If the Government becomes a lawbreaker, it breeds contempt for law; it invites every man to become a law unto himself; it invites anarchy. To declare that in the administration of the criminal law the end justifies the means . . . would bring terrible retribution. Against that pernicious doctrine, this Court should resolutely set its face." (dissenting opinion).

---

[7] The Fourth Amendment contains no express or implied territorial limitations, and the majority does not hold that the Fourth Amendment is inapplicable to searches outside the United States and its territories. It holds that respondent is not protected by the Fourth Amendment because he is not one of "the people." Indeed, the majority's analysis implies that a foreign national who had "developed sufficient connection with this country to be considered part of [our] community" would be protected by the Fourth Amendment regardless of the location of the search. Certainly nothing in the Court's opinion questions the validity of the rule, accepted by every Court of Appeals to have considered the question, that the Fourth Amendment applies to searches conducted by the United States Government against United States citizens abroad. A warrantless, unreasonable search and seizure is no less a violation of the Fourth Amendment because it occurs in Mexicali, Mexico, rather than Calexico, California.

This principle is no different when the United States applies its rules of conduct to foreign nationals. If we seek respect for law and order, we must observe these principles ourselves. Lawlessness breeds lawlessness.

Finally, when United States agents conduct unreasonable searches, whether at home or abroad, they disregard our Nation's values. For over 200 years, our country has considered itself the world's foremost protector of liberties. The privacy and sanctity of the home have been primary tenets of our moral, philosophical, and judicial beliefs. Our national interest is defined by those values and by the need to preserve our own just institutions. We take pride in our commitment to a government that cannot, on mere whim, break down doors and invade the most personal of places. We exhort other nations to follow our example. How can we explain to others—and to ourselves—that these long cherished ideals are suddenly of no consequence when the door being broken belongs to a foreigner?

### B

In its effort to establish that respondent does not have sufficient connection to the United States to be considered one of "the people" protected by the Fourth Amendment, the Court relies on the text of the Amendment, historical evidence, and cases refusing to apply certain constitutional provisions outside the United States. None of these, however, justifies the majority's cramped interpretation of the Fourth Amendment's applicability.

The majority looks to various constitutional provisions and suggests that "'the people' seems to have been a term of art." But the majority admits that its "textual exegesis is by no means conclusive."[9] One Member of the majority even states that he "cannot place any weight on the reference to 'the

---

[9] The majority places an unsupportable reliance on the fact that the drafters used "the people" in the Fourth Amendment while using "person" and "accused" in the Fifth and Sixth Amendments respectively. The drafters purposely did not use the term "accused." As the majority recognizes, the Fourth Amendment is violated at the time of an unreasonable governmental intrusion, even if the victim of unreasonable governmental action is never formally "accused" of any wrongdoing. The majority's suggestion that the drafters could have used "person" ignores the fact that the Fourth Amendment then would have begun quite awkwardly: "The right of persons to be secure in their persons. . . ."

people' in the Fourth Amendment as a source of restricting its protections." (Kennedy, J., concurring). The majority suggests a restrictive interpretation of those with "sufficient connection" to this country to be considered among "the people," but the term "the people" is better understood as a rhetorical counterpoint to "the government," such that rights that were reserved to "the people" were to protect all those subject to "the government." "The people" are "the governed."

### C

The majority's rejection of respondent's claim to Fourth Amendment protection is apparently motivated by its fear that application of the Amendment to law enforcement searches against foreign nationals overseas "could significantly disrupt the ability of the political branches to respond to foreign situations involving our national interest." The majority's doomsday scenario—that American Armed Forces conducting a mission to protect our national security with no law enforcement objective "would have to articulate specific facts giving them probable cause to undertake a search or seizure,"—is fanciful. Verdugo-Urquidez is protected by the Fourth Amendment because our Government, by investigating and prosecuting him, has made him one of "the governed." Accepting respondent as one of "the governed," however, hardly requires the Court to accept enemy aliens in wartime as among "the governed" entitled to invoke the protection of the Fourth Amendment.

Moreover, with respect to non-law-enforcement activities not directed against enemy aliens in wartime but nevertheless implicating national security, doctrinal exceptions to the general requirements of a warrant and probable cause likely would be applicable more frequently abroad, thus lessening the purported tension between the Fourth Amendment's strictures and the Executive's foreign affairs power. Many situations involving sensitive operations abroad likely would involve exigent circumstances such that the warrant requirement would be excused. Therefore, the Government's conduct would be assessed only under the reasonableness standard, the application of which depends on context.

In addition, where the precise contours of a "reasonable" search and seizure are unclear, the Executive Branch will not be "plunge[d] . . . into a sea of uncertainty" that will impair materially its ability to conduct foreign affairs. Doctrines such as official immunity have long protected Government agents from any undue chill on the exercise of lawful discretion. Similarly, the Court has recognized that there may be certain situations in which the offensive use of constitutional rights should be limited. In most cases implicating foreign policy concerns in which the reasonableness of an overseas search or seizure is unclear, application of the Fourth Amendment will not interfere with the Executive's traditional prerogative in foreign affairs because a court will have occasion to decide the constitutionality of such a search only if *the Executive* decides to bring a criminal prosecution and introduce evidence seized abroad. When the Executive decides to conduct a search as part of an ongoing criminal investigation, fails to get a warrant, and then seeks to introduce the fruits of that search at trial, however, the courts must enforce the Constitution.

## II

Because the Fourth Amendment governs the search of respondent's Mexican residences, the District Court properly suppressed the evidence found in that search because the officers conducting the search did not obtain a warrant. I cannot agree with Justice Blackmun and Justice Stevens that the Warrant Clause has no application to searches of noncitizens' homes in foreign jurisdictions because American magistrates lack the power to authorize such searches. The Warrant Clause would serve the same primary functions abroad as it does domestically, and I see no reason to distinguish between foreign and domestic searches.

The Warrant Clause cannot be ignored simply because Congress has not given any United States magistrate authority to issue search warrants for foreign searches. Congress cannot define the contours of the Constitution. If the Warrant Clause applies, Congress cannot excise the Clause from the Constitution by failing to provide a means for United States agents to obtain a warrant.

Nor is the Warrant Clause inapplicable merely because a warrant from a United States magistrate could not "authorize" a search in a foreign country. Although this may be true as a matter of international law, it is irrelevant to our interpretation of the Fourth Amendment. As a matter of United States constitutional law, a warrant serves the same primary function overseas as it does domestically: it assures that a neutral magistrate has authorized the search and limited its scope. The need to protect those suspected of criminal activity from the unbridled discretion of

investigating officers is no less important abroad than at home.

## III

Justice BLACKMUN, dissenting.

I cannot accept the Court of Appeals' conclusion, echoed in some portions of Justice Brennan's dissent, that the Fourth Amendment governs every action by an American official that can be characterized as a search or seizure. American agents acting abroad generally do not purport to exercise *sovereign* authority over the foreign nationals with whom they come in contact. The relationship between these agents and foreign nationals is therefore fundamentally different from the relationship between United States officials and individuals residing within this country.

I am inclined to agree with Justice Brennan, however, that when a foreign national is held accountable for purported violations of United States criminal laws, he has effectively been treated as one of "the governed" and therefore is entitled to Fourth Amendment protections. Although the Government's exercise of *power* abroad does not ordinarily implicate the Fourth Amendment, the enforcement of domestic criminal law seems to me to be the paradigmatic exercise of sovereignty over those who are compelled to obey. In any event, as Justice Stevens notes, respondent was lawfully (though involuntarily) within this country at the time the search occurred. Under these circumstances I believe that respondent is entitled to invoke protections of the Fourth Amendment. I agree with the Government, however, that an American magistrate's lack of power to authorize a search abroad renders the Warrant Clause inapplicable to the search of a noncitizen's residence outside this country.

The Fourth Amendment nevertheless requires that the search be "reasonable." And when the purpose of a search is the procurement of evidence for a criminal prosecution, we have consistently held that the search, to be reasonable, must be based upon probable cause. Neither the District Court nor the Court of Appeals addressed the issue of probable cause, and I do not believe that a reliable determination could be made on the basis of the record before us. I therefore would vacate the judgment of the Court of Appeals and remand the case for further proceedings.

## QUESTIONS AND NOTES

**1.** Does a majority of the Court believe that Verdugo-Urquidez is not one of the people protected by the Fourth Amendment? Explain.

**2.** Do you think that he should be one of "the people" protected by the Fourth Amendment? Why? Why not?

**3.** How does Chief Justice Rehnquist perceive the Fourth Amendment to be different from the Fifth and Sixth Amendments? Do you agree with that distinction? Explain.

**4.** If a United States magistrate lacks power to issue a warrant in Mexico, why should we expect Government officials to seek one (as Brennan suggests)?

**5.** *Could* Congress authorize a magistrate to issue a warrant for the search of a Mexican house? Why? Why not?

**6.** With which of the opinions, if any, did you agree? Explain.

# 9.

# SEIZURES

Heretofore, we have assumed that we have been dealing with a search or seizure, and have sought to determine the circumstances under which that search or seizure was justified. In this chapter (seizure) and the next (search), we shall attempt to define those terms. The question is significant, because if the police conduct does not constitute a search or seizure, the Fourth Amendment is not implicated. A good place to begin our analysis of the concept of "seizure" is Justice Stewart's opinion (for only himself and Justice Rehnquist) in *Mendenhall*.

## United States v. Mendenhall
446 U.S. 544 (1980)

Mr. Justice STEWART delivered the opinion of the Court with respect to parts I, II-B, II-C, and III, concluding:

### I

The respondent arrived at the Detroit Metropolitan Airport on a commercial airline flight from Los Angeles early in the morning on February 10, 1976. As she disembarked from the airplane, she was observed by two agents of the DEA, who were present at the airport for the purpose of detecting unlawful traffic in narcotics. After observing the respondent's conduct, which appeared to the agents to be characteristic of persons unlawfully carrying narcotics,[1] the agents approached her as she was walking through the concourse, identified themselves as federal agents, and asked to see her identification and airline ticket. The respondent produced her driver's license, which was in the name of Sylvia Mendenhall, and, in answer to a question of one of the agents, stated

the agents thought it relevant that (1) the respondent was arriving on a flight from Los Angeles, a city believed by the agents to be the place of origin for much of the heroin brought to Detroit; (2) the respondent was the last person to leave the plane, "appeared to be very nervous," and "completely scanned the whole area where [the agents] were standing"; (3) after leaving the plane the respondent proceeded past the baggage area without claiming any luggage; and (4) the respondent changed airlines for her flight out of Detroit.

---

[1] The agent testified that the respondent's behavior fit the so-called "drug courier profile" — an informally compiled abstract of characteristics thought typical of persons carrying illicit drugs. In this case

that she resided at the address appearing on the license. The airline ticket was issued in the name of "Annette Ford." When asked why the ticket bore a name different from her own, the respondent stated that she "just felt like using that name." In response to a further question, the respondent indicated that she had been in California only two days. Agent Anderson then specifically identified himself as a federal narcotics agent and, according to his testimony, the respondent "became quite shaken, extremely nervous. She had a hard time speaking."

After returning the airline ticket and driver's license to her, Agent Anderson asked the respondent if she would accompany him to the airport DEA office for further questions. She did so, although the record does not indicate a verbal response to the request. The office, which was located up one flight of stairs about 50 feet from where the respondent had first been approached, consisted of a reception area adjoined by three other rooms. At the office the agent asked the respondent if she would allow a search of her person and handbag and told her that she had the right to decline the search if she desired. She responded: "Go ahead." She then handed Agent Anderson her purse, which contained a receipt for an airline ticket that had been issued to "F. Bush" three days earlier for a flight from Pittsburgh through Chicago to Los Angeles. The agent asked whether this was the ticket that she had used for her flight to California, and the respondent stated that it was.

A female police officer then arrived to conduct the search of the respondent's person. She asked the agents if the respondent had consented to be searched. The agents said that she had, and the respondent followed the policewoman into a private room. There the policewoman again asked the respondent if she consented to the search, and the respondent replied that she did. The policewoman explained that the search would require that the respondent remove her clothing. The respondent stated that she had a plane to catch and was assured by the policewoman that if she were carrying no narcotics, there would be no problem. The respondent then began to disrobe without further comment. As the respondent removed her clothing, she took from her undergarments two small packages, one of which appeared to contain heroin, and handed both to the policewoman. The agents then arrested the respondent for possessing heroin.

## II

Here the Government concedes that its agents had neither a warrant nor probable cause to believe that the respondent was carrying narcotics when the agents conducted a search of the respondent's person. It is the Government's position, however, that the search was conducted pursuant to the respondent's consent, and thus was excepted from the requirements of both a warrant and probable cause. See *Schneckloth v. Bustamonte* (Chapter 12, *infra*.). Evidently, the Court of Appeals concluded that the respondent's apparent consent to the search was in fact not voluntarily given and was in any event the product of earlier official conduct violative of the Fourth Amendment. We must first consider, therefore, whether such conduct occurred, either on the concourse or in the DEA office at the airport.

### A

The distinction between an intrusion amounting to a "seizure" of the person and an encounter that intrudes upon no constitutionally protected interest is illustrated by the facts of *Terry*, which the Court recounted as follows: "Officer McFadden approached the three men, identified himself as a police officer and asked for their names. . . . When the men 'mumbled something' in response to his inquiries, Officer McFadden grabbed petitioner Terry, spun him around so that they were facing the other two, with Terry between McFadden and the others, and patted down the outside of his clothing." Obviously the officer "seized" Terry and subjected him to a "search" when he took hold of him, spun him around, and patted down the outer surfaces of his clothing. What was not determined in that case, however, was that a seizure had taken place before the officer physically restrained Terry for purposes of searching his person for weapons. The Court "assume[d] that up to that point no intrusion upon constitutionally protected rights had occurred." The Court's assumption appears entirely correct in view of the fact, noted in the concurring opinion of Mr. Justice White, that "[t]here is nothing in the Constitution which prevents a policeman from addressing questions to anyone on the streets." Police officers enjoy "the liberty (again, possessed by every citizen) to address questions to other persons" (Harlan, J., concurring), although "ordinarily the person addressed has an equal right to ignore his interrogator and walk away."

Similarly, the Court in *Sibron*, a case decided the same day as *Terry*, indicated that not every encounter between a police officer and a citizen is an intrusion requiring an objective justification. In that case, a police officer, before conducting what was later found to have been an unlawful search, approached Sibron in a restaurant and told him to come outside, which Sibron did. The Court had no occasion to decide whether there was a "seizure" of

Sibron inside the restaurant antecedent to the seizure that accompanied the search. The record was "barren of any indication whether Sibron accompanied [the officer] outside in submission to a show of force or authority which left him no choice, or *whether he went voluntarily in a spirit of apparent cooperation* with the officer's investigation." (emphasis added). Plainly, in the latter event, there was no seizure until the police officer in some way demonstrably curtailed Sibron's liberty.

We adhere to the view that a person is "seized" only when, by means of physical force or a show of authority, his freedom of movement is restrained. Only when such restraint is imposed is there any foundation whatever for invoking constitutional safeguards. The purpose of the Fourth Amendment is not to eliminate all contact between the police and the citizenry, but "to prevent arbitrary and oppressive interference by enforcement officials with the privacy and personal security of individuals." As long as the person to whom questions are put remains free to disregard the questions and walk away, there has been no intrusion upon that person's liberty or privacy as would under the Constitution require some particularized and objective justification.

Moreover, characterizing every street encounter between a citizen and the police as a "seizure," while not enhancing any interest secured by the Fourth Amendment, would impose wholly unrealistic restrictions upon a wide variety of legitimate law enforcement practices. The Court has on other occasions referred to the acknowledged need for police questioning as a tool in the effective enforcement of the criminal laws. "Without such investigation, those who were innocent might be falsely accused, those who were guilty might wholly escape prosecution, and many crimes would go unsolved. In short, the security of all would be diminished."

We conclude that a person has been "seized" within the meaning of the Fourth Amendment only if, in view of all of the circumstances surrounding the incident, a reasonable person would have believed that he was not free to leave.[6] Examples of circumstances that might indicate a seizure, even where the person did not attempt to leave, would be the threatening presence of several officers, the display of a weapon by an officer, some physical

---

[6] We agree with the District Court that the subjective intention of the DEA agent in this case to detain the respondent, had she attempted to leave, is irrelevant except insofar as that may have been conveyed to the respondent.

touching of the person of the citizen, or the use of language or tone of voice indicating that compliance with the officer's request might be compelled. In the absence of some such evidence, otherwise inoffensive contact between a member of the public and the police cannot, as a matter of law, amount to a seizure of that person.

On the facts of this case, no "seizure" of the respondent occurred. The events took place in the public concourse. The agents wore no uniforms and displayed no weapons. They did not summon the respondent to their presence, but instead approached her and identified themselves as federal agents. They requested, but did not demand to see the respondent's identification and ticket. Such conduct without more, did not amount to an intrusion upon any constitutionally protected interest. The respondent was not seized simply by reason of the fact that the agents approached her, asked her if she would show them her ticket and identification, and posed to her a few questions. Nor was it enough to establish a seizure that the person asking the questions was a law enforcement official. In short, nothing in the record suggests that the respondent had any objective reason to believe that she was not free to end the conversation in the concourse and proceed on her way, and for that reason we conclude that the agents' initial approach to her was not a seizure.

Our conclusion that no seizure occurred is not affected by the fact that the respondent was not expressly told by the agents that she was free to decline to cooperate with their inquiry, for the voluntariness of her responses does not depend upon her having been so informed. We also reject the argument that the only inference to be drawn from the fact that the respondent acted in a manner so contrary to her self-interest is that she was compelled to answer the agents' questions. It may happen that a person makes statements to law enforcement officials that he later regrets, but the issue in such cases is not whether the statement was self-protective, but rather whether it was made voluntarily.

The Court's decision last Term in *Brown v. Texas*, 443 U.S. 47, on which the respondent relies, is not apposite. It could not have been plainer under the circumstances there presented that Brown was forcibly detained by the officers. In that case, two police officers approached Brown in an alley, and asked him to identify himself and to explain his reason for being there. Brown "refused to identify himself and angrily asserted that the officers had no right to stop him." Up to this point there was no seizure. But after continuing to protest the officers' power to interrogate him, Brown was first frisked, and then arrested for violation of a state statute making it a criminal offense for a person to refuse to give his name and address to an officer "who has lawfully stopped him and requested the information." The Court simply held in that case that because the officers had no reason to suspect Brown of wrongdoing, there was no basis for detaining him, and therefore no permissible foundation for applying the state statute in the circumstances there presented.

### B

Although we have concluded that the initial encounter between the DEA agents and the respondent on the concourse at the Detroit Airport did not constitute an unlawful seizure, it is still arguable that the respondent's Fourth Amendment protections were violated when she went from the concourse to the DEA office. Such a violation might in turn infect the subsequent search of the respondent's person.

The District Court specifically found that the respondent accompanied the agents to the office "'voluntarily in a spirit of apparent cooperation,'" quoting *Sibron*. Notwithstanding this determination by the trial court, the Court of Appeals evidently concluded that the agents' request that the respondent accompany them converted the situation into an arrest requiring probable cause in order to be found lawful. But because the trial court's finding was sustained by the record, the Court of Appeals was mistaken in substituting for that finding its view of the evidence.

The question whether the respondent's consent to accompany the agents was in fact voluntary or was the product of duress or coercion, express or implied, is to be determined by the totality of all the circumstances, and is a matter which the Government has the burden of proving. The respondent herself did not testify at the hearing. The Government's evidence showed that the respondent was not told that she had to go to the office, but was simply asked if she would accompany the officers. There were neither threats nor any show of force. The respondent had been questioned only briefly, and her ticket and identification were returned to her before she was asked to accompany the officers.

On the other hand, it is argued that the incident would reasonably have appeared coercive to the respondent, who was 22 years old and had not been graduated from high school. It is additionally suggested that the respondent, a female and a Negro, may have felt unusually threatened by the officers, who were white males. While these factors were not irrelevant, neither were they decisive, and the totality of the evidence in this case was plainly adequate to support the District Court's finding that the respondent voluntarily consented to accompany the officers to the DEA office.

[The remainder of Justice Stewart's opinion is reproduced in chapter 11.]

Mr. Justice POWELL, with whom the Chief Justice and Mr. Justice BLACKMUN join, concurring in part and concurring in judgment.

I join Parts I, II-B, II-C, and III of the Court's opinion. Because neither of the courts below considered the question, I do not reach the Government's contention that the agents did not "seize" the respondent within the meaning of the Fourth Amendment. In my view, we may assume for present purposes that the stop did constitute a seizure.[1] I would hold—as did the District Court—that the federal agents had reasonable suspicion that the respondent was engaging in criminal activity, and, therefore, that they did not violate the Fourth Amendment by stopping the respondent for routine questioning.

Mr. Justice WHITE, with whom Mr. Justice BRENNAN, Mr. Justice MARSHALL, and Mr. Justice STEVENS join, dissenting.

Mr. Justice Stewart believes that a "seizure" within the meaning of the Fourth Amendment occurs when an individual's freedom of movement is restrained by means of physical force or a show of authority. Although it is undisputed that Ms. Mendenhall was not free to leave after the DEA agents stopped her and inspected her identification, Mr. Justice Stewart concludes that she was not "seized" because he finds that, under the totality of the circumstances, a reasonable person would have believed that she was free to leave. While basing this finding on an alleged absence from the record of objective evidence indicating that Ms. Mendenhall

---

[1] Mr. Justice Stewart concludes in Part II-A that there was no "seizure" within the meaning of the Fourth Amendment. He reasons that such a seizure occurs "only if, in view of all of the circumstances surrounding the incident, a reasonable person would have believed that he was not free to leave." Mr. Justice Stewart also notes that "[t]here is nothing in the Constitution which prevents a policeman from addressing questions to anyone on the streets." I do not necessarily disagree with the views expressed in Part II-A. For me, the question whether the respondent in this case reasonably could have thought she was free to "walk away" when asked by two Government agents for her driver's license and ticket is extremely close.

was not free to ignore the officer's inquiries and continue on her way, Mr. Justice Stewart's opinion brushes off the fact that this asserted evidentiary deficiency may be largely attributable to the fact that the "seizure" question was never raised below. In assessing what the record does reveal, the opinion discounts certain objective factors that would tend to support a "seizure" finding,[3] while relying on contrary factors inconclusive even under its own illustrations of how a "seizure" may be established.[4] Even if one believes the Government should be permitted to raise the "seizure" question in this Court, the proper course would be to direct a remand to the District Court for an evidentiary hearing on the question, rather than to decide it in the first instance in this Court.

### III

Whatever doubt there may be concerning whether Ms. Mendenhall's Fourth Amendment interests were implicated during the initial stages of her confrontation with the DEA agents, she undoubtedly was "seized" within the meaning of the Fourth Amendment when the agents escorted her from the public area of the terminal to the DEA office for questioning and a strip-search of her person. In *Dunaway*, we held that a person who accompanied police officers to a police station for purposes of interrogation undoubtedly "was 'seized' in the Fourth Amendment sense," even though "he was not told he was under arrest." We found it significant that the suspect was taken to a police station, "was never informed that he was 'free to go,'" and "would have been physically restrained if he had refused to accompany the officers or had tried to escape their custody." Like the "seizure" in *Dunaway*, the nature of the intrusion to which Ms. Mendenhall was subjected when she was escorted by DEA agents to

their office and detained there for questioning and a strip-search was so great that it "was in important respects indistinguishable from a traditional arrest." Although Ms. Mendenhall was not told that she was under arrest, she in fact was not free to refuse to go to the DEA office and was not told that she was.[12] Furthermore, once inside the office, Ms. Mendenhall would not have been permitted to leave without submitting to a strip-search.[13] Thus, as in *Dunaway*,

> "[t]he mere facts that [the suspect] was not told he was under arrest, was not 'booked,' and would not have had an arrest record if the interrogation had proved fruitless, while not insignificant for all purposes, . . . obviously do not make [the suspect's] seizure even roughly analogous to the narrowly defined intrusions involved in *Terry* and its progeny."

Because the intrusion to which Ms. Mendenhall was subjected when she was escorted to the DEA office is of the same character as that involved in *Dunaway*, probable cause, which concededly was absent, was required to support the intrusion.

The Court's suggestion that no Fourth Amendment interest possessed by Ms. Mendenhall was implicated because she consented to go to the DEA

---

[3] Not the least of these factors is the fact that the DEA agents for a time took Ms. Mendenhall's plane ticket and driver's license from her. It is doubtful that any reasonable person about to board a plane would feel free to leave when law enforcement officers have her plane ticket.

[4] Mr. Justice Stewart notes, for example, that a "seizure" might be established even if the suspect did not attempt to leave, by the nature of the language or tone of voice used by the officers, factors that were never addressed at the suppression hearing, very likely because the "seizure" question was not raised.

[12] Agent Anderson testified on cross-examination at the suppression hearing:

> "Q. All right. Now, when you asked her to accompany you to the DEA office for further questioning, if she had wanted to walk away, would you have stopped her?
> "A. Once I asked her to accompany me?
> "Q. Yes.
> "A. Yes, I would have stopped her.
> "Q. She was not free to leave, was she?
> "A. Not at that point."

[13] Agent Anderson testified:

> "Q. Had she tried to leave that room when she was being accompanied by the female officer, would you have known?
> "A. If she had attempted to leave the room?
> "Q. Yes.
> "A. Well yes, I could say that I would have known.
> "Q. And if she had tried to leave prior to being searched by the female officer, would you have stopped her?
> "A. Yes."

office is inconsistent with *Dunaway* and unsupported in the record. There was no evidence in the record to support the District Court's speculation, made before *Dunaway* was decided, that Ms. Mendenhall accompanied "Agent Anderson to the airport DEA Office 'voluntarily in a spirit of apparent cooperation with the [agent's] investigation,' *Sibron*." Ms. Mendenhall did not testify at the suppression hearing and the officers presented no testimony concerning what she said, if anything, when informed that the officers wanted her to come with them to the DEA office. Indeed, the only testimony concerning what occurred between Agent Anderson's "request" and Ms. Mendenhall's arrival at the DEA office is the agent's testimony that if Ms. Mendenhall had wanted to leave at that point she would have been forcibly restrained. The evidence of consent here is even flimsier than that we rejected in *Dunaway* where it was claimed that the suspect made an affirmative response when asked if he would accompany the officers to the police station. Also in *Sibron*, from which the District Court culled its description of Ms. Mendenhall's "consent," we described a record in a similar state as "totally barren of any indication whether Sibron accompanied Patrolman Martin outside in submission to a show of force or authority which left him no choice, or whether he went voluntarily in a spirit of apparent cooperation with the officer's investigation."

The Court recognizes that the Government has the burden of proving that Ms. Mendenhall consented to accompany the officers, but it nevertheless holds that the "totality of evidence was plainly adequate" to support a finding of consent. On the record before us, the Court's conclusion can only be based on the notion that consent can be assumed from the absence of proof that a suspect resisted police authority. This is a notion that we have squarely rejected. While the Government need not prove that Ms. Mendenhall knew that she had a right to refuse to accompany the officers, it cannot rely solely on acquiescence to the officers' wishes to establish the requisite consent. The Court of Appeals properly understood this in rejecting the District Court's "findings" of consent.

Since the defendant was not present to testify at the suppression hearing, we can only speculate about her state of mind as her encounter with the DEA agents progressed from surveillance, to detention, to questioning, to seclusion in a private office, to the female officer's command to remove her clothing. Nevertheless, it is unbelievable[15] that this sequence of events involved no invasion of a citizen's constitutionally protected interest in privacy. The rule of law requires a different conclusion.

---

[15] "Will you walk into my parlour?" said the spider to a fly. (You may find you have consented, without ever knowing why.)

## QUESTIONS AND NOTES

**1.** A majority of the Court concluded that Mendenhall was not seized when she "voluntarily" accompanied the officers to the DEA office. Only Justice Stewart and Rehnquist, however, concluded that the initial encounter was voluntary (see fn. 1 of Justice Powell's opinion).

**2.** Do you think that Mendenhall was seized at either or both times? Why? Why not?

**3.** Is the Court saying that even if (1) Agent Anderson thought that Mendenhall was not free to leave, and (2) Sylvia Mendenhall thought that she was not free to leave, a seizure did not occur because a reasonable person would have felt free to leave? If so, does something seem amiss?

**4.** Because the Government did not claim that there was no initial seizure, shouldn't the Court have at least remanded the case for a factual hearing to determine the extent to which the police may have coerced Mendenhall's compliance? Compare *Bostick, infra*.

**5.** We now revisit *Royer*, where on arguably similar facts, the Court, applying Justice Stewart's definition, concluded that Royer *had* been seized.

# Florida v. Royer
## 460 U.S. 491 (1983)

Justice WHITE announced the judgment of the Court and delivered an opinion in which Justices MARSHALL, POWELL and STEVENS joined.

[For a recounting of the facts (which are important), turn to this case in section 7B, *supra*.]

[L]aw enforcement officers do not violate the Fourth Amendment by merely approaching an individual on the street or in another public place, by asking him if he is willing to answer some questions, by putting questions to him if the person is willing to listen, or by offering in evidence in a criminal prosecution his voluntary answers to such questions. Nor would the fact that the officer identifies himself as a police officer, without more, convert the encounter into a seizure requiring some level of objective justification. *Mendenhall* (opinion of Stewart, J.). The person approached, however, need not answer any question put to him; indeed, he may decline to listen to the questions at all and may go on his way. *Terry* (Harlan, J., concurring); (White, J., concurring). He may not be detained even momentarily without reasonable, objective grounds for doing so; and his refusal to listen or answer does not, without more, furnish those grounds. *Mendenhall* (opinion of Stewart, J.). If there is no detention—no seizure within the meaning of the Fourth Amendment—then no constitutional rights have been infringed.

The State [contends] that the entire encounter was consensual and hence Royer was not being held against his will at all. We find this submission untenable. Asking for and examining Royer's ticket and his driver's license were no doubt permissible in themselves, but when the officers identified themselves as narcotics agents, told Royer that he was suspected of transporting narcotics, and asked him to accompany them to the police room, while retaining his ticket and driver's license and without indicating in any way that he was free to depart, Royer was effectively seized for the purposes of the Fourth Amendment. These circumstances surely amount to a show of official authority such that "a reasonable person would have believed he was not free to leave." *Mendenhall* (Opinion of Stewart, J.).

By the time Royer was informed that the officers wished to examine his luggage, he had identified himself when approached by the officers and had attempted to explain the discrepancy between the name shown on his identification and the name under which he had purchased his ticket and identified his luggage. The officers were not satisfied, for they informed him they were narcotics agents and had reason to believe that he was carrying illegal drugs.

They requested him to accompany them to the police room. Royer went with them. He found himself in a small room—a large closet—equipped with a desk and two chairs. He was alone with two police officers who again told him that they thought he was carrying narcotics. He also found that the officers, without his consent, had retrieved his checked luggage from the airlines. What had begun as a consensual inquiry in a public place had escalated into an investigatory procedure in a police interrogation room, where the police, unsatisfied with previous explanations, sought to confirm their suspicions. The officers had Royer's ticket, they had his identification, and they had seized his luggage. Royer was never informed that he was free to board his plane if he so chose, and he reasonably believed that he was being detained. At least as of that moment, any consensual aspects of the encounter had evaporated, and we cannot fault the Florida Court of Appeal for concluding that *Terry* and the cases following it did not justify the restraint to which Royer was then subjected. As a practical matter, Royer was under arrest. Consistent with this conclusion, the State conceded in the Florida courts that Royer would not have been free to leave the interrogation room had he asked to do so.[8] Furthermore, the state's brief in this Court interprets the testimony of the officers at the suppression hearing as indicating that had Royer refused to consent to a search of his luggage, the officers would have held the luggage and sought a warrant to authorize the search.[9]

---

[8] In its brief and at oral argument before this Court, the State contests whether this concession was ever made. We have no basis to question the statement of the Florida court.

[9] Our decision here is consistent with the Court's judgment in *Mendenhall*. In *Mendenhall*, the respondent was walking along an airport concourse when she was approached by two federal Drug Enforcement Agency (DEA) officers. As in the present case, the officers asked for Mendenhall's airline ticket and some identification; the names on the ticket and identification did not match. When one of the agents specifically identified himself as attached to the DEA, Mendenhall became visibly shaken and nervous.

After returning the ticket and identification, one officer asked Mendenhall if she would accompany him to the DEA airport office, 50 feet away for further questions. Once in the office, Mendenhall was asked to consent to a search of her person and her handbag; she was advised of her right to decline.

Justice POWELL, concurring.

This case differs strikingly from *Mendenhall* in the circumstances following the lawful initial questioning and the request that the suspect accompany the officers to a more private place. Royer then found himself in a small, windowless room — described as a "large closet" — alone with two officers who, without his consent, already had obtained possession of his checked luggage. In addition, they had retained his driver's license and airline ticket. Neither the evidence in this case nor common sense suggests that Royer was free to walk away. I agree with the plurality that as a practical matter he then was under arrest, and his surrender of the luggage key to the officers cannot be viewed as consensual.

Justice BRENNAN, concurring in result.

[P]lainly Royer was "seized" for purposes of the Fourth Amendment when the officers asked him to produce his driver's license and airline ticket. *Terry* stated that "whenever a police officer accosts an individual and restrains his freedom to walk away, he has 'seized' that person." Although I agree that "not all personal intercourse between policemen and citizens involves 'seizures' of persons," and that policemen may approach citizens on the street and ask them questions without "seizing" them for purposes of the Fourth Amendment, once an officer has identified himself and asked a traveler for identification and his airline ticket, the traveler has been "seized" within the meaning of the Fourth Amendment. By identifying themselves and asking for Royer's airline ticket and driver's license the officers, as a practical matter, engaged in a "show of authority" and "restrained [Royer's] liberty." It is simply

---

In a private room following further assurance from Mendenhall that she consented to the search, a policewoman began the search of Mendenhall's person by requesting that Mendenhall disrobe. As she began to undress, Mendenhall removed two concealed packages that appeared to contain heroin and handed them to the policewoman.

The case before us differs in important respects. Here, Royer's ticket and identification remained in the possession of the officers throughout the encounter; the officers also seized and had possession of his luggage. As a practical matter, Royer could not leave the airport without them. In *Mendenhall*, no luggage was involved, the ticket and identification were immediately returned, and the officers were careful to advise that the suspect could decline to be searched. Here, the officers had seized Royer's luggage and made no effort to advise him that he need not consent to the search.

wrong to suggest that a traveler feels free to walk away when he has been approached by individuals who have identified themselves as police officers and asked for, and received, his airline ticket and driver's license.

Justice BLACKMUN, dissenting.

I concur in the plurality's adoption of the Fourth Amendment "seizure" standard proposed by Justice Stewart in *Mendenhall*: Fourth Amendment protections apply when "official authority" is exercised "such that 'a reasonable person would have believed he was not free to leave.'" I do not quarrel with the plurality's conclusion that at some point in this encounter, that threshold was passed.

Justice REHNQUIST, with whom the Chief Justice and Justice O'CONNOR join, dissenting.

The facts are similar to those addressed in *Mendenhall*, where a majority of the Court determined that consent to accompany police officers had been voluntary. Royer was not told that he had to go to the room, but was simply asked, after a brief period of questioning, if he would accompany the detectives to the room. Royer was informed as to why the officers wished to question him further. There were neither threats nor any show of force. Detectives Johnson and Magdelena were not in uniform and did not display weapons. The detectives did not touch Royer and made no demands. In fact, Royer admits that the detectives were quite polite.[9]

The plurality concludes that somewhere between the beginning of the 40-foot journey and the resumption of conversation in the room the investigation became so intrusive that Royer's consent "evaporated" leaving him "[a]s a practical matter . . . under arrest." But if Royer was legally approached in the first instance and consented to accompany the detectives to the room, it does not follow that his consent went up in smoke and he was "arrested"

---

[9] Contrary to the Florida court's view, this phase of the encounter contrasts sharply with the circumstances we examined in *Dunaway*. In that case, police officers deliberately sought out the suspect at a neighbor's house and, with a show of force, brought the suspect to police headquarters in a police car, placed him in an interrogation room, and questioned him extensively after giving him a *Miranda* warning. Unlike in *Dunaway*, Royer, after brief questioning, was *asked to cooperate* by accompanying the officers to a room no more than 40 feet away, so that the questioning could proceed out of the view of the general public.

upon entering the room. As we made clear in *Mendenhall*, logical analysis would focus on whether the environment in the room rendered the subsequent consent to a search of the luggage involuntary.

As we said in *Mendenhall*, "the fact that she was [in the room] is little or no evidence that she was in any way coerced." Other than the size of the room, described as "a large storage closet,[10]

---

[10] "The characterization of the room as a "closet" is quite misleading. The room contained one desk and two chairs. It was large enough to allow three persons to enter with two heavy suitcases. It also is relevant that it was the Florida court, not Royer, who focused on the size of the room. It was during rehearing by the court en banc

there is nothing in the record which would indicate that Royer's resistance was overborne by anything about the room. Royer, who was in his fourth year of study at Ithaca College at the time and has since graduated with a degree in *communications*, simply continued to cooperate with the detectives as he had from the beginning of the encounter. Absent any evidence of objective indicia of coercion, and even absent any claim of such indicia by Royer, the size of the room itself does not transform a voluntary consent to search into a coerced consent.

---

that the conviction was reversed with the court finding that when Royer was taken into the private room he was in effect placed under arrest.

## QUESTIONS AND NOTES

**1.** Are you persuaded that a meaningful distinction can be drawn between *Royer* and *Mendenhall* in regard to the question of seizure?

**2.** In that regard, should Royer's status as a near-graduate in communications as contrasted to Mendenhall's 11th grade education have cut in the opposite direction?

**3.** How persuasive is Justice Brennan's observation that "[i]t is simply wrong to suggest that a traveler feels free to walk away when he has been approached by individuals who have identified themselves as police officers and have asked for, and received, his airline ticket and driver's license?"

**4.** Would Brennan's statement be significantly less persuasive if the phrase "and received" were deleted?

**5.** In *Mendenhall* and *Royer*, we considered the plight of captured drug couriers. In *Delgado*, we consider the meaning of "seizure" as applied to innocent people.

### INS v. Delgado
466 U.S. 210 (1984)

Justice REHNQUIST delivered the opinion of the Court.

In the course of enforcing the immigration laws, petitioner Immigration and Naturalization Service (INS) enters employers' work sites to determine whether any illegal aliens may be present as employees. The Court of Appeals for the Ninth Circuit held that the "factory surveys" involved in this case amounted to a seizure of the entire work forces, and further held that the INS could not question individual employees during any of these surveys unless its agents had a reasonable suspicion that the employee

to be questioned was an illegal alien. We conclude that these factory surveys did not result in the seizure of the entire work forces, and that the individual questioning of the respondents in this case by INS agents concerning their citizenship did not amount to a detention or seizure under the Fourth Amendment. Accordingly, we reverse the judgment of the Court of Appeals.

Acting pursuant to two warrants, in January and September, 1977, the INS conducted a survey of the work force at Southern California Davis Pleating Company (Davis Pleating) in search of illegal aliens.

The warrants were issued on a showing of probable cause by the INS that numerous illegal aliens were employed at Davis Pleating, although neither of the search warrants identified any particular illegal aliens by name. A third factory survey was conducted with the employer's consent in October, 1977, at Mr. Pleat, another garment factory.

At the beginning of the surveys several agents positioned themselves near the buildings' exits, while other agents dispersed throughout the factory to question most, but not all, employees at their work stations. The agents displayed badges, carried walkie-talkies, and were armed, although at no point during any of the surveys was a weapon ever drawn. Moving systematically through the factory, the agents approached employees and, after identifying themselves, asked them from one to three questions relating to their citizenship. If the employee gave a credible reply that he was a United States citizen, the questioning ended, and the agent moved on to another employee. If the employee gave an unsatisfactory response or admitted that he was an alien, the employee was asked to produce his immigration papers. During the survey, employees continued with their work and were free to walk around within the factory.

Respondents are four employees questioned in one of the three surveys.[1] In 1978 respondents and their union representative, the International Ladies Garment Workers' Union, filed two actions, later consolidated, in United States District Court for the Central District of California challenging the constitutionality of INS factory surveys and seeking declaratory and injunctive relief. Respondents argued that the factory surveys violated their Fourth Amendment right to be free from unreasonable searches or seizures.

The Fourth Amendment does not proscribe all contact between the police and citizens, but is designed "to prevent arbitrary and oppressive interference by law enforcement officials with the privacy and personal security of individuals." Given the diversity of encounters between police officers and citizens, however, the Court has been cautious in defining the limits imposed by the Fourth Amendment on encounters between the police and

citizens. As we have noted elsewhere, "Obviously, not all personal intercourse between policemen and citizens involves 'seizures' of persons. Only when the officer, by means of physical force or show of authority, has restrained the liberty of a citizen may we conclude that a 'seizure' has occurred." *Terry.* While applying such a test is relatively straightforward in a situation resembling a traditional arrest, the protection against unreasonable seizures also extends to "seizures that involve only a brief detention short of traditional arrest." What has evolved from our cases is a determination that an initially consensual encounter between a police officer and a citizen can be transformed into a seizure or detention within the meaning of the Fourth Amendment, "if, in view of all the circumstances surrounding the incident, a reasonable person would have believed that he was not free to leave." *Mendenhall, Royer.*

What is apparent from *Royer* and *Brown* is that police questioning, by itself, is unlikely to result in a Fourth Amendment violation. While most citizens will respond to a police request, the fact that people do so, and do so without being told they are free not to respond, hardly eliminates the consensual nature of the response. Unless the circumstances of the encounter are so intimidating as to demonstrate that a reasonable person would have believed he was not free to leave if he had not responded, one cannot say that the questioning resulted in a detention under the Fourth Amendment. But if the person refuses to answer and the police take additional steps — such as those taken in *Brown* — to obtain an answer, then the Fourth Amendment imposes some minimal level of objective justification to validate the detention or seizure.

The Court of Appeals held that "the manner in which the factory surveys were conducted in this case constituted a seizure of the workforce" under the Fourth Amendment. While the element of surprise and the systematic questioning of individual workers by several INS agents contributed to the court's holding, the pivotal factor in its decision was the stationing of INS agents near the exits of the factory buildings. According to the Court of Appeals, the stationing of agents near the doors meant that "departures were not to be contemplated," and thus, workers were "not free to leave." In support of the decision below, respondents argue that the INS created an intimidating psychological environment when it intruded unexpectedly into the workplace with such a show of officers. Besides the stationing of agents near the

---

[1] Respondents Herman Delgado, Ramona Correa, and Francisca Labonte worked at Davis Pleating, while Marie Miramontes, the fourth respondent, was employed by Mr. Pleat. Both Delgado and Correa are United States citizens, while Labonte and Miramontes are permanent resident aliens.

exits, respondents add that the length of the survey and the failure to inform workers they were free to leave resulted in a Fourth Amendment seizure of the entire work force.[5]

We reject the claim that the entire work forces of the two factories were seized for the duration of the surveys when the INS placed agents near the exits of the factory sites. Ordinarily, when people are at work their freedom to move about has been meaningfully restricted, not by the actions of law enforcement officials, but by the workers' voluntary obligations to their employers. The record indicates that when these surveys were initiated, the employees were about their ordinary business, operating machinery and performing other job assignments. While the surveys did cause some disruption, including the efforts of some workers to hide, the record also indicates that workers were not prevented by the agents from moving about the factories.

Respondents argue, however, that the stationing of agents near the factory doors showed the INS's intent to prevent people from leaving. But there is nothing in the record indicating that this is what the agents at the doors actually did. The obvious purpose of the agents' presence at the factory doors was to insure that all persons in the factories were questioned. The record indicates that the INS agents' conduct in this case consisted simply of questioning employees and arresting those they had probable cause to believe were unlawfully present in the factory. This conduct should have given respondents no reason to believe that they would be detained if they gave truthful answers to the questions put to them or if they simply refused to answer. If mere questioning does not constitute a seizure when it occurs inside the factory, it is no more a seizure when it occurs at the exits.[6]

A similar conclusion holds true for all other citizens or aliens lawfully present inside the factory buildings during the surveys. The presence of agents by the exits posed no reasonable threat of detention to these workers while they walked throughout the factories on job assignments. Likewise, the mere possibility that they would be questioned if they sought to leave the buildings should not have resulted in any reasonable apprehension by any of them that they would be seized or detained in any meaningful way. Since most workers could have had no reasonable fear that they would be detained upon leaving, we conclude that the work forces as a whole were not seized.[7]

The Court of Appeals also held that "detentive questioning" of individuals could be conducted only if INS agents could articulate "objective facts providing investigators with a reasonable suspicion that each questioned person, so detained, is an alien illegally in the country." Under our analysis, however, since there was no seizure of the work forces by virtue of the method of conducting the factory surveys, the only way the issue of individual questioning could be presented would be if one of the named respondents had in fact been seized or detained. Reviewing the deposition testimony of respondents, we conclude that none were.

The questioning of each respondent by INS agents seems to have been nothing more than a brief encounter. None of the three Davis Pleating employees were questioned during the January survey. During the September survey at Davis Pleating, respondent Delgado was discussing the survey with another employee when two INS agents approached him and asked him where he was from and from what city. When Delgado informed them that he came from Mayaguez, Puerto Rico, the agent made an innocuous observation to his partner and left. Respondent Correa's experience in the September survey was similar. Walking from one part of the factory to another, Correa was stopped by an INS agent and

---

[5] Contrary to respondents' assertion, it also makes no difference in this case that the encounters took place inside a factory, a location usually not accessible to the public. The INS officers were lawfully present pursuant to consent or a warrant, and other people were in the area during the INS agents' questioning. Thus, the same considerations attending contacts between the police and citizens in public places should apply to the questions presented to the individual respondents here.

[6] In her deposition respondent Miramontes described an incident that occurred during the October factory survey at Mr. Pleat, in which an INS agent stationed by an exit attempted to prevent a worker, presumably an illegal alien, from leaving the premises after the survey started. The worker walked out the

---

door and when an agent tried to stop him, the worker pushed the agent aside and ran away. An ambiguous, isolated incident such as this fails to provide any basis on which to conclude that respondents have shown an INS policy entitling them to injunctive relief.

[7] Respondents Delgado and Labonte both left the building during the INS survey, Delgado to load a truck and Labonte to observe INS activities outside the building. Neither of them stated in their depositions that the INS agents in any way restrained them from leaving the building, or even addressed any questions to them upon leaving.

asked where she was born. When she replied "Huntington Park, [California]," the agent walked away and Correa continued about her business. Respondent Labonte, the third Davis Pleating employee, was tapped on the shoulder and asked in Spanish, "Where are your papers?" Labonte responded that she had her papers and without any further request from the INS agents, showed the papers to the agents, who then left. Finally, respondent Miramontes, the sole Mr. Pleat employee involved in this case, encountered an agent en route from an office to her workaday. Questioned concerning her citizenship, Miramontes replied that she was a resident alien, and on the agent's request, produced her work permit. The agent then left.

Respondents argue that the manner in which the surveys were conducted and the attendant disruption caused by the surveys created a psychological environment which made them reasonably afraid they were not free to leave. Consequently, when respondents were approached by INS agents and questioned concerning their citizenship and right to work, they were effectively detained under the Fourth Amendment, since they reasonably feared that refusing to answer would have resulted in their arrest. But it was obvious from the beginning of the surveys that the INS agents were only questioning people. Persons such as respondents who simply went about their business in the workplace were not detained in any way; nothing more occurred than that a question was put to them. While persons who attempted to flee or evade the agents may eventually have been detained for questioning, respondents did not do so and were not in fact detained. The manner in which respondents were questioned, given its obvious purpose, could hardly result in a reasonable fear that respondents were not free to continue working or to move about the factory. Respondents may only litigate what happened to them, and our review of their description of the encounters with the INS agents satisfies us that the encounters were classic consensual encounters rather than Fourth Amendment seizures. See *Royer, Mendenhall*.

Accordingly, the judgment of the Court of Appeals is reversed.

Justice STEVENS, concurring.

A trial has not yet been held in this case. The District Court entered summary judgment against respondents, and the Court of Appeals, in reversing, did not remand the case for trial but rather directed the District Court to enter summary judgment for respondents and a permanent injunction against petitioners. As the case comes to us, therefore, we must construe the record most favorably to petitioners, and resolve all issues of fact in their favor. Because I agree that this record does not establish that there is no genuine issue of fact on the question whether any of the respondents could have reasonably believed that he or she had been detained in some meaningful way, I join the opinion of the Court.

Justice POWELL, concurring in result.

While the Court's opinion is persuasive, I find the question of whether the factory surveys conducted in this case resulted in any Fourth Amendment "seizures" to be a close one. The question turns on a difficult characterization of fact and law: whether a reasonable person in respondents' position would have believed he was free to refuse to answer the questions put to him by INS officers and leave the factory. I believe that the Court need not decide the question, however, because it is clear that any "seizure" that may have taken place was permissible under the reasoning of our decision in *Martinez-Fuerte*.

In that case, we held that stopping automobiles for brief questioning at permanent traffic checkpoints away from the Mexican border is consistent with the Fourth Amendment and need not be authorized by a warrant.[1] We assumed that the stops constituted "seizures" within the meaning of the Fourth Amendment, but upheld them as reasonable. As in prior cases involving the apprehension of aliens illegally in the United States, we weighed the public interest in the practice at issue against the Fourth Amendment interest of the individual. Noting the importance of routine checkpoint stops to controlling the flow of illegal aliens into the interior of the country, we found that the government had a substantial interest in the practice. On the other hand, the intrusion on individual motorists was minimal: the stops were brief, usually involving only a question or two and possibly the production of documents. Moreover, they were public and regularized law enforcement activities vesting limited discretion in officers in the field. Weighing these considerations, we held that the stops and questioning at issue, as well as referrals to a slightly longer secondary inspection, might be made "in the absence of any individualized suspicion" that a particular car contained illegal aliens.

This case is similar. The government's interest

---

[1] This case presents no question as to whether a warrant was required for the entry by the INS officers into the plants. As the majority notes, the INS obtained either a warrant or consent from the factory owners before entering the plants to conduct the surveys.

in using factory surveys is as great if not greater. According to an affidavit by the INS's assistant district director in Los Angeles contained in the record in this case, the surveys account for one-half to three-quarters of the illegal aliens identified and arrested away from the border every day in the Los Angeles district. In that district alone, over 20,000 illegal aliens were arrested in the course of factory surveys in one year. The surveys in this case resulted in the arrest of between 20% and 50% of the employees at each of the factories.[3]

We have noted before the dimensions of the immigration problem in this country. Recent estimates of the number of illegal aliens in this country range between 2 and 12 million, although the consensus appears to be that the number at any one time is between 3 and 6 million. One of the main reasons they come — perhaps *the* main reason — is to seek employment. Factory surveys strike directly at this cause, enabling the INS with relatively few agents to diminish the incentive for the dangerous passage across the border and to apprehend large numbers of those who come. Clearly, the government interest in this enforcement technique is enormous.[5]

The intrusion into the Fourth Amendment interests of the employees, on the other hand, is about the same as it was in *Martinez-Fuerte*. The objective intrusion is actually less: there, cars often were stopped for up to five minutes, while here employees could continue their work as the survey progressed. They were diverted briefly to answer a few questions or to display their registration cards. It is true that the initial entry into the plant in a factory survey is a surprise to the workers, but the obviously authorized

---

[3] During the course of the first survey at Davis Pleating, 78 illegal aliens were arrested out of a work force of approximately 300. The second survey nine months later resulted in the arrest of 39 illegal aliens out of about 200 employees. The survey at Mr. Pleat resulted in the arrest of 45 illegal aliens out of approximately 90 employees.

[5] Despite the vast expenditures by the INS and other agencies to prevent illegal immigration and apprehend aliens illegally in the United States, and despite laws making it a crime for them to be here, our law irrationally continues to permit United States employers to hire them. Many employers actively recruit low-paid illegal immigrant labor, encouraging — with Government tolerance — illegal entry into the United States. This incongruity in our immigration statutes is not calculated to increase respect for the rule of law.

character of the operation, the clear purpose of seeking illegal aliens, and the systematic and public nature of the survey serve to minimize any concern or fright on the part of lawful employees. Moreover, the employees' expectation of privacy in the plant setting here, like that in an automobile, certainly is far less than the traditional expectation of privacy in one's residence. Therefore, for the same reasons that we upheld the checkpoint stops in *Martinez-Fuerte* without any individualized suspicion, I would find the factory surveys here to be reasonable.

Justice BRENNAN, with whom Justice MARSHALL joins, concurring in part and dissenting in part.

As part of its ongoing efforts to enforce the immigration laws, the Immigration and Naturalization Service (INS) conducts "surveys" of those workplaces that it has reason to believe employ large numbers of undocumented aliens who may be subject to deportation. This case presents the question whether the INS's method of carrying out these "factory surveys" violates the rights of the affected factory workers to be secure against unreasonable seizures of one's person as guaranteed by the Fourth Amendment. Answering that question, the Court today holds, first, that the INS surveys involved here did not result in the seizure of the entire factory workforce for the complete duration of the surveys, and, second, that the individual questioning of respondents by INS agents concerning their citizenship did not constitute seizures within the meaning of the Fourth Amendment. Although I generally agree with the Court's first conclusion,[2] I am convinced that a fair application of our prior decisions to the facts of this case compels the conclusion that respondents were unreasonably seized by INS agents in the course of these factory surveys.

---

[2] It seems to me that the Court correctly finds that there was no single continuing seizure of the entire workforce from the moment that the INS agents first secured the factory exits until the completion of the survey. I join the Court's judgment in this respect because it is apparent that in all three factory surveys under review most of the employees were generally free while the survey was being conducted to continue working without interruption and to move about the workplace. Having said that, however, I should emphasize that I find the evidence concerning the conduct of the factory-wide survey highly relevant to determining whether the individual respondents were seized.

At first blush, the Court's opinion appears unremarkable. But what is striking about today's decision is its studied air of unreality. Indeed, it is only through a considerable feat of legerdemain that the Court is able to arrive at the conclusion that the respondents were not seized. The success of the Court's sleight of hand turns on the proposition that the interrogations of respondents by the INS were merely brief "consensual encounters" that posed no threat to respondents' personal security and freedom. The record, however, tells a far different story.

I

[W]e have repeatedly considered whether and, if so, under what circumstances questioning of an individual by law enforcement officers may amount to a seizure within the meaning of the Fourth Amendment. See, *e.g., Terry, Adams, Brown, Mendenhall, Royer.* Of course, as these decisions recognize, the question does not admit of any simple answer. The difficulty springs from the inherent tension between our commitment to safeguarding the precious, and all too fragile, right to go about one's business free from unwarranted government interference, and our recognition that the police must be allowed some latitude in gathering information from those individuals who are willing to cooperate. Given these difficulties, it is perhaps understandable that our efforts to strike an appropriate balance have not produced uniform results. Nevertheless, the outline of what appears to be the appropriate inquiry has been traced over the years with some clarity.

The Court launched its examination of this issue in *Terry*, by explaining that "the Fourth Amendment governs 'seizures' of the person which do not eventuate in a trip to the station house and prosecution for crime—'arrests' in traditional terminology. *It must be recognized that whenever a police officer accosts an individual and restrains his freedom to walk away, he has 'seized' that person."* (emphasis added). Such a seizure, the Court noted, may be evidenced by either "physical force or a show of authority" indicating that the individual's liberty has been restrained. The essential teaching of the Court's decision in *Terry*—that an individual's right to personal security and freedom must be respected even in encounters with the police that fall short of full arrest—has been consistently reaffirmed. [I]n *Brown*, we overturned a conviction for refusing to stop and identify oneself to police, because, in making the stop, the police lacked any "reasonable suspicion, based on objective facts, that the individual [was] involved in criminal activity." The animating principle underlying this unanimous decision was

that the Fourth Amendment protects an individual's personal security and privacy from unreasonable interference by the police, even when that interference amounts to no more than a brief stop and questioning concerning one's identity.

Although it was joined at the time by only one other Member of this Court, Justice Stewart's plurality opinion in *Mendenhall*, offered a helpful, preliminary distillation of the lessons of these cases. Noting first that "as long as the person to whom questions are put remains free to disregard the questions and walk away, there has been no intrusion upon that person's liberty or privacy," Justice Stewart explained that "a person has been 'seized' within the meaning of the Fourth Amendment only if, in view of all the circumstances surrounding the incident, a reasonable person would have believed that he was not free to leave." The opinion also suggested that such circumstances might include "the threatening presence of several officers, the display of a weapon by an officer, some physical touching of the person of the citizen, or the use of language or tone of voice indicating that compliance with the officer's request might be compelled."

A majority of the Court has since adopted that formula as the appropriate standard for determining when inquiries made by the police cross the boundary separating merely consensual encounters from forcible stops to investigate a suspected crime. See *Royer*. This rule properly looks not to the subjective impressions of the person questioned but rather to the objective characteristics of the encounter which may suggest whether or not a reasonable person would believe that he remained free during the course of the questioning to disregard the questions and walk away. The governing principles that should guide us in this difficult area were summarized in the *Royer* plurality opinion:

"[L]aw enforcement officers do not violate the Fourth Amendment by merely approaching an individual on the street or in another public place, by asking him if he is willing to answer some questions, by putting questions to him if the person is willing to listen, or by offering in evidence in a criminal prosecution his voluntary answers to such questions. Nor would the fact that the officer identifies himself as a police officer, without more, convert the encounter into a seizure requiring some level of objective justification. The person approached, however, need not answer any question put to him; indeed, he may decline to listen to the questions at all and may go on his way. *He may not be detained even momentarily without reasonable, objective grounds for doing so; and his refusal to listen or to answer does not, without more, furnish those grounds.*" (emphasis added).

The surrounding circumstances in this case are far different from an isolated encounter between the police and a passerby on the street. Each of the respondents testified at length about the widespread disturbance among the workers that was sparked by the INS surveys and the intimidating atmosphere created by the INS's investigative tactics. First, as the respondents explained, the surveys were carried out by surprise by relatively large numbers of agents, generally from 15 to 25, who moved systematically through the rows of workers who were seated at their work stations. Second, as the INS agents discovered persons whom they suspected of being illegal aliens, they would handcuff these persons and lead them away to waiting vans outside the factory. Third, all of the factory exits were conspicuously guarded by INS agents, stationed there to prevent anyone from leaving while the survey was being conducted. Finally, as the INS agents moved through the rows of workers, they would show their badges and direct pointed questions at the workers. In light of these circumstances, it is simply fantastic to conclude that a reasonable person could ignore all that was occurring throughout the factory and, when the INS agents reached him, have the temerity to believe that he was at liberty to refuse to answer their questions and walk away.

Indeed, the experiences recounted by respondents clearly demonstrate that they did not feel free either to ignore the INS agents or to refuse to answer the questions posed to them. For example, respondent Delgado, a naturalized American citizen, explained that he was standing near his work station when two INS agents approached him, identified themselves as immigration officers, showed him their badges, and asked him to state where he was born. Delgado, of course, had seen all that was going on around him up to that point and naturally he responded. As a final reminder of who controlled the situation, one INS agent remarked as they were leaving Delgado that they would be coming back to check him out again because he spoke English too well. Respondent Miramontes described her encounter with the INS in similar terms: "He told me he was from Immigration, so when I showed him the [work permit] papers I saw his badge. *If I hadn't* [seen his badge], *I wouldn't have shown them to him.*" (emphasis added). She further testified that she was frightened during this interview because "normally you get nervous when you see everybody is scared, everybody is nervous." Respondent Labontes

testified that while she was sitting at her machine an immigration officer came up to her from behind, tapped her on the left shoulder and asked "Where are your papers?" Explaining her response to this demand, she testified that "I turned, *and at the same time I didn't wish to identify myself.* When I saw [the INS agents], I said, 'Yes, yes, I have my papers.'" (emphasis added).

In sum, it is clear from this testimony that respondents felt constrained to answer the questions posed by the INS agents, even though they did not wish to do so. That such a feeling of constraint was reasonable should be beyond question in light of the surrounding circumstances. Indeed, the respondents' testimony paints a frightening picture of people subjected to wholesale interrogation under conditions designed not to respect personal security and privacy, but rather to elicit prompt answers from completely intimidated workers. Nothing could be clearer than that these tactics amounted to seizures of respondents under the Fourth Amendment.

## II

The Court's eagerness to conclude that these interrogations did not represent seizures is to some extent understandable, of course, because such a conclusion permits the Court to avoid the imposing task of justifying these seizures on the basis of reasonable, objective criteria as required by the Fourth Amendment.

In this case, the individual seizures of respondents by the INS agents clearly were neither "based on specific, objective facts indicating that society's legitimate interests require[d] the seizure," nor "carried out pursuant to a plan embodying explicit, neutral limitations on the conduct of individual officers." It is undisputed that the vast majority of the undocumented aliens discovered in the surveyed factories had illegally immigrated from Mexico. Nevertheless, the INS agents involved in this case apparently were instructed, in the words of the INS Assistant District Director in charge of the operations, to interrogate "virtually all persons employed by a company." Consequently, all workers, irrespective of whether they were American citizens, permanent resident aliens, or deportable aliens, were subjected to questioning by INS agents concerning their right to remain in the country. By their own admission, the INS agents did not selectively question persons in these surveys on the basis of any reasonable suspicion that the persons were illegal aliens. That the INS policy is so indiscriminate should not be surprising, however, since many of the employees in the surveyed factories who are lawful residents of the United States may have been born in Mexico, have a Latin appearance, or speak Spanish while at work. What this means, of course, is that the many lawful workers who constitute the clear majority at the surveyed workplaces are subjected to surprise questioning under intimidating circumstances by INS agents who have no reasonable basis for suspecting that they have done anything wrong. To say that such an indiscriminate policy of mass interrogation is constitutional makes a mockery of the words of the Fourth Amendment.

Relying upon *Martinez-Fuerte*, however, Justice Powell would hold that the interrogation of respondents represented a "reasonable" seizure under the Fourth Amendment, even though the INS agents lacked any particularized suspicion of illegal alienage to support the questioning. In my view, reliance on that decision is misplaced. In *Martinez-Fuerte*, the Court held that when the intrusion upon protected privacy interests is extremely limited, the INS, in order to serve the pressing governmental interest in immigration enforcement, may briefly detain travelers at fixed checkpoints for questioning solely on the basis of "apparent Mexican ancestry." In so holding, the Court was careful to distinguish its earlier decision in *Brignoni-Ponce*, which held that Border Patrol agents conducting roving patrols may not stop and question motorists solely on the basis of apparent Mexican ancestry, and may instead make such stops only when their observations lead them "reasonably to suspect that a particular vehicle may contain aliens who are illegally in the country." The "crucial distinction" between the roving patrols and the fixed checkpoints, as the Court later observed in *Prouse*, was "the lesser intrusion upon the motorist's Fourth Amendment interests" caused by the checkpoint operations. Thus, as the Court explained in *Martinez-Fuerte*, "the objective intrusion — the stop itself, the questioning, and the visual inspection — also existed in roving-patrol stops. But we view checkpoint stops in a different light because the subjective intrusion — generating of concern or even fright on the part of lawful travelers — is appreciably less in the case of a checkpoint stop."[6]

The limited departure from *Terry*'s general requirement of particularized suspicion permitted in *Martinez-Fuerte* turned, therefore, largely on the fact that the intrusion upon motorists resulting from the checkpoint operations was extremely modest. In this case, by contrast, there are no equivalent guarantees that the privacy of lawful workers will not be substantially invaded by the factory surveys or that the workers will not be frightened by the INS tactics. Indeed, the opposite is true. First, unlike the fixed checkpoints that were upheld in *Martinez-Fuerte* in part because their location was known to motorists in advance, the INS factory surveys are sprung upon unsuspecting workers completely by surprise. Respondents testified that the sudden arrival of large numbers of INS agents created widespread fear and anxiety among most workers. Respondent Miramontes, for instance, explained that she was afraid during the surveys "[b]ecause if I leave and they think I don't have no papers and they shoot me or something. They see me leaving and they think I'm guilty."[7] In *Martinez-Fuerte*, there was absolutely no evidence of wide-spread fear and anxiety similar to that adduced in this case.

In my view, therefore, the only acceptable alternatives that would adequately safeguard Fourth Amendment values in this context are for the INS either (a) to adopt a firm policy of stopping and questioning only those workers who are reasonably suspected of being illegal aliens, or (b) to develop a factory survey program that is predictably and reliably less intrusive than the current scheme under review. The first alternative would satisfy the requirement of particularized suspicion enunciated in *Terry* — a principle that must control here because the specific conditions that permitted exception to that requirement in *Martinez-Fuerte* are simply not present. The second alternative would seek to redesign the factory survey techniques used by the INS in order to bring them more closely into line with the characteristics found in *Martinez-Fuerte*. Such a scheme might require the INS, before conducting a survey of all workers in a particular plant, to secure

---

[6] Indeed, in *Martinez-Fuerte*, the Court repeatedly emphasized that, in contrast to the roving patrol stops, the fixed checkpoint operations are less likely to frighten motorists. This was so because "[m]otorists using these highways are not taken by surprise as they know . . . the location of the checkpoints and will not be stopped elsewhere," and because the operations "both appear to and actually involve less discretionary enforcement activity."

[7] See also United States Commission on Civil Rights, The Tarnished Golden Door: Civil Rights Issues in Immigration 90-91 (1980) (noting that "[t]estimony received by the Commission indicates that . . . INS area control operations do cause confusion and pandemonium among all factory employees, thereby disrupting a factory's operations and decreasing production").

an administrative warrant based upon a showing that reasonable grounds exist for believing that a substantial number of workers employed at the factory are undocumented aliens subject to deportation, and that there are no practical alternatives to conducting such a survey. Cf. *Camara*. In addition, the surveys could be further tailored in duration and manner so as to be substantially less intrusive.

## QUESTIONS AND NOTES

**1.** How (if at all) does Justice Stevens' opinion differ from the opinion of the Court? To the extent that they are different, with which do you more nearly agree?

**2.** If one is going to uphold the *Delgado* practice, is it better to do so on the ground that there was no seizure (Rehnquist) or on the ground that whatever seizure occurred was reasonable (Powell)?

**3.** Do you agree with the Court's unanimous conclusion that the entire work force was *not* seized? Why? Why not?

**4.** How would you have decided this case? Why?

**5.** In *Bostick*, the Court elaborated upon, and arguably expanded, what does *not* constitute a seizure.

### Florida v. Bostick
### 111 S.Ct. 2382 (1991)

Justice O'CONNOR delivered the opinion of the Court.

We have held that the Fourth Amendment permits police officers to approach individuals at random in airport lobbies and other public places to ask them questions and to request consent to search their luggage, so long as a reasonable person would understand that he or she could refuse to cooperate. This case requires us to determine whether the same rule applies to police encounters that take place on a bus.

I

Drug interdiction efforts have led to the use of police surveillance at airports, train stations, and bus depots. Law enforcement officers stationed at such locations routinely approach individuals, either randomly or because they suspect in some vague way that the individuals may be engaged in criminal activity, and ask them potentially incriminating questions. Broward County has adopted such a program. County Sheriff's Department officers routinely board buses at scheduled stops and ask passengers for permission to search their luggage.

In this case, two officers discovered cocaine when they searched a suitcase belonging to Terrance Bostick. The underlying facts of the search are in dispute, but the Florida Supreme Court, whose decision we review here, stated explicitly the factual premise for its decision:

"Two officers, complete with badges, insignia and one of them holding a recognizable zipper pouch, containing a pistol, boarded a bus bound from Miami to Atlanta during a stopover in Fort Lauderdale. Eyeing the passengers, the officers admittedly without articulable suspicion, picked out the defendant passenger and asked to inspect his ticket and identification. The ticket, from Miami to Atlanta, matched the defendant's identification and both were immediately returned to him as unremarkable. However, the two police officers persisted and explained their presence as narcotics agents on the lookout for illegal drugs. In pursuit of that aim, they then requested the defendant's consent to search his luggage. Needless to say, there is a conflict in the evidence about whether the defendant consented to the search of the second bag in which the contraband was found and as to whether he was informed of his right to refuse consent. However, any conflict must be resolved in favor of the state, it being a question of fact decided by the trial judge."

Two facts are particularly worth noting. First, the police specifically advised Bostick that he had the right to refuse consent. Bostick appears to have disputed the point, but, as the Florida Supreme Court noted explicitly, the trial court resolved this evidentiary conflict in the State's favor. Second, at no time did the officers threaten Bostick with a gun. The Florida Supreme Court indicated that one officer carried a zipper pouch containing a pistol – the equivalent of carrying a gun in a holster – but the court did not suggest that the gun was ever removed from its pouch, pointed at Bostick, or otherwise used in a threatening manner. The dissent's characterization of the officers as "gun-wielding inquisitor[s]," is colorful, but lacks any basis in fact.

Bostick was arrested and charged with trafficking in cocaine. He moved to suppress the cocaine on the grounds that it had been seized in violation of his Fourth Amendment rights. The trial court denied the motion but made no factual findings. Bostick subsequently entered a plea of guilty, but reserved the right to appeal the denial of the motion to suppress.

The Florida Supreme Court reasoned that Bostick had been seized because a reasonable passenger in his situation would not have felt free to leave the bus to avoid questioning by the police. It rephrased and answered the certified question so as to make the bus setting dispositive in every case. It ruled categorically that "an impermissible seizure result[s] when police mount a drug search on buses during scheduled stops and question boarded passengers without articulable reasons for doing so, thereby obtaining consent to search the passengers' luggage." The Florida Supreme Court thus adopted a *per se* rule that the Broward County Sheriff's practice of "working the buses" is unconstitutional.** The result of this decision is that police in Florida, as elsewhere, may approach persons at random in most public places, ask them questions and seek consent to a search, but they may not engage in the same behavior on a bus. We granted certiorari to determine whether the Florida Supreme Court's *per se*

---

** The dissent acknowledges that the Florida Supreme Court's answer to the certified question reads like a *per se* rule, but dismisses as "implausible" the notion that the court would actually apply this rule to "trump" a careful analysis of all the relevant facts. Implausible as it may seem, that is precisely what the Florida Supreme Court does. It routinely grants review in bus search cases and quashes denials of motions to suppress *expressly on the basis of its answer to the certified question in this case*. (Citations omitted.)

rule is consistent with our Fourth Amendment jurisprudence.

## II

The sole issue presented for our review is whether a police encounter on a bus of the type described above necessarily constitutes a "seizure" within the meaning of the Fourth Amendment. The State concedes, and we accept for purposes of this decision, that the officers lacked the reasonable suspicion required to justify a seizure and that, if a seizure took place, the drugs found in Bostick's suitcase must be suppressed as tainted fruit.

Our cases make it clear that a seizure does not occur simply because a police officer approaches an individual and asks a few questions. So long as a reasonable person would feel free "to disregard the police and go about his business," the encounter is consensual and no reasonable suspicion is required. The encounter will not trigger Fourth Amendment scrutiny unless it loses its consensual nature.

There is no doubt that if this same encounter had taken place before Bostick boarded the bus or in the lobby of the bus terminal, it would not rise to the level of a seizure. The Court has dealt with similar encounters in airports and has found them to be "the sort of consensual encounter[s] that implicat[e] no Fourth Amendment interest." We have stated that even when officers have no basis for suspecting a particular individual, they may generally ask questions of that individual, ask to examine the individual's identification, and request consent to search his or her luggage – as long as the police do not convey a message that compliance with their requests is required.

Bostick insists that this case is different because it took place in the cramped confines of a bus. A police encounter is much more intimidating in this setting, he argues, because police tower over a seated passenger and there is little room to move around. Bostick claims to find support in language from cases, indicating that a seizure occurs when a reasonable person would believe that he or she is not "free to leave." Bostick maintains that a reasonable bus passenger would not have felt free to leave under the circumstances of this case because there is nowhere to go on a bus. Also, the bus was about to depart. Had Bostick disembarked, he would have risked being stranded and losing whatever baggage he had locked away in the luggage compartment.

The Florida Supreme Court found this argument persuasive, so much so that it adopted a *per se* rule prohibiting the police from randomly boarding buses as a means of drug interdiction. The state court erred, however, in focusing on whether Bostick was "free to leave" rather than on the principle that those words were intended to capture. When police attempt to question a person who is walking down the street or through an airport lobby, it makes sense to inquire whether a reasonable person would feel free to continue walking. But when the person is seated on a bus and has no desire to leave, the degree to which a reasonable person would feel that he or she could leave is not an accurate measure of the coercive effect of the encounter.

Here, for example, the mere fact that Bostick did not feel free to leave the bus does not mean that the police seized him. Bostick was a passenger on a bus that was scheduled to depart. He would not have felt free to leave the bus even if the police had not been present. Bostick's movements were "confined" in a sense, but this was the natural result of his decision to take the bus; it says nothing about whether or not the police conduct at issue was coercive.

The present case is analytically indistinguishable from *Delgado*. Like the workers in that case, Bostick's freedom of movement was restricted by a factor independent of police conduct — *i.e.*, by his being a passenger on a bus. Accordingly, the "free to leave" analysis on which Bostick relies is inapplicable. In such a situation, the appropriate inquiry is whether a reasonable person would feel free to decline the officers' requests or otherwise terminate the encounter. This formulation follows logically from prior cases and breaks no new ground. We have said before that the crucial test is whether, taking into account all of the circumstances surrounding the encounter, the police conduct would "have communicated to a reasonable person that he was not at liberty to ignore the police presence and go about his business." Where the encounter takes place is one factor, but it is not the only one. And, as the Solicitor General correctly observes, an individual may decline an officer's request without fearing prosecution. We have consistently held that a refusal to cooperate, without more, does not furnish the minimal level of objective justification needed for a detention or seizure.

The facts of this case, as described by the Florida Supreme Court, leave some doubt whether a seizure occurred. Two officers walked up to Bostick on the bus, asked him a few questions, and asked if they could search his bags. As we have explained, no seizure occurs when police ask questions of an individual, ask to examine the individual's identification, and request consent to search his or her luggage — so long as the officers do not convey a message that compliance with their requests is required. Here, the facts recited by the Florida Supreme Court indicate that the officers did not point guns at Bostick or otherwise threaten him and that they specifically advised Bostick that he could refuse consent.

Nevertheless, we refrain from deciding whether or not a seizure occurred in this case. The trial court made no express findings of fact, and the Florida Supreme Court rested its decision on a single fact — that the encounter took place on a bus — rather than on the totality of the circumstances. We remand so that the Florida courts may evaluate the seizure question under the correct legal standard. We do reject, however, Bostick's argument that he must have been seized because no reasonable person would freely consent to a search of luggage that he or she knows contains drugs. This argument cannot prevail because the "reasonable person" test presupposes an *innocent* person. See *Royer* (Blackmun, J., dissenting) ("The fact that [respondent] knew the search was likely to turn up contraband is of course irrelevant; the potential intrusiveness of the officers' conduct must be judged from the viewpoint of an innocent person in [his] position").

The dissent characterizes our decision as holding that police may board buses and by an "*intimidating* show of authority," (emphasis added), demand of passengers their "voluntary" cooperation. That characterization is incorrect. Clearly, a bus passenger's decision to cooperate with law enforcement officers authorizes the police to conduct a search without first obtaining a warrant *only* if the cooperation is voluntary. "Consent" that is the product of official intimidation or harassment is not consent at all. Citizens do not forfeit their constitutional rights when they are coerced to comply with a request that they would prefer to refuse. The question to be decided by the Florida courts on remand is whether Bostick chose to permit the search of his luggage.

The dissent also attempts to characterize our decision as applying a lesser degree of constitutional protection to those individuals who travel by bus, rather than by other forms of transportation. This, too, is an erroneous characterization. Our Fourth Amendment inquiry in this case — whether a reasonable person would have felt free to decline the officers' requests or otherwise terminate the encounter — applies equally to police encounters that take place on trains, planes, and city streets. It is the dissent that would single out this particular mode of travel for differential treatment by adopting a *per se* rule that random bus searches are unconstitutional.

The dissent reserves its strongest criticism for the proposition that police officers can approach individuals as to whom they have no reasonable suspicion and ask them potentially incriminating questions. But this proposition is by no means novel; it has been endorsed by the Court any number of times. *Terry, Royer*, and *Delgado* are just a few examples. As we have explained, today's decision follows logically from those decisions and breaks no new ground. Unless the dissent advocates overruling a long, unbroken line of decisions dating back more than 20 years, its criticism is not well taken.

This Court, as the dissent correctly observes, is not empowered to suspend constitutional guarantees so that the Government may more effectively wage a "war on drugs." If that war is to be fought, those who fight it must respect the rights of individuals, whether or not those individuals are suspected of having committed a crime. By the same token, this Court is not empowered to forbid law enforcement practices simply because it considers them distasteful. The Fourth Amendment proscribes unreasonable searches and seizures; it does not proscribe voluntary cooperation. The cramped confines of a bus are one relevant factor that should be considered in evaluating whether a passenger's consent is voluntary. We cannot agree, however, with the Florida Supreme Court that this single factor will be dispositive in every case.

The judgment of the Florida Supreme Court is reversed, and the case remanded for further proceedings not inconsistent with this opinion.

Justice MARSHALL, with whom Justice BLACKMUN and Justice STEVENS join, dissenting.

Our Nation, we are told, is engaged in a "war on drugs." No one disputes that it is the job of law-enforcement officials to devise effective weapons for fighting this war. But the effectiveness of a law-enforcement technique is not proof of its constitutionality. The general warrant, for example, was certainly an effective means of law enforcement. Yet it was one of the primary aims of the Fourth Amendment to protect citizens from the tyranny of being singled out for search and seizure without particularized suspicion *notwithstanding* the effectiveness of this method. In my view, the law-enforcement technique with which we are confronted in this case—the suspicionless police sweep of buses in intrastate or interstate travel—bears all of the indicia of coercion and unjustified intrusion associated with the general warrant. Because I believe that the bus sweep at issue in this case violates the core values of the Fourth Amendment, I dissent.

I

At issue in this case is a "new and increasingly common tactic in the war on drugs": the suspicionless police sweep of buses in interstate or intrastate travel. Typically under this technique, a group of state or federal officers will board a bus while it is stopped at an intermediate point on its route. Often displaying badges, weapons or other indicia of authority, the officers identify themselves and announce their purpose to intercept drug traffickers. They proceed to approach individual passengers, requesting them to show identification, produce their tickets, and explain the purpose of their travels. Never do the officers advise the passengers that they are free not to speak with the officers. An "interview" of this type ordinarily culminates in a request for consent to search the passenger's luggage.

These sweeps are conducted in "dragnet" style. The police admittedly act without an "articulable suspicion" in deciding which buses to board and which passengers to approach for interviewing.[1] By proceeding systematically in this fashion, the police are able to engage in a tremendously high volume of searches.

To put it mildly, these sweeps "are inconvenient, intrusive, and intimidating." They occur within cramped confines, with officers typically placing themselves in between the passenger selected for an interview and the exit of the bus. Because the bus is only temporarily stationed at a point short of its destination, the passengers are in no position to leave as a means of evading the officers' questioning. Undoubtedly, such a sweep holds up the progress of the bus. Cf. *United States v. Rembert*, 694 F.Supp. 163, 175 (WDNC 1988) (reporting testimony of officer that he makes "every effort in the world not to delay the bus" but that the driver does not leave terminal until sweep is complete). Thus, this "new and increasingly common tactic," burdens the experience of traveling by bus with a degree of governmental interference to which, until now, our society has been proudly unaccustomed. See, *e.g.*, *State ex rel. Ekstrom v. Justice Court*, 136 Ariz. 1, 6, 663 P.2d 992, 997 (1983) (Feldman, J., concurring) ("The thought that an American can be compelled to 'show his papers' before exercising his right to walk the streets, drive the highways or board the trains is repugnant to American institutions and ideals").

---

[1] That is to say, the police who conduct these sweeps decline to offer a reasonable, articulable suspicion of criminal wrongdoing sufficient to justify a warrantless "stop" or "seizure" of the confronted passenger. It does not follow, however, that the approach of passengers during a sweep is completely random. Indeed, at least one officer who routinely confronts interstate travelers candidly admitted that *race* is a factor influencing his decision whom to approach. Thus, the basis of the decision to single out particular passengers during a suspicionless sweep is less likely to be *inarticulable* than *unspeakable*.

This aspect of the suspicionless sweep has not been lost on many of the lower courts called upon to review the constitutionality of this practice. Remarkably, the courts located at the heart of the "drug war" have been the most adamant in condemning this technique. As one Florida court put it:

> "[T]he evidence in this cause has evoked images of other days, under other flags, when no man traveled his nation's roads or railways without fear of unwarranted interruption, by individuals who held temporary power in the Government. The spectre of American citizens being asked, by badge-wielding police, for identification, travel papers—in short a *raison d'etre*—is foreign to *any* fair reading of the Constitution, and its guarantee of human liberties. This is not Hitler's Berlin, nor Stalin's Moscow, nor is it white supremacist South Africa. Yet in Broward County, Florida, these police officers approach every person on board buses and trains ("that time permits") and check identification [and] tickets, [and] ask to search luggage—all in the name of 'voluntary cooperation' with law enforcement. . . ."

The District Court for the District of Columbia spoke in equally pointed words:

> "It seems rather incongruous at this point in the world's history that we find totalitarian states becoming more like our free society while we in this nation are taking on their former trappings of suppressed liberties and freedoms."

. . . . .

"The random indiscriminate stopping and questioning of individuals on interstate busses seems to have gone too far. If this Court approves such 'bus stops' and allows prosecutions to be based on evidence seized as a result of such 'stops,' then we will have stripped our citizens of basic Constitutional protections. Such action would be inconsistent with what this nation has stood for during its 200 years of existence. If passengers on a bus passing through the Capital of this great nation cannot be free from police interference where there is absolutely no basis for the police officers to stop and question them, then the police will be free to accost people on our streets without any reason or cause. In this 'anything goes' war on drugs, random knocks on the doors of our citizens' homes seeking 'consent' to search for drugs cannot be far away. This is not America."

The question for this Court, then, is whether the suspicionless, dragnet-style sweep of buses in intrastate and interstate travel is consistent with the Fourth Amendment. The majority suggests that this latest tactic in the drug war is perfectly compatible with the Constitution. I disagree.

## II

I have no objection to the manner in which the majority frames the test for determining whether a suspicionless bus sweep amounts to a Fourth Amendment "seizure." I agree that the appropriate question is whether a passenger who is approached during such a sweep "would feel free to decline the officers' requests or otherwise terminate the encounter." What I cannot understand is how the majority can possibly suggest an affirmative answer to this question.

The majority reverses what it characterizes as the Florida Supreme Court's "*per se* rule" against suspicionless encounters between the police and bus passengers, suggesting only in dictum its "doubt" that a seizure occurred on the facts of this case. However, the notion that the Florida Supreme Court decided this case on the basis of any "*per se* rule" *independent* of the facts of this case is wholly a product of the majority's imagination. As the majority acknowledges, the Florida Supreme Court "stated explicitly the factual premise for its decision." This factual premise contained *all* of the details of the encounter between respondent and the police. The lower court's analysis of whether respondent was seized drew heavily on these facts, and the court repeatedly emphasized that its conclusion was based on "*all the circumstances*" of this case. (emphasis added); ("*Here, the circumstances indicate* that the officers effectively 'seized' [respondent]" (emphasis added)).

The majority's conclusion that the Florida Supreme Court, contrary to all appearances, *ignored* these facts is based solely on the failure of the lower court to expressly incorporate all of the facts into its reformulation of the certified question on which respondent took his appeal.[2] The majority never explains the basis of its implausible assumption that the Florida Supreme Court intended its phrasing of the certified question to trump its opinion's careful treatment of the facts in this case. Certainly, when *this* Court issues an opinion, it does not intend lower courts and parties to treat as irrelevant the analysis

---

[2] As reformulated, this question read: "Does an impermissible seizure result when police mount a drug search on buses during scheduled stops and question boarded passengers without articulable reasons for doing so, thereby obtaining consent to search the passengers' luggage?"

of facts that the parties neglected to cram into the question presented in the petition for certiorari. But in any case, because the issue whether a seizure has occurred in any given factual setting is a question of law, nothing prevents this Court from deciding on its own whether a seizure occurred based on *all* of the facts of this case as they appear in the opinion of the Florida Supreme Court.

These facts exhibit all of the elements of coercion associated with a typical bus sweep. Two officers boarded the Greyhound bus on which respondent was a passenger while the bus, en route from Miami to Atlanta, was on a brief stop to pick up passengers in Fort Lauderdale. The officers made a visible display of their badges and wore bright green "raid" jackets bearing the insignia of the Broward County Sheriff's Department; one held a gun in a recognizable weapons pouch. These facts alone constitute an intimidating "show of authority." Once on board, the officers approached respondent, who was sitting in the back of the bus, identified themselves as narcotics officers and began to question him. One officer stood in front of respondent's seat, partially blocking the narrow aisle through which respondent would have been required to pass to reach the exit of the bus.

As far as is revealed by facts on which the Florida Supreme Court premised its decision, the officers did not advise respondent that he was free to break off this "interview." Inexplicably, the majority repeatedly stresses the trial court's implicit finding that the police officers advised respondent that he was free to refuse permission to search his travel bag. This aspect of the exchange between respondent and the police is completely irrelevant to the issue before us. For as the State concedes, and as the majority purports to "accept," *if* respondent was unlawfully seized when the officers approached him and initiated questioning, the resulting search was likewise unlawful no matter how well advised respondent was of his right to refuse it. See *Royer.* Consequently, the issue is not whether a passenger in respondent's position would have felt free to deny consent to the search of his bag, but whether such a passenger — without being apprised of his rights — would have felt free to terminate the antecedent encounter with the police.

Unlike the majority, I have no doubt that the answer to this question is no. Apart from trying to accommodate the officers, respondent had only two options. First, he could have remained seated while obstinately refusing to respond to the officers' questioning. But in light of the intimidating show of authority that the officers made upon boarding the bus, respondent reasonably could have believed that such behavior would only arouse the officers' suspicions

and intensify their interrogation. Indeed, officers who carry out bus sweeps like the one at issue here frequently admit that this is the effect of a passenger's refusal to cooperate. The majority's observation that a mere refusal to answer questions, "without more," does not give rise to a reasonable basis for seizing a passenger is utterly beside the point, because a passenger unadvised of his rights and otherwise unversed in constitutional law has *no reason to know* that the police cannot hold his refusal to cooperate against him.

Second, respondent could have tried to escape the officers' presence by leaving the bus altogether. But because doing so would have required respondent to squeeze past the gun-wielding inquisitor who was blocking the aisle of the bus, this hardly seems like a course that respondent reasonably would have viewed as available to him.[3] The majority lamely protests that nothing in the stipulated facts shows that the questioning officer "*point[ed]* [his] gu[n] at [respondent] or otherwise *threatened* him" with the weapon. (emphasis added). Our decisions recognize the obvious point, however, that the choice of the police to "display" their weapons during an encounter exerts significant coercive pressure on the confronted citizen. We have never suggested that the police must go so far as to put a citizen in immediate apprehension of *being shot* before a court can take account of the intimidating effect of being questioned by an officer with weapon in hand.

Even if respondent had perceived that the officers would *let* him leave the bus, moreover, he could not reasonably have been expected to resort to this means of evading their intrusive questioning. For so far as respondent knew, the bus's departure from the terminal was imminent. Unlike a person approached by the police on the street, or at a bus or airport terminal after reaching his destination, a passenger approached by the police at an intermediate point in a long bus journey cannot simply leave the scene and repair to a safe haven to avoid unwanted probing by law-enforcement officials. The vulnerability that an intrastate or interstate traveler experiences when confronted by the police outside of his "own familiar territory" surely aggravates the coercive quality of such an encounter.

The case on which the majority primarily relies, *Delgado,* is distinguishable in every relevant respect. In *Delgado,* this Court held that workers approached

---

[3] As the majority's discussion makes plain, the officer questioning respondent clearly carried a weapons pouch during the interview.

by law-enforcement officials inside of a factory were not "seized" for purposes of the Fourth Amendment. The Court was careful to point out, however, that the presence of the agents did not furnish the workers with a reasonable basis for believing that they were not free to leave the factory, as at least some of them did. Unlike passengers confronted by law-enforcement officials on a bus stopped temporarily at an intermediate point in its journey, workers approached by law-enforcement officials at their workplace need not abandon personal belongings and venture into unfamiliar environs in order to avoid unwanted questioning. Moreover, the workers who did not leave the building in *Delgado* remained free to move about the entire factory, a considerably less confining environment than a bus. Finally, contrary to the officer who confronted respondent, the law-enforcement officials in *Delgado* did not conduct their interviews with guns in hand.

Rather than requiring the police to justify the coercive tactics employed here, the majority blames respondent for his own sensation of constraint. The majority concedes that respondent "did not feel free to leave the bus" as a means of breaking off the interrogation by the Broward County officers. But this experience of confinement, the majority explains, "was the natural result of *his* decision to take the bus." (emphasis added). Thus, in the majority's view, because respondent's "freedom of movement was restricted by a factor independent of police conduct—*i.e.*, by his being a passenger on a bus," respondent was not seized for purposes of the Fourth Amendment.

This reasoning borders on sophism and trivializes the values that underlie the Fourth Amendment. Obviously, a person's "voluntary decision" to place himself in a room with only one exit does not authorize the police to force an encounter upon him by placing themselves in front of the exit. It is no more acceptable for the police to force an encounter on a person by exploiting his "voluntary decision" to

expose himself to perfectly legitimate personal or social constraints. By consciously deciding to single out persons who have undertaken interstate or intrastate travel, officers who conduct suspicionless, dragnet-style sweeps put passengers to the choice of cooperating or of exiting their buses and possibly being stranded in unfamiliar locations. It is exactly because this "choice" is no "choice" at all that police engage this technique.

In my view, the Fourth Amendment clearly condemns the suspicionless, dragnet-style sweep of intrastate or interstate buses. Withdrawing this particular weapon from the government's drug-war arsenal would hardly leave the police without any means of combating the use of buses as instrumentalities of the drug trade. The police would remain free, for example, to approach passengers whom they have a reasonable, articulable basis to suspect of criminal wrongdoing.[4] Alternatively, they could continue to confront passengers without suspicion so long as they took simple steps, like advising the passengers confronted of their right to decline to be questioned, to dispel the aura of coercion and intimidation that pervades such encounters. There is no reason to expect that such requirements would render the Nation's buses law-enforcement-free zones.

### III

The majority attempts to gloss over the violence that today's decision does to the Fourth Amendment with empty admonitions. "If th[e] [war on drugs] is to be fought," the majority intones, "those who fight it must respect the rights of individuals, whether or not those individuals are suspected of having committed a crime." The majority's actions, however, speak louder than its words.

I dissent.

---

[4] Insisting that police officers explain their decision to single out a particular passenger for questioning would help prevent their reliance on impermissible criteria such as race.

## QUESTIONS AND NOTES

**1.** How far apart are the majority and dissent? On remand, would it be appropriate for the Florida Supreme Court to determine that under all of the circumstances, Bostick *was* seized?

**2.** If your answer to question 1 was "yes," is the majority's approach (as opposed to the "*per se*" approach) nevertheless problematic because it invites swearing contests in which the truth may or may not ultimately prevail (*e.g.* was the searchee told that he did not have to permit the search)?

**3.** Is questioning a passenger on a bus inherently different from questioning him at a bus terminal?

**4.** Do you think that the police conducting bus sweeps are likely to make an effort to let the citizenry know that they do *not* have to consent? Or are they more likely to make an effort to convey the *opposite* message?

**5.** Is allowing "bus sweeps" unacceptably analogous to totalitarian practices? If so, is there anything in the Fourth Amendment that can fairly be read to condemn them?

**6.** The Court emphasizes the importance of focusing on a hypothetical "innocent" person. In what way, if at all, might an innocent person have been hurt by the conduct of the policemen in this case? (See Chapter 10, *infra.*)

**7.** We conclude this section with *Hodari D.*, a case dealing with an attempted seizure.

## California v. Hodari D.
### 111 S.Ct. 1547 (1991)

Justice SCALIA delivered the opinion of the Court.

Late one evening in April 1988, Officers Brian McColgin and Jerry Pertoso were on patrol in a high-crime area of Oakland, California. They were dressed in street clothes but wearing jackets with "Police" embossed on both front and back. Their unmarked car proceeded west on Foothill Boulevard, and turned south onto 63rd Avenue. As they rounded the corner, they saw four or five youths huddled around a small red car parked at the curb. When the youths saw the officers' car approaching they apparently panicked, and took flight. The respondent here, Hodari D., and one companion ran west through an alley; the others fled south. The red car also headed south, at a high rate of speed.

The officers were suspicious and gave chase. McColgin remained in the car and continued south on 63rd Avenue; Pertoso left the car, ran back north along 63rd, then west on Foothill Boulevard, and turned south on 62nd Avenue. Hodari, meanwhile, emerged from the alley onto 62nd and ran north. Looking behind as he ran, he did not turn and see Pertoso until the officer was almost upon him, whereupon he tossed away what appeared to be a small rock. A moment later, Pertoso tackled Hodari, handcuffed him, and radioed for assistance. Hodari was found to be carrying $130 in cash and a pager; and the rock he had discarded was found to be crack cocaine.

In the juvenile proceeding brought against him, Hodari moved to suppress the evidence relating to the cocaine. The court denied the motion without opinion. The California Court of Appeal reversed, holding that Hodari had been "seized" when he saw Officer Pertoso running towards him, that this seizure was unreasonable under the Fourth Amendment, and that the evidence of cocaine had to be suppressed as the fruit of that illegal seizure. The California Supreme Court denied the State's application for review. We granted certiorari.

As this case comes to us, the only issue presented is whether, at the time he dropped the drugs, Hodari had been "seized" within the meaning of the Fourth Amendment.[1] If so, respondent argues, the drugs were the fruit of that seizure and the evidence concerning them was properly excluded. If not, the drugs were abandoned by Hodari and lawfully recovered by the police, and the evidence should have been admitted. (In addition, of course, Pertoso's seeing the rock of cocaine, at least if he recognized it as such, would provide reasonable suspicion for the unquestioned seizure that occurred when he tackled Hodari).

We have long understood that the Fourth Amendment's protection against "unreasonable . . . seizures" includes seizure of the person. From the time of the founding to the present, the word "seizure" has meant a "taking possession," 2 N. Webster, An

---

[1] California conceded below that Officer Pertoso did not have the "reasonable suspicion" required to justify stopping Hodari. That it would be unreasonable to stop, for brief inquiry, young men who scatter in panic upon the mere sighting of the police is not self-evident, and arguably contradicts proverbial common sense. See Proverbs 28:1 ("The wicked flee when no man pursueth"). We do not decide that point here, but rely entirely upon the State's concession.

American Dictionary of the English Language 67 (1828); 2 J. Bouvier, A Law Dictionary 510 (6th ed. 1856); Webster's Third New International Dictionary 2057 (1981). For most purposes at common law, the word connoted not merely grasping, or applying physical force to, the animate or inanimate object in question, but actually bringing it within physical control. A ship still fleeing, even though under attack, would not be considered to have been seized as a war prize. To constitute an arrest, however – the quintessential "seizure of the person" under our Fourth Amendment jurisprudence – the mere grasping or application of physical force with lawful authority, whether or not it succeeded in subduing the arrestee, was sufficient. See, *e.g., Whitehead v. Keyes*, 85 Mass. 495, 501 (1862) ("[A]n officer effects an arrest of a person whom he has authority to arrest, by laying his hand on him for the purpose of arresting him, though he may not succeed in stopping and holding him").

To say that an arrest is effected by the slightest application of physical force, despite the arrestee's escape, is not to say that for Fourth Amendment purposes there is a *continuing* arrest during the period of fugitivity. If, for example, Pertoso had laid his hands upon Hodari to arrest him, but Hodari had broken away and had *then* cast away the cocaine, it would hardly be realistic to say that that disclosure had been made during the course of an arrest. The present case, however, is even one step further removed. It does not involve the application of any physical force; Hodari was untouched by Officer Pertoso at the time he discarded the cocaine. His defense relies instead upon the proposition that a seizure occurs "when the officer, by means of physical force *or show of authority*, has in some way restrained the liberty of a citizen." *Terry* (emphasis added). Hodari contends (and we accept as true for purposes of this decision) that Pertoso's pursuit qualified as a "show of authority" calling upon Hodari to halt. The narrow question before us is whether, with respect to a show of authority as with respect to application of physical force, a seizure occurs even though the subject does not yield. We hold that it does not.

The language of the Fourth Amendment, of course, cannot sustain respondent's contention. The word "seizure" readily bears the meaning of a laying on of hands or application of physical force to restrain movement, even when it is ultimately unsuccessful. ("She seized the purse-snatcher, but he broke out of her grasp.") It does not remotely apply, however, to the prospect of a policeman yelling "Stop, in the name of the law!" at a fleeing form

that continues to flee. That is no seizure.[2] Nor can the result respondent wishes to achieve be produced – indirectly, as it were – by suggesting that Pertoso's uncomplied-with show of authority was a common-law arrest, and then appealing to the principle that all common-law arrests are seizures. An arrest requires *either* physical force (as described above) *or*, where that is absent, *submission* to the assertion of authority.

"Mere words will not constitute an arrest, while, on the other hand, no actual, physical touching is essential. The apparent inconsistency in the two parts of this statement is explained by the fact that an assertion of authority and purpose to arrest followed by submission of the arrestee constitutes an arrest. There can be no arrest without either touching or submission." Perkins, The Law of Arrest, 25 Iowa L.Rev. 201, 206 (1940).

We do not think it desirable, even as a policy matter, to stretch the Fourth Amendment beyond its words and beyond the meaning of arrest, as respondent urges. Street pursuits always place the public at some risk, and compliance with police orders to stop should therefore be encouraged. Only a few of those orders, we must presume, will be without adequate basis, and since the addressee has no ready means of identifying the deficient ones it almost invariably is the responsible course to comply. Unlawful orders will not be deterred, moreover, by sanctioning through the exclusionary rule those of them that are *not* obeyed. Since policemen do not command "Stop!" expecting to be ignored, or give chase hoping to be outrun, it fully suffices to apply the deterrent to their genuine, successful seizures.

Respondent contends that his position is sustained by the so-called *Mendenhall* test, formulated by Justice Stewart: "A person has been 'seized' within the

---

[2] For this simple reason – which involves neither "logic-chopping," nor any arcane knowledge of legal history – it is irrelevant that English law proscribed "an unlawful *attempt* to take a presumptively innocent person into custody." We have consulted the common-law to explain the meaning of seizure – and, contrary to the dissent's portrayal, to expand rather than contract that meaning (since one would not normally think that the mere touching of a person would suffice). But neither usage nor common-law tradition makes an *attempted* seizure a seizure. The common-law may have made an attempted seizure unlawful in certain circumstances; but it made many things unlawful, very few of which were elevated to constitutional proscriptions.

meaning of the Fourth Amendment only if, in view of all the circumstances surrounding the incident, a reasonable person would have believed that he was not free to leave." In seeking to rely upon that test here, respondent fails to read it carefully. It says that a person has been seized "only if," not that he has been seized "whenever"; it states a *necessary*, but not a *sufficient* condition for seizure—or, more precisely, for seizure effected through a "show of authority." *Mendenhall* establishes that the test for existence of a "show of authority" is an objective one: not whether the citizen perceived that he was being ordered to restrict his movement, but whether the officer's words and actions would have conveyed that to a reasonable person. Application of this objective test was the basis for our decision in the other case principally relied upon by respondent, *Michigan v. Chesternut*, 486 U.S. 567 (1988), where we concluded that the police cruiser's slow following of the defendant did not convey the message that he was not free to disregard the police and go about his business. We did not address in *Chesternut*, however, the question whether, if the *Mendenhall* test was met—if the message that the defendant was not free to leave *had* been conveyed—a Fourth Amendment seizure would have occurred.

In sum, assuming that Pertoso's pursuit in the present case constituted a "show of authority" enjoining Hodari to halt, since Hodari did not comply with that injunction he was not seized until he was tackled. The cocaine abandoned while he was running was in this case not the fruit of a seizure, and his motion to exclude evidence of it was properly denied. We reverse the decision of the California Court of Appeal, and remand for further proceedings not inconsistent with this opinion.

Justice STEVENS, with whom Justice MARSHALL joins, dissenting.

The Court's narrow construction of the word "seizure" represents a significant, and in my view, unfortunate, departure from prior case law construing the Fourth Amendment. [T]he Court now adopts a definition of "seizure" that is unfaithful to a long line of Fourth Amendment cases. Even if the Court were defining seizure for the first time, which it is not, the definition that it chooses today is profoundly unwise. In its decision, the Court assumes, without acknowledging, that a police officer may now fire his weapon at an innocent citizen and not implicate the Fourth Amendment—as long as he misses his target.

For the purposes of decision, the following propositions are not in dispute. First, when Officer Pertoso began his pursuit of respondent,[4] the officer did not have a lawful basis for either stopping or arresting respondent. Second, the officer's chase amounted to a "show of force" as soon as respondent saw the officer nearly upon him. Third, the act of discarding the rock of cocaine was the direct consequence of the show of force. Fourth, as the Court correctly demonstrates, no common-law arrest occurred until the officer tackled respondent. Thus, the Court is quite right in concluding that the abandonment of the rock was not the fruit of a common-law arrest.

It is equally clear, however, that if the officer had succeeded in touching respondent before he dropped the rock—even if he did not subdue him—an arrest would have occurred. In that event (assuming the touching precipitated the abandonment), the evidence would have been the fruit of an unlawful common-law arrest. The distinction between the actual case and the hypothetical case is the same as the distinction between the common-law torts of assault and battery—a touching converts the former into the latter. Although the distinction between assault and battery was important for pleading purposes, the distinction should not take on constitutional dimensions. The Court mistakenly allows this common-law distinction to define its interpretation of the Fourth Amendment.

At the same time, the Court fails to recognize the existence of another, more telling, common-law distinction—the distinction between an arrest and an attempted arrest. As the Court teaches us, the distinction between battery and assault was critical to a correct understanding of the common law of arrest. However, the facts of this case do not describe an actual arrest, but rather, an unlawful *attempt* to take a presumptively

---

[4] The Court's gratuitous quotation from Proverbs 28:1, mistakenly assumes that innocent residents have no reason to fear the sudden approach of strangers. We have previously considered, and rejected, this ivory-towered analysis of the real world for it fails to describe the experience of many residents, particularly if they are members of a minority. It has long been "a matter of common knowledge that men who are entirely innocent do sometimes fly from the scene of a crime through fear of being apprehended as the guilty parties, or from an unwillingness to appear as witnesses. Nor is it true as an accepted axiom of criminal law that 'the wicked flee when no man pursueth, but the righteous are as bold as a lion.'"

innocent person into custody. Such an attempt was unlawful at common law.[7] Thus, if the Court wants to define the scope of the Fourth Amendment based on the common law, it should look, not to the common law of arrest, but to the common law of attempted arrest, according to the facts of this case.

The first question, then, is whether the common law should define the scope of the outer boundaries of the constitutional protection against unreasonable seizures. Even if, contrary to settled precedent, traditional common-law analysis were controlling, it would still be necessary to decide whether the unlawful attempt to make an arrest should be considered a seizure within the meaning of the Fourth Amendment, and whether the exclusionary rule should apply to unlawful attempts.

## II

The Court today draws the novel conclusion that even though no seizure can occur *unless* the *Mendenhall* reasonable person standard is met, the fact that the standard has been met does not necessarily mean that a seizure has occurred. (*Mendenhall* "states a *necessary*, but not a *sufficient* condition for seizure . . . effected through a 'show of authority'"). If it were true that a seizure requires more than whether a reasonable person felt free to leave, then the following passage from the Court's opinion in *Delgado*, is at best, seriously misleading:

"As we have noted elsewhere: 'Obviously, not all personal intercourse between policemen and citizens involves "seizures" of persons. Only when the officer, by means of physical force or show of authority, has restrained the liberty of a citizen may we conclude that a "seizure" has occurred.' While applying such a test is relatively straightforward in a situation resembling a traditional arrest, the protection against unreasonable seizures also extends to 'seizures that involve only a brief detention short of traditional arrest.' What has evolved from our cases is a determination that an initially consensual encounter between a police officer and a citizen can be transformed into a seizure or detention within the meaning of the Fourth Amendment, 'if, in view of all the circumstances surrounding the incident, a reasonable person would have believed that he was not free to leave.'"

More importantly, in *Royer*, 460 U.S. 491 (1983), a plurality of the Court adopted Justice Stewart's formulation in *Mendenhall* as the appropriate standard for determining when police questioning crosses the threshold from a consensual encounter to a forcible stop. In *Royer*, the Court held that an illegal seizure had occurred. As a predicate for that holding, Justice White, in his opinion for the plurality, explained that the citizen "may not be detained *even momentarily* without reasonable, objective grounds for doing so; and his refusal to listen or answer does not, without more, furnish those grounds." (emphasis added). The rule looks, not to the subjective perceptions of the person questioned, but rather, to the objective characteristics of the encounter that may suggest whether a reasonable person would have felt free to leave.

Finally, it is noteworthy that in *Chesternut*, the State asked us to repudiate the reasonable person standard developed in *Terry, Mendenhall, Delgado*, and *Royer*.[13] We decided, however, to "adhere to our traditional contextual approach." In our opinion, we described Justice Stewart's analysis in *Mendenhall* as "a test to be applied in determining whether 'a person has been "seized" within the meaning of the Fourth Amendment'" and noted that "[t]he Court has since embraced this test." Moreover, in commenting on the virtues of the test, we explained that it focused on the police officer's conduct:

"The test's objective standard—looking to the reasonable man's interpretation of the conduct in question—allows the police to determine in advance whether the conduct contemplated will implicate the Fourth Amendment."

Expressing his approval of the Court's rejection of Michigan's argument in *Chesternut*, Professor LaFave observed:

"The 'free to leave' concept, in other words, has nothing to do with a particular suspect's choice to flee rather than submit or with his assessment of the probability of successful flight. Were it otherwise, police would be encouraged to utilize a very threatening but sufficiently slow chase as an evidence-gathering

---

[7] "[E]ven without touching the other, the officer may subject himself to liability if he undertakes to make an arrest without being privileged by law to do so."

[13] "Petitioner argues that the Fourth Amendment is never implicated until an individual stops in response to the police's show of authority. Thus, petitioner would have us rule that a lack of objective and particularized suspicion would not poison police conduct, no matter how coercive, as long as the police did not succeed in actually apprehending the individual."

technique whenever they lack even the reasonable suspicion needed for a *Terry* stop.''

Whatever else one may think of today's decision, it unquestionably represents a departure from earlier Fourth Amendment case law. The notion that our prior cases contemplated a distinction between seizures effected by a touching on the one hand, and those effected by a show of force on the other hand, and that all of our repeated descriptions of the *Mendenhall* test stated only a necessary, but not a sufficient, condition for finding seizures in the latter category, is nothing if not creative lawmaking. Moreover, by narrowing the definition of the term seizure, instead of enlarging the scope of reasonable justifications for seizures, the Court has significantly limited the protection provided to the ordinary citizen by the Fourth Amendment.

### III

In this case the officer's show of force—taking the form of a head-on chase—adequately conveyed the message that respondent was not free to leave.[14] Whereas in *Mendenhall*, there was "nothing in the record [to] sugges[t] that the respondent had any objective reason to believe that she was not free to end the conversation in the concourse and proceed on her way," here, respondent attempted to end "the conversation" before it began and soon found himself literally "not free to leave" when confronted by an officer running toward him head-on who eventually tackled him to the ground. There was an interval of time between the moment that respondent saw the officer fast approaching and the moment when he was tackled, and thus brought under the control of the officer. The question is whether the Fourth Amendment was implicated at the earlier or the later moment.

Because the facts of this case are somewhat unusual, it is appropriate to note that the same issue would arise if the show of force took the form of a command to "freeze," a warning shot, or the sound of sirens accompanied by a patrol car's flashing lights. In any of these situations, there may be a

---

[14] The California Court of Appeal noted:

"This case involves more than a pursuit, as Officer Pertoso did not pursue [respondent], but ran in such a fashion as to cut him off and confront him head on. Under the rationale of *Chesternut*, this action is reasonably perceived as an intrusion upon one's freedom of movement and as a maneuver intended to block or 'otherwise control the direction or speed' of one's movement."

significant time interval between the initiation of the officer's show of force and the complete submission by the citizen. At least on the facts of this case, the Court concludes that the timing of the seizure is governed by the citizen's reaction, rather than by the officer's conduct. One consequence of this conclusion is that the point at which the interaction between citizen and police officer becomes a seizure occurs, not when a reasonable citizen believes he or she is no longer free to go, but rather, only after the officer exercises control over the citizen.

In my view, our interests in effective law enforcement and in personal liberty would be better served by adhering to a standard that "allows the police to determine in advance whether the conduct contemplated will implicate the Fourth Amendment." The range of possible responses to a police show of force, and the multitude of problems that may arise in determining whether, and at which moment, there has been "submission," can only create uncertainty and generate litigation.

In cases within this new subcategory, there will be a period of time during which the citizen's liberty has been restrained, but he or she has not yet completely submitted to the show of force. A motorist pulled over by a highway patrol car cannot come to an immediate stop, even if the motorist intends to obey the patrol car's signal. If an officer decides to make the kind of random stop forbidden by *Prouse*, and, after flashing his lights, but before the vehicle comes to a complete stop, sees that the license plate has expired, can he justify his action on the ground that the seizure became lawful after it was initiated but before it was completed? In an airport setting, may a drug enforcement agent now approach a group of passengers with his gun drawn, announce a "baggage search," and rely on the passengers' reactions to justify his investigative stops? The holding of today's majority fails to recognize the coercive and intimidating nature of such behavior and creates a rule that may allow such behavior to go unchecked.

The deterrent purposes of the exclusionary rule focus on the conduct of law enforcement officers, and on discouraging improper behavior on their part, and not on the reaction of the citizen to the show of force. In the present case, if Officer Pertoso had succeeded in tackling respondent before he dropped the rock of cocaine, the rock unquestionably would have been excluded as the fruit of the officer's unlawful seizure. Instead, under the Court's logic-chopping analysis, the exclusionary rule has no application because an attempt to make an unconstitutional seizure is beyond the coverage of the Fourth Amendment, no matter how outrageous or unreasonable the officer's conduct may be.

It is too early to know the consequences of the Court's holding. If carried to its logical conclusion, it will encourage unlawful displays of force that will frighten countless innocent citizens into surrendering whatever privacy rights they may still have. It is not too soon, however, to note the irony in the fact that the Court's own justification for its result is its analysis of the rules of the common law of arrest that antedated *Terry*. Yet, even in those days the common law provided the citizen with protection against an attempt to make an unlawful arrest. The central message of *Terry* was that the protection the Fourth Amendment provides to the average citizen is not rigidly confined by ancient common-law precept. The message that today's literal-minded majority conveys is that the common law, rather than our understanding of the Fourth Amendment as it has developed over the last quarter of a century, defines, and limits, the scope of a seizure. The Court today defines a seizure as commencing, not with egregious police conduct, but rather, with submission by the citizen. Thus, it both delays the point at which "the Fourth Amendment becomes relevant" to an encounter and limits the range of encounters that will come under the heading of "seizure." Today's qualification of the Fourth Amendment means that innocent citizens may remain "secure in their persons . . . against unreasonable searches and seizures" only at the discretion of the police.

I respectfully dissent.

## QUESTIONS AND NOTES

**1.** Do you think that the Scalia opinion may have been influenced by his attitude towards California's concession as reflected in his footnote 1? Should it be?

**2.** Who has the better of the semantics, Scalia or Stevens? Explain.

**3.** If a criminal statute forbade rape, would (should) we imply that it intended to punish an attempted rapist?

**4.** Assume that a University forbade employing racial criteria in placing students with roommates. Assume further that a University official had intentionally assigned a black student to room with another black student. Assume that upon the student's complaint, a higher University official placed the student with a roommate on a nonracial criterion. Would (should) the original University official be able to defend himself from being disciplined on the ground that he did *not* place the student on racial grounds, he only attempted to place the student on racial grounds?

**5.** As between Scalia and Stevens, who has the better of the policy argument? Explain.

# 10.

# SEARCHES

In this chapter, we shall attempt to define searches. As with seizures (Chapter 9, *supra*), we have heretofore assumed that all of the alleged searches have in fact been such. Perhaps a threshold question to ask is why we should care whether a particular police activity constitutes a search (or seizure). For example, why don't we just ask, in a case like *Hodari D.*, whether the police conduct was reasonable and not worry about whether it was a seizure? Would it be unduly burdensome for the police to *always* have to act reasonably? Why? Why not?

In fact, it is clear that (at least in the ordinary case) unreasonable police conduct, such as excessive questioning of friends and associates or excessive surveillance, will not constitute a Fourth Amendment violation. So, for example, if after the DEA had questioned Mark Royer (see *Florida v. Royer*, Chapter 7, B, *supra*) and had *not* found evidence of crime, they went to Ithaca College and asked all of Royer's classmates and professors whether they had heard of Royer's drug activities, it is unlikely that the DEA would have been found to have violated the Fourth Amendment. (Whether they would have incurred any other tort or criminal liability is beyond the scope of this book.) Consequently, ascertaining whether particular activity constitutes a search is of critical importance to the Fourth Amendment.

## A.   The Divining Rod Theory of the Fourth Amendment

One of your authors, Arnold Loewy, has developed a theory of the Fourth Amendment (to which your other author, Arthur LaFrance, has substantial reservations) which is presented in the following law review excerpt.

# The Fourth Amendment as a Device
## for Protecting the Innocent*
### 81 Mich. L. Rev. 1229 (1983)
### Arnold H. Loewy

If the Fourth Amendment permits the government to search for and seize evidence of crime (See *Warden v. Hayden*, chapter 9, *infra*), it should follow that an individual has no inherent right to secrete such evidence. Consequently, the Fourth Amendment should be understood as a device to separate the wheat (evidence of crime) from the chaff (that which individuals may possess free from government prying). In a Utopian society,[69] each policeman would be equipped with an evidence-detecting divining rod. He would walk up and down the streets and whenever the divining rod detected evidence of crime, it would locate the evidence. First, it would single out the house, then it would point to the room, then the drawer, and finally the evidence itself. Thus, all evidence of crime would be uncovered in the most efficient possible manner, and no innocent person would be subject to a search. In a real society (such as ours), the Fourth Amendment serves as an imperfect divining rod.

Consider the following hypothetical: Principal X of Y High School, because of a hunch that students A, B, and C each have marijuana in their respective lockers, opens the lockers with a passkey. In A's locker, he finds marijuana, which is subsequently given to the police and used to convict A of possession of marijuana, for which A receives a year's imprisonment. In B's locker he finds a picture of his (Principal X's) head attached to the rear end of a horse with the caption: "X is a Horse's Ass." In C's locker, he finds a picture of C's mother with the caption: "Mom."

Assuming that these searches were unlawful, conventional wisdom suggests that A's rights were violated more than the others since only he suffered a criminal conviction by virtue of the search. Yet B's and C's legitimate privacy interest were more seriously intruded upon. B had a fourth (and probably a first) amendment right to keep his opinion of the principal to himself. His belief that the principal's prying eyes would not see his crude, but arguably cute, caricature is a reasonable one which ought to be protected. Similarly, C's hanging his mother's picture in his locker (though along with apple pie and the flag, the paradigmatic affirmation of true-blue American values) could be a source of embarrassment if made known to the public.

Let us now vary the hypothetical. Assume that instead of searching the three lockers, X decides to confirm his suspicions by having a marijuana-sniffing dog sniff the three lockers. The dog determines that marijuana is present in A's locker, but is not present in either B's or C's locker. X then goes before a magistrate, who issues a search warrant to search A's locker for marijuana, which of course is found.

In this situation, neither B nor C has had his fourth amendment rights violated. Neither's privacy has been invaded. They have not been compelled to share secrets with others. The government has learned nothing about them except that they do not possess marijuana. Any interest they may have in keeping the authorities from learning of their innocence is surely too trivial to protect.

Have A's rights been violated? He would of course like to keep to himself the evidence of his crime. But his claim is not a powerful one. Indeed, in this case, an accurate dog[75] approaches the hypothetical divining rod by separating the innocent from the guilty.

Many students and colleagues with whom I have discussed the divining rod theory have objected to it because of its "1984" overtones. There is a major difference, however, between "Big Brother" watching *everything* and government being able to detect *only* evidence of crime.

I am not contending that any use of any device that in some ways resembles a divining rod is *per se* reasonable. For example, so innocuous a device as a magnetometer cannot distinguish permissible metals (coins, keys, etc.) from impermissible ones (guns, knives, etc.).[78] Furthermore, most magnetometers, such as the one in the United States Supreme Court Building, require that innocent people

---

* Copyright 1983, reprinted with permission of The Michigan Law Review Association.

[69] Ignoring for the moment that nobody commits crime in a Utopia.

---

[75] Obviously, an inaccurate dog would present different problems.

[78] Indeed, so innocent a person as the author of this Article was compelled to empty from his pockets metal-framed glasses, coins and keys in full view of his students after activating the magnetometer at the United States Supreme Court.

be herded like cattle and marched single file through the device. On the other hand, if a device could be invented that accurately detected weapons and did not disrupt the normal movement of people, there could be no fourth amendment objection to its use.[79]

Nor do I suggest *carte blanche* use of marijuana-sniffing dogs. To the extent that the dog is less than perfectly accurate, innocent people run the risk of being searched.[80] Additionally, the very act of being subjected to a body sniff by a German Shepherd may be offensive at best or harrowing at worst to the innocent sniffee.[81]

Another concern expressed about marijuana-sniffing dogs (and presumably other divining rods) is Professor Gardner's contention that people have a right to be free from unwarranted suspicion.[82]

---

[79] This is not to say the use of a magnetometer is impermissible; rather, that it is only permissible when the interest in using it outweighs the offensiveness of the intrusion involved.

[80] For example, in *Doe v. Renfrow*, 475 F. Supp. 1012 (N.D. Ind. 1979), a drug-sniffing dog had "alerted" to a 13-year-old junior high school girl during a school-wide "sniff" of all the students. The dog continued to "alert" to her even after she emptied her pockets. Diane Doe was then subjected to a nude search by two women who examined her clothing and lifted her hair to look for drugs. No drugs were found but it was later discovered that she had been playing that morning with her dog, which was in heat.

To further highlight the inaccuracy of these particular dogs, they "alerted" to some fifty students, only seventeen of whom were found to be in possession of drugs.

[81] In *Doe v. Renfrow*, 475 F. Supp. at 1017, the Highland Town School District Board, the Superintendent of Schools (Omer Renfrow), members of the Highland Police Department and Patricia Little (owner of a dog training school) devised a plan to combat what they feared was a growing drug problem in the Highland Junior and Senior High Schools wherein all 2,780 students were required to remain seated at their desks while a dog sniffed at them as the dog and his trainer walked up and down the aisles. Thus approximately 2,763 innocent students were subjected to this potentially frightening and definitely degrading experience, and some 33 students were wrongly suspected of possessing contraband by the dogs' false alerts.

[82] Gardner, *Sniffing for Drugs in the Classroom-Perspectives on Fourth Amendment Scope*, 74 Nw.U.L.Rev. 803 (1980).

Thus, in our hypothetical locker search, A, B, and C could all argue that they had the right to be free from unwarranted suspicion. B and C, however, were benefited by the dog (divining rod) because it was the dog that freed them from the unwarranted suspicion which otherwise would have continued in the principal's mind.

Student A might have an argument that he, along with students B and C, was singled out for special treatment. If he could introduce additional factors, for example, that half of the students were believed to have marijuana in their lockers and that A, B, and C were the only blacks in an otherwise all-white school, he might have a serious constitutional contention. Apart from this equal protection problem, however, there is no constitutional basis for holding that a person has a right to be free from unjustifiable suspicion.[85] Indeed, as noted, the beauty of the canine sniff is the ability to free one from unjustifiable suspicion.[86]

In sum, the fourth amendment exists to protect the innocent and may normally be invoked by the guilty only when necessary to protect the innocent.

---

[85] Gardner cites no authority to support a constitutional basis for "the right to be free from unjust suspicion." Furthermore, if there were such a rule, neither the principal nor the police could ask questions about students suspected of criminal activity as long as there were no probable cause (or at least no reasonable suspicion) for arrest or search. The result would be a catch-22 in which police could not search because they did not have probable cause and could not investigate in order to establish probable cause because suspicion would thereby be cast on the individual unjustly.

[86] A final objection to the divining rod theory is that if we had a device that would detect evidence of crimes whenever it existed, it would possibly precipitate enforcement of laws that we do not really want enforced. The following quote by Thurman W. Arnold expresses the idea sharply: "Most unenforced criminal laws survive in order to satisfy moral objections to established modes of conduct. They are unenforced because we want to continue our conduct, and unrepealed because we want to preserve our morals." Arnold, *Law Enforcement—An Attempt at Social Dissection*, 42 YALE L.J. 1, 14 (1932). Arguably certain drug laws (*e.g.*, possession of marijuana) are examples of such laws. If so, the better course of action is for the legislatures and perhaps the courts to rethink the propriety of marijuana laws. If the employment of crime-detecting devices such as marijuana-sniffing dogs causes us to rethink that which we outlaw, it is an argument in favor of, and not against, such a use.

# QUESTIONS AND NOTES

**1.** At different times, both the "liberals" and "conservatives" seem to think of the Fourth Amendment as a device for protecting the innocent. For example, in *Bostick*, the conservatives emphasized that their only concern was whether an innocent person would have felt free to refrain from cooperating with the police. On the other hand, in *Montoya DeHernandez*, it was the "liberals" who were concerned with the INS practice on hypothetically innocent people. The "divining rod" theory suggests that we should always focus on the innocent, regardless of whose ox is gored.

**2.** We will first look at judicial attitudes towards the divining rod theory and then focus on its appropriateness as a Fourth Amendment measuring stick.

## United States v. Place
### 462 U.S. 696 (1983)

Justice O'CONNOR delivered the opinion of the Court.

(For a statement of the facts, see Ch. 7, C, *supra*.)

The purpose for which respondent's luggage was seized, of course, was to arrange its exposure to a narcotics detection dog. Obviously, if this investigative procedure is itself a search requiring probable cause, the initial seizure of respondent's luggage for the purpose of subjecting it to the sniff test—no matter how brief—could not be justified on less than probable cause.

The Fourth Amendment "protects people from unreasonable government intrusions into their legitimate expectations of privacy." We have affirmed that a person possesses a privacy interest in the contents of personal luggage that is protected by the Fourth Amendment. A "canine sniff" by a well-trained narcotics detection dog, however, does not require opening the luggage. It does not expose non-contraband items that otherwise would remain hidden from public view, as does, for example, an officer's rummaging through the contents of the luggage. Thus, the manner in which information is obtained through this investigative technique is much less intrusive than a typical search. Moreover, the sniff discloses only the presence or absence of narcotics, a contraband item. Thus, despite the fact that the sniff tells the authorities something about the contents of the luggage, the information obtained is limited. This limited disclosure also ensures that the owner of the property is not subjected to the embarrassment and inconvenience entailed in less discriminate and more intrusive investigative methods.

In these respects, the canine sniff is *sui generis*.

We are aware of no other investigative procedure that is so limited both in the manner in which the information is obtained and in the content of the information revealed by the procedure. Therefore, we conclude that the particular course of investigation that the agents intended to pursue here—exposure of respondent's luggage, which was located in a public place, to a trained canine—did not constitute a "search" within the meaning of the Fourth Amendment.

Justice BRENNAN, with whom Justice MARSHALL joins, concurring in result.

The Court suggests today, in a discussion unnecessary to the judgment, that exposure of respondent's luggage to a narcotics detection dog "did not constitute a 'search' within the meaning of the Fourth Amendment." In the District Court, respondent did "not contest the validity of sniff searches *per se*. . . ." The Court of Appeals did not reach or discuss the issue. It was not briefed or argued in this Court. In short, I agree with Justice Blackmun that the Court should not address the issue.

I also agree with Justice Blackmun's suggestion that the issue is more complex than the Court's discussion would lead one to believe. As Justice Stevens suggested in objecting to "unnecessarily broad dicta" in *United States v. Knotts*, 460 U.S. 276 (1983), the use of electronic detection techniques that enhance human perception implicates "especially sensitive concerns." (opinion concurring in the judgment). Obviously, a narcotics detection dog is not an electronic detection device. Unlike the electronic "beeper" in *Knotts*, however, a dog does more than merely allow the police to do more efficiently what they could do using only their own senses. A dog adds a new and previously unobtainable dimension to human perception. The use of dogs, therefore, represents a greater intrusion into an individual's privacy. Such use implicates concerns that are at least as sensitive as those implicated by the use of certain electronic detection devices.

I have expressed the view that dog sniffs of people constitute searches. See *Doe v. Renfrow*, 451 U.S. 1022, 1025-1026 (1981) (Brennan, J., dissenting from denial of certiorari). In *Doe*, I suggested that sniffs of inanimate objects might present a different case. In any event, I would leave the determination of whether dog sniffs of luggage amount to searches, and the subsidiary question of what standards should govern such intrusions, to a future case providing an appropriate, and more informed, basis for deciding these questions.

## QUESTIONS AND NOTES

**1.** Did the Court, in *Place*, adopt the divining rod theory?

**2.** If not, on what basis did it conclude that a dog sniff did not constitute a search?

**3.** The issue was more clearly joined in *Jacobsen*.

### United States v. Jacobsen
### 466 U.S. 109 (1984)

Justice STEVENS delivered the opinion of the Court.

A chemical test that merely discloses whether or not a particular substance is cocaine does not compromise any legitimate interest in privacy. This conclusion is not dependent on the result of any particular test. It is probably safe to assume that virtually all of the tests conducted under circumstances comparable to those disclosed by this record would result in a positive finding; in such cases, no legitimate interest has been compromised. But even if the results are negative—merely disclosing that the substance is something other than cocaine—such a result reveals nothing of special interest. Congress has decided—and there is no question about its power to do so—to treat the interest in "privately" possessing cocaine as illegitimate; thus governmental conduct that can reveal whether a substance is cocaine, and no other arguably "private" fact, compromises no legitimate privacy interest.[23]

This conclusion is dictated by *Place*, in which the Court held that subjecting luggage to a "sniff test" by a trained narcotics detection dog was not a

"search" within the meaning of the Fourth Amendment:

"A 'canine sniff' by a well-trained narcotics detection dog, however, does not require opening of the luggage. It does not expose noncontraband items that otherwise would remain hidden from public view, as does, for example, an officer's rummaging through the contents of the luggage. Thus, the manner in which information is obtained through this investigative technique is much less intrusive than a typical search. Moreover, the sniff discloses only the presence or absence of narcotics, a contraband item. Thus, despite the fact that the sniff tells the authorities something about the contents of the luggage, the information obtained is limited."[24]

Here, as in *Place*, the likelihood that official conduct of the kind disclosed by the record will actually

[23] See Loewy, The Fourth Amendment as a Device for Protecting the Innocent, 81 Mich.L.Rev. 1229 (1983). Our discussion, of course, is confined to possession of contraband.

[24] Respondents attempt to distinguish *Place* arguing that it involved no physical invasion of Place's effects, unlike the conduct at issue here. However, as the quotation makes clear, the reason this did not intrude upon any legitimate privacy interest was that the governmental conduct could reveal nothing about noncontraband items. That rationale is fully applicable here.

compromise any legitimate interest in privacy seems much too remote to characterize the testing as a search subject to the Fourth Amendment.

Justice BRENNAN, with whom Justice MARSHALL joins, dissenting.

The Court has reached this conclusion (legality of Government conduct) on a much broader ground, relying on two factors alone to support the proposition that the field test was not a search; *first*, the fact that the test revealed only whether or not the substance was cocaine, without providing any further information; and *second*, the assumption that an individual does not have a reasonable expectation of privacy in such a fact.

The Court asserts that its "conclusion is dictated by *Place*," in which the Court stated that a "canine sniff" of a piece of luggage did not constitute a search because it "is less intrusive than a typical search," and because it "discloses only the presence or absence of narcotics, a contraband item." Presumably, the premise of *Place* was that an individual could not have a reasonable expectation of privacy in the presence or absence of narcotics in his luggage. The validity of the canine sniff in that case, however, was neither briefed by the parties nor addressed by the courts below. Indeed, since the Court ultimately held that the defendant's luggage had been impermissibly seized, its discussion of the question was wholly unnecessary to its judgment. In short, as Justice Blackmun pointed out at the time, "the Court [was] certainly in no position to consider all the ramifications of this important issue."

Nonetheless, the Court concluded:

> "the canine sniff is *sui generis*. We are aware of no other investigative procedure that is so limited both in the manner in which the information is obtained and in the content of the information revealed by the procedure. Therefore, we conclude that the particular course of investigation that the agents intended to pursue here—exposure of respondent's luggage, which was located in a public place, to a trained canine—did not constitute a 'search' within the meaning of the Fourth Amendment."

As it turns out, neither the Court's knowledge nor its imagination regarding criminal investigative techniques proved very sophisticated, for within one year we have learned of another investigative procedure that shares with the dog sniff the same defining characteristics that led the Court to suggest that the dog sniff was not a search.

Before continuing along the course that the Court so hastily charted in *Place*, it is only prudent to take this opportunity—in my view, the first real opportunity—to consider the implications of the Court's new Fourth Amendment jurisprudence. Indeed, in light of what these two cases have taught us about contemporary law-enforcement methods, it is particularly important that we analyze the basis upon which the Court has redefined the term "search" to exclude a broad class of surveillance techniques. In my view, such an analysis demonstrates that, although the Court's conclusion is correct in this case, its dictum in *Place* was dangerously incorrect. More important, however, the Court's reasoning in both cases is fundamentally misguided and could potentially lead to the development of a doctrine wholly at odds with the principles embodied in the Fourth Amendment.

Because the requirements of the Fourth Amendment apply only to "searches" and "seizures," an investigative technique that falls within neither category need not be reasonable and may be employed without a warrant and without probable cause, regardless of the circumstances surrounding its use. The prohibitions of the Fourth Amendment are not, however, limited to any preconceived conceptions of what constitutes a search or a seizure; instead we must apply the constitutional language to modern developments according to the fundamental principles that the Fourth Amendment embodies. Before excluding a class of surveillance techniques from the reach of the Fourth Amendment, therefore, we must be certain that none of the techniques so excluded threatens the areas of personal security and privacy that the Amendment is intended to protect.

What is most startling about the Court's interpretation of the term "search," both in this case and in *Place*, is its exclusive focus on the nature of the information or item sought and revealed through the use of a surveillance technique, rather than on the context in which the information or item is concealed. Combining this approach with the blanket assumption, implicit in *Place* and explicit in this case, that individuals in our society have no reasonable expectation of privacy in the fact that they have contraband in their possession, the Court adopts a general rule that a surveillance technique does not constitute a search if it reveals only whether or not an individual possesses contraband.

It is certainly true that a surveillance technique that identifies only the presence or absence of contraband is less intrusive than a technique that reveals the precise nature of an item regardless of whether it is contraband. But by seizing upon this distinction alone to conclude that the first type of technique, as a general matter, is not a search, the Court has foreclosed any consideration of the circumstances under which the technique is used, and may very well have paved the way for technology to override the limits of law in the area of criminal investigation.

For example, under the Court's analysis in these cases, law enforcement officers could release a trained cocaine-sensitive dog—to paraphrase the California Court of Appeal, a "canine cocaine connoisseur"—to roam the streets at random, alerting the officers to people carrying cocaine. Or, if a device were developed that, when aimed at a person, would detect instantaneously whether the person is carrying cocaine, there would be no Fourth Amendment bar, under the Court's approach, to the police setting up such a device on a street corner and scanning all passersby. In fact, the Court's analysis is so unbounded that if a device were developed that could detect, from the outside of a building, the presence of cocaine inside, there would be no constitutional obstacle to the police cruising through a residential neighborhood and using the device to identify all homes in which the drug is present. In short, under the interpretation of the Fourth Amendment first suggested in *Place* and first applied in this case, these surveillance techniques would not constitute searches and therefore could be freely pursued whenever and wherever law enforcement officers desire. Hence, at some point in the future, if the Court stands by the theory it has adopted today, search warrants, probable cause, and even "reasonable suspicion" may very well become notions of the past. Fortunately, we know from precedents such as *Katz v. United States* (chapter 10, B, *infra.*) that this Court ultimately stands ready to prevent this Orwellian world from coming to pass.

Although the Court accepts, as it must, the fundamental proposition that an investigative technique is a search within the meaning of the Fourth Amendment if it intrudes upon a privacy expectation that society considers to be reasonable, the Court has entirely omitted from its discussion the considerations that have always guided our decisions in this area. In determining whether a reasonable expectation of privacy has been violated, we have always looked to the context in which an item is concealed, not to the identity of the concealed item. Thus in cases involving searches for physical items, the Court has framed its analysis first in terms of the expectation of privacy that normally attends the location of the item and ultimately in terms of the legitimacy of that expectation. In *Chadwick*, for example, we held that "no less than one who locks the doors of his home against intruders, one who safeguards

his possessions [by locking them in a footlocker] is due the protection of the Fourth Amendment. . . ." Our holding was based largely on the observation that, "[b]y placing personal effects inside a double-locked footlocker, respondents manifested an expectation that the contents would remain free from public examination." The Court made the same point in *Ross*, where it held that the "Fourth Amendment provides protection to the owner of every container that conceals its contents from plain view." The fact that a container contains contraband, which indeed it usually does in such cases, has never altered our analysis.

Similarly, in *Katz v. United States, infra*, we held that electronic eavesdropping constituted a search under the Fourth Amendment because it violated a reasonable expectation of privacy. In reaching that conclusion, we focused upon the private context in which the conversation in question took place, stating that "[w]hat a person knowingly exposes to the public . . . is not a subject of Fourth Amendment protection. . . . But what he seeks to preserve as private, even in an area accessible to the public, may be constitutionally protected." Again, the fact that the conversations involved in *Katz* were incriminating did not alter our consideration of the privacy issue. Nor did such a consideration affect our analysis in *Payton*, in which we reaffirmed the principle that the home is private even though it may be used to harbor a fugitive.

In sum, until today this Court has always looked to the manner in which an individual has attempted to preserve the private nature of a particular fact before determining whether there is a reasonable expectation of privacy upon which the government may not intrude without substantial justification. And it has always upheld the general conclusion that searches constitute at least "those more extensive intrusions that significantly jeopardize the sense of security which is the paramount concern of Fourth Amendment liberties."

Nonetheless, adopting the suggestion in *Place*, the Court has veered away from this sound and well-settled approach and has focused instead solely on the product of the would-be search. In so doing, the Court has ignored the fundamental principle that "[a] search prosecuted in violation of the Constitution is not made lawful by what it brings to light." The unfortunate product of this departure from precedent is an undifferentiated rule allowing law enforcement officers free rein in utilizing a potentially broad range of surveillance techniques that reveal only whether or not contraband is present in a particular location. The Court's new rule has rendered irrelevant the circumstances surrounding the use of the technique, the accuracy of the technique, and the privacy interest upon which it intrudes. Furthermore, the Court's rule leaves no room to consider whether the surveillance technique is employed randomly or selectively, a consideration that surely implicates Fourth Amendment concerns. Although a technique that reveals only the presence or absence of illegal activity intrudes less into the private life of an individual under investigation than more conventional techniques, the fact remains that such a technique does intrude. In my view, when the investigation intrudes upon a domain over which the individual has a reasonable expectation of privacy, such as his home or a private container, it is plainly a search within the meaning of the Fourth Amendment. Surely it cannot be that the individual's reasonable expectation of privacy dissipates simply because a sophisticated surveillance technique is employed.

This is not to say that the limited nature of the intrusion has no bearing on the general Fourth Amendment inquiry. Although there are very few exceptions to the general rule that warrantless searches are presumptively unreasonable, the isolated exceptions that do exist are based on a "balancing [of] the need to search against the invasion which the search entails." *Camara*. Hence it may be, for example, that the limited intrusion effected by a given surveillance technique renders the employment of the technique, under particular circumstances, a "reasonable" search under the Fourth Amendment. See *Place*, (Blackmun, J., concurring in the judgment) ("a dog sniff may be a search, but a minimally intrusive one that could be justified in this situation under *Terry*"). At least under this well-settled approach, the Fourth Amendment inquiry would be broad enough to allow consideration of the method by which a surveillance technique is employed as well as the circumstances attending its use. More important, however, it is only under this approach that law enforcement procedures, like those involved in this case and in *Place*, may continue to be governed by the safeguards of the Fourth Amendment.

B

In sum, the question whether the employment of a particular surveillance technique constitutes a search depends on whether the technique intrudes upon a reasonable expectation of privacy. This inquiry, in turn, depends primarily on the private nature of the area or item subjected to the intrusion. In cases involving techniques used to locate or identify a physical item, the manner in which a person has attempted to shield the item's existence or identity from public scrutiny will usually be the key to determining whether a reasonable expectation of privacy has been violated. Accordingly, the use of techniques like the dog sniff at issue in *Place* constitutes a search whenever the police employ such techniques to secure any information about an item that is concealed in a container that we are prepared to view as supporting a reasonable expectation of privacy. The same would be true if a more technologically sophisticated method were developed to take the place of the dog.

## QUESTIONS AND NOTES

**1.** Justice Brennan sees an inconsistency between cases like *Chadwick, Ross*, and *Payton* and the divining rod theory of the Fourth Amendment because those cases were not concerned about the guilt of the defendant. Could a defender of the "divining rod" theory answer those objections? How?

**2.** In *Chadwick,* were we trying to protect the right to transport drugs privately? Or, were we trying to protect the right to transport other private things without the police discovering them? Put differently, are the criminals the *intended* beneficiaries of the Fourth Amendment, or necessary incidental beneficiaries of the rights of the innocent?

**3.** Should it be permissible for the police to point an *accurate* cocaine detecting device at everybody who passes a particular (unannounced) street corner? How about some randomly selected people who pass that street corner? Why? Why not?

**4.** While the impact of the police practice on the innocent has appeared to motivate the Court in some cases, the rhetoric that has dominated this area of the law is "reasonable expectation of privacy." As you read the next series of cases, consider whether the police practices involved therein interfere with what you would have thought to have been a legitimate expectation of privacy.

## Lewis v. United States
### 385 U.S. 206 (1966)

Mr. Chief Justice WARREN delivered the opinion of the Court.

The question for resolution here is whether the Fourth Amendment was violated when a federal narcotics agent, by misrepresenting his identity and stating his willingness to purchase narcotics, was invited into petitioner's home where an unlawful narcotics transaction was consummated and the narcotics were thereafter introduced at petitioner's criminal trial over his objection. We hold that under the facts of this case it was not. Those facts are not disputed and may be briefly stated as follows:

On December 3, 1964, Edward Cass, an undercover federal narcotics agent, telephoned petitioner's home to inquire about the possibility of purchasing marihuana. Cass, who previously had not met or dealt with petitioner, falsely identified himself as one "Jimmy the Pollack [*sic*]" and stated that a mutual friend had told him petitioner might be able to supply marihuana. In response, petitioner said, "Yes. I believe, Jimmy, I can take care of you," and then directed Cass to his home where, it was indicated, a sale of marihuana would occur. Cass drove to petitioner's home, knocked on the door, identified himself as "Jim," and was admitted. After discussing the possibility of regular future dealings at a discounted price, petitioner led Cass to a package located on the front porch of his home. Cass gave petitioner $50, took the package, and left the premises. The package contained five bags of marihuana. On December 17, 1964, a similar transaction took place, beginning with a phone conversation in which Cass identified himself as "Jimmy the Pollack" and ending with an invited visit by Cass to petitioner's home where a second sale of marihuana occurred. Once again, Cass paid petitioner $50, but this time he received in return a package containing six bags of marihuana.

Petitioner does not argue that he was entrapped, as he could not on the facts of this case; nor does he contend that a search of his home was made or that anything other than the purchased narcotics was taken away. His only contentions are that, in the absence of a warrant, any official intrusion upon the privacy of a home constitutes a Fourth Amendment violation and that the fact the suspect invited the intrusion cannot be held a waiver when the invitation was induced by fraud and deception.

Petitioner argues that the Government overstepped the constitutional bounds in this case and places principal reliance on *Gouled* v. *United States*, 255 U.S. 298 (1921). But a short statement of that case will demonstrate how misplaced his reliance is. There, a business acquaintance of the petitioner, acting under orders of federal officers, obtained entry into the petitioner's office by falsely representing that he intended only to pay a social visit. In the petitioner's absence, however, the intruder secretly ransacked the office and seized certain private papers of an incriminating nature. This Court had no difficulty concluding that the Fourth Amendment had been violated by the secret and general ransacking, notwithstanding that the initial intrusion was occasioned by a fraudulently obtained invitation rather than by force or stealth.

In the instant case, on the other hand, the petitioner invited the undercover agent to his home for the specific purpose of executing a felonious sale of narcotics. Petitioner's only concern was whether the agent was a willing purchaser who could pay the agreed price. Indeed, in order to convince the agent that his patronage at petitioner's home was desired, petitioner told him that, if he became a regular customer there, he would in the future receive an extra bag of marihuana at no additional cost; and in fact petitioner did hand over an extra bag at a second sale which was consummated at the same place and in precisely the same manner. During neither of his visits to petitioner's home did the agent see, hear, or take anything that was not contemplated, and in fact intended, by petitioner as a necessary part of his illegal business. Were we to hold the deceptions of the agent in this case constitutionally prohibited, we would come near to a rule that the use of undercover agents in any manner is virtually unconstitutional *per se*. Such a rule would, for example, severely hamper the Government in ferreting out those organized criminal activities that are characterized by covert dealings with victims who either cannot or do not protest.[6] A prime example is provided by the narcotics traffic.

The fact that the undercover agent entered petitioner's home does not compel a different conclusion. Without question, the home is accorded the full range of Fourth Amendment protections. But when, as here, the home is converted into a commercial center to which outsiders are invited for purposes of transacting unlawful business, that business is entitled to no greater sanctity than if it were carried on in a store, a garage, a car, or on the street. A government agent, in the same manner as a private person, may accept an invitation to do business and may enter upon the premises for the very purposes contemplated by the occupant. Of course, this does not mean that, whenever entry is obtained by invitation and the locus is characterized as a place of business, an agent is authorized to conduct a general search for incriminating materials; a citation to the *Gouled* case is sufficient to dispose of that contention.

Mr. Justice DOUGLAS, dissenting.

---

[6] "Particularly, in the enforcement of vice, liquor or narcotics laws, it is all but impossible to obtain evidence for prosecution save by the use of decoys. There are rarely complaining witnesses. The participants in the crime enjoy themselves. Misrepresentation by a police officer or agent concerning the identity of the purchaser of illegal narcotics is a practical necessity. . . . Therefore, the law must attempt to distinguish between those deceits and persuasions which are permissible and those which are not." Model Penal Code § 2.10, comment, p. 16 (Tent. Draft No. 9, 1959).

Entering another's home in disguise to obtain evidence is a "search" that should bring into play all the protective features of the Fourth Amendment. When the agent had reason for believing that petitioner possessed narcotics, a search warrant should have been obtained.

Mr. Justice BRENNAN, with whom Mr. Justice FORTAS joins, concurring.

While I concur in the Court's judgment, I vote to affirm solely on the reasoning on which the Court ultimately relies, namely that petitioner's apartment was not an area protected by the Fourth Amendment as related to the transactions in the present case.

The Fourth Amendment protects against governmental intrusion upon "the sanctity of a man's home and the privacies of life." However, the occupant can break the seal of sanctity and waive his right to privacy in the premises. Plainly he does this to the extent that he opens his home to the transaction of business and invites anyone willing to enter to come in to trade with him. When his customer turns out to be a government agent, the seller cannot, then, complain that his privacy has been invaded so long as the agent does no more than buy his wares. Thus the corner grocery with the living quarters in the rear would not be protected with respect to the area set aside for the purchase of groceries, although the living quarters to which shoppers are not privy retain the constitutional immunity.

The petitioner in this case opened his apartment for the conduct of a business, the sale of narcotics; the agent, in the same manner as any private person, entered the premises for the very purpose contemplated by the occupant and took nothing away except what would be taken away by any willing purchaser. There was therefore no intrusion upon the "sanctity" of petitioner's home or the "privacies of life."

## QUESTIONS AND NOTES

**1.** Do you agree with Justice Douglas' assertion that a disguised government agent attempting to find evidence of crime constitutes a search? Why? Why not?

**2.** What do you perceive to be the distinction between *Lewis* and *Gouled*? Do you find it persuasive?

**3.** Could an innocent person be hurt by the *Lewis* procedure? How? Could an innocent person be hurt by the *Gouled* procedure? How?

**4.** Consider whether *Lewis* principles should control *Hoffa*.

## Hoffa v. United States
### 385 U.S. 293 (1966)

Mr. Justice STEWART delivered the opinion of the Court.

Over a period of several weeks in the late autumn of 1962 there took place in a federal court in Nashville, Tennessee, a trial by jury in which James Hoffa was charged with violating a provision of the Taft-Hartley Act. That trial, known in the present record as the Test Fleet trial, ended with a hung jury. The petitioners now before us — James Hoffa, Thomas Parks, Larry Campbell, and Ewing King — were tried and convicted in 1964 for endeavoring to bribe members of that jury. The convictions were affirmed by the Court of Appeals. A substantial element in the Government's proof that led to the convictions of these four petitioners was contributed by a witness named Edward Partin, who testified to several incriminating statements which he said petitioners Hoffa and King had made in his presence during the course of the Test Fleet trial.

The controlling facts can be briefly stated. The Test Fleet trial, in which James Hoffa was the sole individual defendant, was in progress between October 22 and December 23, 1962, in Nashville, Tennessee. James Hoffa was president of the International Brotherhood of Teamsters. During the course of the trial he occupied a three-room suite in the Andrew Jackson Hotel in Nashville. One of his constant companions throughout the trial was the petitioner King, president of the Nashville local of the Teamsters Union. Edward Partin, a resident of Baton Rouge, Louisiana, and a local Teamsters Union official there, made repeated visits to Nashville during the period of the trial. On these visits he frequented the Hoffa hotel suite, and was continually in the company of Hoffa and his associates, including King, in and around the hotel suite, the hotel lobby, the courthouse, and elsewhere in Nashville. During this period Partin made frequent reports to a federal agent named Sheridan concerning conversations he said Hoffa and King had had with him and with each other, disclosing endeavors to bribe members of the Test Fleet jury. Partin's reports and his subsequent testimony at the petitioners' trial unquestionably contributed, directly or indirectly, to the convictions of all four of the petitioners.

The chain of circumstances which led Partin to be in Nashville during the Test Fleet trial extended back at least to September of 1962. At that time Partin was in jail in Baton Rouge on a state criminal charge. He was also under a federal indictment for embezzling union funds, and other indictments for state offenses were pending against him. Between that time and Partin's initial visit to Nashville on October 22 he was released on bail on the state criminal charge, and proceedings under the federal indictment were postponed. On October 8, Partin telephoned Hoffa in Washington, D.C., to discuss local union matters and Partin's difficulties with the authorities. In the course of this conversation Partin asked if he could see Hoffa to confer about these problems, and Hoffa acquiesced. Partin again called Hoffa on October 18 and arranged to meet him in Nashville. During this period Partin also consulted on several occasions with federal law enforcement agents, who told him that Hoffa might attempt to tamper with the Test Fleet jury, and asked him to be on the lookout in Nashville for such attempts and to report to the federal authorities any evidence of wrongdoing that he discovered. Partin agreed to do so.

After the Test Fleet trial was completed, Partin's wife received four monthly installment payments of $300 from government funds, and the state and federal charges against Partin were either dropped or not actively pursued.

[W]hether or not the Government "placed" Partin with Hoffa in Nashville during the Test Fleet trial, we proceed upon the premise that Partin was a government informer from the time he first arrived in Nashville on October 22, and that the Government compensated him for his services as such. It is upon that premise that we consider the constitutional issues presented.

### I.

It is contended that only by violating the petitioner's rights under the Fourth Amendment was Partin able to hear the petitioner's incriminating statements in the hotel suite. The argument is that Partin's failure to disclose his role as a government informer vitiated the consent that the petitioner gave to Partin's repeated entries into the suite, and that by listening to the petitioner's statements Partin conducted an illegal "search" for verbal evidence.

The preliminary steps of this argument are on solid ground. A hotel room can clearly be the object of Fourth Amendment protection as much as a home or an office. *United States v. Jeffers*, 342 U.S. 48. The Fourth Amendment can certainly be violated by guileful as well as by forcible intrusions into a constitutionally protected area. *Gouled v. United States*, 255 U.S. 298. And the protections of the

Fourth Amendment are surely not limited to tangibles, but can extend as well to oral statements. *Silverman v. United States*, 365 U.S. 505.

Where the argument falls is in its misapprehension of the fundamental nature and scope of Fourth Amendment protection. What the Fourth Amendment protects is the security a man relies upon when he places himself or his property within a constitutionally protected area, be it his home or his office, his hotel room or his automobile. There he is protected from unwarranted governmental intrusion. And when he puts something in his filing cabinet, in his desk drawer, or in his pocket, he has the right to know it will be secure from an unreasonable search or an unreasonable seizure. So it was that the Fourth Amendment could not tolerate the warrantless search of the hotel room in *Jeffers*, the purloining of the petitioner's private papers in *Gouled*, or the surreptitious electronic surveillance in *Silverman*. Countless other cases which have come to this Court over the years have involved a myriad of differing factual contexts in which the protections of the Fourth Amendment have been appropriately invoked. No doubt the future will bring countless others. By nothing we say here do we either foresee or foreclose factual situations to which the Fourth Amendment may be applicable.

In the present case, however, it is evident that no interest legitimately protected by the Fourth Amendment is involved. It is obvious that the petitioner was not relying on the security of his hotel suite when he made the incriminating statements to Partin or in Partin's presence. Partin did not enter the suite by force or by stealth. He was not a surreptitious eavesdropper. Partin was in the suite by invitation, and every conversation which he heard was either directed to him or knowingly carried on in his presence. The petitioner, in a word, was not relying on the security of the hotel room; he was relying upon his misplaced confidence that Partin would not reveal his wrongdoing. As counsel for the petitioner himself points out, some of the communications with Partin did not take place in the suite at all, but in the "hall of the hotel," in the "Andrew Jackson Hotel lobby," and "at the courthouse."

Neither this Court nor any member of it has ever expressed the view that the Fourth Amendment protects a wrongdoer's misplaced belief that a person to whom he voluntarily confides his wrongdoing will not reveal it. Indeed, the Court unanimously rejected that very contention less than four years ago in *Lopez v. United States*, 373 U.S. 427. In that case the petitioner had been convicted of attempted bribery of an internal revenue agent named Davis. The Court was divided with regard to the admissibility in evidence of a surreptitious electronic recording of an incriminating conversation Lopez had had in his private office with Davis. But there was no dissent from the view that testimony about the conversation by Davis himself was clearly admissible.

As the Court put it, "Davis was not guilty of an unlawful invasion of petitioner's office simply because his apparent willingness to accept a bribe was not real. He was in the office with petitioner's consent, and while there he did not violate the privacy of the office by seizing something surreptitiously without petitioner's knowledge. The only evidence obtained consisted of statements made by Lopez to Davis, statements which Lopez knew full well could be used against him by Davis if he wished. . . ." In the words of the dissenting opinion in *Lopez*, "The risk of being overheard by an eavesdropper or betrayed by an informer or deceived as to the identity of one with whom one deals is probably inherent in the conditions of human society. It is the kind of risk we necessarily assume whenever we speak."

Adhering to these views, we hold that no right protected by the Fourth Amendment was violated in the present case.

[Mr. Chief Justice WARREN, dissented on the ground that under the Court's Federal supervisory powers it should reverse the conviction because of the inherent unreliability of one whose motivations and propensity to lie is as strong as those of Mr. Partin.]

[Mr. Justice CLARK, joined by Mr. Justice DOUGLAS would have dismissed the writs of certiorari as improvidently granted on the ground that the trial and appellate courts' conclusion that Partin was not placed in Hoffa's hotel room by the government was not clearly erroneous.]

## QUESTIONS AND NOTES

**1.** Is the risk that a friend has been planted by the government as a spy, a different risk than the risk that one who has not been planted by the government will nevertheless decide to turn state's evidence? Explain.

**2.** Does an innocent person run any risk in the *Hoffa* situation? If so, what are they?

**3.** The term reasonable expectation of privacy, which informs so much of our Fourth Amendment jurisprudence was first developed in *Katz*.

### Katz v. United States
### 389 U.S. 347 (1967)

Mr. Justice STEWART delivered the opinion of the Court.

The petitioner was convicted in the District Court for the Southern District of California under an eight-count indictment charging him with transmitting wagering information by telephone from Los Angeles to Miami and Boston in violation of a federal statute. At trial the Government was permitted, over the petitioner's objection, to introduce evidence of the petitioner's end of telephone conversations, overheard by FBI agents who had attached an electronic listening and recording device to the outside of the public telephone booth from which he had placed his calls. In affirming his conviction, the Court of Appeals rejected the contention that the recordings had been obtained in violation of the Fourth Amendment, because "[t]here was no physical entrance into the area occupied by, [the petitioner]." We granted certiorari in order to consider the constitutional questions thus presented.

The petitioner had phrased those questions as follows:

> "A. Whether a public telephone booth is a constitutionally protected area so that evidence obtained by attaching an electronic listening recording device to the top of such a booth is obtained in violation of the right to privacy of the user of the booth.
>
> "B. Whether physical penetration of a constitutionally protected area is necessary before a search and seizure can be said to be violative of the Fourth Amendment to the United States Constitution."

We decline to adopt this formulation of the issues. In the first place the correct solution of Fourth Amendment problems is not necessarily promoted by incantation of the phrase "constitutionally protected area." Secondly, the Fourth Amendment cannot be translated into a general constitutional "right to privacy." That Amendment protects individual privacy against certain kinds of governmental intrusion, but its protections go further, and often have nothing to do with privacy at all. Other provisions of the Constitution protect personal privacy from other forms of governmental invasion. But the protection of a person's *general* right to privacy — his right to be let alone by other people — is, like the protection of his property and of his very life, left largely to the law of the individual States.

Because of the misleading way the issues have been formulated, the parties have attached great significance to the characterization of the telephone booth from which the petitioner placed his calls. The petitioner has strenuously argued that the booth was a "constitutionally protected area." The Government has maintained with equal vigor that it was not. But this effort to decide whether or not a given "area," viewed in the abstract, is "constitutionally protected" deflects attention from the problem presented by this case. For the Fourth Amendment protects people, not places. What a person knowingly exposes to the public, even in his own home or office, is not a subject of Fourth Amendment protection. See *Lewis.* But what he seeks to preserve as private, even in an area accessible to the public, may be constitutionally protected.

The Government stresses the fact that the telephone booth from which the petitioner made his calls was constructed partly of glass, so that he was as visible after he entered it as he would have been if he had remained outside. But what he sought to exclude when he entered the booth was not the intruding eye — it was the uninvited ear. He did not shed his right to do so simply because he made his calls from a place where he might be seen. No less than an individual in a business office, in a friend's apartment, or in a taxicab, a person in a telephone booth may rely upon the protection of the Fourth Amendment. One who occupies it, shuts the door behind him, and pays the toll that permits him to place a call is surely entitled to assume that the words he utters into the mouthpiece will not be broadcast to the world. To read the Constitution more narrowly is to ignore the vital role that the public telephone has come to play in private communication.

The Government contends, however, that the activities of its agents in this case should not be tested by Fourth Amendment requirements, for the surveillance technique they employed involved no physical penetration of the telephone booth from which the petitioner placed his calls. It is true that the absence of such penetration was at one time thought to foreclose further Fourth Amendment inquiry, for that Amendment was thought to limit only searches and seizures of tangible property. But "[t]he premise that property interests control the right of the Government to search and seize has been discredited." *Warden v. Hayden*, 387 U.S. 294.

The fact that the electronic device did not happen to penetrate the wall of the booth can have no constitutional significance.

The question remaining for decision, then, is whether the search and seizure conducted in this case complied with constitutional standards. [The Court then held that the government had probable cause to electronically eavesdrop, but that it did not have a good excuse for dispensing with a warrant. Consequently, it reversed the conviction because of the lack of a warrant.]

Mr. Justice HARLAN, concurring.

I join the opinion of the Court, which I read to hold only (a) that an enclosed telephone booth is an area where, like a home, *Weeks v. United States*, 232 U.S. 383, and unlike a field, *Hester v. United States*, 265 U.S. 57, a person has a constitutionally protected reasonable expectation of privacy; (b) that electronic as well as physical intrusion into a place that is in this sense private may constitute a violation of the Fourth Amendment; and (c) that the invasion of a constitutionally protected area by federal authorities is, as the Court has long held, presumptively unreasonable in the absence of a search warrant.

As the Court's opinion states, "the Fourth Amendment protects people, not places." The question, however, is what protection it affords to those people. Generally, as here, the answer to that question requires reference to a "place." My understanding of the rule that has emerged from prior

decisions is that there is a twofold requirement, first that a person have exhibited an actual (subjective) expectation of privacy and, second, that the expectation be one that society is prepared to recognize as "reasonable." Thus a man's home is, for most purposes, a place where he expects privacy, but objects, activities, or statements that he exposes to the "plain view" of outsiders are not "protected" because no intention to keep them to himself has been exhibited. On the other hand, conversations in the open would not be protected against being overheard, for the expectation of privacy under the circumstances would be unreasonable.

The critical fact in this case is that "[o]ne who occupies it, [a telephone booth] shuts the door behind him, and pays the toll that permits him to place a call is surely entitled to assume" that his conversation is not being intercepted. The point is not that the booth is "accessible to the public" at other times, but that it is a temporarily private place whose momentary occupants' expectations of freedom from intrusion are recognized as reasonable.

Mr. Justice BLACK, dissenting.

If I could agree with the Court that eavesdropping carried on by electronic means (equivalent to wiretapping) constitutes a "search" or "seizure," I would be happy to join the Court's opinion. For on that premise my Brother Stewart sets out methods in accord with the Fourth Amendment to guide States in the enactment and enforcement of laws passed to regulate wiretapping by government.

My basic objection is twofold: (1) I do not believe that the words of the Amendment will bear the meaning given them by today's decision, and (2) I do not believe that it is the proper role of this Court to rewrite the Amendment in order "to bring it into harmony with the times" and thus reach a result that many people believe to be desirable.

While I realize that an argument based on the meaning of words lacks the scope, and no doubt the appeal, of broad policy discussions and philosophical discourses on such nebulous subjects as privacy, for me the language of the Amendment is the crucial place to look in construing a written document such as our Constitution. The Fourth Amendment says that

"The right of the people to be secure in their persons, houses, papers, and effects, against unreasonable searches and seizures, shall not be violated, and no Warrants shall issue, but upon probable cause, supported by Oath or affirmation, and particularly describing the place to be searched, and the persons or things to be seized."

The first clause protects "persons, houses, papers, and effects, against unreasonable searches and seizures. . . ." These words connote the idea of tangible things with size, form, and weight, things capable of being searched, seized, or both. The second clause of the Amendment still further establishes its Framers' purpose to limit its protection to tangible things by providing that no warrants shall issue but those "particularly describing the place to be searched, and the persons or things to be seized." A conversation overheard by eavesdropping, whether by plain snooping or wiretapping, is not tangible and, under the normally accepted meanings of the words, can neither be searched nor seized. In addition the language of the second clause indicates that the Amendment refers not only to something tangible so it can be seized but to something already in existence so it can be described. Yet the Court's interpretation would have the Amendment apply to overhearing future conversations which by their very nature are nonexistent until they take place. How can one "describe" a future conversation, and, if one cannot, how can a magistrate issue a warrant to eavesdrop one in the future? It is argued that information showing what is expected to be said is sufficient to limit the boundaries of what later can be admitted into evidence; but does such general information really meet the specific language of the Amendment which says "particularly describing?" Rather than using language in a completely artificial way, I must conclude that the Fourth Amendment simply does not apply to eavesdropping.

Tapping telephone wires, of course, was an unknown possibility at the time the Fourth Amendment was adopted. But eavesdropping (and wiretapping is nothing more than eavesdropping by telephone) was recognized, "an ancient practice which at common law was condemned as a nuisance. In those days the eavesdropper listened by naked ear under the eaves of houses or their windows, or beyond their walls seeking out private discourse." There can be no doubt that the Framers were aware of this practice, and if they had desired to outlaw or restrict the use of evidence obtained by eavesdropping, I believe that they would have used the appropriate language to do so in the Fourth Amendment.

Since I see no way in which the words of the Fourth Amendment can be construed to apply to eavesdropping, that closes the matter for me. In interpreting the Bill of Rights, I willingly go as far as a liberal construction of the language takes me, but I simply cannot in good conscience give a meaning to words which they have never before been thought to have and which they certainly do not have in common ordinary usage. I will not distort the words of the Amendment in order to "keep the Constitution up to date" or "to bring it into harmony with the times." It was never meant that this Court have such power, which in effect would make us a continuously functioning constitutional convention.

For these reasons I respectfully dissent.

## QUESTIONS AND NOTES

**1.** Is Justice Black's reliance on history, a defensible way to analyze Fourth Amendment issues? A desirable way?

**2.** Whose opinion is best supported by the text of the Fourth Amendment?

**3.** Should one's subjective expectation of privacy be at all relevant? Why? Why not?

**4.** If reasonable expectation of privacy is the key, how is it to be measured? Should empiric data of societal attitudes be relevant? Determinative?

**5.** Is it meaningful to talk about the Fourth Amendment as protecting people rather than places? Isn't the amount of protection that a person gets dependent on where she is? Isn't that inherent in the Fourth Amendment?

**6.** As you read *White*, consider whether it is consistent with or counter to the *Katz* philosophy? How, if at all, does it differ from *Hoffa*?

## United States v. White
### 401 U.S. 745 (1971)

Mr. Justice WHITE announced the judgment of the Court and an opinion in which the Chief Justice, Mr. Justice STEWART, and Mr. Justice BLACKMUN join.

In 1966, respondent James A. White was tried and convicted under two consolidated indictments charging various illegal transactions in narcotics. He was fined and sentenced as a second offender to 25-year concurrent sentences. The issue before us is whether the Fourth Amendment bars from evidence the testimony of governmental agents who related certain conversations which had occurred between defendant White and a government informant, Harvey Jackson, and which the agents overheard by monitoring the frequency of a radio transmitter carried by Jackson and concealed on his person. On four occasions the conversations took place in Jackson's home; each of these conversations was overheard by an agent concealed in a kitchen closet with Jackson's consent and by a second agent outside the house using a radio receiver. Four other conversations—one in respondent's home, one in a restaurant, and two in Jackson's car—were overheard by the use of radio equipment. The prosecution was unable to locate and produce Jackson at the trial and the trial court overruled objections to the testimony of the agents who conducted the electronic surveillance. The jury returned a guilty verdict and defendant appealed.

### I

Until *Katz*, neither wiretapping nor electronic eavesdropping violated a defendant's Fourth Amendment rights "unless there has been an official search and seizure of his person, or such a seizure of his papers or his tangible material effects, or an actual physical invasion of his house 'or curtilage' for the purpose of making a seizure."

*Katz*, however, finally swept away doctrines that electronic eavesdropping is permissible under the Fourth Amendment unless physical invasion of a constitutionally protected area produced the challenged evidence.

The Court of Appeals understood *Katz* to render inadmissible against White the agents' testimony concerning conversations that Jackson broadcast to them. We cannot agree. *Katz* involved no revelation to the Government by a party to conversations with the defendant nor did the Court indicate in any way that a defendant has a justifiable and constitutionally protected expectation that a person with whom he is conversing will not then or later reveal the conversation to the police.

*Hoffa*, which was left undisturbed by *Katz*, held that however strongly a defendant may trust an apparent colleague, his expectations in this respect are not protected by the Fourth Amendment when it turns out that the colleague is a government agent regularly communicating with the authorities. In these circumstances, "no interest legitimately protected by the Fourth Amendment is involved," for that amendment affords no protection to "a wrongdoer's misplaced belief that a person to whom he voluntarily confides his wrongdoing will not reveal it." No warrant to "search and seize" is required in such circumstances, nor is it when the Government sends to defendant's home a secret agent who conceals his identity and makes a purchase of narcotics from the accused, *Lewis*, or when the same agent, unbeknown to the defendant, carries electronic equipment to record the defendant's words and the evidence so gathered is later offered in evidence. *Lopez*.

Conceding that *Hoffa, Lewis,* and *Lopez* remained unaffected by *Katz*, the Court of Appeals nevertheless read both *Katz* and the Fourth Amendment to require a different result if the agent not only records his conversations with the defendant but instantaneously transmits them electronically to other agents equipped with radio receivers. Where this occurs, the Court of Appeals held, the Fourth Amendment is violated and the testimony of the listening agents must be excluded from evidence.

To reach this result it was necessary for the Court of Appeals to hold that *On Lee v. United States, 343v.5, 747 (1952)* was no longer good law. In that case, which involved facts very similar to the case before us, the Court rejected claims of a Fourth Amendment violation [in part] because On Lee "was talking confidentially and indiscreetly with one he trusted, and he was overheard. . . . It would be a dubious service to the genuine liberties protected by the Fourth Amendment to make them bedfellows with spurious liberties improvised by farfetched analogies which would liken eavesdropping on a conversation, with the connivance of one of the parties, to an unreasonable search or seizure. We find no violation of the Fourth Amendment here." 343 U.S., at 753-754. We see no indication in *Katz* that the Court meant to disturb that understanding of the Fourth Amendment or to disturb the result reached in the *On Lee* case, nor are we now inclined to overturn this view of the Fourth Amendment.

Concedely a police agent who conceals his police connections may write down for official use his conversations with a defendant and testify concerning them, without a warrant authorizing his encounters with the defendant and without otherwise violating the latter's Fourth Amendment rights. *Hoffa*. For constitutional purposes, no different result is required if the agent instead of immediately reporting and transcribing his conversations with defendant, either (1) simultaneously records them with electronic equipment which he is carrying on his person, *Lopez*; (2) or carries radio equipment which simultaneously transmits the conversations either to recording equipment located elsewhere or to other agents monitoring the transmitting frequency. *On Lee*. If the conduct and revelations of an agent operating without electronic equipment do not invade the defendant's constitutionally justifiable expectations of privacy, neither does a simultaneous recording of the same conversations made by the agent or by others from transmissions received from the agent to whom the defendant is talking and whose trustworthiness the defendant necessarily risks.

Our problem is not what the privacy expectations of particular defendants in particular situations may be or the extent to which they may in fact have relied on the discretion of their companions. Very probably, individual defendants neither know nor suspect that their colleagues have gone or will go to the police or are carrying recorders or transmitters. Otherwise, conversation would cease and our problem with these encounters would be nonexistent or far different from those now before us. Our problem, in terms of the principles announced in *Katz*, is what expectations of privacy are constitutionally "justifiable" – what expectations the Fourth Amendment will protect in the absence of a warrant. So far, the law permits the frustration of actual expectations of privacy by permitting authorities to use the testimony of those associates who for one reason or another have determined to turn to the police, as well as by authorizing the use of informants in the manner exemplified by *Hoffa* and *Lewis*. If the law gives no protection to the wrongdoer whose trusted accomplice is or becomes a police agent, neither should it protect him when that same agent has recorded or transmitted the conversations which are later offered in evidence to prove the State's case.

Inescapably, one contemplating illegal activities must realize and risk that his companions may be reporting to the police. If he sufficiently doubts their trustworthiness, the association will very probably end or never materialize. But if he has no doubts, or allays them, or risks what doubt he has, the risk is his. In terms of what his course will be, what he will or will not do or say, we are unpersuaded that he would distinguish between probable informers on the one hand and probable informers with transmitters on the other. Given the possibility or probability that one of his colleagues is cooperating with the police, it is only speculation to assert that the defendant's utterances would be substantially different or his sense of security any less if he also thought it possible that the suspected colleague is wired for sound. At least there is no persuasive evidence that the difference in this respect between the electronically equipped and the unequipped agent is substantial enough to require discrete constitutional recognition, particularly under the Fourth Amendment which is ruled by fluid concepts of "reasonableness."

Nor should we be too ready to erect constitutional barriers to relevant and probative evidence which is also accurate and reliable. An electronic recording will many times produce a more reliable rendition of what a defendant has said than will the unaided memory of a police agent. It may also be that with the recording in existence it is less likely that the informant will change his mind, less chance that threat or injury will suppress unfavorable evidence and less chance that cross-examination will confound the testimony. Considerations like these obviously do not favor the defendant, but we are not prepared to hold that a defendant who has no constitutional right to exclude the informer's unaided testimony nevertheless has a Fourth Amendment privilege against a more accurate version of the events in question.

It is thus untenable to consider the activities and reports of the police agent himself, though acting without a warrant, to be a "reasonable" investigative effort and lawful under the Fourth Amendment but to view the same agent with a recorder or transmitter as conducting an "unreasonable" and unconstitutional search and seizure.

The judgment of the Court of Appeals is reversed.

[Mr. Justice BLACK concurred in the judgment of the Court for the reasons set forth in his dissent in *Katz*.]

[Mr. Justice BRENNAN concurred in the result on the ground that *Katz* should not be retroactively applied to this case. He argued, however, that both *On Lee* and *Lopez* should be overruled.]

Mr. Justice DOUGLAS, dissenting.

I

The issue in this case is clouded and concealed by the very discussion of it in legalistic terms. What the ancients knew as "eavesdropping," we now call "electronic surveillance"; but to equate the two is to treat man's first gunpowder on the same level as the nuclear bomb. Electronic surveillance is the greatest leveler of human privacy ever known. How most forms of it can be held "reasonable" within the meaning of the Fourth Amendment is a mystery. To be sure, the Constitution and Bill of Rights are not to be read as covering only the technology known in the 18th century. Otherwise its concept of "commerce" would be hopeless when it comes to the management of modern affairs. At the same time the concepts of privacy which the Founders enshrined in the Fourth Amendment vanish completely when we slavishly allow an all-powerful government, proclaiming law and order, efficiency, and other benign purposes, to penetrate all the walls and doors which men need to shield them from the pressures of a turbulent life around them and give them the health and strength to carry on.

That is why a "strict construction" of the Fourth Amendment is necessary if every man's liberty and privacy are to be constitutionally honored.

## II

*On Lee* and *Lopez* are of a vintage opposed to *Katz*. However they may be explained, they are products of the old common-law notions of trespass. *Katz*, on the other hand, emphasized that with few exceptions "searches conducted outside the judicial process, without prior approval by judge or magistrate, are *per se* unreasonable under the Fourth Amendment."

We have moved far away from the rationale of *On Lee* and *Lopez* and only a retrogressive step of large dimensions would bring us back to it.

The threads of thought running through our recent decisions are that these extensive intrusions into privacy made by electronic surveillance make self-restraint by law enforcement officials an inadequate protection, that the requirement of warrants under the Fourth Amendment is essential to a free society.

Monitoring, if prevalent, certainly kills free discourse and spontaneous utterances. Free discourse — a First Amendment value — may be frivolous or serious, humble or defiant, reactionary or revolutionary, profane or in good taste; but it is not free if there is surveillance. Free discourse liberates the spirit, though it may produce only froth. The individual must keep some facts concerning his thoughts within a small zone of people. At the same time he must be free to pour out his woes or inspirations or dreams to others. He remains the sole judge as to what must be said and what must remain unspoken. This is the essence of the idea of privacy implicit in the First

and Fifth Amendments as well as in the Fourth.

Now that the discredited decisions in *On Lee* and *Lopez* are resuscitated and revived, must everyone live in fear that every word he speaks may be transmitted or recorded[5] and later repeated to the entire world? I can imagine nothing that has a more chilling effect on people speaking their minds and expressing their views on important matters. The advocates of that regime should spend some time in totalitarian countries and learn firsthand the kind of regime they are creating here.

Mr. Justice HARLAN, dissenting.

---

[5] Senator Edward Long, who intensively investigated wiretapping and "bugging" said:

"You would be amazed at the different ways you can now be 'bugged.' There is today a transmitter the size of an aspirin tablet which can help transmit conversations in your room to a listening post up to 10 miles away.

"An expert can devise a bug to fit into almost any piece of furniture in your room. And even if you find the bug, you will have no evidence of who put it there. A United States Senator was bugged by a transmitter secretly placed into a lamp which his wife was having fixed at the shop. When experts searched for the transmitter, it was gone.

"A leading electronics expert told my Subcommittee last year that wiretapping and bugging in industrial espionage triples every year. He said that new bugging devices are so small and cleverly concealed that it takes search equipment costing over one hundred thousand dollars and an expert with 10 years of field experience to discover them. Ten years ago, the same search for bugs could have been done with equipment costing only one-fourth as much.

"In California we found a businessman who had been so frightened by electronic eavesdropping devices which had been concealed in his office, that he is now spending thousands of dollars having his office searched each day, taking his phone apart every morning, and stationing a special guard outside his office 24 hours a day.

"He is one of a growing number of men in industry who live in constant fear that what they say is being listened to by their competitor." 19 Adm.L.Rev. 442, 444. And see E. Long, The Intruders (1966).

I think that a perception of the scope and role of the Fourth Amendment, as elucidated by this Court since *On Lee* was decided, and full comprehension of the precise issue at stake lead to the conclusion that *On Lee* can no longer be regarded as sound law.

### III

#### A.

That the foundations of *On Lee* have been destroyed does not, of course, mean that its result can no longer stand. Indeed, the plurality opinion today fastens upon our decisions in *Lopez, Lewis,* and *Hoffa,* to resist the undercurrents of more recent cases emphasizing the warrant procedure as a safeguard to privacy. But this category provides insufficient support. In each of these cases the risk the general populace faced was different from that surfaced by the instant case. No surreptitious third ear was present, and in each opinion that fact was carefully noted.

In *Lewis,* a federal agent posing as a potential purchaser of narcotics gained access to petitioner's home and there consummated an illegal sale, the fruits of which were admitted at trial along with the testimony of the agent. Chief Justice Warren, writing for the majority, expressly distinguished the third-party overhearing [situation], noting that "there, the conduct proscribed was that of eavesdroppers, unknown and unwanted intruders who furtively listened to conversations occurring in the privacy of a house." Similarly in *Hoffa,* Mr. Justice Stewart took care to mention that "surreptitious" monitoring was not there before the Court, and so too in *Lopez.*

The plurality opinion seeks to erase the crucial distinction between the facts before us and these holdings by the following reasoning: if A can relay verbally what is revealed to him by B (as in *Lewis* and *Hoffa*), or record and later divulge it (as in *Lopez*), what difference does it make if A conspires with another to betray B by contemporaneously transmitting to the other all that is said? The contention is, in essence, an argument that the distinction between third-party monitoring and other undercover techniques is one of form and not substance. The force of the contention depends on the evaluation of two separable but intertwined assumptions: first, that there is no greater invasion of privacy in the third-party situation, and, second, that uncontrolled consensual surveillance in an electronic age is a tolerable technique of law enforcement, given the values and goals of our political system.

The first of these assumptions takes as a point of departure the so-called "risk analysis" approach of *Lewis,* and *Lopez,* and to a lesser extent *On Lee,* or the expectations approach of *Katz.* While these formulations represent an advance over the unsophisticated trespass analysis of the common law, they too have their limitations and can, ultimately, lead to the substitution of words for analysis. The analysis must, in my view, transcend the search for subjective expectations or legal attribution of assumptions of risk. Our expectations, and the risks we assume, are in large part reflections of laws that translate into rules the customs and values of the past and present.

Since it is the task of the law to form and project, as well as mirror and reflect, we should not, as judges, merely recite the expectations and risks without examining the desirability of saddling them upon society. The critical question, therefore, is whether under our system of government, as reflected in the Constitution, we should impose on our citizens the risks of the electronic listener or observer without at least the protection of a warrant requirement.

This question must, in my view, be answered by assessing the nature of a particular practice and the likely extent of its impact on the individual's sense of security balanced against the utility of the conduct as a technique of law enforcement. For those more extensive intrusions that significantly jeopardize the sense of security which is the paramount concern of Fourth Amendment liberties, I am of the view that more than self-restraint by law enforcement officials is required and at the least warrants should be necessary.

#### B.

The impact of the practice of third-party bugging, must, I think, be considered such as to undermine that confidence and sense of security in dealing with one another that is characteristic of individual relationships between citizens in a free society. It goes beyond the impact on privacy occasioned by the ordinary type of "informer" investigation upheld in *Lewis* and *Hoffa.* The argument of the plurality opinion, to the effect that it is irrelevant whether secrets are revealed by the mere tattletale or the transistor, ignores the differences occasioned by third-party monitoring and recording which insures full and accurate disclosure of all that is said, free of the possibility of error and oversight that inheres in human reporting.

Authority is hardly required to support the proposition that words would be measured a good deal more carefully and communication inhibited if one suspected his conversations were being transmitted and transcribed. Were third-party bugging a prevalent practice, it might well smother that spontaneity — reflected in frivolous, impetuous, sacrilegious, and defiant discourse—that liberates daily life. Much off-hand exchange is easily forgotten and one may count on the obscurity of his remarks, protected by the very fact of a limited audience, and the likelihood that the listener will either overlook or forget what is said, as well as the listener's inability to reformulate a conversation without having to contend with a documented record.[24] All these values are sacrificed by a rule of law that permits official monitoring of private discourse limited only by the need to locate a willing assistant.

Finally, it is too easy to forget—and, hence, too

------

[24] From the same standpoint it may also be thought that electronic recording by an informer of a face-to-face conversation with a criminal suspect, as in *Lopez*, should be differentiated from third-party monitoring, as in *On Lee* and the case before us, in that the latter assures revelation to the Government by obviating the possibility that the informer may be tempted to renege in his undertaking to pass on to the Government all that he has learned. While the continuing vitality of *Lopez* is not drawn directly into question by this case, candor compels me to acknowledge that the views expressed in this opinion may impinge upon that part of the reasoning in *Lopez* which suggested that a suspect has no right to anticipate unreliable testimony. I am now persuaded that such an approach misconceives the basic issue, focusing, as it does, on the interests of a particular individual rather than evaluating the impact of a practice on the sense of security that is the true concern of the Fourth Amendment's protection of privacy. Distinctions do, however, exist between *Lopez*, where a known Government agent uses a recording device, and this case which involves third-party overhearing. However unlikely that the participant recorder will not play his tapes, the fact of the matter is that in a third-party situation the intrusion is instantaneous. Moreover, differences in the prior relationship between the investigator and the suspect may provide a focus for future distinctions.

often forgotten—that the issue here is whether to interpose a search warrant procedure between law enforcement agencies engaging in electronic eavesdropping and the public generally. By casting its "risk analysis" solely in terms of the expectations and risks that "wrongdoers" or "one contemplating illegal activities" ought to bear, the plurality opinion, I think, misses the mark entirely. *On Lee* does not simply mandate that criminals must daily run the risk of unknown eavesdroppers prying into their private affairs; it subjects each and every law-abiding member of society to that risk. The very purpose of interposing the Fourth Amendment warrant requirement is to redistribute the privacy risks throughout society in a way that produces the results the plurality opinion ascribes to the *On Lee* rule. Abolition of *On Lee* would not end electronic eavesdropping. It would prevent public officials from engaging in that practice unless they first had probable cause to suspect an individual of involvement in illegal activities and had tested their version of the facts before a detached judicial officer. The interest *On Lee* fails to protect is the expectation of the ordinary citizen, who has never engaged in illegal conduct in his life, that he may carry on his private discourse freely, openly, and spontaneously without measuring his every word against the connotations it might carry when instantaneously heard by others unknown to him and unfamiliar with his situation or analyzed in a cold, formal record played days, months, or years after the conversation. Interposition of a warrant requirement is designed not to shield "wrongdoers," but to secure a measure of privacy and a sense of personal security throughout our society.

The Fourth Amendment does, of course, leave room for the employment of modern technology in criminal law enforcement, but in the stream of current developments in Fourth Amendment law I think it must be held that third-party electronic monitoring, subject only to the self-restraint of law enforcement officials, has no place in our society.

I would hold that *On Lee* is no longer good law and affirm the judgment below.

[Mr. Justice MARSHALL also dissented.]

## QUESTIONS AND NOTES

**1.** Do Justice White and Justice Harlan see the case as raising the same question or different questions? If different, how are they different?

**2.** Is there a difference between the risk run by the wrongdoer in *White vis-a-vis Hoffa*? Is it a difference that we should care about?

**3.** Is there a difference between the risk run by an innocent citizen in *White vis-a-vis Hoffa*? Is that a difference that we should care about?

**4.** Is there a meaningful difference between *White* and *On Lee* on the one hand, and *Lopez*, on the other? Explain.

**5.** As you read *Smith*, consider the extent to which the Court is in tune with most people's expectations of privacy?

## Smith v. Maryland
### 442 U.S. 735 (1979)

Mr. Justice BLACKMUN delivered the opinion of the Court.

This case presents the question whether the installation and use of a pen register[1] constitutes a "search" within the meaning of the Fourth Amendment.

### I

On March 5, 1976, in Baltimore, Md., Patricia McDonough was robbed. She gave the police a description of the robber and of a 1975 Monte Carlo automobile she had observed near the scene of the crime. After the robbery, McDonough began receiving threatening and obscene phone calls from a man identifying himself as the robber. On one occasion, the caller asked that she step out on her front porch; she did so, and saw the 1975 Monte Carlo she had earlier described to police moving slowly past her home. On March 16, police spotted a man who met McDonough's description driving a 1975 Monte Carlo in her neighborhood. By tracing the license plate number, police learned that the car was registered in the name of petitioner, Michael Lee Smith. The next day, the telephone company, at police request, installed a pen register at its central offices to record the numbers dialed from the telephone at petitioner's home. The police did not get a warrant or court order before having the pen register installed. The register revealed that on March 17 a call was placed from petitioner's home to McDonough's

phone. On the basis of this and other evidence, the police obtained a warrant to search petitioner's residence. The search revealed that a page in petitioner's phone book was turned down to the name and number of Patricia McDonough; the phone book was seized. Petitioner was arrested, and a six-man lineup was held on March 19. McDonough identified petitioner as the man who had robbed her.

Petitioner was indicted in the Criminal Court of Baltimore for robbery. By pretrial motion, he sought to suppress "all fruits derived from the pen register" on the ground that the police had failed to secure a warrant prior to its installation. The trial court denied the suppression motion, holding that the warrantless installation of the pen register did not violate the Fourth Amendment. Petitioner then waived a jury, and the case was submitted to the court on an agreed statement of facts. The pen register tape (evidencing the fact that a phone call had been made from petitioner's phone to McDonough's phone) and the phone book seized in the search of petitioner's residence were admitted into evidence against him. Petitioner was convicted and sentenced to six years.

### II

#### A

In determining whether a particular form of government-initiated electronic surveillance is a "search" within the meaning of the Fourth Amendment, our lodestar is *Katz*. Because the Government's monitoring of Katz' conversation "violated the privacy upon which he justifiably relied while using the telephone booth," the Court held that it "constituted a 'search and seizure' within the meaning of the Fourth Amendment."

Consistently with *Katz*, this Court uniformly has held that the application of the Fourth Amendment depends on whether the person invoking its protection can claim a "justifiable," a "reasonable," or a "legitimate expectation of privacy" that has been invaded by government action. This inquiry, as Mr.

---

[1] "A pen register is a mechanical device that records the numbers dialed on a telephone by monitoring the electrical impulses caused when the dial on the telephone is released. It does not overhear oral communications and does not indicate whether calls are actually completed." A pen register is "usually installed at a central telephone facility [and] records on a paper tape all numbers dialed from [the] line" to which it is attached.

Justice Harlan aptly noted in his *Katz* concurrence, normally embraces two discrete questions. The first is whether the individual, by his conduct, has "exhibited an actual (subjective) expectation of privacy," – whether, in the words of the *Katz* majority, the individual has shown that "he seeks to preserve [something] as private." The second question is whether the individual's subjective expectation of privacy is "one that society is prepared to recognize as 'reasonable,'" – whether, in the words of the *Katz* majority, the individual's expectation, viewed objectively, is "justifiable" under the circumstances.[5]

### B

A pen register differs significantly from the listening device employed in *Katz*, for pen registers do not acquire the contents of communications. This Court recently noted:

> "Indeed, a law enforcement official could not even determine from the use of a pen register whether a communication existed. These devices do not hear sound. They disclose only the telephone numbers that have been dialed – a means of establishing communication. Neither the purport of any communication between the caller and the recipient of the call, their identities, nor whether the call was even completed is disclosed by pen registers." *United States v. New York Tel. Co.*, 434 U.S. 159, 167 (1977).

---

[5] Situations can be imagined, of course, in which *Katz*' two-pronged inquiry would provide an inadequate index of Fourth Amendment protection. For example, if the Government were suddenly to announce on nationwide television that all homes henceforth would be subject to warrantless entry, individuals thereafter might not in fact entertain any actual expectation or privacy regarding their homes, papers, and effects. Similarly, if a refugee from a totalitarian country, unaware of this Nation's traditions, erroneously assumed that police were continuously monitoring his telephone conversations, a subjective expectation of privacy regarding the contents of his calls might be lacking as well. In such circumstances, where an individual's subjective expectations had been "conditioned" by influences alien to well-recognized Fourth Amendment freedoms, those subjective expectations obviously could play no meaningful role in ascertaining what the scope of Fourth Amendment protection was. In determining whether a "legitimate expectation of privacy" existed in such cases, a normative inquiry would be proper.

Given a pen register's limited capabilities, therefore, petitioner's argument that its installation and use constituted a "search" necessarily rests upon a claim that he had a "legitimate expectation of privacy" regarding the numbers he dialed on his phone.

This claim must be rejected. First, we doubt that people in general entertain any actual expectation of privacy in the numbers they dial. All telephone users realize that they must "convey" phone numbers to the telephone company, since it is through telephone company switching equipment that their calls are completed. All subscribers realize, moreover, that the phone company has facilities for making permanent records of the numbers they dial, for they see a list of their long-distance (toll) calls on their monthly bills. In fact, pen registers and similar devices are routinely used by telephone companies "for the purposes of checking billing operations, detecting fraud and preventing violations of law." Electronic equipment is used not only to keep billing records of toll calls, but also "to keep a record of all calls dialed from a telephone which is subject to a special rate structure." Pen registers are regularly employed "to determine whether a home phone is being used to conduct a business, to check for a defective dial, or to check for over-billing." Although most people may be oblivious to a pen register's esoteric functions, they presumably have some awareness of one common use: to aid in the identification of persons making annoying or obscene calls. Most phone books tell subscribers, on a page entitled "Consumer Information," that the company "can frequently help in identifying to the authorities the origin of unwelcome and troublesome calls." Telephone users, in sum, typically know that they must convey numerical information to the phone company; that the phone company has facilities for recording this information; and that the phone company does in fact record this information for a variety of legitimate business purposes. Although subjective expectations cannot be scientifically gauged, it is too much to believe that telephone subscribers, under these circumstances, harbor any general expectation that the numbers they dial will remain secret.

Petitioner argues, however, that, whatever the expectations of telephone users in general, he demonstrated an expectation of privacy by his own conduct here, since he "us[ed] the telephone *in his house* to the exclusion of all others." (emphasis added). But the site of the call is immaterial for purposes of analysis in this case. Although petitioner's conduct may have been calculated to keep the contents of his conversation private, his conduct was not and could not have been calculated to preserve the privacy of the number he dialed. Regardless of his location, petitioner had to convey that number to the telephone company in precisely the same way if he wished to complete his call. The fact that he dialed the number on his home phone rather than on some other phone could make no conceivable difference, nor could any subscriber rationally think that it would.

Second, even if petitioner did harbor some subjective expectation that the phone numbers he dialed would remain private, this expectation is not "one that society is prepared to recognize as 'reasonable.'" *Katz*, 389 U.S., at 361. This Court consistently has held that a person has no legitimate expectation of privacy in information he voluntarily turns over to third parties. In *Miller* [*United States v.*, 425 U.S. 435], for example, the Court held that a bank depositor has no "legitimate 'expectation of privacy'" in financial information "voluntarily conveyed to . . . banks and exposed to their employees in the ordinary course of business." The Court explained:

"The depositor takes the risk, in revealing his affairs to another, that the information will be conveyed by that person to the Government. . . . This Court has held repeatedly that the Fourth Amendment does not prohibit the obtaining of information revealed to a third party and conveyed by him to Government authorities, even if the information is revealed on the assumption that it will be used only for a limited purpose and the confidence placed in the third party will not be betrayed."

Because the depositor "assumed the risk" of disclosure, the Court held that it would be unreasonable for him to expect his financial records to remain private.

This analysis dictates that petitioner can claim no legitimate expectation of privacy here. When he used his phone, petitioner voluntarily conveyed numerical information to the telephone company and "exposed" that information to its equipment in the ordinary course of business. In so doing, petitioner assumed the risk that the company would reveal to police the numbers he dialed. The switching equipment that processed those numbers is merely the modern counterpart of the operator who, in an earlier day, personally completed calls for the subscriber. Petitioner concedes that if he had placed his calls through an operator, he could claim no legitimate expectation of privacy. We are not inclined to hold that a different constitutional result is required because the telephone company has decided to automate.

Petitioner argues, however, that automatic switching equipment differs from a live operator in one pertinent respect. An operator, in theory at least, is capable of remembering every number that is conveyed to him by callers. Electronic equipment, by contrast can "remember" only those numbers it is programmed to record, and telephone companies, in view of their present billing practices, usually do not record local calls. Since petitioner, in calling McDonough, was making a local call, his expectation of privacy as to her number, on this theory, would be "legitimate."

This argument does not withstand scrutiny. The fortuity of whether or not the phone company in fact elects to make a quasi-permanent record of a particular number dialed does not in our view, make any constitutional difference. Regardless of the phone company's election, petitioner voluntarily conveyed to it information that it had facilities for recording and that it was free to record. In these circumstances, petitioner assumed the risk that the information would be divulged to police. Under petitioner's theory, Fourth Amendment protection would exist, or not, depending on how the telephone company chose to define local-dialing zones, and depending on how it chose to bill its customers for local calls. Calls placed across town, or dialed directly, would be protected; calls placed across the river, or dialed with operator assistance, might not be. We are not inclined to make a crazy quilt of the Fourth Amendment, especially in circumstances where (as here) the pattern of protection would be dictated by billing practices of a private corporation.

We therefore conclude that petitioner in all probability entertained no actual expectation of privacy in the phone numbers he dialed, and that, even if he did, his expectation was not "legitimate." The installation and use of a pen register, consequently, was not a "search," and no warrant was required. The judgment of the Maryland Court of Appeals is affirmed.

Mr. Justice MARSHALL, with whom Mr. Justice BRENNAN joins, dissenting.

Applying the standards set forth in *Katz* (Harlan, J., concurring), the Court first determines that telephone subscribers have no subjective expectations of privacy concerning the numbers they dial. To reach this conclusion, the Court posits that individuals somehow infer from the long-distance listings on their phone bills, and from the cryptic assurances of "help" in tracing obscene calls included in "most" phone books, that pen registers are regularly used for recording local calls. But even assuming, as I do not, that individuals "typically know" that a phone company monitors calls for internal reasons,[1] it does not follow that they expect this information to be made available to the public in general or the government in particular. Privacy is not a discrete commodity, possessed absolutely or not at all. Those who disclose certain facts to a bank or phone company for a limited business purpose need not assume that this information will be released to other persons for other purposes.

The crux of the Court's holding, however, is that whatever expectation of privacy petitioner may in fact have entertained regarding his calls, it is not one "society is prepared to recognize as 'reasonable.'" In so ruling, the Court determines that individuals who convey information to third parties have "assumed the risk" of disclosure to the government. This analysis is misconceived in two critical respects.

Implicit in the concept of assumption of risk is some notion of choice. At least in the third-party consensual surveillance cases, which first incorporated risk analysis into Fourth Amendment doctrine, the defendant presumably had exercised some discretion in deciding who should enjoy his confidential communications. See, *e.g., Hoffa*; *White* (plurality opinion). By contrast here, unless a person is prepared to forgo use of what for many has become a personal or professional necessity, he cannot help but accept the risk of surveillance. It is idle to speak of "assuming" risks in contexts where, as a practical matter, individuals have no realistic alternative.

More fundamentally, to make risk analysis dispositive in assessing the reasonableness of privacy expectations would allow the government to define the scope of Fourth Amendment protections. For example, law enforcement officials, simply by announcing their intent to monitor the content of random samples of first-class mail or private phone conversations, could put the public on notice of the risks they would thereafter assume in such communications. Yet, although acknowledging this implication of its analysis, the Court is willing to concede only that, in some circumstances, a further "normative inquiry would be proper." No meaningful effort is made to explain what those circumstances might be, or why this case is not among them.

---

[1] Lacking the Court's apparently exhaustive knowledge of this Nation's telephone books and the reading habits of telephone subscribers, I decline to assume general public awareness of how obscene phone calls are traced. Nor am I persuaded that the scope of Fourth Amendment protection should turn on the concededly "esoteric functions" of pen registers in corporate billing, functions with which subscribers are unlikely to have intimate familiarity.

In my view, whether privacy expectations are legitimate within the meaning of *Katz* depends not on the risks an individual can be presumed to accept when imparting information to third parties, but on the risks he should be forced to assume in a free and open society. By its terms, the constitutional prohibition of unreasonable searches and seizures assigns to the judiciary some prescriptive responsibility. As Mr. Justice Harlan, who formulated the standard the Court applies today, himself recognized: "[s]ince it is the task of the law to form and project, as well as mirror and reflect, we should not . . . merely recite . . . risks without examining the desirability of saddling them upon society." *White*, (dissenting opinion). In making this assessment, courts must evaluate the "intrinsic character" of investigative practices with reference to the basic values underlying the Fourth Amendment. And for those "extensive intrusions that significantly jeopardize [individuals'] sense of security . . ., more than self-restraint by law enforcement officials is required."

The use of pen registers, I believe, constitutes such an extensive intrusion. To hold otherwise ignores the vital role telephonic communication plays in our personal and professional relationships, as well as the First and Fourth Amendment interests implicated by unfettered official surveillance. Privacy in placing calls is of value not only to those engaged in criminal activity. The prospect of unregulated governmental monitoring will undoubtedly prove disturbing even to those with nothing illicit to hide. Many individuals, including members of unpopular political organizations or journalists with confidential sources, may legitimately wish to avoid disclosure of their personal contacts. Permitting governmental access to telephone records on less than probable cause may thus impede certain forms of political affiliation and journalistic endeavor that are the hallmark of a truly free society. Particularly given the Government's previous reliance on warrantless telephonic surveillance to trace reporters' sources and monitor protected political activity, I am unwilling to insulate use of pen registers from independent judicial review.

Just as one who enters a public telephone booth is "entitled to assume that the words he utters into the mouthpiece will not be broadcast to the world," *Katz* v. *United States, supra,* 389 U.S., at 352, so too, he should be entitled to assume that the numbers he dials in the privacy of his home will be recorded, if at all, solely for the phone company's business purposes. Accordingly, I would require law enforcement officials to obtain a warrant before they enlist telephone companies to secure information otherwise beyond the government's reach.

(Justice Stewart also dissented.)

## QUESTIONS AND NOTES

**1.** Did the Court deem pen registers to be a nonsearch primarily because they yield virtually no useful information (*i.e.*, one doesn't even know whether the call was completed or if it was an inadvertent wrong number)?

**2.** If that is so, why is it important for the police to acquire the information?

**3.** Did you know that your phone company could record local phone numbers that you dialed?

**4.** If your answer to question 3 was yes, did you assume that the phone company chose to record such numbers?

**5.** In any event, did you assume that the phone company, for no reason except that it was asked to do so, shared such information with the police?

**6.** Would you assume that when the police receive a report of an obscene phone call, they put a pen register on *every* telephone in the city?

**7.** Isn't the knowledge that the police or phone company can track down obscene phone calls a little bit like the police ability to track down robbers? If one robs a bank, he is at risk of having his home searched if, but only if, the police can convince a magistrate to issue a warrant on the basis of probable cause. Likewise, shouldn't the obscene caller be subject to a pen register only if similar conditions are met?

**8.** If the Court had held that the procedure to which Smith was subjected constituted a search, what result would the Court likely reach in a future case that is factually similar to *Smith*? What could the police do about it?

**9.** In *Oliver*, we see that even if the Fourth Amendment protects people rather than places, the place still matters.

### Oliver v. United States
#### 466 U.S. 170 (1984)

Justice POWELL delivered the opinion of the Court.

The "open fields" doctrine, first enunciated by this Court in *Hester v. United States*, 265 U.S. 57 (1924), permits police officers to enter and search a field without a warrant. We granted certiorari in these cases to clarify confusion that has arisen as to the continued vitality of the doctrine.

#### I

Acting on reports that marijuana was being raised on the farm of petitioner Oliver, two narcotics agents of the Kentucky State Police went to the farm to investigate.[1] Arriving at the farm, they drove past

---

[1] It is conceded that the police did not have a warrant authorizing the search, that there was no probable cause for the search and that no exception to the warrant requirement is applicable.

petitioner's house to a locked gate with a "No Trespassing" sign. A footpath led around one side of the gate. The agents walked around the gate and along the road for several hundred yards, passing a barn and a parked camper. At that point, someone standing in front of the camper shouted, "No hunting is allowed, come back here." The officers shouted back that they were Kentucky State Police officers, but found no one when they returned to the camper. The officers resumed their investigation of the farm and found a field of marijuana over a mile from petitioner's home.

#### II

The rule announced in *Hester v. United States* was founded upon the explicit language of the Fourth Amendment. That Amendment indicates with some precision the places and things encompassed by its protections. As Justice Holmes explained for the Court in his characteristically laconic style: "[T]he special protection accorded by the Fourth Amendment to the people in their 'persons, houses, papers, and effects,' is not extended to the open fields. The distinction between the latter and the house is as old as the common law.''

Nor are the open fields "effects" within the meaning of the Fourth Amendment. In this respect, it is suggestive that James Madison's proposed draft of what became the Fourth Amendment preserves "[t]he rights of the people to be secured in their persons, their houses, their papers, and their other property, from all unreasonable searches and seizures. . . ." Although Congress' revisions of Madison's proposal broadened the scope of the Amendment in some respects, the term "effects" is less inclusive than "property" and cannot be said to encompass open fields.[7] We conclude, as did the Court in deciding *Hester*, that the government's intrusion upon the open fields is not one of those "unreasonable searches" proscribed by the text of the Fourth Amendment.

### III

This interpretation of the Fourth Amendment's language is consistent with the understanding of the right to privacy expressed in our Fourth Amendment jurisprudence. Since *Katz*, the touchstone of Fourth Amendment analysis has been the question whether a person has a "constitutionally protected reasonable expectation of privacy." The Amendment does not protect the merely subjective expectation of privacy, but only "those expectations that society is prepared to recognize as 'reasonable.'" See also *Smith*.

### A

No single factor determines whether an individual legitimately may claim under the Fourth Amendment that a place should be free of government intrusion not authorized by warrant. In assessing the degree to which a search infringes upon individual privacy, the Court has given weight to such factors as the intention of the Framers of the Fourth Amendment, [the *Chadwick* test,] 433 U.S. 1, 7-8 (1977), the uses to which the individual has put a location, and our societal understanding that certain areas deserve the most scrupulous protection from government invasion, [the *Payton* test]. These factors are equally relevant to determining whether the government's intrusion upon open fields without a warrant or probable cause violates reasonable expectations of privacy and is therefore a search proscribed by the Amendment.

In this light, the rule of *Hester* that we reaffirm today, may be understood as providing that an individual may not legitimately demand privacy for activities conducted out of doors in fields, except in

the area immediately surrounding the home. This rule is true to the conception of the right to privacy embodied in the Fourth Amendment. The Amendment reflects the recognition of the Founders that certain enclaves should be free from arbitrary government interference. For example, the Court since the enactment of the Fourth Amendment has stressed "the overriding respect for the sanctity of the home that has been embedded in our traditions since the origins of the Republic."[8]

In contrast, open fields do not provide the setting for those intimate activities that the Amendment is intended to shelter from government interference or surveillance. There is no societal interest in protecting the privacy of those activities, such as the cultivation of crops, that occur in open fields. Moreover, as a practical matter these lands usually are accessible to the public and the police in ways that a home, an office or commercial structure would not be. It is not generally true that fences or "No Trespassing" signs effectively bar the public from viewing open fields in rural areas. And petitioner Oliver concede[s] that the public and police lawfully may survey lands from the air.[9] For these reasons, the asserted expectation of privacy in open fields is not an expectation that "society recognizes as reasonable."[10]

---

[8] The Fourth Amendment's protection of offices and commercial buildings, in which there may be legitimate expectations of privacy, is also based upon societal expectations that have deep roots in the history of the Amendment.

[9] In practical terms, Oliver's analysis merely would require law enforcement officers, in most situations, to use aerial surveillance to gather the information necessary to obtain a warrant or to justify warrantless entry onto the property. It is not easy to see how such a requirement would advance legitimate privacy interests.

[10] The dissent conceives of open fields as bustling with private activity as diverse as lovers' trysts and worship services. But in most instances police will disturb no one when they enter upon open fields. These fields, by their very character as open and unoccupied, are unlikely to provide the setting for activities whose privacy is sought to be protected by the Fourth Amendment. One need think only of the vast expanse of some western ranches or of the undeveloped woods of the Northwest to see the unreality of the dissent's conception. Further, the Fourth Amendment provides ample protection to activities in the open fields that might implicate an individual's privacy. An individual who enters a place defined to be "public" for Fourth Amendment analysis does not lose all claims to privacy

---

[7] The Framers would have understood the term "effects" to be limited to personal, rather than real, property.

The historical underpinnings of the "open fields" doctrine also demonstrate that the doctrine is consistent with respect for "reasonable expectations of privacy." As Justice Holmes, writing for the Court, observed in *Hester*, the common law distinguished "open fields" from the "curtilage," the land immediately surrounding and associated with the home. The distinction implies that only the curtilage, not the neighboring open fields, warrants the Fourth Amendment protections that attach to the home. At common law, the curtilage is the area to which extends the intimate activity associated with the "sanctity of a man's home and the privacies of life," and therefore has been considered part of home itself for Fourth Amendment purposes. Thus, courts have extended Fourth Amendment protection to the curtilage; and they have defined the curtilage, as did the common law, by reference to the factors that determine whether an individual reasonably may expect that an area immediately adjacent to the home will remain private. Conversely, the common law implies, as we reaffirm today, that no expectation of privacy legitimately attaches to open fields.[11]

We conclude, from the text of the Fourth Amendment and from the historical and contemporary understanding of its purposes, that an individual has no legitimate expectation that open fields will remain free from warrantless intrusion by government officers.

### B

Oliver contend[s], to the contrary, that the circumstances of a search sometimes may indicate that reasonable expectations of privacy were violated; and that courts therefore should analyze these circumstances on a case-by-case basis. The language of the Fourth Amendment itself answers their contention.

Nor would a case-by-case approach provide a workable accommodation between the needs of law enforcement and the interests protected by the Fourth Amendment. Under this approach, police officers would have to guess before every search whether landowners had erected fences sufficiently high, posted a sufficient number of warning signs, or located contraband in an area sufficiently secluded to establish a right of privacy. The lawfulness of a search would turn on "[a] highly sophisticated set of rules, qualified by all sorts of ifs, ands, and buts and requiring the drawing of subtle nuances and hairline distinctions. . . ." This Court repeatedly has acknowledged the difficulties created for courts, police and citizens by an ad hoc, case-by-case definition of Fourth Amendment standards to be applied in differing factual circumstances. *Belton.* The ad hoc approach not only makes it difficult for the policeman to discern the scope of his authority, it also creates a danger that constitutional rights will be arbitrarily and inequitably enforced.[12]

### IV

In any event, while the factors that Oliver urge[s] the courts to consider may be relevant to Fourth Amendment analysis in some contexts, these factors cannot be decisive on the question whether the search of an open field is subject to the Amendment. Initially, we reject the suggestion that steps taken to protect privacy establish that expectations of privacy in an open field are legitimate. It is true, of course, that Oliver, in order to conceal his criminal activities, planted the marijuana upon secluded land and erected fences and no trespassing signs around the property. And it may be that because of such precautions, few

---

or personal security. For example, the Fourth Amendment's protections against unreasonable arrest or unreasonable seizure of effects upon the person remain fully applicable. See, *e.g., United States v. Watson*, 423 U.S. 411 (1976).

[11] Oliver has [not] contended that the property searched was within the curtilage. Nor is it necessary in [this case] to consider the scope of the curtilage exception to the open fields doctrine or the degree of Fourth Amendment protection afforded the curtilage, as opposed to the home itself. It is clear, however, that the term "open fields" may include any unoccupied or undeveloped area outside of the curtilage. An open field need be neither "open" nor a "field" as those terms are used in common speech. For example, a thickly wooded area nonetheless may be an open field as that term is used in construing the Fourth Amendment.

[12] The clarity of the open fields doctrine that we reaffirm today is not sacrificed, as the dissent suggests, by our recognition that the curtilage remains within the protections of the Fourth Amendment. Most of the many millions of acres that are "open fields" are not close to any structure and so not arguably within the curtilage. And, for most homes, the boundaries of the curtilage will be clearly marked; and the conception defining the curtilage—as the area around the home to which the activity of home life extends—is a familiar one easily understood from our daily experience. The occasional difficulties that courts might have in applying this, like other, legal concepts, do not argue for the unprecedented expansion of the Fourth Amendment advocated by the dissent.

members of the public stumbled upon the marijuana crops seized by the police. Neither of these suppositions demonstrates, however, that the expectation of privacy was *legitimate* in the sense required by the Fourth Amendment. The test of legitimacy is not whether the individual chooses to conceal assertedly "private" activity.[13] Rather, the correct inquiry is whether the government's intrusion infringes upon the personal and societal values protected by the Fourth Amendment. As we have explained, we find no basis for concluding that a police inspection of open fields accomplishes such an infringement.

Nor is the government's intrusion upon an open field a "search" in the constitutional sense because that intrusion is a trespass at common law. The existence of a property right is but one element in determining whether expectations of privacy are legitimate. "[T]he premise that property interests control the right of the Government to search and seize has been discredited." *Katz.* "[E]ven a property interest in premises may not be sufficient to establish a legitimate expectation of privacy with respect to particular items located on the premises or activity conducted thereon."

The common law may guide consideration of what areas are protected by the Fourth Amendment search by defining areas whose invasion by others is wrongful. The law of trespass, however, forbids intrusions upon land that the Fourth Amendment would not proscribe. For trespass law extends to instances where the exercise of the right to exclude vindicates no legitimate privacy interest.[15] Thus, in the case of open fields, the general rights of property protected by the common law of trespass have little or no relevance to the applicability of the Fourth Amendment.

V

We conclude that the open fields doctrine, as enunciated in *Hester*, is consistent with the plain language of the Fourth Amendment and its historical purposes. Moreover, Justice Holmes' interpretation of the Amendment in *Hester* accords with the "reasonable expectation of privacy" analysis developed in subsequent decisions of this Court.

Justice WHITE, concurring in part and in the judgment.

I concur in the judgment and join Parts I and II of the Court's opinion. These parts dispose of the issue before us; there is no need to go further and deal with the expectation of privacy matter. However reasonable a landowner's expectations of privacy may be, those expectations cannot convert a field into a "house" or an "effect."

Justice MARSHALL, with whom Justice BRENNAN and Justice STEVENS join, dissenting.

I

The first ground on which the Court rests its decision is that the Fourth Amendment "indicates with some precision the places and things encompassed by its protections," and that real property is not included in the list of protected spaces and possessions. This line of argument has several flaws. Most obviously, it is inconsistent with the results of many of our previous decisions, none of which the Court purports to overrule. For example, neither a public telephone booth nor a conversation conducted therein can fairly be described as a person, house, paper, or effect;[1] yet we have held that the Fourth Amendment forbids the police without a warrant to eavesdrop on such a conversation. Nor can it plausibly be argued that an office or commercial establishment is covered by the plain language of the Amendment; yet we have held that such premises are entitled to constitutional protection if they are marked in a fashion

---

[13] Certainly the Framers did not intend that the Fourth Amendment should shelter criminal activity wherever persons with criminal intent choose to erect barriers and post "No Trespassing" signs.

[15] The law of trespass recognizes the interest in possession and control of one's property and for that reason permits exclusion of unwanted intruders. But it does not follow that the right to exclude conferred by trespass law embodies a privacy interest also protected by the Fourth Amendment. To the contrary, the common law of trespass furthers a range of interests that have nothing to do with privacy and that would not be served by applying the strictures of trespass law to public officers. Criminal laws against trespass are prophylactic: they protect against intruders who poach, steal livestock and crops or vandalize property. And the civil action of trespass serves the important function of authorizing an owner to defeat claims of prescription by asserting his own title. In any event, unlicensed use of property by others is presumptively unjustified, as anyone who wishes to use the property is free to bargain for the right to

---

do so with the property owner. For these reasons, the law of trespass confers protections from intrusion by others far broader than those required by Fourth Amendment interests.

[1] The Court informs us that the Framers would have understood the term "effects" to encompass only personal property. Such a construction of the term would exclude both a public phone booth and spoken words.

that alerts the public to the fact that they are private.[2]

Indeed, the Court's reading of the plain language of the Fourth Amendment is incapable of explaining even its own holding in this case. The Court rules that the curtilage, a zone of real property surrounding a dwelling, is entitled to constitutional protection. We are not told, however, whether the curtilage is a "house" or an "effect" — or why, if the curtilage can be incorporated into the list of things and spaces shielded by the Amendment, a field cannot.

The Court's inability to reconcile its parsimonious reading of the phrase "persons, houses, papers, and effects" with our prior decisions or even its own holding is a symptom of a more fundamental infirmity in the Court's reasoning. The Fourth Amendment, like the other central provisions of the Bill of Rights that loom large in our modern jurisprudence, was designed, not to prescribe with "precision" permissible and impermissible activities, but to identify a fundamental human liberty that should be shielded forever from government intrusion. We do not construe constitutional provisions of this sort the way we do statutes, whose drafters can be expected to indicate with some comprehensiveness and exactitude the conduct they wish to forbid or control and to change those prescriptions when they become obsolete.[4] Rather, we strive, when interpreting these seminal constitutional provisions, to effectuate their purposes — to lend them meanings that ensure that the liberties the Framers sought to protect are not undermined by the changing activities of government officials.

The liberty shielded by the Fourth Amendment, as we have often acknowledged, is freedom "from unreasonable government intrusions into . . . legitimate expectations of privacy." That freedom would be incompletely protected if only government conduct that impinged upon a person, house, paper, or

effect were subject to constitutional scrutiny. Accordingly, we have repudiated the proposition that the Fourth Amendment applies only to a limited set of locales or kinds of property. In *Katz*, we expressly rejected a proffered locational theory of the coverage of the Amendment, holding that it "protects people, not places." Since that time we have consistently adhered to the view that the applicability of the provision depends solely upon "whether the person invoking its protection can claim a 'justifiable,' a 'reasonable,' or a 'legitimate expectation of privacy' that has been invaded by government action." *Smith*. The Court's contention that, because a field is not a house or effect, it is not covered by the Fourth Amendment is inconsistent with this line of cases and with the understanding of the nature of constitutional adjudication from which it derives.[7]

## II

The second ground for the Court's decision is its contention that any interest a landowner might have in the privacy of his woods and fields is not one that "society is prepared to recognize as 'reasonable.'" The mode of analysis that underlies this assertion is certainly more consistent with our prior decisions than that discussed above. But the Court's conclusion cannot withstand scrutiny.

## A

It is undisputed that Oliver owned the land into which the police intruded. That fact alone provides considerable support for their assertion of legitimate privacy interests in their woods and fields. But even more telling is the nature of the sanctions that Oliver could invoke, under local law, for violation of [his] property rights. In Kentucky, a knowing entry upon fenced or otherwise enclosed land, or upon unenclosed land conspicuously posted with signs excluding the public, constitutes criminal trespass. Thus, positive law not only recognizes the legitimacy of Oliver's insistence that strangers keep off [his] land, but subjects those who refuse to respect [his] wishes to the most severe of penalties — criminal liability.

---

[2] On the other hand, an automobile surely does constitute an "effect." Under the Court's theory, cars should therefore stand on the same constitutional footing as houses. Our cases establish, however, that car owners' diminished expectations that their cars will remain free from prying eyes warrants a corresponding reduction in the constitutional protection accorded cars.

[4] Cf. *McCulloch v. Maryland*, 17 U.S. 316, 407, 4 Wheat. 316, 407 (1819) ("[W]e must never forget, that it is *a constitution* we are expounding." Such a document cannot be as detailed as a "legal code"; "[i]ts nature . . . requires, that only its great outlines should be marked, its important objects designated, and the minor ingredients which compose those objects be deduced from the nature of the objects themselves.") (emphasis in original).

[7] Sensitive to the weakness of its argument that the "persons and things" mentioned in the Fourth Amendment exhaust the coverage of the provision, the Court goes on to analyze at length the privacy interests that might legitimately be asserted in "open fields." The inclusion of Parts III and IV in the opinion, coupled with the Court's reaffirmation of *Katz* and its progeny, strongly suggest that the plain-language theory sketched in Part II of the Court's opinion will have little or no effect on our future decisions in this area.

Under these circumstances, it is hard to credit the Court's assertion that Oliver's expectation of privacy [was] not of a sort that society is prepared to recognize as reasonable.

### B

The uses to which a place is put are highly relevant to the assessment of a privacy interest asserted therein. If, in light of our shared sensibilities, those activities are of a kind in which people should be able to engage without fear of intrusion by private persons or government officials, we extend the protection of the Fourth Amendment to the space in question, even in the absence of any entitlement derived from positive law. *E.g., Katz.*[13]

Privately-owned woods and fields that are not exposed to public view regularly are employed in a variety of ways that society acknowledges deserve privacy. Many landowners like to take solitary walks on their property, confident that they will not be confronted in their rambles by strangers or policemen. Others conduct agricultural businesses on their property.[14] Some landowners use their secluded spaces to meet lovers, others to gather together with fellow worshippers, still others to engage in sustained creative endeavor. Private land is sometimes used as a refuge for wildlife, where flora and fauna are protected from human intervention of any kind.[15] Our respect

for the freedom of landowners to use their posted "open fields" in ways such as these partially explains the seriousness with which the positive law regards deliberate invasions of such spaces, and substantially reinforces the landowners' contention that their expectations of privacy are "reasonable."

### C

Whether a person "took normal precautions to maintain his privacy" in a given space affects whether his interest is one protected by the Fourth Amendment. The reason why such precautions are relevant is that we do not insist that a person who has a right to exclude others exercise that right. A claim to privacy is therefore strengthened by the fact that the claimant somehow manifested to other people his desire that they keep their distance.

Certain spaces are so presumptively private that signals of this sort are unnecessary; a homeowner need not post a "do not enter" sign on his door in order to deny entrance to uninvited guests.[17] Privacy interests in other spaces are more ambiguous, and the taking of precautions is consequently more important; placing a lock on one's footlocker strengthens one's claim that an examination of its contents is impermissible. See *Chadwick.* Still other spaces are, by positive law and social convention, presumed accessible to members of the public *unless* the owner manifests his intention to exclude them.

Undeveloped land falls into the last-mentioned category. If a person has not marked the boundaries of his fields or woods in a way that informs passersby that they are not welcome, he cannot object if members of the public enter onto the property. There is no reason why he should have any greater rights as against government officials. Accordingly, we have held that an official may, without a warrant, enter private land from which the public is not excluded and make observations from that vantage point. *Air Pollution Variance Board v. Western Alfalfa Corp.*, 416 U.S. 861, 865 (1974). Fairly read, the case on which the majority so heavily relies, *Hester*, affirms little more than the foregoing unremarkable proposition. From aught that appears in the opinion in that case, the defendants, fleeing from revenue agents who had observed them committing a crime, abandoned incriminating evidence on private land from which the public had not been excluded. Under such circumstances, it is not surprising that

---

[13] In most circumstances, this inquiry requires analysis of the sorts of uses to which a given space is susceptible, not the manner in which the person asserting an expectation of privacy in the space was in fact employing it. Thus, the majority's contention that, because the cultivation of marijuana is not an activity that society wishes to protect, Oliver had no legitimate privacy interest in [his] fields, reflects a misunderstanding of the level of generality on which the constitutional analysis must proceed.

[14] We accord constitutional protection to businesses conducted in office buildings; it is not apparent why businesses conducted in fields that are not open to the public are less deserving of the benefit of the Fourth Amendment.

[15] This last mentioned use implicates a kind of privacy interest somewhat different from those to which we are accustomed. It involves neither a person's interest in immunity from observation nor a person's interest in shielding from scrutiny the residues and manifestations of his personal life. It derives, rather, from a person's desire to preserve inviolate a portion of his world. The idiosyncrasy of this interest does not, however, render it less deserving of constitutional protection.

---

[17] However, if the homeowner acts affirmatively to invite someone into his abode, he cannot later insist that his privacy interests have been violated. *Lewis.*

the Court was unpersuaded by the defendants' argument that the entry onto their fields by the agents violated the Fourth Amendment.[18]

A very different case is presented when the owner of undeveloped land has taken precautions to exclude the public. As indicated above, a deliberate entry by a private citizen onto private property marked with "No Trespassing" signs will expose him to criminal liability. I see no reason why a government official should not be obliged to respect such unequivocal and universally understood manifestations of a landowner's desire for privacy.[19]

### III

A clear, easily administrable rule emerges from the analysis set forth above: Private land marked in a fashion sufficient to render entry thereon a criminal trespass under the law of the state in which the land lies is protected by the Fourth Amendment's proscription of unreasonable searches and seizures. One of the advantages of the foregoing rule is that it draws upon a doctrine already familiar to both citizens and government officials. In each jurisdiction, a substantial body of statutory and case law defines the precautions a landowner must take in order to avail himself of the sanctions of the criminal law. The police know that body of law, because they are entrusted with responsibility for enforcing it against the public; it therefore would not be difficult for the police to abide by it themselves.

---

[18] An argument supportive of the position taken by the Court today might be constructed on the basis of an examination of the record in *Hester*. It appears that, in his approach to the house, one of the agents crossed a pasture fence. However, the Court, in its opinion, placed no weight upon—indeed, did not even mention—that circumstance.

In any event, to the extent that *Hester* may be read to support a rule any broader than that stated in *Air Pollution Variance Board, supra*, it is undercut by our decision in *Katz*, which repudiated the locational theory of the coverage of the Fourth Amendment.

[19] Indeed, important practical considerations suggest that the police should not be empowered to invade land closed to the public. In many parts of the country, landowners feel entitled to use self-help in expelling trespassers from their posted property. There is thus a serious risk that police officers, making unannounced, warrantless searches of "open fields," will become involved in violent confrontations with irate landowners, with potentially tragic results.

By contrast, the doctrine announced by the Court today is incapable of determinate application. Police officers, making warrantless entries upon private land, will be obliged in the future to make on-the-spot judgments as to how far the curtilage extends, and to stay outside that zone. In addition, we may expect to see a spate of litigation over the question of how much improvement is necessary to remove private land from the category of "unoccupied or undeveloped area" to which the "open fields exception" is now deemed applicable.

The Court's holding not only ill serves the need to make constitutional doctrine "workable for application by rank and file, trained police officers," it withdraws the shield of the Fourth Amendment from privacy interests that clearly deserve protection. By exempting from the coverage of the Amendment large areas of private land, the Court opens the way to investigative activities we would all find repugnant. Cf., *e.g., United States v. Lace*, 669 F.2d 46, 54 (CA2 1982) (Newman, J., concurring in the result) ("[W]hen police officers execute military maneuvers on residential property for three weeks of round-the-clock surveillance, can that be called 'reasonable'?"); *Florida v. Brady*, 406 So.2d 1093, 1094-1095 (Fla.1981) ("In order to position surveillance groups around the ranch's airfield, deputies were forced to cross a dike, ram through one gate and cut the chain lock on another, cut across posted fences, and proceed several hundred yards to their hiding places").[21]

The Fourth Amendment, properly construed, embodies and gives effect to our collective sense of the degree to which men and women, in civilized society, are entitled "to be let alone" by their governments. The Court's opinion bespeaks and will help to promote an impoverished vision of that fundamental right.

I dissent.

---

[21] Perhaps the most serious danger in the decision today is that, if the police are permitted routinely to engage in such behavior, it will gradually become less offensive to us all. As Justice Brandeis once observed: "Our Government is the potent, the omnipresent teacher. For good or for ill, it teaches the whole people by its example. Crime is contagious. If the Government becomes a lawbreaker, it breeds contempt for the law. . . ." *Olmstead v. United States*, 277 U.S. 438, 485 (1928) (dissenting opinion).

## QUESTIONS AND NOTES

**1.** One of your authors, Professor Loewy, wrote an article in which he commented on the *Oliver* Court's invitation to police officers to stop taking the Fourth Amendment so seriously. Arnold H. Loewy, *A Modest Proposal for Fighting Organized Crime: Stop Taking the Fourth Amendment so Seriously*, 16 Rutgers L.J. 831. In the course thereof, he imagined the following dialogue between two different police officers and their respective chief of police:

Captain: Officer A, what did you do last month?

Officer A: Last month while on duty I saw thirty heavily wooded fenced-in areas with "no trespassing" signs. Because they sought privacy, I was somewhat concerned that they might be growing marijuana. So I blasted a hole in each fence, like the Supreme Court said I could, and carefully searched the whole fenced-in area. Fortunately, things were slow last month, so I had plenty of time for these operations.

Captain: Did you find anything?

Officer A: I sure did. In two of the thirty fields, I found marijuana growing. One of them even turned out to be owned by an organized crime leader. I think that we're going to be able to put him away.

Captain: What about the other twenty-eight?

Officer A: Well, in twenty of them, I found nothing. Except for the hole in the fence, nobody would even know I was there. In two other searches, I found couples making love. Unfortunately, they were married, so I couldn't arrest them. In three other searches, I found people meeting at a hideout that they had hoped to keep secret. In another search, I found a group of scientists conducting experiments that they had hoped to keep secret. In the remaining two searches, I just found the owners seeking peace and repose in their woods. I don't think they minded my being there, especially since they couldn't do anything about it.

Captain: Officer B, what did you do last month?

Officer B: I also saw thirty heavily wooded fenced-in areas with "no trespassing" signs. I figured that while one or two of these areas might contain evidence of crime, most would not. Since the owners obviously sought privacy, and since most were innocent and had no outward indicia of guilt, I decided to respect their privacy and not search any of them. Consequently, I have neither made any arrests nor uncovered any evidence this month.

Each police officer reading this article can of course determine for himself whether his department would be more pleased with the performance of Officer A or Officer B. To the extent that I am correct, however, in thinking that most police departments would reward Officer A's performance more than Officer B's, there is a powerful incentive for a police officer to join the Supreme Court in not taking the Fourth Amendment seriously.

In your opinion, is the foregoing fair commentary on *Oliver*?

**2.** Which rule is more manageable, Justice Powell's opinion of the Court, or Justice Marshall's dissent?

**3.** If you think that Marshall's rule is more manageable, how do you deal with the problem of the uncertainty of height of fences or size and visibility of "No Trespassing" signs?

**4.** On the other hand, if you think that the Court's rule is more manageable, how do you deal with the problem of distinguishing open fields from curtilage? (See *Dunn infra*.)

**5.** Justice Marshall contends that freedom protected by the Fourth Amendment would be incomplete "if only government conduct that impinged upon a person, paper, house, or effect were subject to constitutional scrutiny." Is he saying that the Fourth Amendment, as written, incompletely protects Fourth Amendment values? If not, what is he saying?

**6.** Justice Powell says that "[a]n open field need be neither 'open' nor a 'field' as those terms are used in common speech." By that same logic, why do "persons, papers, houses, and effects" have to be defined in the dictionary sense?

**7.** How would you have decided this case? Why?

## PROBLEM

Respondent Ronald Dale Dunn and a codefendant, Robert Lyle Carpenter, were convicted by a jury of conspiring to manufacture phenylacetone and amphetamine, and to possess amphetamine with intent to distribute. Respondent was also convicted of manufacturing these two controlled substances and possessing amphetamine with intent to distribute.

Respondent's ranch comprised approximately 198 acres and was completely encircled by a perimeter fence. The property also contained several interior fences, constructed mainly of posts and multiple strands of barbed wire. The ranch residence was situated ½ mile from a public road. A fence encircled the residence and a nearby small greenhouse. Two barns were located approximately 50 yards from this fence. The front of the larger of the two barns was enclosed by a wooden fence and had an open overhang. Locked, waist-high gates barred entry into the barn proper, and netting material stretched from the ceiling to the top of the wooden gates.

On the evening of November 5, 1980, law enforcement officials made a warrantless entry onto respondent's ranch property. A DEA agent accompanied by an officer from the Houston Police Department crossed over the perimeter fence and one interior fence. Standing approximately midway between the residence and the barns, the DEA agent smelled what he believed to be phenylacetic acid, the odor coming from the direction of the barns. The officers approached the smaller of the barns – crossing over a barbed wire fence – and, looking into the barn, observed only empty boxes. The officers then proceeded to the larger barn, crossing another barbed wire fence as well as a wooden fence that enclosed the front portion of the barn. The officers walked under the barn's overhang to the locked wooden gates and, shining a flashlight through the netting on top of the gates, peered into the barn. They observed what the DEA agent thought to be a phenylacetone laboratory. The officers did not enter the barn. At this point the officers departed from respondent's property, but entered it twice more on November 6 to confirm the presence of the phenylacetone laboratory.

On November 6, 1980, at 8:30 p.m., a Federal Magistrate issued a warrant authorizing a search of respondent's ranch. DEA agents and state law enforcement officials executed the warrant on November 8, 1980. The officers arrested respondent and seized chemicals and equipment, as well as bags of amphetamines they discovered in a closet in the ranch house.

Assuming that the warrant would have been valid if the police had validly discovered the lab, but otherwise would have been invalid, should the Court have sustained the warrant? For the United States Supreme Court's solution, see *United States v. Dunn*, 480 U.S. 294 (1987).

In the next case, *Riley*, we consider the extent to which even curtilage activities can be observed without a Fourth Amendment search.

## Florida v. Riley
### 488 U.S. 445 (1989)

Justice WHITE announced the judgment of the Court and delivered an opinion, in which the Chief Justice, Justice SCALIA and Justice KENNEDY join.

On certification to it by a lower state court, the Florida Supreme Court addressed the following question: "Whether surveillance of the interior of a partially covered greenhouse in a residential backyard from the vantage point of a helicopter located 400 feet above the greenhouse constitutes a 'search' for which a warrant is required under the Fourth Amendment." The court answered the question in the affirmative, and we granted the State's petition for certiorari challenging that conclusion.

Respondent Riley lived in a mobile home located on five acres of rural property. A greenhouse was located 10 to 20 feet behind the mobile home. Two sides of the greenhouse were enclosed. The other two sides were not enclosed but the contents of the greenhouse were obscured from view from surrounding property by trees, shrubs and the mobile home. The greenhouse was covered by corrugated roofing panels, some translucent and some opaque. At the time relevant to this case, two of the panels, amounting to approximately 10% of the roof area, were missing. A wire fence surrounded the mobile home and the greenhouse, and the property was posted with a "DO NOT ENTER" sign.

This case originated with an anonymous tip to the Pasco County Sheriff's office that marijuana was being grown on respondent's property. When an investigating officer discovered that he could not see the contents of the greenhouse from the road, he circled twice over respondent's property in a helicopter at the height of 400 feet. With his naked eye, he was able to see through the openings in the roof and one or more of the open sides of the greenhouse and to identify what he thought was marijuana growing in the structure. A warrant was obtained based on these observations, and the ensuing search revealed marijuana growing in the greenhouse. Respondent was charged with possession of marijuana under Florida law. The trial court granted his motion to suppress; the Florida Court of Appeals reversed but certified the case to the Florida Supreme Court, which quashed the decision of the Court of Appeals and reinstated the trial court's suppression order.

We agree with the State's submission that our decision in *California v. Ciraolo*, 476 U.S. 207 (1986), controls this case. There, acting on a tip, the police inspected the back yard of a particular house while flying in a fixed-wing aircraft at 1,000 feet. With the naked eye the officers saw what they concluded was marijuana growing in the yard. A search warrant was obtained on the strength of this airborne inspection, and marijuana plants were found. We [held] that the inspection was not a search subject to the Fourth Amendment. We recognized that the yard was within the curtilage of the house, that a fence shielded the yard from observation from the street and that the occupant had a subjective expectation of privacy. We held, however, that such an expectation was not reasonable and not one "that society is prepared to honor." Our reasoning was that the home and its curtilage are not necessarily protected from inspection that involves no physical invasion. "What a person knowingly exposes to the public, even in his own home or office, is not a subject of Fourth Amendment protection." As a general proposition, the police may see what may be seen "from a public vantage point where [they have] a right to be." Thus the police, like the public, would have been free to inspect the backyard garden from the street if their view had been unobstructed. They were likewise, free to inspect the yard from the vantage point of an aircraft flying in the navigable airspace as this plane was. "In an age where private and commercial flight in the public airways is routine, it is unreasonable for respondent to expect that his marijuana plants were constitutionally protected from being observed with the naked eye from an altitude of 1,000 feet. The Fourth Amendment simply does not require the police traveling in the public airways at this altitude to obtain a warrant in order to observe what is visible to the naked eye."

We arrive at the same conclusion in the present case. In this case, as in *Ciraolo*, the property surveyed was within the curtilage of respondent's home. Riley no doubt intended and expected that his greenhouse would not be open to public inspection, and the precautions he took protected against ground-level observation. Because the sides and roof of his greenhouse were left partially open, however, what was growing in the greenhouse was subject to viewing from the air. Under the holding in *Ciraolo*, Riley could not reasonably have expected the contents of his greenhouse to be immune from examination by an officer seated in a fixed-wing aircraft flying in navigable airspace at an altitude of 1,000 feet or, as the Florida Supreme Court seemed to recognize, at an altitude of 500 feet, the lower limit of the navigable airspace for such an aircraft. Here, the inspection was made from a helicopter, but as is the case with fixed-wing planes, "private and commercial flight [by helicopter] in the public airways is routine" in this country, and there is no indication that such flights are unheard of in Pasco County, Florida. Riley could not reasonably have expected that his greenhouse was protected from public or official observation from a helicopter had it been flying within the navigable airspace for fixed-wing aircraft.

Nor on the facts before us, does it make a difference for Fourth Amendment purposes that the helicopter was flying at 400 feet when the officer saw what was growing in the greenhouse through the partially open roof and sides of the structure. We would have a different case if flying at that altitude had been contrary to law or regulation. But helicopters are not bound by the lower limits of the navigable airspace allowed to other aircraft. Any member of the public could legally have been flying over Riley's property in a helicopter at the altitude of 400 feet and could have observed Riley's greenhouse. The police officer did no more. This is not to say that an inspection of the curtilage of a house from an aircraft will always pass muster under the Fourth Amendment simply because the plane is within the navigable airspace specified by law. But it is of obvious importance that the helicopter in this case was *not* violating the law, and there is nothing in the record or before us to suggest that helicopters flying at 400 feet are sufficiently rare in this country to lend substance to respondent's claim that he reasonably anticipated that his greenhouse would not be subject to observation from that altitude. Neither is there any intimation here that the helicopter interfered with respondent's normal use of the greenhouse or of other parts of the curtilage. As far as this record reveals, no intimate details connected with the use of the home or curtilage were observed, and there was no undue noise, no wind, dust, or threat of injury. In these circumstances, there was no violation of the Fourth Amendment.

The judgment of the Florida Supreme Court is accordingly reversed.

Justice O'CONNOR, concurring in the judgment.

I concur in the judgment reversing the Supreme Court of Florida because I agree that police observation of the greenhouse in Riley's curtilage from a helicopter passing at an altitude of 400 feet did not violate an expectation of privacy "that society is prepared to recognize as 'reasonable.'" I write separately, however, to clarify the standard I believe follows from *Ciraolo*. In my view, the plurality's approach rests the scope of Fourth Amendment protection too heavily on compliance with FAA regulations whose purpose is to promote air safety not to protect "[t]he right of the people to be secure in their persons, houses, papers, and effects, against unreasonable searches and seizures."

*Ciraolo* involved observation of curtilage by officers flying in an airplane at an altitude of 1,000 feet. In evaluating whether this observation constituted a search for which a warrant was required, we acknowledged the importance of curtilage in Fourth Amendment doctrine: "The protection afforded the curtilage is essentially a protection of families and personal privacy in an area intimately linked to the home, both physically and psychologically, where privacy expectations are most heightened." Although the curtilage is an area to which the private activities of the home extend, all police observation of the curtilage is not necessarily barred by the Fourth Amendment. As we observed: "The Fourth Amendment protection of the home has never been extended to require law enforcement officers to shield their eyes when passing by a home on public thoroughfares." In *Ciraolo*, we likened observation from a plane traveling in "public navigable airspace" at 1,000 feet to observation by police "passing by a home on public thoroughfares." We held that "[i]n an age where private and commercial flight in the public airways is routine," it is unreasonable to expect curtilage to be constitutionally protected from aerial observation with the naked eye from an altitude of 1,000 feet.

*Ciraolo's* expectation of privacy was unreasonable not because the airplane was operating where it had a "right to be," but because public air travel at 1,000 feet is a sufficiently routine part of modern life that it is unreasonable for persons on the ground to expect that their curtilage will not be observed from the air at that altitude. Although "helicopters are not bound by the lower limits of the navigable airspace allowed to other aircraft," there is no reason to assume that compliance with FAA regulations alone determines "whether the government's intrusion infringes upon the personal and societal values protected by the Fourth Amendment." Because the FAA has decided that helicopters can lawfully operate at virtually any altitude so long as they pose no safety hazard, it does not follow that the expectations of privacy "society is prepared to recognize as 'reasonable'" simply mirror the FAA's safety concerns.

Observations of curtilage from helicopters at very

low altitudes are not perfectly analogous to ground-level observations from public roads or sidewalks. While in both cases the police may have a legal right to occupy the physical space from which their observations are made, the two situations are not necessarily comparable in terms of whether expectations of privacy from such vantage points should be considered reasonable. Public roads, even those less traveled by, are clearly demarked public thoroughfares. Individuals who seek privacy can take precautions, tailored to the location of the road, to avoid disclosing private activities to those who pass by. They can build a tall fence, for example, and thus ensure private enjoyment of the curtilage without risking public observation from the road or sidewalk. If they do not take such precautions, they cannot reasonably expect privacy from public observation. In contrast, even individuals who have taken effective precautions to ensure against ground-level observations cannot block off all conceivable aerial views of their outdoor patios and yards without entirely giving up their enjoyment of those areas. To require individuals to completely cover and enclose their curtilage is to demand more than the "precautions customarily taken by those seeking privacy." The fact that a helicopter could conceivably observe the curtilage at virtually any altitude or angle, without violating FAA regulations, does not in itself mean that an individual has no reasonable expectation of privacy from such observation.

In determining whether Riley had a reasonable expectation of privacy from aerial observation, the relevant inquiry after *Ciraolo* is not whether the helicopter was where it had a right to be under FAA regulations. Rather, consistent with *Katz*, we must ask whether the helicopter was in the public airways at an altitude at which members of the public travel with sufficient regularity that Riley's expectation of privacy from aerial observation was not "one that society is prepared to recognize as 'reasonable.'" Thus, in determining "whether the government's intrusion infringes upon the personal and societal values protected by the Fourth Amendment," it is not conclusive to observe, as the plurality does, that "[a]ny member of the public could legally have been flying over Riley's property in a helicopter at the altitude of 400 feet and could have observed Riley's greenhouse." Nor is it conclusive that police helicopters may often fly at 400 feet. If the public rarely, if ever, travels overhead at such altitudes, the observation cannot be said to be from a vantage point generally used by the public and Riley cannot be said to have "knowingly expose[d]" his greenhouse to public view. However, if the public can generally be expected to travel over residential backyards at an altitude of 400 feet, Riley cannot reasonably expect his curtilage to be free from such aerial observation.

In my view, the defendant must bear the burden of proving that his expectation of privacy was a reasonable one, and thus that a "search" within the meaning of the Fourth Amendment even took place.

Because there is reason to believe that there is considerable public use of airspace at altitudes of 400 feet and above, and because Riley introduced no evidence to the contrary before the Florida courts, I conclude that Riley's expectation that his curtilage was protected from naked-eye aerial observation from that altitude was not a reasonable one. However, public use of altitudes lower than that—particularly public observations from helicopters circling over the curtilage of a home—may be sufficiently rare that police surveillance from such altitudes would violate reasonable expectations of privacy, despite compliance with FAA air safety regulations.

Justice BRENNAN, with whom Justice MARSHALL and Justice STEVENS, join, dissenting.

The plurality undertakes no inquiry into whether low-level helicopter surveillance by the police of activities in an enclosed backyard is consistent with the "aims of a free and open society." Instead, it summarily concludes that Riley's expectation of privacy was unreasonable because "[a]ny member of the public could legally have been flying over Riley's property in a helicopter at the altitude of 400 feet and could have observed Riley's greenhouse." This observation is, in turn, based solely on the fact that the police helicopter was within the airspace within which such craft are allowed by federal safety regulations to fly.

I agree, of course, that "[w]hat a person knowingly exposes to the public . . . is not a subject of Fourth Amendment protection." But I cannot agree that one "knowingly exposes [an area] to the public" solely because a helicopter may legally fly above it. Under the plurality's exceedingly grudging Fourth Amendment theory, the expectation of privacy is defeated if a single member of the public could conceivably position herself to see into the area in question without doing anything illegal. It is defeated whatever the difficulty a person would have in so positioning herself, and however infrequently anyone would in fact do so. In taking this view the plurality ignores the very essence of *Katz*. The reason why there is no reasonable expectation of privacy in an area that is exposed to the public is that little diminution in "the amount of privacy and freedom remaining to citizens" will result from police surveillance of something that any passerby readily sees. To pretend, as the plurality opinion does, that the same is true when the police use a helicopter to peer over high fences is, at best, disingenuous. Notwithstanding the plurality's statistics about the number of helicopters registered in this country, can it seriously be questioned that Riley enjoyed virtually complete privacy in his backyard greenhouse, and that that privacy was invaded solely by police helicopter surveillance? Is the theoretical possibility that any member of the public (with sufficient means) could also have hired a helicopter and looked over Riley's fence of any relevance at all in determining whether Riley suffered a serious loss of privacy and personal security through the police action?

In *Ciraolo*, we held that whatever might be observed from the window of an airplane flying at 1000 feet could be deemed unprotected by any reasonable expectation of privacy. That decision was based on the belief that airplane traffic at that altitude was sufficiently common that no expectation of privacy could inure in anything on the ground observable with the naked eye from so high. Indeed, we compared those airways to "public thoroughfares," and made the obvious point that police officers passing by a home on such thoroughfares were not required by the Fourth Amendment to "shield their eyes." Seizing on a reference in *Ciraolo* to the fact that the police officer was in a position "where he ha[d] a right to be," today's plurality professes to find this case indistinguishable because FAA regulations do not impose a minimum altitude requirement on helicopter traffic; thus, the officer in this case too made his observations from a vantage point where he had a right to be.

It is a curious notion that the reach of the Fourth Amendment can be so largely defined by administrative regulations issued for purposes of flight safety.[2] It is more curious still that the plurality relies to such an extent on the legality of the officer's act, when we have consistently refused to

equate police violation of the law with infringement of the Fourth Amendment.[3] But the plurality's willingness to end its inquiry when it finds that the officer was in a position he had a right to be in is misguided for an even more fundamental reason. Finding determinative the fact that the officer was where he had a right to be is, at bottom, an attempt to analogize surveillance from a helicopter to surveillance by a police officer standing on a public road and viewing evidence of crime through an open window or a gap in a fence. In such a situation, the occupant of the home may be said to lack any reasonable expectation of privacy in what can be seen from that road—even if, in fact, people rarely pass that way.

The police officer positioned 400 feet above Riley's backyard was not, however, standing on a public road. The vantage point he enjoyed was not one any citizen could readily share. His ability to see over Riley's fence depended on his use of a very expensive and sophisticated piece of machinery to which few ordinary citizens have access. In such circumstances it makes no more sense to rely on the legality of the officer's position in the skies than it would to judge the constitutionality of the wiretap in *Katz* by the legality of the officer's position outside the telephone booth. The simple inquiry whether the police officer had the legal right to be in the position from which he made his observations cannot suffice, for we cannot assume that Riley's curtilage was so open to the observations of passersby in the skies that he retained little privacy or personal security to be lost to police surveillance. The question before us must be not whether the police were where they had a right to be, but whether public observation of Riley's curtilage was so commonplace that Riley's expectation of privacy in his backyard could not be considered reasonable. To say that an invasion of Riley's privacy from the skies was not impossible is most emphatically not the same as saying that his expectation of privacy within his enclosed curtilage was not "one that society is prepared to recognize as 'reasonable.'" While, as we held in *Ciraolo*, air traffic at elevations of 1000 feet or more

---

[2] The plurality's use of the FAA regulations as a means for determining whether Riley enjoyed a reasonable expectation of privacy produces an incredible result. Fixed-wing aircraft may not be operated below 500 feet (1000 feet over congested areas), while helicopters may be operated below those levels. Therefore, whether Riley's expectation of privacy is reasonable turns on whether the police officer at 400 feet above his curtilage is seated in an airplane or a helicopter. This cannot be the law.

---

[3] In *Oliver*, for example, we held that police officers who trespassed upon posted and fenced private land did not violate the Fourth Amendment, despite the fact that their action was subject to criminal sanctions. We noted that the interests vindicated by the Fourth Amendment were not identical with those served by the common law of trespass.

may be so common that whatever could be seen with the naked eye from that elevation is unprotected by the Fourth Amendment, it is a large step from there to say that the Amendment offers no protection against low-level helicopter surveillance of enclosed curtilage areas. To take this step is error enough. That the plurality does so with little analysis beyond its determination that the police complied with FAA regulations is particularly unfortunate.

### III

Perhaps the most remarkable passage in the plurality opinion is its suggestion that the case might be a different one had any "intimate details connected with the use of the home or curtilage [been] observed." What, one wonders, is meant by "intimate details"? If the police had observed Riley embracing his wife in the backyard greenhouse, would we then say that his reasonable expectation of privacy had been infringed? Where in the Fourth Amendment or in our cases is there any warrant for imposing a requirement that the activity observed must be "intimate" in order to be protected by the Constitution?

It is difficult to avoid the conclusion that the plurality has allowed its analysis of Riley's expectation of privacy to be colored by its distaste for the activity in which he was engaged. It is indeed easy to forget, especially in view of current concern over drug trafficking, that the scope of the Fourth Amendment's protection does not turn on whether the activity disclosed by a search is illegal or innocuous. But we dismiss this as a "drug case" only at the peril of our own liberties. Justice Frankfurter once noted that "[i]t is a fair summary of history to say that the safeguards of liberty have frequently been forged in controversies involving not very nice people," *United States v. Rabinowitz*, 339 U.S. 56, 69 (1950) (dissenting opinion), and nowhere is this observation more apt than in the area of the Fourth Amendment, whose words have necessarily been given meaning largely through decisions suppressing evidence of criminal activity. The principle enunciated in this case determines what limits the Fourth Amendment imposes on aerial surveillance of any person, for any reason. If the Constitution does not protect Riley's marijuana garden against such surveillance, it is hard to see how it will forbid the Government from aerial spying on the activities of a law-abiding citizen on her fully enclosed outdoor patio. As Professor Amsterdam has eloquently written: "The question is not whether you or I must draw the blinds before we commit a crime. It is whether you and I must discipline ourselves to draw the blinds every time we enter a room, under pain of surveillance if we do not." Amsterdam, 58 Minn.L.Rev., at 403.[6]

### IV

I find little to disagree with in the concurring opinion of Justice O'Connor, apart from its closing paragraphs. A majority of the Court thus agrees that the fundamental inquiry is not whether the police were where they had a right to be under FAA regulations, but rather whether Riley's expectation of privacy was rendered illusory by the extent of public observation of his backyard from aerial traffic at 400 feet.

What separates me from Justice O'Connor is essentially an empirical matter concerning the extent of public use of the airspace at that altitude, together with the question of how to resolve that issue. I do not think the constitutional claim should fail simply because "there is reason to believe" that there is "considerable" public flying this close to earth or because Riley "introduced no evidence to the contrary before the Florida courts." I think we could take judicial notice that, while there may be an occasional privately owned helicopter that flies over populated areas at an altitude of 400 feet, such flights are a rarity and are almost entirely limited to approaching or leaving airports or to reporting traffic congestion near major roadways. And, as the concurring opinion agrees, the extent of police surveillance traffic cannot serve as a bootstrap to demonstrate public use of the airspace.

If, however, we are to resolve the issue by considering whether the appropriate party carried its burden of proof, I again think that Riley must prevail. Because the State has greater access to information concerning customary flight patterns and because the coercive power of the State ought not be brought to bear in cases in which it is unclear whether the prosecution is a product of an unconstitutional, warrantless search. The State quite clearly has not carried this burden.

### V

The issue in this case is, ultimately, "how tightly

---

[6] See also *White*, (Harlan, J., dissenting):

"The interest [protected by the Fourth Amendment] is the expectation of the ordinary citizen, who has never engaged in illegal conduct in his life, that he may carry on his private discourse freely, openly, and spontaneously. . . . Interposition of a warrant requirement is designed not to shield 'wrongdoers,' but to secure a measure of privacy and a sense of personal security throughout our society."

the Fourth Amendment permits people to be driven back into the recesses of their lives by the risk of surveillance.'' The Court today approves warrantless helicopter surveillance from an altitude of 400 feet. While Justice O'Connor's opinion gives reason to hope that this altitude may constitute a lower limit, I find considerable cause for concern in the fact that a plurality of four Justices would remove virtually all constitutional barriers to police surveillance from the vantage point of helicopters. The Fourth Amendment demands that we temper our efforts to apprehend criminals with a concern for the impact on our fundamental liberties of the methods we use. I hope it will be a matter of concern to my colleagues that the police surveillance methods they would sanction were among those described forty years ago in George Orwell's dread vision of life in the 1980's:

> "The black-mustachio'd face gazed down from every commanding corner. There was one on the house front immediately opposite. BIG BROTHER IS WATCHING YOU, the caption said. . . . In the far distance a helicopter skimmed down between the roofs, hovered for an instant like a bluebottle, and darted away again with a curving flight. It was the Police Patrol, snooping into people's windows." G. Orwell, Nineteen Eighty-Four 4 (1949).

Who can read this passage without a shudder, and without the instinctive reaction that it depicts life in some country other than ours? I respectfully dissent.

Justice BLACKMUN, dissenting.

The question before the Court is whether the helicopter surveillance over Riley's property constituted a ''search'' within the meaning of the Fourth Amendment. Like Justice Brennan, Justice Marshall, Justice Stevens, and Justice O'Connor, I believe that answering this question depends upon whether Riley has a ''reasonable expectation of privacy'' that no such surveillance would occur, and does not depend upon the fact that the helicopter was flying at a lawful altitude under FAA regulations. A majority of this Court thus agrees to at least this much.

The inquiry then becomes how to determine whether Riley's expectation was a reasonable one. Both Justice Brennan, and the two Justices who have joined him, and Justice O'Connor believe that the reasonableness of Riley's expectation depends, in large measure, on the frequency of nonpolice helicopter flights at an altitude of 400 feet. I agree.

How is this factual issue to be decided? Justice Brennan suggests that we may resolve it ourselves without any evidence in the record on this point. I am wary of this approach. While I, too, suspect that for most American communities it is a rare event when nonpolice helicopters fly over one's curtilage at an altitude of 400 feet, I am not convinced that we should establish a *per se* rule for the entire Nation based on judicial suspicion alone.

But we need not abandon our judicial intuition entirely. The opinions of both Justice Brennan and Justice O'Connor, by their use of ''cf.'' citations, implicitly recognize that none of our prior decisions tells us who has the burden of proving whether Riley's expectation of privacy was reasonable. In the absence of precedent on the point, it is appropriate for us to take into account our estimation of the frequency of nonpolice helicopter flights. Thus, because I believe that private helicopters rarely fly over curtilages at an altitude of 400 feet, I would impose upon the prosecution the burden of proving contrary facts necessary to show that Riley lacked a reasonable expectation of privacy. Indeed, I would establish this burden of proof for any helicopter surveillance case in which the flight occurred below 1000 feet—in other words, for any aerial surveillance case not governed by the Court's decision in *Ciraolo*.

In this case, the prosecution did not meet this burden of proof, as Justice Brennan notes. This failure should compel a finding that a Fourth Amendment search occurred. But because our prior cases gave the parties little guidance on the burden of proof issue, I would remand this case to allow the prosecution an opportunity to meet this burden.

The order of this Court, however, is not to remand the case in this manner. Rather, because Justice O'Connor would impose the burden of proof on Riley and because she would not allow Riley an opportunity to meet this burden, she joins the plurality's view that no Fourth Amendment search occurred. The judgment of the Court, therefore, is to reverse outright on the Fourth Amendment issue. Accordingly, for the reasons set forth above, I respectfully dissent.

## QUESTIONS AND NOTES

**1.** Are *Riley* and *Ciraola* distinguishable in any meaningful way? Explain.

**2.** If your answer to question 1 was "no," were the cases rightly decided? Why? Why not?

**3.** How do the White, O'Connor, Brennan, and Blackmun opinions differ from each other? With which would you most closely align yourself? Why?

**4.** What is the law of the case? Explain.

**5.** The concluding case in this chapter, *Greenwood*, examines one's reasonable expectation of privacy in one's trash.

## California v. Greenwood
### 486 U.S. 35 (1988)

Justice WHITE delivered the opinion of the Court.

The issue here is whether the Fourth Amendment prohibits the warrantless search and seizure of garbage left for collection outside the curtilage of a home. We conclude, in accordance with the vast majority of lower courts that have addressed the issue, that it does not.

### I

In early 1984, Investigator Jenny Stracner of the Laguna Beach Police Department received information indicating that respondent Greenwood might be engaged in narcotics trafficking. Stracner learned that a criminal suspect had informed a federal drug enforcement agent in February 1984 that a truck filled with illegal drugs was en route to the Laguna Beach address at which Greenwood resided. In addition, a neighbor complained of heavy vehicular traffic late at night in front of Greenwood's single-family home. The neighbor reported that the vehicles remained at Greenwood's house for only a few minutes.

Stracner sought to investigate this information by conducting a surveillance of Greenwood's home. She observed several vehicles make brief stops at the house during the late-night and early morning hours, and she followed a truck from the house to a residence that had previously been under investigation as a narcotics-trafficking location.

On April 6, 1984, Stracner asked the neighborhood's regular trash collector to pick up the plastic garbage bags that Greenwood had left on the curb in front of his house and to turn the bags over to her without mixing their contents with garbage from other houses. The trash collector cleaned his truck bin of other refuse, collected the garbage bags from

the street in front of Greenwood's house, and turned the bags over to Stracner. The officer searched through the rubbish and found items indicative of narcotics use. She recited the information that she had gleaned from the trash search in an affidavit in support of a warrant to search Greenwood's home.

Police officers encountered both respondents at the house later that day when they arrived to execute the warrant. The police discovered quantities of cocaine and hashish during their search of the house. Respondents were arrested on felony narcotics charges. They subsequently posted bail.

The police continued to receive reports of many late-night visitors to the Greenwood house. On May 4, Investigator Robert Rahaeuser obtained Greenwood's garbage from the regular trash collector in the same manner as had Stracner. The garbage again contained evidence of narcotics use.

Rahaeuser secured another search warrant for Greenwood's home based on the information from the second trash search. The police found more narcotics and evidence of narcotics trafficking when they executed the warrant. Greenwood was again arrested.

### II

The warrantless search and seizure of the garbage bags left at the curb outside the Greenwood house would violate the Fourth Amendment only if respondents manifested a subjective expectation of privacy in their garbage that society accepts as objectively reasonable. Respondents do not disagree with this standard.

They assert, however, that they had, and exhibited, an expectation of privacy with respect to the trash that was searched by the police: The trash, which was placed on the street for collection at a fixed time, was contained in opaque plastic bags, which the garbage collector was expected to pick up, mingle with the trash of others, and deposit at the garbage dump. The trash was only temporarily on the street, and there was little likelihood that it would be inspected by anyone.

It may well be that respondents did not expect that the contents of their garbage bags would become known to the police or other members of the public. An expectation of privacy does not give rise to Fourth Amendment protection, however, unless society is prepared to accept that expectation as objectively reasonable.

Here, we conclude that respondents exposed their garbage to the public sufficiently to defeat their claim to Fourth Amendment protection. It is common knowledge that plastic garbage bags left on or at the side of a public street are readily accessible to animals, children, scavengers, snoops, and other members of the public. Moreover, respondents placed their refuse at the curb for the express purpose of conveying it to a third party, the trash collector, who might himself have sorted through respondents' trash or permitted others, such as the police, to do so. Accordingly, having deposited their garbage "in an area particularly suited for public inspection and, in a manner of speaking, public consumption, for the express purpose of having strangers take it," respondents could have had no reasonable expectation of privacy in the inculpatory items that they discarded.

Furthermore, as we have held, the police cannot reasonably be expected to avert their eyes from evidence of criminal activity that could have been observed by any member of the public. Hence, "[w]hat a person knowingly exposes to the public, even in his own home or office, is not a subject of Fourth Amendment protection." We held in *Smith*, for example, that the police did not violate the Fourth Amendment by causing a pen register to be installed at the telephone company's offices to record the telephone numbers dialed by a criminal suspect. An individual has no legitimate expectation of privacy in the numbers dialed on his telephone, we reasoned, because he voluntarily conveys those numbers to the telephone company when he uses the telephone. Again, we observed that "a person has no legitimate expectation of privacy in information he voluntarily turns over to third parties."

Similarly, we held in *Ciraolo*, that the police were not required by the Fourth Amendment to obtain a warrant before conducting surveillance of the respondent's fenced backyard from a private plane flying at an altitude of 1,000 feet. We concluded that the respondent's expectation that his yard was protected from such surveillance was unreasonable because "[a]ny member of the public flying in this airspace who glanced down could have seen everything that these officers observed."

Our conclusion that society would not accept as reasonable respondents' claim to an expectation of privacy in trash left for collection in an area accessible to the public is reinforced by the unanimous rejection of similar claims by the Federal Courts of Appeals.[5]

### V

The judgment of the California Court of Appeal is therefore reversed, and this case is remanded for further proceedings not inconsistent with this opinion.

Justice BRENNAN, with whom Justice MARSHALL joins, dissenting.

Every week for two months, and at least once more a month later, the Laguna Beach police clawed through the trash that respondent Greenwood left in opaque, sealed bags on the curb outside his home. Complete strangers minutely scrutinized their bounty, undoubtedly dredging up intimate details of Greenwood's private life and habits. The intrusions proceeded without a warrant, and no court before or since has concluded that the police acted on probable cause to believe Greenwood was engaged in any criminal activity.

Scrutiny of another's trash is contrary to commonly accepted notions of civilized behavior. I suspect, therefore, that members of our society will be shocked to learn that the Court, the ultimate guarantor of liberty, deems unreasonable our expectation that the aspects of our private lives that are concealed safely in a trash bag will not become public.

### I

Our precedent leaves no room to doubt that had respondents been carrying their personal effects in opaque, sealed plastic bags — identical to the ones they placed on the curb — their privacy would have been protected from warrantless police intrusion. So far as Fourth Amendment protection is concerned, opaque plastic bags are every bit as worthy as "packages wrapped in green opaque plastic" and "double-locked footlocker[s]."

---

[5] Given that the dissenters are among the tiny minority of judges whose views are contrary to ours, we are distinctly unimpressed with the dissent's prediction that "society will be shocked to learn" of today's decision.

II

Respondents deserve no less protection just because Greenwood used the bags to discard rather than to transport his personal effects. Their contents are not inherently any less private, and Greenwood's decision to discard them, at least in the manner in which he did, does not diminish his expectation of privacy.

A trash bag, like any of the above-mentioned containers, "is a common repository for one's personal effects" and, even more than many of them, is "therefore . . . inevitably associated with the expectation of privacy." "[A]lmost every human activity ultimately manifests itself in waste products. . . ." A single bag of trash testifies eloquently to the eating, reading, and recreational habits of the person who produced it. A search of trash, like a search of the bedroom, can relate intimate details about sexual practices, health, and personal hygiene. Like rifling through desk drawers or intercepting phone calls, rummaging through trash can divulge the target's financial and professional status, political affiliations and inclinations, private thoughts, personal relationships, and romantic interests. It cannot be doubted that a sealed trash bag harbors telling evidence of the "intimate activity associated with the 'sanctity of a man's home and the privacies of life,'" which the Fourth Amendment is designed to protect.

The Court properly rejects the State's attempt to distinguish trash searches from other searches on the theory that trash is abandoned and therefore not entitled to an expectation of privacy. In evaluating the reasonableness of Greenwood's expectation that his sealed trash bags would not be invaded, the Court has held that we must look to "understandings that are recognized and permitted by society." Most of us, I believe, would be incensed to discover a meddler — whether a neighbor, a reporter, or a detective — scrutinizing our sealed trash containers to discover some detail of our personal lives. That was, quite naturally, the reaction to the sole incident on which the Court bases its conclusion that "snoops" and the like defeat the expectation of privacy in trash. When a tabloid reporter examined then-Secretary of State Henry Kissinger's trash and published his findings, Kissinger was "really revolted" by the intrusion and his wife suffered "grave anguish." The public response roundly condemning the reporter demonstrates that society not only recognized those reactions as reasonable, but shared them as well. Commentators variously characterized his conduct as "a disgusting invasion of personal privacy," "indefensible . . . as civilized behavior," and contrary to "the way decent people behave in relation to each other."

Beyond a generalized expectation of privacy, many municipalities, whether for reasons of privacy, sanitation, or both, reinforce confidence in the integrity of sealed trash containers by "prohibit[ing] anyone, except authorized employees of the Town . . ., to rummage into, pick up, collect, move or otherwise interfere with articles or materials placed on . . . any public street for collection." In fact, the California Constitution, as interpreted by the State's highest court, guarantees a right of privacy in trash vis-a-vis government officials.

That is not to deny that isolated intrusions into opaque, sealed trash containers occur. When, acting on their own, "animals, children, scavengers, snoops, [or] other members of the public," *actually* rummage through a bag of trash and expose its contents to plain view, "police cannot reasonably be expected to avert their eyes from evidence of criminal activity that could have been observed by any member of the public." That much follows from cases like *Jacobsen*, 466 U.S., at 117, 120, n. 17, (emphasis added), which held that police may constitutionally inspect a package whose "integrity" a private carrier has *already* "compromised," because "[t]he Fourth Amendment is implicated only if the authorities use information with respect to which the expectation of privacy has not *already* been frustrated"; and *Ciraolo*, (emphasis added), which held that the Fourth Amendment does not prohibit police from observing what "[a]ny member of the public flying in this airspace who glanced down *could* have seen."

Had Greenwood flaunted his intimate activity by strewing his trash all over the curb for all to see, or had some nongovernmental intruder invaded his privacy and done the same, I could accept the Court's conclusion that an expectation of privacy would have been unreasonable. Similarly, had police searching the city dump run across incriminating evidence that, despite commingling with the trash of others, still retained its identity as Greenwood's, we would have a different case. But all that Greenwood "exposed . . . to the public," were the exteriors of several opaque, sealed containers. Until the bags were opened by police, they hid their contents from the public's view every bit as much as did Chadwick's double-locked footlocker and Robbins' green, plastic wrapping. Faithful application of the warrant requirement does not require police to "avert their eyes from evidence of criminal activity that could have been observed by any member of the public." Rather, it only requires them to adhere to norms of privacy that members of the public plainly acknowledge.

The mere *possibility* that unwelcome meddlers

might open and rummage through the containers does not negate the expectation of privacy in their contents any more than the possibility of a burglary negates an expectation of privacy in the home; or the possibility of a private intrusion negates an expectation of privacy in an unopened package; or the possibility that an operator will listen in on a telephone conversation negates an expectation of privacy in the words spoken on the telephone. "What a person . . . seeks to preserve as private, *even in an area accessible to the public*, may be constitutionally protected." *Katz.*

Nor is it dispositive that "respondents placed their refuse at the curb for the express purpose of conveying it to a third party, . . . who might himself have sorted through respondents' trash or permitted others, such as the police, to do so." In the first place, Greenwood can hardly be faulted for leaving trash on his curb when a county ordinance commanded him to do so, and prohibited him from disposing of it in any other way. Unlike in other circumstances where privacy is compromised, Greenwood could not "avoid exposing personal belongings . . . by simply leaving them at home." More importantly, even the voluntary relinquishment of possession or control over an effect does not necessarily amount to a relinquishment of a privacy expectation in it. Were it otherwise, a letter or package would lose all Fourth Amendment protection when placed in a mailbox or other depository with the

"express purpose" of entrusting it to the postal officer or a private carrier; those bailees are just as likely as trash collectors (and certainly have greater incentive) to "sor[t] through" the personal effects entrusted to them, "or permi[t] others, such as police to do so." Yet, it has been clear for at least 110 years that the possibility of such an intrusion does not justify a warrantless search by police in the first instance.

### III

In holding that the warrantless search of Greenwood's trash was consistent with the Fourth Amendment, the Court paints a grim picture of our society. It depicts a society in which local authorities may command their citizens to dispose of their personal effects in the manner least protective of the "sanctity of [the] home and the privacies of life," and then monitor them arbitrarily and without judicial oversight — a society that is not prepared to recognize as reasonable an individual's expectation of privacy in the most private of personal effects sealed in an opaque container and disposed of in a manner designed to commingle it imminently and inextricably with the trash of others. The American society with which I am familiar "chooses to dwell in reasonable security and freedom from surveillance," *Johnson v. United States*, 333 U.S. 10, 14 (1948), and is more dedicated to individual liberty and more sensitive to intrusions on the sanctity of the home than the Court is willing to acknowledge.

I dissent.

## QUESTIONS AND NOTES

**1.** Do you think that the Court does a very good job of accurately assessing the expectations of privacy that a typical person would be willing to call reasonable?

**2.** If your answer to question 1 was "no," why do you think that the Court cannot (will not) do better? *See* Slobogin and Schumacher, *Reasonable Expectations of Privacy and Autonomy in Fourth Amendment Cases: An Empirical Look at Understandings Recognized and Permitted by Society*, 42 Duke L.J. 727 (1993).

**3.** Could the Court have upheld Greenwood's claim consistent with cases like *Smith, Oliver,* and *Ciraola*? Explain. Should it have?

**4.** California had previously held that the *Greenwood* procedure violated the California Constitution. However, as a matter of California law, the exclusionary rule (see Chapter 10, *infra*) cannot be applied unless the procedure also violates the Federal Constitution. Consequently, it was necessary for the California courts to rely on the Federal Constitution, which, of course, allowed the Supreme Court to overturn the California Supreme Court's decision.

# PROBLEM

Officer Smith learned that Green had offered to purchase eight high-powered lamps from a police informant. The lamps were of a type which is commonly used to grow marijuana inside a dwelling or other premises. Smith obtained the informant's permission to install an electronic monitor on one of the lamps before selling them to Green. Smith used the monitor to track the lamps from the informant's place of business to a house owned by Harris, one of Green's friends. At no time was a warrant obtained to install or track the electronic monitor.

1) Was it an unconstitutional search or seizure to install the electronic monitor?
2) Was it an unconstitutional search or seizure to track the electronic monitor after the lamps were removed from the informant's place of business?
3) Was it an unconstitutional search or seizure to use the monitor to detect the location of the lamp inside Harris' house?
4) If your answers to questions 1-3 are not the same, how do you account for the differences?

For the Court's analysis of this problem see *United States v. Karo*, 468 U.S. 705 (1984).

# 11.

# WHAT ITEMS MAY BE SEIZED?

Heretofore we have assumed that any item which is evidence of crime may be seized. Although current law is moving in that direction, evidence of crime was not always seizable merely because it was evidence. In this chapter, we explore the development of and rationale for rendering "mere evidence" of crime seizable.

## Warden v. Hayden
### 387 U.S. 294 (1967)

Mr. Justice BRENNAN delivered the opinion of the Court.

We review in this case the validity of the proposition that there is under the Fourth Amendment a "distinction between merely evidentiary materials, on the one hand, which may not be seized either under the authority of a search warrant or during the course of a search incident to arrest, and on the other hand, those objects which may validly be seized including the instrumentalities and means by which a crime is committed, the fruits of crime such as stolen property, weapons by which escape of the person arrested might be effected, and property the possession of which is a crime."

A Maryland court sitting without a jury convicted respondent of armed robbery. Items of his clothing, a cap, jacket, and trousers, among other things, were seized during a search of his home, and were admitted in evidence.

I

About 8 a.m. on March 17, 1962, an armed robber entered the business premises of the Diamond Cab Company in Baltimore, Maryland. He took some $363 and ran. Two cab drivers in the vicinity, attracted by shouts of "Holdup," followed the man to 2111 Cocoa Lane. One driver notified the company dispatcher by radio that the man was a Negro about 5'8" tall, wearing a light cap and dark jacket, and that he had entered the house on Cocoa Lane. The dispatcher relayed the information to police who were proceeding to the scene of the robbery. Within minutes, police arrived at the house in a number of patrol cars. An officer knocked and announced their presence. Mrs. Hayden answered, and the officers told her they believed that a robber had entered the house, and asked to search the house. She offered no objection.

The officers spread out through the first and second floors and the cellar in search of the robber. Hayden was found in an upstairs bedroom feigning sleep. He was arrested when the officers on the first floor and in the cellar reported that no other man was in the house. Meanwhile an officer was attracted to an adjoining bathroom by the noise of running water, and discovered a shotgun and a pistol in a flush tank; another officer who, according to the District Court, "was searching the cellar for a man or the money" found in a washing machine a jacket and trousers of the type the fleeing man was said to have worn. A clip of ammunition for the pistol and a cap were found under the mattress of Hayden's bed, and ammunition for the shotgun was found in a bureau drawer in Hayden's room. All these items of evidence were introduced against respondent at his trial.

### III

We come, then, to the question whether, even though the search was lawful [see Chapter 4, Problem p. 87, *supra*], the Court of Appeals was correct in holding that the seizure and introduction of the items of clothing violated the Fourth Amendment because they are "mere evidence." The distinction made by some of our cases between seizure of items of evidential value only and seizure of instrumentalities, fruits, or contraband has been criticized by courts and commentators. The Court of Appeals, however, felt "obligated to adhere to it." We today reject the distinction as based on premises no longer accepted as rules governing the application of the Fourth Amendment.[8]

In *Gouled v. United States*, 255 U.S. 298, 309, the Court said that search warrants "may not be used as a means of gaining access to a man's house or office and papers solely for the purpose of making search to secure evidence to be used against him in a criminal or penal proceeding * * *." The Court derived from *Boyd v. United States*, 116 U.S. 616 the proposition that warrants "may be resorted to only when a primary right to such search and seizure may be found in the interest which the public or the complainant may have in the property to be seized, or in the right to the possession of it, or when a valid exercise of the police power renders possession of the property by the accused unlawful and provides that it may be taken," that is, when the property is an instrumentality or fruit of crime, or contraband. Since it was "impossible to say, on the record * * * that the government had any interest" in the papers involved "other than as evidence against the accused * * *," "to permit them to be used in evidence would be, in effect, as ruled in

the *Boyd Case*, to compel the defendant to become a witness against himself."

The items of clothing involved in this case are not "testimonial" or "communicative" in nature, and their introduction therefore did not compel respondent to become a witness against himself in violation of the Fifth Amendment. This case thus does not require that we consider whether there are items of evidential value whose very nature precludes them from being the object of a reasonable search and seizure.

The Fourth Amendment ruling in *Gouled* was based upon the dual, related premises that historically the right to search for and seize property depended upon the assertion by the Government of a valid claim of superior interest, and that it was not enough that the purpose of the search and seizure was to obtain evidence to use in apprehending and convicting criminals. The common law of search and seizure after *Entick v. Carrington*, 19 How.St.Tr. 1029, reflected Lord Camden's view, derived no doubt from the political thought of his time, that the "great end, for which men entered into society, was to secure their property." Warrants were "allowed only where the primary right to such a search and seizure is in the interest which the public or complainant may have in the property seized." Thus stolen property—the fruits of crime—was always subject to seizure. And the power to search for stolen property was graudually extended to cover "any property which the private citizen was not permitted to possess," which included instrumentalities of crime (because of the early notion that items used in crime were forfeited to the State) and contraband. Kaplan, Search and Seizure: A No-Man's Land in the Criminal Law, 49 Calif.L.Rev. 474, 475. No separate governmental interest in seizing evidence to apprehend and convict criminals was recognized; it was required that some property interest be asserted. The remedial structure also reflected these dual premises. Trespass, replevin, and the other means of redress for persons aggrieved by searches and seizures, depended upon proof of a superior property interest. And since a lawful seizure presupposed a superior claim, it was inconceivable that a person could recover property lawfully seized. As Lord Camden pointed out in *Entick v. Carrington*, a general warrant enabled "the party's own property (to be) seized before and without conviction, and he has no power to reclaim his goods, even after his innocence is cleared by acquittal."

The premise that property interests control the right of the Government to search and seize has been discredited. Searches and seizures may be "unreasonable" within the Fourth Amendment even though the Government asserts a superior property interest

---

[8] This Court has approved the seizure and introduction of items having only evidential value without, however, considering the validity of the distinction rejected today. See *Schmerber v. State of California*, 384 U.S. 757 (seizure of blood).

at common law. We have recognized that the principal object of the Fourth Amendment is the protection of privacy rather than property, and have increasingly discarded fictional and procedural barriers rested on property concepts.

The development of search and seizure law since *Gouled* is replete with examples of the transformation in substantive law brought about through the interaction of the felt need to protect privacy from unreasonable invasions and the flexibility in rulemaking made possible by the remedy of exclusion. We have held, for example, that intangible as well as tangible evidence may be suppressed, and that an actual trespass under local property law is unnecessary to support a remediable violation of the Fourth Amendment. In determining whether someone is a "person aggrieved by an unlawful search and seizure" we have refused "to import into the law * * * subtle distinctions, developed and refined by the common law in evolving the body of private property law which, more than almost any other branch of law, has been shaped by distinctions whose validity is largely historical." And with particular relevance here, we have given recognition to the interest in privacy despite the complete absence of a property claim by suppressing the very items which at common law could be seized with impunity: stolen goods, instrumentalities, and contraband.

The premise in *Gouled* that government may not seize evidence simply for the purpose of proving crime has likewise been discredited. The requirement that the Government assert in addition some property interest in material it seizes has long been a fiction,[11] obscuring the reality that government has an interest in solving crime. *Schmerber* settled the proposition that it is reasonable, within the terms of the Fourth Amendment, to conduct otherwise permissible searches for the purpose of obtaining evidence which would aid in apprehending and convicting criminals. The requirements of the Fourth Amendment can secure the same protection of privacy whether the search is for "mere evidence" or for fruits, instrumentalities or contraband. There must, of course, be a nexus – automatically provided in the case of fruits, instrumentalities or contraband – between the item to be seized and criminal behavior. Thus in the case of "mere evidence," probable cause must be examined in terms of cause to believe that the evidence sought will aid in a particular apprehension or conviction. In so doing, consideration of police purposes will be required. But no such problem is presented in this case. The clothes found in the washing machine matched the description of those worn by the robber and the police therefore could reasonably believe that the items would aid in the identification of the culprit.

The survival of the *Gouled* distinction is attributable more to chance than considered judgment. Legislation has helped perpetuate it. Thus, Congress has never authorized the issuance of search warrants for the seizure of mere evidence of crime. Even in the Espionage Act of 1917, where Congress for the first time granted general authority for the issuance of search warants, the authority was limited to fruits of crime, instrumentalities, and certain contraband. *Gouled* concluded, needlessly it appears, that the Constitution virtually limited searches and seizures to these categories. After *Gouled*, pressure to test this conclusion was slow to mount. Rule 41(b) of the Federal Rules of Criminal Procedure incorporated the *Gouled* categories as limitations on federal authorities to issue warrants, and *Mapp v. Ohio*, 367 U.S. 643, only recently made the "mere evidence" rule a problem in the state courts. Pressure against the rule in the federal courts has taken the form rather of broadening the categories of evidence subject to seizure, thereby creating considerable confusion in the law.

The rationale most frequently suggested for the rule preventing the seizure of evidence is that "limitations upon the fruit to be gathered tend to limit the quest itself." But privacy "would be just as well served by a restriction on search to the even-numbered days of the month. * * * And it would

---

[11] At common law the Government did assert a superior property interest when it searched lawfully for stolen property, since the procedure then followed made it necessary that the true owner swear that his goods had been taken. But no such procedure need be followed today; the Government may demonstrate probable cause and lawfully search for stolen property even though the true owner is unknown or unavailable to request and authorize the Government to assert his interest. As to instrumentalities, the Court in *Gouled* allowed their seizure, not because the Government had some property interest in them (under the ancient, fictitious forfeiture theory), but because they could be used to perpetrate further crime. The same holds true, of course, for "mere evidence"; the prevention of crime is served at least as much by allowing the Government to identify and capture the criminal, as it is by allowing the seizure of his instrumentalities. Finally, contraband is indeed property in which the Government holds a superior interest, but only because the Government decides to vest such an interest in itself. And while there may be limits to what may be declared contraband, the concept is hardly more than a form through which the Government seeks to prevent and deter crime.

have the extra advantage of avoiding hair-splitting questions. * * *'' The ''mere evidence'' limitation has spawned exceptions so numerous and confusion so great, in fact, that it is questionable whether it affords meaningful protection. But if its rejection does enlarge the area of permissible searches, the intrusions are nevertheless made after fulfilling the probable cause and particularity requirements of the Fourth Amendment and after the intervention of ''a neutral and detached magistrate. * * *'' The Fourth Amendment allows intrusions upon privacy under these circumstances, and there is no viable reason to distinguish intrusions to secure ''mere evidence'' from intrusions to secure fruits, instrumentalities, or contraband.

The judgment of the Court of Appeals is Reversed.

Mr. Justice BLACK concurs in the result. Mr. Justice FORTAS, with whom the Chief Justice joins, concurring.

While I agree that the Fourth Amendment should not be held to require exclusion from evidence of the clothing as well as the weapons and ammunition found by the officers during the search, I cannot join in the majority's broad — and in my judgment, totally unnecessary — repudiation of the so-called ''mere evidence'' rule.

Our Constitution envisions that searches will ordinarily follow procurement by police of a valid search warrant. Such warrants are to issue only on probable cause, and must describe with particularity the persons or things to be seized. There are exceptions to this rule. Searches may be made incident to a lawful arrest, and — as today's decision indicates — in the course of ''hot pursuit.'' But searches under each of these exceptions have, until today, been confined to those essential to fulfill the purpose of the exception: that is, we have refused to permit use of articles the seizure of which could not be strictly tied to and justified by the exigencies which excused the warrantless search. The use in evidence of weapons seized in a ''hot pursuit'' search or search incident to arrest satisfies this criterion because of the need to protect the arresting officers from weapons to which the suspect might resort. The search for and seizure of fruits are, of course, justifiable on independent grounds: The fruits are an object of the pursuit or arrest of the suspect, and should be restored to their true owner. The seizure of contraband has been justified on the ground that the suspect has not even a bare possessory right to contraband.

Similarly, we have forbidden the use of articles seized in such a search unless obtained from the person of the suspect or from the immediate vicinity.

Since a warrantless search is justified only as incident to an arrest or ''hot pursuit,'' this Court and others have held that its scope does not include permission to search the entire building in which the arrests occurs, or to rummage through locked drawers and closets, or to search at another time or place.

In the present case, the articles of clothing admitted into evidence are not within any of the traditional categories which describe what materials may be seized, either with or without a warrant. The restrictiveness of these categories has been subjected to telling criticism, and although I believe that we should approach expansion of these categories with the diffidence which their imposing provenance commands, I agree that the use of identifying clothing worn in the commission of a crime and seized during ''hot pursuit'' is within the spirit and intendment of the ''hot pursuit'' exception to the search-warrant requirement. That is because the clothing is pertinent to identification of the person hotly pursued as being, in fact, the person whose pursuit was justified by connection with the crime. I would frankly place the ruling on that basis. I would not drive an enormous and dangerous hole in the Fourth Amendment to accommodate a specific and, I think, reasonable exception.

As my Brother DOUGLAS notes, opposition to general searches is a fundamental of our heritage and of the history of Anglo-Saxon legal principles. Such searches, pursuant to ''writs of assistance,'' were one of the matters over which the American Revolution was fought. The very purpose of the Fourth Amendment was to outlaw such searches, which the Court today sanctions. I fear that in gratuitously striking down the ''mere evidence'' rule, which distinguished members of this Court have acknowledged as essential to enforce the Fourth Amendment's prohibition against general searches, the Court today needlessly destroys, root and branch, a basic part of liberty's heritage.

Mr. Justice DOUGLAS, dissenting.

[The Fourth Amendment] has been thought, until today, to have two faces of privacy:

(1) One creates a zone of privacy that may not be invaded by the police through raids, by the legislators through laws, or by magistrates through the issuance of warrants.

(2) A second creates a zone of privacy that may be invaded either by the police in hot pursuit or by a search incident to arrest or by a warrant issued by a magistrate on a showing of probable cause.

The debates concerning the Bill of Rights did not focus on the precise point with which we here deal. There was much talk about the general warrants and the fear of them. But there was also some reference to the sanctity of one's home and his personal belongings, even including the clothes he wore. Thus in Virginia, Patrick Henry said:

> "The officers of Congress may come upon you now, fortified with all the terrors of paramount federal authority. Excisemen may come in multitudes; for the limitation of their numbers no man knows. They may, unless the general government be restrained by a bill of rights, or some similar restriction, go into your cellars and rooms, and search, ransack, and measure, every thing you eat, drink, and wear. They ought to be restrained within proper bounds." 3 Elliot's Debates 448-449.

[The] twofold classification of zones of privacy was said by Cooley to be reflected in the Fourth Amendment:

> "The warrant is not allowed for the purpose of obtaining evidence of an intended crime; but only after lawful evidence of an offence actually committed. Nor even then is it allowable to invade one's privacy for the sole purpose of obtaining evidence against him, except in a few special cases where that which is the subject of the crime is supposed to be concealed, and the public or the complainant has an interest in it or in its destruction." Constitutional Limitations 431-432 (7th ed. 1903).

That doctrine had its full flowering in *Gouled*, where an opinion was written by Mr. Justice Clarke for a unanimous Court that included both Mr. Justice Holmes and Mr. Justice Brandeis. The prosecution was for defrauding the Government under procurement contracts. Documents were taken from defendant's business office under a search warrant and used at the trial as evidence against him. Stolen or forged papers could be so seized, the Court said; so could lottery tickets; so could contraband; so could property in which the public had an interest, for reasons tracing back to warrants allowing the seizure of stolen property. But the papers or documents fell in none of those categories and the Court therefore held that even though they had been taken under a warrant, they were inadmissible at the trial as not even a warrant, though otherwise proper and regular, could be used "for the purpose of making search to secure evidence" of a crime. The use of those documents against the accused might, of course, violate the Fifth Amendment. But whatever may be the intrinsic nature of the evidence, the owner is then "the unwilling source of the evidence," there being

no difference so far as the Fifth Amendment is concerned "whether he be obliged to supply evidence against himself or whether such evidence be obtained by an illegal search of his premises and seizure of his private papers."

The right of privacy protected by the Fourth Amendment relates in part of course to the precincts of the home or the office. But it does not make them sanctuaries where the law can never reach. There are such places in the world. A mosque in Fez, Morocco, that I have visited, is by custom a sanctuary where any refugee may hide, safe from police intrusion. We have no such sanctuaries here. A policeman in "hot pursuit" or an officer with a search warrant can enter any house, any room, any building, any office. The privacy of those *places* is of course protected against invasion except in limited situations. The full privacy protected by the Fourth Amendment is, however, reached when we come to books, pamphlets, papers, letters, documents, and other personal effects. Unless they are contraband or instruments of the crime, they may not be reached by any warrant nor may they be lawfully seized by the police who are in "hot pursuit." By reason of the Fourth Amendment the police may not rummage around among these personal effects, no matter how formally perfect their authority may appear to be. They may not seize them. If they do, those articles may not be used in evidence. Any invasion whatsoever of those personal effects is "unreasonable" within the meaning of the Fourth Amendment. That is the teaching of *Entick, Boyd*, and *Gouled*.

The constitutional philosophy is, I think, clear. The personal effects and possessions of the individual (all contraband and the like excepted) are sacrosanct from prying eyes, from the long arm of the law, from any rummaging by police. Privacy involves the choice of the individual to disclose or to reveal what he believes, what he thinks, what he possesses. The article may be a nondescript work of art, a manuscript of a book, a personal account book, a diary, invoices, personal clothing, jewelry, or whatnot. Those who wrote the Bill of Rights believed that every individual needs both to communicate with others and to keep his affairs to himself. That dual aspect of privacy means that the individual should have the freedom to select for himself the time and circumstances when he will share his secrets with others and decide the extent of that sharing. This is his prerogative not the States'. The Framers, who were as knowledgeable as we, knew what police surveillance meant and how the practice of rummaging through one's personal effects could destroy freedom.

That there is a zone that no police can enter—

whether in "hot pursuit" or armed with a meticulously proper warrant—has been emphasized by *Boyd* and by *Gouled*. They have been consistently and continuously approved. I would adhere to them and leave with the individual the choice of opening his private effects (apart from contraband and the like) to the police or keeping their contents a secret and their integrity inviolate. The existence of that choice is the very essence of the right of privacy. Without it the Fourth Amendment and the Fifth are ready instruments for the police state that the Framers sought to avoid.

## QUESTIONS AND NOTES

**1.** What do you understand to be the root theory of the "mere evidence" rule?

**2.** Does it have anything to do with the Fifth Amendment? If so, should the Court have been slower to repudiate it?

**3.** If the "mere evidence" rule were not overturned and you had been the prosecutor in this case, could you have legitimately argued that Hayden's jacket and trousers should have been deemed instrumentalities of the crime? If so, how? Is that what Justice Fortas is arguing? If not, what is he arguing?

**4.** Do you like the policy of Justice Douglas's "two-faced" theory of the Fourth Amendment? Does the language of the amendment support his conclusion?

**5.** The extent to which *Hayden* applies to papers was explored in *Andresen*.

### Andresen v. Maryland
### 427 U.S. 463 (1976)

Mr. Justice BLACKMUN delivered the opinion of the Court.

I

In early 1972, a Bi-County Fraud Unit, acting under the joint auspices of the State's Attorneys' Offices of Montgomery and Prince George's Counties, Md., began an investigation of real estate settlement activities in the Washington, D. C., area. At the time, petitioner Andresen was an attorney who, as a sole practitioner, specialized in real estate settlements in Montgomery County.

The investigators, concluding that there was probable cause to believe that petitioner had committed the state crime of false pretenses, applied for warrants to search petitioner's law office and the separate office of Mount Vernon Development Corporation, of which petitioner was incorporator, sole shareholder, resident agent, and director. The application sought permission to search for specified documents pertaining to the sale and conveyance of Lot 13T. A judge of the Sixth Judicial Circuit of Montgomery County concluded that there was probable cause and issued the warrants.

The searches of the two offices were conducted simultaneously during daylight hours on October 31, 1972. Petitioner was present during the search of his law office and was free to move about. Counsel for him was present during the latter half of the search. Between 2% and 3% of the files in the office were seized. A single investigator, in the presence of a police officer, conducted the search of Mount Vernon Development Corporation. This search, taking about four hours, resulted in the seizure of less than 5% of the corporation's files.

Petitioner eventually was charged with the crime of false pretenses concerning Lot 13T, and with fraudulent misappropriation by a fiduciary, based on similar false claims made to three home purchasers.

There is no question that the records seized from petitioner's offices and introduced against him were incriminating. Moreover, it is undisputed that some of these business records contain statements made by petitioner. The question, therefore, is whether the seizure of these business records, and their admission into evidence at his trial, compelled petitioner to testify against himself in violation of the Fifth Amendment. This question may be said to have been reserved in *Warden v. Hayden*.

Petitioner contends that "the Fifth Amendment prohibition against compulsory self-incrimination applies as well to personal business papers seized from his offices as it does to the same papers being required to be produced under a subpoena." He bases his argument, naturally, on dicta in a number of cases which imply, or state, that the search for and seizure of a person's private papers violate the privilege against self-incrimination. Thus, in *Boyd*, the Court said: "(W)e have been unable to perceive that the seizure of a man's private books and papers to be used in evidence against him is substantially different from compelling him to be a witness against himself." And in *Hale v. Henkel*, 201 U.S. 43, 76 (1906), it was observed that "the substance of the offense is the compulsory production of private papers, whether under a search warrant or a *subpoena duces tecum*, against which the person . . . is entitled to protection."

We do not agree, however, that these broad statements compel suppression of this petitioner's business records as a violation of the Fifth Amendment. In the very recent case of *Fisher v. United States*, 425 U.S. 391 (1976), the Court held that an attorney's production, pursuant to a lawful summons, of his client's tax records in his hands did not violate the Fifth Amendment privilege of the taxpayer "because enforcement against a taxpayer's lawyer would not 'compel' the taxpayer to do anything and certainly would not compel him to be a 'witness' against himself." We recognized that the continued validity of the broad statements contained in some of the Court's earlier cases had been discredited by later opinions. In those earlier cases, the legal predicate for the inadmissibility of the evidence seized was a violation of the Fourth Amendment; the unlawfulness of the search and seizure was thought to supply the compulsion of the accused necessary to invoke the Fifth Amendment.[6]

This case thus falls within the principle stated by Mr. Justice Holmes: "A party is privileged from producing the evidence but not from its production."

---

[6] In *Boyd*, for example, it was held that the Government could not, consistently with the Fourth Amendment, obtain "mere evidence" from the accused; accordingly, a subpoena seeking "mere evidence" constituted compulsion of the accused against which he could invoke the Fifth Amendment. The "mere evidence" rule was overturned in *Hayden*.

The "convergence theory" of the Fourth and Fifth Amendments is also illustrated by *Agnello v. United States*, 269 U.S. 20 (1925), where the seizure of contraband pursuant to a search not incident to arrest and otherwise unlawful in violation of the Fourth Amendment was held to permit the accused to invoke the Fifth Amendment when the Government sought to introduce this evidence in a criminal proceeding against him.

*Johnson v. United States*, 228 U.S. 457, 458 (1913).

A contrary determination that the seizure of a person's business records and their introduction into evidence at a criminal trial violates the Fifth Amendment, would undermine the principles announced in earlier cases. Nearly a half century ago, in *Marron v. United States*, 275 U.S. 192 (1927), the Court upheld, against both Fourth and Fifth Amendment claims, the admission into evidence of business records seized during a search of the accused's illegal liquor business. And in *Abel v. United States*, 362 U.S. 217 (1960), the Court again upheld, against both Fourth and Fifth Amendment claims, the introduction into evidence at an espionage trial of false identity papers and a coded message seized during a search of the accused's hotel room. These cases recognize a general rule: "There is no special sanctity in papers, as distinguished from other forms of property, to render them immune from search and seizure, if only they fall within the scope of the principles of the cases in which other property may be seized, and if they be adequately described in the affidavit and warrant." *Gouled*.

Moreover, a contrary determination would prohibit the admission of evidence traditionally used in criminal cases and traditionally admissible despite the Fifth Amendment. For example, it would bar the admission of an accused's gambling records in a prosecution for gambling; a note given temporarily to a bank teller during a robbery and subsequently seized in the accused's automobile or home in a prosecution for bank robbery; and incriminating notes prepared, but not sent, by an accused in a kidnaping or blackmail prosecution.

In this case, the statements seized were voluntarily committed to paper before the police arrived to search for them, and petitioner was not treated discourteously during the search. Also, the "good cause" to "disturb," petitioner was independently determined by the judge who issued the warrants; and the State bore the burden of executing them. Finally, there is no chance in this case, of petitioner's statements being self-deprecatory and untrustworthy because they were extracted from him they were already in existence and had been made voluntarily.

Accordingly, we hold that the search of an individual's office for business records, their seizure, and subsequent introduction into evidence do not offend the Fifth Amendment's proscription that "(n)o person . . . shall be compelled in any criminal case to be a witness against himself."

Mr. Justice BRENNAN, dissenting.

In a concurring opinion earlier this Term in *Fisher v. United States*, 425 U.S. 391 (1976), I stated my view that the Fifth Amendment protects an individual citizen against the compelled production of testimonial matter that might tend to incriminate him, provided it is matter that comes within the zone of privacy recognized by the Amendment to secure to the individual "a private inner sanctum of individual feeling and thought." *Couch v. United States*, 409 U.S. 322, 327 (1973). Accordingly, the production of testimonial material falling within this zone of privacy may not be compelled by subpoena. The Court holds today that the search and seizure, pursuant to a valid warrant, of business records in petitioner's possession and containing statements made by the petitioner does not violate the Fifth Amendment. I can perceive no distinction of meaningful substance between compelling the production of such records through subpoena and seizing such records against the will of the petitioner.

## I

"There is no question that the records seized from petitioner's offices and introduced against him were incriminating. Moreover, it is undisputed that some of these business records contain statements made by petitioner." It also cannot be questioned that these records fall within the zone of privacy protected by the Fifth Amendment. *Bellis v. United States*, 417 U.S. 85, 87-88 (1974), squarely recognized that "(t)he privilege applies to the business records of the sole proprietor or sole practitioner as well as to personal documents containing more intimate information about the individual's private life." The Court today retreats from this view. Though recognizing the value of privacy protected by the Fifth Amendment, and the "right of each individual 'to a private enclave where he may lead a private life,'" the Court declines, without adequate explanation, to include business records within that private zone comprising the mere physical extensions of an individual's thoughts and knowledge. As I noted in *Fisher*, the failure to give effect to such a zone ignores the essential spirit of the Fifth Amendment: "[Business] records are at least an extension of an aspect of a person's activities, though concededly not the more intimate aspects of one's life. Where the privilege would have protected one's mental notes of his business affairs in a less complicated day and age, it would seem that that protection should not fall away because the complexities of another time compel one to keep business records."

As indicated at the outset, today's assault on the Fifth Amendment is not limited to narrowing this view of the scope of privacy respected by it. The Court also sanctions circumvention of the Amendment by indulging an unjustified distinction between production compelled by subpoena and production secured against the will of the petitioner through

warrant. But a privilege protecting against the compelled production of testimonial material is a hollow guarantee where production of that material may be secured through the expedient of search and seizure.

The matter cannot be resolved on any simplistic notion of compulsion. Search and seizure is as rife with elements of compulsion as subpoena. The intrusion occurs under the lawful process of the State. The individual is not free to resist that authority. To be sure, as the Court observes, "[p]etitioner was present during the search of his law office and was free to move about," but I do not believe the Court means to suggest that petitioner was free to obstruct the investigators' search through his files.

As early as *Boyd*, the Court was "unable to perceive that the seizure of a man's private books and papers to be used in evidence against him is substantially different from compelling him to be a witness against himself." Though the Court in *Boyd* held that compelling a person to be a witness against himself was tantamount to an unreasonable search and seizure, it never required a search and seizure to be independently unreasonable in order that it violate the Fifth Amendment. And though the several decisions which have found a Fifth Amendment violation stemming from a search and seizure all involved unreasonable search and seizures, it has never been established, contrary to the Court's assertion, that the unlawfulness of the search and seizure is necessary to invoke the Fifth Amendment. Under *Gouled*, a Fifth Amendment violation exists because the "[accused] is the unwilling source of the evidence," a matter which does not depend on the illegality *vel non* of the search and seizure.

Until today, no decision by this Court had held that the seizure of testimonial evidence by legal process did not violate the Fifth Amendment. Indeed, with few exceptions, the indications were strongly to the contrary. *Hayden* carefully observed that the items of clothing seized in that case were "not 'testimonial' or 'communicative' in nature, and their introduction therefore did not compel respondent to become a witness against himself in violation of the Fifth Amendment."[7] These cases all reflect the root understanding of *Boyd*: "It is not the breaking of his doors, and the rummaging of his drawers, that constitutes the essence of the offence [to the Fifth

---

[7] By further observing that "[t]his case thus does not require that we consider whether there are items of evidential value whose very nature precludes them from being the object of a reasonable search and seizure," *Hayden*, at the very least, clearly left open the question whether lawful seizure of testimonial evidence violated the Fifth Amendment.

Amendment]; but it is the invasion of his indefeasible right of personal security, personal liberty and private property. . . . [A]ny forcible and compulsory extortion of a man's own testimony or of his private papers to be used as evidence to convict him of crime . . ., is within the condemnation of [the Amendment]. In this regard the Fourth and Fifth Amendments run almost into each other.''

## QUESTIONS AND NOTES

**1.** Is (should) *Andresen* (be) limited to business records? What result if the police seize a personal diary? Is there anything that the police should never be permitted to seize? Why? Why not?

**2.** Is Brennan's *Andresen* dissent consistent with his *Hayden* opinion? Explain.

**3.** Is the distinction between seized and subpeonaed evidence valid? Why? Why not?

**4.** In *Zurcher*, we will consider whether there are ever instances in which the government should be required to employ a subpeona rather than a search.

### Zurcher v. Stanford Daily
### 436 U.S. 547 (1978)

Mr. Justice WHITE delivered the opinion of the Court.

As heretofore understood, the [Fourth] Amendment has not been a barrier to warrants to search property on which there is probable cause to believe that fruits, instrumentalities, or evidence of crime is located, whether or not the owner or possessor of the premises to be searched is himself reasonably suspected of complicity in the crime being investigated. We are now asked to reconstrue the Fourth Amendment and to hold for the first time that when the place to be searched is occupied by a person not then a suspect, a warrant to search for criminal objects and evidence reasonably believed to be located there should not issue except in the most unusual circumstances, and that except in such circumstances, a subpoena *duces tecum* must be relied upon to recover the objects or evidence sought.

I

Late in the day on Friday, April 9, 1971, officers of the Palo Alto Police Department and of the Santa Clara County Sheriff's Department responded to a call from the director of the Stanford University Hospital requesting the removal of a large group of demonstrators who had seized the hospital's administrative offices and occupied them since the previous afternoon.

On Sunday, April 11, a special edition of the Stanford Daily (Daily), a student newspaper published at Stanford University, carried articles and photographs devoted to the hospital protest and the violent clash between demonstrators and police. The photographs carried the byline of a Daily staff member and indicated that he had been at the east end of the hospital hallway where he could have photographed the assault on the nine officers. The next day, the Santa Clara County District Attorney's Office secured a warrant from the Municipal Court for an immediate search of the Daily's offices for negatives, film, and pictures showing the events and occurrences at the hospital on the evening of April 9. The warrant issued on a finding of "just, probable and reasonable cause for believing that: Negatives and photographs and films, evidence material and relevant to the identity of the perpetrators of felonies, to wit, Battery on a Peace Officer, and Assault with Deadly Weapon, will be located [on the premises of the Daily].'' The warrant affidavit contained no allegation or indication that members of the Daily staff were in any way involved in unlawful acts at the hospital.

The search pursuant to the warrant was conducted later that day by four police officers and took place in the presence of some members of the Daily staff. The Daily's photographic laboratories, filing cabinets, desks, and wastepaper baskets were searched. Locked drawers and rooms were not opened. The officers apparently had opportunity to read notes and correspondence during the search; but, contrary to claims of the staff, the officers denied that they had exceeded the limits of the warrant.[2] They had not been advised by the staff that the areas they were searching contained confidential materials. The search revealed only the photographs that had already been published on April 11, and no materials were removed from the Daily's office.

A month later the Daily and various members of its staff, respondents here, brought a civil action in the United States District Court for the Northern District of California seeking declaratory and injunctive relief against the police officers who conducted the search, the chief of police, the district attorney and one of his deputies, and the judge who had issued the warrant. The complaint alleged that the search of the Daily's office had deprived respondents under color of state law of rights secured to them by the First, Fourth, and Fourteenth Amendments of the United States Constitution.

The District Court denied the request for an injunction but, on respondents' motion for summary judgment, granted declaratory relief. The court did not question the existence of probable cause to believe that a crime had been committed and to believe that relevant evidence would be found on the Daily's premises. It held, however, that the Fourth and Fourteenth Amendments forbade the issuance of a warrant to search for materials in possession of one not suspected of crime unless there is probable cause to believe, based on facts presented in a sworn affidavit, that a subpoena *duces tecum* would be impracticable. Moreover, the failure to honor a subpoena would not alone justify a warrant; it must also appear that the possessor of the objects sought would disregard a court order not to remove or destroy them. The District Court further held that where the innocent object of the search is a newspaper, First Amendment interests are also involved and that such a search is constitutionally permissible "only in the rare circumstance where there is a *clear showing* that (1) important materials will be destroyed or removed from the jurisdiction; and (2) a restraining order would be futile." Since these preconditions to a valid warrant had not been satisfied here, the search of the Daily's offices was declared to have been illegal. The Court of Appeals affirmed *per curiam*, adopting the opinion of the District Court. We reverse.

## II

It is an understatement to say that there is no direct authority in this or any other federal court for

the District Court's sweeping revision of the Fourth Amendment. Under existing law, valid warrants may be issued to search *any* property, whether or not occupied by a third party, at which there is probable cause to believe that fruits, instrumentalities, or evidence of a crime will be found. Nothing on the face of the Amendment suggests that a third-party search warrant should not normally issue. The Warrant Clause speaks of search warrants issued on "probable cause" and "particularly describing the place to be searched, and the persons or things to be seized." In situations where the State does not seek to seize "persons" but only those "things" which there is probable cause to believe are located on the place to be searched, there is no apparent basis in the language of the Amendment for also imposing the requirements for a valid arrest—probable cause to believe that the third party is implicated in the crime.

This is not to question that "reasonableness" is the overriding test of compliance with the Fourth Amendment or to assert that searches, however or whenever executed, may never be unreasonable if supported by a warrant issued on probable cause and properly identifying the place to be searched and the property to be seized. We do hold, however, that the courts may not, in the name of Fourth Amendment reasonableness, prohibit the States from issuing warrants to search for evidence simply because the owner or possessor of the place to be searched is not then reasonably suspected of criminal involvement.

## III

The reasons presented by the District Court and adopted by the Court of Appeals for arriving at its remarkable conclusion do not withstand analysis. First, as we have said, it is apparent that whether the third-party occupant is suspect or not, the State's interest in enforcing the criminal law and recovering the evidence remains the same; and it is the seeming innocence of the property owner that the District Court relied on to foreclose the warrant to search. But, as respondents themselves now concede, if the third party knows that contraband or other illegal materials are on his property, he is sufficiently culpable to justify the issuance of a search warrant. Similarly, if his ethical stance is the determining factor, it seems to us that whether or not he knows that the sought-after articles are secreted on his property and whether or not he knows that the articles are in fact the fruits, instrumentalities, or evidence of crime, he will be so informed when the search warrant is served, and it is doubtful that he should then be permitted to object to the search, to withhold, if it is there, the evidence of crime reasonably

---

[2] The District Court did not find it necessary to resolve this dispute.

believed to be possessed by him or secreted on his property, and to forbid the search and insist that the officers serve him with a subpoena *duces tecum*.

Second, we are unpersuaded that the District Court's new rule denying search warrants against third parties and insisting on subpoenas would substantially further privacy interests without seriously undermining law enforcement efforts. Because of the fundamental public interest in implementing the criminal law, the search warrant, a heretofore effective and constitutionally acceptable enforcement tool, should not be suppressed on the basis of surmise and without solid evidence supporting the change. As the District Court understands it, denying third-party search warrants would not have substantial adverse effects on criminal investigations because the nonsuspect third party, once served with a subpoena, will preserve the evidence and ultimately lawfully respond. The difficulty with this assumption is that search warrants are often employed early in an investigation, perhaps before the identity of any likely criminal and certainly before all the perpetrators are or could be known. The seemingly blameless third party in possession of the fruits or evidence may not be innocent at all; and if he is, he may nevertheless be so related to or so sympathetic with the culpable that he cannot be relied upon to retain and preserve the articles that may implicate his friends, or at least not to notify those who would be damaged by the evidence that the authorities are aware of its location. In any event, it is likely that the real culprits will have access to the property, and the delay involved in employing the subpoena *duces tecum*, offering as it does the opportunity to litigate its validity, could easily result in the disappearance of the evidence, whatever the good faith of the third party.

Forbidding the warrant and insisting on the subpoena instead when the custodian of the object of the search is not then suspected of crime, involves hazards to criminal investigation much more serious than the District Court believed; and the record is barren of anything but the District Court's assumptions to support its conclusions. At the very least, the burden of justifying a major revision of the Fourth Amendment has not been carried.

We are also not convinced that the net gain to privacy interests by the District Court's new rule would be worth the candle. In the normal course of events, search warrants are more difficult to obtain than subpoenas, since the latter do not involve the judiciary and do not require proof of probable cause. Where, in the real world, subpoenas would suffice, it can be expected that they will be employed by the

rational prosecutor. On the other hand, when choice is available under local law and the prosecutor chooses to use the search warrant, it is unlikely that he has needlessly selected the more difficult course. His choice is more likely to be based on the solid belief, arrived at through experience but difficult, if not impossible, to sustain a specific case, that the warranted search is necessary to secure and to avoid the destruction of evidence.

### IV

The District Court held, and respondents assert here, that whatever may be true of third-party searches generally, where the third party is a newspaper, there are additional factors derived from the First Amendment that justify a nearly *per se* rule forbidding the search warrant and permitting only the subpoena *duces tecum*. The general submission is that searches of newspaper offices for evidence of crime reasonably believed to be on the premises will seriously threaten the ability of the press to gather, analyze, and disseminate news. This is said to be true for several reasons: First, searches will be physically disruptive to such an extent that timely publication will be impeded. Second, confidential sources of information will dry up, and the press will also lose opportunities to cover various events because of fears of the participants that press files will be readily available to the authorities. Third, reporters will be deterred from recording and preserving their recollections for future use if such information is subject to seizure. Fourth, the processing of news and its dissemination will be chilled by the prospects that searches will disclose internal editorial deliberations. Fifth, the press will resort to self-censorship to conceal its possession of information of potential interest to the police.

It is true that the struggle from which the Fourth Amendment emerged "is largely a history of conflict between the Crown and the press," and that in issuing warrants and determining the reasonableness of a search, state and federal magistrates should be aware that "unrestricted power of search and seizure could also be an instrument for stifling liberty of expression." Where the materials sought to be seized may be protected by the First Amendment, the requirements of the Fourth Amendment must be applied with "scrupulous exactitude." "A seizure reasonable as to one type of material in one setting may be unreasonable in a different setting or with respect to another kind of material." *Roaden v. Kentucky*, 413 U.S. 496, 501 (1973). Hence, in *Stanford v. Texas*, 379 U.S. 476 (1965), the Court invalidated a warrant authorizing the search of a private home for all books, records, and other materials relating to the Communist Party, on the ground that whether or not the warrant would have been sufficient in other contexts, it authorized the searchers to rummage among and make judgments about books and papers and was the functional equivalent of a general warrant, one of the principal targets of the Fourth Amendment. Where presumptively protected materials are sought to be seized, the warrant requirement should be administered to leave as little as possible to the discretion or whim of the officer in the field.

Neither the Fourth Amendment nor the cases requiring consideration of First Amendment values in issuing search warrants, however, call for imposing the regime ordered by the District Court. Aware of the long struggle between Crown and press and desiring to curb unjustified official intrusions, the Framers took the enormously important step of subjecting searches to the test of reasonableness and to the general rule requiring search warrants issued by neutral magistrates. They nevertheless did not forbid warrants where the press was involved, did not require special showings that subpoenas would be impractical, and did not insist that the owner of the place to be searched, if connected with the press, must be shown to be implicated in the offense being investigated. Further, the prior cases do no more than insist that the courts apply the warrant requirements with particular exactitude when First Amendment interests would be endangered by the search. As we see it, no more than this is required where the warrant requested is for the seizure of criminal evidence reasonably believed to be on the premises occupied by a newspaper. Properly administered, the preconditions for a warrant—probable cause, specificity with respect to the place to be searched and the things to be seized, and overall reasonableness—should afford sufficient protection against the harms that are assertedly threatened by warrants for searching newspaper offices.

There is no reason to believe, for example, that magistrates cannot guard against searches of the type, scope, and intrusiveness that would actually interfere with the timely publication of a newspaper. Nor, if the requirements of specificity and reasonableness are properly applied, policed, and observed, will there be any occasion or opportunity for officers to rummage at large in newspaper files or to intrude into or to deter normal editorial and publication decisions. The warrant issued in this case authorized nothing of this sort. Nor are we convinced, that confidential sources will disappear and that the press will suppress news because of fears of warranted searches. Whatever incremental effect there may be in this regard if search warrants, as well as subpoenas, are permissible in proper circumstances, it does not make a constitutional difference in our judgment.

The fact is that respondents and *amici* have pointed to only a very few instances in the entire United States since 1971 involving the issuance of warrants for searching newspaper premises. This reality hardly suggests abuse; and if abuse occurs, there will be time enough to deal with it. Furthermore, the press is not only an important, critical, and valuable asset to society, but it is not easily intimidated—nor should it be.

Respondents also insist that the press should be afforded opportunity to litigate the State's entitlement to the material it seeks before it is turned over or seized and that whereas the search warrant procedure is defective in this respect, resort to the subpoena would solve the problem. The Court has held that a restraining order imposing a prior restraint upon free expression is invalid for want of notice and opportunity for a hearing, and that seizures not merely for use as evidence but entirely removing arguably protected materials from circulation may be effected only after an adversary hearing and a judicial finding of obscenity. But presumptively protected materials are not necessarily immune from seizure under warrant for use at a criminal trial. And surely a warrant to search newspaper premises for criminal evidence such as the one issued here for news photographs taken in a public place carries no realistic threat of prior restraint or of any direct restraint whatsoever on the publication of the Daily or on its communication of ideas. The hazards of such warrants can be avoided by a neutral magistrate carrying out his responsibilities under the Fourth Amendment, for he has ample tools at his disposal to confine warrants to search within reasonable limits.

We note finally that if the evidence sought by warrant is sufficiently connected with the crime to satisfy the probable-cause requirement, it will very likely be sufficiently relevant to justify a subpoena and to withstand a motion to quash. Further, Fifth Amendment and state shield-law objections that might be asserted in opposition to compliance with a subpoena are largely irrelevant to determining the legality of a search warrant under the Fourth Amendment. Of course, the Fourth Amendment does not prevent or advise against legislative or executive efforts to establish nonconstitutional protections against possible abuses of the search warrant procedure, but we decline to reinterpret the Amendment to impose a general constitutional barrier against warrants to search newspaper premises, to require resort to subpoenas as a general rule, or to demand prior notice and hearing in connection with the issuance of search warrants.

It follows that the judgment of the Court of Appeals is reversed.

Mr. Justice BRENNAN took no part in the consideration or decision of these cases.

Mr. Justice POWELL, concurring.

I join the opinion of the Court, and I write simply to emphasize what I take to be the fundamental error of Mr. Justice Stewart's dissenting opinion. As I understand that opinion, it would read into the Fourth Amendment, as a new and *per se* exception, the rule that any search of an entity protected by the Press Clause of the First Amendment is unreasonable so long as a subpoena could be used as a substitute procedure. Even aside from the difficulties involved in deciding on a case-by-case basis whether a subpoena can serve as an adequate substitute,[1] I

---

[1] For example, respondents had announced a policy of destroying any photographs that might aid prosecution of protesters. While this policy probably reflected the deep feelings of the Vietnam era, and one may assume that under normal circumstances few, if any, press entities would adopt a policy so hostile to law enforcement, respondents' policy at least illustrates the possibility of such hostility. Use of a subpoena, as proposed by the dissent, would be of no utility in face of a policy of destroying evidence. And unless the policy were publicly announced, it probably would be difficult to show the impracticality of a subpoena as opposed to a search warrant. At oral argument, counsel for respondents stated that the announced policy of the Stanford Daily conceivably could have extended to the destruction of evidence of *any* crime:

"QUESTION: Let us assume you had a picture of the commission of a crime. For example, in banks they take pictures regularly of, not only of robbery but of murder committed in a bank and there have been pictures taken of the actual pulling of the trigger or the pointing of the gun and pulling of the trigger. There is a very famous one related to the assassination of President Kennedy.

"What would the policy of the *Stanford Daily* be with respect to that? Would it feel free to destroy it at any time before a subpoena had been served?

"MR. FALK: The – literally read, the policy of the *Daily* requires me to give an affirmative answer. I find it hard to believe that in an example such as that, that the policy would have been carried out. It was not addressed to a picture of that kind or in that context.

"QUESTION: Well, I am sure you were right. I was just getting to the scope of your theory.

"MR. FALK: Our –

"QUESTION: What is the difference between the pictures Justice Powell just described and the pictures they were thought to have?

"MR. FALK: Well, it simply is a distinction that –

"QUESTION: Attacking police officers instead

---

agree with the Court that there is no constitutional basis for such a reading.

If the Framers had believed that the press was entitled to a special procedure, not available to others, when government authorities required evidence in its possession, one would have expected the terms of the Fourth Amendment to reflect that belief. As the opinion of the Court points out, the struggle from which the Fourth Amendment emerged was that between Crown and press. The Framers were painfully aware of that history, and their response to it was the Fourth Amendment. Hence, there is every reason to believe that the usual procedures contemplated by the Fourth Amendment do indeed apply to the press, as to every other person.

This is not to say that a warrant which would be sufficient to support the search of an apartment or an automobile necessarily would be reasonable in supporting the search of a newspaper office. As the Court's opinion makes clear, the magistrate must judge the reasonableness of every warrant in light of the circumstances of the particular case, carefully considering the description of the evidence sought, the situation of the premises, and the position and interests of the owner or occupant. While there is no justification for the establishment of a separate Fourth Amendment procedure for the press, a magistrate asked to issue a warrant for the search of press offices can and should take cognizance of the independent values protected by the First Amendment – such as those highlighted by Mr. Justice STEWART – when he weighs such factors. If the reasonableness and particularity requirements are thus applied, the dangers are likely to be minimal.[2]

In any event, considerations such as these are the province of the Fourth Amendment. There is no authority either in history or in the Constitution itself

---

of the President. That is the only difference."

While the existence of this policy was not before the magistrate at the time of the warrant's issuance, it illustrates the possible dangers of creating separate standards for the press alone.

[2] Similarly, the magnitude of a proposed search directed at *any* third party and the nature and significance of the material sought, are factors properly considered as bearing on the reasonableness and particularity requirements. Moreover, there is no reason why police officers executing a warrant should not seek the cooperation of the subject party, in order to prevent needless disruption.

for exempting certain classes of persons or entities from its reach.

Mr. Justice STEWART, with whom Mr. Justice MARSHALL joins, dissenting.

Believing that the search by the police of the offices of the Stanford Daily infringed the First and Fourteenth Amendments' guarantee of a free press, I respectfully dissent.[1]

I

It seems to me self-evident that police searches of newspaper offices burden the freedom of the press. The most immediate and obvious First Amendment injury caused by such a visitation by the police is physical disruption of the operation of the newspaper. Policemen occupying a newsroom and searching it thoroughly for what may be an extended period of time[2] will inevitably interrupt its normal operations, and thus impair or even temporarily prevent the processes of newsgathering, writing, editing, and publishing. By contrast, a subpoena would afford the newspaper itself an opportunity to locate whatever material might be requested and produce it.

But there is another and more serious burden on a free press imposed by an unannounced police search of a newspaper office: the possibility of disclosure of information received from confidential sources, or of the identity of the sources themselves. Protection of those sources is necessary to ensure that the press can fulfill its constitutionally designated function of informing the public, because important information can often be obtained only by an assurance that the source will not be revealed.

Today the Court does not question the existence of this constitutional protection, but says only that it is not "convinced . . . that confidential sources will disappear and that the press will suppress news because of fears of warranted searches." This facile conclusion seems to me to ignore common experience. It requires no blind leap of faith to understand that a person who gives information to a journalist only on condition that his identity will not be revealed will be less likely to give that information if he knows that, despite the journalist's assurance his identity may in fact be disclosed. And it cannot be denied that confidential information may be exposed to the eyes of police officers who execute a search warrant by rummaging through the files, cabinets, desks, and wastebaskets of a newsroom.[5] Since the indisputable effect of such searches will thus be to prevent a newsman from being able to promise confidentiality to his potential sources, it seems obvious to me that a journalist's access to information, and thus the public's will thereby be impaired.

A search warrant allows police officers to ransack the files of a newspaper, reading each and every document until they have found the one named in the warrant,[7] while a subpoena would permit the newspaper itself to produce only the specific documents requested. A search, unlike a subpoena, will therefore lead to the needless exposure of confidential information completely unrelated to the purpose of the investigation. The knowledge that police officers can make an unannounced raid on a newsroom is thus bound to have a deterrent effect on the availability of confidential news sources. The end result, wholly inimical to the First Amendment, will be a diminishing flow of potentially important information to the public.

One need not rely on mere intuition to reach this conclusion. The record in this case includes affidavits not only from members of the staff of the Stanford Daily but also from many professional journalists and editors, attesting to precisely such personal

---

[1] I agree with the Court that the *Fourth* Amendment does not forbid the issuance of search warrants "simply because the owner or possessor of the place to be searched is not then reasonably suspected of criminal involvement." Thus, contrary to the understanding expressed in the concurring opinion, I do not "read" anything "into the Fourth Amendment." Instead, I would simply enforce the provisions of the *First* Amendment.

[2] One search of a radio station in Los Angeles lasted over eight hours. Note, Search and Seizure of the Media: A Statutory, Fourth Amendment and First Amendment Analysis, 28 Stan.L.Rev. 957, 957-959 (1976).

[5] In this case, the policemen executing the search warrant were concededly in a position to read confidential material unrelated to the object of their search; whether they in fact did so is disputed.

[7] The Court says that "if the requirements of specificity and reasonableness are properly applied, policed, and observed" there will be no opportunity for the police to "rummage at large in newspaper files." But in order to find a particular document, no matter how specifically it is identified in the warrant, the police will have to search every place where it might be—including, presumably, every file in the office—and to examine each document they find to see if it is the correct one. I thus fail to see how the Fourth Amendment would provide an effective limit to these searches.

experience.[8] Despite the Court's rejection of this un-controverted evidence, I believe it clearly establishes that unannounced police searches of newspaper of-fices will significantly burden the constitutionally protected function of the press to gather news and report it to the public.

## II

It is well to recall the actual circumstances of this litigation. The application for a warrant showed only that there was reason to believe that photo-graphic evidence of assaults on the police would be found in the offices of the Stanford Daily. There was no emergency need to protect life or property by an immediate search. The evidence sought was not contraband, but material obtained by the Daily in the normal exercise of its journalistic function. Neither the Daily nor any member of its staff was suspected of criminal activity. And there was no showing that the Daily would not respond to a sub-poena commanding production of the photographs, or that for any other reason a subpoena could not be obtained. Surely, then, a subpoena *duces tecum* would have been just as effective as a police raid in obtaining the production of the material sought by the Santa Clara County District Attorney.

The District Court and the Court of Appeals clearly recognized that if the affidavits submitted with a search warrant application should demonstrate probable cause to believe that a subpoena would be impractical, the magistrate must have the authority to issue a warrant. In such a case, by definition, a subpoena would not be adequate to protect the rele-vant societal interest. But they held, and I agree, that a warrant should issue only after the magistrate has performed the careful "balanc[ing] of these vital constitutional and societal interests." *Branzburg v.*

*Hayes, supra,* at 710, (Powell, J., concurring).[9]

The decisions of this Court establish that a prior adversary judicial hearing is generally required to as-sess in advance any threatened invasion of First Amendment liberty. A search by police officers affords no timely opportunity for such a hearing, since a search warrant is ordinarily issued *ex parte* upon the affidavit of a policeman or prosecutor. There is no opportunity to challenge the necessity for the search until after it has occurred and the constitutional protection of the newspaper has been irretrievably invaded.

On the other hand, a subpoena would allow a news-paper, through a motion to quash, an opportunity for an adversary hearing with respect to the production of any material which a prosecutor might think is in its possession. If, in the present litigation, the Stanford Daily had been served with a subpoena, it would have had an opportunity to demonstrate to the court what the police ultimately found to be true—that the evi-dence sought did not exist. The legitimate needs of government thus would have been served without in-fringing the freedom of the press.

## III

Perhaps as a matter of abstract policy a newspaper office should receive no more protection from unan-nounced police searches than, say, the office of a doc-tor or the office of a bank. But we are here to uphold a Constitution. And our Constitution does not explicitly protect the practice of medicine or the business of banking from all abridgment by government. It does explicitly protect the freedom of the press.

For these reasons I would affirm the judgment of the Court of Appeals.

Mr. Justice STEVENS, dissenting.

The novel problem presented by this case is an outgrowth of the profound change in Fourth Amend-ment law that occurred in 1967, when *Hayden* was decided. The question is what kind of "probable cause" must be established in order to obtain a warrant to conduct an unannounced search for documentary

---

[8] According to these uncontradicted affidavits, when it becomes known that a newsman cannot guar-antee confidentiality, potential sources of informa-tion often become unavailable. Moreover, efforts are sometimes made, occasionally by force, to prevent reporters and photographers from covering news-worthy events, because of fear that the police will seize the newsman's notes or photographs as evi-dence. The affidavits of the members of the staff of the Stanford Daily give examples of how this very search produced such an impact on the Daily's own journalistic functions.

---

[9] The petitioners have argued here that in fact there was reason to believe that the Daily would not honor a subpoena. Regardless of the probative value of this information, it is irrelevant, since it was not before the magistrate when he issued the warrant. *Whiteley v. Warden*, 401 U.S. 560, 565 n. 8; *Spinelli v. United States*, 393 U.S. 410, 413 n. 3; *Aguilar v. Texas*, 378 U.S. 108, 109 n. 1; see *Johnson v. United States*, 333 U.S. 10, 13-14.

evidence in the private files of a person not suspected of involvement in any criminal activity. The Court holds that a reasonable belief that the files contain relevant evidence is a sufficient justification. This holding rests on a misconstruction of history and of the Fourth Amendment's purposely broad language.

The Amendment contains two Clauses, one protecting "persons, houses, papers, and effects, against unreasonable searches and seizures," the other regulating the issuance of warrants: "no Warrants shall issue, but upon probable cause, supported by Oath or affirmation, and particularly describing the place to be searched, and the persons or things to be seized." When these words were written, the procedures of the Warrant Clause were not the primary protection against oppressive searches. It is unlikely that the authors expected private papers ever to be among the "things" that could be seized with a warrant, for only a few years earlier, in 1765, Lord Camden had delivered his famous opinion denying that any magistrate had power to authorize the seizure of private papers.[1] Because all such seizures were considered unreasonable, the Warrant Clause was not framed to protect against them.

In the pre-*Hayden* era warrants were used to search for contraband,[4] weapons, and plunder, but not for "mere evidence." The practical effect of the rule prohibiting the issuance of warrants to search for mere evidence was to narrowly limit not only the category of objects, but also the category of persons and the character of the privacy interests that

---

[1] "Papers are the owner's goods and chattels: they are his dearest property; and are so far from enduring a seizure, that they will hardly bear an inspection; and though the eye cannot by the laws of England be guilty of a trespass, yet where private papers are removed and carried away, the secret nature of those goods will be an aggravation of the trespass, and demand more considerable damages in that respect. Where is the written law that gives any magistrate such a power? I can safely answer, there is none; and therefore it is too much for us without such authority to pronounce a practice legal, which would be subversive of all the comforts of society." *Entick v. Carrington*, 19 How.St.Tr. 1029, 1066 (1765).

[4] It was stated in 1967 that about 95% of the search warrants obtained by the office of the District Attorney for New York County were for the purpose of seizing narcotics and arresting the possessors. See T. Taylor, Two Studies in Constitutional Interpretation 48, and n. 85 (1969).

might be affected by an unannounced police search.

Just as the witnesses who participate in an investigation or a trial far outnumber the defendants, the persons who possess evidence that may help to identify an offender, or explain an aspect of a criminal transaction, far outnumber those who have custody of weapons or plunder. Countless law-abiding citizens – doctors, lawyers, merchants, customers, bystanders – may have documents in their possession that relate to an ongoing criminal investigation. The consequences of subjecting this large category of persons to unannounced police searches are extremely serious. The *ex parte* warrant procedure enables the prosecutor to obtain access to privileged documents that could not be examined if advance notice gave the custodian an opportunity to object.[6] The search for the documents described in a warrant may involve the inspection of files containing other private matter.[7] The dramatic character of a sudden

---

[6] The suggestion that, instead of setting standards, we should rely on the good judgment of the magistrate to prevent abuse represents an abdication of the responsibilities this Court previously accepted in carefully supervising the performance of the magistrate's warrant-issuing function.

[7] "There are three considerations which support the conclusion that private papers are central to the concerns of the fourth amendment and which suggest that, in accord with the amendment's privacy rationale, private papers should occupy a type of preferred position. The first consideration is the very personal, private nature of such papers. This rationale has been cogently articulated on a number of occasions. Private papers have been said to be 'little more than an extension of [the owner's] person,' their seizure 'a particularly abrasive infringement of privacy,' and their protection 'impelled by the moral and symbolic need to recognize and defend the private aspect of personality.' In this sense, every governmental procurement of private papers regardless of how it is accomplished, is uniquely intrusive. In addition to the nature of the papers themselves, a second reason for according them strict protection concerns the nature of the search for private papers. The fundamental evil at which the fourth amendment was directed was the sweeping, exploratory search conducted pursuant to a general warrant. A search involving private papers, it has been noted, invariably partakes of a similar generality, for 'even a search for a specific, identified paper may involve the same rude intrusion [of an exploratory search] if the quest for it leads to an examination of all of a man's private papers.' Thus, both their contents

search may cause an entirely unjustified injury to the reputation of the persons searched.

Of greatest importance, however, is the question whether the offensive intrusion on the privacy of the ordinary citizen is justified by the law enforcement interest it is intended to vindicate. Possession of contraband or the proceeds or tools of crime gives rise to two inferences: that the custodian is involved in the criminal activity, and that, if given notice of an intended search, he will conceal or destroy what is being sought. The probability of criminal culpability justifies the invasion of his privacy; the need to accomplish the law enforcement purpose of the search justifies acting without advance notice and by force, if necessary. By satisfying the probable-cause standard appropriate for weapons or plunder, the police effectively demonstrate that no less intrusive method of investigation will succeed.

Mere possession of documentary evidence, however, is much less likely to demonstrate that the custodian is guilty of any wrongdoing or that he will not honor a subpoena or informal request to produce it. In the pre-*Hayden* era, evidence of that kind was routinely obtained by procedures that presumed that the custodian would respect his obligation to obey subpoenas and to cooperate in the investigation of crime. These procedures had a constitutional dimension. For the innocent citizen's interest in the privacy of his papers and possessions is an aspect of liberty protected by the Due Process Clause of the Fourteenth Amendment. Notice and an opportunity to object to the deprivation of the citizen's liberty are, therefore, the constitutionally mandated general

rule. An exception to that rule can only be justified by strict compliance with the Fourth Amendment. That Amendment flatly prohibits the issuance of any warrant unless justified by probable cause.

A showing of probable cause that was adequate to justify the issuance of a warrant to search for stolen goods in the 18th century does not automatically satisfy the new dimensions of the Fourth Amendment in the post-*Hayden* era. In *Hayden* itself, the Court recognized that the meaning of probable cause should be reconsidered in the light of the new authority it conferred on the police.[11] The only conceivable justification for an unannounced search of an innocent citizen is the fear that, if notice were given, he would conceal or destroy the object of the search. Probable cause to believe that the custodian is a criminal, or that he holds a criminal's weapons, spoils, or the like, justifies that fear,[12] and therefore such a showing complies with the Clause. But if nothing said under oath in the warrant application demonstrates the need for an unannounced search by force, the probable-cause requirement is not satisfied. In the absence of some other showing of reasonableness, the ensuing search violates the Fourth Amendment.

In this case, the warrant application set forth no facts suggesting that respondents were involved in any wrongdoing or would destroy the desired evidence if given notice of what the police desired. I would therefore hold that the warrant did not comply with the Warrant Clause and that the search was unreasonable within the meaning of the first Clause of the Fourth Amendment.

I respectfully dissent.

---

and the inherently intrusive nature of a search for them militates toward the position that private papers are deserving of the fullest possible fourth amendment protection. Finally, not only is a search involving private papers highly intrusive in fourth amendment terms, but the nature of the papers themselves may implicate the policies of other constitutional protections. In addition to the 'intimate' relation with fifth amendment values, the obtaining of private papers by the government touches upon the first amendment and the generalized right of privacy." McKenna, The Constitutional Protection of Private Papers: The Role of a Hierarchical Fourth Amendment, 53 Ind.L.J. 55, 68-69 (1977-1978) (footnotes omitted).

---

[11] "There must, of course, be a nexus—automatically provided in the case of fruits, instrumentalities or contraband—between the item to be seized and criminal behavior. Thus in the case of 'mere evidence,' probable cause must be examined in terms of cause to believe that the evidence sought will aid in a particular apprehension or conviction. In so doing, consideration of police purposes will be required."

[12] "The danger is all too obvious that a criminal will destroy or hide evidence or fruits of his crime if given any prior notice."

## QUESTIONS AND NOTES

**1.** The Court's opinion treats the respondent's argument as though it were trying to change the law, rather than resolve a heretofore unresolved question. Do you agree with the Court that the question should be so treated? Did the Court's categorization of it in those terms influence its result?

**2.** What, if anything, ought to have to be alleged in addition to probable cause to believe that evidence would be found at the site of the search?

**3.** Is the information contained in footnote 1 of Justice Powell's concurrence relevant to the resolution of this case? If so, how?

**4.** Does the Court overvalue the independence of the magistrate and undervalue his/her need for judicial supervision?

**5.** If you were a D.A., would you ordinarily opt for a subpeona or a search warrant in the *Zurcher* situation?

**6.** If you had been on the Court, would you have concurred with Justice White? Justice Stewart? Justice Stevens? None of the above? Explain.

**7.** Perhaps in response to Justice White's invitation, Congress enacted a statute essentially adopting Justice Stewart's opinion as the law of the land. Consequently, where the third party searchee can raise a First Amendment claim, such as the Stanford Daily, *Zurcher* is no longer to be followed. On the other hand, *Zurcher* is still good law where the third party, though innocent, has no special First Amendment claim. 42 U.S.C. § 2000aa (1994).

# 12.

# CONSENT

It is beyond dispute that a search conducted pursuant to a legally recognized consent is permitted by the Fourth Amendment. What constitutes a legally recognized consent is less clear. Also, less clear is whether consent searches are excepted from the Fourth Amendment because they are not searches at all, or because they are *per se* reasonable. Think about these questions as you read *Schneckloth* and *Rodriguez*.

## Schneckloth v. Bustamonte
### 412 U.S. 218 (1973)

Mr. Justice STEWART delivered the opinion of the Court.

### I

While on routine patrol in Sunnyvale, California, at approximately 2:40 in the morning, Police Officer James Rand stopped an automobile when he observed that one headlight and its license plate light were burned out. Six men were in the vehicle. Joe Alcala and the respondent, Robert Bustamonte, were in the front seat with Joe Gonzales, the driver. Three older men were seated in the rear. When, in response to the policeman's question, Gonzales could not produce a driver's license, Officer Rand asked if any of the other five had any evidence of identification. Only Alcala produced a license, and he explained that the car was his brother's. After the six occupants had stepped out of the car at the officer's request and after two additional policemen had arrived, Officer Rand asked Alcala if he could search the car. Alcala replied, "Sure,

go ahead." Prior to the search no one was threatened with arrest and, according to Officer Rand's uncontradicted testimony, it "was all very congenial at this time." Gonzales testified that Alcala actually helped in the search of the car, by opening the trunk and glove compartment. In Gonzales' words: "[T]he police officer asked Joe [Alcala], he goes, 'Does the trunk open?' And Joe said, 'Yes.' He went to the car and got the keys and opened up the trunk." Wadded up under the left rear seat, the police officers found three checks that had previously been stolen from a car wash.

### II

It is important to make it clear at the outset what is not involved in this case. The respondent concedes that a search conducted pursuant to a valid consent is constitutionally permissible. And similarly the State concedes that "(w)hen a prosecutor seeks to rely upon consent to justify the lawfulness of a search, he has the burden of proving that the consent was, in fact, freely and voluntarily given.''

The precise question in this case, then, is what must the prosecution prove to demonstrate that a consent was ''voluntarily'' given. And upon that question there is a square conflict of views between the state and federal courts that have reviewed the search involved in the case before us. The Court of Appeals for the Ninth Circuit concluded that it is an essential part of the State's initial burden to prove that a person knows he has a right to refuse consent. The California courts have followed the rule that voluntariness is a question of fact to be determined from the totality of all the circumstances, and that the state of a defendant's knowledge is only one factor to be taken into account in assessing the voluntariness of a consent.

### A

The most extensive judicial exposition of the meaning of ''voluntariness'' has been developed in those cases in which the Court has had to determine the ''voluntariness'' of a defendant's confession for purposes of the Fourteenth Amendment. Almost 40 years ago, in *Brown v. Mississippi*, 297 U.S. 278, the Court held that a criminal conviction based upon a confession obtained by brutality and violence was constitutionally invalid under the Due Process Clause of the Fourteenth Amendment. In some 30 different cases decided during the era that intervened between *Brown* and *Escobedo v. Illinois*, 378 U.S. 478, the Court was faced with the necessity of determining whether in fact the confessions in issue had been ''voluntarily'' given. It is to that body of case law to which we turn for initial guidance on the meaning of ''voluntariness'' in the present context.

In determining whether a defendant's will was overborne in a particular case, the Court has assessed the totality of all the surrounding circumstances – both the characteristics of the accused and the details of the interrogation. Some of the factors taken into account have included the youth of the accused, his lack of education, or his low intelligence, the lack of any advice to the accused of his constitutional rights, the length of detention, the repeated and prolonged nature of the questioning, and the use of physical punishment such as the deprivation of food or sleep. In all of these cases, the Court determined the factual circumstances surrounding the confession, assessed the psychological impact on the accused, and evaluated the legal significance of how the accused reacted.

The significant fact about all of these decisions is that none of them turned on the presence or absence of a single controlling criterion; each reflected a careful scrutiny of all the surrounding circumstances. In none of them did the Court rule that the Due Process Clause required the prosecution to prove as part of its initial burden that the defendant knew he had a right to refuse to answer the questions that were put. While the state of the accused's mind, and the failure of the police to advise the accused of his rights, were certainly factors to be evaluated in assessing the ''voluntariness'' of an accused's responses, they were not in and of themselves determinative.

### B

Similar considerations lead us to agree with the courts of California that the question whether a consent to a search was in fact ''voluntary'' or was the product of duress or coercion, express or implied, is a question of fact to be determined from the totality of all the circumstances. While knowledge of the right to refuse consent is one factor to be taken into account, the government need not establish such knowledge as the *sine qua non* of an effective consent. As with police questioning, two competing concerns must be accommodated in determining the meaning of a ''voluntary'' consent – the legitimate need for such searches and the equally important requirement of assuring the absence of coercion.

In situations where the police have some evidence of illicit activity, but lack probable cause to arrest or search, a search authorized by a valid consent may be the only means of obtaining important and reliable evidence. In the present case for example, while the police had reason to stop the car for traffic violations, the State does not contend that there was probable cause to search the vehicle or that the search was incident to a valid arrest of any of the occupants. Yet, the search yielded tangible evidence that served as a basis for a prosecution, and provided some assurance that others, wholly innocent of the crime, were not mistakenly brought to trial. And in those cases where there is probable cause to arrest or search, but where the police lack a warrant, a consent search may still be valuable. If the search is conducted and proves fruitless, that in itself may convince the police that an arrest with its possible stigma and embarrassment is unnecessary, or that a far more extensive search pursuant to a warrant is not justified. In short, a search pursuant to consent may result in considerably less inconvenience for the subject of the search, and, properly conducted, is a constitutionally permissible and wholly legitimate aspect of effective police activity.

The approach of the Court of Appeals for the Ninth Circuit finds no support in any of our decisions that have attempted to define the meaning of "voluntariness." Its ruling, that the State must affirmatively prove that the subject of the search knew that he had a right to refuse consent, would, in practice, create serious doubt whether consent searches could continue to be conducted. There might be rare cases where it could be proved from the record that a person in fact affirmatively knew of his right to refuse — such as a case where he announced to the police that if he didn't sign the consent form, "you (police) are going to get a search warrant;" or a case where by prior experience and training a person had clearly and convincingly demonstrated such knowledge. But more commonly where there was no evidence of any coercion, explicit or implicit, the prosecution would nevertheless be unable to demonstrate that the subject of the search in fact had known of his right to refuse consent.

One alternative that would go far toward proving that the subject of a search did know he had a right to refuse consent would be to advise him of that right before eliciting his consent. That, however, is a suggestion that has been almost universally repudiated by both federal and state courts, and, we think, rightly so. For it would be thoroughly impractical to impose on the normal consent search the detailed requirements of an effective warning. Consent searches are part of the standard investigatory techniques of law enforcement agencies. They normally occur on the highway, or in a person's home or office, and under informal and unstructured conditions. The circumstances that prompt the initial request to search may develop quickly or be a logical extension of investigative police questioning. The police may seek to investigate further suspicious circumstances or to follow up leads developed in questioning persons at the scene of a crime. These situations are a far cry from the structured atmosphere of a trial where, assisted by counsel if he chooses, a defendant is informed of his trial rights. And, while surely a closer question, these situations are still immeasurably, far removed from "custodial interrogation" where, in *Miranda v. Arizona*, 384 U.S. 436, we found that the Constitution required certain now familiar warnings as a prerequisite to police interrogation. Indeed, in language applicable to the typical consent search, we refused to extend the need for warnings:

> "Our decision is not intended to hamper the traditional function of police officers in investigating crime. . . . When an individual is in custody on probable cause, the police may, of course, seek out evidence in the field to be used at trial against him. Such investigation may include inquiry of persons not under

restraint. General on-the-scene questioning as to facts surrounding a crime or other general questioning of citizens in the fact-finding process is not affected by our holding. It is an act of responsible citizenship for individuals to give whatever information they may have to aid in law enforcement."

Consequently, we cannot accept the position of the Court of Appeals in this case that proof of knowledge of the right to refuse consent is a necessary prerequisite to demonstrating a "voluntary" consent. Rather it is only by analyzing all the circumstances of an individual consent that it can be ascertained whether in fact it was voluntary or coerced. It is this careful sifting of the unique facts and circumstances of each case that is evidenced in our prior decisions involving consent searches.

For example in *Davis v. United States*, 328 U.S. 582, federal agents enforcing wartime gasoline-rationing regulations, arrested a filling station operator and asked to see his rationing coupons. He eventually unlocked a room where the agents discovered the coupons that formed the basis for his conviction. The District Court found that the petitioner had consented to the search — that although he had at first refused to turn the coupons over, he had soon been persuaded to do so and that force or threat of force had not been employed to persuade him. Concluding that it could not be said that this finding was erroneous, this Court, in an opinion by Mr. Justice Douglas that looked to all the circumstances surrounding the consent, affirmed the judgment of conviction: "The public character of the property, the fact that the demand was made during business hours at the place of business where the coupons were required to be kept, the existence of the right to inspect, the nature of the request, the fact that the initial refusal to turn the coupons over was soon followed by acquiescence in the demand — these circumstances all support the conclusion of the District Court."

Conversely, if under all the circumstances it has appeared that the consent was not given voluntarily — that it was coerced by threats or force, or granted only in submission to a claim of lawful authority — then we have found the consent invalid and the search unreasonable. *See, e.g., Bumper v. North Carolina*, 391 U.S., at 548-549. In *Bumper*, a 66-year-old Negro widow, who lived in a house located in a rural area at the end of an isolated mile-long dirt road, allowed four white law enforcement officials to search her home after they asserted they had a warrant to search the house. We held the alleged consent to be invalid, noting that "(w)hen a law enforcement officer claims authority to search a home under a warrant, he announces in effect that the occupant has no right to resist the search. The situation is instinct with coercion—albeit colorably lawful coercion. Where there is coercion there cannot be consent.''

Implicit in all of these cases is the recognition that knowledge of a right to refuse is not a prerequisite of a voluntary consent. If the prosecution were required to demonstrate such knowledge, *Davis* could not have found consent without evidence of that knowledge. And similarly if the failure to prove such knowledge were sufficient to show an ineffective consent, the *Bumper* opinion would surely have focused upon the subjective mental state of the person who consented. Yet it did not.

In short, neither this Court's prior cases, nor the traditional definition of "voluntariness" requires proof of knowledge of a right to refuse as the *sine qua non* of an effective consent to a search.

### C

It is said, however, that a "consent" is a "waiver" of a person's rights under the Fourth and Fourteenth Amendments. The argument is that by allowing the police to conduct a search, a person "waives" whatever right he had to prevent the police from searching. It is argued that under the doctrine of *Johnson v. Zerbst*, 304 U.S. 458, 464, to establish such a "waiver" the State must demonstrate "an intentional relinquishment or abandonment of a known right or privilege."

But these standards were enunciated in *Johnson* in the context of the safeguards of a fair criminal trial. Our cases do not reflect an uncritical demand for a knowing and intelligent waiver in every situation where a person has failed to invoke a constitutional protection.

A strict standard of waiver has been applied to those rights guaranteed to a criminal defendant to insure that he will be accorded the greatest possible opportunity to utilize every facet of the constitutional model of a fair criminal trial. Any trial conducted in derogation of that model leaves open the possibility that the trial reached an unfair result precisely because all the protections specified in the Constitution were not provided. A prime example is the right to counsel. For without that right, a wholly innocent accused faces the real and substantial danger that simply because of his lack of legal expertise he may be convicted. As Mr. Justice Harlan once wrote: "The sound reason why (the right to counsel) is so freely extended for a criminal trial is the severe injustice risked by confronting an untrained defendant with a range of technical points of law, evidence, and tactics familiar to the prosecutor but not

to himself.'' The Constitution requires that every effort be made to see to it that a defendant in a criminal case has not unknowingly relinquished the basic protections that the Framers thought indispensable to a fair trial.

The guarantees of the Fourth Amendment stand ''as a protection of quite different constitutional values—values reflecting the concern of our society for the right of each individual to be let alone. To recognize this is no more than to accord those values undiluted respect.''

Nor can it even be said that a search, as opposed to an eventual trial, is somehow "unfair" if a person consents to a search. While the Fourth and Fourteenth Amendments limit the circumstances under which the police can conduct a search, there is nothing constitutionally suspect in a person's voluntarily allowing a search. The actual conduct of the search may be precisely the same as if the police had obtained a warrant. And, unlike those constitutional guarantees that protect a defendant at trial, it cannot be said every reasonable presumption ought to be indulged against voluntary relinquishment. We have only recently stated: ''(I)t is no part of the policy underlying the Fourth and Fourteenth Amendments to discourage citizens from aiding to the utmost of their ability in the apprehension of criminals.'' *Coolidge*. Rather, the community has a real interest in encouraging consent, for the resulting search may yield necessary evidence for the solution and prosecution of crime, evidence that may insure that a wholly innocent person is not wrongly charged with a criminal offense.

It would be unrealistic to expect that in the informal, unstructured context of a consent search, a policeman, upon pain of tainting the evidence obtained, could make the detailed type of examination demanded by *Johnson*.

### D

Much of what has already been said disposes of the argument that the Court's decision in the *Miranda* case requires the conclusion that knowledge of a right to refuse is an indispensable element of a valid consent. The considerations that informed the Court's holding in *Miranda* are simply inapplicable in the present case. In *Miranda* the Court found that the techniques of police questioning and the nature of custodial surroundings produce an inherently coercive situation. The Court concluded that ''(u)nless adequate protective devices are employed to dispel the compulsion inherent in custodial surroundings, no statement obtained from the defendant can truly be the product of his free choice.'' And at another point the Court noted that "without proper safeguards the process of in-custody interrogation of persons suspected or accused of crime contains inherently compelling pressures which work to undermine the individual's will to resist and to compel him to speak where he would not otherwise do so freely."

In this case, there is no evidence of any inherently coercive tactics—either from the nature of the police questioning or the environment in which it took place. Indeed, since consent searches will normally occur on a person's own familiar territory, the specter of incommunicado police interrogation in some remote station house is simply inapposite.[36] There is no reason to believe, under circumstances such as are present here, that the response to a policeman's question is presumptively coerced; and there is, therefore, no reason to reject the traditional test for determining the voluntariness of a person's response. *Miranda*, of course, did not reach investigative questioning of a person not in custody, which is most directly analogous to the situation of a consent search, and it assuredly did not indicate that such questioning ought to be deemed inherently coercive.

It is also argued that the failure to require the Government to establish knowledge as a prerequisite to a valid consent, will relegate the Fourth Amendment to the special province of "the sophisticated, the knowledgeable and the privileged." We cannot agree. The traditional definition of voluntariness we accept today has always taken into account evidence of minimal schooling, low intelligence, and the lack of any effective warnings to a person of his rights; and the voluntariness of any statement taken under those conditions has been carefully scrutinized to determine whether it was in fact voluntarily given.

### E

Our decision today is a narrow one. We hold only that when the subject of a search is not in custody and the State attempts to justify a search on the basis of his consent, the Fourth and Fourteenth Amendments require that it demonstrate that the consent was in fact voluntarily given, and not the result of duress or coercion, express or implied. Voluntariness is a question of fact to be determined from all the circumstances, and while the subject's knowledge of a right to refuse is a factor to be taken into account, the prosecution is not required to demonstrate such

knowledge as a prerequisite to establishing a voluntary consent. Because the California court followed these principles in affirming the respondent's conviction, and because the Court of Appeals for the Ninth Circuit in remanding for an evidentiary hearing required more, its judgment must be reversed.

It is so ordered.

[Justice POWELL, joined by Justice REHNQUIST and Chief Justice BURGER, while concurring in the opinion, would have held that Busamonte's claim was not cognizable on habeas corpus.]

Mr. Justice MARSHALL, dissenting.

### I

I believe that the Court misstates the true issue in this case. That issue is not, as the Court suggests whether the police overbore Alcala's will in eliciting his consent, but rather, whether a simple statement of assent to search, without more, should be sufficient to permit the police to search and thus act as a relinquishment of Alcala's constitutional right to exclude the police. This Court has always scrutinized with great care claims that a person has forgone the opportunity to assert constitutional rights. I see no reason to give the claim that a person consented to a search any less rigorous scrutiny. Every case in this Court involving this kind of search has heretofore spoken of consent as a waiver.[4]

### A

The Court assumes that the issue in this case is:

---

[36] [T]he present case does not require a determination of what effect custodial conditions might have on a search authorized solely by an alleged consent.

---

[4] The Court reads *Davis v. United States*, 328 U.S. 582 (1946), as upholding a search like the one in this case on the basis of consent. But it was central to the reasoning of the Court in that case that the items seized were the property of the Government temporarily in Davis' custody. The agents of the Government were thus simply demanding that property to which they had a lawful claim be returned to them. Because of this, the Court held that "permissible limits of persuasion are not so narrow as where private papers are sought." The opinion of the Court therefore explicitly disclaimed stating a general rule for ordinary searches for evidence. That the distinction, for purposes of Fourth Amendment analysis, between mere evidence and contraband or instrumentalities has now been abolished, *Warden v. Hayden*, 387 U.S. 294 (1967), is no reason to disregard the fact that when *Davis* was decided, that distinction played an important role in shaping analysis.

what are the standards by which courts are to determine that consent is voluntarily given? It then imports into the law of search and seizure standards developed to decide entirely different questions about coerced confessions.[6]

The Fifth Amendment, in terms, provides that no person "shall be compelled in any criminal case to be a witness against himself." Nor is the interest protected by the Due Process Clause of the Fourteenth Amendment any different. The inquiry in a case where a confession is challenged as having been elicited in an unconstitutional manner is, therefore, whether the behavior of the police amounted to compulsion of the defendant. Because of the nature of the right to be free of compulsion, it would be pointless to ask whether a defendant knew of it before he made a statement; no sane person would knowingly relinquish a right to be free of compulsion. Thus, the questions of compulsion and of violation of the right itself are inextricably intertwined. The cases involving coerced confessions, therefore, pass over the question of knowledge of that right as irrelevant, and turn directly to the question of compulsion.

### B

In contrast, this case deals not with "coercion," but with "consent," a subtly different concept to which different standards have been applied in the past. Freedom from coercion is a substantive right, guaranteed by the Fifth and Fourteenth Amendments. Consent, however, is a mechanism by which substantive requirements, otherwise applicable, are avoided. In the context of the Fourth Amendment, the relevant substantive requirements are that searches be conducted only after evidence justifying them has been submitted to an impartial magistrate for a determination of probable cause. There are, of course, exceptions to these requirements based on a variety of exigent circumstances that make it impractical to invalidate a search simply because the police failed to get a warrant. But none of the exceptions relating to the overriding needs of law enforcement are applicable when a search is justified solely by consent. On the contrary, the needs of law enforcement are significantly more attenuated, for probable cause to search may be lacking but a search permitted if the subject's consent has been obtained. Thus,

consent searches are permitted, not because such an exception to the requirements of probable cause and warrant is essential to proper law enforcement, but because we permit our citizens to choose whether or not they wish to exercise their constitutional rights. Our prior decisions simply do not support the view that a meaningful choice has been made solely because no coercion was brought to bear on the subject.

For example, in *Bumper*, four law enforcement officers went to the home of Bumper's grandmother. They announced that they had a search warrant, and she permitted them to enter. Subsequently, the prosecutor chose not to rely on the warrant, but attempted to justify the search by the woman's consent. We held that consent could not be established "by showing no more than acquiescence to a claim of lawful authority." We did not there inquire into all the circumstances, but focused on a single fact, the claim of authority, even though the grandmother testified that no threats were made. It may be that, on the facts of that case, her consent was under all the circumstances involuntary, but it is plain that we did not apply the test adopted by the Court today. And, whatever the posture of the case when it reached this Court, it could not be said that the police in *Bumper* acted in a threatening or coercive manner, for they did have the warrant they said they had; the decision not to rely on it was made long after the search, when the case came into court.

That case makes it clear that police officers may not courteously order the subject of a search simply to stand aside while the officers carry out a search they have settled on. Yet there would be no coercion or brutality in giving that order. No interests that the Court today recognizes would be damaged in such a search. Thus, all the police must do is conduct what will inevitably be a charade of asking for consent. If they display any firmness at all, a verbal expression of assent will undoubtedly be forthcoming. I cannot believe that the protections of the Constitution mean so little.

### II

If consent to search means that a person has chosen to forgo his right to exclude the police from the place they seek to search, it follows that his consent cannot be considered a meaningful choice unless he knew that he could in fact exclude the police. The Court appears, however, to reject even the modest proposition that, if the subject of a search convinces the trier of fact that he did not know of his right to refuse assent to a police request for permission to search, the search must be held unconstitutional. For

---

[6] That this application of the "domino" method of adjudication is misguided is shown, I believe, by the fact that the phrase "voluntary consent" seems redundant in a way that the phrase "voluntary confession" does not.

it says only that "knowledge of the right to refuse consent is one factor to be taken into account." I find this incomprehensible. I can think of no other situation in which we would say that a person agreed to some course of action if he convinced us that he did not know that there was some other course he might have pursued. I would therefore hold, at a minimum, that the prosecution may not rely on a purported consent to search if the subject of the search did not know that he could refuse to give consent. That, I think, is the import of *Bumper*. Where the police claim authority to search yet in fact lack such authority, the subject does not know that he may permissibly refuse them entry, and it is this lack of knowledge that invalidates the consent.

If one accepts this view, the question then is a simple one: must the Government show that the subject knew of his rights, or must the subject show that he lacked such knowledge?

I think that any fair allocation of the burden would require that it be placed on the prosecution. On this question, the Court indulges in what might be called the "straw man" method of adjudication. The Court responds to this suggestion by overinflating the burden. And, when it is suggested that the *prosecution*'s burden of proof could be easily satisfied if the police informed the subject of his rights, the Court responds by refusing to require the *police* to make a "detailed" inquiry. If the Court candidly faced the real question of allocating the burden of proof, neither of these maneuvers would be available to it. If the burden is placed on the defendant, all the subject can do is to testify that he did not know of his rights. And I doubt that many trial judges will find for the defendant simply on the basis of that testimony. Precisely because the evidence is very hard to come by, courts have traditionally been reluctant to require a party to prove negatives such as the lack of knowledge.

In contrast, there are several ways by which the subject's knowledge of his rights may be shown. The subject may affirmatively demonstrate such knowledge by his responses at the time the search took place. Where, as in this case, the person giving consent is someone other than the defendant, the prosecution may require him to testify under oath. Denials of knowledge may be disproved by establishing that the subject had, in the recent past, demonstrated his knowledge of his rights, for example, by refusing entry when it was requested by the police. The prior experience or training of the subject might in some cases support an inference that he knew of his right to exclude the police.

The burden on the prosecutor would disappear, of course, if the police, at the time they requested consent to search, also told the subject that he had a right to refuse consent and that his decision to refuse would be respected. The Court's assertions to the contrary notwithstanding, there is nothing impractical about this method of satisfying the prosecution's burden of proof. It must be emphasized that the decision about informing the subject of his rights would lie with the officers seeking consent. If they believed that providing such information would impede their investigation, they might simply ask for consent, taking the risk that at some later date the prosecutor would be unable to prove that the subject knew of his rights or that some other basis for the search existed.

The Court contends that if an officer paused to inform the subject of his rights, the informality of the exchange would be destroyed. I doubt that a simple statement by an officer of an individual's right to refuse consent would do much to alter the informality of the exchange, except to alert the subject to a fact that he surely is entitled to know. It is not without significance that for many years the agents of the Federal Bureau of Investigation have routinely informed subjects of their right to refuse consent, when they request consent to search. The reported cases in which the police have informed subjects of their right to refuse consent show, also, that the information can be given without disrupting the casual flow of events. What evidence there is, then, rather strongly suggests that nothing disastrous would happen if the police, before requesting consent, informed the subject that he had a right to refuse consent and that his refusal would be respected.[12]

I must conclude with some reluctance that when the Court speaks of practicality, what it really is talking of is the continued ability of the police to

---

[12] The Court's suggestion that it would be "unrealistic" to require the officers to make "the detailed type of examination" involved when a court considers whether a defendant has waived a trial right deserves little comment. The question before us relates to the inquiry to be made in court when the prosecution seeks to establish that consent was given. I therefore do not address the Court's strained argument that one may waive constitutional rights without making a knowing and intentional choice so long as the rights do not relate to the fairness of a criminal trial. I would suggest, however, that that argument is fundamentally inconsistent with the law of unconstitutional conditions. In any event, I do not understand how one can relinquish a right without knowing of its existence, and that is the only issue in this case.

capitalize on the ignorance of citizens so as to accomplish by subterfuge what they could not achieve by relying only on the knowing relinquishment of constitutional rights. Of course it would be "practical" for the police to ignore the commands of the Fourth Amendment, if by practicality we mean that more criminals will be apprehended, even though the constitutional rights of innocent people also go by the board. But such a practical advantage is achieved only at the cost of permitting the police to disregard the limitations that the Constitution places on their behavior, a cost that a constitutional democracy cannot long absorb.

I find nothing in the opinion of the Court to dispel my belief that, in such a case, as the Court of Appeals for the Ninth Circuit said, "[u]nder many circumstances a reasonable person might read an officer's 'May I' as the courteous expression of a demand backed by force of law." Most cases, in my view, are akin to *Bumper*: consent is ordinarily given as acquiescence in an implicit claim of authority to search. Permitting searches in such circumstances, without any assurance at all that the subject of the search knew that, by his consent, he was relinquishing his constitutional rights, is something that I cannot believe is sanctioned by the Constitution.

### III

The proper resolution of this case turns, I believe, on a realistic assessment of the nature of the interchange between citizens and the police, and of the practical import of allocating the burden of proof in one way rather than another. The Court seeks to escape such assessments by escalating its rhetoric to unwarranted heights, but no matter how forceful the adjectives the Court uses, it cannot avoid being judged by how well its image of these interchanges

accords with reality. Although the Court says without real elaboration that it "cannot agree," the holding today confines the protection of the Fourth Amendment against searches conducted without probable cause to the sophisticated, the knowledgeable, and, I might add, the few.[13] In the final analysis, the Court now sanctions a game of blindman's buff, in which the police always have the upper hand, for the sake of nothing more than the convenience of the police. But the guarantees of the Fourth Amendment were never intended to shrink before such an ephemeral and changeable interest. The Framers of the Fourth Amendment struck the balance against this sort of convenience and in favor of certain basic civil rights. It is not for this Court to restrike that balance because of its own views of the needs of law enforcement officers. I fear that that is the effect of the Court's decision today.

It is regrettable that the obsession with validating searches like that conducted in this case, so evident in the Court's hyperbole, has obscured the Court's vision of how the Fourth Amendment was designed to govern the relationship between police and citizen in our society. I believe that experience and careful reflection show how narrow and inaccurate that vision is, and I respectfully dissent.

Justice DOUGLAS and BRENNAN also dissented.

---

[13] The Court's half-hearted defense, that lack of knowledge is to be "taken into account," rings rather hollow, in light of the apparent import of the opinion that even a subject who proves his lack of knowledge may nonetheless have consented "voluntarily," under the Court's peculiar definition of voluntariness.

## QUESTIONS AND NOTES

**1.** Do you believe that the need for consent searches is especially important for the police? Does your answer to this question impact on your judgment about the correctness of the Court's decision?

**2.** What percentage of the populace do you believe would feel free to decline consent in the *Schneckloth* situation? Would you have felt free to refuse consent before you entered law school? Would you feel free to decline consent now?

**3.** If the Marshall opinion had prevailed, and you were a police attorney, could you devise a warning that would not break the informality of the police/citizen dialogue? If you can, would it follow that the majority reached the wrong result?

**4.** Is the concept of "voluntary consent" redundant as Justice Marshall suggests in footnote 6? If so, is he correct in rejecting the voluntary confession cases as appropriate analogues?

**5.** Is there a good reason for rejecting the *Johnson v. Zerbst* waiver standard?

**6.** Assuming that your answer to question 5 was "yes," can you still make an argument against the Court's result?

**7.** Might it not be to an innocent citizen's advantage to consent to a search and thereby dispel suspicion? If so, did the majority reach the correct result?

**8.** Is there a meaningful distinction between *Schneckloth* and *Bumper*?

**9.** Would a good citizen consent to a search?

**10.** In *Rodriguez*, we consider the problem of third party consent.

## Illinois v. Rodriguez
### 497 U.S. 177 (1990)

Justice SCALIA delivered the opinion of the Court.

In *United States v. Matlock*, 415 U.S. 164 (1974), this Court reaffirmed that a warrantless entry and search by law enforcement officers does not violate the Fourth Amendment's proscription of "unreasonable searches and seizures" if the officers have obtained the consent of a third party who possesses common authority over the premises. The present case presents an issue we expressly reserved in *Matlock*: whether a warrantless entry is valid when based upon the consent of a third party whom the police, at the time of the entry, reasonably believe to possess common authority over the premises, but who in fact does not do so.

### I

On July 26, 1985, police were summoned to the residence of Dorothy Jackson on South Wolcott in Chicago. They were met by Ms. Jackson's daughter, Gail Fischer, who showed signs of a severe beating. She told the officers that she had been assaulted by respondent Edward Rodriguez earlier that day in an apartment on South California. Fischer stated that Rodriguez was then asleep in the apartment, and she consented to travel there with the police in order to unlock the door with her key so that the officers could enter and arrest him. During this conversation, Fischer several times referred to the apartment on South California as "our" apartment, and said that she had clothes and furniture there. It is unclear whether she indicated that she currently lived at the apartment, or only that she used to live there.

The police officers drove to the apartment on South California, accompanied by Fischer. They did not obtain an arrest warrant for Rodriguez, nor did they seek a search warrant for the apartment. At the apartment, Fischer unlocked the door with her key and gave the officers permission to enter. They moved through the door into the living room, where they observed in plain view drug paraphernalia and containers filled with white powder that they believed (correctly, as later analysis showed) to be cocaine. They proceeded to the bedroom, where they found Rodriguez asleep and discovered additional containers of white powder in two open attache cases. The officers arrested Rodriguez and seized the drugs and related paraphernalia.

### II

The Fourth Amendment generally prohibits the warrantless entry of a person's home, whether to make an arrest or to search for specific objects. *Payton*. The prohibition does not apply, however, to situations in which voluntary consent has been obtained, either from the individual whose property is searched, see *Schneckloth*, or from a third party who possesses common authority over the premises, see *Matlock*. The State of Illinois contends that that exception applies in the present case.

As we stated in *Matlock*, "[c]ommon authority" rests "on mutual use of the property by persons generally having joint access or control for most purposes. . . ." The burden of establishing that common authority rests upon the State. On the basis of this record, it is clear that burden was not sustained. The evidence showed that although Fischer, with her two small children, had lived with Rodriguez beginning in December 1984, she had moved out on July 1, 1985, almost a month before the search at issue here, and had gone to live with her mother. She took her and her children's clothing with her, though leaving behind some furniture and household effects. During the period after July 1 she sometimes spent the night at Rodriguez's apartment, but never invited her friends there, and never went there herself when he was not home. Her name was not on the lease nor did she contribute to the rent. She had a key to the apartment, which she said at trial she had taken without Rodriguez's knowledge (though she testified at the preliminary hearing that Rodriguez had given her the key). On these facts the State has not established that, with respect to the South California apartment, Fischer had "joint access or control for most purposes." To the contrary, the Appellate Court's determination of no common authority over the apartment was obviously correct.

### III

[R]espondent asserts that permitting a reasonable belief of common authority to validate an entry would cause a defendant's Fourth Amendment rights to be "vicariously waived." We disagree.

What Rodriguez is assured by the trial right of the exclusionary rule, where it applies, is that no evidence seized in violation of the Fourth Amendment will be introduced at his trial unless he consents. What he is assured by the Fourth Amendment itself, however, is not that no government search of his house will occur unless he consents; but that no such search will occur that is "unreasonable." There are various elements, of course, that can make a search of a person's house "reasonable" – one of which is the consent of the person or his cotenant. The essence of respondent's argument is that we should impose upon this element a requirement that we have not imposed upon other elements that regularly compel government officers to exercise judgment regarding the facts: namely, the requirement that their judgment be not only responsible but correct.

The fundamental objective that alone validates all unconsented government searches is, of course, the seizure of persons who have committed or are about to commit crimes, or of evidence related to crimes. But "reasonableness," with respect to this necessary element, does not demand that the government be factually correct in its assessment that that is what a search will produce. Warrants need only be supported by "probable cause," which demands no more than a proper "assessment of probabilities in particular factual contexts. . . ." *Gates*. If a magistrate, based upon seemingly reliable but factually inaccurate information, issues a warrant for the search of a house in which the sought-after felon is not present, has never been present, and was never likely to have been present, the owner of that house suffers one of the inconveniences we all expose ourselves to as the cost of living in a safe society; he does not suffer a violation of the Fourth Amendment.

Another element often, though not invariably, required in order to render an unconsented search "reasonable" is, of course, that the officer be authorized by a valid warrant. Here also we have not

held that "reasonableness" precludes error with respect to those factual judgments that law enforcement officials are expected to make. In *Maryland v. Garrison*, 480 V.5 79 (1987) a warrant supported by probable cause with respect to one apartment was erroneously issued for an entire floor that was divided (though not clearly) into two apartments. We upheld the search of the apartment not properly covered by the warrant. We said:

> "[T]he validity of the search of respondent's apartment pursuant to a warrant authorizing the search of the entire third floor depends on whether the officers' failure to realize the overbreadth of the warrant was objectively understandable and reasonable. Here it unquestionably was. The objective facts available to the officers at the time suggested no distinction between [the suspect's] apartment and the third-floor premises."

The ordinary requirement of a warrant is sometimes supplanted by other elements that render the unconsented search "reasonable." Here also we have not held that the Fourth Amendment requires factual accuracy. A warrant is not needed, for example, where the search is incident to an arrest. In *Hill v. California*, 401 U.S. 797 (1971), we upheld a search incident to an arrest, even though the arrest was made of the wrong person. We said:

> "The upshot was that the officers in good faith believed Miller was Hill and arrested him. They were quite wrong as it turned out, and subjective good-faith belief would not in itself justify either the arrest or the subsequent search. But sufficient probability, not certainty, is the touchstone of reasonableness under the Fourth Amendment and on the record before us the officers' mistake was understandable and the arrest a reasonable response to the situation facing them at the time."

*Stoner v. California*, 376 U.S. 483 (1964) is in our view not to the contrary. There, in holding that police had improperly entered the defendant's hotel room based on the consent of a hotel clerk, we stated that "the rights protected by the Fourth Amendment are not to be eroded . . . by unrealistic doctrines of 'apparent authority.'" It is ambiguous, of course, whether the word "unrealistic" is descriptive or limiting – that is, whether we were condemning as unrealistic all reliance upon apparent authority, or whether we were condemning only such reliance upon apparent authority as is unrealistic. Similarly ambiguous is the opinion's earlier statement that "there [is no] substance to the claim that the search was reasonable because the police, relying upon the night clerk's expressions of consent, had a reasonable basis for the belief that the clerk had authority to consent to the search." Was there no substance to it because it failed as a matter of law, or because the facts could not possibly support it? At one point the opinion does seem to speak clearly:

"It is important to bear in mind that it was the petitioner's constitutional right which was at stake here, and not the night clerk's nor the hotel's. It was a right, therefore, which only the petitioner could waive by word or deed, either directly or through an agent."

But as we have discussed, what is at issue when a claim of apparent consent is raised is not whether the right to be free of searches has been *waived*, but whether the right to be free of *unreasonable* searches has been *violated*. Even if one does not think the *Stoner* opinion had this subtlety in mind, the supposed clarity of its foregoing statement is immediately compromised, as follows:

"It is true that the night clerk clearly and unambiguously consented to the search. But there is nothing in the record to indicate that *the police had any basis whatsoever to believe that* the night clerk had been authorized by the petitioner to permit the police to search the petitioner's room." (emphasis added).

The italicized language should have been deleted, of course, if the statement two sentences earlier meant that an appearance of authority could never validate a search. In the last analysis, one must admit that the rationale of *Stoner* was ambiguous — and perhaps deliberately so. It is at least a reasonable reading of the case, and perhaps a preferable one, that the police could not rely upon the obtained consent because they knew it came from a hotel clerk, knew that the room was rented and exclusively occupied by the defendant, and could not reasonably have believed that the former had general access to or control over the latter.

As *Stoner* demonstrates, what we hold today does not suggest that law enforcement officers may always accept a person's invitation to enter premises. Even when the invitation is accompanied by an explicit assertion that the person lives there, the surrounding circumstances could conceivably be such that a reasonable person would doubt its truth and not act upon it without further inquiry. As with other factual determinations bearing upon search and seizure, determination of consent to enter must "be judged against an objective standard: would the facts available to the officer at the moment . . . 'warrant a man of reasonable caution in the belief'" that the consenting party had authority over the premises? If not, then warrantless entry without further inquiry is unlawful unless authority actually exists. But if so, the search is valid.

In the present case, the Appellate Court found it unnecessary to determine whether the officers reasonably believed that Fischer had the authority to consent, because it ruled as a matter of law that a reasonable belief could not validate the entry. Since we find that ruling to be in error, we remand for consideration of that question. The judgment of the Illinois Appellate Court is reversed and remanded for further proceedings not inconsistent with this opinion.

So ordered.

Justice MARSHALL, with whom Justice BRENNAN and Justice STEVENS join, dissenting.

Dorothy Jackson summoned police officers to her house to report that her daughter Gail Fischer had been beaten. Fischer told police that Ed Rodriguez, her boyfriend, was her assaulter. During an interview with Fischer, one of the officers asked if Rodriguez dealt in narcotics. Fischer did not respond. Fischer did agree, however, to the officers' request to let them into Rodriguez's apartment so that they could arrest him for battery. The police, without a warrant and despite the absence of an exigency, entered Rodriguez's home to arrest him. As a result of their entry, the police discovered narcotics that the State subsequently sought to introduce in a drug prosecution against Rodriguez.

The baseline for the reasonableness of a search or seizure in the home is the presence of a warrant. Indeed, "searches and seizures inside a home without a warrant are presumptively unreasonable." Exceptions to the warrant requirement must therefore serve "compelling" law enforcement goals. Because the sole law enforcement purpose underlying third-party consent searches is avoiding the inconvenience of securing a warrant, a departure from the warrant requirement is not justified simply because an officer reasonably believes a third party has consented to a search of the defendant's home. In holding otherwise, the majority ignores our longstanding view that "the informed and deliberate determinations of magistrates . . . as to what searches and seizures are permissible under the Constitution are to be preferred over the hurried action of officers and others who may happen to make arrests."

I

The Court has tolerated departures from the warrant requirement only when an exigency makes a warrantless search imperative to the safety of the police and of the community. In the absence of an exigency, then, warrantless home searches and seizures are unreasonable under the Fourth Amendment. The weighty constitutional interest in preventing unauthorized intrusions into the home overrides any law enforcement interest in relying on the reasonable but potentially mistaken belief that a third party has authority to consent to such a search or seizure. Indeed, as the present case illustrates, only the minimal interest in avoiding the inconvenience of obtaining a warrant weighs in on the law enforcement side.

Unlike searches conducted pursuant to the recognized exceptions to the warrant requirement, third-party consent searches are not based on an exigency and therefore serve no compelling social goal. Police officers, when faced with the choice of relying on consent by a third party or securing a warrant, should secure a warrant, and must therefore accept the risk of error should they instead choose to rely on consent.

## II

Our prior cases discussing searches based on third-party consent have never suggested that such searches are "reasonable." In *Matlock*, this Court upheld a warrantless search conducted pursuant to the consent of a third party who was living with the defendant. The Court rejected the defendant's challenge to the search, stating that a person who permits others to have "joint access or control for most purposes . . . assume[s] the risk that [such persons] might permit the common area to be searched." As the Court's assumption-of-risk analysis makes clear, third-party consent limits a person's ability to challenge the reasonableness of the search only because that person voluntarily has relinquished some of his expectation of privacy by sharing access or control over his property with another person.

A search conducted pursuant to an officer's reasonable but mistaken belief that a third party had authority to consent is thus on an entirely different constitutional footing from one based on the consent of a third party who in fact has such authority. Even if the officers reasonably believed that Fischer had authority to consent, she did not, and Rodriguez's expectation of privacy was therefore undiminished. Rodriguez accordingly can challenge the warrantless intrusion into his home as a violation of the Fourth Amendment. This conclusion flows directly from *Stoner*. There, the Court required the suppression of evidence seized in reliance on a hotel clerk's consent to a warrantless search of a guest's room. The Court reasoned that the guest's right to be free of unwarranted intrusion "was a right . . . which only [he] could waive by word or deed, either directly or through an agent." Accordingly, the Court rejected resort to "unrealistic doctrines of 'apparent authority' " as a means of upholding the search to which the guest had not consented.

## III

Acknowledging that the third party in this case lacked authority to consent, the majority seeks to rely on cases suggesting that reasonable but mistaken factual judgments by police will not invalidate otherwise reasonable searches. The majority reads these cases as establishing a "general rule" that "what is generally demanded of the many factual determinations that must regularly be made by agents of the government—whether the magistrate issuing a warrant, the police officer executing a warrant, or the police officer conducting a search or seizure under one of the exceptions to the warrant requirement—is not that they always be correct, but that they always be reasonable."

The majority's assertion, however, is premised on the erroneous assumption that third-party consent searches are generally reasonable. Because reasonable factual errors by law enforcement officers will not validate unreasonable searches, the reasonableness of the officer's mistaken belief that the third party had authority to consent is irrelevant.

The majority's reliance on *Garrison* is also misplaced. In *Garrison*, the police obtained a valid warrant for the search of the "third floor apartment" of a building whose third floor in fact housed two apartments. Although the police had probable cause to search only one of the apartments, they entered both apartments because "[t]he objective facts available to the officers at the time suggested no distinction between [the apartment for which they legitimately had the warrant and the entire third floor]." The Court held that the officers' reasonable mistake of fact did not render the search unconstitutional. Because searches based on warrants are generally reasonable, the officers' reasonable mistake of fact did not render their search "unreasonable." This reasoning is evident in the Court's conclusion that little would be gained by adopting additional burdens "over and above the bedrock requirement that, with the exceptions we have traced in our cases, the police may conduct searches only pursuant to a reasonably detailed warrant."

*Garrison* thus tells us nothing about the reasonableness under the Fourth Amendment of a warrantless arrest in the home based on an officer's reasonable but mistaken belief that the third party consenting to the arrest was empowered to do so.

### IV

Our cases demonstrate that third-party consent searches are free from constitutional challenge only to the extent that they rest on consent by a party empowered to do so. The majority's conclusion to the contrary ignores the legitimate expectations of privacy on which individuals are entitled to rely. That a person who allows another joint access over his property thereby limits his expectation of privacy does not justify trampling the rights of a person who has not similarly relinquished any of his privacy expectation.

Instead of judging the validity of consent searches, as we have in the past, based on whether a defendant has in fact limited his expectation of privacy, the Court today carves out an additional exception to the warrant requirement for third-party consent searches without pausing to consider whether " 'the exigencies of the situation' make the needs of law enforcement so compelling that the warrantless search is objectively reasonable under the Fourth Amendment.'' Where this free-floating creation of ''reasonable'' exceptions to the warrant requirement will end, now that the Court has departed from the balancing approach that has long been part of our Fourth Amendment jurisprudence, is unclear. But by allowing a person to be subjected to a warrantless search in his home without his consent and without exigency, the majority has taken away some of the liberty that the Fourth Amendment was designed to protect.

## QUESTIONS AND NOTES

**1.** Is the theory of a consent search that it is not a search at all or that it is a reasonable search? What would Scalia say? What would Marshall say?

**2.** Does your answer to question 1 affect the result in *Rodriguez*?

**3.** Are consent searches to be encouraged because they prevent (or reduce) adversarial police/citizen contact?

**4.** On the other hand, are consent searches to be discouraged because they circumvent the salutary principles of the Fourth Amendment?

**5.** Do your answers to questions 3 and 4 affect your assessment of *Rodriguez*? Explain.

**6.** Had you been on the Court, how would you have resolved *Rodriguez*? Why?

# 13.

# THE EXCLUSIONARY RULE

We have postponed until now an examination of the exclusionary rule. Heretofore, we have simply assumed that unconstitutionally obtained evidence may not be introduced against the victim of the unconstitutional search or seizure. Now that we know what it means to call something an unreasonable search or seizure, it is appropriate to consider whether or not (and under what circumstances) the exclusionary rule ought to apply.

## A.   The Rationale For The Exclusionary Rule

In analyzing the rationale for the exclusionary rule, we begin with a look at the opinion of the Court in the famous case of *Mapp v. Ohio*. At the time that *Mapp* was decided, not all provisions of the Bill of Rights were applicable to the states. Rather, the states were bound by only those provisions deemed fundamental. Bear that in mind as you read *Mapp*.

### Mapp v. Ohio
367 U.S. 643 (1961)

Mr. Justice CLARK delivered the opinion of the Court.

On May 23, 1957, three Cleveland police officers arrived at appellant's residence in that city pursuant to information that "a person (was) hiding out in the home, who was wanted for questioning in connection with a recent bombing, and that there was a large amount of policy paraphernalia being hidden in the home." Miss Mapp and her daughter by a former marriage lived on the top floor of the two-family dwelling. Upon their arrival at that house, the officers knocked on the door and demanded entrance but appellant, after telephoning her attorney, refused to admit them without a search warrant. They advised their headquarters of the situation and undertook a surveillance of the house.

The officers again sought entrance some three hours later when four or more additional officers arrived on the scene. When Miss Mapp did not come to the door immediately, at least one of the several doors to the house was forcibly opened and the policemen gained admittance. Meanwhile Miss Mapp's attorney arrived, but the officers, having secured their own entry, and continuing in their defiance of the law, would permit him neither to see Miss Mapp nor to enter the house. It appears that Miss Mapp was halfway down the stairs from the upper floor to the front door when the officers, in this highhanded manner, broke into the hall. She demanded to see the search warrant. A paper, claimed to be a warrant, was held up by one of the officers. She grabbed the "warrant" and placed it in her bosom. A struggle ensued in which the officers recovered the piece of paper and as a result of which they handcuffed appellant because she had been "belligerent" in resisting their official rescue of the "warrant" from her person. Running roughshod over appellant, a policeman "grabbed" her, "twisted [her] hand," and she "yelled [and] pleaded with him" because "it was hurting." Appellant, in handcuffs, was then forcibly taken upstairs to her bedroom where the officers searched a dresser, a chest of drawers, a closet and some suitcases. They also looked into a photo album and through personal papers belonging to the appellant. The search spread to the rest of the second floor including the child's bedroom, the living room, the kitchen and a dinette. The basement of the building and a trunk found therein were also searched. The obscene materials for possession of which she was ultimately convicted were discovered in the course of that widespread search.

The State says that even if the search were made without authority, or otherwise unreasonably, it is not prevented from using the unconstitutionally seized evidence at trial, citing *Wolf v. Colorado*, 338 U.S. 25 (1949), in which this Court did indeed hold "that in a prosecution in a State court for a State crime the Fourteenth Amendment does not forbid the admission of evidence obtained by an unreasonable search and seizure."

## I

[T]his Court, in *Weeks v. United States*, 232 U.S. 383 (1914), dealing with the use of evidence unconstitutionally seized, concluded:

"If letters and private documents can thus be seized and held and used in evidence against a citizen accused of an offense, the protection of the Fourth Amendment declaring his right to be secure against such searches and seizures is of no value, and, so far as those thus placed are concerned, might as well be stricken from the Constitution. The efforts of the courts and their officials to bring the guilty to punishment,

praiseworthy as they are, are not to be aided by the sacrifice of those great principles established by years of endeavor and suffering which have resulted in their embodiment in the fundamental law of the land."

Finally, the Court in that case clearly stated that use of the seized evidence involved "a denial of the constitutional rights of the accused." Thus, in the year 1914, in the *Weeks* case, this Court "for the first time" held that "in a federal prosecution the Fourth Amendment barred the use of evidence secured through an illegal search and seizure."

There are in the cases of this Court some passing references to the *Weeks* rule as being one of evidence. But the plain and unequivocal language of *Weeks* — and its later paraphrase in *Wolf* — to the effect that the *Weeks* rule is of constitutional origin, remains entirely undisturbed. In *Byars v. United States*, 273 U.S. 28 (1927), a unanimous Court declared that "the doctrine [cannot] . . . be tolerated *under our constitutional system*, that evidences of crime discovered by a federal officer in making a search without lawful warrant may be used against the victim of the unlawful search where a timely challenge has been interposed." (Emphasis added). The Court, in *Olmstead v. United States*, 277 U.S. 438 (1928), in unmistakable language restated the *Weeks* rule:

"The striking outcome of the Weeks case and those which followed it was the sweeping declaration that the Fourth Amendment, although not referring to or limiting the use of evidence in court, really forbade its introduction if obtained by government officers through a violation of the amendment."

## II

In 1949, 35 years after *Weeks* was announced, this Court, in *Wolf*, again for the first time, discussed the effect of the Fourth Amendment upon the States through the operation of the Due Process Clause of the Fourteenth Amendment. It said:

"[W]e have no hesitation in saying that were a State affirmatively to sanction such police incursion into privacy it would run counter to the guaranty of the Fourteenth Amendment."

Nevertheless, after declaring that the "security of one's privacy against arbitrary intrusion by the police" is "implicit in 'the concept of ordered liberty' and as such enforceable against the States through the Due Process Clause," and announcing that it "stoutly adhere(d)" to the *Weeks* decision, the Court decided that the *Weeks* exclusionary rule would not then be imposed upon the States as "an essential ingredient of the right." The Court's reasons for not considering essential to the right to privacy, as a curb imposed upon the States by the Due Process Clause, that which decades before had been posited as part and parcel of the Fourth Amendment's limitations upon federal encroachment of individual privacy, were bottomed on factual considerations.

The Court in *Wolf* first stated that "[t]he contrariety of views of the States" on the adoption of the exclusionary rule of *Weeks* was "particularly impressive" and, in this connection that it could not "brush aside the experience of States which deem the incidence of such conduct by the police too slight to call for a deterrent remedy . . . by overriding the [States'] relevant rules of evidence." While in 1949, prior to the *Wolf* case, almost two-thirds of the States were opposed to the use of the exclusionary rule, now, despite the *Wolf* case, more than half of those since passing upon it, by their own legislative or judicial decision, have wholly or partly adopted or adhered to the *Weeks* rule. Significantly, among those now following the rule is California, which, according to its highest court, was "compelled to reach that conclusion because other remedies have completely failed to secure compliance with the constitutional provisions. . . ." *People v. Cahan*, 282 P.2d 905, 911 (1955). In connection with this California case, we note that the second basis elaborated in *Wolf* in support of its failure to enforce the exclusionary doctrine against the States was that "other means of protection" have been afforded "the right to privacy."[7] The experience of California that such other remedies have been worthless and futile is buttressed by the experience of other States. The obvious futility of relegating the Fourth Amendment to the protection of other remedies has, moreover, been recognized by this Court since *Wolf*.

It, therefore, plainly appears that the factual considerations supporting the failure of the *Wolf* Court to include the *Weeks* exclusionary rule when it recognized the enforceability of the right to privacy against the States in 1949, while not basically relevant to the constitutional consideration, could not, in any analysis, now be deemed controlling.

IV

[I]n extending the substantive protections of due process to all constitutionally unreasonable

searches—state or federal—it was logically and constitutionally necessary that the exclusion doctrine—an essential part of the right to privacy—be also insisted upon as an essential ingredient of the right newly recognized by the *Wolf* case. In short, the admission of the new constitutional right by *Wolf* could not consistently tolerate denial of its most important constitutional privilege, namely, the exclusion of the evidence which an accused had been forced to give by reason of the unlawful seizure. To hold otherwise is to grant the right but in reality to withhold its privilege and enjoyment. Only last year the Court itself recognized that the purpose of the exclusionary rule "is to deter—to compel respect for the constitutional guaranty in the only effectively available way—by removing the incentive to disregard it." *Elkins v. United States*, 364 U.S. 206 (1960).

Indeed, we are aware of no restraint, similar to that rejected today, conditioning the enforcement of any other basic constitutional right. The right to privacy, no less important than any other right carefully and particularly reserved to the people, would stand in marked contrast to all other rights declared as "basic to a free society." *Wolf*. This Court has not hesitated to enforce as strictly against the States as it does against the Federal Government the rights of free speech and of a free press, the rights to notice and to a fair, public trial, including, as it does, the right not to be convicted by use of a coerced confession, however logically relevant it be, and without regard to its reliability. *Rogers v. Richmond*, 365 U.S. 534 (1961). And nothing could be more certain than that when a coerced confession is involved, "the relevant rules of evidence" are overridden without regard to "the incidence of such conduct by the police," slight or frequent. Why should not the same rule apply to what is tantamount to coerced testimony by way of unconstitutional seizure of goods, papers, effect, documents, etc.? We find that, as to the Federal Government, the Fourth and Fifth Amendments and, as to the States, the freedom from unconscionable invasions of privacy and the freedom from convictions based upon coerced confessions do enjoy an "intimate relation" in their perpetuation of "principles of humanity and civil liberty (secured) . . . only after years of struggle." They express "supplementing phases of the same constitutional purpose—to maintain inviolate large areas of personal privacy." The philosophy of each Amendment and of each freedom is complementary to, although not dependent upon, that of the other in its sphere of influence—the very least that together they assure in either sphere is that no man is to be convicted on

---

[7] Less than half of the States have any criminal provisions relating directly to unreasonable searches and seizures.

unconstitutional evidence.

## V

There are those who say, as did Justice (then Judge) Cardozo, that under our constitutional exclusionary doctrine "[t]he criminal is to go free because the constable has blundered." *People v. Defore*, 150 N.E. at page 587. In some cases this will undoubtedly be the result. But, as was said in *Elkins*, "there is another consideration – the imperative of judicial integrity." The criminal goes free, if he must, but it is the law that sets him free. Nothing can destroy a government more quickly than its failure to observe its own laws, or worse, its disregard of the charter of its own existence. As Mr. Justice Brandeis, dissenting, said in *Olmstead v. United States*, 277 U.S. 438 (1928): "Our government is the potent, the omnipresent teacher. For good or for ill, it teaches the whole people by its example. . . . If the government becomes a lawbreaker, it breeds contempt for law; it invites every man to become a law unto himself; it invites anarchy." Nor can it lightly be assumed that, as a practical matter, adoption of the exclusionary rule fetters law enforcement. Only last year this Court expressly considered that contention and found that "pragmatic evidence of a sort" to the contrary was not wanting. *Elkins*. The Court noted that:

> "The federal courts themselves have operated under the exclusionary rule of *Weeks* for almost half a century; yet it has not been suggested either that the Federal Bureau of Investigation has thereby been rendered ineffective, or that the administration of criminal justice in the federal courts has thereby been disrupted. Moreover, the experience of the states is impressive. . . . The movement towards the rule of exclusion has been halting but seemingly inexorable."

The ignoble shortcut to conviction left open to the State tends to destroy the entire system of constitutional restraints on which the liberties of the people rest. Having once recognized that the right to privacy embodied in the Fourth Amendment is enforceable against the States, and that the right to be secure against rude invasions of privacy by state officers is, therefore, constitutional in origin, we can no longer permit that right to remain an empty promise. Because it is enforceable in the same manner and to like effect as other basic rights secured by the Due Process Clause, we can no longer permit it to be revocable at the whim of any police officer who, in the name of law enforcement itself, chooses to suspend its enjoyment. Our decision, founded on reason and truth, gives to the individual no more than that which the Constitution guarantees him, to the police officer no less than that to which honest law enforcement is entitled, and, to the courts, that judicial integrity so necessary in the true administration of justice.

The judgment of the Supreme Court of Ohio is reversed and the cause remanded for further proceedings not inconsistent with this opinion.

Reversed and remanded.

[Justices BLACK and DOUGLAS wrote separate concurring opinions. Justice STEWART concurred in the result on other grounds. Justices FRANKFURTER, WHITTAKER and HARLAN dissented.]

## QUESTIONS AND NOTES

**1.** Is there any logic to not *automatically* applying the exclusionary remedy if there has been a violation? Does it make any sense to say that the police violated your rights in obtaining evidence, but they can use it anyway?

**2.** Which of the following factors influenced the Court's decision: A. The exclusionary rule creates a disincentive for the police to conduct unconstitutional searches, B. The exclusionary rule deters unconstitutional searches, C. The exclusionary rule is an inherent right of the victim of an unconstitutional search or seizure, D. Considerations of judicial integrity compel the exclusionary rule?

**3.** Which of the factors in question 2 do you find most persuasive?

**4.** How, if at all, are factors A and B in question 2 different? To the extent that they are different, which one ought to be deemed more significant?

**5.** Under the exclusionary rule, is it fair to say that "the criminal goes free because the constable has blundered?" Explain.

**6.** Does the benefit of the exclusionary rule necessarily redound solely to the benefit of criminals? If so, is that a good reason for abandoning it?

**7.** In an ideal system of jurisprudence, would we have an exclusionary rule? Explain.

**8.** As you read *Calandra*, consider whether it would change any of your answers to the preceding questions.

## United States v. Calandra
### 414 U.S. 338 (1973)

Mr. Justice POWELL delivered the opinion of the Court.

This case presents the question whether a witness summoned to appear and testify before a grand jury may refuse to answer questions on the ground that they are based on evidence obtained from an unlawful search and seizure. The issue is of considerable importance to the administration of criminal justice.

### III

In the instant case, the Court of Appeals held that the exclusionary rule of the Fourth Amendment limits the grand jury's power to compel a witness to answer questions based on evidence obtained from a prior unlawful search and seizure. The exclusionary rule was adopted to effectuate the Fourth Amendment right of all citizens "to be secure in their persons, houses, papers, and effects, against unreasonable searches and seizures. . . ." Under this rule, evidence obtained in violation of the Fourth Amendment cannot be used in a criminal proceeding against the victim of the illegal search and seizure. This prohibition applies as well to the fruits of the illegally seized evidence.

The purpose of the exclusionary rule is not to redress the injury to the privacy of the search victim:

"[T]he ruptured privacy of the victims' homes and effects cannot be restored. Reparation comes too late." *Linkletter v. Walker*, 381 U.S. 618, 637 (1965).

Instead, the rule's prime purpose is to deter future unlawful police conduct and thereby effectuate the guarantee of the Fourth Amendment against unreasonable searches and seizures:

"The rule is calculated to prevent, not to repair. Its purpose is to deter—to compel respect for the constitutional guaranty in the only effectively available way—by removing the incentive to disregard it." *Elkins v. United States*, 364 U.S. 206, 217 (1960).

In sum, the rule is a judicially created remedy designed to safeguard Fourth Amendment rights generally through its deterrent effect, rather than a personal constitutional right of the party aggrieved.[5]

Despite its broad deterrent purpose, the exclusionary rule has never been interpreted to proscribe the use of illegally seized evidence in all proceedings or against all persons. As with any remedial device, the application of the rule has been restricted to those areas where its remedial objectives are thought most efficaciously served. The balancing process implicit in this approach is expressed in the contours of the standing requirement. Thus, standing to invoke the exclusionary rule has been confined to situations where the Government seeks to use such evidence to incriminate the victim of the unlawful search. This standing rule is premised on a recognition that the need for deterrence and hence the rationale for excluding the evidence are strongest where the Government's unlawful conduct would result in imposition of a criminal sanction on the victim of the search.

### IV

In deciding whether to extend the exclusionary rule to grand jury proceedings, we must weigh the potential injury to the historic role and functions of the grand jury against the potential benefits of the rule as applied in this context. It is evident that this extension of the exclusionary rule would seriously impede the grand jury. Because the grand jury does not finally adjudicate guilt or innocence, it has traditionally been allowed to pursue its investigative and

---

[5] There is some disagreement as to the practical efficacy of the exclusionary rule, and as the Court noted in *Elkins v. United States*, relevant "[e]mpirical statistics are not available." Cf. Oaks, Studying the Exclusionary Rule in Search and Seizure, 37 U.Chi.L.Rev. 665 (1970). We have no occasion in the present case to consider the extent of the rule's efficacy in criminal trials.

accusatorial functions unimpeded by the evidentiary and procedural restrictions applicable to a criminal trial. Permitting witnesses to invoke the exclusionary rule before a grand jury would precipitate adjudication of issues hitherto reserved for the trial on the merits and would delay and disrupt grand jury proceedings. Suppression hearings would halt the orderly progress of an investigation and might necessitate extended litigation of issues only tangentially related to the grand jury's primary objective.[7] The probable result would be "protracted interruption of grand jury proceedings," effectively transforming them into preliminary trials on the merits. In some cases the delay might be fatal to the enforcement of the criminal law. In sum, we believe that allowing a grand jury witness to invoke the exclusionary rule would unduly interfere with the effective and expeditious discharge of the grand jury's duties.

Against this potential damage to the role and functions of the grand jury, we must weigh the benefits to be derived from this proposed extension of the exclusionary rule. Suppression of the use of illegally seized evidence against the search victim in a criminal trial is thought to be an important method of effectuating the Fourth Amendment. But it does not follow that the Fourth Amendment requires adoption of every proposal that might deter police misconduct.

Any incremental deterrent effect which might be achieved by extending the rule to grand jury proceedings is uncertain at best. Whatever deterrence of police misconduct may result from the exclusion of illegally seized evidence from criminal trials, it is unrealistic to assume that application of the rule to grand jury proceedings would significantly further that goal. Such an extension would deter only police investigation consciously directed toward the discovery of evidence solely for use in a grand jury investigation. The incentive to disregard the requirement of the Fourth Amendment solely to obtain an indictment from a grand jury is substantially negated by the inadmissibility of the illegally seized evidence in a subsequent criminal prosecution of the search victim. For the most part, a prosecutor would be unlikely to request an indictment where a conviction

---

[7] The force of this argument is well illustrated by the facts of the present case. As of the date of this decision, almost two and one-half years will have elapsed since respondent was summoned to appear and testify before the grand jury. If respondent's testimony was vital to the grand jury's investigation in August 1971 of extortionate credit transactions, it is possible that this particular investigation has been completely frustrated.

could not be obtained. We therefore decline to embrace a view that would achieve a speculative and undoubtedly minimal advance in the deterrence of police misconduct at the expense of substantially impeding the role of the grand jury.

## V

Respondent also argues that each and every question based on evidence obtained from an illegal search and seizure constitutes a fresh and independent violation of the witness' constitutional rights. Ordinarily, of course, a witness has no right of privacy before the grand jury. Absent some recognized privilege of confidentiality, every man owes his testimony. He may invoke his Fifth Amendment privilege against compulsory self-incrimination, but he may not decline to answer on the grounds that his responses might prove embarrassing or result in an unwelcome disclosure of his personal affairs. Respondent's claim must be, therefore, not merely that the grand jury's questions invade his privacy but that, because those questions are based on illegally obtained evidence, they somehow constitute distinct violations of his Fourth Amendment rights. We disagree.

The purpose of the Fourth Amendment is to prevent unreasonable governmental intrusions into the privacy of one's person, house, papers, or effects. The wrong condemned is the unjustified governmental invasion of these areas of an individual's life. That wrong, committed in this case, is fully accomplished by the original search without probable cause. Grand jury questions based on evidence obtained thereby involve no independent governmental invasion of one's person, house, papers, or effects, but rather the usual abridgment of personal privacy common to all grand jury questioning. Questions based on illegally obtained evidence are only a derivative use of the product of a past unlawful search and seizure. They work no new Fourth Amendment wrong. Whether such derivative use of illegally obtained evidence by a grand jury should be proscribed presents a question, not of rights, but of remedies.

In the usual context of a criminal trial, the defendant is entitled to the suppression of, not only the evidence obtained through an unlawful search and seizure, but also any derivative use of that evidence. The prohibition of the exclusionary rule must reach such derivative use if it is to fulfill its function of deterring police misconduct. In the context of a grand jury proceeding, we believe that the damage to that institution from the unprecedented extension of the exclusionary rule urged by respondent outweighs the benefit of any possible incremental deterrent effect. Our conclusion necessarily controls both the evidence seized during the course of an unlawful search and seizure and any question or evidence derived therefrom (the fruits of the unlawful search).[10] The same considerations of logic and policy apply to both the fruits of an unlawful search and seizure and derivative use of that evidence, and we do not distinguish between them.[11]

The judgment of the Court of Appeals is reversed.

Mr. Justice BRENNAN, with whom Mr. Justice DOUGLAS and Mr. Justice MARSHALL join, dissenting.

The Court holds that the exclusionary rule in search-and-seizure cases does not apply to grand jury proceedings because the principal objective of the rule is "to deter future unlawful police conduct," and "it is unrealistic to assume that application of the rule to grand jury proceedings would significantly further that goal." This downgrading of the exclusionary rule to a determination whether its application in a particular type of proceeding furthers deterrence of future police misconduct reflects a startling misconception, unless it is a purposeful rejection, of the historical objective and purpose of the rule.

---

[10] It should be noted that, even absent the exclusionary rule, a grand jury witness may have other remedies to redress the injury to his privacy and to prevent a further invasion in the future. He may be entitled to maintain a cause of action for damages against the officers who conducted the unlawful search. *Bivens v. Six Unknown Named Agents of Federal Bureau of Narcotics*, 403 U.S. 388 (1971). He may also seek return of the illegally seized property, and exclusion of the property and its fruits from being used as evidence against him in a criminal trial. *Go-Bart Importing Co. v. United States*, 282 U.S. 344 (1931). In these circumstances, we cannot say that such a witness is necessarily left remediless in the face of an unlawful search and seizure.

[11] The dissent voices concern that today's decision will betray "the imperative of judicial integrity," sanction "illegal government conduct," and even "imperil the very foundation of our people's trust in their Government." There is no basis for this alarm. "Illegal conduct" is hardly sanctioned, nor are the foundations of the Republic imperilled, by declining to make an unprecedented extension of the exclusionary rule to grand jury proceedings where the rule's objectives would not be effectively served and where other important and historic values would be unduly prejudiced.

The commands of the Fourth Amendment are, of course, directed solely to public officials. Necessarily, therefore, only official violations of those commands could have created the evil that threatened to make the Amendment a dead letter. But curtailment of the evil, if a consideration at all, was at best only a hoped-for effect of the exclusionary rule, not its ultimate objective. Indeed, there is no evidence that the possible deterrent effect of the rule was given any attention by the judges chiefly responsible for its formulation. Their concern as guardians of the Bill of Rights was to fashion an enforcement tool to give content and meaning to the Fourth Amendment's guarantees. They thus bore out James Madison's prediction in his address to the First Congress on June 8, 1789:

> "If they [the rights] are incorporated into the Constitution, independent tribunals of justice will consider themselves in a peculiar manner the guardians of those rights; they will be an impenetrable bulwark against every assumption of power in the Legislative or Executive; they will be naturally led to resist every encroachment upon rights expressly stipulated for in the Constitution by the declaration of rights." 1 Annals of Cong. 439 (1789).

Since, however, those judges were without power to direct or control the conduct of law enforcement officers, the enforcement tool had necessarily to be one capable of administration by judges. The exclusionary rule, if not perfect, accomplished the twin goals of enabling the judiciary to avoid the taint of partnership in official lawlessness and of assuring the people — all potential victims of unlawful government conduct — that the government would not profit from its lawless behavior, thus minimizing the risk of seriously undermining popular trust in government.

That these considerations, not the rule's possible deterrent effect, were uppermost in the minds of the framers of the rule clearly emerges from the decision which fashioned it:

> "The effect of the Fourth Amendment is to put the courts of the United States and Federal officials, in the exercise of their power and authority, under limitations and restraints as to the exercise of such power and authority, and to forever secure the people, their persons, houses, papers, and effects, against all unreasonable searches and seizures under the guise of law. . . . The tendency of those who execute the criminal laws of the country to obtain conviction by means of unlawful seizures . . . *should find no sanction in the judgments of the courts, which are charged at all*

*times with the support of the Constitution, and to which people of all conditions have a right to appeal for the maintenance of such fundamental rights.* This protection is equally extended to the action of the government and officers of the law acting under it. . . . *To sanction such proceedings would be to affirm by judicial decision a manifest neglect, if not an open defiance, of the prohibitions of the Constitution, intended for the protection of the people against such unauthorized action.*" *Weeks v. United States*, 232 U.S. 383, 391–392, 394 (1914) (emphasis added).

Mr. Justice Brandeis and Mr. Justice Holmes added their enormous influence to these precepts in their notable dissents in *Olmstead v. United States*, 277 U.S. 438 (1928). Mr. Justice Brandeis said:

"In a government of laws, existence of the government will be imperiled if it fails to observe the law scrupulously. Our government is the potent, the omnipresent teacher. For good or for ill, it teaches the whole people by its example. Crime is contagious. If the government becomes a lawbreaker, it breeds contempt for law; it invites every man to become a law unto himself; it invites anarchy."

And Justice Holmes said:

"[W]e must consider the two objects of desire both of which we cannot have, and make up our minds which to choose. It is desirable that criminals should be detected, and to that end that all available evidence should be used. It also is desirable that the government should not itself foster and pay for other crimes, when they are the means by which the evidence is to be obtained. . . . We have to choose, and for my part I think it a less evil that some criminals should escape than that the government should play an ignoble part.

". . . If the existing code does not permit district attorneys to have a hand in such dirty business it does not permit the judge to allow such iniquities to succeed."

The same principles were reiterated less than six years ago. In *Terry v. Ohio*, 392 U.S. 1, 12–13 (1968), Mr. Chief Justice Warren said for the Court:

"The rule also serves another vital function—'the imperative of judicial integrity.' Courts which sit under our Constitution cannot and will not be made party to lawless invasions of the constitutional rights of citizens by permitting unhindered governmental use of the fruits of such invasions."

It is true that deterrence was a prominent consideration in the determination whether *Mapp v. Ohio*, 367 U.S. 643 (1961), which applied the exclusionary rule to the States, should be given retrospective effect. *Linkletter v. Walker*, 381 U.S. 618 (1965). But that lends no support to today's holding that the application of the exclusionary rule depends solely upon whether its invocation in a particular type of proceeding will significantly further the goal of deterrence. The emphasis upon deterrence in *Linkletter* must be understood in the light of the crucial fact that the States had justifiably relied from 1949 to 1961 upon *Wolf*, and consequently, that application of *Mapp* would have required the wholesale release of innumerable convicted prisoners, few of whom could have been successfully retried. In that circumstance, *Linkletter* held not only that retrospective application of *Mapp* would not further the goal of deterrence but also that it would not further "the administration of justice and the integrity of the judicial process."

Thus, the Court seriously errs in describing the exclusionary rule as merely "a judicially created remedy designed to safeguard Fourth Amendment rights generally through its deterrent effect. . . ." Rather, the exclusionary rule is "part and parcel of the Fourth Amendment's limitation upon (governmental) encroachment of individual privacy" and "an essential part of both the Fourth and Fourteenth Amendments," that "gives to the individual no more than that which the Constitution guarantees him, to the police officer no less than that to which honest law enforcement is entitled, and, to the courts, that judicial integrity so necessary in the true administration of justice."

The judges who developed the exclusionary rule were well aware that it embodied a judgment that it is better for some guilty persons to go free than for the police to behave in forbidden fashion.

[T]o allow Calandra to be subjected to questions derived from the illegal search of his office and seizure of his files is "to thwart the [Fourth and Fourteenth Amendments' protection] of . . . individual privacy . . . and to entangle the courts in the illegal acts of Government agents." "And for a court, on petition of the executive department, to sentence a witness who is [himself] the victim of the illegal [search and seizure], to jail for refusal to participate in the exploitation of that [conduct in violation of the explicit command of the Fourth Amendment] is to stand our whole system of criminal justice on its head."

It is no answer, to suggest as the Court does, that the grand jury witnesses' Fourth Amendment rights will be sufficiently protected "by the inadmissibility of the illegally seized evidence in a subsequent criminal prosecution of the search victim." This, of course, is no alternative for Calandra, since he was granted transactional immunity and cannot be criminally prosecuted. But the fundamental flaw of the alternative is that to compel Calandra to testify in the first place under penalty of contempt necessarily "thwarts" his Fourth Amendment protection and "entangle[s] the courts in the illegal acts of Government agents" — consequences that *Silverthorne* condemned as intolerable.

To be sure, the exclusionary rule does not "provide that illegally seized evidence is inadmissible against anyone for any purpose." But clearly there is a crucial distinction between withholding its cover from individuals whose Fourth Amendment rights have not been violated — as has been done in the "standing" cases, and withdrawing its cover from persons whose Fourth Amendment rights have in fact been abridged.

"If constitutional rights are to be anything more than pious pronouncements, then some measurable consequence must be attached to their violation. It would be intolerable if the guarantee against unreasonable search and seizure could be violated without practical consequence. It is likewise imperative to have a practical procedure by which courts can review alleged violations of constitutional rights and articulate the meaning of those rights. The advantage of the exclusionary rule — entirely apart from any direct deterrent effect — is that it provides an occasion for judicial review, and it gives credibility to the constitutional guarantees. By demonstrating that society will attach serious consequences to the violation of constitutional rights, the exclusionary rule invokes and magnifies the moral and educative force of the law. Over the long term this may integrate some fourth amendment ideals into the value system or norms of behavior of law enforcement agencies." Oaks, Studying the Exclusionary Rule in Search and Seizure, 37 U.Chi.L.Rev. 665, 756 (1970). See also Dellinger, Of Rights and Remedies: The Constitution as a Sword, 85 Harv.L.Rev. 1532, 1562-1563 (1972).

I dissent and would affirm the judgment of the Court of Appeals.

## QUESTIONS AND NOTES

**1.** What does the *Calandra* Court perceive the purpose of the exclusionary rule to be? Is the Court's analysis consistent or in conflict with that employed in *Mapp*?

**2.** Should the practical efficacy of the exclusionary rule matter (see footnote 5 of the Court's opinion)? Would (should) evidence that the exclusionary rule does not significantly deter police misconduct be relevant (determinative of) whether or not to retain the rule?

**3.** Do you think that the exclusionary rule is likely to deter police conduct?

**4.** Is *Calandra* too specific in the question it asks; *i.e.,* should we ask whether the exclusionary rule generally deters police misconduct, or should we ask (as *Calandra* did) whether the exclusionary rule will deter the police from obtaining evidence that can be used to compel Calandra to testify before the grand jury against his friends?

**5.** If the police knew before conducting the search against Calandra that what they found could not be used to convict him, but could be used to make him testify against the other criminals or alternatively be held in contempt, would the police have had an incentive to conduct the search?

**6.** If your answer to question 5 was "yes," does it follow that *Calandra* was wrongly decided?

**7.** Do you believe that Calandra was subject to a continuing Fourth Amendment violation each time that he was questioned by the grand jury? Why? Why not?

**8.** If you had been on the Court would you have voted with Powell or Brennan, or in some other way? Explain.

**9.** Applying the *Calandra* cost benefit analysis, the Court has held that evidence unconstitutionally obtained by State police may be used in a Federal civil tax proceeding, *United States v. Janis*, 428 U.S. 433 (1976), and that evidence unconstitutionally obtained by the I.N.S. may be used in a civil deportation hearing against an allegedly deportable alien who was victimized by an unlawful search, *I.N.S. v. Lopez-Mendoza*, 468 U.S. 1032 (1984).

## B.   The Good Faith Exception To The Exclusionary Rule

In *Leon*, we consider when, and under what circumstances, the exclusionary rule can be avoided despite a violation of the Fourth Amendment.

### United States v. Leon
### 468 U.S. 897 (1984)

Justice WHITE delivered the opinion of the Court.

This case presents the question whether the Fourth Amendment exclusionary rule should be modified so as not to bar the use in the prosecution's case-in-chief of evidence obtained by officers acting in reasonable reliance on a search warrant issued by a detached and neutral magistrate but ultimately found to be unsupported by probable cause. To resolve this question, we must consider once again the tension between the sometimes competing goals of, on the one hand, deterring official misconduct and removing inducements to unreasonable invasions of privacy and, on the other, establishing procedures under which criminal defendants are "acquitted or convicted on the basis of all the evidence which exposes the truth."

I

In August 1981, a confidential informant of unproven reliability informed an officer of the Burbank Police Department that two persons known to him as "Armando" and "Patsy" were selling large quantities of cocaine and methaqualone from their residence at 620 Price Drive in Burbank, Cal. The informant also indicated that he had witnessed a sale of methaqualone by "Patsy" at the residence approximately five months earlier and had observed at that time a shoe box containing a large amount of cash that belonged to "Patsy." He further declared that "Armando" and "Patsy" generally kept only small quantities of drugs at their residence and stored the remainder at another location in Burbank.

On the basis of this information, the Burbank police initiated an extensive investigation focusing first on the Price Drive residence and later on two other residences as well. Cars parked at the Price Drive residence were determined to belong to respondents Armando Sanchez, who had previously been arrested for possession of marihuana, and Patsy Stewart, who had no criminal record. During the course of the investigation, officers observed an automobile belonging to respondent Ricardo Del Castillo, who had previously been arrested for possession of 50 pounds of marihuana, arrive at the Price Drive residence. The driver of that car entered the house, exited shortly thereafter carrying a small paper sack, and drove away. A check of Del Castillo's probation records led the officers to respondent Alberto Leon, whose telephone number Del Castillo had listed as his employer's. Leon had been arrested in 1980 on drug charges, and a companion had informed the police at that time that Leon was heavily involved in the importation of drugs into this country. Before the current investigation began, the Burbank officers had learned that an informant had told a Glendale police officer that Leon stored a large quantity of methaqualone at his residence in Glendale. During the course of this investigation, the Burbank officers learned that Leon was living at 716 South Sunset Canyon in Burbank.

Subsequently, the officers observed several persons, at least one of whom had prior drug involvement, arriving at the Price Drive residence and leaving with small packages; observed a variety of other material activity at the two residences as well as at a condominium at 7902 Via Magdalena; and witnessed a variety of relevant activity involving respondents' automobiles. The officers also observed respondents Sanchez and Stewart board separate flights for Miami. The pair later returned to Los Angeles together, consented to a search of their luggage that revealed only a small amount of marihuana, and left the airport. Based on these and other observations summarized in the affidavit, Officer

Cyril Rombach of the Burbank Police Department, an experienced and well-trained narcotics investigator, prepared an application for a warrant to search 620 Price Drive, 716 South Sunset Canyon, 7902 Via Magdalena, and automobiles registered to each of the respondents for an extensive list of items believed to be related to respondents' drug-trafficking activities. Officer Rombach's extensive application was reviewed by several Deputy District Attorneys.

A facially valid search warrant was issued in September 1981 by a state superior court judge. The ensuing searches produced large quantities of drugs at the Via Magdalena and Sunset Canyon addresses and a small quantity at the Price Drive residence. Other evidence was discovered at each of the residences and in Stewart's and Del Castillo's automobiles. Respondents were indicted by a grand jury in the District Court for the Central District of California and charged with conspiracy to possess and distribute cocaine and a variety of substantive counts.

The respondents then filed motions to suppress the evidence seized pursuant to the warrant. The District Court held an evidentiary hearing and, while recognizing that the case was a close one, granted the motions to suppress in part. It concluded that the affidavit was insufficient to establish probable cause,[2] but did not suppress all of the evidence as to all of the respondents because none of the respondents had standing to challenge all of the searches. In response to a request from the Government, the court made clear that Officer Rombach had acted in good faith, but it rejected the Government's suggestion that the Fourth Amendment exclusionary rule should not apply where evidence is seized in reasonable, good-faith reliance on a search warrant.

The Government's petition for certiorari expressly declined to seek review of the lower courts' determinations that the search warrant was unsupported by probable cause and presented only the

---

[2] "I just cannot find this warrant sufficient for a showing of probable cause.

There is no question of the reliability and credibility of the informant as not being established. Some details given tended to corroborate, maybe, the reliability of [the informant's] information about the previous transaction, but if it is not a stale transaction, it comes awfully close to it; and all the other material I think is as consistent with innocence as it is with guilt.

So I just do not think this affidavit can withstand the test. I find, then, that there is no probable cause in this case for the issuance of the search warrant. . . ."

question "[w]hether the Fourth Amendment exclusionary rule should be modified so as not to bar the admission of evidence seized in reasonable, good-faith reliance on a search warrant that is subsequently held to be defective." We granted certiorari to consider the propriety of such a modification. Although it undoubtedly is within our power to consider the question whether probable cause existed under the "totality of the circumstances" test announced last Term in *Illinois v. Gates*, 462 U.S. 213 (1983), that question has not been briefed or argued; and it is also within our authority, which we choose to exercise, to take the case as it comes to us, accepting the Court of Appeals' conclusion that probable cause was lacking under the prevailing legal standards.

We have concluded that, in the Fourth Amendment context, the exclusionary rule can be modified somewhat without jeopardizing its ability to perform its intended functions. Accordingly, we reverse the judgment of the Court of Appeals.

## II

Language in opinions of this Court and of individual Justices has sometimes implied that the exclusionary rule is a necessary corollary of the Fourth Amendment, *Mapp*, or that the rule is required by the conjunction of the Fourth and Fifth Amendments. These implications need not detain us long. The Fifth Amendment theory has not withstood critical analysis or the test of time, see *Andresen*, and the Fourth Amendment "has never been interpreted to proscribe the introduction of illegally seized evidence in all proceedings or against all persons." *Stone v. Powell*, 428 U.S. 465, 486 (1976).

### A

Whether the exclusionary sanction is appropriately imposed in a particular case, our decisions make clear, is "an issue separate from the question whether the Fourth Amendment rights of the party seeking to invoke the rule were violated by police conduct." Only the former question is currently before us, and it must be resolved by weighing the costs and benefits of preventing the use in the prosecution's case-in-chief of inherently trustworthy tangible evidence obtained in reliance on a search warrant issued by a detached and neutral magistrate that ultimately is found to be defective.

### B

Close attention to remedial objectives has characterized our recent decisions concerning the scope of the Fourth Amendment exclusionary rule. The Court has, to be sure, not seriously questioned, "in the absence of a more efficacious sanction, the continued application of the rule to suppress evidence from the [prosecution's] case where a Fourth Amendment violation has been substantial and deliberate. . . .'' Nevertheless, the balancing approach that has evolved in various contexts – including criminal trials – "forcefully suggest[s] that the exclusionary rule be more generally modified to permit the introduction of evidence obtained in the reasonable good-faith belief that a search or seizure was in accord with the Fourth Amendment."

In *Stone v. Powell, supra,* the Court emphasized the costs of the exclusionary rule, expressed its view that limiting the circumstances under which Fourth Amendment claims could be raised in federal habeas corpus proceedings would not reduce the rule's deterrent effect, and held that a state prisoner who has been afforded a full and fair opportunity to litigate a Fourth Amendment claim may not obtain federal habeas relief on the ground that unlawfully obtained evidence had been introduced at his trial. Proposed extensions of the exclusionary rule to proceedings other than the criminal trial itself have been evaluated and rejected under the same analytic approach.

As cases considering the use of unlawfully obtained evidence in criminal trials themselves make clear, it does not follow from the emphasis on the exclusionary rule's deterrent value that "anything which deters illegal searches is thereby commanded by the Fourth Amendment."

We have not required suppression of the fruits of a search incident to an arrest made in good-faith reliance on a substantive criminal statute that subsequently is declared unconstitutional. *Michigan v. De-Fillippo,* 443 U.S. 31 (1979).[8] Similarly, although

***

[8] We have held, however, that the exclusionary rule requires suppression of evidence obtained in searches carried out pursuant to statutes, not yet declared unconstitutional, purporting to authorize searches and seizures without probable cause or search warrants. *See, e.g., Ybarra v. Illinois,* 444 U.S. 85 (1979); *Torres v. Puerto Rico,* 442 U.S. 465 (1979); *Almeida-Sanchez v. United States,* 413 U.S. 266 (1973); *Sibron v. New York,* 392 U.S. 40 (1968); *Berger v. New York,* 388 U.S. 41 (1967). "Those decisions involved statutes which, by their own terms, authorized searches under circumstances which did not satisfy the traditional warrant and probable-cause requirements of the Fourth Amendment." *Michigan v. DeFillippo,* 443 U.S. 31 (1979). The substantive Fourth Amendment principles announced in those cases are fully consistent with our holding here.

the Court has been unwilling to conclude that new Fourth Amendment principles are always to have only prospective effect, *United States v. Johnson,* 457 U.S. 537, 560 (1982), no Fourth Amendment decision marking a "clear break with the past" has been applied retroactively. The propriety of retroactive application of a newly announced Fourth Amendment principle, moreover, has been assessed largely in terms of the contribution retroactivity might make to the deterrence of police misconduct.

As yet, we have not recognized any form of good-faith exception to the Fourth Amendment exclusionary rule. But the balancing approach that has evolved during the years of experience with the rule provides strong support for the modification currently urged upon us. As we discuss below, our evaluation of the costs and benefits of suppressing reliable physical evidence seized by officers reasonably relying on a warrant issued by a detached and neutral magistrate leads to the conclusion that such evidence should be admissible in the prosecution's case-in-chief.

### III

### A

Because a search warrant "provides the detached scrutiny of a neutral magistrate, which is a more reliable safeguard against improper searches than the hurried judgment of a law enforcement officer 'engaged in the often competitive enterprise of ferreting out crime,'" we have expressed a strong preference for warrants and declared that "in a doubtful or marginal case a search under a warrant may be sustainable where without one it would fail." Reasonable minds frequently may differ on the question whether a particular affidavit establishes probable cause, and we have thus concluded that the preference for warrants is most appropriately effectuated by according "great deference" to a magistrate's determination. See *Gates.*

Deference to the magistrate, however, is not boundless. It is clear, first, that the deference accorded to a magistrate's finding of probable cause does not preclude inquiry into the knowing or reckless falsity of the affidavit on which that determination was based. *Franks v. Delaware,* 438 U.S. 154 (1978).[12] Second, the courts must also insist that

***

[12] Indeed, "it would be an unthinkable imposition upon [the magistrate's] authority if a warrant affidavit, revealed after the fact to contain a deliberately or recklessly false statement, were to stand beyond impeachment."

the magistrate purport to "perform his 'neutral and detached' function and not serve merely as a rubber stamp for the police." A magistrate failing to "manifest that neutrality and detachment demanded of a judicial officer when presented with a warrant application" and who acts instead as "an adjunct law enforcement officer" cannot provide valid authorization for an otherwise unconstitutional search. *Lo-Ji Sales, Inc. v. New York*, 442 U.S. 319, 326-327 (1979).

Third, reviewing courts will not defer to a warrant based on an affidavit that does not "provide the magistrate with a substantial basis for determining the existence of probable cause." *Gates*. "Sufficient information must be presented to the magistrate to allow that official to determine probable cause; his action cannot be a mere ratification of the bare conclusions of others." Even if the warrant application was supported by more than a "bare bones" affidavit, a reviewing court may properly conclude that, notwithstanding the deference that magistrates deserve, the warrant was invalid because the magistrate's probable-cause determination reflected an improper analysis of the totality of the circumstances, *Gates*, or because the form of the warrant was improper in some respect.

Only in the first of these three situations, however, has the Court set forth a rationale for suppressing evidence obtained pursuant to a search warrant; in the other areas, it has simply excluded such evidence without considering whether Fourth Amendment interests will be advanced. To the extent that proponents of exclusion rely on its behavioral effects on judges and magistrates in these areas, their reliance is misplaced. First, the exclusionary rule is designed to deter police misconduct rather than to punish the errors of judges and magistrates. Second, there exists no evidence suggesting that judges and magistrates are inclined to ignore or subvert the Fourth Amendment or that lawlessness among these actors requires application of the extreme sanction of exclusion.[14]

Third, and most important, we discern no basis, and are offered none, for believing that exclusion of evidence seized pursuant to a warrant will have a significant deterrent effect on the issuing judge or magistrate. Many of the factors that indicate that the

exclusionary rule cannot provide an effective "special" or "general" deterrent for individual offending law enforcement officers apply as well to judges or magistrates. And, to the extent that the rule is thought to operate as a "systemic" deterrent on a wider audience, it clearly can have no such effect on individuals empowered to issue search warrants. Judges and magistrates are not adjuncts to the law enforcement team; as neutral judicial officers, they have no stake in the outcome of particular criminal prosecutions. The threat of exclusion thus cannot be expected significantly to deter them. Imposition of the exclusionary sanction is not necessary meaningfully to inform judicial officers of their errors, and we cannot conclude that admitting evidence obtained pursuant to a warrant while at the same time declaring that the warrant was somehow defective will in any way reduce judicial officers' professional incentives to comply with the Fourth Amendment, encourage them to repeat their mistakes, or lead to the granting of all colorable warrant requests.

### B

If exclusion of evidence obtained pursuant to a subsequently invalidated warrant is to have any deterrent effect, therefore, it must alter the behavior of individual law enforcement officers or the policies of their departments. One could argue that applying the exclusionary rule in cases where the police failed to demonstrate probable cause in the warrant application deters future inadequate presentations or "magistrate shopping" and thus promotes the ends of the Fourth Amendment. Suppressing evidence obtained pursuant to a technically defective warrant supported by probable cause also might encourage officers to scrutinize more closely the form of the warrant and to point out suspected judicial errors. We find such arguments speculative and conclude that suppression of evidence obtained pursuant to a warrant should be ordered only on a case-by-case basis and only in those unusual cases in which exclusion will further the purposes of the exclusionary rule.

We have frequently questioned whether the exclusionary rule can have any deterrent effect when the offending officers acted in the objectively reasonable belief that their conduct did not violate the Fourth Amendment. "No empirical researcher, proponent or opponent of the rule, has yet been able to establish with any assurance whether the rule has a deterrent effect. . . ." But even assuming that the rule effectively deters some police misconduct and provides incentives for the law enforcement profession as a whole to conduct itself in accord with the

---

[14] Although there are assertions that some magistrates become rubber stamps for the police and others may be unable effectively to screen police conduct, we are not convinced that this is a problem of major proportions.

Fourth Amendment, it cannot be expected, and should not be applied, to deter objectively reasonable law enforcement activity.[20]

In short, where the officer's conduct is objectively reasonable,

> "excluding the evidence will not further the ends of the exclusionary rule in any appreciable way; for it is painfully apparent that . . . the officer is acting as a reasonable officer would and should act under the circumstances. Excluding the evidence can in no way affect his future conduct unless it is to make him less willing to do his duty." *Stone v. Powell*, 428 U.S., at 539-540 (White, J., dissenting).

This is particularly true, we believe, when an officer acting with objective good faith has obtained a search warrant from a judge or magistrate and acted within its scope. In most such cases, there is no police illegality and thus nothing to deter. It is the magistrate's responsibility to determine whether the officer's allegations establish probable cause and, if so, to issue a warrant comporting in form with the requirements of the Fourth Amendment. In the ordinary case, an officer cannot be expected to question the magistrate's probable-cause determination or his judgment that the form of the warrant is technically sufficient. "[O]nce the warrant issues, there is literally nothing more the policeman can do in seeking to comply with the law." Penalizing the officer for the magistrate's error, rather than his own, cannot logically contribute to the deterrence of Fourth Amendment violations.

### C

We conclude that the marginal or nonexistent benefits produced by suppressing evidence obtained in objectively reasonable reliance on a subsequently invalidated search warrant cannot justify the substantial costs of exclusion. We do not suggest, however, that exclusion is always inappropriate in cases where an officer has obtained a warrant and abided by its terms. "[S]earches pursuant to a warrant will rarely require any deep inquiry into reasonableness," *Gates* (White, J., concurring in the judgment), for "a warrant issued by a magistrate normally suffices to establish" that a law enforcement officer has "acted in good faith in conducting the search." Nevertheless, the officer's reliance on the magistrate's probable-cause determination and on the technical sufficiency of the warrant he issues must be objectively reasonable,[23] and it is clear that in some circumstances the officer[24] will have no reasonable grounds for believing that the warrant was properly issued.

Suppression therefore remains an appropriate remedy if the magistrate or judge in issuing a warrant was misled by information in an affidavit that the affiant knew was false or would have known was false except for his reckless disregard of the truth. *Franks v. Delaware*, 438 U.S. 154 (1978). The exception we recognize today will also not apply in cases where the issuing magistrate wholly abandoned his judicial role in the manner condemned in *Lo-Ji Sales, Inc. v. New York*, 442 U.S. 319 (1979); in such circumstances, no reasonably well-trained officer should rely on the warrant. Nor would an officer manifest objective good faith in relying on a warrant based on an affidavit "so lacking in indicia of probable cause as to render official belief in its existence entirely unreasonable." Finally, depending on the

---

[20] We emphasize that the standard of reasonableness we adopt is an objective one. Many objections to a good-faith exception assume that the exception will turn on the subjective good faith of individual officers. "Grounding the modification in objective reasonableness, however, retains the value of the exclusionary rule as an incentive for the law enforcement profession as a whole to conduct themselves in accord with the Fourth Amendment." The objective standard we adopt, moreover, requires officers to have a reasonable knowledge of what the law prohibits.

[23] Accordingly, our good-faith inquiry is confined to the objectively ascertainable question whether a reasonably well-trained officer would have known that the search was illegal despite the magistrate's authorization. In making this determination, all of the circumstances—including whether the warrant application had previously been rejected by a different magistrate—may be considered.

[24] References to "officer" throughout this opinion should not be read too narrowly. It is necessary to consider the objective reasonableness, not only of the officers who eventually executed a warrant, but also of the officers who originally obtained it or who provided information material to the probable-cause determination. Nothing in our opinion suggests, for example, that an officer could obtain a warrant on the basis of a "bare bones" affidavit and then rely on colleagues who are ignorant of the circumstances under which the warrant was obtained to conduct the search. See *Whiteley v. Warden*, 401 U.S. 560, 568, (1971).

circumstances of the particular case, a warrant may be so facially deficient – *i.e.*, in failing to particularize the place to be searched or the things to be seized – that the executing officers cannot reasonably presume it to be valid.

In so limiting the suppression remedy, we leave untouched the probable-cause standard and the various requirements for a valid warrant. Other objections to the modification of the Fourth Amendment exclusionary rule we consider to be insubstantial. The good-faith exception for searches conducted pursuant to warrants is not intended to signal our unwillingness strictly to enforce the requirements of the Fourth Amendment, and we do not believe that it will have this effect. As we have already suggested, the good-faith exception, turning as it does on objective reasonableness, should not be difficult to apply in practice. When officers have acted pursuant to a warrant, the prosecution should ordinarily be able to establish objective good faith without a substantial expenditure of judicial time.

Nor are we persuaded that application of a good-faith exception to searches conducted pursuant to warrants will preclude review of the constitutionality of the search or seizure, deny needed guidance from the courts, or freeze Fourth Amendment law in its present state.[25] There is no need for courts to adopt the inflexible practice of always deciding whether the officers' conduct manifested objective good faith before turning to the question whether the Fourth Amendment has been violated. Defendants seeking suppression of the fruits of allegedly unconstitutional searches or seizures undoubtedly raise live controversies which Article III empowers federal courts to adjudicate.

If the resolution of a particular Fourth Amendment question is necessary to guide future action by law enforcement officers and magistrates, nothing will prevent reviewing courts from deciding that question before turning to the good-faith issue.[26] Indeed, it frequently will be difficult to determine whether the officers acted reasonably without resolving the Fourth Amendment issue. Even if the Fourth Amendment question is not one of broad import, reviewing courts could decide in particular cases that magistrates under their supervision need to be informed of their errors and so evaluate the officers' good faith only after finding a violation. In other circumstances, those courts could reject suppression motions posing no important Fourth Amendment questions by turning immediately to a consideration of the officers' good faith. We have no reason to believe that our Fourth Amendment jurisprudence would suffer by allowing reviewing courts to exercise an informed discretion in making this choice.

## IV

When the principles we have enunciated today are applied to the facts of this case, it is apparent that the judgment of the Court of Appeals cannot stand. The Court of Appeals applied the prevailing legal standards to Officer Rombach's warrant application and concluded that the application could not support the magistrate's probable-cause determination. In so doing, the court clearly informed the magistrate that he had erred in issuing the challenged warrant. This aspect of the court's judgment is not under attack in this proceeding.

Having determined that the warrant should not have issued, the Court of Appeals understandably declined to adopt a modification of the Fourth Amendment exclusionary rule that this Court had not previously sanctioned. Although the modification finds strong support in our previous cases, the Court of Appeals' commendable self-restraint is not to be criticized. We have now re-examined the purposes of the exclusionary rule and the propriety of its application in cases where officers have relied on a subsequently invalidated search warrant. Our conclusion is that the rule's purposes will only rarely be served by applying it in such circumstances.

In the absence of an allegation that the magistrate abandoned his detached and neutral role, suppression is appropriate only if the officers were dishonest or reckless in preparing their affidavit or could not have

---

[25] The argument that defendants will lose their incentive to litigate meritorious Fourth Amendment claims as a result of the good-faith exception we adopt today is unpersuasive. Although the exception might discourage presentation of insubstantial suppression motions, the magnitude of the benefit conferred on defendants by a successful motion makes it unlikely that litigation of colorable claims will be substantially diminished.

[26] It has been suggested, in fact, that "the recognition of a 'penumbral zone,' within which an inadvertent mistake would not call for exclusion, . . .

will make it less tempting for judges to bend fourth amendment standards to avoid releasing a possibly dangerous criminal because of a minor and unintentional miscalculation by the police.'' Schroeder, *supra* n. 14, (footnote omitted); see Ashdown, Good Faith, the Exclusionary Remedy, and Rule-Oriented Adjudication in the Criminal Process, 24 Wm. & Mary L.Rev. 335, 383-384 (1983).

harbored an objectively reasonable belief in the existence of probable cause. Only respondent Leon has contended that no reasonably well-trained police officer could have believed that there existed probable cause to search his house; significantly, the other respondents advance no comparable argument. Officer Rombach's application for a warrant clearly was supported by much more than a "bare bones" affidavit. The affidavit related the results of an extensive investigation and, as the opinions of the divided panel of the Court of Appeals make clear, provided evidence sufficient to create disagreement among thoughtful and competent judges as to the existence of probable cause. Under these circumstances, the officers' reliance on the magistrate's determination of probable cause was objectively reasonable, and application of the extreme sanction of exclusion is inappropriate.

Accordingly, the judgment of the Court of Appeals is Reversed.

Justice BLACKMUN, concurring.

As the Court's opinion in this case makes clear, the Court has narrowed the scope of the exclusionary rule because of an empirical judgment that the rule has little appreciable effect in cases where officers act in objectively reasonable reliance on search warrants. Because I share the view that the exclusionary rule is not a constitutionally compelled corollary of the Fourth Amendment itself, I see no way to avoid making an empirical judgment of this sort, and I am satisfied that the Court has made the correct one on the information before it. Like all courts, we face institutional limitations on our ability to gather information about "legislative facts," and the exclusionary rule itself has exacerbated the shortage of hard data concerning the behavior of police officers in the absence of such a rule. Nonetheless, we cannot escape the responsibility to decide the question before us, however imperfect our information may be, and I am prepared to join the Court on the information now at hand.

What must be stressed, however, is that any empirical judgment about the effect of the exclusionary rule in a particular class of cases necessarily is a provisional one. By their very nature, the assumptions on which we proceed today cannot be cast in stone. To the contrary, they now will be tested in the real world of state and federal law enforcement, and this Court will attend to the results. If it should emerge from experience that, contrary to our expectations, the good faith exception to the exclusionary rule results in a material change in police compliance with the Fourth Amendment, we shall have to reconsider what we have undertaken here. The logic of a decision that rests on untested predictions about police conduct demands no less.

If a single principle may be drawn from this Court's exclusionary rule decisions, from *Weeks* through *Mapp* to the decisions handed down today, it is that the scope of the exclusionary rule is subject to change in light of changing judicial understanding about the effects of the rule outside the confines of the courtroom. It is incumbent on the Nation's law enforcement officers, who must continue to observe the Fourth Amendment in the wake of today's decisions, to recognize the double-edged nature of that principle.

Justice BRENNAN, with whom Justice MARSHALL joins, dissenting.

Ten years ago in *Calandra*. I expressed the fear that the Court's decision "may signal that a majority of my colleagues have positioned themselves to reopen the door [to evidence secured by official lawlessness] still further and abandon altogether the exclusionary rule in search-and-seizure cases." Since then, in case after case, I have witnessed the Court's gradual but determined strangulation of the rule. It now appears that the Court's victory over the Fourth Amendment is complete. That today's decision represents the *piece de resistance* of the Court's past efforts cannot be doubted, for today the Court sanctions the use in the prosecution's case-in-chief of illegally obtained evidence against the individual whose rights have been violated—a result that had previously been thought to be foreclosed.

The Court seeks to justify this result on the ground that the "costs" of adhering to the exclusionary rule in cases like those before us exceed the "benefits." But the language of deterrence and of cost/benefit analysis, if used indiscriminately, can have a narcotic effect. It creates an illusion of technical precision and ineluctability. It suggests that not only constitutional principle but also empirical data supports the majority's result. When the Court's analysis is examined carefully, however, it is clear that we have not been treated to an honest assessment of the merits of the exclusionary rule, but have instead been drawn into a curious world where the "costs" of excluding illegally obtained evidence loom to exaggerated heights and where the "benefits" of such exclusion are made to disappear with a mere wave of the hand.

A proper understanding of the broad purposes sought to be served by the Fourth Amendment demonstrates that the principles embodied in the exclusionary rule rest upon a far firmer constitutional foundation than the shifting sands of the Court's deterrence rationale. But even if I were to accept the Court's chosen method of analyzing the question posed by these cases, I would still conclude that the Court's decision cannot be justified.

## I

### A

At bottom, the Court's decision turns on the proposition that the exclusionary rule is merely a "judicially created remedy designed to safeguard Fourth Amendment rights generally through its deterrent effect, rather than a personal constitutional right."

Such a reading appears plausible, because, as critics of the exclusionary rule never tire of repeating, the Fourth Amendment makes no express provision for the exclusion of evidence secured in violation of its commands. A short answer to this claim, of course, is that many of the Constitution's most vital imperatives are stated in general terms and the task of giving meaning to these precepts is therefore left to subsequent judicial decision-making in the context of concrete cases. The nature of our Constitution, as Chief Justice Marshall long ago explained, "requires that only its great outlines should be marked, its important objects designated, and the minor ingredients which compose those objects be deduced from the nature of the objects themselves." *McCulloch v. Maryland*, 4 Wheat. 316, 407 (1819).

A more direct answer may be supplied by recognizing that the Amendment, like other provisions of the Bill of Rights, restrains the power of the government as a whole; it does not specify only a particular agency and exempt all others. The judiciary is responsible, no less than the executive, for ensuring that constitutional rights are respected.

It is difficult to give any meaning at all to the limitations imposed by the Amendment if they are read to proscribe only certain conduct by the police but to allow other agents of the same government to take advantage of evidence secured by the police in violation of its requirements. The Amendment therefore must be read to condemn not only the initial unconstitutional invasion of privacy—which is done, after all, for the purpose of securing evidence—but also the subsequent use of any evidence so obtained.

The various arguments advanced by the Court in this campaign have only strengthened my conviction that the deterrence theory is both misguided and unworkable. First, the Court has frequently bewailed the "cost" of excluding reliable evidence. In large part, this criticism rests upon a refusal to acknowledge the function of the Fourth Amendment itself. If nothing else, the Amendment plainly operates to disable the government from gathering information and securing evidence in certain ways. In practical terms, of course, this restriction of official power

means that some incriminating evidence inevitably will go undetected if the government obeys these constitutional restraints. It is the loss of that evidence that is the "price" our society pays for enjoying the freedom and privacy safeguarded by the Fourth Amendment. Thus, some criminals will go free *not*, in Justice (then Judge) Cardozo's misleading epigram, "because the constable has blundered," but rather because official compliance with Fourth Amendment requirements makes it more difficult to catch criminals. Understood in this way, the Amendment directly contemplates that some reliable and incriminating evidence will be lost to the government; therefore, it is not the exclusionary rule, but the Amendment itself that has imposed this cost.[8]

In addition, the Court's decisions over the past decade have made plain that the entire enterprise of attempting to assess the benefits and costs of the exclusionary rule in various contexts is a virtually impossible task for the judiciary to perform honestly or accurately. Although the Court's language in those cases suggests that some specific empirical basis may support its analyses, the reality is that the Court's opinions represent inherently unstable compounds of intuition, hunches, and occasional pieces

---

[8] Justice Stewart has explained this point in detail in a recent article:

"Much of the criticism leveled at the exclusionary rule is misdirected; it is more properly directed at the Fourth Amendment itself. It is true that, as many observers have charged, the effect of the rule is to deprive the courts of extremely relevant, often direct evidence of the guilt of the defendant. But these same critics fail to acknowledge that, in many instances, the same extremely relevant evidence would not have been obtained had the police officer complied with the commands of the fourth amendment in the first place. . . .

"The exclusionary rule places no limitations on the actions of the police. The fourth amendment does. The inevitable result of the Constitution's prohibition against unreasonable searches and seizures and its requirements that no warrant shall issue but upon probable cause is that police officers who obey its strictures will catch fewer criminals. . . . [T]hat is the price the framers anticipated and were willing to pay to ensure the sanctity of the person, home, and property against unrestrained governmental power."

of partial and often inconclusive data. In *Calandra*, for example, the Court, in considering whether the exclusionary rule should apply in grand jury proceedings, had before it no concrete evidence whatever concerning the impact that application of the rule in such proceedings would have either in terms of the long-term costs or the expected benefits. To the extent empirical data is available regarding the general costs and benefits of the exclusionary rule, it has shown, on the one hand, as the Court acknowledges today, that the costs are not as substantial as critics have asserted in the past, and, on the other hand, that while the exclusionary rule may well have certain deterrent effects, it is extremely difficult to determine with any degree of precision whether the incidence of unlawful conduct by police is now lower than it was prior to *Mapp*. The Court has sought to turn this uncertainty to its advantage by casting the burden of proof upon proponents of the rule. "Obviously," however, "the assignment of the burden of proof on an issue where evidence does not exist and cannot be obtained is outcome determinative. [The] assignment of the burden is merely a way of announcing a predetermined conclusion."

### III

Even if I were to accept the Court's general approach to the exclusionary rule, I could not agree with today's result.

At the outset, the Court suggests that society has been asked to pay a high price—in terms either of setting guilty persons free or of impeding the proper functioning of trials—as a result of excluding relevant physical evidence in cases where the police, in conducting searches and seizing evidence, have made only an "objectively reasonable" mistake concerning the constitutionality of their actions. But what evidence is there to support such a claim? Significantly, the Court points to none, and, indeed, as the Court acknowledges, recent studies have demonstrated that the "costs" of the exclusionary rule—calculated in terms of dropped prosecutions and lost convictions—are quite low.

What then supports the Court's insistence that this evidence be admitted? Apparently, the Court's only answer is that even though the costs of exclusion are not very substantial, the potential deterrent effect in these circumstances is so marginal that exclusion cannot be justified. The key to the Court's conclusion in this respect is its belief that the prospective deterrent effect of the exclusionary rule operates only in those situations in which police officers, when deciding whether to go forward with some particular search, have reason to know that their planned conduct will violate the requirements of the Fourth Amendment. If these officers in fact

understand (or reasonably should understand because the law is well-settled) that their proposed conduct will offend the Fourth Amendment and that, consequently, any evidence they seize will be suppressed in court, they will refrain from conducting the planned search. In those circumstances, the incentive system created by the exclusionary rule will have the hoped-for deterrent effect. But in situations where police officers reasonably (but mistakenly) believe that their planned conduct satisfies Fourth Amendment requirements—presumably either (a) because they are acting on the basis of an apparently valid warrant, or (b) because their conduct is only later determined to be invalid as a result of a subsequent change in the law or the resolution of an unsettled question of law—then such officers will have no reason to refrain from conducting the search and the exclusionary rule will have no effect.

At first blush, there is some logic to this position. Undoubtedly, in the situation hypothesized by the Court, the existence of the exclusionary rule cannot be expected to have any deterrent effect on the particular officers at the moment they are deciding whether to go forward with the search. Indeed, the subsequent exclusion of any evidence seized under such circumstances appears somehow "unfair" to the particular officers involved. As the Court suggests, these officers have acted in what they thought was an appropriate and constitutionally authorized manner, but then the fruit of their efforts is nullified by the application of the exclusionary rule.

The flaw in the Court's argument, however, is that its logic captures only one comparatively minor element of the generally acknowledged deterrent purposes of the exclusionary rule. To be sure, the rule operates to some extent to deter future misconduct by individual officers who have had evidence suppressed in their own cases. But what the Court overlooks is that the deterrence rationale for the rule is not designed to be, nor should it be thought of as, a form of "punishment" of individual police officers for their failures to obey the restraints imposed by the Fourth Amendment. Instead, the chief deterrent function of the rule is its tendency to promote institutional compliance with Fourth Amendment requirements on the part of law enforcement agencies generally. Thus, as the Court has previously recognized, "over the long term, [the] demonstration [provided by the exclusionary rule] that our society attaches serious consequences to violation of constitutional rights is thought to encourage those who formulate law enforcement policies, and the officers who implement them, to incorporate Fourth Amendment ideals into their value system."

It is only through such an institution-wide mechanism that information concerning Fourth Amendment standards can be effectively communicated to rank and file officers.[13]

If the overall educational effect of the exclusionary rule is considered, application of the rule to even those situations in which individual police officers have acted on the basis of a reasonable but mistaken

---

[13] Although specific empirical data on the systemic deterrent effect of the rule is not conclusive, the testimony of those actually involved in law enforcement suggests that, at the very least, the *Mapp* decision had the effect of increasing police awareness of Fourth Amendment requirements and of prompting prosecutors and police commanders to work towards educating rank and file officers. For example, as former New York Police Commissioner Murphy explained the impact of the *Mapp* decision: "I can think of no decision in recent times in the field of law enforcement which had such a dramatic and traumatic effect. . . . I was immediately caught up in the entire program of reevaluating our procedures, which had followed the *Defore* rule, and modifying, amending, and creating new policies and new instructions for implementing *Mapp*. . . . Retraining sessions had to be held from the very top administrators down to each of the thousands of foot patrolmen." Murphy, Judicial Review of Police Methods in Law Enforcement: The Problem of Compliance by Police Departments, 44 Tex.L.Rev. 939, 941 (1966).

Further testimony about the impact of the *Mapp* decision can be found in the statement of Deputy Commissioner Reisman: "The *Mapp* case was a shock to us. We had to reorganize our thinking, frankly. Before this, nobody bothered to take out search warrants. Although the U.S. Constitution requires warrants in most cases, the U.S. Supreme Court had ruled that evidence obtained without a warrant—illegally, if you will—was admissible in state courts. So the feeling was, why bother? Well, once that rule was changed we knew we had better start teaching our men about it." N.Y. Times, April 28, 1965, at 50, col. 1. A former United States Attorney and now Attorney General of Maryland, Stephen Sachs, has described the impact of the rule on police practices in similar terms: "I have watched the rule deter, routinely, throughout my years as a prosecutor. . . . [P]olice-prosecutor consultation is customary in all our cases when Fourth Amendment concerns arise. . . . In at least three Maryland jurisdictions, for example, prosecutors are on twenty-four hour call to field search and seizure questions presented by police officers."

belief that their conduct was authorized can still be expected to have a considerable long-term deterrent effect. If evidence is consistently excluded in these circumstances, police departments will surely be prompted to instruct their officers to devote greater care and attention to providing sufficient information to establish probable cause when applying for a warrant, and to review with some attention the form of the warrant that they have been issued, rather than automatically assuming that whatever document the magistrate has signed will necessarily comport with Fourth Amendment requirements.

After today's decision, however, that institutional incentive will be lost. Indeed, the Court's "reasonable mistake" exception to the exclusionary rule will tend to put a premium on police ignorance of the law. Armed with the assurance provided by today's decision that evidence will always be admissible whenever an officer has "reasonably" relied upon a warrant, police departments will be encouraged to train officers that if a warrant has simply been signed, it is reasonable, without more, to rely on it. Since in close cases there will no longer be any incentive to err on the side of constitutional behavior, police would have every reason to adopt a "let's-wait-until-its-decided" approach in situations in which there is a question about a warrant's validity or the basis for its issuance.

Although the Court brushes these concerns aside, a host of grave consequences can be expected to result from its decision to carve this new exception out of the exclusionary rule. A chief consequence of today's decision will be to convey a clear and unambiguous message to magistrates that their decisions to issue warrants are now insulated from subsequent judicial review. Creation of this new exception for good faith reliance upon a warrant implicitly tells magistrates that they need not take much care in reviewing warrant applications, since their mistakes will from now on have virtually no consequence: If their decision to issue a warrant was correct, the evidence will be admitted; if their decision was incorrect but the police relied in good faith on the warrant, the evidence will also be admitted. Inevitably, the care and attention devoted to such an inconsequential chore will dwindle. Although the Court is correct to note that magistrates do not share the same stake in the outcome of a criminal case as the police, they nevertheless need to appreciate that their role is of some moment in order to continue performing the important task of carefully reviewing warrant applications. Today's decision effectively removes that incentive.

Finally, even if one were to believe, as the Court apparently does, that police are hobbled by inflexible and hypertechnical warrant procedures, today's decision cannot be justified. This is because, given the relaxed standard for assessing probable cause established just last Term in *Gates*, the Court's newly fashioned good faith exception, when applied in the warrant context, will rarely, if ever, offer any greater flexibility for police than the *Gates* standard already supplies. In *Gates*, the Court held that "the task of an issuing magistrate is simply to make a practical, common-sense decision whether, given all the circumstances set forth in the affidavit before him, . . . there is a fair probability that contraband or evidence of a crime will be found in a particular place." The task of a reviewing court is confined to determining whether "the magistrate had a 'substantial basis' for concluding that probable cause existed." Given such a relaxed standard, it is virtually inconceivable that a reviewing court, when faced with a defendant's motion to suppress, could first find that a warrant was invalid under the new *Gates* standard, but then, at the same time, find that a police officer's reliance on such an invalid warrant was nevertheless "objectively reasonable" under the test announced today. Because the two standards overlap so completely, it is unlikely that a warrant could be found invalid under *Gates* and yet the police reliance upon it could be seen as objectively reasonable; otherwise, we would have to entertain the mind-boggling concept of objectively reasonable reliance upon an objectively unreasonable warrant.

[T]he full impact of the Court's regrettable decision will not be felt until the Court attempts to extend this rule to situations in which the police have conducted a warrantless search solely on the basis of their own judgment about the existence of probable cause and exigent circumstances. When that question is finally posed, I for one will not be surprised if my colleagues decide once again that we simply cannot afford to protect Fourth Amendment rights.

### IV

When the public, as it quite properly has done in the past as well as in the present, demands that those in government increase their efforts to combat crime, it is all too easy for those government officials to seek expedient solutions. In contrast to such costly and difficult measures as building more prisons, improving law enforcement methods, or hiring more prosecutors and judges to relieve the overburdened court systems in the country's metropolitan areas, the relaxation of Fourth Amendment standards seems a tempting, costless means of meeting the public's demand for better law enforcement. In the long run, however, we as a society pay a heavy price for such expediency, because as Justice Jackson observed, the rights guaranteed in the Fourth Amendment "are not mere second-class rights but belong in the catalog of indispensable freedoms." *Brinegar*

*v. United States*, 338 U.S. 160, 180 (1949) (dissenting opinion). Once lost, such rights are difficult to recover. There is hope, however, that in time this or some later Court will restore these precious freedoms to their rightful place as a primary protection for our citizens against overreaching officialdom.

I dissent.

Justice STEVENS dissenting.

The Court assumes that the searches in these cases violated the Fourth Amendment, yet refuses to apply the exclusionary rule because the Court concludes that it was "reasonable" for the police to conduct them. In my opinion an official search and seizure cannot be both "unreasonable" and "reasonable" at the same time. The doctrinal vice in the Court's holding is its failure to consider the separate purposes of the two prohibitory clauses in the Fourth Amendment.

The first clause prohibits unreasonable searches and seizures and the second prohibits the issuance of warrants that are not supported by probable cause or that do not particularly describe the place to be searched and the persons or things to be seized. We have, of course, repeatedly held that warrantless searches are presumptively unreasonable.

The notion that a police officer's reliance on a magistrate's warrant is automatically appropriate is one the Framers of the Fourth Amendment would have vehemently rejected. The precise problem that the Amendment was intended to address was *the unreasonable issuance of warrants*. As we have often observed, the Amendment was actually motivated by the practice of issuing general warrants— warrants which did not satisfy the particularity and probable cause requirements. The resentments which led to the Amendment were directed at the issuance of warrants unjustified by particularized evidence of wrongdoing. Those who sought to amend the Constitution to include a Bill of Rights repeatedly voiced the view that the evil which had to be addressed was the issuance of warrants on insufficient evidence. As Professor Taylor has written:

"[O]ur constitutional fathers were not concerned about warrantless searches, but about overreaching warrants. It is perhaps too much to say that they feared the warrant more than the search, but it is plain enough that the warrant was the prime object of their concern. Far from looking at the warrant as a protection against unreasonable searches, they saw it as an authority for unreasonable and oppressive searches. . . ." T. Taylor, Two Studies in Constitutional Interpretation 41 (1969).

In short, the Framers of the Fourth Amendment were deeply suspicious of warrants; in their minds the paradigm of an abusive search was the execution of a warrant not based on probable cause. The fact that colonial officers had magisterial authorization for their conduct when they engaged in general searches surely did not make their conduct "reasonable." The Court's view that it is consistent with our Constitution to adopt a rule that it is presumptively reasonable to rely on a defective warrant is the product of constitutional amnesia.[27]

### IV

In *Brinegar*, Justice Jackson, after observing that "[i]ndications are not wanting that Fourth Amendment freedoms are tacitly marked as secondary rights, to be relegated to a deferred position," (dissenting opinion), continued:

"These, I protest, are not mere second-class rights but belong in the catalog of indispensable freedoms. Among deprivations of rights, none is so effective in cowing a population, crushing the spirit of the individual and putting terror in every heart. Uncontrolled search and seizure is one of the first and most effective weapons in the arsenal of every arbitrary government. And one need only briefly to have dwelt and worked among a people possessed of many admirable qualities but deprived of these rights to know that the human personality deteriorates and dignity and self-reliance disappear where homes, persons and possessions are subject at any hour to unheralded search and seizure by the police.

"Only occasional and more flagrant abuses come to the attention of the courts, and then only those where the search and seizure yields incriminating evidence and the defendant is at least sufficiently compromised to be indicted. If the officers raid a home, an office, or stop and search an automobile but find nothing incriminating, this invasion of the personal liberty of the innocent too often finds no practical redress. There may be, and I am convinced that there are, many unlawful searches of homes and automobiles of innocent people which turn up nothing incriminating, in which no arrest is made, about which courts do nothing, and about which we never hear.

"Courts can protect the innocent against such invasions only indirectly and through the medium of excluding evidence obtained against those who frequently are guilty. . . . So a search against Brinegar's car must be regarded as a search of the car of Everyman."

Justice Jackson's reference to his experience at Nuremberg should remind us of the importance of considering the consequences of today's decision for "Everyman."

The exclusionary rule is designed to prevent violations of the Fourth Amendment.[28] "Its purpose

---

[27] "It makes all the difference in the world whether one recognizes the central fact about the Fourth Amendment, namely, that it was a safeguard against recurrence of abuses so deeply felt by the Colonies as to be one of the potent causes of the Revolution, or one thinks of it as merely a requirement for a piece of paper." *United States v. Rabinowitz*, 339 U.S. 56, 69 (1950) (Frankfurter, J., dissenting).

---

[28] For at least two reasons, the exclusionary rule is a better remedy than a civil action against an offending officer. Unlike the fear of personal liability, it should not create excessive deterrence; moreover, it avoids the obvious unfairness of subjecting the dedicated officer to the risk of monetary liability for a misstep while endeavoring to enforce the law. Society, rather than the individual officer, should accept the responsibility for inadequate training or supervision of officers engaged in hazardous police work. What the Chief Justice wrote, some two decades ago, remains true today:

"It is the proud claim of a democratic society that the people are masters and all officials of the state are servants of the people. That being so, the ancient rule of *respondeat superior* furnishes us with a simple, direct and reasonable basis for refusing to admit evidence secured in violation of constitutional or statutory provisions. Since the policeman is society's servant, his acts in the execution of his duty are attributable to the master or employer. Society as a whole is thus responsible and society is 'penalized' by refusing it the benefit of evidence secured by the illegal action. This satisfies me more than the other explanations because it seems to me that society—in a country like ours—*is* involved in and *is* responsible for what is done in its name and by its agents. Unlike the Germans of the 1930's and early '40's, we cannot say 'it is all The Leader's doing. I am not responsible.' In a representative democracy

is to deter – to compel respect for the constitutional guaranty in the only effectively available way, by removing the incentive to disregard it.'' If the police cannot use evidence obtained through warrants issued on less than probable cause, they have less incentive to seek those warrants, and magistrates have less incentive to issue them.

Today's decisions do grave damage to that deterrent function. Under the majority's new rule, even when the police know their warrant application is probably insufficient, they retain an incentive to submit it to a magistrate, on the chance that he may take the bait. No longer must they hesitate and seek additional evidence in doubtful cases.

The Court is of course correct that the exclusionary rule cannot deter when the authorities have no reason to know that their conduct is unconstitutional. But when probable cause is lacking, then by definition a reasonable person under the circumstances would not believe there is a fair likelihood that a search will produce evidence of a crime. Under such circumstances well-trained professionals must know that they are violating the Constitution. The Court's approach – which, in effect, encourages the police to seek a warrant even if they know the existence of probable cause is doubtful – can only lead to an increased number of constitutional violations.

Today, for the first time, this Court holds that although the Constitution has been violated, no court should do anything about it at any time and in any proceeding.[35] In my judgment, the Constitution requires more. Courts simply cannot escape their responsibility for redressing constitutional violations if they admit evidence obtained through unreasonable searches and seizures, since the entire point of police

conduct that violates the Fourth Amendment is to obtain evidence for use at trial. If such evidence is admitted, then the courts become not merely the final and necessary link in an unconstitutional chain of events, but its actual motivating force. ''If the existing code does not permit district attorneys to have a hand in such dirty business it does not permit the judge to allow such iniquities to succeed.'' *Olmstead v. United States*, 277 U.S 438, 470 (1928) (Holmes, J., dissenting). Nor should we so easily concede the existence of a constitutional violation for which there is no remedy. To do so is to convert a Bill of *Rights* into an unenforced honor code that the police may follow in their discretion. The Constitution requires more; it requires a *remedy*. If the Court's new rule is to be followed, the Bill of Rights should be renamed.

It is of course true that the exclusionary rule exerts a high price – the loss of probative evidence of guilt. But that price is one courts have often been required to pay to serve important social goals. That price is also one the Fourth Amendment requires us to pay, assuming as we must that the Framers intended that its strictures ''shall not be violated.'' For in all such cases, as Justice Stewart has observed, ''the same extremely relevant evidence would not have been obtained had the police officer complied with the commands of the fourth amendment in the first place.''

> ''[T]he forefathers thought this was not too great a price to pay for that decent privacy of home, papers and effects which is indispensable to individual dignity and self-respect. They may have overvalued privacy, but I am not disposed to set their command at naught.'' *Harris v. United States*, 331 U.S. 145, 198 (1947) (Jackson, J., dissenting).

We could, of course, facilitate the process of administering justice to those who violate the criminal laws by ignoring the commands of the Fourth Amendment – indeed, by ignoring the entire Bill of Rights – but it is the very purpose of a Bill of Rights to identify values that may not be sacrificed to expediency. In a just society those who govern, as well as those who are governed, must obey the law.

I would vacate the judgment in *Leon* and remand the case to the Court of Appeals for reconsideration in the light of *Gates*. Accordingly, I respectfully dissent.

---

we are responsible, whether we like it or not. And so each of us is involved and each is in this sense responsible when a police officer breaks rules of law established for our common protection.'' Burger, Who Will Watch the Watchman?, 14 Am.U.L.Rev. 1, 14 (1964) (emphasis in original) (footnote omitted).

[35] As the majority recognizes in all cases in which its ''good faith'' exception to the exclusionary rule would operate, there will also be immunity from civil damages.

## QUESTIONS AND NOTES

**1.** Do you think that the Court inappropriately balances the costs and benefits of the exclusionary rule?

**2.** Is the dispute between the Court and Justice Brennan anything more than a replay of *Calandra*?

**3.** Do you agree with the Court that indiscriminate application of the exclusionary rule brings the Court into disrespect?

**4.** Is the problem (if there is one) the exclusionary rule or the Fourth Amendment itself?

**5.** Is *Leon* likely to adversely impact on the magistrate's performance? Is it likely to change the manner in which police present warrants? Is it likely to lead to (more) magistrate shopping?

**6.** Is it relevant, as Justice Stevens suggests, that one of the purposes of the Fourth Amendment was to strictly circumscribe the power of magistrates to issue warrants? If he is correct, is *Leon* necessarily wrongly decided?

**7.** If the police are acting in objective good faith, is there anything more that we can expect of them?

**8.** Can you imagine a case in which a warrant would have been invalid under *Gates*, but valid under *Leon*?

**9.** If your answer to question 7 was "no," does that suggest that *Leon* is a lot of fuss about nothing?

**10.** Given that neither money damages nor exclusion of evidence is appropriate when police officer's act in good faith, is it meaningful to call the officer's action a violation of the Fourth Amendment at all?

**11.** Given the implication of question 10, would it have been better for the Court to hold that the Fourth Amendment is satisfied when the police act in good faith reliance on a warrant issued by a magistrate?

**12.** In the companion case, *Sheppard*, the Court found another good faith exception to the exclusionary rule.

## Massachusetts v. Sheppard
### 468 U.S. 981 (1984)

Justice WHITE delivered the opinion of the Court.

This case involves the application of the rules articulated today in *Leon* to a situation in which police officers seize items pursuant to a warrant subsequently invalidated because of a technical error on the part of the issuing judge.

### I

The badly burned body of Sandra Boulware was discovered in a vacant lot in the Roxbury section of Boston at approximately 5 a.m., Saturday, May 5, 1979. An autopsy revealed that Boulware had died of multiple compound skull fractures caused by blows to the head. After a brief investigation, the police decided to question one of the victim's boyfriends, Osborne Sheppard. Sheppard told the police that he had last seen the victim on Tuesday night and that he had been at a local gaming house (where card games were played) from 9 p.m. Friday until 5 a.m. Saturday. He identified several people who would be willing to substantiate the latter claim.

By interviewing the people Sheppard had said were at the gaming house on Friday night, the police learned that although Sheppard was at the gaming house that night, he had borrowed an automobile at about 3 a.m. Saturday morning in order to give two men a ride home. Even though the trip normally took only fifteen minutes, Sheppard did not return with the car until nearly 5 a.m.

On Sunday morning, police officers visited the owner of the car Sheppard had borrowed. He consented to an inspection of the vehicle. Bloodstains and pieces of hair were found on the rear bumper and within the trunk compartment. In addition, the officers noticed strands of wire in the trunk similar to wire strands found on and near the body of the victim. The owner of the car told the officers that when he last used the car on Friday night, shortly before Sheppard borrowed it, he had placed articles in the trunk and had not noticed any stains on the bumper or in the trunk.

On the basis of the evidence gathered thus far in the investigation, Detective Peter O'Malley drafted an affidavit designed to support an application for an arrest warrant and a search warrant authorizing a search of Sheppard's residence. The affidavit set forth the results of the investigation and stated that the police wished to search for:

> "[a] fifth bottle of amaretto liquor, 2 nickel bags of marijuana, a woman's jacket that has been described as black-grey (charcoal), any possessions of Sandra D. Boulware, similar type wire and rope that match those on the body of Sandra D. Boulware, or in the above Thunderbird. A blunt instrument that might have been used on the victim, men's or women's clothing that may have blood, gasoline burns on them. Items that may have fingerprints of the victim."[1]

Detective O'Malley showed the affidavit to the district attorney, the district attorney's first assistant, and a sergeant, who all concluded that it set forth probable cause for the search and the arrest.

Because it was Sunday, the local court was closed, and the police had a difficult time finding a warrant application form. Detective O'Malley finally found a warrant form previously in use in the Dorchester District. The form was entitled "Search Warrant—Controlled Substance G.L. c. 276 §§ 1 through 3A." Realizing that some changes had to be made before the form could be used to authorize the search requested in the affidavit, Detective O'Malley deleted the subtitle "controlled substance" with a typewriter. He also substituted "Roxbury" for the printed "Dorchester" and typed Sheppard's name and address into blank spaces provided

for that information. However, the reference to "controlled substance" was not deleted in the portion of the form that constituted the warrant application and that, when signed, would constitute the warrant itself.

Detective O'Malley then took the affidavit and the warrant form to the residence of a judge who had consented to consider the warrant application. The judge examined the affidavit and stated that he would authorize the search as requested. Detective O'Malley offered the warrant form and stated that he knew the form as presented dealt with controlled substances. He showed the judge where he had crossed out the subtitles. After unsuccessfully searching for a more suitable form, the judge informed O'Malley that he would make the necessary changes so as to provide a proper search warrant. The judge then took the form, made some changes on it, and dated and signed the warrant. However, he did not change the substantive portion of the warrant, which continued to authorize a search for controlled substances; nor did he alter the form so as to incorporate the affidavit. The judge returned the affidavit and the warrant to O'Malley, informing him that the warrant was sufficient authority in form and content to carry out the search as requested. O'Malley took the two documents and, accompanied by other officers, proceeded to Sheppard's residence. The scope of the ensuing search was limited to the items listed in the affidavit, and several incriminating pieces of evidence were discovered.[4] Sheppard was then charged with first degree murder.

II

Having already decided that the exclusionary rule should not be applied when the officer conducting the search acted in objectively reasonable reliance on a warrant issued by a detached and neutral magistrate that subsequently is determined to be invalid, the sole issue before us in this case is whether the officers reasonably believed that the search they conducted was authorized by a valid warrant. There is no dispute that the officers believed that the warrant authorized the search that they conducted. Thus, the only question is whether there was an objectively

---

[1] The liquor and marihuana were included in the request because Sheppard had told the officers that when he was last with the victim, the two had purchased two bags of marihuana and a fifth of amaretto before going to his residence.

[4] The police found a pair of bloodstained boots, blood stains on the concrete floor, a woman's earring with bloodstains on it, a bloodstained envelope, a pair of men's jockey shorts and women's leotards with blood on them, three types of wire, and a woman's hairpiece, subsequently identified as the victim's.

reasonable basis for the officers' mistaken belief. Both the trial court and a majority of the Supreme Judicial Court concluded that there was. We agree.

The officers in this case took every step that could reasonably be expected of them. Detective O'Malley prepared an affidavit which was reviewed and approved by the District Attorney. He presented that affidavit to a neutral judge. The judge concluded that the affidavit established probable cause to search Sheppard's residence and informed O'Malley that he would authorize the search as requested. O'Malley then produced the warrant form and informed the judge that it might need to be changed. He was told by the judge that the necessary changes would be made. He then observed the judge make some changes and received the warrant and the affidavit. At this point, a reasonable police officer would have concluded, as O'Malley did, that the warrant authorized a search for the materials outlined in the affidavit.

Sheppard contends that since O'Malley knew the warrant form was defective, he should have examined it to make sure that the necessary changes had been made. However, that argument is based on the premise that O'Malley had a duty to disregard the judge's assurances that the requested search would be authorized and the necessary changes would be made. Whatever an officer may be required to do when he executes a warrant without knowing beforehand what items are to be seized, we refuse to rule that an officer is required to disbelieve a judge who has just advised him, by word and by action, that the warrant he possesses authorizes him to conduct the search he has requested. In Massachusetts, as in most jurisdictions, the determinations of a judge acting within his jurisdiction, even if erroneous, are valid and binding until they are set aside under some recognized procedure. If an officer is required to accept at face value the judge's conclusion that a warrant form is invalid, there is little reason why he should be expected to disregard assurances that everything is all right, especially when he has alerted the judge to the potential problems.

The judgment of the Supreme Judicial Court is therefore reversed, and the case is remanded for further proceedings not inconsistent with this opinion.

Justice STEVENS concurring.

## II

[T]here is no contention that the police officers did not receive appropriate judicial authorization for their search of respondent's residence. A neutral and detached judicial officer had correctly determined that there was probable cause to conduct a search. Nevertheless, the Supreme Judicial Court suppressed the fruits of the search because the warrant did not particularly describe the place to be searched and the things to be seized.

The particularity requirement of the Fourth Amendment has a manifest purpose—to prevent general searches. By limiting the authorization to search to the specific areas and things for which there is probable cause to search, the requirement ensures that the search is carefully tailored to its justification, and does not resemble the wide-ranging general searches that the Framers intended to prohibit.[4] In this case the warrant did not come close to authorizing a general search.[5]

The affidavit supporting the application for the warrant correctly identified the things to be seized, and on its face the affidavit indicated that it had been presented to the judge who had issued the warrant.[6] Both the police officers and the judge were fully aware of the contents of the affidavit, and therefore knew precisely what the officers were authorized to search for. Since the affidavit was available for after-the-fact review, the Massachusetts courts could readily ascertain the limits of the officers' authority

---

[4] See *Andresen v. Maryland*, 427 U.S. 463, 480 (1976); *Stanley v. Georgia*, 394 U.S. 557, 569-572 (1969) (Stewart, J., concurring in the result); *Stanford v. Texas*, 379 U.S. 476, 481-482, 485 (1965); *Go-Bart Importing Co. v. United States*, 282 U.S. 344, 357 (1931); *Marron v. United States*, 275 U.S. 192, 195-196 (1927).

[5] Indeed, the "defect" in the warrant was that it authorized—albeit mistakenly—a search for quite particular "things to be seized," controlled substances, rather than the evidence described in the affidavit supporting the warrant application. This "defect" posed no risk of a general search. On its face, the warrant correctly identified the place to be searched. Thus, the threshold invasion of privacy—entry into respondent's home—was properly and specifically authorized. Moreover, the four corners of the warrant plainly indicate that it was not intended to authorize a search for controlled substances. On the cover of the warrant the caption "Controlled Substances" had been crossed out, and an "addendum" to the warrant authorized a search for and seizure of a rifle and ammunition, indicating that the warrant was not limited to controlled substances.

[6] The issuing judge attested to the affiant's signature on the affidavit.

under the warrant. In short, the judge who issued the warrant, the police officers who executed it, and the reviewing courts all were able easily to ascertain the precise scope of the authorization provided by the warrant.

All that our cases require is that a warrant contain a description sufficient to enable the officers who execute it to ascertain with reasonable effort where they are to search and what they are to seize. The test is whether the executing officers' discretion has been limited in a way that forbids a general search. Here there was no question that the executing officers' discretion had been limited—they, as well as the reviewing courts, knew the precise limits of their authorization. There was simply no "occasion or opportunity for officers to rummage at large."

The only Fourth Amendment interest that is arguably implicated by the "defect" in the warrant is the citizen's interest in being able to ascertain the limits of the officers' authorization by examining the warrant. Respondent, however, was not home at the time the warrant was executed, and therefore had no occasion to see the warrant. The two persons who were present when the warrant was executed, respondent's mother and sister, did not read the warrant or ask to have it read. "[T]he general rule [is] that Fourth Amendment rights are personal rights which, like some other constitutional rights, may not be vicariously asserted." *Alderman v. United States*, 394 U.S. 165, 174 (1969). Thus, respondent, who

has standing to assert only his own Fourth Amendment interests, cannot complain that his interest in ascertaining the limits of the officers' authority under the search warrant was infringed.[12] In short, our precedents construing the particularity requirement of the Warrant Clause unambiguously demonstrate that this warrant did not violate the Fourth Amendment.

Justice BRENNAN, joined by Justice MARSHALL, dissented. [The *Leon* opinion covered both cases.]

---

[12] Even if respondent had standing to assert his right to be able to ascertain the officers' authority from the four corners of the warrant, it is doubtful that he could succeed. On its face the warrant authorized a search of respondent's residence, "42 Deckard Street." Had respondent read the warrant he would have had no reason to question the officers' right to enter the premises. Moreover, the face of the warrant indicated that the caption "Controlled Substances" had been stricken, and at the bottom on the warrant an addendum authorized the search for and seizure of a rifle and ammunition. The supporting affidavit, which the police had with them when they executed the warrant, and which was attested by the same judge who had issued the warrant, described in detail the items for which the police were authorized to search and to seize.

## QUESTIONS AND NOTES

**1.** Do you think that the evidence should have been admissible against Sheppard? Why? Why not?

**2.** If your answer to question 1 were "yes," or if you were aware that the Court on which you were sitting was prepared to so hold, would you have preferred Justice White's approach or Justice Stevens' approach? Explain.

**3.** Would (should) the good faith exception apply to a police officer's reasonable belief that an unconstitutional search authorized by an unconstitutional statute is constitutional. In a 5-4 decision, the Supreme Court answered that question "yes." See *Illinois v. Krull*, 480 U.S. 340 (1987).

**4.** When considering questions such as those raised in this section (or for that matter, the entire book), the diligent attorney should not ignore State Constitutions or State Statutes. *Commonwealth v. Edmunds*, suggests both of those potential sources.

## Commonwealth v. Edmunds
### 586 A.2d 887 (Pennsylvania, 1991)

CAPPY, Justice.

### I. THE HISTORY OF THE CASE

The issue presented to this court is whether Pennsylvania should adopt the "good faith" exception to the exclusionary rule as articulated by the United States Supreme Court in *Leon*. We conclude that a "good faith" exception to the exclusionary rule would frustrate the guarantees embodied in Article I, Section 8, of the Pennsylvania Constitution. Accordingly, the decision of the Superior Court is reversed.

The defendant in the instant case was found guilty after a non-jury trial on August 18, 1987 of criminal conspiracy, simple possession, possession with intent to deliver, possession with intent to manufacture and manufacture of a controlled substance. The conviction was premised upon the admission into evidence of marijuana seized at the defendant's property pursuant to a search warrant, after information was received from two anonymous informants.

The trial court held that the search warrant failed to establish probable cause that the marijuana would be at the location to be searched on the date it was issued. The trial court found that the warrant failed to set forth with specificity the date upon which the anonymous informants observed the marijuana. See, *Commonwealth v. Conner*, 452 Pa. 333, 305 A.2d 341 (1973). However, the trial court went on to deny the defendant's motion to suppress the marijuana. Applying the rationale of *Leon*, the trial court looked beyond the four corners of the affidavit, in order to establish that the officers executing the warrant acted in "good faith" in relying upon the warrant to conduct the search. In reaching this conclusion the trial court also decided that *Leon* permitted the court to undercut the language of Pa.R.Crim.P. 2003, which prohibits oral testimony outside the four corners of the written affidavit to supplement the finding of probable cause.

The Superior Court in a divided panel decision, opinion by Wieand J., dissent by Popovich J., affirmed the judgment of the trial court, specifically relying upon in *Leon*.

As a preliminary matter, we concur with the inevitable conclusion of the trial court and the Superior Court, that probable cause did not exist on the face of the warrant. In *Conner*, this Court made clear that a search warrant is defective if it is issued without reference to the time when the informant obtained his or her information. Coupled with *Pa.R.Crim.P.*

2003, which mandates that courts in Pennsylvania shall not consider oral testimony outside the four corners of the written affidavit to supplement the finding of probable cause for a search warrant, we are compelled to conclude that the affidavit of probable cause and warrant were facially invalid. As the Superior Court candidly stated, the affidavit in question "did not contain facts from which the date of the hunters' observations could be determined." Indeed, the dissenting opinion of Mr. Justice McDermott concedes that probable cause was lacking.

We are not at liberty to ignore the *Leon* issue as it has been injected into the case by the trial court, and expressly affirmed by the Superior Court. Both lower courts have acknowledged, correctly, that Rule 2003 and our decision in *Conner* render the warrant invalid on its face under Pennsylvania law. The only way to salvage the warrant from facial invalidity is to disregard Rule 2003 and consider oral testimony outside the four corners of the affidavit to establish probable cause, which we are not free to do; or to consider the same oral testimony to establish a "good faith" exception under the federal *Leon* test, which is precisely what the trial court sought to accomplish. The trial judge conducted a supplemental suppression hearing for the express purpose of bringing the *Leon* issue four-square into this case, and the Superior Court affirmed explicitly on that basis. The "good faith" exception issue having thus been joined by both courts below, we are now constrained to address it.

The sole question in this case, therefore, is whether the Constitution of Pennsylvania incorporates a "good faith" exception to the exclusionary rule, which permits the introduction of evidence seized where probable cause is lacking on the face of the warrant.

Put in other terms, the question is whether the federal *Leon* test circumvents the acknowledged deficiencies under Pennsylvania law, and prevents the suppression of evidence seized pursuant to an *invalid search warrant*. For the reasons that follow, we conclude that it does not.

[After analyzing *Leon*, *Sheppard*, and *Krull*, the Court continued.]

### III. FACTORS TO CONSIDER IN UNDERTAKING PENNSYLVANIA CONSTITUTIONAL ANALYSIS

This Court has long emphasized that, in interpreting a provision of the Pennsylvania Constitution, we are not bound by the decisions of the United States Supreme Court which interpret similar (yet distinct) federal constitutional provisions.

As Mr. Chief Justice Nix aptly stated, the federal constitution establishes certain minimum levels which are "equally applicable to the [analogous] state constitutional provision." However, each state has the power to provide broader standards, and go beyond the minimum floor which is established by the federal Constitution. *Commonwealth v. Sell*, 470 A.2d at 467.

The United States Supreme Court has repeatedly affirmed that the states are not only free to, but also encouraged to engage in independent analysis in drawing meaning from their own state constitutions. See *PruneYard Shopping Center v. Robins*, 447 U.S. 74, 80-82 (1980) (Rehnquist, J.). Indeed, this is a positive expression of the jurisprudence which has existed in the United States since the founding of the nation. Alexander Hamilton, lobbying for the ratification of the U.S. Constitution in the Federalist Papers over two hundred years ago, made clear that the Supremacy Clause of the Federal Constitution was never designed to overshadow the states, or prevent them from maintaining their own pockets of autonomy. See, The Federalist No. 33 (A. Hamilton), in *The Federalist Papers* (The New American Library ed.) 204.

The past two decades have witnessed a strong resurgence of independent state constitutional analysis, in Pennsylvania and elsewhere.

Here in Pennsylvania, we have stated with increasing frequency that it is both important and necessary that we undertake an independent analysis of the Pennsylvania Constitution, each time a provision of that fundamental document is implicated. Although we may accord weight to federal decisions where they "are found to be logically persuasive and well reasoned, paying due regard to precedent and the policies underlying specific constitutional guarantees," we are free to reject the conclusions of the United States Supreme Court so long as we remain faithful to the minimum guarantees established by the United States Constitution.

Accordingly, as a general rule it is important that litigants brief and analyze at least the following four factors:

1) text of the Pennsylvania constitutional provision;

2) history of the provision, including Pennsylvania case-law;

3) related case-law from other states;

4) policy considerations, including unique issues of state and local concern, and applicability within modern Pennsylvania jurisprudence.

Depending upon the particular issue presented, an examination of related federal precedent may be useful as part of the state constitutional analysis, not as binding authority, but as one form of guidance. However, it is essential that courts in Pennsylvania undertake an independent analysis under the Pennsylvania Constitution. Utilizing the above four factors, and having reviewed *Leon*, we conclude that a "good faith" exception to the exclusionary rule would frustrate the guarantees embodied in Article I, Section 8 of our Commonwealth's constitution.

## IV. ANALYSIS

### A. Text

The text of Article 1, Section 8 of the Pennsylvania Constitution provides as follows:

*Security from Searches and Seizures*

Section 8. The people shall be secure in their persons, houses, papers and possessions from unreasonable searches and seizures, and no warrant to search any place or to seize any person or things shall issue without describing them as nearly as may be, nor without probable cause, supported by oath or affirmation subscribed to by the affiant.

Although the wording of the Pennsylvania Constitution is similar in language to the Fourth Amendment of the United States Constitution, we are not bound to interpret the two provisions as if they were mirror images, even where the text is similar or identical. Thus, we must next examine the history of Article I, Section 8, in order to draw meaning from that provision and consider the appropriateness of a "good faith" exception to the exclusionary rule in the Pennsylvania constitutional scheme.

### B. History

We have made reference, on repeated occasions, to the unique history of Article 1, Section 8, as well as other provisions of the Pennsylvania Constitution. As we noted in *Sell*: "constitutional protection against unreasonable searches and seizures existed in Pennsylvania more than a decade before the adoption of the federal Constitution, and fifteen years prior to the promulgation of the Fourth Amendment."

Thus, contrary to the popular misconception that state constitutions are somehow patterned after the United States Constitution, the reverse is true. The federal Bill of Rights borrowed heavily from the Declarations of Rights contained in the constitutions of Pennsylvania and other colonies.

With respect to Article 1, Section 8 of the present Pennsylvania Constitution, which relates to freedom from unreasonable searches and seizures, that provision had its origin prior to the 4th Amendment, in Clause 10 of the original Constitution of 1776. Specifically, the original version of the search and seizure provision reads as follows:

The people have a right to hold themselves, their houses, papers and possessions free from search and seizure, and therefore warrants without oaths or affirmations first made, affording sufficient foundation for them, and whereby any officer or messenger may be commanded or required to search suspected places, or to seize any person or persons, his or their property, not particularly described, are contrary to that right and ought not be granted.

The requirement of probable cause in this Commonwealth thus traces its origin to its original Constitution of 1776, drafted by the first convention of delegates chaired by Benjamin Franklin. The primary purpose of the warrant requirement was to abolish "general warrants," which had been used by the British to conduct sweeping searches of residences and businesses, based upon generalized suspicions. Therefore, at the time the Pennsylvania Constitution was drafted in 1776, the issue of searches and seizures unsupported by probable cause was of utmost concern to the constitutional draftsmen.

Moreover, as this Court has stated repeatedly in interpreting Article 1, Section 8, that provision is meant to embody a strong notion of privacy, carefully safeguarded in this Commonwealth for the past two centuries. As we stated in *Sell*: "the survival of the language now employed in Article 1, Section 8 through over 200 years of profound change in other areas demonstrates that the paramount concern for privacy first adopted as part of our organic law in 1776 continues to enjoy the mandate of the people of this Commonwealth."

The history of Article I, Section 8, thus indicates that the purpose underlying the exclusionary rule in this Commonwealth is quite distinct from the purpose underlying the exclusionary rule under the 4th Amendment, as articulated by the majority in *Leon*.

The United States Supreme Court in *Leon* made clear that, in its view, the *sole purpose* for the exclusionary rule under the 4th Amendment was to deter police misconduct. The *Leon* majority also made clear that, under the Federal Constitution, the exclusionary rule operated as "a judicially created remedy designed to safeguard Fourth Amendment rights generally through its deterrent effect, rather than a personal constitutional right of the party aggrieved."

This reinterpretation differs from the way the exclusionary rule has evolved in Pennsylvania since the decision of *Mapp v. Ohio* in 1961 and represents a shift in judicial philosophy from the decisions of the United States Supreme Court dating back to *Weeks v. United States*.

Like many of its sister states, Pennsylvania did not adopt an exclusionary rule until the United States Supreme Court's decision in *Mapp* required it to do so. However, at the time the exclusionary rule was embraced in Pennsylvania, we clearly viewed it as a constitutional mandate. This interpretation was in keeping with a long line of federal cases, beginning with *Weeks* in 1914, which viewed the exclusionary rule as a necessary corollary to the prohibition against unreasonable searches and seizures.

During the first decade after *Mapp*, our decisions in Pennsylvania tended to parallel the cases interpreting the 4th Amendment. However, beginning in 1973, our case-law began to reflect a clear divergence from federal precedent. The United States Supreme Court at this time began moving towards a metamorphosed view, suggesting that the purpose of the exclusionary rule "is not to redress the injury to the *privacy* of the search victim (but, rather) to deter future *unlawful police conduct*." *Calandra*, 414 U.S. at 347 (emphasis added). At the same time this Court began to forge its own path under Article I, Section 8 of the Pennsylvania Constitution, declaring with increasing frequency that Article I, Section 8 of the Pennsylvania Constitution embodied a strong notion of privacy, notwithstanding federal cases to the contrary. In *Commonwealth v. Platou* and *Commonwealth v. DeJohn*, we made explicit that "the right to be free from unreasonable searches and seizures contained in Article I, Section 8 of the Pennsylvania Constitution is tied into the implicit right to privacy in this Commonwealth." In *DeJohn*, we specifically refused to follow the U.S. Supreme Court's decision in *U.S. v. Miller*, 425 U.S. 435 (1976), which had held that a citizen had no standing to object to the seizure of his or her bank records.

From *DeJohn* forward, a steady line of case-law has evolved under the Pennsylvania Constitution, making clear that Article I, Section 8 is unshakably linked to a right of privacy in this Commonwealth.

Most recently, in *Melilli*, 521 Pa. 405, 555 A.2d 1254 (1989), this Court held that Article I, Section 8 of the Pennsylvania Constitution was offended by the installation of a pen register device without probable cause. Mr. Justice Papadakos, in rejecting the holding of the United States Supreme Court in *Smith v. Maryland*, emphasized that "Article I, Section 8 of the Pennsylvania Constitution . . . may be employed to guard *individual privacy* rights against unreasonable searches and seizures more zealously than the federal government does under the Constitution of the United States by serving as an independent source of supplemental rights.'' Mr. Justice Papadakos went on to conclude that, because a pen register ''is the equivalent of a search warrant in its operative effect where the intrusion involves a violation of a privacy interest,'' the affidavit and order ''must comply with the requirements of probable cause required under Pa. Rules of Criminal Procedure Chapter 2000, Search Warrants.''

Thus, the exclusionary rule in Pennsylvania has consistently served to bolster the twin aims of Article I, Section 8; to-wit, the safeguarding of privacy and the fundamental requirement that warrants shall only be issued upon probable cause.

Whether the United States Supreme Court has determined that the exclusionary rule does not advance the 4th Amendment purpose of deterring police conduct is irrelevant. Indeed, we disagree with that Court's suggestion in *Leon* that we in Pennsylvania have been employing the exclusionary rule all these years to deter police corruption. We flatly reject this notion. We have no reason to believe that police officers or district justices in the Commonwealth of Pennsylvania do not engage in ''good faith'' in carrying out their duties. What is significant, however, is that our Constitution has historically been interpreted to incorporate a strong right of privacy, and an equally strong adherence to the requirement of probable cause under Article 1, Section 8. Citizens in this Commonwealth possess such rights, even where a police officer in ''good faith'' carrying out his or her duties inadvertently invades the privacy or circumvents the strictures of probable cause. To adopt a ''good faith'' exception to the exclusionary rule, we believe, would virtually emasculate those clear safeguards which have been carefully developed under the Pennsylvania Constitution over the past 200 years.

### C. Related Case-Law From Other States

A number of states other than Pennsylvania have confronted the issue of whether to apply a ''good faith'' exception to the exclusionary rule, under their own constitutions, in the wake of *Leon*.

The highest courts of at least two states – Arkansas and Missouri – have seemingly embraced the good faith exception under their own constitutions. Intermediary appellate courts in at least four other states – Indiana, Kansas, Maryland and Louisiana – have indicated their acceptance of the ''good faith'' exception. In virtually all of those states embracing

the ''good-faith'' exception under their own constitutions, however, the reasoning is a simple affirmation of the logic of *Leon*, with little additional state constitutional analysis.[11]

On the other hand, the highest courts of at least four states – New Jersey, New York, North Carolina and Connecticut – have chosen to reject the ''good-faith'' exception under their own constitutions, with more detailed analysis of state constitutional principles. The intermediate appellate courts of at least four additional states – Tennessee, Wisconsin, Michigan, and Minnesota – have likewise eschewed the logic of *Leon* under their own state constitutions.

A mere scorecard of those states which have accepted and rejected *Leon* is certainly not dispositive of the issue in Pennsylvania. However, the logic of certain of those opinions bears upon our analysis under the Pennsylvania Constitution, particularly given the unique history of Article 1, Section 8.

In this respect, we draw support from other states which have declined to adopt a ''good faith'' exception, particularly New Jersey, Connecticut and North Carolina.

### D. Policy Considerations

We recognize that, in analyzing any state constitutional provision, it is necessary to go beyond the bare text and history of that provision as it was drafted 200 years ago, and consider its application within the modern scheme of Pennsylvania jurisprudence. An assessment of various policy considerations, however, only supports our conclusion that the good faith exception to the exclusionary rule would be inconsistent with the jurisprudence surrounding Article 1, Section 8.

First, such a rule would effectively negate the judicially created mandate reflected in the Pennsylvania Rules of Criminal Procedure, in Rules 2003, 2005 and 2006. Specifically, Rule 2003 relates to the requirements for the issuance of a warrant, and provides in relevant part:

(a) No search warrant shall issue but upon probable cause supported by one or more affidavits sworn to before the issuing authority. The issuing authority, in determining whether probable cause has been established, may not consider any evidence outside the affidavits.

---

[11] For a complete list of those states which have adopted and rejected *Leon*, with or without analysis, *see*, Uchida *et al*, *Acting In Good Faith: The Effects of United States v. Leon on the Police and Courts*, 30 Ariz.L.Rev. 467, 475-480 (1988).

(b) At any hearing on a motion for the return or suppression of evidence, or for suppression of the fruits of evidence, obtained pursuant to a search warrant, no evidence shall be admissible to establish probable cause other than the affidavits provided for in paragraph (a).

Rule 2003 thus adopts a "four corners" requirement, and provides that only evidence contained within the four corners of the affidavit may be considered to establish probable cause. This Rule, along with Rules 2005 and 2006 which reiterate that probable cause must exist on the face of the affidavit, were promulgated by this Court following this Court's decision in *Commonwealth v. Milliken*, 450 Pa. 310, 300 A.2d 78 (1973). The decision in *Milliken* is significant, because it makes clear that the "four corners" requirement of Rule 2003 was carefully and deliberately established in this Commonwealth.

In *Milliken*, a police officer had obtained a warrant to search the defendant's home for evidence relating to a murder, based upon an informant's tip. The affidavit of probable cause failed to set forth sufficient facts to establish the "reliability" of the informant, under the prevailing *Aguilar-Spinelli* test, rendering the warrant defective. At the suppression hearing, however, the police officer testified that he had given additional sworn oral testimony to the magistrate at the time the warrant was issued, not reduced to writing, which established the informant's reliability. The magistrate admitted that his memory was "dimmed" by the fact the proceeding was "some time ago," but essentially corroborated the officer's story.

This Court in *Milliken* rejected the contention that Article I, Section 8 of the Pennsylvania Constitution itself mandated that all facts relied upon to establish probable cause be reduced to writing; the constitutional language itself contained no such requirement. We therefore held that the sworn oral testimony of the police officer in that case could be used to supplement the affidavit. However, we went on to express deep concern for the fact that "the 'passage of time' inevitably causes 'memories . . . (to) fade.'" We stated that without a transcribed record made contemporaneously with the issuance of the warrant, "subsequent review of the partially unwritten proceeding may become tainted by possible additions of relevant information initially omitted but later supplied by hindsight."

Recognizing this "troublesome" dilemma, this Court in a thoughtful opinion written by the late Mr. Justice Roberts (later Chief Justice Roberts) and joined by then Mr. Justice, now Chief Justice Nix, announced in *Milliken* that we would exercise our supervisory powers to formulate a rule of procedure mandating that "a sufficient written record (be) made contemporaneously with the issuance of search warrants." We held that since this rule was procedural in nature, it could not be applied retroactively to invalidate the warrant in Milliken's case. However, we made clear that: "After the effective date of the rule the determination of probable cause by a suppression hearing court and an appellate court upon review will be made *only* from the written record prepared contemporaneously with the issuance of the search warrant." The result was the adoption of Pa.R.Crim.P. 2003 on March 28, 1973, effective in 60 days, which made explicit that probable cause for search warrants in Pennsylvania may be based only upon materials contained within the four corners of the written affidavit.

A second policy consideration which bolsters our conclusion is that the underlying premise of *Leon* is still open to serious debate. Although it is clear that the exclusionary rule presents some cost to society, in allowing "some guilty defendants (to) . . . go free," the extent of the costs are far from clear. A number of recent studies have indicated that the exclusion of illegally seized evidence has had a marginal effect in allowing guilty criminals to avoid successful prosecution. Indeed, the *Leon* decision itself indicates relatively low statistics with respect to the impact of the exclusionary rule in thwarting legitimate prosecutions. Equally as important, the alternative to the exclusionary rule most commonly advanced – i.e., allowing victims of improper searches to sue police officers directly – has raised serious concern among police officers.

A third policy consideration which compels our decisions is that, given the recent decision of the United States Supreme Court in *Gates*, adopting a "totality of the circumstances test" in assessing probable cause, there is far less reason to adopt a "good faith" exception to the exclusionary rule. We have adopted *Gates* as a matter of Pennsylvania law in the recent case of *Commonwealth v. Gray*. As a number of jurists have pointed out, the flexible *Gates* standard now eliminates much of the prior concern which existed with respect to an overly rigid application of the exclusionary rule.

Finally, the dangers of allowing magistrates to serve as "rubber stamps" and of fostering "magistrate-shopping," are evident under *Leon*. As the instant case illustrates, police officers and magistrates have historically worked closely together in this Commonwealth. Trooper Deise and District Justice Tlumac prepared the warrant and affidavit with Trooper Deise dictating the affidavit while the magistrate typed it verbatim.

There is no suggestion here that Trooper Deise and District Justice Tlumac acted other than in utmost "good faith" when preparing the warrant. Nevertheless, we are mindful of the fact that both state and federal interpretations of the 4th Amendment require a warrant to be issued by a "neutral and detached magistrate," because as Mr. Justice Papadakos noted, there is a requirement of "an independent determination of probable cause."

### CONCLUSION

Thirty years ago, when the exclusionary rule was first introduced, police officers were perhaps plagued with ill-defined, unarticulated rules governing their conduct. However, the past thirty years have seen a gradual sharpening of the process, with police officers adapting well to the exclusionary rule.

The purpose of Rule 2003 is not to exclude *bona fide* evidence based upon technical errors and omissions by police officers or magistrates. Rather, Rule 2003 is meant to provide support for the probable cause requirement of Article I, Section 8, by assuring that there is an objective method for determining when probable cause exists, and when it does not.

In the instant case, the evidence seized from defendant Edmunds was the product of a constitutionally defective search warrant. Article I, Section 8 of the Pennsylvania Constitution does not incorporate a "good faith" exception to the exclusionary rule. Therefore, the marijuana seized from the white corrugated building, the marijuana seized from Edmund's home, and the written and oral statements obtained from Edmunds by the troopers, must be suppressed. We base our decision strictly upon the Pennsylvania Constitution; any reference to the United States Constitution is merely for guidance and does not compel our decision.

Although the exclusionary rule may place a duty of thoroughness and care upon police officers and district justices in this Commonwealth, in order to safeguard the rights of citizens under Article I, Section 8, that is a small price to pay, we believe, for a democracy.

JUDGMENT OF SENTENCE REVERSED. Jurisdiction relinquished.

PAPADAKOS, Justice, concurring.

I am compelled to concur in the result because Rule 2003(a) of the Pa. Rules of Criminal Procedure is absolute in requiring that the affidavit of probable cause supporting the issuance of a search warrant must be complete on its face in every essential detail, and that no testimony is permitted after its execution to fill in the blanks. The affidavit of probable cause

in this case clearly lacks the essential element of the date when the informants saw the contraband growing. Although the affiant orally related to the magistrate, before the preparation of the affidavit of probable cause, the date on which the informants had seen the contraband growing, the magistrate, in acting the role of the scribe in typing the affidavit of probable cause, neglected to include this crucial date and the affiant neglected to spot this omission.

The majority correctly quotes this court's prior pronouncement on the subject:

"After the effective date of the rule the determination of probable cause by a suppression hearing court and an appellate court upon review will be made only from the written record prepared contemporaneously with the issuance of the search warrant."

*Commonwealth v. Milliken*, quoted by the majority opinion.

In view of the clear, unequivocal command of Rule 2003(a), I see no reason for the majority to reinvent the wheel and re-express the rationale underpinning the judicially created rule of procedure. It's all been said before. I see no issue of a good faith exception applicable in this case. I see only a reaffirmation of the dictates of Rule 2003(a) by simple statement to that effect or a change in the rule to accommodate the error committed by the scribe. Since the majority apparently does not wish to change the rule to avoid the absurdity of excluding the evidence obtained by the police through no misconduct on their part, I see no need for the in-depth re-analysis given by the majority.

Were the rule not so absolute on its face, I would gladly join McDermott, J., in dissent, for my sympathies and reason lie in his expression of outrage in the result of cases such as this.

McDERMOTT, Justice, dissenting.

Today we have abandoned the twenty seven (27) year history of this Court's restrictive use of the exclusionary rule to only those instances where its application would deter misconduct by law enforcement authorities. Now that we have ignored that history and have decided to employ it even in cases where police officers have fulfilled their every obligation to protect the individual constitutional rights of citizens, I dissent.

Until this day we have dutifully followed the canons of the Fourth Amendment prescribed by the Supreme Court of the United States through hundreds of cases. We accepted, as we must, their rationale that police procedures had overstepped constitutional bounds and we imposed the sanction of suppression to dissuade illegal search. To teach the lesson, we were obliged to ignore a mountain of illegal contraband that otherwise was palpable indicia of guilt. There is no doubt that the social cost has been more than criminals freed to try again. It has generated a disbelief and a growing disrespect in the efficacy of law that stands mute in the presence of incontrovertible evidence of fire and lets the house burn down because the fireman arrived before he was properly called. *Leon* does not open the gates to unauthorized search, it does not dissolve the need for probable cause. It simply and properly shifts the responsibility for determining probable cause to a neutral magistrate and frees the police of his or her mistakes. The police cannot search on a whim. They must present their cause to a neutral magistrate. The facts they present must be true, the magistrate must act within his bounds, and, as the final test, the police must employ their experience in recognizing whether a warrant is illegal despite the authorization of the magistrate. All of these contentions remain alive and subject to scrutiny at a suppression hearing. The instant case is a classic illustration. The defect in the affidavit of probable cause was that the time of the offense was not specified. What was told the magistrate was that the contraband was "growing," a clear indication of present tense. The informants told the police that they saw it growing and the magistrate was told that it was growing and he issued a search warrant on that premise. When the police arrived it was still growing. All concerned acted in good faith. To suppress the evidence because a date was not specified with exactitude under those circumstances dwindles into practiced absurdity.

The United States Supreme Court has made it abundantly clear that suppression of evidence seized without probable cause is not a constitutional right. This Court has made that clear as well. *See Commonwealth v. Miller*, 513 Pa. 118, 133-134, 518 A.2d 1187, 1195 (1986) ("[T]he exclusionary rule is a judicially created device designed to deter improper governmental action in the course of criminal investigations and prosecutions. It is not a personal right of the accused").

The United States Supreme Court has made it equally clear that suppression of evidence seized without probable cause is mandated to contain police action. Likewise, we have approved the suppression of evidence only where it will have the benefit of deterring similar police misconduct in the future.

In interpreting our Constitution we are, as are our sister states, always free to give more than that allowed under Federal Constitutional interpretation. I would choose to accept the rationale of the Supreme Court and recognize the "good faith exception" of *Leon* to the exclusionary rule as have eighteen of our sister states. My opinion is not merely grounded in the absurdity of excluding this evidence, nor only upon the persuasiveness of *Leon*, but also because it is firmly grounded in Pennsylvania jurisprudence.

[I]n *Commonwealth v. Melilli*, 521 Pa. 405, 555 A.2d 1254 (1989), we held that a pen register device could not be installed unless probable cause to do so was established. We concluded that evidence seized by the installation of pen registers without probable cause, even though the police reasonably relied upon the Federal standard, should nevertheless be suppressed. We explicitly did not disagree with the *Leon* decision. Instead, we determined that the evidence was appropriately suppressed because the judge who issued the order to install the pen registers never considered whether probable cause existed and thereby "wholly abandoned his judicial role," a situation "envisioned" by *Leon* as worthy of suppression.

To now reject the holding of *Leon* for Pennsylvania is mere fiat, an exercise of personal illumination about a need for protection not only from the police but from the judiciary. Like the United States Supreme Court, I find no evidence that the judiciary has run beyond its responsibilities, or that if they do we cannot correct them. The Supreme Court of the United States is a world landmark for the protection of constitutional rights. What they require we enforce; what they allow we ought not deter except upon clear evidence of positive need. The United States Supreme Court has recognized a positive need to allow, under the canons of *Leon*, a good faith exception. To do otherwise is to provide a sanctuary for the lawless elements seeking profit, particularly in the growing human misery of addiction.

I would affirm the Superior Court.

## QUESTIONS AND NOTES

**1.** Given that the deficiency in the *Edmunds* warrant was the failure to put the time of the relevant observations in writing, and given further that the essential nature of both the time (substance) and the writing (procedure) have been the law of Pennsylvania since 1973, how could the police officer possibly claimed to have acted in objective good faith?

**2.** How would you have decided this case if you had been on the Pennsylvania Supreme Court? Why?

**3.** The lesson of *Edmunds* clearly transcends the case itself. The opinion indicates that some, though not all, other Supreme Court cases upholding searches despite the Fourth Amendment have been rejected by the Pennsylvania Supreme Court. One faced with such a question in state court should *never* overlook the possibility of excluding evidence on state constitutional *or statutory* grounds.

**4.** Conversely, as the last case in this section, *Arizona v. Evans,* makes clear, the United States Supreme Court insists that a state court opinion purporting to rest on independent state grounds must do so clearly.

## Arizona v. Evans
### 115 S. Ct. 1185 (1995)

Chief Justice REHNQUIST delivered the opinion of the Court.

In January 1991, Phoenix police officer Bryan Sargent observed respondent Evans driving the wrong way on a one-way street in front of the police station. The officer stopped respondent and asked to see his driver's license. After respondent told him that his license had been suspended, the officer entered respondent's name into a computer data terminal located in his patrol car. The computer inquiry confirmed that respondent's license had been suspended and also indicated that there was an outstanding misdemeanor warrant for his arrest. Based upon the outstanding warrant, Officer Sargent placed respondent under arrest. While being handcuffed, respondent dropped a hand-rolled cigarette that the officers determined smelled of marijuana. Officers proceeded to search his car and discovered a bag of marijuana under the passenger's seat.

The State charged respondent with possession of marijuana. When the police notified the Justice Court that they had arrested him, the Justice Court discovered that the arrest warrant previously had been quashed and so advised the police. Respondent argued that because his arrest was based on a warrant that had been quashed 17 days prior to his arrest, the marijuana seized incident to the arrest should be suppressed as the fruit of an unlawful arrest. Respondent also argued that "[t]he 'good faith' exception to the exclusionary rule [was] inapplicable . . . because it was police error, not judicial error, which caused the invalid arrest."

At the suppression hearing, the Chief Clerk of the Justice Court testified that a Justice of the Peace had issued the arrest warrant on December 13, 1990, because respondent had failed to appear to answer for several traffic violations. On December 19, 1990, respondent appeared before a pro tem Justice of the Peace who entered a notation in respondent's file to "quash warrant."

The Chief Clerk also testified regarding the standard court procedure for quashing a warrant. Under that procedure a justice court clerk calls and informs the warrant section of the Sheriff's Office when a warrant has been quashed. The Sheriff's Office then removes the warrant from its computer records. After calling the Sheriff's Office, the clerk makes a note in the individual's file indicating the clerk who made the phone call and the person at the Sheriff's Office to whom the clerk spoke. The Chief Clerk testified that there was no indication in respondent's file that a clerk had called and notified the Sheriff's Office that his arrest warrant had been quashed. A records clerk from the Sheriff's Office also testified that the Sheriff's Office had no record of a telephone call informing it that respondent's arrest warrant had been quashed. At the close of testimony, respondent argued that the evidence obtained as a result of the arrest should be suppressed because "the purposes of the exclusionary rule would be served here by making the clerks for the court, or the clerk for the Sheriff's Office, whoever is responsible for this mistake, to be more careful about making sure that warrants are removed from the records."

We first must consider whether we have jurisdiction to review the Arizona Supreme Court's decision. Respondent argues that we lack jurisdiction under 28 U.S.C. § 1257 because the Arizona Supreme Court never passed upon the Fourth Amendment issue and instead based its decision on the Arizona good-faith statute, Ariz.Rev.Stat.Ann. § 13-3925 (1993), an adequate and independent state ground. In the alternative, respondent asks that we remand to the Arizona Supreme Court for clarification.

In *Michigan v. Long*, 463 U.S. 1032, we adopted a standard for determining whether a state-court decision rested upon an adequate and independent state ground. When "a state court decision fairly appears to rest primarily on federal law, or to be interwoven with the federal law, and when the adequacy and independence of any possible state law ground is not clear from the face of the opinion, we will accept as the most reasonable explanation that the state court decided the case the way it did because it believed that federal law required it to do so." We adopted this practice, in part, to obviate the "unsatisfactory and intrusive practice of requiring state courts to clarify their decisions to the satisfaction of this Court." We also concluded that this approach would "provide state judges with a clearer opportunity to develop state jurisprudence unimpeded by federal interference, and yet will preserve the integrity of federal law."

Justice GINSBURG would overrule *Long,* supra, because she believes that the rule of that case "impedes the States' ability to serve as laboratories for testing solutions to novel legal problems."

We believe that *Long* properly serves its purpose and should not be disturbed. Under it, state courts are absolutely free to interpret state constitutional provisions to accord greater protection to individual rights than do similar provisions of the United States Constitution.

Applying that standard here, we conclude that we have jurisdiction. In reversing the Court of Appeals, the Arizona Supreme Court stated that "[w]hile it may be inappropriate to invoke the exclusionary rule where a magistrate has issued a facially valid warrant (a discretionary judicial function) based on an erroneous evaluation of the facts, the law, or both, *Leon,* it is useful and proper to do so where negligent record keeping (a purely clerical function) results in an unlawful arrest." Thus, the Arizona Supreme Court's decision to suppress the evidence was based squarely upon its interpretation of federal law.

"The question whether the exclusionary rule's remedy is appropriate in a particular context has long been regarded as an issue separate from the question whether the Fourth Amendment rights of the party seeking to invoke the rule were violated by police conduct."

Where "the exclusionary rule does not result in appreciable deterrence, then, clearly, its use . . . is unwarranted."

In *Leon,* we applied these principles to the context of a police search in which the officers had acted in objectively reasonable reliance on a search warrant, issued by a neutral and detached Magistrate, that later was determined to be invalid. 468 U.S., at 905, 104 S.Ct., at 3411. On the basis of three factors, we determined that there was no sound reason to apply the exclusionary rule as a means of deterring misconduct on the part of judicial officers who are responsible for issuing warrants. First, we noted that the exclusionary rule was historically designed " 'to deter police misconduct rather than to punish the errors of judges and magistrates.' " Second, there was " 'no evidence suggesting that judges and magistrates are inclined to ignore or subvert the Fourth Amendment or that lawlessness among these actors requires the application of the extreme sanction of exclusion.' " Third, and of greatest importance, there was no basis for believing that exclusion of evidence seized pursuant to a warrant would have a significant deterrent effect on the issuing judge or magistrate.

The *Leon* Court then examined whether application of the exclusionary rule could be expected to alter the behavior of the law enforcement officers. We concluded:

> "[W]here the officer's conduct is objectively reasonable, 'excluding the evidence will not further the ends of the exclusionary rule in any appreciable way; for it is painfully apparent that . . . the officer is acting as a reasonable officer would and should act in similar circumstances. Excluding the evidence can in no way affect his future conduct unless it is to make him less willing to do his duty.' "

Respondent relies on *United States v. Hensley,* 469 U.S. 221 (1985), and argues that the evidence seized incident to his arrest should be suppressed because he was the victim of a Fourth Amendment violation. In *Hensley,* the Court determined that evidence uncovered as a result of a *Terry* stop was admissible because the officers who made the stop acted in objectively reasonable reliance on a flyer that had been issued by officers of another police department who possessed a reasonable suspicion to justify a *Terry* stop. Because the *Hensley* Court determined that there had been no Fourth Amendment violation, the Court never considered whether the seized evidence should have been excluded. *Hensley* does not contradict our earlier pronouncements that "[t]he question whether the exclusionary rule's remedy is appropriate in a particular context has long been regarded as an issue separate from the question whether the Fourth Amendment rights of the party seeking to invoke the rule were violated by police conduct."

Respondent also argues that *Whiteley v. Warden*, 401 U.S. 560 (1971), compels exclusion of the evidence. In *Whiteley*, the Court determined that the Fourth Amendment had been violated when police officers arrested Whiteley and recovered inculpatory evidence based upon a radio report that two suspects had been involved in two robberies. Although the "police were entitled to act on the strength of the radio bulletin," the Court determined that there had been a Fourth Amendment violation because the initial complaint, upon which the arrest warrant and subsequent radio bulletin were based, was insufficient to support an independent judicial assessment of probable cause. The Court concluded that "an otherwise illegal arrest cannot be insulated from challenge by the decision of the instigating officer to rely on fellow officers to make the arrest." Because the "arrest violated [Whiteley's] constitutional rights under the Fourth and Fourteenth Amendments; the evidence secured as an incident thereto should have been excluded from his trial."

Although *Whiteley* clearly retains relevance in determining whether police officers have violated the Fourth Amendment, its precedential value regarding application of the exclusionary rule is dubious. In *Whiteley*, the Court treated identification of a Fourth Amendment violation as synonymous with application of the exclusionary rule to evidence secured incident to that violation.

Subsequent case law has rejected this reflexive application of the exclusionary rule. *Sheppard, Leon*, and *Calandra*. These later cases have emphasized that the issue of exclusion is separate from whether the Fourth Amendment has been violated.

Applying the reasoning of *Leon* to the facts of this case, we conclude that the decision of the Arizona Supreme Court must be reversed. The Arizona Supreme Court determined that it could not "support the distinction drawn . . . between clerical errors committed by law enforcement personnel and similar mistakes by court employees," and that "even assuming . . . that responsibility for the error rested with the justice court, it does not follow that the exclusionary rule should be inapplicable to these facts."

This holding is contrary to the reasoning of *Leon* [and] *Sheppard*. If court employees were responsible for the erroneous computer record, the exclusion of evidence at trial would not sufficiently deter future errors so as to warrant such a severe sanction. First, as we noted in *Leon*, the exclusionary rule was historically designed as a means of deterring police misconduct, not mistakes by court employees. Second, respondent offers no evidence that court employees are inclined to ignore or subvert the Fourth

Amendment or that lawlessness among these actors requires application of the extreme sanction of exclusion. To the contrary, the Chief Clerk of the Justice Court testified at the suppression hearing that this type of error occurred once every three or four years.

Finally, and most important, there is no basis for believing that application of the exclusionary rule in these circumstances will have a significant effect on court employees responsible for informing the police that a warrant has been quashed. Because court clerks are not adjuncts to the law enforcement team engaged in the often competitive enterprise of ferreting out crime they have no stake in the outcome of particular criminal prosecutions. The threat of exclusion of evidence could not be expected to deter such individuals from failing to inform police officials that a warrant had been quashed.

If it were indeed a court clerk who was responsible for the erroneous entry on the police computer, application of the exclusionary rule also could not be expected to alter the behavior of the arresting officer. As the trial court in this case stated: "I think the police officer [was] bound to arrest. I think he would [have been] derelict in his duty if he failed to arrest." Excluding the evidence can in no way affect [the officer's] future conduct unless it is to make him less willing to do his duty. The Chief Clerk of the Justice Court testified that this type of error occurred "on[c]e every three or four years." In fact, once the court clerks discovered the error, they immediately corrected it, and then proceeded to search their files to make sure that no similar mistakes had occurred. There is no indication that the arresting officer was not acting objectively reasonably when he relied upon the police computer record. Application of the *Leon* framework supports a categorical exception to the exclusionary rule for clerical errors of court employees.

The judgment of the Supreme Court of Arizona is therefore reversed, and the case is remanded to that court for proceedings not inconsistent with this opinion.

It is so ordered.

Justice SOUTER, with whom Justice BREYER joins, concurring.

In joining the Court's opinion, I share Justice O'CONNOR's understanding of the narrow scope of what we hold today. To her concurrence, which I join as well, I add only that we do not answer another question that may reach us in due course, that is, how far, in dealing with fruits of computerized error, our very concept of deterrence by exclusion of evidence should extend to the government as a whole, not merely the police, on the ground that there would otherwise be no reasonable expectation of keeping the number of resulting false arrests within an acceptable minimum limit.

Justice O'CONNOR, with whom Justice SOUTER and Justice BREYER join, concurring.

The evidence in this case strongly suggests that it was a court employee's departure from established recordkeeping procedures that caused the record of respondent's arrest warrant to remain in the computer system after the warrant had been quashed. Prudently, then, the Court limits itself to the question whether a court employee's departure from such established procedures is the kind of error to which the exclusionary rule should apply. The Court holds that it is not such an error, and I agree with that conclusion and join the Court's opinion. The Court's holding reaffirms that the exclusionary rule imposes significant costs on society's law enforcement interests and thus should apply only where its deterrence purposes are "most efficaciously served."

In limiting itself to that single question, however, the Court does not hold that the court employee's mistake in this case was necessarily the only error that may have occurred and to which the exclusionary rule might apply. While the police were innocent of the court employee's mistake, they may or may not have acted reasonably in their reliance on the recordkeeping system itself. Surely it would not be reasonable for the police to rely, say, on a recordkeeping system, their own or some other agency's, that has no mechanism to ensure its accuracy over time and that routinely leads to false arrests, even years after the probable cause for any such arrest has ceased to exist (if it ever existed).

This is saying nothing new. We have said the same with respect to other information sources police use, informants being an obvious example. Certainly the reliability of recordkeeping systems deserves no less scrutiny than that of informants. Of course, the comparison to informants may be instructive the opposite way as well. So long as an informant's reliability does pass constitutional muster, a finding of probable cause may not be defeated by an after-the-fact showing that the information the informant provided was mistaken.

In recent years, we have witnessed the advent of powerful, computer-based recordkeeping systems that facilitate arrests in ways that have never before been possible. The police, of course, are entitled to enjoy the substantial advantages this technology confers. They may not, however, rely on it blindly. With the benefits of more efficient law enforcement mechanisms comes the burden of corresponding constitutional responsibilities.

Justice STEVENS, dissenting.

The Court seems to assume that the Fourth Amendment—and particularly the exclusionary rule, which effectuates the Amendment's commands—has the limited purpose of deterring police misconduct. Both the constitutional text and the history of its adoption and interpretation identify a more majestic conception. The Amendment protects the fundamental "right of the people to be secure in their persons, houses, papers, and effects," against all official searches and seizures that are unreasonable. The Amendment is a constraint on the power of the sovereign, not merely on some of its agents. The remedy for its violation imposes costs on that sovereign, motivating it to train all of its personnel to avoid future violations. See Stewart, *The Road to Mapp v. Ohio and Beyond: The Origins, Development and Future of the Exclusionary Rule in Search-and-Seizure Cases*, 83 Colum.L.Rev. 1365, 1400 (1983).

The exclusionary rule is not fairly characterized as an "extreme sanction." As Justice Stewart cogently explained, the implementation of this constitutionally mandated sanction merely places the Government in the same position as if it had not conducted the illegal search and seizure in the first place.[1] Given the undisputed fact in this case that the Constitution prohibited the warrantless arrest of petitioner, there is nothing "extreme" about the Arizona Supreme Court's conclusion that the State should not be permitted to profit from its negligent misconduct.

Even if one accepts deterrence as the sole rationale for the exclusionary rule, the Arizona Supreme Court's decision is correct on the merits. The majority's reliance on *Leon* is misplaced. The search in

---

[1] See Stewart, The Road to Mapp v. Ohio and Beyond: The Origins, Development and Future of the Exclusionary Rule in Search-and-Seizure Cases, 83 Colum.L.Rev. 1365, 1392 (1983). I am fully aware of the Court's statements that the question whether the exclusionary rule should be applied is distinct from the question whether the Fourth Amendment has been violated. I would note that such eminent members of this Court as Justices Holmes, Brandeis, Harlan, and Stewart have expressed the opposite view. The majority today candidly acknowledges that Justice Harlan's opinion for the Court in *Whiteley* "treated identification of a Fourth Amendment violation as synonymous with application of the exclusionary rule to evidence secured incident to that violation."

that case had been authorized by a presumptively valid warrant issued by a California Superior Court Judge. In contrast, this case involves a search pursuant to an arrest made when no warrant at all was outstanding against petitioner. The holding in *Leon* rested on the majority's doubt "that exclusion of evidence seized pursuant to a warrant will have a significant deterrent effect on the issuing judge or magistrate." The reasoning in *Leon* assumed the existence of a warrant; it was, and remains, wholly inapplicable to warrantless searches and seizures.

The *Leon* Court's exemption of judges and magistrates from the deterrent ambit of the exclusionary rule rested, consistently with the emphasis on the warrant requirement, on those officials' constitutionally determined role in issuing warrants. Taken on its own terms, *Leon's* logic does not extend to the time after the warrant has issued; nor does it extend to court clerks and functionaries, some of whom work in the same building with police officers and may have more regular and direct contact with police than with judges or magistrates.

The Phoenix Police Department was part of the chain of information that resulted in petitioner's unlawful, warrantless arrest. We should reasonably presume that law enforcement officials, who stand in the best position to monitor such errors as occurred here, can influence mundane communication procedures in order to prevent those errors. That presumption comports with the notion that the exclusionary rule exists to deter future police misconduct systemically. The deterrent purpose extends to law enforcement as a whole, not merely to "the arresting officer." *Whiteley*. Consequently, the Phoenix officers' good faith does not diminish the deterrent value of invalidating their arrest of petitioner.

The Court seeks to minimize the impact of its holding on the security of the citizen by referring to the testimony of the chief clerk of the East Phoenix Number One Justice Court that in her "particular court" this type of error occurred "'maybe [once] every three or four years.'" Apart from the fact that the clerk promptly contradicted herself,[3] this is slim

---

[3] "Q. In your eight years as a chief clerk with the Justice of the Peace, have there been other occasions where a warrant was quashed but the police were not notified?

"A. That does happen on rare occasions.

"Q. And when you say rare occasions, about how many times in your eight years as chief clerk?

"A. In my particular court, they would be like maybe one every three or four years.

"Q. When something like this happens, is anything done by your office to correct that problem?

"A. Well, when this one happened, we searched

evidence on which to base a conclusion that computer error poses no appreciable threat to Fourth Amendment interests. The Court overlooks the reality that computer technology has changed the nature of threats to citizens' privacy over the past half century. What has not changed is the reality that only that fraction of Fourth Amendment violations held to have resulted in unlawful arrests is ever noted and redressed. As Justice Jackson observed: "There may be, and I am convinced that there are, many unlawful searches . . . of innocent people which turn up nothing incriminating, in which no arrest is made, about which courts do nothing, and about which we never hear." *Brinegar v. United States*, 338 U.S. 160 (1949) (dissenting opinion). Moreover, even if errors in computer records of warrants were rare, that would merely minimize the cost of enforcing the exclusionary rule in cases like this.

The use of general warrants to search for evidence of violations of the Crown's revenue laws understandably outraged the authors of the Bill of Rights. The offense to the dignity of the citizen who is arrested, handcuffed, and searched on a public street simply because some bureaucrat has failed to maintain an accurate computer data base strikes me as equally outrageous. In this case, of course, such an error led to the fortuitous detection of respondent's unlawful possession of marijuana, and the suppression of the fruit of the error would prevent the prosecution of his crime. That cost, however, must be weighed against the interest in protecting other, wholly innocent citizens from unwarranted indignity. In my judgment, the cost is amply offset by an appropriately "jealous regard for maintaining the integrity of individual rights." For this reason, as well as those set forth by Justice GINSBURG, I respectfully dissent.

Justice GINSBURG, with whom Justice STEVENS joins, dissenting.

This case portrays the increasing use of computer technology in law enforcement; it illustrates an evolving problem this Court need not, and in my judgment should not, resolve too hastily. The Arizona Supreme Court relied on "the principles of a free society" in reaching its decision. This Court reviews and reverses the Arizona decision on the assumption that Arizona's highest court sought assiduously to apply this Court's Fourth Amendment

---

all the files to make sure that there were no other ones in there, which there were three other ones on that same day that it happened. Fortunately, they weren't all arrested."

jurisprudence. The Court thus follows the presumption announced in *Michigan v. Long*: If it is unclear whether a state court's decision rests on state or federal law, *Long* dictates the assumption that the state court relied on federal law. On the basis of that assumption, the Court asserts jurisdiction to review the decision of the Arizona Supreme Court.

The *Long* presumption, as I see it, impedes the States' ability to serve as laboratories for testing solutions to novel legal problems. I would apply the opposite presumption and assume that Arizona's Supreme Court has ruled for its own State and people, under its own constitutional recognition of individual security against unwarranted state intrusion. Accordingly, I would dismiss the writ of certiorari.

## I

Isaac Evans was arrested because a computer record erroneously identified an outstanding misdemeanor arrest warrant in his name. The Arizona Supreme Court's suppression of evidence obtained from this unlawful arrest did not rest on a close analysis of this Court's Fourth Amendment precedents. Indeed, the court found our most relevant decision, *Leon,* "not helpful." Instead, the Arizona court emphasized its comprehension of the severe curtailment of personal liberty inherent in arrest warrants.

Specifically, the Arizona Supreme Court saw the growing use of computerized records in law enforcement as a development presenting new dangers to individual liberty; excluding evidence seized as a result of incorrect computer data, the Arizona court anticipated, would reduce the incidence of uncorrected records:

"The dissent laments the 'high costs' of the exclusionary rule, and suggests that its application here is 'purposeless' and provides 'no offsetting benefits.' Such an assertion ignores the fact that arrest warrants result in a denial of human liberty, and are therefore among the most important of legal documents. It is repugnant to the principles of a free society that a person should ever be taken into police custody because of a computer error precipitated by government carelessness. As automation increasingly invades modern life, the potential for Orwellian mischief grows. Under such circumstances, the exclusionary rule is a 'cost' we cannot afford to be without."

Thus, the Arizona court did not consider this case to involve simply and only a court employee's slip in failing to communicate with the police, or a police officer's oversight in failing to record information received from a court employee. That court recognized a "potential for Orwellian mischief" in the government's increasing reliance on computer technology in law enforcement. The Arizona Supreme Court concluded that *Leon's* distinction between police conduct and judicial conduct loses force where, as here, the error derives not from a discretionary judicial function, but from inattentive recordkeeping. Application of an exclusionary rule in the circumstances Evans' case presents, the Arizona court said, "will hopefully serve to improve the efficiency of those who keep records in our criminal justice system."

## II

### A

Widespread reliance on computers to store and convey information generates, along with manifold benefits, new possibilities of error, due to both computer malfunctions and operator mistakes. Most germane to this case, computerization greatly amplifies an error's effect, and correspondingly intensifies the need for prompt correction; for inaccurate data can infect not only one agency, but the many agencies that share access to the data-base. The computerized databases of the FBI's National Crime Information Center (NCIC), to take a conspicuous example, contain over 23 million records, identifying, among other things, persons and vehicles sought by law enforcement agencies nationwide. Thus, any mistake entered into the NCIC spreads nationwide in an instant.

Isaac Evans' arrest exemplifies the risks associated with computerization of arrest warrants. Though his arrest was in fact warrantless – the warrant once issued having been quashed over two weeks before the episode in suit – the computer reported otherwise. Evans' case is not idiosyncratic. *Rogan v. Los Angeles*, 668 F.Supp. 1384 (CD Cal.1987), similarly indicates the problem. There, the Los Angeles Police Department, in 1982, had entered into the NCIC computer an arrest warrant for a man suspected of robbery and murder. Because the suspect had been impersonating Terry Dean Rogan, the arrest warrant erroneously named Rogan. Compounding the error, the Los Angeles Police Department had failed to include a description of the suspect's physical characteristics. During the next two years, this incorrect and incomplete information caused Rogan to be arrested four times, three times at gunpoint, after stops for minor traffic infractions in Michigan and Oklahoma. In another case of the same genre, the District Court observed:

"Because of the inaccurate listing in the

NCIC computer, defendant was a 'marked man' for the five months prior to his arrest. . . . At any time . . . a routine check by the police could well result in defendant's arrest, booking, search and detention. . . . Moreover, this could happen anywhere in the United States where law enforcement officers had access to NCIC information. Defendant was subject to being deprived of his liberty at any time and without any legal basis." *United States v. Mackey*, 387 F.Supp. 1121, 1124 (Nev.1975).

In the instant case, the Court features testimony of the chief clerk of the justice court in East Phoenix to the effect that errors of the kind Evans encountered are reported only "on[c]e every three or four years." But the same witness also recounted that, when the error concerning Evans came to light, an immediate check revealed that three other errors of the very same kind had occurred on "that same day." see n. 3 (STEVENS, J., dissenting).

### B

This Court and the Arizona Supreme Court hold diverse views on the question whether application of an exclusionary rule will reduce the incidence of erroneous computer data left without prompt correction. Observing that "court clerks are not adjuncts to the law enforcement team engaged in the often competitive enterprise of ferreting out crime," the Court reasons that "there is no basis for believing that application of the exclusionary rule in these circumstances will have a significant effect on court employees responsible for informing the police that a warrant has been quashed." In the Court's view, exclusion of evidence, even if capable of deterring police officer errors, cannot deter the carelessness of other governmental actors.[5] Whatever federal

precedents may indicate—an issue on which I voice no opinion—the Court's conclusion is not the lesson inevitably to be drawn from logic or experience.

In this electronic age, particularly with respect to recordkeeping, court personnel and police officers are not neatly compartmentalized actors. Instead, they serve together to carry out the State's information-gathering objectives. Whether particular records are maintained by the police or the courts should not be dispositive where a single computer database can answer all calls. Not only is it artificial to distinguish between court clerk and police clerk slips; in practice, it may be difficult to pinpoint whether one official, e.g., a court employee, or another, e.g., a police officer, caused the error to exist or to persist. Applying an exclusionary rule as the Arizona court did may well supply a powerful incentive to the State to promote the prompt updating of computer records. That was the Arizona Supreme Court's hardly unreasonable expectation. The incentive to update promptly would be diminished if court-initiated records were exempt from the rule's sway.

### C

The debate over the efficacy of an exclusionary rule reveals that deterrence is an empirical question, not a logical one. "It is one of the happy incidents of the federal system that a single courageous State may, if its citizens choose, serve as a laboratory; and try novel social and economic experiments without risk to the rest of the country." *New State Ice Co. v. Liebmann*, 285 U.S. 262, 311 (1932) (Brandeis, J., dissenting). With that facet of our federalism in mind, this Court should select a jurisdictional presumption that encourages States to explore different means to secure respect for individual rights in modern times.

### III

Under *Long*, when state courts engage in the essential process of developing state constitutional law, they may insulate their decisions from this Court's review by means of a plain statement of intent to rest upon an independent state ground. The plain statement option does not, however, make pleas for reconsideration of the *Long* presumption much ado

---

[5] It has been suggested that an exclusionary rule cannot deter carelessness, but can affect only intentional or reckless misconduct. This suggestion runs counter to a premise underlying all of negligence law—that imposing liability for negligence, i.e., lack of due care, creates an incentive to act with greater care.

That the mistake may have been made by a clerical worker does not alter the conclusion that application of the exclusionary rule has deterrent value. Just as the risk of respondeat superior liability encourages employers to supervise more closely their employees' conduct, so the risk of exclusion of evidence encourages policymakers and systems managers to monitor the performance of the systems they

install and the personnel employed to operate those systems. In the words of the trial court, the mistake in Evans' case was "perhaps the negligence of the Justice Court, or the negligence of the Sheriff's Office. But it is still the negligence of the State."

about nothing. Both on a practical and on a symbolic level, the presumption chosen matters.

Application of the *Long* presumption has increased the incidence of nondispositive U.S. Supreme Court determinations—instances in which state courts, on remand, have reinstated their prior judgments after clarifying their reliance on state grounds.

The Arizona Supreme Court found it "repugnant to the principles of a free society," to take a person "into police custody because of a computer error precipitated by government carelessness." Few, I believe, would disagree. Whether, in order to guard against such errors, "the exclusionary rule is a 'cost' we cannot afford to be without," seems to me a question this Court should not rush to decide. The Court errs, as I see it, in presuming that Arizona rested its decision on federal grounds. I would abandon the *Long* presumption and dismiss the writ because the generally applicable obligation affirmatively to establish the Court's jurisdiction has not been satisfied.

## QUESTIONS AND NOTES

1. Do you think that excluding the evidence against Evans would serve any deterrent purpose? If so, how?

2. On remand, is there any way that Evans could win on Federal Constitutional grounds? Explain.

3. Is it still open for the Arizona Supreme Court to release Evans on State grounds? Explain.

4. Is the *Long* presumption soundly premised? Why? Why not?

## C.   Standing

One limitation that the Court has always put on the exclusionary rule is "standing." That is, in addition to establishing a Fourth Amendment violation, the defendant must establish that he was the victim of the violation. How that rule developed, its scope and limitations, and the normative desirability of continuing to adhere to it, are all questions that you should think about as you read *Rakas, Salvucci, Rawlings*, and *Payner*.

### Rakas v. Illinois
### 439 U.S. 128 (1978)

Mr. Justice REHNQUIST delivered the opinion of the Court.

Petitioners were convicted of armed robbery in the Circuit Court of Kankakee County, Ill., and their convictions were affirmed on appeal. At their trial, the prosecution offered into evidence a sawed-off rifle and rifle shells that had been seized by police during a search of an automobile in which petitioners had been passengers. Neither petitioner is the owner of the automobile and neither has ever asserted that he owned the rifle or shells seized. The Illinois Appellate Court held that petitioners lacked standing to object to the allegedly unlawful search and seizure and denied their motion to suppress the evidence.

We granted certiorari in light of the obvious importance of the issues raised to the administration of criminal justice, and now affirm.

I

Because we are not here concerned with the issue of probable cause, a brief description of the events leading to the search of the automobile will suffice. A police officer on a routine patrol received a radio call notifying him of a robbery of a clothing store in Bourbonnais, Ill., and describing the getaway car. Shortly thereafter, the officer spotted an automobile which he thought might be the getaway car. After following the car for some time and after the arrival of assistance, he and several other officers stopped the vehicle. The occupants of the automobile, petitioners and two female companions, were ordered out of the car and, after the occupants had left the car, two officers searched the interior of the vehicle. They discovered a box of rifle shells in the glove compartment, which had been locked, and a sawed-off rifle under the front passenger seat. After discovering the rifle and the shells, the officers took petitioners to the station and placed them under arrest.

## II

Petitioners first urge us to relax or broaden the rule of standing enunciated in *Jones v. United States*, 362 U.S. 257 (1960), so that any criminal defendant at whom a search was "directed" would have standing to contest the legality of that search and object to the admission at trial of evidence obtained as a result of the search. Alternatively, petitioners argue that they have standing to object to the search under *Jones* because they were "legitimately on [the] premises" at the time of the search.

The concept of standing discussed in *Jones* focuses on whether the person seeking to challenge the legality of a search as a basis for suppressing evidence was himself the "victim" of the search or seizure. Adoption of the so-called "target" theory advanced by petitioners would in effect permit a defendant to assert that a violation of the Fourth Amendment rights of a third party entitled him to have evidence suppressed at his trial. If we reject petitioners' request for a broadened rule of standing such as this, and reaffirm the holding of *Jones* and other cases that Fourth Amendment rights are personal rights that may not be asserted vicariously, we will have occasion to re-examine the "standing" terminology emphasized in *Jones*. For we are not at all sure that the determination of a motion to suppress is materially aided by labeling the inquiry identified in *Jones* as one of standing, rather than simply recognizing it as one involving the substantive question of whether or not the proponent of the motion to suppress has had his own Fourth Amendment rights infringed by the search and seizure which he seeks to challenge. We shall therefore consider in turn petitioners' target theory, the necessity for continued adherence to the notion of standing discussed in *Jones* as a concept that is theoretically distinct from the merits of a defendant's Fourth Amendment claim, and, finally, the proper disposition of petitioners' ultimate claim in this case.

## A

We decline to extend the rule of standing in Fourth Amendment cases in the manner suggested by petitioners. As we stated in *Alderman v. United States*, 394 U.S. 165 (1969). "Fourth Amendment rights are personal rights which, like some other constitutional rights, may not be vicariously asserted." A person who is aggrieved by an illegal search and seizure only through the introduction of damaging evidence secured by a search of a third person's premises or property has not had any of his Fourth Amendment rights infringed. And since the exclusionary rule is an attempt to effectuate the guarantees of the Fourth Amendment, *Calandra*, it is proper to permit only defendants whose Fourth Amendment rights have been violated to benefit from the rule's protections.[3] There is no reason to think that a party whose rights have been infringed will not, if evidence is used against him, have ample motivation to move to suppress it. Even if such a person is not a defendant in the action, he may be able to recover damages for the violation of his Fourth Amendment rights, see *Monroe v. Pape*, 365 U.S. 167 (1961), or seek redress under state law for invasion of privacy or trespass.

In support of their target theory, petitioners rely on the following quotation from *Jones*:

"In order to qualify as a 'person aggrieved by an unlawful search and seizure' one must have been a victim of a search or seizure, *one against whom the search was directed*, as distinguished from one who claims prejudice only through the use of evidence gathered as a consequence of a search or seizure directed at someone else." (emphasis added).

The above-quoted statement from *Jones* suggests that the italicized language was meant merely as a parenthetical equivalent of the previous phrase "a victim of a search or seizure." To the extent that the language might be read more broadly, it is dictum which was impliedly repudiated in *Alderman*, and which we now expressly reject. In *Jones*, the Court set forth two alternative holdings: It established a rule of "automatic" standing to contest an

---

[3] The necessity for a showing of a violation of personal rights is not obviated by recognizing the deterrent purpose of the exclusionary rule. Despite the deterrent aim of the exclusionary rule, we never have held that unlawfully seized evidence is inadmissible in all proceedings or against all persons. "[T]he application of the rule has been restricted to those areas where its remedial objectives are thought most efficaciously served."

allegedly illegal search where the same possession needed to establish standing is an essential element of the offense charged; and second, it stated that "anyone legitimately on premises where a search occurs may challenge its legality by way of a motion to suppress." Had the Court intended to adopt the target theory now put forth by petitioners, neither of the above two holdings would have been necessary since Jones was the "target" of the police search in that case.[5]

Conferring standing to raise vicarious Fourth Amendment claims would necessarily mean a more widespread invocation of the exclusionary rule during criminal trials. The Court's opinion in *Alderman* counseled against such an extension of the exclusionary rule:

> "The deterrent values of preventing the incrimination of those whose rights the police have violated have been considered sufficient to justify the suppression of probative evidence even though the case against the defendant is weakened or destroyed. We adhere to that judgment. But we are not convinced that the additional benefits of extending the exclusionary rule to other defendants would justify further encroachment upon the public interest in prosecuting those accused of crime and having them acquitted or convicted on the basis of all the evidence which exposes the truth."

Each time the exclusionary rule is applied it exacts a substantial social cost for the vindication of Fourth Amendment rights. Relevant and reliable evidence is kept from the trier of fact and the search for truth at trial is deflected. Since our cases generally have held that one whose Fourth Amendment rights are violated may successfully suppress evidence obtained in the course of an illegal search and seizure, misgivings as to the benefit of enlarging the class of persons who may invoke that rule are properly considered when deciding whether to expand standing to assert Fourth Amendment violations.[6]

B

Had we accepted petitioners' request to allow persons other than those whose own Fourth Amendment rights were violated by a challenged search and seizure to suppress evidence obtained in the course of such police activity, it would be appropriate to retain *Jones'* use of standing in Fourth Amendment analysis. Under petitioners' target theory, a court could determine that a defendant had standing to invoke the exclusionary rule without having to inquire into the substantive question of whether the challenged search or seizure violated the Fourth Amendment rights of that particular defendant. However, having rejected petitioners' target theory and reaffirmed the principle that the "rights assured by the Fourth Amendment are personal rights,[8] [which] . . . may be enforced by exclusion of evidence only at the instance of one whose own protection was infringed by the search and seizure," the question necessarily arises whether it serves any useful analytical purpose to consider this principle a matter of standing, distinct from the merits of a defendant's Fourth Amendment claim. We can think of no decided cases of this Court that would have come out differently had we concluded, as we do now, that the type of standing requirement discussed in *Jones* and reaffirmed today is more properly subsumed under substantive Fourth Amendment doctrine.

Analyzed in these terms, the question is whether the challenged search or seizure violated the Fourth Amendment rights of a criminal defendant who seeks to exclude the evidence obtained during it. That inquiry in turn requires a determination of whether the disputed search and seizure has infringed an interest of the defendant which the Fourth Amendment was designed to protect. We are under no illusion that by dispensing with the rubric of standing used in *Jones* we have rendered any simpler the determination of whether the proponent of a motion to suppress is entitled to contest the legality of a search

---

[5] The search of the apartment in *Jones* was pursuant to a search warrant naming Jones and another woman as occupants of the apartment. The affidavit submitted in support of the search warrant alleged that Jones and the woman were involved in illicit narcotics traffic and kept a supply of heroin and narcotics paraphernalia in the apartment.

[6] For these same prudential reasons, the Court in *Alderman* rejected the argument that *any* defendant should be enabled to apprise the court of unconstitutional searches and seizures and to exclude all such

unlawfully seized evidence from trial, regardless of whether his Fourth Amendment rights were violated by the search *or* whether he was the "target" of the search. This expansive reading of the Fourth Amendment also was advanced by the petitioner in *Jones* and implicitly rejected by the Court.

[8] This approach is consonant with that which the Court already has taken with respect to the Fifth Amendment privilege against self-incrimination, which also is a purely personal right. (footnote repositioned ed.)

and seizure. But by frankly recognizing that this aspect of the analysis belongs more properly under the heading of substantive Fourth Amendment doctrine than under the heading of standing, we think the decision of this issue will rest on sounder logical footing.

### C

Here petitioners, who were passengers occupying a car which they neither owned nor leased, seek to analogize their position to that of the defendant in *Jones*. In *Jones*, petitioner was present at the time of the search of an apartment which was owned by a friend. The friend had given Jones permission to use the apartment and a key to it, with which Jones had admitted himself on the day of the search. He had a suit and shirt at the apartment and had slept there "maybe a night," but his home was elsewhere. At the time of the search, Jones was the only occupant of the apartment because the lessee was away for a period of several days. Under these circumstances, this Court stated that while one wrongfully on the premises could not move to suppress evidence obtained as a result of searching them, "anyone legitimately on premises where a search occurs may challenge its legality." Petitioners argue that their occupancy of the automobile in question was comparable to that of Jones in the apartment and that they therefore have standing to contest the legality of the search—or as we have rephrased the inquiry, that they, like Jones, had their Fourth Amendment rights violated by the search.

We do not question the conclusion in *Jones* that the defendant in that case suffered a violation of his personal Fourth Amendment rights if the search in question was unlawful. Nonetheless, we believe that the phrase "legitimately on premises" coined in *Jones* creates too broad a gauge for measurement of Fourth Amendment rights. For example, applied literally, this statement would permit a casual visitor who has never seen, or been permitted to visit, the basement of another's house to object to a search of the basement if the visitor happened to be in the kitchen of the house at the time of the search. Likewise, a casual visitor who walks into a house one minute before a search of the house commences and leaves one minute after the search ends would be able to contest the legality of the search. The first visitor would have absolutely no interest or legitimate expectation of privacy in the basement, the second would have none in the house, and it advances no purpose served by the Fourth Amendment

to permit either of them to object to the lawfulness of the search.[11]

We think that *Jones* on its facts merely stands for the unremarkable proposition that a person can have a legally sufficient interest in a place other than his own home so that the Fourth Amendment protects him from unreasonable governmental intrusion into that place. In defining the scope of that interest, we adhere to the view expressed in *Jones* and echoed in later cases that arcane distinctions developed in property and tort law between guests, licensees, invitees, and the like, ought not to control. But the *Jones* statement that a person need only be "legitimately on premises" in order to challenge the validity of the search of a dwelling place cannot be taken in its full sweep beyond the facts of that case.

*Katz* provides guidance in defining the scope of the interest protected by the Fourth Amendment. [T]he Court in *Katz* held that capacity to claim the protection of the Fourth Amendment depends not upon a property right in the invaded place but upon whether the person who claims the protection of the Amendment has a legitimate expectation of privacy in the invaded place. Viewed in this manner, the holding in *Jones* can best be explained by the fact that Jones had a legitimate expectation of privacy in the premises he was using and therefore could claim the protection of the Fourth Amendment with respect to a governmental invasion of those premises, even though his "interest" in those premises might not have been a recognized property interest at common law.

### D

Judged by the foregoing analysis, petitioners' claims must fail. They asserted neither a property nor a possessory interest in the automobile, nor an interest in the property seized. And as we have previously indicated, the fact that they were "legitimately on [the] premises" in the sense that they were in the car with the permission of its owner is not determinative of whether they had a legitimate expectation of privacy in the particular areas of the automobile searched. It is unnecessary for us to decide here whether the same expectations of privacy are warranted in a car as would be justified in a dwelling place in analogous circumstances. We have on numerous occasions pointed out that cars are not

---

[11] This is not to say that such visitors could not contest the lawfulness of the seizure of evidence or the search if their own property were seized during the search.

to be treated identically with houses or apartments for Fourth Amendment purposes. But here petitioners' claim is one which would fail even in an analogous situation in a dwelling place, since they made no showing that they had any legitimate expectation of privacy in the glove compartment or area under the seat of the car in which they were merely passengers. Like the trunk of an automobile, these are areas in which a passenger *qua* passenger simply would not normally have a legitimate expectation of privacy.

*Jones* and *Katz* involved significantly different factual circumstances. Jones not only had permission to use the apartment of his friend, but also had a key to the apartment with which he admitted himself on the day of the search and kept possessions in the apartment. Except with respect to his friend, Jones had complete dominion and control over the apartment and could exclude others from it. Likewise in *Katz*, the defendant occupied the telephone booth, shut the door behind him to exclude all others and paid the toll, which "entitled [him] to assume that the words he utter[ed] into the mouthpiece [would] not be broadcast to the world."[16] Katz and Jones could legitimately expect privacy in the areas which were the subject of the search and seizure each sought to contest. No such showing was made by these petitioners with respect to those portions of the automobile which were searched and from which incriminating evidence was seized.[17]

---

[16] The dissent states that *Katz v. United States* expressly recognized protection for passengers of taxicabs and asks why that protection should not also extend to these petitioners. *Katz* relied on *Rios v. United States*, 364 U.S. 253 (1960), as support for that proposition. The question of Rios' right to contest the search was not presented to or addressed by the Court and the property seized appears to have belonged to Rios. Additionally, the facts of that case are quite different from those of the present case. Rios had hired the cab and occupied the rear passenger section. When police stopped the cab, he placed a package he had been holding on the floor of the rear section. The police saw the package and seized it after defendant was removed from the cab.

[17] For reasons which they do not explain, our dissenting Brethren repeatedly criticize our "holding" that unless one has a common-law property interest in the premises searched, one cannot object to the search. We have rendered no such "holding," however. To the contrary, we have taken pains to reaffirm the statements in *Jones* and *Katz* that "arcane distinctions developed in property . . . law

## III

The Illinois courts were therefore correct in concluding that it was unnecessary to decide whether the search of the car might have violated the rights secured to someone else by the Fourth and Fourteenth Amendments to the United States Constitution. Since it did not violate any rights of these petitioners, their judgment of conviction is Affirmed.

Mr. Justice POWELL, with whom the Chief Justice joins, concurring.

The petitioners do not challenge the constitutionality of the police action in stopping the automobile in which they were riding; nor do they complain of being made to get out of the vehicle. Rather, petitioners assert that their constitutionally protected interest in privacy was violated when the police, after stopping the automobile and making them get out, searched the vehicle's interior, where they discovered a sawed-off rifle under the front seat and rifle shells in the locked glove compartment. The question before the Court, therefore, is a narrow one: Did the search of their friend's automobile after they had left it violate any Fourth Amendment right of the petitioners?

The dissenting opinion urges the Court to answer this question by considering only the talisman of legitimate presence on the premises.

This Court's decisions since *Jones* have emphasized a sounder standard for determining the scope of a person's Fourth Amendment rights: Only legitimate expectations of privacy are protected by the

---

. . . ought not to control." In a similar vein, the dissenters repeatedly state or imply that we now "hold" that a passenger lawfully in an automobile "may not invoke the exclusionary rule and challenge a search of that vehicle unless he happens to own or have a possessory interest in it." It is not without significance that these statements of today's "holding" come from the dissenting opinion, and not from the Court's opinion. The case before us involves the search of and seizure of property from the glove compartment and area under the seat of a car in which petitioners were riding as passengers. Petitioners claimed only that they were "legitimately on [the] premises" and did not claim that they had any legitimate expectation of privacy in the areas of the car which were searched. We cannot, therefore, agree with the dissenters' insistence that our decision will encourage the police to violate the Fourth Amendment.

Constitution. As Mr. Justice Harlan pointed out in his concurrence [in *Katz*], however, it is not enough that an individual desired or anticipated that he would be free from governmental intrusion. Rather, for an expectation to deserve the protection of the Fourth Amendment, it must "be one that society is prepared to recognize as 'reasonable.'"[1]

We are concerned here with an automobile search. Nothing is better established in Fourth Amendment jurisprudence than the distinction between one's expectation of privacy in an automobile and one's expectation when in other locations.[2]

Here there were three passengers and a driver in the automobile searched. None of the passengers is said to have had control of the vehicle or the keys. It is unrealistic – as the shared experience of us all bears witness – to suggest that these passengers had any reasonable expectation that the car in which they had been riding would not be searched after they were lawfully stopped and made to get out. The minimal privacy that existed simply is not comparable to that, for example, of an individual in his place of abode, of one who secludes himself in a telephone booth, or of the traveler who secures his belongings in a locked suitcase or footlocker.[4]

This is not an area of the law in which any "bright line" rule would safeguard both Fourth Amendment rights and the public interest in a fair and effective criminal justice system. The range of variables in the fact situations of search and seizure is almost infinite. Rather than seek facile solutions, it is best to apply principles broadly faithful to Fourth Amendment purposes. I believe the Court has identified these principles.

Mr. Justice WHITE, with whom Mr. Justice BRENNAN, Mr. Justice MARSHALL, and Mr. Justice STEVENS join, dissenting.

The Court today holds that the Fourth Amendment protects property, not people, and specifically that a legitimate occupant of an automobile may not invoke the exclusionary rule and challenge a search of that vehicle unless he happens to own or have a possessory interest in it. Though professing to acknowledge that the primary purpose of the Fourth Amendment's prohibition of unreasonable searches is the protection of privacy – not property – the Court nonetheless effectively ties the application of the Fourth Amendment and the exclusionary rule in this situation to property law concepts. Insofar as passengers are concerned, the Court's opinion today declares an "open season" on automobiles. However

---

[1] I do not share the dissenters' concern that the Court's ruling will "invit[e] police to engage in patently unreasonable searches every time an automobile contains more than one occupant." A police officer observing an automobile carrying several passengers will not know the circumstances surrounding each occupant's presence in the automobile, and certainly will not know whether an occupant will be able to establish that he had a reasonable expectation of privacy. Thus, there will continue to be a significant incentive for the police to comply with the requirements of the Fourth Amendment, lest otherwise valid prosecutions be voided. Moreover, any marginal diminution in this incentive that might result from the Court's decision today is more than justified by society's interest in restricting the scope of the exclusionary rule to those cases where in fact there is a reasonable expectation of privacy. (footnote repositioned ed.)

[2] There are sound reasons for this distinction: Automobiles operate on public streets; they are serviced in public places; they stop frequently; they are usually parked in public places; their interiors are highly visible; and they are subject to extensive regulation and inspection. The rationale of the automobile distinction does not apply, of course, to objects on the person of an occupant.

[4] The sawed-off rifle in this case was merely pushed beneath the front seat, presumably by one of the petitioners. In that position, it could have slipped into full or partial view in the event of an accident, or indeed upon any sudden stop. As the rifle shells were in the locked glove compartment, this might have presented a closer case if it had been shown that one of the petitioners possessed the keys or if a rifle had not been found in the automobile. The dissenting opinion suggests that the petitioners here took the same actions to preserve their privacy as did the defendant in *Katz* : Just as Katz closed the door to the telephone booth after him, petitioners closed the doors to their automobile. Last Term, this Court determined in *Pennsylvania v. Mimms*, 434 U.S. 106 (1977), that passengers in automobiles have no Fourth Amendment right not to be ordered from their vehicle, once a proper stop is made. The dissenting opinion concedes that there is no question here of the propriety of the stopping of the automobile in which the petitioners were riding. Thus, the closing of the doors of a vehicle, even if there were only one occupant, cannot have the same significance as it might in other contexts.

unlawful stopping and searching a car may be, absent a possessory or ownership interest, no "mere" passenger may object, regardless of his relationship to the owner. Because the majority's conclusion has no support in the Court's controlling decisions, in the logic of the Fourth Amendment, or in common sense, I must respectfully dissent. If the Court is troubled by the practical impact of the exclusionary rule, it should face the issue of that rule's continued validity squarely instead of distorting other doctrines in an attempt to reach what are perceived as the correct results in specific cases.

### I

Two intersecting doctrines long established in this Court's opinions control here. The first is the recognition of some cognizable level of privacy in the interior of an automobile. Though the reasonableness of the expectation of privacy in a vehicle may be somewhat weaker than that in a home, "[a] search even of an automobile, is a substantial invasion of privacy. To protect that privacy from official arbitrariness, the Court always has regarded probable cause as the minimum requirement for a lawful search." *United States v. Ortiz*, 422 U.S. 891, 896 (1975).

The second tenet is that when a person is legitimately present in a private place, his right to privacy is protected from unreasonable governmental interference even if he does not own the premises. Just a few years ago, the Chief Justice, for a unanimous Court, wrote that the "[p]resence of the defendant at the search and seizure was held, in *Jones*, to be a sufficient source of standing in itself." The Court in *Jones* itself was unanimous in this regard, and its holding is not the less binding because it was an alternative one.

These two fundamental aspects of Fourth Amendment law demand that petitioners be permitted to challenge the search and seizure of the automobile in this case. It is of no significance that a car is different for Fourth Amendment purposes from a house, for if there is some protection for the privacy of an automobile then the only relevant analogy is between a person legitimately in someone else's vehicle and a person legitimately in someone else's home. If both strands of the Fourth Amendment doctrine adumbrated above are valid, the Court must reach a different result. Instead, it chooses to eviscerate the *Jones* principle, an action in which I am unwilling to participate.

### II

Though we had reserved the very issue over 50 years ago, see *Carroll v. United States*, 267 U.S. 132, 162 (1925), and never expressly dealt with it again until today, many of our opinions have assumed that a mere passenger in an automobile is entitled to protection against unreasonable searches occurring in his presence. In decisions upholding the validity of automobile searches, we have gone directly to the merits even though some of the petitioners did not own or possess the vehicles in question. *E.g.*, *Schneckloth* (sole petitioner was not owner; in fact, owner was not in the automobile at all). Similarly, in *Preston v. United States*, 376 U.S. 364 (1964), the Court unanimously overturned a search though the single petitioner was not the owner of the automobile. The Court's silence on this issue in light of its actions can only mean that, until now, we, like most lower courts, had assumed that *Jones* foreclosed the answer now supplied by the majority. That assumption was perfectly understandable, since all private premises would seem to be the same for the purposes of the analysis set out in *Jones*.

### III

The logic of Fourth Amendment jurisprudence compels the result reached by the above decisions. Our starting point is "[t]he established principle . . . that suppression of the product of a Fourth Amendment violation can be successfully urged only by those whose rights were violated by the search itself. . . ." Though the Amendment protects one's liberty and property interests against unreasonable seizures of self and effects, "the primary object of the Fourth Amendment [is] . . . the protection of privacy." And privacy is the interest asserted here, so the first step is to ascertain whether the premises searched "fall within a protected zone of privacy." My Brethren in the majority assertedly do not deny that automobiles warrant at least some protection from official interference with privacy. Thus, the next step is to decide who is entitled, vis-a-vis the State, to enjoy that privacy. The answer to that question must be found by determining "whether petitioner had an interest in connection with the searched premises that gave rise to 'a reasonable expectation [on his part] of freedom from governmental intrusion' upon those premises."

[O]ne consistent theme in our decisions under the Fourth Amendment has been, until now, that "the Amendment does not shield only those who have title to the searched premises." Though there comes a point when use of an area is shared with so many that one simply cannot reasonably expect seclusion, short of that limit a person legitimately on private premises knows the others allowed there and, though his privacy is not absolute, is entitled to expect that he is sharing it only with those persons and that governmental officials will intrude only with consent or by complying with the Fourth Amendment.

The Court approves the result in *Jones*, but it fails to give any explanation why the facts in *Jones* differ, in a fashion material to the Fourth Amendment, from the facts here.[5] More importantly, how is the Court able to avoid answering the question why presence in a private place with the owner's permission is insufficient? If it is "tautological to fall back on the notion that those expectations of privacy which are legitimate depend primarily on cases deciding exclusionary rule issues in criminal cases," then it surely must be tautological to decide that issue simply by unadorned fiat.

As a control on governmental power, the Fourth Amendment assures that some expectations of privacy are justified and will be protected from official intrusion. That should be true in this instance, for if protected zones of privacy can only be purchased or obtained by possession of property, then much of our daily lives will be unshielded from unreasonable governmental prying, and the reach of the Fourth Amendment will have been narrowed to protect chiefly those with possessory interests in real or personal property. I had thought that *Katz* firmly established that the Fourth Amendment was intended as more than simply a trespass law applicable to the government. Katz had no possessory interest in the public telephone booth, at least no more than petitioners had in their friend's car; Katz was simply legitimately present. And the decision in *Katz* was based not on property rights, but on the theory that it was essential to securing "conditions favorable to the pursuit of happiness" that the expectation of privacy in question be recognized.

---

[5] Jones had permission to use the apartment, had slept in it one night, had a key, had left a suit and a shirt there, and was the only occupant at the time of the search. Petitioners here had permission to be in the car and were occupying it at the time of the search. Thus the only distinguishing fact is that Jones could exclude others from the apartment by using his friend's key. But petitioners and their friend the owner had excluded others by entering the automobile and shutting the doors. Petitioners did not need a key because the owner was present. Similarly, the Court attempts to distinguish *Katz* on the theory that Katz had "shut the door behind him to exclude all others," but petitioners here did exactly the same. The car doors remained closed until the police ordered them opened at gunpoint.

At most, one could say that perhaps the Constitution provides some degree less protection for the personal freedom from unreasonable governmental intrusion when one does not have a possessory interest in the invaded private place. But that would only change the extent of the protection; it would not free police to do the unreasonable, as does the decision today. And since the accused should be entitled to litigate the application of the Fourth Amendment where his privacy interest is merely arguable, the failure to allow such litigation here is the more incomprehensible.

### IV

The Court's holding is contrary not only to our past decisions and the logic of the Fourth Amendment but also to the everyday expectations of privacy that we all share. Because of that, it is unworkable in all the various situations that arise in real life. If the owner of the car had not only invited petitioners to join her but had said to them, "I give you a temporary possessory interest in my vehicle so that you will share the right to privacy that the Supreme Court says that I own," then apparently the majority would reverse. But people seldom say such things, though they may mean their invitation to encompass them if only they had thought of the problem.[19] If the nonowner were the spouse or child of the owner,[20] would the Court recognize a sufficient interest? If so, would distant relatives somehow have more of an expectation of privacy than close friends? What if the nonowner were driving with the owner's permission? Would nonowning drivers have more of an expectation of privacy than mere passengers? What about a passenger in a taxicab? *Katz* expressly recognized protection for such passengers. Why should Fourth Amendment rights be present when one pays a cabdriver for a ride but be absent when one is given a ride by a friend?

---

[19] So far as we know, the owner of the automobile in question might have expressly granted or intended to grant exactly such an interest. Apparently not contemplating today's radical change in the law, petitioners did not know at the suppression hearing that the precise form of the invitation extended by the owner to the petitioners would be dispositive of their rights against governmental intrusion.

[20] In fact, though it was not brought out at the suppression hearing, one of the petitioners is the former husband of the owner and driver of the car. He did testify at the suppression hearing that he was with her when she purchased it.

[T]he ruling today undercuts the force of the exclusionary rule in the one area in which its use is most certainly justified – the deterrence of bad-faith violations of the Fourth Amendment. This decision invites police to engage in patently unreasonable searches every time an automobile contains more than one occupant. Should something be found, only the owner of the vehicle, or of the item, will have standing to seek suppression, and the evidence will presumably be usable against the other occupants. The danger of such bad faith is especially high in cases such as this one where the officers are only after the passengers and can usually infer accurately that the driver is the owner. The suppression remedy for those owners in whose vehicles something is found and who are charged with crime is small consolation for all those owners *and* occupants whose privacy will be needlessly invaded by officers following mistaken hunches not rising to the level of probable cause but operated on in the knowledge that someone in a crowded car will probably be unprotected if contraband or incriminating evidence happens to be found. After this decision, police will have little to lose by unreasonably searching vehicles occupied by more than one person.

Of course, most police officers will decline the Court's invitation and will continue to do their jobs as best they can in accord with the Fourth Amendment. But the very purpose of the Bill of Rights was to answer the justified fear that governmental agents cannot be left totally to their own devices, and the Bill of Rights is enforceable in the courts because human experience teaches that not all such officials will otherwise adhere to the stated precepts. Some policemen simply do act in bad faith, even if for understandable ends, and some deterrent is needed. In the rush to limit the applicability of the exclusionary rule somewhere, anywhere, the Court ignores precedent, logic, and common sense to exclude the rule's operation from situations in which, paradoxically, it is justified and needed.

## QUESTIONS AND NOTES

**1.** Should only those whose personal Fourth Amendment rights have been violated be permitted to invoke the exclusionary rule? Discuss all of the arguments that can be made on both sides of the question.

**2.** Assuming that you agree with (or at least accept) the Court's conclusion that Fourth Amendment rights are personal, should the Court adopt a broad view of standing (*Jones*) or a narrower view (*Rakas*)? Explain.

**3.** After *Rakas*, how much of *Jones* is still good law?

**4.** Is *Rakas* an exclusionary rule case or a substantive Fourth Amendment case? If Rakas and King sued the officers who searched the car, would they win? Why? Why not?

**5.** Assuming that Fourth Amendment rights are personal, does merging the standing and substantive questions improve or retard analysis?

**6.** Why did Rakas and King not have standing to challenge the search and seizure?

**7.** In view of Justice Powell's opinions and Justice White's, how would you assess defense counsel's performance?

**8.** Should the fact that this search involved an automobile rather than a house have been relevant to the resolution of the question in *Rakas*?

**9.** *Rakas* emphasizes that the defendants never alleged that they owned the guns or the shell casings. After *Salvucci* and *Rawlings*, it is doubtful that such an allegation would have done much good.

## United States v. Salvucci
### 448 U.S. 83 (1980)

Mr. Justice REHNQUIST delivered the opinion of the Court.

Relying on *Jones*, the Court of Appeals for the First Circuit held that since respondents were charged with crimes of possession, they were entitled to claim "automatic standing" to challenge the legality of the search which produced the evidence against them, without regard to whether they had an expectation of privacy in the premises searched. Today we hold that defendants charged with crimes of possession may only claim the benefits of the exclusionary rule if their own Fourth Amendment rights have in fact been violated. The automatic standing rule of *Jones* is therefore overruled.

### I

Respondents, John Salvucci and Joseph Zackular, were charged in a federal indictment with 12 counts of unlawful possession of stolen mail. The 12 checks which formed the basis of the indictment had been seized by the Massachusetts police during the search of an apartment rented by respondent Zackular's mother. The search was conducted pursuant to a warrant.

Respondents filed a motion to suppress the checks on the ground that the affidavit supporting the application for the search warrant was inadequate to demonstrate probable cause. The District Court granted respondents' motions and ordered that the checks be suppressed.

### II

[A]ttempts to vicariously assert violations of the Fourth Amendment rights of others have been repeatedly rejected by this Court. Most recently, in *Rakas*, we held that "it is proper to permit only defendants whose Fourth Amendment rights have been violated to benefit from the [exclusionary] rule's protections."

Even though the Court in *Jones* recognized that the exclusionary rule should only be available to protect defendants who have been the victims of an illegal search or seizure, the Court thought it necessary to establish an exception. In cases where possession of the seized evidence was an essential element of the offense charged, the Court held that the defendant was not obligated to establish that his own Fourth Amendment rights have been violated, but only that the search and seizure of the evidence was unconstitutional. Upon such a showing, the exclusionary rule would be available to prevent the admission of the evidence against the defendant.

The Court found that the prosecution of such possessory offenses presented a "special problem" which necessitated the departure from the then settled principles of Fourth Amendment "standing."[4] Two circumstances were found to require this exception. First, the Court found that in order to establish standing at a hearing on a motion to suppress, the defendant would often be "forced to allege facts the proof of which would tend, if indeed not be sufficient, to convict him," since several Courts of Appeals had "pinioned a defendant within this dilemma" by holding that evidence adduced at the motion to suppress could be used against the defendant at trial. The Court declined to embrace any rule which would require a defendant to assert his Fourth Amendment claims only at the risk of providing the prosecution with self-incriminating statements admissible at trial. The Court sought resolution of this dilemma by relieving the defendant of the obligation of establishing that his Fourth Amendment rights were violated by an illegal search or seizure.

The Court also commented that this rule would be beneficial for a second reason. Without a rule prohibiting a Government challenge to a defendant's "standing" to invoke the exclusionary rule in a possessory offense prosecution, the Government would be allowed the "advantage of contradictory positions." The Court reasoned that the Government ought not to be allowed to assert that the defendant possessed the goods for purposes of criminal liability, while simultaneously asserting that he did not possess them for the purposes of claiming the protections of the Fourth Amendment. The Court found that "[i]t is not consonant with the amenities, to put it mildly, of the administration of criminal justice to sanction such squarely contradictory assertions of power by the Government." Thus in order to prevent both the risk that self-incrimination would attach to the assertion of Fourth Amendment rights,

---

[4] In *Rakas*, this Court discarded reliance on concepts of "standing" in determining whether a defendant is entitled to claim the protections of the exclusionary rule. The inquiry, after *Rakas*, is simply whether the defendant's rights were violated by the allegedly illegal search or seizure. Because *Jones* was decided at a time when "standing" was designated as a separate inquiry, we use that term for the purposes of re-examining that opinion.

as well as to prevent the "vice of prosecutorial self-contradiction," the Court adopted the rule of "automatic standing."

In the 20 years which have lapsed since the Court's decision in *Jones*, the two reasons which led the Court to the rule of automatic standing have likewise been affected by time. This Court has held that testimony given by a defendant in support of a motion to suppress cannot be admitted as evidence of his guilt at trial. *Simmons v. United States*, 390 U.S. 377 (1968). Developments in the principles of Fourth Amendment standing, as well, clarify that a prosecutor may, with legal consistency and legitimacy, assert that a defendant charged with possession of a seized item did not have a privacy interest violated in the course of the search and seizure. We are convinced not only that the original tenets of the *Jones* decision have eroded, but also that no alternative principles exist to support retention of the rule.

### B

We need not belabor the question of whether the "vice" of prosecutorial contradiction could alone support a rule countenancing the exclusion of probative evidence on the grounds that someone other than the defendant was denied a Fourth Amendment right. The simple answer is that the decisions of this Court, especially our most recent decision in *Rakas*, clearly establish that a prosecutor may simultaneously maintain that a defendant criminally possessed the seized good, but was not subject to a Fourth Amendment deprivation, without legal contradiction. To conclude that a prosecutor engaged in self-contradiction in *Jones*, the Court necessarily relied on the unexamined assumption that a defendant's possession of a seized good sufficient to establish criminal culpability was also sufficient to establish Fourth Amendment "standing." This assumption, however, even if correct at the time, is no longer so.

The person in legal possession of a good seized during an illegal search has not necessarily been subject to a Fourth Amendment deprivation.[6] As we hold today in *Rawlings v. Kentucky*, legal possession of a seized good is not a proxy for determining

---

[6] Legal possession of the seized good may be sufficient in some circumstances to entitle a defendant to seek the return of the seized property if the seizure, as opposed to the search, was illegal. We need not explore this issue since respondents did not challenge the constitutionality of the seizure of the evidence.

whether the owner had a Fourth Amendment interest, for it does not invariably represent the protected Fourth Amendment interest. This Court has repeatedly repudiated the notion that "arcane distinctions developed in property and tort law" ought to control our Fourth Amendment inquiry. *Rakas*.

We simply decline to use possession of a seized good as a substitute for a factual finding that the owner of the good had a legitimate expectation of privacy in the area searched. In *Jones*, the Court held not only that automatic standing should be conferred on defendants charged with crimes of possession, but, alternatively, that Jones had actual standing because he was "legitimately on the premises" at the time of the search. In *Rakas*, this Court rejected the adequacy of this second *Jones* standard, finding that it was "too broad a gauge for measurement of Fourth Amendment rights." As in *Rakas*, we again reject "blind adherence" to the other underlying assumption in *Jones* that possession of the seized good is an acceptable measure of Fourth Amendment interests. As in *Rakas*, we find that the *Jones* standard "creates too broad a gauge for measurement of Fourth Amendment rights" and that we must instead engage in a "conscientious effort to apply the Fourth Amendment" by asking not merely whether the defendant had a possessory interest in the items seized, but whether he had an expectation of privacy in the area searched. Thus neither prosecutorial "vice," nor the underlying assumption of *Jones* that possession of a seized good is the equivalent of Fourth Amendment "standing" to challenge the search, can save the automatic standing rule.

### C

This action comes to us as a challenge to a pretrial decision suppressing evidence. The respondents relied on automatic standing and did not attempt to establish that they had a legitimate expectation of privacy in the areas of Zackular's mother's home where the goods were seized. We therefore think it appropriate to remand so that respondents will have an opportunity to demonstrate, if they can, that their own Fourth Amendment rights were violated.

Reversed and remanded.

Mr. Justice MARSHALL, with whom Mr. Justice BRENNAN joins, dissenting.

Today the Court overrules the "automatic standing" rule of *Jones*, because it concludes that the rationale underpinning the rule has been "eroded." I do not share that view.

A ground for relieving the defendant charged with possession from the necessity of showing "an interest in the premises searched or the property seized'' was that ''to hold to the contrary . . . would be to permit the Government to have the advantage of contradictory positions as a basis for conviction,'' *Jones*. That is, since ''possession both convicts and confers standing,'' the Government, which had charged the defendant with possession, would not be permitted to deny that he had standing. By holding today in *Rawlings* that a person may assert a Fourth Amendment claim only if he has a privacy interest in the area that was searched, the Court has, to be sure, done away with that logical inconsistency. For

reasons stated in my dissenting opinion in that case, I believe that holding is diametrically opposed to the meaning of the Fourth Amendment as it has always been understood.

The automatic standing rule is a salutary one which protects the rights of defendants and eliminates the wasteful requirement of making a preliminary showing of standing in pretrial proceedings involving possessory offenses, where the charge itself alleges an interest sufficient to support a Fourth Amendment claim. I dissent.

## QUESTIONS AND NOTES

**1.** Explain how the government can consistently argue that the defendant possessed the items seized, but lacked standing to challenge the search?

**2.** Does *Rakas* support or oppose the *Salvucci* result?

## Rawlings v. Kentucky
### 448 U.S. 98 (1980)

Mr. Justice REHNQUIST delivered the opinion of the Court.

### I

In the middle of the afternoon on October 18, 1976, six police officers armed with a warrant for the arrest of one Lawrence Marquess on charges of drug distribution arrived at Marquess' house in Bowling Green, Ky. In the house at the time the police arrived were one of Marquess' housemates, Dennis Saddler, and four visitors, Keith Northern, Linda Braden, Vanessa Cox, and petitioner David Rawlings. While searching unsuccessfully in the house for Marquess, several police officers smelled marihuana smoke and saw marihuana seeds on the mantel in one of the bedrooms. After conferring briefly, Officers Eddie Railey and John Bruce left to obtain a search warrant. While Railey and Bruce were gone, the other four officers detained the occupants of the house in the living room, allowing them to leave only if they consented to a body search. Northern and Braden did consent to such a search and were permitted to depart. Saddler, Cox, and petitioner remained seated in the living room.

Approximately 45 minutes later, Railey and Bruce returned with a warrant authorizing them to search the house. Railey read the warrant to Saddler, Cox, and petitioner, and also read ''*Miranda*'' warnings from a card he carried in his pocket. At that

time, Cox was seated on a couch with petitioner seated to her left. In the space between them was Cox's handbag.

After Railey finished his recitation, he approached petitioner and told him to stand. Officer Don Bivens simultaneously approached Cox and ordered her to empty the contents of her purse onto a coffee table in front of the couch. Among those contents were a jar containing 1,800 tablets of LSD and a number of smaller vials containing benzphetamine, methamphetamine, methyprylan, and pentobarbital, all of which are controlled substances under Kentucky law.

Upon pouring these objects out onto the coffee table, Cox turned to petitioner and told him ''to take what was his.'' Petitioner, who was standing in response to Officer Railey's command, immediately claimed ownership of the controlled substances. At that time, Railey searched petitioner's person and found $4,500 in cash in petitioner's shirt pocket and a knife in a sheath at petitioner's side. Railey then placed petitioner under formal arrest.

Petitioner was indicted for possession with intent to sell the various controlled substances recovered from Cox's purse. At the suppression hearing, he testified that he had flown into Bowling Green about a week before his arrest to look for a job and perhaps to attend the local university. He brought with him at that time the drugs later found in Cox's purse.

Initially, petitioner stayed in the house where the arrest took place as the guest of Michael Swank, who shared the house with Marquess and Saddler. While at a party at that house, he met Cox and spent at least two nights of the next week on a couch at Cox's house.

On the morning of petitioner's arrest, Cox had dropped him off at Swank's house where he waited for her to return from class. At that time, he was carrying the drugs in a green bank bag. When Cox returned to the house to meet him, petitioner dumped the contents of the bank bag into Cox's purse. Although there is dispute over the discussion that took place, petitioner testified that he "asked her if she would carry this for me, and she said, 'yes'. . . ."[1] Petitioner then left the room to use the bathroom and, by the time he returned, discovered that the police had arrived to arrest Marquess.

---

[1] At petitioner's trial, Vanessa Cox described the transfer of possession quite differently. She testified that, as she and petitioner were getting ready to leave the house, petitioner asked "would you please carry this for me" and simultaneously dumped the drugs into her purse. According to Cox, she looked into her purse, saw the drugs, and said "would you please take this, I do not want this in my purse." Petitioner allegedly replied "okay, just a minute, I will," and then went out of the room. At that point the police entered the house. David Saddler, who was in the next room at the time of the transfer, corroborated Cox's version of the events, testifying that he heard Cox say "I do not want this in my purse" and that he heard petitioner reply "don't worry" or something to that effect.

Although none of the lower courts specifically found that Cox did not consent to the bailment, the trial court clearly was skeptical about petitioner's version of events:

"The Court finds it unbelievable that just of his own volition, David Rawlings put the contraband in the purse of Mrs. Cox just a minute before the officers knocked on the door. He had been carrying these things around Bowling Green in a bank deposit sack for days, either on his person or in his pocket, and it is unworthy of belief that just immediately before the officers knocked on the door that he put them in the purse of Vanessa Cox.

It is far more plausible to believe that he saw the officers pull up out front and then elected to 'push them off' on Vanessa Cox, believing that search was probable, possible, and emminent [*sic*]."

The trial court denied petitioner's motion to suppress the drugs and the money and to exclude the statements made by petitioner when the police discovered the drugs. According to the trial court, the warrant obtained by the police authorized them to search Cox's purse. Moreover, even if the search of the purse was illegal, the trial court believed that petitioner lacked "standing" to contest that search. Finally, the trial court believed that the search that revealed the money and the knife was permissible "under the exigencies of the situation."

The Kentucky Court of Appeals affirmed. Disagreeing with the trial court, the appellate court held that petitioner did have "standing" to dispute the legality of the search of Cox's purse but that the detention of the five persons present in the house and the subsequent searches were legitimate because the police had probable cause to arrest all five people in the house when they smelled the marihuana smoke and saw the marihuana seeds.

The Supreme Court of Kentucky in turn affirmed, but again on a somewhat different rationale. According to the Supreme Court, petitioner had no "standing" because he had no "legitimate or reasonable expectation of freedom from governmental intrusion" into Cox's purse. *Rakas*. Moreover, according to the Supreme Court, the search uncovering the money in petitioner's pocket, which search followed petitioner's admission that he owned the drugs in Cox's purse, was justifiable as incident to a lawful arrest based on probable cause.

## II

In this Court, petitioner claims that he did have a reasonable expectation of privacy in Cox's purse so as to allow him to challenge the legality of the search of that purse.[2]

In holding that petitioner could not challenge the legality of the search of Cox's purse, the Supreme Court of Kentucky looked primarily to our then recent decision in *Rakas* where we abandoned a separate inquiry into a defendant's "standing" to contest an allegedly illegal search in favor of an inquiry that focused directly on the substance of the defendant's claim that he or she possessed a "legitimate expectation of privacy" in the area searched. In the present case, the Supreme Court of Kentucky looked to the "totality of the circumstances," including petitioner's own admission at the suppression hearing that he did not believe that Cox's purse would be free

---

[2] Petitioner also claims that he is entitled to "automatic standing" to contest the legality of the search that uncovered the drugs. Our decision today in *Salvucci* disposes of this contention adversely to him.

from governmental intrusion,[3] and held that petitioner "[had] not made a sufficient showing that his legitimate or reasonable expectations of privacy were violated" by the search of the purse.

We believe that the record in this case supports that conclusion. Petitioner, of course, bears the burden of proving not only that the search of Cox's purse was illegal, but also that he had a legitimate expectation of privacy in that purse. At the time petitioner dumped thousands of dollars worth of illegal drugs into Cox's purse, he had known her for only a few days. According to Cox's uncontested testimony, petitioner had never sought or received access to her purse prior to that sudden bailment. Contrast *Jones*. Nor did petitioner have any right to exclude other persons from access to Cox's purse. See *Rakas*. In fact, Cox testified that Bob Stallons, a longtime acquaintance and frequent companion of Cox's, had free access to her purse and on the very morning of the arrest had rummaged through its contents in search of a hairbrush. Moreover, even assuming that petitioner's version of the bailment is correct and that Cox did consent to the transfer of possession, the precipitous nature of the transaction hardly supports a reasonable inference that petitioner took normal precautions to maintain his privacy. In addition to all the foregoing facts, the record also contains a frank admission by petitioner that he had no subjective expectation that Cox's purse would remain free from governmental intrusion, an admission credited by both the trial court and the Supreme Court of Kentucky.

Petitioner contends nevertheless that, because he claimed ownership of the drugs in Cox's purse, he should be entitled to challenge the search regardless of his expectation of privacy. We disagree. While petitioner's ownership of the drugs is undoubtedly one fact to be considered in this case, *Rakas* emphatically rejected the notion that "arcane" concepts of property law ought to control the ability to claim the protections of the Fourth Amendment. Had petitioner placed his drugs in plain view, he would still have owned them, but he could not claim any legitimate expectation of privacy. Prior to *Rakas*, petitioner might have been given "standing" in such a

case to challenge a "search" that netted those drugs but probably would have lost his claim on the merits. After *Rakas*, the two inquiries merge into one: whether governmental officials violated any legitimate expectation of privacy held by petitioner.

In sum, we find no reason to overturn the lower court's conclusion that petitioner had no legitimate expectation of privacy in Cox's purse at the time of the search.

Mr. Justice BLACKMUN, concurring.

I join the Court's opinion, but I write separately to explain my somewhat different approach.

In my view, *Rakas* recognized two analytically distinct but "invariably intertwined" issues of substantive Fourth Amendment jurisprudence. The first is "whether [a] disputed search or seizure has infringed an interest of the defendant which the Fourth Amendment was designed to protect;" the second is whether "the challenged search or seizure violated [that] Fourth Amendment righ[t]." The first of these questions is answered by determining whether the defendant has a "legitimate expectation of privacy" that has been invaded by a governmental search or seizure. The second is answered by determining whether applicable cause and warrant requirements have been properly observed.

I agree with the Court that these two inquiries "merge into one," in the sense that both are to be addressed under the principles of Fourth Amendment analysis developed in *Katz* and its progeny. But I do not read today's decision, or *Rakas*, as holding that it is improper for lower courts to treat these inquiries as distinct components of a Fourth Amendment claim. Indeed, I am convinced that it would invite confusion to hold otherwise. It remains possible for a defendant to prove that his legitimate interest of privacy was invaded, and yet fail to prove that the police acted illegally in doing so. And it is equally possible for a defendant to prove that the police acted illegally, and yet fail to prove that his own privacy interest was affected.

Nor do I read this Court's decisions to hold that property interests cannot be, in some circumstances at least, weighty factors in establishing the existence of fourth Amendment rights. Not every concept of ownership or possession is "arcane." Not every interest in property exists only in the desiccated atmosphere of ancient maxims and dusty books. Earlier this Term the Court recognized that "the right to exclude" is an essential element of modern property rights. *Kaiser Aetna v. United States*, 444 U.S. 164, at 179-180 (1979). In my view, that "right to exclude" often may be a principal determinant in the

---

[3] Under questioning by his own counsel, petitioner testified as follows:

"Q Did you feel that Vannessa [*sic*] Cox's purse would be free from the intrusion of the officers as you sat there? When you put the pills in her purse, did you feel that they would be free from governmental intrusion?

"A No sir."

establishment of a legitimate Fourth Amendment interest. Accordingly, I would confine analysis to the facts of this case. On those facts, however, I agree that petitioner's possessory interest in the vials of controlled substances is not sufficient to create a privacy interest in Vanessa Cox's purse, and that such an interest was not otherwise conferred by any agreement between petitioner and Cox.

Mr. Justice MARSHALL, with whom Mr. Justice BRENNAN joins, dissenting.

The vials of pills found in Vanessa Cox's purse and petitioner's admission that they belonged to him established his guilt conclusively. The State concedes, as it must, that the search of the purse was unreasonable and in violation of the Fourth Amendment, see *Ybarra*, and the Court assumes that the detention which led to the search, the seizure, and the admissions also violated the Fourth Amendment. Nevertheless, the Court upholds the conviction. I dissent.

### I

The Court holds first that petitioner may not object to the introduction of the pills into evidence because the unconstitutional actions of the police officers did not violate his personal Fourth Amendment rights. To reach this result, the Court holds that the Constitution protects an individual against unreasonable searches and seizures only if he has "a 'legitimate expectation of privacy' in the area searched." This holding cavalierly rejects the fundamental principle, unquestioned until today, that an interest in either the place searched or the property seized is sufficient to invoke the Constitution's protections against unreasonable searches and seizures.

The Court's examination of previous Fourth Amendment cases begins and ends—as it must if it is to reach its desired conclusion—with *Rakas*. Contrary to the Court's assertion, however, *Rakas* did not establish that the Fourth Amendment protects individuals against unreasonable searches and seizures only if they have a privacy interest in the place searched. The question before the Court in *Rakas* was whether the defendants could establish their right to Fourth Amendment protection simply by showing that they were "legitimately on [the] premises" searched. Overruling that portion of *Jones*, the Court held that when a Fourth Amendment objection is based on an interest in the place searched, the defendant must show an actual invasion of his personal privacy interest. The petitioners in *Rakas* did not claim that they had standing either under the *Jones* automatic standing rule for persons charged with possessory offenses, which the Court overrules

today, see *Salvucci*, or because their possessory interest in the items seized gave them "actual standing." No Fourth Amendment claim based on an interest in the property seized was before the Court, and, consequently, the Court did not and could not have decided whether such a claim could be maintained. In fact, the Court expressly disavowed any intention to foreclose such a claim ("This is not to say that such [casual] visitors could not contest the lawfulness of the seizure of evidence or the search if their own property were seized during the search," and suggested its continuing validity ("[P]etitioners' claims must fail. They asserted neither a property nor a possessory interest in the automobile, *nor an interest in the property seized*," (emphasis supplied)).

The decision today, then, is not supported by the only case directly cited in its favor. Further, the Court has ignored a long tradition embodying the opposite view. *United States v. Jeffers*, 342 U.S. 48 (1951), for example, involved a seizure of contraband alleged to belong to the defendant from a hotel room occupied by his two aunts. The Court rejected the Government's argument that because the search of the room did not invade Jeffers' privacy he lacked standing to suppress the evidence. It held that standing to object to the seizure could not be separated from standing to object to the search, for "[t]he search and seizure are . . . incapable of being untied." The Court then concluded that Jeffers "unquestionably had standing . . . unless the contraband nature of the narcotics seized precluded his assertion, for purposes of the exclusionary rule, of *a property interest therein*." (emphasis supplied).

Similarly, *Jones* is quite plainly premised on the understanding that an interest in the seized property is sufficient to establish that the defendant "himself was the victim of an invasion of privacy." The Court observed that the "conventional standing requirement" required the defendant to "claim either to have *owned or possessed the seized property* or to have had a substantial possessory interest in the premises searched," (emphasis supplied). The Court relaxed that rule for defendants charged with possessory offenses because "[t]he same element . . . which has caused a dilemma, *i.e.*, that *possession both convicts and confers standing*, eliminates any necessity for a preliminary showing of an interest in the premises searched *or the property seized*, which ordinarily is required when standing is challenged." (emphasis supplied). Instead, "[t]he possession on the basis of which petitioner is to be and was convicted suffices to give him standing,".

The Court's decision today is not wrong, however, simply because it is contrary to our previous cases. It is wrong because it is contrary to the Fourth Amendment, which guarantees that "[t]he right of the people to be secure in their persons, houses, papers, and effects, against unreasonable searches and seizures, shall not be violated." The Court's reading of the Amendment is far too narrow. The Court misreads the guarantee of security *"in* their persons, houses, papers, and effects, *against* unreasonable searches and seizures" to afford protection only against unreasonable searches and seizures *of* persons and places.

The Fourth Amendment, it seems to me, provides in plain language that if one's security in one's "effects" is disturbed by an unreasonable search and seizure, one has been the victim of a constitutional violation; and so it has always been understood. Therefore the Court's insistence that in order to challenge the legality of the search one must also assert a protected interest in the premises is misplaced. The interest in the item seized is quite enough to establish that the defendant's personal Fourth Amendment rights have been invaded by the government's conduct.

The idea that a person cannot object to a search unless he can show an interest in the premises, even though he is the owner of the seized property, was squarely rejected almost 30 years ago in *Jeffers*. There the Court stated:

> "The Government argues . . . that the search did not invade respondent's privacy and that he, therefore, lacked the necessary standing to suppress the evidence seized. The significant act, it says, is the seizure of the goods of the respondent without a warrant. We do not believe the events are so easily isolable. Rather they are bound together by one sole purpose – to locate and seize the narcotics of respondent. The search and seizure are, therefore, incapable of being untied. To hold that this search and seizure were lawful as to the respondent would permit a quibbling distinction to overturn a principle which was designed to protect a fundamental right."

When the government seizes a person's property, it interferes with his constitutionally protected right to be secure in his effects. That interference gives him the right to challenge the reasonableness of the government's conduct, including the seizure. If the defendant's property was seized as the result of an unreasonable search, the seizure cannot be other than unreasonable.

In holding that the Fourth Amendment protects only those with a privacy interest in the place searched, and not those with an ownership or possessory interest in the things seized, the Court has turned the development of the law of search and seizure on its head. The history of the Fourth Amendment shows that it was designed to protect property interests as well as privacy interests; in fact, until *Jones* the question whether a person's Fourth Amendment rights had been violated turned on whether he had a property interest in the place searched or the items seized. *Jones* and *Katz* expanded our view of the protections afforded by the Fourth Amendment by recognizing that privacy interests are protected even if they do not arise from property rights. But that recognition was never intended to exclude interests that had historically been sheltered by the Fourth Amendment from its protection. Neither *Jones* nor *Katz* purported to provide an exclusive definition of the interests protected by the Fourth Amendment. Indeed, as *Katz* recognized: "That Amendment protects individual privacy against certain kinds of governmental intrusion, but its protections go further, and often have nothing to do with privacy at all." Those decisions freed Fourth Amendment jurisprudence from the constraints of "subtle distinctions, developed and refined by the common law in evolving the body of private property law which, more than almost any other branch of law, has been shaped by distinctions whose validity is largely historical." Rejection of those finely drawn distinctions as irrelevant to the concerns of the Fourth Amendment did not render property rights wholly outside its protection, however. Not every concept involving property rights, we should remember, is "arcane."

In fact, the Court rather inconsistently denies that property rights may, by themselves, entitle one to the protection of the Fourth Amendment, but simultaneously suggests that a person may claim such protection only if his expectation of privacy in the premises searched is so strong that he may exclude all others from that place. Such a harsh threshold requirement was not imposed even in the heyday of a property rights oriented Fourth Amendment.

### III

In the words of Mr. Justice Frankfurter: "A decision [of a Fourth Amendment claim] may turn on whether one gives that Amendment a place second to none in the Bill of Rights, or considers it on the whole a kind of nuisance, a serious impediment in the war against crime." *Harris v. United States*, 331 U.S. 145, 157 (1947) (dissenting opinion). Today a majority of the Court has substantially cut back the protection afforded by the Fourth Amendment and the ability of the people to claim that protection, apparently out of concern lest the government's ability to obtain criminal convictions be impeded. A slow and steady erosion of the ability of victims of unconstitutional searches and seizures to obtain a remedy for the invasion of their rights saps the constitutional guarantee of its life just as surely as would a substantive limitation. Because we are called on to decide whether evidence should be excluded only when a search has been "successful," it is easy to forget that the standards we announce determine what government conduct is reasonable in searches and seizures directed at persons who turn out to be innocent as well as those who are guilty. I continue to believe that ungrudging application of the Fourth Amendment is indispensable to preserving the liberties of a democratic society. Accordingly, I dissent.

## QUESTIONS AND NOTES

**1.** Is it clear to you that the search which produced the drugs was unlawful? If you represented the government could you have made a case that the search was lawful?

**2.** If the Government could have established that the search was lawful, why do you suppose that it did not try?

**3.** Why was Rawlings' expectation of privacy in Cox's purse unreasonable?

**4.** Would (should) the case have been different if Rawlings had (with Cox's permission) placed a nude photograph of himself in her purse because he was embarrassed for a stranger to see it, and sued the police officer for violating his constitutional rights?

**5.** In *Payner* we examine the question of whether a bad faith exploitation of the standing doctrine can warrant a different result.

### United States v. Payner
### 447 U.S. 727 (1980)

Mr. Justice POWELL delivered the opinion of the Court.

The question is whether the District Court properly suppressed the fruits of an unlawful search that did not invade the respondent's Fourth Amendment rights.

I

Respondent Jack Payner was indicted in September 1976 on a charge of falsifying his 1972 federal income tax return. The indictment alleged that respondent denied maintaining a foreign bank account at a time when he knew that he had such an account at the Castle Bank and Trust Company of Nassau, Bahama Islands. The Government's case rested heavily on a loan guarantee agreement dated April 28, 1972, in which respondent pledged the funds in his Castle Bank account as security for a $100,000 loan.

The events leading up to the 1973 search are not in dispute. In 1965, the Internal Revenue Service launched an investigation into the financial activities of American citizens in the Bahamas. The project, known as "Operation Trade Winds," was headquartered in Jacksonville, Fla. Suspicion focused on the Castle Bank in 1972, when investigators learned that a suspected narcotics trafficker had an account there. Special Agent Richard Jaffe of the Jacksonville office asked Norman Casper, a private investigator and occasional informant, to learn what he could about the Castle Bank and its depositors. To that end, Casper cultivated his friendship with Castle Bank vice president Michael Wolstencroft. Casper introduced Wolstencroft to Sybol Kennedy, a private investigator and former employee. When Casper discovered that the banker intended to spend a few days in Miami in January 1973, he devised a scheme to gain access to the bank records he knew Wolstencroft would be carrying in his briefcase. Agent Jaffe approved the basic outline of the plan.

Wolstencroft arrived in Miami on January 15 and went directly to Kennedy's apartment. At about 7:30 p. m., the two left for dinner at a Key Buskin restaurant. Shortly thereafter, Casper entered the apartment using a key supplied by Kennedy. He removed the briefcase and delivered it to Jaffe. While the agent supervised the copying of approximately 400 documents taken from the briefcase, a "lookout" observed Kennedy and Wolstencroft at dinner. The observer notified Casper when the pair left the restaurant, and the briefcase was replaced. The documents photographed that evening included papers evidencing a close working relationship between the Castle Bank and the Bank of Perrine, Fla. Subpoenas issued to the Bank of Perrine ultimately uncovered the loan guarantee agreement at issue in this case.

The District Court found that the United States, acting through Jaffe, "knowingly and willfully participated in the unlawful seizure of Michael Wolstencroft's briefcase. . . ." According to that court, "the Government affirmatively counsels its agents that the Fourth Amendment standing limitation permits them to purposefully conduct an unconstitutional search and seizure of one individual in order to obtain evidence against third parties. . . ." The District Court also found that the documents seized from Wolstencroft provided the leads that ultimately led to the discovery of the critical loan guarantee agreement.[3] Although the search did not impinge upon the respondent's Fourth Amendment rights, the District Court believed that the Due Process Clause of the Fifth Amendment and the inherent supervisory power of the federal courts required it to exclude evidence tainted by the Government's "knowing and purposeful *bad faith hostility* to any person's fundamental constitutional rights."

## II

This Court discussed the doctrine of "standing to invoke the [Fourth Amendment] exclusionary rule" in some detail last Term. *Rakas*. We reaffirmed the established rule that a court may not exclude evidence under the Fourth Amendment unless it finds that an unlawful search or seizure violated the defendant's own constitutional rights. And the defendant's Fourth Amendment rights are violated only when the challenged conduct invaded his legitimate expectation of privacy rather than that of a third party.

---

[3] The United States argued in the District Court and the Court of Appeals that the guarantee agreement was discovered through an independent investigation untainted by the briefcase search. The Government also denied that its agents willfully encouraged Casper's illegal behavior. For purposes of this opinion, we need not question the District Court's contrary findings on either point.

The foregoing authorities establish, as the District Court recognized, that respondent lacks standing under the Fourth Amendment to suppress the documents illegally seized from Wolstencroft. The Court of Appeals did not disturb the District Court's conclusion that "Jack Payner possessed no privacy interest in the Castle Bank documents that were seized from Wolstencroft." Nor do we.

The District Court and the Court of Appeals believed, however, that a federal court should use its supervisory power to suppress evidence tainted by gross illegalities that did not infringe the defendant's constitutional rights. The United States contends that this approach—as applied in this case—upsets the careful balance of interests embodied in the Fourth Amendment decisions of this Court. In the Government's view, such an extension of the supervisory power would enable federal courts to exercise a standardless discretion in their application of the exclusionary rule to enforce the Fourth Amendment. We agree with the Government.

## III

We certainly can understand the District Court's commendable desire to deter deliberate intrusions into the privacy of persons who are unlikely to become defendants in a criminal prosecution. No court should condone the unconstitutional and possibly criminal behavior of those who planned and executed this "briefcase caper."[5] Indeed, the decisions of this

---

[5] "The security of persons and property remains a fundamental value which law enforcement officers must respect. Nor should those who flout the rules escape unscathed." *Alderman*. We note that in 1976 Congress investigated the improprieties revealed in this record. See Oversight Hearings into the Operations of the IRS before a Subcommittee of the House Committee on Government Operations (Operation Tradewinds, Project Haven, and Narcotics Traffickers Tax Program), 94th Cong., 1st Sess. (1975). As a result, the Commissioner of Internal Revenue "called off" Operation Trade Winds. The Commissioner also adopted guidelines that require agents to instruct informants on the requirements of the law and to report known illegalities to a supervisory officer, who is in turn directed to notify appropriate state authorities. Although these measures appear on their face to be less positive than one might expect from an agency charged with upholding the law, they do indicate disapproval of the practices found to have been implemented in this case. We cannot assume that similar lawless conduct, if brought to the attention of responsible officials, would not be

Court are replete with denunciations of willfully lawless activities undertaken in the name of law enforcement. But our cases also show that these unexceptional principles do not command the exclusion of evidence in every case of illegality. Instead, they must be weighed against the considerable harm that would flow from indiscriminate application of an exclusionary rule.

Thus, the exclusionary rule "has been restricted to those areas where its remedial objectives are most efficaciously served." *Calandra*. The Court has acknowledged that the suppression of probative but tainted evidence exacts a costly toll upon the ability of courts to ascertain the truth in a criminal case. Our cases have consistently recognized that unbending application of the exclusionary sanction to enforce ideals of governmental rectitude would impede unacceptably the truth-finding functions of judge and jury. After all, it is the defendant, and not the constable, who stands trial.

The same societal interests are at risk when a criminal defendant invokes the supervisory power to suppress evidence seized in violation of a third party's constitutional rights. The supervisory power is applied with some caution even when the defendant asserts a violation of his own rights.

We conclude that the supervisory power does not authorize a federal court to suppress otherwise admissible evidence on the ground that it was seized unlawfully from a third party not before the court. Our Fourth Amendment decisions have established beyond any doubt that the interest in deterring illegal searches does not justify the exclusion of tainted evidence at the instance of a party who was not the victim of the challenged practices. *Rakas*; *Alderman*.[8] The values assigned to the competing interests

---

dealt with appropriately. To require in addition the suppression of highly probative evidence in a trial against a third party would penalize society unnecessarily.

[8] "The deterrent values of preventing the incrimination of those whose rights the police have violated have been considered sufficient to justify the suppression of probative evidence even though the case against the defendant is weakened or destroyed. We adhere to that judgment. But we are not convinced that the additional benefits of extending the exclusionary rule to other defendants would justify further encroachment upon the public interest in prosecuting those accused of crime and having them acquitted or convicted on the basis of all the evidence which exposes the truth." *Alderman*.

The dissent urges that the balance of interests

do not change because a court has elected to analyze the question under the supervisory power instead of the Fourth Amendment. In either case, the need to deter the underlying conduct and the detrimental impact of excluding the evidence remain precisely the same.

The District Court erred, therefore, when it concluded that "society's interest in deterring [bad faith] conduct by exclusion outweigh[s] society's interest in furnishing the trier of fact with all relevant evidence." This reasoning, which the Court of Appeals affirmed, amounts to a substitution of individual judgment for the controlling decisions of this Court. Were we to accept this use of the supervisory power, we would confer on the judiciary discretionary power to disregard the considered limitations of the law it is charged with enforcing. We hold that the supervisory power does not extend so far.

The judgment of the Court of Appeals is Reversed.

Mr. Chief Justice BURGER, concurring.

I join the Court's opinion because Payner — whose

---

under the supervisory power differs from that considered in *Alderman* and like cases, because the supervisory power focuses upon the "need to protect the integrity of the federal courts." Although the District Court in this case relied upon a deterrent rationale, we agree that the supervisory power serves the "twofold" purpose of deterring illegality and protecting judicial integrity. As the dissent recognizes, however, the Fourth Amendment exclusionary rule serves precisely the same purposes. Thus, the Fourth Amendment exclusionary rule, like the supervisory power, is applied in part "to protect the integrity of the *court*, rather than to vindicate the constitutional rights of the defendant. . . ." *Calandra*.

In this case, where the illegal conduct did not violate the respondent's rights, the interest in preserving judicial integrity and in deterring such conduct is outweighed by the societal interest in presenting probative evidence to the trier of fact. None of the cases cited by the dissent supports a contrary view, since none of those cases involved criminal defendants who were not themselves the victims of the challenged practices. Thus, our decision today does not limit the traditional scope of the supervisory power in any way; nor does it render that power "superfluous." We merely reject its use as a substitute for established Fourth Amendment doctrine.

guilt is not in doubt—cannot take advantage of the Government's violation of the constitutional rights of Wolstencroft, for he is not a party to this case. The Court's opinion makes clear the reason for that sound rule.

Orderly government under our system of separate powers calls for internal self-restraint and discipline in each Branch; this Court has no general supervisory authority over operations of the Executive Branch, as it has with respect to the federal courts. I agree fully with the Court that the exclusionary rule is inapplicable to a case of this kind, but that should not be read as condoning the conduct of the IRS "private investigators" as disclosed by this record, or as approval of their evidence-gathering methods.

Mr. Justice MARSHALL, with whom Mr. Justice BRENNAN and Mr. Justice BLACKMUN join, dissenting.

The Court today holds that a federal court is unable to exercise its supervisory powers to prevent the use of evidence in a criminal prosecution in that court, even though that evidence was obtained through intentional illegal and unconstitutional conduct by agents of the United States, because the defendant does not satisfy the standing requirement of the Fourth Amendment. That holding effectively turns the standing rules created by this Court for assertions of Fourth Amendment violations into a sword to be used by the Government to permit it deliberately to invade one person's Fourth Amendment rights in order to obtain evidence against another person. Unlike the Court, I do not believe that the federal courts are unable to protect the integrity of the judicial system from such gross Government misconduct.

I

The facts as found by the District Court need to be more fully stated in order to establish the level of purposeful misconduct to which agents of the United States have sunk in this case. Operation Trade Winds was initiated by the Internal Revenue Service (IRS) in 1965 to gather information about the financial activities of American citizens in the Bahamas. The investigation was supervised by Special Agent Richard Jaffe in the Jacksonville, Fla., office. It was not until June 1972 that the investigation focused on the Castle Bank and Trust Company of the Bahamas. In late October 1972 Jaffe asked one of his informants, Norman Casper, to obtain the names and addresses of the individuals holding accounts with the Castle Bank. Casper set to work soon thereafter. He was already an acquaintance of Michael Wolstencroft,

vice president and trust officer of the Castle Bank. Casper knew that Wolstencroft frequently visited the United States carrying a briefcase with documents from the Castle Bank. Casper therefore introduced Wolstencroft to Sybol Kennedy, a private detective who worked for Casper. In early January 1973, Casper learned that Wolstencroft planned a business trip to the United States on January 15, 1973, and that he would have Castle Bank records with him on that trip. Plans for the "briefcase caper," as Casper called it, began in earnest.

As found by the District Court, Casper discussed the details of the plan with Jaffe on several occasions during the week before Wolstencroft's trip.[1] Casper told Jaffe that he could get the needed documents from Wolstencroft, but that Jaffe would have to supply photographic services. On January 11, Casper specifically informed Jaffe that he planned to enter an apartment and take Wolstencroft's briefcase. Jaffe then stated that he would have to clear the operation with his superior, Troy Register, Jr., Chief of the IRS Intelligence Division in Jacksonville. Clearance was obtained, and Jaffe told Casper to proceed with the plan.[2] Casper called Jaffe the following day and asked if the IRS could refer him to a locksmith who could be "trusted." Jaffe gave him such a referral.[3]

---

[1] The Court rather blandly states that "Agent Jaffe approved the basic outline of the plan." Such a characterization is misleading in light of the findings of the District Court. As is noted in the text *infra*, Jaffe knew explicit details of the operation in advance and helped to make the arrangements by recommending a locksmith who could be "trusted," by providing a safe and convenient location for the photographing of the documents, and by providing a photographer from the IRS.

[2] Jaffe testified in the District Court that "[w]hatever I knew, he [Register] knew."

[3] It was clear why Casper needed a locksmith who could be "trusted." Casper testified as follows in the District Court:

"Q. Isn't it a fact, Mr. Casper, you knew you were committing an illegal act, and you wanted somebody who could be trusted to keep his mouth shut about it?

"A. There is that possibility, yes.

"Q. Isn't that the fact?

"A. Yes."

It is interesting to note that even the locksmith who could be "trusted" refused to enter Kennedy's apartment with Casper.

The Government contends that when Agent Jaffe made the referral he did not know what use Casper

The plans were finalized by the time of Wolstencroft's arrival on January 15. Wolstencroft went directly to Sybol Kennedy's apartment. The couple eventually went to a restaurant for dinner.[4] Using a key provided by Kennedy, Casper entered the apartment and *stole* Wolstencroft's briefcase. Casper then rendezvoused with the IRS-recommended locksmith in a parking lot five blocks from the apartment; the locksmith made a key to fit the lock on the case. Casper took the briefcase and newly made key to the home of an IRS agent. Jaffe had selected that location for the photographing because it was only eight blocks from the parking lot where Casper met the locksmith and Jaffe knew there was a need to act with haste. The briefcase was opened in Jaffe's presence. Jaffe, Casper, and an IRS photography expert then photographed over 400 documents. Casper had arranged for Kennedy and Wolstencroft to be watched on their date, and this lookout called Casper at the IRS agent's home when the couple finished their dinner. After all the documents had been copied, Casper relocked the briefcase and returned it to Kennedy's apartment. The entire "caper" lasted approximately one and one-half hours.

The illegalities of agents of the United States did not stop even at that point, however. During the following two weeks, Jaffe told Casper that the IRS needed additional information. Casper therefore sent Kennedy to visit Wolstencroft in the Bahamas. While there, acting pursuant to Casper's instructions, Kennedy stole a Rolodex file from Wolstencroft's office. This file was turned over to Jaffe, who testified in the District Court that he had not cared how the rolodex file had been obtained.

---

intended to make of such a locksmith. The District Court found, however, that Jaffe already knew at the time of the referral that Casper intended to enter Kennedy's apartment and to take and open Wolstencroft's briefcase. There were, then, only two logical alternatives why Casper would want such a locksmith: to make a key to enter the briefcase, or to make a key to enter the apartment. Either way, Jaffe must have known that Casper's conduct was improper, and yet Jaffe made the referral anyway.

[4] It was not established at trial what occurred in Kennedy's apartment prior to the couple's departure for dinner. Since it was peculiarly within the power of the United States to produce Kennedy as a witness and since the Government did not explain her absence from the trial, the District Court inferred that Kennedy's testimony "would be unfavorable to the Government by further delineating the improprieties" of the "briefcase caper."

The IRS paid Casper $8,000 in cash for the services he rendered in obtaining the information about Castle Bank. Casper in turn paid approximately $1,000 of this money to Kennedy for her role in the "briefcase caper" and the theft of the rolodex file.

The "briefcase caper" revealed papers which showed a close relationship between the Castle Bank and a Florida bank. Subpoenas issued to that Florida bank resulted in the uncovering of the loan guarantee agreement which was the principal piece of evidence against respondent at trial. It is that loan agreement and the evidence discovered as a result of it that the District Court reluctantly suppressed under the Due Process Clause of the Fifth Amendment and under its supervisory powers.

The District Court made several key findings concerning the level of misconduct of agents of the United States in these activities. The District Court found that "the United States, through its agents, Richard Jaffe, and others, knowingly and willfully participated in the unlawful seizure of Michael Wolstencroft's briefcase, and encouraged its informant, Norman Casper, to arrange the theft of a rolodex from the offices of Castle Bank." The District Court concluded that "the United States was an active participant in the admittedly criminal conduct in which Casper engaged. . . ." The District Court found that "the illegal conduct of the government officials involved in this case compels the conclusion that they knowingly and purposefully obtained the briefcase materials with *bad faith hostility* toward the strictures imposed on their activities by the Constitution." (emphasis in original). The District Court considered the actions of Jaffe and Casper "outrageous" because they "plotted, schemed and ultimately acted in contravention of the United States Constitution and laws of Florida, knowing that their conduct was illegal."

The most disturbing finding by the District Court, however, related to the intentional manipulation of the standing requirements of the Fourth Amendment by agents of the United States, who are, of course, supposed to uphold and enforce the Constitution and laws of this country. The District Court found:

"It is evident that the Government and its agents, including Richard Jaffe, were, and are, well aware that under the standing requirement of the Fourth Amendment, evidence obtained from a party pursuant to an unconstitutional search is admissible against third parties who's [*sic*] own privacy expectations are not subject to the search, even though the cause for the unconstitutional search was to obtain evidence incriminating those third parties. This Court finds that, in its desire to apprehend tax evaders, a desire the Court fully shares, the Government affirmatively counsels its agents that the Fourth Amendment standing limitation permits them to purposefully conduct an unconstitutional search and seizure of one individual in order to obtain evidence against third parties, who are the real targets of the governmental intrusion, and that the IRS agents in this case acted, and will act in the future, according to that counsel. Such governmental conduct compels the conclusion that Jaffe and Casper transacted the 'briefcase caper' with a purposeful, bad faith hostility toward the Fourth Amendment rights of Wolstencroft in order to obtain evidence against persons like Payner.''

The Court of Appeals did not disturb any of these findings. Nor does the Court today purport to set them aside. It is in the context of these findings—intentional illegal actions by Government agents taken in bad-faith hostility toward the constitutional rights of Wolstencroft for the purpose of obtaining evidence against persons such as the respondent through manipulation of the standing requirements of the Fourth Amendment—that the suppression issue must be considered.

## II

The need to use the Court's supervisory powers to suppress evidence obtained through governmental misconduct was perhaps best expressed by Mr. Justice Brandeis in his famous dissenting opinion in *Olmstead v. United States*, 277 U.S. 438, 485 (1928):

> "Decency, security and liberty alike demand that government officials shall be subjected to the same rules of conduct that are commands to the citizen. In a government of laws, existence of the government will be imperilled if it fails to observe the law scrupulously. Our Government is the potent, the omnipresent teacher. For good or for ill, it teaches the whole people by its example. Crime is contagious. If the Government becomes a lawbreaker, it breeds contempt for law; it invites every man to become a law unto himself; it invites anarchy. To declare that in the administration of the criminal law the end justifies the means—to declare that the Government may commit crimes in order to secure the conviction of a private criminal—would bring terrible retribution. Against that

pernicious doctrine this Court should resolutely set its face.''

The reason for this emphasis on the need to protect the integrity of the federal courts through the use of supervisory powers can be derived from the factual contexts in which supervisory powers have been exercised. In large part when supervisory powers have been invoked the Court has been faced with intentional illegal conduct. It has not been the case that "[t]he criminal is to go free because the constable has blundered.'' In these cases there has been no "blunder'' by the Government agent at all; rather, the agent has intentionally violated the law for the explicit purpose of obtaining the evidence in question.

The present case falls within that category. The District Court found, and the record establishes, a deliberate decision by Government agents to violate the constitutional rights of Wolstencroft for the explicit purpose of obtaining evidence against persons such as Payner. The Government knew exactly what information it wanted, and it was that information which was stolen from Wolstencroft. Similarly, the Government knew that it wanted to prosecute persons such as Payner, and it made a conscious decision to forgo any opportunity to prosecute Wolstencroft in order to obtain illegally the evidence against Payner and others.[13]

Since the supervisory powers are exercised to protect the integrity of the *court*, rather than to vindicate the constitutional rights of the defendant, it is hard to see why the Court today bases its analysis entirely on Fourth Amendment standing rules. The point is that the federal judiciary should not be made accomplices to the crimes of Casper, Jaffe, and others. The only way the IRS can benefit from the evidence it chose to obtain illegally is if the evidence is admitted at trial against persons such as Payner; that was the very point of the criminal exercise in

---

[13] Wolstencroft in fact was indicted for aiding and abetting Payner. However, Wolstencroft is a Bahamian resident, and did not return to the United States to answer the indictment. The mere fact that the Government went through the steps of indicting Wolstencroft does not in any way undermine the District Court's finding, based on substantial evidence in the record, that Wolstencroft was never the target of the IRS investigation. In light of the Government's concession that Wolstencroft's Fourth Amendment rights were violated, it is hard to see how the banker could be successfully prosecuted on the aiding and abetting charge.

the first place. If the IRS is permitted to obtain a conviction in federal court based almost entirely on that illegally obtained evidence and its fruits, then the judiciary has given full effect to the deliberate wrongdoings of the Government. The federal court does indeed become the accomplice of the Government lawbreaker, an accessory after the fact, for without judicial use of the evidence the "caper" would have been for nought. Such a pollution of the federal courts should not be permitted.[14]

It is particularly disturbing that the Court today chooses to allow the IRS deliberately to manipulate the standing rules of the Fourth Amendment to achieve its ends. As previously noted, the District Court found that "the Government affirmatively counsels its agents that the Fourth Amendment standing limitation permits them to purposefully conduct an unconstitutional search and seizure of one individual in order to obtain evidence against third parties, who are the real targets of the governmental intrusion, and that the IRS agents in this case acted, *and will act in the future,* according to that counsel." (emphasis supplied). Whatever role those standing limitations may play, it is clear that they were never intended to be a sword to be used by the Government in its deliberate choice to sacrifice the constitutional rights of one person in order to prosecute another.

Contrary to the Court's characterization, this is also not a case in which there has been "indiscriminate" or "unbending" application of the exclusionary rule. The District Court noted that "exclusion on the basis of supervisory power is only done as a last resort." That court concluded that suppression was proper only where there had been "purposefully illegal" conduct by the Government to obtain the evidence or where the Government's conduct was "motivated by an intentional bad faith hostility to a constitutional right." In this case, both those threshold requirements were met, and the District Court in addition concluded that absent suppression there was no deterrent to continued lawless conduct undertaken by the IRS to facilitate these types of prosecutions.[16] This is not "a 'chancellor's foot' veto [by the District Court] over law enforcement practices of which it did not approve." As my Brother Powell noted on a prior occasion: "The fact that there is sometimes no sharply defined standard against which to make these judgments [of fundamental fairness] is not itself a sufficient reason to deny the federal judiciary's power to make them when warranted by the circumstances. . . . Nor do I despair of our ability in an appropriate case to identify appropriate standards for police practices without relying on the 'chancellor's' 'fastidious squeamishness or private sentimentalism.'" *Hampton v. United States,* 425 U.S. 484, 495, n.6 (1976) (concurring in judgment). That appropriate case has arrived, and the Court should prevent the Government from profiting by use in the federal courts of evidence deliberately obtained by illegal actions taken in bad-faith hostility to constitutional rights.

I would affirm the judgment of the Court of Appeals and suppress the fruits of the Government's illegal action under the Court's supervisory powers. Accordingly, I dissent.

---

[14] It is simply not a sufficient cure for the Court to denounce the actions of the IRS, while at the same time rewarding the Government for this conduct by permitting the IRS to use the evidence in the very manner which was the purpose of the illegal and unconstitutional activities.

[16] There is no suggestion by the Government that any action has been taken against Casper, Jaffe, or others for the conduct exposed in this case. The Court admits that the corrective measures taken by the IRS "appear on their face to be less positive than one might expect from an agency charged with upholding the law." The District Court specifically found that the Government agents knew they were violating the Constitution at the time, and that continued manipulation of the standing limitations of the Fourth Amendment by the IRS could be deterred only by suppression of the evidence.

## QUESTIONS AND NOTES

**1.** Does *Payner* appear to you to have carefully balanced the equities? Explain.

**2.** Just as we have a good faith exception to the exclusionary rule (*Leon*), should there be a bad-faith exception to the nonexclusionary rule? Why? Why not? If so, would *Payner* be a good case to apply one?

**3.** If you were an IRS employee (such as Jaffe), what lesson would you learn from *Payner*? Is that a lesson that the Court ought to be teaching IRS employees?

**4.** If you had been on the Court, how would you have decided this case? Why?

# 14.

# CONFESSIONS, VOLUNTARINESS

Although the privilege against self-incrimination precludes legal compulsion to testify, it was not available to invalidate coerced confessions for most of the nation's history for two reasons. First, until the 1960s, the privilege was thought to apply only to the Federal government. Second, the privilege was not thought to apply to interrogation because no *legal* process was applied to the arrestee to compel him to speak. Consequently, most of the coerced confession cases were analyzed under the Due Process Clause. In this chapter, we analyze four of them, *Brown, Watts, Crooker*, and *Spano*.

## Brown v. Mississippi
### 297 U.S. 278 (1936)

Mr. Chief Justice HUGHES delivered the opinion of the Court.

The question in this case is whether convictions, which rest solely upon confessions shown to have been extorted by officers of the state by brutality and violence, are consistent with the due process of law required by the Fourteenth Amendment of the Constitution of the United States.

Petitioners were indicted for the murder of one Raymond Stewart, whose death occurred on March 30, 1934. They were indicted on April 4, 1934, and were then arraigned and pleaded not guilty. Counsel were appointed by the court to defend them. Trial was begun the next morning and was concluded on the following day, when they were found guilty and sentenced to death.

"The crime with which these defendants, all ignorant negroes, are charged, was discovered about 1 o'clock p.m. on Friday, March 30, 1934. On that night one Dial, a deputy sheriff, accompanied by others, came to the home of Ellington, one of the defendants, and requested him to accompany them to the house of the deceased, and there a number of white men were gathered, who began to accuse the defendant of the crime. Upon his denial they seized him, and with the participation of the deputy they hanged him by a rope to the limb of a tree, and, having let him down, they hung him again, and when he was let down the second time, and he still protested his innocence, he was tied to a tree and whipped, and, still declining to accede to the demands that he confess, he was finally released, and he returned with some difficulty to his home, suffering intense pain and agony. The record of the testimony shows that the signs of the rope on his neck were plainly visible during the so-called trial. A day or two thereafter the said deputy, accompanied by another, returned to the home of the said defendant and arrested him, and departed with the prisoner towards the jail in an adjoining county, but went by a route which led into the state of Alabama; and while on the way, in that state, the deputy stopped and again severely whipped the defendant, declaring that he would continue the whipping until he confessed, and the defendant then agreed to confess to such a statement as the deputy would dictate, and he did so, after which he was delivered to jail.

"The other two defendants, Ed Brown and Henry Shields, were also arrested and taken to the same jail. On Sunday night, April 1, 1934, the same deputy, accompanied by a number of white men, one of whom was also an officer, and by the jailer, came to the jail, and the two last named defendants were made to strip and they were laid over chairs and their backs were cut to pieces with a leather strap with buckles on it, and they were likewise made by the said deputy definitely to understand that the whipping would be continued unless and until they confessed, and not only confessed, but confessed in every matter of detail as demanded by those present; and in this manner the defendants confessed the crime, and, as the whippings progressed and were repeated, they changed or adjusted their confession in all particulars of detail so as to conform to the demands of their torturers. When the confessions had been obtained in the exact form and contents as desired by the mob, they left with the parting admonition and warning that, if the defendants changed their story at any time in any respect from that last stated, the perpetrators of the outrage would administer the same or equally effective treatment.

"Further details of the brutal treatment to which these helpless prisoners were subjected need not be pursued. It is sufficient to say that in pertinent respects the transcript reads more like pages torn from some medieval account than a record made within the confines of a modern civilization which aspires to an enlightened constitutional government.

"All this having been accomplished, on the next day, that is, on Monday, April 2, when the defendants had been given time to recuperate somewhat from the tortures to which they had been subjected, the two sheriffs, one of the county where the crime was committed, and the other of the county of the jail in which the prisoners were confined, came to the jail, accompanied by eight other persons, some of them deputies, there to hear the free and voluntary confession of these miserable and abject defendants. The sheriff of the county of the crime admitted that

he had heard of the whipping, but averred that he had no personal knowledge of it. He admitted that one of the defendants, when brought before him to confess, was limping and did not sit down, and that this particular defendant then and there stated that he had been strapped so severely that he could not sit down, and, as already stated, the signs of the rope on the neck of another of the defendants were plainly visible to all. Nevertheless the solemn farce of hearing the free and voluntary confessions was gone through with, and these two sheriffs and one other person then present were the three witnesses used in court to establish the so-called confessions, which were received by the court and admitted in evidence over the objections of the defendants duly entered of record as each of the said three witnesses delivered their alleged testimony. There was thus enough before the court when these confessions were first offered to make known to the court that they were not, beyond all reasonable doubt, free and voluntary; and the failure of the court then to exclude the confessions is sufficient to reverse the judgment, under every rule of procedure that has heretofore been prescribed, and hence it was not necessary subsequently to renew the objections by motion or otherwise.

"The spurious confessions having been obtained — and the farce last mentioned having been gone through with on Monday, April 2d — the court, then in session, on the following day, Tuesday, April 3, 1934, ordered the grand jury to reassemble on the succeeding day, April 4, 1934, at 9 o'clock, and on the morning of the day last mentioned the grand jury returned an indictment against the defendants for murder. Late that afternoon the defendants were brought from the jail in the adjoining county and arraigned, when one or more of them offered to plead guilty, which the court declined to accept, and, upon inquiry whether they had or desired counsel, they stated that they had none, and did not suppose that counsel could be of any assistance to them. The court thereupon appointed counsel, and set the case for trial for the following morning at 9 o'clock, and the defendants were returned to the jail in the adjoining county about thirty miles away.

"The defendants were brought to the courthouse of the county on the following morning, April 5th, and the so-called trial was opened, and was concluded on the next day, April 6, 1934, and resulted in a pretended conviction with death sentences. The evidence upon which the conviction was obtained was the so-called confessions. Without this evidence, a peremptory instruction to find for the defendants would have been inescapable. The defendants were put on the stand, and by their testimony the facts and the details thereof as to the manner by which the confessions were extorted from them were fully developed, and it is further disclosed by the record that the same deputy, Dial, under whose guiding hand and active participation the tortures to coerce the confessions were administered, was actively in the performance of the supposed duties of a court deputy in the courthouse and in the presence of the prisoners during what is denominated, in complimentary terms, the trial of these defendants. This deputy was put on the stand by the state in rebuttal, and admitted the whippings. It is interesting to note that in his testimony with reference to the whipping of the defendant Ellington, and in response to the inquiry as to how severely he was whipped, the deputy stated, 'Not too much for a negro; not as much as I would have done if it were left to me.' Two others who had participated in these whippings were introduced and admitted it—not a single witness was introduced who denied it. The facts are not only undisputed, they are admitted, and admitted to have been done by officers of the state, in conjunction with other participants, and all this was definitely well known to everybody connected with the trial, and during the trial, including the state's prosecuting attorney and the trial judge presiding.''

The state stresses the statement in *Twining v. New Jersey*, 211 U.S. 78, 114, that "exemption from compulsory self-incrimination in the courts of the states is not secured by any part of the Federal Constitution,'' and the statement in *Snyder v. Massachusetts*, 291 U.S. 97, 105, that "the privilege against self-incrimination may be withdrawn and the accused put upon the stand as a witness for the state.'' But the question of the right of the state to withdraw the privilege against self-incrimination is not here involved. The compulsion to which the quoted statements refer is that of the processes of justice by which the accused may be called as a witness and

required to testify. Compulsion by torture to extort a confession is a different matter.

The state is free to regulate the procedure of its courts in accordance with its own conceptions of policy, unless in so doing it "offends some principle of justice so rooted in the traditions and conscience of our people as to be ranked as fundamental.'' The state may abolish trial by jury. It may dispense with indictment by a grand jury and substitute complaint or information. But the freedom of the state in establishing its policy is the freedom of constitutional government and is limited by the requirement of due process of law. Because a state may dispense with a jury trial, it does not follow that it may substitute trial by ordeal. The rack and torture chamber may not be substituted for the witness stand. The state may not permit an accused to be hurried to conviction under mob domination—where the whole proceeding is but a mask—without supplying corrective process. The state may not deny to the accused the aid of counsel. Nor may a state, through the action of its officers, contrive a conviction through the pretense of a trial which in truth is "but used as a means of depriving a defendant of liberty through a deliberate deception of court and jury by the presentation of testimony known to be perjured.'' *Mooney v. Holohan*, 294 U.S. 103, 112. And the trial equally is a mere pretense where the state authorities have contrived a conviction resting solely upon confessions obtained by violence. The due process clause requires "that state action, whether through one agency or another, shall be consistent with the fundamental principles of liberty and justice which lie at the base of all our civil and political institutions.'' *Hebert v. Louisiana*, 272 U.S. 312, 316. It would be difficult to conceive of methods more revolting to the sense of justice than those taken to procure the confessions of these petitioners, and the use of the confessions thus obtained as the basis for conviction and sentence was a clear denial of due process.

## QUESTIONS AND NOTES

**1.** Are the convictions in this case reversed to compensate the victims for their torture, or because they never had a fair trial? Does it matter?

**2.** Should there be a *per se* rule denying the admissibility of confessions where the arrestee has been beaten?

**3.** If your answer to question 2 was ''yes,'' how should the Court determine from frequently conflicting stories whether or not a beating occurred?

**4.** Can any conceivable argument be made in favor of the State in this case?

**5.** Without physical torture, the cases get much more difficult as will become apparent from reading *Watts*.

## Watts v. Indiana
### 338 U.S. 49 (1949)

Mr. Justice FRANKFURTER announced the judgment of the Court and an opinion in which Mr. Justice MURPHY and Mr. Justice RUTLEDGE join.

In the application of so embracing a constitutional concept as "due process," it would be idle to expect at all times unanimity of views. Nevertheless, in all the cases that have come here during the last decade from the courts of the various States in which it was claimed that the admission of coerced confessions vitiated convictions for murder, there has been complete agreement that any conflict in testimony as to what actually led to a contested confession is not this Court's concern. Such conflict comes here authoritatively resolved by the State's adjudication. Therefore only those elements of the events and circumstances in which a confession was involved that are unquestioned in the State's version of what happened are relevant to the constitutional issue here. But if force has been applied, this Court does not leave to local determination whether or not the confession was voluntary. There is torture of mind as well as body; the will is as much affected by fear as by force. And there comes a point where this Court should not be ignorant as judges of what we know as men.

This brings us to the undisputed circumstances which must determine the issue of due process in this case. Thanks to the forthrightness of counsel for Indiana, these circumstances may be briefly stated.

On November 12, 1947, a Wednesday, petitioner was arrested and held as the suspected perpetrator of an alleged criminal assault earlier in the day. Later the same day, in the vicinity of this occurrence, a woman was found dead under conditions suggesting murder in the course of an attempted criminal assault. Suspicion of murder quickly turned towards petitioner and the police began to question him. They took him from the county jail to State Police Headquarters, where he was questioned by officers in relays from about eleven thirty that night until sometime between 2:30 and 3 o'clock the following morning. The same procedure of persistent interrogation from about 5:30 in the afternoon until about 3 o'clock the following morning, by a relay of six to eight officers, was pursued on Thursday the 13th, Friday the 14th, Saturday

the 15th, Monday the 17th. Sunday was a day of rest from interrogation. About 3 o'clock on Tuesday morning, November 18, the petitioner made an incriminating statement after continuous questioning since 6 o'clock of the preceding evening. The statement did not satisfy the prosecutor who had been called in and he then took petitioner in hand. Petitioner, questioned by an interrogator of twenty years' experience as lawyer, judge and prosecutor, yielded a more incriminating document.

Until his inculpatory statements were secured, the petitioner was a prisoner in the exclusive control of the prosecuting authorities. He was kept for the first two days in solitary confinement in a cell aptly enough called "the hole" in view of its physical conditions as described by the State's witnesses. Apart from the five night sessions, the police intermittently interrogated Watts during the day and on three days drove him around town, hours at a time, with a view to eliciting identifications and other disclosures. Although the law of Indiana required that petitioner be given a prompt preliminary hearing before a magistrate, with all the protection a hearing was intended to give him, the petitioner was not only given no hearing during the entire period of interrogation but was without friendly or professional aid and without advice as to his constitutional rights. Disregard of rudimentary needs of life—opportunities for sleep and a decent allowance of food—are also relevant, not as aggravating elements of petitioner's treatment, but as part of the total situation out of which his confessions came and which stamped their character.

A confession by which life becomes forfeit must be the expression of free choice. A statement to be voluntary of course need not be volunteered. But if it is the product of sustained pressure by the police it does not issue from a free choice. When a suspect speaks because he is overborne, it is immaterial whether he has been subjected to a physical or a mental ordeal. Eventual yielding to questioning under such circumstances is plainly the product of the suction process of interrogation and therefore the reverse of voluntary. We would have to shut our minds to the plain significance of what here transpired to deny that this was a calculated endeavor to secure a confession through the pressure of unrelenting interrogation. The very relentlessness of such interrogation implies that it is better for the prisoner to answer than to persist in the refusal of disclosure which is his constitutional right. To turn the detention of an accused into a process of wrenching from him evidence which could not be extorted in open court with all its safeguards, is so grave an abuse of the power of arrest as to offend the procedural standards of due process.

This is so because it violates the underlying principle in our enforcement of the criminal law. Ours is the accusatorial as opposed to the inquisitorial system. Such has been the characteristic of Anglo-American criminal justice since it freed itself from practices borrowed by the Star Chamber from the Continent whereby an accused was interrogated in secret for hours on end. Under our system society carries the burden of proving its charge against the accused not out of his own mouth. It must establish its case, not by interrogation of the accused even under judicial safeguards, but by evidence independently secured through skillful investigation. "The law will not suffer a prisoner to be made the deluded instrument of his own conviction." 2 Hawkins, Pleas of the Crown c. 46, § 34 (8th ed., 1824). The requirement of specific charges, their proof beyond a reasonable doubt, the protection of the accused from confessions extorted through whatever form of police pressures, the right to a prompt hearing before a magistrate, the right to assistance of counsel, to be supplied by government when circumstances make it necessary, the duty to advise an accused of his constitutional rights—these are all characteristics of the accusatorial system and manifestations of its demands. Protracted, systematic and uncontrolled subjection of an accused to interrogation by the police for the purpose of eliciting disclosures or confessions is subversive of the accusatorial system. It is the inquisitorial system without its safeguards. For while under that system the accused is subjected to judicial interrogation, he is protected by the disinterestedness of the judge in the presence of counsel. See Keedy, *The Preliminary Investigation of Crime in France*, 88 U. of Pa. L. Rev., 692, 708-712 (1940).

In holding that the Due Process Clause bars police procedure which violates the basic notions of our accusatorial mode of prosecuting crime and vitiates a conviction based on the fruits of such procedure, we apply the Due Process Clause to its historic function of assuring appropriate procedure before liberty is curtailed or life is taken. We are deeply mindful of the anguishing problems which the incidence of crime presents to the States. But the history of the criminal law proves overwhelmingly that brutal methods of law enforcement are essentially self-defeating, whatever may be their effect in a particular case. Law triumphs when the natural impulses aroused by a shocking crime yield to the safeguards which our civilization has evolved for an administration of criminal justice at once rational and effective.

Mr. Justice BLACK concurs in the judgment of the Court on the authority of *Chambers v. Florida*, 309 U.S. 227; *Ashcraft v. Tennessee*, 322 U.S. 143.

On the record before us and in view of the consideration given by the state courts and the conclusion reached, The Chief Justice, Mr. Justice REED and Mr. Justice BURTON believe that the judgement should be affirmed.

Mr. Justice DOUGLAS, concurring.

It would be naive to think that this protective custody was less than the inquisition. The man was held until he broke. Then and only then was he arraigned and given the protection which the law provides all accused. Detention without arraignment is a time-honored method for keeping an accused under the exclusive control of the police. They can then operate at their leisure. The accused is wholly at their mercy. He is without the aid of counsel or friends; and he is denied the protection of the magistrate. We should unequivocally condemn the procedure and stand ready to outlaw any confession obtained during the period of the unlawful detention. The procedure breeds coerced confessions. It is the root of the evil. It is the procedure without which the inquisition could not flourish in the country.

Mr. Justice JACKSON concurring in the result in [*Watts*] and dissenting in [*Harris v. South Carolina*] and [*Turner v. Pennsylvania*].

These three cases, [*Watts, Harris*, 338 U.S. 68 (1949), and *Turner*, 338 U.S. 62 (1949)], from widely separated states, present essentially the same problem. Its recurrence suggests that it has roots in some condition fundamental and general to our criminal system.

In each case police were confronted with one or more brutal murders which the authorities were under the highest duty to solve. Each of these murders was unwitnessed, and the only positive knowledge on which a solution could be based was possessed by the killer. In each there was reasonable ground to *suspect* an individual but not enough legal evidence to *charge* him with guilt. In each the police attempted to meet the situation by taking the suspect into custody and interrogating him. This extended over varying periods. In each, confessions were made and received in evidence at the trial. Checked with external evidence, they are inherently believable, and were not shaken as to truth by anything that occurred at the trial. Each confessor was convicted by a jury and state courts affirmed. This Court sets all three convictions aside.

The seriousness of the Court's judgment is that no one suggests that any course held promise of solution of these murders other than to take the suspect into custody for questioning. The alternative was to close the books on the crime and forget it, with the suspect at large. This is a grave choice for a society in which two-thirds of the murders already are closed out as insoluble.

A concurring opinion, however, goes to the very limit and seems to declare for outlawing any confession, however freely given, if obtained during a period of custody between arrest and arraignment—which, in practice, means all of them.

Others would strike down these confessions because of conditions which they say make them "involuntary." In this, on only a printed record, they pit their judgment against that of the trial judge and the jury. Both, with the great advantage of hearing and seeing the confessor and also the officers whose conduct and bearing toward him is in question, have found that the confessions were voluntary. In addition, the majority overrule in each case one or more state appellate courts, which have the same limited opportunity to know the truth that we do.

Amid much that is irrelevant or trivial one serious situation seems to me to stand out in these cases. The suspect neither had nor was advised of his right to get counsel. This presents a real dilemma in a free society. To subject one without counsel to questioning which may and is intended to convict him, is a real peril to individual freedom. To bring in a lawyer means a real peril to solution of the crime because, under our adversary system, he deems that his sole duty is to protect his client—guilty or innocent—and that in such a capacity he owes no duty whatever to help society solve its crime problem. Under this conception of criminal procedure, any lawyer worth his salt will tell the suspect in no uncertain terms to make no statement to police under any circumstances.

If the State may arrest on suspicion and interrogate without counsel, there is no denying the fact that it largely negates the benefits of the constitutional guaranty of the right to assistance of counsel. Any lawyer who has ever been called into a case after his client has "told all" and turned any evidence he has over to the Government, knows how helpless he is to protect his client against the facts thus disclosed.

I suppose the view one takes will turn on what one thinks should be the right of an accused person against the State. Is it his right to have the judgment on the facts? Or is it his right to have a judgment based on only such evidence as he cannot conceal from the authorities, who cannot compel him to testify in court and also cannot question him before? Our system comes close to the latter by any interpretation, for the defendant is shielded by such safeguards as no system to law except the Anglo-American concedes to him.

Of course, no confession that has been obtained by any form of physical violence to the person is reliable and hence no conviction should rest upon one obtained in that manner. Such treatment not only breaks the will to conceal or lie, but may even break the will to stand by the truth. Nor is it questioned that the same result can sometimes be achieved by threats, promises, or inducements, which torture the mind but put no scar on the body. If the opinion of Mr. Justice Frankfurter in the *Watts* case were based solely on the State's admissions as to the treatment of Watts, I should not disagree. But if the ultimate quest in a criminal trial is the truth and if the circumstances indicate no violence or threats of it, should society be deprived of the suspect's help in solving a crime merely because he was confined and questioned when uncounseled?

We must not overlook that in these, as in some previous cases, once a confession is obtained it supplies ways of verifying its trustworthiness. In these cases before us the verification is sufficient to leave me in no doubt that the admissions of guilt were genuine and truthful. Such corroboration consists in one case of finding a weapon where the accused has said he hid it, and in others that conditions which could only have been known to one who was implicated correspond with his story. It is possible, but it is rare, that a confession, if repudiated on the trial, standing alone will convict unless there is external proof of its verity.

In all such cases, along with other conditions criticized, the continuity and duration of the questioning is invoked and it is called an "inquiry," "inquest" or "inquisition," depending mainly on the emotional state of the writer. But as in some of the cases here, if interrogation is permissible at all, there are sound reasons for prolonging it—which the opinions here ignore. The suspect at first perhaps makes an effort to exculpate himself by alibis or other statements. These are verified, found false, and he is then confronted with his falsehood. Sometimes (though such cases do not reach us) verification proves them true or credible and the suspect is released. Sometimes, as here, more than one crime is involved. The duration of an interrogation may well depend on the temperament, shrewdness and cunning of the accused and the competence of the examiner. But assuming a right to examine at all, the right must include what is made reasonably necessary by the facts of the particular case.

If the right of interrogation be admitted, then it seems to me that we must leave it to trial judges and juries and state appellate courts to decide individual cases, unless they show some want of proper standards of decision.

I suppose no one would doubt that our Constitution and Bill of Rights, grounded in revolt against the arbitrary measures of George III and in the philosophy of the French Revolution, represent the maximum restrictions upon the power of organized society over the individual that are compatible with the maintenance of organized society itself. They were so intended and should be so interpreted. It cannot be denied that, even if construed as these

provisions traditionally have been, they contain an aggregate of restrictions which seriously limit the power of society to solve such crimes as confront us in these cases. Those restrictions we should not for that reason cast aside, but that is good reason for indulging in no unnecessary expansion of them.

I doubt very much if they require us to hold that the State may not take into custody and question one suspected reasonably of an unwitnessed murder. If it does, the people of this country must discipline themselves to seeing their police stand by helplessly while those suspected of murder prowl about unmolested. Is it a necessary price to pay for the fairness which we know as "due process of law"? And if not a necessary one, should it be demanded by this Court? I do not know the ultimate answer to these questions; but, for the present, I should not increase the handicap on society.

## QUESTIONS AND NOTES

**1.** Do you see anything wrong with the *Watts* procedure? Explain.

**2.** If one takes the Frankfurter opinion seriously, does it necessarily lead to the conclusion that Justice Douglas is correct?

**3.** The Court says: "The law will not suffer a prisoner to be made the deluded instrument of his own conviction." Do we really believe that? Should we really believe that?

**4.** How would you resolve the dilemma identified by Justice Jackson?

**5.** Do you think that the system is too pro-defendant? Why? Why not?

**6.** As you read *Crooker*, consider whether Justice Frankfurter's *Watts'* observations were taken seriously. It is worth noting that Frankfurter was necessary for a five-four majority in *Crooker*.

### Crooker v. California
357 U.S. 433 (1958)

Mr. Justice CLARK delivered the opinion of the Court.

Petitioner, under sentence of death for the murder of his paramour, claims that his conviction in a California court violates Fourteenth Amendment due process of law because (1) the confession admitted into evidence over his objection had been coerced from him by state authorities, and (2) even if his confession was voluntary it occurred while he was without counsel because of the previous denial of his request therefor.

The record here clearly reveals that prior to petitioner's confession he asked for and was denied opportunity to call his lawyer. We first consider that

denial in connection with petitioner's contention that his subsequent confession was involuntary in nature.

It is well established that the Fourteenth Amendment prohibits use of coerced confessions in state prosecutions. *E.g., Brown; Watts.*

The victim's son discovered her body the morning of July 5, 1955, stabbed and strangled to death in the bedroom of her Los Angeles home. She was last known to be alive about 1 a.m. the same day, when she talked with a friend by telephone.

Petitioner was arrested in his apartment at 1:30 that afternoon and subsequently was charged with the murder. He was then 31 years of age, a college graduate who had attended the first year of law school. While going to law school he had been a house boy in the home of the victim. That position led to an illicit relationship with her, which she had attempted several times to terminate in the month preceding her death. The week of her death, after telling petitioner they had been found out, she had requested, and he had agreed, that he would never see her again.

Despite this understanding, he returned to her house late in the afternoon of July 4. Finding no one at home, he hid nearby for the ostensible purpose of discovering who was "threatening" her. From his hiding place he watched the victim return home with an escort around midnight. Shortly thereafter he saw the escort leave and watched the victim talk on the telephone. He claims that he then left the vicinity to return to his apartment, never having entered the house that evening.

At the time of his arrest, petitioner was questioned about scratches that were evident on his neck and hands. He attributed the former to shaving and the latter to a traffic mishap on his way to the beach on July 4. However he refused to reveal where the accident occurred. After his apartment was searched, petitioner was taken to the Los Angeles Police Station, where he was photographed and asked to take a lie detector test. He refused to submit to the test, and indicated that he wanted to call an attorney. At no time, however, does it appear that petitioner was offered the use of a telephone. Aside from sporadic questioning at his apartment, petitioner was interrogated for the first time from 8:30-9:30 p.m., the questioning being conducted by four officers and centering around his refusal of the lie detector test. During this time he asked for an opportunity to get a lawyer, naming a specific attorney whom he thought might represent him, but was told that "after [the] investigation was concluded he could call an attorney."

At 9:30 p.m. petitioner was transferred to the West Los Angeles Police Station, where five officers questioned him from 11 p.m. until shortly after midnight. He then was formally "booked," and given a physical examination by a police physician. The third and last questioning period was conducted by the same five men from approximately 1-2 a.m. July 6. For the next hour petitioner wrote and signed a detailed confession of the murder. Afterward, he was taken to the victim's home to re-enact the crime. At 5 a.m. he was put in jail and permitted to sleep.

That afternoon, a full day after his arrest, he was taken to the office of the Los Angeles County District Attorney to orally repeat the written confession. Petitioner balked at doing so and again asked that his attorney be called. Thereupon the District Attorney

placed the call for him and listened to the conversation while petitioner talked on an extension phone with the attorney. Neither petitioner nor his attorney was aware that a tape recording was being made of everything that transpired in the office. The District Attorney interrupted at one point to deny that petitioner was forced to answer police questions, and later to advise that the most convenient time for the attorney to see petitioner would be at 7 p.m. back at the West Los Angeles Police Station. After the phone call, petitioner was returned to jail to meet his attorney that evening. From that time forward, through both arraignment and trial, he was represented by his own counsel.

In the 14 hours between his arrest and confession, petitioner was given coffee and allowed to smoke whenever he liked. He also was given milk and a sandwich a few hours after his arrest. Before being transferred to the West Los Angeles Police Station he was advised by a police lieutenant, "You don't have to say anything that you don't want to," and he in fact refused to answer many questions both before and after the transfer. At such times he simply stated he "would rather not answer, or rather not make a statement about that."

The bare fact of police "detention and police examination in private of one in official state custody" does not render involuntary a confession by the one so detained. Neither does an admonition by the police to tell the truth, nor the failure of state authorities to comply with local statutes requiring that an accused promptly be brought before a magistrate.[2]

Petitioner's claim of coercion, then, depends almost entirely on denial of his request to contact counsel.[3] This Court has not previously had occasion to determine the character of a confession obtained after

---

[2] Section 849 of the California Penal Code provides that a person arrested without a warrant must be brought before the nearest or most accessible magistrate in the county of arrest "without unnecessary delay. Cal.Penal Code, 1956, § 849.

[3] Even if within the scope of the limited grant of certiorari, claims of physical violence—"third degree" methods—were denied by witnesses for the State, and hence are not part of the undisputed portions of the record which we consider here. The ambiguous reply by one police officer, "I don't think we hurt you," in response to petitioner's assertion in the District Attorney's office that the officer struck him, cannot alter the contradicted state of the evidence when the same officer categorically denied the claim on cross-examination at the trial.

such a denial. But we have held that confessions made by indigent defendants prior to state appointment of counsel are not thereby rendered involuntary, even in prosecutions where conviction without counsel would violate due process under the Fourteenth Amendment. To be sure, coercion seems more likely to result from state denial of a specific request for opportunity to engage counsel than it does from state failure to appoint counsel immediately upon arrest. That greater possibility, however, is not decisive. It is negated here by petitioner's age, intelligence, and education. While in law school he had studied criminal law; indeed, when asked to take the lie detector test, he informed the operator that the results of such a test would not be admissible at trial absent a stipulation by the parties. Supplementing that background is the police statement to petitioner well before his confession that he did not have to answer questions. Moreover, the manner of his refusals to answer indicates full awareness of the right to be silent. On this record we are unable to say that petitioner's confession was anything other than voluntary.

We turn now to the contention that even if the confession be voluntary, its use violates due process because it was obtained after denial of petitioner's request to contact his attorney. Petitioner reaches this position by reasoning first that he has been denied a due process right to representation and advice from his attorney,[4] and secondly that the use of any confession obtained from him during the time of such a denial would itself be barred by the Due Process Clause, even though freely made. We think petitioner fails to sustain the first point, and therefore we do not reach the second.

In *House v. Mayo*, 324 U.S. 42 (1945), an uneducated man in his twenties, a stranger to the area, was brought before a court to be sentenced on two convictions previously returned against him. He was there presented for the first time with a burglary information filed by the State, asked for and was denied opportunity to engage counsel, and finally

---

[4] At times petitioner appears to urge "a rule" barring use of a voluntary confession obtained after state denial of a request to contact counsel regardless of whether any violation of a due process right to counsel occurred. That contention is simply an appeal to the supervisory power of this Court over the administration of justice in the federal courts. See *McNabb v. United States*, 318 U.S. 332 (1943), which, significantly enough, petitioner cites. The short answer to such a contention here is that this conviction was had in a state, not a federal, court.

pleaded guilty to the information, thereby obviating any necessity for trial of the charge on the merits. We held that a due process right to counsel was denied.

In contrast, the sum total of the circumstances here during the time petitioner was without counsel is a voluntary confession by a college-educated man with law school training who knew of his right to keep silent. Such facts, while perhaps a violation of California law,[5] do not approach the prejudicial impact in *House v. Mayo*, and do not show petitioner to have been so "taken advantage of" as to violate due process of law.

Mr. Justice DOUGLAS, with whom THE CHIEF JUSTICE, Mr. Justice BLACK and Mr. Justice BRENNAN concur, dissenting.

When petitioner was first arrested, and before any real interrogation took place, he asked that his attorney be present. "I had no objection to talking with them about whatever they had to talk about, but . . . I wanted counsel with me. . . . I wanted an attorney with me before I would talk with them."

That was petitioner's testimony; and it is verified by the testimony of Sergeant Gotch of the police.

"A. I stated to him that after our investigation was concluded he could call an attorney, and if he didn't have funds to hire an attorney, when he went to Court a public defender would be assigned to handle his case.

"He then stated that he had a friend who had been an instructor at Pepperdine College that would probably handle the case for him. I asked him who the name was, and he said it was a man by the name of Simpson, who lived in Long Beach.

"Q. He asked you if he could call an attorney at that time, and you told him that he could call after your investigation was completed, is that right?

"A. I told him, after I was through with the investigation, he could make a call."

This demand for an attorney was made over and again prior to the time a confession was extracted from the accused. Its denial was in my view a denial of that due process of law guaranteed the citizen by the Fourteenth Amendment.

---

[5] Section 825 of the California Penal Code provides that after an arrest, an attorney "may at the request of the prisoner or any relative of such prisoner, visit the person so arrested." Any officer in charge of the prisoner who wilfully refuses to let the attorney see the prisoner is made guilty of a misdemeanor. Cal.Penal Code, 1956, § 825.

The Court properly concedes that the right to counsel extends to pretrial proceedings as well as to the trial itself. The need is as great then as at any time. The right to have counsel at the pretrial stage is often necessary to give meaning and protection to the right to be heard at the trial itself. It may also be necessary as a restraint on the coercive power of the police. The pattern of the third degree runs through our cases: a lone suspect unrepresented by counsel against whom the full coercive force of a secret inquisition is brought to bear. See *Watts*. The third degree flourishes only in secrecy. One who feels the need of a lawyer and asks for one is asking for some protection which the law can give him against a coerced confession. No matter what care is taken innocent people are convicted of crimes they did not commit. We should not lower the barriers and deny the accused any procedural safeguard against coercive police practices. The trial of the issue of coercion is seldom helpful. Law officers usually testify one way, the accused another. The citizen who has been the victim of these secret inquisitions has little chance to prove coercion. The mischief and abuse of the third degree will continue as long as an accused can be denied the right to counsel at this the most critical period of his ordeal. For what takes place in the secret confines of the police station may be more critical than what takes place at the trial.

[A]s stated by a Committee headed by Prof. Zechariah Chafee, "A person accused of crime needs a lawyer right after his arrest probably more than at any other time."

The Court speaks of the education of this petitioner and his ability to take care of himself. In an opinion written by Mr. Justice Sutherland the Court said, "Even the intelligent and educated layman has small and sometimes no skill in the science of law. . . . He requires the guiding hand of counsel at every step in the proceedings against him." *Powell v. Alabama*, 287 U.S. 45, 69. Mr. Justice Sutherland spoke of the trial itself. But what is true of the trial is true of the preparation for trial and of the period commencing with the arrest of the accused. No matter how well educated, and how well trained in the law an accused may be, he is sorely in need of legal advice once he is arrested for an offense that may exact his life. The innocent as well as the guilty may be caught in a web of circumstantial evidence that is difficult to break. A man may be guilty of indiscretions but not of the crime. He may be implicated by ambiguous circumstances difficult to explain away. He desperately needs a lawyer to help extricate him if he's innocent. He has the right to receive the benefit of the advice of his own counsel at the trial. That same right should extend to the pretrial stage.

## QUESTIONS AND NOTES

**1.** Do you agree that the bare fact of detention, coupled with an admonition to tell the truth and a failure to bring the accused promptly before a magistrate, does not render a confession involuntary? Was Frankfurter consistent with his *Watts* opinion in accepting that statement?

**2.** Should petitioner's education have been relevant? Would you have felt uncoerced under these circumstances? Explain.

**3.** How should the problem suggested by footnote 3 of the Court's opinion be resolved? Apparently if Crooker had been hit (even if not hurt too much) his confession would have been involuntary. However, the Court is willing to accept the findings of the lower court unless there is no evidence to support them.

**4.** Should the fact that California violated its own statutes have been relevant? Why? Why not?

**5.** What do you understand to be the difference between supervisory powers and constitutional adjudication.

**6.** We conclude this section with *Spano*, where the entire Court appears to be growing impatient with, at least some aspects of, police practices in obtaining confessions.

## Spano v. New York
### 360 U.S. 315 (1959)

Mr. Chief Justice WARREN delivered the opinion of the Court.

This is another in the long line of cases presenting the question whether a confession was properly admitted into evidence under the Fourteenth Amendment. As in all such cases, we are forced to resolve a conflict between two fundamental interests of society; its interest in prompt and efficient law enforcement, and its interest in preventing the rights of its individual members from being abridged by unconstitutional methods of law enforcement.

The State's evidence reveals the following: Petitioner Vincent Joseph Spano is a derivative citizen of this country, having been born in Messina, Italy. He was 25 years old at the time of the shooting in question and had graduated from junior high school. He had a record of regular employment. The shooting took place on January 22, 1957.

On that day, petitioner was drinking in a bar. The decedent, a former professional boxer weighing almost 200 pounds who had fought in Madison Square Garden, took some of petitioner's money from the bar. Petitioner followed him out of the bar to recover it. A fight ensued, with the decedent knocking petitioner down and then kicking him in the head three or four times. Shock from the force of these blow caused petitioner to vomit. After the bartender applied some ice to his head, petitioner left the bar, walked to his apartment, secured a gun, and walked eight or nine blocks to a candy store where the decedent was frequently to be found. He entered the store in which decedent, three friends of decedent, at least two of whom were ex-convicts, and a boy who was supervising the store were present. He fired five shots, two of which entered the decedent's body, causing his death. The boy was the only eyewitness; the three friends of decedent did not see the person who fired the shot. Petitioner then disappeared for the next week or so.

On February 1, 1957, the Bronx County Grand Jury returned an indictment for first-degree murder against petitioner. Accordingly, a bench warrant was issued for his arrest, commanding that he be forthwith brought before the court to answer the indictment, or, if the court had adjourned for the term, that he be delivered into the custody of the Sheriff of Bronx County.

On February 3, 1957, petitioner called one Gaspar Bruno, a close friend of 8 or 10 years' standing who had attended school with him. Bruno was a fledgling police officer, having at that time not yet finished attending police academy. According to Bruno's testimony, petitioner told him "that he took a terrific beating, that the deceased hurt him real bad and he dropped him a couple of times and he was dazed; he didn't know what he was doing and that he went and shot at him." Petitioner told Bruno that he intended to get a lawyer and give himself up. Bruno relayed this information to his superiors.

The following day, February 4, at 7:10 p.m., petitioner, accompanied by counsel, surrendered himself to the authorities in front of the Bronx County Building, where both the office of the Assistant District Attorney who ultimately prosecuted his case and the court-room in which he was ultimately tried were located. His attorney had cautioned him to answer no questions, and left him in the custody of the officers. He was promptly taken to the office of the Assistant District Attorney and at 7:15 p.m. the questioning began, being conducted by Assistant District Attorney Goldsmith, Lt. Gannon, Detectives Farrell, Lehrer and Motta, and Sgt. Clarke. The record reveals that the questioning was both persistent and continuous. Petitioner, in accordance with his attorney's instructions, steadfastly refused to answer. Detective Motta testified: "He refused to talk to me." "He just looked up to the ceiling and refused to talk to me." Detective Farrell testified:

"Q. And you started to interrogate him?
"A. That is right.
"Q. What did he say?
"A. He said 'you would have to see my attorney. I tell you nothing but my name.'
"Q. Did you continue to examine him?
"A. Verbally, yes, sir."

He asked one officer, Detective Ciccone, if he could speak to his attorney, but that request was denied. Detective Ciccone testified that he could not find the attorney's name in the telephone book.[1] He was given two sandwiches, coffee and cake at 11 p.m.

At 12:15 a.m. on the morning of February 5, after five hours of questioning in which it became

---

[1] How this could be so when the attorney's name, Tobias Russo, was concededly in the telephone book does not appear. The trial judge sustained objections by the Assistant District Attorney to questions designed to delve into this mystery.

evident that petitioner was following his attorney's instructions, on the Assistant District Attorney's orders petitioner was transferred to the 46th Squad, Ryer Avenue Police Station. The Assistant District Attorney also went to the police station and to some extent continued to participate in the interrogation. Petitioner arrived at 12:30 and questioning was resumed at 12:40. The character of the questioning is revealed by the testimony of Detective Farrell:

> "Q. Who did you leave him in the room with?
>
> "A. With Detective Lehrer and Sergeant Clarke came in and Mr. Goldsmith came in or Inspector Halk came in. It was back and forth. People just came in, spoke a few words to the defendant or they listened a few minutes and they left."

But petitioner persisted in his refusal to answer, and again requested permission to see his attorney, this time from Detective Lehrer. His request was again denied.

It was then that those in charge of the investigation decided that petitioner's close friend, Bruno, could be of use. He had been called out on the case around 10 or 11 p.m., although he was not connected with the 46th Squad or Precinct in any way. Although, in fact, his job was in no way threatened, Bruno was told to tell petitioner that petitioner's telephone call had gotten him "in a lot of trouble," and that he should seek to extract sympathy from petitioner for Bruno's pregnant wife and three children. Bruno developed this theme with petitioner without success, and petitioner, also without success, again sought to see his attorney, a request which Bruno relayed unavailingly to his superiors. After this first session with petitioner, Bruno was again directed by Lt. Gannon to play on petitioner's sympathies, but again no confession was forthcoming. But the Lieutenant a third time ordered Bruno falsely to importune his friend to confess but again petitioner clung to his attorney's advice. Inevitably, in the fourth such session directed by the Lieutenant, lasting a full hour, petitioner succumbed to his friend's prevarications and agreed to make a statement. Accordingly, at 3:25 a.m. the Assistant District Attorney, a stenographer, and several other law enforcement officials entered the room where petitioner was being questioned, and took his statement in question and answer form with the Assistant District Attorney asking the questions. The statement was completed at 4:05 a.m.

But this was not the end. At 4:30 a.m. three detectives took petitioner to Police Headquarters in Manhattan. On the way they attempted to find the bridge from which petitioner said he had thrown the murder weapon. They crossed the Triborough Bridge into Manhattan, arriving at Police Headquarters at 5 a.m., and left Manhattan for the Bronx at 5:40 a.m. via the Willis Avenue Bridge. When petitioner recognized neither bridge as the one from which he had thrown the weapon, they re-entered Manhattan via the Third Avenue Bridge, which petitioner stated was the right one, and then returned to the Bronx well after 6 a.m. During that trip the officers also elicited a statement from petitioner that the deceased was always "on [his] back," "always pushing" him and that he was "not sorry" he had shot the deceased. All three detectives testified to that statement at the trial.

Petitioner's first contention is that his absolute right to counsel in a capital case became operative on the return of an indictment against him, for at that time he was in every sense a defendant in a criminal case, the grand jury having found sufficient cause to believe that he had committed the crime. He argues accordingly that following indictment no confession obtained in the absence of counsel can be used without violating the Fourteenth Amendment. He seeks to distinguish *Crooker* on the ground that in those cases no indictment had been returned. We find it unnecessary to reach that contention, for we find use of the confession obtained here inconsistent with the Fourteenth Amendment under traditional principles.

The abhorrence of society to the use of involuntary confessions does not turn alone on their inherent untrustworthiness. It also turns on the deep-rooted feeling that the police must obey the law while enforcing the law; that in the end life and liberty can be as much endangered from illegal methods used to convict those thought to be criminals as from the actual criminals themselves. Accordingly, the actions of police in obtaining confessions have come under scrutiny in a long series of cases. Those cases suggest that in recent years law enforcement officials have become increasingly aware of the burden which they share, along with our courts, in protecting fundamental rights of our citizenry, including that portion of our citizenry suspected of crime. The facts of no case recently in this Court have quite approached the brutal beatings in *Brown*, or the 36 consecutive hours of questioning present in *Ashcraft v. Tennessee*, 322 U.S. 143 (1944). But as law enforcement officers become more responsible, and the methods used to extract confessions more sophisticated, our duty to enforce federal constitutional protections does not cease. It only becomes more difficult because of the more delicate judgments to be made. Our judgment here is that, on all the facts, this conviction cannot stand.

Petitioner was a foreign-born young man of 25 with no past history of law violation or of subjection to official interrogation, at least insofar as the record shows. He had progressed only one-half year into high school and the record indicates that he had a history of emotional instability. He did not make a narrative statement, but was subject to the leading questions of a skillful prosecutor in a question and answer confession. He was subjected to questioning not by a few men, but by many. They included Assistant District Attorney Goldsmith, one Hyland of the District Attorney's Office, Deputy Inspector Halks, Lieutenant Gannon, Detective Ciccone, Detective Motta, Detective Lehrer, Detective Marshal, Detective Farrell, Detective Leira, Detective Murphy, Detective Murtha, Sergeant Clarke, Patrolman Bruno and Stenographer Baldwin. All played some part, and the effect of such massive official interrogation must have been felt. Petitioner was questioned for virtually eight straight hours before he confessed, with his only respite being a transfer to an arena presumably considered more appropriate by the police for the task at hand. Nor was the questioning conducted during normal business hours, but began in early evening, continued into the night, and did not bear fruition until the not-too-early morning. The drama was not played out, with the final admissions obtained, until almost sunrise. In such circumstances slowly mounting fatigue does, and is calculated to, play its part. The questioners persisted in the face of his repeated refusals to answer on the advice of his attorney, and they ignored his reasonable requests to contact the local attorney whom he had already retained and who had personally delivered him into the custody of these officers in obedience to the bench warrant.

The use of Bruno, characterized in this Court by counsel for the State as a "childhood friend" of petitioner's, is another factor which deserves mention in the totality of the situation. Bruno's was the one face visible to petitioner in which he could put some trust. There was a bond of friendship between them going back a decade into adolescence. It was with this material that the officers felt that they could overcome petitioner's will. They instructed Bruno falsely to state that petitioner's telephone call had gotten him into trouble, that his job was in jeopardy, and that loss of his job would be disastrous to his three children, his wife and his unborn child. And Bruno played this part of a worried father, harried by his superiors, in not one, but four different acts,

the final one lasting an hour. Petitioner was apparently unaware of John Gay's famous couplet:

> "An open foe may prove a curse,
> But a pretended friend is worse,"

and he yielded to his false friend's entreaties.

We conclude that petitioner's will was overborne by official pressure, fatigue and sympathy falsely aroused after considering all the facts in their post-indictment setting. Here a grand jury had already found sufficient cause to require petitioner to face trial on a charge of first-degree murder, and the police had an eyewitness to the shooting. The police were not therefore merely trying to solve a crime, or even to absolve a suspect. Compare *Crooker*. They were rather concerned primarily with securing a statement from defendant on which they could convict him. The undeviating intent of the officers to extract a confession from petitioner is therefore patent. When such an intent is shown, this Court has held that the confession obtained must be examined with the most careful scrutiny, and has reversed a conviction on facts less compelling than these. Accordingly, we hold that petitioner's conviction cannot stand under the Fourteenth Amendment.

The judgment must be reversed.

Mr. Justice DOUGLAS, with whom Mr. Justice BLACK and Mr. Justice BRENNAN join, concurring.

While I join the opinion of the Court, I add what for me is an even more important ground of decision.

We have often divided on whether state authorities may question a suspect for hours on end when he has no lawyer present and when he has demanded that he have the benefit of legal advice. See *Crooker*. But here we deal not with a suspect but with a man who has been formally charged with a crime. The question is whether after the indictment and before the trial the Government can interrogate the accused *in secret* when he asked for his lawyer and when his request was denied.

Depriving a person, formally charged with a crime, of counsel during the period prior to trial may be more damaging than denial of counsel during the trial itself.

We do not have here mere suspects who are being secretly interrogated by the police as in *Crooker*. This is a case of an accused, who is scheduled to be tried by a judge and jury, being tried in a preliminary way by the police. This is a kangaroo court procedure whereby the police produce the vital evidence in the form of a confession which is useful or necessary to obtain a conviction. They in effect deny him effective representation by counsel. This seems to me to be a flagrant violation of the principle that the right of counsel extends to the preparation for trial, as well as to the trial itself. As Professor Chafee once said, "A person accused of crime needs a lawyer right after his arrest probably more than at any other time."

Mr. Justice STEWART, whom Mr. Justice DOUGLAS and Mr. Justice BRENNAN join, concurring.

While I concur in the opinion of the Court, it is my view that the absence of counsel when this confession was elicited was alone enough to render it inadmissible under the Fourteenth Amendment.

Let it be emphasized at the outset that this is not a case where the police were questioning a suspect in the course of investigating an unsolved crime. See *Crooker*. When the petitioner surrendered to the New York authorities he was under indictment for first degree murder.

Under our system of justice an indictment is supposed to be followed by an arraignment and a trial.

[T]he right to the assistance of counsel whom the accused has himself retained is absolute.

What followed the petitioner's surrender in this case was not arraignment in a court of law, but an all-night inquisition in a prosecutor's office, a police station, and an automobile. Throughout the night the petitioner repeatedly asked to be allowed to send for his lawyer, and his requests were repeatedly denied. He finally was induced to make a confession. That confession was used to secure a verdict sending him to the electric chair.

Our Constitution guarantees the assistance of counsel to a man on trial for his life in an orderly courtroom, presided over by a judge, open to the public, and protected by all the procedural safeguards of the law. Surely a Constitution which promises that much can vouchsafe no less to the same man under midnight inquisition in the squad room of a police station.

## QUESTIONS AND NOTES

**1.** Why do you suppose that the Court unanimously reversed this conviction?

**2.** Why do you suppose that the New York Court of Appeals affirmed it?

**3.** How significant is the indictment? How significant should it be? Why?

**4.** After this case, probably a majority of the Court (the four concurring Justices plus Warren, who had dissented in *Crooker*) believed that there was an absolute right to counsel after indictment.

**5.** Is there an inherent "kangaroo court" problem with police interrogation? Is there a solution? What might it be?

# 15.

# RIGHT TO COUNSEL

The right to counsel was first used to invalidate a confession in *Massiah*, a 1964 decision. *Massiah*'s fact pattern, on one level, does not appear to be about the right to counsel at all.

## Massiah v. United States
### 377 U.S. 201 (1964)

Mr. Justice STEWART delivered the opinion of the Court.

The petitioner, a merchant seaman, was in 1958 a member of the crew of the S. S. *Santa Maria*. In April of that year federal customs officials in New York received information that he was going to transport a quantity of narcotics aboard that ship from South America to the United States. As a result of this and other information, the agents searched the *Santa Maria* upon its arrival in New York and found in the afterpeak of the vessel five packages containing about three and a half pounds of cocaine. They also learned of circumstances, not here relevant, tending to connect the petitioner with the cocaine. He was arrested, promptly arraigned, and subsequently indicted for possession of narcotics aboard a United States vessel. In July a superseding indictment was returned, charging the petitioner and a man named Colson with the same substantive offense, and in separate counts charging the petitioner, Colson, and others with having conspired to possess narcotics aboard a United States vessel, and to import, conceal, and facilitate the sale of narcotics. The petitioner, who had retained a lawyer, pleaded

not guilty and was released on bail, along with Colson.

A few days later, and quite without the petitioner's knowledge, Colson decided to cooperate with the government agents in their continuing investigation of the narcotics activities in which the petitioner, Colson, and others had allegedly been engaged. Colson permitted an agent named Murphy to install a Schmidt radio transmitter under the front seat of Colson's automobile, by means of which Murphy, equipped with an appropriate receiving device, could overhear from some distance away conversations carried on in Colson's car.

On the evening of November 19, 1959, Colson and the petitioner held a lengthy conversation while sitting in Colson's automobile, parked on a New York street. By prearrangement with Colson, and totally unbeknown to the petitioner, the agent Murphy sat in a car parked out of sight down the street and listened over the radio to the entire conversation. The petitioner made several incriminating statements during the course of this conversation. At the petitioner's trial these incriminating statements were brought before the jury through Murphy's testimony, despite the insistent objection of defense counsel. The jury convicted the petitioner of several related narcotics offenses, and the convictions were affirmed by the Court of Appeals.

The petitioner argues that it was an error of constitutional dimensions to permit the agent Murphy at the trial to testify to the petitioner's incriminating statements which Murphy had overheard under the circumstances disclosed by this record. This argument is based upon two distinct and independent grounds. First, we are told that Murphy's use of the radio equipment violated the petitioner's rights under the Fourth Amendment, and, consequently, that all evidence which Murphy thereby obtained was inadmissible against the petitioner at the trial. Secondly, it is said that the petitioner's Fifth and Sixth Amendment rights were violated by the use in evidence against him of incriminating statements which government agents had deliberately elicited from him after he had been indicted and in the absence of his retained counsel. Because of the way we dispose of the case, we do not reach the Fourth Amendment issue.

In *Spano*, this Court reversed a state criminal conviction because a confession had been wrongly admitted into evidence against the defendant at his trial. In that case the defendant had already been indicted for first-degree murder at the time he confessed. The Court held that the defendant's conviction could not stand under the Fourteenth Amendment. While the Court's opinion relied upon the totality of the circumstances under which the confession had been obtained, four concurring Justices pointed out that the Constitution required reversal of the conviction upon the sole and specific ground that the confession had been deliberately elicited by the police after the defendant had been indicted, and therefore at a time when he was clearly entitled to a lawyer's help.

Here we deal not with a state court conviction, but with a federal case, where the specific guarantee of the Sixth Amendment directly applies.[6] *Johnson v. Zerbst*. We hold that the petitioner was denied the basic protections of that guarantee when there was used against him at his trial evidence of his own incriminating words, which federal agents had deliberately elicited from him after he had been indicted and in the absence of his counsel. It is true

---

[6] "In all criminal prosecutions, the accused shall enjoy the right . . . to have the Assistance of Counsel for his defence."

that in the *Spano* case the defendant was interrogated in a police station, while here the damaging testimony was elicited from the defendant without his knowledge while he was free on bail. But, as Judge Hays pointed out in his dissent in the Court of Appeals, "if such a rule is to have any efficacy it must apply to indirect and surreptitious interrogations as well as those conducted in the jailhouse. In this case, Massiah was more seriously imposed upon . . . because he did not even know that he was under interrogation by a government agent."

The Solicitor General, in his brief and oral argument, has strenuously contended that the federal law enforcement agents had the right, if not indeed the duty, to continue their investigation of the petitioner and his alleged criminal associates even though the petitioner had been indicted. He points out that the Government was continuing its investigation in order to uncover not only the source of narcotics found on the S. S. *Santa Maria*, but also their intended buyer. He says that the quantity of narcotics involved was such as to suggest that the petitioner was part of a large and well-organized ring, and indeed that the continuing investigation confirmed this suspicion, since it resulted in criminal charges against many defendants. Under these circumstances the Solicitor General concludes that the Government agents were completely "justified in making use of Colson's cooperation by having Colson continue his normal associations and by surveilling them."

We may accept and, at least for present purposes, completely approve all that this argument implies, Fourth Amendment problems to one side. We do not question that in this case, as in many cases, it was entirely proper to continue an investigation of the suspected criminal activities of the defendant and his alleged confederates, even though the defendant had already been indicted. All that we hold is that the defendant's own incriminating statements, obtained by federal agents under the circumstances here disclosed, could not constitutionally be used by the prosecution as evidence against *him* at his trial.

Reversed.

Mr. Justice WHITE, with whom Mr. Justice CLARK and Mr. Justice HARLAN join, dissenting.

The current incidence of serious violations of the law represents not only an appalling waste of the potentially happy and useful lives of those who engage in such conduct but also an overhanging, dangerous threat to those unidentified and innocent people who will be the victims of crime today and tomorrow. This is a festering problem for which no adequate cures have yet been devised. At the very least there is much room for discontent with remedial measures so far undertaken. And admittedly there remains much to be settled concerning the disposition to be made of those who violate the law.

But dissatisfaction with preventive programs aimed at eliminating crime and profound dispute about whether we should punish, deter, rehabilitate or cure cannot excuse concealing one of our most menacing problems until the millennium has arrived. In my view, a civilized society must maintain its capacity to discover transgressions of the law and to identify those who flout it. This much is necessary even to know the scope of the problem, much less to formulate intelligent counter-measures. It will just not do to sweep these disagreeable matters under the rug or to pretend they are not there at all.

It is therefore a rather portentous occasion when a constitutional rule is established barring the use of evidence which is relevant, reliable and highly probative of the issue which the trial court has before it—whether the accused committed the act with which he is charged. Without the evidence, the quest for truth may be seriously impeded and in many cases the trial court, although aware of proof showing defendant's guilt, must nevertheless release him because the crucial evidence is deemed inadmissible. This result is entirely justified in some circumstances because exclusion serves other policies of overriding importance, as where evidence seized in an illegal search is excluded, not because of the quality of the proof, but to secure meaningful enforcement of the Fourth Amendment. *Weeks, Mapp.* But this only emphasizes that the soundest of reasons is necessary to warrant the exclusion of evidence otherwise admissible and the creation of another area of privileged testimony. With all due deference, I am not at all convinced that the additional barriers to the pursuit of truth which the Court today erects rest on anything like the solid foundations which decisions of this gravity should require.

The importance of the matter should not be underestimated, for today's rule promises to have wide application well beyond the facts of this case. The reason given for the result here—the admissions were obtained in the absence of counsel—would seem equally pertinent to statements obtained at any time after the right to counsel attaches, whether there has been an indictment or not; to admissions made prior to arraignment, at least where the defendant has counsel or asks for it; to the fruits of admissions improperly obtained under the new rule; to criminal proceedings in state courts; and to defendants long since convicted upon evidence including such admissions. The new rule will immediately do service in a great many cases.

Whatever the content or scope of the rule may

prove to be, I am unable to see how this case presents an unconstitutional interference with Massiah's right to counsel. Massiah was not prevented from consulting with counsel as often as he wished. No meetings with counsel were disturbed or spied upon. Preparation for trial was in no way obstructed. It is only a sterile syllogism—an unsound one, besides—to say that because Massiah had a right to counsel's aid before and during the trial, his out-of-court conversations and admissions must be excluded if obtained without counsel's consent or presence. The right to counsel has never meant as much before, *Crooker*, and its extension in this case requires some further explanation, so far unarticulated by the Court.

Since the new rule would exclude all admissions made to the police, no matter how voluntary and reliable, the requirement of counsel's presence or approval would seem to rest upon the probability that counsel would foreclose any admissions at all. This is nothing more than a thinly disguised constitutional policy of minimizing or entirely prohibiting the use in evidence of voluntary out-of-court admissions and confessions made by the accused. Carried as far as blind logic may compel some to go, the notion that statements from the mouth of the defendant should not be used in evidence would have a severe and unfortunate impact upon the great bulk of criminal cases.

Viewed in this light, the Court's newly fashioned exclusionary principle goes far beyond the constitutional privilege against self-incrimination, which neither requires nor suggests the barring of voluntary pretrial admissions. The Fifth Amendment states that no person "shall be compelled in any criminal case to be a witness against himself. . . ." The defendant may thus not be compelled to testify at his trial, but he may if he wishes. Likewise he may not be compelled or coerced into saying anything before trial; but until today he could if he wished to, and if he did, it could be used against him. Whether as a matter of self-incrimination or of due process, the proscription is against compulsion-coerced incrimination. Under the prior law, announced in countless cases in this Court, the defendant's pretrial statements were admissible evidence if voluntarily made; inadmissible if not the product of his free will. Hardly any constitutional area has been more carefully patrolled by this Court, and until now the Court has expressly rejected the argument that admissions are to be deemed involuntary if made outside the presence of counsel.[*]

---

[*] Today's rule picks up where the Fifth Amendment ends and bars wholly voluntary admissions. I would assume, although one cannot be sure, that the new rule would not have a similar supplemental role

The Court presents no facts, no objective evidence, no reasons to warrant scrapping the voluntary-involuntary test for admissibility in this area. Without such evidence I would retain it in its present form.

This case cannot be analogized to the American Bar Association's rule forbidding an attorney to talk to the opposing party litigant outside the presence of his counsel. Aside from the fact that the Association's canons are not of constitutional dimensions, the specific canon argued is inapposite because it deals with the conduct of lawyers and not with the conduct of investigators. Lawyers are forbidden to interview the opposing party because of the supposed imbalance of legal skill and acumen between the lawyer and the party litigant; the reason for the rule does not apply to non-lawyers and certainly not to Colson, Massiah's codefendant.

Applying the new exclusionary rule is peculiarly inappropriate in this case. At the time of the conversation in question, petitioner was not in custody but free on bail. He was not questioned in what anyone could call an atmosphere of official coercion. What he said was said to his partner in crime who had also been indicted. There was no suggestion or any possibility of coercion. What petitioner did not know was that Colson had decided to report the conversation to the police. Had there been no prior arrangements between Colson and the police, had Colson simply gone to the police after the conversation had occurred, his testimony relating Massiah's statements would be readily admissible at the trial, as would a recording which he might have made of the conversation. In such event, it would simply be said that Massiah risked talking to a friend who decided to disclose what he knew of Massiah's criminal activities. But, if, as occurred here, Colson had been cooperating with the police prior to his meeting with Massiah, both his evidence and the recorded conversation are somehow transformed into inadmissible evidence despite the fact that the hazard to Massiah remains precisely the same—the defection of a confederate in crime.

---

in connection with the Fourth Amendment. While the Fifth Amendment bars only compelled incrimination, the Fourth Amendment bars only unreasonable searches. It could be argued, fruitlessly I would hope, that if the police must stay away from the defendant they must also stay away from his house once the right to counsel has attached and that a court must exclude the products of a reasonable search made pursuant to a properly issued warrant but without the consent or presence of the accused's counsel.

Reporting criminal behavior is expected or even demanded of the ordinary citizen. Friends may be subpoenaed to testify about friends, relatives about relatives and partners about partners. I therefore question the soundness of insulating Massiah from the apostasy of his partner in crime and of furnishing constitutional sanction for the strict secrecy and discipline of criminal organizations. Neither the ordinary citizen nor the confessed criminal should be discouraged from reporting what he knows to the authorities and from lending his aid to secure evidence of crime. Certainly after this case the Colsons will be few and far between; and the Massiahs can breathe much more easily, secure in the knowledge that the Constitution furnishes an important measure of protection against faithless compatriots and guarantees sporting treatment for sporting peddlers of narcotics.

Meanwhile, of course, the public will again be the loser and law enforcement will be presented with another serious dilemma. The general issue lurking in the background of the Court's opinion is the legitimacy of penetrating or obtaining confederates in criminal organizations. For the law enforcement agency, the answer for the time being can only be in the form of a prediction about the future application of today's new constitutional doctrine. More narrowly, and posed by the precise situation involved here, the question is this: when the police have arrested and released on bail one member of a criminal ring and another member, a confederate, is cooperating with the police, can the confederate be allowed to continue his association with the ring or must he somehow be withdrawn to avoid challenge to trial evidence on the ground that it was acquired after rather than before the arrest, after rather than before the indictment?

Defendants who are out on bail have been known to continue their illicit operations. That an attorney is advising them should not constitutionally immunize their statements made in furtherance of these operations and relevant to the question of their guilt at the pending prosecution. In this very case there is evidence that after indictment defendant Aiken tried to persuade Agent Murphy to go into the narcotics business with him. Under today's decision, Murphy may neither testify as to the content of this conversation nor seize for introduction in evidence any narcotics whose location Aiken may have made known.

Undoubtedly, the evidence excluded in this case would not have been available but for the conduct of Colson in cooperation with Agent Murphy, but is it this kind of conduct which should be forbidden to those charged with law enforcement? It is one thing to establish safeguards against procedures fraught with the potentiality of coercion and to outlaw "easy but self-defeating ways in which brutality is substituted for brains as an instrument of crime detection.'' But here there was no substitution of brutality for brains, no inherent danger of police coercion justifying the prophylactic effect of another exclusionary rule. Massiah was not being interrogated in a police station, was not surrounded by numerous officers or questioned in relays, and was not forbidden access to others. Law enforcement may have the elements of a contest about it, but it is not a game. Massiah and those like him receive ample protection from the long line of precedents in this Court holding that confessions may not be introduced unless they are voluntary. In making these determinations the courts must consider the absence of counsel as one of several factors by which voluntariness is to be judged. This is a wiser rule than the automatic rule announced by the Court, which requires courts and juries to disregard voluntary admissions which they might well find to be the best possible evidence in discharging their responsibility for ascertaining truth.

## QUESTIONS AND NOTES

**1.** How would the Fourth Amendment question in *Massiah* have been decided if the case were before the Court today? Why?

**2.** The Court ends its opinion in seeming agreement with the Government's position that it did nothing wrong. If that is true, why should the evidence have been excluded?

**3.** Is it significant that Massiah's counsel was not present at the time he confessed? Would the case be significantly easier for the Government if Massiah's lawyer were with him in Colson's car when he made his incriminating statements? Why? Why not? Compare *Weatherford, infra.*

**4.** How did the Government deliberately elicit a confession? Did it not simply overhear an incriminating statement?

**5.** Is Justice White overly apocalyptic in his view of *Massiah*'s potential? Was not the fact of indictment a core part of the majority's opinion?

**6.** Justice White suggests that codefendant Aiken's attempt to recruit Officer Murphy into the drug smuggling business is inadmissable according to *Massiah*. Do you agree? Explain.

**7.** In *Weatherford*, the Court explores the extent to which it may be possible to spy on conversations between the defendant and defendant's counsel.

### Weatherford v. Bursey
### 429 U.S. 545 (1977)

Mr. Justice WHITE delivered the opinion of the Court.

The issue here is whether in the circumstances present in this case the conduct of an undercover agent for a state law enforcement agency deprived respondent Bursey of his right to the effective assistance of counsel guaranteed him by the Sixth and Fourteenth Amendments of the United States Constitution or deprived him of due process of law in violation of the Fourteenth Amendment.

I

This case began when respondent Bursey filed suit under 42 U.S.C. § 1983 against petitioners Weatherford and Strom, respectively an undercover agent for and the head of the South Carolina State Law Enforcement Division, asserting that the defendants had deprived him of certain constitutional rights. The case was tried without a jury. The following facts are taken from the District Court's findings, which were not disturbed by the Court of Appeals.

During the early morning hours of March 20, 1970, Bursey and Weatherford, along with two others, vandalized the offices of the Richland County Selective Service in Columbia, S. C. Police were advised of the incident by Weatherford, who, in order to maintain his undercover status and his capability of working on other current matters in that capacity, was arrested and charged along with Bursey.

Weatherford was immediately released on bond and, continuing the masquerade, retained an attorney, Frank Taylor, Sr. Bursey, who was later released on bond, retained his own counsel, C. Rauch Wise.

On two occasions thereafter and prior to trial, Weatherford met with Bursey and Wise, and the approaching trial was discussed. With respect to these meetings, the District Court found as follows:

"On neither of these occasions did the defendant Weatherford seek information from the plaintiff or his attorney, and on neither occasion did he initiate or ask for the meeting. He was brought into the meetings by the plaintiff and plaintiff's attorney in an effort to obtain information, ideas or suggestions as to the plaintiff's defense. From the beginning Weatherford advised plaintiff and plaintiff's attorney that Weatherford would obtain a severance of his case from that of the plaintiff. This severance was to be upon the ground that Weatherford might be prejudiced in going to trial with Bursey as a codefendant, because of Bursey's reputation and participation in other activities which had been covered by the news media. On no occasion did Bursey or his attorney question the granting of a severance, nor did they seem to concern themselves with whether the prosecutor would consent to a severance, although such consent is quite unusual where codefendants are charged with the same crime and proof will be from the same witnesses based upon identical facts. At those meetings between plaintiff, plaintiff's attorney and defendant Weatherford the plaintiff and his attorney raised the question of a possible informer being used to prove the case, but they never asked Weatherford if he were an informer and he never specifically denied being an informer, since he was never asked or accused."

At no time did Weatherford discuss with or pass on to his superiors or to the prosecuting attorney or any of the attorney's staff "any details or information regarding the plaintiff's trial plans, strategy, or anything having to do with the criminal action pending against plaintiff." Until the day of trial the prosecuting attorney did not plan to use Weatherford as a witness. Consequently, until then, Weatherford had not expected to be a witness and had anticipated continuing his undercover work. However, Weatherford had lost some of his effectiveness as an agent in the weeks preceding trial because he had been seen in the company of police officers, and he was called for the prosecution. He testified as to his undercover activities and gave an eyewitness account of the events of March 20, 1970. Bursey took the stand, was convicted, and then disappeared until apprehended some two years later, at which time he was incarcerated and forced to serve his 18-month sentence.

II

The exact contours of the Court of Appeals' *per se* right-to-counsel rule are difficult to discern; but as the Court of Appeals applied the rule in this case, it would appear that if an undercover agent meets with a criminal defendant who is awaiting trial and with his attorney and if the forthcoming trial is discussed without the agent's revealing his identity, a violation of the defendant's constitutional rights has occurred, whatever was the purpose of the agent in attending the meeting, whether or not he reported on the meeting to his superiors, and whether or not any specific prejudice to the defendant's preparation for or conduct of the trial is demonstrated or otherwise threatened. The Court of Appeals was of the view that this Court "establish[ed] such a per se rule" in *Black v. United States*, 385 U.S. 26 (1966), and *O'Brien v. United States*, 386 U.S. 345 (1967).

We cannot agree that these cases, individually or together, either require or suggest the rule announced by the Court of Appeals and now urged by Bursey. Both *Black* and *O'Brien* involved surreptitious electronic surveillance by the Government, which was discovered after trial and conviction and which was plainly illegal under the Fourth Amendment. In each case, some, but not all, of the conversations overheard were between the criminal defendant and his counsel during trial preparation. The conviction in each case was set aside and a new trial ordered.

At the same time, we need not agree with petitioners that whenever a defendant converses with his counsel in the presence of a third party thought to be a confederate and ally, the defendant assumes the risk and cannot complain if the third party turns out to be an informer for the government who has reported on the conversations to the prosecution and who testifies about them at the defendant's trial. Had Weatherford testified at Bursey's trial as to the conversation between Bursey and Wise; had any of the State's evidence originated in these conversations; had those overheard conversations been used in any other way to the substantial detriment of Bursey; or even had the prosecution learned from Weatherford, an undercover agent, the details of the Bursey-Wise conversations about trial preparations, Bursey would have a much stronger case.

None of these elements is present here, however. Weatherford's testimony for the prosecution about the events of March and April 1970 revealed nothing said or done at the meetings between Bursey and Wise that he attended. None of the Government's evidence was obtained as a consequence of Weatherford's participation in those meetings. Nevertheless, it might be argued that Weatherford, a dutiful agent, surely communicated to the prosecutors Bursey's defense plans and strategy and his attorney's efforts to prepare for trial, all of which was inherently detrimental to Bursey, unfairly advantaged the prosecution, and threatened to subvert the adversary system of criminal justice.

The argument founders on the District Court's express finding that Weatherford communicated nothing at all to his superiors or to the prosecution about Bursey's trial plans or about the upcoming trial. The Court of Appeals did not disturb this finding, but sought to surmount it by declaring Weatherford himself to have been a member of the prosecuting team whose knowledge of Bursey's trial plans was alone enough to violate Bursey's constitutional right to counsel and to vitiate Bursey's conviction. Though imaginative, this reasoning is not a realistic assessment of the relationship of Weatherford to the prosecuting staff or of the potential for detriment to Bursey or benefit to the State that Weatherford's uncommunicated knowledge might pose. If the fact was, as found by the District Court, that Weatherford communicated nothing about the two meetings to anyone else, we are quite unconvinced that a constitutional claim under the Sixth and Fourteenth Amendments was made out.

This is consistent with the Court's approach in the *Hoffa* case. There, the informant overheard several conversations between Hoffa and his attorneys, but the Court found it necessary to deal with the Sixth Amendment right-to-counsel claim only after noting that the informant had reported to the Government about at least some of the activities of Hoffa's defense counsel. As long as the information possessed by Weatherford remained uncommunicated, he posed no substantial threat to Bursey's Sixth Amendment rights. Nor do we believe that federal or state prosecutors will be so prone to lie or the difficulties of proof will be so great that we must always assume not only that an informant communicates what he learns from an encounter with the defendant and his counsel but also that what he communicates has the potential for detriment to the defendant or benefit to the prosecutor's case.

Moreover, this is not a situation where the State's purpose was to learn what it could about the defendant's defense plans and the informant was instructed to intrude on the lawyer-client relationship or where the informant has assumed for himself that task and acted accordingly. Weatherford, the District Court found, did not intrude at all; he was invited to the meeting, apparently not for his benefit but for the benefit of Bursey and his lawyer. Weatherford went, not to spy, but because he was asked and because the State was interested in retaining his undercover services on other matters and it was therefore necessary to avoid raising the suspicion that he was in fact the informant whose existence Bursey and Wise already suspected.

That the *per se* rule adopted by the Court of Appeals would operate prophylactically and effectively is very likely true; but it would require the informant to refuse to participate in attorney-client meetings, even though invited, and thus for all practical purposes to unmask himself. Our cases, however, have recognized the unfortunate necessity of undercover work and the value it often is to effective law enforcement. We have also recognized the desirability and legality of continued secrecy even after arrest. We have no general oversight authority with respect to state police investigations. We may disapprove an investigatory practice only if it violates the Constitution; and judged in this light, the Court of Appeals' *per se* rule cuts much too broadly. If, for example, Weatherford at Bursey's invitation had attended a meeting between Bursey and Wise but Wise had become suspicious and the conversation was confined to the weather or other harmless subjects, the Court of Appeals' rule, literally read, would cloud Bursey's subsequent conviction, although there would have been no constitutional violation. The same would have been true if Wise had merely asked whether Weatherford was an informant, Weatherford had denied it, and the meeting then had ended; likewise if the entire conversation had consisted of Wise's questions and Weatherford's answers about Weatherford's own defense plans. Also, and more cogently for present purposes, unless Weatherford communicated the substance of the Bursey-Wise conversations and thereby created at least a realistic possibility of injury to Bursey or benefit to the State, there can be no Sixth Amendment violation. Yet under the Court of Appeals' rule, Bursey's conviction would have been set aside on appeal.

There being no tainted evidence in this case, no communication of defense strategy to the prosecution, and no purposeful intrusion by Weatherford, there was no violation of the Sixth Amendment insofar as it is applicable to the States by virtue of the

Fourteenth Amendment. The proof in this case thus fell short of making out a § 1983 claim, and the judgment of the District Court should have been affirmed in this respect.

It is also apparent that neither Weatherford's trial testimony nor the fact of his testifying added anything to the Sixth Amendment claim. Weatherford's testimony for the prosecution related only to events prior to the meetings with Wise and Bursey and referred to nothing that was said at those meetings. There is no indication that any of this testimony was prompted by or was the product of those meetings. Weatherford's testimony was surely very damaging, but the mere fact that he had met with Bursey and his lawyer prior to trial did not violate Bursey's right to counsel any more than the informant's meetings with Hoffa and Hoffa's lawyers rendered inadmissible the informer's testimony having no connection with those conversations.

The judgment of the Court of Appeals is reversed.

Mr. Justice MARSHALL, with whom Mr. Justice BRENNAN joins, dissenting.

It is easy to minimize the significance of the incursion into the lawyer-client relationship that the Court sanctions today. After all, as the Court observes, there is no evidence that Weatherford went to the meetings between Bursey and his lawyer with an intent to spy; that he reported to the prosecutor on those meetings; or that what he learned was used to develop evidence against Bursey. But while what occurred here may be "the obnoxious thing in its mildest and least repulsive form . . . illegitimate and unconstitutional practices get their first footing in that way, namely, by silent approaches and slight deviations from legal modes of procedure." I cannot join in providing even the narrowest of openings to the practice of spying upon attorney-client communications.

In *Wardius v. Oregon*, 412 U.S. 470 (1973), this Court made clear that while "the Due Process Clause has little to say regarding the amount of discovery which the parties must be afforded . . . it does speak to the balance of forces between the accused and his accuser." Due process requires that discovery "be a two-way street."

> "The State may not insist that trials be run as a 'search for truth' so far as defense witnesses are concerned, while maintaining 'poker game' secrecy for its own witnesses. It is fundamentally unfair to require a defendant to divulge the details of his own case while at the same time subjecting him to the

hazard of surprise concerning refutation of the very pieces of evidence which he disclosed to the State." *Id.*, at 475-476.

At issue in *Wardius* was a statute compelling defendants to provide certain information about their case to the prosecution. But the same concerns are implicated when the State seeks such information, not by force of law, but by surreptitious invasions and deceit.

Of equal concern, governmental incursions into confidential lawyer-client communications threaten criminal defendants' right to the effective assistance of counsel. Only last Term we held that the right to counsel encompasses the right to confer with one's lawyer. But "[a]s a practical matter, if the client knows that damaging information could more readily be obtained from the attorney following disclosure than from himself in the absence of disclosure, the client would be reluctant to confide in his lawyer and it would be difficult to obtain fully informed legal advice." For this reason, it has long been recognized that "the essence of the Sixth Amendment right is . . . privacy of communication with counsel."

The Court today apparently concludes that neither of these constitutional values is infringed when as here, the State does not act with a purpose to intercept information about the defense, and the information that is uncovered is neither transmitted to the prosecutor nor used by him to the defendant's detriment. I respectfully disagree. In my view, the "balance of forces between the accused and his accuser" is sharply skewed in favor of the accuser if the government's key witnesses are permitted to discover the defense strategy by intercepting attorney-client communications, even if the witnesses cannot divulge the information to the prosecution. With this information, the witnesses are in a position to formulate in advance answers to anticipated questions and even to shade their testimony to meet expected defenses.[1] Furthermore, because of these dangers defendants may be deterred from exercising

---

[1] If, for example, Weatherford had learned that Bursey would use an entrapment defense against whoever admitted to being a government agent, Weatherford could have planned his testimony so as to minimize his own role and emphasize Bursey's predisposition. Bursey, on the other hand, would have had little time to reconstruct in his mind Weatherford's role in the decision to commit the crime once Weatherford testified that he was the state agent.

their right to communicate candidly with their lawyers if government witnesses can intrude upon the lawyer-client relationship with impunity so long as they do not discuss what they learn with the prosecutor.[2] And insofar as the Sixth Amendment establishes an independent right to confidential communications with a lawyer, that right by definition is invaded when a government agent attends meetings of the defense team at which defense plans are reviewed.[3]

But even if I were to agree that unintended and undisclosed interceptions by government witness-employees affect neither the fairness of trials nor the effectiveness of defense counsel, I still could not join in upholding the practice. For in my view, the precious constitutional rights at stake here, like other constitutional rights, need "breathing space to survive," and a prophylactic prohibition on all intrusions of this sort is therefore essential. A rule that offers defendants relief only when they can prove "intent" or "disclosure" is, I fear, little better than no rule at all. Establishing that a desire to intercept confidential communications was a factor in a State's decision to keep an agent under cover will seldom be possible, since the State always can argue plausibly that its sole purpose was to continue to enjoy the legitimate services of the undercover agent. Proving that an informer reported to the prosecution on defense strategy will be equally difficult, not only because such proof requires an informer or prosecutor to admit his own wrongdoing (and open the door to damages suits and attacks on convictions), but also because an informer's failure to make a report after overhearing a lawyer-client session oftentimes can be an effective means of communicating to the prosecutor that nothing surprising was uncovered.[4] Given these problems of proof, the only way to assure that defendants will feel free to communicate candidly with their lawyers is to prohibit the government from intercepting such confidential communications, at least absent a compelling justification for doing so.[5]

Like the Court of Appeals, and unlike the majority today, I believe a *per se* rule of this sort is fully supported, if not compelled, by our decisions in *Black* and *O'Brien*.

Rather than retreating from *Black* and *O'Brien*, I would reaffirm them and would affirm the judgment of the Court of Appeals.

---

[2] The Court suggests that defendants can protect themselves against intrusions by third parties by excluding them from meetings at which defense strategy is discussed. But when, as here, the third party is an indicted codefendant, exclusion is not practicable; codefendants need to be informed of each other's strategy if only to determine whether joinder is prejudicial. Indeed, because of the interdependence of codefendants, communications between a lawyer and his client generally remain privileged even when disclosed to a codefendant or his attorney.

[3] Of course, the fact that Weatherford did not reveal what he learned may be relevant to the amount of damages Bursey can recover, as the Court of Appeals acknowledged. No damages assessment has been made in this case, however, since the District Court found no liability.

[4] In this case, for example, the prosecutor might have assumed that Weatherford had been privy to Bursey's defense plans, and that Weatherford's acquiescence when told of the prosecutor's decision to use him as a witness meant that the defense did not suspect Weatherford or have any damaging information about him.

[5] There is no evidence in this record that Weatherford's life would have been jeopardized or any ongoing investigations compromised had Weatherford given up his cover on March 20, 1970, after the crime was committed, rather than on July 27, 1970, after trial began. To the contrary, the fact that Weatherford felt no need for police protection after trial, suggests that there was no danger at any time. And the Chief of the South Carolina State Law Enforcement Division conceded that Weatherford was not working on "anything particular" between the time of the crime and the time of the trial. Indeed the Chief admitted that he "wasn't concerned" about losing Weatherford's cover because after breaking the case "his identity is going to be known anyway." Thus the only legitimate justification the State had for arresting and indicting Weatherford, and for retaining a lawyer and manufacturing a story for him was to postpone for several months the date at which a new agent would have to be assigned again.

## QUESTIONS AND NOTES

**1.** After reading *Weatherford*, rethink question 3 after *Massiah*. Would Massiah's case have been strengthened or weakened if his lawyer had been present during the conversations overheard by Murphy?

**2.** Do you believe that Weatherford never communicated anything that he learned from Bursey and Bursey's attorney to his superiors? Upon what do you predicate your belief?

**3.** Assuming that the Court's prior decisions permit, but do not compel, the rule urged by Bursey, should the Court have adopted it?

**4.** In an ideal system of jurisprudence, what would we want somebody like Weatherford to do when asked to meet someone like Bursey and Bursey's attorney?

**5.** Was (should) Bursey's case (have been) stronger or weaker because it arose in the context of a civil suit for damages rather than a criminal prosecution?

**6.** We now turn to *Escobedo*, which arguably constitutes the high water mark for the right to counsel during interrogation.

## Escobedo v. Illinois
### 378 U.S. 478 (1964)

Mr. Justice GOLDBERG delivered the opinion of the Court.

The critical question in this case is whether, under the circumstances, the refusal by the police to honor petitioner's request to consult with his lawyer during the course of an interrogation constitutes a denial of "the Assistance of Counsel" in violation of the Sixth Amendment to the Constitution as "made obligatory upon the States by the Fourteenth Amendment," *Gideon v. Wainwright*, 372 U.S. 335, 342, and thereby renders inadmissible in a state criminal trial any incriminating statement elicited by the police during the interrogation.

On the night of January 19, 1960, petitioner's brother-in-law was fatally shot. In the early hours of the next morning, at 2:30 a.m., petitioner was arrested without a warrant and interrogated. Petitioner made no statement to the police and was released at 5 that afternoon pursuant to a state court writ of habeas corpus obtained by Mr. Warren Wolfson, a lawyer who had been retained by petitioner.

On January 30, Benedict DiGerlando, who was then in police custody and who was later indicted for the murder along with petitioner, told the police that petitioner had fired the fatal shots. Between 8 and 9 that evening, petitioner and his sister, the widow of the deceased, were arrested and taken to police headquarters. En route to the police station, the police "had handcuffed the defendant behind his back," and "one of the arresting officers told defendant that DiGerlando had named him as the one who shot" the deceased. Petitioner testified, without contradiction, that the "detectives said they had us pretty well, up pretty tight, and we might as well admit to this crime," and that he replied, "I am sorry but I would like to have advice from my lawyer." A police officer testified that although petitioner was not formally charged "he was in custody" and "couldn't walk out the door."

Shortly after petitioner reached police headquarters, his retained lawyer arrived. The lawyer described the ensuing events in the following terms:

"On that day I received a phone call [from 'the mother of another defendant'] and pursuant to that phone call I went to the Detective Bureau at 11th and State. The first person I talked to was the Sergeant on duty at the Bureau Desk, Sergeant Pidgeon. I asked Sergeant Pidgeon for permission to speak to my client, Danny Escobedo. . . . Sergeant Pidgeon made a call to the Bureau lockup and informed me that the boy had been taken from the lockup to the Homicide Bureau. This was between 9:30 and 10:00 in the evening. Before I went anywhere, he called the Homicide Bureau and told them there was an attorney waiting to see Escobedo. He told me I could not see him. Then I went upstairs to the Homicide Bureau. There were several Homicide Detectives around and I talked to them. I identified myself as Escobedo's attorney and asked permission to see him. They said I could not. . . . The police officer told me to see Chief Flynn who was on duty. I identified myself to Chief Flynn and asked permission to see my client. He said I could not. . . . I think it was approximately 11:00 o'clock. He said I couldn't see him because they hadn't completed questioning. . . . [F]or a second or two I spotted him in an office in the Homicide Bureau. The door was open and I could see through the office. . . . I waved to him and he waved back and then the door was closed, by one of the officers at Homicide.[1] There were four or five officers milling around the Homicide Detail that night. As to whether I talked to Captain Flynn any later that day, I waited around for another hour or two and went back again and renewed by [*sic*] request to see my client. He again told me I could not. . . . I filed an official complaint with Commissioner Phelan of the Chicago Police Department. I had a conversation with every police officer I could find. I was told at Homicide that I couldn't see him and I would have to get a writ of habeas corpus. I left the Homicide Bureau and from the Detective Bureau at 11th and State at approximately 1:00 A.M. [Sunday morning] I had no opportunity to talk to my client that night. I quoted to Captain Flynn the Section of the Criminal Code which allows an attorney the right to see his client.''[2]

Petitioner testified that during the course of the interrogation he repeatedly asked to speak to his lawyer and that the police said that his lawyer ''didn't want to see'' him. The testimony of the police officers confirmed these accounts in substantial detail.

Notwithstanding repeated requests by each, petitioner and his retained lawyer were afforded no opportunity to consult during the course of the entire

---

[1] Petitioner testified that this ambiguous gesture ''could have meant most anything,'' but that he ''took it upon [his] own to think that [the lawyer was telling him] not to say anything,'' and that the lawyer ''wanted to talk'' to him.

[2] The statute then in effect provided in pertinent part that: ''All public officers . . . having the custody of any person . . . restrained of his liberty for any alleged cause whatever, shall, except in cases of imminent danger of escape, admit any practicing attorney . . . whom such person . . . may desire to see or consult. . . .'' Ill.Rev.Stat. (1959), c. 38, § 477.

interrogation. At one point, as previously noted, petitioner and his attorney came into each other's view for a few moments but the attorney was quickly ushered away. Petitioner testified ''that he heard a detective telling the attorney the latter would not be allowed to talk to [him] 'until they were done' '' and that he heard the attorney being refused permission to remain in the adjoining room. A police officer testified that he had told the lawyer that he could not see petitioner until ''we were through interrogating'' him.

There is testimony by the police that during the interrogation, petitioner, a 22-year-old of Mexican extraction with no record of previous experience with the police, ''was handcuffed'' in a standing position and that he ''was nervous, he had circles under his eyes and he was upset'' and was ''agitated'' because ''he had not slept well in over a week.''

It is undisputed that during the course of the interrogation Officer Montejano, who ''grew up'' in petitioner's neighborhood, who knew his family, and who uses ''Spanish language in [his] police work,'' conferred alone with petitioner ''for about a quarter of an hour. . . .'' Petitioner testified that the officer said to him ''in Spanish that my sister and I could go home if I pinned it on Benedict DiGerlando,'' that ''he would see to it that we would go home and be held only as witnesses, if anything, if we had made a statement against DiGerlando . . ., that we would be able to go home that night.'' Petitioner testified that he made the statement in issue because of this assurance. Officer Montejano denied offering any such assurance.

A police officer testified that during the interrogation the following occurred:

> ''I informed him of what DiGerlando told me and when I did, he told me that DiGerlando was [lying] and I said, 'Would you care to tell DiGerlando that?' and he said, 'Yes, I will.' So, I brought . . . Escobedo in and he confronted DiGerlando and he told him that he was lying and said, 'I didn't shoot Manuel, you did it.' ''

In this way, petitioner, for the first time admitted to some knowledge of the crime.

The Supreme Court of Illinois, in its original opinion of February 1, 1963, held the statement inadmissible and reversed the conviction. The court said:

> ''[I]t seems manifest to us, from the undisputed evidence and the circumstances surrounding defendant at the time of his statement and shortly prior thereto, that the defendant understood he would be permitted to go

home if he gave the statement and would be granted an immunity from prosecution.''

The State petitioned for, and the court granted, rehearing. The court then affirmed the conviction. It said: "[T]he officer denied making the promise and the trier of fact believed him. We find no reason for disturbing the trial court's finding that the confession was voluntary."[4] The court also held, on the authority of this Court's decisions in *Crooker*, that the confession was admissible even though "it was obtained after he had requested the assistance of counsel, which request was denied."

In *Massiah*, this Court observed that "a Constitution which guarantees a defendant the aid of counsel at . . . trial could surely vouchsafe no less to an indicted defendant under interrogation by the police in a completely extrajudicial proceeding. Anything less . . . might deny a defendant 'effective representation by counsel at the only stage when legal aid and advice would help him." Quoting Douglas, J., concurring in *Spano*.

The interrogation here was conducted before petitioner was formally indicted. But in the context of this case, that fact should make no difference. When petitioner requested, and was denied, an opportunity to consult with his lawyer, the investigation had ceased to be a general investigation of "an unsolved crime." *Spano* (Stewart, J., concurring). Petitioner had become the accused, and the purpose of the interrogation was to "get him" to confess his guilt despite his constitutional right not to do so. At the time of his arrest and throughout the course of the interrogation, the police told petitioner that they had

---

[4] Compare *Haynes v. Washington*, 373 U.S. 503, 515 (decided on the same day as the decision of the Illinois Supreme Court here), where we said:

"Our conclusion is in no way foreclosed, as the State contends, by the fact that the state trial judge or the jury may have reached a different result on this issue.

"It is well settled that the duty of constitutional adjudication resting upon this Court requires that the question whether the Due Process Clause of the Fourteenth Amendment has been violated by admission into evidence of a coerced confession be the subject of an *independent* determination here, see, *e.g.*, *Ashcraft v. Tennessee*, 322 U.S. 143, 147-148; 'we cannot escape the responsibility of making our own examination of the record,' *Spano v. New York*, 360 U.S. 315, 316." (Emphasis in original.)

convincing evidence that he had fired the fatal shots. Without informing him of his absolute right to remain silent in the face of this accusation, the police urged him to make a statement.[5] As this Court observed many years ago:

"It cannot be doubted that, placed in the position in which the accused was when the statement was made to him that the other suspected person had charged him with crime, the result was to produce upon his mind the fear that, if he remained silent, it would be considered an admission of guilt, and therefore render certain his being committed for trial as the guilty person, and it cannot be conceived that the converse impression would not also have naturally arisen that, by denying, there was hope of removing the suspicion from himself." *Bram v. United States*, 168 U.S. 532, 562.

Petitioner, a layman, was undoubtedly unaware that under Illinois law an admission of "mere" complicity in the murder plot was legally as damaging as an admission of firing of the fatal shots. The "guiding hand of counsel" was essential to advise petitioner of his rights in this delicate situation. *Powell v. Alabama*, 287 U.S. 45, 69. This was the "stage when legal aid and advice" were most critical to petitioner. *Massiah*. It was a stage surely as critical as was the arraignment in *Hamilton v. Alabama*, 368 U.S. 52, and the preliminary hearing in *White v. Maryland*, 373 U.S. 59. What happened at this interrogation could certainly "affect the whole trial," since rights "may be as irretrievably lost, if not then and there asserted, as they are when an accused represented by counsel waives a right for strategic purposes." It would exalt form over substance to make the right to counsel, under these circumstances, depend on whether at the time of the interrogation, the authorities had secured a formal indictment. Petitioner had, for all practical purposes, already been charged with murder.

In *Gideon v. Wainwright*, 372 U.S. 335, we held that every person accused of a crime, whether state or federal, is entitled to a lawyer at trial.[8] The rule

---

[5] Although there is testimony in the record that petitioner and his lawyer had previously discussed what petitioner should do in the event of interrogation, there is no evidence that they discussed what petitioner should, or could, do in the face of a false accusation that he had fired the fatal bullets.

[8] Twenty-two States, including Illinois, urged us so to hold.

sought by the State here, however, would make the trial no more than an appeal from the interrogation; and the "right to use counsel at the formal trial (would be) a very hollow thing (if), for all practical purposes, the conviction is already assured by pre-trial examination." "One can imagine a cynical prosecutor saying: 'Let them have the most illustrious counsel, now. They can't escape the noose. There is nothing that counsel can do for them at the trial.'" *Ex parte Sullivan*, 107 F.Supp. 514, 517-518.[9]

It is argued that if the right to counsel is afforded prior to indictment, the number of confessions obtained by the police will diminish significantly, because most confessions are obtained during the period between arrest and indictment, and "any lawyer worth his salt will tell the suspect in no uncertain terms to make no statement to police under any circumstances." *Watts* (Jackson, J., concurring in part and dissenting in part). This argument, of course, cuts two ways. The fact that many confessions are obtained during this period points up its critical nature as a "stage when legal aid and advice" are surely needed. The right to counsel would indeed be hollow if it began at a period when few confessions were obtained. There is necessarily a direct relationship between the importance of a stage to the police in their quest for a confession and the criticalness of that stage to the accused in his need for legal advice. Our Constitution, unlike some others, strikes the balance in favor of the right of the accused to be advised by his lawyer of his privilege against self-incrimination.

We have learned the lesson of history, ancient and modern, that a system of criminal law enforcement which comes to depend on the "confession" will, in the long run, be less reliable and more subject to abuses than a system which depends on extrinsic evidence independently secured through skillful investigation. As Dean Wigmore so wisely said:

> "[A]ny system of administration which permits the prosecution to trust habitually to compulsory self-disclosure as a source of proof must itself suffer morally thereby. The inclination develops to rely mainly upon such evidence, and to be satisfied with an incomplete investigation of the other sources. The

exercise of the power to extract answers begets a forgetfulness of the just limitations of that power. The simple and peaceful process of questioning breeds a readiness to resort to bullying and to physical force and torture. If there is a right to an answer, there soon seems to be a right to the expected answer, – that is, to a confession of guilt. Thus the legitimate use grows into the unjust abuse; ultimately, the innocent are jeopardized by the encroachments of a bad system. Such seems to have been the course of experience in those legal systems where the privilege was not recognized." 8 Wigmore, Evidence (3d ed. 1940), 309. (Emphasis in original.)

This Court also has recognized that "history amply shows that confessions have often been extorted to save law enforcement officials the trouble and effort of obtaining valid and independent evidence. . . ."

We have also learned the companion lesson of history that no system of criminal justice can, or should, survive if it comes to depend for its continued effectiveness on the citizens' abdication through unawareness of their constitutional rights. No system worth preserving should have to *fear* that if an accused is permitted to consult with a lawyer, he will become aware of, and exercise, these rights. If the exercise of constitutional rights will thwart the effectiveness of a system of law enforcement, then there is something very wrong with that system.[14]

We hold, therefore, that where, as here, the investigation is no longer a general inquiry into an unsolved crime but has begun to focus on a particular suspect, the suspect has been taken into police custody, the police carry out a process of interrogations that lends itself to eliciting incriminating statements, the suspect has requested and been denied an opportunity to consult with his lawyer, and the police have not effectively warned him of his absolute constitutional right to remain silent, the accused has been denied "The Assistance of Counsel" in violation of the Sixth Amendment to the Constitution as "made obligatory upon the States by the Fourteenth Amendment," *Gideon v. Wainwright*, 372 U.S., at 342, and that no statement elicited by the police during

---

[9] The Soviet criminal code does not permit a lawyer to be present during the investigation. The Soviet Trial has thus been aptly described as "an appeal from the pretrial investigation." Feifer, Justice in Moscow (1964), 86.

[14] The accused may, of course, intelligently and knowingly waive his privilege against self-incrimination and his right to counsel either at a pretrial stage or at the trial. But no knowing and intelligent waiver of any constitutional right can be said to have occurred under the circumstances of this case.

the interrogation may be used against him at a criminal trial.

*Crooker* does not compel a contrary result. In that case the Court merely rejected the absolute rule sought by petitioner, that "every state denial of a request to contact counsel [is] an infringement of the constitutional right *without regard to the circumstances of the case.*" (Emphasis in original.) In its place, the following rule was announced:

> "[S]tate refusal of a request to engage counsel violates due process not only if the accused is deprived of counsel at trial on the merits, . . . *but also if he is deprived of counsel for any part of the pretrial proceedings*, provided that he is so prejudiced thereby as to infect his subsequent trial with an absence of 'that fundamental fairness essential to the very concept of justice. . . .' The latter determination necessarily depends upon all the circumstances of the case." (Emphasis added.)

The Court, applying "these principles" to "the sum total of the circumstances [there] during the time petitioner was without counsel," concluded that he had not been fundamentally prejudiced by the denial of his request for counsel. Among the critical circumstances which distinguish that case from this one are that the petitioner there, but not here, was explicitly advised by the police of his constitutional right to remain silent and not to "say anything" in response to the questions, and that petitioner there, but not here, was a well-educated man who had studied criminal law while attending law school for a year. The Court's opinion in *Cicenia v. Lagay*, 357 U.S. 504, decided the same day, merely said that the "contention that petitioner had a constitutional right to confer with counsel is disposed of by *Crooker v. California*. . . ." That case adds nothing, therefore, to *Crooker*. In any event, to the extent that *Cicenia* or *Crooker* may be inconsistent with the principles announced today, they are not to be regarded as controlling.

Nothing we have said today affects the powers of the police to investigate "an unsolved crime," *Spano* (Stewart, J., concurring), by gathering information from witnesses and by other "proper investigative efforts." We hold only that when the process shifts from investigatory to accusatory—when its focus is on the accused and its purpose is to elicit a confession—our adversary system begins to operate, and, under the circumstances here, the accused must be permitted to consult with his lawyer.

The judgment of the Illinois Supreme Court is reversed and the case remanded for proceedings not inconsistent with this opinion.

Mr. Justice HARLAN, dissenting.

I would affirm the judgment of the Supreme Court of Illinois on the basis of *Cicenia v. Lagay*, 357 U.S. 504, decided by this Court only six years ago. Like my Brother White, I think the rule announced today is most ill-conceived and that it seriously and unjustifiably fetters perfectly legitimate methods of criminal law enforcement.

Mr. Justice STEWART, dissenting.

I think this case is directly controlled by *Cicenia v. Lagay*, 357 U.S. 504, and I would therefore affirm the judgment.

*Massiah*, is not in point here. In that case a federal grand jury had indicted Massiah. He had retained a lawyer and entered a formal plea of not guilty. Under our system of federal justice an indictment and arraignment are followed by a trial, at which the Sixth Amendment guarantees the defendant the assistance of counsel. But Massiah was released on bail, and thereafter agents of the Federal Government deliberately elicited incriminating statements from him in the absence of his lawyer. We held that the use of these statements against him at his trial denied him the basic protections of the Sixth Amendment guarantee. Putting to one side the fact that the case now before us is not a federal case, the vital fact remains that this case does not involve the deliberate interrogation of a defendant after the initiation of judicial proceedings against him. The Court disregards this basic difference between the present case and Massiah's, with the bland assertion that "that fact should make no difference."

It is "that fact," I submit, which makes all the difference. Under our system of criminal justice the institution of formal, meaningful judicial proceedings, by way of indictment, information, or arraignment, marks the point at which a criminal investigation has ended and adversary proceedings have commenced. It is at this point that the constitutional guarantees attach which pertain to a criminal trial. Among those guarantees are the right to a speedy trial, the right of confrontation, and the right to trial by jury. Another is the guarantee of the assistance of counsel.

The confession which the Court today holds inadmissible was a voluntary one. It was given during the course of a perfectly legitimate police investigation of an unsolved murder. The Court says that what happened during this investigation "affected" the trial. I had always supposed that the whole purpose of a police investigation of a murder was to "affect" the trial of the murderer, and that it would be only an incompetent, unsuccessful, or corrupt investigation which would not do so. The Court further says that the Illinois police officers did not advise the petitioner of his "constitutional rights" before he confessed to the murder. This Court has never held that the Constitution requires the police to give any "advice" under circumstances such as these.

Supported by no stronger authority than its own rhetoric, the Court today converts a routine police investigation of an unsolved murder into a distorted analogue of a judicial trial. It imports into this investigation constitutional concepts historically applicable only after the onset of formal prosecutorial proceedings. By doing so, I think the Court perverts those precious constitutional guarantees, and frustrates the vital interests of society in preserving the legitimate and proper function of honest and purposeful police investigation.

Like my Brother Clark, I cannot escape the logic of my Brother White's conclusions as to the extraordinary implications which emanate from the Court's opinion in this case, and I share their views as to the untold and highly unfortunate impact today's decision may have upon the fair administration of criminal justice. I can only hope we have completely misunderstood what the Court has said.

Mr. Justice WHITE, with whom Mr. Justice CLARK and Mr. Justice STEWART join, dissenting.

In *Massiah*, the Court held that as of the date of the indictment the prosecution is disentitled to secure admissions from the accused. The Court now moves that date back to the time when the prosecution begins to "focus" on the accused. Although the opinion purports to be limited to the facts of this case, it would be naive to think that the new constitutional right announced will depend upon whether the accused has retained his own counsel, or has asked to consult with counsel in the course of interrogation. At the very least the Court holds that once the accused becomes a suspect and, presumably, is arrested, any admission made to the police thereafter is inadmissible in evidence unless the accused has waived his right to counsel. The decision is thus another major step in the direction of the goal which the Court seemingly has in mind—to bar from evidence all admissions obtained from an individual suspected of crime, whether involuntarily made or not. It does of course put us one step "ahead" of the English judges who have had the good sense to leave the matter a discretionary one with the trial court. I reject this step and the invitation to go farther which the Court has now issued.

By abandoning the voluntary-involuntary test for admissibility of confessions, the Court seems driven by the notion that it is uncivilized law enforcement to use an accused's own admissions against him at his trial. It attempts to find a home for this new and nebulous rule of due process by attaching it to the right to counsel guaranteed in the federal system by the Sixth Amendment and binding upon the States by virtue of the due process guarantee of the Fourteenth Amendment. *Gideon*. The right to counsel now not only entitles the accused to counsel's advice and aid in preparing for trial but stands as an impenetrable barrier to any interrogation once the accused has become a suspect. From that very moment apparently his right to counsel attaches, a rule wholly unworkable and impossible to administer unless police cars are equipped with public defenders and undercover agents and police informants have defense counsel at their side. I would not abandon the Court's prior cases defining with some care and analysis the circumstances requiring the presence or aid of counsel and substitute the amorphous and wholly unworkable principle that counsel is constitutionally required whenever he would or could be helpful. Under this new approach one might just as well argue that a potential defendant is constitutionally entitled to a lawyer before, not after, he commits a crime, since it is then that crucial incriminating evidence is put within the reach of the Government by the would-be accused. Until now there simply has been no right guaranteed by the Federal Constitution to be free from the use at trial of a voluntary admission made prior to indictment.

Today's decision cannot be squared with other provisions of the Constitution which, in my view, define the system of criminal justice this Court is empowered to administer. The Fourth Amendment permits upon probable cause even compulsory searches of the suspect and his possessions and the use of the fruits of the search at trial, all in the absence of counsel. The Fifth Amendment and state constitutional provisions authorize, indeed require, inquisitorial grand jury proceedings at which a potential defendant, in the absence of counsel, is shielded against no more than compulsory incrimination. A grand jury witness, who may be a suspect, is interrogated and his answers, at least until today, are admissible in evidence at trial. And these provisions have been thought of as constitutional safeguards to persons suspected of an offense. Furthermore, until now, the Constitution has permitted the accused to be fingerprinted and to be identified in a line-up or in the courtroom itself.

The Court chooses to ignore these matters and

to rely on the virtues and morality of a system of criminal law enforcement which does not depend on the "confession." No such judgment is to be found in the Constitution. It might be appropriate for a legislature to provide that a suspect should not be consulted during a criminal investigation; that an accused should never be called before a grand jury to answer, even if he wants to, what may well be incriminating questions; and that no person, whether he be a suspect, guilty criminal or innocent bystander, should be put to the ordeal of responding to orderly noncompulsory inquiry by the State. But this is not the system our Constitution requires. The only "inquisitions" the Constitution forbids are those which compel incrimination. Escobedo's statements were not compelled and the Court does not hold that they were.

The Court may be concerned with a narrower matter: the unknowing defendant who responds to police questioning because he mistakenly believes that he must and that his admissions will not be used against him. But this worry hardly calls for the broadside the Court has now fired. The failure to inform an accused that he need not answer and that his answers may be used against him is very relevant indeed to whether the disclosures are compelled. Cases in this Court, to say the least, have never placed a premium on ignorance of constitutional rights. If an accused is told he must answer and does not know better, it would be very doubtful that the resulting admissions could be used against him. When the accused has not been informed of his rights at all the Court characteristically and properly looks very closely at the surrounding circumstances. I would continue to do so. But, in this case Danny Escobedo knew full well that he did not have to answer and knew full well that his lawyer had advised him not to answer.

I do not suggest for a moment that law enforcement will be destroyed by the rule announced today. The need for peace and order is too insistent for that. But it will be crippled and its task made a great deal more difficult, all in my opinion, for unsound, unstated reasons, which can find no home in any of the provisions of the Constitution.

## QUESTIONS AND NOTES

**1.** Prior to *Escobedo*, the Court had held that the right to counsel (*Gideon*), and the privilege against self-incrimination (*Malloy*) were both applicable to the States. Given that both of these decisions were rendered within a year of *Escobedo* does it surprise you that the Court opted for the Sixth Amendment right to counsel as the grounds for its decision? Why do you suppose the Court relied on the Sixth rather than the Fifth Amendment?

**2.** Do you think that Escobedo's confession was (should have been) involuntary under traditional coerced confession law? Would (should) it matter whether Officer Montejano made the statements attributed to him by Escobedo? How and at what level should a question like that be resolved?

**3.** Is the Court outlawing (or casting doubt upon) *all* confessions? Explain. Should it?

**4.** Is the Court opting for a Utopian rule or a constitutionally mandated one?

**5.** Is Justice Stewart's angry tone justified? Was his *Massiah* opinion justified by anything stronger than *his* own rhetoric?

**6.** When would a person be questioned under circumstances that are *not* accusatory?

**7.** Do you agree with the Court that "if the exercise of constitutional rights will thwart the effectiveness of a system of law enforcement, then there is something very wrong with that system?"

**8.** Should the Court have forthrightly overruled *Crooker* and its companion case, *Cicenia v. Lagay*, which involved a less sophisticated defendant than Crooker, rather than try to distinguish the cases?

# 16.

# MIRANDA

If ever one case stood for an entire area of the law, it is *Miranda*. As we shall see over the next several classes, the text of *Miranda* has been construed as though it, itself, was constitutional language. We begin with the case itself.

## A.  The Case Itself

### Miranda v. Arizona
### 384 U.S. 436 (1966)

Mr. Chief Justice WARREN delivered the opinion of the Court.

The cases before us raise questions which go to the roots of our concepts of American criminal jurisprudence: the restraints society must observe consistent with the Federal Constitution in prosecuting individuals for crime. More specifically, we deal with the admissibility of statements obtained from an individual who is subjected to custodial police interrogation and the necessity for procedures which assure that the individual is accorded his privilege under the Fifth Amendment to the Constitution not to be compelled to incriminate himself.

We dealt with certain phases of this problem recently in *Escobedo*. There, as in the four cases before us, law enforcement officials took the defendant into custody and interrogated him in a police station for the purpose of obtaining a confession. The police did not effectively advise him of his right to remain silent or of his right to consult with his attorney. We held that the statements thus made were constitutionally inadmissible.

We start here, as we did in *Escobedo*, with the premise that our holding is not an innovation in our jurisprudence, but is an application of principles long recognized and applied in other settings. We have undertaken a thorough re-examination of the *Escobedo* decision and the principles it announced, and we reaffirm it. That case was but an explication of basic rights that are enshrined in our Constitution — that "No person . . . shall be compelled in any criminal case to be a witness against himself," and that "the accused shall . . . have the Assistance of Counsel" — rights which were put in jeopardy in that case through official overbearing. These precious rights were fixed in our Constitution only after centuries of persecution and struggle. And in the words of Chief Justice Marshall, they were secured "for ages to come, and . . . designed to approach immortality as nearly as human institutions can approach it," *Cohens v. Virginia*, 6 Wheat. 264, 387 (1821).

This was the spirit in which we delineated, in meaningful language, the manner in which the constitutional rights of the individual could be enforced against overzealous police practices. It was necessary in *Escobedo*, as here, to insure that what was proclaimed in the Constitution had not become but a "form of words," *Silverthorn Lumber Co. v. United States*, 251 U.S. 385, 392 (1920), in the hands of government officials. And it is in this spirit, consistent with our role as judges, that we adhere to the principles of *Escobedo* today.

Our holding will be spelled out with some specificity in the pages which follow but briefly stated it is this: the prosecution may not use statements, whether exculpatory or inculpatory, stemming from custodial interrogation of the defendant unless it demonstrates the use of procedural safeguards effective to secure the privilege against self-incrimination. By custodial interrogation, we mean questioning initiated by law enforcement officers after a person has been taken into custody or otherwise deprived of his freedom of action in any significant way.[4] As for the procedural safeguards to be employed, unless other fully effective means are devised to inform accused persons of their right of silence and to assure a continuous opportunity to exercise it, the following measures are required. Prior to any questioning, the person must be warned that he has a right to remain silent, that any statement he does make may be used as evidence against him, and that he has a right to the presence of an attorney, either retained or appointed. The defendant may waive effectuation of these rights, provided the waiver is made voluntarily, knowingly and intelligently. If, however, he indicates in any manner and at any stage of the process that he wishes to consult with an attorney before speaking there can be no questioning. Likewise, if the individual is alone and indicates in any manner that he does not wish to be interrogated, the police may not question him. The mere fact that he may have answered some questions or volunteered some statements on his own does not deprive him of the right to refrain from answering any further inquiries until he has consulted with an attorney and thereafter consents to be questioned.

## I.

An understanding of the nature and setting of

---

[4] This is what we meant in *Escobedo* when we spoke of an investigation which had focused on an accused.

in-custody interrogation is essential to our decisions today. The difficulty in depicting what transpires at such interrogations stems from the fact that in this country they have largely taken place incommunicado. From extensive factual studies undertaken in the early 1930's, including the famous Wickersham Report to Congress by a Presidential Commission, it is clear that police violence and the "third degree" flourished at that time. In a series of cases decided by this Court long after these studies, the police resorted to physical brutality – beatings, hanging, whipping – and to sustained and protracted questioning incommunicado in order to extort confessions. The Commission on Civil Rights in 1961 found much evidence to indicate that "some policemen still resort to physical force to obtain confessions." The use of physical brutality and violence is not, unfortunately, relegated to the past or to any part of the country. Only recently in Kings County, New York, the police brutally beat, kicked and placed lighted cigarette butts on the back of a potential witness under interrogation for the purpose of securing a statement incriminating a third party. *People v. Portelli*, 15 N.Y.2d 235, 257 N.Y.S.2d 931, 205 N.E.2d 857 (1965).[7]

The examples given above are undoubtedly the

---

[7] In addition, see *People v. Wakat*, 415 Ill. 610, 114 N.E.2d 706 (1953); *Wakat v. Harlib*, 253 F.2d 59 (C.A.7th Cir.1958) (defendant suffering from broken bones, multiple bruises and injuries sufficiently serious to require eight months' medical treatment after being manhandled by five policemen); *Kier v. State*, 213 Md. 556, 132 A.2d 494 (1957) (police doctor told accused, who was strapped to a chair completely nude, that he proposed to take hair and skin scrapings from anything that looked like blood or sperm from various parts of his body); *Bruner v. People*, 113 Colo. 194, 156 P.2d 111 (1945) (defendant held in custody over two months, deprived of food for 15 hours, forced to submit to a lie detector test when he wanted to go to the toilet); *People v. Matlock*, 51 Cal.2d 682, 336 P.2d 505, 71 A.L.R.2d 605 (1959) (defendant questioned incessantly over an evening's time, made to lie on cold board and to answer questions whenever it appeared he was getting sleepy). Other cases are documented in American Civil Liberties Union, Illinois Division, Secret Detention by the Chicago Police (1959); Potts, The Preliminary Examination and "The Third Degree," 2 Baylor L.Rev. 131 (1950); Sterling, Police Interrogation and the Psychology of Confession, 14 J.Pub.L. 25 (1965).

exception now, but they are sufficiently widespread to be the object of concern. Unless a proper limitation upon custodial interrogation is achieved—such as these decisions will advance—there can be no assurance that practices of this nature will be eradicated in the foreseeable future.

Again we stress that the modern practice of in-custody interrogation is psychologically rather than physically oriented. As we have stated before, "Since *Chambers v. Florida*, 309 U.S. 227, this Court has recognized that coercion can be mental as well as physical, and that the blood of the accused is not the only hallmark of an unconstitutional inquisition." *Blackburn v. Alabama*, 361 U.S. 199, 206 (1960). Interrogation still takes place in privacy. Privacy results in secrecy and this in turn results in a gap in our knowledge as to what in fact goes on in the interrogation rooms. A valuable source of information about present police practices, however, may be found in various police manuals and texts which document procedures employed with success in the past, and which recommend various other effective tactics. These texts are used by law enforcement agencies themselves as guides. It should be noted that these texts professedly present the most enlightened and effective means presently used to obtain statements through custodial interrogation. By considering these texts and other data, it is possible to describe procedures observed and noted around the country.

The officers are told by the manuals that the "principal psychological factor contributing to a successful interrogation is privacy—being alone with the person under interrogation." The efficacy of this tactic has been explained as follows:

> "If at all practicable, the interrogation should take place in the investigator's office or at least in a room of his own choice. The subject should be deprived of every psychological advantage. In his own home he may be confident, indignant, or recalcitrant. He is more keenly aware of his rights and more reluctant to tell of his indiscretions of criminal behavior within the walls of his home. Moreover his family and other friends are nearby, their presence lending moral support. In his office, the investigator possesses all the advantages. The atmosphere suggests the invincibility of the forces of the law."

To highlight the isolation and unfamiliar surroundings, the manuals instruct the police to display an air of confidence in the suspect's guilt and from outward appearance to maintain only an interest in confirming certain details. The guilt of the subject is to be posited as a fact. The interrogator should direct his comments toward the reasons why the subject committed the act, rather than court failure by asking the subject whether he did it. Like other men, perhaps the subject has had a bad family life, had an unhappy childhood, had too much to drink, had an unrequited desire for women. The officers are instructed to minimize the moral seriousness of the offense,[12] to cast blame on the victim or on society. These tactics are designed to put the subject in a psychological state where his story is but an elaboration of what the police purport to know already—that he is guilty. Explanations to the contrary are dismissed and discouraged.

The texts thus stress that the major qualities an interrogator should possess are patience and perseverance. One writer describes the efficacy of these characteristics in this manner:

> "In the preceding paragraphs emphasis has been placed on kindness and stratagems. The investigator will, however, encounter many situations where the sheer weight of his personality will be the deciding factor. Where emotional appeals and tricks are employed to no avail, he must rely on an oppressive atmosphere of dogged persistence. He must interrogate steadily and without relent, leaving the subject no prospect of surcease. He must dominate his subject and overwhelm him with his inexorable will to obtain the truth. He should interrogate for a spell of several hours pausing only for the subject's necessities in acknowledgment of the need to avoid a charge of duress that can be technically substantiated. In a serious case, the interrogation may continue for days, with the required intervals for food and sleep, but with no respite from the atmosphere of domination. It is possible in this way to induce the subject to talk without resorting to duress or coercion. The method should be used only when the guilt of the subject appears highly probable."

The manuals suggest that the suspect be offered legal excuses for his actions in order to obtain an

---

12 For example, in *Leyra v. Denno*, 347 U.S. 556 (1954), the interrogator-psychiatrist told the accused, "We do sometimes things that are not right, but in a fit of temper or anger we sometimes do things we aren't really responsible for," and again, "We know that morally you were just in anger. Morally, you are not to be condemned."

initial admission of guilt. Where there is a suspected revenge-killing, for example, the interrogator may say:

> "Joe, you probably didn't go out looking for this fellow with the purpose of shooting him. My guess is, however, that you expected something from him and that's why you carried a gun—for your own protection. You knew him for what he was, no good. Then when you met him he probably started using foul, abusive language and he gave some indication that he was about to pull a gun on you, and that's when you had to act to save your own life. That's about it, isn't it, Joe?"

Having then obtained the admission of shooting, the interrogator is advised to refer to circumstantial evidence which negates the self-defense explanation. This should enable him to secure the entire story. One text notes that "Even if he fails to do so, the inconsistency between the subject's original denial of the shooting and his present admission of at least doing the shooting will serve to deprive him of a self-defense 'out' at the time of trial."

When the techniques described above prove unavailing, the texts recommend they be alternated with a show of some hostility. One ploy often used has been termed the "friendly-unfriendly" or the "Mutt and Jeff" act:

> ". . . In this technique, two agents are employed. Mutt, the relentless investigator, who knows the subject is guilty and is not going to waste any time. He's sent a dozen men away for this crime and he's going to send the subject away for the full term. Jeff, on the other hand, is obviously a kindhearted man. He has a family himself. He has a brother who was involved in a little scrape like this. He disapproves of Mutt and his tactics and will arrange to get him off the case if the subject will cooperate. He can't hold Mutt off for very long. The subject would be wise to make a quick decision. The technique is applied by having both investigators present while Mutt acts out his role. Jeff may stand by quietly and demur at some of Mutt's tactics. When Jeff makes his plea for cooperation, Mutt is not present in the room."[17]

---

[17] A variant on the technique of creating hostility is one of engendering fear. This is perhaps best described by the prosecuting attorney in *Malinski v. New York*, 324 U.S. 401, 407 (1945): "Why this talk about being undressed? Of course, they had a right to undress him to look for bullet scars, and keep the clothes off him. That was quite proper police

The interrogators sometimes are instructed to induce a confession out of trickery. The technique here is quite effective in crimes which require identification or which run in series. In the identification situation, the interrogator may take a break in his questioning to place the subject among a group of men in a line-up. "The witness or complainant (previously coached, if necessary) studies the line-up and confidently points out the subject as the guilty party." Then the questioning resumes "as though there were now no doubt about the guilt of the subject." A variation on this technique is called the "reverse line-up":

> "The accused is placed in a line-up, but this time he is identified by several fictitious witnesses or victims who associated him with different offenses. It is expected that the subject will become desperate and confess to the offense under investigation in order to escape from the false accusations."

The manuals also contain instructions for police on how to handle the individual who refuses to discuss the matter entirely, or who asks for an attorney or relatives. The examiner is to concede him the right to remain silent. "This usually has a very undermining effect. First of all, he is disappointed in his expectation of an unfavorable reaction on the part of the interrogator. Secondly, a concession of this right to remain silent impresses the subject with the apparent fairness of his interrogator." After this psychological conditioning, however, the officer is told to point out the incriminating significance of the suspect's refusal to talk:

> "Joe, you have a right to remain silent. That's your privilege and I'm the last person in the world who'll try to take it away from you. If that's the way you want to leave this, O.K. But let me ask you this. Suppose you were in my shoes and I were in yours and you called me in to ask me about this and I told you, 'I don't want to answer any of your questions.' You'd think I had something to hide, and you'd probably be right in thinking that. That's exactly what I'll have to think about you, and so will everybody else. So let's sit here and talk this whole thing over."

---

procedure. That is some more psychology—let him sit around with a blanket on him, humiliate him there for a while; let him sit in the corner, let him think he is going to get a shellacking."

Few will persist in their initial refusal to talk, it is said, if this monologue is employed correctly.

In the event that the subject wishes to speak to a relative or an attorney, the following advice is tendered:

> "[T]he interrogator should respond by suggesting that the subject first tell the truth to the interrogator himself rather than get anyone else involved in the matter. If the request is for an attorney, the interrogator may suggest that the subject save himself or his family the expense of any such professional service, particularly if he is innocent of the offense under investigation. The interrogator may also add, 'Joe, I'm only looking for the truth, and if you're telling the truth, that's it. You can handle this by yourself.'"

From these representative samples of interrogation techniques, the setting prescribed by the manuals and observed in practice becomes clear. In essence, it is this: To be alone with the subject is essential to prevent distraction and to deprive him of any outside support. The aura of confidence in his guilt undermines his will to resist. He merely confirms the preconceived story the police seek to have him describe. Patience and persistence, at times relentless questioning, are employed. To obtain a confession, the interrogator must "patiently maneuver himself or his quarry into a position from which the desired objective may be attained."[23] When normal procedures fail to produce the needed result, the police may resort to deceptive stratagems such as giving false legal advice. It is important to keep the subject off balance, for example, by trading on his insecurity about himself or his surroundings. The police then persuade, trick, or cajole him out of exercising his constitutional rights.

Even without employing brutality, the "third degree" or the specific stratagems described above, the very fact of custodial interrogation exacts a heavy toll on individual liberty and trades on the weakness of individuals.[24]

---

[23] Inbau & Reid, Lie Detection and Criminal Interrogation 185 (3d ed. 1953).

[24] Interrogation procedures may even give rise to a false confession. The most recent conspicuous example occurred in New York, in 1964, when a Negro of limited intelligence confessed to two brutal murders and a rape which he had not committed. When this was discovered, the prosecutor was reported as saying: "Call it what you want—brain-

It is obvious that such an interrogation environment is created for no purpose other than to subjugate the individual to the will of his examiner. This atmosphere carries its own badge of intimidation. To be sure, this is not physical intimidation, but it is equally destructive of human dignity.[26] The current practice of incommunicado interrogation is at odds with one of our Nation's most cherished principles— that the individual may not be compelled to incriminate himself. Unless adequate protective devices are employed to dispel the compulsion inherent in custodial surroundings, no statement obtained from the defendant can truly be the product of his free choice.

### III.

It is impossible for us to foresee the potential alternatives for protecting the privilege which might be devised by Congress or the States in the exercise of their creative rule-making capacities. Therefore we cannot say that the Constitution necessarily requires adherence to any particular solution for the inherent compulsions of the interrogation process as it is presently conducted. Our decision in no way creates a constitutional straitjacket which will handicap sound efforts at reform, nor is it intended to

---

washing, hypnosis, fright. They made him give an untrue confession. The only thing I don't believe is that Whitmore was beaten." N.Y. Times, Jan. 28, 1965, p. 1, col. 5.

[26] The absurdity of denying that a confession obtained under these circumstances is compelled is aptly portrayed by an example in Professor Sutherland's recent article, Crime and Confession, 79 Harv.L.Rev. 21, 37 (1965):

> "Suppose a well-to-do testatrix says she intends to will her property to Elizabeth. John and James want her to bequeath it to them instead. They capture the testatrix, put her in a carefully designed room, out of touch with everyone but themselves and their convenient 'witnesses,' keep her secluded there for hours while they make insistent demands, weary her with contradictions of her assertions that she wants to leave her money to Elizabeth, and finally induce her to execute the will in their favor. Assume that John and James are deeply and correctly convinced that Elizabeth is unworthy and will make base use of the property if she gets her hands on it, whereas John and James have the noblest and most righteous intentions. Would any judge of probate accept the will so procured as the 'voluntary' act of the testatrix?"

have this effect. We encourage Congress and the States to continue their laudable search for increasingly effective ways of protecting the rights of the individual while promoting efficient enforcement of our criminal laws. However, unless we are shown other procedures which are at least as effective in apprising accused persons of their right of silence and in assuring a continuous opportunity to exercise it, the following safeguards must be observed.

At the outset, if a person in custody is to be subjected to interrogation, he must first be informed in clear and unequivocal terms that he has the right to remain silent. For those unaware of the privilege, the warning is needed simply to make them aware of it—the threshold requirement for an intelligent decision as to its exercise. More important, such a warning is an absolute prerequisite in overcoming the inherent pressures of the interrogation atmosphere. It is not just the subnormal or woefully ignorant who succumb to an interrogator's imprecations, whether implied or expressly stated, that the interrogation will continue until a confession is obtained or that silence in the face of accusation is itself damning and will bode ill when presented to a jury.[37] Further, the warning will show the individual that his interrogators are prepared to recognize his privilege should he choose to exercise it.

The Fifth Amendment privilege is so fundamental to our system of constitutional rule and the expedient of giving an adequate warning as to the availability of the privilege so simple, we will not pause to inquire in individual cases whether the defendant was aware of his rights without a warning being given. Assessments of the knowledge the defendant possessed, based on information as to his age, education, intelligence, or prior contact with authorities, can never be more than speculation; a warning is a clear-cut fact. More important, whatever the background of the person interrogated, a warning at the time of the interrogation is indispensable to overcome its pressures and to insure that the individual knows he is free to exercise the privilege at that point in time.

The warning of the right to remain silent must be accompanied by the explanation that anything said

---

[37] In accord with our decision today, it is impermissible to penalize an individual for exercising his Fifth Amendment privilege when he is under police custodial interrogation. The prosecution may not, therefore, use at trial the fact that he stood mute or claimed his privilege in the face of accusation. Cf. *Griffin v. California*, 380 U.S. 609 (1965).

can and will be used against the individual in court. This warning is needed in order to make him aware not only of the privilege, but also of the consequences of forgoing it. It is only through an awareness of these consequences that there can be any assurance of real understanding and intelligent exercise of the privilege. Moreover, this warning may serve to make the individual more acutely aware that he is faced with a phase of the adversary system—that he is not in the presence of persons acting solely in his interest.

The circumstances surrounding in-custody interrogation can operate very quickly to overbear the will of one merely made aware of his privilege by his interrogators. Therefore, the right to have counsel present at the interrogation is indispensable to the protection of the Fifth Amendment privilege under the system we delineate today. Our aim is to assure that the individual's right to choose between silence and speech remains unfettered throughout the interrogation process. A once-stated warning, delivered by those who will conduct the interrogation, cannot itself suffice to that end among those who most require knowledge of their rights. A mere warning given by the interrogators is not alone sufficient to accomplish that end. Prosecutors themselves claim that the admonishment of the right to remain silent without more "will benefit only the recidivist and the professional." Brief for the National District Attorneys Association as *amicus curiae*, p. 14. Even preliminary advice given to the accused by his own attorney can be swiftly overcome by the secret interrogation process. Cf. *Escobedo*. Thus, the need for counsel to protect the Fifth Amendment privilege comprehends not merely a right to consult with counsel prior to questioning, but also to have counsel present during any questioning if the defendant so desires.

The presence of counsel at the interrogation may serve several significant subsidiary functions as well. If the accused decides to talk to his interrogators, the assistance of counsel can mitigate the dangers of untrustworthiness. With a lawyer present the likelihood that the police will practice coercion is reduced, and if coercion is nevertheless exercised the lawyer can testify to it in court. The presence of a lawyer can also help to guarantee that the accused gives a fully accurate statement to the police and that the statement is rightly reported by the prosecution at trial.

An individual need not make a pre-interrogation request for a lawyer. While such request affirmatively secures his right to have one, his failure to ask for a lawyer does not constitute a waiver. No effective waiver of the right to counsel during interrogation can be recognized unless specifically made after the warnings we here delineate have been given. The accused who does not know his rights and therefore does not make a request may be the person who most needs counsel.

If an individual indicates that he wishes the assistance of counsel before any interrogation occurs, the authorities cannot rationally ignore or deny his request on the basis that the individual does not have or cannot afford a retained attorney. The financial ability of the individual has no relationship to the scope of the rights involved here. The privilege against self-incrimination secured by the Constitution applies to all individuals. The need for counsel in order to protect the privilege exists for the indigent as well as the affluent. In fact, were we to limit these constitutional rights to those who can retain an attorney, our decisions today would be of little significance. The cases before us as well as the vast majority of confession cases with which we have dealt in the past involve those unable to retain counsel. While authorities are not required to relieve the accused of his poverty, they have the obligation not to take advantage of indigence in the administration of justice. Denial of counsel to the indigent at the time of interrogation while allowing an attorney to those who can afford one would be no more supportable by reason or logic than the similar situation at trial and on appeal struck down in *Gideon v. Wainwright*, 372 U.S. 335 (1963), and *Douglas v. California*, 372 U.S. 353 (1963).[43]

Once warnings have been given, the subsequent procedure is clear. If the individual indicates in any manner, at any time prior to or during questioning, that he wishes to remain silent, the interrogation must cease.[44] At this point he has shown that he

---

[43] While a warning that the indigent may have counsel appointed need not be given to the person who is known to have an attorney or is known to have ample funds to secure one, the expedient of giving a warning is too simple and the rights involved too important to engage in *ex post facto* inquiries into financial ability when there is any doubt at all on that score. (Repositioned, ed.)

[44] If an individual indicates his desire to remain silent, but has an attorney present, there may be some circumstances in which further questioning would be permissible. In the absence of evidence of overbearing, statements then made in the presence of counsel might be free of the compelling influence of the interrogation process and might fairly be construed as a waiver of the privilege for purposes of these statements.

intends to exercise his Fifth Amendment privilege; any statement taken after the person invokes his privilege cannot be other than the product of compulsion, subtle or otherwise. Without the right to cut off questioning, the setting of in-custody interrogation operates on the individual to overcome free choice in producing a statement after the privilege has been once invoked. If the individual states that he wants an attorney, the interrogation must cease until an attorney is present. At that time, the individual must have an opportunity to confer with the attorney and to have him present during any subsequent questioning. If the individual cannot obtain an attorney and he indicates that he wants one before speaking to police, they must respect his decision to remain silent.

If the interrogation continues without the presence of an attorney and a statement is taken, a heavy burden rests on the government to demonstrate that the defendant knowingly and intelligently waived his privilege against self-incrimination and his right to retained or appointed counsel. *Escobedo*. This Court has always set high standards of proof for the waiver of constitutional rights, *Johnson v. Zerbst*, 304 U.S. 458 (1938), and we reassert these standards as applied to in-custody interrogation. Since the State is responsible for establishing the isolated circumstances under which the interrogation takes place and has the only means of making available corroborated evidence of warnings given during incommunicado interrogation, the burden is rightly on its shoulders.

An express statement that the individual is willing to make a statement and does not want an attorney followed closely by a statement could constitute a waiver. But a valid waiver will not be presumed simply from the silence of the accused after warnings are given or simply from the fact that a confession was in fact eventually obtained. Moreover, where in-custody interrogation is involved, there is no room for the contention that the privilege is waived if the individual answers some questions or gives some information on his own prior to invoking his right to remain silent when interrogated.

Whatever the testimony of the authorities as to waiver of rights by an accused, the fact of lengthy interrogation or incommunicado incarceration before a statement is made is strong evidence that the accused did not validly waive his rights. In these circumstances the fact that the individual eventually made a statement is consistent with the conclusion that the compelling influence of the interrogation finally forced him to do so. It is inconsistent with any notion of a voluntary relinquishment of the privilege. Moreover, any evidence that the accused was threatened, tricked, or cajoled into a waiver will, of course, show that the defendant did not voluntarily waive his privilege. The requirement of warnings and waiver of rights is a fundamental with respect to the Fifth Amendment privilege and not simply a preliminary ritual to existing methods of interrogation.

The warnings required and the waiver necessary in accordance with our opinion today are, in the absence of a fully effective equivalent, prerequisites to the admissibility of any statement made by a defendant. No distinction can be drawn between statements which are direct confessions and statements which amount to "admissions" of part or all of an offense. The privilege against self-incrimination protects the individual from being compelled to incriminate himself in any manner; it does not distinguish degrees of incrimination. Similarly, for precisely the same reason, no distinction may be drawn between inculpatory statements and statements alleged to be merely "exculpatory." If a statement made were in fact truly exculpatory it would, of course, never be used by the prosecution. In fact, statements merely intended to be exculpatory by the defendant are often used to impeach his testimony at trial or to demonstrate untruths in the statement given under interrogation and thus to prove guilt by implication. These statements are incriminating in any meaningful sense of the word and may not be used without the full warnings and effective waiver required for any other statement. In *Escobedo* itself, the defendant fully intended his accusation of another as the slayer to be exculpatory as to himself.

The principles announced today deal with the protection which must be given to the privilege against self-incrimination when the individual is first subjected to police interrogation while in custody at the station or otherwise deprived of his freedom of action in any significant way. It is at this point that our adversary system of criminal proceedings commences, distinguishing itself at the outset from the inquisitorial system recognized in some countries. Under the system of warnings we delineate today or under any other system which may be devised and found effective, the safeguards to be erected about the privilege must come into play at this point.

Our decision is not intended to hamper the traditional function of police officers in investigating crime. When an individual is in custody on probable cause, the police may, of course, seek out evidence in the field to be used at trial against him. Such investigation may include inquiry of persons not under restraint. General on-the-scene questioning as to facts surrounding a crime or other general questioning of citizens in the fact-finding process is not

affected by our holding. It is an act of responsible citizenship for individuals to give whatever information they may have to aid in law enforcement. In such situations the compelling atmosphere inherent in the process of in-custody interrogation is not necessarily present.[46]

In dealing with statements obtained through interrogation, we do not purport to find all confessions inadmissible. Confessions remain a proper element in law enforcement. Any statement given freely and voluntarily without any compelling influences is, of course, admissible in evidence. The fundamental import of the privilege while an individual is in custody is not whether he is allowed to talk to the police without the benefit of warnings and counsel, but whether he can be interrogated.[48] There is no requirement that police stop a person who enters a police station and states that he wishes to confess to a crime, or a person who calls the police to offer a confession or any other statement he desires to make. Volunteered statements of any kind are not barred by the Fifth Amendment and their admissibility is not affected by our holding today.

IV.

If the individual desires to exercise his privilege, he has the right to do so. This is not for the authorities to decide. An attorney may advise his client not to talk to police until he has had an opportunity to investigate the case, or he may wish to be present with his client during any police questioning. In doing so an attorney is merely exercising the good professional judgment he has been taught. This is not cause for considering the attorney a menace to law enforcement. He is merely carrying out what he is sworn to do under his oath—to protect to the extent of his ability the rights of his client. In fulfilling this responsibility the attorney plays a vital role in the

---

[46] The distinction and its significance has been aptly described in the opinion of a Scottish court:

"In former times such questioning, if undertaken, would be conducted by police officers visiting the house or place of business of the suspect and there questioning him, probably in the presence of a relation or friend. However convenient the modern practice may be, it must normally create a situation very unfavorable to the suspect." *Chalmers v. H. M. Advocate*, (1954) Sess.Cas. 66, 78 (J.C.).

[48] In accordance with our holdings today and in *Escobedo, Crooker v. California*, and *Cicenia* are not to be followed. (Repositioned, ed)

administration of criminal justice under our Constitution.

In announcing these principles, we are not unmindful of the burdens which law enforcement officials must bear, often under trying circumstances. We also fully recognize the obligation of all citizens to aid in enforcing the criminal laws. This Court, while protecting individual rights, has always given ample latitude to law enforcement agencies in the legitimate exercise of their duties. The limits we have placed on the interrogation process should not constitute an undue interference with a proper system of law enforcement. As we have noted, our decision does not in any way preclude police from carrying out their traditional investigatory functions. Although confessions may play an important role in some convictions, the cases before us present graphic examples of the overstatement of the "need" for confessions. In each case authorities conducted interrogations ranging up to five days in duration despite the presence, through standard investigating practices, of considerable evidence against each defendant.[49] Further examples are chronicled in our prior cases.

It is also urged that an unfettered right to detention for interrogation should be allowed because it will often redound to the benefit of the person questioned. When police inquiry determines that there is no reason to believe that the person has committed any crime, it is said, he will be released without need for further formal procedures. The person who has committed no offense, however, will be better able to clear himself after warnings with counsel present than without. It can be assumed that in such circumstances a lawyer would advise his client to talk freely to police in order to clear himself.

Custodial interrogation, by contrast, does not necessarily afford the innocent an opportunity to clear themselves. A serious consequence of the present practice of the interrogation alleged to be beneficial for the innocent is that many arrests "for investigation" subject large numbers of innocent persons to detention and interrogation. In one of the cases before us, *California v. Stewart*, police held four persons, who were in the defendant's house at the time of the arrest, in jail for five days until

defendant confessed. At that time they were finally released. Police stated that there was "no evidence to connect them with any crime." Available statistics on the extent of this practice where it is condoned indicate that these four are far from alone in being subjected to arrest, prolonged detention, and interrogation without the requisite probable cause.[53]

Over the years the Federal Bureau of Investigation has compiled an exemplary record of effective law enforcement while advising any suspect or arrested person, at the outset of an interview, that he is not required to make a statement, that any statement may be used against him in court, that the individual may obtain the services of an attorney of his own choice and, more recently, that he has a right to free counsel if he is unable to pay.[54]

---

[49] Miranda, Vignera, and Westover were identified by eyewitnesses. Marked bills from the bank robbed were found in Westover's car. Articles stolen from the victim as well as from several other robbery victims were found in Stewart's home at the outset of the investigation.

[53] An extreme example of this practice occurred in the District of Columbia in 1958. Seeking three "stocky" young Negroes who had robbed a restaurant, police rounded up 90 persons of that general description. Sixth-three were held overnight before being released for lack of evidence. A man not among the 90 arrested was ultimately charged with the crime. Washington Daily News, January 21, 1958, p. 5, col. 1; Hearings before a Subcommittee of the Senate Judiciary Committee on H.R. 11477, S. 2970, S. 3325, and S. 3355, 85th Cong., 2d Sess. (July 1958), pp. 40, 78.

[54] In 1952, J. Edgar Hoover, Director of the Federal Bureau of Investigation, stated:

"Law enforcement, however, in defeating the criminal, must maintain inviolate the historic liberties of the individual. To turn back the criminal, yet, by so doing, destroy the dignity of the individual, would be a hollow victory.

"We can have the Constitution, the best laws in the land, and the most honest reviews by courts—but unless the law enforcement profession is steeped in the democratic tradition, maintains the highest in ethics, and makes its work a career of honor, civil liberties will continually—and without end be violated. . . . The best protection of civil liberties is an alert, intelligent and honest law enforcement agency. There can be no alternative.

". . . Special Agents are taught that any suspect or arrested person, at the outset of an interview, must be advised that he is not required to make a statement and that any statement given can be used against him in court. Moreover, the individual must be informed that, if he desires, he may obtain the

V.

Because of the nature of the problem and because of its recurrent significance in numerous cases, we have to this point discussed the relationship of the Fifth Amendment privilege to police interrogation without specific concentration on the facts of the cases before us. We turn now to these facts to consider the application to these cases of the constitutional principles discussed above. In each instance, we have concluded that statements were obtained from the defendant under circumstances that did not meet constitutional standards for protection of the privilege.

*Miranda v. Arizona.*

On March 13, 1963, petitioner, Ernesto Miranda, was arrested at his home and taken in custody to a Phoenix police station. He was there identified by the complaining witness. The police then took him to "Interrogation Room No. 2" of the detective bureau. There he was questioned by two police officers. The officers admitted at trial that Miranda was not advised that he had a right to have an attorney present. Two hours later, the officers emerged from the interrogation room with a written confession signed by Miranda. At the top of the statement was a typed paragraph stating that the confession was made voluntarily, without threats or promises of immunity and "with full knowledge of my legal rights, understanding any statement I make may be used against me."[67]

At his trial before a jury, the written confession was admitted into evidence over the objection of defense counsel, and the officers testified to the prior oral confession made by Miranda during the interrogation. Miranda was found guilty of kidnapping and rape. He was sentenced to 20 to 30 years' imprisonment on each count, the sentences to run concurrently. On appeal, the Supreme Court of Arizona held that Miranda's constitutional rights were not violated in obtaining the confession and affirmed the conviction. In reaching its decision, the court emphasized heavily the fact that Miranda did not specifically request counsel.

We reverse. From the testimony of the officers

and by the admission of respondent, it is clear that Miranda was not in any way apprised of his right to consult with an attorney and to have one present during the interrogation, nor was his right not to be compelled to incriminate himself effectively protected in any other manner. Without these warnings the statements were inadmissible. The mere fact that he signed a statement which contained a typed-in clause stating that he had "full knowledge" of his "legal rights" does not approach the knowing and intelligent waiver required to relinquish constitutional rights.

*Vignera v. New York.*

Petitioner, Michael Vignera, was picked up by New York police on October 14, 1960, in connection with the robbery three days earlier of a Brooklyn dress shop. They took him to the 17th Detective Squad headquarters in Manhattan. Sometime thereafter he was taken to the 66th Detective Squad. There a detective questioned Vignera with respect to the robbery. Vignera orally admitted the robbery to the detective. The detective was asked on cross-examination at trial by defense counsel whether Vignera was warned of his right to counsel before being interrogated. The prosecution objected to the question and the trial judge sustained the objection. Thus, the defense was precluded from making any showing that warnings had not been given. While at the 66th Detective Squad, Vignera was identified by the store owner and a saleslady as the man who robbed the dress shop. At about 3 p.m. he was formally arrested. The police then transported him to still another station, the 70th Precinct in Brooklyn, "for detention." At 11 p.m. Vignera was questioned by an assistant district attorney in the presence of a hearing reporter who transcribed the questions and Vignera's answers. This verbatim account of these proceedings contains no statement of any warnings given by the assistant district attorney. At Vignera's trial on a charge of first degree robbery, the detective testified as to the oral confession. The transcription of the statement taken was also introduced in evidence. At the conclusion of the testimony, the trial judge charged the jury in part as follows:

> "The law doesn't say that the confession is void or invalidated because the police officer didn't advise the defendant as to his rights. Did you hear what I said? I am telling you what the law of the State of New York is."

Vignera was found guilty of first degree robbery. He was subsequently adjudged a third-felony offender and sentenced to 30 to 60 years' imprisonment.

---

services of an attorney of his own choice."
Hoover, Civil Liberties and Law Enforcement: The Role of the FBI, 37 Iowa L.Rev. 175, 177-182 (1952).

[67] One of the officers testified that he read this paragraph to Miranda. Apparently, however, he did not do so until after Miranda had confessed orally.

We reverse. The foregoing indicates that Vignera was not warned of any of his rights before the questioning by the detective and by the assistant district attorney. No other steps were taken to protect these rights. Thus he was not effectively apprised of his Fifth Amendment privilege or of his right to have counsel present and his statements are inadmissible.

*Westover v. United States.*

At approximately 9:45 p.m. on March 20, 1963, petitioner, Carl Calvin Westover, was arrested by local police in Kansas City as a suspect in two Kansas City robberies. A report was also received from the FBI that he was wanted on a felony charge in California. The local authorities took him to a police station and placed him in a line-up on the local charges, and at about 11:45 p.m. he was booked. Kansas City police interrogated Westover on the night of his arrest. He denied any knowledge of criminal activities. The next day local officers interrogated him again throughout the morning. Shortly before noon they informed the FBI that they were through interrogating Westover and that the FBI could proceed to interrogate him. There is nothing in the record to indicate that Westover was ever given any warning as to his rights by local police. At noon, three special agents of the FBI continued the interrogation in a private interview room of the Kansas City Police Department, this time with respect to the robbery of a savings and loan association and a bank in Sacramento, California. After two or two and one-half hours, Westover signed separate confessions to each of these two robberies which had been prepared by one of the agents during the interrogation. At trial one of the agents testified, and a paragraph on each of the statements states, that the agents advised Westover that he did not have to make a statement, that any statement he made could be used against him, and that he had the right to see an attorney.

On the facts of this case we cannot find that Westover knowingly and intelligently waived his right to remain silent and his right to consult with counsel prior to the time he made the statement. At the time the FBI agents began questioning Westover, he had been in custody for over 14 hours and had been interrogated at length during that period. The FBI interrogation began immediately upon the conclusion of the interrogation by Kansas City police and was conducted in local police headquarters. Although the two law enforcement authorities are legally distinct and the crimes for which they interrogated Westover were different, the impact on him was that of a continuous period of questioning. There is no evidence of any warning given prior to the FBI interrogation nor is there any evidence of an articulated waiver of rights after the FBI commenced its interrogation. The record simply shows that the defendant did in fact confess a short time after being turned over to the FBI following interrogation by local police. Despite the fact that the FBI agents gave warnings at the outset of their interview, from Westover's point of view the warnings came at the end of the interrogation process. In these circumstances an intelligent waiver of constitutional rights cannot be assumed.

We do not suggest that law enforcement authorities are precluded from questioning any individual who has been held for a period of time by other authorities and interrogated by them without appropriate warnings. A different case would be presented if an accused were taken into custody by the second authority, removed both in time and place from his original surroundings, and then adequately advised of his rights and given an opportunity to exercise them. But here the FBI interrogation was conducted immediately following the state interrogation in the same police station—in the same compelling surroundings. Thus, in obtaining a confession from Westover the federal authorities were the beneficiaries of the pressure applied by the local in-custody interrogation. In these circumstances the giving of warnings alone was not sufficient to protect the privilege.

*California v. Stewart.*

In the course of investigating a series of purse-snatch robberies in which one of the victims had died of injuries inflicted by her assailant, respondent, Roy Allen Stewart, was pointed out to Los Angeles police as the endorser of dividend checks taken in one of the robberies. At about 7:15 p.m., January 31, 1963, police officers went to Stewart's house and arrested him. One of the officers asked Stewart if they could search the house, to which he replied, "Go ahead." The search turned up various items taken from the five robbery victims. At the time of Stewart's arrest, police also arrested Stewart's wife and three other persons who were visiting him. These four were jailed along with Stewart and were interrogated. Stewart was taken to the University Station of the Los Angeles Police Department where he was placed in a cell. During the next five days, police interrogated Stewart on nine different occasions. Except during the first interrogation session, when he was confronted with an accusing witness, Stewart was isolated with his interrogators.

During the ninth interrogation session, Stewart

admitted that he had robbed the deceased and stated that he had not meant to hurt her. Police then brought Stewart before a magistrate for the first time. Since there was no evidence to connect them with any crime, the police then released the other four persons arrested with him.

Nothing in the record specifically indicates whether Stewart was or was not advised of his right to remain silent or his right to counsel. In a number of instances, however, the interrogating officers were asked to recount everything that was said during the interrogations. None indicated that Stewart was ever advised of his rights.

Stewart was charged with kidnapping to commit robbery, rape, and murder. At his trial, transcripts of the first interrogation and the confession at the last interrogation were introduced in evidence. The jury found Stewart guilty of robbery and first degree murder and fixed the penalty as death. On appeal, the Supreme Court of California reversed. It held that under this Court's decision in *Escobedo*, Stewart should have been advised of his right to remain silent and of his right to counsel and that it would not presume in the face of a silent record that the police advised Stewart of his rights.[70]

We affirm. In dealing with custodial interrogation, we will not presume that a defendant has been effectively apprised of his rights and that his privilege against self-incrimination has been adequately safeguarded on a record that does not show that any warnings have been given or that any effective alternative has been employed. Nor can a knowing and intelligent waiver of these rights be assumed on a silent record. Furthermore, Stewart's steadfast denial of the alleged offenses through eight of the nine interrogations over a period of five days is subject to no other construction than that he was compelled by persistent interrogation to forgo his Fifth Amendment privilege.

Therefore, in accordance with the foregoing, the judgments of the Supreme Court of Arizona, of the New York Court of Appeals, and of the Court of Appeals for the Ninth Circuit are reversed. The judgment of the Supreme Court of California is affirmed.

Mr. Justice CLARK, dissenting in [*Miranda, Vignera* and *Westover,*] and concurring in the result in [*Stewart*].

It is with regret that I find it necessary to write in these cases. However, I am unable to join the majority because its opinion goes too far on too little, while my dissenting brethren do not go quite far enough. Nor can I join in the Court's criticism of the present practices of police and investigatory agencies as to custodial interrogation. The materials it refers to as "police manuals"[1] are, as I read them, merely writings in this field by professors and some police officers. Not one is shown by the record here to be the official manual of any police department, much less in universal use in crime detection. Moreover the examples of police brutality mentioned by the Court are rare exceptions to the thousands of cases that appear every year in the law reports. The police agencies – all the way from municipal and state forces to the federal bureaus – are responsible for law enforcement and public safety in this country. I am proud of their efforts, which in my view are not fairly characterized by the Court's opinion.

The *ipse dixit* of the majority has no support in our cases. Indeed, the Court admits that "we might not find the defendants' statements [here] to have been involuntary in traditional terms." The Court holds that failure to follow the new procedures requires inexorably the exclusion of any statement by the accused, as well as the fruits thereof. Such a strict constitutional specific inserted at the nerve center of crime detection may well kill the patient. Since there is at this time a paucity of information and an almost total lack of empirical knowledge on the practical operation of requirements truly comparable to those announced by the majority, I would be more restrained lest we go too far too fast.

Custodial interrogation has long been recognized as "undoubtedly an essential tool in effective law enforcement." Recognition of this fact should put us on guard against the promulgation of doctrinaire rules. Especially is this true where the Court finds that "the Constitution has prescribed" its holding and where the light of our past cases is to the contrary. Indeed, even in *Escobedo* the Court never hinted that an affirmative "waiver" was a prerequisite to questioning; that the burden of proof as to waiver was on the prosecution; that the presence of counsel – absent a waiver – during interrogation was required; that a waiver can be withdrawn at the will

---

[70] Because of this disposition of the case, the California Supreme Court did not reach the claims that the confession was coerced by police threats to hold his ailing wife in custody until he confessed.

[1] *E.g.*, Inbau & Reid, Criminal Interrogation and Confessions (1962); O'Hara, Fundamentals of Criminal Investigation (1956); Dienstein, Technics for the Crime Investigator (1952); Mulbar, Interrogation (1951); Kidd, Police Interrogation (1940).

of the accused; that counsel must be furnished during an accusatory stage to those unable to pay; nor that admissions and exculpatory statements are "confessions." To require all those things at one gulp should cause the Court to choke over more cases than *Crooker* and *Cicenia*, which it expressly overrules today.

Rather than employing the arbitrary Fifth Amendment rule which the Court lays down I would follow the more pliable dictates of the Due Process Clauses of the Fifth and Fourteenth Amendments which we are accustomed to administering and which we know from our cases are effective instruments in protecting persons in police custody. In this way we would not be acting in the dark nor in one full sweep changing the traditional rules of custodial interrogation which this Court has for so long recognized as a justifiable and proper tool in balancing individual rights against the rights of society. It will be soon enough to go further when we are able to appraise with somewhat better accuracy the effect of such a holding.

I would affirm the convictions in *Miranda, Vignera,* and *Westover.* In each of those cases I find from the circumstances no warrant for reversal. In *Stewart,* I would dismiss the writ of certiorari for want of a final judgment, but if the merits are to be reached I would affirm on the ground that the State failed to fulfill its burden, in the absence of a showing that appropriate warnings were given, of proving a waiver or a totality of circumstances showing voluntariness. Should there be a retrial, I would leave the State free to attempt to prove these elements.

Mr. Justice HARLAN, whom Mr. Justice STEWART and Mr. Justice WHITE join, dissenting.

I believe the decision of the Court represents poor constitutional law and entails harmful consequences for the country at large. How serious these consequences may prove to be only time can tell. But the basic flaws in the Court's justification seem to me readily apparent now once all sides of the problem are considered.

## I. INTRODUCTION

The new rules are not designed to guard against police brutality or other unmistakably banned forms of coercion. Those who use third-degree tactics and deny them in court are equally able and destined to lie as skillfully about warnings and waivers. Rather, the thrust of the new rules is to negate all pressures, to reinforce the nervous or ignorant suspect, and ultimately to discourage any confession at all. The aim in short is toward "voluntariness" in a utopian sense, or to view it from a different angle, voluntariness with a vengeance.

To incorporate this notion into the Constitution requires a strained reading of history and precedent and a disregard of the very pragmatic concerns that alone may on occasion justify such strains. I believe that reasoned examination will show that the Due Process Clauses provide an adequate tool for coping with confessions and that, even if the Fifth Amendment privilege against self-incrimination be invoked, its precedents taken as a whole do not sustain the present rules. Viewed as a choice based on pure policy, these new rules prove to be a highly debatable, if not one-sided, appraisal of the competing interests, imposed over widespread objection, at the very time when judicial restraint is most called for by the circumstances.

## II. CONSTITUTIONAL PREMISES.

It is most fitting to begin an inquiry into the constitutional precedents by surveying the limits on confessions the Court has evolved under the Due Process Clause of the Fourteenth Amendment. This is so because these cases show that there exists a workable and effective means of dealing with confessions in a judicial manner; because the cases are the baseline from which the Court now departs and so serve to measure the actual as opposed to the professed distance it travels; and because examination of them helps reveal how the Court has coasted into its present position.

Apart from direct physical coercion no single default or fixed combination of defaults guaranteed exclusion, and synopses of the cases would serve little use because the overall gauge has been steadily changing, usually in the direction of restricting admissibility. But to mark just what point had been reached before the Court jumped the rails in *Escobedo,* it is worth capsulizing the then-recent case of *Haynes v. Washington,* 373 U.S. 503. There, Haynes had been held some 16 or more hours in violation of state law before signing the disputed confession, had received no warnings of any kind, and despite requests had been refused access to his wife or to counsel, the police indicating that access would be allowed after a confession. Emphasizing especially this last inducement and rejecting some contrary indicia of voluntariness, the Court in a 5-to-4 decision held the confession inadmissible.

There are several relevant lessons to be drawn from this constitutional history. The first is that with over 25 years of precedent the Court has developed an elaborate, sophisticated, and sensitive approach to admissibility of confessions. It is "judicial" in its treatment of one case at a time, flexible in its ability to respond to the endless mutations of fact presented, and ever more familiar to the lower courts. Of course, strict certainty is not obtained in this developing process, but this is often so with constitutional principles, and disagreement is usually confined to that borderland of close cases where it matters least.

The second point is that in practice and from time to time in principle, the Court has given ample recognition to society's interest in suspect questioning as an instrument of law enforcement. Cases countenancing quite significant pressures can be cited without difficulty,[5] and the lower courts may often have been yet more tolerant. Of course the limitations imposed today were rejected by necessary implication in case after case, the right to warnings having been explicitly rebuffed in this Court many years ago.

Finally, the cases disclose that the language in many of the opinions overstates the actual course of decision. It has been said, for example, that an admissible confession must be made by the suspect "in the unfettered exercise of his own will," and that "a prisoner is not 'to be made the deluded instrument of his own conviction.'" Though often repeated, such principles are rarely observed in full measure. Even the word "voluntary" may be deemed somewhat misleading, especially when one considers many of the confessions that have been brought under its umbrella. The tendency to overstate may be laid in part to the flagrant facts often before the Court; but in any event one must recognize how it has tempered attitudes and lent some color of authority to the approach now taken by the Court.

I turn now to the Court's asserted reliance on the Fifth Amendment, an approach which I frankly regard as a *trompe l'oeil*. The Court's opinion in my view reveals no adequate basis for extending the Fifth Amendment's privilege against self-incrimination to the police station. Far more important, it fails to show that the Court's new rules are well supported, let alone compelled, by Fifth Amendment precedents. Instead, the new rules actually derive from quotation and analogy drawn from

---

[5] One not too distant example is *Stroble v. California*, 343 U.S. 181 (1952), in which the suspect was kicked and threatened after his arrest, questioned a little later for two hours, and isolated from a lawyer trying to see him; the resulting confession was held admissible.

precedents under the Sixth Amendment, which should properly have no bearing on police interrogation.

The Court's opening contention, that the Fifth Amendment governs police station confessions, is perhaps not an impermissible extension of the law but it has little to commend itself in the present circumstances. Historically, the privilege against self-incrimination did not bear at all on the use of extra-legal confessions, for which distinct standards evolved; indeed, "the history of the two principles is wide apart, differing by one hundred years in origin, and derived through separate lines of precedents. . . ." Practice under the two doctrines has also differed in a number of important respects. Even those who would readily enlarge the privilege must concede some linguistic difficulties since the Fifth Amendment in terms proscribes only compelling any person "in any criminal case to be a witness against himself."

Though weighty, I do not say these points and similar ones are conclusive, for, as the Court reiterates, the privilege embodies basic principles always capable of expansion. Certainly the privilege does represent a protective concern for the accused and an emphasis upon accusatorial rather than inquisitorial values in law enforcement, although this is similarly true of other limitations such as the grand jury requirement and the reasonable doubt standard. Accusatorial values, however, have openly been absorbed into the due process standard governing confessions; this indeed is why at present "the kinship of the two rules (governing confessions and self-incrimination) is too apparent for denial." Since extension of the general principle has already occurred, to insist that the privilege applies as such serves only to carry over inapposite historical details and engaging rhetoric and to obscure the policy choices to be made in regulating confessions.

Having decided that the Fifth Amendment privilege does apply in the police station, the Court reveals that the privilege imposes more exacting restrictions than does the Fourteenth Amendment's voluntariness test. It then emerges from a discussion of *Escobedo* that the Fifth Amendment requires for an admissible confession that it be given by one distinctly aware of his right not to speak and shielded from "the compelling atmosphere" of interrogation. From these key premises, the Court finally develops the safeguards of warning, counsel, and so forth. I do not believe these premises are sustained by precedents under the Fifth Amendment.

The more important premise is that pressure on the suspect must be eliminated though it be only the subtle influence of the atmosphere and surroundings. The Fifth Amendment, however, has never been thought to forbid *all* pressure to incriminate one's self in the situations covered by it. On the contrary, it has been held that failure to incriminate one's self can result in denial of removal of one's case from state to federal court, in refusal of a military commission, in denial of a discharge in bankruptcy, and in numerous other adverse consequences. This is not to say that short of jail or torture any sanction is permissible in any case; policy and history alike may impose sharp limits. However, the Court's unspoken assumption that *any* pressure violates the privilege is not supported by the precedents and it has failed to show why the Fifth Amendment prohibits that relatively mild pressure the Due Process Clause permits.

The Court appears similarly wrong in thinking that precise knowledge of one's rights is a settled prerequisite under the Fifth Amendment to the loss of its protections. A number of lower federal court cases have held that grand jury witnesses need not always be warned of their privilege, and Wigmore states this to be the better rule for trial witnesses. No Fifth Amendment precedent is cited for the Court's contrary view. There might of course be reasons apart from Fifth Amendment precedent for requiring warning or any other safeguard on questioning but that is a different matter entirely.

A closing word must be said about the Assistance of Counsel Clause of the Sixth Amendment, which is never expressly relied on by the Court but whose judicial precedents turn out to be linchpins of the confession rules announced today. To support its requirement of a knowing and intelligent waiver, the Court cites cases imparting glosses to the Sixth Amendment, concern[ing] counsel at trial or on appeal. While the Court finds no pertinent difference between judicial proceedings and police interrogation, I believe the differences are so vast as to disqualify wholly the Sixth Amendment precedents as suitable analogies in the present cases.

The only attempt in this Court to carry the right to counsel into the station house occurred in *Escobedo*, the Court repeating several times that that stage was no less "critical" than trial itself. This is hardly persuasive when we consider that a grand jury inquiry, the filing of a certiorari petition, and certainly the purchase of narcotics by an undercover agent from a prospective defendant may all be equally "critical" yet provision of counsel and advice on the score have never been thought compelled by the Constitution in such cases. The sound reason why this right is so freely extended for a criminal trial is the severe injustice risked by confronting an untrained defendant with a range of technical points of law, evidence, and tactics familiar to the prosecutor but not to himself. This danger shrinks markedly in the police station where indeed the lawyer in fulfilling his professional responsibilities of necessity may become an obstacle to truth-finding. The Court's summary citation of the Sixth Amendment cases here seems to me best described as "the domino method of constitutional adjudication . . . wherein every explanatory statement in a previous opinion is made the basis for extension to a wholly different situation."

### III. POLICY CONSIDERATIONS.

Without at all subscribing to the generally black picture of police conduct painted by the Court, I think it must be frankly recognized at the outset that police questioning allowable under due process precedents may inherently entail some pressure on the suspect and may seek advantage in his ignorance or weaknesses. The atmosphere and questioning techniques, proper and fair though they be, can in themselves exert a tug on the suspect to confess, and in this light "[t]o speak of any confessions of crime made after arrest as being 'voluntary' or 'uncoerced' is somewhat inaccurate, although traditional. A confession is wholly and incontestably voluntary only if a guilty person gives himself up to the law and becomes his own accuser." Until today, the role of the Constitution has been only to sift out *undue* pressure, not to assure spontaneous confessions.

The Court's new rules aim to offset these minor pressures and disadvantages intrinsic to any kind of police interrogation. The rules do not serve due process interests in preventing blatant coercion since, as I noted earlier, they do nothing to contain the policeman who is prepared to lie from the start. The rules work for reliability in confessions almost only in the Pickwickian sense that they can prevent some from being given at all.[12] In short, the benefit of this new regime is simply to lessen or wipe out the inherent compulsion and inequalities to which the Court devotes some nine pages of description.

---

[12] The Court's vision of a lawyer "mitigat[ing] the dangers of untrustworthiness" by witnessing coercion and assisting accuracy in the confession is largely a fancy; for if counsel arrives, there is rarely going to be a police station confession. *Watts v. Indiana*, (separate opinion of Jackson, J.):

> "[A]ny lawyer worth his salt will tell the suspect in no uncertain terms to make no statement to police under any circumstances."

What the Court largely ignores is that its rules impair, if they will not eventually serve wholly to frustrate, an instrument of law enforcement that has long and quite reasonably been thought worth the price paid for it.[13] There can be little doubt that the Court's new code would markedly decrease the number of confessions. To warn the suspect that he may remain silent and remind him that his confession may be used in court are minor obstructions. To require also an express waiver by the suspect and an end to questioning whenever he demurs must heavily handicap questioning. And to suggest or provide counsel for the suspect simply invites the end of the interrogation.

While passing over the costs and risks of its experiment, the Court portrays the evils of normal police questioning in terms which I think are exaggerated. Albeit stringently confined by the due process standards interrogation is no doubt often inconvenient and unpleasant for the suspect. However, it is no less so for a man to be arrested and jailed, to have his house searched, or to stand trial in court, yet all this may properly happen to the most innocent given probable cause, a warrant, or an indictment. Society has always paid a stiff price for law and order, and peaceful interrogation is not one of the dark moments of the law.

This brief statement of the competing considerations seems to me ample proof that the Court's preference is highly debatable at best and therefore not to be read into the Constitution. However, it may make the analysis more graphic to consider the actual facts of one of the four cases reversed by the Court. *Miranda v. Arizona* serves best, being neither the hardest nor easiest of the four under the Court's standards.[15]

On March 3, 1963, an 18-year-old girl was kidnapped and forcibly raped near Phoenix, Arizona.

---

[13] This need is, of course, what makes so misleading the Court's comparison of a probate judge readily setting aside as involuntary the will of an old lady badgered and beleaguered by the new heirs. With wills, there is no public interest save in a totally free choice; with confessions, the solution of crime is a countervailing gain, however the balance is resolved.

[15] In *Westover*, a seasoned criminal was practically given the Court's full complement of warnings and did not heed them. The *Stewart* case, on the other hand, involves long detention and successive questioning. In *Vignera*, the facts are complicated and the record somewhat incomplete.

Ten days later, on the morning of March 13, petitioner Miranda was arrested and taken to the police station. At this time Miranda was 23 years old, indigent, and educated to the extent of completing half the ninth grade. He had "an emotional illness" of the schizophrenic type, according to the doctor who eventually examined him; the doctor's report also stated that Miranda was "alert and oriented as to time, place, and person," intelligent within normal limits, competent to stand trial, and sane within the legal definition. At the police station, the victim picked Miranda out of a lineup, and two officers then took him into a separate room to interrogate him, starting about 11:30 a.m. Though at first denying his guilt, within a short time Miranda gave a detailed oral confession and then wrote out in his own hand and signed a brief statement admitting and describing the crime. All this was accomplished in two hours or less without any force, threats or promises and—I will assume this though the record is uncertain,—without any effective warnings at all.

Miranda's oral and written confessions are now held inadmissible under the Court's new rules. One is entitled to feel astonished that the Constitution can be read to produce this result. These confessions were obtained during brief, daytime questioning conducted by two officers and unmarked by any of the traditional indicia of coercion. They assured a conviction for a brutal and unsettling crime, for which the police had and quite possibly could obtain little evidence other than the victim's identifications, evidence which is frequently unreliable. There was, in sum, a legitimate purpose, no perceptible unfairness, and certainly little risk of injustice in the interrogation. Yet the resulting confessions, and the responsible course of police practice they represent, are to be sacrificed to the Court's own finespun conception of fairness which I seriously doubt is shared by many thinking citizens in this country.

Mr. Justice WHITE, with whom Mr. Justice HARLAN and Mr. Justice STEWART join, dissenting.

II.

That the Court's holding today is neither compelled nor even strongly suggested by the language of the Fifth Amendment, is at odds with American and English legal history, and involves a departure from a long line of precedent does not prove either that the Court has exceeded its powers or that the Court is wrong or unwise in its present reinterpretation of the Fifth Amendment. It does, however, underscore the obvious—that the Court has not discovered or found the law in making today's decision, nor has it derived it from some irrefutable sources; what it has done is to make new law and new public policy in much the same way that it has in the course of interpreting other great clauses of the Constitution. This is what the Court historically has done. Indeed, it is what it must do and will continue to do until and unless there is some fundamental change in the constitutional distribution of governmental powers.

But if the Court is here and now to announce new and fundamental policy to govern certain aspects of our affairs, it is wholly legitimate to examine the mode of this or any other constitutional decision in this Court and to inquire into the advisability of its end product in terms of the long-range interest of the country. At the very least, the Court's text and reasoning should withstand analysis and be a fair exposition of the constitutional provision which its opinion interprets. Decisions like these cannot rest alone on syllogism, metaphysics or some ill-defined notions of natural justice, although each will perhaps play its part. In proceeding to such constructions as it now announces, the Court should also duly consider all the factors and interests bearing upon the cases, at least insofar as the relevant materials are available; and if the necessary considerations are not treated in the record or obtainable from some other reliable source, the Court should not proceed to formulate fundamental policies based on speculation alone.

### III.

First, we may inquire what are the textual and factual bases of this new fundamental rule. To reach the result announced on the grounds it does, the Court must stay within the confines of the Fifth Amendment, which forbids self-incrimination only if *compelled*. Hence the core of the Court's opinion is that because of the "compulsion inherent in custodial surroundings, no statement obtained from [a] defendant [in custody] can truly be the product of his free choice," absent the use of adequate protective devices as described by the Court. However, the Court does not point to any sudden inrush of new knowledge requiring the rejection of 70 years' experience. Nor does it assert that its novel conclusion reflects a changing consensus among state courts, see *Mapp*, or that a succession of cases had steadily eroded the old rule and proved it unworkable, see *Gideon v. Wainwright*, 372 U.S. 335. Rather than asserting new knowledge, the Court concedes that it cannot truly know what occurs during custodial questioning, because of the innate secrecy of such proceedings. It extrapolates a picture of what it conceives to be the norm from police investigatorial

manuals, published in 1959 and 1962 or earlier, without any attempt to allow for adjustments in police practices that may have occurred in the wake of more recent decisions of state appellate tribunals or this Court. But even if the relentless application of the described procedures could lead to involuntary confessions, it most assuredly does not follow that each and every case will disclose this kind of interrogation or this kind of consequence. Insofar as appears from the Court's opinion, it has not examined a single transcript of any police interrogation, let alone the interrogation that took place in any one of these cases which it decides today. Judged by any of the standards for empirical investigation utilized in the social sciences the factual basis for the Court's premise is patently inadequate.

Although in the Court's view in-custody interrogation is inherently coercive, the Court says that the spontaneous product of the coercion of arrest and detention is still to be deemed voluntary. An accused, arrested on probable cause, may blurt out a confession which will be admissible despite the fact that he is alone and in custody, without any showing that he had any notion of his right to remain silent or of the consequences of his admission. Yet, under the Court's rule, if the police ask him a single question such as "Do you have anything to say?" or "Did you kill your wife?" his response, if there is one, has somehow been compelled, even if the accused has been clearly warned of his right to remain silent. Common sense informs us to the contrary. While one may say that the response was "involuntary" in the sense the question provoked or was the occasion for the response and thus the defendant was induced to speak out when he might have remained silent if not arrested and not questioned, it is patently unsound to say the response is compelled.

The duration and nature of incommunicado custody, the presence or absence of advice concerning the defendant's constitutional rights, and the granting or refusal of requests to communicate with lawyers, relatives or friends have all been rightly regarded as important data bearing on the basic inquiry. But it has never been suggested, until today, that such questioning was so coercive and accused persons so lacking in hardihood that the very first response to the very first question following the commencement of custody must be conclusively presumed to be the product of an overborne will.

If the rule announced today were truly based on a conclusion that all confessions resulting from custodial interrogation are coerced, then it would simply have no rational foundation. *A fortiori* that would be true of the extension of the rule to exculpatory statements, which the Court effects after a brief discussion of why, in the Court's view, they must be deemed incriminatory but without any discussion of why they must be deemed coerced. Even if one were to postulate that the Court's concern is not that all confessions induced by police interrogation are coerced but rather that some such confessions are coerced and present judicial procedures are believed to be inadequate to identify the confessions that are coerced and those that are not, it would still not be essential to impose the rule that the Court has now fashioned. Transcripts or observers could be required, specific time limits, tailored to fit the cause, could be imposed, or other devices could be utilized to reduce the chances that otherwise indiscernible coercion will produce an inadmissible confession.

## IV.

Criticism of the Court's opinion, however, cannot stop with a demonstration that the factual and textual bases for the rule it propounds are, at best, less than compelling. Equally relevant is an assessment of the rule's consequences measured against community values. The Court's duty to assess the consequences of its action is not satisfied by the utterance of the truth that a value of our system of criminal justice is "to respect the inviolability of the human personality" and to require government to produce the evidence against the accused by its own independent labors. More than the human dignity of the accused is involved; the human personality of others in the society must also be preserved. Thus the values reflected by the privilege are not the sole desideratum; society's interest in the general security is of equal weight.

The obvious underpinning of the Court's decision is a deep-seated distrust of all confessions. As the Court declares that the accused may not be interrogated without counsel present, absent a waiver of the right to counsel, and as the Court all but admonishes the lawyer to advise the accused to remain silent, the result adds up to a judicial judgment that evidence from the accused should not be used against him in any way, whether compelled or not. This is the not so subtle overtone of the opinion—that it is inherently wrong for the police to gather evidence from the accused himself. And this is precisely the nub of this dissent. I see nothing wrong or immoral, and certainly nothing unconstitutional, in the police's asking a suspect whom they have reasonable cause to arrest whether or not he killed his wife or in confronting him with the evidence on which the arrest was based, at least where he has been plainly advised that he may remain completely silent, see

*Escobedo* (dissenting opinion). Until today, "the admissions or confessions of the prisoner, when voluntarily and freely made, have always ranked high in the scale of incriminating evidence." Particularly when corroborated, as where the police have confirmed the accused's disclosure of the hiding place of implements or fruits of the crime, such confessions have the highest reliability and significantly contribute to the certitude with which we may believe the accused is guilty. Moreover, it is by no means certain that the process of confessing is injurious to the accused. To the contrary it may provide psychological relief and enhance the prospects for rehabilitation.

This is not to say that the value of respect for the inviolability of the accused's individual personality should be accorded no weight or that all confessions should be indiscriminately admitted. This Court has long read the Constitution to proscribe compelled confessions, a salutary rule from which there should be no retreat. But I see no sound basis, factual or otherwise, and the Court gives none, for concluding that the present rule against the receipt of coerced confessions is inadequate for the task of sorting out inadmissible evidence and must be replaced by the *per se* rule which is now imposed. Even if the new concept can be said to have advantages of some sort over the present law, they are far outweighed by its likely undesirable impact on other very relevant and important interests.

The most basic function of any government is to provide for the security of the individual and of his property. These ends of society are served by the criminal laws which for the most part are aimed at the prevention of crime. Without the reasonably effective performance of the task of preventing private violence and retaliation, it is idle to talk about human dignity and civilized values.

In some unknown number of cases the Court's rule will return a killer, a rapist or other criminal to the streets and to the environment which produced him, to repeat his crime whenever it pleases him. As a consequence, there will not be a gain, but a loss, in human dignity. The real concern is not the unfortunate consequences of this new decision on the criminal law as an abstract, disembodied series of authoritative proscriptions, but the impact on those who rely on the public authority for protection and who without it can only engage in violent self-help with guns, knives and the help of their neighbors similarly inclined. There is, of course, a saving factor: the next victims are uncertain, unnamed and unrepresented in this case.

Nor can this decision do other than have a corrosive effect on the criminal laws as an effective device

Chapter 16 Miranda 507

to prevent crime. A major component in its effectiveness in this regard is its swift and sure enforcement. The easier it is to get away with rape and murder, the less the deterrent effect on those who are inclined to attempt it. This is still good common sense. If it were not, we should posthaste liquidate the whole law enforcement establishment as a useless, misguided effort to control human conduct.

And what about the accused who has confessed or would confess in response to simple, noncoercive questioning and whose guilt could not otherwise be proved? Is it so clear that release is the best thing for him in every case? Has it so unquestionably been resolved that in each and every case it would be better for him not to confess and to return to his environment with no attempt whatsoever to help him? I think not. It may well be that in many cases it will be no less than a callous disregard for his own welfare as well as for the interests of his next victim.

There is another aspect to the effect of the Court's rule on the person whom the police have arrested on probable cause. The fact is that he may not be guilty at all and may be able to extricate himself quickly and simply if he were told the circumstances of his arrest and were asked to explain. This effort, and his release, must now await the hiring of a lawyer or his appointment by the court, consultation with counsel and then a session with the police or the prosecutor. Similarly, where probable cause exists to arrest several suspects, as where the body of the victim is discovered in a house having several residents, it will often be true that a suspect may be cleared only through the results of interrogation of other suspects. Here too the release of the innocent may be delayed by the Court's rule.

Nor can it be claimed that judicial time and effort, assuming that is a relevant consideration, will be conserved because of the ease of application of the new rule. Today's decision leaves open such questions as whether the accused was in custody, whether his statements were spontaneous or the product of interrogation, whether the accused has effectively waived his rights, and whether nontestimonial evidence introduced at trial is the fruit of statements made during a prohibited interrogation, all of which are certain to prove productive of uncertainty during investigation and litigation during prosecution. For all these reasons, if further restrictions on police interrogation are desirable at this time, a more flexible approach makes much more sense than the Court's constitutional straitjacket which forecloses more discriminating treatment by legislative or rule-making pronouncements.

Applying the traditional standards to the cases before the Court, I would hold these confessions voluntary.

## QUESTIONS AND NOTES

**1.** What were the available constitutional provisions upon which to predicate *Miranda*? 4th Amendment? 5th Amendment? 6th Amendment? 14th Amendment? Which did the Court choose? Why? If you wished to reach the Court's result, which would you have chosen? Why?

**2.** Which opinion does the best job of balancing the interests that need to be balanced in cases like *Miranda*? Why?

**3.** The majority is opting for a strict set of rules (bright-line, if you will) whereas the dissenters seem to prefer standards (*i.e.,* guidelines). What are the advantages and disadvantages of each approach? Which do you generally prefer? Why? Which do you prefer in this instance? Why?

**4.** The Court begins by announcing that "our holding is not an innovation in our jurisprudence." Do you agree? Do you think that the quoted observation makes the opinion more or less persuasive to the neutral observer?

**5.** Does footnote 4 narrow *Escobedo*? If so, is it a desirable narrowing?

**6.** Is *Miranda* likely to stop or significantly reduce the amount of police brutality? In that regard, what would be the post-*Miranda* result in *People v. Portelli* (text accompanying Court's footnote 7)?

**7.** What, if any, relevance should the police manuals play? What relevance do they play?

**8.** Was *Miranda* intended to stop the various psychological ploys (such as "Mutt and Jeff") referred to in the opinion? Do you think that it in fact stopped them?

**9.** Do you think that the testatrix hypothetical in footnote 26 of the Court's opinion is a valid analogy? Is Justice Harlan's criticism of the analogy, in his dissent, well-taken?

**10.** Is there any good reason to require the warnings for sophisticated defendants who know their rights?

**11.** Is footnote 44 realistic? If you were representing a defendant under those circumstances would you permit him to speak? If so, when? If not, why not?

**12.** In regard to question 10, do you think that Justice Harlan got it right in dissent when he suggested that "the rules work for reliability only in the Pickwickian sense that they prevent some from being given at all?"

**13.** What should (or could) the F.B.I. have done to legitimate the interrogation and subsequent confession in *Westover*?

**14.** Justice White suggests that confessions may be good for a defendant psychologically and rehabilitatively. Are you persuaded? What, if any, impact should that possibility have had on the result in this case?

**15.** Do you agree with Justice White's suggestions that *Miranda* might retard the achievement of some of the basic purposes of the criminal law?

**16.** We now turn to cases examining particular aspects of *Miranda*, starting with the specificity of the warnings.

## B. The Nature of the Warnings

One of the many questions left open by *Miranda* was how closely the actual warnings must parallel the manner in which they were spelled out in *Miranda*. Like so much else about *Miranda*, it depends on which paragraph of the opinion one reads. The issue was joined in *Duckworth v. Eagan*, where a very different Court from the one that delivered *Miranda* split five to four.

### Duckworth v. Eagan
### 492 U.S. 195 (1989)

Chief Justice REHNQUIST delivered the opinion of the Court.

Respondent confessed to stabbing a woman nine times after she refused to have sexual relations with him, and he was convicted of attempted murder. Before confessing, respondent was given warnings by the police, which included the advice that a lawyer would be appointed "if and when you go to court." The United States Court of Appeals for the Seventh Circuit held that such advice did not comply with the requirements of *Miranda*. We disagree and reverse.

Late on May 16, 1982, respondent contacted a Chicago police officer he knew to report that he had seen the naked body of a dead woman lying on a Lake Michigan beach. Respondent denied any involvement in criminal activity. He then took several Chicago police officers to the beach, where the woman was crying for help. When she saw respondent, the woman exclaimed: "Why did you stab me? Why did you stab me?" Respondent told the officers that he had been with the woman earlier that night, but that they had been attacked by several men who abducted the woman in a van.

The next morning, after realizing that the crime had been committed in Indiana, the Chicago police turned the investigation over to the Hammond, Indiana, Police Department. Respondent repeated to the Hammond police officers his story that he had been attacked on the lakefront, and that the woman had been abducted by several men. After he filled out a battery complaint at a local police station, respondent agreed to go to the Hammond police headquarters for further questioning.

At about 11 a.m., the Hammond police questioned respondent. Before doing so, the police read to respondent a waiver form, entitled "Voluntary Appearance; Advice of Rights," and they asked him to sign it. The form provided:

> "Before we ask you any questions, you must understand your rights. You have the right to remain silent. Anything you say can be used against you in court. *You have a right to talk to a lawyer for advice before we ask you any questions, and to have him with you during questioning.* You have this right to the advice and presence of a lawyer even if you cannot afford to hire one. *We have no way of giving you a lawyer, but one will be appointed for you, if you wish, if and when you go to court.* If you wish to answer questions now without a lawyer present, you have the right to stop answering questions at any time. You also have the right to stop answering at any time until you've talked to a lawyer." (emphasis added).[1]

Respondent signed the form and repeated his exculpatory explanation for his activities of the previous evening.

Respondent was then placed in the "lock up" at the Hammond police headquarters. Some 29 hours later, at about 4 p.m. on May 18, the police again interviewed respondent. Before this questioning, one of the officers read the following waiver form to respondent:

> "1. Before making this statement, I was advised that I have the right to remain silent and that anything I might say may or will be used against me in a court of law.
>
> "2. That I have the right to consult with an attorney of my own choice before saying

---

[1] The remainder of the form signed by respondent provided: "I, *[Gary Eagan,]* have come to the Detective Bureau of the Hammond, Indiana Police Department, of my own choice to talk with Officers . . . In [sic] regard to an investigation they are conducting. I know that I am not under arrest and that I can leave this office if I wish to do so.

"Prior to any questioning, I was furnished with the above statement of my rights. . . . I have (read) (had read to me) this statement of my rights. I understand what my rights are. I am willing to answer questions and make a statement. I do not want a lawyer. I understand and know what I am doing. No promises or threats have been made to me and no pressure of any kind has been used against me."

anything, and that an attorney may be present while I am making any statement or throughout the course of any conversation with any police officer if I so choose.

> "3. That I can stop and request an attorney at any time during the course of the taking of any statement or during the course of any such conversation.
>
> "4. That in the course of any conversation I can refuse to answer any further questions and remain silent, thereby terminating the conversation.
>
> "5. That if I do not hire an attorney, one will be provided for me."

Respondent read the form back to the officers and signed it. He proceeded to confess to stabbing the woman. The next morning, respondent led the officers to the Lake Michigan beach where they recovered the knife he had used in the stabbing and several items of clothing.

At trial, over respondent's objection, the state court admitted his confession, his first statement denying any involvement in the crime, the knife, and the clothing. The jury found respondent guilty of attempted murder, but acquitted him of rape. He was sentenced to 35 years' imprisonment. The conviction was upheld on appeal.

Respondent sought a writ of habeas corpus in the United States District Court for the Northern District of Indiana, claiming, *inter alia*, that his confession was inadmissible because the first waiver form did not comply with *Miranda*. The District Court denied the petition, holding that the record "clearly manifests adherence to *Miranda* . . . especially as to the so-called second statement."

A divided United States Court of Appeals for the Seventh Circuit reversed. The majority held that the advice that counsel would be appointed "if and when you go to court," which was included in the first warnings given to respondent, was "constitutionally defective because it denies an accused indigent a clear and unequivocal warning of the right to appointed counsel before any interrogation," and "link[s] an indigent's right to counsel before interrogation with a future event."

We have never insisted that *Miranda* warnings be given in the exact form described in that decision.[4] In

---

[4] For example, the standard *Miranda* warnings used by the Federal Bureau of Investigation provide as follows:

"Before we ask you any questions, you must understand your rights.

"You have the right to remain silent.

*Miranda* itself, the Court said that "[t]he warnings required and the waiver necessary in accordance with our opinion today are, *in the absence of a fully effective equivalent*, prerequisites to the admissibility of any statement made by a defendant." (emphasis added). In *California v. Prysock*, 453 U.S. 355 (1981) (*per curiam*), we stated that "the 'rigidity' of *Miranda* [does not] exten[d] to the precise formulation of the warnings given a criminal defendant," and that "no talismanic incantation [is] required to satisfy its strictures."

*Miranda* has not been limited to station house questioning, and the officer in the field may not always have access to printed *Miranda* warnings, or he may inadvertently depart from routine practice, particularly if a suspect requests an elaboration of the warnings. The prophylactic *Miranda* warnings are "not themselves rights protected by the Constitution but [are] instead measures to insure that the right against compulsory self-incrimination [is] protected." *Michigan v. Tucker*, 417 U.S. 433 (1974). Reviewing courts therefore need not examine *Miranda* warnings as if construing a will or defining the terms of an easement. The inquiry is simply whether the warnings reasonably "conve[y] to [a suspect] his rights as required by *Miranda*." *Prysock*.

We think the initial warnings given to respondent touched all of the bases required by *Miranda*. The police told respondent that he had the right to remain silent, that anything he said could be used against him in court, that he had the right to speak to an attorney before and during questioning, that he had "this right to the advice and presence of a lawyer even if [he could] not afford to hire one," and that he had the "right to stop answering at any time until [he] talked to a lawyer." As noted, the police also added that they could not provide respondent with

---

"Anything you say can be used against you in court.

"You have the right to talk to a lawyer for advice before we ask you any questions and to have a lawyer with you during questioning.

"If you cannot afford a lawyer, one will be appointed for you before any questioning if you wish.

"If you decide to answer questions now without a lawyer present, you will still have the right to stop answering at any time. You also have the right to stop answering at any time until you talk to a lawyer."

a lawyer, but that one would be appointed "if and when you go to court." The Court of Appeals thought this "if and when you go to court" language suggested that "only those accused who can afford an attorney have the right to have one present before answering any questions," and "implie[d] that if the accused does not 'go to court,' *i.e.*[,] the government does not file charges, the accused is not entitled to [counsel] at all."

In our view, the Court of Appeals misapprehended the effect of the inclusion of "if and when you go to court" language in *Miranda* warnings. First, this instruction accurately described the procedure for the appointment of counsel in Indiana. Under Indiana law, counsel is appointed at the defendant's initial appearance in court, and formal charges must be filed at or before that hearing. We think it must be relatively commonplace for a suspect, after receiving *Miranda* warnings, to ask *when* he will obtain counsel. The "if and when you go to court" advice simply anticipates that question. Second, *Miranda* does not require that attorneys be producible on call, but only that the suspect be informed, as here, that he has the right to an attorney before and during questioning, and that an attorney would be appointed for him if he could not afford one.[7] The Court in *Miranda* emphasized that it was not suggesting that "each police station must have a 'station house lawyer' present at all times to advise prisoners." If the police cannot provide appointed counsel, *Miranda* requires only that the police not question a suspect unless he waives his right to counsel. Here, respondent did just that.

Respondent relies on language in *California v. Prysock*, where we suggested that *Miranda* warnings would not be sufficient "if the reference to the right to appointed counsel was linked [to a] future point in time *after* the police interrogation." (emphasis added). The Court of Appeals also referred to *Prysock* in finding deficient the initial warnings given to respondent. But the vice referred to in *Prysock* was that such warnings would not apprise the accused of his right to have an attorney present if he chose to answer questions. The warnings in this case did not suffer from that defect. Of the eight sentences in the initial warnings, one described respondent's

---

[7] In *Miranda*, the Court stated that the FBI's then-current practice of informing suspects "of a right to free counsel *if* they are unable to pay, and the availability of such counsel from the Judge" was "consistent with the procedure which we delineate today."

right to counsel "before [the police] ask[ed] [him] questions," while another stated his right to "stop answering at any time until [he] talk [ed] to a lawyer." We hold that the initial warnings given to respondent, in their totality, satisfied *Miranda*, and therefore that his first statement denying his involvement in the crime, as well as the knife and the clothing, was properly admitted into evidence.

The Court of Appeals thought it necessary to remand this case for consideration of whether respondent's second statement was tainted by the first warnings. In view of our disposition of this case, we need not reach that question.[8] The judgment of the Court of Appeals is accordingly reversed, and the case is remanded for further proceedings not inconsistent with our decision.

Justice MARSHALL, with whom Justice BRENNAN joins, and with whom Justice BLACKMUN and Justice STEVENS join, dissenting.

The majority holds today that a police warning advising a suspect that he is entitled to an appointed lawyer only "if and when he goes to court" satisfies the requirements of *Miranda*. The majority reaches this result by seriously mischaracterizing that decision. Under *Miranda*, a police warning must "*clearly infor[m]*" a suspect taken into custody "that if he cannot afford an attorney one will be appointed for him *prior to any questioning* if he so desires." (emphasis added). A warning qualified by an "if and when you go to court" caveat does nothing of the kind; instead, it leads the suspect to believe that a lawyer will not be provided until some indeterminate time in the future *after questioning*.

In *Miranda*, the Court held that law enforcement officers who take a suspect into custody must inform the suspect of, among other things, his right to have counsel appointed to represent him before and during interrogation:

"In order fully to apprise a person interrogated of the extent of his rights . . ., it is necessary to warn him not only that he has the right to consult with an attorney, but also that if he is indigent a lawyer will be appointed to represent him. Without this additional warning, the admonition of the right to consult with counsel would often be understood as

meaning only that he can consult with a lawyer if he has one or has the funds to obtain one. The warning of a right to counsel would be hollow if not couched in terms that would convey to the indigent – the person most often subjected to interrogation – the knowledge that he too has a right to have counsel present. As with the warning of the right to remain silent and of the general right to counsel, only by effective and express explanation to the indigent of this right can there be assurance that he was truly in a position to exercise it."

*Miranda* mandated no specific verbal formulation that police must use, but the Court, speaking through Chief Justice Warren, emphasized repeatedly that the offer of appointed counsel must be "effective and express." A clear and unequivocal offer to provide appointed counsel prior to questioning is, in short, an "absolute prerequisite to interrogation."

In concluding that the first warning given to respondent Eagan satisfies the dictates of *Miranda*, the majority makes a mockery of that decision. Eagan was initially advised that he had the right to the presence of counsel before and during questioning. But in the very next breath, the police informed Eagan that, if he could not afford a lawyer, one would be appointed to represent him only "if and when" he went to court. As the Court of Appeals found, Eagan could easily have concluded from the "if and when" caveat that only "those accused who can afford an attorney have the right to have one present before answering any questions; those who are not so fortunate must wait." Eagan was, after all, never told that questioning would be *delayed* until a lawyer was appointed "if and when" Eagan did, in fact, go to court. Thus, the "if and when" caveat may well have had the effect of negating the initial promise that counsel could be present. At best, a suspect like Eagan "would not know . . . whether or not he had a right to the services of a lawyer."

In lawyerlike fashion, the Chief Justice parses the initial warnings given Eagan and finds that the most plausible interpretation is that Eagan would not be questioned until a lawyer was appointed when he later appeared in court. What goes wholly overlooked in the Chief Justice's analysis is that the recipients of police warnings are often frightened suspects unlettered in the law, not lawyers or judges or others schooled in interpreting legal or semantic nuance. Such suspects can hardly be expected to interpret, in as facile a manner as the Chief Justice, "the pretzel-like warnings here – intertwining, contradictory, and ambiguous as they are." The majority thus refuses to recognize that "[t]he warning of

---

[8] Respondent argues that the second set of *Miranda* warnings he received were deficient. These specific warnings have been upheld by the Seventh Circuit, and the Indiana Supreme Court, and we think they plainly comply with *Miranda*.

a right to counsel would be hollow if not couched in terms that would convey to the indigent—the person most often subjected to interrogation—the knowledge that he too has the right to have counsel present." *Miranda*.

Even if the typical suspect could draw the inference the majority does—that questioning will not commence until a lawyer is provided at a later court appearance—a warning qualified by an "if and when" caveat still fails to give a suspect any indication of *when* he will be taken to court. Upon hearing the warnings given in this case, a suspect would likely conclude that no lawyer would be provided until trial. In common parlance, "going to court" is synonymous with "going to trial." Furthermore, the negative implication of the caveat is that, if the suspect is never taken to court, he "is not entitled to an attorney at all." An unwitting suspect harboring uncertainty on this score is precisely the sort of person who may feel compelled to talk "voluntarily" to the police, without the presence of counsel, in an effort to extricate himself from his predicament:

> "[The suspect] is effectively told that he can talk now or remain in custody—in an alien, friendless, harsh world—for an indeterminate length of time. To the average accused, still hoping at this stage to be home on time for dinner or to make it to work on time, the implication that his choice is to answer questions right away or remain in custody until that nebulous time 'if and when' he goes to court is a coerced choice of the most obvious kind." *Dickerson v. State*, 257 Ind. 562, 276 N.E.2d 845, 852 (1972) (DeBruler, J., concurring in result) (finding inadequate a warning identical to the one in this case).

That the warning given to Eagan "accurately described the procedure for the appointment of counsel in Indiana," does nothing to mitigate the possibility that he would feel coerced into talking to the police. *Miranda*, it is true, does not require the police to have a "station house lawyer" ready at all times to counsel suspects taken into custody. But if a suspect does not understand that a lawyer will be made available within a reasonable period of time after he has been taken into custody and advised of his rights, the suspect may decide to talk to the police *for that reason alone*. The threat of an indefinite deferral of interrogation, in a system like Indiana's, thus constitutes an effective means by which the police can pressure a suspect to speak without the presence of counsel. Sanctioning such police practices simply because the warnings given do not misrepresent state

law does nothing more than let the state-law tail wag the federal constitutional dog.[2]

The majority's misreading of *Miranda*—stating that police warnings need only "touc[h] all of the bases required by *Miranda*," that *Miranda* warnings need only be "reasonably 'conve[yed]'" to a suspect, and that *Miranda* warnings are to be measured not point by point but "in their totality,"—is exacerbated by its interpretation of *California v. Prysock*, a decision that squarely supports Eagan's claim in this case. The juvenile suspect in *Prysock* was initially told that he had the right to have a lawyer present before and during questioning. He then was told that he had the right to have his parents present as well. At this point the suspect was informed that a lawyer would be appointed to represent him at no cost if he could not afford one. The California Court of Appeal ruled these warnings insufficient because the suspect was not expressly told of his right to an appointed attorney before and during questioning. This Court reversed, finding that "nothing in the warnings given respondent suggested any limitation on the right to the presence of appointed counsel."

In reaching this result, the *Prysock* Court pointedly distinguished a series of lower court decisions that had found inadequate warnings in which "the reference to the right to appointed counsel was linked with some future point in time." In *United States v. Garcia*, 431 F.2d 134 (CA9 1970) (*per curiam*), for example, the suspect had been informed on one occasion that she had the right to appointed counsel "when she answered any questions," and on another occasion that she could "have an attorney appointed to represent [her] when [she] first appear[ed] before the U.S. Commissioner or the Court." Similarly, in *People v. Bolinski*, 260 Cal.App.2d 705, 718, 67 Cal.Rptr. 347, 355 (1968), the suspect was advised that counsel would be appointed "if he was charged." These lower courts had correctly found these warnings defective, the *Prysock* Court explained, because "[i]n both instances the reference to appointed counsel was linked to a future point in time after police interrogation," and therefore did not clearly advise the suspect of his right to appointed counsel before such interrogation. The initial, conditional warning given Eagan suffers from

---

[2] Nothing in *Miranda*, nor any of our other cases for that matter, supports the notion that the police may indefinitely delay the point at which counsel is appointed. On the contrary, the Court indicated in *Miranda* that the police could detain a person without providing counsel for no more than "a reasonable period of time."

precisely the same fatal defect. It is highly disingenuous for the majority to ignore this fact, characterizing *Prysock* as involving only the question whether a particular warning "apprise[d] the accused of his right to have an attorney present if he chose to answer questions."

It poses no great burden on law enforcement officers to eradicate the confusion stemming from the "if and when" caveat. Deleting the sentence containing the offending language is all that needs to be done. Purged of this language, the warning tells the suspect in a straightforward fashion that he has the right to the presence of a lawyer before and during questioning, and that a lawyer will be appointed if he cannot afford one. The suspect is given no reason to believe that the appointment of an attorney may come after interrogation. To the extent one doubts that it is the "if and when" caveat that is the source of the confusion, compare the initial warning given Eagan, and the crystal-clear warning currently used by the FBI, quoted at n. 4. The majority's claim that the two warnings are indistinguishable in the message conveyed to a suspect defies belief. I dissent.[4]

_____

[4] With no analysis whatsoever, the majority also

holds that the second set of warnings read to Eagan and included in a waiver form that he signed prior to his second interrogation, "plainly comply with *Miranda*." This proposition is subject to dispute given the presence of the "of my own choice" language. See *Sotelo v. State*, 264 Ind. 298, 342 N.E.2d 844, 851 (1976) (DeBruler, J. concurring). But even assuming the second set of warnings complied with *Miranda*, it does not necessarily follow that Eagan's subsequent waiver of rights was knowing and intelligent. Given "the misapprehension caused by the initial warning," the issue is not whether the second warnings were adequate standing alone, but rather whether under the circumstances the mistaken impression Eagan was initially given was corrected. While various factors might inform this inquiry, such as the passage of time, the principal question must be whether the new warnings were sufficiently clear to correct the effect of the earlier, defective warning. As there is little in the record on "the factual circumstances surrounding these events because the state courts did not directly examine this issue," I agree with the Court of Appeals that "remand for a determination of whether [Eagan] knowingly and intelligently waived his right to the presence of an attorney during the second interrogation" is the appropriate course.

## QUESTIONS AND NOTES

**1.** Two of the Justices, O'Connor and Scalia, argued that *Miranda* claims should not be cognizable on habeas corpus. Two others, Marshall and Brennan, argued that they should be. The Court simply assumed that they should be without deciding. Four years later, a sharply divided Supreme Court ruled that *Miranda* claims are cognizable in habeas corpus. *Withrow v. Williams*, 507 U.S. ___, 113 S.Ct. 1745, 123 L.Ed.2d 407 (1993). Rehnquist, O'Connor, Scalia, and Thomas dissented. Do you think that the uncertain procedural status of Eagan's claim may have influenced the Court to decide against him?

**2.** Was the portion of the statement signed by Eagan indicating that he was not in custody obviously false (see fn. 1)? If so, should that have influenced the Court to have resolved the case against the State?

**3.** Which opinion (majority or dissent) comes closer to capturing the spirit of *Miranda*? Explain.

**4.** Which opinion comes closer to establishing the spirit of the Fifth Amendment? Explain.

**5.** Does the defendant have a *right* to an interview with the police so that he can get home for dinner or whatever?

**6.** If your answer to question 5 is "no," is Marshall's dissent undercut to the extent that he suggests that the suspect will be coerced into talking to the police because he does not know when, if ever, he will be brought to trial?

**7.** Is the defendant entitled to counsel during questioning or just not to be questioned in the absence of counsel? Is there a difference between those two concepts? Is the difference significant in terms relevant to the resolution of this case?

**8.** Would somebody in Gary Eagan's position understand the difference between Rehnquist's reading of the warnings and Marshall's somewhat contrary reading of them? Would he understand the questions raised by your author? To the extent that your answer is "no," what does that tell us about the type of warning that he should be given?

**9.** Should the time of appointment of counsel according to Indiana law have been relevant? If so, should the police at least have been required to say that you will go to court in a few hours?

**10.** Should the police at least have been required to say that counsel will be appointed for you "when you go to Court" rather than "if and when you go to court?" For that matter in the second statement, should the fact that the form said that "anything I might say *may* or will be used against me" rather than simply "will be used against me" as *Miranda* mandates have made a difference?

**11.** In *Spring*, we will consider whether failure to inform the defendant as to what he is being questioned about can invalidate an otherwise effective waiver.

## Colorado v. Spring
### 479 U.S. 564 (1987)

Justice POWELL delivered the opinion of the Court.

In *Miranda* the Court held that a suspect's waiver of the Fifth Amendment privilege against self-incrimination is valid only if it is made voluntarily, knowingly, and intelligently. This case presents the question whether the suspect's awareness of all the crimes about which he may be questioned is relevant to determining the validity of his decision to waive the Fifth Amendment privilege.

### I

In February 1979, respondent John Leroy Spring and a companion shot and killed Donald Walker during a hunting trip in Colorado. Shortly thereafter, an informant told agents of the Bureau of Alcohol, Tobacco, and Firearms (ATF) that Spring was engaged in the interstate transportation of stolen firearms. The informant also told the agents that Spring had discussed his participation in the Colorado killing. At the time the ATF agents received this information, Walker's body had not been found and the police had received no report of his disappearance. Based on the information received from the informant relating to the firearms violations, the ATF agents set up an undercover operation to purchase firearms from Spring. On March 30, 1979, ATF agents arrested Spring in Kansas City, Missouri, during the undercover purchase.

An ATF agent on the scene of the arrest advised

Spring of his *Miranda* rights. Spring was advised of his *Miranda* rights a second time after he was transported to the ATF office in Kansas City. At the ATF office, the agents also advised Spring that he had the right to stop the questioning at any time or to stop the questioning until the presence of an attorney could be secured. Spring then signed a written form stating that he understood and waived his rights, and that he was willing to make a statement and answer questions.

ATF agents first questioned Spring about the firearms transactions that led to his arrest. They then asked Spring if he had a criminal record. He admitted that he had a juvenile record for shooting his aunt when he was 10 years old. The agents asked if Spring had ever shot anyone else. Spring ducked his head and mumbled, "I shot another guy once." The agents asked Spring if he had ever been to Colorado. Spring said no. The agents asked Spring whether he had shot a man named Walker in Colorado and thrown his body into a snowbank. Spring paused and then ducked his head again and said no. The interview ended at this point.

On May 26, 1979, Colorado law enforcement officials visited Spring while he was in jail in Kansas City pursuant to his arrest on the firearms offenses. The officers gave Spring the *Miranda* warnings, and Spring again signed a written form indicating that he understood his rights and was willing to waive them. The officers informed Spring that they wanted to question him about the Colorado homicide. Spring indicated that he "wanted to get it off his chest." In an interview that lasted approximately 1½ hours, Spring confessed to the Colorado murder. During that time, Spring talked freely to the officers, did not indicate a desire to terminate the questioning, and never requested counsel. The officers prepared a written statement summarizing the interview. Spring read, edited, and signed the statement.

Spring was charged in Colorado state court with first-degree murder. Spring moved to suppress both statements on the ground that his waiver of *Miranda* rights was invalid.

The Colorado Supreme Court found:

"[T]he validity of Spring's waiver of constitutional rights must be determined upon an examination of the totality of the circumstances surrounding the making of the statement to determine if the waiver was voluntary, knowing and intelligent. No one factor is always determinative in that analysis. Whether, and to what extent, a suspect has been informed or is aware of the subject matter of the interrogation prior to its commencement is simply one factor in the court's evaluation of the total circumstances, although it may be a major or even a determinative factor in some situations."

The court concluded:

"Here, the absence of an advisement to Spring that he would be questioned about the Colorado homicide, and the lack of any basis to conclude that at the time of the execution of the waiver, he reasonably could have expected that the interrogation would extend to that subject, *are* determinative factors in undermining the validity of the waiver."

## II

There is no dispute that the police obtained the May 26 confession after complete *Miranda* warnings and after informing Spring that he would be questioned about the Colorado homicide. The Colorado Supreme Court nevertheless held that the confession should have been suppressed because it was the illegal "fruit" of the March 30 statement. A confession cannot be "fruit of the poisonous tree" if the tree itself is not poisonous. Our inquiry, therefore, centers on the validity of the March 30 statement.

### A

In this case, the law enforcement officials twice informed Spring of his Fifth Amendment privilege in precisely the manner specified by *Miranda*. As we have noted, Spring indicated that he understood the enumerated rights and signed a written form expressing his intention to waive his Fifth Amendment privilege. The trial court specifically found that "there was no element of duress or coercion used to induce Spring's statements [on March 30, 1978]." Despite the explicit warnings and the finding by the trial court, Spring argues that his March 30 statement was in effect compelled in violation of his Fifth Amendment privilege because he signed the waiver form without being aware that he would be questioned about the Colorado homicide. Spring's argument strains the meaning of compulsion past the breaking point.

### B

A statement is not "compelled" within the meaning of the Fifth Amendment if an individual "voluntarily, knowingly and intelligently" waives his constitutional privilege. *Miranda*. The inquiry whether a waiver is coerced "has two distinct dimensions." *Moran v. Burbine*, 475 U.S. 412, 421 (1986):

"First the relinquishment of the right must have been voluntary in the sense that it was the product of a free and deliberate choice rather than intimidation, coercion, or deception. Second, the waiver must have been made with a full awareness both of the nature of the right being abandoned and the consequences of the decision to abandon it. Only if the 'totality of the circumstances surrounding the interrogation' reveal both an uncoerced choice and the requisite level of comprehension may a court properly conclude that the *Miranda* rights have been waived."

There is no doubt that Spring's decision to waive his Fifth Amendment privilege was voluntary. He alleges no "coercion of a confession by physical violence or other deliberate means calculated to break [his] will," and the trial court found none. His allegation that the police failed to supply him with certain information does not relate to any of the traditional indicia of coercion: "the duration and conditions of detention . . ., the manifest attitude of the police toward him, his physical and mental state, the diverse pressures which sap or sustain his powers of resistance and self-control." *Culombe v. Connecticut*, 367 U.S. 568, 602 (1961) (opinion of Frankfurter, J.). Absent evidence that Spring's "will [was] overborne and his capacity for self-determination critically impaired" because of coercive police conduct, his waiver of his Fifth Amendment privilege was voluntary under this Court's decision in *Miranda*.

There also is no doubt that Spring's waiver of his Fifth Amendment privilege was knowingly and intelligently made: that is, that Spring understood that he had the right to remain silent and that anything he said could be used as evidence against him. The Constitution does not require that a criminal suspect know and understand every possible consequence of a waiver of the Fifth Amendment privilege. The Fifth Amendment's guarantee is both simpler and more fundamental: A defendant may not be compelled to be a witness against himself in any respect. The *Miranda* warnings protect this privilege by ensuring that a suspect knows that he may choose not to talk to law enforcement officers, to talk only with counsel present, or to discontinue talking at any time. The *Miranda* warnings ensure that a waiver of these rights is knowing and intelligent by requiring that the suspect be fully advised of this constitutional privilege, including the critical advice that whatever he chooses to say may be used as evidence against him.

In this case there is no allegation that Spring failed to understand the basic privilege guaranteed by the Fifth Amendment. Nor is there any allegation that he misunderstood the consequences of speaking freely to the law enforcement officials. In sum, we think that the trial court was indisputably correct in finding that Spring's waiver was made knowingly and intelligently within the meaning of *Miranda*.

### III

### A

Spring relies on this Court's statement in *Miranda* that "any evidence that the accused was threatened, tricked, or cajoled into a waiver will . . . show that the defendant did not voluntarily waive his privilege." He contends that the failure to inform him of the potential subjects of interrogation constitutes the police trickery and deception condemned in *Miranda*, thus rendering his waiver of *Miranda* rights invalid. Spring, however, reads this statement in *Miranda* out of context and without due regard to the constitutional privilege the *Miranda* warnings were designed to protect.

We note first that the Colorado courts made no finding of official trickery. In fact, as noted above, the trial court expressly found that "there was no element of duress or coercion used to induce Spring's statements." Spring nevertheless insists that the failure of the ATF agents to inform him that he would be questioned about the murder constituted official "trickery" sufficient to invalidate his waiver

of his Fifth Amendment privilege, even if the official conduct did not amount to "coercion." Even assuming that Spring's proposed distinction has merit, we reject his conclusion. This Court has never held that mere silence by law enforcement officials as to the subject matter of an interrogation is "trickery" sufficient to invalidate a suspect's waiver of *Miranda* rights, and we expressly decline so to hold today.[8]

Once *Miranda* warnings are given, it is difficult to see how official silence could cause a suspect to misunderstand the nature of his constitutional right— "his right to refuse to answer any question which might incriminate him." "Indeed, it seems self-evident that one who is told he is free to refuse to answer questions is in a curious posture to later complain that his answers were compelled." We have held that a valid waiver does not require that an individual be informed of all information "useful" in making his decision or all information that "might . . . affec[t] his decision to confess." *Moran v. Burbine*, 475 U.S., at 422. "[W]e have never read the Constitution to require that the police supply a suspect with a flow of information to help him calibrate his self-interest in deciding whether to speak or stand by his rights."[9] Here, the additional information could affect only the wisdom of a *Miranda* waiver, not its essentially voluntary and

---

[8] In certain circumstances, the Court has found affirmative misrepresentations by the police sufficient to invalidate a suspect's waiver of the Fifth Amendment privilege. See, *e.g., Lynumn v. Illinois*, 372 U.S. 528 (1963) (misrepresentation by police officers that a suspect would be deprived of state financial aid for her dependent child if she failed to cooperate with authorities rendered the subsequent confession involuntary); *Spano v. New York*, 360 U.S. 315 (1959) (misrepresentation by the suspect's friend that the friend would lose his job as a police officer if the suspect failed to cooperate rendered his statement involuntary). In this case, we are not confronted with an affirmative misrepresentation by law enforcement officials as to the scope of the interrogation and do not reach the question whether a waiver of *Miranda* rights would be valid in such a circumstance.

[9] Such an extension of *Miranda* would spawn numerous problems of interpretation because any number of factors could affect a suspect's decision to waive his *Miranda* rights. The requirement would also vitiate to a great extent the *Miranda* rule's important "virtue of informing police and prosecutors with specificity" as to how a pretrial questioning of a suspect must be conducted.

knowing nature. Accordingly, the failure of the law enforcement officials to inform Spring of the subject matter of the interrogation could not affect Spring's decision to waive his Fifth Amendment privilege in a constitutionally significant manner.

### B

This Court's holding in *Miranda* specifically required that the police inform a criminal suspect that he has the right to remain silent and that *anything* he says may be used against him. There is no qualification of this broad and explicit warning. The warning, as formulated in *Miranda*, conveys to a suspect the nature of his constitutional privilege and the consequences of abandoning it. Accordingly, we hold that a suspect's awareness of all the possible subjects of questioning in advance of interrogation is not relevant to determining whether the suspect voluntarily, knowingly, and intelligently waived his Fifth Amendment privilege.

### IV

The judgment of the Colorado Supreme Court is reversed, and the case is remanded for further proceedings not inconsistent with this opinion.

Justice MARSHALL, with whom Justice BRENNAN joins, dissenting.

The Court asserts there is "no doubt" that respondent Spring's decision to waive his Fifth Amendment privilege was voluntarily, knowingly, and intelligently made. I agree, however, with the Colorado Supreme Court that a significant doubt exists in the circumstances of this case and thus the State has failed to carry the "heavy burden" recognized in *Miranda* for establishing the constitutional validity of Spring's alleged waiver.

Consistent with our prior decisions, the Court acknowledges that a suspect's waiver of fundamental constitutional rights, such as *Miranda*'s protections against self-incrimination during a custodial interrogation, must be examined in light of the "totality of the circumstances." Nonetheless, the Court proceeds to hold that the specific crimes and topics of investigation known to the interrogating officers before questioning begins are "not relevant" to, and in this case "could not affect," the validity of the suspect's decision to waive his Fifth Amendment privilege. It seems to me self-evident that a suspect's decision to waive this privilege will necessarily be influenced by his awareness of the scope and seriousness of the matters under investigation.

To attempt to minimize the relevance of such information by saying that it "could affect only the wisdom of" the suspect's waiver, as opposed to the validity of that waiver, ventures an inapposite distinction. Wisdom and validity in this context are overlapping concepts, as circumstances relevant to assessing the validity of a waiver may also be highly relevant to its wisdom in any given context. Indeed, the admittedly "critical" piece of advice the Court recognizes today—that the suspect be informed that whatever he says may be used as evidence against him—is certainly relevant to the wisdom of any suspect's decision to submit to custodial interrogation without first consulting his lawyer. The Court offers no principled basis for concluding that this is a relevant factor for determining the validity of a waiver but that, under what it calls a *totality* of the circumstances analysis, a suspect's knowledge of the specific crimes and other topics previously identified for questioning can never be.

The Court quotes *Moran v. Burbine* as holding that "a valid waiver does not require that an individual be informed of all information 'useful' in making his decision or *all* information that 'might . . . affec[t] his decision to confess.'" (emphasis added). Noticeably similar is the Court's holding today: "[A] suspect's awareness of *all* the possible subjects of questioning in advance of interrogation is not relevant to determining" the validity of his waiver. (emphasis added). This careful phraseology avoids the important question whether the lack of *any* indication of the identified subjects for questioning *is* relevant to determining the validity of the suspect's waiver.

I would include among the relevant factors for consideration whether before waiving his Fifth Amendment rights the suspect was aware, either through the circumstances surrounding his arrest or through a specific advisement from the arresting or interrogating officers, of the crime or crimes he was suspected of committing and about which they intended to ask questions. To hold that such knowledge is relevant would not undermine the "'virtue of informing police and prosecutors with specificity' as to how a pretrial questioning of a suspect must be conducted," nor would it interfere with the use of legitimate interrogation techniques.

The interrogation tactics utilized in this case demonstrate the relevance of the information Spring did not receive. The agents evidently hoped to obtain from Spring a valid confession to the federal firearms charge for which he was arrested and then parlay this admission into an additional confession of first-degree murder. Spring could not have expected questions about the latter, separate offense when he agreed to waive his rights, as it occurred in a different State and was a violation of state law outside the normal investigative focus of federal Alcohol, Tobacco, and Firearms agents.

"Interrogators describe the point of the first admission as the 'breakthrough' and the 'beachhead,' which once obtained will give them enormous 'tactical advantages.'" The coercive aspects of the psychological ploy intended in this case, when combined with an element of surprise which may far too easily rise to a level of deception,[1] cannot be justified in light of *Miranda*'s strict requirements that the suspect's waiver and confession be voluntary, knowing, and intelligent. If a suspect has signed a waiver form with the intention of making a statement regarding a specifically alleged crime, the Court today would hold this waiver valid with respect to questioning about any other crime, regardless of its relation to the charges the suspect believes he will be asked to address. Yet once this waiver is given and the intended statement made, the protections afforded by *Miranda* against the "inherently compelling pressures" of the custodial interrogation have effectively dissipated. Additional questioning about entirely separate and more serious suspicions of criminal activity can take unfair advantage of the suspect's psychological state, as the unexpected questions cause the compulsive pressures suddenly to reappear. Given this technique of interrogation, a suspect's understanding of the topics planned for questioning is, therefore, at the very least "relevant" to assessing whether his decision to talk to the officers was voluntarily, knowingly, and intelligently made.

Not only is the suspect's awareness of the suspected criminal conduct relevant, its absence may be determinative in a given case. The State's burden of proving that a suspect's waiver was voluntary, knowing, and intelligent is a "heavy" one. We are to "'indulge every reasonable presumption against waiver' of fundamental constitutional rights" and we shall "'not presume acquiescence in the loss of fundamental rights.'" It is reasonable to conclude that, had Spring known of the federal agents' intent to ask questions about a murder unrelated to the offense for which he was arrested, he would not have consented to interrogation without first consulting his attorney. In this case, I would therefore accept the determination of the Colorado Supreme Court that Spring did not voluntarily, knowingly, and intelligently waive his Fifth Amendment rights.[2]

I dissent.

---

[1] The Court rejects, for now, the notion that "mere silence" by law enforcement officials may deprive the suspect of information so relevant to his decision to waive his *Miranda* rights as to constitute deception, though it does acknowledge that circumstances can arise in which an affirmative misrepresentation by the officers will invalidate the suspect's waiver. In *Moran v. Burbine*, 475 U.S. 412, 453 (1986), I joined Justice Stevens' dissenting opinion, which stated that "there can be no constitutional distinction . . . between a deceptive misstatement and the concealment by the police of the critical fact that an attorney retained by the accused or his family has offered assistance. . . ." I would hold the officers' failure in the present case to inform Spring of their intent to question him about the Colorado murder equally critical. *Miranda* places an especially heavy burden on the State to show that a suspect waived his privilege against self-incrimination: "*[A]ny* evidence that the accused was threatened, *tricked*, or cajoled into a waiver will, of course, show that the defendant did not voluntarily waive his privilege." (emphasis added). I would hold that the interrogating officers' preconceived plan in this case to obtain a waiver from Spring with reference to a particular federal offense and then ask about a separate, unrelated state offense precludes the State from carrying that heavy burden.

[2] Nothing in the Court's decision today precludes the courts of Colorado from interpreting that State's Constitution as independently recognizing a suspect's knowledge of the intended scope of interrogation as a relevant factor for determining whether he validly waived his right against self-incrimination under state law. See Colo. Const., Art. II, § 18.

## QUESTIONS AND NOTES

**1.** The Colorado Supreme Court seems to prefer a "standard" to a "rule" in regard to ascertaining what warnings ought to be given. Apart from the issue of whether the warning was adequate in this case, do you think that this would be a good idea?

**2.** If the dissent had prevailed, would the police have been deprived of a legitimate stratagem for bringing a murderer to justice? Explain.

**3.** Should the fact that the defendant is free to stop questioning whenever he doesn't like the topic be a complete answer to the dissent?

**4.** In the context of this case, should "wisdom" and "validity" or "voluntariness" be separated from one another as the majority has done?

**5.** A competent defense attorney should carefully heed Justice Marshall's suggestion in footnote 2.

## C.   Invoking Miranda

**Fare v. Michael C.**

442 U.S. 707 (1979)

Mr. Justice BLACKMUN delivered the opinion of the Court.

In *Miranda*, this Court established certain procedural safeguards designed to protect the rights of an accused, under the Fifth and Fourteenth Amendments, to be free from compelled self-incrimination during custodial interrogation. The Court specified, among other things, that if the accused indicates in any manner that he wishes to remain silent or to consult an attorney, interrogation must cease, and any statement obtained from him during interrogation thereafter may not be admitted against him at his trial.

In this case, the State of California, in the person of its acting chief probation officer, attacks the conclusion of the Supreme Court of California that a juvenile's request, made while undergoing custodial interrogation, to see his *probation officer* is *per se* an invocation of the juvenile's Fifth Amendment rights as pronounced in *Miranda*.

I

Respondent Michael C. was implicated in the murder of Robert Yeager. The murder occurred during a robbery of the victim's home on January 19, 1976. A small truck registered in the name of respondent's mother was identified as having been near the Yeager home at the time of the killing, and a young man answering respondent's description was seen by witnesses near the truck and near the home shortly before Yeager was murdered.

On the basis of this information, Van Nuys, Cal., police took respondent into custody at approximately 6:30 p.m. on February 4. Respondent then was 16½ years old and on probation to the Juvenile Court. He had been on probation since the age of 12. Approximately one year earlier he had served a term in a youth corrections camp under the supervision of the Juvenile Court. He had a record of several previous offenses, including burglary of guns and purse snatching, stretching back over several years.

Upon respondent's arrival at the Van Nuys station house two police officers began to interrogate him. The officers and respondent were the only persons in the room during the interrogation. The conversation was tape-recorded. One of the officers initiated the interview by informing respondent that he had been brought in for questioning in relation to a murder. The officer fully advised respondent of his *Miranda* rights. The following exchange then occurred, as set out in the opinion of the California Supreme Court, *In re Michael C.*, (emphasis added by that court):

"Q. . . . Do you understand all of these rights as I have explained them to you?

"A. Yeah.

"Q. Okay, do you wish to give up your right to remain silent and talk to us about this murder?

"A. What murder? I don't know about no murder.

"Q. I'll explain to you which one it is if you want to talk to us about it.

"A. Yeah, I might talk to you.

"Q. Do you want to give up your right to have an attorney present here while we talk about it?

"A. Can I have my probation officer here?

"Q. Well I can't get a hold of your probation officer right now. You have the right to an attorney.

"A. How I know you guys won't pull no police officer in and tell me he's an attorney?

"Q. Huh?

"A. [How I know you guys won't pull no police officer in and tell me he's an attorney?]

"Q. Your probation officer is Mr. Christiansen.

"A. Yeah.

"Q. Well I'm not going to call Mr. Christiansen tonight. There's a good chance we can talk to him later, but I'm not going to call him right now. If you want to talk to us without an attorney present, you can. If you don't want to, you don't have to. But if you want to say something, you can, and if you don't want to say something you don't have to. That's your right. You understand that right?

"A. Yeah.

"Q. Okay, will you talk to us without an attorney present?

"A. Yeah I want to talk to you."

Respondent thereupon proceeded to answer questions put to him by the officers. He made statements and drew sketches that incriminated him in the Yeager murder.

[Respondent] alleged that the statements had been obtained in violation of *Miranda* in that his request to see his probation officer at the outset of the questioning constituted an invocation of his Fifth Amendment right to remain silent, just as if he had requested the assistance of an attorney. Accordingly, respondent argued that since the interrogation did not cease until he had a chance to confer with his probation officer, the statements and sketches could not be admitted against him in the Juvenile Court proceedings. In so arguing, respondent relied by analogy on the decision in *People v. Burton*, 6 Cal.3d 375, 99 Cal.Rptr. 1, 491 P.2d 793 (1971), where the Supreme Court of California had held that a minor's request, made during custodial interrogation, to see his parents constituted an invocation of the minor's Fifth Amendment rights.

In support of his suppression motion, respondent called his probation officer, Charles P. Christiansen, as a witness. Christiansen testified that he had instructed respondent that if at any time he had "a concern with his family," or ever had "a police contact," he should get in touch with his probation officer immediately. The witness stated that, on a previous occasion, when respondent had had a police contact and had failed to communicate with Christiansen, the probation officer had reprimanded him. This testimony, respondent argued, indicated that when he asked for his probation officer, he was in fact asserting his right to remain silent in the face of further questioning.

## II

We note at the outset that it is clear that the judgment of the California Supreme Court rests firmly on that court's interpretation of federal law.

This Court, however, has not heretofore extended the *per se* aspects of the *Miranda* safeguards beyond the scope of the holding in the *Miranda* case itself.[4] We therefore must examine the California court's decision to determine whether that court's conclusion so to extend *Miranda* is in harmony with *Miranda*'s underlying principles. For it is clear that "a State may not impose . . . greater restrictions as a matter of *federal constitutional law* when this Court specifically refrains from imposing them."

The rule the Court established in *Miranda* is clear. In order to be able to use statements obtained during custodial interrogation of the accused, the State must warn the accused prior to such questioning of his right to remain silent and of his right to have counsel, retained or appointed, present during interrogation. "Once [such] warnings have been given, the subsequent procedure is clear."

"If the individual indicates in any manner, at any time prior to or during questioning, that he wishes to remain silent, the interrogation must cease. At this point he has shown that he intends to exercise his Fifth Amendment privilege; any statement taken after the person invokes his privilege cannot be other than the product of compulsion, subtle or otherwise. . . . If the individual states that he wants an attorney, the interrogation must cease until an attorney is present. At that time, the individual must have an opportunity to confer with the attorney and to have him present during any subsequent questioning. If the individual cannot obtain an attorney and he indicates that he wants one before speaking to police, they must respect his decision to remain silent."

Any statements obtained during custodial interrogation conducted in violation of these rules may not be admitted against the accused, at least during the State's case in chief.

---

[4] Indeed, this Court has not yet held that *Miranda* applies with full force to exclude evidence obtained in violation of its proscriptions from consideration in juvenile proceedings, which for certain purposes have been distinguished from formal criminal prosecutions. See *McKeiver v. Pennsylvania*, 403 U.S. 528, 540-541 (1971) (plurality opinion). We do not decide that issue today. In view of our disposition of this case, we assume without deciding that the *Miranda* principles were fully applicable to the present proceedings.

Whatever the defects, if any, of this relatively rigid requirement that interrogation must cease upon the accused's request for an attorney, *Miranda*'s holding has the virtue of informing police and prosecutors with specificity as to what they may do in conducting custodial interrogation, and of informing courts under what circumstances statements obtained during such interrogation are not admissible. This gain in specificity, which benefits the accused and the State alike, has been thought to outweigh the burdens that the decision in *Miranda* imposes on law enforcement agencies and the courts by requiring the suppression of trustworthy and highly probative evidence even though the confession might be voluntary under traditional Fifth Amendment analysis.

The California court in this case, however, significantly has extended this rule by providing that a request by a juvenile for his probation officer has the same effect as a request for an attorney. Based on the court's belief that the probation officer occupies a position as a trusted guardian figure in the minor's life that would make it normal for the minor to turn to the officer when apprehended by the police, and based as well on the state-law requirement that the officer represent the interest of the juvenile, the California decision found that consultation with a probation officer fulfilled the role for the juvenile that consultation with an attorney does in general, acting as a "protective [device] . . . to dispel the compulsion inherent in custodial surroundings."

The rule in *Miranda*, however, was based on this Court's perception that the lawyer occupies a critical position in our legal system because of his unique ability to protect the Fifth Amendment rights of a client undergoing custodial interrogation. Because of this special ability of the lawyer to help the client preserve his Fifth Amendment rights once the client becomes enmeshed in the adversary process, the Court found that "the right to have counsel present at the interrogation is indispensable to the protection of the Fifth Amendment privilege under the system" established by the Court. Moreover, the lawyer's presence helps guard against overreaching by the police and ensures that any statements actually obtained are accurately transcribed for presentation into evidence.

A probation officer is not in the same posture with regard to either the accused or the system of justice as a whole. Often he is not trained in the law, and so is not in a position to advise the accused as to his legal rights. Neither is he a trained advocate, skilled in the representation of the interests of his client before both police and courts. He does not assume the power to act on behalf of his client by

virtue of his status as adviser, nor are the communications of the accused to the probation officer shielded by the lawyer-client privilege.

Moreover, the probation officer is the employee of the State which seeks to prosecute the alleged offender. He is a peace officer, and as such is allied, to a greater or lesser extent, with his fellow peace officers. He owes an obligation to the State, notwithstanding the obligation he may also owe the juvenile under his supervision. In most cases, the probation officer is duty bound to report wrongdoing by the juvenile when it comes to his attention, even if by communication from the juvenile himself. Indeed, when this case arose, the probation officer had the responsibility for filing the petition alleging wrongdoing by the juvenile and seeking to have him taken into the custody of the Juvenile Court. It was respondent's probation officer who filed the petition against him, and it is the acting chief of probation for the State of California, a probation officer, who is petitioner in this Court today.

In these circumstances, it cannot be said that the probation officer is able to offer the type of independent advice that an accused would expect from a lawyer retained or assigned to assist him during questioning. Indeed, the probation officer's duty to his employer in many, if not most, cases would conflict sharply with the interests of the juvenile. For where an attorney might well advise his client to remain silent in the face of interrogation by the police, and in doing so would be "exercising [his] good professional judgment . . . to protect to the extent of his ability the rights of his client," a probation officer would be bound to advise his charge to cooperate with the police. The justices who concurred in the opinion of the California Supreme Court in this case aptly noted: "Where a conflict between the minor and the law arises, the probation officer can be neither neutral nor in the minor's corner." It thus is doubtful that a general rule can be established that a juvenile, in every case, looks to his probation officer as a "trusted guardian figure" rather than as an officer of the court system that imposes punishment.

We thus believe it clear that the probation officer is not in a position to offer the type of legal assistance necessary to protect the Fifth Amendment rights of an accused undergoing custodial interrogation that a lawyer can offer. The Court in *Miranda* recognized that "the attorney plays a vital role in the administration of criminal justice under our Constitution." It is this pivotal role of legal counsel that justifies the *per se* rule established in *Miranda*, and that distinguishes the request for counsel from the request for a probation officer, a clergyman, or a close friend. A probation officer simply is not necessary, in the way an attorney is, for the protection of the legal rights of the accused, juvenile or adult. He is significantly handicapped by the position he occupies in the juvenile system from serving as an effective protector of the rights of a juvenile suspected of a crime.

Similarly, the fact that the State has created a statutory duty on the part of the probation officer to protect the interests of the juvenile does not render the probation officer any more capable of rendering legal assistance to the juvenile or of protecting his legal rights, especially in light of the fact that the State has also legislated a duty on the part of the officer to report wrongdoing by the juvenile and serve the ends of the juvenile court system. The State cannot transmute the relationship between probation officer and juvenile offender into the type of relationship between attorney and client that was essential to the holding of *Miranda* simply by legislating an amorphous "duty to advise and care for the juvenile defendant." Though such a statutory duty might serve to distinguish to some degree the probation officer from the coach and the clergyman, it does not justify the extension of *Miranda* to requests to see probation officers. If it did, the State could expand the class of persons covered by the *Miranda per se* rule simply by creating a duty to care for the juvenile on the part of other persons, regardless of whether the logic of *Miranda* would justify that extension.

We hold, therefore, that it was error to find that the request by respondent to speak with his probation officer *per se* constituted an invocation of respondent's Fifth Amendment right to be free from compelled self-incrimination. It therefore was also error to hold that because the police did not then cease interrogating respondent the statements he made during interrogation should have been suppressed.

### III

In this case, we conclude that the California Supreme Court should have determined the issue of waiver on the basis of all the circumstances surrounding the interrogation of respondent. The Juvenile Court found that under this approach, respondent in fact had waived his Fifth Amendment rights and consented to interrogation by the police after his request to see his probation officer was denied. Given its view of the case, of course, the California Supreme Court did not consider this issue, though it did hold that the State had failed to prove that, notwithstanding respondent's request to see his probation officer, respondent had not intended to invoke his Fifth Amendment rights.

We feel that the conclusion of the Juvenile Court was correct. The transcript of the interrogation reveals that the police officers conducting the interrogation took care to ensure that respondent understood his rights. They fully explained to respondent that he was being questioned in connection with a murder. They then informed him of all the rights delineated in *Miranda*, and ascertained that respondent understood those rights. There is no indication in the record that respondent failed to understand what the officers told him. Moreover, after his request to see his probation officer had been denied, and after the police officer once more had explained his rights to him, respondent clearly expressed his willingness to waive his rights and continue the interrogation.

Further, no special factors indicate that respondent was unable to understand the nature of his actions. He was a 16½-year-old juvenile with considerable experience with the police. He had a record of several arrests. He had served time in a youth camp, and he had been on probation for several years. He was under the full-time supervision of probation authorities. There is no indication that he was of insufficient intelligence to understand the rights he was waiving, or what the consequences of that waiver would be. He was not worn down by improper interrogation tactics or lengthy questioning or by trickery or deceit.

On these facts, we think it clear that respondent voluntarily and knowingly waived his Fifth Amendment rights. Respondent argues, however, that any statements he made during interrogation were coerced. Specifically, respondent alleges that the police made threats and promises during the interrogation to pressure him into cooperating in the hope of obtaining leniency for his cooperative attitude. He notes also that he repeatedly told the officers during his interrogation that he wished to stop answering their questions, but that the officers ignored his pleas. He argues further that the record reveals that he was afraid that the police would coerce him, and that this fear caused him to cooperate. He points out that at one point the transcript revealed that he wept during the interrogation.

Review of the entire transcript reveals that respondent's claims of coercion are without merit. As noted, the police took care to inform respondent of his rights and to ensure that he understood them. The officers did not intimidate or threaten respondent in any way. Their questioning was restrained and free from the abuses that so concerned the Court in *Miranda*. The police did indeed indicate that a cooperative attitude would be to respondent's benefit, but their remarks in this regard were far from threatening or coercive. And respondent's allegation that he repeatedly asked that the interrogation cease goes too far: at some points he did state that he did not know the answer to a question put to him or that he could not, or would not, answer the question, but these statements were not assertions of his right to remain silent.

### IV

We hold, in short, that the California Supreme Court erred in finding that a juvenile's request for his probation officer was a *per se* invocation of that juvenile's Fifth Amendment rights under *Miranda*. We conclude, rather, that whether the statements obtained during subsequent interrogation of a juvenile who has asked to see his probation officer, but who has not asked to consult an attorney or expressly asserted his right to remain silent, are admissible on the basis of waiver remains a question to be resolved on the totality of the circumstances surrounding the interrogation. On the basis of the record in this case, we hold that the Juvenile Court's findings that respondent voluntarily and knowingly waived his rights and consented to continued interrogation, and that the statements obtained from him were voluntary, were proper, and that the admission of those statements in the proceeding against respondent in Juvenile Court was correct. The judgment of the Supreme Court of California is reversed, and the case is remanded for further proceedings not inconsistent with this opinion.

Mr. Justice MARSHALL, with whom Mr. Justice BRENNAN and Mr. Justice STEVENS join, dissenting.

In *Miranda*, this Court sought to ensure that the inherently coercive pressures of custodial interrogation would not vitiate a suspect's privilege against self-incrimination. Noting that these pressures "can operate very quickly to overbear the will of one merely made aware of his privilege," the Court held:

> "If [a suspect in custody] indicates in any manner, at any time prior to or during questioning, that he wishes to remain silent, the interrogation must cease. At this point he has shown that he intends to exercise his Fifth Amendment privilege; any statement taken after the person invokes his privilege cannot be other than the product of compulsion, subtle or otherwise. . . . If the individual states that he wants an attorney, the interrogation must cease until an attorney is present."

As this Court has consistently recognized, the coerciveness of the custodial setting is of heightened concern where, as here, a juvenile is under investigation. In *Haley v. Ohio*, 332 U.S. 596 (1948), the plurality reasoned that because a 15½-year-old minor was particularly susceptible to overbearing interrogation tactics, the voluntariness of his confession could not "be judged by the more exacting standards of maturity."

It is therefore critical in the present context that we construe *Miranda*'s prophylactic requirements broadly to accomplish their intended purpose—"dispel[ling] the compulsion inherent in custodial surroundings." To effectuate this purpose, the Court must ensure that the "protective device" of legal counsel be readily available, and that any intimation of a desire to preclude questioning be scrupulously honored. Thus, I believe *Miranda* requires that interrogation cease whenever a juvenile requests an adult who is obligated to represent his interests. Such a request, in my judgment, constitutes both an attempt to obtain advice and a general invocation of the right to silence. For, as the California Supreme Court recognized, "[i]t is fatuous to assume that a minor in custody will be in a position to call an attorney for assistance," or that he will trust the police to obtain a lawyer for him.[1] A juvenile in these circumstances will likely turn to his parents, or another adult responsible for his welfare, as the only means of securing legal counsel. Moreover, a request for such adult assistance is surely inconsistent with a present desire to speak freely. Requiring a strict verbal formula to invoke the protections of *Miranda* would "protect the knowledgeable accused from station house coercion while abandoning the young person who knows no more than to ask for the . . . person he trusts."

On my reading of *Miranda*, a California juvenile's request for his probation officer should be treated as a *per se* assertion of Fifth Amendment rights. The California Supreme Court determined that probation officers have a statutory duty to represent minors' interests and, indeed, are "trusted guardian figure[s]" to whom a juvenile would likely turn for assistance. In addition, the court found, probation officers are particularly well suited to assist

---

[1] The facts of the instant case are illustrative. When the police offered to obtain an attorney for respondent, he replied: "How I know you guys won't pull no police officer in and tell me he's an attorney?" Significantly, the police made no attempt to allay that concern.

a juvenile "on such matters as to whether or not he should obtain an attorney" and "how to conduct himself with police." Hence, a juvenile's request for a probation officer may frequently be an attempt to secure protection from the coercive aspects of custodial questioning.[2]

This Court concludes, however, that because a probation officer has law enforcement duties, juveniles generally would not call upon him to represent their interests, and if they did, would not be well served. But that conclusion ignores the California Supreme Court's express determination that the officer's responsibility to initiate juvenile proceedings did not negate his function as personal adviser to his wards. I decline to second-guess that court's assessment of state law.[4] Further, although the majority here speculates that probation officers have a duty to advise cooperation with the police—a proposition suggested only in the concurring opinion of two justices below—respondent's probation officer instructed all his charges "not to go and admit openly to an offense, [but rather] to get some type of advice from . . . parents or a lawyer." Absent an explicit statutory provision or judicial holding, the officer's assessment of the obligations imposed by state law is entitled to deference by this Court.

Thus, given the role of probation officers under California law, a juvenile's request to see his officer may reflect a desire for precisely the kind of assistance *Miranda* guarantees an accused before he waives his Fifth Amendment rights. At the very least, such a request signals a desire to remain silent

---

[2] The Court intimates that construing a request for a probation officer as an invocation of the Fifth Amendment privilege would undermine the specificity of *Miranda*'s prophylactic rules. Yet the Court concedes that the statutory duty to "advise and care for the juvenile defendant" distinguishes probation officers from other adults, such as coaches and clergymen. Since law enforcement officials should be on notice of such legal relationships, they would presumably have no difficulty determining whether a suspect has asserted his Fifth Amendment rights.

Although I agree with my Brother Powell that, on the facts here, respondent was not "subjected to a fair interrogation free from inherently coercive circumstances," I do not believe a case-by-case approach provides police sufficient guidance, or affords juveniles adequate protection.

[4] One thing is certain. The California Supreme Court is more familiar with the duties and performance of its probation officers than we are.

until contact with the officer is made. Because the Court's contrary determination withdraws the safeguards of *Miranda* from those most in need of protection, I respectfully dissent.

Mr. Justice POWELL, dissenting.

Although I agree with the Court that the Supreme Court of California misconstrued *Miranda*, I would not reverse the California court's judgment. This Court repeatedly has recognized that "the greatest care" must be taken to assure that an alleged confession of a juvenile was voluntary. Respondent was a young person, 16 years old at the time of his arrest and the subsequent prolonged interrogation at the station house. Although respondent had had prior brushes with the law, and was under supervision by a probation officer, the taped transcript of his interrogation—as well as his testimony at the suppression hearing—demonstrates that he was immature, emotional,[2] and uneducated, and therefore was likely to be vulnerable to the skillful, two-on-one, repetitive style of interrogation to which he was subjected.

When given *Miranda* warnings and asked whether he desired an attorney, respondent requested permission to "have my probation officer here," a request that was refused. That officer testified later that he had communicated frequently with respondent, that respondent had serious and "extensive" family problems, and that the officer had instructed respondent to call him immediately "at any time he has a police contact, even if they stop him and talk to him on the street."[3] The reasons given by the probation officer for having so instructed his charge were substantially the same reasons that prompt this Court to examine with special care the circumstances under which a minor's alleged confession was obtained. After stating that respondent had been "going through problems," the officer observed that "many times the kids don't understand what is going on, and what they are supposed to do relative to police. . . ." This view of the limited

---

[2] The Juvenile Court Judge observed that he had "heard the tapes" of the interrogation, and was "aware of the fact that Michael [respondent] was crying at the time he talked to the police officers."

[3] The Supreme Court of California stated that a "probation officer is an official appointed pursuant to legislative enactment 'to represent the interests' of the juvenile [and] . . . has borne the duty to advise and care for the juvenile defendant." 21 Cal.3d, at 477, 146 Cal.Rptr., at 361, 579 P.2d, at 10.

understanding of the average 16-year-old was borne out by respondent's question when, during interrogation, he was advised of his right to an attorney: "How I know you guys won't pull no police officer in and tell me he's an attorney?" It was during this part of the interrogation that the police had denied respondent's request to "have my probation officer here."

The police then proceeded, despite respondent's repeated denial of any connection to the murder under investigation, persistently to press interrogation until they extracted a confession. In *In re Gault*, in addressing police interrogation of detained juveniles, the Court stated:

> "If counsel was not present for some permissible reason when an admission was obtained [from a child], the greatest care must be taken to assure that the admission was voluntary, in the sense not only that it was not coerced or suggested, but also that it was not the product of ignorance of rights or of adolescent fantasy, fright or despair." 387 U.S., at 55.

It is clear that the interrogating police did not exercise "the greatest care" to assure that respondent's "admission was voluntary."[4] In the absence of counsel, and having refused to call the probation officer, they nevertheless engaged in protracted interrogation.

Although I view the case as close, I am not satisfied that this particular 16-year-old boy, in this particular situation, was subjected to a fair interrogation free from inherently coercive circumstances. For these reasons, I would affirm the judgment of the Supreme Court of California.

---

[4] Minors who become embroiled with the law range from the very young up to those on the brink of majority. Some of the older minors become fully "street-wise," hardened criminals, deserving no greater consideration than that properly accorded all persons suspected of crime. Other minors are more of a child than an adult. As the Court indicated in *In re Gault*, 387 U.S. 1 (1967), the facts relevant to the care to be exercised in a particular case vary widely. They include the minor's age, actual maturity, family environment, education, emotional and mental stability, and, of course, any prior record he might have.

## QUESTIONS AND NOTES

**1.** With whom would you have sided had you been on the Court (Blackmun, Marshall, Powell, or none of the above)? Why?

**2.** After *Fare*, if a juvenile asks to see a parent would (should) that be viewed as a *per se* invocation of *Miranda*?

**3.** Even Justice Marshall apparently concedes that a request to see a football coach or clergyman is distinguishable from a request to see a probation officer and that a denial of such a request would not necessarily lead to a *per se* finding of involuntariness. Do you agree? Is there any good reason to deny a suspect access to *anybody* that she or he desires to see?

**4.** Even if the specifics of *Miranda* does not cover this case, does its underlying philosophy?

**5.** Is *Fare*, like *Miranda*, a battle over whether to use rules or standards? Is there any good reason for standards to prevail in *Fare*, and rules to apply in *Miranda*?

**6.** Do you think that the police acted wisely in *not* calling Michael C's probation officer? If you had been the police attorney and had been asked whether he should have been allowed to call his officer, what would you have advised? Why?

**7.** Is there any good reason *not* to apply *Miranda* to juveniles? Conversely, should *Miranda* apply *more* strictly to juveniles? Why?

**8.** In *Mosely*, we will examine the significance of invoking the right to silence. In the cases that follow, we will contrast the rule governing the right to counsel.

## Michigan v. Mosley
### 423 U.S. 96 (1975)

Mr. Justice STEWART delivered the opinion of the Court.

The respondent, Richard Bert Mosley, was arrested in Detroit, Mich., in the early afternoon of April 8, 1971, in connection with robberies that had recently occurred at the Blue Goose Bar and the White Tower Restaurant on that city's lower east side. After effecting the arrest, Detective Cowie brought Mosley to the Robbery, Breaking and Entering Bureau of the Police Department, located on the fourth floor of the departmental headquarters building. The officer advised Mosley of his rights under this Court's decision in *Miranda*, and had him read and sign the department's constitutional rights notification certificate. After filling out the necessary arrest papers, Cowie began questioning Mosley about the robbery of the White Tower Restaurant. When Mosley said he did not want to answer any questions about the robberies, Cowie promptly ceased the interrogation. The completion of the arrest papers and the questioning of Mosley together took approximately 20 minutes. At no time during the questioning did Mosley indicate a desire to consult with a lawyer, and there is no claim that the procedures followed to this point did not fully comply with the strictures of the *Miranda* opinion. Mosley was then taken to a ninth-floor cell block.

Shortly after 6 p.m., Detective Hill of the Detroit Police Department Homicide Bureau brought Mosley from the cell block to the fifth-floor office of the Homicide Bureau for questioning about the fatal shooting of a man named Leroy Williams. Williams had been killed on January 9, 1971, during a holdup attempt outside the 101 Ranch Bar in Detroit. Mosley had not been arrested on this charge or interrogated about it by Detective Cowie.[2] Before questioning Mosley about this homicide, Detective Hill carefully advised him of his "*Miranda* rights." Mosley read the notification form both silently and aloud, and Detective Hill then read and explained the warnings to him and had him sign the form. Mosley at first denied any involvement in the Williams murder, but after the officer told him that Anthony Smith had confessed to participating in the

slaying and had named him as the "shooter," Mosley made a statement implicating himself in the homicide.[3] The interrogation by Detective Hill lasted approximately 15 minutes, and at no time during its course did Mosley ask to consult with a lawyer or indicate that he did not want to discuss the homicide. In short, there is no claim that the procedures followed during Detective Hill's interrogation of Mosley, standing alone, did not fully comply with the strictures of the *Miranda* opinion.

Mosley was subsequently charged in a one-count information with first-degree murder. Before the trial he moved to suppress his incriminating statement on a number of grounds, among them the claim that under the doctrine of the *Miranda* case it was constitutionally impermissible for Detective Hill to question him about the Williams murder after he had told Detective Cowie that he did not want to answer any questions about the robberies.[5] The trial court denied the motion to suppress after an evidentiary hearing, and the incriminating statement was subsequently introduced in evidence against Mosley at his trial. The jury convicted Mosley of first-degree murder, and the court imposed a mandatory sentence of life imprisonment.

The appellate court reversed the judgment of conviction, holding that Detective Hill's interrogation of Mosley had been a *per se* violation of the *Miranda* doctrine. Accordingly, without reaching Mosley's other contentions, the Court remanded the case for a new trial with instructions that Mosley's statement be suppressed as evidence.

Neither party in the present case challenges the continuing validity of the *Miranda* decision, or of

---

[2] The original tip to Detective Cowie had, however, implicated Mosley in the Williams murder.

[3] During cross-examination by Mosley's counsel at the evidentiary hearing, Detective Hill conceded that Smith in fact had not confessed but had "denied a physical participation in the robbery."

[5] In addition to the claim that Detective Hill's questioning violated *Miranda*, Mosley contended that the statement was the product of an illegal arrest, that the statement was inadmissible because he had not been taken before a judicial officer without unnecessary delay, and that it had been obtained through trickery and promises of leniency. He argued that these circumstances, either independently or in combination, required the suppression of his incriminating statement.

any of the so-called guidelines it established to protect what the Court there said was a person's constitutional privilege against compulsory self-incrimination. The issue in this case, rather, is whether the conduct of the Detroit police that led to Mosley's incriminating statement did in fact violate the *Miranda* "guidelines," so as to render the statement inadmissible in evidence against Mosley at his trial. Resolution of the question turns almost entirely on the interpretation of a single passage in the *Miranda* opinion, upon which the Michigan appellate court relied in finding a *per se* violation of *Miranda*:

> "Once warnings have been given, the subsequent procedure is clear. If the individual indicates in any manner, at any time prior to or during questioning, that he wishes to remain silent, the interrogation must cease. At this point he has shown that he intends to exercise his Fifth Amendment privilege; any statement taken after the person invokes his privilege cannot be other than the product of compulsion, subtle or otherwise. Without the right to cut off questioning, the setting of in-custody interrogation operates on the individual to overcome free choice in producing a statement after the privilege has been once invoked."

This passage states that "the interrogation must cease" when the person in custody indicates that "he wishes to remain silent." It does not state under what circumstances, if any, a resumption of questioning is permissible.[8] The passage could be literally read to mean that a person who has invoked his "right to silence" can never again be subjected to custodial interrogation by any police officer at any time or place on any subject. Another possible construction of the passage would characterize "any

---

[8] The Court did state in a footnote:

"If an individual indicates his desire to remain silent, but has an attorney present, there may be some circumstances in which further questioning would be permissible. In the absence of evidence of overbearing, statements then made in the presence of counsel might be free of the compelling influence of the interrogation process and might fairly be construed as a waiver of the privilege for purposes of these statements."

This footnote in the *Miranda* opinion is not relevant to the present case, since Mosley did not have an attorney present at the time he declined to answer Detective Cowie's questions, and the officer did not continue to question Mosley but instead ceased the interrogation in compliance with *Miranda*'s dictates.

statement taken after the person invokes his privilege" as "the product of compulsion" and would therefore mandate its exclusion from evidence, even if it were volunteered by the person in custody without any further interrogation whatever. Or the passage could be interpreted to require only the immediate cessation of questioning, and to permit a resumption of interrogation after a momentary respite.

It is evident that any of these possible literal interpretations would lead to absurd and unintended results. To permit the continuation of custodial interrogation after a momentary cessation would clearly frustrate the purposes of *Miranda* by allowing repeated rounds of questioning to undermine the will of the person being questioned. At the other extreme, a blanket prohibition against the taking of voluntary statements or a permanent immunity from further interrogation, regardless of the circumstances, would transform the *Miranda* safeguards into wholly irrational obstacles to legitimate police investigative activity, and deprive suspects of an opportunity to make informed and intelligent assessments of their interests. Clearly, therefore, neither this passage nor any other passage in the *Miranda* opinion can sensibly be read to create a *per se* proscription of indefinite duration upon any further questioning by any police officer on any subject, once the person in custody has indicated a desire to remain silent.

A reasonable and faithful interpretation of the *Miranda* opinion must rest on the intention of the Court in that case to adopt "fully effective means . . . to notify the person of his right of silence and to assure that the exercise of the right will be scrupulously honored. . . ." The critical safeguard identified in the passage at issue is a person's "right to cut off questioning." Through the exercise of his option to terminate questioning he can control the time at which questioning occurs, the subjects discussed, and the duration of the interrogation. The requirement that law enforcement authorities must respect a person's exercise of that option counteracts the coercive pressures of the custodial setting. We therefore conclude that the admissibility of statements obtained after the person in custody has decided to remain silent depends under *Miranda* on whether his "right to cut off questioning" was "scrupulously honored."[10]

---

[10] The dissenting opinion asserts that *Miranda* established a requirement that once a person has indicated a desire to remain silent, questioning may be resumed only when counsel is present. But clearly the Court in *Miranda* imposed no such requirement,

A review of the circumstances leading to Mosley's confession reveals that his "right to cut off questioning" was fully respected in this case. Before his initial interrogation, Mosley was carefully advised that he was under no obligation to answer any questions and could remain silent if he wished. He orally acknowledged that he understood the *Miranda* warnings and then signed a printed notification-of-rights form. When Mosley stated that he did not want to discuss the robberies, Detective Cowie immediately ceased the interrogation and did not try either to resume the questioning or in any way to persuade Mosley to reconsider his position. After an interval of more than two hours, Mosley was questioned by another police officer at another location about an unrelated holdup murder. He was given full and complete *Miranda* warnings at the outset of the second interrogation. He was thus reminded again that he could remain silent and could consult with a lawyer, and was carefully given a full and fair opportunity to exercise these options. The subsequent questioning did not undercut Mosley's previous decision not to answer Detective Cowie's inquiries. Detective Hill did not resume the interrogation about the White Tower Restaurant robbery or inquire about the Blue Goose Bar robbery, but instead focused exclusively on the Leroy Williams homicide, a crime different in nature and in time and place of occurrence from the robberies for which Mosley had been arrested and interrogated by Detective Cowie. Although it is not clear from the record how much Detective Hill knew about the earlier interrogation, his questioning of Mosley about an unrelated homicide was quite consistent with a reasonable interpretation of Mosley's earlier refusal to answer any questions about the robberies.

This is not a case, therefore, where the police failed to honor a decision of a person in custody to cut off questioning, either by refusing to discontinue the interrogation upon request or by persisting in repeated efforts to wear down his resistance and make him change his mind. In contrast to such practices, the police here immediately ceased the interrogation, resumed questioning only after the passage of a significant period of time and the provision of a fresh set of warnings, and restricted the second interrogation to a crime that had not been a subject of the earlier interrogation.

for it distinguished between the procedural safeguards triggered by a request to remain silent and a request for an attorney and directed that "the interrogation must cease until an attorney is present" only "[i]f the individual states that he wants an attorney."

The Michigan Court of Appeals viewed this case as factually similar to *Westover*, a companion case to *Miranda*. But the controlling facts of the two cases are strikingly different.

In *Westover*, the petitioner was arrested by the Kansas City police at 9:45 p.m. and taken to the police station. Without giving any advisory warnings of any kind to Westover, the police questioned him that night and throughout the next morning about various local robberies. At noon, three FBI agents took over, gave advisory warnings to Westover, and proceeded to question him about two California bank robberies. After two hours of questioning, the petitioner confessed to the California crimes. The Court held that the confession obtained by the FBI was inadmissible because the interrogation leading to the petitioner's statement followed on the heels of prolonged questioning that was commenced and continued by the Kansas City police without preliminary warnings to Westover of any kind. The Court found that "the federal authorities were the beneficiaries of the pressure applied by the local in-custody interrogation" and that the belated warnings given by the federal officers were "not sufficient to protect" Westover because from his point of view "the warnings came at the end of the interrogation process."

Here, by contrast, the police gave full "*Miranda* warnings" to Mosley at the very outset of each interrogation, subjected him to only a brief period of initial questioning, and suspended questioning entirely for a significant period before beginning the interrogation that led to his incriminating statement. The cardinal fact of *Westover*—the failure of the police officers to give any warnings whatever to the person in their custody before embarking on an intense and prolonged interrogation of him—was simply not present in this case. The Michigan Court of Appeals was mistaken, therefore, in believing that Detective Hill's questioning of Mosley was "not permitted" by the *Westover* decision. For these reasons, we conclude that the admission in evidence of Mosley's incriminating statement did not violate the principles of *Miranda*. Accordingly, the judgment of the Michigan Court of Appeals is vacated, and the case is remanded to that court for further proceedings not inconsistent with this opinion.

Mr. Justice WHITE, concurring.

I concur in the result and in much of the majority's reasoning. However, it appears to me that in an effort to make only a limited holding in this case, the majority has implied that some custodial confessions will be suppressed even though they follow an informed and voluntary waiver of the defendant's rights. The majority seems to say that a statement obtained within some unspecified time after an assertion by an individual of his "right to silence" is always inadmissible, even if it was the result of an informed and voluntary decision following, for example, a disclosure to such an individual of a piece of information bearing on his waiver decision which the police had failed to give him prior to his assertion of the privilege but which they gave him immediately thereafter. Indeed, the majority characterizes as "absurd" any contrary rule. I disagree. I do not think the majority's conclusion is compelled by *Miranda*, and I suspect that in the final analysis the majority will adopt voluntariness as the standard by which to judge the waiver of the right to silence by a properly informed defendant. I think the Court should say so now.

*Miranda* holds that custody creates an inherent compulsion on an individual to incriminate himself in response to questions, and that statements obtained under such circumstances are therefore obtained in violation of the Fifth Amendment privilege against compelled testimonial self-incrimination unless the privilege is "knowingly and intelligently waived." It also holds that an individual will not be deemed to have made a knowing and intelligent waiver of his "right to silence" unless the authorities have first informed him, *inter alia*, of that right—"the threshold requirement for an intelligent decision as to its exercise." I am no more convinced that *Miranda* was required by the United States Constitution than I was when it was decided. However, there is at least some support in the law both before and after *Miranda* for the proposition that some rights will never be deemed waived unless the defendant is first expressly advised of their existence. There is little support in the law or in common sense for the proposition that an informed waiver of a right may be ineffective even where voluntarily made. Indeed, the law is exactly to the contrary. Unless an individual is incompetent, we have in the past rejected any paternalistic rule protecting a defendant from his intelligent and voluntary decisions about his own criminal case. To do so would be to "imprison a man in his privileges,"[1] and to disregard " 'that respect for the individual which is the lifeblood of the

law.' " I am very reluctant to conclude that *Miranda* stands for such a proposition.

The language of *Miranda* no more compels such a result than does its basic rationale. As the majority points out, the statement in *Miranda* requiring interrogation to *cease* after an assertion of the "right to silence" tells us nothing because it does not indicate how soon this interrogation may resume. The Court showed in the very next paragraph, moreover, that when it wanted to create a *per se* rule against further interrogation after assertion of a right, it knew how to do so. The Court there said "[i]f the individual states that he wants an attorney, the interrogation must cease *until an attorney is present.*"[2] However, when the individual indicates that he will decide unaided by counsel whether or not to assert his "right to silence" the situation is different. In such a situation, the Court in *Miranda* simply said: "If the interrogation continues without the presence of an attorney and a statement is taken, a heavy burden rests on the government to demonstrate that the defendant knowingly and intelligently waived his privilege

---

[1] The majority's rule may cause an accused injury. Although a recently arrested individual may have indicated an initial desire not to answer questions, he would nonetheless want to know immediately if it were true that his ability to explain a particular incriminating fact or to supply an alibi for a particular time period would result in his immediate release. Similarly, he might wish to know if it were true that (1) the case against him was unusually strong and that (2) his immediate cooperation with the authorities in the apprehension and conviction of others or in the recovery of property would redound to his benefit in the form of a reduced charge. Certainly the individual's lawyer, if he had one, would be interested in such information, even if communication of such information followed closely on an assertion of the "right to silence." Where the individual has not requested counsel and has chosen instead to make his own decisions regarding his conversations with the authorities, he should not be deprived even temporarily of any information relevant to the decision.

[2] The question of the proper procedure following expression by an individual of his desire to consult counsel is not presented in this case. It is sufficient to note that the reasons to keep the lines of communication between the authorities and the accused open when the accused has chosen to make his own decisions are not present when he indicates instead that he wishes legal advice with respect thereto. The authorities may then communicate with him through an attorney. More to the point, the accused having expressed his own view that he is not competent to deal with the authorities without legal advice, a later decision at the authorities' insistence to make a statement without counsel's presence may properly be viewed with skepticism.

against self-incrimination and his right to retained or appointed counsel.'' Apparently, although placing a heavy burden on the government, *Miranda* intended waiver of the ''right to silence'' to be tested by the normal standards. In any event, insofar as the *Miranda* decision might be read to require interrogation to cease for some magical and unspecified period of time following an assertion of the ''right to silence,'' and to reject voluntariness as the standard by which to judge informed waivers of that right, it should be disapproved as inconsistent with otherwise uniformly applied legal principles.

In justifying the implication that questioning must inevitably cease for some unspecified period of time following an exercise of the ''right to silence,'' the majority says only that such a requirement would be necessary to avoid ''undermining'' ''the will of the person being questioned.'' Yet, surely a waiver of the ''right to silence'' obtained by ''undermining the will'' of the person being questioned would be considered an involuntary waiver. Thus, in order to achieve the majority's only stated purpose, it is sufficient to exclude all confessions which are the result of involuntary waivers. To exclude any others is to deprive the fact finding process of highly probative information for no reason at all. The ''repeated rounds'' of questioning following an assertion of the privilege, which the majority is worried about, would, of course, count heavily against the State in any determination of voluntariness particularly if no reason (such as new facts communicated to the accused or a new incident being inquired about) appeared for repeated questioning. There is no reason, however, to rob the accused of the choice to answer questions voluntarily for some unspecified period of time following his own previous contrary decision. The Court should now so state.

Mr. Justice BRENNAN, with whom Mr. Justice MARSHALL joins, dissenting.

The *Miranda* guidelines were necessitated by the inherently coercive nature of in-custody questioning. To assure safeguards that promised to dispel the ''inherently compelling pressures'' of in-custody interrogation, a prophylactic rule was fashioned to supplement the traditional determination of voluntariness on the facts of each case. *Miranda* held that any confession obtained when not preceded by the required warnings or an adequate substitute safeguard was *per se* inadmissible in evidence. Satisfaction of this prophylactic rule, therefore, was necessary, though not sufficient, for the admission of a confession.

We observed in *Miranda*: ''Whatever the testimony of the authorities as to waiver of rights by an accused, the fact of lengthy interrogation or incommunicado incarceration before a statement is made

is strong evidence that the accused did not validly waive his rights. In these circumstances the fact that the individual eventually made a statement is consistent with the conclusion that the compelling influence of the interrogation finally forced him to do so. It is inconsistent with any notion of a voluntary relinquishment of the privilege.'' And, as that portion of *Miranda* which the majority finds controlling observed, ''the setting of in-custody interrogation operates on the individual to overcome free choice in producing a statement after the privilege has been once invoked.'' Thus, as to statements which are the product of renewed questioning, *Miranda* established a virtually irrebuttable presumption of compulsion, and that presumption stands strongest where, as in this case, a suspect, having initially determined to remain silent, is subsequently brought to confess his crime. Only by adequate procedural safeguards could the presumption be rebutted.

In formulating its procedural safeguard, the Court skirts the problem of compulsion and thereby fails to join issue with the dictates of *Miranda*. The language which the Court finds controlling in this case teaches that renewed questioning itself is part of the process which invariably operates to overcome the will of a suspect. That teaching is embodied in the form of a proscription on any further questioning once the suspect has exercised his right to remain silent. Today's decision uncritically abandons that teaching. The Court assumes, contrary to the controlling language, that ''scrupulously honoring'' an initial exercise of the right to remain silent preserves the efficaciousness of initial and future warnings despite the fact that the suspect has once been subjected to interrogation and then has been detained for a lengthy period of time.

For the Court it is enough conclusorily to assert that ''[t]he subsequent questioning did not undercut Mosley's previous decision not to answer Detective Cowie's inquiries.'' Under *Miranda*, however, Mosley's failure to exercise the right upon renewed questioning is presumptively the consequence of an overbearing in which detention and that subsequent questioning played central roles.

I agree that *Miranda* is not to be read, on the one hand, to impose an absolute ban on resumption of questioning ''at any time or place on any subject,'' or on the other hand, ''to permit a resumption of interrogation after a momentary respite.'' But this surely cannot justify adoption of a vague and ineffective procedural standard that falls somewhere between those absurd extremes, for *Miranda* in flat and unambiguous terms requires that questioning ''cease'' when a suspect exercises the right to remain silent. *Miranda*'s terms, however, are not so uncompromising as to preclude the fashioning of guidelines to govern this case. Those guidelines must, of course, necessarily be sensitive to the reality that "[a]s a practical matter, the compulsion to speak in the isolated setting of the police station may well be greater than in courts or other official investigations, where there are often impartial observers to guard against intimidation or trickery."

The fashioning of guidelines for this case is an easy task. Adequate procedures are readily available. Michigan law requires that the suspect be arraigned before a judicial officer "without unnecessary delay,"[2] certainly not a burdensome requirement. Alternatively, a requirement that resumption of questioning should await appointment and arrival of counsel for the suspect would be an acceptable and readily satisfied precondition to resumption. *Miranda* expressly held that "[t]he presence of counsel . . . would be the adequate protective device necessary to make the process of police interrogation conform to the dictates of the privilege [against self-incrimination]." The Court expediently bypasses this alternative in its search for circumstances where renewed questioning would be permissible.[4]

Indeed, language in *Miranda* suggests that the presence of counsel is the only appropriate alternative. In categorical language we held in *Miranda*: "If the individual indicates in any manner, at any time prior to or during questioning, that he wishes to remain silent, the interrogation must cease." We then immediately observed:

"If an individual indicates his desire to remain silent, but has an attorney present,

there *may* be some circumstances in which further questioning would be permissible. In the absence of evidence of overbearing, statements then made in the presence of counsel *might* be free of the compelling influence of the interrogation process and *might* fairly be construed as a waiver of the privilege for purposes of these statements." (emphasis added).

This was the only circumstance in which we at all suggested that questioning could be resumed, and even then, further questioning was not permissible in all such circumstances, for compulsion was still the presumption not easily dissipated.[5]

These procedures would be wholly consistent with the Court's rejection of a "*per se* proscription of indefinite duration," a rejection to which I fully subscribe. Today's decision, however, virtually empties *Miranda* of principle, for plainly the decision encourages police asked to cease interrogation to continue the suspect's detention until the police station's coercive atmosphere does its work and the suspect responds to resumed questioning.[6] I can only conclude that today's decision signals rejection of *Miranda*'s basic premise.

---

[2] Detective Cowie's testimony indicated that a judge was available across the street from the police station in which Mosley was held from 2:15 p.m. until 4 p.m. or 4:30 p.m. The actual interrogation of Mosley, however, covered only 15 or 20 minutes of this time. The failure to comply with a simple state-law requirement in these circumstances is totally at odds with the holding that the police "scrupulously honored" Mosley's rights.

[4] I do not mean to imply that counsel may be forced on a suspect who does not request an attorney. I suggest only that either arraignment or counsel must be provided before resumption of questioning to eliminate the coercive atmosphere of in-custody interrogation. The Court itself apparently proscribes resuming questioning until counsel is present if an accused has exercised the right to have an attorney present at questioning.

[5] The Court asserts that this language is not relevant to the present case, for "Mosley did not have an attorney present at the time he declined to answer Detective Cowie's questions." The language, however, does not compel a reading that it is applicable only if counsel is present when the suspect initially exercises his right to remain silent. Even if it did, this would only indicate that *Miranda* placed even stiffer limits on the circumstances when questioning may be resumed than I suggest here. Moreover, since the concern in *Miranda* was with assuring the absence of compulsion upon renewed questioning, it makes little difference whether counsel is initially present. Thus, even if the language does not specifically address the situation where counsel is not initially present, it certainly contemplates that situation.

The Court also asserts that *Miranda* "directed that 'the interrogation must cease until an attorney is present' only '[i]f the individual states that he wants an attorney.'" This is patently inaccurate. The language from the quoted portion of *Miranda* actually reads: "If the individual states that he wants an attorney, the interrogation must cease until an attorney is present."

[6] I do not suggest that the Court's opinion is to be read as permitting unreasonably lengthy detention without arraignment so long as any exercise of rights by a suspect is "scrupulously honored."

## QUESTIONS AND NOTES

**1.** Does the *Mosley* Court appear to be distancing itself from *Miranda*? Explain.

**2.** Do you agree that the alternatives suggested by Justice Stewart to his result are "absurd"? Are there any sensible alternatives other than his? Why do you suppose that he did not opt for one of them?

**3.** Are you persuaded by the Court's distinction between *Mosley* and *Westover*? Why? Why not?

**4.** In regard to Justice White's opinion, is it meaningful to talk in terms of "rob[bing] the accused of the choice to answer questions. . . .?" Is Justice White's footnote 1 helpful in analyzing this question?

**5.** Justice Brennan concluded in his dissent that "[i]n these circumstances the fact that the individual made a statement is consistent with the conclusion that the compelling influences of the interrogation finally forced him to do so." Do you agree? How could interrogation have affected his decision at all, when he was not being interrogated until he agreed to it?

**6.** Is Justice Brennan's footnote 4 suggesting that after arraignment an accused, who has previously invoked her right to silence, can be questioned without counsel? If so, do you agree?

**7.** How would you have voted had you been on the Court? Why?

**8.** In *Edwards*, we will examine the difference between invoking the right to remain silent and invoking the right to counsel.

### Edwards v. Arizona
### 451 U.S. 477 (1981)

Justice WHITE delivered the opinion of the Court.

#### I

On January 19, 1976, a sworn complaint was filed against Edwards in Arizona state court charging him with robbery, burglary, and first-degree murder. An arrest warrant was issued pursuant to the complaint, and Edwards was arrested at his home later that same day. At the police station, he was informed of his rights as required by *Miranda*. Petitioner stated that he understood his rights, and was willing to submit to questioning. After being told that another suspect already in custody had implicated him in the crime, Edwards denied involvement and gave a taped statement presenting an alibi defense. He then sought to "make a deal." The interrogating officer told him that he wanted a statement, but that he did not have the authority to negotiate a deal. The officer provided Edwards with the telephone number of a county attorney. Petitioner made the call, but hung up after a few moments. Edwards then said: "I want an attorney before making a deal." At that point, questioning ceased and Edwards was taken to county jail.

At 9:15 the next morning, two detectives, colleagues of the officer who had interrogated Edwards the previous night, came to the jail and asked to see Edwards. When the detention officer informed Edwards that the detectives wished to speak with him, he replied that he did not want to talk to anyone. The guard told him that "he had" to talk and then took him to meet with the detectives. The officers identified themselves, stated they wanted to talk to him, and informed him of his *Miranda* rights. Edwards was willing to talk, but he first wanted to hear the taped statement of the alleged accomplice who had implicated him.[2] After listening to the tape for several minutes, petitioner said that he would make a statement so long as it was not tape-recorded. The detectives informed him that the recording was irrelevant since they could testify in court concerning whatever he said. Edwards replied: "I'll tell you anything you want to know, but I don't want it on tape." He thereupon implicated himself in the crime.

Prior to trial, Edwards moved to suppress his

---

[2] It appears from the record that the detectives had brought the tape-recording with them.

confession on the ground that his *Miranda* rights had been violated when the officers returned to question him after he had invoked his right to counsel. The trial court initially granted the motion to suppress, but reversed its ruling when presented with a supposedly controlling decision of a higher Arizona court. The court stated without explanation that it found Edwards' statement to be voluntary. Edwards was tried twice and convicted.[5] Evidence concerning his confession was admitted at both trials.

On appeal, the Arizona Supreme Court held that Edwards had invoked both his right to remain silent and his right to counsel during the interrogation conducted on the night of January 19.[6] The court then went on to determine, however, that Edwards had waived both rights during the January 20 meeting when he voluntarily gave his statement to the detectives after again being informed that he need not answer questions and that he need not answer without the advice of counsel: "The trial court's finding that the waiver and confession were voluntarily and knowingly made is upheld."

II

We hold that an accused, such as Edwards, having expressed his desire to deal with the police only through counsel, is not subject to further interrogation by the authorities until counsel has been made available to him, unless the accused himself initiates further communication, exchanges, or conversations with the police.

*Miranda* itself indicated that the assertion of the right to counsel was a significant event and that once exercised by the accused, "the interrogation must cease until an attorney is present." Our later cases have not abandoned that view. In *Mosley*, the Court noted that *Miranda* had distinguished between the procedural safeguards triggered by a request to remain silent and a request for an attorney and had required that interrogation cease until an attorney was present only if the individual stated that he wanted counsel. In *Fare v. Michael C.*, the Court referred to Miranda's "rigid rule that an accused's

request for an attorney is *per se* an invocation of his Fifth Amendment rights, requiring that all interrogation cease." We reconfirm these views and, to lend them substance, emphasize that it is inconsistent with *Miranda* and its progeny for the authorities, at their instance, to reinterrogate an accused in custody if he has clearly asserted his right to counsel.

In concluding that the fruits of the interrogation initiated by the police on January 20 could not be used against Edwards, we do not hold or imply that Edwards was powerless to countermand his election or that the authorities could in no event use any incriminating statements made by Edwards prior to his having access to counsel. Had Edwards initiated the meeting on January 20, nothing in the Fifth and Fourteenth Amendments would prohibit the police from merely listening to his voluntary, volunteered statements and using them against him at the trial. The Fifth Amendment right identified in *Miranda* is the right to have counsel present at any custodial interrogation. Absent such interrogation, there would have been no infringement of the right that Edwards invoked and there would be no occasion to determine whether there had been a valid waiver.[9]

But this is not what the facts of this case show. Here, the officers conducting the interrogation on the evening of January 19 ceased interrogation when Edwards requested counsel as he had been advised he had the right to do. The Arizona Supreme Court was of the opinion that this was a sufficient invocation of his *Miranda* rights, and we are in accord. It is also clear that without making counsel available to Edwards, the police returned to him the next day. This was not at his suggestion or request. Indeed, Edwards informed the detention officer that he did not want to talk to anyone. At the meeting, the detectives told Edwards that they wanted to talk to him and again advised him of his *Miranda* rights. Edwards stated that he would talk, but what prompted this action does not appear. He listened at his own

---

[5] The jury in the first trial was unable to reach a verdict.

[6] This issue was disputed by the State. The court, while finding that the question was arguable, held that Edwards' request for an attorney to assist him in negotiating a deal was "sufficiently clear" within the context of the interrogation that it "must be interpreted as a request for counsel and as a request to remain silent until counsel was present."

[9] If, as frequently would occur in the course of a meeting initiated by the accused, the conversation is not wholly one-sided, it is likely that the officers will say or do something that clearly would be "interrogation." In that event, the question would be whether a valid waiver of the right to counsel and the right to silence had occurred, that is, whether the purported waiver was knowing and intelligent and found to be so under the totality of the circumstances, including the necessary fact that the accused, not the police, reopened the dialogue with the authorities.

request to part of the taped statement made by one of his alleged accomplices and then made an incriminating statement, which was used against him at his trial. We think it is clear that Edwards was subjected to custodial interrogation on January 20 and that this occurred at the instance of the authorities. His statement made without having had access to counsel, did not amount to a valid waiver and hence was inadmissible.

Accordingly, the holding of the Arizona Supreme Court that Edwards had waived his right to counsel was infirm, and the judgment of that court is reversed.

Chief Justice BURGER, concurring in the judgment.

I concur only in the judgment because I do not agree that either any constitutional standard or the holding of *Miranda* — as distinguished from its dicta — calls for a special rule as to how an accused in custody may waive the right to be free from interrogation. The extraordinary protections afforded a person in custody suspected of criminal conduct are not without a valid basis, but as with all "good" things they can be carried too far. The notion that any "prompting" of a person in custody is somehow evil *per se* has been rejected. For me, the inquiry in this setting is whether resumption of interrogation is a result of a voluntary waiver, and that inquiry should be resolved under the traditional standards established in *Johnson v. Zerbst*:

"A waiver is ordinarily an intentional relinquishment or abandonment of a known right or privilege. The determination of whether there has been an intelligent waiver . . . must depend, in each case, upon the particular facts and circumstances surrounding that case, including the background, experience, and conduct of the accused."

In this case, the Supreme Court of Arizona described the situation as follows:

"When the detention officer told Edwards that the detectives were there to see him, he told the officer that he did not wish to speak to anyone. The officer told him *that he had to.*" (emphasis added).

This is enough for me, and on this record the Supreme Court of Arizona erred in holding that the resumption of interrogation was the product of a voluntary waiver.

Justice POWELL, with whom Justice REHNQUIST joins, concurring in the result.

Although I agree that the judgment of the Arizona Supreme Court must be reversed, I do not join the Court's opinion because I am not sure what it means.

I can agree with much of the opinion. It states the settled rule:

"It is reasonably clear under our cases that waivers of counsel must not only be voluntary, but must also constitute a knowing and intelligent relinquishment or abandonment of a known right or privilege, a matter which depends in each case 'upon the particular facts and circumstances surrounding that case, including the background, experience and conduct of the accused.'"

I have thought it settled law that one accused of crime may waive *any* of the constitutional safeguards — including the right to remain silent, to jury trial, to call witnesses, to cross-examine one's accusers, to testify in one's own behalf, and — of course — to have counsel. Whatever the right, the standard for waiver is whether the actor fully understands the right in question and voluntarily intends to relinquish it.

In its opinion today, however, the Court — after reiterating the familiar principles of waiver — goes on to say:

"We further hold that an accused, such as Edwards, having expressed his desire to deal with the police only through counsel, is not subject to further interrogation by the authorities until counsel has been made available to him, *unless the accused [has] himself initiate[d] further communication, exchanges, or conversations with the police.*" (emphasis added).

In view of the emphasis placed on "initiation," I find the Court's opinion unclear. If read to create a new *per se* rule, requiring a threshold inquiry as to precisely who opened any conversation between an accused and state officials, I cannot agree. I would not superimpose a new element of proof on the established doctrine of waiver of counsel.

Perhaps the Court's opinion can be read as not departing from established doctrine. Accepting the formulation quoted above, two questions are identifiable: (i) was there in fact "interrogation," and (ii) did the police "initiate" it? Each of these questions is, of course, relevant to the admissibility of a confession. In this case, for example, it is clear that Edwards was taken from his cell against his will and subjected to renewed interrogation. Whether this is described as police-"initiated" interrogation or in some other way, it clearly was questioning under circumstances incompatible with a voluntary waiver of the fundamental right to counsel.

But few cases will be as clear as this one. Communications between police and a suspect in custody are common-place. It is useful to contrast the circumstances of this case with typical, and permissible, custodial communications between police and a suspect who has asked for counsel. For example, police do not impermissibly "initiate" renewed interrogation by engaging in routine conversations with suspects about unrelated matters. And police legitimately may inquire whether a suspect has changed his mind about speaking to them without an attorney. It is not unusual for a person in custody who previously has expressed an unwillingness to talk or a desire to have a lawyer, to change his mind and even welcome an opportunity to talk. Nothing in the Constitution erects obstacles that preclude police from ascertaining whether a suspect has reconsidered his original decision. As Justice White has observed, this Court consistently has "rejected any paternalistic rule protecting a defendant from his intelligent and voluntary decisions about his own criminal case." *Mosley* (White, J., concurring in result).[1]

In sum, once warnings have been given and the right to counsel has been invoked, the relevant inquiry—whether the suspect now desires to talk to police without counsel—is a question of fact to be determined in light of all of the circumstances. Who "initiated" a conversation may be relevant to the question of waiver, but it is not the *sine qua non* to the inquiry. The ultimate question is whether there was a free and knowing waiver of counsel before interrogation commenced.

---

[1] In *Mosley*, of course, the question was whether a suspect who had invoked his right to *remain silent* later could change his mind and speak to police. The facts of *Mosley* differ somewhat from the present case because here petitioner had *requested counsel*. It is nevertheless true in both cases that "a blanket prohibition against the taking of voluntary statements or a permanent immunity from further interrogation, regardless of the circumstances, would transform the *Miranda* safeguards into wholly irrational obstacles to legitimate police investigative activity, and deprive suspects of an opportunity to make informed and intelligent assessments of their interests." (opinion of Stewart, J.).

## QUESTIONS AND NOTES

**1.** Whatever might be said of either *Edwards* or *Mosley* standing alone, do they make sense when considered together? Explain.

**2.** If you were a suspect, would you think that you were invoking a different and superior right by invoking the right to counsel as opposed to the right to silence? If your answer is "no" would either *Mosley* or *Edwards* have to be wrong?

**3.** May the police ask a suspect if he has changed his mind? Should they be able to? Why? Why not?

**4.** Is Chief Justice Burger's opinion sounder than that of the majority? Explain.

**5.** In *Bradshaw*, the Court confronted the question of a suspect's "initiated" conversation with the police after having once invoked his right to counsel.

### Oregon v. Bradshaw
### 462 U.S. 1039 (1983)

Justice REHNQUIST announced the judgment of the Court and delivered an opinion in which THE CHIEF JUSTICE, Justice WHITE, and Justice O'CONNOR joined.

After a bench trial in an Oregon trial court, respondent James Edward Bradshaw was convicted of the offenses of first degree manslaughter, driving while under the influence of intoxicants, and driving while his license was revoked. The Oregon Court of Appeals reversed his conviction, holding that an inquiry he made of a police officer at the time he was in custody did not "initiate" a conversation with the officer, and that therefore statements by the respondent growing out of that conversation should have been excluded from evidence under *Edwards*.

In September, 1980, Oregon police were investigating the death of one Lowell Reynolds in Tillamook County. Reynolds' body had been found in his wrecked pickup truck, in which he appeared to have been a passenger at the time the vehicle left the roadway, struck a tree and an embankment, and finally came to rest on its side in a shallow creek. Reynolds had died from traumatic injury, coupled with asphyxia by drowning. During the investigation of Reynolds' death, respondent was asked to accompany a police officer to the Rockaway Police Station for questioning.

Once at the station, respondent was advised of his rights as required by *Miranda*. Respondent then repeated to the police his earlier account of the events of the evening of Reynolds' death, admitting that he had provided Reynolds and others with liquor for a party at Reynolds' house, but denying involvement in the traffic accident that apparently killed Reynolds. Respondent suggested that Reynolds might have met with foul play at the hands of the assailant whom respondent alleged had struck him at the party.

At this point, respondent was placed under arrest for furnishing liquor to Reynolds, a minor, and again advised of his *Miranda* rights. A police officer then told respondent the officer's theory of how the traffic accident that killed Reynolds occurred; a theory which placed respondent behind the wheel of the vehicle. Respondent again denied his involvement, and said "I do want an attorney before it goes very much further." The officer immediately terminated the conversation.

Sometime later respondent was transferred from the Rockaway Police Station to the Tillamook County Jail, a distance of some ten or fifteen miles. Either just before, or during, his trip from Rockaway to Tillamook, respondent inquired of a police officer, "Well, what is going to happen to me now?" The officer answered by saying "You do not have to talk to me. You have requested an attorney and I don't want you talking to me unless you so desire because anything you say—because—since you have requested an attorney, you know, it has to be at your own free will." Respondent said he understood. There followed a discussion between respondent and the officer concerning where respondent was being taken and the offense with which he would be charged. The officer suggested that respondent might help himself by taking a polygraph examination. Respondent agreed to take such an examination, saying that he was willing to do whatever he could to clear up the matter.

The next day, following another reading to respondent of his *Miranda* rights, and respondent's signing a written waiver of those rights, the polygraph was administered. At its conclusion, the examiner told respondent that he did not believe respondent was telling the truth. Respondent then recanted his earlier story, admitting that he had been at the wheel of the vehicle in which Reynolds was killed, that he had consumed a considerable amount of alcohol, and that he had passed out at the wheel before the vehicle left the roadway and came to rest in the creek.

Respondent was charged with first degree manslaughter, driving while under the influence of intoxicants, and driving while his license was revoked. His motion to suppress the statements described above was denied, and he was found guilty after a bench trial. The Oregon Court of Appeals, relying on our decision in *Edwards*, reversed, concluding that the statements had been obtained in violation of respondent's Fifth Amendment rights. We now conclude that the Oregon Court of Appeals misapplied our decision in *Edwards*.

In *Edwards*, we stated:

> "We hold that *an accused, such as [the defendant], having expressed his desire to deal with the police only through counsel, is not subject to further interrogation by the authorities until counsel has been made available to him, unless the accused himself initiates further communication, exchanges, or conversations with the police.*" (emphasis added).

Respondent's question in the present case, "Well, what is going to happen to me now?", admittedly was asked prior to respondent being "subject[ed] to further interrogation by the authorities." The Oregon Court of Appeals stated that it did not "construe defendant's question about what was going to happen to him to have been a waiver of his right to counsel, invoked only minutes before. . . ." The Court of Appeals, after quoting relevant language from *Edwards*, concluded that "under the reasoning enunciated in *Edwards*, defendant did not make a valid waiver of his Fifth Amendment rights, and his statements were inadmissible."

We think the Oregon Court of Appeals misapprehended the test laid down in *Edwards*. We did not there hold that the "initiation" of a conversation by a defendant such as respondent would amount to a waiver of a previously invoked right to counsel; we held that after the right to counsel had been asserted by an accused, further interrogation of the accused should not take place "unless the accused himself initiates further communication, exchanges, or conversations with the police." This was in effect a prophylactic rule, designed to protect an accused in police custody from being badgered by police officers in the manner in which the defendant in *Edwards* was. We recently restated the requirement in *Wyrick v. Fields*, 459 U.S. 42, 46 (1982) (*per curiam*), to be that before a suspect in custody can be subjected to further interrogation after he requests an attorney there must be a showing that the "suspect himself initiates dialogue with the authorities."

But even if a conversation taking place after the accused has "expressed his desire to deal with the police only through counsel," is initiated by the accused, where reinterrogation follows, the burden remains upon the prosecution to show that subsequent events indicated a waiver of the Fifth Amendment right to have counsel present during the interrogation. This is made clear in the following footnote to our *Edwards* opinion:

> "If, as frequently would occur in the course of a meeting initiated by the accused, the conversation is not wholly one-sided, it is likely that the officers will say or do something that clearly would be 'interrogation.' In that event, the question would be whether a valid waiver of the right to counsel and the right to silence had occurred, that is, *whether the purported waiver was knowing and intelligent and found to be so under the totality of the circumstances*, including the necessary fact that the accused, not the police, reopened the dialogue with the authorities." (emphasis added).

Thus, the Oregon Court of Appeals was wrong in thinking that an "initiation" of a conversation or discussion by an accused not only satisfied the *Edwards* rule, but *ex proprio vigore* sufficed to show a waiver of the previously asserted right to counsel. The inquiries are separate, and clarity of application is not gained by melding them together.

There can be no doubt in this case that in asking, "Well, what is going to happen to me now?", respondent "initiated" further conversation in the ordinary dictionary sense of that word. While we doubt that it would be desirable to build a superstructure of legal refinements around the word "initiate" in this context, there are undoubtedly situations where a bare inquiry by either a defendant or by a police officer should not be held to "initiate" any conversation or dialogue. There are some inquiries, such

as a request for a drink of water or a request to use a telephone that are so routine that they cannot be fairly said to represent a desire on the part of an accused to open up a more generalized discussion relating directly or indirectly to the investigation. Such inquiries or statements, by either an accused or a police officer, relating to routine incidents of the custodial relationship, will not generally "initiate" a conversation in the sense in which that word was used in *Edwards*.

Although ambiguous, the respondent's question in this case as to what was going to happen to him evinced a willingness and a desire for a generalized discussion about the investigation; it was not merely a necessary inquiry arising out of the incidents of the custodial relationship. It could reasonably have been interpreted by the officer as relating generally to the investigation. That the police officer so understood it is apparent from the fact that he immediately reminded the accused that "you do not have to talk to me," and only after the accused told him that he "understood" did they have a generalized conversation. On these facts we believe that there was not a violation of the *Edwards* rule.

Justice POWELL, concurring in the judgment.

The Court's recent decision in *Edwards v. Arizona* has resulted in disagreement as to whether it announced a new *per se* rule. My hope had been that this case would afford an opportunity to clarify the confusion. As evidenced by the differing readings of *Edwards* by Justices Marshall and Rehnquist in their respective opinions, my hope has not been fully realized. Justice Marshall, and the three Justices who join his opinion, would affirm the Oregon Court of Appeals because it "properly applied *Edwards*." Justice Rehnquist, and the three Justices who join him, would "conclude that the Oregon Court of Appeals misapplied our decision in *Edwards*." In view of the disagreement here, it is not surprising that courts have differed as to whether *Edwards* announced a *per se* rule, and if so what rule. I joined the judgment in *Edwards* because on the facts "it [was] clear that Edwards [had been] taken from his cell against his will and [improperly] subjected to renewed interrogation." I did not join the Court's opinion because I was "not sure what it mean[t]."

Justice Rehnquist's opinion observes that the initiation and the voluntariness of the waiver under *Zerbst* "are separate, and clarity of application is not gained by melding them together."

This bifurcating of the *Zerbst* standard is not

compelled by *Edwards* or any of our other cases. The inquiry in *Edwards* did focus on the reopening of communication with the accused by the police — a reopening that properly was held to be coercive. As there were no other significant facts or circumstances bearing upon the waiver question, there was no occasion for the Court to consider whether a two-step analysis is required in the more customary case. An incarcerated person, accused of crime, does not remain silent and speak only when conversation is initiated by others, whether by fellow prisoners, guards, or law enforcement officers. Jail or prison confinements prior to indictment or trial may extend over days and weeks, and numerous conversations customarily occur, often accompanied by collateral facts and circumstances. Rarely can a Court properly focus on a particular conversation, and intelligently base a judgment on the simplistic inquiry as to who spoke first.

In this case, for example, Bradshaw's initiating question ("what is going to happen to me now?") was not an isolated event. It was immediately followed by a renewal of *Miranda* warnings and additional conversation. The following day there was further conversation, a third reading of *Miranda* rights, and finally Bradshaw's signing of a written waiver of those rights. Only then did he confess. Justice Marshall would hold that there can be no waiver of the right to counsel unless the accused himself opens a dialogue "about the subject matter of the criminal investigation." He states that "unless the accused himself initiates further communication with the police, a valid waiver of the right to counsel cannot be established." Under this view of the two-step analysis, a court never gets to the second step — however relevant subsequent facts and circumstances may be to a waiver — unless the accused was the first to speak and to say the right thing. This is illustrated by the reasoning in the dissenting opinion in this case. Since Justice Marshall concludes that Bradshaw had not initiated the dialogue, he does not consider the subsequent facts and circumstances that were found by the trial court to satisfy the *Zerbst* standard. Justice Rehnquist, however, moves from the first to the second step to conclude that the facts and circumstances, when viewed in their entirety, clearly establish a valid waiver of the right to counsel. To this extent, I agree with his plurality opinion.

The *Zerbst* standard is one that is widely understood and followed. It also comports with common sense. Fragmenting the standard into a novel two-step analysis — if followed literally — often would frustrate justice as well as common sense.[4] Courts should engage in more substantive inquiries than "who said what first." The holding of the Court in *Edwards* cannot in my view fairly be reduced to this.

We are unanimous in agreeing in this case, as in *Edwards*, that "the right to counsel [is] a prime example of those rights requiring the special protection of the knowing and intelligent waiver standard." We also agree that once the accused has requested counsel this right requires additional safeguards, particularly against any coercive form of custodial interrogation. But the question of whether a suspect has waived this important right to counsel is uniquely one of fact, and usually must and should be left to the judgment of the trial court that has had the benefit of hearing the evidence and assessing the weight and credibility of testimony. In the circumstances of this case, I agree that Bradshaw knowingly and intelligently waived his right to counsel, and that the judgment below therefore should be reversed.

Justice MARSHALL, with whom Justice BRENNAN, Justice BLACKMUN, and Justice STEVENS join, dissenting.

Because in my view the plurality has misapplied *Edwards*, I respectfully dissent.

I

In *Miranda*, this Court recognized that "[u]nless adequate protective devices are employed to dispel the compulsion inherent in custodial surroundings, no statement obtained from the defendant can truly be the product of his free choice." Access to counsel was held essential to secure the Fifth Amendment privilege against self-incrimination. "If the individual states that he wants an attorney, *the interrogation must cease until an attorney is present*." (emphasis added). *Miranda* thus created a "rigid rule that an accused's request for an attorney is *per se* an invocation of his Fifth Amendment rights, requiring that all interrogation cease." *Fare v. Michael C.*

The Oregon Court of Appeals properly applied *Edwards*.[1] When this Court in *Edwards* spoke of

---

[4] I therefore prefer to read Justice Rehnquist's opinion merely as an analytical framework that — except in a case like *Edwards* — would not inhibit courts from a full examination of all relevant facts and circumstances.

[1] In rebuking the Oregon Court of Appeals for failing to distinguish between the initiation of a conversation and a valid waiver of the right to counsel, the plurality is attacking a straw man. Because it concluded that respondent had not initiated any conversation, the Oregon Court never even undertook

"initiat[ing] further communication" with the police and "reopen[ing] the dialogue with the authorities," it obviously had in mind communication or dialogue *about the subject matter of the criminal investigation.* The rule announced in *Edwards* was designed to ensure that any interrogation subsequent to an invocation of the right to counsel be at the instance of the accused, not the authorities. Thus, a question or statement which does not invite further interrogation before an attorney is present cannot qualify as "initiation" under *Edwards*. To hold otherwise would drastically undermine the safeguards that *Miranda* and *Edwards* carefully erected around the right to counsel in the custodial setting.

The safeguards identified in *Edwards* hardly pose an insurmountable obstacle to an accused who truly wishes to waive his rights after invoking his right to counsel. A waiver can be established, however, only when the accused himself reopens the dialogue about the subject matter of the criminal investigation. Since our decision in *Edwards*, the lower courts have had no difficulty in identifying such situations. See, *e.g., McCree v. Housewright,* 689 F.2d 797 (CA8 1982) (defendant initiated reinterrogation by knocking on cell door and telling police officer that he wanted to make a statement); *United States v. Gordon,* 655 F.2d 478 (CA2 1981) (defendant reopened dialogue by expressing a desire to provide information about someone else who should also be arrested); *State v. Brezee,* 66 Haw. 163, 657 P.2d 1044 (1983) (defendant asked detective to come back to his cell and then expressed desire to make a statement); *Payne v. State,* 424 So.2d 722 (Ala.-Cr.App.1982) (defendant asked for a meeting with police at which statements were made); *People v. Thomas,* 98 Ill.App.3d 852, 54 Ill.Dec. 235, 424 N.E.2d 985 (1982), cert. denied, 456 U.S. 993, 102 S.Ct. 2276, 73 L.Ed.2d 1289 (1982) (defendant initiated further communication by inquiring about accomplice's statements linking him to the crime);

---

the distinct inquiry into the existence of a knowing and intelligent waiver. *Edwards* makes clear that, in the absence of "initiation" by an accused, there can be no valid waiver regardless of whatever else the accused may say or do. Having concluded that respondent did not initiate further conversation, the Oregon Court thus stated that there was no valid waiver in this case. This conclusion is entirely consistent with *Edwards*. Indeed, the Oregon Court's decision contains lengthy quotations from *Edwards*. Unless we are to assume that the State Court did not read the very portions of *Edwards* that it quotes, the plurality's attack is completely unjustified.

*State v. Pittman,* 210 Neb. 117, 313 N.W.2d 252 (1981) (defendant initiated further conversation by stating that he was being "railroaded" by his codefendants).[2]

## II

I agree with the plurality that, in order to constitute "initiation" under *Edwards*, an accused's inquiry must demonstrate a desire to discuss the subject matter of the criminal investigation. I am baffled, however, at the plurality's application of that standard to the facts of this case. The plurality asserts that respondent's question, "What is going to happen to me now?", evinced both "a willingness and a desire for a generalized discussion about the investigation." If respondent's question had been posed by Jean-Paul Sartre before a class of philosophy students, it might well have evinced a desire for a "generalized" discussion. But under the circumstances of this case, it is plain that respondent's only "desire" was to find out where the police were going to take him. As the Oregon Court of Appeals stated, respondent's query came only minutes after his invocation of the right to counsel and was simply "a normal reaction to being taken from the police station and placed in a police car, obviously for transport to some destination."[3] On these facts, I fail

---

[2] In his opinion concurring in the judgment, Justice Powell suggests that there is confusion as to whether *Edwards* announced a *per se* rule. In my view, *Edwards* unambiguously established such a rule. In any event, no confusion on this point can remain after today's decision for eight Justices manifestly agree that *Edwards* did create a *per se* rule.

[3] The plurality seems to place some reliance on the police officer's reaction to respondent's question. The officer described his response as follows:

"I says, 'You do not have to talk to me. You have requested an attorney and I don't want you talking to me unless you so desire because anything you say—because—since you have requested an attorney, you know, it has to be at your own free will.' I says, 'I can't prevent you from talking, but you understand where your place—you know, where your standing is here?' and he agreed. He says 'I understand.'"

As the officer's testimony indicates, respondent's statement was at best ambiguous. In any event, as the Oregon Court of Appeals noted, the officer clearly took advantage of respondent's inquiry to commence once again his questioning—a practice squarely at odds with *Edwards*.

to see how respondent's question can be considered "initiation" of a conversation about the subject matter of the criminal investigation.

To hold that respondent's question in this case opened a dialogue with the authorities flies in the face of the basic purpose of the *Miranda* safeguards. When someone in custody asks, "What is going to happen to me now?", he is surely responding to his custodial surroundings. The very essence of custody is the loss of control over one's freedom of movement. The authorities exercise virtually unfettered control over the accused. To allow the authorities to recommence an interrogation based on such a question is to permit them to capitalize on the custodial setting. Yet *Miranda*'s procedural protections were adopted precisely in order "to dispel the compulsion inherent in custodial surroundings."

Accordingly, I dissent.

## QUESTIONS AND NOTES

**1.** With which (if any) of the three opinions do you agree? Explain.

**2.** Do you think that Bradshaw's question initiated further discussion?

**3.** What significance (if any) do you attach to the officer's immediately telling Bradshaw that he did not have to speak to them? Is it a point in favor of admissibility or inadmissibility of the confession? Explain.

**4.** Even if Bradshaw had initiated discussion, did he ever agree to be questioned? If so, when?

**5.** In *Roberson*, the Court amplified and arguably expanded the *Edwards* right.

### Arizona v. Roberson
### 486 U.S. 675 (1988)

Justice STEVENS delivered the opinion of the Court.

In *Edwards*, we held that a suspect who has "expressed his desire to deal with the police only through counsel is not subject to further interrogation by the authorities until counsel has been made available to him, unless the accused himself initiates further communication, exchanges, or conversations with the police." In this case Arizona asks us to craft an exception to that rule for cases in which the police want to interrogate a suspect about an offense that is unrelated to the subject of their initial interrogation. Several years ago the Arizona Supreme Court considered, and rejected, a similar argument, stating:

"The only difference between Edwards and the appellant is that Edwards was questioned about the same offense after a request for counsel while the appellant was reinterrogated about an unrelated offense. We do not believe that this factual distinction holds any legal significance for fifth amendment purposes." *State v. Routhier*, 137 Ariz. 90, 97, 669 P.2d 68, 75 (1983), cert. denied, 464 U.S. 1073, 104 S.Ct. 985, 79 L.Ed.2d 221 (1984).

We agree with the Arizona Supreme Court's conclusion.

#### I

On April 16, 1985, respondent was arrested at the scene of a just-completed burglary. The arresting officer advised him that he had a constitutional right to remain silent and also the right to have an attorney present during any interrogation. Respondent replied that he "wanted a lawyer before answering any questions." This fact was duly recorded in the officer's written report of the incident. In due course, respondent was convicted of the April 16, 1985, burglary.

On April 19, 1985, while respondent was still in custody pursuant to the arrest three days earlier, a different officer interrogated him about a different burglary that had occurred on April 15. That officer was not aware of the fact that respondent had requested the assistance of counsel three days earlier. After advising respondent of his rights, the officer obtained an incriminating statement concerning the April 15 burglary. In the prosecution for that offense, the trial court suppressed that statement. In explaining his ruling, the trial judge relied squarely on the Arizona Supreme Court's opinion in *Routhier*, characterizing the rule of the *Edwards* case as "clear and unequivocal."

We now affirm.

### III

Petitioner points to our holding in *Mosley*, that when a suspect asserts his right to cut off questioning, the police may "scrupulously honor" that right by "immediately ceas[ing] the interrogation, resum[ing] questioning only after the passage of a significant period of time and the provision of a fresh set of warnings, and restrict[ing] the second interrogation to a crime that had not been a subject of the earlier interrogation." The police in this case followed precisely that course, claims the State. However, as *Mosley* made clear, a suspect's decision to cut off questioning, unlike his request for counsel, does not raise the presumption that he is unable to proceed without a lawyer's advice.

Petitioner argues that Roberson's request for counsel was limited to the investigation pursuant to which the request was made. This argument is flawed both factually and legally. As a matter of fact, according to the initial police report, respondent stated that "he wanted a lawyer before answering *any* questions." As a matter of law, the presumption raised by a suspect's request for counsel — that he considers himself unable to deal with the pressures of custodial interrogation without legal assistance — does not disappear simply because the police have approached the suspect, still in custody, still without counsel, about a separate investigation.

That a suspect's request for counsel should apply to any questions the police wish to pose follows, we think, not only from *Edwards* and *Miranda*, but also *Spring*. In *Spring*, we held that "a suspect's awareness of all the possible subjects of questioning in advance of interrogation is not relevant to determining whether the suspect voluntarily, knowingly, and intelligently waived his Fifth Amendment privilege." In the face of the warning that anything he said could be used as evidence against him, Spring's willingness to answer questions, without limiting such a waiver, indicated that he felt comfortable enough with the pressures of custodial interrogation both to answer questions and to do so without an attorney. Since there is "no qualification of [the] broad and explicit warning" that "*anything* [a suspect] says may be used against him," (emphasis in

original), Spring's decision to talk was properly considered to be equally unqualified. Conversely, Roberson's unwillingness to answer any questions without the advice of counsel, without limiting his request for counsel, indicated that he did not feel sufficiently comfortable with the pressures of custodial interrogation to answer questions without an attorney. This discomfort is precisely the state of mind that *Edwards* presumes to persist unless the suspect himself initiates further conversation about the investigation; unless he otherwise states, there is no reason to assume that a suspect's state of mind is in any way investigation-specific. *Spring*.

### IV

Petitioner's attempts at distinguishing the factual setting here from that in *Edwards* are equally unavailing. Petitioner first relies on the plurality opinion in *Bradshaw*, (Rehnquist, J.), which stated that *Edwards* laid down "a prophylactic rule, designed to protect an accused in police custody from being badgered by police officers in the manner in which the defendant in *Edwards* was." Petitioner reasons that "the chances that an accused will be questioned so repeatedly and in such quick succession that it will 'undermine the will' of the person questioned, or will constitute 'badger[ing],' are so minute as not to warrant consideration, if the officers are truly pursuing separate investigations." It is by no means clear, though, that police engaged in separate investigations will be any less eager than police involved in only one inquiry to question a suspect in custody. Further, to a suspect who has indicated his inability to cope with the pressures of custodial interrogation by requesting counsel, any further interrogation without counsel having been provided will surely exacerbate whatever compulsion to speak the suspect may be feeling. Thus, we also disagree with petitioner's contention that fresh sets of *Miranda* warnings will "reassure" a suspect who has been denied the counsel he has clearly requested that his rights have remained untrammeled. Especially in a case such as this, in which a period of three days elapsed between the unsatisfied request for counsel and the interrogation about a second offense, there is a serious risk that the mere repetition of the *Miranda* warnings would not overcome the presumption of coercion that is created by prolonged police custody.[6]

---

[6] The United States, as *amicus curiae* supporting petitioner, suggests similarly that "respondent's failure to reiterate his request for counsel to [the officer involved in the second investigation], even after [that officer] gave respondent complete *Miranda* warnings, could not have been the result of any doubt on

The United States, as *amicus curiae* supporting petitioner, suggests that a suspect in custody might have "good reasons for wanting to speak with the police about the offenses involved in the new investigation, or at least to learn from the police what the new investigation is about so that he can decide whether it is in his interest to make a statement about that matter without the assistance of counsel." The simple answer is that the suspect, having requested counsel, can determine how to deal with the separate investigations with counsel's advice. Further, even if the police have decided temporarily not to provide counsel, they are free to inform the suspect of the facts of the second investigation as long as such communication does not constitute interrogation. As we have made clear, any "further communication, exchanges, or conversations with the police" that the suspect himself initiates, *Edwards*, are perfectly valid.

Finally, we attach no significance to the fact that the officer who conducted the second interrogation did not know that respondent had made a request for counsel. In addition to the fact that *Edwards* focuses on the state of mind of the suspect and not of the police, custodial interrogation must be conducted pursuant to established procedures, and those procedures in turn must enable an officer who proposes to initiate an interrogation to determine whether the suspect has previously requested counsel. In this case respondent's request had been properly memorialized in a written report but the officer who conducted the interrogation simply failed to examine that report. Whether a contemplated reinterrogation concerns the same or a different offense, or whether the same or different law enforcement authorities are involved in the second investigation, the same need to determine whether the suspect has requested

---

respondent's part that the police would honor a request for counsel if one were made." This conclusion is surprising, considering that respondent had not been provided with the attorney he had already requested, despite having been subjected to police-initiated interrogation with respect to the first investigation as well. We reiterate here, though, that the "right" to counsel to protect the Fifth Amendment right against self-incrimination is not absolute; that is, "[i]f authorities conclude that they will not provide counsel during a reasonable period of time in which investigation in the field is carried out, they may refrain from doing so without violating the person's Fifth Amendment privilege so long as they do not question him during that time." *Miranda*.

counsel exists.[7] The police department's failure to honor that request cannot be justified by the lack of diligence of a particular officer.

The judgment of the Arizona Court of Appeals is *Affirmed*.

Justice KENNEDY, with whom the Chief Justice joins, dissenting.

The majority frames the case as one in which we are asked to "craft an exception" to *Edwards*. The implication from this, it would seem, is that the burden of proof falls on those who say no constitutional or preventative purpose is served by prohibiting the police from asking a suspect, once he has requested counsel, if he chooses to waive that right in a new and independent investigation of a different crime. But the rule of *Edwards* is our rule, not a constitutional command; and it is our obligation to justify its expansion. Our justification must be consistent with the practical realities of suspects' rights and police investigations. With all respect, I suggest the majority does not have a convincing case. The majority's rule is not necessary to protect the rights of suspects, and it will in many instances deprive our nationwide law enforcement network of a legitimate investigative technique now routinely used to resolve major crimes.

When a suspect is in custody for even the most minor offense, his name and fingerprints are checked against master files. It is a frequent occurrence that the suspect is wanted for questioning with respect to crimes unrelated to the one for which he has been apprehended. The rule announced today will bar law enforcement officials, even those from some other city or other jurisdiction, from questioning a suspect about an unrelated matter if he is in custody and has requested counsel to assist in answering questions put to him about the crime for which he was arrested.

This is the first case in which we are asked to apply *Edwards* to separate and independent investigations. The statements deemed inadmissible in *Edwards* and in our later cases applying its doctrine were statements relating to the same investigation in

---

[7] Indeed, the facts of this case indicate that different officers investigating the same offense are just as likely to bypass proper procedures as an officer investigating a different offense, inasmuch as the record discloses no less than five violations of the *Edwards* rule, four concerning the April 16 burglary and only one concerning the April 15 burglary. It is only the last violation that is at issue in this case.

which the right to counsel was invoked. The majority's extension of the *Edwards* rule to separate and independent investigations is unwarranted.

Our ultimate concern in *Edwards*, and in the cases which follow it, is whether the suspect knows and understands his rights and is willing to waive them, and whether courts can be assured that coercion did not induce the waiver. That concern does not dictate the result reached by the Court today, for the dangers present in *Edwards* and later cases are insubstantial here.

The rule in *Edwards* "was in effect a prophylactic rule, designed to protect an accused in police custody from being badgered by police officers in the manner in which the defendant in *Edwards* was." *Bradshaw*, (plurality opinion). Where the subsequent questioning is confined to an entirely independent investigation, there is little risk that the suspect will be badgered into submission.

The Court reasons that it is "by no means clear" that "police engaged in separate investigations will be any less eager than police involved in only one inquiry to question a suspect in custody." That misses the point. Unless there are so many separate investigations that fresh teams of police are regularly turning up to question the suspect, the danger of badgering is minimal, and insufficient to justify a rigid *per se* rule. Whatever their eagerness, the police in a separate investigation may not commence any questioning unless the suspect is readvised of his *Miranda* rights and consents to the interrogation, and they are required by *Edwards* to cease questioning him if he invokes his right to counsel. Consequently, the legitimate interest of the suspect in not being subjected to coercive badgering is already protected. The reason for the *Edwards* rule is not that confessions are disfavored but that coercion is feared. The rule announced today, however, prohibits the police from resuming questions, after a second *Miranda* warning, when there is no more likelihood of coercion than when the first interrogation began.

The Court suggests that the suspect may believe his rights are fictitious if he must assert them a second time, but the support for this suggestion is weak. The suspect, having observed that his earlier invocation of rights was effective in terminating questioning and having been advised that further questioning may not relate to that crime, would understand that he may invoke his rights again with respect to the new investigation, and so terminate questioning regarding that investigation as well. Indeed, the new warnings and explanations will reinforce his comprehension of a suspect's rights.

I note that the conduct of the police in this case was hardly exemplary; they reinitiated questioning of respondent regarding the first investigation after he had asserted his right to counsel in that investigation. The statements he gave in response, however, properly were excluded at trial for all purposes except impeachment. Any sense of coercion generated by this violation which carried over into the questioning on the second offense would of course be taken into account by a court reviewing whether the waiver of *Miranda* rights in the second investigation was voluntary, and the *per se* rule announced today is therefore not necessary to respond to such misconduct.

Allowing authorities who conduct a separate investigation to read the suspect his *Miranda* rights and ask him whether he wishes to invoke them strikes an appropriate balance, which protects the suspect's freedom from coercion without unnecessarily disrupting legitimate law enforcement efforts. Balance is essential when the Court fashions rules which are preventative and do not themselves stem from violations of a constitutional right. By contrast with the Fourth Amendment exclusionary rule, for instance, the rule here operates even absent constitutional violation, and we should be cautious in extending it. The Court expresses a preference for bright lines, but the line it draws here is far more restrictive than necessary to protect the interests at stake.

By prohibiting the police from questioning the suspect regarding a separate investigation, the Court chooses to presume that a suspect has made the decision that he does not wish to talk about that investigation without counsel present, although that decision was made when the suspect was unaware of even the existence of a separate investigation. The underlying premise seems to be that there are two types of people: those who never talk without a lawyer and those who always talk without a lawyer. The more realistic view of human nature suggests that a suspect will want the opportunity, when he learns of the separate investigations, to decide whether he wishes to speak to the authorities in a particular investigation with or without representation.

In other contexts, we have taken a more realistic approach to separate and independent investigations. [W]e held in *Mosley* that a suspect who had been arrested on charges of committing robbery and who had invoked his right to silence could be questioned later about an unrelated murder, if first read his *Miranda* rights. The Court correctly points out that *Mosley* involved the Fifth Amendment right to silence, while this case involves the Fifth Amendment right to counsel. *Mosley* nevertheless reflected an understanding that the invocation of a criminal suspect's constitutional rights could be respected, and the opportunities for unfair coercion restricted, without the establishment of a broad-brush rule by which the assertion of a right in one investigation is automatically applied to a separate and independent one.

In considering whether to extend the *Edwards* rule to this case, the choice is not between holding, as the Court does, that such statements will never be admissible, and holding that such statements will always be admissible. The choice is between the Court's absolute rule establishing an irrebuttable presumption of coercion, and one which relies upon known and tested warnings, applied to each investigation as required by *Edwards* and *Miranda*, to insure that a waiver is voluntary. The problems to which *Edwards* was addressed are not present here in any substantial degree. Today's rule will neither serve the interest of law enforcement nor give necessary protection to the rights of those suspected of crime. I respectfully dissent.

## QUESTIONS AND NOTES

**1.** If when given his warnings, Roberson had said: "I want a lawyer before answering any questions about this burglary," would the result have been different? Should it have been different?

**2.** Do you think that this case is analogous to *Spring*? Explain.

**3.** Should this case be treated as an exception to *Edwards*, or as an exception to the voluntariness standard? Why? Would your conclusion likely be dictated by which of those premises you began the case?

**4.** Is the *Roberson* corollary to *Edwards* really necessary to prevent coercion? Why? Why not?

**5.** Explain the distinction between a prophylactic rule and a constitutional rule. Which is *Roberson*?

**6.** In *Minnick*, we explore what happens after a suspect who has invoked his right to counsel has an opportunity to speak with his attorney.

### Minnick v. Mississippi
498 U.S. 146 (1990).

Justice KENNEDY delivered the opinion of the Court.

The issue in the case before us is whether *Edwards*' protection ceases once the suspect has consulted with an attorney.

Petitioner Robert Minnick and fellow prisoner James Dyess escaped from a county jail in Mississippi and, a day later, broke into a mobile home in search of weapons. In the course of the burglary they were interrupted by the arrival of the trailer's owner, Ellis Thomas, accompanied by Lamar Lafferty and Lafferty's infant son. Dyess and Minnick used the stolen weapons to kill Thomas and the senior Lafferty. Minnick's story is that Dyess murdered one victim and forced Minnick to shoot the other. Before the escapees could get away, two young women arrived at the mobile home. They were held at gunpoint, then bound hand and foot.

Dyess and Minnick fled in Thomas' truck, abandoning the vehicle in New Orleans. The fugitives continued to Mexico, where they fought, and Minnick then proceeded alone to California. Minnick was arrested in Lemon Grove, California, on a Mississippi warrant, some four months after the murders.

The confession at issue here resulted from the last interrogation of Minnick while he was held in the San Diego jail, but we first recount the events which preceded it. Minnick was arrested on Friday, August 22, 1986. Petitioner testified that he was mistreated by local police during and after the arrest. The day following the arrest, Saturday, two FBI agents came to the jail to interview him. Petitioner testified that he refused to go to the interview, but was told he would "have to go down or else." The FBI report indicates that the agents read petitioner his *Miranda* warnings, and that he acknowledged he understood his rights. He refused to sign a rights waiver form, however, and said he would not answer "very many" questions. Minnick told the agents about the jail break and the flight, and described how Dyess threatened and beat him. Early in the interview, he sobbed "[i]t was my life or theirs," but otherwise he hesitated to tell what happened at the trailer. The agents reminded him he did not have to answer questions without a lawyer present. According to the report, "Minnick stated 'Come back Monday when I have a lawyer,' and stated that he would make a more complete statement then with his lawyer present." The FBI interview ended.

After the FBI interview, an appointed attorney met with petitioner. Petitioner spoke with the lawyer on two or three occasions, though it is not clear from the record whether all of these conferences were in person.

On Monday, August 25, Deputy Sheriff J.C. Denham of Clarke County, Mississippi, came to the San Diego jail to question Minnick. Minnick testified that his jailers again told him he would "have to talk" to Denham and that he "could not refuse." Denham advised petitioner of his rights, and petitioner again declined to sign a rights waiver form. Petitioner told Denham about the escape and then proceeded to describe the events at the mobile home. According to petitioner, Dyess jumped out of the mobile home and shot the first of the two victims, once in the back with a shotgun and once in the head with a pistol. Dyess then handed the pistol to petitioner and ordered him to shoot the other victim, holding the shotgun on petitioner until he did so. Petitioner also said that when the two girls arrived, he talked Dyess out of raping or otherwise hurting them.

Minnick was tried for murder in Mississippi. He moved to suppress all statements given to the FBI or other police officers, including Denham. The trial court denied the motion with respect to petitioner's statements to Denham, but suppressed his other statements. Petitioner was convicted on two counts of capital murder and sentenced to death.

*Edwards* is "designed to prevent police from badgering a defendant into waiving his previously asserted *Miranda* rights." The rule ensures that any statement made in subsequent interrogation is not the result of coercive pressures. *Edwards* conserves judicial resources which would otherwise be expended in making difficult determinations of voluntariness, and implements the protections of *Miranda* in practical and straightforward terms.

The merit of the *Edwards* decision lies in the clarity of its command and the certainty of its application. We have confirmed that the *Edwards* rule

provides "'clear and unequivocal' guidelines to the law enforcement profession." *Roberson*. Even before *Edwards*, we noted that *Miranda*'s "relatively rigid requirement that interrogation must cease upon the accused's request for an attorney . . . has the virtue of informing police and prosecutors with specificity as to what they may do in conducting custodial interrogation, and of informing courts under what circumstances statements obtained during such interrogation are not admissible. This gain in specificity, which benefits the accused and the State alike, has been thought to outweigh the burdens that the decision in *Miranda* imposes on law enforcement agencies and the courts by requiring the suppression of trustworthy and highly probative evidence even though the confession might be voluntary under traditional Fifth Amendment analysis." *Fare v. Michael C.* This pre-*Edwards* explanation applies as well to *Edwards* and its progeny. *Roberson*.

The Mississippi Supreme Court relied on our statement in *Edwards* that an accused who invokes his right to counsel "is not subject to further interrogation by the authorities until counsel has been made available to him. . . ." We do not interpret this language to mean, as the Mississippi court thought, that the protection of *Edwards* terminates once counsel has consulted with the suspect. In context, the requirement that counsel be "made available" to the accused refers to more than an opportunity to consult with an attorney outside the interrogation room.

In *Edwards*, we focused on *Miranda*'s instruction that when the accused invokes his right to counsel, "the interrogation must cease until an attorney is *present*," (emphasis added), agreeing with Edwards' contention that he had not waived his right "to have counsel *present* during custodial interrogation." (emphasis added). In the sentence preceding the language quoted by the Mississippi Supreme Court, we referred to the "right to have counsel *present* during custodial interrogation," and in the sentence following, we again quoted the phrase "interrogation must cease until an attorney is present." *Miranda* (emphasis added). The full sentence relied on by the Mississippi Supreme Court, moreover, says: "We further hold that an accused, such as Edwards, *having expressed his desire to deal with the police only through counsel*, is not subject to further interrogation by the authorities until counsel has been made available to him, unless the accused himself initiates further communication, exchanges, or conversations with the police." (emphasis added).

Our emphasis on counsel's *presence* at interrogation is not unique to *Edwards*. It derives from *Miranda*, where we said that in the cases before us "[t]he presence of counsel . . . would be the adequate protective device necessary to make the process of police interrogation conform to the dictates of the [Fifth Amendment] privilege. Writing for a plurality of the Court, for instance, then-Justice Rehnquist described the holding of *Edwards* to be "that subsequent incriminating statements made *without [Edwards'] attorney present* violated the rights secured to the defendant by the Fifth and Fourteenth Amendments to the United States Constitution." *Bradshaw* (emphasis added). In our view, a fair reading of *Edwards* and subsequent cases demonstrates that we have interpreted the rule to bar police-initiated interrogation unless the accused has counsel with him at the time of questioning. Whatever the ambiguities of our earlier cases on this point, we now hold that when counsel is requested, interrogation must cease, and officials may not reinitiate interrogation without counsel present, whether or not the accused has consulted with his attorney.

We consider our ruling to be an appropriate and necessary application of the *Edwards* rule. A single consultation with an attorney does not remove the suspect from persistent attempts by officials to persuade him to waive his rights, or from the coercive pressures that accompany custody and that may increase as custody is prolonged. The case before us well illustrates the pressures, and abuses, that may be concomitants of custody. Petitioner testified that though he resisted, he was required to submit to both the FBI and the Denham interviews. In the latter instance, the compulsion to submit to interrogation followed petitioner's unequivocal request during the FBI interview that questioning cease until counsel was present. The case illustrates also that consultation is not always effective in instructing the suspect of his rights. One plausible interpretation of the record is that petitioner thought he could keep his admissions out of evidence by refusing to sign a formal waiver of rights. If the authorities had complied with Minnick's request to have counsel present during interrogation, the attorney could have corrected Minnick's misunderstanding, or indeed counseled him that he need not make a statement at all. We decline to remove protection from police-initiated questioning based on isolated consultations with counsel who is absent when the interrogation resumes.

The exception to *Edwards* here proposed is inconsistent with *Edwards'* purpose to protect the suspect's right to have counsel present at custodial interrogation. It is inconsistent as well with *Miranda*, where we specifically rejected respondent's theory that the opportunity to consult with one's attorney would substantially counteract the compulsion created by custodial interrogation. We noted in *Miranda* that "[e]ven preliminary advice given to the accused by his own attorney can be swiftly overcome by the secret interrogation process. Thus the need for counsel to protect the Fifth Amendment privilege comprehends not merely a right to consult with counsel prior to questioning, but also to have counsel present during any questioning if the defendant so desires."

[A]dopting the rule proposed would leave far from certain the sort of consultation required to displace *Edwards*. Consultation is not a precise concept, for it may encompass variations from a telephone call to say that the attorney is in route, to a hurried interchange between the attorney and client in a detention facility corridor, to a lengthy in-person conference in which the attorney gives full and adequate advice respecting all matters that might be covered in further interrogations. And even with the necessary scope of consultation settled, the officials in charge of the case would have to confirm the occurrence and, possibly, the extent of consultation to determine whether further interrogation is permissible. The necessary inquiries could interfere with the attorney-client privilege.

Added to these difficulties in definition and application of the proposed rule is our concern over its consequence that the suspect whose counsel is prompt would lose the protection of *Edwards*, while the one whose counsel is dilatory would not. There is more than irony to this result. There is a strong possibility that it would distort the proper conception of the attorney's duty to the client and set us on a course at odds with what ought to be effective representation.

Both waiver of rights and admission of guilt are consistent with the affirmation of individual responsibility that is a principle of the criminal justice system. It does not detract from this principle, however, to insist that neither admissions nor waivers are effective unless there are both particular and systemic assurances that the coercive pressures of custody were not the inducing cause. The *Edwards* rule sets forth a specific standard to fulfill these purposes, and we have declined to confine it in other instances. It would detract from the efficacy of the rule to remove its protections based on consultation with counsel.

*Edwards* does not foreclose finding a waiver of Fifth Amendment protections after counsel has been requested, provided the accused has initiated the conversation or discussions with the authorities; but that is not the case before us. There can be no doubt that the interrogation in question was initiated by the police; it was a formal interview which petitioner was compelled to attend. Since petitioner made a specific request for counsel before the interview, the police-initiated interrogation was impermissible. Petitioner's statement to Denham was not admissible at trial.

The judgment is reversed and the case remanded for further proceedings not inconsistent with this opinion.

Justice SCALIA, with whom the CHIEF JUSTICE joins, dissenting.

The Court today establishes an irrebuttable presumption that a criminal suspect, after invoking his *Miranda* right to counsel, can *never* validly waive that right during any police-initiated encounter, even after the suspect has been provided multiple *Miranda* warnings and has actually consulted his attorney. This holding builds on foundations already established in *Edwards*, but "the rule of *Edwards* is our rule, not a constitutional command; and it is our obligation to justify its expansion." *Roberson*. Because I see no justification for applying the *Edwards* irrebuttable presumption when a criminal suspect has actually consulted with his attorney, I respectfully dissent.

### I

Some recapitulation of pertinent facts is in order, given the Court's contention that "[t]he case before us well illustrates the pressures, and abuses, that may be concomitants of custody." It is undisputed that the FBI agents who first interviewed Minnick on Saturday, August 23, 1986, advised him of his *Miranda* rights before any questioning began. Although he refused to sign a waiver form, he agreed to talk to the agents, and described his escape from prison in Mississippi and the ensuing events. When he came to what happened at the trailer, however, Minnick hesitated. The FBI agents then reminded him that he did not have to answer questions without a lawyer present. Minnick indicated that he would finish his account on Monday, when he had a lawyer, and the FBI agents terminated the interview forthwith.

Minnick was then provided with an attorney, with whom he consulted several times over the weekend. As Minnick testified at a subsequent suppression hearing:

"I talked to [my attorney] two different times and—it might have been three different times. . . . He told me that first day that he was my lawyer and that he was appointed to

me and not to talk to nobody and not tell nobody nothing and to not sign no waivers and not sign no extradition papers or sign anything and that he was going to get a court order to have any of the police—I advised him of the FBI talking to me and he advised me not to tell anybody anything that he was going to get a court order drawn up to restrict anybody talking to me outside of the San Diego Police Department."

On Monday morning, Minnick was interviewed by Deputy Sheriff J.C. Denham, who had come to San Diego from Mississippi. Before the interview, Denham reminded Minnick of his *Miranda* rights. Minnick again refused to sign a waiver form, but he did talk with Denham, and did not ask for his attorney. As Minnick recalled at the hearing, he and Denham "went through several different conversations about—first, about how everybody was back in the county jail and what everybody was doing, had he heard from Mama and had he went and talked to Mama and had he seen my brother, Tracy, and several different other questions pertaining to such things as that. And, we went off into how the escape went down at the county jail. . . ." Minnick then proceeded to describe his participation in the double murder at the trailer.

The Court today holds that, because Minnick had asked for counsel during the interview with the FBI agents, he could not—as a matter of law—validly waive the right to have counsel present during the conversation initiated by Denham. That Minnick's original request to see an attorney had been honored, that Minnick had consulted with his attorney on several occasions, and that the attorney had specifically warned Minnick not to speak to the authorities, are irrelevant. That Minnick was familiar with the criminal justice system in general or *Miranda* warnings in particular (he had previously been convicted of robbery in Mississippi and assault with a deadly weapon in California) is also beside the point. The confession must be suppressed, not because it was "compelled," nor even because it was obtained from an individual who could realistically be assumed to be unaware of his rights, but simply because this Court sees fit to prescribe as a "systemic assuranc[e]," that a person in custody who has once asked for counsel cannot thereafter be approached by the police unless counsel is present. Of course the Constitution's proscription of compelled testimony does not remotely authorize this incursion upon state practices; and even our recent precedents are not a valid excuse.

The value of any prophylactic rule (assuming the

authority to adopt a prophylactic rule) must be assessed not only on the basis of what is gained, but also on the basis of what is lost. "Admissions of guilt," we have said, "are more than merely 'desirable'; they are essential to society's compelling interest in finding, convicting, and punishing those who violate the law."

### III

In this case, of course, we have not been called upon to reconsider *Edwards*, but simply to determine whether its irrebuttable presumption should continue after a suspect has actually consulted with his attorney. Whatever justifications might support *Edwards* are even less convincing in this context.

Most of the Court's discussion of *Edwards* — which stresses repeatedly, in various formulations, the case's emphasis upon "the 'right to have counsel *present* during custodial interrogation,'" (emphasis added by the Court) — is beside the point. The existence and the importance of the *Miranda*-created right "to have counsel *present*" are unquestioned here. What *is* questioned is why a State should not be given the opportunity to prove (under *Zerbst*) that the right was *voluntarily waived* by a suspect who, after having been read his *Miranda* rights twice and having consulted with counsel at least twice, chose to speak to a police officer (and to admit his involvement in two murders) without counsel present.

*Edwards* did not assert the principle that no waiver of the *Miranda* right "to have counsel *present*" is possible. It simply adopted the presumption that no waiver is *voluntary* in certain circumstances, and the issue before us today is how broadly those circumstances are to be defined. They should not, in my view, extend beyond the circumstances present in *Edwards* itself — where the suspect in custody asked to consult an attorney, and was interrogated before that attorney had ever been provided. In those circumstances, the *Edwards* rule rests upon an assumption similar to that of *Miranda* itself: that when a suspect in police custody is first questioned he is likely to be ignorant of his rights and to feel isolated in a hostile environment. This likelihood is thought to justify special protection against unknowing or coerced waiver of rights. After a suspect has seen his request for an attorney honored, however, and has actually spoken with that attorney, the probabilities change. The suspect then knows that he has an advocate on his side, and that the police will permit him to consult that advocate. He almost certainly also has a heightened awareness (above what the *Miranda* warning itself will provide) of his right to remain silent — since at the earliest opportunity

"any lawyer worth his salt will tell the suspect in no uncertain terms to make no statement to the police under any circumstances." *Watts v. Indiana* (Opinion of Jackson, J.).

One should not underestimate the extent to which the Court's expansion of *Edwards* constricts law enforcement. Today's ruling, that the invocation of a right to counsel permanently prevents a police-initiated waiver, makes it largely impossible for the police to urge a prisoner who has initially declined to confess to change his mind — or indeed, even to ask whether he has changed his mind. Many persons in custody will invoke the *Miranda* right to counsel during the first interrogation, so that the permanent prohibition will attach at once. Those who do not do so will almost certainly request or obtain counsel at arraignment. I presume that the perpetuality of prohibition announced in today's opinion applies in that context as well. "Perpetuality" is not too strong a term, since, although the Court rejects one logical moment at which the *Edwards* presumption might end, it suggests no alternative. In this case Minnick was reapproached by the police three days after he requested counsel, but the result would presumably be the same if it had been three months, or three years, or even three decades. This perpetual irrebuttable presumption will apply, I might add, not merely to interrogations involving the original crime but to those involving other subjects as well. *Roberson*.

The rest of the Court's arguments can be answered briefly. The suggestion that it will either be impossible or ethically impermissible to determine whether a "consultation" between the suspect and his attorney has occurred is alarmist. Since, as I have described above, the main purpose of the consultation requirement is to eliminate the suspect's feeling of isolation and to assure him the presence of legal assistance, any discussion between him and an attorney whom he asks to contact, or who is provided to him, in connection with his arrest, will suffice. The precise content of the discussion is irrelevant.

As for the "irony" that "the suspect whose counsel is prompt would lose the protection of *Edwards*, while the one whose counsel is dilatory would not": There seems to me no irony in applying a special protection only when it is needed. The *Edwards* rule is premised on an (already tenuous) assumption about the suspect's psychological state, and when the event of consultation renders that assumption invalid the rule should no longer apply. One searching for ironies in the state of our law should consider, first, the irony created by *Edwards* itself: The suspect in custody who says categorically "I do not wish to discuss this matter'' can be asked to change his mind; but if he should say, more tentatively, ''I do not think I should discuss this matter without my attorney present'' he can no longer be approached. To that there is added, by today's decision, the irony that it will be far harder for the state to establish a knowing and voluntary waiver of Fifth Amendment rights by a prisoner who has already consulted with counsel than by a newly arrested suspect.

Today's extension of the *Edwards* prohibition is the latest stage of prophylaxis built upon prophylaxis, producing a veritable fairyland castle of imagined constitutional restriction upon law enforcement. This newest tower, according to the Court, is needed to avoid ''inconsisten[cy] with [the] purpose'' of *Edwards*' prophylactic rule, which was needed to protect *Miranda*'s prophylactic right to have counsel present, which was needed to protect the right against *compelled self-incrimination* found (at last!) in the Constitution.

It seems obvious to me that, even in *Edwards* itself but surely in today's decision, we have gone far beyond any genuine concern about suspects who do not *know* their right to remain silent, or who have been *coerced* to abandon it. Both holdings are explicable, in my view, only as an effort to protect suspects against what is regarded as their own folly. The sharp-witted criminal would know better than to confess; why should the dull-witted suffer for his lack of mental endowment? Providing him an attorney at every stage where he might be induced or persuaded (though not coerced) to incriminate himself will even the odds. Apart from the fact that this protective enterprise is beyond our authority under the Fifth Amendment or any other provision of the Constitution, it is unwise. The procedural protections of the Constitution protect the guilty as well

as the innocent, but it is not their objective to set the guilty free. That some clever criminals may employ those protections to their advantage is poor reason to allow criminals who have not done so to escape justice.

Thus, even if I were to concede that an honest confession is a foolish mistake, I would welcome rather than reject it; a rule that foolish mistakes do not count would leave most offenders not only unconvicted but undetected. More fundamentally, however, it is wrong, and subtly corrosive of our criminal justice system, to regard an honest confession as a ''mistake.'' While every person is entitled to stand silent, it is more virtuous for the wrongdoer to admit his offense and accept the punishment he deserves. Not only for society, but for the wrongdoer himself, ''admissio[n] of guilt . . ., if not coerced, [is] inherently desirable,'' because it advances the goals of both ''justice *and* rehabilitation.'' (emphasis added). A confession is rightly regarded by the sentencing guidelines as warranting a reduction of sentence, because it ''demonstrates a recognition and affirmative acceptance of personal responsibility for . . . criminal conduct,'' U.S. Sentencing Commission, Guidelines Manual § 3E1.1 (1988), which is the beginning of reform. We should, then, rejoice at an honest confession, rather than pity the ''poor fool'' who has made it; and we should regret the attempted retraction of that good act, rather than seek to facilitate and encourage it. To design our laws on premises contrary to these is to abandon belief in either personal responsibility or the moral claim of just government to obedience. Today's decision is misguided, it seems to me, in so readily exchanging, for marginal, *super-Zerbst* protection against genuinely compelled testimony, investigators' ability to urge, or even ask, a person in custody to do what is right.

## QUESTIONS AND NOTES

**1.** Is Justice Kennedy consistent in dissenting in *Roberson* and writing *Minnick*? Conversely, is Justice Scalia consistent in dissenting in *Minnick* after having joined the *Roberson* majority? Explain.

**2.** Is there anything wrong with the dissent's approach to the case? Explain.

**3.** Is the dissent principally predicated on not wanting to expand a mistake? If the dissent thought that *Edwards* and *Miranda* were correctly decided, would it have reached the same result?

**4.** Would the dissent's rule reward dilatory counsel? Would it encourage counsel to be dilatory?

**5.** Apart from *Edwards*, should the statements in *Minnick* be inadmissible? Why? Why not?

# PROBLEM

Lowell Green originally was arrested on July 18, 1989, on a charge of possessing a controlled substance with intent to distribute. He signed a police advice-of-rights (PD 47) form that day and answered "No" in writing to the question whether he was willing to answer questions without having an attorney present. Green was presented in court the next day and an attorney was appointed to represent him. He was held on bond until July 28, 1989, when the drug case was dismissed at preliminary hearing. It appears that he was then remanded to the custody of juvenile authorities, presumably in connection with a juvenile matter pending against him at the time. He was subsequently indicted on the drug charge, but failed to appear for his arraignment on August 22, 1989, apparently because he was in the custody of juvenile authorities. When eventually located, he was arraigned in the drug case on September 7, 1989. A bond was imposed and he remained in custody on the bond until September 27, 1989, when he pled guilty to the lesser included offense of attempted possession with intent to distribute cocaine. Following the plea, he was held in the Youth Center at the Lorton Reformatory while a Youth Act Study was conducted. On February 26, 1990, he was sentenced to fifteen months' incarceration under the Youth Act.

Meanwhile, on January 4, 1990, while defendant was at Lorton, Detective Donald Gossage of the Metropolitan Police Department obtained an arrest warrant charging him with the murder of Cheaver Herriott on December 30, 1988. Also on January 4, Detective Gossage obtained an order directing that defendant be brought up the next day from the Youth Center to be booked and formally presented on the murder warrant. On January 5, defendant was brought to the police Homicide Office to be booked. Detective Gossage advised him of his *Miranda* rights by reading to him both sides of the PD 47 form. Defendant chose to waive his *Miranda* rights, so indicating by his answers to the four questions on the form. After he discussed with Gossage his involvement in the murder of Cheaver Herriott, defendant was again advised of his rights and agreed to make a videotaped statement, in which he confessed involvement in the robbery and killing of Herriott.

Following his indictment on April 17, 1990 on various charges including first-degree murder, defendant moved to suppress his confession on several grounds, chief among them that it had been obtained in violation of *Edwards* in view of his original refusal—at the time of his arrest on the drug charge—to answer questions without counsel being present. The trial judge heard testimony and initially denied the motion to suppress, concluding that "none of the reasons which underlie [the Supreme] Court's decision[s] which have addressed a criminal defendant's right not to incriminate himself under the 5th Amendment[ ] would be served by suppression" of defendant's murder confession. The judge emphasized three points. First, an "extraordinary amount of time [over five months] . . . [had] elapsed between" defendant's invocation of rights in the drug case and his waiver of rights in connection with his confession to murder. Second, although he was under some form of restraint of liberty during the entire five or more months, during the last part of that period he was not being held in jail but rather in the presumably less coercive environment of the Youth Center. Finally, defendant had had the opportunity to consult repeatedly with counsel during the period between his invocation of rights in the drug case and his waiver of rights before his murder confession.

Three days after the court's initial ruling, however, the Supreme Court decided *Minnick*. The judge reconsidered his ruling on the Fifth Amendment issue in light of *Minnick*, noting in particular that the "most significant[ ]" ground of his ruling had been the appointment of counsel and the opportunity defendant had had to consult counsel in the months prior to the reinitiation of questioning by the police—a factor specifically addressed by *Minnick*, and held not to justify a departure from *Edwards*. On the strength of *Minnick*'s specific holding and its reaffirmation of the "bright-line" test established by *Edwards*, the judge reversed his earlier ruling and ordered the confession suppressed.

How should the Supreme Court decide this case? Why?

The Supreme Court in fact granted certiorari in this case at the behest of the government (which had lost by a 2-1 vote in the lower court). 112 S.Ct. 1935, 118 L.Ed.2d 542 (1992). It subsequently dismissed the case as moot because of Lowell Green's death. 113 S.Ct. 1835, 123 L.Ed.2d 260 (1993).

In *Davis*, the Supreme Court considered under what circumstances, a request for counsel will be deemed sufficiently unequivocal to preclude further questioning.

## Davis v. United States
### 114 S.Ct. 2350 (1994)

Justice O'CONNOR delivered the opinion of the Court.

### I

Pool brought trouble—not to River City, but to the Charleston Naval Base. Petitioner, a member of the United States Navy, spent the evening of October 2, 1988, shooting pool at a club on the base. Another sailor, Keith Shackleford, lost a game and a $30 wager to petitioner, but Shackleford refused to pay. After the club closed, Shackleford was beaten to death with a pool cue on a loading dock behind the commissary. The body was found early the next morning.

The investigation by the Naval Investigative Service (NIS) gradually focused on petitioner. Investigative agents determined that petitioner was at the club that evening, and that he was absent without authorization from his duty station the next morning. The agents also learned that only privately owned pool cues could be removed from the club premises, and that petitioner owned two cues—one of which had a bloodstain on it. The agents were told by various people that petitioner either had admitted committing the crime or had recounted details that clearly indicated his involvement in the killing. On November 4, 1988, petitioner was interviewed at the NIS office. As required by military law, the agents advised petitioner that he was a suspect in the killing, that he was not required to make a statement, that any statement could be used against him at a trial by court-martial, and that he was entitled to speak with an attorney and have an attorney present during questioning. Petitioner waived his rights to remain silent and to counsel, both orally and in writing.

About an hour and a half into the interview, petitioner said, "Maybe I should talk to a lawyer." According to the uncontradicted testimony of one of the interviewing agents, the interview then proceeded as follows: "[We m]ade it very clear that we're not here to violate his rights, that if he wants a lawyer, then we will stop any kind of questioning with him, that we weren't going to pursue the matter unless we have it clarified is he asking for a lawyer or is he just making a comment about a lawyer, and he said, [']No, I'm not asking for a lawyer,' and then he continued on, and said, 'No, I don't want a lawyer.'" After a short break, the agents reminded petitioner of his rights to remain silent and to counsel. The interview then continued for another hour, until petitioner said, "I think I want a lawyer before I say anything else." At that point, questioning ceased.

### II

The right to counsel recognized in *Miranda* is sufficiently important to suspects in criminal investigations, we have held, that it "requir[es] the special protection of the knowing and intelligent waiver standard." *Edwards, Bradshaw.* If the suspect effectively waives his right to counsel after receiving the Miranda warnings, law enforcement officers are free to question him. *North Carolina v. Butler, infra.* But if a suspect requests counsel at any time during the interview, he is not subject to further questioning until a lawyer has been made available or the suspect himself reinitiates conversation. *Edwards*. This "second layer of prophylaxis for the Miranda right to counsel" is "designed to prevent police from badgering a defendant into waiving his previously asserted Miranda rights." To that end, we have held that a suspect who has invoked the right to counsel cannot be questioned regarding any offense unless an attorney is actually present. *Minnick, Roberson*. "It remains clear, however, that this prohibition on further questioning – like other aspects of Miranda – is not itself required by the Fifth Amendment's prohibition on coerced confessions, but is instead justified only by reference to its prophylactic purpose."

The applicability of the " 'rigid' prophylactic rule" of *Edwards* requires courts to "determine whether the accused actually invoked his right to counsel." To avoid difficulties of proof and to provide guidance to officers conducting interrogations, this is an objective inquiry. Invocation of the *Miranda* right to counsel "requires, at a minimum, some statement that can reasonably be construed to be an expression of a desire for the assistance of an attorney." But if a suspect makes a reference to an attorney that is ambiguous or equivocal in that a reasonable officer in light of the circumstances would have understood only that the suspect *might* be invoking the right to counsel, our precedents do not require the cessation of questioning. ("the *likelihood* that a suspect would wish counsel to be present is not the test for applicability of *Edwards*"); (impermissible for authorities "to reinterrogate an accused in custody if he has *clearly asserted* his right to counsel") (emphasis added).

Rather, the suspect must unambiguously request counsel. As we have observed, "a statement either is such an assertion of the right to counsel or it is not." *Smith v. Illinois*, 469 U.S., at 97-98. Although a suspect need not "speak with the discrimination of an Oxford don," (SOUTER, J., concurring in judgment), he must articulate his desire to have counsel present sufficiently clearly that a reasonable police officer in the circumstances would understand the statement to be a request for an attorney. If the statement fails to meet the requisite level of clarity, *Edwards* does not require that the officers stop questioning the suspect.

We decline petitioner's invitation to extend *Edwards* and require law enforcement officers to cease questioning immediately upon the making of an ambiguous or equivocal reference to an attorney. See *Roberson* (KENNEDY, J., dissenting) ("the rule of *Edwards* is our rule, not a constitutional command; and it is our obligation to justify its expansion"). The rationale underlying Edwards is that the police

must respect a suspect's wishes regarding his right to have an attorney present during custodial interrogation. But when the officers conducting the questioning reasonably do not know whether or not the suspect wants a lawyer, a rule requiring the immediate cessation of questioning "would transform the Miranda safeguards into wholly irrational obstacles to legitimate police investigative activity," *Mosley*, because it would needlessly prevent the police from questioning a suspect in the absence of counsel even if the suspect did not wish to have a lawyer present. Nothing in *Edwards* requires the provision of counsel to a suspect who consents to answer questions without the assistance of a lawyer.

We recognize that requiring a clear assertion of the right to counsel might disadvantage some suspects who – because of fear, intimidation, lack of linguistic skills, or a variety of other reasons – will not clearly articulate their right to counsel although they actually want to have a lawyer present. But the primary protection afforded suspects subject to custodial interrogation is the *Miranda* warnings themselves. A suspect who knowingly and voluntarily waives his right to counsel after having that right explained to him has indicated his willingness to deal with the police unassisted. Although *Edwards* provides an additional protection – if a suspect subsequently requests an attorney, questioning must cease – it is one that must be affirmatively invoked by the suspect.

In considering how a suspect must invoke the right to counsel, we must consider the other side of the *Miranda* equation: the need for effective law enforcement. Although the courts ensure compliance with the *Miranda* requirements through the exclusionary rule, it is police officers who must actually decide whether or not they can question a suspect. The *Edwards* rule – questioning must cease if the suspect asks for a lawyer – provides a bright line that can be applied by officers in the real world of investigation and interrogation without unduly hampering the gathering of information. But if we were to require questioning to cease if a suspect makes a statement that might be a request for an attorney, this clarity and ease of application would be lost. Police officers would be forced to make difficult judgment calls about whether the suspect in fact wants a lawyer even though he hasn't said so, with the threat of suppression if they guess wrong. We therefore hold that, after a knowing and voluntary waiver of the *Miranda* rights, law enforcement officers may continue questioning until and unless the suspect clearly requests an attorney.

Of course, when a suspect makes an ambiguous

or equivocal statement it will often be good police practice for the interviewing officers to clarify whether or not he actually wants an attorney. That was the procedure followed by the NIS agents in this case. Clarifying questions help protect the rights of the suspect by ensuring that he gets an attorney if he wants one, and will minimize the chance of a confession being suppressed due to subsequent judicial second-guessing as to the meaning of the suspect's statement regarding counsel. But we decline to adopt a rule requiring officers to ask clarifying questions. If the suspect's statement is not an unambiguous or unequivocal request for counsel, the officers have no obligation to stop questioning him.

To recapitulate: We held in *Miranda* that a suspect is entitled to the assistance of counsel during custodial interrogation even though the Constitution does not provide for such assistance. We held in *Edwards* that if the suspect invokes the right to counsel at any time, the police must immediately cease questioning him until an attorney is present. But we are unwilling to create a third layer of prophylaxis to prevent police questioning when the suspect might want a lawyer. Unless the suspect actually requests an attorney, questioning may continue.The courts below found that petitioner's remark to the NIS agents—"Maybe I should talk to a lawyer"—was not a request for counsel, and we see no reason to disturb that conclusion. The NIS agents therefore were not required to stop questioning petitioner, though it was entirely proper for them to clarify whether petitioner in fact wanted a lawyer. Because there is no ground for suppression of petitioner's statements, the judgment of the Court of Military Appeals is

Affirmed.

Justice SCALIA, concurring.

(Although fully concurring in the opinion, Justice Scalia suggested that the Government should not have conceded the inapplicability of Section 3501 of Title 18, which was adopted by Congress shortly after and in response to *Miranda*. Among other things, the statute requires that the admissibility of confessions in Federal Courts be determined on the basis of voluntariness, rather than in accordance with the *Miranda* strictures. Justice Scalia indicated that he would consider that statute in the next Federal prosecution potentially raising that issue, whether or not the Government chose to push the issue.)

Justice SOUTER, with whom Justice BLACKMUN, Justice STEVENS, and Justice GINSBURG join, concurring in the judgment.

I agree with the majority that the Constitution does not forbid law enforcement officers to pose questions (like those directed at Davis) aimed solely at clarifying whether a suspect's ambiguous reference to counsel was meant to assert his Fifth Amendment right. Accordingly I concur in the judgment affirming Davis's conviction, resting partly on evidence of statements given after agents ascertained that he did not wish to deal with them through counsel. I cannot, however, join in my colleagues' further conclusion that if the investigators here had been so inclined, they were at liberty to disregard Davis's reference to a lawyer entirely, in accordance with a general rule that interrogators have no legal obligation to discover what a custodial subject meant by an ambiguous statement that could reasonably be understood to express a desire to consult a lawyer.

Our own precedent, the reasonable judgments of the majority of the many courts already to have addressed the issue before us, and the advocacy of a considerable body of law enforcement officials are to the contrary. All argue against the Court's approach today, which draws a sharp line between interrogated suspects who "clearly" assert their right to counsel, ante, and those who say something that may, but may not, express a desire for counsel's presence, the former suspects being assured that questioning will not resume without counsel present, the latter being left to fend for themselves. The concerns of fairness and practicality that have long anchored our Miranda case law point to a different response: when law enforcement officials "reasonably do not know whether or not the suspect wants a lawyer," they should stop their interrogation and ask him to make his choice clear.

I

A

While the question we address today is an open one, its answer requires coherence with nearly three decades of case law addressing the relationship between police and criminal suspects in custodial interrogation. Throughout that period, two precepts have commanded broad assent: that the Miranda safeguards exist "to assure that *the individual's right to choose* between speech and silence remains unfettered throughout the interrogation process," see *Connecticut v. Barrett, infra* (quoting *Miranda*, and supplying emphasis), and that the justification for *Miranda* rules, intended to operate in the real world, "must be consistent with . . . practical realities." *Roberson* (KENNEDY, J., dissenting). A rule barring government agents from further interrogation until they determine whether a suspect's ambiguous statement was meant as a request for counsel fulfills both ambitions. It assures that a suspect's choice whether or not to deal with police through counsel will be "scrupulously honored," *Mosley* (White, J., concurring in result), and it faces both the real-world reasons why misunderstandings arise between suspect and interrogator and the real-world limitations on the capacity of police and trial courts to apply fine distinctions and intricate rules.

### B

Tested against the same two principles, the approach the Court adopts does not fare so well. First, as the majority expressly acknowledges, criminal suspects who may (in *Miranda's* words) be "thrust into an unfamiliar atmosphere and run through menacing police interrogation procedures," would seem an odd group to single out for the Court's demand of heightened linguistic care. A substantial percentage of them lack anything like a confident command of the English language, many are "woefully ignorant," and many more will be sufficiently intimidated by the interrogation process or overwhelmed by the uncertainty of their predicament that the ability to speak assertively will abandon them.[4] Indeed, the awareness of just these realities has, in the past, dissuaded the Court from placing any burden of clarity upon individuals in custody, but has led it instead to require that requests for counsel be "give [n] a broad, rather than a narrow, interpretation," and that courts "indulge every reasonable presumption" that a suspect has not waived his right to counsel under Miranda.

Nor may the standard governing waivers be deflected away by drawing a distinction between initial waivers of *Miranda* rights and subsequent decisions to reinvoke them, on the theory that so long as the burden to demonstrate waiver rests on the government, it is only fair to make the suspect shoulder a burden of showing a clear subsequent assertion. *Miranda* itself discredited the legitimacy of any such distinction. The opinion described the object of the warning as being to assure "a continuous opportunity to exercise [the right of silence]."

The Court defends as tolerable the certainty that some poorly expressed requests for counsel will be disregarded on the ground that Miranda warnings suffice to alleviate the inherent coercion of the custodial interrogation. But, "a once-stated warning, delivered by those who will conduct the interrogation cannot itself suffice" to "assure that the . . . right to choose between silence and speech remains unfettered throughout the interrogation process."

Indeed, it is easy, amidst the discussion of layers of protection, to lose sight of a real risk in the majority's approach, going close to the core of what the Court has held that the Fifth Amendment provides. The experience of the timid or verbally inept suspect (whose existence the Court acknowledges) may not always closely follow that of the defendant in *Edwards* (whose purported waiver of his right to counsel, made after having invoked the right, was held ineffective, lest police be tempted to "badge[r]" others like him. Indeed, it may be more like that of the defendant in *Escobedo*, whose sense of dilemma was heightened by his interrogators' denial of his requests to talk to a lawyer. When a suspect understands his (expressed) wishes to have been ignored (and by hypothesis, he has said something that an objective listener could "reasonably," although not necessarily, take to be a request), in contravention of the "rights" just read to him by his interrogator, he may well see further objection as futile and confession (true or not) as the only way to end his interrogation.[5]

Nor is it enough to say that a "'statement either is . . . an assertion of the right to counsel or it is not.'" While it might be fair to say that every statement is meant either to express a desire to deal with police through counsel or not, this fact does not dictate the rule that interrogators who hear a statement consistent with either possibility may presume

---

[4] Social science confirms what common sense would suggest, that individuals who feel intimidated or powerless are more likely to speak in equivocal or nonstandard terms when no ambiguity or equivocation is meant. See W. O'Barr, Linguistic Evidence: Language, Power and Strategy in the Courtroom 61-71 (1982).

[5] See People v. Harper, 94 Ill.App.3d 298, 300, 49 Ill.Dec. 874, 876, 418 N.E.2d 894, 896 (1981) (defendant who asked interrogator to retrieve an attorney's business card from his wallet but was told that it " 'wouldn't be necessary' " held not to have "availed himself" of right to counsel); see also Cooper v. Dupnik, 963 F.2d 1220, 1225 (CA9 1992) (en banc) (describing elaborate police Task Force plan to ignore systematically a suspect's requests for counsel, on the theory that such would induce hopelessness and thereby elicit an admission, which would then be used to keep the suspect off the witness stand, see Oregon v. Haas, 420 U.S. 714, 95 S.Ct. 1215, 43 L.Ed.2d 570 (1975) (statements obtained in violation of Miranda rules admissible for impeachment purposes)).

the latter and forge ahead; on the contrary, clarification is the intuitively sensible course.

The other justifications offered for the "requisite level of clarity" rule are that, whatever its costs, it will further society's strong interest in "effective law enforcement," and maintain the "ease of application" that has long been a concern of our *Miranda* jurisprudence. With respect to the first point, the margin of difference between the clarification approach advocated here and the one the Court adopts is defined by the class of cases in which a suspect, if asked, would make it plain that he meant to request counsel (at which point questioning would cease). While these lost confessions do extract a real price from society, it is one that Miranda itself determined should be borne.

As for practical application, while every approach, including the majority's, will involve some "difficult judgment calls,"[7] the rule argued for here would relieve the officer of any responsibility for guessing "whether the suspect in fact wants a lawyer even though he hasn't said so." To the contrary, it would assure that the "judgment call" will be made by the party most competent to resolve the ambiguity, who our case law has always assumed should

---

[7] In the abstract, nothing may seem more clear than a "clear statement" rule, but in police stations and trial courts the question, "how clear is clear?" is not so readily answered. When a suspect says, "uh, yeah, I'd like to do that" after being told he has a right to a lawyer, has he "clearly asserted" his right? Compare *Smith v. Illinois*, 469 U.S. 91, 97 (statement was " 'neither indecisive nor ambiguous' ") (citation omitted)), with id., at 101, 105 S.Ct., at 495-496 (REHNQUIST, J., dissenting) (questioning clarity); see also *Bradshaw* (plurality opinion) ("I do want an attorney before it goes very much further"); *Edwards* (" 'I want an attorney before making a deal' "). Indeed, in this case, when Davis finally said, "I think I want a lawyer before I say anything else," the agents ceased questioning; but see *People v. Kendricks*, 121 Ill.App.3d 442, 446, 77 Ill.Dec. 41, 43, 459 N.E.2d 1137, 1139 (1984) (agents need not stop interrogation when suspect says, " 'I think I might need a lawyer' "); Cf. *People v. Santiago*, 133 App.Div.2d 429, 430-431, 519 N.Y.S.2d 413, 414-415 (1987) (" 'Will you supply [a lawyer] now so that I may ask him should I continue with this interview at this moment?' " held "not . . . an unequivocal invocation"). See generally Smith, supra, 469 U.S., at 101, 105 S.Ct., at 495-496 (REHNQUIST, J., dissenting) (noting that

make it: the individual suspect.

## II

Although I am convinced that the Court has taken the wrong path, I am not persuaded by the petitioner's contention, that even ambiguous statements require an end to all police questioning. I recognize that the approach petitioner urges on us can claim some support from our case law, most notably in the "indicates in any manner" language of *Miranda*, and I do not deny that the rule I endorse could be abused by "clarifying" questions that shade subtly into illicitly badgering a suspect who wants counsel. But the petitioner's proposal is not entirely in harmony with all the major themes of *Miranda* case law, its virtues and demerits being the reverse images of those that mark the Court's rule. While it is plainly wrong, for example, to continue interrogation when the suspect wants it to stop (and so indicates), the strong bias in favor of individual choice may also be disserved by stopping questioning when a suspect wants it to continue (but where his statement might be understood otherwise), see *Mosley* (White, J., concurring in result) ("[W]e have . . . rejected [the] paternalistic rule protecting a defendant from his intelligent and voluntary decisions about his own criminal case"). The costs to society of losing confessions would, moreover, be especially hard to bear where the suspect, if asked for his choice, would have chosen to continue. One need not sign the majority's opinion here to agree that resort to the rule petitioner argues for should be had only if experience shows that less drastic means of safeguarding suspects' constitutional rights are not up to the job.

Our cases are best respected by a rule that when a suspect under custodial interrogation makes an ambiguous statement that might reasonably be understood as expressing a wish that a lawyer be summoned (and questioning cease), interrogators' questions should be confined to verifying whether the individual meant to ask for a lawyer. While there is

---

statements are rarely "crystal-clear. . . . [D]ifferences between certainty and hesitancy may well turn on the inflection with which words are spoken, especially where [a] statement is isolated from the statements surrounding it"). As a practical matter, of course, the primary arbiters of "clarity" will be the interrogators themselves, who tend as well to be courts' preferred source in determining the precise words a suspect used. And when an inculpatory statement has been obtained as a result of an unrecorded, incommunicado interrogation, these officers rarely lose "swearing matches" against criminal defendants at suppression hearings.

reason to expect that trial courts will apply today's ruling sensibly (without requiring criminal suspects to speak with the discrimination of an Oxford don) and that interrogators will continue to follow what the Court rightly calls "good police practice" (compelled up to now by a substantial body of state and Circuit law), I believe that the case law under *Miranda* does not allow them to do otherwise.

## QUESTIONS AND NOTES

**1.** Do you perceive the Court's decision as one which will contribute to *Miranda's* utility as a bright-line rule? Why? Why not?

**2.** Is the Court's decision likely to have a discriminatory impact on less articulate and less assertive members of society? (See fn. 4 of Justice Souter's opinion, and Ainsworth, *In a Different Register: The Pragmatics of Powerlessness in Police Interrogation,* 103 Yale L.J. 259 (1993).) Do you think that the Court desired such a result?

**3.** Is the majority more concerned with protecting police or protecting suspects? If the former, is it true to the *Miranda* philosophy?

**4.** The Court seems to assume that the *Miranda* warnings simpliciter are enough to dispel the inherent coercion of police interrogation? Do you agree? If the Court thought otherwise, would it have reached a different result?

**5.** Why do you suppose that there were no votes on the Court for reversal of Davis' conviction? Would you have voted for reversal? Explain.

**6.** Should Justice Scalia's suggestion that a statute might prevail over *Miranda* in regard to the admissibility of confessions in Federal Court be taken seriously? Why? Why not?

## PROBLEM

Shortly after his arrest, 18-year-old Steven Smith was taken to an interrogation room at the Logan County Safety Complex for questioning by two police detectives. The session began as follows:

"Q. Steve, I want to talk with you in reference to the armed robbery that took place at McDonald's restaurant on the morning of the 19th. Are you familiar with this?

"A. Yeah. My cousin Greg was.

"Q. Okay. But before I do that I must advise you of your rights. Okay? You have a right to remain silent. You do not have to talk to me unless you want to do so. Do you understand that?

"A. Uh. She told me to get my lawyer. She said you guys would railroad me.[1]

"Q. Do you understand that as I gave it to you, Steve?

"A. Yeah.

"Q. If you do want to talk to me I must advise you that whatever you say can and will be used against you in court. Do you understand that?

"A. Yeah.

"Q. You have a right to consult with a lawyer and to have a lawyer present with you when you're being questioned. Do you understand that?

---

[1] According to the Illinois Supreme Court, the "she" that Smith referred to was an unidentified woman named Chico.

"A. *Uh, yeah. I'd like to do that.*

"Q. Okay."

Instead of terminating the questioning at this point, the interrogating officers proceeded to finish reading Smith his *Miranda* rights and then pressed him again to answer their questions:

"Q. . . .If you want a lawyer and you're unable to pay for one a lawyer will be appointed to represent you free of cost, do you understand that?

"A. Okay.

"Q. Do you wish to talk to me at this time without a lawyer being present?

"A. *Yeah and no, uh, I don't know what's what, really.*

"Q. *Well. You either have [to agree] to talk to me this time without a lawyer being present* and if you do agree to talk with me without a lawyer being present you can stop at any time you want to.

"Q. All right. I'll talk to you then."

Smith then told the detectives that he knew in advance about the planned robbery, but contended that he had not been a participant. After considerable probing by the detectives, Smith confessed that "I committed it," but he then returned to his earlier story that he had only known about the planned crime. Upon further questioning, Smith again insisted that "I wanta get a lawyer." This time the detectives honored the request and terminated the interrogation.

Smith moved at trial to suppress his incriminating statements, but the trial judge denied the motion. A transcript of the interrogation was introduced as part of the State's case in chief, and Smith was convicted.

How should this case be resolved? For the Supreme Court's answer, see *Smith v. Illinois*, 469 U.S. 91 (1984).

## D.  Waiver

A closely related question to assertion of *Miranda* rights is waiver of them. Indeed, the issue in a case is frequently whether the right was asserted, on the one hand, or waived, on the other. Nevertheless, the waiver issue is sufficiently distinct analytically that it deserves a separate analysis. Towards that end, we examine *Butler, Tague*, and *Barrett*.

### North Carolina v. Butler
### 441 U.S. 369 (1979)

Mr. Justice STEWART delivered the opinion of the Court.

In evident conflict with the present view of every other court that has considered the issue, the North Carolina Supreme Court has held that *Miranda* requires that no statement of a person under custodial interrogation may be admitted in evidence against him unless, at the time the statement was made, he explicitly waived the right to the presence of a lawyer. We granted certiorari to consider whether this *per se* rule reflects a proper understanding of the *Miranda* decision.

The respondent was convicted in a North Carolina trial court of kidnaping, armed robbery, and felonious assault. The evidence at his trial showed that he and a man named Elmer Lee had robbed a gas station in Goldsboro, N. C., in December 1976, and had shot the station attendant as he was attempting to escape. The attendant was paralyzed, but survived to testify against the respondent.

The prosecution also produced evidence of incriminating statements made by the respondent shortly after his arrest by Federal Bureau of Investigation agents in the Bronx, N. Y., on the basis of a North Carolina fugitive warrant. Outside the presence of the jury, FBI Agent Martinez testified that at the time of the arrest he fully advised the respondent of the rights delineated in the *Miranda* case. According to the uncontroverted testimony of Martinez, the agents then took the respondent to the FBI office in nearby New Rochelle, N. Y. There, after the agents determined that the respondent had an 11th grade education and was literate, he was given the Bureau's "Advice of Rights" form which he read.[1] When asked if he understood his rights, he replied that he did. The respondent refused to sign the waiver at the bottom of the form. He was told that he need neither speak nor sign the form, but that the agents would like him to talk to them. The respondent replied: "I will talk to you but I am not signing any form." He then made inculpatory statements.[2] Agent Martinez testified that the respondent said nothing when advised of his right to the assistance of a lawyer. At no time did the respondent request counsel or attempt to terminate the agents' questioning.

At the conclusion of this testimony the respondent moved to suppress the evidence of his incriminating statements on the ground that he had not waived his right to the assistance of counsel at the time the statements were made. The court denied the motion, finding that

---

[1] The parties disagree over whether the respondent was also orally advised of his *Miranda* rights at the New Rochelle office. There is no dispute that he was given those warnings orally at the scene of the arrest, or that he read the "Advice of Rights" form in the New Rochelle office. This factual controversy, therefore, is not relevant to the basic issue in this case.

The dissenting opinion points out that at oral argument the respondent's counsel disputed the fact that the respondent is literate. But the trial court specifically found that "it had been . . . determined by Agent Martinez that the defendant has an Eleventh Grade Education and that he could read and write. . . ." This finding, based upon uncontroverted evidence, is binding on this Court.

[2] The respondent admitted to the agents that he and Lee had been drinking heavily on the day of the robbery. He acknowledged that they had decided to rob a gas station, but denied that he had actually participated in the robbery. His friend, he said, had shot the attendant.

"the statement made by the defendant, William Thomas Butler, to Agent David C. Martinez, was made freely and voluntarily to said agent after having been advised of his rights as required by the *Miranda* ruling, including his right to an attorney being present at the time of the inquiry and that the defendant, Butler, understood his rights; [and] that he effectively waived his rights, including the right to have an attorney present during the questioning by his indication that he was willing to answer questions, having read the rights form together with the Waiver of Rights. . . ."

The respondent's statements were then admitted into evidence, and the jury ultimately found the respondent guilty of each offense charged.

On appeal, the North Carolina Supreme Court reversed the convictions and ordered a new trial. It found that the statements had been admitted in violation of the requirements of the *Miranda* decision, noting that the respondent had refused to waive in writing his right to have counsel present and that there had not been a *specific* oral waiver. The court read the *Miranda* opinion as

"provid[ing] in plain language that waiver of the right to counsel during interrogation will not be recognized unless such waiver is 'specifically made' after the *Miranda* warnings have been given."

We conclude that the North Carolina Supreme Court erred in its reading of the *Miranda* opinion. There, this Court said:

"If the interrogation continues without the presence of an attorney and a statement is taken, a heavy burden rests on the government to demonstrate that the defendant knowingly and intelligently waived his privilege against self-incrimination and his right to retained or appointed counsel."

The Court's opinion went on to say:

"An express statement that the individual is willing to make a statement and does not want an attorney followed closely by a statement could constitute a waiver. But a valid waiver will not be presumed simply from the silence of the accused after warnings are given or simply from the fact that a confession was in fact eventually obtained."

As was unequivocally said in *Miranda*, mere silence is not enough. That does not mean that the defendant's silence, coupled with an understanding of his rights and a course of conduct indicating waiver, may never support a conclusion that a defendant has waived his rights. The courts must presume that a defendant did not waive his rights; the prosecution's burden is great; but in at least some cases waiver can be clearly inferred from the actions and words of the person interrogated.

There is no doubt that this respondent was adequately and effectively apprised of his rights. The only question is whether he waived the exercise of one of those rights, the right to the presence of a lawyer. Neither the state court nor the respondent has offered any reason why there must be a negative answer to that question in the absence of an *express* waiver. This is not the first criminal case to question whether a defendant waived his constitutional rights. It is an issue with which courts must repeatedly deal. Even when a right so fundamental as that to counsel at trial is involved, the question of waiver must be determined on "the particular facts and circumstances surrounding that case, including the background, experience, and conduct of the accused."

We see no reason to discard that standard and replace it with an inflexible *per se* rule in a case such as this. As stated at the outset of this opinion, it appears that every court that has considered this question has now reached the same conclusion. Ten of the eleven United States Courts of Appeals and the courts of at least 17 States have held that an explicit statement of waiver is not invariably necessary to support a finding that the defendant waived the right to remain silent or the right to counsel guaranteed by the *Miranda* case. By creating an inflexible rule that no implicit waiver can ever suffice, the North Carolina Supreme Court has gone beyond the requirements of federal organic law. It follows that its judgment cannot stand, since a state court can neither add to nor subtract from the mandates of the United States Constitution.[7]

Accordingly, the judgment is vacated, and the case is remanded to the North Carolina Supreme Court for further proceedings not inconsistent with this opinion.

Mr. Justice BRENNAN, with whom Mr. Justice MARSHALL and Mr. Justice STEVENS joins, dissenting.

There is no allegation of an affirmative waiver in this case. As the Court concedes, the respondent here refused to sign the waiver form, and "said

[7] By the same token this Court must accept whatever construction of a state constitution is placed upon it by the highest court of the State.

nothing when advised of his right to the assistance of a lawyer." Thus, there was no "disputed fact question requiring a hearing," and the trial court erred in holding one. In the absence of an "affirmative waiver" in the form of an express written or oral statement, the Supreme Court of North Carolina correctly granted a new trial. I would, therefore, affirm its decision.

The rule announced by the Court today allows a finding of waiver based upon "infer[ence] from the actions and words of the person interrogated." The Court thus shrouds in half-light the question of waiver, allowing courts to construct inferences from ambiguous words and gestures. But the very premise of *Miranda* requires that ambiguity be interpreted against the interrogator. That premise is the recognition of the "compulsion inherent in custodial" interrogation, and of its purpose "to subjugate the individual to the will of [his] examiner." Under such conditions, only the most explicit waivers of rights can be considered knowingly and freely given.

The instant case presents a clear example of the need for an express waiver requirement. As the Court acknowledges, there is a disagreement over whether respondent was orally advised of his rights at the time he made his statement. The fact that Butler received a written copy of his rights is deemed by the Court to be sufficient basis to resolve the disagreement. But, unfortunately, there is also a dispute over whether Butler could read. And, obviously, if Butler did not have his rights read to him, and could not read them himself, there could be no basis upon which to conclude that he knowingly waived them. Indeed, even if Butler could read there is no reason to believe that his oral statements, which followed a refusal to sign a written waiver form, were intended to signify relinquishment of his rights. Faced with "actions and words" of uncertain meaning, some judges may find waivers where none occurred. Others may fail to find them where they did. In the former case, the defendant's rights will have been violated; in the latter, society's interest in effective law enforcement will have been frustrated. A simple prophylactic rule requiring the police to obtain an express waiver of the right to counsel before proceeding with interrogation eliminates these difficulties. And since the Court agrees that *Miranda* requires the police to obtain some kind of waiver— whether express or implied—the requirement of an express waiver would impose no burden on the police not imposed by the Court's interpretation. It would merely make that burden explicit. Had Agent Martinez simply elicited a clear answer from Willie Butler to the question, "Do you waive your right to a lawyer?" this journey through three courts would not have been necessary.

## QUESTIONS AND NOTES

**1.** Did the Supreme Court find that Butler had waived his right to counsel, or only that the North Carolina Supreme Court erred in its *per se* determination that there was no waiver? Why does it matter?

**2.** Is the *Butler* issue essentially the old rule vs. standard battle? If so, is there any good reason for "standards" winning in this case?

**3.** Is the *Butler* issue the mirror-image of *Davis, i.e.* how to deal with an ambiguous waiver of rights *vis-a-vis* how to deal with an ambiguous assertion of rights?

**4.** On remand, how do you think the case will be resolved? Why?

**5.** In *Tague*, the Court made clear that "waiver" is a concept to be taken seriously.

### Tague v. Louisiana
444 U.S. 469 (1980)

PER CURIAM.

Petitioner was charged with armed robbery. He was convicted by a jury and sentenced to 65 years at hard labor without benefit of parole.

At the suppression hearing in the trial court, the arresting officer testified that he read petitioner his *Miranda* rights from a card, that he could not presently remember what those rights were, that he could not recall whether he asked petitioner whether he understood the rights as read to him, and that he "couldn't say yes or no" whether he rendered any tests to determine whether petitioner was literate or otherwise capable of understanding his rights.

A majority of the Supreme Court of Louisiana held that an arresting officer is not

"compelled to give an intelligence test to a person who has been advised of his rights to determine if he understands them. . . .

"Absent a clear and readily apparent lack thereof, it can be presumed that a person has capacity to understand, and the burden is on the one claiming a lack of capacity to show that lack."

Justice Dennis in dissent wrote that

"[c]ontrary to the explicit requirements of the United States Supreme Court in *Miranda*, the majority today creates a presumption that the defendant understood his constitutional rights and places the burden of proof upon the defendant, instead of the state, to demonstrate whether the defendant knowingly and intelligently waived his privilege against self-incrimination and his right to retained or appointed counsel."

We agree. The majority's error is readily apparent. *Miranda* clearly stated the principles that govern once the required warnings have been given.

"If the interrogation continues without the presence of an attorney and a statement is taken, a heavy burden rests on the government to demonstrate that the defendant knowingly and intelligently waived his privilege against self-incrimination and his right to retained or appointed counsel. This Court has always set high standards of proof for the waiver of constitutional rights, *Johnson v. Zerbst*, 304 U.S. 458 (1938), and we re-assert these standards as applied to. in-custody interrogation. Since the State is responsible for establishing the isolated circumstances under which the interrogation takes place and has the only means of making available corroborated evidence of warnings given during incommunicado interrogation, the burden is rightly on its shoulders."

Just last Term, in holding that a waiver of *Miranda* rights need not be explicit but may be inferred from the actions and words of a person interrogated, we firmly reiterated that

"[t]he courts must presume that a defendant did not waive his rights; the prosecution's burden is great. . . ." *Butler.*

In this case no evidence at all was introduced to prove that petitioner knowingly and intelligently waived his rights before making the inculpatory statement. The statement was therefore inadmissible.

Accordingly, the case is remanded to the Supreme Court of Louisiana for further proceedings not inconsistent with this opinion.

[The CHIEF JUSTICE would set the case for oral argument.]

[Mr. Justice REHNQUIST dissents. He thinks that, under the circumstances described in the opinion of the Supreme Court of Louisiana, the judgment of that court was fully consistent with *Butler*, and not inconsistent with any other decision of this Court.]

# QUESTIONS AND NOTES

**1.** How is *Tague* different from *Butler*?

**2.** After *Butler* would you have expected the result in *Tague*?

**3.** *Tague* was the first case since the departure of Chief Justice Warren to reverse a conviction on the basis of *Miranda*. What might there have been about this case to warrant such treatment?

**4.** Who should have the burden of proof on the issue of waiver? Why?

**5.** We conclude this section with *Barrett*, where we consider the extent to which a sufficiently specific invocation of the right to counsel for some purposes may constitute a waiver of that right for other purposes.

## Connecticut v. Barrett
### 479 U.S. 523 (1987)

Chief Justice REHNQUIST delivered the opinion of the Court.

In the early morning of October 24, 1980, [Respondent William] Barrett was transported from New Haven, Connecticut, to Wallingford, where he was a suspect in a sexual assault that had occurred the previous evening. Upon arrival at the Wallingford police station, Officer Peter Cameron advised Barrett of his rights, and Barrett signed and dated an acknowledgment that he had received the warnings required by *Miranda*. Barrett stated that "he would not give the police any written statements but he had no problem in talking about the incident."

We think that the Connecticut Supreme Court erred in holding that the United States Constitution required suppression of Barrett's statement. Barrett made clear to police his willingness to talk about the crime for which he was a suspect. The trial court found that this decision was a voluntary waiver of his rights, and there is no evidence that Barrett was "threatened, tricked, or cajoled" into this waiver. The Connecticut Supreme Court nevertheless held as a matter of law that respondent's limited invocation of his right to counsel prohibited all interrogation absent initiation of further discussion by Barrett. Nothing in our decisions, however, or in the rationale of *Miranda*, requires authorities to ignore the

tenor or sense of a defendant's response to these warnings.

The fundamental purpose of the Court's decision in *Miranda* was "to assure that *the individual's right to choose* between speech and silence remains unfettered throughout the interrogation process." (emphasis added). To this end, the *Miranda* Court adopted prophylactic rules designed to insulate the exercise of Fifth Amendment rights from the government "compulsion, subtle or otherwise," that "operates on the individual to overcome free choice in producing a statement after the privilege has been once invoked." One such rule requires that, once the accused "states that he wants an attorney, the interrogation must cease until an attorney is present." By prohibiting further interrogation after the invocation of these rights, we erect an auxiliary barrier against police coercion.

But we know of no constitutional objective that would be served by suppression in this case. It is undisputed that Barrett desired the presence of counsel before making a written statement. Had the police obtained such a statement without meeting the waiver standards of *Edwards*, it would clearly be inadmissible. Barrett's limited requests for counsel, however, were accompanied by affirmative announcements of his willingness to speak with the authorities. The fact that officials took the opportunity provided by Barrett to obtain an oral confession is quite consistent with the Fifth Amendment. *Miranda* gives the defendant a right to choose between speech and silence, and Barrett chose to speak.

The Connecticut Supreme Court's decision to the contrary rested on the view that requests for counsel are not to be narrowly construed. In support of this premise, respondent observes that our prior decisions have given broad effect to requests for counsel that were less than all-inclusive. See *Bradshaw*, ("I do want an attorney before it goes very much further"); *Edwards*, ("I want an attorney before making a deal"). We do not denigrate the "settled approach to questions of waiver [that] requires us to give a broad, rather than a narrow, interpretation to a defendant's request for counsel," when we observe that this approach does little to aid respondent's cause. Interpretation is only required where the defendant's words, understood as ordinary people would understand them, are ambiguous. Here, however, Barrett made clear his intentions, and they were honored by police. To conclude that respondent invoked his right to counsel for all purposes requires not a broad interpretation of an ambiguous statement, but a disregard of the ordinary meaning of respondent's statement.

We also reject the contention that the distinction drawn by Barrett between oral and written statements indicates an understanding of the consequences so incomplete that we should deem his limited invocation of the right to counsel effective for all purposes. This suggestion ignores Barrett's testimony—and the finding of the trial court not questioned by the Connecticut Supreme Court—that respondent fully understood the *Miranda* warnings. These warnings, of course, made clear to Barrett that "[i]f you talk to any police officers, anything you say can and will be used against you in court." The fact that some might find Barrett's decision illogical[4] is irrelevant, for we have never "embraced the theory that a defendant's ignorance of the full consequences of his decisions vitiates their voluntariness." *Spring*.

For the reasons stated, the judgment of the Connecticut Supreme Court is reversed, and the case is remanded for further proceedings not inconsistent with this opinion.

Justice BRENNAN, concurring in the judgment.

---

[4] We do not suggest that the distinction drawn by Barrett is in fact illogical, for there may be several strategic reasons why a defendant willing to speak to the police would still refuse to write out his answers to questions, or to sign a transcript of his answers prepared by the police, a statement that may be used against him.

I concur in the judgment that the Constitution does not require the suppression of Barrett's statements to the police, but for reasons different from those set forth in the opinion of the Court. Barrett's contemporaneous waiver of his right to silence and limited invocation of his right to counsel (for the purpose of making a written statement) suggested that he did not understand that anything he *said* could be used against him. However, the State eliminated this apparent ambiguity when it demonstrated that Barrett's waiver of his right to silence was voluntary, knowing, and intelligent. Barrett testified at trial that he understood his *Miranda* rights, *i.e.*, he knew that he need not talk to the police without a lawyer present and that anything he said could be used against him. Under these circumstances, the waiver of the right to silence and the limited invocation of the right to counsel were valid.

I

The language and tenor of the *Miranda* opinion suggested that the Court would require that a waiver of the rights at stake be "specifically made." While the Court retreated from that position in *Butler*, I continue to believe that the Court should require the police to obtain an "affirmative waiver" of *Miranda* rights before proceeding with interrogation.

In this case, Barrett affirmatively waived his *Miranda* rights. Unlike the defendant in *Butler*, Barrett orally expressed his willingness to talk with the police *and* willingly signed a form indicating that he understood his rights. The police obtained an explicit oral waiver of the right to silence. Furthermore, the officer who administered the *Miranda* warnings to Barrett testified that the latter understood his rights "[c]ompletely": "I asked [Barrett] several times during my administration of those rights, if, in fact, he understood them; if there were points he wanted me to clarify, and he indicated to me, no, he understood everything fairly well." At trial, one issue was whether Barrett voluntarily, knowingly, and intelligently waived his *Miranda* rights, and Barrett himself testified that he understood his rights as they were read to him.[1]

---

[1] The trial judge denied Barrett's motion to suppress the statements made following administration of the *Miranda* warnings, holding:

"[T]he Court concludes from the evidence it heard that [Barrett] indicated he understood perfectly what was being read to him. Not only did he indicate that he understood, he offered the statements that he did not need anything explained to him because he understood. So it was not merely a passive acquies-

Had the State been without Barrett's testimony at trial, where he was represented by counsel, I could not reach this conclusion. Barrett's statement to police – that he would talk to them, but allow nothing in writing without counsel – created doubt about whether he actually understood that anything he *said* could be used against him. In other words, the statement is not, on its face, a knowing and intelligent waiver of the right to silence. But Barrett's testimony revealed that he understood that he had rights to remain silent and to have an attorney present, and that anything he said could be used against him; nevertheless he chose to speak.

In sum, the State has carried its "heavy burden" of demonstrating waiver. It has shown that Barrett received the *Miranda* warnings, that he had the capacity to understand them[4] and *in fact* understood them, and that he expressly waived his right to silence, saying that he "had no problem in talking about the incident." In my view, each of these findings was essential to the conclusion that a voluntary, knowing, and intelligent waiver of the *Miranda* rights occurred.

## II

Barrett argues that his refusal to make a written statement without an attorney present constituted an invocation of the right to counsel for all purposes and that any further interrogation after this mention of his desire for an attorney was impermissible under *Edwards*. It is settled that any plain reference, however glancing, to a need or a desire for representation must result in the cessation of questioning.

I believe that a partial invocation of the right to counsel, without more, invariably will be ambiguous. It gives rise to doubts about the defendant's precise wishes regarding representation and about his or her understanding of the nature and scope of the right to counsel. Thus, the police may not infer from a partial invocation of the right to counsel *alone* that the defendant has waived any of his or her rights not specifically invoked.

However, circumstances may clarify an otherwise ambiguous situation. If the partial invocation

is accompanied by an explicit waiver of the right to silence that is voluntary, knowing, and intelligent, it may lose its ambiguity. It may become clear that the portion of the right to counsel that was not invoked was in fact waived, when, for example, a knowing and intelligent waiver of the right to silence necessarily includes a waiver of the right to have counsel present at questioning. This is such a case. Here Barrett's limited invocation was not ambiguous: It was accompanied by an express waiver of his right to silence, the validity of which was plainly established by his subsequent trial testimony. The accompaniment of Barrett's reference to his limited desire for counsel with an explicit waiver of his right to silence rendered permissible the authorities' use of his statements.[7]

For these reasons, I concur in the judgment of the Court.

Justice STEVENS, with whom Justice MARSHALL joins, dissenting.

The Court's disposition of this case raises two troublesome questions.

First, why did the Court decide to exercise its discretion to grant review in this case? The facts of the case are surely unique. They do not give rise to any issue of general or recurring significance. There is no conflict among the state or federal courts on

---

cence and his agreement that he understood, he did go on to explain that he did not need anything explained to him because he perfectly understood."

[4] It is undisputed that the defendant here, unlike the defendant in *Butler*, had the capacity to understand his rights: the police ascertained that Barrett had a 12th-grade education, while in *Butler* there was a dispute over whether the defendant could read.

[7] It is undisputed that "[h]ad the police obtained [a written] statement without meeting the waiver standards of *Edwards*, it would clearly be inadmissible." Barrett's invocation of his rights demonstrates that he opposed any immediate preservation of statements made without counsel. If the attempt to tape Barrett's statements had succeeded, the recording would have been inadmissible. [The attempt was unsuccessful – ed.]

In addition, the police attempted to persuade Barrett to waive the right he had asserted not to make a written statement without the assistance of counsel, not once, but twice, absent any indication from Barrett that he had changed his mind on this point. In *Edwards* we held that once an accused invokes the right to counsel, he or she is not subject to further custodial interrogation "until counsel has been made available to him [or her], unless the accused . . . initiates further communication, exchanges, or conversations with the police." Here the police failed to respect Barrett's limited assertion of his right to counsel. Had a written statement been obtained as a result of these persistent efforts to change Barrett's mind, it would have been inadmissible.

how the narrow question presented should be resolved. It is merely a case in which one State Supreme Court arguably granted more protection to a citizen accused of crime than the Federal Constitution requires. The State "asks us to rule that the state court interpreted federal rights too broadly and 'overprotected' the citizen." If this is a sufficient reason for adding a case to our already overcrowded docket, we will need, not one, but several newly fashioned "intercircuit tribunals" to keep abreast of our work.

Second, why was respondent's request for the assistance of counsel any less ambiguous than the request in *Edwards*? In that case, the defendant said that he wanted an attorney "before making a deal." He also said he would talk to the police "but I don't want it on tape." The police interrogation complied with the everyday meaning of both of those conditions; it occurred before Edwards made any "deal" – indeed, he never made a deal – and no tape recording of the session was made. The Court nevertheless found the interrogation objectionable. In this case, respondent requested an attorney before signing a written statement. Why the police's compliance with the literal terms of that request makes the request – as opposed to the subsequent waiver – any less of a request for the assistance of counsel than Edwards' is not adequately explained in the Court's opinion. In all events, the Court does not purport to change the governing rule of law that judges must "give a broad, rather than a narrow, interpretation to a defendant's request for counsel."

I would dismiss the writ of certiorari as improvidently granted.

## QUESTIONS AND NOTES

**1.** Why do you suppose that the Connecticut Supreme Court found in favor of Barrett? Would you?

**2.** In view of Brennan's concurrence and the dissent's half-hearted jurisdictional argument, do you think that Barrett's lawyer was incompetent in allowing him to testify as to his understanding of the warnings?

**3.** Why do you suppose that Barrett drew the distinction between oral and written statements? Should we speculate on that? Is the Court's footnote 4 helpful on that score?

**4.** Do you think that *Barrett* is consistent with *Edwards* given that Edwards had just asked for counsel before making a deal?

## E.   Custody

A major issue in regard to custodial interrogation is, of course, custody. Without custody, or its functional equivalent, there can be no custodial interrogation. However, as the next several cases demonstrate, the concept of custody is anything but simple.

### Mathis v. United States
### 391 U.S. 1 (1968)

Mr. Justice BLACK delivered the opinion of the Court.

Petitioner was convicted by a jury in a United States District Court on two counts charging that he knowingly filed false claims against the Government. A part of the evidence on which the conviction rested consisted of documents and oral statements obtained from petitioner by a government agent while petitioner was in prison serving a state sentence. Before eliciting this information, the government agent did not warn petitioner that any evidence he gave the Government could be used against him, and that he had a right to remain silent if he desired as well as a right to the presence of counsel and that if he was unable to afford counsel one would be appointed for him. At trial petitioner sought several times without success to have the judge hold hearings out of the presence of the jury to prove that his statements to the revenue agent were given without these warnings and should therefore not be used as evidence against him. For this contention he relied exclusively on *Miranda*. The District Court rejected this contention as did the Court of Appeals in affirming. We granted certiorari to decide whether the *Miranda* case calls for reversal. We hold that it does.

There can be no doubt that the documents and oral statements given by petitioner to the government agent and used against him were strongly incriminating. In the *Miranda* case this Court's opinion stated at some length the constitutional reasons why one in custody who is interrogated by officers about matters that might tend to incriminate him is entitled to be warned "that he has the right to remain silent, that anything he says can be used against him in a court of law, that he has the right to the presence of an attorney, and that if he cannot afford an attorney one will be appointed for him prior to any questioning, if he so desires." The Government here seeks to escape application of the *Miranda* warnings on two arguments: (1) that these questions were asked as a part of a routine tax investigation where no criminal proceedings might even be brought, and (2) that the petitioner had not been put in jail by the officers questioning him, but was there for an entirely separate offense. These differences are too minor and shadowy to justify a departure from the well-considered conclusions of *Miranda* with reference to warnings to be given to a person held in custody.

It is true that a "routine tax investigation" may be initiated for the purpose of a civil action rather than criminal prosecution. To this extent tax investigations differ from investigations of murder, robbery, and other crimes. But tax investigations frequently lead to criminal prosecutions, just as the one here did. In fact, the last visit of the revenue agent to the jail to question petitioner took place only eight days before the full-fledged criminal investigation concededly began. And as the investigating revenue agent was compelled to admit, there was always the possibility during his investigation that his work would end up in a criminal prosecution. We reject the contention that tax investigations are immune from the *Miranda* requirements for warnings to be given a person in custody.

The Government also seeks to narrow the scope of the *Miranda* holding by making it applicable only to questioning one who is "in custody" in connection with the very case under investigation. There

is no substance to such a distinction, and in effect it goes against the whole purpose of the *Miranda* decision which was designed to give meaningful protection to Fifth Amendment rights. We find nothing in the *Miranda* opinion which calls for a curtailment of the warnings to be given persons under interrogation by officers based on the reason why the person is in custody. In speaking of "custody" the language of the *Miranda* opinion is clear and unequivocal:

> "To summarize, we hold that when an individual is taken into custody or otherwise deprived of his freedom by the authorities in any significant way and is subjected to questioning, the privilege against self-incrimination is jeopardized."

And the opinion goes on to say that the person so held must be given the warnings about his right to be silent and his right to have a lawyer.

Thus, the courts below were wrong in permitting the introduction of petitioner's self-incriminating evidence given without warning of his right to be silent and right to counsel. The cause is reversed and remanded for further proceedings consistent with this opinion.

Mr. Justice MARSHALL took no part in the consideration or decision of this case.

Mr. Justice WHITE, with whom Mr. Justice HARLAN and Mr. Justice STEWART join, dissenting.

[E]ven were I to agree that *Miranda* was correctly decided, I would not join the unexplained extension which the Court gives *Miranda* in this case. At issue are two questions[1] asked of petitioner by an Internal Revenue agent in the course of a civil investigation. The interview was indistinguishable from the thousands of inquiries into tax liability made annually as a necessary adjunct to operation of our tax system. The Court said in *Miranda* that "proper safeguards" were needed for "in-custody interrogation of persons suspected or accused of crime." In this case the majority states that criminal investigation of Mathis began soon after the second of the visits to him of Revenue Agent Lawless. This suggests a view, unsupported by the record before us, that the civil investigation had raised suspicions of criminal conduct

---

[1] Petitioner was asked whether tax returns received by the Government bearing his name had in fact been prepared by him and whether he would consent to an extension of the statute of limitations for causes of action arising from those returns.

by Mathis at the time of this visit.[2] However, the majority also says that "tax investigations frequently lead to criminal prosecutions," a hint that any in-custody questioning by an employee of the Government must be preceded by warnings if it is within the immensely broad area of investigations which "frequently lead" to criminal inquiries. Fortunately, voluntary compliance with civil regulation is widespread in this country. Nevertheless, compliance must be supplemented and encouraged by constant and widespread investigations, during which questions are asked and data are required by employees of the Government whose goal is only to settle fairly the civil accounts between the United States and its citizens. Sometimes, of course, the possibility of a criminal violation is discovered through such inquiries. I had not thought that *Miranda* extended its

---

[2] A civil investigator is required, whenever and as soon as he finds "definite indications of fraud or criminal potential," to refer a case to the Intelligence Division for investigation by a different agent who works regularly on criminal matters. In the case before us, such a reference was made eight days after the second visit to petitioner by Agent Lawless. The criminal agent visited petitioner, gave him the full set of "*Miranda* warnings," and was told petitioner did not wish to discuss the case with him. No further questions were asked.

checklist of warnings to these civil investigations. Certainly the explanation of the need for warnings given in the *Miranda* opinion does not cover civil investigations, and the Court's opinion in this case furnishes no additional support.

The Court is equally cavalier in concluding that petitioner was "in custody" in the sense in which that phrase was used in *Miranda*. The State of Florida was confining petitioner at the time he answered Agent Lawless' questions. But *Miranda* rested not on the mere fact of physical restriction but on a conclusion that coercion — pressure to answer questions — usually flows from a certain type of custody, police station interrogation of someone charged with or suspected of a crime. Although petitioner was confined, he was at the time of interrogation in familiar surroundings. Neither the record nor the Court suggests reasons why petitioner was "coerced" into answering Lawless' questions any more than is the citizen interviewed at home by a revenue agent or interviewed in a Revenue Service office to which citizens are requested to come for interviews. The rationale of *Miranda* has no relevance to inquiries conducted outside the allegedly hostile and forbidding atmosphere surrounding police station interrogation of a criminal suspect. The Court's willingness to reverse without explaining why the reasons given for the *Miranda* decision have any relevance to the facts of this case is deeply troubling.

## QUESTIONS AND NOTES

**1.** Do you think that *Miranda* should have any relevance to the facts of this case? Explain.

**2.** Should this case have been treated as custodial interrogation? Were not Mathis' surroundings totally familiar?

**3.** One of the things that makes custodial interrogation so coercive is that the arrestee does not know how long he will be held in custody. Should it be significant that that was not the case in *Mathis*?

**4.** In what way is *Mathis* meaningfully different from an interview held at home?

**5.** As you read *Orozco*, consider whether it is a stronger or weaker case for finding custody.

## Orozco v. Texas
### 394 U.S. 324 (1969)

Mr. Justice BLACK delivered the opinion of the Court.

The petitioner, Reyes Arias Orozco, was convicted in the Criminal District Court of Dallas County, Texas, of murder without malice and was

sentenced to serve in the state prison not less than two nor more than 10 years.

The evidence introduced at trial showed that petitioner and the deceased had quarreled outside the El Farleto Cafe in Dallas shortly before midnight on the date of the shooting. The deceased had apparently spoken to petitioner's female companion inside the restaurant. In the heat of the quarrel outside, the deceased is said to have beaten petitioner about the face and called him "Mexican Grease." A shot was fired killing the deceased. Petitioner left the scene and returned to his boardinghouse to sleep. At about 4 a.m. four police officers arrived at petitioner's boardinghouse, were admitted by an unidentified woman, and were told that petitioner was asleep in the bedroom. All four officers entered the bedroom and began to question petitioner. From the moment he gave his name, according to the testimony of one of the officers, petitioner was not free to go where he pleased but was "under arrest." The officers asked him if he had been to the El Farleto restaurant that night and when he answered "yes" he was asked if he owned a pistol. Petitioner admitted owning one. After being asked a second time where the pistol was located, he admitted that it was in the washing machine in a backroom of the boardinghouse. Ballistics tests indicated that the gun found in the washing machine was the gun that fired the fatal shot. At petitioner's trial, held after the effective date of this Court's decision in *Miranda*, the trial court allowed one of the officers, over the objection of petitioner's lawyer, to relate the statements made by petitioner concerning the gun and petitioner's presence at the scene of the shooting. The trial testimony clearly shows that the officers questioned petitioner about incriminating facts without first informing him of his right to remain silent, his right to have the advice of a lawyer before making any statement, and his right to have a lawyer appointed to assist him if he could not afford to hire one. The Texas Court of Criminal Appeals held, with one judge dissenting, that the admission of testimony concerning the statements petitioner had made without the above warnings was not precluded by *Miranda*. We disagree and hold that the use of these admissions obtained in the absence of the required warnings was a flat violation of the Self-Incrimination Clause of the Fifth Amendment as construed in *Miranda*.

The State has argued here that since petitioner was interrogated on his own bed, in familiar surroundings, our *Miranda* holding should not apply. It is true that the Court did say in *Miranda* that "compulsion to speak in the isolated setting of the police station may well be greater than in courts or other official investigations, where there are often impartial observers to guard against intimidation or trickery." But the opinion iterated and reiterated the absolute necessity for officers interrogating people

"in custody" to give the described warnings. See *Mathis*. According to the officer's testimony, petitioner was under arrest and not free to leave when he was questioned in his bedroom in the early hours of the morning. The *Miranda* opinion declared that the warnings were required when the person being interrogated was "in custody at the station *or otherwise deprived of his freedom of action in any significant way.*" (Emphasis supplied.) The decision of this Court in *Miranda* was reached after careful consideration and lengthy opinions were announced by both the majority and dissenting Justices. There is no need to canvass those arguments again. We do not, as the dissent implies, expand or extend to the slightest extent our *Miranda* decision. We do adhere to our well-considered holding in that case and therefore reverse[4] the conviction below.

Mr. Justice HARLAN, concurring.

The passage of time has not made the *Miranda* case any more palatable to me than it was when the case was decided.

Yet, despite my strong inclination to join in the dissent of my Brother White, I can find no acceptable avenue of escape from *Miranda* in judging this case, especially in light of *Mathis v. United States*, 391 U.S. 1 (1968), which has already extended the *Miranda* rules beyond the police station, over the protest of Justices Stewart, White, and myself. Therefore, and purely out of respect for *stare decisis*, I reluctantly feel compelled to acquiesce in today's decision of the Court, at the same time observing that the constitutional condemnation of this perfectly understandable, sensible, proper, and indeed commendable piece of police work highlights the unsoundness of *Miranda*.

Mr. Justice WHITE, with whom Mr. Justice STEWART joins, dissenting.

This decision carries the rule of *Miranda* to a new and unwarranted extreme. I continue to believe that the original rule amounted to a "constitutional straitjacket" on law enforcement which was justified neither by the words or history of the Constitution, nor by any reasonable view of the likely benefits of the rule as against its disadvantages. Even accepting

---

[4] In light of some apparent misunderstanding on this point, it is perhaps appropriate to point out once again that a reversal by this Court of a conviction based in part on unconstitutional evidence leaves the State free to retry the defendant without the tainted evidence.

*Miranda*, the Court extends the rule here and draws the straitjacket even tighter.

The opinion of the Court in *Miranda* was devoted in large part to an elaborate discussion of the subtle forms of psychological pressure which could be brought to bear when an accused person is interrogated at length in unfamiliar surroundings. The "salient features" of the cases decided in *Miranda* were "incommunicado interrogation of individuals in a police-dominated atmosphere." The danger was that in such circumstances the confidence of the prisoner could be eroded by techniques such as successive interrogations by police acting out friendly or unfriendly roles. These techniques are best developed in "isolation and unfamiliar surroundings." And they take time: "the major qualities an interrogator should possess are patience and perseverance." The techniques of an extended period of isolation, repeated interrogation, cajolery, and trickery often enough produced admissions which were actually coerced in the traditional sense so that new safeguards were deemed essential.

The Court now extends the same rules to all instances of in-custody questioning outside the station house. Once arrest occurs, the application of *Miranda* is automatic. The rule is simple but it ignores the purpose of *Miranda* to guard against what was thought to be the corrosive influence of practices which station house interrogation makes feasible. The Court wholly ignores the question whether similar hazards exist or even are possible when police arrest and interrogate on the spot, whether it be on the street corner or in the home, as in this case. No predicate is laid for believing that practices outside the station house are normally prolonged, carried out in isolation, or often productive of the physical or psychological coercion made so much of in *Miranda*. It is difficult to imagine the police duplicating in a person's home or on the street those conditions and practices which the Court found prevalent in the station house and which were thought so threatening to the right to silence. Without such a demonstration, *Miranda* hardly reaches this case or any cases similar to it.

Here, there was no prolonged interrogation, no unfamiliar surroundings, no opportunity for the police to invoke those procedures which moved the majority in *Miranda*. In fact, the conversation was by all accounts a very brief one. According to uncontradicted testimony, petitioner was awake when the officers entered his room, and they asked him four questions: his name, whether he had been at the El

Farleto, whether he owned a pistol, and where it was. He gave his name, said he had been at the El Farleto, and admitted he owned a pistol without hesitation. He was slow in telling where the pistol was, and the question was repeated. He then took the police to the nearby washing machine where the gun was hidden.

It is unquestioned that this sequence of events in their totality would not constitute coercion in the traditional sense or lead any court to view the admissions as involuntary within the meaning of the rules by which we even now adjudicate claims of coercion relating to pre-*Miranda* trials. And, realistically, had Orozco refused to answer the questions asked of him, it seems most unlikely that prolonged interrogation would have followed in petitioner's own quarters; nothing similar to the station house model invoked by the court would have occurred here. The police had petitioner's name and description, had ample evidence that he had been at the night club and suspected that he had a gun. Surely had he refused to give his name or answer any other questions, they would have arrested him anyway, searched the house and found the gun, which would have been clearly admissible under all relevant authorities. But the Court insists that this case be reversed for failure to give *Miranda* warnings.

I cannot accept the dilution of the custody requirements of *Miranda* to this level, where the hazards to the right to silence are so equivocal and unsupported by experience in a recurring number of cases. Orozco was apprehended in the most familiar quarters, the questioning was brief, and no admissions were made which were not backed up by other evidence. This case does not involve the confession of an innocent man, or even of a guilty man from whom a confession has been wrung by physical abuse or the modern psychological methods discussed in *Miranda*. These are simply the terse remarks of a man who has been caught, almost in the act. Even if there were reason to encourage suspects to consult lawyers to tell them to be silent before quizzing at the station house, there is no reason why police in the field should have to preface every casual question of a suspect with the full panoply of *Miranda* warnings. The same danger of coercion is simply not present in such circumstances, and the answers to the questions may as often clear a suspect as help convict him. If the *Miranda* warnings have their intended effect, and the police are able to get no answers from suspects, innocent or guilty, without arresting them, then a great many more innocent men will be making unnecessary trips to the station house. Ultimately it may be necessary to arrest a man, bring him to the police station, and provide a lawyer, just to discover his name. Even if the man is innocent the process will be an unpleasant one.

Since the Court's extension of *Miranda*'s rule takes it into territory where even what rationale there originally was disappears, I dissent.

Memorandum of Mr. Justice STEWART.

Although there is much to be said for Mr. Justice Harlan's position, I join my Brother White in dissent. It seems to me that those of us who dissented in *Miranda* remain free not only to express our continuing disagreement with that decision, but also to oppose any broadening of its impact.

## QUESTIONS AND NOTES

**1.** Is *Orozco* a stronger or weaker case than *Mathis* for finding custody? Why?

**2.** Do you consider *Orozco* to be an application of *Miranda* or an expansion of it? Explain.

**3.** Do you think that Orozco was in fact compelled to incriminate himself? *I.e.,* what result would (should) have been reached without the *Miranda* presumption?

**4.** In *Beckwith*, the Court begins to show an unwillingness to expand the concept of custody.

### Beckwith v. United States
### 425 U.S. 341 (1977)

Mr. Chief Justice BURGER delivered the opinion of the Court.

The important issue presented in this case is whether a special agent of the Internal Revenue Service, investigating potential criminal income tax violations, must, in an interview with a taxpayer, not in custody, give the warnings called for by this Court's decision in *Miranda*.

The District Court conducted a thorough inquiry into the facts surrounding the interview of petitioner before ruling on his motion to suppress the statements at issue. After a considerable amount of investigation, two special agents of the Intelligence Division of the Internal Revenue Service met with petitioner in a private home where petitioner occasionally stayed. The senior agent testified that they went to see petitioner at this private residence at 8 a.m. in order to spare petitioner the possible embarrassment of being interviewed at his place of employment which opened at 10 a.m. Upon their arrival, they identified themselves to the person answering the door and asked to speak to petitioner. The agents were invited into the house and, when petitioner entered the room where they were waiting, they introduced themselves and, according to the testimony of the senior agent, Beckwith then excused himself for a period in excess of five minutes, to

finish dressing.[3] Petitioner then sat down at the dining room table with the agents; they presented their credentials and stated they were attached to the Intelligence Division and that one of their functions was to investigate the possibility of criminal tax fraud. They then informed petitioner that they were assigned to investigate his federal income tax liability for the years 1966 through 1971. The senior agent then read to petitioner from a printed card the following:

"As a special agent, one of my functions is to investigate the possibility of criminal violations of the Internal Revenue laws, and related offenses.

"Under the Fifth Amendment to the Constitution of the United States, I cannot compel you to answer any questions or to submit any information if such answers or information might tend to incriminate you in any way. I also advise you that anything which you say and any information which you submit may be used against you in any criminal proceeding which may be undertaken. I advise you further

---

[3] Petitioner claimed at the suppression hearing that he was fully dressed when he first met the agents. The District Court did not explicitly resolve this conflict in testimony.

that you may, if you wish, seek the assistance of an attorney before responding.''

Petitioner acknowledged that he understood his rights. The agents then interviewed him until about 11 o'clock. The agents described the conversation as "friendly" and "relaxed." The petitioner noted that the agents did not "press" him on any question he could not or chose not to answer.

Prior to the conclusion of the interview, the senior agent requested that petitioner permit the agents to inspect certain records. Petitioner indicated that they were at his place of employment. The agents asked if they could meet him there later. Having traveled separately from petitioner, the agents met petitioner approximately 45 minutes later and the senior agent advised the petitioner that he was not required to furnish any books or records; petitioner, however, supplied the books to the agents.

Petitioner contends that the "entire starting point" for the criminal prosecution brought against him was secured from his own statements and disclosures during the interview with the Internal Revenue agents from the Intelligence Division.[4] He correctly points out that cases are assigned to the Intelligence Division only when there is some indication of criminal fraud and that, especially since tax offenses rarely result in pretrial custody, the taxpayer is clearly the "focus" of a criminal investigation when a matter is assigned to the Intelligence Division. Given the complexity of the tax structure and the confusion on the part of taxpayers between the civil and criminal function of the Internal Revenue Service, such a confrontation, argues petitioner, places the taxpayer under "psychological restraints" which are the functional, and, therefore, the legal, equivalent of custody. In short we agree with Chief Judge Bazelon, speaking for a unanimous Court of Appeals, that

> "[t]he major thrust of Beckwith's argument is that the principle of *Miranda* and *Mathis* should be extended to cover interrogation in non-custodial circumstances after a police investigation has focused on the suspect."

With the Court of Appeals, we "are not impressed with this argument in the abstract nor as applied to the particular facts of Beckwith's interrogation." It goes far beyond the reasons for that holding and such an extension of the *Miranda* requirements

would cut this Court's holding in that case completely loose from its own explicitly stated rationale. The narrow issue before the Court in *Miranda* was presented very precisely in the opening paragraph of that opinion "the admissibility of statements obtained from an individual who is subjected to *custodial* police interrogation." (Emphasis supplied.) The Court concluded that compulsion is "inherent in custodial surroundings," and, consequently, that special safeguards were required in the case of "incommunicado interrogation of individuals in a police-dominated atmosphere, resulting in self-incriminating statements without full warnings of constitutional rights." In subsequent decisions, the Court specifically stressed that it was the *custodial* nature of the interrogation which triggered the necessity for adherence to the specific requirements of its *Miranda* holding. *Orozco*; *Mathis*.

Petitioner's argument that he was placed in the functional, and, therefore, legal, equivalent of the *Miranda* situation asks us now to ignore completely that *Miranda* was grounded squarely in the Court's explicit and detailed assessment of the peculiar "nature and setting of . . . in-custody interrogation." *Mathis* directly supports this conclusion in holding that the *Miranda* requirements are applicable to interviews with Internal Revenue agents concerning tax liability, *when the subject is in custody*; the Court thus squarely grounded its holding on the custodial aspects of the situation, not the subject matter of the interview.[8]

An interview with Government agents in a situation such as the one shown by this record simply does not present the elements which the *Miranda* Court found so inherently coercive as to require its holding. Although the "focus" of an investigation may indeed have been on Beckwith at the time of the interview in the sense that it was his tax liability which was under scrutiny, he hardly found himself in the custodial situation described by the *Miranda* Court as the basis for its holding. *Miranda* implicitly defined "focus," for its purposes, as "questioning initiated by law enforcement officers *after* a person has been taken into custody or otherwise deprived of his freedom of action in any significant way." (Emphasis supplied.) It may well be true, as petitioner contends that the "starting point" for the

---

[4] [He] does not challenge the holding of the Court of Appeals that, the *Miranda* question aside, the "entire interview was free of coercion."

[8] Four Members of the Court joined Mr. Justice Black; the dissenters regarded *Mathis* as an extension of *Miranda* largely because the custody and the interrogation were in no way related and because a prisoner interrogated in prison was not in unfamiliar surroundings.

criminal prosecution was the information obtained from petitioner and the records exhibited by him. But this amounts to no more than saying that a tax return signed by a taxpayer can be the "starting point" for a prosecution.

We recognize, of course, that noncustodial interrogation might possibly in some situations, by virtue of some special circumstances, be characterized as one where "the behavior of . . . law enforcement officials was such as to overbear petitioner's will to resist and bring about confessions not freely self-determined. . . ." When such a claim is raised, it is the duty of an appellate court, including this Court, "to examine the entire record and make an independent determination of the ultimate issue of voluntariness." Proof that some kind of warnings were given or that none were given would be relevant evidence only on the issue of whether the questioning was in fact coercive. In the present case, however, as Chief Judge Bazelon noted, "[t]he entire interview was free of coercion."

Accordingly, the judgment of the Court of Appeals is Affirmed.

Mr. Justice STEVENS took no part in the consideration or decision of this case.

Mr. Justice MARSHALL, concurring in the judgment.

While the Internal Revenue Service agents in this case did not give petitioner the full warnings prescribed in *Miranda*, they did give him the following warning before questioning him:

[See warning given in opinion of Court]

Under the circumstances of this case, in which petitioner was not under arrest and the interview took place in a private home where petitioner occasionally stayed, the warning recited above satisfied the requirements of the Fifth Amendment. If this warning had not been given, however, I would not join the judgment of the Court.

Mr. Justice BRENNAN, dissenting.

*United States v. Oliver*, 505 F.2d 301 (1974) states the analysis with which I agree and which requires suppression of Beckwith's statements:

"The application of *Miranda* does not turn on such a simple axis as whether or not the suspect is in custody when he is being questioned. As the Court repeatedly indicated, the prescribed warnings are required if the defendant is in custody 'or otherwise deprived of his freedom of action in any significant way.' The fact of custody is emphasized in the [*Miranda*] opinion as having the practical consequence of compelling the accused to make disclosures. But the test also differentiates between the questioning of a mere witness and the interrogation of an accused for the purpose of securing his conviction; the test serves the purpose 'of determining when the adversary process has begun, i.e., when the investigative machinery of the government is directed toward the ultimate conviction of a particular individual and when, therefore, a suspect should be advised of his rights.'

"Since the constitutional protection is expressly applicable to testimony in the criminal case itself, for the purpose of determining when warnings are required, the *Miranda* analysis treats the adversary proceeding as though it commences when a prospective defendant is taken into custody or otherwise significantly restrained. After that point is reached, it is not unreasonable to treat any compelled disclosure as protected by the Fifth Amendment unless, of course, the constitutional protection has been waived. Adequate warnings, or the advise [*sic*] of counsel, are essential if such a waiver is to be effective.

" 'Incriminating statements elicited in reliance upon the taxpayer's misapprehension as to *the nature of the inquiry, his obligation to respond, and the possible consequences of doing so* must be regarded as equally violative of constitutional protections as a custodial confession extracted without proper warnings.' (emphasis added).

"The practical effect of these misapprehensions during questioning of a taxpayer was to 'compel' him to provide information that could be used to obtain his conviction in a criminal tax fraud proceeding, in much the same way that placing a suspect under physical restraint leads to psychological compulsion. Thus, the misapprehensions are tantamount to the deprivation of the suspect's 'freedom of action in any significant way,' repeatedly referred to in *Miranda*."

I would reverse the judgment of conviction and remand to the District Court for a new trial.

## QUESTIONS AND NOTES

**1.** With whom would you have concurred, Burger, Marshall, Brennan, or none of the above? Explain.

**2.** Do you think that Beckwith was subject to custodial interrogation? If not, was the procedure to which he was subjected similarly coercive?

**3.** Was the procedure to which Beckwith was subjected more or less coercive than that to which Mathis had been subjected?

**4.** In *Mathiason*, we will see that even police station interrogation is not always deemed to be custodial, or inherently coercive.

### Oregon v. Mathiason
### 429 U.S. 492 (1977)

PER CURIAM.

Respondent Carl Mathiason was convicted of first-degree burglary after a bench trial in which his confession was critical to the State's case. At trial he moved to suppress the confession as the fruit of questioning by the police not preceded by the warnings required in *Miranda*. The trial court refused to exclude the confession because it found that Mathiason was not in custody at the time of the confession.

The Supreme Court of Oregon described the factual situation surrounding the confession as follows:

"An officer of the State Police investigated a theft at a residence near Pendleton. He asked the lady of the house which had been burglarized if she suspected anyone. She replied that the defendant was the only one she could think of. The defendant was a parolee and a 'close associate' of her son. The officer tried to contact defendant on three or four occasions with no success. Finally, about 25 days after the burglary, the officer left his card at defendant's apartment with a note asking him to call because 'I'd like to discuss something with you.' The next afternoon the defendant did call. The officer asked where it would be convenient to meet. The defendant had no preference; so the officer asked if the defendant could meet him at the state patrol office in about an hour and a half, about 5:00 p.m. The patrol office was about two blocks from defendant's apartment. The building housed several state agencies.

"The officer met defendant in the hallway, shook hands and took him into an office. The defendant was told he was not under arrest.

The door was closed. The two sat across a desk. The police radio in another room could be heard. The officer told defendant he wanted to talk to him about a burglary and that his truthfulness would possibly be considered by the district attorney or judge. The officer further advised that the police believed defendant was involved in the burglary and [falsely stated that] defendant's fingerprints were found at the scene. The defendant sat for a few minutes and then said he had taken the property. This occurred within five minutes after defendant had come to the office. The officer then advised defendant of his *Miranda* rights and took a taped confession.

"At the end of the taped conversation the officer told defendant he was not arresting him at this time; he was released to go about his job and return to his family. The officer said he was referring the case to the district attorney for him to determine whether criminal charges would be brought. It was 5:30 p. m. when the defendant left the office.

"The officer gave all the testimony relevant to this issue. The defendant did not take the stand either at the hearing on the motion to suppress or at the trial."

The Supreme Court of Oregon reasoned from these facts that:

"We hold the interrogation took place in a 'coercive environment.' The parties were in the offices of the State Police; they were alone behind closed doors; the officer informed the defendant he was a suspect in a theft and the authorities had evidence incriminating him in the crime; and the defendant was a parolee under supervision. We are of the opinion that this evidence is not overcome by the evidence that the defendant came to the office in response to a request and was told he was not under arrest."

Our decision in *Miranda* set forth rules of police procedure applicable to "custodial interrogation." "By custodial interrogation, we mean questioning initiated by law enforcement officers after a person has been taken into custody or otherwise deprived of his freedom of action in any significant way." Subsequently we have found the *Miranda* principle applicable to questioning which takes place in a prison setting during a suspect's term of imprisonment on a separate offense, *Mathis*, and to questioning taking place in a suspect's home, after he has been arrested and is no longer free to go where he pleases, *Orozco*.

In the present case, however, there is no indication that the questioning took place in a context where respondent's freedom to depart was restricted in any way. He came voluntarily to the police station, where he was immediately informed that he was not under arrest. At the close of a ½-hour interview respondent did in fact leave the police station without hindrance. It is clear from these facts that Mathiason was not in custody "or otherwise deprived of his freedom of action in any significant way."

Such a noncustodial situation is not converted to one in which *Miranda* applies simply because a reviewing court concludes that, even in the absence of any formal arrest or restraint on freedom of movement, the questioning took place in a "coercive environment." Any interview of one suspected of a crime by a police officer will have coercive aspects to it, simply by virtue of the fact that the police officer is part of a law enforcement system which may ultimately cause the suspect to be charged with a crime. But police officers are not required to administer *Miranda* warnings to everyone whom they question. Nor is the requirement of warnings to be imposed simply because the questioning takes place in the station house, or because the questioned person is one whom the police suspect. *Miranda* warnings are required only where there has been such a restriction on a person's freedom as to render him "in custody." It was *that* sort of coercive environment to which *Miranda* by its terms was made applicable, and to which it is limited.

The officer's false statement about having discovered Mathiason's fingerprints at the scene was found

by the Supreme Court of Oregon to be another circumstance contributing to the coercive environment which makes the *Miranda* rationale applicable. Whatever relevance this fact may have to other issues in the case, it has nothing to do with whether respondent was in custody for purposes of the *Miranda* rule.

The petition for certiorari is granted, the judgment of the Oregon Supreme Court is reversed, and the case is remanded for proceedings not inconsistent with this opinion.

[Mr. Justice BRENNAN would grant the writ but dissents from the summary disposition and would set the case for oral argument.]

Mr. Justice MARSHALL, dissenting.

The respondent in this case was interrogated behind closed doors at police headquarters in connection with a burglary investigation. He had been named by the victim of the burglary as a suspect, and was told by the police that they believed he was involved. He was falsely informed that his fingerprints had been found at the scene, and in effect was advised that by cooperating with the police he could help himself. Not until after he had confessed was he given the warnings set forth in *Miranda*.

The Court today holds that for constitutional purposes all this is irrelevant because respondent had not "been taken into custody or otherwise deprived of his freedom of action in any significant way." I do not believe that such a determination is possible on the record before us. It is true that respondent was not formally placed under arrest, but surely formalities alone cannot control. At the very least, if respondent entertained an objectively reasonable belief that he was not free to leave during the questioning, then he was "deprived of his freedom of action in a significant way."[1] Plainly the respondent could have so believed, after being told by the police that they thought he was involved in a burglary and that his fingerprints had been found at the scene. Yet the majority is content to note that "there is no

---

[1] It has been noted that as a logical matter, a person who honestly but unreasonably believes he is in custody is subject to the same coercive pressures as one whose belief is reasonable; this suggests that such persons also are entitled to warnings. See, *e.g.*, LaFave, "Street Encounters" and the Constitution: Terry, Sibron, Peters, and Beyond, 67 Mich.L.Rev. 39, 105 (1968); Smith, The Threshold Question in Applying Miranda: What Constitutes Custodial Interrogation?, 25 S.C.L.Rev. 699, 711-714 (1974).

indication that . . . respondent's freedom to depart was restricted in any way,'' as if a silent record (and no state-court findings) means that the State has sustained its burden of demonstrating that respondent received his constitutional due.

More fundamentally, however, I cannot agree with the Court's conclusion that if respondent were not in custody no warnings were required. I recognize that *Miranda* is limited to custodial interrogations, but that is because, as we noted last Term, the facts in the *Miranda* cases raised only this "narrow issue." *Beckwith*. The rationale of *Miranda*, however, is not so easily cabined.

*Miranda* requires warnings to "combat" a situation in which there are "inherently compelling pressures which work to undermine the individual's will to resist and to compel him to speak where he would not otherwise do so freely." It is of course true, as the Court notes, that "[a]ny interview of one suspected of a crime by a police officer will have coercive aspects to it." But it does not follow that because police "are not required to administer *Miranda* warnings to everyone whom they question," that they need not administer warnings to anyone, unless the factual setting of the *Miranda* cases is replicated. Rather, faithfulness to *Miranda* requires us to distinguish situations that resemble the "coercive aspects" of custodial interrogation from those that more nearly resemble "[g]eneral on-the-scene questioning . . . or other general questioning of citizens in the fact-finding process" which *Miranda* states usually can take place without warnings.

In my view, even if respondent were not in custody, the coercive elements in the instant case were so pervasive as to require *Miranda*-type warnings.[3] Respondent was interrogated in "privacy" and in "unfamiliar surroundings," factors on which *Miranda* places great stress. [S]ee also *Beckwith*. The investigation had focused on respondent. And respondent was subjected to some of the "deceptive stratagems," which called forth the *Miranda* decision. I therefore agree with the Oregon Supreme Court that to excuse the absence of warnings given

these facts is "contrary to the rationale expressed in *Miranda*."

The privilege against self-incrimination "has always been 'as broad as the mischief against which it seeks to guard.'" *Miranda*, quoting *Counselman v. Hitchcock*, 142 U.S. 547, 562 (1892). Today's decision means, however, that the Fifth Amendment privilege does not provide full protection against mischiefs equivalent to, but different from, custodial interrogation.[5] It is therefore important to note that the state courts remain free, in interpreting state constitutions, to guard against the evil clearly identified by this case.

I respectfully dissent.

Mr. Justice STEVENS, dissenting.

In my opinion the issues presented by this case are too important to be decided summarily. Of particular importance is the fact that the respondent was on parole at the time of his interrogation in the police station. This fact lends support to inconsistent conclusions.

On the one hand, the State surely has greater power to question a parolee about his activities than to question someone else. Moreover, as a practical matter, it seems unlikely that a *Miranda* warning would have much effect on a parolee's choice between silence and responding to police interrogation. Arguably, therefore, *Miranda* warnings are entirely inappropriate in the parole context.

On the other hand, a parolee is technically in legal custody continuously until his sentence has been served. Therefore, if a formalistic analysis of the custody question is to determine when the *Miranda* warning is necessary, a parolee should always be warned. Moreover, *Miranda* teaches that even if a suspect is not in custody, warnings are necessary if he is "otherwise deprived of his freedom of action in any significant way." If a parolee being questioned in a police station is not described by that language, today's decision qualifies that part of *Miranda* to some extent. I believe we would have a better understanding of the extent of that qualification, and therefore of the situations in which warnings must be given to a suspect who is not technically in custody, if we had the benefit of full argument and plenary consideration.

I therefore respectfully dissent from the Court's summary disposition.

---

[3] I do not rule out the possibility that lesser warnings would suffice when a suspect is not in custody but is subjected to a highly coercive atmosphere. See, *e. g., Beckwith* (Marshall, J., concurring in judgment); ALI, Model Code of Pre-Arraignment Procedure § 110.1(2) (Approved Draft 1975) (suspects interrogated at police station must be advised of their right to leave and right to consult with counsel, relatives, or friends).

---

[5] I trust today's decision does not suggest that police officers can circumvent *Miranda* by deliberately postponing the official "arrest" and the giving of *Miranda* warnings until the necessary incriminating statements have been obtained.

## QUESTIONS AND NOTES

**1.** Is (should) a parolee (be) deemed to be in custody by the mere fact of that status? Compare *Mathis*.

**2.** Does *Mathiason* invite the police to postpone an arrest in order to obtain a confession as Justice Marshall feared in footnote 5? If so, is that such a bad thing?

**3.** Would (should) it be permissible for the police to "interview" a suspect at a local restaurant over coffee and doughnuts? Would your answer be any different if the officer had formed the intent to arrest him before conducting the interview, but did not communicate that intent until after the confession?

**4.** Why do you suppose that the officer released Mathiason after his confession? Do you consider that to be good police work?

## PROBLEM

On Saturday June 3 at 1 p.m., Officer Joe Rogers made the following phone call to Fred Flowers:

Rogers: Fred Flowers, this is Police Officer Joe Rogers. I have a warrant for your arrest for harassing Raleigh Birdsong. Will you come in on your own or do I have to come out there and arrest you?

Flowers: My sister is getting married at 4 o'clock this afternoon. The wedding should be over by 8 this evening, can I turn myself in then?

Rogers: I'll tell you what I'll do. If you voluntarily come to the police station now to talk to me, I'll let you go at 3, and I won't arrest you until after the wedding.

Flowers: Can I bring my lawyer with me?

Rogers: No, if you were under arrest you would be entitled to counsel, but since I'm not going to arrest you until 8, you won't be entitled to counsel until then.

Flowers: Do I have to answer all of your questions?

Rogers: Well, if you're guilty, you don't have to answer any question that might incriminate you. But, you can't refuse to answer just because you don't want to talk to me. If you do that, I'll arrest you.

When Flowers arrived at the police station, Rogers played a tape of somebody making a threatening phone call to Raleigh Birdsong, whereupon the following conversation transpired:

Rogers: O.K. Fred, why did you do it?

Flowers: It wasn't me.

Rogers: If you don't start giving me some straight answers, I'm going to arrest you now.

Flowers: O.K., Harlan Applewhite made me do it.

Rogers: Thank you very much, you can go to the wedding now.

Should Flowers' confession be admissible? Why? Why not? In *Murphy*, the Court continued to read the concept of "custody" narrowly.

# Minnesota v. Murphy
## 465 U.S. 420 (1984)

Justice WHITE delivered the opinion of the Court.

In this case, respondent Murphy, who was on probation, made incriminating admissions during a meeting with his probation officer. The issue before us is whether the Fifth and Fourteenth Amendments prohibit the introduction into evidence of the admissions in Murphy's subsequent criminal prosecution.

### I

In 1974, Marshall Murphy was twice questioned by Minneapolis Police concerning the rape and murder of a teenage girl. No charges were then brought. In 1980, in connection with a prosecution for criminal sexual conduct arising out of an unrelated incident, Murphy pleaded guilty to a reduced charge of false imprisonment. He was sentenced to a prison term of 16 months, which was suspended, and three years' probation. The terms of Murphy's probation required, among other things, that he participate in a treatment program for sexual offenders at Alpha House, report to his probation officer as directed, and be truthful with the probation officer "in all matters." Failure to comply with these conditions, Murphy was informed, could result in his return to the sentencing court for a probation revocation hearing.

Murphy met with his probation officer at her office approximately once a month, and his probation continued without incident until July 1981, when the officer learned that he had abandoned the treatment program. The probation officer then wrote to Murphy and informed him that failure to set up a meeting would "result in an immediate request for a warrant." At a meeting in late July, the officer agreed not to seek revocation of probation for nonparticipation in the treatment program since Murphy was employed and doing well in other areas.

In September 1981, an Alpha House counselor informed the probation officer that, during the course of treatment, Murphy had admitted to a rape and murder in 1974. After discussions with her superior, the officer determined that the police should have this information.[1] She then wrote to Murphy and asked him to contact her to discuss a treatment plan for the remainder of his probationary period.[2] Although she did not contact the police before the meeting, the probation officer knew in advance that she would report any incriminating statements.

Upon receipt of the letter, Murphy arranged to meet with his probation officer in her office on September 28, 1981. The officer opened the meeting by telling Murphy about the information she had received from the Alpha House counselor and expressing her belief that this information evinced his continued need for treatment. Murphy became angry about what he considered to be a breach of his confidences and stated that he "felt like calling a lawyer."[3] The probation officer replied that Murphy would have to deal with that problem outside the office; for the moment, their primary concern was the relationship between the crimes that Murphy had admitted to the Alpha House counselor and the incident that led to his conviction for false imprisonment.

During the course of the meeting, Murphy denied the false imprisonment charge, admitted that he had committed the rape and murder, and attempted to persuade the probation officer that further treatment was unnecessary because several extenuating circumstances explained the prior crimes. At the conclusion of the meeting, the officer told Murphy that

---

[1] The parties stipulated in the trial court that Alpha House was covered by federal statutes providing for the confidentiality of patient records in federally assisted drug and alcohol rehabilitation programs, and the regulations adopted pursuant thereto. Although the Alpha House counselor legitimately informed Murphy's probation officer of his incriminating admissions, we assume, without deciding, that the counselor could not have provided the information to the police. We assume, as well, that the probation officer could not have made the counselor's information available for use in a criminal prosecution.

[2] It is unclear whether the probation officer could have ordered Murphy to pursue additional treatment as a condition of probation. But there is no evidence that she used treatment as a subterfuge or that her sole purpose was to obtain incriminating statements for the police. Under our view of the case, such a purpose would not change the result.

[3] The trial court concluded that Murphy's statement did not constitute an invocation of the privilege against self-incrimination: "[W]hatever his real intent may have been, we are persuaded by the probation officer's testimony that he did not express [the] desire [to talk to an attorney] in any context other than a civil suit for the breach of confidentiality."

she had a duty to relay the information to the authorities and encouraged him to turn himself in. Murphy then left the office. Two days later, Murphy called his probation officer and told her that he had been advised by counsel not to surrender himself to the police. The officer then procured the issuance of an arrest and detention order from the judge who had sentenced Murphy on the false imprisonment charge. On October 29, 1981, a State grand jury returned an indictment charging Murphy with first-degree murder.

## II

The Fifth Amendment, in relevant part, provides that no person "shall be compelled in any criminal case to be a witness against himself." It has long been held that this prohibition not only permits a person to refuse to testify against himself at a criminal trial in which he is a defendant, but also "privileges him not to answer official questions put to him in any other proceeding, civil or criminal, formal or informal, where the answers might incriminate him in future criminal proceedings." A defendant does not lose this protection by reason of his conviction of a crime; notwithstanding that a defendant is imprisoned or on probation at the time he makes incriminating statements, if those statements are compelled they are inadmissible in a subsequent trial for a crime other than that for which he has been convicted. The issue in this case is whether the Fifth Amendment right that Murphy enjoyed was violated by the admission into evidence at his trial for another crime of the prior statements made by him to his probation officer.

### B

[A] witness confronted with questions that the government should reasonably expect to elicit incriminating evidence ordinarily must assert the privilege rather than answer if he desires not to incriminate himself. If he asserts the privilege, he "may not be required to answer a question if there is some rational basis for believing that it will incriminate him, at least without *at that time* being assured that neither it nor its fruits may be used against him" in a subsequent criminal proceeding. *Maness v. Meyers*, 419 U.S. 449, 473 (1976) (White, J., concurring in the result) (emphasis in original). But if he chooses to answer, his choice is considered to be voluntary since he was free to claim the privilege and would suffer no penalty as the result of his decision to do so. As the Minnesota Supreme Court recognized, application of this general rule is inappropriate in certain well-defined situations. In each of those situations, however, some identifiable factor

"was held to deny the individual a 'free choice to admit, to deny, or to refuse to answer.'" Because we conclude that no such factor was present here, we hold that the Minnesota Supreme Court erred in excluding the probation officer's testimony.

### 1

A well-known exception to the general rule addresses the problem of confessions obtained from suspects in police custody.[5] Not only is custodial interrogation ordinarily conducted by officers who are "acutely aware of the potentially incriminatory nature of the disclosures sought," but also the custodial setting is thought to contain "inherently compelling pressures which work to undermine the individual's will to resist and to compel him to speak where he would not otherwise do so freely." *Miranda*. To dissipate "the overbearing compulsion . . . caused by isolation of a suspect in police custody," the *Miranda* Court required the exclusion of incriminating statements obtained during custodial interrogation unless the suspect fails to claim the Fifth Amendment privilege after being suitably warned of his right to remain silent and of the consequences of his failure to assert it. We have consistently held, however, that this extraordinary safeguard "does not apply outside the context of the inherently coercive custodial interrogations for which it was designed."

The Minnesota Supreme Court recognized that Murphy was not "in custody" when he made his incriminating admissions. He was, to be sure, subject to a number of restrictive conditions governing various aspects of his life, and he would be regarded as "in custody" for purposes of federal habeas corpus. But custody in that context has been defined broadly to effectuate the purposes of the writ, and custody for *Miranda* purposes has been more narrowly circumscribed. See *Mathiason*. Under the narrower standard appropriate in the *Miranda* context, it is clear that Murphy was not "in custody" for purposes of receiving *Miranda* protection since there was no "'formal arrest or restraint on freedom of movement' of the degree associated with a formal arrest."

Notwithstanding the inapplicability of *Miranda*, the Minnesota Supreme Court held that the probation

---

[5] We emphasize that Murphy was not under arrest and that he was free to leave at the end of the meeting. A different question would be presented if he had been interviewed by his probation officer while being held in police custody or by the police themselves in a custodial setting.

officer's failure to inform Murphy of the Fifth Amendment privilege barred use of his confession at trial. Four factors have been advanced in support of this conclusion, but we find them, alone or in combination, insufficient to excuse Murphy's failure to claim the privilege in a timely manner.

First, the probation officer could compel Murphy's attendance and truthful answers. The Minnesota Supreme Court failed to explain how this transformed a routine interview into an inherently coercive setting. In our view, this factor subjected Murphy to less intimidating pressure than is imposed on grand jury witnesses, who are sworn to tell the truth and placed in a setting conducive to truth-telling. Although warnings in both contexts might serve to dissipate "any possible coercion or unfairness resulting from a witness' misimpression that he must answer truthfully even questions with incriminating aspects," we have never held that they must be given to grand jury witnesses, and we decline to require them here since the totality of the circumstances is not such as to overbear a probationer's free will.

Second, the probation officer consciously sought incriminating evidence. We have already explained that this factor does not give rise to a self-executing privilege, and we pause here only to emphasize that police officers questioning persons suspected of crimes often consciously seek incriminating statements. The mere fact that an investigation has focused on a suspect does not trigger the need for *Miranda* warnings in noncustodial settings, *Beckwith*, and the probation officer's knowledge and intent have no bearing on the outcome of this case.

Third, Murphy did not expect questions about prior criminal conduct and could not seek counsel before attending the meeting. But the nature of probation is such that probationers should expect to be questioned on a wide range of topics relating to their past criminality. Moreover, the probation officer's letter, which suggested a need to discuss treatment from which Murphy had already been excused, would have led a reasonable probationer to conclude that new information had come to her attention. In any event, Murphy's situation was in this regard indistinguishable from that facing suspects who are questioned in noncustodial settings and grand jury witnesses who are unaware of the scope of an investigation or that they are considered potential defendants. See *Beckwith*.

Fourth, there were no observers to guard against abuse or trickery. Again, this often will be true when a suspect is subjected to noncustodial interrogation, where no warnings are required. Murphy does not allege that the probation officer was not legitimately

concerned with the need for further treatment, and we cannot conclude that her actions would have led a reasonable probationer to believe that his statements to her would remain confidential. A probationer cannot pretend ignorance of the fact that his probation officer "is a peace officer, and as such is allied, to a greater or lesser extent, with his fellow peace officers." *Michael C.* Absent some express or implied promise to the contrary, he may also be charged with knowledge that "the probation officer is duty bound to report wrongdoing by the [probationer] when it comes to his attention, even if by communication from the [probationer] himself." *Michael C.* The fact that Murphy apparently expressed no surprise on being informed that his statements would be made available to the police, moreover, strongly suggests that he was not misled by any expectation that his statements would remain confidential.

Even a cursory comparison of custodial interrogation and probation interviews reveals the inaptness of the Minnesota Supreme Court's analogy to *Miranda*. Custodial arrest is said to convey to the suspect a message that he has no choice but to submit to the officers' will and to confess. It is unlikely that a probation interview, arranged by appointment at a mutually convenient time, would give rise to a similar impression. Moreover, custodial arrest thrusts an individual into "an unfamiliar atmosphere" or "an interrogation environment . . . created for no purpose other than to subjugate the individual to the will of his examiner." Many of the psychological ploys discussed in *Miranda* capitalize on the suspect's unfamiliarity with the officers and the environment. Murphy's regular meetings with his probation officer should have served to familiarize him with her and her office and to insulate him from psychological intimidation that might overbear his desire to claim the privilege. Finally, the coercion inherent in custodial interrogation derives in large measure from an interrogator's insinuations that the interrogation will continue until a confession is obtained. Since Murphy was not physically restrained and could have left the office, any compulsion he might have felt from the possibility that terminating the meeting would have led to revocation of probation was not comparable to the pressure on a suspect who is painfully aware that he literally cannot escape a persistent custodial interrogator.[6]

---

[6] Neither the trial court nor the Minnesota Supreme Court found that Murphy believed that his probation could have been revoked for leaving the meeting or that he remained in the office for this reason. Since the meeting was scheduled at a mutu-

We conclude, therefore, that Murphy cannot claim the benefit of the first exception to the general rule that the Fifth Amendment privilege is not self-executing.

### 2

The general rule that the privilege must be claimed when self-incrimination is threatened has also been deemed inapplicable in cases where the assertion of the privilege is penalized so as to "forceclos[e] a free choice to remain silent, and . . . compe[l] . . . incriminating testimony." Because revocation of his probation was threatened if he was untruthful with his probation officer, Murphy argues that he was compelled to make incriminating disclosures instead of claiming the privilege. Although this contention is not without force, we find it unpersuasive on close examination.

Murphy was informed that he was required to be truthful with his probation officer in all matters and that failure to do so could result in revocation of probation. The opinion of the Minnesota Supreme Court made clear that this was indeed the case, but its conclusion that the probation officer's failure to give Murphy adequate warnings barred the use of his incriminating statements in the criminal trial did not rest on the ground that a refusal to furnish incriminating information would have justified revocation of probation. Although the court recognized that imposing a penalty for a valid exercise of the Fifth Amendment privilege could impermissibly foreclose a free choice to remain silent, it did not purport to find that Minnesota's probation revocation statute had such an effect. The court relied instead on the fact that Murphy was under legal compulsion to attend the meeting and to answer truthfully the questions of a probation officer who anticipated incriminating answers. Such compulsion, however, is indistinguishable from that felt by any witness who is required to appear and give testimony, and, as we have already made clear, it is insufficient to excuse Murphy's failure to exercise the privilege in a timely manner.

The State court did not attempt to define the precise contours of Murphy's obligation to respond to questions. On its face, Murphy's probation condition proscribed only false statements; it said nothing about his freedom to decline to answer particular

___

ally convenient time and was arranged pursuant to a request that did not include any threat, it is unlikely that Murphy believed that terminating the meeting would have jeopardized his probationary status.

questions and certainly contained no suggestion that his probation was conditional on his waiving his Fifth Amendment privilege with respect to further criminal prosecution. "At this point in our history virtually every schoolboy is familiar with the concept, if not the language, of the [Fifth Amendment]." Yet Murphy, although he had a right to do so, did not seek clarification of the condition. Without the benefit of an authoritative state-court construction of the condition, we are hesitant to read into the truthfulness requirement an additional obligation that Murphy refrain from raising legitimate objections to furnishing information that might lead to his conviction for another crime.

Whether we employ a subjective or an objective test, there is no reasonable basis for concluding that Minnesota attempted to attach an impermissible penalty to the exercise of the privilege against self-incrimination. There is no direct evidence that Murphy confessed because he feared that his probation would be revoked if he remained silent. Murphy was not expressly informed during the crucial meeting with his probation officer that an assertion of the privilege would result in the imposition of a penalty. And the fact that Murphy apparently felt no compunction about adamantly denying the false imprisonment charge on which he had been convicted before admitting to the rape and murder strongly suggests that the "threat" of revocation did not overwhelm his resistance.

If Murphy did harbor a belief that his probation might be revoked for exercising the Fifth Amendment privilege, that belief would not have been reasonable. Our decisions have made clear that the State could not constitutionally carry out a threat to revoke probation for the legitimate exercise of the Fifth Amendment privilege. It is not surprising, then, that neither the State court nor any State officer has suggested otherwise. Indeed, in its brief in this Court, the State submits that it would not, and legally could not, revoke probation for refusing to answer questions calling for information that would incriminate in separate criminal proceedings.

### III

We conclude, in summary, that since Murphy revealed incriminating information instead of timely asserting his Fifth Amendment privilege, his disclosures were not compelled incriminations. Because he had not been compelled to incriminate himself, Murphy could not successfully invoke the privilege to prevent the information he volunteered to his probation officer from being used against him in a criminal prosecution.

The judgment of the Minnesota Supreme Court is reversed.

Justice MARSHALL, with whom Justice STEVENS joins, and with whom Justice BRENNAN joins except as to Part II-A, dissenting.

The opinion of the Court helpfully clarifies the scope of the privilege against self-incrimination that may be asserted by a probationer when asked questions by an officer of the State.

If a truthful response might reveal that he has violated a condition of his probation but would not subject him to criminal prosecution, the state may insist that he respond and may penalize him for refusing to do so.[1] By contrast, if there is a chance that a truthful answer to a given question would expose the probationer to liability for a crime different from the crime for which he has already been convicted, he has a right to refuse to answer and the state may not attempt to coerce him to forgo that right.[2] As the majority points out, if the answer to a question might lead both to criminal sanctions and to probation revocation, the state has the option of insisting that the probationer respond, in return for an express guarantee of immunity from criminal liability. Unless it exercises that option, however, the state may not interfere with the probationer's right "to remain silent unless he chooses to speak in the unfettered exercise of his own will."

The flaw in the opinion of the Court lies not in its analysis of the constitutional rights available to a probationer, but in its finding that those rights were not violated in this case. The majority concludes that, "since Murphy revealed incriminating information instead of timely asserting his Fifth Amendment privilege, his disclosures were not compelled incriminations." In my view, that conclusion is inconsistent with our prior cases dealing with invocations of the Fifth Amendment.

When Murphy was placed on probation, he was given a letter setting forth the conditions under which he was discharged. The pertinent portions of the letter provide:

"For the present, you are only conditionally released. If you comply with the conditions of your probation you may expect to be discharged at the expiration of the period stated. If you fail to comply with the requirements you may be returned to Court at any time for further hearing or commitment. . . .

"It will be necessary for you to obey strictly the following conditions:

"BE TRUTHFUL to your Probation Officer in all matters." (emphasis in original).

Murphy was required to sign the letter, attesting that he had read and understood the instructions.

The majority contends that the foregoing passages merely required Murphy to answer nonincriminating questions and forbade him to make false statements to his probation officer. The majority's interpretation, which is essential to its result, is simply incredible. A reasonable layman would interpret the imperative, "be truthful . . . in all matters," as a command to answer honestly all questions presented. Any ambiguity inherent in the language of the directive is dispelled by its context. The duty to be truthful in dealings with the probation officer is listed as the first term of the conditions of probation. The critical phrase is capitalized. And the injunction is immediately preceded by an instruction "to obey strictly the following conditions."[9]

## II

Even if Minnesota had not impaired Murphy's freedom to respond or to refuse to respond to incriminating questions regarding the 1974 murder, I would hold his confession inadmissible because, in view of the circumstances under which he was interrogated, the State had a duty to prove that Murphy waived his privilege against self-incrimination, and it has not made such a showing.

### A

It is now settled that, in most contexts, the privilege against self-incrimination is not self-executing.

---

[1] This is not to suggest that a State must or should organize its probation system in a fashion that compels probationers to respond under these circumstances, only that a State is not prevented by the Federal Constitution from doing so.

[2] It makes no difference whether the criminal conduct that the probationer might reveal was committed before or after the crime for which he was convicted or before or after the conviction itself.

[9] The Solicitor General observes: "Citizens are often required to be truthful in their dealings with the government; any person commits a crime if, for example, he makes a false statement to a federal law enforcement officer in connection with a matter within the officer's jurisdiction. It is precisely because such proscriptions on lying to government officials are so common that the emphatic injunction contained in Murphy's probation conditions must be interpreted to impose on him more extensive obligations.

"[I]n the ordinary case," if a person questioned by an officer of the state makes damaging disclosures instead of asserting his privilege, he forfeits his right to object to subsequent use of his admissions against him. This forfeiture occurs even if the person is subject to a general legal duty to respond to the officer's questions. And it occurs regardless of whether the person's failure to claim the privilege was founded upon a knowing and intelligent decision to waive his constitutional right not to answer those questions that might incriminate him.

It should be apparent that these considerations do not apply with equal force in all contexts. Until today, the Court has been sensitive to variations in their relevance and strength. Accordingly, we have adhered to the general principle that a defendant forfeits his privilege if he fails to assert it before making incriminating statements only in situations implicating several of the factors that support the principle. More specifically, we have applied the principle only in cases in which at least two of the following statements have been true: (a) At the time the damaging disclosures were made, the defendant's constitutional right not to make them was clearly established. (b) The defendant was given sufficient warning that he would be asked potentially incriminating questions to be able to secure legal advice and to reflect upon how he would respond. (c) The environment in which the questions were asked did not impair the defendant's ability intelligently to exercise his rights. (d) The questioner had no reason to assume that truthful responses would be self-incriminating.

By contrast, in cases in which only one of the statements enumerated above has been true, the Court has refused to adhere to the general rule that a privilege not claimed is lost, and instead has insisted upon a showing that the defendant made a knowing and intelligent decision to forgo his constitutional right not to incriminate himself. The classic situation of this sort is custodial interrogation. In *Miranda*, the Court acknowledged that the right of a suspect in police custody not to answer questions is well established. However, we stressed that other aspects of the situation impair the ability of the suspect to exercise his rights and threaten the values underlying the Fifth Amendment: the suspect is unable to consult with counsel regarding how he should respond to questions; the environment in which the questions are presented (the police station, from which the suspect is forbidden to leave) "work[s] to undermine the individual's will to resist and to compel him to speak where he would not otherwise do so freely," and the interrogators are well aware that truthful answers to their questions are likely to incriminate the suspect. In short, only one of the four circumstances favoring application of the general principle exist in the context of custodial interrogation. To mitigate the risk that suspects would ignorantly or involuntarily fail to claim their privilege against self-incrimination under these circumstances, the Court in *Miranda* imposed a requirement that they be shown to have freely waived their rights after being fully apprised of them.

B

If we remain sensitive to the concerns implicit in the foregoing pattern of cases, we should insist that the State, in the instant case, demonstrate that Murphy intelligently waived his right to remain silent. None of the four conditions that favor application of the principle that a defendant forfeits his privilege if he fails to claim it before confessing can be found in the circumstances under which Murphy was interrogated. First, the existence and scope of Murphy's constitutional right to refuse to testify were at best unclear when he appeared in the probation officer's office. It is undisputed that the conditions of Murphy's probation imposed on him a duty to answer all questions presented by his probation officer except those implicating his Fifth Amendment rights. What exactly those rights were was far from apparent. The majority opinion in this case constitutes the first authoritative analysis of the privilege against self-incrimination available to a probationer. The ambiguity of scope of that privilege prior to today is suggested by the fact the Solicitor General, appearing as *amicus curiae*, seriously misconceived the rights that might have been asserted by Murphy when examined by his probation officer.[23] If, after being afforded substantial opportunity for research and reflection, the lawyers who represent the Nation err in their explication of the relevant constitutional principles, Murphy surely cannot be charged with knowledge of his entitlements.

Second, contrary to the suggestion of the majority, Murphy was given no warning that he would be

---

[23] The Solicitor argued in the alternative that, "[w]hen a person has been convicted of a crime, his constitutional rights can be limited to the extent reasonably necessary to accommodate the government's penal and rehabilitative interests," and therefore that the government may constitutionally exert upon a probationer pressures to incriminate himself that it could not exert upon a citizen who had not been convicted of a crime. That proposition is rejected by the Court today.

asked potentially incriminating questions. The letter in which Murphy's probation officer instructed him to make an appointment informed him that the purpose of the meeting was "[t]o further discuss a treatment plan for the remainder of [his] probation." In view of the fact that Murphy remained under a legal obligation to attend treatment sessions,[25] there was no reason why he should have assumed from the letter that the officer planned to question him regarding prior criminal activity.[26] In short, prior to the moment he was asked whether he had committed the murder, Murphy had no reason to suspect that he would be obliged to respond to incriminating questions. He thus had no opportunity to consult a lawyer, or even to consider how he should proceed.

Third, the environment in which the questioning occurred impaired Murphy's ability to recognize and claim his constitutional rights. It is true, as the majority points out, that the discussion between a probation officer and a probationer is likely to be less coercive and intimidating than a discussion between a police officer and a suspect in custody. But it is precisely in that fact that the danger lies. In contrast to the inherently adversarial relationship between a suspect and a policeman, the relationship between a probationer and the officer to whom he reports is likely to incorporate elements of confidentiality, even friendship. Indeed, many probation officers deliberately cultivate such bonds with their charges. The point should not be overstated; undoubtedly, few probationers are entirely blind to the fact that their probation officers are "peace officer[s], . . . allied, to a greater or lesser extent, with [their] fellow peace officers." *Michael C.*. On the other hand, many probationers develop "relationship[s] of trust and confidence" with their officers. Through abuse of that trust, a probation officer can elicit admissions from a probationer that the probationer would be unlikely to make to a hostile police interrogator.

The instant case aptly illustrates the danger. Before she sent her letter to Murphy asking him to make an appointment, the probation officer had decided to try to induce him to confess to the 1974

killing and to turn over that information to the police. She was aware that, if she were successful, Murphy would soon be arrested and tried for murder.[29] There was thus no prospect whatsoever that the information she elicited would be used to design a treatment program to be followed by Murphy during the remainder of his probation. Yet, in her letter, she described the purpose of the meeting as that of "discuss[ing] a treatment plan." When Murphy arrived at the meeting, she persisted in the deceit; instead of informing him at once what she intended to do with his anticipated confession to the 1974 murder, she told him that "her main concern was to talk to him about the relationship of the prior crime and the one of which he was convicted and about his need for treatment under the circumstances." That Murphy succumbed to the deception is apparent from the sequence of his responses. Instead of denying responsibility for the 1974 killing, he admitted his guilt but sought to explain that extenuating circumstances accounted for that crime. Because those circumstances no longer existed, he argued, he had no need for further treatment. Only after Murphy had made his confession did the officer inform him of her intent to transmit that information to the police. In short, the environment in which the interview was conducted afforded the probation officer opportunities to reinforce and capitalize on Murphy's ignorance that he had a right to refuse to answer incriminating questions, and the officer deliberately and effectively exploited those opportunities.

Finally, it is indisputable that the probation officer had reason to know that truthful responses to her questions would expose Murphy to criminal liability. This case does not arise out of a spontaneous confession to a routine question innocently asked by a government official. Rather, it originates in precisely the sort of situation the Fifth Amendment was designed to prevent—in which a government, instead of establishing a defendant's guilt through independent investigation, seeks to induce him, against his will, to convict himself out of his own mouth.

In sum, none of the factors that, in most contexts, justify application of the principle that a defendant loses his Fifth Amendment privilege unless he claims it in a timely fashion are present in this case. Accordingly, the State should be obliged to demonstrate that Murphy knew of his constitutional rights and freely waived them. Because the State has made no such

---

[25] Contrary to the majority's suggestion, nothing in the record indicates that the probation officer had "excused" Murphy from the condition of probation that required him "to pursue . . . Alpha treatment," the Minnesota Supreme Court found merely that she had agreed not to seek revocation of his probation because of his breach of that condition.

[26] Indeed, it appears that the letter was shrewdly designed to prevent Murphy from discerning in advance the true purpose of the meeting.

---

[29] Indeed, when Murphy refused to turn himself in, it was his probation officer who secured the order for his arrest.

showing, I would hold his confession inadmissible.

### III

The criminal justice system contains safeguards that should minimize the damage done by the Court's decision today. In the future, responsible criminal defense attorneys whose clients are given probation will inform those clients, in their final interviews, that they may disregard probation conditions insofar as those conditions are inconsistent with probationers' Fifth Amendment rights. The attorneys will then carefully instruct their clients on the nuances of those rights as we have now explicated them.[30] Armed with this knowledge,

---

[30] It is to be hoped, moreover, that persons currently on probation who are no longer represented by counsel will somehow be informed of the cen-

few probationers will succumb to the sort of pressure and deceit that overwhelmed Murphy.

Because Murphy himself had the benefit of none of the safeguards just described, I would affirm the judgment of the Supreme Court of Minnesota that the admission into evidence of the disclosures he made to his probation officer violated the Constitution.

I respectfully dissent.

---

tral principle established by the Court's decision: that a probationer has a right to refuse to respond to a question the answer to which might expose him to criminal liability unless he is granted immunity from the use of his answer against him in a subsequent criminal prosecution.

## QUESTIONS AND NOTES

**1.** Did the Court hold the Fifth Amendment to be applicable to probation revocation proceedings?

**2.** Did the Court hold *Miranda* to be applicable to probation revocation proceedings?

**3.** Assuming that your answer to question 1 is ''yes'' and your answer to question 2 is ''no,'' explain the dichotomy.

**4.** Why did the Court find that Murphy was not in custody for purposes of *Miranda*? Do you agree? Explain.

**5.** Do you think that the *Murphy* and *Beckwith* situations are analogous? Explain.

**6.** Do you think that Murphy believed that terminating the meeting with his probation officer would have jeopardized his probation? If so, would such a belief be reasonable?

**7.** If your answer to both parts of question 6 is ''yes,'' would it follow that the Court reached the wrong result?

**8.** Did (should) Murphy have the right to be represented by counsel during his interview with his probation officer?

**9.** Assuming that your answer to question 8 was ''no,'' should he nevertheless have been informed of his right to remain silent?

**10.** Do you think that Murphy's probation officer cared about getting him further treatment? Should that matter? Why?

**11.** Justice Marshall seems to think that few people will be hurt by *Murphy* in the future because counsel will warn their clients that the Fifth Amendment is applicable during probation revocation proceedings. Do you agree? Explain.

**12.** In *McCarty*, decided just a few months after *Murphy*, the Court adopted a rather strict objective test for determining custody, but clearly held that *Miranda* was applicable to misdemeanors as well as felonies.

# Berkemer v. McCarty
## 468 U.S. 420 (1984)

Justice MARSHALL delivered the opinion of the Court.

This case presents two related questions: First, does our decision in *Miranda* govern the admissibility of statements made during custodial interrogation by a suspect accused of a misdemeanor traffic offense? Second, does the roadside questioning of a motorist detained pursuant to a traffic stop constitute custodial interrogation for the purposes of the doctrine enunciated in *Miranda*?

## I

### A

The parties have stipulated to the essential facts. On the evening of March 31, 1980, Trooper Williams of the Ohio State Highway Patrol observed respondent's car weaving in and out of a lane on Interstate Highway 270. After following the car for two miles, Williams forced respondent to stop and asked him to get out of the vehicle. When respondent complied, Williams noticed that he was having difficulty standing. At that point, "Williams concluded that [respondent] would be charged with a traffic offense and, therefore, his freedom to leave the scene was terminated." However, respondent was not told that he would be taken into custody. Williams then asked respondent to perform a field sobriety test, commonly known as a "balancing test." Respondent could not do so without falling.

While still at the scene of the traffic stop, Williams asked respondent whether he had been using intoxicants. Respondent replied that "he had consumed two beers and had smoked several joints of marijuana a short time before." Respondent's speech was slurred, and Williams had difficulty understanding him. Williams thereupon formally placed respondent under arrest and transported him in the patrol car to the Franklin County Jail.

At the jail, respondent was given an intoxilyzer test to determine the concentration of alcohol in his blood. The test did not detect any alcohol whatsoever in respondent's system. Williams then resumed questioning respondent in order to obtain information for inclusion in the State Highway Patrol Alcohol Influence Report. Respondent answered affirmatively a question whether he had been drinking. When then asked if he was under the influence of alcohol, he said, "I guess, barely." Williams next asked respondent to indicate on the form whether the marihuana he had smoked had been treated with

any chemicals. In the section of the report headed "Remarks," respondent wrote, "No ang[el] dust or PCP in the pot. Rick McCarty."

At no point in this sequence of events did Williams or anyone else tell respondent that he had a right to remain silent, to consult with an attorney, and to have an attorney appointed for him if he could not afford one.

### B

Respondent was charged with operating a motor vehicle while under the influence of alcohol and/or drugs. Under Ohio law, that offense is a first-degree misdemeanor and is punishable by fine or imprisonment for up to 6 months. Incarceration for a minimum of 3 days is mandatory.

Respondent moved to exclude the various incriminating statements he had made to Patrolman Williams on the ground that introduction into evidence of those statements would violate the Fifth Amendment insofar as he had not been informed of his constitutional rights prior to his interrogation. When the trial court denied the motion, respondent pleaded "no contest" and was found guilty. He was sentenced to 90 days in jail, 80 of which were suspended, and was fined $300, $100 of which were suspended.

In the years since the decision in *Miranda*, we have frequently reaffirmed the central principle established by that case: if the police take a suspect into custody and then ask him questions without informing him of the rights enumerated above, his responses cannot be introduced into evidence to establish his guilt.

Petitioner asks us to carve an exception out of the foregoing principle. When the police arrest a person for allegedly committing a misdemeanor traffic offense and then ask him questions without telling him his constitutional rights, petitioner argues, his responses should be admissible against him. We cannot agree.

One of the principal advantages of the doctrine that suspects must be given warnings before being interrogated while in custody is the clarity of that rule. "*Miranda*'s holding has the virtue of informing police and prosecutors with specificity as to what they may do in conducting custodial interrogation, and of informing courts under what circumstances statements obtained during such interrogation are not admissible. This gain in specificity, which benefits the accused and the State alike, has been thought to outweigh the burdens that the decision in *Miranda* imposes on law enforcement agencies and the courts by requiring the suppression of trustworthy and highly probative evidence even though the confession might be voluntary under traditional Fifth Amendment analysis." *Fare v. Michael C.*

The exception to *Miranda* proposed by petitioner would substantially undermine this crucial advantage of the doctrine. The police often are unaware when they arrest a person whether he may have committed a misdemeanor or a felony. Consider, for example, the reasonably common situation in which the driver of a car involved in an accident is taken into custody. Under Ohio law, both driving while under the influence of intoxicants and negligent vehicular homicide are misdemeanors, while reckless vehicular homicide is a felony. When arresting a person for causing a collision, the police may not know which of these offenses he may have committed. Indeed, the nature of his offense may depend upon circumstances unknowable to the police, such as whether the suspect has previously committed a similar offense or has a criminal record of some other kind. It may even turn upon events yet to happen, such as whether a victim of the accident dies. It would be unreasonable to expect the police to make guesses as to the nature of the criminal conduct at issue before deciding how they may interrogate the suspect.

Absent a compelling justification we surely would be unwilling so seriously to impair the simplicity and clarity of the holding of *Miranda*. Petitioner contends that *Miranda* warnings are unnecessary when a suspect is questioned about a misdemeanor traffic offense, because the police have no reason to subject such a suspect to the sort of interrogation that most troubled the Court in *Miranda*. We cannot agree that the dangers of police abuse are so slight in this context. For example, the offense of driving while intoxicated is increasingly regarded in many jurisdictions as a very serious matter. Especially when the intoxicant at issue is a narcotic drug rather than alcohol, the police sometimes have difficulty obtaining evidence of this crime. Under such circumstances, the incentive for the police to try to induce the defendant to incriminate himself may well be substantial. Similar incentives are likely to be present when a person is arrested for a minor offense but the police suspect that a more serious crime may have been committed.

### III

To assess the admissibility of the self-incriminating statements made by respondent prior to his formal arrest, we are obliged to address a second issue concerning the scope of our decision in *Miranda*: whether the roadside questioning of a motorist detained pursuant to a routine traffic stop should be considered "custodial interrogation." Respondent urges that it should, on the ground that *Miranda* by its terms applies whenever "a person has been taken into custody *or otherwise deprived of his freedom of action in any significant way*," (emphasis added). Petitioner contends that a holding that every detained motorist must be advised of his rights before being questioned would constitute an unwarranted extension of the *Miranda* doctrine.

It must be acknowledged at the outset that a traffic stop significantly curtails the "freedom of action" of the driver and the passengers, if any, of the detained vehicle. Under the law of most States, it is a crime either to ignore a policeman's signal to stop one's car or, once having stopped, to drive away without permission. Certainly few motorists would feel free either to disobey a directive to pull over or to leave the scene of a traffic stop without being told they might do so.[25] Partly for these reasons, we have long acknowledged that "stopping an automobile and detaining its occupants constitute a 'seizure' within the meaning of [the Fourth] Amendmen[t], even though the purpose of the stop is limited and the resulting detention quite brief." *Delaware v. Prouse*.

However, we decline to accord talismanic power to the phrase in the *Miranda* opinion emphasized by respondent. Fidelity to the doctrine announced in *Miranda* requires that it be enforced strictly, but only in those types of situations in which the concerns that powered the decision are implicated. Thus, we must decide whether a traffic stop exerts upon a detained person pressures that sufficiently impair his free exercise of his privilege against self-incrimination to require that he be warned of his constitutional rights.

Two features of an ordinary traffic stop mitigate the danger that a person questioned will be induced "to speak where he would not otherwise do so freely," *Miranda*. First, detention of a motorist pursuant to a traffic stop is presumptively temporary and brief. The vast majority of roadside detentions

---

[25] Indeed, petitioner frankly admits that "[n]o reasonable person would feel that he was free to ignore the visible and audible signal of a traffic safety enforcement officer. . . . Moreover, it is nothing short of sophistic to state that a motorist ordered by a police officer to step out of his vehicle would reasonabl[y] or prudently believe that he was at liberty to ignore that command."

last only a few minutes. A motorist's expectations, when he sees a policeman's light flashing behind him, are that he will be obliged to spend a short period of time answering questions and waiting while the officer checks his license and registration, that he may then be given a citation, but that in the end he most likely will be allowed to continue on his way. In this respect, questioning incident to an ordinary traffic stop is quite different from stationhouse interrogation, which frequently is prolonged, and in which the detainee often is aware that questioning will continue until he provides his interrogators the answers they seek.[27]

Second, circumstances associated with the typical traffic stop are not such that the motorist feels completely at the mercy of the police. To be sure, the aura of authority surrounding an armed, uniformed officer and the knowledge that the officer has some discretion in deciding whether to issue a citation, in combination, exert some pressure on the detainee to respond to questions. But other aspects of the situation substantially offset these forces. Perhaps most importantly, the typical traffic stop is public, at least to some degree. Passersby, on foot or in other cars, witness the interaction of officer and motorist. This exposure to public view both reduces the ability of an unscrupulous policeman to use illegitimate means to elicit self-incriminating statements and diminishes the motorist's fear that, if he does not cooperate, he will be subjected to abuse. The fact that the detained motorist typically is confronted by only one or at most two policemen further mutes his sense of vulnerability. In short, the atmosphere surrounding an ordinary traffic stop is substantially less "police dominated" than that surrounding the kinds of interrogation at issue in *Miranda* itself, and in the subsequent cases in which we have applied *Miranda*.[28]

In both of these respects, the usual traffic stop is more analogous to a so-called "*Terry* stop" than

to a formal arrest.[29] Typically, this means that the officer may ask the detainee a moderate number of questions to determine his identity and to try to obtain information confirming or dispelling the officer's suspicions. But the detainee is not obliged to respond. And, unless the detainee's answers provide the officer with probable cause to arrest him, he must then be released. The comparatively nonthreatening character of detentions of this sort explains the absence of any suggestion in our opinions that *Terry* stops are subject to the dictates of *Miranda*. The similarly noncoercive aspect of ordinary traffic stops prompts us to hold that persons temporarily detained pursuant to such stops are not "in custody" for the purposes of *Miranda*.

Respondent contends that to "exempt" traffic stops from the coverage of *Miranda* will open the way to widespread abuse. Policemen will simply delay formally arresting detained motorists, and will subject them to sustained and intimidating interrogation at the scene of their initial detention. The net result, respondent contends, will be a serious threat to the rights that the *Miranda* doctrine is designed to protect.

We are confident that the state of affairs projected by respondent will not come to pass. It is settled that the safeguards prescribed by *Miranda* become applicable as soon as a suspect's freedom of action is curtailed to a "degree associated with formal arrest." If a motorist who has been detained pursuant to a traffic stop thereafter is subjected to treatment that renders him "in custody" for practical purposes, he will be entitled to the full panoply of protections prescribed by *Miranda*. See *Mathiason*.

Admittedly, our adherence to the doctrine just recounted will mean that the police and lower courts will continue occasionally to have difficulty deciding exactly when a suspect has been taken into custody. Either a rule that *Miranda* applies to all traffic stops or a rule that a suspect need not be advised of his rights until he is formally placed under arrest would provide a clearer, more easily administered line. However, each of these two alternatives has drawbacks that make it unacceptable. The first would substantially impede the enforcement of the nation's

---

[27] The brevity and spontaneity of an ordinary traffic stop also reduces the danger that the driver through subterfuge will be made to incriminate himself. One of the investigative techniques that *Miranda* was designed to guard against was the use by police of various kinds of trickery — such as "Mutt and Jeff" routines — to elicit confessions from suspects. A police officer who stops a suspect on the highway has little chance to develop or implement a plan of this sort.

[28] See *Orozco* (suspect arrested and questioned in his bedroom by four police officers); *Mathis* (defendant questioned by a government agent while in jail).

---

[29] No more is implied by this analogy than that most traffic stops resemble, in duration and atmosphere, the kind of brief detention authorized in *Terry*. We of course do not suggest that a traffic stop supported by probable cause may not exceed the bounds set by the Fourth Amendment on the scope of a *Terry* stop.

traffic laws — by compelling the police either to take the time to warn all detained motorists of their constitutional rights or to forgo use of self-incriminating statements made by those motorists — while doing little to protect citizens' Fifth Amendment rights.[33] The second would enable the police to circumvent the constraints on custodial interrogations established by *Miranda*.

Turning to the case before us, we find nothing in the record that indicates that respondent should have been given *Miranda* warnings at any point prior to the time Trooper Williams placed him under arrest. For the reasons indicated above, we reject the contention that the initial stop of respondent's car, by itself, rendered him "in custody." And respondent has failed to demonstrate that, at any time between the initial stop and the arrest, he was subjected to restraints comparable to those associated with a formal arrest. Only a short period of time elapsed between the stop and the arrest.[34] At no point during that interval was respondent informed that his detention would not be temporary. Although Trooper Williams apparently decided as soon as respondent stepped out of his car that respondent would be taken into custody and charged with a traffic offense, Williams never communicated his intention to respondent. A policeman's unarticulated plan has no bearing on the question whether a suspect was "in custody" at a particular time; the only relevant inquiry is how a reasonable man in the suspect's position would have understood his situation.[35] Nor do other aspects of the interaction of Williams and respondent support the contention that respondent was exposed to "custodial interrogation" at the scene of the stop. From aught that appears in the stipulation of facts, a single police officer asked respondent a modest number of questions and requested him to perform a simple balancing test at a location visible to passing motorists. Treatment of this sort cannot fairly be characterized as the functional equivalent of formal arrest.

We conclude, in short, that respondent was not taken into custody for the purposes of *Miranda* until Williams arrested him. Consequently, the statements respondent made prior to that point were admissible against him.

Affirmed.

Justice STEVENS, concurring in part and concurring in the judgment.

The only question presented by the petition for certiorari reads as follows:

"Whether law enforcement officers must give '*Miranda* warnings' to individuals arrested for misdemeanor traffic offenses."

In Parts I, II and IV of its opinion, the Court answers that question in the affirmative and explains why that answer requires that the judgment of the Court of Appeals be affirmed. Part III of the Court's opinion is written for the purpose of discussing the admissibility of statements made by respondent "prior to his formal arrest." That discussion is not necessary to the disposition of the case, nor necessary to answer the only question presented by the certiorari petition. Indeed, the Court of Appeals quite properly did not pass on the question answered in Part III since it was entirely unnecessary to the judgment in this case. It thus wisely followed the cardinal rule that a court should not pass on a constitutional question in advance of the necessity of deciding it.

Lamentably, this Court fails to follow the course of judicial restraint that we have set for the entire federal judiciary. In this case, it appears the reason for reaching out to decide a question not passed upon below and unnecessary to the judgment is that the answer to the question upon which we granted review is so clear under our settled precedents that the majority — its appetite for deciding constitutional

---

[33] Contrast the minor burdens on law enforcement and significant protection of citizens' rights effected by our holding that *Miranda* governs custodial interrogation of persons accused of misdemeanor traffic offenses.

[34] Cf. *Commonwealth v. Meyer*, 488 Pa., at 301, 307, 412 A.2d, at 518-519, 522 (driver who was detained for over one-half hour, part of the time in a patrol car, held to have been in custody for the purposes of *Miranda* by the time he was questioned concerning the circumstances of an accident).

[35] Cf. *Beckwith* ("It was the compulsive aspect of custodial interrogation, and not the strength or content of the government's suspicions at the time the questioning was conducted, which led the Court to impose the *Miranda* requirements with regard to custodial questioning"); *People v. P.*, 21 N.Y.2d 1, 9-10, 286 N.Y.S.2d 225, 232, 233 N.E.2d 255, 260 (1967) (an objective, reasonable-man test is appropriate because, unlike a subjective test, it "is not solely dependent either on the self-serving declara-

tions of the police officers or the defendant nor does it place upon the police the burden of anticipating the frailties or idiosyncracies of every person whom they question").

questions only whetted — is driven to serve up a more delectable issue to satiate it. I had thought it clear, however, that no matter how interesting or potentially important a determination on a question of constitutional law may be, "broad considerations of the appropriate exercise of judicial power prevent such determinations unless actually compelled by the litigation before the Court." Indeed, this principle of restraint grows in importance the more problematic the constitutional issue is.

Because I remain convinced that the Court should abjure the practice of reaching out to decide cases on the broadest grounds possible, I do not join Part III of the Court's opinion.

## QUESTIONS AND NOTES

**1.** Do parts II and III of the opinion appear to take the same approach to *Miranda*? Would you have concurred in both parts of the opinion? In one part? In neither part? Explain.

**2.** If you were in McCarty's position would you feel compelled to respond? Explain.

**3.** Does part III of *McCarty* blur *Miranda*'s bright line? If so, is it justifiable? Unavoidable?

**4.** Is objectivity carried too far in this opinion? *I.e.*, does it make sense to treat the suspect as not being in custody when the policeman in fact intended to arrest him? Suppose that McCarty knew or believed that the policeman intended to arrest him when he was first stopped?

## PROBLEM

Ten-year old Robyn Jackson disappeared from a playground in Baldwin Park, California, at around 6:30 p.m. on September 28, 1982. Early the next morning, about 10 miles away in Pasadena, Andrew Zimmerman observed a large man emerge from a turquoise American sedan and throw something into a nearby flood control channel. Zimmerman called the police, who arrived at the scene and discovered the girl's body in the channel. There was evidence that she had been raped, and the cause of death was determined to be asphyxia complicated by blunt force trauma to the head.

Lieutenant Thomas Johnston, a detective with the Los Angeles County Sheriff's Department, investigated the homicide. From witnesses interviewed on the day the body was discovered, he learned that Robyn had talked to two ice cream truck drivers, one being petitioner Robert Edward Stansbury, in the hours before her disappearance. Given these contacts, Johnston thought Stansbury and the other driver might have some connection with the homicide or knowledge thereof, but for reasons unimportant here Johnston considered only the other driver to be a leading suspect. After the suspect driver was brought in for interrogation, Johnston asked Officer Lee of the Baldwin Park Police Department to contact Stansbury to see if he would come in for questioning as a potential witness.

Lee and three other plainclothes officers arrived at Stansbury's trailer home at about 11:00 that evening. The officers surrounded the door and Lee knocked. When Stansbury answered, Lee told him the officers were investigating a homicide to which Stansbury was a possible witness and asked if he would accompany them to the police station to answer some questions. Stansbury agreed to the interview and accepted a ride to the station in the front seat of Lee's police car.

At the station, Lieutenant Johnston, in the presence of another officer, questioned Stansbury about his whereabouts and activities during the afternoon and evening of September 28. Neither Johnston nor the other officer issued Miranda warnings. Stansbury told the officers (among other things) that on the evening of the 28th he spoke with the victim at about 6:00, returned to his trailer home after work at 9:00, and left the trailer at about midnight in his housemate's turquoise,

American-made car. This last detail aroused Johnston's suspicions, as the turquoise car matched the description of the one Andrew Zimmerman had observed in Pasadena. When Stansbury, in response to a further question, admitted to prior convictions for rape, kidnaping and child molestation, Johnston terminated the interview and another officer advised Stansbury of his Miranda rights. Stansbury declined to make further statements, requested an attorney, and was arrested. Respondent State of California charged Stansbury with first-degree murder and other crimes.

Stansbury filed a pretrial motion to suppress all statements made at the station, and the evidence discovered as a result of those statements. The trial court denied the motion in relevant part, ruling that Stansbury was not "in custody" – and thus not entitled to Miranda warnings – until he mentioned that he had taken his housemate's turquoise car for a midnight drive. Before that stage of the interview, the trial court reasoned, "the focus in [Lieutenant Johnston's] mind certainly was on the other ice cream [truck] driver"; only "after Mr. Stansbury made the comment . . . describing the . . . turquoise-colored automobile" did Johnston's suspicions "shif[t] to Mr. Stansbury." Based upon its conclusion that Stansbury was not in custody until Johnston's suspicions had focused on him, the trial court permitted the prosecution to introduce in its case-in-chief the statements Stansbury made before that time. At trial, the jury convicted Stansbury of first-degree murder, rape, kidnaping, and lewd act on a child under the age of 14, and fixed the penalty for the first-degree murder at death.

The California Supreme Court affirmed. Before determining whether Stansbury was in custody during the interview at the station, the court set out what it viewed as the applicable legal standard: "In deciding the custody issue, the totality of the circumstances is relevant, and no one factor is dispositive. However, the most important considerations include (1) the site of the interrogation, (2) whether the investigation has focused on the subject, (3) whether the objective indicia of arrest are present, and (4) the length and form of questioning." The court proceeded to analyze the second factor in detail, in the end accepting the trial court's factual determination "that suspicion focused on [Stansbury] only when he mentioned that he had driven a turquoise car on the night of the crime." The court "conclude[d] that [Stansbury] was not subject to custodial interrogation before he mentioned the turquoise car," and thus approved the trial court's ruling that *Miranda* did not bar the admission of statements Stansbury made before that point.

How should the United States Supreme Court resolve this case? Why? Assuming that the Supreme Court remands the case to a California court, what factors should determine its resolution of the issue?

For the Supreme Court's resolution, see *Stansbury v. California*, 114 S.Ct. 1526 (1994).

In *Perkins*, we see that not all forms of custodial interrogation are covered by *Miranda*.

## Illinois v. Perkins
### 496 U.S. 292 (1990)

Justice KENNEDY delivered the opinion of the Court.

An undercover government agent was placed in the cell of respondent Perkins, who was incarcerated on charges unrelated to the subject of the agent's investigation. Respondent made statements that implicated him in the crime that the agent sought to solve. Respondent claims that the statements should be inadmissible because he had not been given *Miranda* warnings by the agent. We hold that the statements are admissible. *Miranda* warnings are not required when the suspect is unaware that he is speaking to a law enforcement officer and gives a voluntary statement.

I

In November 1984, Richard Stephenson was

murdered in a suburb of East St. Louis, Illinois. The murder remained unsolved until March 1986, when one Donald Charlton told police that he had learned about a homicide from a fellow inmate at the Graham Correctional Facility, where Charlton had been serving a sentence for burglary. The fellow inmate was Lloyd Perkins, who is the respondent here. Charlton told police that, while at Graham, he had befriended respondent, who told him in detail about a murder that respondent had committed in East St. Louis. On hearing Charlton's account, the police recognized details of the Stephenson murder that were not well known, and so they treated Charlton's story as a credible one.

By the time the police heard Charlton's account, respondent had been released from Graham, but police traced him to a jail in Montgomery County, Illinois, where he was being held pending trial on a charge of aggravated battery, unrelated to the Stephenson murder. The police wanted to investigate further respondent's connection to the Stephenson murder, but feared that the use of an eavesdropping device would prove impractical and unsafe. They decided instead to place an undercover agent in the cellblock with respondent and Charlton. The plan was for Charlton and undercover agent John Parisi to pose as escapees from a work release program who had been arrested in the course of a burglary. Parisi and Charlton were instructed to engage respondent in casual conversation and report anything he said about the Stephenson murder.

Parisi, using the alias "Vito Bianco," and Charlton, both clothed in jail garb, were placed in the cellblock with respondent at the Montgomery County jail. The cellblock consisted of 12 separate cells that opened onto a common room. Respondent greeted Charlton who, after a brief conversation with respondent, introduced Parisi by his alias. Parisi told respondent that he "wasn't going to do any more time" and suggested that the three of them escape. Respondent replied that the Montgomery County jail was "rinky-dink" and that they could "break out." The trio met in respondent's cell later that evening, after the other inmates were asleep, to refine their plan. Respondent said that his girlfriend could smuggle in a pistol. Charlton said: "Hey, I'm not a murderer, I'm a burglar. That's your guys' profession." After telling Charlton that he would be responsible for any murder that occurred, Parisi asked respondent if he had ever "done" anybody. Respondent said that he had and proceeded to describe at length the events of the Stephenson murder. Parisi and respondent then engaged in some casual conversation before respondent went to sleep. Parisi did not give

respondent *Miranda* warnings before the conversations.

## II

In *Miranda*, the Court held that the Fifth Amendment privilege against self-incrimination prohibits admitting statements given by a suspect during "custodial interrogation" without a prior warning. Custodial interrogation means "questioning initiated by law enforcement officers after a person has been taken into custody. . . ." The warning mandated by *Miranda* was meant to preserve the privilege during "incommunicado interrogation of individuals in a police-dominated atmosphere." That atmosphere is said to generate "inherently compelling pressures which work to undermine the individual's will to resist and to compel him to speak where he would not otherwise do so freely." "Fidelity to the doctrine announced in *Miranda* requires that it be enforced strictly, but only in those types of situations in which the concerns that powered the decision are implicated." *McCarty*.

Conversations between suspects and undercover agents do not implicate the concerns underlying *Miranda*. The essential ingredients of a "police-dominated atmosphere" and compulsion are not present when an incarcerated person speaks freely to someone whom he believes to be a fellow inmate. Coercion is determined from the perspective of the suspect. *McCarty*. When a suspect considers himself in the company of cellmates and not officers, the coercive atmosphere is lacking. *Miranda* ("[T]he 'principal psychological factor contributing to a successful interrogation is *privacy* – being alone with the person under interrogation'"). There is no empirical basis for the assumption that a suspect speaking to those whom he assumes are not officers will feel compelled to speak by the fear of reprisal for remaining silent or in the hope of more lenient treatment should he confess.

It is the premise of *Miranda* that the danger of coercion results from the interaction of custody and official interrogation. We reject the argument that *Miranda* warnings are required whenever a suspect is in custody in a technical sense and converses with someone who happens to be a government agent. Questioning by captors, who appear to control the suspect's fate, may create mutually reinforcing pressures that the Court has assumed will weaken the suspect's will, but where a suspect does not know that he is conversing with a government agent, these pressures do not exist. The state court here mistakenly assumed that because the suspect was in custody, no undercover questioning could take place.

When the suspect has no reason to think that the listeners have official power over him, it should not be assumed that his words are motivated by the reaction he expects from his listeners. "[W]hen the agent carries neither badge nor gun and wears not 'police blue,' but the same prison gray" as the suspect, there is no "*interplay* between police interrogation and police custody." Kamisar, *Brewer v. Williams, Massiah* and *Miranda*: What is "Interrogation"? When Does it Matter?, 67 Geo.L.J. 1, 67, 63 (1978).

*Miranda* forbids coercion, not mere strategic deception by taking advantage of a suspect's misplaced trust in one he supposes to be a fellow prisoner. As we recognized in *Miranda*, "[c]onfessions remain a proper element in law enforcement. Any statement given freely and voluntarily without any compelling influences is, of course, admissible in evidence." Ploys to mislead a suspect or lull him into a false sense of security that do not rise to the level of compulsion or coercion to speak are not within *Miranda*'s concerns. Cf. *Mathiason*.

*Miranda* was not meant to protect suspects from boasting about their criminal activities in front of persons whom they believe to be their cellmates. This case is illustrative. Respondent had no reason to feel that undercover agent Parisi had any legal authority to force him to answer questions or that Parisi could affect respondent's future treatment. Respondent viewed the cellmate-agent as an equal and showed no hint of being intimidated by the atmosphere of the jail. In recounting the details of the Stephenson murder, respondent was motivated solely by the desire to impress his fellow inmates. He spoke at his own peril.

The tactic employed here to elicit a voluntary confession from a suspect does not violate the Self-Incrimination Clause. We held in *Hoffa*, that placing an undercover agent near a suspect in order to gather incriminating information was permissible under the Fifth Amendment. In *Hoffa*, while petitioner Hoffa was on trial, he met often with one Partin, who, unbeknownst to Hoffa, was cooperating with law enforcement officials. Partin reported to officials that Hoffa had divulged his attempts to bribe jury members. We approved using Hoffa's statements at his subsequent trial for jury tampering, on the rationale that "no claim ha[d] been or could [have been] made that [Hoffa's] incriminating statements were the product of any sort of coercion, legal or factual." In addition, we found that the fact that Partin had fooled Hoffa into thinking that Partin was a sympathetic colleague did not affect the voluntariness of the statements. Cf. *Mathiason* (officer's falsely telling

suspect that suspect's fingerprints had been found at crime scene did not render interview "custodial" under *Miranda*). The only difference between this case and Hoffa is that the suspect here was incarcerated, but detention, whether or not for the crime in question, does not warrant a presumption that the use of an undercover agent to speak with an incarcerated suspect makes any confession thus obtained involuntary.

Our decision in *Mathis* is distinguishable. In *Mathis*, an inmate in a state prison was interviewed by an Internal Revenue Service agent about possible tax violations. No *Miranda* warning was given before questioning. The Court held that the suspect's incriminating statements were not admissible at his subsequent trial on tax fraud charges. The suspect in *Mathis* was aware that the agent was a Government official, investigating the possibility of noncompliance with the tax laws. The case before us now is different. Where the suspect does not know that he is speaking to a government agent there is no reason to assume the possibility that the suspect might feel coerced. (The bare fact of custody may not in every instance require a warning even when the suspect is aware that he is speaking to an official, but we do not have occasion to explore that issue here.)

Respondent can seek no help from his argument that a bright-line rule for the application of *Miranda* is desirable. Law enforcement officers will have little difficulty putting into practice our holding that undercover agents need not give *Miranda* warnings to incarcerated suspects. The use of undercover agents is a recognized law enforcement technique, often employed in the prison context to detect violence against correctional officials or inmates, as well as for the purposes served here. The interests protected by *Miranda* are not implicated in these cases, and the warnings are not required to safeguard the constitutional rights of inmates who make voluntary statements to undercover agents.

We hold that an undercover law enforcement officer posing as a fellow inmate need not give *Miranda* warnings to an incarcerated suspect before asking questions that may elicit an incriminating response. The statements at issue in this case were voluntary, and there is no federal obstacle to their admissibility at trial. We now reverse and remand for proceedings not inconsistent with our opinion.

Justice BRENNAN, concurring in the judgment.

The Court holds that *Miranda* does not require suppression of a statement made by an incarcerated suspect to an undercover agent. Although I do not subscribe to the majority's characterization of *Miranda* in its entirety, I do agree that when a suspect does not know that his questioner is a police agent, such questioning does not amount to "interrogation" in an "inherently coercive" environment so as to require application of *Miranda*. Since the only issue raised at this stage of the litigation is the applicability of *Miranda*,* I concur in the judgment of the Court.

This is not to say that I believe the Constitution condones the method by which the police extracted the confession in this case. To the contrary, the deception and manipulation practiced on respondent raise a substantial claim that the confession was obtained in violation of the Due Process Clause.

The method used to elicit the confession in this case deserves close scrutiny. The police devised a ruse to lure respondent into incriminating himself when he was in jail on an unrelated charge. A police agent, posing as a fellow inmate and proposing a sham escape plot, tricked respondent into confessing that he had once committed a murder, as a way of proving that he would be willing to do so again should the need arise during the escape. The testimony of the undercover officer and a police informant at the suppression hearing reveal the deliberate manner in which the two elicited incriminating statements from respondent. We have recognized that "the mere fact of custody imposes pressures on the accused; confinement may bring into play subtle influences that will make him particularly susceptible

---

* As the case comes to us, it involves only the question whether *Miranda* applies to the questioning of an incarcerated suspect by an undercover agent. Nothing in the Court's opinion suggests that, had respondent previously invoked his Fifth Amendment right to counsel or right to silence, his statements would be admissible. If respondent had invoked either right, the inquiry would focus on whether he subsequently waived the particular right. See *Edwards v. Arizona*, 451 U.S. 477 (1981); *Michigan v. Mosley*, 423 U.S. 96, 104 (1975). As the Court made clear in *Moran v. Burbine*, 475 U.S. 412, 421 (1986), the waiver of *Miranda* rights "must [be] voluntary in the sense that it [must be] the product of a free and deliberate choice rather than *intimidation, coercion or deception*." (Emphasis added.) Since respondent was in custody on an unrelated charge when he was questioned, he may be able to challenge the admission of these statements if he previously had invoked his *Miranda* rights with respect to that charge. See *Arizona v. Roberson*, 486 U.S. 675 (1988); *Mosley*.

to the ploys of undercover Government agents." As Justice Marshall points out, the pressures of custody make a suspect more likely to confide in others and to engage in "jailhouse bravado." The State is in a unique position to exploit this vulnerability because it has virtually complete control over the suspect's environment. Thus, the State can ensure that a suspect is barraged with questions from an undercover agent until the suspect confesses. The testimony in this case suggests the State did just that.

The deliberate use of deception and manipulation by the police appears to be incompatible "with a system that presumes innocence and assures that a conviction will not be secured by inquisitorial means," and raises serious concerns that respondent's will was overborne. It is open to the lower court on remand to determine whether, under the totality of the circumstances, respondent's confession was elicited in a manner that violated the Due Process Clause. That the confession was not elicited through means of physical torture, see *Brown*, or overt psychological pressure, does not end the inquiry. "[A]s law enforcement officers become more responsible, and the methods used to extract confessions more sophisticated, [a court's] duty to enforce federal constitutional protections does not cease. It only becomes more difficult because of the more delicate judgments to be made." *Spano*.

Justice MARSHALL, dissenting.

This Court clearly and simply stated its holding in *Miranda*: "[T]he prosecution may not use statements, whether exculpatory or inculpatory, stemming from custodial interrogation of the defendant unless it demonstrates the use of procedural safeguards effective to secure the privilege against self-incrimination." The conditions that require the police to apprise a defendant of his constitutional rights – custodial interrogation conducted by an agent of the police – were present in this case. Because Lloyd Perkins received no *Miranda* warnings before he was subjected to custodial interrogation, his confession was not admissible.

The Court reaches the contrary conclusion by fashioning an exception to the *Miranda* rule that applies whenever "an undercover law enforcement officer posing as a fellow inmate . . . ask[s] questions that may elicit an incriminating response" from an incarcerated suspect. This exception is inconsistent with the rationale supporting *Miranda* and allows police officers intentionally to take advantage of suspects unaware of their constitutional rights. I therefore dissent.

The Court does not dispute that the police officer

here conducted a custodial interrogation of a criminal suspect. Perkins was incarcerated in county jail during the questioning at issue here; under these circumstances, he was in custody as that term is defined in *Miranda*. *Mathis* (holding that defendant incarcerated on charges different from the crime about which he is questioned was in custody for purposes of *Miranda*). The United States argues that Perkins was not in custody for purpose of *Miranda* because he was familiar with the custodial environment as a result of being in jail for two days and previously spending time in prison. Perkins' familiarity with confinement, however, does not transform his incarceration into some sort of noncustodial arrangement. Cf. *Orozco* (holding that suspect who had been arrested in his home and then questioned in his bedroom was in custody, notwithstanding his familiarity with the surroundings).

While Perkins was confined, an undercover police officer, with the help of a police informant, questioned him about a serious crime. Although the Court does not dispute that Perkins was interrogated, it downplays the nature of the 35-minute questioning by disingenuously referring to it as a "conversatio[n]." The officer's narration of the "conversation" at Perkins' suppression hearing however, reveals that it clearly was an interrogation.

"[Agent:] You ever do anyone?"
"[Perkins:] Yeah, once in East St. Louis, in a rich white neighborhood."
"Informant: I didn't know they had any rich white neighborhoods in East St. Louis."
"Perkins: It wasn't in East St. Louis, it was by a race track in Fairview Heights. . . ."
"[Agent]: You did a guy in Fairview Heights?"
"Perkins: Yeah in a rich white section where most of the houses look the same."
"[Informant]: If all the houses look the same, how did you know you had the right house?"
"Perkins: Me and two guys cased the house for about a week. I knew exactly which house, the second house on the left from the corner.
"[Agent]: How long ago did this happen?"
"Perkins: Approximately about two years ago. I got paid $5,000 for that job."
"[Agent]: How did it go down?"
"Perkins: I walked up [to] this guy['s] house with a sawed-off under my trench coat."
"[Agent]: What type gun[?]"
"Perkins: A .12 gauge Remmington [sic] Automatic Model 1100 sawed-off.''

The police officer continued the inquiry, asking a series of questions designed to elicit specific information about the victim, the crime scene, the weapon, Perkins' motive, and his actions during and after the shooting. This interaction was not a "conversation"; Perkins, the officer, and the informant were not equal participants in a free-ranging discussion, with each man offering his views on different topics. Rather, it was an interrogation: Perkins was subjected to express questioning likely to evoke an incriminating response.

Because Perkins was interrogated by police while he was in custody, *Miranda* required that the officer inform him of his rights. In rejecting that conclusion, the Court finds that "conversations" between undercover agents and suspects are devoid of the coercion inherent in station house interrogations conducted by law enforcement officials who openly represent the State. *Miranda* was not, however, concerned solely with police *coercion*. It dealt with *any* police tactics that may operate to compel a suspect in custody to make incriminating statements without full awareness of his constitutional rights. Thus, when a law enforcement agent structures a custodial interrogation so that a suspect feels compelled to reveal incriminating information, he must inform the suspect of his constitutional rights and give him an opportunity to decide whether or not to talk.

The compulsion proscribed by *Miranda* includes deception by the police. See *Miranda* (indicting police tactics "to induce a confession out of trickery," such as using fictitious witnesses or false accusations); *McCarty* ("The purposes of the safeguards prescribed by *Miranda* are to ensure that the police do not coerce *or* trick captive suspects into confessing") (emphasis deleted and added). Although the Court did not find trickery by itself sufficient to constitute compulsion in *Hoffa*, the defendant in that case was not in custody. Perkins, however, was interrogated while incarcerated. As the Court has acknowledged in the Sixth Amendment context: "[T]he mere fact of custody imposes pressures on the accused; confinement may bring into play subtle influences that will make him particularly susceptible to the ploys of undercover Government agents." See also *Massiah* (holding, in the context of the Sixth Amendment, that defendant's constitutional privilege against self-incrimination was "more seriously imposed upon . . . because he did not even know that he was under interrogation by a government agent").

Custody works to the State's advantage in obtaining incriminating information. The psychological pressures inherent in confinement increase the suspect's anxiety, making him likely to seek relief by talking with others. The inmate is thus more susceptible to efforts by undercover agents to elicit information from him. Similarly, where the suspect is incarcerated, the constant threat of physical danger peculiar to the prison environment may make him demonstrate his toughness to other inmates by recounting or inventing past violent acts. "Because the suspect's ability to select people with whom he can confide is completely within their control, the police have a unique opportunity to exploit the suspect's vulnerability. In short, the police can insure that if the pressures of confinement lead the suspect to confide in anyone, it will be a police agent." In this case, the police deceptively took advantage of Perkins' psychological vulnerability by including him in a sham escape plot, a situation in which he would feel compelled to demonstrate his willingness to shoot a prison guard by revealing his past involvement in a murder. ([The] agent stressed that a killing might be necessary in the escape and then asked Perkins if he had ever murdered someone).

Thus, the pressures unique to custody allow the police to use deceptive interrogation tactics to compel a suspect to make an incriminating statement. The compulsion is not eliminated by the suspect's ignorance of his interrogator's true identity. The Court therefore need not inquire past the bare facts of custody and interrogation to determine whether *Miranda* warnings are required.

The Court's adoption of an exception to the *Miranda* doctrine is incompatible with the principle, consistently applied by this Court, that the doctrine should remain simple and clear. We explained the benefits of a bright-line rule in *Michael C.*: "*Miranda*'s holding has the virtue of informing police and prosecutors with specificity as to what they may do in conducting custodial interrogation, and of informing courts under what circumstances statements obtained during such interrogation are not admissible."

The Court's holding today complicates a previously clear and straightforward doctrine. The Court opines that "[l]aw enforcement officers will have little difficulty putting into practice our holding that undercover agents need not give *Miranda* warnings to incarcerated suspects." Perhaps this prediction is true with respect to fact patterns virtually identical to the one before the Court today. But the outer boundaries of the exception created by the Court are by no means clear. Would *Miranda* be violated, for instance, if an undercover police officer beat a confession out of a suspect, but the suspect thought the officer was another prisoner who wanted the information for his own purposes?

Even if *Miranda*, as interpreted by the Court, would not permit such obviously compelled confessions, the ramifications of today's opinion are still disturbing. The exception carved out of the *Miranda* doctrine today may well result in a proliferation of departmental policies to encourage police officers to conduct interrogations of confined suspects through undercover agents, thereby circumventing the need to administer *Miranda* warnings. Indeed, if *Miranda* now requires a police officer to issue warnings only in those situations in which the suspect might feel compelled "to speak by the fear of reprisal for remaining silent or in the hope of more lenient treatment should he confess," presumably it allows custodial interrogation by an undercover officer posing as a member of the clergy or a suspect's defense attorney. Although such abhorrent tricks would play on a suspect's need to confide in a trusted adviser, neither would cause the suspect to "think that the listeners have official power over him." The Court's adoption of the "undercover agent" exception to the *Miranda* rule thus is necessarily also the adoption of a substantial loophole in our jurisprudence protecting suspects' Fifth Amendment rights.

I dissent.

## QUESTIONS AND NOTES

**1.** Does the Court find that Perkins was not in custody? Was not subject to interrogation? Something else? Explain.

**2.** Is the process by which the police obtained the confession in this case something that should be applauded or condemned? Why?

**3.** Does Justice Brennan's footnote make any sense? If the procedure to which Perkins was subjected does not constitute custodial interrogation, why should it matter whether he invoked his right to counsel *during custodial interrogation*?

**4.** Is Justice Marshall's concept of custody too wooden?

**5.** Conversely, is it fair to say that custody *per se*, even without interrogation, is inherently coercive?

**6.** Under the Court's opinion, would it be possible for the police to disguise one of their own as a priest or attorney and thereby obtain a confession? Should the Fifth Amendment forbid such a practice? Should any other amendment forbid such a practice? If so, which Amendment? Explain.

**7.** In the next section, we will explore the Court's conception of "interrogation."

# F.  Interrogation

## Rhode Island v. Innis
### 446 U.S. 291 (1980)

Mr. Justice STEWART delivered the opinion of the Court.

In *Miranda*, the Court held that, once a defendant in custody asks to speak with a lawyer, all interrogation must cease until a lawyer is present. The issue in this case is whether the respondent was "interrogated" in violation of the standards promulgated in the *Miranda* opinion.

### I

On the night of January 12, 1975, John Mulvaney, a Providence, R.I., taxicab driver, disappeared after being dispatched to pick up a customer. His body was discovered four days later buried in a shallow grave in Coventry, R.I. He had died from a shotgun blast aimed at the back of his head.

On January 17, 1975, shortly after midnight, the Providence police received a telephone call from Gerald Aubin, also a taxicab driver, who reported that he had just been robbed by a man wielding a sawed-off shotgun. Aubin further reported that he had dropped off his assailant near Rhode Island College in a section of Providence known as Mount Pleasant. While at the Providence police station waiting to give a statement, Aubin noticed a picture of his assailant on a bulletin board. Aubin so informed one of the police officers present. The officer prepared a photo array, and again Aubin identified a picture of the same person. That person was the respondent. Shortly thereafter, the Providence police began a search of the Mount Pleasant area.

At approximately 4:30 a.m. on the same date, Patrolman Lovell, while cruising the streets of Mount Pleasant in a patrol car, spotted the respondent standing in the street facing him. When Patrolman Lovell stopped his car, the respondent walked towards it. Patrolman Lovell then arrested the respondent, who was unarmed, and advised him of his so-called *Miranda* rights. While the two men waited in the patrol car for other police officers to arrive, Patrolman Lovell did not converse with the respondent other than to respond to the latter's request for a cigarette.

Within minutes, Sergeant Sears arrived at the scene of the arrest, and he also gave the respondent the *Miranda* warnings. Immediately thereafter, Captain Leyden and other police officers arrived. Captain Leyden advised the respondent of his *Miranda* rights. The respondent stated that he understood those rights and wanted to speak with a lawyer. Captain Leyden then directed that the respondent be placed in a "caged wagon," a four-door police car with a wire screen mesh between the front and rear seats, and be driven to the central police station. Three officers, Patrolmen Gleckman, Williams, and McKenna, were assigned to accompany the respondent to the central station. They placed the respondent in the vehicle and shut the doors. Captain Leyden then instructed the officers not to question the respondent or intimidate or coerce him in any way. The three officers then entered the vehicle, and it departed.

While en route to the central station, Patrolman Gleckman initiated a conversation with Patrolman McKenna concerning the missing shotgun.[1] As Patrolman Gleckman later testified:

> "A. At this point, I was talking back and forth with Patrolman McKenna stating that I frequent this area while on patrol and [that because a school for handicapped children is located nearby,] there's a lot of handicapped

---

[1] Although there was conflicting testimony about the exact seating arrangements, it is clear that everyone in the vehicle heard the conversation.

children running around in this area, and God forbid one of them might find a weapon with shells and they might hurt themselves.''

Patrolman McKenna apparently shared his fellow officer's concern:

"A. I more or less concurred with him [Gleckman] that it was a safety factor and that we should, you know, continue to search for the weapon and try to find it.''

While Patrolman Williams said nothing, he overheard the conversation between the two officers:

"A. He [Gleckman] said it would be too bad if the little−I believe he said a girl− would pick up the gun, maybe kill herself.''

The respondent then interrupted the conversation, stating that the officers should turn the car around so he could show them where the gun was located. At this point, Patrolman McKenna radioed back to Captain Leyden that they were returning to the scene of the arrest and that the respondent would inform them of the location of the gun. At the time the respondent indicated that the officers should turn back, they had traveled no more than a mile, a trip encompassing only a few minutes.

The police vehicle then returned to the scene of the arrest where a search for the shotgun was in progress. There, Captain Leyden again advised the respondent of his *Miranda* rights. The respondent replied that he understood those rights but that he "wanted to get the gun out of the way because of the kids in the area in the school.'' The respondent then led the police to a nearby field, where he pointed out the shotgun under some rocks by the side of the road.

## II

In the present case, the parties are in agreement that the respondent was fully informed of his *Miranda* rights and that he invoked his *Miranda* right to counsel when he told Captain Leyden that he wished to consult with a lawyer. It is also uncontested that the respondent was "in custody" while being transported to the police station.

The issue, therefore, is whether the respondent was "interrogated" by the police officers in violation of the respondent's undisputed right under *Miranda* to remain silent until he had consulted with a lawyer.[2] In resolving this issue, we first define the

term "interrogation" under *Miranda* before turning to a consideration of the facts of this case.

### A

The starting point for defining "interrogation" in this context is, of course, the Court's *Miranda* opinion. There the Court observed that "[b]y custodial interrogation, we mean *questioning* initiated by law enforcement officers after a person has been taken into custody or otherwise deprived of his freedom of action in any significant way." (emphasis added). This passage and other references throughout the opinion to "questioning" might suggest that the *Miranda* rules were to apply only to those police interrogation practices that involve express questioning of a defendant while in custody.

We do not, however, construe the *Miranda* opinion so narrowly. The concern of the Court in *Miranda* was that the "interrogation environment" created by the interplay of interrogation and custody would "subjugate the individual to the will of his examiner" and thereby undermine the privilege against compulsory self-incrimination. The police practices that evoked this concern included several that did not involve express questioning. For example, one of the practices discussed in *Miranda* was the use of line-ups in which a coached witness would pick the defendant as the perpetrator. This was designed to establish that the defendant was in fact guilty as a predicate for further interrogation. A variation on this theme discussed in *Miranda* was the so-called "reverse line-up" in which a defendant would be identified by coached witnesses as the perpetrator of a fictitious crime, with the object of inducing him to confess to the actual crime of which he was suspected in order to escape the false prosecution. The Court in *Miranda* also included in its survey of interrogation practices the use of psychological ploys, such as to "posi[t]" "the guilt of the subject," to "minimize the moral seriousness of the offense," and "to cast blame on the victim or on society." It is clear that these techniques of persuasion, no less than express questioning, were thought, in a custodial setting, to amount to interrogation.[3]

This is not to say, however, that all statements obtained by the police after a person has been taken

---

[2] Since we conclude that the respondent was not "interrogated" for *Miranda* purposes, we do not reach the question whether the respondent waived his right under *Miranda* to be free from interrogation until counsel was present.

[3] To limit the ambit of *Miranda* to express questioning would "place a premium on the ingenuity of the police to devise methods of indirect interrogation, rather than to implement the plain mandate of *Miranda*." *Commonwealth v. Hamilton*, 445 Pa. 292, 297, 285 A.2d 172, 175.

into custody are to be considered the product of interrogation. As the Court in *Miranda* noted:

> "Confessions remain a proper element in law enforcement. Any statement given freely and voluntarily without any compelling influences is, of course, admissible in evidence. *The fundamental import of the privilege while an individual is in custody is not whether he is allowed to talk to the police without the benefit of warnings and counsel, but whether he can be interrogated.* . . . Volunteered statements of any kind are not barred by the Fifth Amendment and their admissibility is not affected by our holding today." (emphasis added).

It is clear therefore that the special procedural safeguards outlined in *Miranda* are required not where a suspect is simply taken into custody, but rather where a suspect in custody is subjected to interrogation. "Interrogation," as conceptualized in the *Miranda* opinion, must reflect a measure of compulsion above and beyond that inherent in custody itself.

We conclude that the *Miranda* safeguards come into play whenever a person in custody is subjected to either express questioning or its functional equivalent. That is to say, the term "interrogation" under *Miranda* refers not only to express questioning, but also to any words or actions on the part of the police (other than those normally attendant to arrest and custody) that the police should know are reasonably likely to elicit an incriminating response[5] from the suspect.[6] The latter portion of this definition focuses primarily upon the perceptions of the suspect, rather than the intent of the police. This focus reflects the fact that the *Miranda* safeguards were designed to vest a suspect in custody with an added measure of protection against coercive police practices, without regard to objective proof of the underlying intent of the police. A practice that the police should know is reasonably likely to evoke an incriminating response

from a suspect thus amounts to interrogation.[7] But, since the police surely cannot be held accountable for the unforeseeable results of their words or actions, the definition of interrogation can extend only to words or actions on the part of police officers that they *should have known* were reasonably likely to elicit an incriminating response.[8]

### B

Turning to the facts of the present case, we conclude that the respondent was not "interrogated" within the meaning of *Miranda*. It is undisputed that the first prong of the definition of "interrogation" was not satisfied, for the conversation between Patrolmen Gleckman and McKenna included no express questioning of the respondent. Rather, that conversation was, at least in form, nothing more than a dialogue between the two officers to which no response from the respondent was invited.

Moreover, it cannot be fairly concluded that the respondent was subjected to the "functional equivalent" of questioning. It cannot be said, in short, that Patrolmen Gleckman and McKenna should have known that their conversation was reasonably likely to elicit an incriminating response from the respondent. There is nothing in the record to suggest that the officers were aware that the respondent was peculiarly susceptible to an appeal to his conscience concerning the safety of handicapped children. Nor is there anything in the record to suggest that the police knew that the respondent was unusually disoriented or upset at the time of his arrest.[9]

---

[7] This is not to say that the intent of the police is irrelevant, for it may well have a bearing on whether the police should have known that their words or actions were reasonably likely to evoke an incriminating response. In particular, where a police practice is designed to elicit an incriminating response from the accused, it is unlikely that the practice will not also be one which the police should have known was reasonably likely to have that effect.

[8] Any knowledge the police may have had concerning the unusual susceptibility of a defendant to a particular form of persuasion might be an important factor in determining whether the police should have known that their words or actions were reasonably likely to elicit an incriminating response from the suspect.

[9] The record in no way suggests that the officers' remarks were *designed* to elicit a response. See n.7, *supra*. It is significant that the trial judge, after hear-

---

[5] By "incriminating response" we refer to any response – whether inculpatory or exculpatory – that the *prosecution* may seek to introduce at trial.

[6] One of the dissenting opinions seems totally to misapprehend this definition in suggesting that it "will almost certainly exclude every statement [of the police] that is not punctuated with a question mark."

The case thus boils down to whether, in the context of a brief conversation, the officers should have known that the respondent would suddenly be moved to make a self-incriminating response. Given the fact that the entire conversation appears to have consisted of no more than a few off hand remarks, we cannot say that the officers should have known that it was reasonably likely that Innis would so respond. This is not a case where the police carried on a lengthy harangue in the presence of the suspect. Nor does the record support the respondent's contention that, under the circumstances, the officers' comments were particularly "evocative." It is our view, therefore, that the respondent was not subjected by the police to words or actions that the police should have known were reasonably likely to elicit an incriminating response from him.

The Rhode Island Supreme Court erred, in short, in equating "subtle compulsion" with interrogation. That the officers' comments struck a responsive chord is readily apparent. Thus, it may be said, as the Rhode Island Supreme Court did say, that the respondent was subjected to "subtle compulsion." But that is not the end of the inquiry. It must also be established that a suspect's incriminating response was the product of words or actions on the part of the police that they should have known were reasonably likely to elicit an incriminating response.[10] This was not established in the present case.

For the reasons stated, the judgment of the Supreme Court of Rhode Island is vacated, and the case is remanded to that court for further proceedings not inconsistent with this opinion.

Mr. Chief Justice BURGER, concurring in the judgment.

Since the result is not inconsistent with *Miranda*, I concur in the judgment. The meaning of *Miranda*

---

ing the officers' testimony, concluded that it was "entirely understandable that [the officers] would voice their concern [for the safety of the handicapped children] to each other."

10 By way of example, if the police had done no more than to drive past the site of the concealed weapon while taking the most direct route to the police station, and if the respondent, upon noticing for the first time the proximity of the school for handicapped children, had blurted out that he would show the officers where the gun was located, it could not seriously be argued that this "subtle compulsion" would have constituted "interrogation" within the meaning of the *Miranda* opinion.

has become reasonably clear and law enforcement practices have adjusted to its strictures; I would neither overrule *Miranda*, disparage it, nor extend it at this late date. I fear, however, that the rationale in Parts II-A and II-B, of the Court's opinion may introduce new elements of uncertainty; under the Court's test, a police officer, in the brief time available, apparently must evaluate the suggestibility and susceptibility of an accused. See, *e.g.*, n. 8. Few, if any, police officers are competent to make the kind of evaluation seemingly contemplated; even a psychiatrist asked to express an expert opinion on these aspects of a suspect in custody would very likely employ extensive questioning and observation to make the judgment now charged to police officers.

Trial judges have enough difficulty discerning the boundaries and nuances flowing from post-*Miranda* opinions, and we do not clarify that situation today.

Mr. Justice MARSHALL, with whom Mr. Justice BRENNAN joins, dissenting.

I am substantially in agreement with the Court's definition of "interrogation" within the meaning of *Miranda*. In my view, the *Miranda* safeguards apply whenever police conduct is intended or likely to produce a response from a suspect in custody. As I read the Court's opinion, its definition of "interrogation" for *Miranda* purposes is equivalent, for practical purposes, to my formulation, since it contemplates that "where a police practice is designed to elicit an incriminating response from the accused, it is unlikely that the practice will not also be one which the police should have known was reasonably likely to have that effect." Thus, the Court requires an objective inquiry into the likely effect of police conduct on a typical individual, taking into account any special susceptibility of the suspect to certain kinds of pressure of which the police know or have reason to know.

I am utterly at a loss, however, to understand how this objective standard as applied to the facts before us can rationally lead to the conclusion that there was no interrogation. Innis was arrested at 4:30 a.m., handcuffed, searched, advised of his rights, and placed in the back seat of a patrol car. Within a short time he had been twice more advised of his rights and driven away in a four-door sedan with three police officers. Two officers sat in the front seat and one sat beside Innis in the back seat. Since the car traveled no more than a mile before Innis agreed to point out the location of the murder weapon, Officer Gleckman must have begun almost immediately to talk about the search for the shotgun. The Court attempts to characterize Gleckman's statements as "no more than a few off hand re-marks" which could not reasonably have been ex-pected to elicit a response. If the statements had been addressed to respondent, it would be impossible to draw such a conclusion. The simple message of the "talking back and forth" between Gleckman and McKenna was that they had to find the shotgun to avert a child's death.

One can scarcely imagine a stronger appeal to the conscience of a suspect—*any* suspect—than the assertion that if the weapon is not found an innocent person will be hurt or killed. And not just any inno-cent person, but an innocent child—a little girl—a helpless, handicapped little girl on her way to school. The notion that such an appeal could not be expected to have any effect unless the suspect were known to have some special interest in handicapped children verges on the ludicrous. As a matter of fact, the appeal to a suspect to confess for the sake of others, to "display some evidence of decency and honor," is a classic interrogation technique.

Gleckman's remarks would obviously have con-stituted interrogation if they had been explicitly di-rected to respondent, and the result should not be different because they were nominally addressed to McKenna. This is not a case where police officers speaking among themselves are accidentally over-heard by a suspect. These officers were "talking back and forth" in close quarters with the hand-cuffed suspect, traveling past the very place where they believed the weapon was located. They knew respondent would hear and attend to their conversa-tion, and they are chargeable with knowledge of and responsibility for the pressures to speak which they created.

I firmly believe that this case is simply an aberra-tion, and that in future cases the Court will apply the standard adopted today in accordance with its plain meaning.

Mr. Justice STEVENS, dissenting.

I

As the Court recognizes, *Miranda* makes it clear that, once respondent requested an attorney, he had an absolute right to have any type of interrogation cease until an attorney was present. As it also recog-nizes, *Miranda* requires that the term "interroga-tion" be broadly construed to include "either ex-press questioning or its functional equivalent."[4] In

---

[4] As the Court points out, the Court in *Miranda* was acutely aware of the fact that police interroga-tion techniques are not limited to direct questioning.

my view any statement that would normally be un-derstood by the average listener as calling for a re-sponse is the functional equivalent of a direct ques-tion, whether or not it is punctuated by a question mark. The Court, however, takes a much narrower view. It holds that police conduct is not the "func-tional equivalent" of direct questioning unless the police should have known that what they were saying or doing was likely to elicit an incriminating re-sponse from the suspect.[5] This holding represents a plain departure from the principles set forth in *Miranda*.

[I]f after being told that he has a right to have an attorney present during interrogation, a suspect chooses to cut off questioning until counsel can be obtained, his choice must be "scrupulously hon-ored" by the police. See *Mosley* (White, J., concur-ring in result). At the least this must mean that the police are prohibited from making deliberate at-tempts to elicit statements from the suspect. Yet the Court is unwilling to characterize all such attempts as "interrogation," noting only that "where a police practice is designed to elicit an incriminating re-sponse from the accused, it is unlikely that the prac-tice will not also be one which the police should have known was reasonably likely to have that effect."[8]

From the suspect's point of view, the effective-ness of the warnings depends on whether it appears that the police are scrupulously honoring his rights. Apparent attempts to elicit information from a sus-pect after he has invoked his right to cut off ques-tioning necessarily demean that right and tend to reinstate the imbalance between police and suspect that the *Miranda* warnings are designed to correct. Thus, if the rationale for requiring those warnings

---

[5] In limiting its test to police statements "likely to elicit an incriminating response," the Court con-fuses the scope of the exclusionary rule with the definition of "interrogation." Of course, any in-criminating statement as defined in *Miranda*, must be excluded from evidence if it is the product of impermissible interrogation. But I fail to see how this rule helps in deciding whether a particular state-ment or tactic constitutes "interrogation." After all, *Miranda* protects a suspect in Innis' position not simply from interrogation that is likely to be success-ful, but from any interrogation at all.

[8] This factual assumption is extremely dubious. I would assume that police often interrogate suspects without any reason to believe that their efforts are likely to be successful in the hope that a statement will nevertheless be forthcoming.

in the first place is to be respected, any police conduct or statements that would appear to a reasonable person in the suspect's position to call for a response must be considered "interrogation."[10]

In short, in order to give full protection to a suspect's right to be free from any interrogation at all, the definition of "interrogation" must include any police statement or conduct that has the same purpose or effect as a direct question. Statements that appear to call for a response from the suspect, as well as those that are designed to do so, should be considered interrogation. By prohibiting only those relatively few statements or actions that a police officer should know are likely to elicit an incriminating response, the Court today accords a suspect considerably less protection. Indeed, since I suppose most suspects are unlikely to incriminate themselves even when questioned directly, this new definition will almost certainly exclude every statement that is not punctuated with a question mark from the concept of "interrogation."[11]

The difference between the approach required by a faithful adherence to *Miranda* and the stinted test applied by the Court today can be illustrated by comparing three different ways in which Officer Gleckman could have communicated his fears about the possible dangers posed by the shotgun to handicapped children. He could have:

(1) directly asked Innis:

Will you please tell me where the shotgun is so we can protect handicapped school children from danger?

(2) announced to the other officers in the wagon:

If the man sitting in the back seat with me should decide to tell us where the gun is, we can protect handicapped children from danger.

or (3) stated to the other officers:

It would be too bad if a little handicapped girl would pick up the gun that this man left in the area and maybe kill herself.

In my opinion, all three of these statements should be considered interrogation because all three

appear to be designed to elicit a response from anyone who in fact knew where the gun was located.[12] Under the Court's test, on the other hand, the form of the statements would be critical. The third statement would not be interrogation because in the Court's view there was no reason for Officer Gleckman to believe that Innis was susceptible to this type of an implied appeal, therefore, the statement would not be reasonably likely to elicit an incriminating response. Assuming that this is true, then it seems to me that the first two statements, which would be just as unlikely to elicit such a response, should also not be considered interrogation. But, because the first statement is clearly an express question, it *would* be considered interrogation under the Court's test. The second statement, although just as clearly a deliberate appeal to Innis to reveal the location of the gun, would presumably not be interrogation because (a) it was not in form a direct question and (b) it does not fit within the "reasonably likely to elicit an incriminating response" category that applies to indirect interrogation.

As this example illustrates, the Court's test creates an incentive for police to ignore a suspect's invocation of his rights in order to make continued attempts to extract information from him. If a suspect does not appear to be susceptible to a particular type of psychological pressure,[13] the police are apparently free to exert that pressure on him despite his request for counsel, so long as they are careful not to punctuate their statements with question

---

[10] I would use an objective standard both to avoid the difficulties of proof inherent in a subjective standard and to give police adequate guidance in their dealings with suspects who have requested counsel.

[11] The Court's suggestion, n. 6, that I totally misapprehend the import of its definition is belied by its application of the new standard to the facts of this case.

[12] See White, *Rhode Island v. Innis*: The Significance of a Suspect's Assertion of His Right to Counsel, 17 Am.Crim.L.Rev. 53, 68 (1979), where the author proposes the same test and applies it to the facts of this case, stating:"Under the proposed objective standard, the result is obvious. Since the conversation indicates a strong desire to know the location of the shotgun, any person with knowledge of the weapon's location would be likely to believe that the officers wanted him to disclose its location. Thus, a reasonable person in Innis's position would believe that the officers were seeking to solicit precisely the type of response that was given."

[13] As The Chief Justice points out in his concurring opinion, "[f]ew, if any, police officers are competent to make the kind of evaluation seemingly contemplated [by the Court's opinion]" except by close and careful observation. Under these circumstances, courts might well find themselves deferring to what appeared to be good-faith judgments on the part of the police.

marks. And if, contrary to all reasonable expectations, the suspect makes an incriminating statement, that statement can be used against him at trial. The Court thus turns *Miranda*'s unequivocal rule against any interrogation at all into a trap in which unwary suspects may be caught by police deception.

## II

I think the Court is clearly wrong in holding, as a matter of law, that Officer Gleckman should not have realized that his statement was likely to elicit an incriminating response. The Court implicitly assumes that, at least in the absence of a lengthy harangue, a criminal suspect will not be likely to respond to indirect appeals to his humanitarian impulses. It then goes on to state that the officers in this case had no reason to believe that respondent would be unusually susceptible to such appeals. Finally, although the significance of the officer's intentions is not clear under its objective test, the Court states in a footnote that the record "in no way suggests" that Officer Gleckman's remarks were designed to elicit a response.

The Court's assumption that criminal suspects are not susceptible to appeals to conscience is directly contrary to the teachings of police interrogation manuals, which recommend appealing to a suspect's sense of morality as a standard and often successful interrogation technique. Surely the practical experience embodied in such manuals should not be ignored in a case such as this in which the record is devoid of any evidence – one way or the other – as to the susceptibility of suspects in general or of Innis in particular.

Moreover, there is evidence in the record to support the view that Officer Gleckman's statement was intended to elicit a response from Innis. Officer Gleckman, who was not regularly assigned to the caged wagon, was directed by a police captain to ride with respondent to the police station. Although there is a dispute in the testimony, it appears that Gleckman may well have been riding in the back seat with Innis.[16] The record does not explain why, notwithstanding the fact that respondent was handcuffed, unarmed, and had offered no resistance when

arrested by an officer acting alone, the captain ordered Officer Gleckman to ride with respondent.[17] It is not inconceivable that two professionally trained police officers concluded that a few well-chosen remarks might induce respondent to disclose the whereabouts of the shotgun.[18] This conclusion becomes even more plausible in light of the emotionally charged words chosen by Officer Gleckman ("God forbid" that a "little girl" should find the gun and hurt herself).[19]

## III

Under my view of the correct standard, the judgment of the Rhode Island Supreme Court should be affirmed because the statements made within Innis' hearing were as likely to elicit a response as a direct question. However, even if I were to agree with the Court's much narrower standard, I would disagree with its disposition of this particular case because the Rhode Island courts should be given an opportunity to apply the new standard to the facts of this case.

---

[16] Officer Gleckman testified that he was riding in the front seat with the driver. However, Officer McKenna, who had also ridden in the wagon, and the police captain both testified that Gleckman rode in the back seat with the suspect. Thereafter, the third officer in the wagon corroborated Gleckman's testimony.

[17] This was apparently a somewhat unusual procedure. Officer McKenna testified that:

"If I remember correctly, the vehicle – Innis was placed in it and the vehicle door was closed, and we were waiting for instructions from Captain Leyden. . . . At that point, Captain Leyden instructed Patrolman Gleckman to accompany us. There's usually two men assigned to the wagon, but in this particular case he wanted a third man to accompany us, and Gleckman got in the rear seat. In other words, the door was closed. Gleckman opened the door and got in the vehicle with the subject. Myself, I went over to the other side and got in the passenger's side in the front."

[18] Although Officer Gleckman testified that the captain told him not to interrogate, intimidate or coerce respondent on the way back, this does not rule out the possibility that either or both of them thought an indirect psychological ploy would be permissible.

[19] In his article quoted in n. 12, *supra*, Professor White also points out that the officers were probably aware that the chances of a handicapped child's finding the weapon at a time when police were not present were relatively slim. Thus, he concluded that it was unlikely that the true purpose of the conversation was to voice a genuine concern over the children's welfare. See 17 Am.Crim.L.Rev., at 68.

## QUESTIONS AND NOTES

**1.** Do you think that *Innis* takes a broad or narrow view of interrogation within the meaning of *Miranda*? Explain. If you think that it takes a broad view, how do you explain Justice Stewart's (a *Miranda* dissenter) authorship of the opinion, and Justice Rehnquist's concurrence?

**2.** If the police had *intentionally* driven out of the way to pass the suspected hiding place (compare n. 10) or had intentionally driven out of their way to pass the state's prison, would (should) that constitute interrogation?

**3.** Suppose the police left the items obtained from a burglary in front of the defendant's jail cell, and said nothing. Interrogation?

**4.** Is interrogation *vel non* determined from the perspective of the policeman or the suspect? Explain.

**5.** Does the Court adopt an objective or subjective view of interrogation? Which one should it have adopted?

**6.** Was Officer Gleckman's professed concern reasonably *likely* to elicit an incriminating response? Was it reasonably *calculated* to elicit an incriminating response? Which of those questions was (should have been) the more relevant?

**7.** Which (if any) of Justice Stevens three hypotheticals calls for a response? Which (if any) would be deemed interrogation by the majority? How (if at all) are they different from Gleckman's actual statements in the case?

## PROBLEM

Police officers Jim Rogers and Joe Martin arrested Johnny Jones for burglary. After handcuffing him, placing him in the police car and driving him off to jail (Martin driving with Rogers sitting beside him in the front seat, and Jones sitting alone in the back seat), the following conversation transpired:

Rogers (looking at Jones): Johnny Jones: You have the right to remain silent; anything you say can and will be used against you in a court of law; you have the right to an attorney before I ask you any questions; if you cannot afford an attorney one will be appointed for you before any questions are asked if you so desire. Do you understand these rights?

Jones: Yes I do.

Rogers: What would you like to do?

Jones: I think that I better talk to my attorney before you ask me any questions.

Rogers (turning to Martin): Thank goodness he invoked his right to counsel. If he talked to us the judge would probably go easy on him. Since we have him dead to rights anyway, we won't have to worry about the judge giving him a lighter sentence.

Jones: Maybe I should talk to you.

Rogers (looking back at Jones): Not till you talk to your lawyer.

Jones: But wouldn't the judge go easier on me if I talked?

Rogers: That's not for me to say son; ask your lawyer. He's on your side. I'm out to get you.

Jones: But you think that the judge would go easier on me if I talked.

Rogers: True.

Jones: Then I want to talk to you.

Rogers: Sorry son, you waived your right to be questioned.

Jones: Couldn't I just waive my right to counsel?

Rogers: Yes, I suppose you could. Read this and sign right here.

Rogers then handed Jones a waiver of counsel and silence form which Jones (a college graduate who had no prior experience with the law) read and signed. The dialogue continued:

Rogers: Why did you burglarize Jewel's jewelry store?

Jones: Because Jewel ripped me off last week and I wanted to get back at her.

At Jones' trial for burglary, should his last statement be admissible? Explain thoroughly.

## G.    The Public Safety Exception

### New York v. Quarles
### 467 U.S. 649 (1984)

Justice REHNQUIST delivered the opinion of the Court.

Respondent Benjamin Quarles was charged in the New York trial court with criminal possession of a weapon. The trial court suppressed the gun in question, and a statement made by respondent, because the statement was obtained by police before they read respondent his "*Miranda* rights." That ruling was affirmed on appeal through the New York Court of Appeals. We granted certiorari, and we now reverse. We conclude that under the circumstances involved in this case, overriding considerations of public safety justify the officer's failure to provide *Miranda* warnings before he asked questions devoted to locating the abandoned weapon.

On September 11, 1980, at approximately 12:30 a.m., Officer Frank Kraft and Officer Sal Scarring were on road patrol in Queens, New York, when a young woman approached their car. She told them that she had just been raped by a black male, approximately six feet tall, who was wearing a black jacket with the name "Big Ben" printed in yellow letters on the back. She told the officers that the man had just entered an A & P supermarket located nearby and that the man was carrying a gun.

The officers drove the woman to the supermarket, and Officer Kraft entered the store while Officer

Scarring radioed for assistance. Officer Kraft quickly spotted respondent, who matched the description given by the woman, approaching a checkout counter. Apparently upon seeing the officer, respondent turned and ran toward the rear of the store, and Officer Kraft pursued him with a drawn gun. When respondent turned the corner at the end of an aisle, Officer Kraft lost sight of him for several seconds, and upon regaining sight of respondent, ordered him to stop and put his hands over his head.

Although more than three other officers had arrived on the scene by that time, Officer Kraft was the first to reach respondent. He frisked him and discovered that he was wearing a shoulder holster which was then empty. After handcuffing him, Officer Kraft asked him where the gun was. Respondent nodded in the direction of some empty cartons and responded, "the gun is over there." Officer Kraft thereafter retrieved a loaded .38-caliber revolver from one of the cartons, formally placed respondent under arrest, and read him his *Miranda* rights from a printed card. Respondent indicated that he would be willing to answer questions without an attorney present. Officer Kraft then asked respondent if he owned the gun and where he had purchased it. Respondent answered that he did own it and that he had purchased it in Miami, Florida.

In the subsequent prosecution of respondent for criminal possession of a weapon,[2] the judge excluded the statement, "the gun is over there," and the gun because the officer had not given respondent the warnings required by *Miranda* before asking him where the gun was located. The judge excluded the other statements about respondent's ownership of the gun and the place of purchase, as evidence tainted by the prior *Miranda* violation.

The Court of Appeals affirmed by a 4-3 vote. It concluded that respondent was in "custody" within the meaning of *Miranda* during all questioning and rejected the state's argument that the exigencies of the situation justified Officer Kraft's failure to read respondent his *Miranda* rights until after he had located the gun. The court declined to recognize an exigency exception to the usual requirements of *Miranda* because it found no indication from Officer Kraft's testimony at the suppression hearing that his subjective motivation in asking the question was to protect his own safety or the safety of the public. For the reasons which follow, we believe that this case presents a situation where concern for public safety must be paramount to adherence to the literal language of the prophylactic rules enunciated in *Miranda*.[3]

In this case we have before us no claim that respondent's statements were actually compelled by police conduct which overcame his will to resist. Thus the only issue before us is whether Officer Kraft was justified in failing to make available to respondent the procedural safeguards associated with the privilege against compulsory self-incrimination since *Miranda*.[5]

The New York Court of Appeals was undoubtedly correct in deciding that the facts of this case come within the ambit of the *Miranda* decision as we have subsequently interpreted it. We agree that respondent was in police custody because we have noted that "the ultimate inquiry is simply whether there is a 'formal arrest or restraint on freedom of movement' of the degree associated with a formal arrest." *Mathiason*. Here Quarles was surrounded by at least four police officers and was handcuffed when the questioning at issue took place. As the New York Court of Appeals observed, there was nothing to suggest that any of the officers were any longer concerned for their own physical safety. The New York Court of Appeals' majority declined to express an opinion as to whether there might be an exception to the *Miranda* rule if the police had been acting to protect the public, because the lower courts in New York had made no factual determination that the police had acted with that motive.

We hold that on these facts there is a "public safety" exception to the requirement that *Miranda* warnings be given before a suspect's answers may be admitted into evidence, and that the availability of that exception does not depend upon the motivation of the individual officers involved. In a kaleidoscopic situation such as the one confronting these officers, where spontaneity rather than adherence to a police manual is necessarily the order of the day, the application of the exception which we recognize today should not be made to depend on *post hoc* findings at a suppression hearing concerning the subjective motivation of the arresting officer.[6] Undoubtedly most police officers, if placed in Officer Kraft's

---

[2] The state originally charged respondent with rape, but the record provides no information as to why the state failed to pursue that charge.

[3] We have long recognized an exigent-circumstances exception to the warrant requirement in the Fourth Amendment context. We have found the warrant requirement of the Fourth Amendment inapplicable in cases where the "'exigencies of the situation' make the needs of law enforcement so compelling that the warrantless search is objectively reasonable under the Fourth Amendment." Although "the Fifth Amendment's strictures, unlike the Fourth's, are not removed by showing reasonableness," we conclude today that there are limited circumstances where the judicially imposed strictures of *Miranda* are inapplicable.

[5] The dissent curiously takes us to task for "endors[ing] the introduction of coerced self-incriminating statements in criminal prosecutions," and for "sanctioning *sub silentio* criminal prosecu-

tions based on compelled self-incriminating statements." Of course our decision today does nothing of the kind. As the *Miranda* Court itself recognized, the failure to provide *Miranda* warnings in and of itself does not render a confession involuntary, and respondent is certainly free on remand to argue that his statement was coerced under traditional due process standards. Today we merely reject the only argument that respondent has raised to support the exclusion of his statement, that the statement must be *presumed* compelled because of Officer Kraft's failure to read him his *Miranda* warnings.

[6] Similar approaches have been rejected in other contexts. See *Innis* (officer's subjective intent to incriminate not determinative of whether "interrogation" occurred); *United States v. Mendenhall*, (opinion of Stewart, J.) (officer's subjective intent to detain not determinative of whether a "seizure" occurred within the meaning of the Fourth Amendment).

position, would act out of a host of different, instinctive, and largely unverifiable motives – their own safety, the safety of others, and perhaps as well the desire to obtain incriminating evidence from the suspect.

Whatever the motivation of individual officers in such a situation, we do not believe that the doctrinal underpinnings of *Miranda* require that it be applied in all its rigor to a situation in which police officers ask questions reasonably prompted by a concern for the public safety. The *Miranda* decision was based in large part on this Court's view that the warnings which it required police to give to suspects in custody would reduce the likelihood that the suspects would fall victim to constitutionally impermissible practices of police interrogation in the presumptively coercive environment of the station house. The dissenters warned that the requirement of *Miranda* warnings would have the effect of decreasing the number of suspects who respond to police questioning. The *Miranda* majority, however, apparently felt that whatever the cost to society in terms of fewer convictions of guilty suspects, that cost would simply have to be borne in the interest of enlarged protection for the Fifth Amendment privilege.

The police in this case, in the very act of apprehending a suspect, were confronted with the immediate necessity of ascertaining the whereabouts of a gun which they had every reason to believe the suspect had just removed from his empty holster and discarded in the supermarket. So long as the gun was concealed somewhere in the supermarket, with its actual whereabouts unknown, it obviously posed more than one danger to the public safety: an accomplice might make use of it, a customer or employee might later come upon it.

In such a situation, if the police are required to recite the familiar *Miranda* warnings before asking the whereabouts of the gun, suspects in Quarles' position might well be deterred from responding. Procedural safeguards which deter a suspect from responding were deemed acceptable in *Miranda* in order to protect the Fifth Amendment privilege; when the primary social cost of those added protections is the possibility of fewer convictions, the *Miranda* majority was willing to bear that cost. Here, had *Miranda* warnings deterred Quarles from responding to Officer Kraft's question about the whereabouts of the gun, the cost would have been something more than merely the failure to obtain evidence useful in convicting Quarles. Officer Kraft needed an answer to his question not simply to make

his case against Quarles but to insure that further danger to the public did not result from the concealment of the gun in a public area.

We conclude that the need for answers to questions in a situation posing a threat to the public safety outweighs the need for the prophylactic rule protecting the Fifth Amendment's privilege against self-incrimination. We decline to place officers such as Officer Kraft in the untenable position of having to consider, often in a matter of seconds, whether it best serves society for them to ask the necessary questions without the *Miranda* warnings and render whatever probative evidence they uncover inadmissible, or for them to give the warnings in order to preserve the admissibility of evidence they might uncover but possibly damage or destroy their ability to obtain that evidence and neutralize the volatile situation confronting them.[7]

In recognizing a narrow exception to the *Miranda* rule in this case, we acknowledge that to some degree we lessen the desirable clarity of that rule. At least in part in order to preserve its clarity, we have over the years refused to sanction attempts to expand our *Miranda* holding. See, *e.g.*, *Murphy* (refusal to extend *Miranda* requirements to interviews with probation officers); *Michael C.* (refusal to equate request to see a probation officer with request to see a lawyer for *Miranda* purposes); *Beckwith* (refusal to extend *Miranda* requirements to questioning in non-custodial circumstances). As we have in other contexts, we recognize here the importance of a workable rule "to guide police officers, who have only limited time and expertise to reflect on and balance the social and individual interests involved in the specific circumstances they confront." But as we have pointed out, we believe that the exception which we recognize today lessens the necessity of that on-the-scene balancing process. The exception

---

[7] The dissent argues that a public safety exception to *Miranda* is unnecessary because in every case an officer can simply ask the necessary questions to protect himself or the public, and then the prosecution can decline to introduce any incriminating responses at a subsequent trial. But absent actual coercion by the officer, there is no constitutional imperative requiring the exclusion of the evidence that results from police inquiry of this kind; and we do not believe that the doctrinal underpinnings of *Miranda* require us to exclude the evidence, thus penalizing officers for asking the very questions which are the most crucial to their efforts to protect themselves and the public.

will not be difficult for police officers to apply because in each case it will be circumscribed by the exigency which justifies it. We think police officers can and will distinguish almost instinctively between questions necessary to secure their own safety or the safety of the public and questions designed solely to elicit testimonial evidence from a suspect.

The facts of this case clearly demonstrate that distinction and an officer's ability to recognize it. Officer Kraft asked only the question necessary to locate the missing gun before advising respondent of his rights. It was only after securing the loaded revolver and giving the warnings that he continued with investigatory questions about the ownership and place of purchase of the gun. The exception which we recognize today, far from complicating the thought processes and the on-the-scene judgments of police officers, will simply free them to follow their legitimate instincts when confronting situations presenting a danger to the public safety.[8]

We hold that the Court of Appeals in this case erred in excluding the statement, "the gun is over there," and the gun because of the officer's failure to read respondent his *Miranda* rights before attempting to locate the weapon. Accordingly we hold

---

[8] Although it involves police questions in part relating to the whereabouts of a gun, *Orozco*, is in no sense inconsistent with our disposition of this case. In *Orozco* four hours after a murder had been committed at a restaurant, four police officers entered the defendant's boardinghouse and awakened the defendant, who was sleeping in his bedroom. Without giving him *Miranda* warnings, they began vigorously to interrogate him about whether he had been present at the scene of the shooting and whether he owned a gun. The defendant eventually admitted that he had been present at the scene and directed the officers to a washing machine in the backroom of the boardinghouse where he had hidden the gun. We held that all the statements should have been suppressed. In *Orozco*, however, the questions about the gun were clearly investigatory; they did not in any way relate to an objectively reasonable need to protect the police or the public from any immediate danger associated with the weapon. In short there was no exigency requiring immediate action by the officers beyond the normal need expeditiously to solve a serious crime.

*Innis* also involved the whereabouts of a missing weapon, but our holding in that case depended entirely on our conclusion that no police interrogation took place so as to require consideration of the applicability of the *Miranda* prophylactic.

that it also erred in excluding the subsequent statements as illegal fruits of a *Miranda* violation.[9] We therefore reverse and remand for further proceedings not inconsistent with this opinion.

Justice O'CONNOR, concurring in the judgment in part and dissenting in part.

Were the Court writing from a clean slate, I could agree with its holding. But *Miranda* is now the law and, in my view, the Court has not provided sufficient justification for departing from it or for blurring its now clear strictures. Accordingly, I would require suppression of the initial statement taken from respondent in this case. On the other hand, nothing in *Miranda* or the privilege itself requires exclusion of nontestimonial evidence derived from informal custodial interrogation, and I therefore agree with the Court that admission of the gun in evidence is proper.

I

The *Miranda* Court itself considered objections akin to those raised by the Court today. In dissent, Justice White protested that the *Miranda* rules would "operate indiscriminately in all criminal cases, regardless of the severity of the crime or the circumstances involved." But the *Miranda* Court would not accept any suggestion "that society's need for interrogation [could] outweig[h] the privilege." To that Court, the privilege against self-incrimination was absolute and therefore could not be "abridged."

Since the time *Miranda* was decided, the Court has repeatedly refused to bend the literal terms of that decision. To be sure, the Court has been sensitive to the substantial burden the *Miranda* rules place on local law enforcement efforts, and consequently has refused to extend the decision or to increase its strictures on law enforcement agencies in almost any way.

In my view, a "public safety" exception unnecessarily blurs the edges of the clear line heretofore established and makes *Miranda*'s requirements more difficult to understand. In some cases, police will benefit because a reviewing court will find that an

---

[9] Because we hold that there is no violation of *Miranda* in this case, we have no occasion to reach arguments made by the state and the United States as *amicus curiae* that the gun is admissible either because it is non-testimonial or because the police would inevitably have discovered it absent their questioning.

exigency excused their failure to administer the required warnings. But in other cases, police will suffer because, though they thought an exigency excused their noncompliance, a reviewing court will view the "objective" circumstances differently and require exclusion of admissions thereby obtained. The end result will be a finespun new doctrine on public safety exigencies incident to custodial interrogation, complete with the hair-splitting distinctions that currently plague our Fourth Amendment jurisprudence. "While the rigidity of the prophylactic rules was a principal weakness in the view of dissenters and critics outside the Court, . . . that rigidity [has also been called a] strength of the decision. It [has] afforded police and courts clear guidance on the manner in which to conduct a custodial investigation: if it was rigid, it was also precise. . . . [T]his core virtue of *Miranda* would be eviscerated if the prophylactic rules were freely [ignored] by . . . courts under the guise of [reinterpreting] *Miranda*. . . ." *Fare v. Michael C.* (Rehnquist, J., in chambers on application for stay).

The justification the Court provides for upsetting the equilibrium that has finally been achieved—that police cannot and should not balance considerations of public safety against the individual's interest in avoiding compulsory testimonial self-incrimination—really misses the critical question to be decided. *Miranda* has never been read to prohibit the police from asking questions to secure the public safety. Rather, the critical question *Miranda* addresses is who shall bear the cost of securing the public safety when such questions are asked and answered: the defendant or the State. *Miranda*, for better or worse, found the resolution of that question implicit in the prohibition against compulsory self-incrimination and placed the burden on the State. When police ask custodial questions without administering the required warnings, *Miranda* quite clearly requires that the answers received be presumed compelled and that they be excluded from evidence at trial.

The Court concedes, as it must, both that respondent was in "custody" and subject to "interrogation" and that his statement "the gun is over there" was compelled within the meaning of our precedent. In my view, since there is nothing about an exigency that makes custodial interrogation any less compelling, a principled application of *Miranda* requires that respondent's statement be suppressed.

[Justice O'Connor then explained why, in her view, the gun was admissible. That issue will be discussed in Chapter 21, *infra*.]

Justice MARSHALL, with whom Justice BRENNAN and Justice STEVENS join, dissenting.

The police in this case arrested a man suspected of possessing a firearm in violation of New York law. Once the suspect was in custody and found to be unarmed, the arresting officer initiated an interrogation. Without being advised of his right not to respond, the suspect incriminated himself by locating the gun. The majority concludes that the State may rely on this incriminating statement to convict the suspect of possessing a weapon. I disagree. The arresting officers had no legitimate reason to interrogate the suspect without advising him of his rights to remain silent and to obtain assistance of counsel. By finding on these facts justification for unconsented interrogation, the majority abandons the clear guidelines enunciated in *Miranda* and condemns the American judiciary to a new era of *post hoc* inquiry into the propriety of custodial interrogations. More significantly and in direct conflict with this Court's long-standing interpretation of the Fifth Amendment, the majority has endorsed the introduction of coerced self-incriminating statements in criminal prosecutions. I dissent.

I

The majority's entire analysis rests on the factual assumption that the public was at risk during Quarles' interrogation. This assumption is completely in conflict with the facts as found by New York's highest court. Before the interrogation began, Quarles had been "reduced to a condition of physical powerlessness." Contrary to the majority's speculations, Quarles was not believed to have, nor did he in fact have, an accomplice to come to his rescue. When the questioning began, the arresting officers were sufficiently confident of their safety to put away their guns. As Officer Kraft acknowledged at the suppression hearing, "the situation was under control." Based on Officer Kraft's own testimony, the New York Court of Appeals found: "Nothing suggests that any of the officers was by that time concerned for his own physical safety." The Court of Appeals also determined that there was no evidence that the interrogation was prompted by the arresting officers' concern for the public's safety.

The majority attempts to slip away from these unambiguous findings of New York's highest court by proposing that danger be measured by objective facts rather than the subjective intentions of arresting officers. Though clever, this ploy was anticipated by the New York Court of Appeals: "[T]here is no evidence in the record before us that there were exigent circumstances posing a risk to the public safety. . . ."

The New York court's conclusion that neither Quarles nor his missing gun posed a threat to the public's safety is amply supported by the evidence presented at the suppression hearing. Again contrary to the majority's intimations, no customers or employees were wandering about the store in danger of coming across Quarles' discarded weapon. Although the supermarket was open to the public, Quarles' arrest took place during the middle of the night when the store was apparently deserted except for the clerks at the checkout counter. The police could easily have cordoned off the store and searched for the missing gun. Had they done so, they would have found the gun forthwith. The police were well aware that Quarles had discarded his weapon somewhere near the scene of the arrest. As the State acknowledged before the New York Court of Appeals: "After Officer Kraft had handcuffed and frisked the defendant in the supermarket, *he knew with a high degree of certainty that the defendant's gun was within the immediate vicinity of the encounter.* He undoubtedly would have searched for it in the carton a few feet away without the defendant having looked in that direction and saying that it was there." Brief for Appellant, p.11 (emphasis added).

In this case, there was convincing, indeed almost overwhelming, evidence to support the New York court's conclusion that Quarles' hidden weapon did not pose a risk either to the arresting officers or to the public. The majority ignores this evidence and sets aside the factual findings of the New York Court of Appeals. More cynical observers might well conclude that a state court's findings of fact "deserv[e] a 'high measure of deference,'" only when deference works against the interests of a criminal defendant.

## II

The majority's treatment of the legal issues presented in this case is no less troubling than its abuse of the facts. Before today's opinion, the Court had twice concluded that, under *Miranda*, police officers conducting custodial interrogations must advise suspects of their rights before any questions concerning the whereabouts of incriminating weapons can be asked. *Innis*, (dicta); *Orozco*, (holding).[2] Now the

majority departs from these cases and rules that police may withhold *Miranda* warnings whenever custodial interrogations concern matters of public safety.

The majority contends that the law, as it currently stands, places police officers in a dilemma whenever they interrogate a suspect who appears to know of some threat to the public's safety. If the police interrogate the suspect without advising him of his rights, the suspect may reveal information that the authorities can use to defuse the threat, but the suspect's statements will be inadmissible at trial. If, on the other hand, the police advise the suspect of his rights, the suspect may be deterred from responding to the police's questions, and the risk to the public may continue unabated. According to the majority, the police must now choose between establishing the suspect's guilt and safeguarding the public from danger.

The majority proposes to eliminate this dilemma by creating an exception to *Miranda* for custodial interrogations concerning matters of public safety. Under the majority's exception, police would be permitted to interrogate suspects about such matters before the suspects have been advised of their constitutional rights. Without being "deterred" by the knowledge that they have a constitutional right not to respond, these suspects will be likely to answer the questions. Should the answers also be incriminating, the State would be free to introduce them as evidence in a criminal prosecution. Through this "narrow exception to the *Miranda* rule," the majority proposes to protect the public's safety without jeopardizing the prosecution of criminal defendants. I find in this reasoning an unwise and unprincipled departure from our Fifth Amendment precedents.

Before today's opinion, the procedures established in *Miranda* had "the virtue of informing police and prosecutors with specificity as to what they may do in conducting custodial interrogation, and of informing courts under what circumstances statements obtained during such interrogations are not admissible." In a chimerical quest for public safety, the majority has abandoned the rule that brought eighteen years of doctrinal tranquility to the field of custodial interrogations. As the majority candidly concedes, a public-safety exception destroys forever

---

[2] The majority attempts to distinguish *Orozco* by stressing the fact that the interrogation in this case immediately followed the Quarles' arrest whereas the interrogation in *Orozco* occurred some four hours after the crime and was investigatory. I fail to comprehend the distinction. In both cases, a group of police officers had taken a suspect into custody

and questioned the suspect about the location of a missing gun. In both cases a dangerous weapon was missing, and in neither case was there any direct evidence where the weapon was hidden.

the clarity of *Miranda* for both law enforcement officers and members of the judiciary. The Court's candor cannot mask what a serious loss the administration of justice has incurred.

This case is illustrative of the chaos the "publicsafety" exception will unleash. The circumstances of Quarles' arrest have never been in dispute. After the benefit of briefing and oral argument, the New York Court of Appeals concluded that there was "no evidence in the record before us that there were exigent circumstances posing a risk to the public safety." Upon reviewing the same facts and hearing the same arguments, a majority of this Court has come to precisely the opposite conclusion: "So long as the gun was concealed somewhere in the supermarket, with its actual whereabouts unknown, it obviously posed more than one danger to the public safety. . . ."

If after plenary review two appellate courts so fundamentally differ over the threat to public safety presented by the simple and uncontested facts of this case, one must seriously question how law enforcement officers will respond to the majority's new rule in the confusion and haste of the real world. As The Chief Justice wrote in a similar context, "Few, if any, police officers are competent to make the kind of evaluation seemingly contemplated. . . ." *Innis*, (concurring in the judgment). Not only will police officers have to decide whether the objective facts of an arrest justify an unconsented custodial interrogation; they will also have to remember to interrupt the interrogation and read the suspect his *Miranda* warnings once the focus of the inquiry shifts from protecting the public's safety to ascertaining the suspect's guilt. Disagreements of the scope of the "public-safety" exception and mistakes in its application are inevitable.[4]

The end result, as Justice O'Connor predicts, will be "a finespun new doctrine of public safety exigencies incident to custodial interrogation, complete with the hair-splitting distinctions that currently plague our Fourth Amendment jurisprudence." In

---

[4] One of the peculiarities of the majority's decision is its suggestion that police officers can "distinguish almost instinctively" questions tied to public safety and questions designed to elicit testimonial evidence. Obviously, these distinctions are extraordinarily difficult to draw. In many cases—like this one—custodial questioning may serve both purposes. It is therefore wishful thinking for the majority to suggest that the intuitions of police officers will render its decision self-executing.

the meantime, the courts will have to dedicate themselves to spinning this new web of doctrines, and the country's law enforcement agencies will have to suffer patiently through the frustrations of another period of constitutional uncertainty.

### III

Though unfortunate, the difficulty of administering the "public-safety" exception is not the most profound flaw in the majority's decision. The majority has lost sight of the fact that *Miranda* and our earlier custodial-interrogation cases all implemented a constitutional privilege against self-incrimination. The rules established in these cases were designed to protect criminal defendants against prosecutions based on coerced self-incriminating statements. The majority today turns its back on these constitutional considerations, and invites the government to prosecute through the use of what necessarily are coerced statements.

### A

The majority's error stems from a serious misunderstanding of *Miranda* and of the Fifth Amendment upon which that decision was based. The majority implies that *Miranda* consisted of no more than a judicial balancing act in which the benefits of "enlarged protection for the Fifth Amendment privilege" were weighed against "the cost to society in terms of fewer convictions of guilty suspects." Supposedly because the scales tipped in favor of the privilege against self-incrimination, the *Miranda* Court erected a prophylactic barrier around statements made during custodial interrogations. The majority now proposes to return to the scales of social utility to calculate whether *Miranda*'s prophylactic rule remains cost-effective when threats to public's safety are added to the balance. The results of the majority's "test" are announced with pseudoscientific precision:

> "We conclude that the need for answers
> to questions in a situation posing a threat to
> the public safety outweighs the need for the
> prophylactic rule protecting the Fifth Amend
> ment's privilege against self-incrimination."

The majority misreads *Miranda*. Though the *Miranda* dissent prophesized dire consequences, the *Miranda* Court refused to allow such concerns to weaken the protections of the Constitution:

> "A recurrent argument made in these
> cases is that society's need for interrogation
> outweighs the privilege. This argument is not
> unfamiliar to this Court. The whole thrust of

our foregoing discussion demonstrates that the Constitution has prescribed the rights of the individual when confronted with the power of government when it provided in the Fifth Amendment that an individual cannot be compelled to be a witness against himself. That right cannot be abridged.''

Whether society would be better off if the police warned suspects of their rights before beginning an interrogation or whether the advantages of giving such warnings would outweigh their costs did not inform the *Miranda* decision. On the contrary, the *Miranda* Court was concerned with the proscriptions of the Fifth Amendment, and, in particular, whether the Self-Incrimination Clause permits the government to prosecute individuals based on statements made in the course of custodial interrogations.

After a detailed examination of police practices and a review of its previous decisions in the area, the Court in *Miranda* determined that custodial interrogations are inherently coercive. The Court therefore created a constitutional presumption that statements made during custodial interrogations are compelled in violation of the Fifth Amendment and are thus inadmissible in criminal prosecutions. As a result of the Court's decision in *Miranda*, a statement made during a custodial interrogation may be introduced as proof of a defendant's guilt only if the prosecution demonstrates that the defendant knowingly and intelligently waived his constitutional rights before making the statement. The now-familiar *Miranda* warnings offer law-enforcement authorities a clear, easily administered device for ensuring that criminal suspects understand their constitutional rights well enough to waive them and to engage in consensual custodial interrogation.

In fashioning its "public-safety" exception to *Miranda*, the majority makes no attempt to deal with the constitutional presumption established by that case. The majority does not argue that police questioning about issues of public safety is any less coercive than custodial interrogations into other matters. The majority's only contention is that police officers could more easily protect the public if *Miranda* did not apply to custodial interrogations concerning the public's safety. But *Miranda* was not a decision about public safety; it was a decision about coerced confessions. Without establishing that interrogations concerning the public's safety are less likely to be coercive than other interrogations, the majority cannot endorse the "public-safety" exception and remain faithful to the logic of *Miranda*.

### B

The majority's avoidance of the issue of coercion

may not have been inadvertent. It would strain credulity to contend that Officer Kraft's questioning of respondent Quarles was not coercive.[8] In the middle of the night and in the back of an empty supermarket, Quarles was surrounded by four armed police officers. His hands were handcuffed behind his back. The first words out of the mouth of the arresting officer were: "Where is the gun?" In the majority's phrase, the situation was "kaleidoscopic." Police and suspect were acting on instinct. Officer Kraft's abrupt and pointed question pressured Quarles in precisely the way that the *Miranda* Court feared the custodial interrogations would coerce self-incriminating testimony.

That the application of the "public-safety" exception in this case entailed coercion is no happenstance. The majority's *ratio decidendi* is that interrogating suspects about matters of public safety *will* be coercive. In its cost-benefit analysis, the Court's strongest argument in favor of a public-safety exception to *Miranda* is that the police would be better able to protect the public's safety if they were not always required to give suspects their *Miranda* warnings. The crux of this argument is that, by deliberately withholding *Miranda* warnings, the police can get information out of suspects who would refuse to respond to police questioning were they advised of their constitutional rights. The "public-safety" exception is efficacious precisely because it permits police officers to coerce criminal defendants into making involuntary statements.

Indeed, in the efficacy of the "public-safety" exception lies a fundamental and constitutional defect. Until today, this Court could truthfully state that the Fifth Amendment is given "broad scope" "where there has been genuine compulsion of testimony." Coerced confessions were simply inadmissible in criminal prosecutions. The "public-safety" exception departs from this principle by expressly inviting police officers to coerce defendants into making incriminating statements, and then permitting prosecutors to introduce those statements at

---

[8] The majority's reliance on respondent's failure to claim that his testimony was compelled by police conduct can only be disingenuous. Before today's opinion, respondent had no need to claim actual compulsion. Heretofore, it was sufficient to demonstrate that the police had conducted nonconsensual custodial interrogation. But now that the law has changed, it is only fair to examine the facts of the case to determine whether coercion probably was involved.

trial. Though the majority's opinion is cloaked in the beguiling language of utilitarianism, the Court has sanctioned *sub silentio* criminal prosecutions based on compelled self-incriminating statements. I find this result in direct conflict with the Fifth Amendment's dictate that "No person . . . shall be compelled in any criminal case to be a witness against himself."

The irony of the majority's decision is that the public's safety can be perfectly well protected without abridging the Fifth Amendment. If a bomb is about to explode or the public is otherwise imminently imperiled, the police are free to interrogate suspects without advising them of their constitutional rights. Such unconsented questioning may take place not only when police officers act on instinct but also when higher faculties lead them to believe that advising a suspect of his constitutional rights might decrease the likelihood that the suspect would reveal life-saving information. If trickery is necessary to protect the public, then the police may trick a suspect into confessing. While the Fourteenth Amendment sets limits on such behavior, nothing in the Fifth Amendment or our decision in *Miranda* proscribes this sort of emergency questioning. All the Fifth Amendment forbids is the introduction of coerced statements at trial. Cf. *Weatherford v. Bursey* (Sixth Amendment violated only if trial affected).

To a limited degree, the majority is correct that there is a cost associated with the Fifth Amendment's ban on introducing coerced self-incriminating statements at trial. Without a "public-safety" exception, there would be occasions when a defendant incriminated himself by revealing a threat to the public, and the State was unable to prosecute because the defendant retracted his statement after consulting with counsel and the police cannot find independent proof of guilt. Such occasions would not, however, be common. The prosecution does not always lose the use of incriminating information revealed in these situations. After consulting with counsel, a suspect may well volunteer to repeat his statement in hopes of gaining a favorable plea bargain or more lenient sentence. The majority thus overstates its

case when it suggests that a police officer must necessarily choose between public safety and admissibility.[9]

But however frequently or infrequently such cases arise, their regularity is irrelevant. The Fifth Amendment prohibits compelled self-incrimination.[10] As the Court has explained on numerous occasions, this prohibition is the mainstay of our adversarial system of criminal justice. Not only does it protect us against the inherent unreliability of compelled testimony, but it also ensures that criminal investigations will be conducted with integrity and that the judiciary will avoid the taint of official lawlessness. The policies underlying the Fifth Amendment's privilege against self-incrimination are not diminished simply because testimony is compelled to protect the public's safety. The majority should not be permitted to elude the Amendment's absolute prohibition simply by calculating special costs that arise when the public's safety is at issue. Indeed, were constitutional adjudication always conducted in such an ad hoc manner, the Bill of Rights would be a most unreliable protector of individual liberties.

---

[9] I also seriously question how often a statement linking a suspect to the threat to the public ends up being the crucial and otherwise unprovable element of a criminal prosecution. The facts of the current case illustrate this point. The police arrested respondent Quarles not because he was suspected of carcommitted rape. Had the State elected to prosecute on the rape count alone, petitioner's incriminating statement about the gun would have had no role in the prosecution. Only because the State dropped the rape count and chose to proceed to trial solely on the criminal-possession charge did respondent's answer to Officer Kraft's question become critical.

[10] In this sense, the Fifth Amendment differs fundamentally from the Fourth Amendment, which only cordingly, the various exceptions to the Fourth Amendment permitting warrantless searches under various circumstances should have no analogy in the Fifth Amendment context. Curiously, the majority accepts this point, but persists in limiting the protections of the Fifth Amendment.

## QUESTIONS AND NOTES

**1.** Should the defense attorney have claimed that the confession was involuntary? Why do you suppose he failed to do so?

**2.** Do you think that there was in fact an issue of public safety here? Why? Why not? Should the Supreme Court have substituted its judgment for that of the New York courts on this question?

**3.** If the concern is public safety, are we worried about the time that it takes to administer *Miranda* warnings? If that is not the concern, what is?

**4.** Do you think that the presumption of coercion that *Miranda* created is more or less valid in an emergency situation? Explain.

**5.** Even in the ordinary situation, does a police officer who fails to give *Miranda* warnings flout the Constitution, or is the Constitution only flouted by introducing the confessions at trial?

**6.** If the Constitution leaves room for the police officer to make a calculated choice between administering *Miranda* and using a subsequently obtained confession, or not administering *Miranda* and deriving the benefit of quickly finding the location of a gun, is it accurate (helpful) to think of the officer as being "penalized?"

**7.** How do you calculate the costs and benefits of blurring the theretofore "bright line" *Miranda* rule? Explain.

**8.** Would (should) *Innis* have been resolved as a public safety case if only the State or the Court had though of the argument?

# 17.

# THE RIGHT TO COUNSEL
# AND CONFESSIONS

## A. *Massiah* Revisited

Although *Massiah*, along with *Escobedo*, was generally thought to have been relegated to the scrap heap of history by *Miranda*, in fact, as the following cases show, *Massiah* retains a good deal of vitality. As you read the cases in this chapter, think about what different values *Massiah* and *Miranda* serve. Also think about what triggers a *Massiah* as opposed to a *Miranda* violation, and how, if at all, are the results different. Obviously, if you have forgotten *Massiah*, or if your memory of it is a bit fuzzy, you would be well-advised to reread it. We start with *Brewer v. Williams*.

### Brewer v. Williams
### 430 U.S. 387 (1977)

Mr. Justice STEWART delivered the opinion of the Court.

An Iowa trial jury found the respondent, Robert Williams, guilty of murder. The judgment of conviction was affirmed in the Iowa Supreme Court by a closely divided vote. In a subsequent habeas corpus proceeding a Federal District Court ruled that under the United States Constitution Williams is entitled to a new trial, and a divided Court of Appeals for the Eighth Circuit agreed. The question before us is whether the District Court and the Court of Appeals were wrong.

I

On the afternoon of December 24, 1968, a 10-year-old girl named Pamela Powers went with her family to the YMCA in Des Moines, Iowa, to watch a wrestling tournament in which her brother was participating. When she failed to return from a trip to the washroom, a search for her began. The search was unsuccessful.

Robert Williams, who had recently escaped from a mental hospital, was a resident of the YMCA. Soon after the girl's disappearance Williams was seen in the YMCA lobby carrying some clothing and a large bundle wrapped in a blanket. He obtained help from a 14-year-old boy in opening the street door of the YMCA and the door to his automobile parked outside. When Williams placed the bundle in the front seat of his car the boy "saw two legs in it and they were skinny and white." Before anyone could see what was in the bundle Williams drove away. His abandoned car was found the following day in Davenport, Iowa, roughly 160 miles east of Des Moines. A warrant was then issued in Des Moines for his arrest on a charge of abduction.

On the morning of December 26, a Des Moines lawyer named Henry McKnight went to the Des Moines police station and informed the officers present that he had just received a long-distance call from Williams, and that he had advised Williams to turn himself in to the Davenport police. Williams did surrender that morning to the police in Davenport, and they booked him on the charge specified in the arrest warrant and gave him the warnings required by *Miranda*. The Davenport police then telephoned their counterparts in Des Moines to inform them that Williams had surrendered. McKnight, the lawyer, was still at the Des Moines police headquarters, and Williams conversed with McKnight on the telephone. In the presence of the Des Moines chief of police and a police detective named Leaming, McKnight advised Williams that Des Moines police officers would be driving to Davenport to pick him up, that the officers would not interrogate him or mistreat him, and that Williams was not to talk to the officers about Pamela Powers until after consulting with McKnight upon his return to Des Moines. As a result of these conversations, it was agreed between McKnight and the Des Moines police officials that Detective Leaming and a fellow officer would drive to Davenport to pick up Williams, that they would bring him directly back to Des Moines, and that they would not question him during the trip.

In the meantime Williams was arraigned before a judge in Davenport on the outstanding arrest warrant. The judge advised him of his *Miranda* rights and committed him to jail. Before leaving the courtroom, Williams conferred with a lawyer named Kelly, who advised him not to make any statements until consulting with McKnight back in Des Moines.

Detective Leaming and his fellow officer arrived in Davenport about noon to pick up Williams and return him to Des Moines. Soon after their arrival they met with Williams and Kelly, who, they understood, was acting as Williams' lawyer. Detective Leaming repeated the *Miranda* warnings, and told Williams:

"[W]e both know that you're being represented here by Mr. Kelly and you're being represented by Mr. McKnight in Des Moines, and . . . I want you to remember this because we'll be visiting between here and Des Moines."

Williams then conferred again with Kelly alone, and after this conference Kelly reiterated to Detective Leaming that Williams was not to be questioned about the disappearance of Pamela Powers until after he had consulted with McKnight back in Des Moines. When Leaming expressed some reservations, Kelly firmly stated that the agreement with McKnight was to be carried out that there was to be no interrogation of Williams during the automobile journey to Des Moines. Kelly was denied permission to ride in the police car back to Des Moines with Williams and the two officers.

The two detectives, with Williams in their charge, then set out on the 160-mile drive. At no time during the trip did Williams express a willingness to be interrogated in the absence of an attorney. Instead, he stated several times that "[w]hen I get to Des Moines and see Mr. McKnight, I am going to tell you the whole story." Detective Leaming knew that Williams was a former mental patient, and knew also that he was deeply religious.

The detective and his prisoner soon embarked on a wide-ranging conversation covering a variety of topics, including the subject of religion. Then, not long after leaving Davenport and reaching the interstate highway, Detective Leaming delivered what has been referred to in the briefs and oral arguments as the "Christian burial speech." Addressing Williams as "Reverend," the detective said:

"I want to give you something to think about while we're traveling down the road. . . . Number one, I want you to observe the weather conditions, it's raining, it's sleeting, it's freezing, driving is very treacherous, visibility is poor, it's going to be dark early this evening. They are predicting several inches of snow for tonight, and I feel that you yourself are the only person that knows where this little girl's body is, that you yourself have only been there once, and if you get a snow on top of it you yourself may be unable to find it. And, since we will be going right past the area on the way into Des Moines, I feel that we could stop and locate the body, that the parents of this little girl should be entitled to a Christian burial for the little girl who was snatched away from them on Christmas [E]ve and murdered. And I feel we should stop and locate it on the way in rather than waiting until morning and trying to come back out after a snow storm and possibly not being able to find it at all.''

Williams asked Detective Leaming why he thought their route to Des Moines would be taking them past the girl's body, and Leaming responded that he knew the body was in the area of Mitchellville a town they would be passing on the way to Des Moines.[1] Leaming then stated: ''I do not want you to answer me. I don't want to discuss it any further. Just think about it as we're riding down the road.''

As the car approached Grinnell, a town approximately 100 miles west of Davenport, Williams asked whether the police had found the victim's shoes. When Detective Leaming replied that he was unsure, Williams directed the officers to a service station where he said he had left the shoes; a search for them proved unsuccessful. As they continued towards Des Moines, Williams asked whether the police had found the blanket, and directed the officers to a rest area where he said he had disposed of the blanket. Nothing was found. The car continued towards Des Moines, and as it approached Mitchellville, Williams said that he would show the officers where the body was. He then directed the police to the body of Pamela Powers.

## II

### B

[T]here is no need to review in this case the doctrine of *Miranda*, a doctrine designed to secure the constitutional privilege against compulsory self-incrimination. It is equally unnecessary to evaluate the ruling of the District Court that Williams' self-incriminating statements were, indeed, involuntarily made. Cf. *Spano.* For it is clear that the judgment before us must in any event be affirmed upon the ground that Williams was deprived of a different constitutional right—the right to the assistance of counsel.

There has occasionally been a difference of opinion within the Court as to the peripheral scope of this constitutional right. But its basic contours, which are identical in state and federal contexts, are too well established to require extensive elaboration here. Whatever else it may mean, the right to counsel granted by the Sixth and Fourteenth Amendments

means at least that a person is entitled to the help of a lawyer at or after the time that judicial proceedings have been initiated against him ''whether by way of formal charge, preliminary hearing, indictment, information, or arraignment.'' *Massiah.*

There can be no doubt in the present case that judicial proceedings had been initiated against Williams before the start of the automobile ride from Davenport to Des Moines. A warrant had been issued for his arrest, he had been arraigned on that warrant before a judge in a Davenport courtroom, and he had been committed by the court to confinement in jail. The State does not contend otherwise.

There can be no serious doubt, either, that Detective Leaming deliberately and designedly set out to elicit information from Williams just as surely as—and perhaps more effectively than—if he had formally interrogated him. Detective Leaming was fully aware before departing for Des Moines that Williams was being represented in Davenport by Kelly and in Des Moines by McKnight. Yet he purposely sought during Williams' isolation from his lawyers to obtain as much incriminating information as possible. Indeed, Detective Leaming conceded as much when he testified at Williams' trial:

> ''Q. In fact, Captain, whether he was a mental patient or not, you were trying to get all the information you could before he got to his lawyer, weren't you?
>
> ''A. I was sure hoping to find out where that little girl was, yes, sir.
>
> ''Q. Well, I'll put it this way: You was [*sic*] hoping to get all the information you could before Williams got back to McKnight, weren't you?
>
> ''A. Yes, sir.''[2]

The state courts clearly proceeded upon the hypothesis that Detective Leaming's ''Christian burial

---

[1] The fact of the matter, of course, was that Detective Leaming possessed no such knowledge.

[2] Counsel for petitioner, in the course of oral argument in this Court, acknowledged that the ''Christian burial speech'' was tantamount to interrogation:

> ''Q: But isn't the point, really, Mr. Attorney General, what you indicated earlier, and that is that the officer wanted to elicit information from Williams—
>
> ''A: Yes, sir.
>
> ''Q: —by whatever techniques he used, I would suppose a lawyer would consider that he were pursuing interrogation.
>
> ''A: It is, but it was very brief.''

speech'' had been tantamount to interrogation. Both courts recognized that Williams had been entitled to the assistance of counsel at the time he made the incriminating statements. Yet no such constitutional protection would have come into play if there had been no interrogation.

That the incriminating statements were elicited surreptitiously in the *Massiah* case, and otherwise here, is constitutionally irrelevant. Rather, the clear rule of *Massiah* is that once adversary proceedings have commenced against an individual, he has a right to legal representation when the government interrogates him.[8] It thus requires no wooden or technical application of the *Massiah* doctrine to conclude that Williams was entitled to the assistance of counsel guaranteed to him by the Sixth and Fourteenth Amendments.

### III

The Iowa courts recognized that Williams had been denied the constitutional right to the assistance of counsel. They held, however, that he had waived that right during the course of the automobile trip from Davenport to Des Moines. The state trial court explained its determination of waiver as follows:

> "The time element involved on the trip, the general circumstances of it, and more importantly the absence on the Defendant's part of any assertion of his right or desire not to give information absent the presence of his attorney, are the main foundations for the Court's conclusion that he voluntarily waived such right."

We conclude that the Court of Appeals was correct in holding that the record in this case falls far

---

[8] The only other significant factual difference between the present case and *Massiah* is that here the police had *agreed* that they would not interrogate Williams in the absence of his counsel. This circumstance plainly provides petitioner with no argument for distinguishing away the protection afforded by *Massiah*.

It is argued that this agreement may not have been an enforceable one. But we do not deal here with notions of offer, acceptance, consideration, or other concepts of the law of contracts. We deal with constitutional law. And every court that has looked at this case has found an "agreement" in the sense of a commitment made by the Des Moines police officers that Williams would not be questioned about Pamela Powers in the absence of his counsel.

short of sustaining petitioner's burden [of proving waiver]. It is true that Williams had been informed of and appeared to understand his right to counsel. But waiver requires not merely comprehension but relinquishment, and Williams' consistent reliance upon the advice of counsel in dealing with the authorities refutes any suggestion that he waived that right. He consulted McKnight by long-distance telephone before turning himself in. He spoke with McKnight by telephone again shortly after being booked. After he was arraigned, Williams sought out and obtained legal advice from Kelly. Williams again consulted with Kelly after Detective Leaming and his fellow officer arrived in Davenport. Throughout, Williams was advised not to make any statements before seeing McKnight in Des Moines, and was assured that the police had agreed not to question him. His statements while in the car that he would tell the whole story *after* seeing McKnight in Des Moines were the clearest expressions by Williams himself that he desired the presence of an attorney before any interrogation took place. But even before making these statements, Williams had effectively asserted his right to counsel by having secured attorneys at both ends of the automobile trip, both of whom, acting as his agents, had made clear to the police that no interrogation was to occur during the journey. Williams knew of that agreement and, particularly in view of his consistent reliance on counsel, there is no basis for concluding that he disavowed it.[10]

Despite Williams' express and implicit assertions of his right to counsel, Detective Leaming proceeded to elicit incriminating statements from Williams. Leaming did not preface this effort by telling Williams that he had a right to the presence of a lawyer, and made no effort at all to ascertain whether Williams wished to relinquish that right. The circumstances of record in this case thus provide no reasonable basis for finding that Williams waived his right to the assistance of counsel.

---

[10] Cf. *Mosley*, (White, J., concurring in result):

"[T]he reasons to keep the lines of communication between the authorities and the accused open when the accused has chosen to make his own decisions are not present when he indicates instead that he wishes legal advice with respect thereto. The authorities may then communicate with him through an attorney. More to the point, the accused having expressed his own view that he is not competent to deal with the authorities without legal ad-

The Court of Appeals did not hold, nor do we, that under the circumstances of this case Williams *could not*, without notice to counsel, have waived his rights under the Sixth and Fourteenth Amendments. It only held, as do we, that he did not.

### IV

The crime of which Williams was convicted was senseless and brutal, calling for swift and energetic action by the police to apprehend the perpetrator and gather evidence with which he could be convicted. No mission of law enforcement officials is more important. Yet "[d]isinterested zeal for the public good does not assure either wisdom or right in the methods it pursues." Although we do not lightly affirm the issuance of a writ of habeas corpus in this case, so clear a violation of the Sixth and Fourteenth Amendments as here occurred cannot be condoned. The pressures on state executive and judicial officers charged with the administration of the criminal law are great, especially when the crime is murder and the victim a small child. But it is precisely the predictability of those pressures that makes imperative a resolute loyalty to the guarantees that the Constitution extends to us all.

The judgment of the Court of Appeals is affirmed.[12]

---

vice, a later decision at the authorities' insistence to make a statement without counsel's presence may properly be viewed with skepticism."

[12] The District Court stated that its decision "does not touch upon the issue of what evidence, if any, beyond the incriminating statements themselves must be excluded as 'fruit of the poisonous tree.'" We, too, have no occasion to address this issue, and in the present posture of the case there is no basis for the view of our dissenting Brethren, that any attempt to retry the respondent would probably be futile. While neither Williams' incriminating statements themselves nor any testimony describing his having led the police to the victim's body can constitutionally be admitted into evidence, evidence of where the body was found and of its condition might well be admissible on the theory that the body would have been discovered in any event, even had incriminating statements not been elicited from Williams. Cf. *Killough v. United States*, 119 U.S.App.D.C. 10, 336 F.2d 929. In the event that a retrial is instituted, it will be for the state courts in the first instance to determine whether particular items of evidence may be admitted.

Mr. Justice MARSHALL, concurring.

I concur wholeheartedly in my Brother Stewart's opinion for the Court, but add these words in light of the dissenting opinions filed today. The dissenters have, I believe, lost sight of the fundamental constitutional backbone of our criminal law. They seem to think that Detective Leaming's actions were perfectly proper, indeed laudable, examples of "good police work." In my view, good police work is something far different from catching the criminal at any price. It is equally important that the police, as guardians of the law, fulfill their responsibility to obey its commands scrupulously. For "in the end life and liberty can be as much endangered from illegal methods used to convict those thought to be criminals as from the actual criminals themselves." *Spano*.

In this case, there can be no doubt that Detective Leaming consciously and knowingly set out to violate Williams' Sixth Amendment right to counsel and his Fifth Amendment privilege against self-incrimination, as Leaming himself understood those rights. Leaming knew that Williams had been advised by two lawyers not to make any statements to police until he conferred in Des Moines with his attorney there, Mr. McKnight. Leaming surely understood, because he had overheard McKnight tell Williams as much, that the location of the body would be revealed to police. Undoubtedly Leaming realized the way in which that information would be conveyed to the police: McKnight would learn it from his client and then he would lead police to the body. Williams would thereby be protected by the attorney-client privilege from incriminating himself by directly demonstrating his knowledge of the body's location, and the unfortunate Powers child could be given a "Christian burial."

Of course, this scenario would accomplish all that Leaming sought from his investigation except that it would not produce incriminating statements or actions from Williams. Accordingly, Leaming undertook his charade to pry such evidence from Williams. After invoking the no-passengers rule to prevent attorney Kelly from accompanying the prisoner, Leaming had Williams at his mercy: during the three- or four-hour trip he could do anything he wished to elicit a confession. The detective demonstrated once again "that the efficiency of the rack and the thumbscrew can be matched, given the proper subject by more sophisticated modes of 'persuasion.'"

Leaming knowingly isolated Williams from the protection of his lawyers and during that period he intentionally "persuaded" him to give incriminating evidence. It is this intentional police misconduct — not good police practice — that the Court rightly condemns. The heinous nature of the crime is no excuse, as the dissenters would have it, for condoning knowing and intentional police transgression of the constitutional rights of a defendant. If Williams is to go free — and given the ingenuity of Iowa prosecutors on retrial or in a civil commitment proceeding, I doubt very much that there is any chance a dangerous criminal will be loosed on the streets, the bloodcurdling cries of the dissents notwithstanding — it will hardly be because he deserves it. It will be because Detective Leaming, knowing full well that he risked reversal of Williams' conviction, intentionally denied Williams the right of *every* American under the Sixth Amendment to have the protective shield of a lawyer between himself and the awesome power of the State.

Mr. Justice POWELL, concurring.

As the dissenting opinion of The Chief Justice sharply illustrates, resolution of the issues in this case turns primarily on one's perception of the facts. There is little difference of opinion, among the several courts and numerous judges who have reviewed the case, as to the relevant constitutional principles: (i) Williams had the right to assistance of counsel; (ii) once that right attached (it is conceded that it had in this case), the State could not properly interrogate Williams in the absence of counsel unless he voluntarily and knowingly waived the right; and (iii) the burden was on the State to show that Williams in fact had waived the right before the police interrogated him.

After finding, upon a full review of the facts, that there had been "interrogation," the District Court addressed the ultimate issue of "waiver" and concluded not only that the State had failed to carry its burden but also that

> "there is *nothing* in the record to indicate that [Williams] waived his Fifth and Sixth Amendment rights *except* the fact that statements eventually were obtained." (Emphasis in original.)

The Court of Appeals stated affirmatively that "the facts as found by the District Court had substantial basis in the record."[1]

---

[1] Before concluding that the police had engaged in interrogation, the District Court summarized the factual background:

> "Detective Leaming obtained statements from Petitioner in the absence of counsel (1) after making, and then breaking, an agree-

I join the opinion of the Court which also finds that the efforts of Detective Leaming "to elicit information from Williams," as conceded by counsel for petitioner at oral argument, were a skillful and effective form of interrogation. Moreover, the entire setting was conducive to the psychological coercion that was successfully exploited. Williams was known by the police to be a young man with quixotic religious convictions and a history of mental disorders. The date was the day after Christmas, the weather was ominous, and the setting appropriate for Detective Leaming's talk of snow concealing the body and preventing a "Christian burial." Williams was alone in the automobile with two police officers for several hours. It is clear from the record, as both of the federal courts below found, that there was no evidence of a knowing and voluntary waiver of the right to have counsel present beyond the fact that Williams ultimately confessed. It is settled law that an inferred waiver of a constitutional right is disfavored. I find no basis in the record of this case — or in the dissenting opinions — for disagreeing with the conclusion of the District Court that "the State has produced no affirmative evidence whatsoever to support its claim of waiver."

The dissenting opinion of The Chief Justice states that the Court's holding today "conclusively presumes a suspect is legally incompetent to change his mind and tell the truth until an attorney is present." I find no justification for this view. On the contrary, the opinion of the Court is explicitly clear that the right to assistance of counsel may be waived, after it has attached, without notice to or consultation with counsel. We would have such a case here if petitioner had proved that the police officers refrained

---

ment with Mr. McKnight that Petitioner would not be questioned until he arrived in Des Moines and saw Mr. McKnight; (2) after being told by both Mr. McKnight and Mr. Kelly that Petitioner was not to be questioned until he reached Des Moines; (3) after refusing to allow Mr. Kelly, whom Detective Leaming himself regarded as Petitioner's co-counsel, to ride to Des Moines with Petitioner; and (4) after being told by Petitioner that he would talk *after* he reached Des Moines and Mr. McKnight. By violating or ignoring these several, clear indications that Petitioner was to have counsel during interrogation, Detective Leaming deprived Petitioner of his right to counsel in a way similar to, if not more objectionable than, that utilized against the defendant in *Massiah*."

from coercion and interrogation, as they had agreed, and that Williams freely on his own initiative had confessed the crime.

Mr. Justice STEVENS, concurring.

Mr. Justice Stewart, in his opinion for the Court which I join, Mr. Justice Powell, and Mr. Justice Marshall have accurately explained the reasons why the law requires the result we reach today. Nevertheless, the strong language in the dissenting opinions prompts me to add this brief comment about the Court's function in a case such as this.

Nothing that we write, no matter how well reasoned or forcefully expressed, can bring back the victim of this tragedy or undo the consequences of the official neglect which led to the respondent's escape from a state mental institution. The emotional aspects of the case make it difficult to decide dispassionately, but do not qualify our obligation to apply the law with an eye to the future as well as with concern for the result in the particular case before us.

Underlying the surface issues in this case is the question whether a fugitive from justice can rely on his lawyer's advice given in connection with a decision to surrender voluntarily. The defendant placed his trust in an experienced Iowa trial lawyer who in turn trusted the Iowa law enforcement authorities to honor a commitment made during negotiations which led to the apprehension of a potentially dangerous person. Under any analysis, this was a critical stage of the proceeding in which the participation of an independent professional was of vital importance to the accused and to society. At this stage—as in countless others in which the law profoundly affects the life of the individual—the lawyer is the essential medium through which the demands and commitments of the sovereign are communicated to the citizen. If, in the long run, we are seriously concerned about the individuals effective representation by counsel, the State cannot be permitted to dishonor its promise to this lawyer.*

Mr. Chief Justice BURGER, dissenting.

The result in this case ought to be intolerable in any society which purports to call itself an organized society. It continues the Court—by the narrowest margin—on the much-criticized course of punishing the public for the mistakes and misdeeds of law enforcement officers, instead of punishing the officer

---

* The importance of this point is emphasized by the State's refusal to permit counsel to accompany his client on the trip from Davenport to Des Moines.

directly, if in fact he is guilty of wrongdoing. It mechanically and blindly keeps reliable evidence from juries whether the claimed constitutional violation involves gross police misconduct or honest human error.

Williams is guilty of the savage murder of a small child; no member of the Court contends he is not. While in custody, and after no fewer than *five* warnings of his rights to silence and to counsel, he led police to the concealed body of his victim. The Court concedes Williams was not threatened or coerced and that he spoke and acted voluntarily and with full awareness of his constitutional rights. In the face of all this, the Court now holds that because Williams was prompted by the detective's statement—not interrogation but a statement—the jury must not be told how the police found the body.

Today's holding fulfills Judge (later Mr. Justice) Cardozo's grim prophecy that someday some court might carry the exclusionary rule to the absurd extent that its operative effect would exclude evidence relating to the body of a murder victim because of the means by which it was found.[1] In so ruling the Court regresses to playing a grisly game of "hide and seek," once more exalting the sporting theory

---

[1] "The criminal is to go free because the constable has blundered. . . . A room is searched against the law, and the body of a murdered man is found. . . . The privacy of the home has been infringed, and the murderer goes free." *People v. Defore*, 242 N.Y. 13, 21, 23-24, 150 N.E. 585, 587, 588 (1926).

The Court protests, *ante*, n.12, that its holding excludes only "Williams' incriminating statements themselves [as well as] any testimony describing his having led the police to the victim's body," thus hinting that successful retrial of this palpably guilty felon is realistically possible. Even if this were all, and the *corpus delicti* could be used to establish the fact and manner of the victim's death, the Court's holding clearly bars all efforts to let the jury know how the police found the body. But the Court's further and remarkable statement that "evidence of where the body was found and of its condition" could be admitted *only* "on the theory that the body would have been discovered in any event" makes clear that the Court is determined to keep the truth from the jurors pledged to find the truth. If all use of the *corpus delicti* is to be barred by the Court as "fruit of the poisonous tree," except on the unlikely theory suggested by the Court, the Court renders the prospects of doing justice in this case exceedingly remote.

of criminal justice which has been experiencing a decline in our jurisprudence. With Justices White, Blackmun, and Rehnquist, I categorically reject the remarkable notion that the police in this case were guilty of unconstitutional misconduct, or any conduct justifying the bizarre result reached by the Court.

Under well-settled precedents which the Court freely acknowledges, it is very clear that Williams had made a valid waiver of his Fifth Amendment right to silence and his Sixth Amendment right to counsel when he led police to the child's body. Indeed, even under the Court's analysis I do not understand how a contrary conclusion is possible.

One plausible but unarticulated basis for the result reached is that once a suspect has asserted his right not to talk without the presence of an attorney, it becomes legally impossible for him to waive that right until he has seen an attorney. But constitutional rights are *personal*, and an otherwise valid waiver should not be brushed aside by judges simply because an attorney was not present. The Court's holding operates to "imprison a man in his privileges; " it conclusively presumes a suspect is legally incompetent to change his mind and tell the truth until an attorney is present. It denigrates an individual to a nonperson whose free will has become hostage to a lawyer so that until the lawyer consents, the suspect is deprived of any legal right or power to decide for himself that he wishes to make a disclosure. It denies that the rights to counsel and silence are personal, nondelegable, and subject to a waiver only by that individual. The opinions in support of the Court's judgment do not enlighten us as to why police conduct whether good or bad should operate to suspend Williams' right to change his mind and "tell all" at once rather than waiting until he reached Des Moines.

In any case, the Court assures us this is not at all what it intends, and that a valid waiver was *possible* in these circumstances, but was not quite made. Here, of course, Williams did not confess to the murder in so many words; it was his conduct in guiding police to the body, not his words, which incriminated him. And the record is replete with evidence that Williams knew precisely what he was doing when he guided police to the body. The human urge to confess wrongdoing is, of course, normal in all save hardened, professional criminals, as psychiatrists and analysts have demonstrated.

Mr. Justice WHITE, with whom Mr. Justice BLACKMUN and Mr. Justice REHNQUIST join, dissenting.

The respondent in this case killed a 10-year-old child. The majority sets aside his conviction, holding that certain statements of unquestioned reliability were unconstitutionally obtained from him, and under the circumstances probably makes it impossible to retry him. Because there is nothing in the Constitution or in our previous cases which requires the Court's action, I dissent.

The majority recognizes that even after his "assertion" of his right to counsel, it would have found that respondent waived his right not to talk in counsel's absence if his waiver had been express — *i.e.*, if the officers had asked him in the car whether he would be willing to answer questions in counsel's absence and if he had answered "yes."[1] But waiver is not a formalistic concept. Waiver is shown whenever the facts establish that an accused knew of a right and intended to relinquish it. Such waiver, even if not express, was plainly shown here. The only other conceivable basis for the majority's holding is the implicit suggestion that the right involved in *Massiah*, as distinguished from the right involved in *Miranda*, is a right not to be *asked* any questions in counsel's absence rather than a right not to *answer* any questions in counsel's absence, and that the right not to be *asked* questions must be waived *before* the questions are asked. Such wafer-thin distinctions cannot determine whether a guilty murderer should go free. The only conceivable purpose for the presence of counsel during questioning is to protect an accused from making incriminating *answers*. Questions, unanswered, have no significance at all. Absent coercion[6] — no matter how the right involved is

---

[1] It does not matter whether the right not to make statements in the absence of counsel stems from *Massiah* or *Miranda*. In either case the question is one of waiver. Waiver was not addressed in *Massiah* because there the statements were being made to an informant and the defendant had no way of knowing that he had a right not to talk to him without counsel. (footnote repositioned - ed.)

[6] There is a rigid prophylactic rule set forth in *Miranda* that once an arrestee requests presence of counsel at questioning, *questioning* must cease. The rule depends on an indication by the accused that he will be unable to handle the decision whether or not to answer questions without advice of counsel, see *Mosley*, (White, J., concurring), and is inapplicable to this case for two reasons. First, at no time did

defined—an accused is amply protected by a rule requiring waiver before or simultaneously with the giving by him of an answer or the making by him of a statement.

The consequence of the majority's decision is, as the majority recognizes, extremely serious. A mentally disturbed killer whose guilt is not in question may be released. Why? Apparently the answer is that the majority believes that the law enforcement officers acted in a way which involves some risk of injury to society and that such conduct should be deterred. However, the officers' conduct did not, and was not likely to, jeopardize the fairness of respondent's trial or in any way risk the conviction of an innocent man—the risk against which the Sixth Amendment guarantee of assistance of counsel is designed to protect. The police did nothing "wrong," let alone anything "unconstitutional." To anyone not lost in the intricacies of the prophylactic rules of *Miranda*, the result in this case seems utterly senseless; and for the reasons stated, *supra*, even applying those rules as well as the rule of *Massiah*, the statements made by respondent were properly admitted. In light of these considerations, the majority's protest that the result in this case is justified by a "clear violation" of the Sixth and Fourteenth Amendments has a distressing hollow ring. I respectfully dissent.

Mr. Justice BLACKMUN, with whom Mr. Justice WHITE and Mr. Justice REHNQUIST join, dissenting.

---

*respondent* indicate a desire not to be asked questions outside the presence of his counsel—notwithstanding the fact that he was told that he and the officers would be "visiting in the car." The majority concludes, although studiously avoiding reliance on *Miranda*, that respondent *asserted* his right to counsel. This he did in some respects, but he never, himself, asserted a right not to be questioned in the absence of counsel. Second, as is noted in the dissenting opinion of Mr. Justice Blackmun, respondent was not questioned. The rigid prophylactic rule as the majority implicitly recognizes is designed solely to prevent involuntary waivers of the right against self-incrimination and is not to be applied to a statement by a law enforcement officer accompanied by a request by the officer that the accused make no response followed by more than an hour of silence and an apparently spontaneous statement on a subject—the victim's shoes—not broached in the "speech." Under such circumstances there is not even a small risk that the waiver will be involuntary.

I disagree that respondent Williams' situation was in the mold of *Massiah*, that is, that it was dominated by a denial to Williams of his Sixth Amendment right to counsel after criminal proceedings had been instituted against him. The Court rules that the Sixth Amendment was violated because Detective Leaming "purposely sought during Williams' isolation from his lawyers to obtain as much incriminating information as possible." I cannot regard that as unconstitutional *per se*.

First, the police did not deliberately seek to isolate Williams from his lawyers so as to deprive him of the assistance of counsel. Cf. *Escobedo*. The isolation in this case was a necessary incident of transporting Williams to the county where the crime was committed.

Second, Leaming's purpose was not solely to obtain incriminating evidence. The victim had been missing for only two days, and the police could not be certain that she was dead. Leaming, of course, and in accord with his duty, was "hoping to find out where that little girl was," but such motivation does not equate with an intention to evade the Sixth Amendment. Moreover, the Court seems to me to place an undue emphasis and aspersion on what it and the lower courts have chosen to call the "Christian burial speech," and on Williams' "deeply religious" convictions.

Third, not every attempt to elicit information should be regarded as "tantamount to interrogation." I am not persuaded that Leaming's observations and comments, made as the police car traversed the snowy and slippery miles between Davenport and Des Moines that winter afternoon, were an interrogation, direct or subtle, of Williams. Contrary to this Court's statement, the Iowa Supreme Court appears to me to have thought and held otherwise, and I agree. Williams, after all, was counseled by lawyers, and warned by the arraigning judge in Davenport and by the police, and yet it was he who started the travel conversations and brought up the subject of the criminal investigation. Without further reviewing the circumstances of the trip, I would say it is clear there was no interrogation. In this respect, I am in full accord with Judge Webster in his vigorous dissent, and with the views implicitly indicated by Chief Judge Gibson and Judge Stephenson, who joined him in voting for rehearing en banc.

In summary, it seems to me that the Court is holding that *Massiah* is violated whenever police engage in any conduct, in the absence of counsel, with the subjective desire to obtain information from a suspect after arraignment. Such a rule is far too broad. Persons in custody frequently volunteer statements in response to stimuli other than interrogation. When there is no interrogation, such statements should be admissible as long as they are truly voluntary.[3]

The *Massiah* point thus being of no consequence, I would vacate the judgment of the Court of Appeals and remand the case for consideration of the issue of voluntariness, in the constitutional sense, of Williams' statements, an issue the Court of Appeals did not reach when the case was before it.

---

[3] With all deference to the Court, I do not agree that *Massiah* regarded it as "constitutionally irrelevant" that the statements in that case were surreptitiously obtained. The *Massiah* opinion quoted with approval the dissenting Circuit Judge's statement that "Massiah was more seriously imposed upon . . . because he did not even know that he was under interrogation by a government agent."

One final word: I can understand the discomfiture the Court obviously suffers and expresses in Part IV of its opinion. This was a brutal, tragic, and heinous crime inflicted upon a young girl on the afternoon of the day before Christmas. With the exclusionary rule operating as the Court effectuates it, the decision today probably means that, as a practical matter, no new trial will be possible at this date eight years after the crime, and that this respondent necessarily will go free. That, of course, is not the standard by which a case of this kind strictly is to be judged. But, as Judge Webster in dissent below observed, placing the case in sensible and proper perspective: "The evidence of Williams' guilt was overwhelming. No challenge is made to the reliability of the fact finding process." I am in full agreement with that observation.

## QUESTIONS AND NOTES

**1.** Do you think that Leaming's course of conduct constituted good police work? Would your answer be any different if the dissent had prevailed?

**2.** Did Leaming break his promise to defense counsel? Explain. Should your answer to this question have any relevance to the resolution of the ultimate issue?

**3.** In any event, should Williams' statements about the shoes and blanket be admissible? Why? Why not?

**4.** How would (should) this case have been decided if it were a *Miranda* case? Explain.

**5.** What makes this case a *Massiah* case?

**6.** Is it clear that the "Christian burial speech" was a charade? Explain.

**7.** Is it clear that Williams intended to confess to murder? Is it even clear that he was guilty? Explain. Should your answer to this question be relevant to the resolution of this case? Why? Why not?

**8.** Do you think that Williams waived his right to counsel? Why? Why not?

**9.** In conjunction with question 8, consider Justice White's footnote 6, and surrounding and preceding text. Is Justice White or the Court more guilty of drawing wafer-thin distinctions?

**10.** We will return to the next phase of this case later (*Nix v. Williams*, Chapter 22, *infra*) to examine the admissibility of the victim's body.

**11.** We next turn to *Moulton*, which revives, and arguably expands, *Massiah*.

# Maine v. Moulton
## 474 U.S. 159 (1985)

Justice BRENNAN delivered the opinion of the Court.

The question presented in this case is whether respondent's Sixth Amendment right to the assistance of counsel was violated by the admission at trial of incriminating statements made by him to his codefendant, a secret government informant, after indictment and at a meeting of the two to plan defense strategy for the upcoming trial.

### I

On the night of January 15, 1981, police officers in Belfast, Maine, responded to a fire call in the vicinity of the Belfast Dodge automobile dealership. Arriving at the scene, the officers discovered a burning Chevrolet dump truck which they recognized as a vehicle that had been reported stolen. After examining the burning truck, the officers searched a building located on the Belfast Dodge property. This building was not part of the dealership, but was leased to respondent Perley Moulton and his codefendant Gary Colson who were using the space to restore and sell old Ford Mustangs. Inside, the officers discovered evidence of several recent automobile and automobile-related thefts.

On April 7, 1981, a Waldo County grand jury returned indictments charging Moulton and Colson with four counts of theft. Specifically, the indictments alleged that Moulton and Colson received, retained, or disposed of a 1978 Ford pickup truck, a 1978 Chevrolet dump truck, a 1970 Ford Mustang automobile, and assorted Ford Motor Company automotive parts knowing these to be stolen and intending to deprive the owners of possession. On April 9, Moulton and Colson, represented by retained counsel, appeared before the Maine Superior Court for Waldo County and entered pleas of not guilty. Both were enlarged on bail pending trial. Numerous proceedings, unnecessary to detail here, occurred during the ensuing year and a half.

On November 4, 1982, Colson complained by telephone to Robert Keating, Chief of the Belfast Police Department, that he had received anonymous threatening telephone calls regarding the charges pending against him and Moulton, and indicated that he wished to talk to the police about the charges. Keating told Colson to speak with his lawyer and to call back.

On November 6, Colson met with Moulton at a Belfast restaurant to plan for their upcoming trial. According to Colson, Moulton suggested the possibility of killing Gary Elwell, a State's witness, and they discussed how to commit the murder.

On November 9 and 10, Colson, accompanied by his lawyer, met with Police Chief Keating and State Police Detective Rexford Kelley. At these meetings, Colson gave full confessions of his participation with Moulton in committing the crimes for which they had been indicted. In addition, Colson admitted that he and Moulton had not merely received stolen automotive parts, but also had broken into the local Ford dealership to steal the parts. Colson also stated that he and Moulton had set fire to the dump truck and had committed other thefts. The officers offered Colson a deal: no further charges would be brought against him if he would testify against Moulton and otherwise cooperate in the prosecution of Moulton on the pending charges. Colson agreed to cooperate.[2]

Moulton asked Colson to set aside an entire day so that the two of them could meet and plan their defense. They agreed to meet on Sunday, December 26. [T]he police obtained Colson's consent to be equipped with a body wire transmitter to record what was said at the meeting. Chief Keating later testified that he did this for Colson's safety in case Moulton realized that Colson was cooperating with the police, and to record any further conversation concerning threats to witnesses. Keating also testified that he was aware that Moulton and Colson were meeting to discuss the charges for which Moulton was already under indictment. Colson was instructed "not to attempt to question Perley Moulton, just be himself in his conversation. . . ."

The December 26 meeting, as was to be expected, consisted of a prolonged discussion of the pending charges—what actually had occurred, what the State's evidence would show, and what Moulton and Colson should do to obtain a verdict of acquittal.

---

[2] Seven months after the conclusion of Moulton's trial, Colson pleaded guilty to two counts of theft. The prosecutor recommended that Colson be sentenced to 2 years' imprisonment, all but 15 days to be suspended, and placed on probation for 2 years. Colson also agreed to make restitution up to $2,000 during the probationary period. The trial court accepted this recommendation and sentenced Colson accordingly.

The idea of eliminating witnesses was briefly mentioned early in the conversation. After a short discussion, encouraged by Colson,[3] Moulton concluded that he did not think the plan would work. The remainder of the lengthy meeting was spent discussing the case. Moulton and Colson decided to create false alibis as their defense at trial. Because they sought to conform these alibis as closely as possible to what really happened, much of their discussion involved recounting the crimes. Although Colson had described what had happened in detail when he confessed to the police a month earlier, he now frequently professed to be unable to recall the events. Apologizing for his poor memory, he repeatedly asked Moulton to remind him about the details of what had happened, and this technique caused Moulton to make numerous incriminating statements.[4] Nor were all of Colson's memory lapses related to events that required discussion to fabricate convincing alibis. Colson also "reminisced" about events

---

[3] The exchange went as follows:

"[Moulton:] You know I thought of a way to eliminate them. Remember we were talking about it before?

"[Colson:] Yes, you thought of a way?

"[Moulton:] Yeah, but . . . I don't think we ought to go for it."

"[Colson:] Is it foolproof?

"[Moulton:] No.

"[Colson:] Is it, is it fairly foolproof?

"[Moulton:] I like it. I think its just for the . . .

"[Colson:] Well let me [hear it]."

Moulton explained that he had considered using air rifles to shoot poisoned darts and the conversation then turned to joking about a magazine that instructed readers how to build bombs to kill large numbers of people.

[4] Colson began doing this immediately after Moulton vetoed the plan to eliminate witnesses. Colson indicated that he did not have copies of all the discovery materials, and Moulton went outside to his car to get his copies. While Moulton was gone, Colson sighed heavily and whispered "[o]h boy, I just hope I can make it through this" into the microphone. Then, when Moulton returned moments later, Colson immediately stated, slowly and deliberately: "I want you to help me with some dates. One date I cannot remember Caps [Moulton's nickname], just can't remember, I know it was in December, what night did we break into Lothrop Ford? What date?"

surrounding the various thefts, and this technique too elicited additional incriminating statements from Moulton. For example, Colson asked Moulton how many locks they had drilled to steal a truck, a fact obviously not relevant to developing an alibi. Similarly, Colson questioned Moulton about whether it was the Mustang or the pickup truck that did not have a heater. Later, Colson jokingly drew forth admissions from Moulton concerning the dumping of a stolen truck into a pond after it had been scavenged for parts, and the dumping of a load of potatoes from another stolen truck onto the road. Each of these statements was later admitted into evidence against Moulton at trial.

## II

### A

Once the right to counsel has attached and been asserted, the State must of course honor it. This means more than simply that the State cannot prevent the accused from obtaining the assistance of counsel. The Sixth Amendment also imposes on the State an affirmative obligation to respect and preserve the accused's choice to seek this assistance. We have on several occasions been called upon to clarify the scope of the State's obligation in this regard, and have made clear that, at the very least, the prosecutor and police have an affirmative obligation not to act in a manner that circumvents and thereby dilutes the protection afforded by the right to counsel.

[In *Massiah*,] Massiah was indicted, along with a man named Colson,[8] for conspiracy to possess and to distribute cocaine. Massiah retained a lawyer, pleaded not guilty and was released on bail. Colson, meanwhile, decided to cooperate with Government agents in their continuing investigation of the narcotics activity in which Massiah and others were thought to be engaged. Colson permitted a Government agent to install a radio transmitter under the front seat of his automobile. Massiah held a lengthy conversation with Colson in this automobile while a Government agent listened over the radio. Massiah made several incriminating statements, and these were brought before the jury through the testimony of the Government agent. We reversed Massiah's conviction on the ground that the incriminating statements were obtained in violation of Massiah's rights under the Sixth Amendment. The Court stressed the fact that the interview took place after indictment,

---

[8] The parties have taken pains to assure us that Massiah's friend Colson and Moulton's friend Colson are unrelated.

at a time when Massiah was clearly entitled to the assistance of counsel. Relying on Justice Douglas' *Spano* concurrence, the Court concluded that the need for, and consequently the right to, the assistance of counsel applied equally in this extrajudicial setting as at the trial itself. Consequently, the Court held:

> "[Massiah] was denied the basic protections of [the right to the assistance of counsel] when there was used against him at trial evidence of his own incriminating words, which federal agents had deliberately elicited from him after he had been indicted and in the absence of his counsel."

### B

The State contends that the decisive fact in *Massiah* and *United States v. Henry*, 447 U.S. 264 (1980), (discussed in *Kuhlmann v. Wilson, infra*) was that the police set up the confrontation between the accused and a police agent at which incriminating statements were elicited. Supported by the United States as *amicus curiae*, the State maintains that the Sixth Amendment is violated only when police intentionally take this or some equivalent step. Because Moulton rather than Colson requested the December 26 meeting, the State concludes that Moulton's Sixth Amendment rights were not violated here.

[T]he State's attempt to limit our holdings in *Massiah* and *Henry* fundamentally misunderstands the nature of the right we recognized in those cases. The Sixth Amendment guarantees the accused, at least after the initiation of formal charges, the right to rely on counsel as a "medium" between him and the State. As noted above, this guarantee includes the State's affirmative obligation not to act in a manner that circumvents the protections accorded the accused by invoking this right. The determination whether particular action by state agents violates the accused's right to the assistance of counsel must be made in light of this obligation. Thus, the Sixth Amendment is not violated whenever—by luck or happenstance—the State obtains incriminating statements from the accused after the right to counsel has attached. See *Henry*, (Powell, J., concurring). However, knowing exploitation by the State of an opportunity to confront the accused without counsel being present is as much a breach of the State's obligation not to circumvent the right to the assistance of counsel as is the intentional creation of such an opportunity. Accordingly, the Sixth Amendment is violated when the State obtains incriminating statements by knowingly circumventing the accused's

right to have counsel present in a confrontation between the accused and a state agent.[12]

### III

Applying this principle to the case at hand, it is clear that the State violated Moulton's Sixth Amendment right when it arranged to record conversations between Moulton and its undercover informant, Colson. It was the police who suggested to Colson that he record his telephone conversations with Moulton. Having learned from these recordings that Moulton and Colson were going to meet, the police asked Colson to let them put a body wire transmitter on him to record what was said. Police Chief Keating admitted that, when they made this request, the police knew—as they must have known from the recorded telephone conversations—that Moulton and Colson were meeting for the express purpose of discussing the pending charges and planning a defense for the trial.[13] The police thus knew that Moulton would make statements that he had a constitutional right not to make to their agent prior to consulting with counsel. As in *Henry*, the fact that the police were "fortunate enough to have an undercover informant already in close proximity to the accused" does not excuse their conduct under these circumstances. By concealing the fact that Colson was an agent of the State, the police denied Moulton the opportunity

---

[12] Direct proof of the State's knowledge will seldom be available to the accused. However, as *Henry* makes clear, proof that the State "must have known" that its agent was likely to obtain incriminating statements from the accused in the absence of counsel suffices to establish a Sixth Amendment violation.

[13] Because Moulton thought of Colson only as his codefendant, Colson's engaging Moulton in active conversation about their upcoming trial was certain to elicit statements that Moulton would not intentionally reveal—and had a constitutional right not to reveal—to persons known to be police agents. Under these circumstances, Colson's merely participating in this conversation was "the functional equivalent of interrogation." In addition, the tapes disclose and the Supreme Judicial Court of Maine found that Colson "frequently pressed Moulton for details of various thefts and in so doing elicited much incriminating information that the State later used at trial." Thus, as in *Henry*, we need not reach the situation where the "listening post" cannot or does not participate in active conversation and prompt particular replies.

to consult with counsel and thus denied him the assistance of counsel guaranteed by the Sixth Amendment.

## IV

The Solicitor General argues that the incriminating statements obtained by the Maine police nevertheless should not be suppressed because the police had other, legitimate reasons for listening to Moulton's conversations with Colson, namely, to investigate Moulton's alleged plan to kill Gary Elwell and to insure Colson's safety. In *Massiah*, the Government also contended that incriminating statements obtained as a result of its deliberate efforts should not be excluded because law enforcement agents had "the right, if not indeed the duty, to continue their investigation of [Massiah] and his alleged criminal associates. . . ." There, as here, the Government argued that this circumstance justified its surveillance and cured any improper acts or purposes. We rejected this argument, and held:

> "We do not question that in this case, as in many cases, it was entirely proper to continue an investigation of the suspected criminal activities of the defendant and his alleged confederates, even though the defendant had already been indicted. All that we hold is that the defendant's own incriminating statements, obtained by federal agents under the circumstances here disclosed, could not constitutionally be used by the prosecution as evidence against him at his trial."

We reaffirm this holding, which states a sensible solution to a difficult problem. The police have an interest in the thorough investigation of crimes for which formal charges have already been filed. They also have an interest in investigating new or additional crimes. Investigations of either type of crime may require surveillance of individuals already under indictment. Moreover, law enforcement officials investigating an individual suspected of committing one crime and formally charged with having committed another crime obviously seek to discover evidence useful at a trial of either crime. In seeking evidence pertaining to pending charges, however, the Government's investigative powers are limited by the Sixth Amendment rights of the accused. To allow the admission of evidence obtained from the accused in violation of his Sixth Amendment rights whenever the police assert an alternative, legitimate reason for their surveillance invites abuse by law enforcement personnel in the form of fabricated investigations and risks the evisceration of the Sixth

Amendment right recognized in *Massiah*. On the other hand, to exclude evidence pertaining to charges as to which the Sixth Amendment right to counsel had not attached at the time the evidence was obtained, simply because other charges were pending at that time, would unnecessarily frustrate the public's interest in the investigation of criminal activities. Consequently, incriminating statements pertaining to pending charges are inadmissible at the trial of those charges, notwithstanding the fact that the police were also investigating other crimes, if, in obtaining this evidence, the State violated the Sixth Amendment by knowingly circumventing the accused's right to the assistance of counsel.[16]

Because we hold that the Maine police knowingly circumvented Moulton's right to have counsel present at a confrontation between Moulton and a police agent, the fact that the police had additional reasons for recording Moulton's meeting with Colson is irrelevant. The decision of the Supreme Judicial Court of Maine is affirmed.

Chief Justice BURGER, with whom Justice WHITE and Justice REHNQUIST join, and with whom Justice O'CONNOR joins as to Parts I and III, dissenting.

Today the Court holds that the Sixth Amendment prohibits the use at trial of postindictment statements made to a government informant, even where those statements were recorded as part of a good-faith investigation of entirely separate crimes. Nothing whatever in the Constitution or our prior opinions supports this bizarre result, which creates a new "right" only for those possibly habitual offenders who persist in criminal activity even while under indictment for other crimes. I dissent and would reverse.

## II

The Court today concludes that "[t]o allow the admission of evidence obtained from an accused in violation of his Sixth Amendment rights whenever the police assert an alternative, legitimate reason for their surveillance . . . risks the evisceration of the Sixth Amendment right recognized in *Massiah*." With all deference I am bound to state that this conclusion turns the Sixth Amendment on its head by first positing a constitutional violation and then asking whether "alternative, legitimate reasons" for the

---

[16] Incriminating statements pertaining to other crimes, as to which the Sixth Amendment right has not yet attached, are, of course, admissible at a trial of those offenses.

police surveillance are sufficient to justify that constitutional violation. As I see it, if "alternative, legitimate reasons" motivated the surveillance, then no Sixth Amendment violation has occurred. Indeed, if the police had failed to take the steps they took here knowing that Colson was endangering his life by talking to them, in my view they would be subject to censure.

Analysis of this issue must begin with *Hoffa*, not cited in the Court's opinion. In *Hoffa*, the Court held that postindictment statements obtained by a Government informant "relat[ing] to the commission of a quite separate offense" were properly admitted at a subsequent trial for the separate crime. Other courts have also held that *Massiah*, viewed in light of the later-decided *Hoffa* case, does not prohibit the introduction of incriminating statements obtained in good faith by the Government even after an indictment at a trial involving an offense different from that covered by the indictment.

Applying *Hoffa* to the facts of this case, it is clear that the statements obtained by Colson could have been introduced against respondent at a subsequent trial for crimes apart from those for which respondent had already been indicted, such as conspiracy to commit murder or to obstruct justice. The majority concedes as much: "Incriminating statements pertaining to other crimes, as to which the Sixth Amendment right has not yet attached, are, of course, admissible at a trial of those offenses." It follows from this that the State engaged in no impermissible conduct in its investigation of respondent based on Colson's revelations. By recording conversations between respondent and Colson, Chief Keating and Detective Kelley succeeded in obtaining evidence that the Court's opinion concedes could have been used to convict respondent of further crimes. In fact this record shows clearly that, based on the recordings, the State was able to obtain additional indictments against respondent for burglary, arson, and three more thefts. The Court's opinion notes that respondent pleaded guilty to several of the additional indictments secured as a result of pursuing Colson's leads.

Courts ought to applaud the kind of careful and diligent efforts of the police shown by this record. Indeed, the Court's opinion does not suggest that the police should have—or could have—conducted their investigation in any other way. Yet, inexplicably, the Court holds that the highly probative and reliable evidence produced by this wholly legitimate investigation must be excluded from respondent's trial for theft. The anomaly of this position, then, is that the evidence at issue in this case should have

been excluded from respondent's theft trial even though the *same evidence* could have been introduced against *respondent himself* at a trial for separate crimes. Far from being "a sensible solution to a difficult problem," as the Court modestly suggests, it is a judicial aberration conferring a windfall benefit to those who are the subject of criminal investigations for one set of crimes while already under indictment for another. I can think of no reason to turn the Sixth Amendment into a "magic cloak" to protect criminals who engage in multiple offenses that are the subject of separate police investigations.

We have held that no Sixth Amendment violation occurs unless the State "deliberately elicit[s]" comments from the defendant. See *Massiah*; *Henry*. As the foregoing amply demonstrates, however, a finding of "deliberate elicitation" is not the end of the inquiry. In using the phrase "deliberate elicitation," we surely must have intended to denote elicitation for the purpose of using such statements against the defendant in connection with charges for which the Sixth Amendment right to counsel had attached. Here the State indeed set out to elicit information from a defendant, but it was an investigation with respect to crimes other than those for which the defendant then stood indicted. As two courts found, the State recorded the conversations "for legitimate purposes not related to the gathering of evidence concerning the crime for which [respondent] had been indicted."

No prior holding of this Court recognizes a Sixth Amendment violation in such circumstances. As one court has put it, the Sixth Amendment "speaks only to the situation where in the absence of retained counsel, statements are deliberately elicited from a defendant in connection with a crime for which he has already been indicted."[17] Thus, in *Henry, supra*,

---

[17] The Court's opinion seems to read *Massiah* as if it definitively addresses situations where the police are investigating a separate crime. This reading is belied by the *Massiah* Court's statement of its own holding:

"We do not question that in this case, as in many cases, it was entirely proper to continue an investigation of the suspected criminal activities of the defendant and his alleged confederates, even though the defendant had already been indicted. All that we hold is that the defendant's own incriminating statements, obtained by federal agents *under the circumstances here disclosed*, could not constitutionally be used by the prosecution as evidence against *him* at his trial." (first emphasis added).

n. 14, we quoted Disciplinary Rule 7-104(A)(1) of the American Bar Association's Code of Professional Responsibility, which provides that "a lawyer shall not . . . [c]ommunicate or cause another to communicate *on the subject of the representation* with a party he knows to be represented by a lawyer in that matter" (emphasis added). Our reference in *Henry* to this rule illustrates that we have framed the Sixth Amendment issue in terms of whether the State deliberately circumvented counsel with regard to the "subject of representation." But where, as here, the incriminating statements are gathered for "an alternative, legitimate reason," wholly apart from the pending charges, no such deliberate circumvention exists.

The Court's opinion seems to rest on the notion that the evidence here is excludable because "the State 'must have known' that its agent was likely to obtain incriminating statements from the accused" with respect to the crimes for which he was already indicted. But the inquiry mandated by our holdings is whether the State recorded the statements not merely *in spite of*, but *because of* that consequence. If the State is not seeking to elicit information with respect to the crime for which the defendant is already indicted, it cannot rationally be said that the State has "planned an impermissible interference with the right to the assistance of counsel."

This case is a particularly inappropriate one for invoking the right to counsel. The right to counsel recognized in *Massiah* was designed to preserve the integrity of the trial. Here respondent was under investigation because of his plans to obstruct justice by killing an essential witness. There is no right to consult an attorney for advice on committing crimes. Indeed, any attorney who undertook to offer such advice would undoubtedly be subject to sanction. Thus there is no warrant for vindicating respondent's right to consult counsel. An observation of this Court in connection with the attorney-client evidentiary privilege bears mention here: "The privilege takes flight if the relation is abused. A client who consults an attorney for advice that will serve him in the commission of a fraud will have no help from the law. He must let the truth be told." I would let the

truth be told in this case rather than exclude evidence that was the product of this police investigation into activities designed to thwart the judicial process.

Even though the *Massiah* rule is inapplicable to situations where the government is gathering information related to a separate crime, police misconduct need not be countenanced. Accordingly, evidence obtained through a separate crimes investigation should be admitted only "so long as investigating officers show no bad faith and do not institute the investigation of the separate offense as a pretext for avoiding the dictates of *Massiah*." Here the careful actions of Chief Keating and Detective Kelley steered well clear of these prohibitions.

Until today, the clearly prevailing view in the federal and state courts was that *Massiah* and its successors did not protect a defendant from the introduction of postindictment statements deliberately elicited when the police undertook an investigation of separate crimes. As two leading commentators have observed:

> "Even before [*Brewer v.*] *Williams*, [430 U.S. 387 (1977),] it was generally accepted that the right to counsel did not bar contact with the defendant concerning *other offenses*, particularly if the offenses were clearly unrelated and it did not appear the charge was simply a pretext to gain custody in order to facilitate the investigation. The more recent cases recognize that [*Massiah* and its progeny do] not confer upon charged defendants immunity from investigation concerning other crimes. This is especially true when the offense under investigation is a new or ongoing one, such as illegal efforts to thwart the forthcoming prosecution." 1 W. LaFave & J. Israel, Criminal Procedure § 6.4, p. 470 (1984) (emphasis added).

Rather than expand *Massiah* beyond boundaries currently recognized, I would take note of the observation that "*Massiah* certainly is the decision in which Sixth Amendment protections have been extended to their outermost point." *Henry*, (Blackmun, J., dissenting). I would not expand them more and well beyond the limits of precedent and logic.

### III

Even if I were prepared to join the Court in this enlargement of the protections of the Sixth Amendment, I would have serious doubts about also extending the reach of the exclusionary rule to cover this case. "Cases involving Sixth Amendment deprivations are subject to the general rule that remedies

---

The reference to the "circumstances here disclosed" must be to the fact that the Government, far from pursuing a good-faith investigation of different crimes, had "instructed the informant to engage [Massiah] in conversation relating to the crimes [for which he had already been indicted]." *Henry*, (Powell, J., concurring); Brief for Petitioner in *Massiah*.

should be tailored to the injury suffered from the constitutional violation and should not unnecessarily infringe on competing interests.'' Application of the exclusionary rule here makes little sense, as demonstrated by ''weighing the costs and benefits of preventing the use in the prosecution's case in chief of inherently trustworthy tangible evidence.'' *Leon.*

With respect to the costs, applying the rule to cases where the State deliberately elicits statements from a defendant in the course of investigating a separate crime excludes evidence that is ''typically reliable and often the most probative information bearing on the guilt or innocence of the defendant.'' Moreover, because of the trustworthy nature of the evidence, its admission will not threaten ''the fairness of a trial or . . . the integrity of the fact finding process.'' *Brewer*, (Powell, J., concurring). Hence, application of the rule to cases like this one ''deflects the truth-finding process,'' ''often frees the guilty,'' and may well ''generat[e] disrespect for the law and [the] administration of justice.''

Against these costs, applying the rule here appears to create precious little in the way of offsetting ''benefits.'' Like searches in violation of the Fourth Amendment, the ''wrong'' that the Court condemns was ''fully accomplished'' by the elicitation of comments from the defendant and ''the exclusionary rule is neither intended nor able to cure the invasion of the defendant's rights which he has already suffered.'' *Leon.*

The application of the exclusionary rule here must therefore be premised on deterrence of certain types of conduct by the police. We have explained,

however, that ''[t]he deterrent purpose of the exclusionary rule necessarily assumes that the police have engaged in willful, or at the very least negligent, conduct which has deprived the defendant of some right.'' Here the trial court found that the State obtained statements from respondent ''for legitimate purposes not related to the gathering of evidence concerning the crime for which [respondent] had been indicted.'' Since the State was not trying to build its theft case against respondent in obtaining the evidence, excluding the evidence from the theft trial will not affect police behavior at all. The exclusion of evidence ''cannot be expected, and should not be applied, to deter objectively reasonable law enforcement activity.'' *Leon.* Indeed, as noted above, it is impossible to identify any police ''misconduct'' to deter in this case. In fact, if anything, actions by the police of the type at issue here should be encouraged. The diligent investigation of the police in this case may have saved the lives of several potential witnesses and certainly led to the prosecution and conviction of respondent for additional serious crimes.

It seems, then, that the Sixth Amendment claims at issue here ''closely parallel claims under the Fourth Amendment,'' where we have found the exclusionary rule to be inapplicable by weighing the costs and benefits of its applications. If anything, the argument for admission of the evidence here is even stronger because ''[t]his is not a case where . . . 'the constable . . . blundered.'''

Because the Court today significantly and unjustifiably departs from our prior holdings, I respectfully dissent.

## QUESTIONS AND NOTES

**1.** Did the police perpetrate any wrong in obtaining the disputed evidence? Explain.

**2.** If your answer to question 1 was ''no,'' does it necessarily follow that Chief Justice Burger's dissent was correct? Why? Why not?

**3.** Is Chief Justice Burger's evaluation of the value of the exclusionary rule appropriate for this type of case? Explain.

**4.** If *Moulton* were a *Miranda* case how would it have been decided? Why? If you concluded that it would have been decided differently, what is there about *Moulton* that warrants more protection than is afforded by *Miranda*?

**5.** We conclude this section with *Kuhlmann v. Wilson*, a case that explores the impact of *Massiah* as applied to those confined in jail or prison.

# Kuhlmann v. Wilson
## 477 U.S. 436 (1986)

Justice POWELL announced the judgment of the Court and delivered the opinion of the Court with respect to Parts I, IV, and V, and an opinion with respect to Parts II and III in which the Chief Justice, Justice REHNQUIST, and Justice O'CONNOR join.

### I

In the early morning of July 4, 1970, respondent and two confederates robbed the Star Taxicab Garage in the Bronx, New York, and fatally shot the night dispatcher. Shortly before, employees of the garage had observed respondent, a former employee there, on the premises conversing with two other men. They also witnessed respondent fleeing after the robbery, carrying loose money in his arms. After eluding the police for four days, respondent turned himself in. Respondent admitted that he had been present when the crimes took place, claimed that he had witnessed the robbery, gave the police a description of the robbers, but denied knowing them. Respondent also denied any involvement in the robbery or murder, claiming that he had fled because he was afraid of being blamed for the crimes.

After his arraignment, respondent was confined in the Bronx House of Detention, where he was placed in a cell with a prisoner named Benny Lee. Unknown to respondent, Lee had agreed to act as a police informant. Respondent made incriminating statements that Lee reported to the police. Prior to trial, respondent moved to suppress the statements on the ground that they were obtained in violation of his right to counsel. The trial court held an evidentiary hearing on the suppression motion, which revealed that the statements were made under the following circumstances.

Before respondent arrived in the jail, Lee had entered into an arrangement with Detective Cullen, according to which Lee agreed to listen to respondent's conversations and report his remarks to Cullen. Since the police had positive evidence of respondent's participation, the purpose of placing Lee in the cell was to determine the identities of respondent's confederates. Cullen instructed Lee not to ask respondent any questions, but simply to "keep his ears open" for the names of the other perpetrators. Respondent first spoke to Lee about the crimes after he looked out the cellblock window at the Star Taxicab Garage, where the crimes had occurred. Respondent said, "someone's messing with me," and began talking to Lee about the robbery, narrating the same story that he had given the police at the time of his arrest. Lee advised respondent that this explanation "didn't sound too good,"[1] but respondent did not alter his story. Over the next few days, however, respondent changed details of his original account. Respondent then received a visit from his brother, who mentioned that members of his family were upset because they believed that respondent had murdered the dispatcher. After the visit, respondent again described the crimes to Lee. Respondent now admitted that he and two other men, whom he never identified, had planned and carried out the robbery, and had murdered the dispatcher. Lee informed Cullen of respondent's statements and furnished Cullen with notes that he had written surreptitiously while sharing the cell with respondent.

After hearing the testimony of Cullen and Lee, the trial court found that Cullen had instructed Lee "to ask no questions of [respondent] about the crime but merely to listen as to what [respondent] might say in his presence." The court determined that Lee obeyed these instructions, that he "at no time asked any questions with respect to the crime," and that he "only listened to [respondent] and made notes regarding what [respondent] had to say." The trial court also found that respondent's statements to Lee were "spontaneous" and "unsolicited." Under state precedent, a defendant's volunteered statements to a police agent were admissible in evidence because the police were not required to prevent talkative defendants from making incriminating statements. The trial court accordingly denied the suppression motion.

The jury convicted respondent of common-law murder and felonious possession of a weapon. On May 18, 1972, the trial court sentenced him to a term of 20 years to life on the murder count and to a concurrent term of up to 7 years on the weapons count. The Appellate Division affirmed without opinion, and the New York Court of Appeals denied respondent leave to appeal.

---

[1] At the suppression hearing, Lee testified that, after hearing respondent's initial version of his participation in the crimes, "I think I remember telling him that the story wasn't—it didn't sound too good. Things didn't look too good for him." At trial, Lee testified to a somewhat different version of his remark: "Well, I said, look, you better come up with a better story than that because that one doesn't sound too cool to me, that's what I said."

[Subsequently, on habeas corpus, the Second Circuit upheld Wilson's claim.]

## IV

As the District Court observed, *Henry* left open the question whether the Sixth Amendment forbids admission in evidence of an accused's statements to a jailhouse informant who was "placed in close proximity but [made] no effort to stimulate conversations about the crime charged."[19] Our review of the line of cases beginning with *Massiah* shows that this question must, as the District Court properly decided, be answered negatively.

### A

The Court in *Massiah* adopted the reasoning of the concurring opinions in *Spano* and held that, once a defendant's Sixth Amendment right to counsel has attached, he is denied that right when federal agents "deliberately elicit" incriminating statements from him in the absence of his lawyer. The Court adopted this test, rather than one that turned simply on whether the statements were obtained in an "interrogation," to protect accused persons from "indirect and surreptitious interrogations as well as those conducted in the jailhouse. In this case, Massiah was more seriously imposed upon . . . because he did not even know that he was under interrogation by a government agent." Thus, the Court made clear that it was concerned with interrogation or investigative techniques that were equivalent to interrogation, and that it so viewed the technique in issue in *Massiah*.

In *Henry*, the Court applied the *Massiah* test to incriminating statements made to a jailhouse informant. The Court of Appeals in that case found a violation of *Massiah* because the informant had engaged the defendant in conversations and "had developed a relationship of trust and confidence with [the defendant] such that [the defendant] revealed incriminating information." This Court affirmed, holding that the Court of Appeals reasonably concluded that the Government informant "deliberately used his position to secure incriminating information from [the defendant] when counsel was not present." Although the informant had not questioned the defendant, the informant had "stimulated" conversations with the defendant in order to "elicit" incriminating information. The Court emphasized

---

[19] In *Moulton*, we again reserved this question, declining to reach the situation where the informant acts simply as a "listening post" without "participat[ing] in active conversation and prompt[ing] particular replies."

that those facts, like the facts of *Massiah*, amounted to "indirect and surreptitious interrogatio[n]" of the defendant.

Earlier this Term, we applied the *Massiah* standard in a case involving incriminating statements made under circumstances substantially similar to the facts of *Massiah* itself. In *Moulton*, the defendant made incriminating statements in a meeting with his accomplice, who had agreed to cooperate with the police. During that meeting, the accomplice, who wore a wire transmitter to record the conversation, discussed with the defendant the charges pending against him, repeatedly asked the defendant to remind him of the details of the crime, and encouraged the defendant to describe his plan for killing witnesses. The Court concluded that these investigatory techniques denied the defendant his right to counsel on the pending charges. Significantly, the Court emphasized that, because of the relationship between the defendant and the informant, the informant's engaging the defendant "in active conversation about their upcoming trial was certain to elicit" incriminating statements from the defendant. Thus, the informant's participation "in this conversation was 'the functional equivalent of interrogation.'"

As our recent examination of this Sixth Amendment issue in *Moulton* makes clear, the primary concern of the *Massiah* line of decisions is secret interrogation by investigatory techniques that are the equivalent of direct police interrogation. Since "the Sixth Amendment is not violated whenever—by luck or happenstance—the State obtains incriminating statements from the accused after the right to counsel has attached," a defendant does not make out a violation of that right simply by showing that an informant, either through prior arrangement or voluntarily, reported his incriminating statements to the police. Rather, the defendant must demonstrate that the police and their informant took some action, beyond merely listening, that was designed deliberately to elicit incriminating remarks.

### B

It is thus apparent that the Court of Appeals erred in concluding that respondent's right to counsel was violated under the circumstances of this case. Its error did not stem from any disagreement with the District Court over appropriate resolution of the question reserved in *Henry*, but rather from its implicit conclusion that this case did not present that open question. That conclusion was based on a fundamental mistake, namely, the Court of Appeals' failure to accord to the state trial court's factual findings the presumption of correctness expressly required by 28 U.S.C. § 2254(d).

The state court found that Officer Cullen had instructed Lee only to listen to respondent for the purpose of determining the identities of the other participants in the robbery and murder. The police already had solid evidence of respondent's participation.[22] The court further found that Lee followed those instructions, that he "at no time asked any questions" of respondent concerning the pending charges, and that he "only listened" to respondent's "spontaneous" and "unsolicited" statements. The only remark made by Lee that has any support in this record was his comment that respondent's initial version of his participation in the crimes "didn't sound too good." Without holding that any of the state court's findings were not entitled to the presumption of correctness under § 2254(d), the Court of Appeals focused on that one remark and gave a description of Lee's interaction with respondent that is completely at odds with the facts found by the trial court. In the Court of Appeals' view, "[s]ubtly and slowly, but surely, Lee's ongoing verbal intercourse with [respondent] served to exacerbate [respondent's] already troubled state of mind."[24] After thus revising some of the trial court's findings, and ignoring other more relevant findings, the Court of Appeals concluded that the police "deliberately elicited" respondent's incriminating statements. This conclusion conflicts with the decision of every other state and federal judge who reviewed this record, and is clear error in light of the provisions and intent of § 2254(d).

V

The judgment of the Court of Appeals is reversed, and the case is remanded for further proceedings consistent with this opinion.

Chief Justice BURGER, concurring.

I agree fully with the Court's opinion and judgment. This case is clearly distinguishable from *Henry*. There is a vast difference between placing an "ear" in the suspect's cell and placing a voice

---

[22] Eyewitnesses had identified respondent as the man they saw fleeing from the garage with an armful of money.

[24] Curiously, the Court of Appeals expressed concern that respondent was placed in a cell that overlooked the scene of his crimes. For all the record shows, however, that fact was sheer coincidence. Nor do we perceive any reason to require police to isolate one charged with crime so that he cannot view the scene, whatever it may be, from his cell window.

in the cell to encourage conversation for the "ear" to record.

Furthermore, the abuse of the Great Writ needs to be curbed so as to limit, if not put a stop to, the "sporting contest" theory of criminal justice so widely practiced today.

Justice BRENNAN, with whom Justice MARSHALL joins, dissenting.

Because I believe that *Henry* directly controls the merits of this case, I dissent.

According to the Court, the Court of Appeals failed to accord § 2254(d)'s presumption of correctness to the state trial court's findings that respondent's cellmate, Lee, "at no time asked any questions" of respondent concerning the pending charges, and that Lee only listened to respondent's "spontaneous" and "unsolicited" statements. As a result, the Court concludes, the Court of Appeals failed to recognize that this case presents the question, reserved in *Henry*, whether the Sixth Amendment forbids the admission into evidence of an accused's statements to a jailhouse informant who was "placed in close proximity but [made] no effort to stimulate conversations about the crime charged." I disagree with the Court's characterization of the Court of Appeals' treatment of the state court's findings and, consequently, I disagree with the Court that the instant case presents the "listening post" question.

The state trial court simply found that Lee did not ask respondent any direct questions about the crime for which respondent was incarcerated. The trial court considered the significance of this fact only under state precedents, which the court interpreted to require affirmative "interrogation" by the informant as a prerequisite to a constitutional violation. The court did not indicate whether it referred to a Fifth Amendment or to a Sixth Amendment violation in identifying "interrogation" as a precondition to a violation; it merely stated that "the utterances made by [respondent] to Lee were unsolicited, and voluntarily made and did not violate the defendant's Constitutional rights."

The Court of Appeals did not disregard the state court's finding that Lee asked respondent no direct questions regarding the crime. Rather, the Court of Appeals *expressly* accepted that finding, but concluded that, as a matter of law, the deliberate elicitation standard of *Henry* and *Massiah* encompasses other, more subtle forms of stimulating incriminating admissions than overt questioning. The court suggested that the police deliberately placed respondent in a cell that overlooked the scene of the crime, hoping that the view would trigger an inculpatory comment to respondent's cellmate.[8] The court also observed that, while Lee asked respondent no questions, Lee nonetheless stimulated conversation concerning respondents' role in the Star Taxicab Garage robbery and murder by remarking that respondent's exculpatory story did not "sound too good" and that he had better come up with a better one. Thus, the Court of Appeals concluded that respondent's case did not present the situation reserved in *Henry*, where an accused makes an incriminating remark within the hearing of a jailhouse informant, who "makes no effort to stimulate conversations about the crime charged." Instead, the court determined this case to be virtually indistinguishable from *Henry*.

In *Henry*, we found that the Federal Government had "deliberately elicited" incriminating statements from Henry based on the following circumstances. The jailhouse informant, Nichols, had apparently followed instructions to obtain information without directly questioning Henry and without initiating conversations concerning the charges pending against Henry. We rejected the Government's argument that because Henry initiated the discussion of his crime, no Sixth Amendment violation had occurred. We pointed out that under *Massiah*, it is irrelevant whether the informant asks pointed questions about the crime or "merely engage[s] in general conversation about it." Nichols, we noted, "was not a passive listener; . . . he had 'some conversations with Mr. Henry' while he was in jail and Henry's incriminatory statements were 'the product of this conversation.'"

In deciding that Nichols' role in these conversations amounted to deliberate elicitation, we also found three other factors important. First, Nichols was to be paid for any information he produced and thus had an incentive to extract inculpatory admissions from Henry. Second, Henry was not aware that Nichols was acting as an informant. "Conversation stimulated in such circumstances," we observed, "may elicit information that an accused would not intentionally reveal to persons known to be Government agents." Third, Henry was in custody at the time he spoke with Nichols. This last fact is significant, we stated, because "custody imposes pressures on the accused [and] confinement may bring into play subtle influences that will make him particularly susceptible to the ploys of undercover Government agents." We concluded that by "intentionally creating a situation likely to induce Henry to make incriminating statements without the assistance of counsel, the Government violated Henry's Sixth Amendment right to counsel."

In the instant case, as in *Henry*, the accused was incarcerated and therefore was "susceptible to the ploys of undercover Government agents." Like Nichols [in *Henry*], Lee was a secret informant, usually received consideration for the services he rendered the police, and therefore had an incentive to produce the information which he knew the police hoped to obtain. Just as Nichols had done, Lee obeyed instructions not to question respondent and to report to the police any statements made by the respondent in Lee's presence about the crime in question. And, like Nichols, Lee encouraged respondent to talk about his crime by conversing with him on the subject over the course of several days and by telling respondent that his exculpatory story would not convince anyone without more work. However, unlike the situation in *Henry*, a disturbing visit from respondent's brother, rather than a conversation with the informant, seems to have been the immediate catalyst for respondent's confession to Lee. While it might appear from this sequence of events that Lee's comment regarding respondent's story and his general willingness to converse with respondent about the crime were not the *immediate* causes of respondent's admission, I think that the deliberate-elicitation standard requires consideration of the entire course of government behavior.

The State intentionally created a situation in which it was foreseeable that respondent would make incriminating statements without the assistance of counsel — it assigned respondent to a cell overlooking the scene of the crime and designated a secret informant to be respondent's cellmate. The informant, while avoiding direct questions, nonetheless developed a relationship of cellmate camaraderie with respondent and encouraged him to talk about his crime. While the *coup de grace* was delivered by respondent's brother, the groundwork for respondent's confession was laid by the State. Clearly the State's actions had a sufficient nexus with respondent's admission of guilt to constitute deliberate elicitation within the meaning of *Henry*. I would affirm the judgment of the Court of Appeals.

Justice STEVENS also dissented.

---

[8] The Court of Appeals noted that "[a]s soon as Wilson arrived and viewed the garage, he became upset and stated that 'someone's messing with me.'"

## QUESTIONS AND NOTES

**1.** Do you think that *Kuhlmann*, and the earlier *Henry* case are consistent with one another? Explain. (Incidently, Chief Justice Burger wrote *Henry*.)

**2.** If your answer to question 1 was "no," which one got the right result? Explain.

**3.** Does (should) it matter whether Wilson was *intentionally* jailed overlooking the scene of his crime?

**4.** Do you think that Lee was merely a listening post? Explain.

**5.** Should a mere listening post be forbidden under the Sixth Amendment? Why is it not forbidden?

**6.** How would *Kuhlmann* and *Henry* be decided under *Miranda*? Why?

**7.** In the next section, we will specifically contrast *Massiah* and *Miranda* cases.

## B.   Contrasting *Massiah* and *Miranda*

### Michigan v. Jackson
### 475 U.S. 625 (1986)

Justice STEVENS delivered the opinion of the Court.

I

The relevant facts may be briefly stated. Respondent Bladel was convicted of the murder of three railroad employees at the Amtrak Station in Jackson, Michigan, on December 31, 1978. Bladel, a disgruntled former employee, was arrested on January 1, 1979, and, after being questioned on two occasions, was released on January 3. He was arrested again on March 22, 1979, and agreed to talk to the police that evening without counsel. On the following morning, Friday, March 23, 1979, Bladel was arraigned. He requested that counsel be appointed for him because he was indigent. The detective in charge of the Bladel investigation was present at the arraignment. A notice of appointment was promptly mailed to a law firm, but the law firm did not receive it until Tuesday, March 27. In the interim, on March 26, 1979, two police officers interviewed Bladel in the county jail and obtained a confession from him. Prior to that questioning, the officers properly advised Bladel of his *Miranda* rights. Although he had inquired about his representation several times since the arraignment, Bladel was not told that a law firm had been appointed to represent him.

Respondent Jackson was convicted of second-degree murder and conspiracy to commit second-degree murder. He was one of four participants in a wife's plan to have her husband killed on July 12, 1979. Arrested on an unrelated charge on July 30, 1979, he made a series of six statements in response to police questioning prior to his arraignment at 4:30 p.m. on August 1. During the arraignment, Jackson requested that counsel be appointed for him. The police involved in his investigation were present at the arraignment. On the following morning, before he had an opportunity to consult with counsel, two police officers obtained another statement from Jackson to "confirm" that he was the person who had shot the victim. As was true of the six prearraignment statements, the questioning was preceded by advice of his *Miranda* rights and Jackson's agreement to proceed without counsel being present.

The Michigan Supreme Court held that the post-arraignment statements in both cases should have been suppressed. Noting that the Sixth Amendment right to counsel attached at the time of the arraignments, the court concluded that the *Edwards* rule "applies by analogy to those situations where an accused requests counsel before the arraigning magistrate. Once this request occurs, the police may not conduct further interrogations until counsel has been made available to the accused, unless the accused initiates further communications, exchanges, or conversations with the police. . . . The police cannot simply ignore a defendant's unequivocal request for counsel." We granted certiorari, and we now affirm.

## II

The question is not whether respondents had a right to counsel at their postarraignment, custodial interrogations. The existence of that right is clear. It has two sources. The Fifth Amendment protection against compelled self-incrimination provides the right to counsel at custodial interrogations. *Edwards*, *Miranda*. The Sixth Amendment guarantee of the assistance of counsel also provides the right to counsel at postarraignment interrogations. The arraignment signals "the initiation of adversary judicial proceedings" and thus the attachment of the Sixth Amendment; thereafter, government efforts to elicit information from the accused, including interrogation, represent "critical stages" at which the Sixth Amendment applies. *Moulton, Henry, Brewer, Massiah*. The question in these cases is whether respondents validly waived their right to counsel at the postarraignment custodial interrogations.

The State contends that differences in the legal principles underlying the Fifth and Sixth Amendments compel the conclusion that the *Edwards* rule should not apply to a Sixth Amendment claim. *Edwards* flows from the Fifth Amendment's right to counsel at custodial interrogations, the State argues; its relevance to the Sixth Amendment's provision of the assistance of counsel is far less clear, and thus the *Edwards* principle for assessing waivers is unnecessary and inappropriate.

In our opinion, however, the reasons for prohibiting the interrogation of an uncounseled prisoner who has asked for the help of a lawyer are even stronger after he has been formally charged with an offense than before. Indeed, after a formal accusation has been made—and a person who had previously been just a "suspect" has become an "accused" within the meaning of the Sixth Amendment—the constitutional right to the assistance of counsel is of such importance that the police may no longer employ techniques for eliciting information from an uncounseled defendant that might have been entirely proper at an earlier stage of their investigation. Thus, the surreptitious employment of a cellmate, see *Henry*, or the electronic surveillance of conversations with third parties, see *Moulton*, *Massiah*, may violate the defendant's Sixth Amendment right to counsel even though the same methods of investigation might have been permissible before arraignment or indictment. Far from undermining

the *Edwards* rule, the difference between the legal basis for the rule applied in *Edwards* and the Sixth Amendment claim asserted in these cases actually provides additional support for the application of the rule in these circumstances.

The State also relies on the factual differences between a request for counsel during custodial interrogation and a request for counsel at an arraignment. The State maintains that respondents may not have actually intended their request for counsel to encompass representation during any further questioning by the police. This argument, however, must be considered against the backdrop of our standard for assessing waivers of constitutional rights. Doubts must be resolved in favor of protecting the constitutional claim. This settled approach to questions of waiver requires us to give a broad, rather than a narrow, interpretation to a defendant's request for counsel—we presume that the defendant requests the lawyer's services at every critical stage of the prosecution.[6] We thus reject the State's suggestion that respondents' requests for the appointment of counsel should be construed to apply only to representation in formal legal proceedings.[7]

---

[6] In construing respondents' request for counsel, we do not, of course, suggest that the right to counsel turns on such a request. See *Brewer* ("[T]he right to counsel does not depend upon a request by the defendant"). Rather, we construe the defendant's request for counsel as an extremely important fact in considering the validity of a subsequent waiver in response to police-initiated interrogation.

[7] We also agree with the comments of the Michigan Supreme Court about the nature of an accused's request for counsel:

"Although judges and lawyers may understand and appreciate the subtle distinctions between the Fifth and Sixth Amendment rights to counsel, the average person does not. When an accused requests an attorney, either before a police officer or a magistrate, he does not know which constitutional right he is invoking; he therefore should not be expected to articulate exactly why or for what purposes he is seeking counsel. It makes little sense to afford relief from further interrogation to a defendant who asks a police officer for an attorney, but permit further interrogation to a defendant who makes an identical request to a judge. The simple fact that defendant has requested an attorney indicates that he does not believe that he is sufficiently capable of dealing with his adversaries singlehandedly."

The State points to another factual difference: the police may not know of the defendant's request for attorney at the arraignment. That claimed distinction is similarly unavailing. In the cases at bar, in which the officers in charge of the investigations of respondents were present at the arraignments, the argument is particularly unconvincing. More generally, however, Sixth Amendment principles require that we impute the State's knowledge from one state actor to another. For the Sixth Amendment concerns the confrontation between the State and the individual. One set of state actors (the police) may not claim ignorance of defendants' unequivocal request for counsel to another state actor (the court).

Finally, the State maintains that each of the respondents made a valid waiver of his Sixth Amendment rights by signing a postarraignment confession after again being advised of his constitutional rights. In *Edwards*, however, we rejected the notion that, after a suspect's request for counsel, advice of rights and acquiescence in police-initiated questioning could establish a valid waiver. We find no warrant for a different view under a Sixth Amendment analysis. Just as written waivers are insufficient to justify police-initiated interrogations after the request for counsel in a Fifth Amendment analysis, so too they are insufficient to justify police-initiated interrogations after the request for counsel in a Sixth Amendment analysis.

### III

*Edwards* is grounded in the understanding that "the assertion of the right to counsel [is] a significant event," and that "additional safeguards are necessary when the accused asks for counsel." We conclude that the assertion is no less significant, and the need for additional safeguards no less clear, when the request for counsel is made at an arraignment and when the basis for the claim is the Sixth Amendment. We thus hold that, if police initiate interrogation after a defendant's assertion, at an arraignment or similar proceeding, of his right to counsel, any waiver of the defendant's right to counsel for that police-initiated interrogation is invalid.

The judgments are accordingly affirmed.

Chief Justice BURGER, concurring in the judgment.

I concurred only in the judgment in *Edwards*, and in doing so I observed:

"The extraordinary protections afforded a person in custody suspected of criminal conduct are not without a valid basis, but as with all 'good' things they can be carried too far."

The urge for "bright-line" rules readily applicable to a host of varying situations would likely relieve this Court somewhat from more than a doubling of the Court's work in recent decades, but this urge seems to be leading the Court to an absolutist, mechanical treatment of the subject. At times, it seems, the judicial mind is in conflict with what behavioral—and theological—specialists have long recognized as a natural human urge of people to confess wrongdoing. See, *e.g.*, T. Reik, The Compulsion to Confess (1959).

We must, of course, protect persons in custody from coercion, but step by step we have carried this concept well beyond sound, common-sense boundaries. The Court's treatment of this subject is an example of the infirmity of trying to perform the rule making function on a case-by-case basis, ignoring the reality that the criminal cases coming to this Court, far from typical, are the "hard" cases. This invokes the ancient axiom that hard cases can make bad law.

*Stare decisis* calls for my following the rule of *Edwards* in this context, but plainly the subject calls for reexamination. Increasingly, to borrow from Justice Cardozo, more and more "criminal[s] . . . go free because the constable has blundered."

Justice REHNQUIST, with whom Justice POWELL and Justice O'CONNOR join, dissenting.

The Court's decision today rests on the following deceptively simple line of reasoning: *Edwards* created a bright-line rule to protect a defendant's Fifth Amendment rights; Sixth Amendment rights are even more important than Fifth Amendment rights; therefore, we must also apply the *Edwards* rule to the Sixth Amendment. The Court prefers this neat syllogism to an effort to discuss or answer the only relevant question: Does the *Edwards* rule make sense in the context of the Sixth Amendment? I think it does not, and I therefore dissent from the Court's unjustified extension of the *Edwards* rule to the Sixth Amendment.

My disagreement with the Court stems from our differing understandings of *Edwards*. In *Edwards*, this Court held that once a defendant has invoked his right under *Miranda* to have counsel present during custodial interrogation, "a valid waiver of that right cannot be established by showing only that he responded to further police-initiated custodial interrogation even if he has been advised of his rights." This "prophylactic rule" was deemed necessary to prevent the police from effectively "overriding" a defendant's assertion of his *Miranda* rights by "badgering" him into waiving those rights. In short, as we explained in later cases, "*Edwards* did not confer a substantive constitutional right that had not existed before; it 'created a protective umbrella serving to enhance a constitutional guarantee.'"

What the Court today either forgets or chooses to ignore is that the "constitutional guarantee" is the Fifth Amendment's prohibition on compelled self-incrimination. This prohibition, of course, is also the constitutional underpinning for the set of prophylactic rules announced in *Miranda* itself.[2] *Edwards*, like *Miranda*, imposes on the police a bright-line standard of conduct intended to help ensure that confessions obtained through custodial interrogation will not be "coerced" or "involuntary." Seen in this proper light, *Edwards* provides nothing more than a second layer of protection, in addition to those rights conferred by *Miranda*, for a defendant who might otherwise be compelled by the police to incriminate himself in violation of the Fifth Amendment.

The dispositive question in the instant cases, and the question the Court should address in its opinion, is whether the same kind of prophylactic rule is needed to protect a defendant's right to counsel under the Sixth Amendment. The answer to this question, it seems to me, is clearly "no." The Court does not even suggest that the police commonly deny defendants their Sixth Amendment right to counsel. Nor, I suspect, would such a claim likely be borne out by empirical evidence. Thus, the justification for the prophylactic rules this Court created in *Miranda* and *Edwards*, namely, the perceived widespread problem that the police were violating, and would probably continue to violate, the Fifth Amendment rights of defendants during the course of custodial interrogations, is conspicuously absent in the Sixth Amendment context. To put it simply, the prophylactic rule set forth in *Edwards* makes no sense at all except when linked to the Fifth Amendment's prohibition against compelled self-incrimination.

Not only does the Court today cut the *Edwards*

rule loose from its analytical moorings, it does so in a manner that graphically reveals the illogic of the Court's position. The Court phrases the question presented in these cases as whether the *Edwards* rule applies "to a defendant who has been formally charged with a crime *and who has requested appointment of counsel at his arraignment.*" (emphasis added). And the Court ultimately limits its holding to those situations where the police "initiate interrogation *after a defendant's assertion, at an arraignment or similar proceeding, of his right to counsel.*" (emphasis added).

In other words, the Court most assuredly does *not* hold that the *Edwards per se* rule prohibiting all police-initiated interrogations applies from the moment the defendant's Sixth Amendment right to counsel attaches, with or without a request for counsel by the defendant. Such a holding would represent, after all, a shockingly dramatic restructuring of the balance this Court has traditionally struck between the rights of the defendant and those of the larger society. Applying the *Edwards* rule to situations in which a defendant has not made an explicit request for counsel would also render completely nugatory the extensive discussion of "waiver" in such prior Sixth Amendment cases as *Brewer*.

This leaves the Court, however, in an analytical straitjacket. The problem with the limitation the Court places on the Sixth Amendment version of the *Edwards* rule is that, unlike a defendant's "right to counsel" under *Miranda*, which does not arise until affirmatively invoked by the defendant during custodial interrogation, a defendant's Sixth Amendment right to counsel does not depend at all on whether the defendant has requested counsel. The Court acknowledges as much in footnote six of its opinion, where it stresses that "we do not, of course, suggest that the right to counsel turns on . . . a request [for counsel]."

The Court provides no satisfactory explanation for its decision to extend the *Edwards* rule to the Sixth Amendment, yet limit that rule to those defendants foresighted enough, or just plain lucky enough, to have made an explicit request for counsel which we have always understood to be completely unnecessary for Sixth Amendment purposes. The Court attempts to justify its emphasis on the otherwise legally insignificant request for counsel by stating that "we construe the defendant's request for counsel as an extremely important fact in considering the validity of a subsequent waiver in response to police-initiated interrogation." This statement sounds reasonable, but it is flatly inconsistent with the remainder of the Court's opinion, in which the Court holds

---

[2] The Court suggests, in dictum, that the Fifth Amendment also provides defendants with a "right to counsel." But our cases make clear that the Fifth Amendment itself provides no such "right." Instead, *Miranda* confers upon a defendant a "right to counsel," *but only when such counsel is requested during custodial interrogations.* Even under *Miranda*, the "right to counsel" exists solely as a means of protecting the defendant's Fifth Amendment right not to be compelled to incriminate himself.

that there can be no waiver of the Sixth Amendment right to counsel after a request for counsel has been made. It is obvious that, for the Court, the defendant's request for counsel is not merely an "extremely important fact"; rather, it is the *only* fact that counts.

The truth is that there is no satisfactory explanation for the position the Court adopts in these cases. The glaring inconsistencies in the Court's opinion arise precisely because the Court lacks a coherent, analytically sound basis for its decision. The prophylactic rule of *Edwards*, designed from its inception to protect a defendant's right under the Fifth Amendment not to be compelled to incriminate himself, simply does not meaningfully apply to the Sixth Amendment. I would hold that *Edwards* has no application outside the context of the Fifth Amendment, and would therefore reverse the judgment of the court below.

## QUESTIONS AND NOTES

**1.** Do you think that the assertion of the right to counsel at the preliminary hearing necessarily, or even probably, meant that the suspects, who previously agreed to be questioned, no longer wished to be subject to custodial interrogation? Why?

**2.** Might *Jackson* discourage prompt arraignments in that once the defendant asserts his right to counsel at arraignment, the opportunity for interrogation will be gone?

**3.** If your answer to question 2 is "yes," does it necessarily follow that *Jackson* was wrongly decided? Explain.

**4.** Should footnote 7 of the Court's opinion be taken seriously? If so, are all of the cases in this chapter that purport to draw a distinction between the Fifth and Sixth Amendment right to counsel fundamentally flawed?

**5.** In regard to Chief Justice Burger's opinion, is it accurate to think of this as a case in which the criminal goes free because the constable has blundered? Explain.

**6.** Under the Court's opinion, is it possible for a suspect who has asserted her right to counsel to ever be questioned without counsel? If so, how?

**7.** In *McNeil*, the Court explored some of the differences between *Jackson* and *Edwards*.

### McNeil v. Wisconsin
### 111 S.Ct. 2204 (1991)

Justice SCALIA delivered the opinion of the Court.

This case presents the question whether an accused's invocation of his Sixth Amendment right to counsel during a judicial proceeding constitutes an invocation of his *Miranda* right to counsel.

### I

Petitioner Paul McNeil was arrested in Omaha, Nebraska, in May 1987, pursuant to a warrant charging him with an armed robbery in West Allis, Wisconsin, a suburb of Milwaukee. Shortly after his arrest, two Milwaukee County deputy sheriffs arrived in Omaha to retrieve him. After advising him of his *Miranda* rights, the deputies sought to question him. He refused to answer any questions, but did not request an attorney. The deputies promptly ended the interview.

Once back in Wisconsin, petitioner was brought before a Milwaukee County court commissioner on the armed robbery charge. The Commissioner set bail and scheduled a preliminary examination. An attorney from the Wisconsin Public Defender's office represented petitioner at this initial appearance.

Later that evening, Detective Joseph Butts of the Milwaukee County Sheriff's Department visited petitioner in jail. Butts had been assisting the Racine County, Wisconsin, police in their investigation of a murder, attempted murder, and armed burglary in the town of Caledonia; petitioner was a suspect. Butts advised petitioner of his *Miranda* rights, and petitioner signed a form waiving them. In this first interview, petitioner did not deny knowledge of the

Caledonia crimes, but said that he had not been involved.

Butts returned two days later with detectives from Caledonia. He again began the encounter by advising petitioner of his *Miranda* rights, and providing a waiver form. Petitioner placed his initials next to each of the warnings and signed the form. This time, petitioner admitted that he had been involved in the Caledonia crimes, which he described in detail. He also implicated two other men, Willie Pope and Lloyd Crowley. The statement was typed up by a detective and given to petitioner to review. Petitioner placed his initials next to every reference to himself and signed every page.

Butts and the Caledonia Police returned two days later, having in the meantime found and questioned Pope, who convinced them that he had not been involved in the Caledonia crimes. They again began the interview by administering the *Miranda* warnings, and obtaining petitioner's signature and initials on the waiver form. Petitioner acknowledged that he had lied about Pope's involvement to minimize his own role in the Caledonia crimes, and provided another statement recounting the events, which was transcribed, signed, and initialed as before.

The following day, petitioner was formally charged with the Caledonia crimes and transferred to that jurisdiction. His pretrial motion to suppress the three incriminating statements was denied. He was convicted of second-degree murder, attempted first-degree murder, and armed robbery, and sentenced to 60 years in prison.

On appeal, petitioner argued that the trial court's refusal to suppress the statements was reversible error. He contended that his courtroom appearance with an attorney for the West Allis crime constituted an invocation of the *Miranda* right to counsel, and that any subsequent waiver of that right during police-initiated questioning regarding *any* offense was invalid. Observing that the State's Supreme Court had never addressed this issue, the Court of Appeals certified to that court the following question:

> "Does an accused's request for counsel at an initial appearance on a charged offense constitute an invocation of his fifth amendment right to counsel that precludes police interrogation on unrelated, uncharged offenses?"

The Wisconsin Supreme Court answered "no." We granted certiorari.

## II

The Sixth Amendment right is offense-specific. It cannot be invoked once for all future prosecutions, for it does not attach until a prosecution is commenced, that is, "at or after the initiation of adversary judicial criminal proceedings—whether by way of formal charge, preliminary hearing, indictment, information, or arraignment." And just as the right is offense-specific, so also its *Jackson* effect of invalidating subsequent waivers in police-initiated interviews is offense-specific.

> "The police have an interest . . . in investigating new or additional crimes [after an individual is formally charged with one crime.] . . . [T]o exclude evidence pertaining to charges as to which the Sixth Amendment right to counsel had not attached at the time the evidence was obtained, simply because other charges were pending at that time, would unnecessarily frustrate the public's interest in the investigation of criminal activities. . . ." *Moulton.*

> "Incriminating statements pertaining to other crimes, as to which the Sixth Amendment right has not yet attached, are, of course, admissible at a trial of those offenses."

Because petitioner provided the statements at issue here before his Sixth Amendment right to counsel with respect to the *Caledonia offenses* had been (or even could have been) invoked, that right poses no bar to the admission of the statements in this case.

Petitioner relies, however, upon a different "right to counsel," found not in the text of the Sixth Amendment, but in this Court's jurisprudence relating to the Fifth Amendment guarantee that "[n]o person . . . shall be compelled in any criminal case to be a witness against himself." In *Miranda*, we established a number of prophylactic rights designed to counteract the "inherently compelling pressures" of custodial interrogation, including the right to have counsel present. *Miranda* did not hold, however, that those rights could not be waived. On the contrary, the opinion recognized that statements elicited during custodial interrogation would be admissible if the prosecution could establish that the suspect "knowingly and intelligently waived his privilege against self-incrimination and his right to retained or appointed counsel."

In *Edwards*, we established a second layer of prophylaxis for the *Miranda* right to counsel: once a suspect asserts the right, not only must the current interrogation cease, but he may not be approached for further interrogation "until counsel has been made available to him,"—which means, we have most recently held, that counsel must be present, *Minnick*. If the police do subsequently initiate an encounter in the absence of counsel (assuming there has been no break in custody), the suspect's statements are presumed involuntary and therefore inadmissible as substantive evidence at trial, even where the suspect executes a waiver and his statements would be considered voluntary under traditional standards. This is "designed to prevent police from badgering a defendant into waiving his previously asserted *Miranda* rights." The *Edwards* rule, moreover, is *not* offense-specific: once a suspect invokes the *Miranda* right to counsel for interrogation regarding one offense, he may not be reapproached regarding *any* offense unless counsel is present. *Roberson.*

Having described the nature and effects of both the Sixth Amendment right to counsel and the *Miranda-Edwards* "Fifth Amendment" right to counsel, we come at last to the issue here: Petitioner seeks to prevail by combining the two of them. He contends that, although he expressly waived his *Miranda* right to counsel on every occasion he was interrogated, those waivers were the invalid product of impermissible approaches, because his prior invocation of the offense-specific Sixth Amendment right with regard to the West Allis burglary was also an invocation of the non-offense-specific *Miranda-Edwards* right. We think that is false as a matter of fact and inadvisable (if even permissible) as a contrary-to-fact presumption of policy.

As to the former: The purpose of the Sixth Amendment counsel guarantee — and hence the purpose of invoking it — is to "protec[t] the unaided layman at critical confrontations" with his "expert adversary," the government, *after* "the adverse positions of government and defendant have solidified" with respect to a particular alleged crime. The purpose of the *Miranda-Edwards* guarantee, on the other hand — and hence the purpose of invoking it — is to protect a quite different interest: the suspect's "desire to deal with the police only through counsel." This is in one respect narrower than the interest protected by the Sixth Amendment guarantee (because it relates only to custodial interrogation) and in another respect broader (because it relates to interrogation regarding *any* suspected crime and attaches whether or not the "adversarial relationship" produced by a pending prosecution has yet arisen). To invoke the Sixth Amendment interest is, as a matter of *fact, not* to invoke the *Miranda-Edwards* interest. One might be quite willing to speak to the police without counsel present concerning many matters, but not the matter under prosecution. It can be said, perhaps, that it is *likely* that one who has asked for counsel's assistance in defending against a prosecution would want counsel present for all custodial interrogation, even interrogation unrelated to the charge. That is not necessarily true, since suspects often believe that they can avoid the laying of charges by demonstrating an assurance of innocence through frank and unassisted answers to questions. But even if it were true, the *likelihood* that a suspect would wish counsel to be present is not the test for applicability of *Edwards*. The rule of that case applies only when the suspect "ha[s] *expressed* " his wish for the particular sort of lawyerly assistance that is the subject of *Miranda*. *Edwards* (emphasis added). It requires, at a minimum, some statement that can reasonably be construed to be expression of a desire for the assistance of an attorney *in dealing with custodial interrogation by the police.* Requesting the assistance of an attorney at a bail hearing does not bear that construction. "[T]o find that [the defendant] invoked his Fifth Amendment right to counsel on the present charges merely by requesting the appointment of counsel at his arraignment on the unrelated charge is to disregard the ordinary meaning of that request."

Our holding in *Jackson* does not, as petitioner asserts, contradict the foregoing distinction; to the contrary, it *rests* upon it. That case, it will be recalled, held that after the Sixth Amendment right to counsel attaches and is invoked, any statements obtained from the accused during subsequent police-initiated custodial questioning regarding the charge at issue (even if the accused purports to waive his rights) are inadmissible. The State in *Jackson* opposed that outcome on the ground that assertion of the Sixth Amendment right to counsel did not realistically constitute the *expression* (as *Edwards* required) of a wish to have counsel present during custodial interrogation. Our response to that contention was not that it *did* constitute such an expression, but that it *did not have to*, since the relevant question was not whether the *Miranda* "Fifth Amendment" right had been *asserted*, but whether the Sixth Amendment right to counsel had been *waived*. We said that since our "settled approach to questions of waiver requires us to give a broad, rather than a narrow, interpretation to a defendant's request for counsel, . . . we *presume* that the defendant requests the lawyer's services at every critical stage of the prosecution." (emphasis added). The holding of *Jackson* implicitly rejects any equivalence in fact between invocation of the Sixth Amendment right to counsel and the expression necessary to trigger *Edwards*. If such invocation constituted a real (as opposed to merely a legally presumed) request for the assistance of counsel in custodial interrogation, it would have been quite unnecessary for *Jackson* to go on to establish, as it did, a new Sixth

641 Chapter 17 The Right to Counsel and Confessions

Amendment rule of no police-initiated interrogation; we could simply have cited and relied upon *Edwards*.[1]

There remains to be considered the possibility that, even though the assertion of the Sixth Amendment right to counsel does not *in fact* imply an assertion of the *Miranda* "Fifth Amendment" right, we should declare it to be such as a matter of sound policy. Assuming we have such an expansive power under the Constitution, it would not wisely be exercised. Petitioner's proposed rule has only insignificant advantages. If a suspect does not wish to communicate with the police except through an attorney, he can simply tell them that when they give him the *Miranda* warnings. There is not the remotest chance that he will feel "badgered" by their asking to talk to him without counsel present, since the subject will not be the charge on which he has already requested counsel's assistance (for in that event *Jackson* would preclude initiation of the interview) and he will not have rejected uncounseled interrogation on *any* subject before (for in that event *Edwards* would preclude initiation of the interview). The proposed rule would, however, seriously impede effective law enforcement. The Sixth Amendment right to counsel attaches at the first formal proceeding against an accused, and in most States, at least with respect to serious offenses, free counsel is made available at that time and ordinarily requested. Thus, if we were to adopt petitioner's rule, most persons in pretrial

custody for serious offenses would be *unapproachable* by police officers suspecting them of involvement in other crimes, *even though they have never expressed any unwillingness to be questioned*. Since the ready ability to obtain uncoerced confessions is not an evil but an unmitigated good, society would be the loser. Admissions of guilt resulting from valid *Miranda* waivers "are more than merely 'desirable'; they are essential to society's compelling interest in finding, convicting, and punishing those who violate the law."[2]

Petitioner urges upon us the desirability of providing a "clear and unequivocal" guideline for the police: no police-initiated questioning of any person in custody who has requested counsel to assist him in defense or in interrogation. But the police do not need our assistance to establish such a guideline; they are free, if they wish, to adopt it on their own. Of course it *is* our task to establish guidelines for judicial review. We like *them* to be "clear and unequivocal," see, *e.g.*, *Roberson*, but only when they guide sensibly, and in a direction we are authorized to go. Petitioner's proposal would in our view do much more harm than good, and is not contained within, or even in furtherance of, the Sixth Amendment's right to counsel or the Fifth Amendment's

---

[1] A footnote in *Jackson* quoted with approval statements by the Michigan Supreme Court to the effect that the average person does not "understand and appreciate the subtle distinctions between the Fifth and Sixth Amendment rights to counsel," that it "makes little sense to afford relief from further interrogation to a defendant who asks a police officer for an attorney, but permit further interrogation to a defendant who makes an identical request to a judge," and that "[t]he simple fact that defendant has requested an attorney indicates that he does not believe that he is sufficiently capable of dealing with his adversaries singlehandedly." Those observations were perhaps true in the context of deciding whether a request for the assistance of counsel in defending against a particular charge implied a desire to have that counsel serve as an "intermediary" for all further interrogation on that charge. They are assuredly not true in the quite different context of deciding whether such a request implies a desire never to undergo custodial interrogation, about anything, without counsel present.

[2] The dissent condemns these sentiments as "revealing a preference for an inquisitorial system of justice." We cannot imagine what this means. What makes a system adversarial rather than inquisitorial is not the presence of counsel, much less the presence of counsel where the defendant has not requested it; but rather, the presence of a judge who does not (as an inquisitor does) conduct the factual and legal investigation himself, but instead decides on the basis of facts and arguments pro and con adduced by the parties. In the inquisitorial criminal process of the civil law, the defendant ordinarily has counsel; and in the adversarial criminal process of the common law, he sometimes does not. Our system of justice is, and has always been, an inquisitorial one at the investigatory stage (even the grand jury is an inquisitorial body), and no other disposition is conceivable. Even if detectives were to bring impartial magistrates around with them to all interrogations, there would be no decision for the impartial magistrate to umpire. If all the dissent means by a "preference for an inquisitorial system" is a preference not to require the presence of counsel during an investigatory interview where the interviewee has not requested it – that is a strange way to put it, but we are guilty.

right against compelled self-incrimination.[3]

"This Court is forever adding new stories to the temples of constitutional law, and the temples have a way of collapsing when one story too many is added." *Douglas v. Jeannette*, 319 U.S. 157, 181 (1943) (opinion of Jackson, J.). We decline to add yet another story to *Miranda*. The judgment of the Wisconsin Supreme Court is affirmed.

Justice KENNEDY, concurring.

I join the opinion of the Court in all respects. Its sensible recognition that invocation of the Sixth Amendment right to counsel is specific to the offense in question should apply as well to requests for counsel under the Fifth Amendment. See *Roberson*, (Kennedy, J., dissenting). For those in custody, *Edwards* and its progeny go far to protect an individual who desires the assistance of counsel during interrogation. Limiting the extraordinary protections of *Edwards* to a particular investigation would not increase the risk of confessions induced by official efforts to wear down the will of a suspect. Having adopted an offense-specific rule for invocation of the Sixth Amendment right to counsel, the Court should

---

[3] The dissent predicts that the result in this case will routinely be circumvented when, "[i]n future preliminary hearings, competent counsel . . . make sure that they, or their clients, make a statement on the record" invoking the *Miranda* right to counsel. We have in fact never held that a person can invoke his *Miranda* rights anticipatorily, in a context other than "custodial interrogation" – which a preliminary hearing will not always, or even usually, involve. If the *Miranda* right to counsel can be invoked at a preliminary hearing, it could be argued, there is no logical reason why it could not be invoked by a letter prior to arrest, or indeed even prior to identification as a suspect. Most rights must be asserted when the government seeks to take the action they protect against. The fact that we have allowed the *Miranda* right to counsel, once asserted, to be effective with respect to future custodial interrogation does not necessarily mean that we will allow it to be asserted initially outside the context of custodial interrogation, with similar future effect. Assuming, however, that an assertion at arraignment would be effective, and would be routinely made, the mere fact that adherence to the principle of our decisions will not have substantial consequences is no reason to abandon that principle. It would remain intolerable that a person in custody who had expressed *no* objection to being questioned would be unapproachable.

devote some attention to bringing its Fifth and Sixth Amendment jurisprudence into a logical alignment, and should give uniform, fair, and workable guidelines for the criminal justice system.

Even if petitioner had invoked his Fifth Amendment right with respect to the West Allis armed robbery, I do not believe the authorities should have been prohibited from questioning him in connection with the Caledonia offenses.

Justice STEVENS, with whom Justice MARSHALL and Justice BLACKMUN join, dissenting.

The Court's opinion demeans the importance of the right to counsel. As a practical matter, the opinion probably will have only a slight impact on current custodial interrogation procedures. As a theoretical matter, the Court's innovative development of an "offense-specific" limitation on the scope of the attorney-client relationship can only generate confusion in the law and undermine the protections that undergird our adversarial system of justice. As a symbolic matter, today's decision is ominous because it reflects a preference for an inquisitorial system that regards the defense lawyer as an impediment rather than a servant to the cause of justice.

I

The predicate for the Court's entire analysis is the failure of the defendant at the preliminary hearing to make a "statement that can reasonably be construed to be expression of a desire for the assistance of an attorney *in dealing with custodial interrogation by the police*." If petitioner in this case had made such a statement indicating that he was invoking his Fifth Amendment right to counsel as well as his Sixth Amendment right to counsel, the entire offense-specific house of cards that the Court has erected today would collapse, pursuant to our holding in *Roberson*, that a defendant who invokes the right to counsel for interrogation on one offense may not be reapproached regarding any offense unless counsel is present.

In future preliminary hearings, competent counsel can be expected to make sure that they, or their clients, make a statement on the record that will obviate the consequences of today's holding. That is why I think this decision will have little, if any, practical effect on police practices.

II

The outcome of this case is determined by the Court's parsimonious "offense-specific" description of the right to counsel guaranteed by the Sixth Amendment. The Court's definition is inconsistent with the high value our prior cases have placed on this right, with the ordinary understanding of the scope of the right, and with the accepted practice of the legal profession.

In *Jackson*, we held that the defendant's invocation of his right to the assistance of counsel at arraignment prohibited the police from initiating a postarraignment custodial interrogation without notice to his lawyer. After explaining that our prior cases required us "to give a broad, rather than a narrow, interpretation to a defendant's request for counsel," we squarely rejected "the State's suggestion that respondents' requests for the appointment of counsel should be construed to apply only to representation in formal legal proceedings." Instead, we noted that "it is the State that has the burden of establishing a valid waiver [of the right to counsel]. Doubts must be resolved in favor of protecting the constitutional claim."

Today, however, the Court accepts a narrow, rather than a broad, interpretation of the same right. The Court's holding today moreover rejects the common sense evaluation of the nature of an accused's request for counsel that we expressly endorsed in *Jackson*:

"We also agree with the comments of the Michigan Supreme Court about the nature of an accused's request for counsel:

"'Although judges and lawyers may understand and appreciate the subtle distinctions between the Fifth and Sixth Amendment rights to counsel, the average person does not. When an accused requests an attorney, either before a police officer or a magistrate, he does not know which constitutional right he is invoking; he therefore should not be expected to articulate exactly why or for what purposes he is seeking counsel. It makes little sense to afford relief from further interrogation to a defendant who asks a police officer for an attorney, but permit further interrogation to a defendant who makes an identical request to a judge. The simple fact that defendant has requested an attorney indicates that he does not believe that he is sufficiently capable of dealing with his adversaries singlehandedly.'"

### III

In the final analysis, the Court's decision is explained by its fear that making counsel available to persons held in custody would "seriously impede effective law enforcement." The magnitude of the Court's alarm is illuminated by its use of italics:

"Thus, if we were to adopt petitioner's rule, most persons in pretrial custody for serious offenses would be *unapproachable* by police officers suspecting them of involvement in other crimes, *even though they have never expressed any unwillingness to be questioned.*"

Of course, the Court is quite wrong and its fears are grossly exaggerated. The fears are exaggerated because, as I have explained, today's holding will probably affect very few cases in the future. The fears are misguided because a contrary rule would not make all pretrial detainees "unapproachable"; it would merely serve to ensure that a suspect's statements during custodial interrogation are truly voluntary.

A contrary rule would also comport with respect to tradition. Undergirding our entire line of cases requiring the police to follow fair procedures when they interrogate presumptively innocent citizens suspected of criminal wrongdoing is the longstanding recognition that an adversarial system of justice can function effectively only when the adversaries communicate with one another through counsel and when laypersons are protected from overreaching by more experienced and skilled professionals. Whenever the Court ignores the importance of fair procedure in this context and describes the societal interest in obtaining "uncoerced confessions" from pretrial detainees as an "unmitigated good," the Court is revealing a preference for an inquisitorial system of justice. As I suggested in *Moran v. Burbine, infra*:

"This case turns on a proper appraisal of the role of the lawyer in our society. If a lawyer is seen as a nettlesome obstacle to the pursuit of wrongdoers—as in an inquisitorial society—then the Court's decision today makes a good deal of sense. If a lawyer is seen as an aid to the understanding and protection of constitutional rights—as in an accusatorial society—then today's decision makes no sense at all." (Stevens, J., dissenting).

The Court's refusal to acknowledge any "danger of 'subtle compulsion'" in a case of this kind evidences an inability to recognize the difference between an inquisitorial and an adversarial system of justice. Accordingly, I respectfully dissent.

## QUESTIONS AND NOTES

**1.** How is the *McNeil* issue different from that presented in *Jackson*?

**2.** Do you agree that an uncoerced confession is an unmitigated good? If so, should we consider revamping all of the jurisprudence emanating from *Massiah*?

**3.** Assess footnote 3 of the majority opinion. Will lawyers routinely assert *Miranda* rights for their clients as soon as the attorney is appointed? Will (should) such an assertion be effective? Why? Why not?

**4.** The last paragraph of the Court's *McNeil* opinion looks very much like the nub of Justice Scalia's dissent in *Minnick*. Does he now have the votes to implement that viewpoint, or is *McNeil* just a different case from *Minnick*?

**5.** If the dissent had prevailed would suspects be essentially unapproachable to be questioned about any crime? Assuming that your answer is "yes," does it follow that the majority correctly decided the case?

**6.** Does the Court view a lawyer as an impediment to justice? Does it undervalue the adversary system? Continue to think about these questions as you read *Moran v. Burbine*.

## Moran v. Burbine
### 475 U.S. 412 (1986)

Justice O'CONNOR delivered the opinion of the Court.

After being informed of his rights pursuant to *Miranda*, and after executing a series of written waivers, respondent confessed to the murder of a young woman. At no point during the course of the interrogation, which occurred prior to arraignment, did he request an attorney. While he was in police custody, his sister attempted to retain a lawyer to represent him. The attorney telephoned the police station and received assurances that respondent would not be questioned further until the next day. In fact, the interrogation session that yielded the inculpatory statements began later that evening. The question presented is whether either the conduct of the police or respondent's ignorance of the attorney's efforts to reach him taints the validity of the waivers and therefore requires exclusion of the confessions.

I

On the morning of March 3, 1977, Mary Jo Hickey was found unconscious in a factory parking lot in Providence, Rhode Island. Suffering from injuries to her skull apparently inflicted by a metal pipe found at the scene, she was rushed to a nearby hospital. Three weeks later she died from her wounds.

Several months after her death, the Cranston, Rhode Island, police arrested respondent and two others in connection with a local burglary. Shortly before the arrest, Detective Ferranti of the Cranston police force had learned from a confidential informant that the man responsible for Ms. Hickey's death lived at a certain address and went by the name of "Butch." Upon discovering that respondent lived at that address and was known by that name, Detective Ferranti informed respondent of his *Miranda* rights. When respondent refused to execute a written waiver, Detective Ferranti spoke separately with the two other suspects arrested on the breaking and entering charge and obtained statements further implicating respondent in Ms. Hickey's murder. At approximately 6 p.m., Detective Ferranti telephoned the police in Providence to convey the information he had uncovered. An hour later, three officers from that department arrived at the Cranston headquarters for the purpose of questioning respondent about the murder.

That same evening, at about 7:45 p.m., respondent's sister telephoned the Public Defender's Office to obtain legal assistance for her brother. Her sole concern was the breaking and entering charge, as she was unaware that respondent was then under suspicion for murder. She asked for Richard Casparian who had been scheduled to meet with respondent earlier that afternoon to discuss another charge unrelated to either the break-in or the murder. As soon as the conversation ended, the attorney who took the call attempted to reach Mr. Casparian. When those efforts were unsuccessful, she telephoned Allegra Munson, another Assistant Public Defender, and told her about respondent's arrest and his sister's subsequent request that the office represent him.

At 8:15 p.m., Ms. Munson telephoned the Cranston police station and asked that her call be transferred to the detective division. In the words of the Supreme Court of Rhode Island, whose factual findings we treat as presumptively correct, the conversation proceeded as follows:

> "A male voice responded with the word 'Detectives.' Ms. Munson identified herself and asked if Brian Burbine was being held; the person responded affirmatively. Ms. Munson explained to the person that Burbine was represented by attorney Casparian who was not available; she further stated that she would act as Burbine's legal counsel in the event that the police intended to place him in a lineup or question him. The unidentified person told Ms. Munson that the police would not be questioning Burbine or putting him in a lineup and that they were through with him for the night. Ms. Munson was not informed that the Providence Police were at the Cranston police station or that Burbine was a suspect in Mary's murder."

At all relevant times, respondent was unaware of his sister's efforts to retain counsel and of the fact and contents of Ms. Munson's telephone conversation.

Less than an hour later, the police brought respondent to an interrogation room and conducted the first of a series of interviews concerning the murder. Prior to each session, respondent was informed of his *Miranda* rights, and on three separate occasions he signed a written form acknowledging that he understood his right to the presence of an attorney and explicitly indicating that he "[did] not want an attorney called or appointed for [him]" before he gave a statement. Uncontradicted evidence at the suppression hearing indicated that at least twice during the course of the evening, respondent was left in a room where he had access to a telephone, which he apparently declined to use. Eventually, respondent signed three written statements fully admitting to the murder.

## II

Respondent does not dispute that the Providence police followed [*Miranda's*] procedures with precision. The record amply supports the state-court findings that the police administered the required warnings, sought to assure that respondent understood his rights, and obtained an express written waiver prior to eliciting each of the three statements. Nor does respondent contest the Rhode Island courts' determination that he at no point requested the presence of a lawyer. He contends instead that the confessions must be suppressed because the police's failure to inform him of the attorney's telephone call deprived him of information essential to his ability to knowingly waive his Fifth Amendment rights. In the alternative, he suggests that to fully protect the Fifth Amendment values served by *Miranda*, we should extend that decision to condemn the conduct of the Providence police. We address each contention in turn.

### A

The voluntariness of the waiver is not at issue. As the Court of Appeals correctly acknowledged, the record is devoid of any suggestion that police resorted to physical or psychological pressure to elicit the statements. Indeed it appears that it was respondent, and not the police, who spontaneously initiated the conversation that led to the first and most damaging confession. Nor is there any question about respondent's comprehension of the full panoply of rights set out in the *Miranda* warnings and of the potential consequences of a decision to relinquish them. Nonetheless, the Court of Appeals believed that the "[d]eliberate or reckless" conduct of the police, in particular their failure to inform respondent of the telephone call, fatally undermined the validity of the otherwise proper waiver. We find this conclusion untenable as a matter of both logic and precedent.

Events occurring outside of the presence of the suspect and entirely unknown to him surely can have no bearing on the capacity to comprehend and knowingly relinquish a constitutional right. Under the analysis of the Court of Appeals, the same defendant, armed with the same information and confronted with precisely the same police conduct, would have knowingly waived his *Miranda* rights had a lawyer not telephoned the police station to inquire about his status. Nothing in any of our waiver decisions or in our understanding of the essential components of a valid waiver requires so incongruous a result. No doubt the additional information would have been useful to respondent; perhaps even it might have affected his decision to confess. But we have never read the Constitution to require that the police supply a suspect with a flow of information to help him calibrate his self-interest in deciding whether to speak or stand by his rights. Once it is determined that a suspect's decision not to rely on his rights was uncoerced, that he at all times knew he could stand mute and request a lawyer, and that he was aware of the State's intention to use his statements to secure a conviction, the analysis is complete and the waiver is valid as a matter of law.[1] The Court of Appeals' conclusion to the contrary was in error.

Nor do we believe that the level of the police's culpability in failing to inform respondent of the telephone call has any bearing on the validity of the waivers. In light of the state-court findings that there was no "conspiracy or collusion" on the part of the police, we have serious doubts about whether the Court of Appeals was free to conclude that their conduct constituted "deliberate or reckless irresponsibility." But whether intentional or inadvertent, the state of mind of the police is irrelevant to the question of the intelligence and voluntariness of respondent's election to abandon his rights. Although highly inappropriate, even deliberate deception of an attorney could not possibly affect a suspect's decision to waive his *Miranda* rights unless he were at least aware of the incident. Compare *Escobedo* (excluding confession where police incorrectly told the *suspect* that his lawyer "'didn't want to see' him"). Nor was the failure to inform respondent of the telephone call the kind of "trick[ery]" that can vitiate the validity of a waiver. Granting that the "deliberate or reckless" withholding of information is objectionable as a matter of ethics, such conduct is only relevant to the constitutional validity of a waiver if it deprives a defendant of knowledge essential to his ability to understand the nature of his

---

[1] The dissent incorrectly reads our analysis of the components of a valid waiver to be inconsistent with the Court's holding in *Edwards*. When a suspect *has* requested counsel, the interrogation must cease, regardless of any question of waiver, unless the suspect himself initiates the conversation. In the course of its lengthy exposition, however, the dissent never comes to grips with the crucial distinguishing feature of this case—that Burbine at no point requested the presence of counsel, as was his right under *Miranda* to do. We do not quarrel with the dissent's characterization of police interrogation as a "privilege terminable at the will of the suspect." We reject, however, the dissent's entirely undefended suggestion that the Fifth Amendment "right to counsel" requires anything more than that the police inform suspect of his right to representation and honor his request that the interrogation cease until his attorney is present.

rights and the consequences of abandoning them. Because respondent's voluntary decision to speak was made with full awareness and comprehension of all the information *Miranda* requires the police to convey, the waivers were valid.

B

At oral argument respondent acknowledged that a constitutional rule requiring the police to inform a suspect of an attorney's efforts to reach him would represent a significant extension of our precedents. He contends, however, that the conduct of the Providence police was so inimical to the Fifth Amendment values *Miranda* seeks to protect that we should read that decision to condemn their behavior. Regardless of any issue of waiver, he urges, the Fifth Amendment requires the reversal of a conviction if the police are less than forthright in their dealings with an attorney or if they fail to tell a suspect of a lawyer's unilateral efforts to contact him. Because the proposed modification ignores the underlying purposes of the *Miranda* rules and because we think that the decision as written strikes the proper balance between society's legitimate law enforcement interests and the protection of the defendant's Fifth Amendment rights, we decline the invitation to further extend *Miranda*'s reach.

Nothing in the Constitution vests in us the authority to mandate a code of behavior for state officials wholly unconnected to any federal right or privilege. The purpose of the *Miranda* warnings instead is to dissipate the compulsion inherent in custodial interrogation and, in so doing, guard against abridgment of the suspect's Fifth Amendment rights. Clearly, a rule that focuses on how the police treat an attorney—conduct that has no relevance at all to the degree of compulsion experienced by the defendant during interrogation—would ignore both *Miranda*'s mission and its only source of legitimacy.

Nor are we prepared to adopt a rule requiring that the police inform a suspect of an attorney's efforts to reach him. While such a rule might add marginally to *Miranda*'s goal of dispelling the compulsion inherent in custodial interrogation, overriding practical considerations counsel against its adoption. As we have stressed on numerous occasions, "[o]ne of the principal advantages" of *Miranda* is the ease and clarity of its application. We have little doubt that the approach urged by respondent and endorsed by the Court of Appeals would have the inevitable consequence of muddying *Miranda*'s otherwise relatively clear waters. The legal questions it would spawn are legion: To what extent should the police be held accountable for knowing that the accused has counsel? Is it enough that someone in the station house knows, or must the interrogating officer himself know of counsel's efforts to contact the suspect? Do counsel's efforts to talk to the suspect concerning one criminal investigation trigger the obligation to inform the defendant before interrogation may proceed on a wholly separate matter? We are unwilling to modify *Miranda* in a manner that would so clearly undermine the decision's central "virtue of informing police and prosecutors with specificity . . . what they may do in conducting [a] custodial interrogation, and of informing courts under what circumstances statements obtained during such interrogation are not admissible."

Moreover, problems of clarity to one side, reading *Miranda* to require the police in each instance to inform a suspect of an attorney's efforts to reach him would work a substantial and, we think, inappropriate shift in the subtle balance struck in that decision. Custodial interrogations implicate two competing concerns. On the one hand, "the need for police questioning as a tool for effective enforcement of criminal laws" cannot be doubted. Admissions of guilt are more than merely "desirable," they are essential to society's compelling interest in finding, convicting, and punishing those who violate the law. On the other hand, the Court has recognized that the interrogation process is "inherently coercive" and that, as a consequence, there exists a substantial risk that the police will inadvertently traverse the fine line between legitimate efforts to elicit admissions and constitutionally impermissible compulsion. *Quarles*. *Miranda* attempted to reconcile these opposing concerns by giving the *defendant* the power to exert some control over the course of the interrogation. Declining to adopt the more extreme position that the actual presence of a lawyer was necessary to dispel the coercion inherent in custodial interrogation, the Court found that the suspect's Fifth Amendment rights could be adequately protected by less intrusive means. Police questioning, often an essential part of the investigatory process, could continue in its traditional form, the Court held, but only if the suspect clearly understood that, at any time, he could bring the proceeding to a halt or, short of that, call in an attorney to give advice and monitor the conduct of his interrogators.

The position urged by respondent would upset this carefully drawn approach in a manner that is both unnecessary for the protection of the Fifth Amendment privilege and injurious to legitimate law enforcement. Because, as *Miranda* holds, full comprehension of the rights to remain silent and request an attorney are sufficient to dispel whatever coercion is inherent in the interrogation process, a rule requiring the police to inform the suspect of an attorney's efforts to contact him would contribute to the protection of the Fifth Amendment privilege only incidentally, if at all. This minimal benefit, however, would come at a substantial cost to society's legitimate and substantial interest in securing admissions of guilt. Indeed, the very premise of the Court of Appeals was not that awareness of Ms. Munson's phone call would have dissipated the coercion of the interrogation room, but that it might have convinced respondent not to speak at all. Because neither the letter nor purposes of *Miranda* require this additional handicap on otherwise permissible investigatory efforts, we are unwilling to expand the *Miranda* rules to require the police to keep the suspect abreast of the status of his legal representation.

### III

Respondent also contends that the Sixth Amendment requires exclusion of his three confessions.[2] It is clear, of course, that, absent a valid waiver, the defendant has the right to the presence of an attorney during any interrogation occurring after the first formal charging proceeding, the point at which the Sixth Amendment right to counsel initially attaches. And we readily agree that once the right *has* attached, it follows that the police may not interfere with the efforts of a defendant's attorney to act as a "'medium' between [the suspect] and the State" during the interrogation. *Moulton*, see *Brewer*. The difficulty for respondent is that the interrogation sessions that yielded the inculpatory statements took place *before* the initiation of "adversary judicial proceedings." He contends, however, that this circumstance is not fatal to his Sixth Amendment claim. At least in some situations, he argues, the Sixth Amendment protects the integrity of the attorney-client relationship regardless of whether the prosecution has in fact commenced "by way of formal charge, preliminary hearing, indictment, information or arraignment." Placing principal reliance on a footnote in *Miranda*, n. 35, and on *Escobedo*, he maintains that our "critical stage" cases, concern

---

[2] Petitioner does not argue that respondent's valid waiver of his Fifth Amendment right to counsel necessarily served to waive his parallel rights under the Sixth Amendment. Accordingly, we have no occasion to consider whether a waiver for one purpose necessarily operates as a general waiver of the right to counsel for all purposes.

only the narrow question of when the right *to* counsel — that is, to the appointment or presence of counsel — attaches. The right to noninterference with an attorney's dealings with a criminal suspect, he asserts, arises the moment that the relationship is formed, or, at the very least, once the defendant is placed in custodial interrogation.

We are not persuaded. At the outset, subsequent decisions foreclose any reliance on *Escobedo* and *Miranda* for the proposition that the Sixth Amendment right, in any of its manifestations, applies prior to the initiation of adversary judicial proceedings. Although *Escobedo* was originally decided as a Sixth Amendment case, "the Court in retrospect perceived that the 'prime purpose' of *Escobedo* was not to vindicate the constitutional right to counsel as such, but, like *Miranda*, 'to guarantee full effectuation of the privilege against self-incrimination. . . .'" Clearly then, *Escobedo* provides no support for respondent's argument. Nor, of course, does *Miranda*, the holding of which rested exclusively on the Fifth Amendment. Thus, the decision's brief observation about the reach of *Escobedo*'s Sixth Amendment analysis is not only dictum, but reflects an understanding of the case that the Court has expressly disavowed.

Questions of precedent to one side, we find respondent's understanding of the Sixth Amendment both practically and theoretically unsound. As a practical matter, it makes little sense to say that the Sixth Amendment right to counsel attaches at different times depending on the fortuity of whether the suspect or his family happens to have retained counsel prior to interrogation. More importantly, the suggestion that the existence of an attorney-client relationship itself triggers the protections of the Sixth Amendment misconceives the underlying purposes of the right to counsel. The Sixth Amendment's intended function is not to wrap a protective cloak around the attorney-client relationship for its own sake any more than it is to protect a suspect from the consequences of his own candor. Its purpose, rather, is to assure that in any "criminal prosecutio[n]," the accused shall not be left to his own devices in facing the "prosecutorial forces of organized society." *Moulton.* By its very terms, it becomes applicable only when the government's role shifts from investigation to accusation. For it is only then that the assistance of one versed in the "intricacies . . . of law," is needed to assure that the prosecution's case encounters "the crucible of meaningful adversarial testing."

Indeed, in *Moulton*, decided this Term, the Court

again confirmed that looking to the initiation of adversary judicial proceedings, far from being mere formalism, is fundamental to the proper application of the Sixth Amendment right to counsel. There, we considered the constitutional implications of a surreptitious investigation that yielded evidence pertaining to two crimes. For one, the defendant had been indicted; for the other, he had not. Concerning the former, the Court reaffirmed that after the first charging proceeding the government may not deliberately elicit incriminating statements from an accused out of the presence of counsel. The Court made clear, however, that the evidence concerning the crime for which the defendant had not been indicted — evidence obtained in precisely the same manner from the identical suspect — would be admissible at a trial limited to those charges. The clear implication of the holding is that the Sixth Amendment right to counsel does not attach until after the initiation of formal charges. Moreover, because Moulton already had legal representation, the decision all but forecloses respondent's argument that the attorney-client relationship itself triggers the Sixth Amendment right.

## IV

Finally, respondent contends that the conduct of the police was so offensive as to deprive him of the fundamental fairness guaranteed by the Due Process Clause of the Fourteenth Amendment. Focusing primarily on the impropriety of conveying false information to an attorney, he invites us to declare that such behavior should be condemned as violative of canons fundamental to the "traditions and conscience of our people." *Rochin v. California, infra.* We do not question that on facts more egregious than those presented here police deception might rise to a level of a due process violation. Accordingly, Justice Stevens' apocalyptic suggestion that we have approved any and all forms of police misconduct is demonstrably incorrect.[3] We hold only that, on these

---

[3] [T]he dissent's misreading of *Miranda* itself is breathtaking in its scope. For example, it reads *Miranda* as creating an undifferentiated right to the presence of an attorney that is triggered automatically by the initiation of the interrogation itself. Yet, as both *Miranda* and subsequent decisions construing *Miranda* make clear beyond refute, "'the interrogation must cease until an attorney is present' *only* '[i]f the individual states that he wants an attorney.'" *Mosley,* (emphasis added), quoting *Miranda.* The dissent condemns us for embracing "incommunicado questioning . . . as a societal goal of the highest

facts, the challenged conduct falls short of the kind of misbehavior that so shocks the sensibilities of civilized society as to warrant a federal intrusion into the criminal processes of the States.

We hold therefore that the Court of Appeals erred in finding that the Federal Constitution required the exclusion of the three inculpatory statements. Accordingly, we reverse and remand for proceedings consistent with this opinion.

Justice STEVENS, with whom Justice BRENNAN and Justice MARSHALL join, dissenting.

This case poses fundamental questions about our system of justice. As this Court has long recognized, and reaffirmed only weeks ago, "ours is an accusatorial and not an inquisitorial system." The Court's opinion today represents a startling departure from that basic insight.

The Court concludes that the police may deceive an attorney by giving her false information about whether her client will be questioned, and that the police may deceive a suspect by failing to inform him of his attorney's communications and efforts to represent him. For the majority, this conclusion, though "distaste[ful]," is not even debatable. The deception of the attorney is irrelevant because the attorney has no right to information, accuracy, honesty, or fairness in the police response to her questions about her client. The deception of the client is acceptable, because, although the information would affect the client's assertion of his rights, the client's actions in ignorance of the availability of his attorney are voluntary, knowing, and intelligent; additionally, society's interest in apprehending, prosecuting,

and punishing criminals outweighs the suspect's interest in information regarding his attorney's efforts to communicate with him. Finally, even mendacious police interference in the communications between a suspect and his lawyer does not violate any notion of fundamental fairness because it does not shock the conscience of the majority.

The murder of Mary Jo Hickey was a vicious crime, fully meriting a sense of outrage and a desire to find and prosecute the perpetrator swiftly and effectively. Indeed, by the time Burbine was arrested on an unrelated breaking-and-entering charge, the Hickey murder had been the subject of a local television special. Not surprisingly, Detective Ferranti, the Cranston Detective who "broke" the case, was rewarded with a special commendation for his efforts.

The recognition that ours is an accusatorial, and not an inquisitorial system nevertheless requires that the government's actions, even in responding to this brutal crime, respect those liberties and rights that distinguish this society from most others. As Justice Jackson observed shortly after his return from Nuremberg, cases of this kind present "a real dilemma in a free society . . . for the defendant is shielded by such safeguards as no system of law except the Anglo-American concedes to him."[5] Justice Frankfurter similarly emphasized that it is "a fair summary of history to say that the safeguards of liberty have been forged in controversies involving not very nice people." And, almost a century and a half ago, Macaulay observed that the guilt of Titus Oates could not justify his conviction by improper methods: "That Oates was a bad man is not a sufficient excuse; for the guilty are almost always the first to suffer those hardships which are afterwards used as precedents against the innocent."

The Court's holding focuses on the period after a suspect has been taken into custody and before he has been charged with an offense. The core of the Court's holding is that police interference with an attorney's access to her client during that period is not unconstitutional. The Court reasons that a State has a compelling interest, not simply in custodial interrogation, but in lawyer-free, incommunicado custodial interrogation. Such incommunicado interrogation is so important that a lawyer may be given false information that prevents her presence and representation; it is so important that police may refuse to inform a suspect of his attorney's communications and immediate availability. This conclusion flies in

---

order that justifies police deception of the shabbiest kind." We, of course, do nothing of the kind. As any reading of *Miranda* reveals, the decision, rather than proceeding from the premise that the rights and needs of the defendant are paramount to all others, embodies a carefully crafted balance designed to fully protect *both* the defendant's and society's interests. The dissent may not share our view that the Fifth Amendment rights of the defendant are amply protected by application of *Miranda as written*. But the dissent is "simply wrong" in suggesting that exclusion of Burbine's three confessions follows perfunctorily from *Miranda*'s mandate.

Quite understandably, the dissent is outraged by the very idea of police deception of a lawyer. Significantly less understandable is its willingness to misconstrue this Court's constitutional holdings in order to implement its subjective notions of sound policy.

---

[5] *Watts*, (Jackson, J., concurring in result).

the face of this Court's repeated expressions of deep concern about incommunicado questioning. Until today, incommunicado questioning has been viewed with the strictest scrutiny by this Court; today, incommunicado questioning is embraced as a societal goal of the highest order that justifies police deception of the shabbiest kind.

Police interference with communications between an attorney and his client is a recurrent problem. The factual variations in the many state-court opinions condemning this interference as a violation of the Federal Constitution suggest the variety of contexts in which the problem emerges. In Oklahoma, police led a lawyer to several different locations while they interrogated the suspect; in Oregon, police moved a suspect to a new location when they learned that his lawyer was on his way; in Illinois, authorities failed to tell a suspect that his lawyer had arrived at the jail and asked to see him; in Massachusetts, police did not tell suspects that their lawyers were at or near the police station. In all these cases, the police not only failed to inform the suspect, but also misled the attorneys. The scenarios vary, but the core problem of police interference remains. "Its recurrence suggests that it has roots in some condition fundamental and general to our criminal system."

The exact reach of the Court's opinion is not entirely clear because, on the one hand, it indicates that more egregious forms of police deception might violate the Constitution, while, on the other hand, it endeavors to make its disposition of this case palatable by making findings of fact concerning the voluntariness of Burbine's confessions that the trial judge who heard the evidence declined to make. Before addressing the legal issues, it therefore seems appropriate to make certain additional comments about what the record discloses concerning the incriminating statements made by Burbine during the 21-hour period that he was detained by the Cranston and Providence police on June 29 and June 30, 1977.

I

[A]lthough there are a number of ambiguities in the record, the state-court findings established (1) that attorney Munson made her call at about 8:15 p.m.; (2) that she was given false information; (3) that Burbine was not told of her call; and (4) that he was thereafter given the *Miranda* warnings, waived his rights, and signed three incriminating statements without receiving any advice from an attorney. The remainder of the record underscores two points. The first is the context of the call—a context in which two Police Departments were on the verge of resolving a highly publicized, hauntingly brutal

homicide and in which, as Lieutenant Gannon testified, the police were aware that counsel's advice to remain silent might be an obstacle to obtaining a confession. The second is the extent of the uncertainty about the events that motivated Burbine's decision to waive his rights. The lawyer-free privacy of the interrogation room, so exalted by the majority, provides great difficulties in determining what actually transpired. It is not simply the ambiguity that is troublesome; if so, the problem would be not unlike other difficult evidentiary problems. Rather, the particularly troublesome aspect is that the ambiguity arises in the very situation—incommunicado interrogation—for which this Court has developed strict presumptions and for which this Court has, in the past, imposed the heaviest burden of justification on the government. It is in this context, and the larger context of our accusatorial system, that the deceptive conduct of the police must be evaluated.

II

Well-settled principles of law lead inexorably to the conclusion that the failure to inform Burbine of the call from his attorney makes the subsequent waiver of his constitutional rights invalid. Analysis should begin with an acknowledgment that the burden of proving the validity of a waiver of constitutional rights is always on the *government*. When such a waiver occurs in a custodial setting, that burden is an especially heavy one because custodial interrogation is inherently coercive, because disinterested witnesses are seldom available to describe what actually happened,[34] and because history has taught us that the danger of overreaching during incommunicado interrogation is so real.

In light of our decision in *Edwards*, the Court is simply wrong in stating that "the analysis is complete and the waiver is valid as a matter of law" when these facts have been established. Like the failure to give warnings and like police initiation of interrogation after a request for counsel, police

---

[34] There is a natural tendency to discredit the testimony of the suspect because of his obvious interest, but it is also true that there have been cases in which the desire to insure a conviction of an apparently guilty suspect has led police officers to color their testimony. As Judge Wilkey observed in a different context, a police officer may "feel that he has a 'higher duty' than the truth. He may perjure himself to convict the defendant." Wilkey, The Exclusionary Rule, 62 Judicature 215, 226 (1978).

deception of a suspect through omission of information regarding attorney communications greatly exacerbates the inherent problems of incommunicado interrogation and requires a clear principle to safeguard the presumption against the waiver of constitutional rights. As in those situations, the police deception should render a subsequent waiver invalid.

Indeed, as *Miranda* itself makes clear, proof that the required warnings have been given is a necessary, but by no means sufficient, condition for establishing a valid waiver. As the Court plainly stated in *Miranda*, "any evidence that the accused was threatened, tricked, or cajoled into a waiver will, of course, show that the defendant did not voluntarily waive his privilege. The requirement of warnings and waiver of rights is a fundamental with respect to the Fifth Amendment privilege and not simply a preliminary ritual to existing methods of interrogation."

In this case it would be perfectly clear that Burbine's waiver was invalid if, for example, Detective Ferranti had "threatened, tricked, or cajoled" Burbine in their private preconfession meeting—perhaps by misdescribing the statements obtained from Di-Orio and Sparks—even though, under the Court's truncated analysis of the issue, Burbine fully understood his rights. For *Miranda* clearly condemns threats or trickery that cause a suspect to make an unwise waiver of his rights even though he fully understands those rights. In my opinion there can be no constitutional distinction—as the Court appears to draw—between a deceptive misstatement and the concealment by the police of the critical fact that an attorney retained by the accused or his family has offered assistance, either by telephone or in person.[39]

As the Court notes, the question is whether the deceptive police conduct "deprives a defendant of

---

[39] It is thus clear that the majority's comparison of a suspect in Burbine's position with "the same defendant . . . had a lawyer not telephoned the police station," sets up a false comparison. For *Miranda*'s condemnation of trickery and cajolery requires that an assessment of police conduct figure importantly in the assessment of a suspect's decision to waive his fundamental constitutional rights. In the majority's comparison, however, the police conduct is irrelevant. In contrast, the appropriate comparison is between a suspect in Burbine's position and a suspect who is otherwise tricked and deceived into a waiver of his rights. *Miranda* itself, as well as the long-established presumption against the waiver of constitutional rights, requires that both kinds of waiver be held invalid. (Repositioned - ed.)

knowledge essential to his ability to understand the nature of his rights and the consequences of abandoning them." Unlike the majority, the state courts have realized that attorney communication to the police about the client is an event that has a direct "bearing" on the knowing and intelligent waiver of constitutional rights. As the Oregon Supreme Court has explained: "To pass up an abstract offer to call some unknown lawyer is very different from refusing to talk with an identified attorney actually available to provide at least initial assistance and advice, whatever might be arranged in the long run. A suspect indifferent to the first offer may well react quite differently to the second." *State v. Haynes*, 288 Ore. 59, 72, 602 P.2d 272, 278 (1979), cert. denied, 446 U.S. 945 (1980).

In short, settled principles about construing waivers of constitutional rights and about the need for strict presumptions in custodial interrogations, as well as a plain reading of the *Miranda* opinion itself, overwhelmingly support the conclusion reached by almost every state court that has considered the matter—a suspect's waiver of his right to counsel is invalid if police refuse to inform the suspect of his counsel's communications.

### III

The Court makes the alternative argument that requiring police to inform a suspect of his attorney's communications to and about him is not required because it would upset the careful "balance" of *Miranda*. Despite its earlier notion that the attorney's call is an "outside event" that has "no bearing" on a knowing and intelligent waiver, the majority does acknowledge that information of attorney Munson's call "would have been useful to respondent" and "might have affected his decision to confess."[43] Thus, a rule requiring the police to inform a suspect of an attorney's call would have two predictable effects. It would serve "*Miranda*'s goal of dispelling the compulsion inherent in custodial interrogation," and it would disserve the goal of custodial interrogation because it would result in fewer confessions. By a process of balancing these two concerns, the Court finds the benefit to the individual outweighed by the "substantial cost to society's legitimate and substantial interest in securing admissions of guilt."

The Court's balancing approach is profoundly

---

[43] In contrast, the theory of the Rhode Island Supreme Court's decision was that, as a matter of fact, knowledge of attorney Munson's call would not have affected Burbine's decision to confess.

misguided. The cost of suppressing evidence of guilt will always make the value of a procedural safeguard appear "minimal," "marginal," or "incremental." Indeed, the value of any trial at all seems like a "procedural technicality" when balanced against the interest in administering prompt justice to a murderer or a rapist caught redhanded. The individual interest in procedural safeguards that minimize the risk of error is easily discounted when the fact of guilt appears certain beyond doubt.

What is the cost of requiring the police to inform a suspect of his attorney's call? It would decrease the likelihood that custodial interrogation will enable the police to obtain a confession. This is certainly a real cost, but it is the same cost that this Court has repeatedly found necessary to preserve the character of our free society and our rejection of an inquisitorial system. Three examples illustrate the point.

In *Escobedo*, we excluded a confession by a defendant who had not been permitted to consult with his lawyer, and whose lawyer had not been permitted to see him. We emphasized the "lesson of history" that our system of justice is not founded on a fear that a suspect will exercise his rights. "If the exercise of constitutional rights will thwart the effectiveness of a system of law enforcement, then there is something very wrong with that system." In *Miranda*, we similarly stressed this character of our system, despite its "cost," by unequivocally holding that an individual has an absolute right to refuse to respond to police interrogation and to have the assistance of counsel during any questioning. Thus, as a matter of law, the assumed right of the police to interrogate a suspect is no right at all; at best, it is a mere privilege terminable at the will of the suspect. And, more recently in *Dunaway v. New York*, 442 U.S. 200 (1979), the Court corrected the long-held but mistaken view of the police that they have some sort of right to take any suspect into custody for the purpose of questioning him even though they may not have probable cause to arrest.[45]

Just as the "cost" does not justify taking a suspect into custody or interrogating him without giving him warnings simply because police desire to question him, so too the "cost" does not justify permitting police to withhold from a suspect knowledge of an attorney's communication, even though that communication would have an unquestionable effect on the suspect's exercise of his rights. The "cost" that concerns the Court amounts to nothing more than an acknowledgment that the law enforcement interest in obtaining convictions suffers whenever a suspect exercises the rights that are afforded by our system of criminal justice. In other words, it is the fear that an individual may exercise his rights that tips the scales of justice for the Court today. The principle that ours is an accusatorial, not an inquisitorial, system, however, has repeatedly led the Court to reject that fear as a valid reason for inhibiting the invocation of rights.

### IV

The Court also argues that a rule requiring the police to inform a suspect of an attorney's efforts to reach him would have an additional cost: it would undermine the "clarity" of the rule of the *Miranda* case. This argument is not supported by any reference to the experience in the States that have adopted such a rule. The Court merely professes concern about its ability to answer three quite simple questions.[46]

Moreover, the Court's evaluation of the interest in "clarity" is rather one-sided. For a police officer

---

[45] A recent treatise describes the significant effect of *Dunaway*:

"Over the years, the impression generally prevailed that the police could 'pick-up' suspects for questioning. In 1979, however, the Supreme Court of the United States held, in *Dunaway v. New York*, that a confession obtained after a 'pick-up' without probable cause (i.e., without reasonable grounds) to make an actual arrest could not be used as evidence." F. Inbau, J. Reid, & J. Buckley, Criminal Interrogation and Confessions 211 (3d ed. 1986).

[46] Thus, the Court asks itself:

(1) "To what extent should the police be held accountable for knowing that the accused has counsel?" The simple answer is that police should be held accountable to the extent that the attorney or the suspect informs the police of the representation.

(2) "Is it enough that someone in the station house knows, or must the interrogating officer himself know of counsel's efforts to contact the suspect?" Obviously, police should be held responsible for getting a message of this importance from one officer to another.

(3) "Do counsel's efforts to talk to the suspect concerning one criminal investigation trigger the obligation to inform the defendant before interrogation may proceed on a wholly separate matter?" As the facts of this case forcefully demonstrate, the answer is "yes."

with a printed card containing the exact text he is supposed to recite, perhaps the rule is clear. But the interest in clarity that the *Miranda* decision was intended to serve is not merely for the benefit of the police. Rather, the decision was also, and primarily, intended to provide adequate guidance to the person in custody who is being asked to waive the protections afforded by the Constitution. Inevitably, the *Miranda* decision also serves the judicial interest in clarifying the inquiry into what actually transpired during a custodial interrogation.[48] Under the Court's conception of the interest in clarity, however, the police would presumably prevail whenever they could convince the trier of fact that a required ritual was performed before the confession was obtained.

## V

At the time attorney Munson made her call to the Cranston police station, she was acting as Burbine's attorney. Under ordinary principles of agency law the deliberate deception of Munson was tantamount to deliberate deception of her client. If an attorney makes a mistake in the course of her representation of her client, the client must accept the consequences of that mistake. It is equally clear that when an attorney makes an inquiry on behalf of her client, the client is entitled to a truthful answer. Surely the client must have the same remedy for a false representation to his lawyer that he would have if he were acting *pro se* and had propounded the question himself.

The majority brushes aside the police deception involved in the misinformation of attorney Munson. It is irrelevant to the Fifth Amendment analysis, concludes the majority, because that right is personal; it is irrelevant to the Sixth Amendment analysis, continues the majority, because the Sixth Amendment does not apply until formal adversary proceedings have begun.

In my view, as a matter of law, the police deception of Munson was tantamount to deception of Burbine himself. It constituted a violation of Burbine's right to have an attorney present during the questioning that began shortly thereafter. The existence

of that right is undisputed.[51] Whether the source of that right is the Sixth Amendment, the Fifth Amendment, or a combination of the two is of no special importance, for I do not understand the Court to deny the existence of the right.

In sharp contrast to the majority, I firmly believe that the right to counsel at custodial interrogation is infringed by police treatment of an attorney that prevents or impedes the attorney's representation of the suspect at that interrogation.

## VI

The Court devotes precisely five sentences to its conclusion that the police interference in the attorney's representation of Burbine did not violate the Due Process Clause. In the majority's view, the due process analysis is a simple "shock the conscience" test. Finding its conscience troubled, but not shocked, the majority rejects the due process challenge.

In a variety of circumstances, however, the Court has given a more thoughtful consideration to the requirements of due process. What emerges from these cases is not the majority's simple "shock the conscience" test, but the principle that due process requires fairness, integrity, and honor in the operation of the criminal justice system, and in its treatment of the citizen's cardinal constitutional protections.

In my judgment, police interference in the attorney-client relationship is the type of governmental misconduct on a matter of central importance to the administration of justice that the Due Process Clause prohibits. Just as the police cannot impliedly promise a suspect that his silence will not be used against him and then proceed to break that promise, so too police cannot tell a suspect's attorney that they will not question the suspect and then proceed to question him. Just as the government cannot conceal from a

---

[48] Indeed, in contrast to the majority's remarks about clarity, the operation of the principle expressed by almost all the state courts would be far clearer than the operation of the Court's contrary principle. For it is surely easier to administer a rule that applies to an external event, such as an attorney's telephone call or a visit to the police station, than a rule that requires an evaluation of the state of mind of a person undergoing custodial interrogation.

[51] In his argument for the United States as *amicus curiae*, the Solicitor General advanced the remarkable suggestion that *Miranda*'s requirement that an individual be told that he has a right to consult with counsel while in custody is "a sort of a white lie" that is "harmless" and "useful." He contended that "police do not have to provide a lawyer if he asks for a lawyer. They need simply terminate the interrogation." I find this view completely untenable, and I take it that the Court's opinion, in today's sanctioning of police deception, does not in any way accept the suggestion that this Court's required warnings are themselves a constitutionally compelled form of deception, or "white lie."

suspect material and exculpatory evidence, so too the government cannot conceal from a suspect the material fact of his attorney's communication.

Police interference with communications between an attorney and his client violates the due process requirement of fundamental fairness. Burbine's attorney was given completely false information about the lack of questioning; moreover, she was not told that her client would be questioned regarding a murder charge about which she was unaware. Burbine, in turn, was not told that his attorney had phoned and that she had been informed that he would not be questioned. Quite simply, the Rhode Island police effectively drove a wedge between an attorney and a suspect through misinformation and omissions.

The majority does not "question that on facts more egregious than those presented here police deception might rise to a level of a due process violation." In my view, the police deception disclosed by this record plainly does rise to that level.

VII

This case turns on a proper appraisal of the role of the lawyer in our society. If a lawyer is seen as a nettlesome obstacle to the pursuit of wrongdoers — as in an inquisitorial society — then the Court's decision today makes a good deal of sense. If a lawyer is seen as an aid to the understanding and protection of constitutional rights — as in an accusatorial society — then today's decision makes no sense at all.

Like the conduct of the police in the Cranston station on the evening of June 29, 1977, the Court's opinion today serves the goal of insuring that the perpetrator of a vile crime is punished. Like the police on that June night as well, however, the Court has trampled on well-established legal principles and flouted the spirit of our accusatorial system of justice.

I respectfully dissent.

## QUESTIONS AND NOTES

**1.** If Burbine had been indicted for the burglary prior to the questioning that led to the confession, would the result have been different? Explain.

**2.** If Burbine had prevailed, would *Miranda*'s carefully drawn balance have been upset? Would the clarity of the *Miranda* rules have been compromised?

**3.** Was there an attorney/client relationship between Munson and Burbine? Is (should) the answer to that question (be) relevant to the resolution of the case?

**4.** In Volume 2 of this book (which those of you who are enrolled only in a police practices course will not have), your authors have reproduced *Burbine* in a section focusing on the duties of the prosecutor. Why do you suppose they did that?

**5.** Did (should) it matter whether the police acted knowingly, recklessly, or without fault in regard to the misinformation conveyed to Munson? How would one prove the police officer's state of mind? Are you satisfied with Justice Stevens' resolution of this question in his footnote 46?

**6.** Does Justice Stevens overstate the right to counsel in his footnote 51? Is it not absolutely true that the police can delay counsel (at least appointed counsel) so long as they discontinue questioning? *Cf. Duckworth v. Eagan*, Chapter 16, B, *supra*.

**7.** Does (should) police trickery affect the voluntariness of a waiver? If so, is there a higher standard for assessing the voluntariness of a waiver from the voluntariness of a confession? Should there be? For more on voluntariness of confessions, see Chapter 18, *infra*.

**8.** If the dissent had prevailed, would there have been an inequity between two otherwise similarly-situated arrestees, one of whom had an unbeknownst lawyer waiting for him, and the other of whom, did not?

**9.** We conclude this section with *Patterson v. Illinois*, where a bare majority of the Court, to the benefit of the State, concluded that *Miranda* warnings were enough to protect a defendant's Sixth, as well as Fifth, Amendment interest in freedom from custodial interrogation.

# Patterson v. Illinois
## 487 U.S. 285 (1988)

Justice WHITE delivered the opinion of the Court.

In this case, we are called on to determine whether the interrogation of petitioner after his indictment violated his Sixth Amendment right to counsel.

### I

Before dawn on August 21, 1983, petitioner and other members of the "Vice Lords" street gang became involved in a fight with members of a rival gang, the "Black Mobsters." Some time after the fight, a former member of the Black Mobsters, James Jackson, went to the home where the Vice Lords had fled. A second fight broke out there, with petitioner and three other Vice Lords beating Jackson severely. The Vice Lords then put Jackson into a car, drove to the end of a nearby street, and left him face down in a puddle of water. Later that morning, police discovered Jackson, dead, where he had been left.

That afternoon, local police officers obtained warrants for the arrest of the Vice Lords, on charges of battery and mob action, in connection with the first fight. One of the gang members who was arrested gave the police a statement concerning the first fight; the statement also implicated several of the Vice Lords (including petitioner) in Jackson's murder. A few hours later, petitioner was apprehended. Petitioner was informed of his rights under *Miranda* and volunteered to answer questions put to him by the police. Petitioner gave a statement concerning the initial fight between the rival gangs, but denied knowing anything about Jackson's death. Petitioner was held in custody the following day, August 22, as law enforcement authorities completed their investigation of the Jackson murder.

On August 23, a Cook County grand jury indicted petitioner and two other gang members for the murder of James Jackson. Police Officer Michael Gresham, who had questioned petitioner earlier, removed him from the lockup where he was being held, and told petitioner that because he had been indicted he was being transferred to the Cook County jail. Petitioner asked Gresham which of the gang members had been charged with Jackson's murder, and upon learning that one particular Vice Lord had been omitted from the indictments, asked: "[W]hy wasn't he indicted, he did everything." Petitioner also began to explain that there was a witness who would support his account of the crime.

At this point, Gresham interrupted petitioner, and handed him a *Miranda* waiver form. The form contained five specific warnings, as suggested by this Court's *Miranda* decision, to make petitioner aware of his right to counsel and of the consequences of any statement he might make to police. Gresham read the warnings aloud, as petitioner read along with him. Petitioner initialed each of the five warnings, and signed the waiver form. Petitioner then gave a lengthy statement to police officers concerning the Jackson murder; petitioner's statement described in detail the role of each of the Vice Lords— including himself— in the murder of James Jackson.

Later that day, petitioner confessed involvement in the murder for a second time. This confession came in an interview with Assistant State's Attorney (ASA) George Smith. At the outset of the interview, Smith reviewed with petitioner the *Miranda* waiver he had previously signed, and petitioner confirmed that he had signed the waiver and understood his rights. Smith went through the waiver procedure once again: reading petitioner his rights, having petitioner initial each one, and sign a waiver form. In addition, Smith informed petitioner that he was a lawyer working with the police investigating the Jackson case. Petitioner then gave another inculpatory statement concerning the crime.

Before trial, petitioner moved to suppress his statements, arguing that they were obtained in a manner at odds with various constitutional guarantees. The trial court denied these motions, and the statements were used against petitioner at his trial. The jury found petitioner guilty of murder, and petitioner was sentenced to a 24-year prison term.

On appeal, petitioner argued that he had not "knowingly and intelligently" waived his Sixth Amendment right to counsel before he gave his uncounseled postindictment confessions. Petitioner contended that the warnings he received, while adequate for the purposes of protecting his *Fifth* Amendment rights as guaranteed by *Miranda*, did not adequately inform him of his *Sixth* Amendment right to counsel. The Illinois Supreme Court, however, rejected this theory, [holding] that *Miranda* warnings were sufficient to make a defendant aware of his Sixth Amendment right to counsel during postindictment questioning.

In reaching this conclusion, the Illinois Supreme Court noted that this Court had reserved decision on this question on several previous occasions[2] and that the lower courts are divided on the issue. We granted this petition for certiorari to resolve this split of authority and to address the issues we had previously left open.

## II

There can be no doubt that petitioner had the right to have the assistance of counsel at his postindictment interviews with law enforcement authorities. Our cases make it plain that the Sixth Amendment guarantees this right to criminal defendants. *Jackson, Brewer, Massiah.*[3] Petitioner asserts that the questioning that produced his incriminating statements violated his Sixth Amendment right to counsel in two ways.

### A

Petitioner's first claim is that because his Sixth Amendment right to counsel arose with his indictment, the police were thereafter barred from initiating a meeting with him. He equates himself with a preindictment suspect who, while being interrogated, asserts his Fifth Amendment right to counsel; under *Edwards*, such a suspect may not be questioned again unless he initiates the meeting.

Petitioner, however, at no time sought to exercise his right to have counsel present. The fact that petitioner's Sixth Amendment right came into existence with his indictment, *i.e.*, that he had such a right at the time of his questioning, does not distinguish him from the preindictment interrogatee whose right to counsel is in existence and available for his exercise while he is questioned. Had petitioner indicated he wanted the assistance of counsel, the authorities' interview with him would have stopped, and further questioning would have been forbidden (unless petitioner called for such a meeting). This was our holding in *Jackson*, which applied *Edwards* to the Sixth Amendment context. We observe that the analysis in *Jackson* is rendered wholly unnecessary if petitioner's position is correct: under petitioner's theory,

---

[2] See, *e.g., Jackson*; *Burbine*; *Brewer*.

[3] We note as a matter of some significance that petitioner had not retained, or accepted by appointment, a lawyer to represent him at the time he was questioned by authorities. Once an accused has a lawyer, a distinct set of constitutional safeguards aimed at preserving the sanctity of the attorney-client relationship takes effect. See *Moulton*. The State conceded as much at argument.

Indeed, the analysis changes markedly once an accused even *requests* the assistance of counsel. See *Jackson*.

the officers in *Jackson* would have been completely barred from approaching the accused in that case unless he called for them. Our decision in *Jackson*, however, turned on the fact that the accused "ha[d] asked for the help of a lawyer" in dealing with the police.

At bottom, petitioner's theory cannot be squared with our rationale in *Edwards*, the case he relies on for support. *Edwards* rested on the view that once "an accused . . . ha[s] expressed his desire to deal with the police only through counsel" he should "not [be] subject to further interrogation by the authorities until counsel has been made available to him, unless the accused himself initiates further communication." Preserving the integrity of an accused's choice to communicate with police only through counsel is the essence of *Edwards* and its progeny—not barring an accused from making an *initial* election as to whether he will face the State's officers during questioning with the aid of counsel, or go it alone. If an accused "knowingly and intelligently" pursues the latter course, we see no reason why the uncounseled statements he then makes must be excluded at his trial.

### B

Petitioner's principal and more substantial claim is that questioning him without counsel present violated the Sixth Amendment because he did not validly waive his right to have counsel present during the interviews. Since it is clear that after the *Miranda* warnings were given to petitioner, he not only voluntarily answered questions without claiming his right to silence or his right to have a lawyer present to advise him but also executed a written waiver of his right to counsel during questioning, the specific issue posed here is whether this waiver was a "knowing and intelligent" waiver of his Sixth Amendment right.

In the past, this Court has held that a waiver of the Sixth Amendment right to counsel is valid only when it reflects "an intentional relinquishment or abandonment of a known right or privilege." In a case arising under the Fifth Amendment, we described this requirement as "a full awareness of both the nature of the right being abandoned and the consequences of the decision to abandon it." *Burbine*. Whichever of these formulations is used, the key inquiry in a case such as this one must be: Was the accused, who waived his Sixth Amendment rights during postindictment questioning, made sufficiently aware of his right to have counsel present during the questioning, and of the possible consequences of a decision to forgo the aid of counsel? In this case, we are convinced that by admonishing petitioner with the *Miranda* warnings, respondent has met this burden and that petitioner's waiver of his right to counsel at the questioning was valid.[5]

First, the *Miranda* warnings given petitioner made him aware of his right to have counsel present during the questioning. By telling petitioner that he had a right to consult with an attorney, to have a lawyer present while he was questioned, and even to have a lawyer appointed for him if he could not afford to retain one on his own, Officer Gresham and ASA Smith conveyed to petitioner the sum and substance of the rights that the Sixth Amendment provided him. "Indeed, it seems self-evident that one who is told he" has such rights to counsel "is in a curious posture to later complain" that his waiver of these rights was unknowing. There is little more petitioner could have possibly been told in an effort to satisfy this portion of the waiver inquiry.

Second, the *Miranda* warnings also served to make petitioner aware of the consequences of a decision by him to waive his Sixth Amendment rights during postindictment questioning. Petitioner knew that any statement that he made could be used against him in subsequent criminal proceedings. This is the ultimate adverse consequence petitioner could have suffered by virtue of his choice to make uncounseled admissions to the authorities. This warning also sufficed—contrary to petitioner's claim here—to let petitioner know what a lawyer could "do for him" during the postindictment questioning: namely, advise petitioner to refrain from making any such statements.[6] By knowing what could be done with any statements he might make, and therefore, what benefit could be obtained by having the aid of counsel

while making such statements, petitioner was essentially informed of the possible consequences of going without counsel during questioning. If petitioner nonetheless lacked "a full and complete appreciation of all of the consequences flowing" from his waiver, it does not defeat the State's showing that the information it provided to him satisfied the constitutional minimum.

Our conclusion is supported by petitioner's inability, in the proceedings before this Court, to articulate with precision what additional information should have been provided to him before he would have been competent to waive his right to counsel. All that petitioner's brief and reply brief suggest is petitioner should have been made aware of his "right under the Sixth Amendment to the broad protection of counsel"—a rather nebulous suggestion—and the "gravity of [his] situation." But surely this latter "requirement" (if it is one) was met when Officer Gresham informed petitioner that he had been formally charged with the murder of James Jackson. Under close questioning on this same point at argument, petitioner likewise failed to suggest any meaningful additional information that he should have been, but was not, provided in advance of his decision to waive his right to counsel.[7] The discussions

---

[5] We emphasize the significance of the fact that petitioner's waiver of counsel was only for this limited aspect of the criminal proceedings against him—only for postindictment questioning. Our decision on the validity of petitioner's waiver extends only so far.

Moreover, even within this limited context, we note that petitioner's waiver was binding on him *only* so long as he wished it to be. Under this Court's precedents, at any time during the questioning petitioner could have changed his mind, elected to have the assistance of counsel, and immediately dissolve the effectiveness of his waiver with respect to any subsequent statements. Our decision today does nothing to change this rule.

[6] An important basis for our analysis is our understanding that an attorney's role at postindictment questioning is rather limited, and substantially different from the attorney's role in later phases of criminal proceedings. At trial, an accused needs an attorney to perform several varied functions—some of which are entirely beyond even the most intelligent

layman. Yet during postindictment questioning, a lawyer's role is rather unidimensional: largely limited to advising his client as to what questions to answer and which ones to decline to answer.

[7] Representative excerpts from the relevant portions of argument include the following:

"QUESTION: [Petitioner] . . . was told that he had a right to counsel.

"MR. HONCHELL [petitioner's counsel]: He was told—the word 'counsel' was used. He was told he had a right to counsel. But not through information by which it would become meaningful to him, because the method that was used was not designed to alert the accused to the Sixth Amendment rights to counsel. . . .

"QUESTION: . . . You mean they should have said you have a Sixth Amendment right to counsel instead of just, you have a right to counsel?

"He knew he had a right to have counsel present before [he] made the confession. Now, what in addition did he have to know to make the waiver an intelligent one?

"MR. HONCHELL: He had to meaningfully know he had a Sixth Amendment right to counsel present because—

"QUESTION: What is the difference between meaningfully knowing and knowing?

found in favorable court decisions, on which petitioner relies, are similarly lacking.

As a general matter, then, an accused who is admonished with the warnings prescribed by this Court in *Miranda*, has been sufficiently apprised of the nature of his Sixth Amendment rights, and of the consequences of abandoning those rights, so that his waiver on this basis will be considered a knowing and intelligent one.[9] We feel that our conclusion in

---

"MR. HONCHELL: Because the warning here used did not convey or express what counsel was intended to do for him after indictment.

"QUESTION: So then you say . . . [that] he would have had to be told more about what counsel would do for him after indictment before he could intelligently waive?

"MR. HONCHELL: That there is a right to counsel who would act on his behalf and represent him.

"QUESTION: Well, okay. So it should have said, in addition to saying counsel, counsel who would act on your behalf and represent you? That would have been the magic solution?

"MR. HONCHELL: That is a possible method, yes." Tr. of Oral Arg. 7-8.

We do not believe that adding the words "who would act on your behalf and represent you" in Sixth Amendment cases would provide any meaningful improvement in the *Miranda* warnings.

[9] This does not mean, of course, that all Sixth Amendment challenges to the conduct of postindictment questioning will fail whenever the challenged practice would pass constitutional muster under *Miranda*. For example, we have permitted a *Miranda* waiver to stand where a suspect was not told that his lawyer was trying to reach him during questioning; in the Sixth Amendment context, this waiver would not be valid. *Burbine*. Likewise a surreptitious conversation between an undercover police officer and an unindicted suspect would not give rise to any *Miranda* violation as long as the "interrogation" was not in a custodial setting; however, once the accused is indicted, such questioning would be prohibited. See *Henry*.

Thus, because the Sixth Amendment's protection of the attorney-client relationship — "the right to rely on counsel as a 'medium' between [the accused] and the State" — extends beyond *Miranda*'s protection of the Fifth Amendment right to counsel, see *Moulton*, there will be cases where a waiver which would be valid under *Miranda* will not suffice for Sixth Amendment purposes. See also *Jackson*.

a recent Fifth Amendment case is equally apposite here: "Once it is determined that a suspect's decision not to rely on his rights was uncoerced, that he at all times knew he could stand mute and request a lawyer, and that he was aware of the State's intention to use his statements to secure a conviction, the analysis is complete and the waiver is valid as a matter of law." See *Burbine*.

### C

We consequently reject petitioner's argument, which has some acceptance from courts and commentators, that since "the sixth amendment right [to counsel] is far superior to that of the fifth amendment right" and since "[t]he greater the right the greater the loss from a waiver of that right," waiver of an accused's Sixth Amendment right to counsel should be "more difficult" to effectuate than waiver of a suspect's Fifth Amendment rights. While our cases have recognized a "difference" between the Fifth Amendment and Sixth Amendment rights to counsel, and the "policies" behind these constitutional guarantees, we have never suggested that one right is "superior" or "greater" than the other, nor is there any support in our cases for the notion that because a Sixth Amendment right may be involved, it is more difficult to waive than the Fifth Amendment counterpart.

Instead, we have taken a more pragmatic approach to the waiver question — asking what purposes a lawyer can serve at the particular stage of the proceedings in question, and what assistance he could provide to an accused at that stage — to determine the scope of the Sixth Amendment right to counsel, and the type of warnings and procedures that should be required before a waiver of that right will be recognized.

Applying this approach, it is our view that whatever warnings suffice for *Miranda*'s purposes will also be sufficient in the context of postindictment questioning. The State's decision to take an additional step and commence formal adversarial proceedings against the accused does not substantially increase the value of counsel to the accused at questioning, or expand the limited purpose that an attorney serves when the accused is questioned by authorities. With respect to this inquiry, we do not discern a substantial difference between the usefulness of a lawyer to a suspect during custodial interrogation, and his value to an accused at postindictment questioning.

Thus, we require a more searching or formal inquiry before permitting an accused to waive his right to counsel at trial than we require for a Sixth Amendment waiver during postindictment questioning — *not* because postindictment questioning is "less important" than a trial (the analysis that petitioner's "hierarchical" approach would suggest) — but because the full "dangers and disadvantages of self-representation," during questioning are less substantial and more obvious to an accused than they are at trial.[13] Because the role of counsel at questioning is relatively simple and limited, we see no problem in having a waiver procedure at that stage which is likewise simple and limited. So long as the accused is made aware of the "dangers and disadvantages of self-representation" during postindictment questioning, by use of the *Miranda* warnings, his waiver of his Sixth Amendment right to counsel at such questioning is "knowing and intelligent."

### III

Before confessing to the murder of James Jackson, petitioner was meticulously informed by authorities of his right to counsel, and of the consequences of any choice not to exercise that right. On two separate occasions, petitioner elected to forgo the assistance of counsel, and speak directly to officials concerning his role in the murder. Because we believe that petitioner's waiver of his Sixth Amendment rights was "knowing and intelligent," we find no error in the decision of the trial court to permit petitioner's confessions to be used against him. Consequently, the judgment of the Illinois Supreme Court is affirmed.

Justice BLACKMUN, dissenting.

I agree with most of what Justice Stevens says in his dissenting opinion. I, however, merely would hold that after formal adversary proceedings against a defendant have been commenced, the Sixth Amendment mandates that the defendant not be "'subject to further interrogation by the authorities until counsel has been made available to him, unless the accused himself initiates further communication, exchanges, or conversations with the police.'" *Jackson*, quoting *Edwards*.

The Court's majority concludes: "The fact that petitioner's Sixth Amendment right came into existence with his indictment . . . does not distinguish him from the preindictment interrogatee whose right

to counsel is in existence and available for his exercise while he is questioned." I must disagree. "[W]hen the Constitution grants protection against criminal proceedings without the assistance of counsel, counsel must be furnished whether or not the accused requested the appointment of counsel." In my view, the Sixth Amendment does not allow the prosecution to take undue advantage of any gap between the commencement of the adversary process and the time at which counsel is appointed for a defendant.

Justice STEVENS, with whom Justice BRENNAN and Justice MARSHALL join, dissenting.

The Court should not condone unethical forms of trial preparation by prosecutors or their investigators. In civil litigation it is improper for a lawyer to communicate with his or her adversary's client without either notice to opposing counsel or the permission of the court. An attempt to obtain evidence for use at trial by going behind the back of one's adversary would be not only a serious breach of professional ethics but also a manifestly unfair form of trial practice. In the criminal context, the same ethical rules apply and, in my opinion, notions of fairness that are at least as demanding should also be enforced.

The question that this case raises is at what point in the adversary process does it become impermissible for the prosecutor, or his or her agents, to conduct such private interviews with the opposing party? Several alternatives are conceivable: when the trial commences, when the defendant has actually met and accepted representation by his or her appointed counsel, when counsel is appointed, or when the adversary process commences. In my opinion, the Sixth Amendment right to counsel demands that a firm and unequivocal line be drawn at the point at which adversary proceedings commence.

In prior cases this Court has used strong language to emphasize the significance of the formal commencement of adversary proceedings. Such language has been employed to explain decisions denying the defendant the benefit of the protection of the Sixth Amendment in preindictment settings, but an even-handed interpretation of the Amendment would support the view that additional protection should automatically attach the moment the formal proceedings begin. One such example is *Kirby v. Illinois*, 406 U.S. 682 (1972). Justice Stewart's plurality opinion explained the significance of the formal charge:

"The initiation of judicial criminal proceedings is far from a mere formalism. It is

---

[13] [A]n attorney's role at questioning is relatively limited. But at trial, counsel is required to help even the most gifted layman adhere to the rules of procedure and evidence, comprehend the subtleties of *voir dire*, examine and cross-examine witnesses effectively (including the accused), object to improper prosecution questions, and much more.

the starting point of our whole system of adversary criminal justice. For it is only then that the government has committed itself to prosecute, and only then that the adverse positions of government and defendant have solidified. It is then that a defendant finds himself faced with the prosecutorial forces of organized society, and immersed in the intricacies of substantive and procedural criminal law. It is this point, therefore, that marks the commencement of the 'criminal prosecutions' to which alone the explicit guarantees of the Sixth Amendment are applicable.''

[R]ecently, in *Burbine*, the Court upheld a waiver of the right to counsel in a pretrial context even though the waiver "would not be valid" if the same situation had arisen after indictment. Today, however, in reaching a decision similarly favorable to the interest in law enforcement unfettered by process concerns, the Court backs away from the significance previously attributed to the initiation of formal proceedings. In the majority's view, the purported waiver of counsel in this case is properly equated with that of an unindicted suspect. Yet, as recognized in [our prior cases], important differences separate the two. The return of an indictment, or like instrument, substantially alters the relationship between the state and the accused. Only after a formal accusation has "the government . . . committed itself to prosecute, and only then [have] the adverse positions of government and defendant . . . solidified." Moreover, the return of an indictment also presumably signals the government's conclusion that it has sufficient evidence to establish a prima facie case. As a result, any further interrogation can only be designed to buttress the government's case; authorities are no longer simply attempting "to solve a crime." Given the significance of the initiation of formal proceedings and the concomitant shift in the relationship between the state and the accused, I think it quite wrong to suggest that *Miranda* warnings—or for that matter, any warnings offered by an adverse party—provide a sufficient basis for permitting the undoubtedly prejudicial—and, in my view, unfair—practice of permitting trained law enforcement personnel and prosecuting attorneys to communicate with as-of-yet unrepresented criminal defendants.

The majority premises its conclusion that *Miranda* warnings lay a sufficient basis for accepting a waiver of the right to counsel on the assumption that those warnings make clear to an accused "what a lawyer could 'do for him' during the postindictment questioning: namely, advise [him] to refrain

from making any [incriminating] statements.'' Yet, this is surely a gross understatement of the disadvantage of proceeding without a lawyer and an understatement of what a defendant must understand to make a knowing waiver.[5] The *Miranda* warnings do not, for example, inform the accused that a lawyer might examine the indictment for legal sufficiency before submitting his or her client to interrogation or that a lawyer is likely to be considerably more skillful at negotiating a plea bargain and that such negotiations may be most fruitful if initiated prior to any interrogation. Rather, the warnings do not even go so far as to explain to the accused the nature of the charges pending against him—advice that a court would insist upon before allowing a defendant to enter a guilty plea with or without the presence of an attorney. Without defining precisely the nature of the inquiry required to establish a valid waiver of the Sixth Amendment right to counsel, it must be conceded that at least minimal advice is necessary—the accused must be told of the "dangers and disadvantages of self-representation.''

Yet, once it is conceded that certain advice is required and that after indictment the adversary relationship between the state and the accused has solidified, it inescapably follows that a prosecutor may not conduct private interviews with a charged defendant. As at least one Court of Appeals has recognized, there are ethical constraints that prevent a prosecutor from giving legal advice to an uncounseled adversary. Thus, neither the prosecutor nor his or her agents can ethically provide the unrepresented

---

[5] Respondent, and the United States as *amicus curiae*, argue that the comprehensive inquiry required by *Faretta v. California*, 422 U.S. 806 (1975), should not be extended to pretrial waivers because the role of counsel—and conversely the difficulty of proceeding without counsel—is more important at trial. I reject the premise that a lawyer's skills are more likely to sit idle at a pretrial interrogation than at trial. Both events require considerable experience and expertise and I would be reluctant to rank one over the other. Moreover, as we recognized in *Escobedo*:

"[T]he 'right to use counsel at the formal trial [would be] a very hollow thing [if], for all practical purposes, the conviction is already assured by pretrial examination.' 'One can imagine a cynical prosecutor saying: "Let them have the most illustrious counsel, now. They can't escape the noose. There is nothing that counsel can do for them at the trial.'''

defendant with the kind of advice that should precede an evidence-gathering interview after formal proceedings have been commenced. Indeed, in my opinion even the *Miranda* warnings themselves are a species of legal advice that is improper when given by the prosecutor after indictment.

Moreover, there are good reasons why such advice is deemed unethical, reasons that extend to the custodial, postindictment setting with unequaled strength. First, the offering of legal advice may lead an accused to underestimate the prosecuting authorities' true adversary posture. For an incarcerated defendant—in this case, a 17-year-old who had been in custody for 44 hours at the time he was told of the indictment—the assistance of someone to explain why he is being held, the nature of the charges against him, and the extent of his legal rights, may be of such importance as to overcome what is perhaps obvious to most, that the prosecutor is a foe and not a friend. Second, the adversary posture of the parties, which is not fully solidified until formal charges are brought, will inevitably tend to color the advice offered. As hard as a prosecutor might try, I doubt that it is possible for one to wear the hat of an effective adviser to a criminal defendant while at the same time wearing the hat of a law enforcement authority. Finally, regardless of whether or not the accused actually understands the legal and factual issues involved and the state's role as an adversary party, advice offered by a lawyer (or his or her agents) with such an evident conflict of interest cannot help but create a public perception of unfairness and unethical conduct.

In sum, without a careful discussion of the pitfalls of proceeding without counsel, the Sixth Amendment right cannot properly be waived. An adversary party, moreover, cannot adequately provide such advice. As a result, once the right to counsel attaches and the adversary relationship between the state and the accused solidifies, a prosecutor cannot conduct a private interview with an accused party without "dilut[ing] the protection afforded by the right to counsel," *Moulton*. Although this ground alone is reason enough to never permit such private interviews, the rule also presents the added virtue of drawing a clear and easily identifiable line at the point between the investigatory and adversary stages of a criminal proceeding. Such clarity in definition of constitutional rules that govern criminal proceedings is important to the law enforcement profession as well as to the private citizen. See *Roberson*. It is true, of course, that the interest in effective law enforcement would benefit from an opportunity to engage in incommunicado questioning of defendants who, for reasons beyond their control, have not been able to receive the legal advice from counsel to which they are constitutionally entitled. But the Court's singleminded concentration on that interest might also lead to the toleration of similar practices at any stage of the trial. I think it clear that such private communications are intolerable not simply during trial, but at any point after adversary proceedings have commenced.

I therefore respectfully dissent.

## QUESTIONS AND NOTES

**1.** Is Patterson's argument that he was given insufficient warnings by the police, or that he should not have been approached by the police at all? Which of these arguments is more powerful? Explain.

**2.** Could you have developed more powerful answers to the questions put to Patterson's attorney in Court footnote 7? What might they have been?

**3.** Is the attorney's role as important during custodial interrogation as it is during trial? If your answer was "yes," is *Patterson* wrongly decided?

**4.** If counsel does no more for his client after indictment in regard to custodial interrogation than he did before such indictment, does it follow that *Miranda* should have been a Sixth Amendment case?

# 18.

# VOLUNTARINESS REVISITED

With confessions being vulnerable under both *Miranda* and *Massiah*, it is easy to assume that the abstract issue of coerced or involuntary confessions (*e.g. Brown, Watts, Cooker*, and *Spano*) can be relegated to a legal history course. In fact, that is not the case.

Among other times when voluntariness is relevant are cases in which *Miranda* warnings are not required either because of an emergency (*e.g. Quarles*) or because the defendant was not in custody (*e.g. Mathiason, Perkins*). Other confessions might be deemed involuntary despite *Miranda* because of the police coercion exercised after the warnings were given and a waiver was obtained. Still other confessions might be inadmissible because of either the failure to give *Miranda* warnings, or the disregard of the warnings when given. But the subsequently obtained statements, if otherwise voluntary, could be admitted to impeach the defendant's credibility at trial. *Mincey* raised such a question.

## Mincey v. Arizona
### 437 U.S. 385 (1978)

Mr. Justice STEWART delivered the opinion of the Court.

On the afternoon of October 28, 1974, under-cover police officer Barry Headricks of the Metropolitan Area Narcotics Squad knocked on the door of an apartment in Tucson, Ariz., occupied by the petitioner, Rufus Mincey. Earlier in the day, Officer Headricks had allegedly arranged to purchase a quantity of heroin from Mincey and had left, ostensibly to obtain money. On his return he was accompanied by nine other plainclothes policemen and a deputy county attorney. The door was opened by John Hodgman, one of three acquaintances of Mincey who were in the living room of the apartment. Officer Headricks slipped inside and moved quickly into the bedroom. Hodgman attempted to slam the door in order to keep the other officers from entering, but was pushed back against the wall. As the police entered the apartment, a rapid volley of shots was heard from the bedroom. Officer Headricks emerged and collapsed on the floor. When other officers entered the bedroom they found Mincey lying on the floor, wounded and semiconscious. Officer Headricks died a few hours later in the hospital.

The petitioner was indicted for murder, assault,[1] and three counts of narcotics offenses. He was tried at a single trial and convicted on all the charges. At his trial and on appeal, he contended that statements used to impeach his credibility were inadmissible because they had not been made voluntarily. The Arizona Supreme Court reversed the murder and assault convictions on state-law grounds,[2] but affirmed the narcotics convictions. It held that Mincey's statements were voluntary.

## II

Since there will presumably be a new trial in this case, it is appropriate to consider the petitioner's contention that statements he made from a hospital bed were involuntary, and therefore could not constitutionally be used against him at his trial.

Mincey was brought to the hospital after the shooting and taken immediately to the emergency room where he was examined and treated. He had sustained a wound in his hip, resulting in damage to the sciatic nerve and partial paralysis of his right leg. Tubes were inserted into his throat to help him breathe, and through his nose into his stomach to keep him from vomiting; a catheter was inserted into his bladder. He received various drugs, and a device was attached to his arm so that he could be fed intravenously. He was then taken to the intensive care unit.

At about eight o'clock that evening, Detective Hust of the Tucson Police Department came to the intensive care unit to interrogate him. Mincey was unable to talk because of the tube in his mouth, and so he responded to Detective Hust's questions by writing answers on pieces of paper provided by the hospital.[11] Hust told Mincey he was under arrest for

the murder of a police officer, gave him the warnings required by *Miranda*, and began to ask questions about the events that had taken place in Mincey's apartment a few hours earlier. Although Mincey asked repeatedly that the interrogation stop until he could get a lawyer, Hust continued to question him until almost midnight.

Statements made by a defendant in circumstances violating the strictures of *Miranda* are admissible for impeachment if their "trustworthiness . . . satisfies legal standards." *Harris v. New York*, 401 U.S., at 224; *Oregon v. Hass*, 420 U.S., at 722. But *any* criminal trial use against a defendant of his *involuntary* statement is a denial of due process of law, "even though there is ample evidence aside from the confession to support the conviction." If therefore, Mincey's statements to Detective Hust were not "the product of a rational intellect and a free will," his conviction cannot stand. In making this critical determination, we are not bound by the Arizona Supreme Court's holding that the statements were voluntary. Instead, this Court is under a duty to make an independent evaluation of the record.

It is hard to imagine a situation less conducive to the exercise of "a rational intellect and a free will" than Mincey's. He had been seriously wounded just a few hours earlier, and had arrived at the hospital "depressed almost to the point of coma," according to his attending physician. Although he had received some treatment, his condition at the time of Hust's interrogation was still sufficiently serious that he was in the intensive care unit.[14] He complained to Hust that the pain in his leg was "unbearable." He was evidently confused and unable to think clearly about either the events of that afternoon or the circumstances of his interrogation, since some of his written answers were on their face not entirely coherent.[15] Finally, while

---

[1] The assault charge was based on the wounding of a person in the living room who was hit by a bullet that came through the wall.

[2] The state appellate court held that the jury had been improperly instructed on criminal intent. It appears from the record in this case that the retrial of the petitioner on the murder and assault charges was stayed by the trial court after certiorari was granted by this Court.

[11] Because of the way in which the interrogation was conducted, the only contemporaneous record consisted of Mincey's written answers. Hust testified that the next day he went over this document and made a few notes to help him reconstruct the conversation. In a written report dated about a week later, Hust transcribed Mincey's answers and added the questions he believed he had asked. It was this written report that was used to cross-examine Mincey at his subsequent trial.

---

[14] A nurse testified at the suppression hearing that the device used to aid Mincey's respiration was reserved for "more critical" patients. Moreover, Mincey apparently remained hospitalized for almost a month after the shooting. According to docket entries in the trial court his arraignment was postponed several times because he was still in the hospital; he was not arraigned until November 26, 1974.

[15] For example, two of the answers written by Mincey were: "Do you me Did he give me some money (no)" and "Every body know Every body." And Mincey apparently believed he was being questioned by several different policemen, not Hust alone; although it was Hust who told Mincey he had killed a policeman, later in the interrogation Mincey indicated he thought it was someone else.

Mincey was being questioned he was lying on his back on a hospital bed, encumbered by tubes, needles, and breathing apparatus. He was, in short, "at the complete mercy" of Detective Hust, unable to escape or resist the thrust of Hust's interrogation.

In this debilitated and helpless condition, Mincey clearly expressed his wish not to be interrogated. As soon as Hust's questions turned to the details of the afternoon's events, Mincey wrote: "This is all I can say without a lawyer." Hust nonetheless continued to question him, and a nurse who was present suggested it would be best if Mincey answered. Mincey gave unresponsive or uninformative answers to several more questions, and then said again that he did not want to talk without a lawyer. Hust ignored that request and another made immediately thereafter.[16]

---

[16] In his reconstruction of the interrogation, see n. 11, *supra*, Hust stated that, after he asked Mincey some questions to try to identify one of the other victims, the following ensued:

"HUST: . . . What do you remember that happened?

"MINCEY: I remember somebody standing over me saying 'move nigger, move.' I was on the floor beside the bed.

"HUST: Do you remember shooting anyone or firing a gun?

"MINCEY: *This is all I can say without a lawyer.*

"HUST: If you want a lawyer now, I cannot talk to you any longer, however, you don't have to answer any questions if you don't want to. Do you still want to talk to me?

"MINCEY: (Shook his head in an affirmative manner.)

"HUST: What else can you remember?

"MINCEY: I'm going to have to put my head together. There are so many things that I don't remember I. Like how did they get into the apartment?

"HUST: How did who get into the apartment?

"MINCEY: Police.

"HUST: Did you sell some narcotics to the guy that was shot?

"MINCEY: Do you mean, did he give me some money?

"HUST: Yes.

"MINCEY: No.

"HUST: Did you give him a sample?

"MINCEY: What do you call a sample?

"HUST: A small amount of drug or narcotic to test?

Indeed, throughout the interrogation Mincey vainly asked Hust to desist. Moreover, he complained several times that he was confused or unable to think clearly, or that he could answer more accurately the next day. But despite Mincey's entreaties to be let alone, Hust ceased the interrogation only during intervals when Mincey lost consciousness or received medical treatment, and after each such interruption returned relentlessly to his task. The statements at issue were thus the result of virtually continuous questioning of a seriously and painfully wounded man on the edge of consciousness.

There were not present in this case some of the gross abuses that have led the Court in other cases to find confessions involuntary, such as beatings, see *Brown v. Mississippi*, or "truth serums," see *Townsend v. Sain*, 372 U.S. 293. But "the blood of the accused is not the only hallmark of an unconstitutional inquisition." *Blackburn v. Alabama*, 361 U.S., at 206. Determination of whether a statement is involuntary "requires more than a mere color-matching of cases." It requires careful evaluation of

---

"MINCEY: *I can't say without a lawyer.*

"HUST: Did anyone say police or narcs when they came into apartment?

"MINCEY: Let me get myself together first. You see, I'm not for sure everything happened so fast. I can't answer at this time because I don't think so, but I can't say for sure. Some questions aren't clear to me at the present time.

"HUST: Did you shoot anyone?

"MINCEY: *I can't say, I have to see a lawyer.*" (Emphasis supplied.)

While some of Mincey's answers seem relatively responsive to the questions, it must be remembered that Hust added the questions at a later date, with the answers in front of him. See n. 11, *supra*. The reliability of Hust's report is uncertain. For example, Hust claimed that immediately after Mincey first expressed a desire to remain silent, Hust said Mincey need not answer any questions but Mincey responded by indicating that he wanted to continue. There is no contemporaneous record supporting Hust's statement that Mincey acted so inconsistently immediately after asserting his wish not to respond further, nor did the nurse who was present during the interrogation corroborate Hust. The Arizona Supreme Court apparently disbelieved Hust in this respect, since it stated that "after *each* indication from [Mincey] that he wanted to consult an attorney or that he wanted to stop answering questions, the police officer continued to question [him]." (emphasis supplied).

all the circumstances of the interrogation.

It is apparent from the record in this case that Mincey's statements were not "the product of his free and rational choice." To the contrary, the undisputed evidence makes clear that Mincey wanted *not* to answer Detective Hust. But Mincey was weakened by pain and shock, isolated from family, friends, and legal counsel, and barely conscious, and his will was simply overborne. Due process of law requires that statements obtained as these were cannot be used in any way against a defendant at his trial.

### III

For the foregoing reasons, the judgment of the Arizona Supreme Court is reversed, and the case is remanded for further proceedings not inconsistent with this opinion.

Mr. Justice REHNQUIST, concurring in part and dissenting in part.

I dissent from the Court's holding that Mincey's statements were involuntary and thus inadmissible.

### II

The Court in Part II of its opinion advises the Arizona courts on the admissibility of certain statements made by Mincey that are relevant only to the murder charge. Because Mincey's murder conviction was reversed by the Arizona Supreme Court, and it is not certain that there will be a retrial, I would not reach this issue. Since the Court addresses the issue, however, I must register my disagreement with its conclusion.

Before trial, Mincey moved to suppress as involuntary certain statements that he had made while confined in an intensive care unit some hours after the shooting. As the Court acknowledges, the trial court found "with unmistakable clarity" that the statements were voluntary, and the Supreme Court of Arizona, unanimously affirmed. This Court now disagrees and holds that "Mincey's statements were not 'the product of his free and rational choice'" and therefore "cannot be used in any way against [him] at his trial." Because I believe that the Court both has failed to accord the state-court finding the deference that the Court has always found such findings due and also misapplied our past precedents, I dissent.

The Court in this case ignores entirely some evidence of voluntariness and distinguishes away yet other testimony. There can be no discounting that Mincey was seriously wounded and laden down with medical equipment. Mincey was certainly not able to move about and, because of the breathing tube in his mouth, had to answer Detective Hust's questions

on paper. But the trial court was certainly not required to find, as the Court would imply, that Mincey was "a seriously and painfully wounded man on the edge of consciousness." Nor is it accurate to conclude that Detective Hust "ceased the interrogation only during intervals when Mincey lost consciousness or received medical treatment, and after each such interruption returned relentlessly to his task."

As the Arizona Supreme Court observed in affirming the trial court's finding of voluntariness, Mincey's nurse

> "testified that she had not given [Mincey] any medication and that [he] was alert and able to understand the officer's questions. . . . She said that [Mincey] was in moderate pain but was very cooperative with everyone. The interrogating officer also testified that [Mincey] did not appear to be under the influence of drugs and that [his] answers were generally responsive to the questions."[1]

The uncontradicted testimony of Detective Hust also reveals a questioning that was far from "relentless." While the interviews took place over a three-hour time span, the interviews were not "very long; probably not more than an hour total for everything." Hust would leave the room whenever Mincey received medical treatment "or if it looked like he was getting a little bit exhausted." According to Detective Hust, Mincey never "los[t] consciousness at any time."

As the Court openly concedes, there were in this case none of the "gross abuses that have led the Court in other cases to find confessions involuntary, such as beatings . . . or 'truth serums.'" Neither is this a case, however, where the defendant's will was "simply overborne" by "mental coercion." As the Supreme Court of Arizona observed, it was the testimony of both Detective Hust and Nurse Graham

---

[1] The Supreme Court of Arizona also emphasized "the fact that [Mincey] was able to write his answers in a legible and fairly sensible fashion." The Court concedes that "Mincey's answers seem relatively responsive to the questions," but chooses to ignore this evidence on the ground that the "reliability of Hust's report is uncertain." Despite the contrary impression given by the Court, the Arizona Supreme Court's opinion casts no doubt on the testimony or report of Detective Hust. The Court is thus left solely with its own conclusion as to the reliability of various witnesses based on a re-examination of the record on appeal.

"that neither mental or physical force nor abuse was used on [Mincey]. . . . Nor were any promises made." According to Mincey's own testimony, he wanted to help Hust "the best I could" and tried to answer each question "to the best of my recollection at the time that this was going on." Mincey did not claim that he felt compelled by Detective Hust to answer the questions propounded.[2]

By all of these standards enunciated in our previous cases, I think the Court today goes too far in substituting its own judgment for the judgment of a trial court and the highest court of a State, both of which decided these disputed issues differently than does this Court, and both of which were a good deal closer to the factual occurrences than is this Court. Admittedly we may not abdicate our duty to decide

---

[2] While Mincey asked at several points to see a lawyer, he also expressed his willingness to continue talking to Detective Hust even without a lawyer. As the Court notes, since Mincey's statements were not

questions of constitutional law under the guise of wholly remitting to state courts the function of fact finding which is a necessary ingredient of the process of constitutional decision. But the authorities previously cited likewise counsel us against going to the other extreme, and attempting to extract from a cold record bits and pieces of evidence which we then treat as the "facts" of the case. I believe that the trial court was entitled to conclude that, notwithstanding Mincey's medical condition, his statements in the intensive care unit were admissible. The fact that the same court might have been equally entitled to reach the opposite conclusion does not justify this Court's adopting the opposite conclusion.

I therefore dissent from Part II of the Court's opinion.

---

used as part of the prosecution's case in chief but only in impeachment, any violation of *Miranda* was irrelevant.

## QUESTIONS AND NOTES

**1.** Should the voluntariness issue have been decided in this case? Why? Why not?

**2.** In your view, should factual doubts in a case such as *Mincey* be resolved against the State or against the defendant? Why?

**3.** Do you think that Mincey's statements were voluntarily given? Explain.

**4.** Sometimes, the involuntariness of a confession will not be caused by the State. In *Connelly*, the Court explored the question of how much of a difference that should make.

### Colorado v. Connelly
### 479 U.S. 157 (1986)

Chief Justice REHNQUIST delivered the opinion of the Court.

In this case, the Supreme Court of Colorado held that the United States Constitution requires a court to suppress a confession when the mental state of the defendant, at the time he made the confession, interfered with his "rational intellect" and his "free will." Because this decision seemed to conflict with prior holdings of this Court, we granted certiorari. We conclude that the admissibility of this kind of statement is governed by state rules of evidence, rather than by our previous decisions regarding coerced confessions and *Miranda* waivers. We therefore reverse.

I

On August 18, 1983, Officer Patrick Anderson of the Denver Police Department was in uniform, working in an off-duty capacity in downtown Denver. Respondent Francis Connelly approached Officer Anderson and, without any prompting, stated that he had murdered someone and wanted to talk about it. Anderson immediately advised respondent that he had the right to remain silent, that anything he said could be used against him in court, and that he had the right to an attorney prior to any police questioning. See *Miranda*. Respondent stated that he understood these rights but he still wanted to talk about the murder. Understandably bewildered by this confession, Officer Anderson asked respondent several questions. Connelly denied that he had been drinking, denied that he had been taking any drugs, and stated that, in the past, he had been a patient in several mental hospitals. Officer Anderson again told Connelly that he was under no obligation to say anything. Connelly replied that it was "all right," and that he would talk to Officer Anderson because his conscience had been bothering him. To Officer Anderson, respondent appeared to understand fully the nature of his acts.

Shortly thereafter, Homicide Detective Stephen Antuna arrived. Respondent was again advised of his rights, and Detective Antuna asked him "what he had on his mind." Respondent answered that he had come all the way from Boston to confess to the murder of Mary Ann Junta, a young girl whom he had killed in Denver sometime during November 1982. Respondent was taken to police headquarters, and a search of police records revealed that the body of an unidentified female had been found in April 1983. Respondent openly detailed his story to Detective Antuna and Sergeant Thomas Haney, and readily agreed to take the officers to the scene of the killing. Under Connelly's sole direction, the two officers and respondent proceeded in a police vehicle to the location of the crime. Respondent pointed out the exact location of the murder. Throughout this episode, Detective Antuna perceived no indication whatsoever that respondent was suffering from any kind of mental illness.

Respondent was held overnight. During an interview with the public defender's office the following morning, he became visibly disoriented. He began giving confused answers to questions, and for the first time, stated that "voices" had told him to come to Denver and that he had followed the directions of these voices in confessing. Respondent was sent to a state hospital for evaluation. He was initially found incompetent to assist in his own defense. By March 1984, however, the doctors evaluating respondent determined that he was competent to proceed to trial.

At a preliminary hearing, respondent moved to suppress all of his statements. Dr. Jeffrey Metzner, a psychiatrist employed by the state hospital, testified that respondent was suffering from chronic schizophrenia and was in a psychotic state at least as of August 17, 1983, the day before he confessed. Metzner's interviews with respondent revealed that respondent was following the "voice of God." This voice instructed respondent to withdraw money from the bank, to buy an airplane ticket, and to fly from Boston to Denver. When respondent arrived from Boston, God's voice became stronger and told respondent either to confess to the killing or to commit suicide. Reluctantly following the command of the voices, respondent approached Officer Anderson and confessed.

Dr. Metzner testified that, in his expert opinion, respondent was experiencing "command hallucinations." This condition interfered with respondent's "volitional abilities; that is, his ability to make free and rational choices." Dr. Metzner further testified that Connelly's illness did not significantly impair his cognitive abilities. Thus, respondent understood the rights he had when Officer Anderson and Detective Antuna advised him that he need not speak. Dr. Metzner admitted that the "voices" could in reality be Connelly's interpretation of his own guilt, but explained that in his opinion, Connelly's psychosis motivated his confession.

## II

Respondent relies on *Blackburn v. Alabama*, 361 U.S. 199 (1960), and *Townsend v. Sain*, 372 U.S. 293 (1963) for the proposition that the "deficient mental condition of the defendants in those cases was sufficient to render their confessions involuntary." But respondent's reading of *Blackburn* and *Townsend* ignores the integral element of police overreaching present in both cases. In *Blackburn*, the Court found that the petitioner was probably insane at the time of his confession and the police learned during the interrogation that he had a history of mental problems. The police exploited this weakness with coercive tactics: "the eight-to nine-hour sustained interrogation in a tiny room which was upon occasion literally filled with police officers; the absence of Blackburn's friends, relatives, or legal counsel; [and] the composition of the confession by the Deputy Sheriff rather than by Blackburn." These tactics supported a finding that the confession was involuntary. Indeed, the Court specifically condemned police activity that "wrings a confession out of an accused against his will." *Townsend* presented a similar instance of police wrongdoing. In that case, a police physician had given Townsend a drug with truth-serum properties. The subsequent confession, obtained by officers who knew that Townsend had been given drugs, was held involuntary. These two cases demonstrate that while mental condition is surely relevant to an individual's susceptibility to police coercion, mere examination of the confessant's state of mind can never conclude the due process inquiry.

Our "involuntary confession" jurisprudence is entirely consistent with the settled law requiring some sort of "state action" to support a claim of violation of the Due Process Clause of the Fourteenth Amendment. The Colorado trial court, of course, found that the police committed no wrongful acts, and that finding has been neither challenged by respondent nor disturbed by the Supreme Court of Colorado. The latter court, however, concluded that sufficient state action was present by virtue of the admission of the confession into evidence in a court of the State.

The difficulty with the approach of the Supreme Court of Colorado is that it fails to recognize the essential link between coercive activity of the State, on the one hand, and a resulting confession by a defendant, on the other. The flaw in respondent's constitutional argument is that it would expand our previous line of "voluntariness" cases into a far-ranging requirement that courts must divine a defendant's motivation for speaking or acting as he did even though there be no claim that governmental conduct coerced his decision.

The most outrageous behavior by a private party seeking to secure evidence against a defendant does not make that evidence inadmissible under the Due Process Clause. See *Walter v. United States*, 447 U.S. 649, 656 (1980); *Coolidge v. New Hampshire*, 403 U.S. 443, 487-488 (1971); *Burdeau v. McDowell*, 256 U.S. 465, 476 (1921). We have also observed that "[j]urists and scholars uniformly have recognized that the exclusionary rule imposes a substantial cost on the societal interest in law enforcement by its proscription of what concededly is relevant evidence." *United States v. Janis*, 428 U.S. 433, 448-449 (1976). See also *United States v. Havens*, 446 U.S. 620, 627 (1980); *Calandra*, 414 U.S. 338 (1974). Moreover, suppressing respondent's statements would serve absolutely no purpose in enforcing constitutional guarantees. The purpose of excluding evidence seized in violation of the Constitution is to substantially deter future violations of the Constitution. See *Leon*. Only if we were to establish a brand new constitutional right—the right of a criminal defendant to confess his crime only when totally rational and properly motivated—could respondent's present claim be sustained.

We have previously cautioned against expanding "currently applicable exclusionary rules by erecting additional barriers to placing truthful and probative evidence before state juries. . . ." We abide by that counsel now. "[T]he central purpose of a criminal trial is to decide the factual question of the defendant's guilt or innocence," *Delaware v. Van Arsdall*, 475 U.S. 673, 681 (1986), and while we have previously held that exclusion of evidence may be necessary to protect constitutional guarantees, both the necessity for the collateral inquiry and the exclusion of evidence deflect a criminal trial from its basic purpose. Respondent would now have us require sweeping inquiries into the state of mind of a criminal defendant who has confessed, inquiries quite divorced from any coercion brought to bear on the defendant by the State. We think the Constitution rightly leaves this sort of inquiry to be resolved by state laws governing the admission of evidence and erects no standard of its own in this area. A statement rendered by one in the condition of respondent might be proved to be quite unreliable, but this is a matter to be governed by the evidentiary laws of the forum, and not by the Due Process Clause of the Fourteenth Amendment. "The aim of the requirement of due process is not to exclude presumptively false evidence, but to prevent fundamental unfairness in the use of evidence, whether true or false." *Lisenba v. California*, 314 U.S. 219, 236 (1941).

We hold that coercive police activity is a necessary predicate to the finding that a confession is not "voluntary" within the meaning of the Due Process Clause of the Fourteenth Amendment. We also conclude that the taking of respondent's statements, and their admission into evidence, constitute no violation of that Clause.

### IV

The judgment of the Supreme Court of Colorado is accordingly reversed, and the cause is remanded for further proceedings not inconsistent with this opinion.

Justice STEVENS, concurring in the judgment in part and dissenting in part.

Respondent made incriminatory statements both before and after he was handcuffed and taken into custody. The only question presented by the Colorado District Attorney in his certiorari petition concerned the admissibility of respondent's precustodial statements. I agree with the State of Colorado that the United States Constitution does not require suppression of those statements, but in reaching that conclusion, unlike the Court, I am perfectly willing to accept the state trial court's finding that the statements were involuntary.

The state trial court found that, in view of the "overwhelming evidence presented by the Defense," the prosecution did not meet its burden of demonstrating that respondent's initial statements to Officer Anderson were voluntary. Nevertheless, in my opinion, the use of these involuntary precustodial statements does not violate the Fifth Amendment because they were not the product of state compulsion.

Although they may well be so unreliable that they could not support a conviction, at this stage of the proceeding I could not say that they have no probative force whatever. The fact that the statements were involuntary—just as the product of Lady Macbeth's nightmare was involuntary[2]—does not mean that their use for whatever evidentiary value they may have is fundamentally unfair or a denial of due process.

Accordingly, I concur in the judgment insofar as it applies to respondent's precustodial statements.

Justice BRENNAN, with whom Justice MARSHALL joins, dissenting.

Today the Court denies Mr. Connelly his fundamental right to make a vital choice with a sane mind, involving a determination that could allow the State to deprive him of liberty or even life. This holding is unprecedented: "Surely in the present stage of our civilization a most basic sense of justice is affronted by the spectacle of incarcerating a human being upon the basis of a statement he made while insane. . . ." *Blackburn.* Because I believe that the use of a mentally ill person's involuntary confession is antithetical to the notion of fundamental fairness embodied in the Due Process Clause, I dissent.

### I

The respondent's seriously impaired mental condition is clear on the record of this case. At the time of his confession, Mr. Connelly suffered from a "longstanding severe mental disorder," diagnosed as chronic paranoid schizophrenia. He had been hospitalized for psychiatric reasons five times prior to his confession; his longest hospitalization lasted for seven months. Mr. Connelly heard imaginary voices and saw nonexistent objects. He believed that his father was God, and that he was a reincarnation of Jesus.

At the time of his confession, Mr. Connelly's mental problems included "grandiose and delusional thinking." He had a known history of "thought withdrawal and insertion." Although physicians had treated Mr. Connelly "with a wide variety of medications in the past including antipsychotic medications," he had not taken any antipsychotic medications for at least six months prior to his confession.

---

[2] "What, will these hands ne'er be clean?

"Here's the smell of the blood still: all the perfumes of Arabia will not sweeten this little hand." W. Shakespeare, Macbeth, Act V, scene 1, lines 41, 47.

Lady Macbeth's "eyes are open," "but their sense is shut."

Following his arrest, Mr. Connelly initially was found incompetent to stand trial because the court-appointed psychiatrist, Dr. Metzner, "wasn't very confident that he could consistently relate accurate information." Dr. Metzner testified that Mr. Connelly was unable "to make free and rational choices" due to auditory hallucinations: "[W]hen he was read his *Miranda* rights, he probably had the capacity to know that he was being read his *Miranda* rights [but] he wasn't able to use that information because of the command hallucinations that he had experienced." He achieved competency to stand trial only after six months of hospitalization and treatment with antipsychotic and sedative medications.

The state trial court found that the "overwhelming evidence presented by the Defense" indicated that the prosecution did not meet its burden of demonstrating by a preponderance of the evidence that the initial statement to Officer Anderson was voluntary. While the court found no police misconduct, it held:

> "[T]here's no question that the Defendant did not exercise free will in choosing to talk to the police. He exercised a choice both [*sic*] of which were mandated by auditory hallucination, had no basis in reality, and were the product of a psychotic break with reality. The Defendant at the time of the confession had absolutely in the Court's estimation no volition or choice to make."

The trial court also held that the State had not shown by clear and convincing evidence that the defendant had waived his *Miranda* right to counsel and to self-incrimination "voluntarily, knowingly and intelligently."

The Supreme Court of Colorado affirmed after evaluating "the totality of circumstances" surrounding the unsolicited confession and the waiver of *Miranda* rights.

### II

The absence of police wrongdoing should not, by itself, determine the voluntariness of a confession by a mentally ill person. The requirement that a confession be voluntary reflects a recognition of the importance of free will and of reliability in determining the admissibility of a confession, and thus demands an inquiry into the totality of the circumstances surrounding the confession.

### A

Today's decision restricts the application of the term "involuntary" to those confessions obtained by police coercion. Confessions by mentally ill individuals or by persons coerced by parties other than police officers are now considered "voluntary." The Court's failure to recognize all forms of involuntariness or coercion as antithetical to due process reflects a refusal to acknowledge free will as a value of constitutional consequence. But due process derives much of its meaning from a conception of fundamental fairness that emphasizes the right to make vital choices voluntarily.

This Court's assertion that we would be required "to establish a brand new constitutional right" to recognize the respondent's claim ignores 200 years of constitutional jurisprudence.[1] As we stated in *Culombe v. Connecticut*, 367 U.S. 568 (1961):

> "The ultimate test remains that which has been the only clearly established test in Anglo-American courts for two hundred years: the test of voluntariness. Is the confession the product of an essentially free and unconstrained choice by its maker? . . . The line of distinction is that at which governing self-direction is lost *and compulsion, of whatever nature or however infused*, propels or helps to propel the confession." (emphasis added).

A true commitment to fundamental fairness requires that the inquiry be "not whether the conduct of state officers in obtaining the confession is shocking, but whether the confession was 'free and voluntary'. . . ." *Malloy v. Hogan*, 378 U.S., at 7.

This Court abandons this precedent in favor of the view that only confessions rendered involuntary by some state action are inadmissible, and that the only relevant form of state action is police conduct. But even if state action is required, police overreaching is not its only relevant form. The Colorado Supreme Court held that the trial court's admission of the involuntary confession into evidence is also state

---

[1] Cf. *Bram v. United States*, 168 U.S. 532, 547-548 (1897) (reviewing the "rule [of law] in England at the time of the adoption of the Constitution and of the Fifth Amendment" and citing W. Hawkins, Pleas of the Crown: "[a] confession, therefore, whether made upon an official examination or *in discourse with private persons*, which is obtained from a defendant, either by the flattery of hope, or by the impressions of fear, however slightly the emotions may be implanted, . . . is not admissible evidence; for the law will not suffer a prisoner to be made the deluded instrument of his own conviction") (emphasis added).

action. The state court's analysis is consistent with *Brown v. Mississippi* on which this Court so heavily relies. *Brown*, a case involving the use of confessions at trial, makes clear that "[t]he due process clause requires 'that state action, *whether through one agency or another*, shall be consistent with the fundamental principles of liberty and justice which lie at the base of all our civil and political institutions.'" Police conduct constitutes but one form of state action. "The objective of deterring improper police conduct is only part of the larger objective of safeguarding the integrity of our adversary system."

The only logical "flaw" which the Court detects in this argument is that it would require courts to "divine a defendant's motivation for speaking or acting as he did even though there be no claim that governmental conduct coerced his decision." Such a criticism, however, ignores the fact that we have traditionally examined the totality of the circumstances, including the motivation and competence of the defendant, in determining whether a confession is voluntary. Even today's Court admits that "as interrogators have turned to more subtle forms of psychological persuasion, courts have found the mental condition of the defendant a more significant factor in the 'voluntariness' calculus." The Court's holding that involuntary confessions are only those procured through police misconduct is thus inconsistent with the Court's historical insistence that only confessions reflecting an exercise of free will be admitted into evidence.

B

Since the Court redefines voluntary confessions to include confessions by mentally ill individuals, the reliability of these confessions becomes a central concern. A concern for reliability is inherent in our criminal justice system, which relies upon accusatorial rather than inquisitorial practices. While an inquisitorial system prefers obtaining confessions from criminal defendants, an accusatorial system must place its faith in determinations of "guilt by evidence independently and freely secured." In *Escobedo*, we justified our reliance upon accusatorial practices:

> "We have learned the lesson of history, ancient and modern, that a system of criminal law enforcement which comes to depend on the 'confession' will, in the long run, be less reliable and more subject to abuses than a system which depends on extrinsic evidence independently secured through skillful investigation."

Our distrust for reliance on confessions is due, in part, to their decisive impact upon the adversarial process. Triers of fact accord confessions such heavy weight in their determinations that "the introduction of a confession makes the other aspects of a trial in court superfluous, and the real trial, for all practical purposes, occurs when the confession is obtained."

Because the admission of a confession so strongly tips the balance against the defendant in the adversarial process, we must be especially careful about a confession's reliability. We have to date not required a finding of reliability for involuntary confessions only because *all* such confessions have been excluded upon a finding of involuntariness, regardless of reliability.[4] The Court's adoption today of a restrictive definition of an "involuntary" confession will require heightened scrutiny of a confession's reliability.

The instant case starkly highlights the danger of admitting a confession by a person with a severe mental illness. The trial court made no findings concerning the reliability of Mr. Connelly's involuntary

confession, since it believed that the confession was excludable on the basis of involuntariness. However, the overwhelming evidence in the record points to the unreliability of Mr. Connelly's delusional mind. Mr. Connelly was found incompetent to stand trial because he was unable to relate accurate information, and the court-appointed psychiatrist indicated that Mr. Connelly was actively hallucinating and exhibited delusional thinking at the time of his confession. The Court, in fact, concedes that "[a] statement rendered by one in the condition of respondent might be proved to be quite unreliable. . . ."

Moreover, the record is barren of any corroboration of the mentally ill defendant's confession. No physical evidence links the defendant to the alleged crime. Police did not identify the alleged victim's body as the woman named by the defendant. Mr. Connelly identified the alleged scene of the crime, but it has not been verified that the unidentified body was found there or that a crime actually occurred there. There is not a shred of competent evidence in this record linking the defendant to the charged homicide. There is only Mr. Connelly's confession.

Minimum standards of due process should require that the trial court find substantial indicia of reliability, on the basis of evidence extrinsic to the confession itself, before admitting the confession of a mentally ill person into evidence. I would require the trial court to make such a finding on remand. To hold otherwise allows the State to imprison and possibly to execute a mentally ill defendant based solely upon an inherently unreliable confession.

---

[4] Prior to establishing this rule excluding all involuntary confessions, we held the view that the Fifth Amendment, at bottom, served as "a guarantee against conviction on inherently untrustworthy evidence." *Stein v. New York*, 346 U.S. 156, 192 (1953).

## QUESTIONS AND NOTES

**1.** Should the Constitution be concerned about the admission of an inaccurate confession? Is it satisfactory to say that it is merely a matter of state law?

**2.** Is the quote from *Lisenba* ("The aim of the requirement of due process is not to exclude presumptively false evidence, but to prevent fundamental unfairness in the use of evidence whether true or false.") decisive in answering question 1?

**3.** Is it significant that most of the Court's exclusionary rule cites are Fourth Amendment cases? How? Why?

**4.** How should *Connelly* have been resolved? Why?

**5.** Perhaps the most interesting recent case in regard to coerced confessions is *Fulminante*.

## Arizona v. Fulminante
## 111 S.Ct. 1246 (1991)

Justice WHITE delivered the opinion of the Court.

The Arizona Supreme Court ruled in this case that respondent Oreste Fulminante's confession, received in evidence at his trial for murder, had been coerced and that its use against him was barred by the Fifth and Fourteenth Amendments to the United States Constitution. The court also held that the harmless-error rule could not be used to save the conviction. We affirm the judgment of the Arizona court, although for different reasons than those upon which that court relied.

### I

Early in the morning of September 14, 1982, Fulminante called the Mesa, Arizona, Police Department to report that his 11-year-old stepdaughter, Jeneane Michelle Hunt, was missing. He had been caring for Jeneane while his wife, Jeneane's mother, was in the hospital. Two days later, Jeneane's body was found in the desert east of Mesa. She had been shot twice in the head at close range with a large caliber weapon, and a ligature was around her neck. Because of the decomposed condition of the body, it was impossible to tell whether she had been sexually assaulted.

Fulminante's statements to police concerning Jeneane's disappearance and his relationship with her contained a number of inconsistencies, and he became a suspect in her killing. When no charges were filed against him, Fulminante left Arizona for New Jersey. Fulminante was later convicted in New Jersey on federal charges of possession of a firearm by a felon.

Fulminante was incarcerated in the Ray Brook Federal Correctional Institution in New York. There he became friends with another inmate, Anthony Sarivola, then serving a 60-day sentence for extortion. The two men came to spend several hours a day together. Sarivola, a former police officer, had been involved in loansharking for organized crime but then became a paid informant for the Federal Bureau of Investigation. While at Ray Brook, he masqueraded as an organized crime figure. After becoming friends with Fulminante, Sarivola heard a rumor that Fulminante was suspected of killing a child in Arizona. Sarivola then raised the subject with Fulminante in several conversations, but Fulminante repeatedly denied any involvement in Jeneane's death. During one conversation, he told Sarivola that Jeneane had been killed by bikers looking

for drugs; on another occasion, he said he did not know what had happened. Sarivola passed this information on to an agent of the Federal Bureau of Investigation, who instructed Sarivola to find out more.

Sarivola learned more one evening in October 1983, as he and Fulminante walked together around the prison track. Sarivola said that he knew Fulminante was "starting to get some tough treatment and whatnot" from other inmates because of the rumor. Sarivola offered to protect Fulminante from his fellow inmates, but told him, "'You have to tell me about it,' you know. I mean, in other words, 'For me to give you any help.'" Fulminante then admitted to Sarivola that he had driven Jeneane to the desert on his motorcycle, where he choked her, sexually assaulted her, and made her beg for her life, before shooting her twice in the head.

Sarivola was released from prison in November 1983. Fulminante was released the following May, only to be arrested the next month for another weapons violation. On September 4, 1984, Fulminante was indicted in Arizona for the first-degree murder of Jeneane.

Prior to trial, Fulminante moved to suppress the statement he had given Sarivola in prison, as well as a second confession he had given to Donna Sarivola, then Anthony Sarivola's fiancee and later his wife, following his May 1984 release from prison. He asserted that the confession to Sarivola was coerced, and that the second confession was the "fruit" of the first. Following the hearing, the trial court denied the motion to suppress, specifically finding that, based on the stipulated facts, the confessions were voluntary. The State introduced both confessions as evidence at trial, and on December 19, 1985, Fulminante was convicted of Jeneane's murder. He was subsequently sentenced to death.

Fulminante appealed, arguing, among other things, that his confession to Sarivola was the product of coercion and that its admission at trial violated his rights to due process under the Fifth and Fourteenth Amendments of the United States Constitution. After considering the evidence at trial as well as the stipulated facts before the trial court on the motion to suppress, the Arizona Supreme Court held that the confession was coerced, but initially determined that the admission of the confession at trial was harmless error, because of the overwhelming nature of the evidence against Fulminante. Upon Fulminante's motion for reconsideration, however, the court ruled that this Court's precedent precluded the use of the harmless-error analysis in the case of a coerced confession. The court therefore reversed the conviction and ordered that Fulminante be retried without the use of the confession to Sarivola.[1] Because of differing views in the state and federal courts over whether the admission at trial of a coerced confession is subject to a harmless-error analysis, we granted the State's petition for certiorari. Although a majority of this Court finds that such a confession is subject to a harmless-error analysis, for the reasons set forth below, we affirm the judgment of the Arizona court.

## II

We deal first with the State's contention that the court below erred in holding Fulminante's confession to have been coerced. The State argues that it is the totality of the circumstances that determines whether Fulminante's confession was coerced, but contends that rather than apply this standard, the Arizona court applied a "but for" test, under which the court found that but for the promise given by Sarivola, Fulminante would not have confessed. In support of this argument, the State points to the Arizona court's reference to *Bram v. United States*, 168 U.S. 532 (1897). Although the Court noted in *Bram* that a confession cannot be obtained by "any direct or implied promises, however slight, nor by the exertion of any improper influence," it is clear this passage from *Bram*, which under current precedent does not state the standard for determining the voluntariness of a confession, was not relied on by the Arizona court in reaching its conclusion. Rather, the court cited this language as part of a longer quotation from an Arizona case which accurately described the State's burden of proof for establishing voluntariness. Indeed, the Arizona Supreme Court stated that a "determination regarding the voluntariness of a confession . . . must be viewed in a totality of the circumstances," and under that standard plainly

---

[1] In its initial opinion, the Arizona Supreme Court had determined that the second confession, to Donna Sarivola was not the "fruit of the poisonous tree," because it was made six months after the confession to Sarivola; it occurred after Fulminante's need for protection from Sarivola presumably had ended; and it took place in the course of a casual conversation with someone who was not an agent of the State. This court adhered to this determination in its supplemental opinion. This aspect of the Arizona Supreme Court's decision is not challenged here.

found that Fulminante's statement to Sarivola had been coerced.

In applying the totality of the circumstances test to determine that the confession to Sarivola was coerced, the Arizona Supreme Court focused on a number of relevant facts. First, the court noted that "because [Fulminante] was an alleged child murderer, he was in danger of physical harm at the hands of other inmates." In addition, Sarivola was aware that Fulminante had been receiving "rough treatment from the guys." Using his knowledge of these threats, Sarivola offered to protect Fulminante in exchange for a confession to Jeneane's murder, and "[i]n response to Sarivola's offer of protection, [Fulminante] confessed." Agreeing with Fulminante that "Sarivola's promise was 'extremely coercive,'" the Arizona Court declared: "[T]he confession was obtained as a direct result of extreme coercion and was tendered in the belief that the defendant's life was in jeopardy if he did not confess. This is a true coerced confession in every sense of the word."[2]

We normally give great deference to the factual findings of the state court. Nevertheless, "the ultimate issue of 'voluntariness' is a legal question requiring independent federal determination."

Although the question is a close one, we agree with the Arizona Supreme Court's conclusion that Fulminante's confession was coerced.[3] The Arizona Supreme Court found a credible threat of

---

[2] There are additional facts in the record, not relied upon by the Arizona Supreme Court, which also support a finding of coercion. Fulminante possesses low average to average intelligence; he dropped out of school in the fourth grade. He is short in stature and slight in build. Although he had been in prison before, he had not always adapted well to the stress of prison life. While incarcerated at the age of 26, he had "felt threatened by the [prison] population," and he therefore requested that he be placed in protective custody. Once there, however, he was unable to cope with the isolation and was admitted to a psychiatric hospital. The Court has previously recognized that factors such as these are relevant in determining whether a defendant's will has been overborne. In addition, we note that Sarivola's position as Fulminante's friend might well have made the latter particularly susceptible to the former's entreaties. See *Spano*.

[3] Our prior cases have used the terms "coerced confession" and "involuntary confession" interchangeably "by way of convenient shorthand." We use the former term throughout this opinion, as that is the term used by the Arizona Supreme Court.

physical violence unless Fulminante confessed. Our cases have made clear that a finding of coercion need not depend upon actual violence by a government agent;[4] a credible threat is sufficient. As in *Payne v. Arkansas*, 356 U.S. 560 (1958), where the Court found that a confession was coerced because the interrogating police officer had promised that if the accused confessed, the officer would protect the accused from an angry mob outside the jailhouse door, so too here, the Arizona Supreme Court found that it was fear of physical violence, absent protection from his friend (and Government agent) Sarivola, which motivated Fulminante to confess. Accepting the Arizona court's finding, permissible on this record, that there was a credible threat of physical violence, we agree with its conclusion that Fulminante's will was overborne in such a way as to render his confession the product of coercion.

### III

[Justice White, speaking only for Justices Marshall, Blackmun, and Stevens, would have held that admission of a coerced confession can *never* be harmless error. However, they were outvoted by the other five Justices on this point.]

### IV

Since five Justices have determined that harmless error analysis applies to coerced confessions, it becomes necessary to evaluate under that ruling the admissibility of Fulminante's confession to Sarivola. *Chapman v. California*, 386 U.S., at 24, made clear that "before a federal constitutional error can be held harmless, the court must be able to declare a belief that it was harmless beyond a reasonable doubt." The Court has the power to review the record *de novo* in order to determine an error's harmlessness. In so doing, it must be determined whether the State has met its burden of demonstrating that the admission of the confession to Sarivola did not contribute to Fulminante's conviction. Five of us are of the view that the State has not carried its burden and accordingly affirm the judgment of the court below reversing petitioner's conviction.

A confession is like no other evidence. Indeed, "the defendant's own confession is probably the most probative and damaging evidence that can be admitted against him. . . . [T]he admissions of a defendant come from the actor himself, the most

knowledgeable and unimpeachable source of information about his past conduct. Certainly, confessions have profound impact on the jury, so much so that we may justifiably doubt its ability to put them out of mind even if told to do so." While some statements by a defendant may concern isolated aspects of the crime or may be incriminating only when linked to other evidence, a full confession in which the defendant discloses the motive for and means of the crime may tempt the jury to rely upon that evidence alone in reaching its decision. In the case of a coerced confession such as that given by Fulminante to Sarivola, the risk that the confession is unreliable, coupled with the profound impact that confession has upon the jury, requires a reviewing court to exercise extreme caution before determining that the admission of the confession at trial was harmless.

In the Arizona Supreme Court's initial opinion, in which it determined that harmless-error analysis could be applied to the confession, the court found that the admissible second confession to Donna Sarivola rendered the first confession to Anthony Sarivola cumulative. The court also noted that circumstantial physical evidence concerning the wounds, the ligature around Jeneane's neck, the location of the body, and the presence of motorcycle tracks at the scene corroborated the second confession. The court concluded that "due to the overwhelming evidence adduced from the second confession, if there had not been a first confession, the jury would still have had the same basic evidence to convict" Fulminante.

We have a quite different evaluation of the evidence. Our review of the record leads us to conclude that the State has failed to meet its burden of establishing, beyond a reasonable doubt, that the admission of Fulminante's confession to Anthony Sarivola was harmless error. Three considerations compel this result.

First, the transcript discloses that both the trial court and the State recognized that a successful prosecution depended on the jury believing the two confessions. Absent the confessions, it is unlikely that Fulminante would have been prosecuted at all, because the physical evidence from the scene and other circumstantial evidence would have been insufficient to convict. Indeed, no indictment was filed until nearly two years after the murder.[8] Although the

---

[4] The parties agree that Sarivola acted as an agent of the Government when he questioned Fulminante about the murder and elicited the confession.

[8] Although Fulminante had allegedly confessed to Donna Sarivola several months previously, police did not yet know of this confession, which Anthony

police had suspected Fulminante from the beginning, as the prosecutor acknowledged in his opening statement to the jury, "[W]hat brings us to Court, what makes this case fileable, and prosecutable and triable is that later, Mr. Fulminante confesses this crime to Anthony Sarivola and later, to Donna Sarivola, his wife." After trial began, during a renewed hearing on Fulminante's motion to suppress, the trial court opined, "You know, I think from what little I know about this trial, the character of this man [Sarivola] for truthfulness or untruthfulness and his credibility is the centerpiece of this case, is it not?," to which the prosecutor responded, "It's very important, there's no doubt." Finally, in his closing argument, the prosecutor prefaced his discussion of the two confessions by conceding, "[W]e have a lot of [circumstantial] evidence that indicates that this is our suspect, this is the fellow that did it, but it's a little short as far as saying that it's proof that he actually put the gun to the girl's head and killed her. So it's a little short of that. We recognize that."

Second, the jury's assessment of the confession to Donna Sarivola could easily have depended in large part on the presence of the confession to Anthony Sarivola. Absent the admission at trial of the first confession, the jurors might have found Donna Sarivola's story unbelievable. Fulminante's confession to Donna Sarivola allegedly occurred in May 1984, on the day he was released from Ray Brook, as she and Anthony Sarivola drove Fulminante from New York to Pennsylvania. Donna Sarivola testified that Fulminante, whom she had never before met, confessed in detail about Jeneane's brutal murder in response to her casual question concerning why he was going to visit friends in Pennsylvania instead of returning to his family in Arizona. Although she testified that she was "disgusted" by Fulminante's disclosures, she stated that she took no steps to notify authorities of what she had learned. In fact, she claimed that she barely discussed the matter with Anthony Sarivola, who was in the car and overheard Fulminante's entire conversation with Donna. Despite her disgust for Fulminante, Donna Sarivola later went on a second trip with him. Although Sarivola informed authorities that he had driven Fulminante to Pennsylvania, he did not mention Donna's presence in the car or her conversation with Fulminante. Only when questioned by authorities in June

1985 did Anthony Sarivola belatedly recall the confession to Donna more than a year before, and only then did he ask if she would be willing to discuss the matter with authorities.

Although some of the details in the confession to Donna Sarivola were corroborated by circumstantial evidence, many, including details that Jeneane was choked and sexually assaulted, were not. As to other aspects of the second confession, including Fulminante's motive and state of mind, the only corroborating evidence was the first confession to Anthony Sarivola.[9] Thus, contrary to what the Arizona Supreme Court found, it is clear that the jury might have believed that the two confessions reinforced and corroborated each other. For this reason, one confession was *not* merely cumulative of the other. While in some cases two confessions, delivered on different occasions to different listeners, might be viewed as being independent of each other, it strains credulity to think that the jury so viewed the two confessions in this case, especially given the close relationship between Donna and Anthony Sarivola.

The jurors could also have believed that Donna Sarivola had a motive to lie about the confession in order to assist her husband. Anthony Sarivola received significant benefits from federal authorities,

---

[9] The inadmissible confession to Anthony Sarivola was itself subject to serious challenge. Sarivola's lack of moral integrity was demonstrated by his testimony that he had worked for organized crime during the time he was a uniformed police officer. His overzealous approach to gathering information for which he would be paid by authorities, was revealed by his admission that he had fabricated a tape recording in connection with an earlier, unrelated FBI investigation. He received immunity in connection with the information he provided. His eagerness to get in and stay in the federal Witness Protection Program provided a motive for giving detailed information to authorities. During his first report of the confession, Sarivola failed to hint at numerous details concerning an alleged sexual assault on Jeneane; he mentioned them for the first time more than a year later during further interrogation, at which he also recalled, for the first time, the confession to Donna Sarivola. The impeaching affect of each of these factors was undoubtedly undercut by the presence of the second confession, which, not surprisingly, recounted a quite similar story and thus corroborated the first confession. Thus, each confession, though easily impeachable if viewed in isolation, became difficult to discount when viewed in conjunction with the other.

---

Sarivola did not mention to them until June 1985. They did, however, know of the first confession, which Fulminante had given to Anthony Sarivola nearly a year before.

including payment for information, immunity from prosecution, and eventual placement in the federal Witness Protection Program. In addition, the jury might have found Donna motivated by her own desire for favorable treatment, for she, too, was ultimately placed in the Witness Protection Program.

Third, the admission of the first confession led to the admission of other evidence prejudicial to Fulminante. For example, the State introduced evidence that Fulminante knew of Sarivola's connections with organized crime in an attempt to explain why Fulminante would have been motivated to confess to Sarivola in seeking protection. Absent the confession, this evidence would have had no relevance and would have been inadmissible at trial. The Arizona Supreme Court found that the evidence of Sarivola's connections with organized crime reflected on Sarivola's character, not Fulminante's, and noted that the evidence could have been used to impeach Sarivola. This analysis overlooks the fact that had the confession not been admitted, there would have been no reason for Sarivola to testify and thus no need to impeach his testimony. Moreover, we cannot agree that the evidence did not reflect on Fulminante's character as well, for it depicted him as someone who willingly sought out the company of criminals. It is quite possible that this evidence led the jury to view Fulminante as capable of murder.[10]

Although our concern here is with the effect of the erroneous admission of the confession on Fulminante's conviction, it is clear that the presence of the confession also influenced the sentencing phase of the trial. Under Arizona law, the trial judge is the sentencer. At the sentencing hearing, the admissibility of information regarding aggravating circumstances is governed by the rules of evidence applicable to criminal trials. In this case, "based upon admissible evidence produced at the trial," the judge found that only one aggravating circumstance existed beyond a reasonable doubt, *i.e.*, that the murder was committed in "an *especially* heinous, cruel, and depraved manner." In reaching this conclusion, the judge relied heavily on evidence concerning the

---

[10] Fulminante asserts that other prejudicial evidence, including his prior felony convictions and incarcerations, and his prison reputation for untruthfulness, likewise would not have been admitted had the confession to Sarivola been excluded. Because we find that the admission of the confession was not harmless in any event, we express no opinion as to the effect any of this evidence might have had on Fulminante's conviction.

manner of the killing and Fulminante's motives and state of mind which could only be found in the two confessions. For example, in labeling the murder "cruel," the judge focused in part on Fulminante's alleged statements that he choked Jeneane and made her get on her knees and beg before killing her. Although the circumstantial evidence was not inconsistent with this determination, neither was it sufficient to make such a finding beyond a reasonable doubt. Indeed, the sentencing judge acknowledged that the confessions were only partly corroborated by other evidence.

Finally, [i]n declaring that Fulminante "acted with an especially heinous and depraved state of mind," the sentencing judge relied solely on the two confessions. While the judge found that the statements in the confessions regarding the alleged sexual assault on Jeneane should not be considered on the issue of cruelty because they were not corroborated by other evidence, the judge determined that they were worthy of belief on the issue of Fulminante's state of mind. The judge then focused on Anthony Sarivola's statement that Fulminante had made vulgar references to Jeneane during the first confession, and on Donna Sarivola's statement that Fulminante had made similar comments to her. Finally, the judge stressed that Fulminante's alleged comments to the Sarivolas concerning torture, choking, and sexual assault, "whether they all occurred or not," depicted "a man who was bragging and relishing the crime he committed."

Because a majority of the Court has determined that Fulminante's confession to Anthony Sarivola was coerced and because a majority has determined that admitting this confession was not harmless beyond a reasonable doubt, we agree with the Arizona Supreme Court's conclusion that Fulminante is entitled to a new trial at which the confession is not admitted. Accordingly the judgment of the Arizona Supreme Court is affirmed.

Chief Justice REHNQUIST, with whom Justice O'CONNOR joins, Justice KENNEDY and Justice SOUTER join as to Parts I and II, and Justice SCALIA joins as to Parts II and III, delivering the opinion of the Court as to Part II, and dissenting as to Parts I and III.

I

The question of whether respondent Fulminante's confession was voluntary is one of federal law. "Without exception, the Court's confession cases hold that the ultimate issue of 'voluntariness' is a legal question requiring independent federal determination." In *Mincey*, we overturned a determination by the Supreme Court of Arizona that a statement of the defendant was voluntary, saying "we are not bound by the Arizona Supreme Court's holding that the statements were voluntary. Instead, this Court is under a duty to make an independent evaluation of the record."

Exercising our responsibility to make the independent examination of the record necessary to decide this federal question, I am at a loss to see how the Supreme Court of Arizona reached the conclusion that it did. Fulminante offered no evidence that he believed that his life was in danger or that he in fact confessed to Sarivola in order to obtain the proffered protection. Indeed, he had stipulated that "[a]t no time did the defendant indicate he was in fear of other inmates nor did he ever seek Mr. Sarivola's 'protection.'" Sarivola's testimony that he told Fulminante that "if [he] would tell the truth, he could be protected," adds little if anything to the substance of the parties' stipulation. The decision of the Supreme Court of Arizona rests on an assumption that is squarely contrary to this stipulation, and one that is not supported by any testimony of Fulminante.

The facts of record in the present case are quite different from those present in cases where we have found confessions to be coerced and involuntary. Since Fulminante was unaware that Sarivola was an FBI informant, there existed none of "the danger of coercion result[ing] from the interaction of custody and official interrogation." *Perkins*. The fact that Sarivola was a government informant does not by itself render Fulminante's confession involuntary, since we have consistently accepted the use of informants in the discovery of evidence of a crime as a legitimate investigatory procedure consistent with the Constitution. The conversations between Sarivola and Fulminante were not lengthy, and the defendant was free at all times to leave Sarivola's company. Sarivola at no time threatened him or demanded that he confess; he simply requested that he speak the truth about the matter. Fulminante was an experienced habitue of prisons, and presumably able to fend for himself. In concluding on these facts that Fulminante's confession was involuntary, the Court today embraces a more expansive definition of that term than is warranted by any of our decided cases.

## II

[This portion of the opinion is the opinion of the Court.]

Since this Court's landmark decision in *Chapman v. California*, 386 U.S. 18 (1967), in which we adopted the general rule that a constitutional error does not automatically require reversal of a conviction, the Court has applied harmless error analysis to a wide range of errors and has recognized that most constitutional errors can be harmless.

Of course an involuntary confession may have a more dramatic effect on the course of a trial than do other trial errors — in particular cases it may be devastating to a defendant — but this simply means that a reviewing court will conclude in such a case that its admission was not harmless error; it is not a reason for eschewing the harmless error test entirely. The Supreme Court of Arizona, in its first opinion in the present case, concluded that the admission of Fulminante's confession was harmless error. That court concluded that a second and more explicit confession of the crime made by Fulminante after he was released from prison was not tainted by the first confession, and that the second confession, together with physical evidence from the wounds (the victim had been shot twice in the head with a large caliber weapon at close range and a ligature was found around her neck) and other evidence introduced at trial rendered the admission of the first confession harmless beyond a reasonable doubt.

## III

I would agree with the finding of the Supreme Court of Arizona in its initial opinion — in which it believed harmless-error analysis was applicable to the admission of involuntary confessions — that the admission of Fulminante's confession was harmless. Indeed, this seems to me to be a classic case of harmless error: a second confession giving more details of the crime than the first was admitted in evidence and found to be free of any constitutional objection. Accordingly, I would affirm the holding of the Supreme Court of Arizona in its initial opinion, and reverse the judgment which it ultimately rendered in this case.

Justice KENNEDY, concurring in the judgment.

For the reasons stated by the Chief Justice, I agree that Fulminante's confession to Anthony Sarivola was not coerced. In my view, the trial court did not err in admitting this testimony. A majority of the Court, however, finds the confession coerced and proceeds to consider whether harmless-error analysis may be used when a coerced confession has been admitted at trial. With the case in this posture, it is appropriate for me to address the harmless-error issue.

Again for the reasons stated by the Chief Justice, I agree that harmless-error analysis should apply in the case of a coerced confession. That said, the court conducting a harmless-error inquiry must appreciate the indelible impact a full confession may have on the trier of fact, as distinguished, for instance, from the impact of an isolated statement that incriminates the defendant only when connected with other evidence. If the jury believes that a defendant has admitted the crime, it doubtless will be tempted to rest its decision on that evidence alone, without careful consideration of the other evidence in the case. Apart, perhaps, from a videotape of the crime, one would have difficulty finding evidence more damaging to a criminal defendant's plea of innocence. For the reasons given by Justice White in Part IV of his opinion, I cannot with confidence find admission of Fulminante's confession to Anthony Sarivola to be harmless error.

The same majority of the Court does not agree on the three issues presented by the trial court's determination to admit Fulminante's first confession: whether the confession was inadmissible because coerced; whether harmless error analysis is appropriate; and if so whether any error was harmless here. My own view that the confession was not coerced does not command a majority.

In the interests of providing a clear mandate to the Arizona Supreme Court in this capital case, I deem it proper to accept in the case now before us the holding of five Justices that the confession was coerced and inadmissible. I agree with a majority of the Court that admission of the confession could not be harmless error when viewed in light of all the other evidence; and so I concur in the judgment to affirm the ruling of the Arizona Supreme Court.

## QUESTIONS AND NOTES

**1.** What three issues did the Court resolve? What was the breakdown of the Court on each of the issues? How many of the Justices were in the majority on all three issues?

**2.** Why was the confession not invalidated because of *Miranda*?

**3.** Do you think that the confession was coerced/involuntary? Explain. Do those terms have different legal meanings than factual meanings? Should they?

**4.** Should the fact that Sarivola appeared to be a friend of Fulminante's cut for or against the voluntariness of his confession?

**5.** Should a coerced confession ever be treated as harmless error? Why? Why not?

**6.** Do you agree with the Court that admission of this confession (if it was involuntary) was not harmless beyond a reasonable doubt? Explain.

## PROBLEM

The following dialogue comes from a case called *Miller v. Fenton*, 796 F.2d 598 (3rd Cir. 1986) in which the third circuit, by a 2-1 vote, held the confession to be voluntary. Do you agree?

BOYCE: Testing 1 2 3. Testing 1 2 3. (Cough) Testing 1 2 3. Testing

BOYCE: Tuesday (cough), Tuesday, August 14, 1973, 1:47 A.M., Flemington State Police Barracks, Detectives' room, this is the start of an interrogation between Detective William Doyle, 1884, New Jersey State Police, Detective Boyce, 2097, also from the New Jersey State Police, and one Frank Melvin Miller, and this interrogation is in reference to the investigation now being conducted which involves the death of Miss Deborah Selma Margolin, white female, age 17, Brown Station Road, R.D. Ringoes, New Jersey. That's a correction, that's Bowne Station Road. This death occurring sometime approximately between 11:15 A.M., 8/13/73, and 5:45 P.M., 8/13/73.

BOYCE: Now, Mr. Miller, uh Frank, I talked to you earlier.

MILLER: Yeah, at PFD.

BOYCE: At PFD where you're employed. I was accompanied by Trooper Robert Scott at that time.

MILLER: Yes, sir.

BOYCE: We identified ourselves and we spoke to you on a voluntary basis in which you extended your cooperation to us, uh, in regards to this investigation of the death of the girl that I have just mentioned.

MILLER: Yes, sir.

BOYCE: You agreed at that time, voluntarily, to speak with us in regards to this matter . . .

MILLER: Yes, sir.

BOYCE: . . .also gave us permission while we were there to look at your vehicle . . .

MILLER: Yes, sir.

BOYCE: . . . to take clothing from your locker . . .

MILLER: Yes, sir.

BOYCE: . . . which is located inside the PFD plant, all of this being done, of course, with the cooperation that was extended to us from you on a voluntary basis.

MILLER: Right.

BOYCE: Now, Frank, you've been here since approximately 11, 11:49 P.M. which would actually be yesterday, 8/13/73. What I'm going to do at this time and, of course, let me just reiterate here, you, you, you came down, you accompanied Trooper Scott and myself here on a voluntary basis . . . that correct?

MILLER: Right.

BOYCE: Okay, and of your own free will?

MILLER: Yes, sir.

BOYCE: Without duress?

MILLER: Yes, sir.

BOYCE: Or having been threatened to do so.

MILLER: Right.

BOYCE: Okay, and while you were here you've been conversing again on a voluntary basis, with Trooper Scott, is that not right?

MILLER: Yes, sir.

BOYCE: Okay (cough). What I'm going to do at this time, as I've indicated already, you've been here for awhile, it is now almost 2:00 A.M. on the 14th, which puts you here approximately 2 hours. I'm going to advise you at this time of your constitutional rights, which you are entitled to, and start off by saying: Number 1, you have the right to remain silent and not to answer any questions, Number 2, if you decide to waive your right to remain silent, anything you say will be used against you if it is incriminating in nature. You have the right to be represented by an attorney before and during any questioning. If you want an attorney and cannot afford one, an attorney will be provided for you free by the State of New Jersey. Do you understand these rights, Frank?

MILLER: Yes, sir.

BOYCE: Are you willing to talk to us without having an attorney? In reference . . .

MILLER: Yes.

BOYCE: . . . to the, what we have talked about?

MILLER: Yes.

BOYCE: Okay, fine.

MILLER: But, at any time though, I can, uh, say no, right? I mean, you know . . .

BOYCE: Yes, Frank, let me go over that again.

MILLER: Yeah, I understand that, that . . .

BOYCE: You understand your rights, Frank?

MILLER: Yeah.

BOYCE: Okay. (cough). You may stop at anytime during this interrogation . . .

MILLER: Yeah.

BOYCE: . . . and request to remain silent and we will honor your request.

MILLER: Yes.

BOYCE: Okay?

MILLER: Yeah.

BOYCE: Now, we're talking about the death of a young girl, Frank, right?

MILLER: Yes, sir.

BOYCE: . . . very attractive, a very attractive young girl, who apparently at the time of her death was wearing nothing but a bathing suit, two piece bathing suit. We feel that there's a sexual aspect at this time is a good indication that there is some type of sexual assault that's associated with this crime . . . Before we continue, Frank, what I would like to ask you to do is, I'm going to ask you to sign the back of this card, okay, with your rights on it, indicating that you in fact have been . . .

MILLER: Yeah, yeah . . .

BOYCE: . . . advised of your rights.

MILLER: I got a pen right here.

BOYCE: Just sign the back of that and date it. (Clanging noises.) Today's the 14th.

MILLER: You want it signed the 14th?

BOYCE: Yes, please.

MILLER: Alright.

BOYCE: Okay.

MILLER: Alright?

BOYCE: Thank you. Now, getting back to the, uh, the death of Miss Margolin, which we were discussing, you already related to me and Trooper Scott at the time in which you did it that as to where you were and what your activities were yesterday.

MILLER: Right, right.

BOYCE: You indicated you came back into the Ringoes area about 11:00 A.M., is that correct?

MILLER: It was somewheres in there, yeah, give or take a little bit of time.

BOYCE: Let's try and narrow that down, Frank. Can you think of anything that would give you any indication as to why you say now you came back into the area sometime around 11 o'clock.

MILLER: Well, this is what I told you at the barracks, or I mean at PFD. I figured it was between 11, uh, around 11 o'clock, because I figured I got home around 11:30, quarter to 12, back to my parents' house and I had stopped at the Post Office in Ringoes to mail a letter which I forgot to mail this morning, or yesterday morning.

BOYCE: Alright, but, in other words what I'm saying Frank is how can you substantiate in your mind, in your mind . . .

MILLER: Uh, huh.

BOYCE: . . . as to wh . . . how, why you feel at this time that you arrived in Ringoes, went to the Post Office around 11 o'clock, can you tell me how you come to this conclusion, or what was, what activity you were involved in prior to getting, getting into Ringoes that would come to your mind as, you know, making you think that you arrived in Ringoes at 11 o'clock?

MILLER: Well, because I was home around 11:30, quarter to 12, because, uh, so I figured, uh, it had to be somewheres around 11 o'clock that I was in Ringoes, that's about the only thing I can think of.

BOYCE: Alright, now, before, when I confronted you with the time element, you said that you were in Ringoes at 11, you got home around 12 o'clock, now, you say 11:30 or quarter to 12. Now, I'm going to ask you a question, how long does it take you to drive your vehicle from the Ringoes Post Office to your father's house?

MILLER: That depends on how fast you go.

BOYCE: Okay, let's say if you drive at a normal rate of speed.

MILLER: I'd say maybe 20 minutes.

BOYCE: 20 minutes. How far would you say it is, Frank?

MILLER: Oh, 6, 7 miles, maybe.

BOYCE: 6, 7 miles. Now, you've indicated once prior to this interrogation that you got home around 12. Now you've indicated 11:30, quarter to 12. Now, what time did you get home, Frank?

MILLER: I'm not exactly sure.

BOYCE: Now that, now you're not sure.

MILLER: Well, I, I say, uh, I figure anywheres from 11:30 to 12 o'clock, quarter to 12, somewheres around there . . .

BOYCE: Alright . . .

MILLER: . . . because I didn't look at the clock.

BOYCE: Okay. Why do you think it was somewhere around there?

MILLER: Because I got myself something to eat and, uh, got my stuff together to get ready to go to work, and I wanted to stop up the hospital to see how this fella was . . .

BOYCE: What time did you leave, how long were you, what time did you arrive at the Post Office? Approximately?

MILLER: I'd say around 11 o'clock.

BOYCE: Okay, how long were you in the Post Office, Frank?

MILLER: A few minutes is all.

BOYCE: A few minutes. What did you do when you walked outside, Frank?

MILLER: Got in my car.

BOYCE: And went where?

MILLER: Home.

BOYCE: Okay, Frank. You indicated it takes approximately 20 minutes to drive home.

MILLER: Approximately, yeah.

BOYCE: Therefore, you would have arrived home in the area of 11:15, 11:20 A.M., but you indicated to me on 4, 5, maybe 6, 7, 8, 9 occasions already that you arrived home between quarter to 12, 12 o'clock. Now, I'm . . . am I right?

MILLER: Yeah.

BOYCE: Okay, now, this is a problem.

MILLER: I realize this . . .

BOYCE: This creates a very serious problem.

MILLER: Times, I uh, you know, I uh . . .

BOYCE: Oh, well, you know, it's not so much times, knowing what time it is, but you do know how long it takes you to get from point A to point B, you've already indicated . . .

MILLER: Yeah, approximately.

BOYCE: Approximately 20 minutes.

MILLER: Right.

BOYCE: So that's 11:15, 11:20

MILLER: Right.

BOYCE: 12 o'clock comes to your mind and I see a 40 minute, anywhere from a half hour to a 40 minute period . . . where are we, where are you, is what I should say?

MILLER: Yeah.

BOYCE: And I, I just, you know, this, this, I have a big question mark in my mind right now.

MILLER: Right.

BOYCE: Do you see my point, Frank?

MILLER: Yes, sir.

BOYCE: That's point one. Your car, right now

MILLER: Yeah.

BOYCE: . . . is dented on the right side?

MILLER: Right.

BOYCE: Your trunk is, I should, may be I should use the words sprang down, because this is some type of a metal spring . . .

MILLER: Right, yeah.

BOYCE: . . . securing the trunk of your vehicle. There is red dust on the vehicle, red dust that is visible to the naked eye . . .

MILLER: Yeah.

BOYCE: . . . when someone looks at it. It's got red clay or dirt in and around the wheel covers . . .

MILLER: Uh, huh.

BOYCE: . . . tires. I'll bet you right now, Frank, there is not another vehicle in Hunterdon County that fits the physical description that we, that Trooper Scott and I saw your vehicle in when we saw it up there tonight. I'll bet you, that I, I can call up a thousand people right now and there will not be another vehicle that fits the description of your vehicle. Am I right?

MILLER: There shouldn't be, no, not with the right side of it dented in like that.

BOYCE: That's the second point. You're with me now, right?

MILLER: Yeah.

BOYCE: Okay. Your vehicle was involved in an accident, was involved in two accidents.

MILLER: Two accidents.

BOYCE: There was blood found on the left front interior portion of your vehicle, tonight, fresh blood.

MILLER: Fresh blood?

BOYCE: Yes, sir. This is very, very serious.

MILLER: I realize this.

BOYCE: That's point 3. Now, you live a few miles from the scene where this young, innocent girl was found.

MILLER: Uh, huh.

BOYCE: You indicate that between 11 and 12 yesterday morning, between 11 and 12, one hour, 60 minutes, you went from, according to your statement . . .

MILLER: Right.

BOYCE: . . . the Ringoes Post Office to your house, a trip admitted to me by yourself that takes maybe 20 minutes.

MILLER: About 20 minutes, right.

BOYCE: You wear, and you have a lot of, dark blue trousers.

MILLER: Right.

BOYCE: You have a lot of light blue shirts.

MILLER: Right.

BOYCE: I know, I have a lot of them in my custody now. We went to your house last night and found blood stains on the front stoop.

MILLER: On the front stoop?

BOYCE: Yes, sir.

MILLER: Well, how did it get there?

BOYCE: I don't know Frank. Let me ask you, how did it get there?

MILLER: I have no idea.

BOYCE: We obtained a sample of the blood.

MILLER: Right.

BOYCE: Obtained a sample from the vehicle.

MILLER: Uh, huh.

BOYCE: We have a witness, Frank, now this is point 4. We have a witness who identified your car, who, no, I'm, I'm sorry, let me, I shouldn't say your car, who identified a vehicle that fits the description of your car, at this girl's home, speaking with her, telling her something about a cow being loose. Someone who was there who wanted to help her, they didn't want to hurt this girl, they didn't want to hurt this girl, Frank, they wanted to help her. You see, I know this, I know that, . . .

MILLER: Yeah.

BOYCE: . . . because I can appreciate that, because I would have done the same thing. If there was something to be rectified, or if somebody had a problem, I would have done the same thing. I would have wanted to help her. The vehicle that came onto her property.

MILLER: Right.

BOYCE: . . . fits the description of your vehicle.

MILLER: It does.

BOYCE: Yes. Now, that's the fourth point. And when I say fits the description, what I mean, Frank, is it fits the description to a 't,' and as we talked about before, how many other vehicles are there like yours in the County right now?

MILLER: There shouldn't be too many, if any . . .

BOYCE: If any . . .

MILLER: Because of the damage on the right-hand side.

BOYCE: Now, what would your conclusion be under those circumstances, if someone told you that?

MILLER: I'd probably, uh, have the same conclusion you got.

BOYCE: Which is what?

MILLER: That I'm the guy that did this.

BOYCE: That did what?

MILLER: Committed this crime.

BOYCE: What crime?

MILLER: Well, you said before the girl was dead, killed, killed this girl.

BOYCE: Who killed this girl?

MILLER: The guy driving this car.

BOYCE: I think the guy driving this car . . . wait, let me, I forgot something . . . We have a physical description . . .

MILLER: Un huh.

BOYCE: . . . of this individual from another witness. The physical description Frank, . . .

MILLER: Yeah.

BOYCE: . . . Fits you and the clothes you were wearing. Frank, I don't think you're a criminal. I don't think you're a criminal. I don't think you have a criminal mind. As a matter of fact, I know you don't have a criminal mind, because we've been talking now for a few hours together, haven't we?

MILLER: Right.

BOYCE: Right?

MILLER: Yeah.

BOYCE: You don't have a criminal mind.

MILLER: No.

BOYCE: I know you don't. But, like I noted before, we all have problems.

MILLER: Right.

BOYCE: Am I right?

MILLER: Yeah, you said this over there at the plant.

BOYCE: And you agree with me?

MILLER: Yes, sir.

BOYCE: I have problems and you have.

MILLER: Right.

BOYCE: Now, how do you solve a problem?

MILLER: That depends on the problem.

BOYCE: Your problem how do we solve it? How are we going to solve it?

MILLER: This I don't know.

BOYCE: Do you want me to help you solve it?

MILLER: Yeah.

BOYCE: You want me to extend all the help I can possibly give you, don't you?

MILLER: Right.

BOYCE: Are you willing to do the same to me?

MILLER: Yeah.

BOYCE: Now, I feel . . .

MILLER: Yeah.

BOYCE: . . . who is ever, whoever is responsible for this act . . .

MILLER: Yeah.

BOYCE: He's not a criminal. Does not have a criminal mind. I think they have a problem.

MILLER: Uh, huh.

BOYCE: Do you agree with me?

MILLER: Yeah.

BOYCE: They have a problem.

MILLER: Right.

BOYCE: A problem, and a good thing about that Frank, is a problem can be rectified.

MILLER: Yeah.

BOYCE: I want to help you. I mean I really want to help you, but you know what they say, God helps those who help themselves, Frank.

MILLER: Right.

BOYCE: We've got to get together on this. You know what I'm talking about, don't you?

MILLER: Yeah, especially if they're trying to say that, you know, that like you say, I'm identified and my car's identified, and uh, we got to get together on this.

BOYCE: Yes we do. Now, that only a few of the items . . .

MILLER: Uh, huh.

BOYCE: . . . that we have now. Your problem, I'm not, let's forget this incident, okay . . .

MILLER: Yeah.

BOYCE: . . . let's forget this incident, let's talk about your problem. This is what, this is what I'm concerned with, Frank, your problem.

MILLER: Right.

BOYCE: If I had a problem like your problem, I would want you to help me with my problem.

MILLER: Uh, huh.

BOYCE: Now, you know what I'm talking about.

MILLER: Yeah.

BOYCE: And I know, and I think that, uh, a lot of other people know. You know what I'm talking about. I don't think you're a criminal, Frank.

MILLER: No, but you're trying to make me one.

BOYCE: No I'm not, no I'm not, but I want you to talk to me so we can get this thing worked out. This is what I want, this is what I want, Frank. I mean it's all there, it's all there. I'm not saying . . .

MILLER: Let me ask you a question.

BOYCE: Sure.

MILLER: Now you say this girl's dead, right?

BOYCE: She died just a few minutes ago. I just got . . . that's what the call was about.

MILLER: Cause Officer Scott said she was in the hospital and I said well then let's go, you know, go right over there.

BOYCE: She was in the hospital . . .

MILLER: And, uh . . .

BOYCE: . . . the call that Detective Doyle got, that's, that's what that call was.

MILLER: Cause, I told him . . .

BOYCE: Are you, do you feel what I feel right now?

MILLER: I feel pretty bad.

BOYCE: Do you want to talk to me about it?

MILLER: There's nothing I can tell . . .

BOYCE: About how you feel?

MILLER: . . . there's nothing I can talk, I mean I feel sorry for this girl, I mean, uh, this is something that, you know . . .

BOYCE: That what?

MILLER: Well, it's a shame, uh . . .

BOYCE: What did she say to you?

MILLER: Beg your pardon?

BOYCE: What did she say to you?

MILLER: Who?

BOYCE: This girl?

MILLER: I never talked to this girl. If she was to walk in here now, I wouldn't know, know that she was the girl that, uh, you're talking about.

BOYCE: But you were identified as being there talking to her minutes before she was . . . probably this thing that happened to her. How can you explain that?

MILLER: I can't.

BOYCE: Why?

MILLER: I don't know why, but I, I, you know, how can I explain something that I don't know anything about.

BOYCE: Frank, look, you want, you want help, don't you Frank?

MILLER: Yes, uh huh, yes, but yet I'm, I'm not going to admit to something that, that I wasn't involved in.

BOYCE: We don't want you to, all I want you to do is talk to me, that's all. I'm not talking about admitting to anything, Frank, I want you to talk to me. I want you to tell me what you think. I want you to tell me how you think about this, what you think about this?

MILLER: What I think about it?

BOYCE: Yeah.

MILLER: I think whoever did it really needs help.

BOYCE: And that's what I think and that's what I know. They don't, they don't need punishment, right? Like you said, they need help.

MILLER: Right.

BOYCE: They don't need punishment. They need help, good medical help.

MILLER: That's right.

BOYCE: . . . to rectify their problem. Putting them in, in a prison isn't going to solve it, is it?

MILLER: No sir. I know, I was in there for three and a half years.

BOYCE: That's right. That's the, that's not going to solve your problem is it?

MILLER: No, you get no help down there. The only thing you learn is how to, you know . . .

BOYCE: Well, let's say this Frank, suppose you were the person who needed help. What would you want somebody to do for you?

MILLER: Help me.

BOYCE: In what way?

MILLER: In any way that they, they see, you know, fit, that it would help me.

BOYCE: What, what do you think compels somebody to do something like this. What do you think it is, Frank?

MILLER: Well, it could be a number of things.

BOYCE: Give me an example.

MILLER: It could be a person that, that drinks, uh, you know, a lot, and just, you know, don't know what they, what they did once they been drinking. It could be somebody with narcotics that, that don't know what they're, you know, what they're doing once they shot up or took some pills or whatever they do, I don't know, I'm not a drug addict and never intend to be.

BOYCE: What else Frank? What other type of person would do something like this?

MILLER: Somebody with a mental problem.

BOYCE: Right. Somebody with a . . .

MILLER: Mental problem . . .

BOYCE: . . . serious mental problem, and you know what I'm interested in, I'm not, I'm interested in, in preventing this in the future.

MILLER: Right.

BOYCE: Now, don't you think it's better if someone knows that he or she has a mental problem to come forward with it and say, look, I've, I've, I've done these acts. I'm responsible for this, but I want to be helped, I couldn't help myself, I had no control of myself and if I'm examined properly you'll find out that's the case. Is that right or wrong?

MILLER: Yeah, that, they should be examined and, uh, you know, maybe a doctor could find out what's wrong with em.

BOYCE: Have you ever been examined?

MILLER: Yes.

BOYCE: And did you have a problem?

MILLER: Well, when I come, uh, made parole in, uh, September, the uh stipulation was, uh, that I see a psychiatrist.

BOYCE: Alright . . .

MILLER: Dr. Taylor over here at the Medical Center, I seen him, two, maybe three times and last time I was there he gave me a test . . .

BOYCE: Uh, huh.

MILLER: . . . uh, it was a bunch of bull shit, in plain English. If the big wheel turns one way, what way does the little wheel turn? So I took that test. He says, alright, he says, I say when do I come back, because this is part of my parole.

BOYCE: I see.

MILLER: And he says, uh, I'll call you and let you know, he says I want to get this, work this test out first. He up to this date, the man has never called me, uh . . .

BOYCE: How do you feel about this?

MILLER: Well, I think it's wrong.

BOYCE: Would you, do you, did you feel that after not finding out the results of that test that you might do something that you might not be responsible for?

MILLER: No.

BOYCE: Did you feel that you were capable, maybe, of doing something because you didn't get the results of this .. because they didn't like, help you, did they?

MILLER: No.

BOYCE: Well, then did you still feel this way that something might happen it would be their fault because, as far as I'm concerned if something did happen, it's not your fault, it's their fault . . .

MILLER: Right.

BOYCE: . . . because that was a part of your parole . . .

MILLER: Right.

BOYCE: . . . and they didn't live up to it.

MILLER: Right.

BOYCE: You agree with me?

MILLER: Yeah, that . . .

BOYCE: So, therefore, if you did commit an act, actually they're the ones that are to blame, in my eyes . . .

MILLER: Right.

BOYCE: . . . not you as an individual. You were there seeking help. You went there, they didn't right, you went there voluntarily, right?

MILLER: Right. It was, uh, it was all set up through . . .

BOYCE: It was all set up.

MILLER: . . . the parole board, or well, my parole officer, I believe set it up. At that time it was, uh, Gene, uh, DiGennie, I believe his name was.

BOYCE: DiGianni.

MILLER: DiGianni.

BOYCE: Frank, you're very, very nervous. Now, I, I don't, you know, you, you're, you understand what I'm saying?

MILLER: Yeah, I know what you're saying.

BOYCE: Now, there's a reason for that, isn't there?

MILLER: Yes.

BOYCE: Do you want to tell me about it?

MILLER: Being involved in something like this is . . .

BOYCE: Is what, does it, does it, does it visibly shake you physically?

MILLER: Yes, it does, because, well, Officer Scott can tell you, it ain't been not even a month ago I sat right in the same room . . .

BOYCE: Uh, huh.

MILLER: . . . behind the girl that I really loved, because she was a minor her father forced her into making statements, which, she didn't lie on the statements. I tried to cover up with Officer Scott until I heard from her and she said yes, she says, I did tell him, she says, I had to tell him. So, then when I talked to my lawyer, you know, I admitted to him, I admitted to my parole officer, I said I'm not making a liar out of the girl, cause I love her too much and so I admitted, you know, he asked me if we were having sex . . .

BOYCE: Alright. What . . .

MILLER: . . . and, uh, I had no intentions of making a liar out of her.

BOYCE: Now listen to me Frank. This hurts me more than it hurts you, because I love people.

MILLER: It can't hurt you anymore than it hurts me.

BOYCE: Okay, listen Frank, I want you . . .

MILLER: I mean even being involved in something like this.

BOYCE: Okay. listen Frank, If I promise to, you know, do all I can with the psychiatrist and everything, and we get the proper help for you, and get the proper help for you, will you talk to me about it?

MILLER: I can't talk to you about something I'm not . . .

BOYCE: Alright, listen Frank, alright, honest. I know, I know what's going on inside you, Frank. I want to help you, you know, between us right now. I know what going on inside you. Frank, you've got to come forward and tell me that you want to help yourself. You've got to talk to me about it. This is the only way we'll be able to work it out. I mean, you know, listen, I want to help you, because you are in my mind, you are not responsible. You are not responsible, Frank. Frank, what's the matter?

MILLER: I feel bad.

BOYCE: Frank, listen to me, honest to God, I'm, I'm telling you, Frank (inaudible). I know, it's going to bother you. Frank, it's going to bother you. It's there, it's not going to go away, it's there. It's right in front of you, Frank. Am I right or wrong?

MILLER: Yeah.

BOYCE: You can see it Frank, you can feel it, you can feel it but you are not responsible. This is what I'm trying to tell you, but you've got to come forward and tell me. Don't, don't, don't let it eat you up, don't, don't fight it. You've got to rectify it, Frank. We've got to get together on this thing, or I, I mean really, you need help, you need proper help and you know it, my God, you know, in God's name, you, you know it. You are not a criminal, you are not a criminal.

MILLER: Alright. Yes, I was over there and I talked to her about the cow and left. I left in my car and I stopped up on the road where, you know, where the cow had been and she followed me in her car . . .

BOYCE: Right.

MILLER: . . . and the cow wasn't down there and we started walking through the fields and stuff, and you could see where the cow was.

BOYCE: Uh, huh.

MILLER: Now, I don't know . . .

BOYCE: Now, Frank please . . .

MILLER: Wait, wait a minute.

BOYCE: I'm sorry, I'm sorry.

MILLER: Okay, okay.

BOYCE: Go ahead, I'm sorry.

MILLER: I don't know where this guy come from . . .

BOYCE: Tell me about him, I'm sorry, go ahead.

MILLER: But . . .

BOYCE: Tell me about him Frank . . .

MILLER: Alright, he, alright, he grabbed her . . .

BOYCE: Right.

MILLER: . . . that's how I got the cut on my hand, I didn't get cut in the car.

BOYCE: Alright, tell me what happened. Tell me what happened. Let it come out, Frank, let it come out. This is what you need, Frank. I'm, it's you and me, now listen.

MILLER: Alright now, he, you know I, tried to get ahold of him and he cut me in the hand with the knife, and he'd already cut her, and then he ran.

BOYCE: Alright.

MILLER: So first thing I thought, you know, try and help her. I got her in the car and she just, you know, she just fell over and I got scared because, you know, I thought she was dead.

BOYCE: Alright.

MILLER: So, I got down by the bridge, I just, you know, laid her off there and got the hell out of there because I was scared, because, you know . . .

BOYCE: Let it come out, Frank. I'm here, I'm here with you now. I'm on your side, I'm on your side, Frank. I'm your brother, you and I are brothers Frank. We are brothers and I want to help my brother.

MILLER: If I hadn't went down on that road I wouldn't even have been involved in it.

BOYCE: Frank, listen . . .

MILLER: It was a shorter way home from, from the Post Office. I'm not lying about that

Post Office or nothing. I came out past that cemetery and up that, up that dirt road . . .

BOYCE: Alright, let's . . .

MILLER: . . . because I could have, you know, swung off at the Whitehall area, I could have swung off and went through the back way to the house.

BOYCE: Let's, Frank, listen. Let's go back to the Post Office, okay? Did you go to the Post Office?

MILLER: Yes.

BOYCE: Okay . . .

MILLER: There was one . . .

BOYCE: Tell me . . .

MILLER: . . . one woman there, I don't, I don't, I couldn't even begin to describe.

BOYCE: Now tell me where you went. Tell me again about this incident, okay?

MILLER: Right.

BOYCE: Alright Frank, tell me what happened.

MILLER: I left the Post Office, you want to go from the Post Office, right?

BOYCE: Uh, huh.

MILLER: Alright. Alright, then I stuck the letter in the mailbox, the out of town mail, and I left there and I could, went up, was gonna go up the back way because it was a shorter way home. Then I seen this cow along the road and there was a farm there so I figured, you know, it must be their cow. So, I went in there, and I started to get out of the car and the dogs barked so I blew the horn . . .

BOYCE: Right.

MILLER: . . . because I wasn't about, I didn't know whether this dog would bite or not. And, I blew the horn two or three times and then this girl come out.

BOYCE: Do you remember what the girl looked like? What she was wearing?

MILLER: She was wearing a two piece bathing suit, like you said.

BOYCE: Go ahead.

MILLER: I told her there was a cow out there and she said, yeah it's probably one that's always getting out. And I said well do you need a help, you got anybody here to help you get it in and she says, uh, I don't need no help, she says I can get it back myself. So, I went out, went up the road there, out the driveway, she was following me in her car. I think a Corvair, or. So, I stop up the road there where I, where I had seen the cow and, uh, the cow wasn't there. She pulled up behind me, she got out of the car and I said the cow was here. Well, you can see the marks where the cow had been and we started walking through the, through the field there, uh, it's be on your lefthand side. And, like I say, I don't know where this guy come from.

BOYCE: Tell me what happened.

MILLER: Well, I heard her scream. She, I was walking more or less along the hedgerow there, or trees, whatever you want to call it. I heard her scream and I turned around and I seen a guy there, I'd say he was maybe my height, maybe a little taller, a little smaller, and I don't know, when, when I ran up there he whipped on me, that's how I got this, and . . .

BOYCE: Listen Frank, this guy, do you know him? Do you know where he lives?

MILLER: No, I don't know where he lives. (inaudible)

BOYCE: You killed this girl didn't you?

MILLER: No, I didn't.

BOYCE: Honest, Frank? It's got to come out. You can't leave it in. It's hard for you, I realize that, how hard it is, how difficult it is, I realize that, but you've got to help yourself before anybody else can help you. And we're going to see to it that you get the proper help. This is our job, Frank. This is our job. This is what I want to do.

MILLER: By sending me back down there.

BOYCE: Wait a second now, don't talk about going back down there. First thing we have to do is let it all come out. Don't fight it because it's worse, Frank, it's worse. It's hurting me because I feel it. I feel it wanting to come out, but it's hurting me, Frank. You're my brother, I mean we're brothers. All men on this, all men on the face of this earth are brothers, Frank, but you got to be completely honest with me.

MILLER: I'm trying to be, but you don't want to believe me.

BOYCE: I want to believe you, Frank, but I want you to tell me the truth, Frank, and you know what I'm talking about and I know what you're talking about. You've got to tell me the truth. I can't help you without the truth.

MILLER: I'm telling you the truth. Sure, that's her blood in the car because when I seen the way she was cut I wanted to help her, and then when she fell over I got scared to even be involved in something like this, being on parole and . . .

BOYCE: I realize this, Frank, it may have been an accident. Isn't that possible, Frank? Isn't that possible?

MILLER: Sure, it's possible.

BOYCE: Well, this is what I'm trying to bring out, Frank. It may be something that, that you did that you can't be held accountable for. This, I can help you, I can help you once you tell me the truth. You know what I'm talking about. I want to help you, Frank. I like you. You've been honest with me. You've been sincere and I've been the same way with you. Now this is the kind of relationship we have, but I can't help you unless you tell me the complete truth. I'll listen to you. I understand, Frank. You have to believe that, I understand. I understand how you feel. I understand how much it must hurt you inside. I know how you feel because I feel it too. Because some day I may be in the same situation Frank, but you've got to help yourself. Tell me exactly what happened, tell me the truth, Frank, please.

MILLER: I'm trying to tell you the truth.

BOYCE: Let me help you. It could have been an accident. You, you've got to tell me the truth, Frank. You know what I'm talking about. I can't help you without the truth. Now you know and I know that's, that's, that's all that counts, Frank. You know and I know that's what counts, that's what it's all about. We can't hide it from each other because we both know, but you've got to be willing to help yourself. You know, I don't think you're a criminal. You have this problem like we talked about before, right?

MILLER: Yeah, you, you say this now, but this thing goes to court and everything and you . . .

BOYCE: No. listen to me, Frank, please listen to me. The issue now is what happened. The issue now is truth. Truth is the issue now. You've got to believe this, and the truth prevails in the end, Frank. You have to believe that and I'm sincere when I'm saying it to you. You've got to be truthful with yourself.

MILLER: Yeah, truth, you say in the end, right? That's why I done three and a half years for . . .

BOYCE: Wait, whoa . . .

MILLER: . . . for a crime that I never committed because of one stinking detective framing me . . .

BOYCE: Frank, Frank.

MILLER: . . . by the name of Rocco.

BOYCE: Frank, you're talking to me now. We have, we have a relationship, don't we? Have I been sincere with you, Frank?

MILLER: Yeah, you . . .

BOYCE: . . . Have I been honest?

MILLER: . . . Yes.

BOYCE: Have I defined your problem, Frank? Have I been willing to help you? Have I stated I'm willing to help you all I can?

MILLER: Yes.

BOYCE: Do I mean it?

MILLER: Yes.

BOYCE: Whenever I talk to anybody I talk the same way, because you have a very, very serious problem, and we want to prevent anything in the future. This is what's important, Frank, not what happened in the past. It's right now, we're living now, Frank, we want to help you now. You've got a lot more, a lot more years to live.

MILLER: No, I don't.

BOYCE: Yes, you do.

MILLER: No, I don't.

BOYCE: Don't say you don't. Now you've got to tell me.

MILLER: Not after all this, because this is going to kill my father.

BOYCE: Listen, Frank. There is where you, the truth comes out. Your father will understand. This is what you have to understand, Frank. If the truth is out he will understand. That's the most important thing, not, not what has happened, Frank. The fact that you were truthful, you came forward and you said, look I have a problem. I didn't mean to do what I did. I have a problem, this is what's important, Frank. This is very important, I got, I, I got to get closer to you, Frank, I got to make you believe this and I'm and I'm sincere when I tell you this. You got to tell me exactly what happened, Frank. That's very important. I know how you feel inside, Frank, it's eating you up, am I right? It's eating you up, Frank. You've got to come forward. You've got to do it for yourself, for your family, for your father, this is what's important Frank. Just tell me. You didn't mean to kill her did you?

MILLER: I thought she was dead or I'd have never dropped her off like that.

BOYCE: Why, Frank? Frank, look at me, okay? I'm looking at your problem now. Just picture this, okay? I'm looking at your problem, okay? You follow me?

MILLER: Uhm.

BOYCE: What made you do this, please tell me. Please tell me now. What made you do this?

MILLER: I don't know.

BOYCE: Alright, explain to me, how, exactly how it happened and then we'll see, maybe we can find out why it happened, alright? Is that fair? Just tell me how it happened and then we'll talk about why it could have happened. This is what's important to me.

MILLER: I don't even know.

BOYCE: Well, just tell me what happened, tell me the truth this time. Please, I can't help you without the truth.

MILLER: Like I said I went, I went there because the cow was out . . .

BOYCE: I know that and . . .

MILLER: Wait, wait, alright, wait a minute. She followed me out the driveway. We stopped up there on the road. The cow wasn't around and we were talking. She got in my car. We figured the cow might be down on the other road, or down further.

BOYCE: You want it to happen.

MILLER: Yes.

BOYCE: Okay. When you got down there, Frank, when you went down there, something happened inside you. This is what I'm interested in, now please tell me, you've got to, you've got to get the proper help, Frank, we want to help you. Please tell me, Frank.

MILLER: I don't know what happened, I really don't.

BOYCE: Alright, but tell me, tell me how it happened, the truth this time, Frank.

MILLER: I can't even tell ya that.

BOYCE: Well, tell me, tell me Frank, (inaudible) . . . have to be completely truthful with me the way I am with you. It's so important, Frank, honest to God, because people believe truth. I mean, Frank, this is hurting me, God listen. I just want you to come out and tell me, so I can help you, that's all. Listen, it's the right way.

MILLER: I, I swear to God, I don't know what happened down there.

BOYCE: Why? Why did you do it?

MILLER: I don't even know that.

BOYCE: What did you, what did you cut the girl with? What did you use, Frank?

MILLER: A penknife.

BOYCE: Your penknife?

MILLER: Yes, sir.

BOYCE: Which penknife?

MILLER: The one you have.

BOYCE: The one I have?

MILLER: Yes.

BOYCE: Where did you cut her, Frank?

MILLER: In the throat.

BOYCE: In the throat?

MILLER: Uh, huh.

BOYCE: Now, right before you cut her in the throat, what, why did you cut, did, was she fighting you off?

MILLER: No.

BOYCE: She wasn't fighting you?

MILLER: No.

BOYCE: Why do you think, where were you when you cut her in the throat? Where were you, where were you at, at that moment?

MILLER: Down by the bridge.

BOYCE: Down by the bridge?

MILLER: Yes.

BOYCE: Were you in the vehicle or were you outside the vehicle?

MILLER: In the car.

BOYCE: You were in the car?

MILLER: Yes.

BOYCE: Okay, now, you were in the car, right?

MILLER: Uh, huh.

BOYCE: Did she get in the car voluntarily?

MILLER: Yes.

BOYCE: She did?

MILLER: Yes.

BOYCE: Did you ask her to get into the car?

MILLER: Yes.

BOYCE: What did you say to her, Frank?

MILLER: I said, why don't we go on down the road and see if the cow's down there.

BOYCE: And she got in the car with you?

MILLER: Yes.

BOYCE: Where did she get in the car with you?

MILLER: Up on the main road.

BOYCE: Where she parked her car?

MILLER: Yes.

BOYCE: Alright. Then you drove down by the bridge.

MILLER: Right.

BOYCE: Okay, now. What happened in the car? Where did you have your knife?

MILLER: In my pocket.

BOYCE: In your pocket?

MILLER: Yes.

BOYCE: And, when did you take it out?

MILLER: From there everything's a blank.

BOYCE: Well . . .

MILLER: I didn't, as far as what, you know, what really . . .

BOYCE: Alright, well where did you cut her with the knife?

MILLER: In the car.

BOYCE: Did she fight you in any way.

MILLER: No.

BOYCE: Did you cut any other part of her body, Frank?

MILLER: No, not that I, no, not that I know of.

BOYCE: Did you bite her in any way, Frank?

MILLER: No, not that I know of.

BOYCE: Not that you know of?

MILLER: No.

BOYCE: Did she bleed a lot in the car, Frank?

MILLER: Some, yes.

BOYCE: What happened to the blood that was in the car, Frank? Did you clean the car, Frank? Did you clean the car out after the blood was in the vehicle?

MILLER: There wasn't really, no, I, I just, you know, wiped what little bit was on the seat.

BOYCE: Alright. After you cut her throat, now, what did you do then? After that, after that happened, what did you do then, Frank?

MILLER: I don't know, I, everything just, everything's a blank, really.

BOYCE: Well, try and remember now. What, did you get out of the vehicle?

MILLER: I guess. Yeah, I, I got, I got out of the car and I took her out of the car . . .

BOYCE: Alright, then what did you do?

MILLER: Carried her over the bridge.

BOYCE: Threw her over the bridge?

MILLER: Yes.

BOYCE: Did, then, after you threw her over the bridge, then what did you do, Frank?

MILLER: I didn't do, I don't know.

BOYCE: Did you drag, did you drag her any further after you threw her over the bridge?

MILLER: I don't think so, no.

BOYCE: Try and remember now, it's very important. I'm sure you can understand that, right?

MILLER: Yeah.

BOYCE: Try and remember now. You threw her over the bridge . . .

MILLER: Yeah.

BOYCE: . . . Now, did you go down and look at her again?

MILLER: I don't really know.

BOYCE: Okay. Did you, did you have sexual relations with her, Frank?

MILLER: Not that I know of.

BOYCE: Are you sure now? Think hard. Think hard now, while you were in the car?

MILLER: I don't think so.

BOYCE: Alright. After she, after you threw her out over the bridge?

MILLER: Yeah.

BOYCE: Is that where you had the sexual relations with her?

MILLER: I don't think I did.

BOYCE: Did you remove any of her clothing, Frank?

MILLER: I don't believe so, no. I don't really know.

BOYCE: Alright. Now think about, did you try and drag her body anywhere?

MILLER: I don't think so.

BOYCE: Did you drag the body up towards the water anywhere?

MILLER: I don't think so, no. I say I, I don't know, I . . .

BOYCE: Where, once again now, you're in the car with her right?

MILLER: Uh, huh.

BOYCE: Now, did you pull the knife out right away? What did you say to her, Frank, before you pulled the knife out? Did you ask her anything?

MILLER: I don't know if I did or not.

BOYCE: And you said the pocket knife, what pocket knife were you referring to now, that you used.

MILLER: The one you have.

BOYCE: The one that you gave me at PFD Plastics?

MILLER: Yeah.

BOYCE: And whereabouts did you cut her?

MILLER: In the throat.

BOYCE: In the throat? Is there any reason why you cut her in the throat, Frank?

MILLER: No, not that I know of.

BOYCE: Did you, did you caress her breasts in any way?

MILLER: No.

BOYCE: Was she an attractive girl?

MILLER: Um, I'd say so, yes.

BOYCE: About what time was that, Frank?

MILLER: I'm not sure.

BOYCE: About what time?

MILLER: Well, I was at the Post Office around, I figure 11 o'clock, so it had to be after that.

BOYCE: It happened sometime after that, about, about how long?

MILLER: I'd say maybe five after, ten after, something like this. That's about all the time it would take to go from the Post Office to there.

BOYCE: And what road were you on when this, when you cut her throat in the vehicle, what road were you on?

MILLER: I don't know the road exactly.

BOYCE: Was it a dirt road, Frank?

MILLER: Yes.

BOYCE: It was a dirt road?

MILLER: Yes.

BOYCE: Did you see anybody at the house when you were there?

MILLER: Just her.

BOYCE: Did you see any of her brothers?

MILLER: No.

BOYCE: Did you see anyone else?

MILLER: No. No one came out but her.

BOYCE: Did you cut any other portion of her body, Frank? Just, just think hard, now, take your time, ah. You know, I realize that, you know, that, just take your time and think, did you cut any portion of her body? Did you cut her breasts?

MILLER: No.

BOYCE: Are you sure, Frank?

MILLER: Positive.

BOYCE: Did you bite her in anyway?

MILLER: I don't think . . .

BOYCE: Tell me the truth, Frank. Honest? You've been so honest with me so far, you've been truthful, you've been honest, you've been sincere. Now, after you threw, how did you, which car, which car did you, uh, side of the car did you drag her out of?

MILLER: The driver's side.

BOYCE: Driver's side?

MILLER: Yeah.

BOYCE: I see. Did you clean your car in anyway?

MILLER: Yeah.

BOYCE: Where, where did you clean your car, Frank?

MILLER: I used the hose at home.

BOYCE: At home?

MILLER: Yeah, in the driveway.

BOYCE: And did you enter your house through the front door, Frank?

MILLER: Through the breezeway.

BOYCE: Through the breezeway?

MILLER: Yeah.

BOYCE: Where are the rags? What did you use to clean the car out with?

MILLER: I just used the hose.

BOYCE: The hose?

MILLER: Yeah.

BOYCE: You washed it out?

MILLER: Yes.

BOYCE: Where was the vehicle when you washed it out, Frank?

MILLER: In the driveway.

BOYCE: In the driveway? Did you use any type of rag on the inside of the car?

MILLER: Just a . . . no.

BOYCE: Are you sure, Frank?

MILLER: There was a . . . I had a paper bag, a brown paper bag and the . . . I just wiped some of the water off of the seat and stuff.

BOYCE: Where is the brown paper bag now, Frank? What did you do with it?

MILLER: I threw it away.

BOYCE: Where did you throw it, Frank?

MILLER: Driving along the road on my way up to Flemington.

BOYCE: Where, do you remember on which road you were, or how far you were away from the house when you threw it out the window?

MILLER: No, I don't.

BOYCE: You don't have any idea, Frank?

MILLER: No.

BOYCE: Now, did you actually throw her over the, uh, the fence then the rail?

MILLER: Yes.

BOYCE: You did?

MILLER: Yes.

BOYCE: Did you go, after you threw her over the fence, did you go and look at her again to see if she was dead?

MILLER: I don't believe I did, no.

BOYCE: Was there anyone with you, Frank, when this occurred, or were you alone? You indicated before that you were alone, were you alone with her when this happened?

MILLER: Yeah.

BOYCE: I see. Were you driving your car, Frank?

MILLER: Yeah.

BOYCE: What kind of a car do you drive?

MILLER: a white Mercury.

BOYCE: What year is that Mercury?

MILLER: '69.

BOYCE: '69? Is there any damage, is there any damage to your vehicle?

MILLER: Yes.

BOYCE: Where is the damage?

MILLER: Right-hand side.

BOYCE: Is your trunk tied down?

MILLER: Yes.

BOYCE: Alright. I've indicated before that you would be willing to sit down with me and the Assistant Prosecutor and indicate to him, like you said, that you have a problem.

MILLER: uh, huh.

BOYCE: Would you be willing to sit down with us while we take a statement from you?

MILLER: Yes.

BOYCE: So it can be incorporated, you follow me?

MILLER: Yeah.

BOYCE: In order to help you.

MILLER: Uh, huh.

BOYCE: Would you be willing to do that?

MILLER: Uh, huh.

BOYCE: Now, is there anything I can get you now? You want coffee?

MILLER: No.

BOYCE: You want to just sit here for awhile?

MILLER: Yes.

The time now is 2:45 A.M. Statement concluded at this time. Statement and interrogation concluded at this time.

At the end of this interrogation, Miller collapsed into a catatonic state, whereupon he was hospitalized.

# 19.

# DUE PROCESS OUTSIDE OF THE CONFESSION CONTEXT

Under current constitutional dogma, virtually all significant provisions of the Bill of Rights concerning criminal procedure are applicable to the states. That was not always the case, however. Prior to 1961, the exclusionary rule of the Fourth Amendment was not applicable to the states, and the privilege against self-incrimination was not applied to the states until 1964.

Before that time, virtually all constitutional criminal procedure applicable to the states had to be justified under the rubric of due process. Today, of course, that is not the case. Nevertheless, as cases like *Fulminante* demonstrate, the due process clause remains one of major import. In terms of strategy, a criminal defense lawyer is generally better off if she can persuade a judge that the complained of procedure violates a specific constitutional prohibition. However, she would be downright incompetent if she fails to raise a due process claim when one is possibly available.

In this chapter, we will examine due process in two cases (*Rochin* and *Irvine*) decided prior to the applicability of specific provisions of the Bill of Rights to the states and one due process plus specific provision case (*Schmerber*) decided after the Fourth, Fifth, and Sixth Amendment criminal procedure provisions were held applicable to the states.

## Rochin v. California
### 342 U.S. 165 (1952)

Mr. Justice FRANKFURTER delivered the opinion of the Court.

Having "some information that [the petitioner here] was selling narcotics," three deputy sheriffs of the County of Los Angeles, on the morning of July 1, 1949, made for the two-story dwelling house in which Rochin lived with his mother, common-law wife, brothers and sisters. Finding the outside door open, they entered and then forced open the door to Rochin's room on the second floor. Inside they found petitioner sitting partly dressed on the side of the bed, upon which his wife was lying. On a "night stand" beside the bed the deputies spied two capsules. When asked "Whose stuff is this?" Rochin seized the capsules and put them in his mouth. A struggle ensued, in the course of which the three officers "jumped upon him" and attempted to extract the capsules. The force they applied proved unavailing against Rochin's resistance. He was handcuffed and taken to a hospital. At the direction of one of the officers a doctor forced an emetic solution through a tube into Rochin's stomach against his will. This "stomach pumping" produced vomiting. In the vomited matter were found two capsules which proved to contain morphine.

Regard for the requirements of the Due Process Clause "inescapably imposes upon this Court an exercise of judgment upon the whole course of the proceedings [resulting in a conviction] in order to ascertain whether they offend those canons of decency and fairness which express the notions of justice of English-speaking peoples even toward those charged with the most heinous offenses." These standards of justice are not authoritatively formulated anywhere as though they were specifics. Due process of law is a summarized constitutional guarantee of respect for those personal immunities which, as Mr. Justice Cardozo twice wrote for the Court, are "so rooted in the traditions and conscience of our people as to be ranked as fundamental," *Snyder v. Commonwealth of Massachusetts*, 291 U.S. 97, 105, or are "implicit in the concept of ordered liberty." *Palko v. State of Connecticut*, 302 U.S. 319, 325.

The vague contours of the Due Process Clause do not leave judges at large. We may not draw on our merely personal and private notions and disregard the limits that bind judges in their judicial function. Even though the concept of due process of law is not final and fixed, these limits are derived from considerations that are fused in the whole nature of our judicial process. These are considerations deeply rooted in reason and in the compelling traditions of the legal profession. The Due Process Clause places upon this Court the duty of exercising a judgment, within the narrow confines of judicial power in reviewing State convictions, upon interests of society pushing in opposite directions.

To practice the requisite detachment and to achieve sufficient objectivity no doubt demands of judges the habit of self-discipline and self-criticism, incertitude that one's own views are incontestable and alert tolerance toward views not shared. But these are precisely the presuppositions of our judicial process. They are precisely the qualities society has a right to expect from those entrusted with ultimate judicial power.

Applying these general considerations to the circumstances of the present case, we are compelled to conclude that the proceedings by which this conviction

was obtained do more than offend some fastidious squeamishness or private sentimentalism about combating crime too energetically. This is conduct that shocks the conscience. Illegally breaking into the privacy of the petitioner, the struggle to open his mouth and remove what was there, the forcible extraction of his stomach's contents—this course of proceeding by agents of government to obtain evidence is bound to offend even hardened sensibilities. They are methods too close to the rack and the screw to permit of constitutional differentiation.

It has long since ceased to be true that due process of law is heedless of the means by which otherwise relevant and credible evidence is obtained. This was not true even before the series of recent cases enforced the constitutional principle that the States may not base convictions upon confessions, however much verified, obtained by coercion. These decisions are not arbitrary exceptions to the comprehensive right of States to fashion their own rules of evidence for criminal trials. They are not sports in our constitutional law but applications of a general principle. They are only instances of the general requirement that States in their prosecutions respect certain decencies of civilized conduct. Due process of law, as a historic and generative principle, precludes defining, and thereby confining, these standards of conduct more precisely than to say that convictions cannot be brought about by methods that offend "a sense of justice." See Mr. Chief Justice Hughes, speaking for a unanimous Court in *Brown v. State of Mississippi*. It would be a stultification of the responsibility which the course of constitutional history has cast upon this Court to hold that in order to convict a man the police cannot extract by force what is in his mind but can extract what is in his stomach.

To attempt in this case to distinguish what lawyers call "real evidence" from verbal evidence is to ignore the reasons for excluding coerced confessions. Use of involuntary verbal confessions in State criminal trials is constitutionally obnoxious not only because of their unreliability. They are inadmissible under the Due Process Clause even though statements contained in them may be independently established as true. Coerced confessions offend the community's sense of fair play and decency. So here, to sanction the brutal conduct which naturally enough was condemned by the court whose judgment is before us, would be to afford brutality the cloak of law. Nothing would be more calculated to discredit law and thereby to brutalize the temper of a society.

We are not unmindful that hypothetical situations can be conjured up, standing imperceptibly from the circumstances of this case and by gradations producing practical differences despite seemingly logical extensions. But the Constitution is "intended to preserve practical and substantial rights, not to maintain theories."

On the facts of this case the conviction of the petitioner has been obtained by methods that offend the Due Process Clause. The judgment below must be Reversed.

Mr. Justice BLACK, concurring.

In the view of a majority of the Court, the Fifth Amendment imposes no restraint of any kind on the states. They nevertheless hold that California's use of this evidence violated the Due Process Clause of the Fourteenth Amendment. Since they hold as I do in this case, I regret my inability to accept their interpretation without protest. But I believe that faithful adherence to the specific guarantees in the Bill of Rights insures a more permanent protection of individual liberty than that which can be afforded by the nebulous standards stated by the majority.

What the majority hold is that the Due Process Clause empowers this Court to nullify any state law if its application "shocks the conscience," offends "a sense of justice" or runs counter to the "decencies of civilized conduct." The majority emphasize that these statements do not refer to their own consciences or to their senses of justice and decency. For we are told that "we may not draw on our merely personal and private notions"; our judgment must be grounded on "considerations deeply rooted in reason and in the compelling traditions of the legal profession." We are further admonished to measure the validity of state practices, not by our reason, or by the traditions of the legal profession, but by "the community's sense of fair play and decency"; by the "traditions and conscience of our people"; or by "those canons of decency and fairness which express the notions of justice of English-speaking peoples." These canons are made necessary, it is said, because of "interests of society pushing in opposite directions."

If the Due Process Clause does vest this Court with such unlimited power to invalidate laws, I am still in doubt as to why we should consider only the notions of English-speaking peoples to determine what are immutable and fundamental principles of justice. Moreover, one may well ask what avenues of investigation are open to discover "canons" of conduct so universally favored that this Court should write them into the Constitution? All we are told is that the discovery must be made by an "evaluation based on a disinterested inquiry pursued in the spirit of science, on a balanced order of facts."

Some constitutional provisions are stated in absolute and unqualified language such, for illustration, as the First Amendment stating that no law shall be passed prohibiting the free exercise of religion or abridging the freedom of speech or press. Other constitutional provisions do require courts to choose between competing policies, such as the Fourth Amendment which, by its terms, necessitates a judicial decision as to what is an "unreasonable" search or seizure. There is, however, no express constitutional language granting judicial power to invalidate *every* state law of *every* kind deemed "unreasonable" or contrary to the Court's notion of civilized decencies; yet the constitutional philosophy used by the majority has, in the past, been used to deny a state the right to fix the price of gasoline, and even the right to prevent bakers from palming off smaller for larger loaves of bread, *Jay Burns Baking Co. v. Bryan*, 264 U.S. 504. These cases, and others, show the extent to which the evanescent standards of the majority's philosophy have been used to nullify state legislative programs passed to suppress evil economic practices. What paralyzing role this same philosophy will play in the future economic affairs of this country is impossible to predict. Of even graver concern, however, is the use of the philosophy to nullify the Bill of Rights. I long ago concluded that the accordion-like qualities of this philosophy must inevitably imperil all the individual liberty safeguards specifically enumerated in the Bill of Rights. Reflection and recent decisions of this Court sanctioning abridgment of the freedom of speech and press have strengthened this conclusion.

Mr. Justice DOUGLAS, concurring.

The evidence obtained from this accused's stomach would be admissible in the majority of states where the question has been raised. So far as the reported cases reveal, the only states which would probably exclude the evidence would be Arkansas, Iowa, Michigan, and Missouri. Yet the Court now says that the rule which the majority of the states have fashioned violates the "decencies of civilized conduct." To that I cannot agree. It is a rule formulated by responsible courts with judges as sensitive as we are to the proper standards for law administration.

As an original matter it might be debatable whether the provision in the Fifth Amendment that no person "shall be compelled in any criminal case to be a witness against himself" serves the ends of justice. Not all civilized legal procedures recognize it. But the Choice was made by the Framers, a choice which sets a standard for legal trials in this country. The Framers made it a standard of due process for prosecutions by the Federal Government. If it is a requirement of due process for a trial in the federal courthouse, it is impossible for me to say it is not a requirement of due process for a trial in the state courthouse.

## QUESTIONS AND NOTES

**1.** What was so shocking about the police behavior in *Rochin*? Was it not desirable to remove morphine (which presumably is not good for people) from the defendant's stomach?

**2.** Is the *Rochin* problem more nearly analogous to the Fourth or Fifth Amendment?

**3.** Was the nature of the police "wrong" in *Rochin* obtaining the evidence or using the evidence? If the former, how, if at all, does it differ from a Fourth Amendment violation?

**4.** Do you think that judges can (should) achieve the level of objectivity suggested by Frankfurter?

**5.** The uncertainty of the *Wolf/Rochin* approach was illustrated in *Irvine*.

### Irvine v. California
### 347 U.S. 128 (1954)

Mr. Justice JACKSON announced the judgment of the Court and an opinion in which the Chief Justice, Mr. Justice REED and Mr. Justice MINTON join.

This case involves constitutional questions growing out of methods employed to convict petitioner on charges of horse race bookmaking and related offenses against the anti-gambling laws of California. Petitioner exhausted all avenues to relief under state procedures and then sought review here of duly raised federal issues.

[T]he questions raised by the officers' conduct while investigating this case are serious. The police strongly suspected petitioner of illegal bookmaking but were without proof of it. On December 1, 1951, while Irvine and his wife were absent from their home, an officer arranged to have a locksmith go there and make a door key. Two days later, again in the absence of occupants, officers and a technician made entry into the home by the use of this key and installed a concealed microphone in the hall. A hole was bored in the roof of the house and wires were strung to transmit to a neighboring garage whatever sounds the microphone might pick up. Officers were posted in the garage to listen. On December 8, police again made surreptitious entry and moved the microphone, this time hiding it in the bedroom. Twenty days later they again entered and placed the microphone in a closet, where the device remained until its purpose of enabling the officers to overhear incriminating statements was accomplished.

At the trial, officers were allowed to testify to conversations heard through their listening installations. The snatches of conversation which the prosecution thought useful were received in evidence. They were in the lingo of the race track and need not be recited, but the jury might well have regarded them as incriminating. The testimony was received under objection, properly raising the question that it was constitutionally inadmissible since obtained by methods which violate the Fourteenth Amendment.

Each of these repeated entries of petitioner's home without a search warrant or other process was a trespass, and probably a burglary, for which any unofficial person should be, and probably would be, severely punished. Science has perfected amplifying and recording devices to become frightening instruments of surveillance and invasion of privacy, whether by the policeman, the blackmailer, or the busy-body. That officers of the law would break and enter a home, secrete such a device, even in a bedroom, and listen to the conversation of the occupants for over a month would be almost incredible if it were not admitted. Few police measures have come to our attention that more flagrantly, deliberately, and persistently violated the fundamental principle declared by the Fourth Amendment as a restriction on the Federal Government that "The right of the people to be secure in their persons, houses, papers, and effects, against unreasonable searches and seizures, shall not be violated, and no Warrants shall issue, but upon probable cause, supported by Oath or affirmation, and particularly describing the place to be searched, and the persons or things to be seized." The decision in *Wolf v. Colorado* for the first time established that "[t]he security of one's privacy against arbitrary intrusion by the police" is embodied in the concept of due process found in the Fourteenth Amendment.

But *Wolf*, for reasons set forth therein, declined to make the subsidiary procedural and evidentiary doctrines developed by the federal courts limitations on the states. On the contrary, it declared, "We, hold, therefore, that in a prosecution in a State court for a State crime the Fourteenth Amendment does not forbid the admission of evidence obtained by an unreasonable search and seizure." That holding would seem to control here.

An effort is made, however, to bring this case under the sway of *Rochin*. That case involved, among other things, an illegal search of the defendant's person. But it also presented an element totally lacking here—coercion, applied by a physical assault upon his person to compel submission to the use of a stomach pump. This was the feature which led to a result in *Rochin* contrary to that in *Wolf*. Although *Rochin* raised the search-and-seizure question, this Court studiously avoided it and never once mentioned the *Wolf* case. Obviously, it thought that illegal search and seizure alone did not call for reversal. However obnoxious are the facts in the case before us, they do not involve coercion, violence or brutality to the person, but rather a trespass to property, plus eavesdropping.

It is suggested, however, that although we affirmed the conviction in *Wolf*, we should reverse here because this invasion of privacy is more shocking, more offensive, than the one involved there. The opinions in *Wolf* were written entirely in the abstract and did not disclose the details of the constitutional violation. Actually, the search was offensive to the law in the same respect, if not the same degree, as here. A deputy sheriff and others went to a doctor's office without a warrant and seized his appointment book, searched through it to learn the names of all his patients, looked up and interrogated certain of them, and filed an information against the doctor on the information that the District Attorney had obtained from the books. The books also were introduced in evidence against the doctor at his trial.

We are urged to make inroads upon *Wolf* by holding that it applies only to searches and seizures which produce on our minds a mild shock, while if the shock is more serious, the states must exclude the evidence or we will reverse the conviction. We think that the *Wolf* decision should not be overruled, for the reasons so persuasively stated therein. We think, too, that a distinction of the kind urged would leave the rule so indefinite that no state court could know what it should rule in order to keep its processes on solid constitutional ground.

It appears to the writer, in which view he is supported by the Chief Justice, that there is no lack of remedy if an unconstitutional wrong has been done in this instance without upsetting a justifiable conviction of this common gambler. If the officials have

willfully deprived a citizen of the United States of a right or privilege secured to him by the Fourteenth Amendment, that being the right to be secure in his home against unreasonable searches, their conduct may constitute a federal crime under 62 Stat. 696, 18 U.S.C. (Supp. III) § 242. This section provides that whoever, under color of any law, statute, ordinance, regulation or custom, willfully subjects any inhabitant of any state to the deprivation of any rights, privileges or immunities secured or protected by the Constitution of the United States shall be fined or imprisoned. It does not appear that the statute of limitations yet bars prosecutions. We believe the Clerk of this Court should be directed to forward a copy of the record in this case, together with a copy of this opinion, for attention of the Attorney General of the United States. However, Mr. Justice Reed and Mr. Justice Minton do not join in this paragraph.

Judgment affirmed.

Mr. Justice CLARK, concurring.

Had I been here in 1949 when *Wolf* was decided I would have applied the doctrine of *Weeks v. United States*, 232 U.S. 383 (1914), to the states. But the Court refused to do so then, and it still refuses today. Thus *Wolf* remains the law and, as such, is entitled to the respect of this Court's membership.

Of course, we could sterilize the rule announced in *Wolf* by adopting a case-by-case approach to due process in which inchoate notions of propriety concerning local police conduct guide our decisions. But this makes for such uncertainty and unpredictability that it would be impossible to foretell—other than by guess-work—just how brazen the invasion of the intimate privacies of one's home must be in order to shock itself into the protective arms of the Constitution. In truth, the practical result of this *ad hoc* approach is simply that when five Justices are sufficiently revolted by local police action a conviction is overturned and a guilty man may go free. *Rochin* bears witness to this. We may thus vindicate the abstract principle of due process, but we do not shape the conduct of local police one whit; unpredictable reversals on dissimilar fact situations are not likely to curb the zeal of those police and prosecutors who may be intent on racking up a high percentage of successful prosecutions. I do not believe that the extension of such a vacillating course beyond the clear cases of physical coercion and brutality, such as *Rochin*, would serve a useful purpose.

In light of the "incredible" activity of the police here it is with great reluctance that I follow *Wolf*. Perhaps strict adherence to the tenor of that decision may produce needed converts for its extinction. Thus

I merely concur in the judgment of affirmance.

Mr. Justice FRANKFURTER, whom Mr. Justice BURTON joins, dissenting.

Mere failure to have an appropriate warrant for arrest or search, without aggravating circumstances of misconduct in obtaining evidence, invalidates a federal conviction helped by such an unreasonable search and seizure. But *Wolf* held that the [exclusionary] rule was not to be deemed part of the Due Process Clause of the Fourteenth Amendment and hence was not binding upon the States. Still more recently, however, in *Rochin*, the Court held that "stomach pumping" to obtain morphine capsules, later used as evidence in a trial, was offensive to prevailing notions of fairness in the conduct of a prosecution and therefore invalidated a resulting conviction as contrary to the Due Process Clause.

The comprehending principle of these two cases is at the heart of "due process." The judicial enforcement of the Due Process Clause is the very antithesis of a Procrustean rule. In its first full-dress discussion of the Due Process Clause of the Fourteenth Amendment, the Court defined the nature of the problem as a "gradual process of judicial inclusion and exclusion, as the cases presented for decision shall require, with the reasoning on which such decisions may be founded."

In the *Wolf* case, the Court rejected one absolute. In *Rochin*, it rejected another.

In holding that not all conduct which by federal law is an unreasonable search and seizure vitiates a conviction in connection with which it transpires, *Wolf* did not and could not decide that as long as relevant evidence adequately supports a conviction, it is immaterial how such evidence was acquired.

*Rochin* decided that the Due Process Clause of the Fourteenth Amendment does not leave States free in their prosecutions for crime. The Clause puts limits on the wide discretion of a State in the process of enforcing its criminal law. The holding of the case is that a State cannot resort to methods that offend civilized standards of decency and fairness. The conviction in the *Rochin* case was found to offend due process not because evidence had been obtained through an unauthorized search and seizure or was the fruit of compulsory self-incrimination. Neither of these concepts, relevant to federal prosecutions, was invoked by the Court in *Rochin*, so of course the *Wolf* case was not mentioned. While there is in the case before us, as there was in *Rochin*, an element of unreasonable search and seizure, what is decisive here, as in *Rochin*, is additional aggravating conduct which the Court finds repulsive.

Thus, the basis on which this case should be adjudicated is laid down in *Rochin*: "Regard for the requirements of the Due Process Clause 'inescapably imposes upon this Court an exercise of judgment upon the whole course of the proceedings [resulting in a conviction] in order to ascertain whether they offend those canons of decency and fairness which express the notions of justice of English-speaking peoples even toward those charged with the most heinous offenses.'"

This brings us to the specific circumstances of this case. This is a summary of the conduct of the police:

(1) They secretly made a key to the Irvines' front door.

(2) By boring a hole in the roof of the house and using the key they had made to enter, they installed a secret microphone in the Irvine house with a listening post in a neighboring garage where officers listened in relays.

(3) Using their key, they entered the house twice again to move the microphone in order to cut out interference from a fluorescent lamp. The first time they moved it into Mr. and Mrs. Irvine's bedroom, and later into their bedroom closet.

(4) Using their key, they entered the house on the night of the arrest and in the course of the arrest made a search for which they had no warrant.

There was lacking here physical violence, even to the restricted extent employed in *Rochin*. We have here, however, a more powerful and offensive control over the Irvines' life than a single, limited physical trespass. Certainly the conduct of the police here went far beyond a bare search and seizure. The police devised means to hear every word that was said in the Irvine household for more than a month. Those affirming the conviction find that this conduct, in its entirety, is "almost incredible if it were not admitted."

The underlying reasoning of *Rochin* rejected the notion that States may secure a conviction by any form of skulduggery so long as it does not involve physical violence. The cases in which coercive or physical infringements of the dignity and privacy of the individual were involved were not deemed "sports in our constitutional law but applications of a general principle. They are only instances of the general requirement that States in their prosecutions respect certain decencies of civilized conduct. Due process of law, as a historic and generative principle, precludes defining, and thereby confining, these standards of conduct more precisely than to say that convictions cannot be brought about by methods that offend 'a sense of justice.'"

"Our people may tolerate many mistakes of both intent and performance, but, with unerring instinct, they know that when any person is intentionally deprived of his constitutional rights those responsible have committed no ordinary offense. A crime of this nature, if subtly encouraged by failure to condemn and punish, certainly leads down the road to totalitarianism."[2]

(Justice Black dissented on Fifth Amendment grounds. Justice Douglas dissented on Fourth Amendment grounds.)

---

[2] Statement by Director J. Edgar Hoover of the Federal Bureau of Investigation in FBI Law Enforcement Bulletin, September 1952.

## QUESTIONS AND NOTES

**1.** Why does Frankfurter think that *Rochin* rather than *Wolf* controlled *Irvine*?

**2.** Was he saying that the search in *Wolf* was *not* a violation of due process? If not, what was he saying?

**3.** Do you see any constitutionally significant difference between *Irvine* and any other Fourth Amendment case?

**4.** Given *Wolf* and *Rochin* do you think that *Irvine* was correctly decided?

**5.** We conclude this chapter by looking at *Schmerber*, a due process plus Fifth Amendment case decided *after* the Fifth Amendment had been held applicable to the states.

### Schmerber v. California
#### 384 U.S. 757 (1966)

Mr. Justice BRENNAN delivered the opinion of the Court.

Petitioner was convicted in Los Angeles Municipal Court of the criminal offense of driving an automobile while under the influence of intoxicating liquor. He had been arrested at a hospital while receiving treatment for injuries suffered in an accident involving the automobile that he had apparently been driving. At the direction of a police officer, a blood sample was then withdrawn from petitioner's body by a physician at the hospital. The chemical analysis of this sample revealed a percent by weight of alcohol in his blood at the time of the offense which indicated intoxication, and the report of this analysis was admitted in evidence at the trial. Petitioner objected to receipt of this evidence of the analysis on the ground that the blood had been withdrawn despite his refusal, on the advice of his counsel, to consent to the test. He contended that in that circumstance the withdrawal of the blood and the admission of the analysis in evidence denied him due process of law under the Fourteenth Amendment.

I
THE DUE PROCESS CLAUSE CLAIM
*Breithaupt* [v. *Abram*, 352 U.S. 432 (1957),] was

also a case in which police officers caused blood to be withdrawn from the driver of an automobile involved in an accident, and in which there was ample justification for the officer's conclusion that the driver was under the influence of alcohol. There, as here, the extraction was made by a physician in a simple, medically acceptable manner in a hospital environment. There, however, the driver was unconscious at the time the blood was withdrawn and hence had no opportunity to object to the procedure. We affirmed the conviction there resulting from the use of the test in evidence, holding that under such circumstances the withdrawal did not offend "that 'sense of justice' of which we spoke in *Rochin*." *Breithaupt* thus requires the rejection of petitioner's due process argument, and nothing in the circumstances of this case[4] or in supervening events persuades us that this aspect of *Breithaupt* should be overruled.

---

[4] We "cannot see that it should make any difference whether one states unequivocally that he objects or resorts to physical violence in protest or is in such condition that he is unable to protest." It would

## II
## THE PRIVILEGE AGAINST
## SELF-INCRIMINATION CLAIM

*Breithaupt* summarily rejected an argument that the withdrawal of blood and the admission of the analysis report involved in that state case violated the Fifth Amendment privilege of any person not to "be compelled in any criminal case to be a witness against himself," citing *Twining v. State of New Jersey*, 211 U.S. 78. But that case, holding that the protections of the Fourteenth Amendment do not embrace this Fifth Amendment privilege, has been succeeded by *Malloy v. Hogan*, 378 U.S. 1, 8. We there held that "[t]he Fourteenth Amendment secures against state invasion the same privilege that the Fifth Amendment guarantees against federal infringement—the right of a person to remain silent unless he chooses to speak in the unfettered exercise of his own will, and to suffer no penalty . . . for such silence." We therefore must now decide whether the withdrawal of the blood and admission in evidence of the analysis involved in this case violated petitioner's privilege. We hold that the privilege protects an accused only from being compelled to testify against himself, or otherwise provide the State with evidence of a testimonial or communicative nature,[5] and that the withdrawal of blood and use of the analysis in question in this case did not involve compulsion to these ends.

It could not be denied that in requiring petitioner to submit to the withdrawal and chemical analysis of his blood the State compelled him to submit to an attempt to discover evidence that might be used

---

be a different case if the police initiated the violence, refused to respect a reasonable request to undergo a different form of testing, or responded to resistance with inappropriate force.

[5] A dissent suggests that the report of the blood test was "testimonial" or "communicative," because the test was performed in order to obtain the testimony of others, communicating to the jury facts about petitioner's condition. Of course, all evidence received in court is "testimonial" or "communicative" if these words are thus used. But the Fifth Amendment relates only to acts on the part of the person to whom the privilege applies, and we use these words subject to the same limitations. A nod or headshake is as much a "testimonial" or "communicative" act in this sense as are spoken words. But the terms as we use them do not apply to evidence of acts noncommunicative in nature as to the person asserting the privilege, even though, as here, such acts are compelled to obtain the testimony of others.

to prosecute him for a criminal offense. He submitted only after the police officer rejected his objection and directed the physician to proceed. The officer's direction to the physician to administer the test over petitioner's objection constituted compulsion for the purposes of the privilege. The critical question, then, is whether petitioner was thus compelled "to be a witness against himself."

[T]he privilege has never been given the full scope which the values it helps to protect suggest. History and a long line of authorities in lower courts have consistently limited its protection to situations in which the State seeks to submerge those values by obtaining the evidence against an accused through "the cruel, simple expedient of compelling it from his own mouth. . . . In sum, the privilege is fulfilled only when the person is guaranteed the right 'to remain silent unless he chooses to speak in the unfettered exercise of his own will.'" The leading case in this Court is *Holt v. United States*, 218 U.S. 245. There the question was whether evidence was admissible that the accused, prior to trial and over his protest, put on a blouse that fitted him. It was contended that compelling the accused to submit to the demand that he model the blouse violated the privilege. Mr. Justice Holmes, speaking for the Court, rejected the argument as "based upon an extravagant extension of the Fifth Amendment," and went on to say: "[T]he prohibition of compelling a man in a criminal court to be witness against himself is a prohibition of the use of physical or moral compulsion to extort communications from him, not an exclusion of his body as evidence when it may be material. The objection in principle would forbid a jury to look at a prisoner and compare his features with a photograph in proof."

It is clear that the protection of the privilege reaches an accused's communications, whatever form they might take, and the compulsion of responses which are also communications, for example, compliance with a subpoena to produce one's papers. *Boyd v. United States*, 116 U.S. 616. On the other hand, both federal and state courts have usually held that it offers no protection against compulsion to submit to fingerprinting, photographing, or measurements, to write or speak for identification, to appear in court, to stand, to assume a stance, to walk, or to make a particular gesture. The distinction which has emerged, often expressed in different ways, is that the privilege is a bar against compelling "communications" or "testimony," but that compulsion which makes a suspect or accused the source of "real or physical evidence" does not violate it.

Although we agree that this distinction is a helpful framework for analysis, we are not to be understood to agree with past applications in all instances.

There will be many cases in which such a distinction is not readily drawn. Some tests seemingly directed to obtain "physical evidence," for example, lie detector tests measuring changes in body function during interrogation, may actually be directed to eliciting responses which are essentially testimonial. To compel a person to submit to testing in which an effort will be made to determine his guilt or innocence on the basis of physiological responses, whether willed or not, is to evoke the spirit and history of the Fifth Amendment. Such situations call to mind the principle that the protection of the privilege "is as broad as the mischief against which it seeks to guard." *Counselman v. Hitchcock*, 142 U.S. 547, 562.

In the present case, however, no such problem of application is presented. Not even a shadow of testimonial compulsion upon or enforced communication by the accused was involved either in the extraction or in the chemical analysis. Petitioner's testimonial capacities were in no way implicated; indeed, his participation, except as a donor, was irrelevant to the results of the test, which depend on chemical analysis and on that alone.[9] Since the blood

---

[9] This conclusion would not necessarily govern had the State tried to show that the accused had incriminated himself when told that he would have to be tested. Such incriminating evidence may be an unavoidable by-product of the compulsion to take the test, especially for an individual who fears the extraction or opposes it on religious grounds. If it wishes to compel persons to submit to such attempts to discover evidence, the State may have to forgo the advantage of any *testimonial* products of administering the test— products which would fall within the privilege. Indeed, there may be circumstances in which the pain, danger, or severity of an operation would almost inevitably cause a person to prefer confession to undergoing the "search," and nothing we say today should be taken as establishing the permissibility of compulsion in that case. But no such situation is presented in this case. Petitioner has raised a similar issue in this case, in connection with a police request that he submit to a "breathalyzer" test of air expelled from his lungs for alcohol content. He refused the request, and evidence of his refusal was admitted in evidence without objection. He argues that the introduction of this evidence and a comment by the prosecutor in closing argument upon his refusal is ground for reversal. Since trial here was conducted after our decision in *Malloy*, making those principles applicable to the States, we think petitioner's contention is foreclosed by his failure to object on this ground to the prosecutor's question and state-

test evidence, although an incriminating product of compulsion, was neither petitioner's testimony nor evidence relating to some communicative act or writing by the petitioner, it was not inadmissible on privilege grounds.

## III
### THE RIGHT TO COUNSEL CLAIM

This conclusion also answers petitioner's claim that, in compelling him to submit to the test in face of the fact that his objection was made on the advice of counsel, he was denied his Sixth Amendment right to the assistance of counsel. Since petitioner was not entitled to assert the privilege, he has no greater right because counsel erroneously advised him that he could assert it. His claim is strictly limited to the failure of the police to respect his wish, reinforced by counsel's advice, to be left inviolate. No issue of counsel's ability to assist petitioner in respect of any rights he did possess is presented. The limited claim thus made must be rejected.

Affirmed.

Mr. Chief Justice WARREN, dissenting.

While there are other important constitutional issues in this case, I believe it is sufficient for me to reiterate my dissenting opinion in *Breithaupt* as the basis on which to reverse this conviction.

Mr. Justice BLACK with whom Mr. Justice DOUGLAS joins, dissenting.

I would reverse petitioner's conviction.

The Court admits that "the State compelled [petitioner] to submit to an attempt to discover evidence [in his blood] that might be [and was] used to prosecute him for a criminal offense." To reach the conclusion that compelling a person to give his blood to help the State convict him is not equivalent to compelling him to be a witness against himself strikes me as quite an extraordinary feat. The Court, however, overcomes what had seemed to me to be an insuperable obstacle to its conclusion by holding that

> ". . . the privilege protects an accused only from being compelled to testify against himself, or otherwise provide the State with evidence of a testimonial or communicative nature, and that the withdrawal of blood and use of the analysis in question in this case did not involve compulsion to these ends."

I cannot agree that this distinction and reasoning of

---

ments. [Several years later the court held that the procedure described in this paragraph did not violate the privilege against self-incrimination. *South Dakota v. Neville*, 459 U.S. 553 (1983) - ed.]

the Court justify denying petitioner his Bill of Rights' guarantee that he must not be compelled to be a witness against himself.

In the first place it seems to me that the compulsory extraction of petitioner's blood for analysis so that the person who analyzed it could give evidence to convict him had both a "testimonial" and a "communicative nature." The sole purpose of this project which proved to be successful was to obtain "testimony" from some person to prove that petitioner had alcohol in his blood at the time he was arrested. And the purpose of the project was certainly "communicative" in that the analysis of the blood was to supply information to enable a witness to communicate to the court and jury that petitioner was more or less drunk.

[T]he Court concedes, as it must so long as *Boyd* stands, that the Fifth Amendment bars a State from compelling a person to produce papers he has that might tend to incriminate him. It is a strange hierarchy of values that allows the State to extract a human being's blood to convict him of a crime because of the blood's content but proscribes compelled production of his lifeless papers. Certainly there could be few papers that would have any more "testimonial" value to convict a man of drunken driving than would an analysis of the alcoholic content of a human being's blood introduced in evidence at a trial for driving while under the influence of alcohol. In such a situation blood, of course, is not oral testimony given by an accused but it can certainly "communicate" to a court and jury the fact of guilt.

The Court itself expresses its own doubts, if not fears, of its own shadowy distinction between compelling "physical evidence" like blood which it holds does not amount to compelled self-incrimination, and "eliciting responses which are essentially testimonial." And in explanation of its fears the Court goes on to warn that

> "To compel a person to submit to testing [by lie detectors for example] in which an effort will be made to determine his guilt or innocence on the basis of physiological responses, whether willed or not, is to evoke the spirit and history of the Fifth Amendment. Such situations call to mind the principle that the protection of the privilege 'is as broad as the mischief against which it seeks to guard.'"

A basic error in the Court's holding and opinion is its failure to give the Fifth Amendment's protection against compulsory self-incrimination the broad and liberal construction that *Counselman* and other opinions of this Court have declared it ought to have.

"A close and literal construction [of constitutional provisions for the security of persons and property] deprives them of half their efficacy, and leads to gradual depreciation of the right, as if it consisted more in sound than in substance. It is the duty of courts to be watchful for the constitutional rights of the citizen, and against any stealthy encroachments thereon." *Boyd*.

The Court went on to say that to require "an owner to produce his private books and papers, in order to prove his breach of the laws, and thus to establish the forfeiture of his property, is surely compelling him to furnish evidence against himself." The Court today departs from the teachings of *Boyd*. Petitioner Schmerber has undoubtedly been compelled to give his blood "to furnish evidence against himself," yet the Court holds that this is not forbidden by the Fifth Amendment. With all deference I must say that the Court here gives the Bill of Rights' safeguard against compulsory self-incrimination a construction that would generally be considered too narrow and technical even in the interpretation of an ordinary commercial contract.

I think the interpretive constitutional philosophy used in *Miranda*, unlike that used in this case, gives the Fifth Amendment's prohibition against compelled self-incrimination a broad and liberal construction in line with the wholesome admonitions in the *Boyd* case. The closing sentence in the Fifth Amendment section of the Court's opinion in the present case is enough by itself, I think, to expose the unsoundness of what the Court here holds. That sentence reads:

> "Since the blood test evidence, although an incriminating product of compulsion, was neither petitioner's testimony nor evidence relating to some communicative act or writing by the petitioner, it was not inadmissible on privilege grounds."

How can it reasonably be doubted that the blood test evidence was not in all respects the actual equivalent of "testimony" taken from petitioner when the result of the test was offered as testimony, was considered by the jury as testimony, and the jury's verdict of guilt rests in part on that testimony? The refined, subtle reasoning and balancing process used here to narrow the scope of the Bill of Rights' safeguard against self-incrimination provides a handy instrument for further narrowing of that constitutional protection, as well as others, in the future. Believing with the Framers that these constitutional safeguards broadly construed by independent tribunals of justice provide our best hope for keeping our people free from governmental oppression, I deeply regret the Court's holding. I dissent from the Court's holding and opinion in this case.

Mr. Justice DOUGLAS, dissenting.

We are dealing with the right of privacy which, since the *Breithaupt* case, we have held to be within the penumbra of some specific guarantees of the Bill of Rights. *Griswold v. Connecticut*, 381 U.S. 479. Thus, the Fifth Amendment marks "a zone of privacy" which the Government may not force a person to surrender. Likewise the Fourth Amendment recognizes that right when it guarantees the right of the people to be secure "in their persons." No clearer invasion of this right of privacy can be imagined than forcible bloodletting of the kind involved here.

Mr. Justice FORTAS, dissenting.

I would reverse. In my view, petitioner's privilege against self-incrimination applies. I would add that, under the Due Process Clause, the State, in its role as prosecutor, has no right to extract blood from an accused or anyone else, over his protest. As prosecutor, the State has no right to commit any kind of violence upon the person, or to utilize the results of such a tort, and the extraction of blood, over protest, is an act of violence.

## QUESTIONS AND NOTES

**1.** Why was the due process standard of *Rochin* not violated in this case? Do you agree?

**2.** In an edited portion of the opinion, the Court held that the Fourth amendment was not violated because there was probable cause to "search" for the blood and insufficient time to obtain a warrant.

**3.** Does the Court intend to construe the Fifth Amendment as broadly as necessary to combat the mischief it was intended to correct?

**4.** Is the standard of testimonial or communicative evidence a meaningful way to limit the Fifth Amendment? Is it desirable?

**5.** Suppose the police ask a D.U.I. suspect the date of his sixth birthday and introduce his ignorance of the date to prove his intoxication. Is his ignorance "testimonial"? For the Supreme Court's resolution, see *Pennsylvania v. Muniz*, 496 U.S. 582 (1990).

**6.** Is there something wrong with a system that values lifeless papers more than blood?

**7.** Even lifeless papers are not protected to the same extent today as they were at the time of *Boyd*. See *Fisher v. United States*, 425 U.S. 391 (1976).

# 20.

# IDENTIFICATION PROCEDURES

## A. The Right To Counsel

Identification procedures can raise Fifth Amendment, Sixth Amendment, and Due Process claims. *Wade* raises both Fifth and Sixth Amendment claims. *Kirby, Moore*, and *Ash* raise only Sixth Amendment claims. In part B of this chapter, we will look at due process cases.

### United States v. Wade
### 388 U.S. 218 (1967)

Mr. Justice BRENNAN delivered the opinion of the Court.

The question here is whether courtroom identifications of an accused at trial are to be excluded from evidence because the accused was exhibited to the witnesses before trial at a post-indictment lineup conducted for identification purposes without notice to and in the absence of the accused's appointed counsel.

The federally insured bank in Eustace, Texas, was robbed on September 21, 1964. A man with a small strip of tape on each side of his face entered the bank, pointed a pistol at the female cashier and the vice president, the only persons in the bank at the time, and forced them to fill a pillowcase with the bank's money. The man then drove away with an accomplice who had been waiting in a stolen car outside the bank. On March 23, 1965, an indictment was returned against respondent, Wade, and two others for conspiring to rob the bank, and against Wade

and the accomplice for the robbery itself. Wade was arrested on April 2, and counsel was appointed to represent him on April 26. Fifteen days later an FBI agent, without notice to Wade's lawyer, arranged to have the two bank employees observe a lineup made up of Wade and five or six other prisoners and conducted in a courtroom of the local county courthouse. Each person in the line wore strips of tape such as allegedly worn by the robber and upon direction each said something like "put the money in the bag," the words allegedly uttered by the robber. Both bank employees identified Wade in the lineup as the bank robber.

At trial the two employees, when asked on direct examination if the robber was in the courtroom, pointed to Wade. The prior lineup identification was then elicited from both employees on cross-examination. At the close of testimony, Wade's counsel moved for a judgment of acquittal or, alternatively, to strike the bank officials' courtroom identifications on the ground that conduct of the lineup, without notice to and in the absence of his appointed counsel, violated his Fifth Amendment privilege against self-incrimination and his Sixth Amendment right to the assistance of counsel. The motion was denied, and Wade was convicted. The Court of Appeals for the Fifth Circuit reversed the conviction and ordered a new trial at which the in-court identification evidence was to be excluded, holding that, though the lineup did not violate Wade's Fifth Amendment rights, "the lineup, held as it was, in the absence of counsel, already chosen to represent appellant, was a violation of his Sixth Amendment rights. . . ." We granted certiorari, and set the case for oral argument with *Gilbert v. California*. We reverse the judgment of the Court of Appeals and remand to that court with direction to enter a new judgment vacating the conviction and remanding the case to the District Court for further proceedings consistent with this opinion.

## I

Neither the lineup itself nor anything shown by this record that Wade was required to do in the lineup violated his privilege against self-incrimination. We have only recently reaffirmed that the privilege "protects an accused only from being compelled to testify against himself, or otherwise provide the State with evidence of a testimonial or communicative nature. . . ." *Schmerber*. We there held that compelling a suspect to submit to a withdrawal of a sample of his blood for analysis for alcohol content and the admission in evidence of the analysis report were not compulsion to those ends. That holding was supported by the opinion in *Holt*, in which case a question arose as to whether a blouse belonged to the defendant. A witness testified at trial that the defendant put on the blouse and it had fit him. The defendant argued that the admission of the testimony was error because compelling him to put on the blouse was a violation of his privilege. The Court rejected the claim as "an extravagant extension of the Fifth Amendment," Mr. Justice Holmes saying for the Court:

"[T]he prohibition of compelling a man in a criminal court to be witness against himself is a prohibition of the use of physical or moral compulsion to extort communications from him, not an exclusion of his body as evidence when it may be material."

The Court in *Holt*, however, put aside any constitutional questions which might be involved in compelling an accused, as here, to exhibit himself before victims of or witnesses to an alleged crime; the Court stated, "we need now consider how far a court would go in compelling a man to exhibit himself."

We have no doubt that compelling the accused merely to exhibit his person for observation by a prosecution witness prior to trial involves no compulsion of the accused to give evidence having testimonial significance. It is compulsion of the accused to exhibit his physical characteristics, not compulsion to disclose any knowledge he might have. It is no different from compelling Schmerber to provide a blood sample or Holt to wear the blouse, and, as in those instances, is not within the cover of the privilege. Similarly, compelling Wade to speak within hearing distance of the witnesses, even to utter words purportedly uttered by the robber, was not compulsion to utter statements of a "testimonial" nature; he was required to use his voice as an identifying physical characteristic, not to speak his guilt. We held in *Schmerber*, that the distinction to be drawn under the Fifth Amendment privilege against self-incrimination is one between an accused's "communications" in whatever form, vocal or physical, and "compulsion which makes a suspect or accused the source of 'real or physical evidence.'" We recognized that "both federal and state courts have usually held that . . . [the privilege] offers no protection against compulsion to submit to fingerprinting, photography, or measurements, to write or speak for identification, to appear in court, to stand, to assume a stance, to walk, or to make a particular gesture." None of these activities becomes testimonial within the scope of the privilege because required of the accused in a pretrial lineup.

Moreover, it deserves emphasis that this case presents no question of the admissibility in evidence of anything Wade said or did at the lineup which implicates his privilege. The Government offered no such evidence as part of its case, and what came out about the lineup proceedings on Wade's cross-examination of the bank employees involved no violation of Wade's privilege.

## II

The fact that the lineup involved no violation of Wade's privilege against self-incrimination does not, however, dispose of his contention that the courtroom identifications should have been excluded because the lineup was conducted without notice to and in the absence of his counsel. Our rejection of the right to counsel claim in *Schmerber* rested on our conclusion in that case that "[n]o issue of counsel's ability to assist petitioner in respect of any rights he did possess is presented." In contrast, in this case it is urged that the assistance of counsel at the lineup was indispensable to protect Wade's most basic right as a criminal defendant—his right to a fair trial at which the witnesses against him might be meaningfully cross-examined.

[The Sixth Amendment] requires that we scrutinize *any* pretrial confrontation of the accused to determine whether the presence of his counsel is necessary to preserve the defendant's basic right to a fair trial as affected by his right meaningfully to cross-examine the witnesses against him and to have effective assistance of counsel at the trial itself. It calls upon us to analyze whether potential substantial prejudice to defendant's rights inheres in the particular confrontation and the ability of counsel to help avoid that prejudice.

### III

The Government characterizes the lineup as a mere preparatory step in the gathering of the prosecution's evidence, not different—for Sixth Amendment purposes—from various other preparatory steps, such as systematized or scientific analyzing of the accused's fingerprints, blood sample, clothing, hair, and the like. We think there are differences which preclude such stages being characterized as critical stages at which the accused has the right to the presence of his counsel. Knowledge of the techniques of science and technology is sufficiently available, and the variables in techniques few enough, that the accused has the opportunity for a meaningful confrontation of the Government's case at trial through the ordinary processes of cross-examination of the Government's expert witnesses and the presentation of the evidence of his own experts. The denial of a right to have his counsel present at such analyses does not therefore violate the Sixth Amendment; they are not critical stages since there is minimal risk that his counsel's absence at such stages might derogate from his right to a fair trial.

### IV

But the confrontation compelled by the State between the accused and the victim or witnesses to a crime to elicit identification evidence is peculiarly riddled with innumerable dangers and variable factors which might seriously, even crucially, derogate from a fair trial. The vagaries of eyewitness identification are well-known; the annals of criminal law are rife with instances of mistaken identification. Mr. Justice Frankfurter once said: "What is the worth of identification testimony even when uncontradicted? The identification of strangers is proverbially untrustworthy. The hazards of such testimony are established by a formidable number of instances in the records of English and American trials. These instances are recent—not due to the brutalities of

ancient criminal procedure.'' The Case of Sacco and Vanzetti 30 (1927). A major factor contributing to the high incidence of miscarriage of justice from mistaken identification has been the degree of suggestion inherent in the manner in which the prosecution presents the suspect to witnesses for pretrial identification. A commentator has observed that ''[t]he influence of improper suggestion upon identifying witnesses probably accounts for more miscarriages of justice than any other single factor—perhaps it is responsible for more such errors than all other factors combined.'' Wall, Eye-Witness Identification in Criminal Cases 26. Suggestion can be created intentionally or unintentionally in many subtle ways. And the dangers for the suspect are particularly grave when the witness' opportunity for observation was insubstantial, and thus his susceptibility to suggestion the greatest.

Moreover, ''[i]t is a matter of common experience that, once a witness has picked out the accused at the line-up, he is not likely to go back on his word later on, so that in practice the issue of identity may (in the absence of other relevant evidence) for all practical purposes be determined there and then, before the trial.''

The pretrial confrontation for purpose of identification may take the form of a lineup, also known as an ''identification parade'' or ''showup,'' as in the present case, or presentation of the suspect alone to the witness. It is obvious that risks of suggestion attend either form of confrontation and increase the dangers inhering in eyewitness identification. But as is the case with secret interrogations, there is serious difficulty in depicting what transpires at lineups and other forms of identification confrontations. ''Privacy results in secrecy and this in turn results in a gap in our knowledge as to what in fact goes on. . . .'' *Miranda*. For the same reasons, the defense can seldom reconstruct the manner and mode of lineup identification for judge or jury at trial. Those participating in a lineup with the accused may often be police officers; in any event, the participants' names are rarely recorded or divulged at trial. The impediments to an objective observation are increased when the victim is the witness. Lineups are prevalent in rape and robbery prosecutions and present a particular hazard that a victim's understandable outrage may excite vengeful or spiteful motives. In any event, neither witnesses nor lineup participants are apt to be alert for conditions prejudicial to the suspect. And if they were, it would likely be of scant benefit to the suspect since neither witnesses nor lineup participants are likely to be schooled in the detection of suggestive influences.[13] Improper influences may go undetected by a suspect, guilty or not, who experiences the emotional tension which we might expect in one being confronted with potential accusers. Even when he does observe abuse, if he has a criminal record he may be reluctant to take the stand and open up the admission of prior convictions. Moreover any protestations by the suspect of the fairness of the lineup made at trial are likely to be in vain; the jury's choice is between the accused's unsupported version and that of the police officers present.[16] In short, the accused's inability effectively to reconstruct at trial any unfairness that occurred at the lineup may deprive him of his only opportunity meaningfully to attack the credibility of the witness' courtroom identification.

What facts have been disclosed in specific cases about the conduct of pretrial confrontations for identification illustrate both the potential for substantial

---

[13] An additional impediment to the detection of such influences by participants, including the suspect, is the physical conditions often surrounding the conduct of the lineup. In many, lights shine on the stage in such a way that the suspect cannot see the witness. In some a one-way mirror is used and what is said on the witness' side cannot be heard.

[16] An instructive example of the defendant's predicament may be found in *Proctor v. State*, 223 Md. 394, 164 A.2d 708 (1960). A prior identification is admissible in Maryland only under the salutary rule that it cannot have been made "under conditions of unfairness or unreliability." Against the defendant's contention that these conditions had not been met, the Court stated:

"In the instant case, there are no such facts as, in our judgment, would call for a finding that the identification . . . was made under conditions of unfairness or unreliability. The relatively large number of persons put into the room together for [the victim] to look at is one circumstance indicating fairness, and the fact that the police officer was unable to remember the appearances of the others and could not recall if they had physical characteristics similar to [the defendant's] or not is at least suggestive that they were not of any one type or that they all differed markedly in looks from the defendant. There is no evidence that the Police Sergeant gave the complaining witness any indication as to which of the thirteen men was the defendant; the Sergeant's testimony is simply that he asked [the victim] if he could identify [the defendant] after having put the thirteen men in the courtroom."

prejudice to the accused at that stage and the need for its revelation at trial. A commentator provides some striking examples:

"In a Canadian case . . . the defendant had been picked out of a lineup of six men, of which he was the only Oriental. On other cases, a black-haired suspect was placed among a group of light-haired persons, tall suspects have been made to stand with short nonsuspects, and, in a case where the perpetrator of the crime was known to be a youth, a suspect under twenty was placed in a lineup with five other persons, all of whom were forty or over."

The potential for improper influence is illustrated by the circumstances, insofar as they appear, surrounding the prior identifications in the cases we decide today. In the present case, the testimony of the identifying witnesses elicited on cross-examination revealed that those witnesses were taken to the courthouse and seated in the courtroom to await assembly of the lineup. The courtroom faced on a hallway observable to the witnesses through an open door. The cashier testified that she saw Wade "standing in the hall" within sight of an FBI agent. Five or six other prisoners later appeared in the hall. The vice president testified that he saw a person in the hall in the custody of the agent who "resembled the person that we identified as the one that had entered the bank."

The lineup in *Gilbert* was conducted in an auditorium in which some 100 witnesses to several alleged state and federal robberies charged to Gilbert made wholesale identifications of Gilbert as the robber in each other's presence, a procedure said to be fraught with dangers of suggestion.

Since it appears that there is grave potential for prejudice, intentional or not, in the pretrial lineup, which may not be capable of reconstruction at trial, and since presence of counsel itself can often avert prejudice and assure a meaningful confrontation at trial, there can be little doubt that for Wade the postindictment lineup was a critical stage of the prosecution at which he was "as much entitled to such aid [of counsel] . . . as at the trial itself." Thus both Wade and his counsel should have been notified of the impending lineup, and counsel's presence should have been a requisite to conduct of the lineup, absent an "intelligent waiver." No substantial countervailing policy considerations have been advanced against the requirement of the presence of counsel. Concern is expressed that the requirement will forestall prompt identifications and result in obstruction of the confrontations. As for the first, we note that in the two cases in which the right to counsel is today held to apply, counsel had already been appointed and no argument is made in either case that notice to counsel would have prejudicially delayed the confrontations. Moreover, we leave open the question whether the presence of substitute counsel might not suffice where notification and presence of the suspect's own counsel would result in prejudicial delay.[27] And to refuse to recognize the right to counsel for fear that counsel will obstruct the course of justice is contrary to the basic assumptions upon which this Court has operated in Sixth Amendment cases. We rejected similar logic in *Miranda* concerning presence of counsel during custodial interrogation.

In our view counsel can hardly impede legitimate law enforcement; on the contrary, for the reasons expressed, law enforcement may be assisted by preventing the infiltration of taint in the prosecution's identification evidence.[28] That result cannot help the guilty avoid conviction but can only help assure that the right man has been brought to justice.

Legislative or other regulations, such as those of local police departments, which eliminate the risks of abuse and unintentional suggestion at lineup proceedings and the impediments to meaningful confrontation at trial may also remove the basis for regarding the stage as "critical."[30] But neither Congress nor the federal authorities have seen fit to provide a solution. What we hold today "in no way

---

[27] Although the right to counsel usually means a right to the suspect's own counsel, provision for substitute counsel may be justified on the ground that the substitute counsel's presence may eliminate the hazards which render the lineup a critical stage for the presence of the suspect's *own* counsel.

[28] Concern is also expressed that the presence of counsel will force divulgence of the identity of government witnesses whose identity the Government may want to conceal. To the extent that this is a valid or significant state interest there are police practices commonly used to effect concealment, for example, masking the face.

[30] Thirty years ago Wigmore suggested a "scientific method" of pretrial identification "to reduce the risk of error hitherto inherent in such proceedings." Wigmore, The Science of Judicial Proof 541 (3d ed. 1937). Under this approach, at least 100 talking films would be prepared of men from various occupations, races, etc. Each would be photographed in a number of stock movements, with and without hat and coat, and would read aloud a standard passage. The suspect would be filmed in the same manner. Some 25 of the films would be shown in succession in a special projection room in which each witness would be provided an electric button which would

creates a constitutional straitjacket which will handicap sound efforts at reform, nor is it intended to have this effect.''

## V

We come now to the question whether the denial of Wade's motion to strike the courtroom identification by the bank witnesses at trial because of the absence of his counsel at the lineup required, as the Court of Appeals held, the grant of a new trial at which such evidence is to be excluded. We do not think this disposition can be justified without first giving the Government the opportunity to establish by clear and convincing evidence that the in-court identifications were based upon observations of the suspect other than the lineup identification. Where, as here, the admissibility of evidence of the lineup identification itself is not involved, a *per se* rule of exclusion of courtroom identification would be unjustified. A rule limited solely to the exclusion of testimony concerning identification at the lineup itself, without regard to admissibility of the courtroom identification, would render the right to counsel an empty one. The lineup is most often used, as in the present case, to crystallize the witnesses' identification of the defendant for future reference. We have already noted that the lineup identification will have that effect. The State may then rest upon the witnesses' unequivocal courtroom identifications, and not mention the pretrial identification as part of the State's case at trial. Counsel is then in the predicament in which Wade's counsel found himself—realizing that possible unfairness at the lineup may be the sole means of attack upon the unequivocal courtroom identification, and having to probe in the dark in an attempt to discover and reveal unfairness, while bolstering the government witness' courtroom identification by bringing out and dwelling upon his prior identification. Since counsel's presence at the lineup would equip him to attack not only the lineup identification but the courtroom identification as well, limiting the impact of violation of the right to counsel to exclusion of evidence only

---

activate a board backstage when pressed to indicate that the witness had identified a given person. Provision would be made for the degree of hesitancy in the identification to be indicated by the number of presses. Of course, the more systematic and scientific a process or proceeding, including one for purposes of identification, the less the impediment to reconstruction of the conditions bearing upon the reliability of that process or proceeding at trial.

of identification at the lineup itself disregards a critical element of that right.

We think it follows that the proper test to be applied in these situations is that quoted in *Wong Sun v. United States*, 371 U.S. 471, 488, "[W]hether, granting establishment of the primary illegality, the evidence to which instant objection is made has been come at by exploitation of that illegality or instead by means sufficiently distinguishable to be purged of the primary taint." Application of this test in the present context requires consideration of various factors; for example, the prior opportunity to observe the alleged criminal act, the existence of any discrepancy between any pre-lineup description and the defendant's actual description, any identification prior to lineup of another person, the identification by picture of the defendant prior to the lineup, failure to identify the defendant on a prior occasion, and the lapse of time between the alleged act and the lineup identification. It is also relevant to consider those facts which, despite the absence of counsel, are disclosed concerning the conduct of the lineup.

On the record now before us we cannot make the determination whether the in-court identifications had an independent origin. This was not an issue at trial, although there is some evidence relevant to a determination. That inquiry is most properly made in the District Court. We therefore think the appropriate procedure to be followed is to vacate the conviction pending a hearing to determine whether the in-court identifications had an independent source, or whether, in any event, the introduction of the evidence was harmless error, and for the District Court to reinstate the conviction or order a new trial, as may be proper.

Mr. Justice DOUGLAS joins the opinion of the Court except for Part I. On that phase of the case he adheres to the dissenting views in *Schmerber*, since he believes that compulsory lineup violates the privilege against self-incrimination contained in the Fifth Amendment.

Mr. Justice CLARK, concurring.

With reference to the lineup point involved in this case I cannot, for the life of me, see why a lineup is not a critical stage of the prosecution. Identification of the suspect—a prerequisite to establishment of guilt—occurs at this stage, and with *Miranda* on the books, the requirement of the presence of counsel arises, unless waived by the suspect. I dissented in *Miranda* but I am bound by it now, as we all are. *Schmerber* precludes petitioner's claim of self-incrimination. I therefore join the opinion of the Court.

Mr. Justice BLACK, dissenting in part and concurring in part.

The Court in Part I of its opinion rejects Wade's Fifth Amendment contention. From that I dissent. In Parts II-IV of its opinion, the Court sustains Wade's claim of denial of right to counsel in the out-of-court lineup, and in that I concur. In Part V, the Court remands the case to the District Court to consider whether the courtroom identification of Wade was the fruit of the illegal lineup, and, if it was, to grant him a new trial unless the court concludes that the courtroom identification was harmless error. I would reverse the Court of Appeals' reversal of Wade's conviction, but I would not remand for further proceedings since the prosecution not having used the out-of-court lineup identification against Wade at his trial, I believe the conviction should be affirmed.

I

In rejecting Wade's claim that his privilege against self-incrimination was violated by compelling him to appear in the lineup wearing the tape and uttering the words given him by the police, the Court relies on the recent holding in *Schmerber*. I dissented from that holding, and [I] still dissent. [H]ere, having Wade in its custody awaiting trial to see if he could or would be convicted of crime, the Government forced him to stand in a lineup, wear strips on his face, and speak certain words, in order to make it possible for government witnesses to identify him as a criminal. Had Wade been compelled to utter these or any other words in open court, it is plain that he would have been entitled to a new trial because of having been compelled to be a witness against himself. Being forced by the Government to help convict himself and to supply evidence against himself by talking outside the courtroom is equally violative of his constitutional right not to be compelled to be a witness against himself. Consequently, because of this violation of the Fifth Amendment, and not because of my own personal view that the Government's conduct was "unfair," "prejudicial," or "improper," I would prohibit the prosecution's use of lineup identification at trial.

III

I would reverse Wade's conviction without further ado had the prosecution at trial made use of his lineup identification either in place of courtroom identification or to bolster in a harmful manner crucial courtroom identification. But the prosecution here did neither of these things. After prosecution witnesses under oath identified Wade in the courtroom, it was the defense, and not the prosecution, which brought out the prior lineup identification. While stating that "a *per se* rule of exclusion of courtroom identification would be unjustified," the Court, nevertheless remands this case for "a hearing to determine whether the in-court identifications had an independent source," or were the tainted fruits of the invalidly conducted lineup. From this holding I dissent.

In the first place, even if this Court has power to establish such a rule of evidence, I think the rule fashioned by the Court is unsound. The "tainted fruit" determination required by the Court involves more than considerable difficulty. I think it is practically impossible. How is a witness capable of probing the recesses of his mind to draw a sharp line between a courtroom identification due exclusively to an earlier lineup and a courtroom identification due to memory not based on the lineup? What kind of "clear and convincing evidence" can the prosecution offer to prove upon what particular events memories resulting in an in-court identification rest? How long will trials be delayed while judges turn psychologists to probe the subconscious minds of witnesses? All these questions are posed but not answered by the Court's opinion. In my view, the Fifth and Sixth Amendments are satisfied if the prosecution is precluded from using lineup identification as either an alternative to or corroboration of courtroom identification. If the prosecution does neither and its witnesses under oath identify the defendant in the courtroom, then I can find no justification for stopping the trial in midstream to hold a lengthy "tainted fruit" hearing. The fact of and circumstances surrounding a prior lineup identification might be used by the defense to impeach the credibility of the in-court identifications, but not to exclude them completely.

I would affirm Wade's conviction.

Mr. Justice WHITE, whom Mr. Justice HARLAN and Mr. Justice STEWART join, dissenting in part and concurring in part.

The Court has again propounded a broad constitutional rule barring the use of a wide spectrum of relevant and probative evidence, solely because a step in its ascertainment or discovery occurs outside the presence of defense counsel. This was the approach of the Court in *Miranda*. I objected then to what I thought was an uncritical and doctrinaire approach without satisfactory factual foundation. I have much the same view of the present ruling and therefore dissent from the judgment and from Parts II, IV, and V of the Court's opinion.

The Court's opinion is far-reaching. It proceeds first by creating a new *per se* rule of constitutional law: a criminal suspect cannot be subjected to a pre-trial identification process in the absence of his counsel without violating the Sixth Amendment. If he is, the State may buttress a later courtroom identification, of the witness by any reference to the previous identification. Furthermore, the courtroom identification is not admissible at all unless the State can establish by clear and convincing proof that the testimony is not the fruit of the earlier identification made in the absence of defendant's counsel – admittedly a heavy burden for the State and probably an impossible one. To all intents and purposes, courtroom identifications are barred if pretrial identifications have occurred without counsel being present.

The rule applies to any lineup, to any other techniques employed to produce an identification and *a fortiori* to a face-to-face encounter between the witness and the suspect alone, regardless of when the identification occurs, in time or place, and whether before or after indictment or information. It matters not how well the witness knows the suspect, whether the witness is the suspect's mother, brother, or long-time associate, and no matter how long or well the witness observed the perpetrator at the scene of the crime. The kidnap victim who has lived for days with his abductor is in the same category as the witness who has had only a fleeting glimpse of the criminal. Neither may identify the suspect without defendant's counsel being present. The same strictures apply regardless of the number of other witnesses who positively identify the defendant and regardless of the corroborative evidence showing that it was the defendant who had committed the crime.

The premise for the Court's rule is not the general unreliability of eyewitness identifications nor the difficulties inherent in observation, recall, and recognition. The Court assumes a narrower evil as the basis for its rule – improper police suggestion which contributes to erroneous identifications. The Court apparently believes that improper police procedures are so widespread that a broad prophylactic rule must be laid down, requiring the presence of counsel at all pretrial identifications, in order to detect recurring instances of police misconduct. I do not share this pervasive distrust of all official investigations. None of the materials the Court relies upon supports it. Certainly, I would bow to solid fact, but the Court quite obviously does not have before it any reliable, comprehensive survey of current police practices on which to base its new rule. Until it does, the Court should avoid excluding relevant evidence from state criminal trials.

There are several striking aspects to the Court's

holding. First, the rule does not bar courtroom identifications where there have been no previous identifications in the presence of the police, although when identified in the courtroom, the defendant is known to be in custody and charged with the commission of a crime. Second, the Court seems to say that if suitable legislative standards were adopted for the conduct of pretrial identifications, thereby lessening the hazards in such confrontations, it would not insist on the presence of counsel. But if this is true, why does not the Court simply fashion what it deems to be constitutionally acceptable procedures for the authorities to follow? Certainly the Court is correct in suggesting that the new rule will be wholly inapplicable where police departments themselves have established suitable safeguards.

Third, courtroom identification may be barred, absent counsel at a prior identification, regardless of the extent of counsel's information concerning the circumstances of the previous confrontation between witness and defendant—apparently even if there were recordings or sound-movies of the events as they occurred. But if the rule is premised on the defendant's right to have his counsel know, there seems little basis for not accepting other means to inform. A disinterested observer, recordings, photographs—any one of them would seem adequate to furnish the basis for a meaningful cross-examination of the eyewitness who identifies the defendant in the courtroom.

I share the Court's view that the criminal trial, at the very least, should aim at truthful fact finding, including accurate eyewitness identifications. I doubt, however, on the basis of our present information, that the tragic mistakes which have occurred in criminal trials are as much the product of improper police conduct as they are the consequence of the difficulties inherent in eyewitness testimony and in resolving evidentiary conflicts by court or jury. I doubt that the Court's new rule will obviate these difficulties, or that the situation will be measurably improved by inserting defense counsel into the investigative processes of police departments everywhere.

But, it may be asked, what possible state interest militates against requiring the presence of defense counsel at lineups? After all, the argument goes, he *may* do some good, he *may* upgrade the quality of identification evidence in state courts and he can scarcely do any harm. [H]owever, requiring counsel at pretrial identifications as an invariable rule trenches on other valid state interests. One of them is its concern with the prompt and efficient enforcement of its criminal laws. Identifications frequently take place after arrest but before an indictment is returned or an information is filed. The police may have arrested a suspect on probable cause but may still have the wrong man. Both the suspect and the State have every interest in a prompt identification at that stage, the suspect in order to secure his immediate release and the State because prompt and early identification enhances *accurate* identification and because it must know whether it is on the right investigative track. Unavoidably, however, the absolute rule requiring the presence of counsel will cause significant delay and it may very well result in no pretrial identification at all. Counsel must be appointed and a time arranged convenient for him and the witnesses. Meanwhile, it may be necessary to file charges against the suspect who may then be released on bail, in the federal system very often on his own recognizance, with neither the State nor the defendant having the benefit of a properly conducted identification procedure.

Nor do I think the witnesses themselves can be ignored. They will now be required to be present at the convenience of counsel rather than their own. Many may be much less willing to participate if the identification stage is transformed into an adversary proceeding not under the control of a judge. Others may fear for their own safety if their identity is known at an early date, especially when there is no way of knowing until the lineup occurs whether or not the police really have the right man.

Finally, I think the Court's new rule is vulnerable in terms of its own unimpeachable purpose of increasing the reliability of identification testimony.

Law enforcement officers have the obligation to convict the guilty and to make sure they do not convict the innocent. They must be dedicated to making the criminal trial a procedure for the ascertainment of the true facts surrounding the commission of the crime.[5] To this extent, our so-called adversary system is not adversary at all; nor should it be. But

---

[5] "The United States Attorney is the representative not of an ordinary party to a controversy, but of a sovereignty whose obligation to govern impartially is as compelling as its obligation to govern at all; and whose interest, therefore, in a criminal prosecution is not that it shall win a case, but that justice shall be done. As such, he is in a peculiar and very definite sense the servant of the law, the twofold aim of which is that guilt shall not escape or innocence suffer. He may prosecute with earnestness and vigor—indeed, he should do so. But, while he may strike hard blows, he is not at liberty to strike

defense counsel has no comparable obligation to ascertain or present the truth. Our system assigns him a different mission. He must be and is interested in preventing the conviction of the innocent, but, absent a voluntary plea of guilty, we also insist that he defend his client whether he is innocent or guilty. The State has the obligation to present the evidence. Defense counsel need present nothing, even if he knows what the truth is. He need not furnish any witnesses to the police, or reveal any confidences of his client, or furnish any other information to help the prosecution's case. If he can confuse a witness, even a truthful one, or make him appear at a disadvantage, unsure or indecisive, that will be his normal course. Our interest in not convicting the innocent permits counsel to put the State to its proof, to put the State's case in the worst possible light, regardless of what he thinks or knows to be the truth. Undoubtedly there are some limits which defense counsel must observe but more often than not, defense counsel will cross-examine a prosecution witness, and impeach him if he can, even if he thinks the witness is telling the truth, just as he will attempt to destroy a witness who he thinks is lying. In this respect, as part of our modified adversary system and as part of the duty imposed on the most honorable defense counsel, we countenance or require conduct which in many instances has little, if any, relation to the search for truth.

I would not extend this system, at least as it presently operates, to police investigations and would not require counsel's presence at pretrial identification procedures. Counsel's interest is in not having his client placed at the scene of the crime, regardless of his whereabouts. Some counsel may advise their clients to refuse to make any movements or to speak any words in a lineup or even to appear in one. To that extent the impact on truthful fact finding is quite obvious. Others will not only observe what occurs and develop possibility for later cross-examination but will hover over witnesses and begin their cross-examination then, menacing truthful fact finding as thoroughly as the Court fears the police now do. Certainly there is an implicit invitation to counsel to suggest rules for the lineup and to manage and produce it as best he can. I therefore doubt that the Court's new rule, at least absent some clearly defined limits on counsel's role, will measurably contribute to more reliable pretrial identifications. My

---

foul ones. It is as much his duty to refrain from improper methods calculated to produce a wrongful conviction as it is to use every legitimate means to bring about a just one.''

fears are that it will have precisely the opposite result. It may well produce fewer convictions, but that is hardly a proper measure of its long-run acceptability. In my view, the State is entitled to investigate and develop its case outside the presence of defense counsel. This includes the right to have private conversations with identification witnesses, just as defense counsel may have his own consultations with these and other witnesses without having the prosecutor present.

Whether today's judgment would be an acceptable exercise of supervisory power over federal courts is another question. But as a constitutional matter, the judgment in this case is erroneous and although I concur in Parts I and III of the Court's opinion I respectfully register this dissent.

Mr. Justice FORTAS, with whom the Chief Justice and Mr. Justice DOUGLAS join, concurring in part and dissenting in part.

1. I agree with the Court that the exhibition of the person of the accused at a lineup is not itself a violation of the privilege against self-incrimination. In itself, it is no more subject to constitutional objection than the exhibition of the person of the accused in the courtroom for identification purposes. It is an incident of the State's power to arrest, and a reasonable and justifiable aspect of the State's custody resulting from arrest. It does not require that the accused take affirmative, volitional action, but only that, having been duly arrested he may be seen for identification purposes. It is, however, a "critical stage" in the prosecution, and I agree with the Court that the opportunity to have counsel present must be made available.

2. In my view, however, the accused may not be compelled in a lineup to speak the words uttered by the person who committed the crime. I am confident that it could not be compelled in court. It cannot be compelled in a lineup. It is more than passive, mute assistance to the eyes of the victim or of witnesses. It is the kind of volitional act—the kind of forced cooperation by the accused—which is within the historical perimeter of the privilege against compelled self-incrimination.

Our history and tradition teach and command that an accused may stand mute. The privilege means just that; not less than that. According to the Court, an accused may be jailed—indefinitely—until he is willing to say, for an identifying audience, whatever was said in the course of the commission of the crime. Presumably this would include, "Your money or your life"—or perhaps, words of assault in a rape case. This is intolerable under our constitutional system.

I completely agree that the accused must be advised of and given the right to counsel before a lineup – and I join in that part of the Court's opinion; but this is an empty right unless we mean to insist upon the accused's fundamental constitutional immunities. One of these is that the accused may not be compelled to speak. To compel him to speak would violate the privilege against self-incrimination, which is incorporated in the Fifth Amendment.

This great privilege is not merely a shield for the accused. It is also a prescription of technique designed to guide the State's investigation. History teaches us that self-accusation is an unreliable instrument of detection, apt to inculpate the innocent-but-weak and to enable the guilty to escape. But this is not the end of the story. The privilege historically goes to the roots of democratic and religious principle. It prevents the debasement of the citizen which would result from compelling him to "accuse" himself before the power of the state. The roots of the privilege are deeper than the rack and the screw used to extort confessions. They go to the nature of a free man and to his relationship to the state.

An accused cannot be compelled to utter the words spoken by the criminal in the course of the crime. I thoroughly disagree with the Court's statement that such compulsion does not violate the Fifth Amendment. The Court relies upon *Schmerber* to support this. I dissented in *Schmerber* but if it were controlling here, I should, of course, acknowledge its binding effect unless we were prepared to overrule it. But *Schmerber*, which authorized the forced extraction of blood from the veins of an unwilling human being, did not compel the person actively to cooperate – to accuse himself by a volitional act which differs only in degree from compelling him

to act out the crime, which, I assume, would be rebuffed by the Court. It is the latter feature which places the compelled utterance by the accused squarely within the history and noble purpose of the Fifth Amendment's commandment.

To permit *Schmerber* to apply in any respect beyond its holding is, in my opinion, indefensible. To permit its insidious doctrine to extend beyond the invasion of the body, which it permits, to compulsion of the will of a man, is to deny and defy a precious part of our historical faith and to discard one of the most profoundly cherished instruments by which we have established the freedom and dignity of the individual. We should not so alter the balance between the rights of the individual and of the state, achieved over centuries of conflict.

3. While the Court holds that the accused must be advised of and given the right to counsel at the lineup, it makes the privilege meaningless in this important respect. Unless counsel has been waived or, being present, has not objected to the accused's utterance of words used in the course of committing the crime, to compel such an utterance is constitutional error.[*]

Accordingly, while I join the Court in requiring vacating of the judgment below for a determination as to whether the identification of respondent was based upon factors independent of the lineup, I would do so not only because of the failure to offer counsel before the lineup but also because of the violation of respondent's Fifth Amendment rights.

---

[*] While it is conceivable that legislation might provide a meticulous lineup procedure which would *satisfy* constitutional requirements, I do not agree with the Court that this would "remove the basis for regarding the [lineup] stage as 'critical.'"

## QUESTIONS AND NOTES

**1.** Succinctly stated, what are all of the holdings in *Wade*?

**2.** Succinctly stated, how would Justice Black have resolved all of the issues in this case? Do you think that his opinion was more or less astute than Justice Brennan's? Explain.

**3.** Given *Schmerber*, how can Justice Fortas seriously contend that the *Wade* procedure violates the Fifth Amendment?

**4.** Precisely what role does *Wade* envision for lawyers? Is it significant? Would a videotape work as well?

**5.** Is there more reason to require counsel here or in *Miranda*?

**6.** Is Justice White's fear of defense counsel overstated?

**7.** Do you think that the police and District Attorneys are as neutral as Justice White suggests?

## PROBLEM

Gilbert was required by the police to give a handwriting exemplar without counsel being present. He was also identified at a post-indictment lineup that was held without counsel. At trial the State introduced the handwriting exemplar (to prove that Gilbert wrote the robbery note) as well as the lineup identification. The jury convicted Gilbert at trial. How should the United States Supreme Court resolve his case? See *Gilbert v. California*, 388 U.S. 263 (1967).

The next case, *Kirby*, deals with a pre-indictment lineup.

## B.  The Decline Of *Wade*

### Kirby v. Illinois
### 406 U.S. 682 (1972)

Mr. Justice STEWART announced the judgment of the Court and an opinion in which the Chief Justice, Mr. Justice BLACKMUN, and Mr. Justice REHNQUIST join.

In *Wade* and *Gilbert* this Court held "that a post-indictment pretrial lineup at which the accused is exhibited to identifying witnesses is a critical stage of the criminal prosecution; that police conduct of such a lineup without notice to and in the absence of his counsel denies the accused his Sixth [and Fourteenth] Amendment right to counsel and calls in question the admissibility at trial of the in-court identifications of the accused by witnesses who attended the lineup." Those cases further held that no "in-court identifications" are admissible in evidence if their "source" is a lineup conducted in violation of this constitutional standard. "Only a *per se* exclusionary rule as to such testimony can be an effective sanction," the Court said, "to assure that law enforcement authorities will respect the accused's constitutional right to the presence of his counsel at the critical lineup." In the present case we are asked to extend the *Wade-Gilbert per se* exclusionary rule to identification testimony based upon a police station showup that took place *before* the defendant had been indicted or otherwise formally charged with any criminal offense.

On February 21, 1968, a man named Willie Shard reported to the Chicago police that the previous day two men had robbed him on a Chicago street of a wallet containing, among other things, traveler's checks and a Social Security card. On February 22, two police officers stopped the petitioner and a companion, Ralph Bean, on West Madison Street in Chicago.[1] When asked for identification, the petitioner produced a wallet that contained three traveler's checks and a Social Security card, all bearing the name of Willie Shard. Papers with Shard's name on them were also found in Bean's possession. When asked to explain his possession of Shard's property, the petitioner first said that the traveler's checks were "play money," and then told the officers that he had won them in a crap game. The officers then arrested the petitioner and Bean and took them to a police station.

Only after arriving at the police station, and checking the records there, did the arresting officers learn of the Shard robbery. A police car was then dispatched to Shard's place of employment, where it picked up Shard and brought him to the police station. Immediately upon entering the room in the police station where the petitioner and Bean were seated at a table, Shard positively identified them as the men who had robbed him two days earlier. No lawyer was present in the room, and neither the petitioner nor Bean had asked for legal assistance, or been advised of any right to the presence of counsel.

More than six weeks later, the petitioner and Bean were indicted for the robbery of Willie Shard. Upon arraignment, counsel was appointed to represent them, and they pleaded not guilty. A pretrial motion to suppress Shard's identification testimony

---

[1] The officers stopped the petitioner and his companion because they thought the petitioner was a man named Hampton, who was "wanted" in connection with an unrelated criminal offense. The legitimacy of this stop and the subsequent arrest is not before us.

was denied, and at the trial Shard testified as a witness for the prosecution. In his testimony he described his identification of the two men at the police station on February 22, and identified them again in the courtroom as the men who had robbed him on February 20. He was cross-examined at length regarding the circumstances of his identification of the two defendants. The jury found both defendants guilty, and the petitioner's conviction was affirmed on appeal.[4] The Illinois appellate court held that the admission of Shard's testimony was not error, relying upon an earlier decision of the Illinois Supreme Court, holding that the *Wade-Gilbert per se* exclusionary rule is not applicable to pre-indictment confrontations. We granted certiorari, limited to this question.

### I

We note at the outset that the constitutional privilege against compulsory self-incrimination is in no way implicated here. The Court emphatically rejected the claimed applicability of that constitutional guarantee in *Wade* itself.

It follows that *Miranda* has no applicability whatever to the issue before us; for the *Miranda* decision was based exclusively upon the Fifth and Fourteenth Amendment privilege against compulsory self-incrimination, upon the theory that custodial *interrogation* is inherently coercive.

The *Wade-Gilbert* exclusionary rule, by contrast, stems from a quite different constitutional guarantee—the guarantee of the right to counsel contained in the Sixth and Fourteenth Amendments. Unless all semblance of principled constitutional adjudication is to be abandoned, therefore, it is to the decisions construing that guarantee that we must look in determining the present controversy.

In a line of constitutional cases in this Court stemming back to the Court's landmark opinion in *Powell v. Alabama*, 287 U.S. 45, it has been firmly established that a person's Sixth and Fourteenth Amendment right to counsel attaches only at or after the time that adversary judicial proceedings have been initiated against him.

This is not to say that a defendant in a criminal case has a constitutional right to counsel only at the trial itself. The *Powell* case makes clear that the right attaches at the time of arraignment, and the Court has recently held that it exists also at the time of a preliminary hearing. But the point is that, while members of the Court have differed as to existence of the right to counsel in the contexts of some of the above cases, *all* of those cases have involved points of time at or after the initiation of adversary judicial criminal proceedings—whether by way of formal charge, preliminary hearing, indictment, information, or arraignment.

The only seeming deviation from this long line of constitutional decisions was *Escobedo*. But *Escobedo* is not apposite here for two distinct reasons. First, the Court in retrospect perceived that the "prime purpose" of *Escobedo* was not to vindicate the constitutional right to counsel as such, but, like *Miranda*, "to guarantee full effectuation of the privilege against self-incrimination. . . ." Secondly, and perhaps even more important for purely practical purposes, the Court has limited the holding of *Escobedo* to its own facts, and those facts are not remotely akin to the facts of the case before us.

The initiation of judicial criminal proceedings is far from a mere formalism. It is the starting point of our whole system of adversary criminal justice. For it is only then that the government has committed itself to prosecute, and only then that the adverse positions of government and defendant have solidified. It is then that a defendant finds himself faced with the prosecutorial forces of organized society, and immersed in the intricacies of substantive and procedural criminal law. It is this point, therefore, that marks the commencement of the "criminal prosecutions" to which alone the explicit guarantees of the Sixth Amendment are applicable.

In this case we are asked to import into a routine police investigation an absolute constitutional guarantee historically and rationally applicable only after the onset of formal prosecutorial proceedings. We decline to do so. Less than a year after *Wade* and *Gilbert* were decided, the Court explained the rule of those decisions as follows: "The rationale of those cases was that an accused is entitled to counsel at any 'critical stage of the *prosecution*,' and that a post-indictment lineup is such a 'critical stage.'" (Emphasis supplied.) *Simmons v. United States*, 390 U.S. 377, 382-383. We decline to depart from that rationale today by imposing a *per se* exclusionary rule upon testimony concerning an identification that took place long before the commencement of any prosecution whatever.

### II

What has been said is not to suggest that there may not be occasions during the course of a criminal investigation when the police do abuse identification procedures. Such abuses are not beyond the reach of the Constitution. As the Court pointed out in *Wade* itself, it is always necessary to "scrutinize *any* pretrial confrontation. . . ." The Due Process

---

[4] Bean's conviction was reversed. *People v. Bean*, 121 Ill.App.2d 332, 257 N.E.2d 562.

Clause of the Fifth and Fourteenth Amendments forbids a lineup that is unnecessarily suggestive and conducive to irreparable mistaken identification.[8] When a person has not been formally charged with a criminal offense, *Stovall* strikes the appropriate constitutional balance between the right of a suspect to be protected from prejudicial procedures and the interest of society in the prompt and purposeful investigation of an unsolved crime.

Mr. Justice POWELL, concurring in the result.

As I would not extend the *Wade-Gilbert per se* exclusionary rule, I concur in the result reached by the Court.

Mr. Justice BRENNAN, with whom Mr. Justice DOUGLAS and Mr. Justice MARSHALL join, dissenting.

While it should go without saying, it appears necessary, in view of the plurality opinion today, to re-emphasize that *Wade* did not require the presence of counsel at pretrial confrontations for identification purposes simply on the basis of an abstract consideration of the words "criminal prosecutions" in the Sixth Amendment. Counsel is required at those confrontations because "the dangers inherent in eyewitness identification and the suggestibility inherent in the context of the pretrial identification,"[4] mean that

protection must be afforded to the "most basic right [of] a criminal defendant—his right to a fair trial at which the witnesses against him might be meaningfully cross-examined." Indeed, the Court expressly stated that "[l]egislative or other regulations, such as those of local police departments, which eliminate the risks of abuse and unintentional suggestion at lineup proceedings and the impediments to meaningful confrontation at trial may also remove the basis for regarding the stage as 'critical.'" Hence, "the initiation of adversary judicial criminal proceedings" is completely irrelevant to whether counsel is necessary at a pretrial confrontation for identification in order to safeguard the accused's constitutional rights to confrontation and the effective assistance of counsel at his trial.

In view of *Wade*, it is plain, and the plurality today does not attempt to dispute it, that there inhere in a confrontation for identification conducted after arrest[5] the identical hazards to a fair trial that inhere in such a confrontation conducted "after the onset of formal prosecutional proceedings." The plurality apparently considers an arrest, which for present purposes we must assume to be based upon probable cause, to be nothing more than part of "a routine police investigation," and thus not "the starting point of our whole system of adversary criminal justice."[6] An arrest, according to the plurality, does not face the accused "with the prosecutional forces of organized society," nor immerse him "in the intricacies of substantive and procedural criminal law." Those consequences ensue, says the plurality, only with "[t]he initiation of judicial criminal proceedings," "[f]or it is only then that the government has committed itself to prosecute, and only then that the adverse positions of government and defendant

---

[8] In view of our limited grant of certiorari, we do not consider whether there might have been a deprivation of due process in the particularized circumstances of this case. That question remains open for inquiry in a federal habeas corpus proceeding.

[4] The plurality refers to "occasions during the course of a criminal investigation when the police do abuse identification procedures" and asserts that "[s]uch abuses are not beyond the reach of the Constitution." The constitutional principles established in *Wade*, however, are not addressed solely to police "abuses," as *Wade* explicitly pointed out:

"The few cases that have surfaced therefore reveal the existence of a process attended with hazards of serious unfairness to the criminal accused and strongly suggest the plight of the more numerous defendants who are unable to ferret out suggestive influences in the secrecy of the confrontation. We do not assume that these risks are the result of police procedures intentionally designed to prejudice an accused. Rather we assume they derive from the dangers inherent in eyewitness identification and the suggestibility inherent in the context of the pretrial identification."

---

[5] This case does not require me to consider confrontations that take place before custody, nor accidental confrontations not arranged by the police, nor on-the-scene encounters shortly after the crime.

[6] Cf. *Miranda* (emphasis added):

"The principles announced today deal with the protection which must be given to the privilege against self-incrimination when the individual is first subjected to police interrogation *while in custody at the station or otherwise deprived of his freedom of action in any significant way. It is at this point that our adversary system of criminal proceedings commences,* distinguishing itself at the outset from the inquisitorial system recognized in some countries."

have solidified." If these propositions do not amount to "mere formalism," it is difficult to know how to characterize them.[8] An arrest evidences the belief of the police that the perpetrator of a crime has been caught. A post-arrest confrontation for identification is not "a mere preparatory step in the gathering of the prosecution's evidence." A primary, and frequently sole, purpose of the confrontation for identification at that stage is to accumulate proof to buttress the conclusion of the police that they have the offender in hand. The plurality offers no reason, and I can think of none, for concluding that a post-arrest confrontation for identification, unlike a post-charge confrontation, is not among those "critical confrontations of the accused by the prosecution at pretrial proceedings where the results might well settle the accused's fate and reduce the trial itself to a mere formality."

The highly suggestive form of confrontation employed in this case underscores the point. This showup was particularly fraught with the peril of mistaken identification. In the setting of a police station squad room where all present except petitioner and Bean were police officers, the danger was quite real that Shard's understandable resentment might lead him too readily to agree with the police that the pair under arrest, and the only persons exhibited to him, were indeed the robbers. "It is hard to imagine a situation more clearly conveying the suggestion to the witness that the one presented is believed guilty by the police." The State had no case without Shard's identification testimony,[9] and

safeguards against that consequence were therefore of critical importance. Shard's testimony itself demonstrates the necessity for such safeguards. On direct examination, Shard identified petitioner and Bean not as the alleged robbers on trial in the courtroom, but as the pair he saw at the police station. His testimony thus lends strong support to the observation, quoted by the Court in *Wade*, that "[i]t is a matter of common experience that, once a witness has picked out the accused at the line-up, he is not likely to go back on his word later on, so that in practice the issue of identity may (in the absence of other relevant evidence) for all practical purposes be determined there and then, before the trial."

*Wade* and *Gilbert*, of course, happened to involve post-indictment confrontations. Yet even a cursory perusal of the opinions in those cases reveals that nothing at all turned upon that particular circumstance.[13] In short, it is fair to conclude that rather than "declin[ing] to depart from [the] rationale" of *Wade* and *Gilbert*, the plurality today, albeit purporting to be engaged in "principled constitutional adjudication," refuses even to recognize that "rationale." For my part, I do not agree that we "extend" *Wade* and *Gilbert* by holding that the principles of those cases apply to confrontations for identification conducted after arrest. Because Shard testified at trial about his identification of petitioner at the police station showup, the exclusionary rule of *Gilbert* requires reversal.

Mr. Justice WHITE, dissenting.

*Wade* and *Gilbert* govern this case and compel reversal of the judgment below.

---

[8] As the California Supreme Court pointed out, with an eye toward the real world, "the establishment of the date of formal accusation as the time wherein the right to counsel at lineup attaches could only lead to a situation wherein substantially all lineups would be conducted prior to indictment or information." *People v. Fowler*, 1 Cal.3d 335, 344, 82 Cal.Rptr. 363, 370, 461 P.2d 643, 650 (1969).

[9] Bean took the stand and testified that he and petitioner found Shard's traveler's checks and Social Security card two hours before their arrest strewn upon the ground in an alley.

[13] The *Wade* dissenters found no such limitation: "The rule applies to any lineup, to any other techniques employed to produce an identification and *a fortiori* to a face-to-face encounter between the witness and the suspect alone, regardless of when the identification occurs, in time or place, and whether before or after indictment or information." (White, J., joined by Harlan and Stewart, JJ., dissenting in part and concurring in part).

## QUESTIONS AND NOTES

**1.** Do you think that the majority or dissent was truer to the spirit of *Wade*? Why?

**2.** Should the fact of arrest rather than indictment trigger the right to counsel? Why? Why not?

**3.** Is the question essentially the same as the *Miranda/Massiah* dichotomy? Or are different factors at work? Explain. Should it matter that the *Wade* rule was designed to further the truth-seeking process?

**4.** Are there any good pragmatic reasons for the majority's line? Explain.

**5.** In any event, was this identification procedure unduly suggestive? Consider in conjunction with *Manson v. Brathwaite, infra*.


# PROBLEM

Petitioner was convicted of rape and related offenses. At trial the complaining witness testified on direct examination by the prosecution that she had identified petitioner at a preliminary hearing at which he was not represented by counsel.

The victim of the offenses in question lived in an apartment on the South Side of Chicago. Shortly after noon on December 14, 1967, she awakened from a nap to find a man standing in the doorway to her bedroom holding a knife. The man entered the bedroom threw her face down on the bed, and choked her until she was quiet. After covering his face with a bandana, the intruder partially undressed the victim, forced her to commit oral sodomy, and raped her. Then he left, taking a guitar and a flute from the apartment.

When police arrived, the victim gave them a description of her assailant. Although she did not know who he was and had seen his face for only 10 to 15 seconds during the attack, she thought he was the same man who had made offensive remarks to her in a neighborhood bar the night before. She also gave police a notebook she had found next to her bed after the attack.

In the week that followed, police showed the victim two groups of photographs of men. From the first group of 200 she picked about 30 who resembled her assailant in height, weight, and build. From the second group of about 10, she picked two or three. One of these was of petitioner. Police also found a letter in the notebook that the victim had given them. Investigation revealed that it was written by a woman with whom petitioner had been staying. The letter had been taken from the woman's home in her absence, and petitioner appeared to be the only other person who had access to the home.

On the evening of December 20, 1967, police arrested petitioner at his apartment and held him overnight pending a preliminary hearing to determine whether he should be bound over to the grand jury and to set bail. The next morning, a policeman accompanied the victim to the Circuit Court of Cook County (First Municipal District) for the hearing. The policeman told her she was going to view a suspect and should identify him if she could. He also had her sign a complaint that named petitioner as her assailant. At the hearing, petitioner's name was called and he was led before the bench. The judge told petitioner that he was charged with rape and deviate sexual behavior. The judge then called the victim, who had been in the courtroom waiting for the case to be called, to come before the bench. The State's Attorney stated that police had found evidence linking petitioner with the offenses charged. He asked the victim whether she saw her assailant in the courtroom, and she pointed at petitioner.

Should she be able to testify at trial to her preliminary hearing identification? Why? Why not? For the Supreme Court's solution, see *Moore v. Illinois*, 434 U.S. 220 (1977).

In *Ash*, we will see that post-indictment pictorial lineups are not necessarily the same as post-indictment corporeal lineups.

# United States v. Ash
## 413 U.S. 300 (1973)

Mr. Justice BLACKMUN delivered the opinion of the Court.

In this case the Court is called upon to decide whether the Sixth Amendment grants an accused the right to have counsel present whenever the Government conducts a post-indictment photographic display, containing a picture of the accused, for the purpose of allowing a witness to attempt an identification of the offender.

### I

On the morning of August 26, 1965, a man with a stocking mask entered a bank in Washington, D.C., and began waving a pistol. He ordered an employee to hang up the telephone and instructed all others present not to move. Seconds later a second man, also wearing a stocking mask, entered the bank, scooped up money from tellers' drawers into a bag, and left. The gunman followed, and both men escaped through an alley. The robbery lasted three or four minutes.

A Government informer, Clarence McFarland, told authorities that he had discussed the robbery with Charles J. Ash, Jr., the respondent here. Acting on this information, an FBI agent, in February 1966, showed five black-and-white mug shots of Negro males of generally the same age, height, and weight, one of which was of Ash, to four witnesses. All four made uncertain identifications of Ash's picture. At this time Ash was not in custody and had not been charged. On April 1, 1966, an indictment was returned charging Ash and a codefendant, John L. Bailey, in five counts related to this bank robbery.

Trial was finally set for May 1968, almost three years after the crime. In preparing for trial, the prosecutor decided to use a photographic display to determine whether the witnesses he planned to call would be able to make in-court identifications. Shortly before the trial, an FBI agent and the prosecutor showed five color photographs to the four witnesses who previously had tentatively identified the black-and-white photograph of Ash. Three of the witnesses selected the picture of Ash, but one was unable to make any selection. None of the witnesses selected the picture of Bailey which was in the group. This post-indictment[3] identification provides the basis for

respondent Ash's claim that he was denied the right to counsel at a "critical stage" of the prosecution.

### II

In *Powell v. Alabama*, 287 U.S. 45, 60-66 (1932), the Court discussed the English common-law rule that severely limited the right of a person accused of a felony to consult with counsel at trial. The Court examined colonial constitutions and statutes and noted that "in at least twelve of the thirteen colonies the rule of the English common law, in the respect now under consideration, had been definitely rejected and the right to counsel fully recognized in all criminal prosecutions, save that in one or two instances the right was limited to capital offenses or to the more serious crimes." The Sixth Amendment counsel guarantee, thus, was derived from colonial statutes and constitutional provisions designed to reject the English common-law rule.

This historical background suggests that the core purpose of the counsel guarantee was to assure "Assistance" at trial, when the accused was confronted with both the intricacies of the law and the advocacy of the public prosecutor. Later developments have led this Court to recognize that "Assistance" would be less than meaningful if it were limited to the formal trial itself.

This extension of the right to counsel to events before trial has resulted from changing patterns of criminal procedure and investigation that have tended to generate pretrial events that might appropriately be considered to be parts of the trial itself. At these newly emerging and significant events, the accused was confronted, just as at trial, by the procedural system, or by his expert adversary, or by both.

The function of counsel in rendering "Assistance" continued at the lineup under consideration in *Wade* and its companion cases. Although the accused was not confronted there with legal questions, the lineup offered opportunities for prosecuting authorities to take advantage of the accused. Counsel was seen by the Court as being more sensitive to, and aware of, suggestive influences than the accused himself, and as better able to reconstruct the events at trial. Counsel present at lineup would be able to remove disabilities of the accused in precisely the same fashion that counsel compensated for the disabilities of the layman at trial. Thus, the Court mentioned that the accused's memory might be dimmed by "emotional tension," that the accused's credibility at trial would be diminished by his status as defendant, and that the accused might be unable to

---

[3] Respondent Ash does not assert a right to counsel at the black-and-white photographic display in February 1966 because he recognizes that *Kirby v. Illinois*, 406 U.S. 682 (1972), forecloses application of the Sixth Amendment to events before the initiation of adversary criminal proceedings.

present his version effectively without giving up his privilege against compulsory self-incrimination. It was in order to compensate for these deficiencies that the Court found the need for the assistance of counsel.

### III

Although the Court of Appeals' majority recognized the argument that "a major purpose behind the right to counsel is to protect the defendant from errors that he himself might make if he appeared in court alone," the court concluded that "other forms of prejudice," mentioned and recognized in *Wade*, could also give rise to a right to counsel. These forms of prejudice were felt by the court to flow from the possibilities for mistaken identification inherent in the photographic display.[8]

After the Court in *Wade* held that a lineup constituted a trial-like confrontation requiring counsel, a more difficult issue remained in the case for consideration. The same changes in law enforcement that led to lineups and pretrial hearings also generated other events at which the accused was confronted by the prosecution. The Government had argued in *Wade* that if counsel was required at a lineup, the same forceful considerations would mandate counsel at other preparatory steps in the "gathering of the

---

[8] "[T]he dangers of mistaken identification from uncounseled lineup identifications set forth in *Wade* are applicable in large measure to photographic as well as corporeal identifications. These include, notably, the possibilities of suggestive influence or mistake—particularly where witnesses had little or no opportunity for detailed observation during the crime; the difficulty of reconstructing suggestivity—even greater when the defendant is not even present; the tendency of a witness's identification, once given under these circumstances, to be frozen. While these difficulties may be somewhat mitigated by preserving the photograph shown, it may also be said that a photograph can preserve the record of a lineup; yet this does not justify a lineup without counsel. The same may be said of the opportunity to examine the participants as to what went on in the course of the identification, whether at lineup or on photograph. Sometimes this may suffice to bring out all pertinent facts, even at a lineup, but this would not suffice under *Wade* to offset the constitutional infringement wrought by proceeding without counsel. The presence of counsel avoids possibilities of suggestiveness in the manner of presentation that are otherwise ineradicable."

prosecution's evidence," such as, for particular example, the taking of fingerprints or blood samples.

The Court concluded that there were differences. Rather than distinguishing these situations from the lineup in terms of the need for counsel to assure an equal confrontation at the time, the Court recognized that there were times when the subsequent trial would cure a one-sided confrontation between prosecuting authorities and the uncounseled defendant. In other words, such stages were not "critical." Referring to fingerprints, hair, clothing, and other blood samples, the Court explained:

> "Knowledge of the techniques of science and technology is sufficiently available, and the variables in techniques few enough, that the accused has the opportunity for a meaningful confrontation of the Government's case at trial through the ordinary processes of cross-examination of the Government's expert witnesses and the presentation of the evidence of his own experts."

The structure of *Wade*, viewed in light of the careful limitation of the Court's language to "confrontations," makes it clear that lack of scientific precision and inability to reconstruct an event are not the tests for requiring counsel in the first instance. These are, instead, the tests to determine whether confrontation with counsel at trial can serve as a substitute for counsel at the pretrial confrontation. If accurate reconstruction is possible, the risks inherent in any confrontation still remain, but the opportunity to cure defects at trial causes the confrontation to cease to be "critical." The opinion of the Court even indicated that changes in procedure might cause a lineup to cease to be a "critical" confrontation.

The Court of Appeals considered its analysis complete after it decided that a photographic display lacks scientific precision and ease of accurate reconstruction at trial. That analysis, under *Wade*, however, merely carries one to the point where one must establish that the trial itself can provide no substitute for counsel if a pretrial confrontation is conducted in the absence of counsel. Judge Friendly, writing for the Second Circuit in *United States v. Bennett*, 409 F.2d 888 (1969), recognized that the "criticality" test of *Wade*, if applied outside the confrontation context, would result in drastic expansion of the right to counsel:

> "None of the classical analyses of the assistance to be given by counsel, Justice Sutherland's in *Powell v. Alabama* . . . and Justice Black's in *Johnson v. Zerbst* . . . and *Gideon*

*v. Wainwright* . . . suggests that counsel must be present when the prosecution is interrogating witnesses in the defendant's absence even when, as here, the defendant is under arrest; counsel is rather to be provided to prevent the defendant himself from falling into traps devised by a lawyer on the other side and to see to it that all available defenses are proffered. Many other aspects of the prosecution's interviews with a victim or a witness to a crime afford just as much opportunity for undue suggestion as the display of photographs; so, too, do the defense's interviews, notably with alibi witnesses.''

We now undertake the threshold analysis that must be addressed.

### IV

A substantial departure from the historical test would be necessary if the Sixth Amendment were interpreted to give Ash a right to counsel at the photographic identification in this case. Since the accused himself is not present at the time of the photographic display, and asserts no right to be present, no possibility arises that the accused might be misled by his lack of familiarity with the law or overpowered by his professional adversary. Similarly, the counsel guarantee would not be used to produce equality in a trial-like adversary confrontation. Rather, the guarantee was used by the Court of Appeals to produce confrontation at an event that previously was not analogous to an adversary trial.

The argument has been advanced that requiring counsel might compel the police to observe more scientific procedures or might encourage them to utilize corporeal rather than photographic displays.[14] This Court has recognized that improved procedures can minimize the dangers of suggestion.

Pretrial photographic identifications, however, are hardly unique in offering possibilities for the actions of the prosecutor unfairly to prejudice the accused. Evidence favorable to the accused may be withheld; testimony of witnesses may be manipulated; the results of laboratory tests may be contrived. In many ways the prosecutor, by accident or by design, may improperly subvert the trial. The primary safeguard against abuses of this kind is the ethical responsibility of the prosecutor, who, as so often has been said, may ''strike hard blows'' but not

---

[14] A variant of this argument is that photographic identifications may be used to circumvent the need for counsel at lineups.

''foul ones.'' If that safeguard fails, review remains available under due process standards. These same safeguards apply to misuse of photographs.

We are not persuaded that the risks inherent in the use of photographic displays are so pernicious that an extraordinary system of safeguards is required. We hold, then, that the Sixth Amendment does not grant the right to counsel at photographic displays conducted by the Government for the purpose of allowing a witness to attempt an identification of the offender.

Reversed and remanded.

Mr. Justice STEWART, concurring in the judgment.

Since the photographic identification in the present case occurred after the accused had been indicted, and thus clearly after adversary judicial proceedings had been initiated, the only question is whether that procedure was such a ''critical stage'' that the Constitution required the presence of counsel.

In *Wade*, the Court determined that a pretrial proceeding is a ''critical stage'' if ''the presence of . . . counsel is necessary to preserve the defendant's . . . right meaningfully to cross-examine the witnesses against him and to have effective assistance of counsel at the trial itself.'' Pretrial proceedings are ''critical,'' then, if the presence of counsel is essential ''to protect the fairness of the trial itself.''

The Court stressed in *Wade* that the danger of mistaken identification at trial was appreciably heightened by the ''degree of suggestion inherent in the manner in which the prosecution presents the suspect to witnesses for pretrial identification.'' There are numerous and subtle possibilities for such improper suggestion in the dynamic context of a lineup. Judge Wilkey, dissenting in the present case, accurately described a lineup as:

''a little drama, stretching over an appreciable span of time. The accused is there in the flesh, three-dimensional and always full-length. Further, he isn't merely there, he acts. He walks on stage, he blinks in the glare of lights, he turns and twists, often muttering asides to those sharing the spotlight. He can be required to utter significant words, to turn a profile or back, to walk back and forth, to doff one costume and don another. All the while the potentially identifying witness is watching, a prosecuting attorney and a police detective at his elbow, ready to record the witness' every word and reaction.''

With no attorney for the accused present at this "little drama," defense counsel at trial could seldom convincingly discredit a witness' courtroom identification by showing it to be based on an impermissibly suggestive lineup. In addition to the problems posed by the fluid nature of a lineup, the Court in *Wade* pointed out that neither the witnesses nor the lineup participants were likely to be alert for suggestive influences or schooled in their detection. "In short, the accused's inability effectively to reconstruct at trial any unfairness that occurred at the lineup may deprive him of his only opportunity meaningfully to attack the credibility of the witness' courtroom identification."

The Court held, therefore, that counsel was required at a lineup, primarily as an observer, to ensure that defense counsel could effectively confront the prosecution's evidence at trial. Attuned to the possibilities of suggestive influences, a lawyer could see any unfairness at a lineup, question the witnesses about it at trial, and effectively reconstruct what had gone on for the benefit of the jury or trial judge.[*]

A photographic identification is quite different from a lineup, for there are substantially fewer possibilities of impermissible suggestion when photographs are used, and those unfair influences can be readily reconstructed at trial. It is true that the defendant's photograph may be markedly different from the others displayed, but this unfairness can be demonstrated at trial from an actual comparison of the photographs used or from the witness' description of the display. Similarly, it is possible that the photographs could be arranged in a suggestive manner, or that by comment or gesture the prosecuting authorities might single out the defendant's picture. But these are the kinds of overt influence that a witness can easily recount and that would serve to impeach the identification testimony. In short, there are few possibilities for unfair suggestiveness—and those rather blatant and easily reconstructed. Accordingly, an accused would not be foreclosed from an effective cross-examination of an identification

witness simply because his counsel was not present at the photographic display. For this reason, a photographic display cannot fairly be considered a "critical stage" of the prosecution.

Preparing witnesses for trial by checking their identification testimony against a photographic display is little different, in my view, from the prosecutor's other interviews with the victim or other witnesses before trial. While these procedures can be improperly conducted, the possibility of irretrievable prejudice is remote, since any unfairness that does occur can usually be flushed out at trial through cross-examination of the prosecution witnesses. The presence of defense counsel at such pretrial preparatory sessions is neither appropriate nor necessary under our adversary system of justice "to preserve the defendant's basic right to a fair trial as affected by his right meaningfully to cross-examine the witnesses against him and to have effective assistance of counsel at the trial itself." *Wade.*

Mr. Justice BRENNAN, with whom Mr. Justice DOUGLAS and Mr. Justice MARSHALL join, dissenting.

The Court holds today that a pretrial display of photographs to the witnesses of a crime for the purpose of identifying the accused, unlike a lineup, does not constitute a "critical stage" of the prosecution at which the accused is constitutionally entitled to the presence of counsel. In my view, today's decision is wholly unsupportable in terms of such considerations as logic, consistency, and, indeed, fairness. As a result, I must reluctantly conclude that today's decision marks simply another[1] step towards the complete evisceration of the fundamental constitutional principles established by this Court, only six years ago, in *Wade.* I dissent.

### III

As the Court of Appeals recognized, "the dangers of mistaken identification . . . set forth in *Wade* are applicable in large measure to photographic as well as corporeal identifications." To the extent that misidentification may be attributable to a witness' faulty memory or perception, or inadequate opportunity for detailed observation during the crime, the risks are obviously as great at a photographic display as at a lineup.[8] But "[b]ecause of the inherent limitations of photography, which presents its subject in

---

[*] I do not read *Wade* as requiring counsel because a lineup is a "trial-type" situation, nor do I understand that the Court required the presence of an attorney because of the advice or assistance he could give to his client at the lineup itself. Rather, I had thought the reasoning of *Wade* was that the right to counsel is essentially a protection for the defendant at trial, and that counsel is necessary at a lineup in order to ensure a meaningful confrontation and the effective assistance of counsel at trial.

---

[1] See *Kirby.*

[8] Thus, "[a] witness may have obtained only a brief glimpse of a criminal, or may have seen him under poor conditions. Even if the police subsequently follow the most correct photographic identi-

two dimensions rather than the three dimensions of reality, . . . a photographic identification, even when properly obtained, is clearly inferior to a properly obtained corporeal identification." P. Wall, Eye-witness Identification in Criminal Cases 70 (1965). Indeed, noting "the hazards of initial identification by photograph," we have expressly recognized that "a corporeal identification . . . is normally more accurate" than a photographic identification. Thus, in this sense at least, the dangers of misidentification are even greater at a photographic display than at a lineup.

Moreover, as in the lineup situation, the possibilities for impermissible suggestion in the context of a photographic display are manifold. Such suggestion, intentional or unintentional, may derive from three possible sources. First, the photographs themselves might tend to suggest which of the pictures is that of the suspect. For example, differences in age, pose, or other physical characteristics of the persons represented, and variations in the mounting, background, lighting, or markings of the photographs all might have the effect of singling out the accused.

Second, impermissible suggestion may inhere in the manner in which the photographs are displayed to the witness. The danger of misidentification is, of course, "increased if the police display to the witness . . . the pictures of several persons among which the photograph of a single such individual recurs or is in some way emphasized." And, if the photographs are arranged in an asymmetrical pattern, or if they are displayed in a time sequence that tends to emphasize a particular photograph, "any identification of the photograph which stands out from the rest is no more reliable than an identification of a single photograph, exhibited alone."

Third, gestures or comments of the prosecutor at the time of the display may lead an otherwise uncertain witness to select the "correct" photograph. For example, the prosecutor might "indicate to the witness that [he has] other evidence that one of the persons pictured committed the crime," and might even point to a particular photograph and ask whether the person pictured "looks familiar." More subtly, the prosecutor's inflection, facial expressions, physical motions, and myriad other almost imperceptible means of communication might tend, intentionally or unintentionally, to compromise the

fication procedures . . . there is some danger that the witness may make an incorrect identification." *Simmons v. United States*, 390 U.S. 377, 383 (1968).

witness' objectivity. Thus, as is the case with lineups, "[i]mproper photographic identification procedures, . . . by exerting a suggestive influence upon the witnesses, can often lead to an erroneous identification. . . ."[12] And "[r]egardless of how the initial misidentification comes about, the witness thereafter is apt to retain in his memory the image of the photograph rather than of the person actually seen. . . ." As a result, "the issue of identity may (in the absence of other relevant evidence) for all practical purposes be determined there and then, before the trial."

Moreover, as with lineups, the defense can "seldom reconstruct" at trial the mode and manner of photographic identification. It is true, of course, that the photographs used at the pretrial display might be preserved for examination at trial. But "it may also be said that a photograph can preserve the record of a lineup; yet this does not justify a lineup without counsel." Indeed, in reality, preservation of the photographs affords little protection to the unrepresented accused. For, although retention of the photographs may mitigate the dangers of misidentification due to the suggestiveness of the photographs themselves, it cannot in any sense reveal to defense counsel the more subtle, and therefore more dangerous, suggestiveness that might derive from the manner in which he photographs were displayed

---

[12] The Court maintains that "the ethical responsibility of the prosecutor" is in itself a sufficient "safeguard" against impermissible suggestion at a photographic display. The same argument might, of course, be made with respect to lineups. Moreover, it is clear that the "prosecutor" is not always present at such pretrial displays. Indeed, in this very case, one of the four eye-witnesses was shown the color photographs on the morning of trial by an agent of the FBI, *not* in the presence of the "prosecutor." And even though "the ethical responsibility of the prosecutor" might be an adequate "safeguard" against *intentional* suggestion, it can hardly be doubted that a "prosecutor" is, after all, only human. His behavior may be fraught with wholly *unintentional* and indeed unconscious nuances that might effectively suggest the "proper" response. And, of course, as *Wade* itself makes clear, unlike other forms of unintentional prosecutorial "manipulation," even unintentional suggestiveness at an identification procedure involves serious risks of "freezing" the witness' mistaken identification and creates almost insurmountable obstacles to reconstruction at trial.

or any accompanying comments or gestures. Moreover, the accused cannot rely upon the witnesses themselves to expose these latter sources of suggestion, for the witnesses are not "apt to be alert for conditions prejudicial to the suspect. And if they were, it would likely be of scant benefit to the suspect" since the witnesses are hardly "likely to be schooled in the detection of suggestive influences."

Finally, and *unlike* the lineup situation, the accused himself is not even present at the photographic identification, thereby reducing the likelihood that irregularities in the procedures will ever come to light. Indeed, in *Wade*, the Government itself observed:

> "When the defendant is present – as he is during a lineup – he may personally observe the circumstances, report them to his attorney, and (if he chooses to take the stand) testify about them at trial. . . . [I]n the absence of an accused, on the other hand, there is no one present to verify the fairness of the interview or to report any irregularities. If the prosecution were tempted to engage in "sloppy or biased or fraudulent" conduct . . ., it would be far more likely to do so when the accused is absent than when he is himself being 'used.'"

Thus, the difficulties of reconstructing at trial an uncounseled photographic display are at least equal to, and possibly greater than, those involved in reconstructing an uncounseled lineup.[15] And, as the

---

[15] The Court's assertion that these difficulties of reconstruction are somehow minimized because the defense can "duplicate" a photographic identification reflects a complete misunderstanding of the issues in this case. Aside from the fact that lineups can also be "duplicated," the Court's assertion is wholly inconsistent with the underlying premises of both *Wade* and *Gilbert*. For, unlike the Court today, the Court in both of those decisions recognized a critical difference between "systematized or scientific analyzing of the accused's fingerprints, blood sample, clothing, hair, and the like," on the one hand, and eyewitness identification, on the other. In essence, the Court noted in *Wade* and *Gilbert* that, in the former situations, the accused can preserve his right to a fair trial simply by "duplicating" the tests of the Government, thereby enabling him to expose any errors in the Government's analysis. Such "duplication" is possible, however, *only* because the accused's tests can be made *independently* of those of the Government – that is, any errors in the Government's analyses cannot affect the reliability of the accused's tests. That simply is not the case,

Government argued in *Wade*, in terms of the need for counsel, "[t]here is no meaningful difference between a witness' pretrial identification from photographs and a similar identification made at a lineup." For in both situations, "the accused's inability effectively to reconstruct at trial any unfairness that occurred at the [pretrial identification] may deprive him of his only opportunity meaningfully to attack the credibility of the witness' courtroom identification." As a result, both photographic and corporeal identifications create grave dangers that an innocent defendant might be convicted simply because of his inability to expose a tainted identification. This being so, considerations of logic, consistency, and, indeed, fairness compel the conclusion that a pretrial photographic identification, like a pretrial corporeal identification, is a "critical stage of the prosecution at which [the accused is] 'as much entitled to such aid [of counsel] . . . as at the trial itself.'"

### IV

Ironically, the Court does not seriously challenge the proposition that presence of counsel at a pretrial photographic display is essential to preserve the accused's right to a fair trial on the issue of identification. Rather, in what I can only characterize a triumph of form over substance, the Court seeks to justify its result by engrafting a wholly unprecedented – and wholly unsupportable-limitation on the Sixth Amendment right of "the accused . . . to have the Assistance of Counsel for his defense." Although apparently conceding that the right to counsel attaches, not only at the trial itself, but at all "critical stages" of the prosecution, the Court holds today that, in order to be deemed "critical," the particular "stage of the prosecution" under consideration must, at the very least, involve the physical "presence of the accused," at a "trial-like confrontation" with the Government, at which the accused requires the "guiding hand of counsel." According to the Court a pretrial photographic identification does not, of course, meet these criteria.

---

however, with respect to eyewitness identifications, whether corporeal or photographic. Due to the "freezing effect" recognized in *Wade*, once suggestion has tainted the identification, its mark is virtually indelible. For once a witness has made a mistaken identification, "he is not likely to go back on his word later on." *Wade*. As a result, any effort of the accused to "duplicate" the initial photographic display will almost necessarily lead to a reaffirmation of the initial misidentification.

[The] established conception of the Sixth Amendment guarantee is, of course, in no sense dependent upon the physical "presence of the accused," at a "trial-like confrontation" with the Government, at which the accused requires the "guiding hand of counsel." On the contrary, in *Powell v. Alabama*, 287 U.S. 45 (1932), the seminal decision in this area, we explicitly held the right to counsel applicable at a stage of the pretrial proceedings involving *none* of the three criteria set forth by the Court today. In *Powell*, the defendants in a state felony prosecution were not appointed counsel until the very eve of trial. This Court held, in no uncertain terms, that such an appointment could not satisfy the demands of the Sixth Amendment, for "[i]t is vain . . . to guarantee [the accused] counsel without giving the latter any opportunity to acquaint himself with the facts or law of the case." In other words, *Powell* made clear that, in order to preserve the accused's right to a fair trial and to "effective and substantial" assistance of counsel at the trial, the Sixth Amendment guarantee necessarily encompasses a reasonable period of time before trial during which counsel might prepare the defense. Yet it can hardly be said that this preparatory period of research and investigation involves the physical "presence of the accused," at a "trial-like confrontation" with the Government, at which the accused requires the "guiding hand of counsel."

Moreover, despite the Court's efforts to rewrite *Wade* so as to suggest a precedential basis for its own analysis, the rationale of *Wade* lends no support whatever to today's decision. In *Wade*, after concluding that compelled participation in a lineup does not violate the accused's right against self-incrimination, the Court addressed the argument "that the assistance of counsel at the lineup was indispensable to protect Wade's most basic right as a criminal defendant—his right to a fair trial at which the witnesses against him might be meaningfully cross-examined." The Court then surveyed the history of the Sixth Amendment, and specifically concluded that that Amendment guarantees "counsel's assistance *whenever* necessary to assure a meaningful

'defense.'" (emphasis added). Then, after examining this Court's prior decisions concerning the applicability of the counsel guarantee, the Court stressed once again that a pretrial proceeding is a "critical stage" of the prosecution if "the presence of his counsel is necessary to preserve the defendant's basic right to a fair trial as affected by his right meaningfully to cross-examine the witnesses against him and to have effective assistance of counsel at the trial itself."

Thus, contrary to the suggestion of the Court, the conclusion in *Wade* that a pretrial lineup is a "critical stage" of the prosecution did not in any sense turn on the fact that a lineup involves the physical "presence of the accused" at a "trial-like confrontation" with the Government. And that conclusion most certainly did not turn on the notion that presence of counsel was necessary so that counsel could offer legal advice or "guidance" to the accused at the lineup. On the contrary, *Wade* envisioned counsel's function at the lineup to be primarily that of a trained observer, able to detect the existence of any suggestive influences and capable of understanding the legal implications of the events that transpire. Having witnessed the proceedings, counsel would then be in a position effectively to reconstruct at trial any unfairness that occurred at the lineup, thereby preserving the accused's fundamental right to a fair trial on the issue of identification.

There is something ironic about the Court's conclusion today that a pretrial lineup identification is a "critical stage" of the prosecution because counsel's presence can help to compensate for the accused's deficiencies as an observer, but that a pretrial photographic identification is not a "critical stage" of the prosecution because the accused is not able to observe at all. In my view, there simply is no meaningful difference, in terms of the need for attendance of counsel, between corporeal and photographic identifications. And applying established and well-reasoned Sixth Amendment principles, I can only conclude that a pretrial photographic display, like a pretrial lineup, is a "critical stage" of the prosecution at which the accused is constitutionally entitled to the presence of counsel.

## QUESTIONS AND NOTES

**1.** After *Ash*, would it be possible for the police to videotape a post-indictment corporeal lineup without counsel present? Explain. Should that be possible? Why? Would it matter whether one adhered to the Blackmun rationale or the Stewart rationale?

**2.** Does the absence of the defendant at a pictorial lineup, weaken or strengthen his need for counsel?

**3.** Is a photo identification significantly easier to reconstruct than a corporeal lineup?

**4.** Does the *Ash* Court see counsel merely as a trained observer? Would the *Wade* Court have concurred?

**5.** After *Ash*, how likely is it that there ever will be a post-indictment corporeal lineup? As a prosecutor would you hold one?

**6.** Should a defendant ever be *entitled* to a lineup? On what ground?


## C.   The Due Process Backup

Quite apart from the right to counsel, a lineup identification which was obtained under fundamentally unfair circumstances may not be introduced. In *Manson v. Brathwaite*, the Court explores the various tests considered by the Court and settles on the one it finds most appropriate. As you read *Manson*, consider whether the Court adopted the best possible standard for measuring due process.


**Manson v. Brathwaite**

432 U.S. 98 (1977)

Mr. Justice BLACKMUN delivered the opinion of the Court.

This case presents the issue as to whether the Due Process Clause of the Fourteenth Amendment compels the exclusion, in a state criminal trial, apart from any consideration of reliability, of pretrial identification evidence obtained by a police procedure that was both suggestive and unnecessary.

I

Jimmy D. Glover, a full-time trooper of the Connecticut State Police, in 1970 was assigned to the Narcotics Division in an undercover capacity. On May 5 of that year, about 7:45 p.m., e.d.t., and while there was still daylight, Glover and Henry Alton Brown, an informant, went to an apartment building at 201 Westland, in Hartford, for the purpose of purchasing narcotics from "Dickie Boy" Cicero, a known narcotics dealer. Cicero, it was thought, lived on the third floor of that apartment building. Glover and Brown entered the building, observed by back-up Officers D'Onofrio and Gaffey, and proceeded by stairs to the third floor. Glover knocked at the door of one of the two apartments served by the stairway.[2] The area was illuminated by natural light from a window in the third

floor hallway. The door was opened 12 to 18 inches in response to the knock. Glover observed a man standing at the door and, behind him, a woman. Brown identified himself. Glover then asked for "two things" of narcotics. The man at the door held out his hand, and Glover gave him two $10 bills. The door closed. Soon the man returned and handed Glover two glassine bags. While the door was open, Glover stood within two feet of the person from whom he made the purchase and observed his face. Five to seven minutes elapsed from the time the door first opened until it closed the second time.

Glover and Brown then left the building. This was about eight minutes after their arrival. Glover drove to headquarters where he described the seller to D'Onofrio and Gaffey. Glover at that time did not know the identity of the seller. He described him as being "a colored man, approximately five feet eleven inches tall, dark complexion, black hair, short Afro style, and having high cheekbones, and of heavy build. He was wearing at the time blue pants and a plaid shirt." D'Onofrio, suspecting from this description that respondent might be the seller, obtained a photograph of respondent from the Records Division of the Hartford Police Department. He left it at Glover's office. D'Onofrio was not acquainted with respondent personally but did know him by sight and had seen him "[s]everal times" prior to May 5. Glover, when alone, viewed the photograph for the first time upon his return to headquarters on May 7; he identified the person shown as the one from whom he had purchased the narcotics.

Respondent was arrested on July 27 while visiting

---

[2] It appears that the door on which Glover knocked may not have been that of the Cicero apartment. Petitioner concedes, in any event, that the transaction effected "was with some other person than had been intended."

at the apartment of a Mrs. Ramsey on the third floor of 201 Westland. This was the apartment at which the narcotics sale had taken place on May 5.[4]

At his trial in January 1971, the photograph from which Glover had identified respondent was received in evidence without objection on the part of the defense. Glover also testified that, although he had not seen respondent in the eight months that had elapsed since the sale, "there [was] no doubt whatsoever" in his mind that the person shown on the photograph was respondent. Glover also made a positive in-court identification without objection.

No explanation was offered by the prosecution for the failure to utilize a photographic array or to conduct a lineup.

Respondent, who took the stand in his own defense, testified that on May 5, the day in question, he had been ill at his Albany Avenue apartment ("a lot of back pains, muscle spasms . . . a bad heart . . . high blood pressure . . . neuralgia in my face, and sinus," and that at no time on that particular day had he been at 201 Westland. His wife testified that she recalled, after her husband had refreshed her memory, that he was home all day on May 5. Doctor Wesley M. Vietzke, an internist and assistant professor of medicine at the University of Connecticut, testified that respondent had consulted him on April 15, 1970, and that he took a medical history from him, heard his complaints about his back and facial pain, and discovered that he had high blood pressure. The physician found respondent, subjectively, "in great discomfort." Respondent in fact underwent surgery for a herniated disc on August 17.

The jury found respondent guilty on both counts of the information. He received a sentence of not less than six nor more than nine years. His conviction was affirmed *per curiam* by the Supreme Court of Connecticut. That court noted the absence of an objection to Glover's in-court identification and concluded that respondent "has not shown that substantial injustice resulted from the admission of this evidence." Under Connecticut law, substantial injustice must be shown before a claim of error not made or passed on by the trial court will be considered on appeal.

---

[4] Respondent testified: "Lots of times I have been there before in that building." He also testified that Mrs. Ramsey was a friend of his wife, that her apartment was the only one in the building he ever visited, and that he and his family, consisting of his wife and five children, did not live there but at 453 Albany Avenue, Hartford.

Fourteen months later, respondent filed a petition for habeas corpus in the United States District Court for the District of Connecticut. He alleged that the admission of the identification testimony at his state trial deprived him of due process of law to which he was entitled under the Fourteenth Amendment. The District Court, by an unreported written opinion based on the court's review of the state trial transcript, dismissed respondent's petition. On appeal, the United States Court of Appeals for the Second Circuit reversed, with instructions to issue the writ unless the State gave notice of a desire to retry respondent and the new trial occurred within a reasonable time to be fixed by the District Judge.

In brief summary, the court felt that evidence as to the photograph should have been excluded, regardless of reliability, because the examination of the single photograph was unnecessary and suggestive. And, in the court's view, the evidence was unreliable in any event. We granted certiorari.

## II

*Stovall v. Denno*, decided in 1967, concerned a petitioner who had been convicted in a New York court of murder. He was arrested the day following the crime and was taken by the police to a hospital where the victim's wife, also wounded in the assault, was a patient. After observing Stovall and hearing him speak, she identified him as the murderer. She later made an in-court identification. On federal habeas, Stovall claimed the identification testimony violated his Fifth, Sixth, and Fourteenth Amendment rights. The District Court dismissed the petition, and the Court of Appeals, en banc, affirmed. This Court also affirmed. On the identification issue, the Court reviewed the practice of showing a suspect singly for purposes of identification, and the claim that this was so unnecessarily suggestive and conducive to irreparable mistaken identification that it constituted a denial of due process of law. The Court noted that the practice "has been widely condemned," but it concluded that "a claimed violation of due process of law in the conduct of a confrontation depends on the totality of the circumstances surrounding it." In that case, showing Stovall to the victim's spouse "was imperative." The Court then quoted the observations of the Court of Appeals, to the effect that the spouse was the only person who could possibly exonerate the accused; that the hospital was not far from the courthouse and jail; that no one knew how long she might live; that she was not able to visit the jail; and that taking Stovall to the hospital room was the only feasible procedure, and, under the circumstances, "the usual police station line-up . . . was out of the question."

*Neil v. Biggers*, decided in 1972, concerned a respondent who had been convicted in a Tennessee court of rape, on evidence consisting in part of the victim's visual and voice identification of Biggers at a station-house showup seven months after the crime. The victim had been in her assailant's presence for some time and had directly observed him indoors and under a full moon outdoors. She testified that she had "no doubt" that Biggers was her assailant. She previously had given the police a description of the assailant. She had made no identification of others presented at previous showups, lineups, or through photographs. On federal habeas, the District Court held that the confrontation was so suggestive as to violate due process. The Court of Appeals affirmed. This Court reversed on that issue, and held that the evidence properly had been allowed to go to the jury. The Court reviewed *Stovall* and certain later cases where it had considered the scope of due process protection against the admission of evidence derived from suggestive identification procedures, namely, *Simmons v. United States*, 390 U.S. 377 (1968) [and] *Foster v. California*, 394 U.S. 440 (1969).[8] The Court concluded that general guidelines emerged from these cases "as to the relationship between suggestiveness and misidentification." The "admission of evidence of a showup without

more does not violate due process." The Court expressed concern about the lapse of seven months between the crime and the confrontation and observed that this "would be a seriously negative factor in most cases." The "central question," however, was "whether under the 'totality of the circumstances' the identification was reliable even though the confrontation procedure was suggestive." Applying that test, the Court found "no substantial likelihood of misidentification. The evidence was properly allowed to go to the jury."

*Biggers* well might be seen to provide an unambiguous answer to the question before us: The admission of testimony concerning a suggestive and unnecessary identification procedure does not violate due process so long as the identification possesses sufficient aspects of reliability.[9] In one passage, however, the Court observed that the challenged procedure occurred pre-*Stovall* and that a strict rule would make little sense with regard to a confrontation that preceded the Court's first indication that a suggestive procedure might lead to the exclusion of evidence.

---

[8] *Simmons* involved photographs, mostly group ones, shown to bank-teller victims who made in-court identifications. The Court discussed the "chance of misidentification," declined to prohibit the procedure "either in the exercise of our supervisory power or, still less, as a matter of constitutional requirement," and held that each case must be considered on its facts and that a conviction would be set aside only if the identification procedure "was so impermissibly suggestive as to give rise to a very substantial likelihood of irreparable misidentification." The out-of-court identification was not offered. Mr. Justice Black would have denied Simmons' due process claim as frivolous.

*Foster* concerned repeated confrontations between a suspect and the manager of an office that had been robbed. At a second lineup, but not at the first and not at a personal one-to-one confrontation, the manager identified the suspect. At trial he testified as to this and made an in-court identification. The Court reaffirmed the *Stovall* standard and then concluded that the repeated confrontations were so suggestive as to violate due process. The case was remanded for the state courts to consider the question of harmless error.

---

[9] Mr. Justice Marshall argues in dissent that our cases have "established two different due process tests for two very different situations." Pretrial identifications are to be covered by *Stovall*, which is said to require exclusion of evidence concerning unnecessarily suggestive pretrial identifications without regard to reliability. In-court identifications, on the other hand, are to be governed by *Simmons* and admissibility turns on reliability. The Court's cases are sorted into one category or the other. *Biggers*, which clearly adopts the reliability of the identification as the guiding factor in the admissibility of both pretrial and in-court identifications, is condemned for mixing the two lines and for adopting a uniform rule.

Although it must be acknowledged that our cases are not uniform in their emphasis, they hardly suggest the formal structure the dissent would impose on them. If our cases truly established two different rules, one might expect at some point at least passing reference to the fact. There is none. And if *Biggers* departed so grievously from the past cases, it is surprising that there was not at least some mention of the point in Mr. Justice Brennan's dissent. In fact, the cases are not so readily sorted as the dissent suggests. Although *Foster* involved both in-court and out-of-court identifications, the Court seemed to apply only a single standard for both. Thus, *Biggers* is not properly seen as a departure from the past cases, but as a synthesis of them.

One perhaps might argue that, by implication, the Court suggested that a different rule could apply post-*Stovall*. The question before us, then, is simply whether the *Biggers* analysis applies to post-*Stovall* confrontations as well as to those pre-*Stovall*.

### III

In the present case the District Court observed that the "sole evidence tying Brathwaite to the possession and sale of the heroin consisted in his identifications by the police undercover agent, Jimmy Glover." On the constitutional issue, the court stated that the first inquiry was whether the police used an impermissibly suggestive procedure in obtaining the out-of-court identification. If so, the second inquiry is whether, under all the circumstances, that suggestive procedure gave rise to a substantial likelihood of irreparable misidentification. *Biggers* and *Simmons* were cited. The court noted that in the Second Circuit, its controlling court, it was clear that "this type of identification procedure [display of a single photograph] is impermissibly suggestive," and turned to the second inquiry. The factors *Biggers* specified for consideration were recited and applied. The court concluded that there was no substantial likelihood of irreparable misidentification. It referred to the facts: Glover was within two feet of the seller. The duration of the confrontation was at least a "couple of minutes." There was natural light from a window or skylight and there was adequate light to see clearly in the hall. Glover "certainly was paying attention to identify the seller." He was a trained police officer who realized that later he would have to find and arrest the person with whom he was dealing. He gave a detailed description to D'Onofrio. The reliability of this description was supported by the fact that it enabled D'Onofrio to pick out a single photograph that was thereafter positively identified by Glover. Only two days elapsed between the crime and the photographic identification. Despite the fact that another eight months passed before the in-court identification, Glover had "no doubt" that Brathwaite was the person who had sold him heroin.

The Court of Appeals confirmed that the exhibition of the single photograph to Glover was "impermissibly suggestive," and felt that, in addition, "it was unnecessarily so." There was no emergency and little urgency. The court said that prior to the decision in *Biggers*, except in cases of harmless error, "a conviction secured as the result of admitting an identification obtained by impermissibly suggestive and unnecessary measures could not stand." It noted what it felt might be opposing inferences to

be drawn from passages in *Biggers*, but concluded that the case preserved the principle "requiring the exclusion of identifications resulting from 'unnecessarily suggestive confrontation'" in post-*Stovall* situations. The court also concluded that for post-*Stovall* identifications, *Biggers* had not changed the existing rule. Thus: "Evidence of an identification unnecessarily obtained by impermissibly suggestive means must be excluded under *Stovall*. . . . No rules less stringent than these can force police administrators and prosecutors to adopt procedures that will give fair assurance against the awful risks of misidentification." Finally, the court said, even if this conclusion were wrong, the writ, nevertheless, should issue. It took judicial notice that on May 5, 1970, sunset at Hartford was at 7:53 p.m. It characterized Glover's duty as an undercover agent as one "to cause arrests to be made," and his description of the suspect as one that "could have applied to hundreds of Hartford black males." The in-court identification had "little meaning," for Brathwaite was at the counsel table. The fact that respondent was arrested in the very apartment where the sale was made was subject to a "not implausible" explanation from the respondent, "although evidently not credited by the jury." And the court was troubled by "the long and unexplained delay" in the arrest. It was too great a danger that the respondent was convicted because he was a man D'Onofrio had previously observed near the scene, was thought to be a likely offender, and was arrested when he was known to be in Mrs. Ramsey's apartment, rather than because Glover "really remembered him as the seller."

### IV

Petitioner at the outset acknowledges that "the procedure in the instant case was suggestive [because only one photograph was used] and unnecessary" [because there was no emergency or exigent circumstance]. The respondent, in agreement with the Court of Appeals, proposes a *per se* rule of exclusion that he claims is dictated by the demands of the Fourteenth Amendment's guarantee of due process. He rightly observes that this is the first case in which this Court has had occasion to rule upon strictly post-*Stovall* out-of-court identification evidence of the challenged kind.

Since the decision in *Biggers*, the Courts of Appeals appear to have developed at least two approaches to such evidence. The first, or *per se* approach, employed by the Second Circuit in the present case, focuses on the procedures employed and requires exclusion of the out-of-court identification evidence, without regard to reliability, whenever it has been obtained through unnecessarily suggested confrontation procedures.[10] The justifications advanced are the elimination of evidence of uncertain reliability, deterrence of the police and prosecutors, and the stated "fair assurance against the awful risks of misidentification."

The second, or more lenient, approach is one that continues to rely on the totality of the circumstances. It permits the admission of the confrontation evidence if, despite the suggestive aspect, the out-of-court identification possesses certain features of reliability. Its adherents feel that the *per se* approach is not mandated by the Due Process Clause of the Fourteenth Amendment. This second approach, in contrast to the other, is ad hoc and serves to limit the societal costs imposed by a sanction that excludes relevant evidence from consideration and evaluation by the trier of fact.

There are, of course, several interests to be considered and taken into account. The driving force behind *Wade, Gilbert*, and *Stovall*, all decided on the same day, was the Court's concern with the problems of eyewitness identification. Usually the witness must testify about an encounter with a total stranger under circumstances of emergency or emotional stress. The witness' recollection of the stranger can be distorted easily by the circumstances or by later actions of the police. Thus, *Wade* and its companion cases reflect the concern that the jury not hear eyewitness testimony unless that evidence has aspects of reliability. It must be observed that both approaches before us are responsive to this concern. The *per se* rule, however, goes too far since its application automatically and peremptorily, and without consideration of alleviating factors, keeps evidence from the jury that is reliable and relevant.

The second factor is deterrence. Although the *per se* approach has the more significant deterrent effect, the totality approach also has an influence on police behavior. The police will guard against unnecessarily suggestive procedures under the totality rule, as well as the *per se* one, for fear that their actions will lead to the exclusion of identifications as unreliable.[12]

The third factor is the effect on the administration of justice. Here the *per se* approach suffers serious drawbacks. Since it denies the trier reliable evidence, it may result, on occasion, in the guilty going free. Also, because of its rigidity, the *per se* approach may make error by the trial judge more likely than the totality approach. And in those cases in which the admission of identification evidence is error under the *per se* approach but not under the totality approach—cases in which the identification is reliable despite an unnecessarily suggestive identification procedure—reversal is a Draconian sanction.[13] Certainly, inflexible rules of exclusion that may frustrate rather than promote justice have not been viewed recently by this Court with unlimited enthusiasm.

We therefore conclude that reliability is the linchpin in determining the admissibility of identification testimony for both pre- and post-*Stovall* confrontations. The factors to be considered are set out in *Biggers*. These include the opportunity of the witness to view the criminal at the time of the crime, the witness' degree of attention, the accuracy of his prior description of the criminal, the level of certainty demonstrated at the confrontation, and the time between the crime and the confrontation. Against these factors is to be weighed the corrupting effect of the suggestive identification itself.

V

We turn, then, to the facts of this case and apply the analysis:

1. The opportunity to view. Glover testified that for two to three minutes he stood at the apartment door, within two feet of the respondent. The door opened twice, and each time the man stood at the door. The moments passed, the conversation took place, and payment was made. Glover looked directly at his vendor. It was near sunset, to be sure, but the sun had not yet set, so it was not dark or even dusk or twilight. Natural light from outside

---

[10] Although the *per se* approach demands the exclusion of testimony concerning unnecessarily suggestive identifications, it does permit the admission of testimony concerning a subsequent identification, including an in-court identification, if the subsequent identification is determined to be reliable. The totality approach, in contrast, is simpler: if the challenged identification is reliable, then testimony as to it and any identification in its wake is admissible.

[12] The interest in obtaining convictions of the guilty also urges the police to adopt procedures that show the resulting identification to be accurate. Suggestive procedures often will vitiate the weight of the evidence at trial and the jury may tend to discount such evidence.

[13] Unlike a warrantless search, a suggestive pre-indictment identification procedure does not in itself intrude upon a constitutionally protected interest. Thus, considerations urging the exclusion of evidence deriving from a constitutional violation do not bear on the instant problem.

entered the hallway through a window. There was natural light, as well, from inside the apartment.

2. The degree of attention. Glover was not a casual or passing observer, as is so often the case with eyewitness identification. Trooper Glover was a trained police officer on duty—and specialized and dangerous duty—when he called at the third floor of 201 Westland in Hartford on May 5, 1970. Glover himself was a Negro and unlikely to perceive only general features of "hundreds of Hartford black males," as the Court of Appeals stated. It is true that Glover's duty was that of ferreting out narcotics offenders and that he would be expected in his work to produce results. But it is also true that, as a specially trained, assigned, and experienced officer, he could be expected to pay scrupulous attention to detail, for he knew that subsequently he would have to find and arrest his vendor. In addition, he knew that his claimed observations would be subject later to close scrutiny and examination at any trial.

3. The accuracy of the description. Glover's description was given to D'Onofrio within minutes after the transaction. It included the vendor's race, his height, his build, the color and style of his hair, and the high cheekbone facial feature. It also included clothing the vendor wore. No claim has been made that respondent did not possess the physical characteristics so described. D'Onofrio reacted positively at once. Two days later, when Glover was alone, he viewed the photograph D'Onofrio produced and identified its subject as the narcotics seller.

4. The witness' level of certainty. There is no dispute that the photograph in question was that of respondent. Glover, in response to a question whether the photograph was that of the person from whom he made the purchase, testified: "There is no question whatsoever." This positive assurance was repeated.

5. The time between the crime and the confrontation. Glover's description of his vendor was given to D'Onofrio within minutes of the crime. The photographic identification took place only two days later. We do not have here the passage of weeks or months between the crime and the viewing of the photograph.

These indicators of Glover's ability to make an accurate identification are hardly outweighed by the corrupting effect of the challenged identification itself. Although identifications arising from single-photograph displays may be viewed in general with suspicion, we find in the instant case little pressure on the witness to acquiesce in the suggestion that such a display entails. D'Onofrio had left the photograph at Glover's office and was not present when Glover first viewed it two days after the event. There thus was little urgency and Glover could view the

photograph at his leisure. And since Glover examined the photograph alone, there was no coercive pressure to make an identification arising from the presence of another. The identification was made in circumstances allowing care and reflection.

Although it plays no part in our analysis, all this assurance as to the reliability of the identification is hardly undermined by the facts that respondent was arrested in the very apartment where the sale had taken place, and that he acknowledged his frequent visits to that apartment.

Surely, we cannot say that under all the circumstances of this case there is "a very substantial likelihood of irreparable misidentification." Short of that point, such evidence is for the jury to weigh. We are content to rely upon the good sense and judgment of American juries, for evidence with some element of untrustworthiness is customary grist for the jury mill. Juries are not so susceptible that they cannot measure intelligently the weight of identification testimony that has some questionable feature.

Of course, it would have been better had D'Onofrio presented Glover with a photographic array including "so far as practicable . . . a reasonable number of persons similar to any person then suspected whose likeness is included in the array." Model Code, § 160.2(2). The use of that procedure would have enhanced the force of the identification at trial and would have avoided the risk that the evidence would be excluded as unreliable. But we are not disposed to view D'Onofrio's failure as one of constitutional dimension to be enforced by a rigorous and unbending exclusionary rule. The defect, if there be one, goes to weight and not to substance.

The judgment of the Court of Appeals is reversed.

Mr. Justice STEVENS, concurring.

While I join the Court's opinion, I would emphasize two points.

First, as I indicated in my opinion in *United States ex rel. Kirby v. Sturges*, 510 F.2d 397, 405-406 (CA7 1975), the arguments in favor of fashioning new rules to minimize the danger of convicting the innocent on the basis of unreliable eyewitness testimony carry substantial force. Nevertheless, for the reasons stated in that opinion, as well as those stated by the Court today. I am persuaded that this rule making function can be performed "more effectively by the legislative process than by a somewhat clumsy judicial fiat," and that the Federal Constitution does not foreclose experimentation by the States in the development of such rules.

Second, in evaluating the admissibility of particular identification testimony it is sometimes difficult to put other evidence of guilt entirely to one side.[*] Mr. Justice Blackmun's opinion for the Court carefully avoids this pitfall and correctly relies only on appropriate indicia of the reliability of the identification itself. Although I consider the factual question in this case extremely close, I am persuaded that the Court has resolved it properly.

Mr. Justice MARSHALL, with whom Mr. Justice BRENNAN joins, dissenting.

Today's decision can come as no surprise to those who have been watching the Court dismantle the protections against mistaken eyewitness testimony erected a decade ago in *Wade, Gilbert*, and *Stovall*. But it is still distressing to see the Court virtually ignore the teaching of experience embodied in those decisions and blindly uphold the conviction of a defendant who may well be innocent.

I

*Stovall*, while holding that the *Wade* prophylactic rules were not retroactive, was decided at the same time and reflects the same concerns about the reliability of identification testimony. *Stovall* recognized that, regardless of Sixth Amendment principles, "the conduct of a confrontation" may be "so unnecessarily suggestive and conducive to irreparable mistaken identification" as to deny due process of law. The pretrial confrontation in *Stovall* was plainly suggestive,[2] and evidence of it was introduced at trial along with the witness' in-court identification. The

---

[*] In this case, for example, the fact that the defendant was a regular visitor to the apartment where the drug transaction occurred tends to confirm his guilt. In the *Kirby* case, where the conviction was for robbery, the fact that papers from the victim's wallet were found in the possession of the defendant made it difficult to question the reliability of the identification. These facts should not, however, be considered to support the admissibility of eyewitness testimony when applying the criteria identified in *Neil v. Biggers*. Properly analyzed, however, such facts would be relevant to a question whether error, if any, in admitting identification testimony was harmless.

[2] The accused, a Negro, was brought handcuffed by seven white police officers and employees of the District Attorney to the hospital room of the only witness to a murder. As the Court said of this encounter: "It is hard to imagine a situation more clearly conveying the suggestion to the witness that the one presented is believed to be guilty by the police."

Court ruled that there had been no violation of due process, however, because the unusual necessity for the procedure[3] outweighed the danger of suggestion.

The development of due process protections against mistaken identification evidence, begun in *Stovall*, was continued in *Simmons v. United States*, 390 U.S. 377 (1968). There, the Court developed a different rule to deal with the admission of in-court identification testimony that the accused claimed had been fatally tainted by a previous suggestive confrontation. In *Simmons*, the exclusionary effect of *Stovall* had already been accomplished, since the prosecution made no use of the suggestive confrontation. *Simmons*, therefore, did not deal with the constitutionality of the pretrial identification procedure. The only question was the impact of the Due Process Clause on an in-court identification that was not itself unnecessarily suggestive. *Simmons* held that due process was violated by the later identification if the pretrial procedure had been "so impermissibly suggestive as to give rise to a very substantial likelihood of irreparable misidentification." This test focused, not on the necessity for the challenged pretrial procedure, but on the degree of suggestiveness that it entailed. In applying this test, the Court understandably considered the circumstances surrounding the witnesses' initial opportunity to view the crime. Finding that any suggestion in the pretrial confrontation had not affected the fairness of the in-court identification, *Simmons* rejected petitioner's due process attack on his conviction.

Thus, *Stovall* and *Simmons* established two different due process tests for two very different situations. Where the prosecution sought to use evidence of a questionable pretrial identification, *Stovall* required its exclusion, because due process had been violated by the confrontation, unless the necessity for the unduly suggestive procedure outweighed its potential for generating an irreparably mistaken identification. The *Simmons* test, on the other hand, was directed to ascertaining due process violations in the introduction of in-court identification testimony that the defendant claimed was tainted by pretrial procedures. In the latter situation, a court could consider the reliability of the identification under all the circumstances.

The Court inexplicably seemed to erase the distinction between *Stovall* and *Simmons* situations in

---

[3] The police reasonably feared that the witness might die before any less suggestive confrontation could be arranged.

*Neil v. Biggers.* In *Biggers* there was a pretrial confrontation that was clearly both suggestive and unnecessary.[6] Evidence of this, together with an in-court identification, was admitted at trial. *Biggers* was, in short, a case plainly cast in the *Stovall* mold. Yet the Court, without explanation or apparent recognition of the distinction, applied the *Simmons* test. The Court stated: "[T]he primary evil to be avoided is 'a very substantial likelihood of irreparable misidentification.' It is the likelihood of misidentification which violates a defendant's right to due process. . . ." While this statement accurately describes the lesson of *Simmons*, it plainly ignores the teaching of *Stovall* and *Foster* that an unnecessarily suggestive pretrial confrontation itself violates due process.

## II

Apparently, the Court does not consider *Biggers* controlling in this case. I entirely agree, since I believe that *Biggers* was wrongly decided. The Court, however, concludes that *Biggers* is distinguishable because it, like the identification decisions that preceded it, involved a pre-*Stovall* confrontation, and because a paragraph in *Biggers* itself, seems to distinguish between pre- and post-*Stovall* confrontations. Accordingly, in determining the admissibility of the post-*Stovall* identification in this case, the Court considers two alternatives, a *per se* exclusionary rule and a totality-of-the-circumstances approach. The Court weighs three factors in deciding that the totality approach, which is essentially the test used in *Biggers*, should be applied. In my view, the Court wrongly evaluates the impact of these factors.

First, the Court acknowledges that one of the factors, deterrence of police use of unnecessarily suggestive identification procedures, favors the *per se* rule. Indeed, it does so heavily, for such a rule would make it unquestionably clear to the police they must never use a suggestive procedure when a fairer alternative is available. I have no doubt that conduct would quickly conform to the rule.

Second, the Court gives passing consideration to the dangers of eyewitness identification recognized in the *Wade* trilogy. It concludes, however, that the

grave risk of error does not justify adoption of the *per se* approach because that would too often result in exclusion of relevant evidence. In my view, this conclusion totally ignores the lessons of *Wade*. The dangers of mistaken identification are, as *Stovall* held, simply too great to permit unnecessarily suggestive identifications. Neither *Biggers* nor the Court's opinion today points to any contrary empirical evidence. Studies since *Wade* have only reinforced the validity of its assessment of the dangers of identification testimony. While the Court is "content to rely on the good sense and judgment of American juries," the impetus for *Stovall* and *Wade* was repeated miscarriages of justice resulting from juries' willingness to credit inaccurate eyewitness testimony.

Finally, the Court errs in its assessment of the relative impact of the two approaches on the administration of justice. The Court relies most heavily on this factor, finding that "reversal is a Draconian sanction" in cases where the identification is reliable despite an unnecessarily suggestive procedure used to obtain it. Relying on little more than a strong distaste for "inflexible rules of exclusion," the Court rejects the *per se* test. In so doing, the Court disregards two significant distinctions between the *per se* rule advocated in this case and the exclusionary remedies for certain other constitutional violations.

First, the *per se* rule here is not "inflexible." Where evidence is suppressed, for example, as the fruit of an unlawful search, it may well be forever lost to the prosecution. Identification evidence, however, can by its very nature be readily and effectively reproduced. The in-court identification, permitted under *Wade* and *Simmons* if it has a source independent of an uncounseled or suggestive procedure, is one example. Similarly, when a prosecuting attorney learns that there has been a suggestive confrontation, he can easily arrange another lineup conducted under scrupulously fair conditions. Since the same factors are evaluated in applying both the Court's totality test and the *Wade-Simmons* independent-source inquiry, any identification which is "reliable" under the Court's test will support admission of evidence concerning such a fairly conducted lineup. The evidence of an additional, properly conducted confrontation will be more persuasive to a jury, thereby increasing the chance of a justified conviction where a reliable identification was tainted by a suggestive confrontation. At the same time, however, the effect of an unnecessarily suggestive identification—which has no value whatsoever in the law enforcement process—will be completely eliminated.

---

[6] "The showup itself consisted of two detectives walking respondent past the victim." The police also ordered respondent to repeat the words used by the criminal. Inadequate efforts were made to secure participants for a lineup, and there was no pressing need to use a showup.

Second, other exclusionary rules have been criticized for preventing jury consideration of relevant and usually reliable evidence in order to serve interest unrelated to guilt or innocence, such as discouraging illegal searches or denial of counsel. Suggestively obtained eyewitness testimony is excluded, in contrast, precisely because of its unreliability and concomitant irrelevance. Its exclusion both protects the integrity of the truth-seeking function of the trial and discourages police use of needlessly inaccurate and ineffective investigatory methods.

Indeed, impermissibly suggestive identifications are not merely worthless law enforcement tools. They pose a grave threat to society at large in a more direct way than most governmental disobedience of the law. For if the police and the public erroneously conclude, on the basis of an unnecessarily suggestive confrontation, that the right man has been caught and convicted, the real outlaw must still remain at large. Law enforcement has failed in its primary function and has left society unprotected from the depredations of an active criminal.

For these reasons, I conclude that adoption of the *per se* rule would enhance, rather than detract from, the effective administration of justice. In my view, the Court's totality test will allow seriously unreliable and misleading evidence to be put before juries. Equally important, it will allow dangerous criminals to remain on the streets while citizens assume that police action has given them protection. According to my calculus, all three of the factors upon which the Court relies point to acceptance of the *per se* approach.

### III

Despite my strong disagreement with the Court over the proper standards to be applied in this case, I am pleased that its application of the totality test does recognize the continuing vitality of *Stovall*. In assessing the reliability of the identification, the Court mandates weighing "the corrupting effect of the suggestive identification itself" against the "indicators of [a witness'] ability to make an accurate identification." The Court holds, as *Neil v. Biggers* failed to, that a due process identification inquiry must take account of the suggestiveness of a confrontation and the likelihood that it led to misidentification, as recognized in *Stovall* and *Wade*. Thus, even if a witness did have an otherwise adequate opportunity to view a criminal, the later use of a highly suggestive identification procedure can render his testimony inadmissible. Indeed, it is my view that, assuming applicability of the totality test enunciated by the Court, the facts of the present case require that result.

I consider first the opportunity that Officer Glover had to view the suspect. Careful review of the record shows that he could see the heroin seller only for the time it took to speak three sentences of four or five short words, to hand over some money, and later after the door reopened, to receive the drugs in return. The entire face-to-face transaction could have taken as little as 15 or 20 seconds. But during this time, Glover's attention was not focused exclusively on the seller's face. He observed that the door was opened 12 to 18 inches, that there was a window in the room behind the door, and, most importantly, that there was a woman standing behind the man. Glover was, of course, also concentrating on the details of the transaction he must have looked away from the seller's face to hand him the money and receive the drugs. The observation during the conversation thus may have been as brief as 5 or 10 seconds.

As the Court notes, Glover was a police officer trained in and attentive to the need for making accurate identifications. Nevertheless, both common sense and scholarly study indicate that while a trained observer such as a police officer "is somewhat less likely to make an erroneous identification than the average untrained observer, the mere fact that he has been so trained is no guarantee that he is correct in a specific case. His identification testimony should be scrutinized just as carefully as that of the normal witness." Moreover, "identifications made by policemen in highly competitive activities, such as undercover narcotic agents . . ., should be scrutinized with special care." Yet it is just such a searching inquiry that the Court fails to make here.

Another factor on which the Court relies—the witness' degree of certainty in making the identification—is worthless as an indicator that he is correct. Even if Glover had been unsure initially about his identification of respondent's picture, by the time he was called at trial to present a key piece of evidence for the State that paid his salary, it is impossible to imagine his responding negatively to such questions as "is there any doubt in your mind whatsoever" that the identification was correct. As the Court noted in *Wade*: "It is a matter of common experience that, once a witness has picked out the accused at the [pretrial confrontation], he is not likely to go back on his word later on."

Next, the Court finds that because the identification procedure took place two days after the crime, its reliability is enhanced. While such temporal proximity makes the identification more reliable than one occurring months later, the fact is that the greatest memory loss occurs within hours after an event.

After that, the drop-off continues much more slowly. Thus, the reliability of an identification is increased only if it was made within several hours of the crime. If the time gap is any greater, reliability necessarily decreases.

Finally, the Court makes much of the fact that Glover gave a description of the seller to D'Onofrio shortly after the incident. Despite the Court's assertion that because "Glover himself was a Negro and unlikely to perceive only general features of 'hundreds of Hartford black males,' as the Court of Appeals stated," the description given by Glover was actually no more than a general summary of the seller's appearance. We may discount entirely the seller's clothing, for that was of no significance later in the proceeding. Indeed, to the extent that Glover noticed clothes, his attention was diverted from the seller's face. Otherwise, Glover merely described vaguely the seller's height, skin color, hairstyle, and build. He did say that the seller had "high cheekbones," but there is no other mention of facial features, nor even an estimate of age. Conspicuously absent is any indication that the seller was a native of the West Indies, certainly something which a member of the black community could immediately recognize from both appearance and accent.[12]

From all of this, I must conclude that the evidence of Glover's ability to make an accurate identification is far weaker than the Court finds it. In contrast, the procedure used to identify respondent was both extraordinarily suggestive and strongly conducive to error. In dismissing "the corrupting effect of the suggestive identification" procedure here, the Court virtually grants the police license to convict the innocent. By displaying a single photograph of respondent to the witness Glover under the circumstances in this record almost everything that could have been done wrong was done wrong.

In the first place, there was no need to use a photograph at all. Because photos are static, two-dimensional, and often outdated, they are "clearly inferior in reliability" to corporeal procedures. While the use of photographs is justifiable and often essential where the police have no knowledge of an offender's identity, the poor reliability of photos makes their use inexcusable where any other means of identification is available. Here, since Detective D'Onofrio believed that he knew the seller's identity, further investigation without resort to a photographic showup was easily possible. With little inconvenience, a corporeal lineup including Brathwaite might have been arranged.[13] Properly conducted, such a procedure would have gone far to remove any doubt about the fairness and accuracy of the identification.[14]

The use of a single picture (or the display of a single live suspect, for that matter) is a grave error, of course, because it dramatically suggests to the witness that the person shown must be the culprit. Why else would the police choose the person? And it is deeply ingrained in human nature to agree with the expressed opinions of others — particularly others who should be more knowledgeable — when making a difficult decision. In this case, moreover, the pressure was not limited to that inherent in the display of a single photograph. Glover, the identifying witness, was a state police officer on special assignment. He knew that D'Onofrio, an experienced Hartford narcotics detective, presumably familiar with local drug operations, believed respondent to be the seller. There was at work, then, both loyalty to another police officer and deference to a better-informed colleague.[16] Finally, of course, there was Glover's

---

[12] Brathwaite had come to the United States from his native Barbados as an adult. It is also noteworthy that the informant who witnessed the transaction and was described by Glover as "trustworthy," disagreed with Glover's recollection of the event. The informant testified that it was a woman in the apartment who took the money from Glover and gave him the drugs in return.

[13] Indeed, the police carefully staged Brathwaite's arrest in the same apartment that was used for the sale, indicating that they were fully capable of keeping track of his whereabouts and using this information in their investigation.

[14] It should be noted that this was not a case where the witness knew the person whom he saw committing a crime, or had an unusually long time to observe the criminal, so that the identification procedure was merely used to confirm the suspect's identity. Cf. *Wade* (White, J., dissenting). For example, had this been an ongoing narcotics investigation in which Glover had met the seller a number of times, the procedure would have been less objectionable.

[16] In fact, the trial record indicates that D'Onofrio was remarkably ill-informed, although it does not appear that Glover knew this at the time of the identification. While the Court is impressed by D'Onofrio's immediate response to Glover's description, that cannot alter the fact that the detective, who had not witnessed the transaction, acted on a wild guess that respondent was the seller. D'Onofrio had seen respondent only "[s]everal times, mostly in his vehi-

knowledge that without an identification and arrest, government funds used to buy heroin had been wasted.

The Court discounts this overwhelming evidence of suggestiveness, however. It reasons that because D'Onofrio was not present when Glover viewed the photograph, there was "little pressure on the witness to acquiesce in the suggestion." That conclusion blinks psychological reality. There is no doubt in my mind that even in D'Onofrio's absence, a clear and powerful message was telegraphed to Glover as he looked at respondent's photograph. He was emphatically told that "*this* is the man," and he responded by identifying respondent then and at trial "whether or not he was in fact 'the man.'" *Foster v. California.*[18]

cle." There was no evidence that respondent was even a suspected narcotics dealer, and D'Onofrio thought that the drugs had been purchased at a different apartment from the one Glover actually went to. The identification of respondent provides a perfect example of the investigator and the witness bolstering each other's inadequate knowledge to produce a seemingly accurate but worthless identification.

[18] This discussion does not imply any lack of respect for the honesty and dedication of the police. We all share the frailties of human nature that create the problem. Justice Frank O'Connor of the New York Supreme Court decried the dangers of eyewitness testimony in a recent article that began with this caveat:

I must conclude that this record presents compelling evidence that there was "a very substantial likelihood of misidentification" of respondent Brathwaite. The suggestive display of respondent's photograph to the witness Glover likely erased any independent memory that Glover had retained of the seller from his barely adequate opportunity to observe the criminal.

IV

Since I agree with the distinguished panel of the Court of Appeals that the legal standard of *Stovall* should govern this case, but that even if it does not, the facts here reveal a substantial likelihood of misidentification in violation of respondent's right to due process of law, I would affirm the grant of habeas corpus relief. Accordingly, I dissent from the Court's reinstatement of respondent's conviction.

---

"From the vantage point of ten years as District Attorney of Queens County(1956-1966) and six years on the trial bench (1969 to (1974)), the writer holds in high regard the professional competence and personal integrity of most policemen. Laudable instances of police efforts to clear a doubtful suspect are legion. Deliberate, willful efforts to frame or railroad an innocent man are totally unknown, at least to me. Yet, once the best-intentioned officer becomes honestly convinced that he has the right man, human nature being what it is, corners may be cut, some of the niceties forgotten, and serious error committed."

## QUESTIONS AND NOTES

**1.** Do you think that the identification procedure in *Brathwaite* was unnecessarily suggestive? If so, why does the Court allow it?

**2.** Are unnecessarily suggestive procedures necessarily *excessively* suggestive? Was the *Neil v. Biggers* procedure excessively suggestive?

**3.** Is the dissent correct in asserting that unnecessarily suggestive identifications can be overcome with scrupulously fair identification procedures? Could that have been done in *Foster* (fn. 8)?

**4.** If Glover had been allowed to identify Brathwaite at trial, but not introduce the arguably tainted identification, how do you suppose that the defense attorney would have cross-examined him?

**5.** If you answered question 4 by saying that the attorney would have confronted him with his prior tainted identification, does that not establish the wisdom of the Court in allowing the arguably tainted identification to be introduced in the first place?

# 21.

# ATTENUATION

## A. Fourth Amendment

In the cases in this chapter, the presence of a constitutional violation is not in issue. Such a violation has either been established, conceded, or assumed. The question upon which we now focus is whether notwithstanding the initial violation, the evidence is nevertheless admissible because it was obtained by means sufficiently attenuated to dissipate the unit.

### Wong Sun v. United States
### 371 U.S. 471 (1963)

Mr. Justice BRENNAN delivered the opinion of the Court.

About 2 a.m. on the morning of June 4, 1959, federal narcotics agents in San Francisco, after having had one Hom Way under surveillance for six weeks, arrested him and found heroin in his possession. Hom Way, who had not before been an informant, stated after his arrest that he had bought an ounce of heroin the night before from one known to him only as 'Blackie Toy,' proprietor of a laundry on Leavenworth Street.

About 6 a.m. that morning six or seven federal agents went to a laundry at 1733 Leavenworth Street. The sign above the door of this establishment said "Oye's Laundry." It was operated by the petitioner James Wah Toy. There is, however, nothing in the record which identifies James Wah Toy and "Blackie Toy" as the same person. The other federal officers remained nearby out of sight while Agent Alton Wong,

who was of Chinese ancestry, rang the bell. When petitioner Toy appeared and opened the door, Agent Wong told him that he was calling for laundry and dry cleaning. Toy replied that he didn't open until 8 o'clock and told the agent to come back at that time. Toy started to close the door. Agent Wong thereupon took his badge from his pocket and said, 'I am a federal narcotics agent.' Toy immediately 'slammed the door and started running' down the hallway through the laundry to his living quarters at the back where his wife and child were sleeping in a bedroom. Agent Wong and the other federal officers broke open the door and followed Toy down the hallway to the living quarters and into the bedroom. Toy reached into a nightstand drawer. Agent Wong thereupon drew his pistol, pulled Toy's hand out of the drawer, placed him under arrest and handcuffed him. There was nothing in the drawer and a search of the premises uncovered no narcotics.

One of the agents said to Toy '. . . [Hom Way]

says he got narcotics from you.' Toy responded, 'No, I haven't been selling any narcotics at all. However, I do know somebody who has.' When asked who that was, Toy said, 'I only know him as Johnny. I don't know his last name.' However, Toy described a house on Eleventh Avenue where he said Johnny lived; he also described a bedroom in the house where he said 'Johnny kept about a piece'[2] of heroin, and where he and Johnny had smoked some of the drug the night before. The agents left immediately for Eleventh Avenue and located the house. They entered and found one Johnny Yee in the bedroom. After a discussion with the agents, Yee took from a bureau drawer several tubes containing in all just less than one ounce of heroin, and surrendered them. Within the hour Yee and Toy were taken to the Office of the Bureau of Narcotics. Yee there stated that the heroin had been brought to him some four days earlier by petitioner Toy and another Chinese known to him only as "Sea Dog."

Toy was questioned as to the identity of "Sea Dog" and said that "Sea Dog" was Wong Sun. Some agents, including Agent Alton Wong, took Toy to Wong Sun's neighborhood where Toy pointed out a multifamily dwelling where he said Wong Sun lived. Agent Wong rang a downstairs door bell and a buzzer sounded, opening the door. The officer identified himself as a narcotics agent to a woman on the landing and asked for Mr. Wong. The woman was the wife of petitioner Wong Sun. She said that Wong Sun was in the back room sleeping. Alton Wong and some six other officers climbed the stairs and entered the apartment. One of the officers went into the back room and brought petitioner Wong Sun from the bedroom in handcuffs. A thorough search of the apartment followed, but no narcotics were discovered.

Petitioner Toy and Johnny Yee were arraigned before a United States Commissioner on June 4 on a complaint charging a violation of 21 U.S.C. § 174. Later that day, each was released on his own recognizance. Petitioner Wong Sun was arraigned on a similar complaint filed the next day and was also released on his own recognizance. Within a few days, both petitioners and Yee were interrogated at the office of the Narcotics Bureau by Agent William Wong, also of Chinese ancestry. The agent advised each of the three of his right to withhold information which might be used against him, and stated to each that he was entitled to the advice of counsel, though it does not appear that any attorney was present during the questioning of any of the three. The officer

also explained to each that no promises or offers of immunity or leniency were being or could be made.

The agent interrogated each of the three separately. After each had been interrogated the agent prepared a statement in English from rough notes. The agent read petitioner Toy's statement to him in English and interpreted certain portions of it for him in Chinese. Toy also read the statement in English aloud to the agent, said there were corrections to be made, and made the corrections in his own hand. Toy would not sign the statement, however; in the agent's words 'he wanted to know first if the other persons involved in the case had signed theirs.' Wong Sun had considerable difficulty understanding the statement in English and the agent restated its substance in Chinese. Wong Sun refused to sign the statement although he admitted the accuracy of its contents.

The Government's evidence tending to prove the petitioners' possession consisted of four items which the trial court admitted over timely objections that they were inadmissible as 'fruits' of unlawful arrests or of attendant searches: (1) the statements made orally by petitioner Toy in his bedroom at the time of his arrest; (2) the heroin surrendered to the agents by Johnny Yee; (3) petitioner Toy's pretrial unsigned statement; and (4) petitioner Wong Sun's similar statement. The dispute below and here has centered around the correctness of the rulings of the trial judge allowing these items in evidence.

The Court of Appeals held that the arrests of both petitioners were illegal because not based on "probable cause' within the meaning of the Fourth Amendment nor reasonable grounds within the meaning of the Narcotic Control Act of 1956. The court said as to Toy's arrest, There is no showing in this case that the agent knew Hom Way to be reliable, and, furthermore, found nothing in the circumstances occurring at Toy's premises that would provide sufficient justification for his arrest without a warrant. As to Wong Sun's arrest, the court said there is no showing that Johnnie Yee was a reliable informer. The Court of Appeals nevertheless held that the four items of proof were not the fruits of the illegal arrests and that they were therefore properly admitted in evidence.

We believe that significant differences between the cases of the two petitioners require separate discussion of each. We shall first consider the case of petitioner Toy.

I

[The Court found that Toy's arrest was unlawful].

---

[2] A "piece" is approximately one ounce.

## II

It is conceded that Toy's declarations in his bedroom are to be excluded if they are held to be fruits of the agents unlawful action. The exclusionary prohibition extends as well to the indirect as the direct products of such invasions. *Silverthorne Lumber Co.* v. *United States*, 251 U.S. 385. Mr. Justice Holmes, speaking for the Court in that case, in holding that the Government might not make use of information obtained during an unlawful search to subpoena from the victims the very documents illegally viewed, expressed succinctly the policy of the broad exclusionary rule:

"The essence of a provision forbidding the acquisition of evidence in a certain way is that not merely evidence so acquired shall not be used before the Court but that it shall not be used at all. Of course this does not mean that the facts thus obtained become sacred and inaccessible. If knowledge of them is gained from an independent source they may be proved like any others, but the knowledge gained by the Government's own wrong cannot be used by it in the way proposed.

[V]erbal evidence which derives so immediately from an unlawful entry and an unauthorized arrest as the officers' action in the present case is no less the 'fruit' of official illegality than the more common tangible fruits of the unwarranted intrusion.

The Government argues that Toy's statements to the officers in his bedroom, although closely consequent upon the invasion which we hold unlawful, were nevertheless admissible because they resulted from 'an intervening independent act of a free will.' This contention, however, takes insufficient account of the circumstances. Six or seven officers had broken the door and followed on Toy's heels into the bedroom where his wife and child were sleeping. He had been almost immediately handcuffed and arrested. Under such circumstances it is unreasonable to infer that Toy's response was sufficiently an act of free will to purge the primary taint of the unlawful invasion.[12]

The Government also contends that Toy's declarations should be admissible because they were ostensibly exculpatory rather than incriminating. There are

---

[12] See Lord Devlin's comment: "It is probable that even today, when there is much less ignorance about these matters than formerly, there is still a general belief that you must answer all questions put to you by a policeman, or at least that it will be the worse for you if you do not." Devlin, The Criminal Prosecution in England (1958), 32.

two answers to this argument. First, the statements soon turned out to be incriminating, for they led directly to the evidence which implicated Toy. Second, when circumstances are shown such as those which induced these declarations, it is immaterial whether the declarations be termed "exculpatory." Thus we find no substantial reason to omit Toy's declarations from the protection of the exclusionary rule.

## III

We now consider whether the exclusion of Toy's declarations requires also the exclusion of the narcotics taken from Yee, to which those declarations led the police. The prosecutor candidly told the trial court that 'we wouldn't have found those drugs except that Mr. Toy helped us to. Hence this is not the case envisioned by this Court where the exclusionary rule has no application because the Government learned of the evidence 'from an independent source, *Silverthorne* nor is this a case in which the connection between the lawless conduct of the police and the discovery of the challenged evidence has become so attenuated as to dissipate the taint. *Nardone* v. *United States*, 308 U.S. 338, 341. We need not hold that all evidence is 'fruit of the poisonous tree' simply because it would not have come to light but for the illegal actions of the police. Rather, the more apt question in such a case is' whether, granting establishment of the primary illegality, the evidence to which instant objection is made has been come at by exploitation of that illegality or instead by means sufficiently distinguishable to be purged of the primary taint. We think it clear that the narcotics were come at by the exploitation of that illegality and hence that they may not be used against Toy.

## IV

It remains only to consider Toy's unsigned statement. We need not decide whether, in light of the fact that Toy was free on his own recognizance when he made the statement, that statement was a fruit of the illegal arrest. Since we have concluded that his declarations in the bedroom and the narcotics surrendered by Yee should not have been admitted in evidence against him, the only proofs remaining to sustain his conviction are his and Wong Sun's unsigned statements. Without scrutinizing the contents of Toy's ambiguous recitals, we conclude that no reference to Toy in Wong Sun's statement constitutes admissible evidence corroborating any admission by Toy. We arrive at this conclusion upon two clear lines of decisions which converge to require it. One line of our decisions establishes that criminal confessions and admissions of guilt require extrinsic corroboration; the other line of precedents holds that an out-of-court declaration made after arrest may not be used at trial against one of the declarant's partners in crime.

Thus as to Toy the only possible source of corroboration is removed and his conviction must be set aside for lack of competent evidence to support it.

### V

We turn now to the case of the other petitioner, Wong Sun. We have no occasion to disagree with the finding of the Court of Appeals that his arrest, also, was without probable cause or reasonable grounds. At all events no evidentiary consequences turn upon that question. For Wong Sun's unsigned confession was not the fruit of that arrest, and was therefore properly admitted at trial. On the evidence that Wong Sun had been released on his own recognizance after a lawful arraignment, and had returned voluntarily several days later to make the statement, we hold that the connection between the arrest and the statement had become so attenuated as to dissipate the taint. *Nardone* v. *United States*, 308 U.S. 338, 341.

We must then consider the admissibility of the narcotics surrendered by Yee. Our holding, supra, that this ounce of heroin was inadmissible against Toy does not compel a like result with respect to Wong Sun. The exclusion of the narcotics as to Toy was required solely by their tainted relationship to information unlawfully obtained from Toy, and not by any official impropriety connected with their surrender by Yee. The seizure of this heroin invaded no right of privacy of person or premises which would entitle Wong Sun to object to its use at his trial.

However, for the reasons that Wong Sun's statement was incompetent to corroborate Toy's admissions contained in Toy's own statement, any references to Wong Sun in Toy's statement were incompetent to corroborate Wong Sun's admissions. Thus, the only competent source of corroboration for Wong Sun's statement was the heroin itself. We cannot be certain, however, on this state of the record, that the trial judge may not also have considered the contents of Toy's statement as a source of corroboration.

We therefore hold that petitioner Wong Sun is also entitled to a new trial.

MR. JUSTICE CLARK, with whom MR. JUSTICE HARLAN, MR. JUSTICE STEWART and MR. JUSTICE WHITE join, dissenting. [The dissenting opinion believed that the arrest was lawful and consequently the evidence was admissible.]

## QUESTIONS AND NOTES

**1.** What does the phrase "so attenuated as to dissipate the taint" mean?

**2.** Upon which of the evidence was the taint dissipated? Upon which was it not dissipated? Why?

**3.** *Toy's* conviction was apparently reversed outright whereas *Wong Sun's* case was remanded for a new trial. Why the distinction?

**4.** In *Taylor*, we see that sometimes even *Miranda* warnings are insufficient to dissipate the taint.

### Taylor v. Alabama
### 457 U.S. 687 (1982)

JUSTICE MARSHALL delivered the opinion of the Court.

This case presents the narrow question whether petitioner's confession should have been suppressed as the fruit of an illegal arrest. The Supreme Court of Alabama held that the evidence was properly admitted. Because the decision below is inconsistent with our decisions in *Dunaway* v. *New York*, 442 U.S. 200 (1979), and *Brown* v. *Illinois*, 422 U.S. 590 (1975), we reserve.

### I

In 1978, a grocery store in Montgomery, Ala., was robbed. There had been a number of robberies in this area and the police had initiated an intensive manhunt in an effort to apprehend the robbers. An individual who was at that time incarcerated on unrelated charges told a police officer that "he had heard that [petitioner] Omar Taylor was involved in the robbery." This individual had never before given similar information to this officer, did not tell the officer where he had heard this information, and did not provide any details of the crime. This tip was insufficient to give the police probable cause to obtain a warrant or to arrest petitioner.

Nonetheless, on the basis of this information, two officers arrested petitioner without a warrant. They told petitioner that he was being arrested in connection with the grocery-store robbery, searched him, and took him to the station for questioning. Petitioner was given the warnings required by *Miranda*. At the station, he was fingerprinted, readvised of his *Miranda* rights, questioned, and placed in a lineup. The victims of the robbery were unable to identify him in the lineup. The police told petitioner that his fingerprints matched those on some grocery items that had been handled by one of the participants in the robbery. After a short visit with his girlfriend and a male companion, petitioner signed a waiver-of-rights form and executed a written confession. The form and the signed confession were admitted into evidence.

Petitioner objected to the admission of this evidence at his trial. He argued that his warrantless arrest was not supported by probable cause, that he had been involuntarily transported to the police station, and that the confession must be suppressed as the fruit of this illegal arrest. The trial court overruled this objection, and petitioner was convicted.

## II

In *Brown* and *Dunaway*, the police arrested suspects without probable cause. The suspects were transported to police headquarters, advised of their *Miranda* rights, and interrogated. They confessed within two hours of their arrest. This Court held that the confessions were not admissible at trial, reasoning that a confession obtained through custodial interrogation after an illegal arrest should be excluded unless intervening events break the causal connection between the illegal arrest and the confession so that the confession is " 'sufficiently an act of free will to purge the primary taint.' " *Brown* (quoting *Wong Sun*). See also *Dunaway*. This Court identified several factors that should be considered in determining whether a confession has been purged of the taint of the illegal arrest: "[t]he temporal proximity of the arrest and the confession, the presence of intervening circumstances, . . . and, particularly, the purpose and flagrancy of the official misconduct." The State bears the burden of proving that a confession is admissible.

In *Brown* and *Dunaway*, this Court firmly established that the fact that the confession may be "voluntary" for purposes of the Fifth Amendment, in

the sense that *Miranda* warnings were given and understood, is not by itself sufficient to purge the taint of the illegal arrest. In this situation, a finding of "voluntariness" for purposes of the Fifth Amendment is merely a threshold requirement for Fourth Amendment analysis. The reason for this approach is clear: "[t]he exclusionary rule, . . . when utilized to effectuate the Fourth Amendment, serves interests and policies that are distinct from those it serves under the Fifth" Amendment. If *Miranda* warnings were viewed as a talisman that cured all Fourth Amendment violations, then the constitutional guarantee against unlawful searches and seizures would be reduced to a mere " 'form of words.' "

This case is a virtual replica of both *Brown* and *Dunaway*. Petitioner was arrested without probable cause in the hope that something would turn up, and he confessed shortly thereafter without any meaningful intervening event. The State's arguments to the contrary are unpersuasive. The State begins by focusing on the temporal proximity of the arrest and the confession. It observes that the length of time between the illegal arrest and the confession was six hours in this case, while in *Brown* and *Dunaway* the incriminating statements were obtained within two hours. However, a difference of a few hours is not significant where, as here, petitioner was in police custody, unrepresented by counsel, and he was questioned on several occasions, finger-printed, and subjected to a lineup. The State has not even demonstrated the amount of this time that was spent in interrogation, arguing only that petitioner "had every opportunity to consider his situation, to organize his thoughts, to contemplate his constitutional rights, and to exercise his free will."

The State points to several intervening events that it argues are sufficient to break the connection between the illegal arrest and petitioner's confession. It observes that petitioner was given *Miranda* warnings three times. As our foregoing discussion of *Brown* and *Dunaway* demonstrates, however, the State's reliance on the giving of *Miranda* warnings is misplaced. The State also observes that petitioner visited with his girlfriend and a male companion before he confessed. This claim fares no better. According to the officer and petitioner, these two visitors were outside the interrogation room where petitioner was being questioned. After petitioner signed a waiver-of-rights form, he was allowed to meet with these visitors. The State fails to explain how this 5- to 10-minute visit, after which petitioner immediately recanted his former statements that he knew nothing about the robbery and signed the confession, could possibly have contributed to his ability to consider carefully and objectively his options and to exercise his free will. This suggestion is particularly dubious in light of petitioner's uncontroverted testimony that his girlfriend was emotionally upset at the time of this visit.[1] If any inference could be drawn, it would be that this visit had just the opposite effect.

The State points to an arrest warrant filed after petitioner had been arrested and while he was being interrogated as another significant "intervening event." While petitioner was in custody, the police determined that the fingerprints on some grocery items matched those that they had taken from petitioner immediately after his arrest. Based on this comparison, an arrest warrant was filed. The filing of this warrant, however, is irrelevant to whether the confession was the fruit of the illegal arrest. This case is not like *Johnson v. Louisiana*, 406 U.S. 356 (1972), where the defendant was brought before a committing Magistrate who advised him of his rights and set bail. Here, the arrest warrant was filed *ex parte*, based on the comparison of the fingerprints found at the scene of the crime and petitioner's fingerprints, which had been taken immediately after his arrest. The initial fingerprints, which were themselves fruit of petitioner's illegal arrest, see *Davis v. Mississippi*, 394 U.S. 721 (1969), and which were used to extract the confession from petitioner, cannot be deemed sufficient "attenuation" to break the connection between the illegal arrest and the confession merely because they also formed the basis for an arrest warrant that was filed while petitioner was being interrogated.

Finally, the State argues that the police conduct here was not flagrant or purposeful, and that we should not follow our decisions in *Brown* and *Dunaway* for that reason. However, we fail to see any relevant distinction between the conduct here and that in *Dunaway*. In this case, as in Dunaway, the police effectuated an investigatory arrest without probable cause, based on an uncorroborated informant's tip, and involuntarily transported petitioner to the station for interrogation in the hope that something would turn up. The fact that the police did not physically abuse petitioner, or that the confession they obtained may have been "voluntary" for purposes of the Fifth Amendment, does not cure the illegality of the initial arrest. Alternatively, the State contends that the police conduct here argues for adopting a "good faith" exception to the exclusionary rule. To date, we have not recognized such an exception, and we decline to do so here.[a]

JUSTICE O'CONNOR, with whom THE CHIEF JUSTICE, JUSTICE POWELL, and JUSTICE REHNQUIST join, dissenting.

The Court holds today that Omar Taylor's detailed confession was the fruit of an illegal arrest, and consequently, should be suppressed. Because I conclude that neither the facts nor the law supports the Court's analysis, I respectfully dissent.

II

Although the Court misapprehends the facts of the present case, it has stated correctly the controlling substantive law. In the Court's words, "a confession obtained through custodial interrogation after an illegal arrest should be excluded unless intervening events break the causal connection between the illegal arrest and the confession so that the confession is 'sufficiently an act of free will to purge the primary taint.'"

In *Brown*, this Court emphasized that "*Miranda* warnings are an important factor . . . in determining whether the confession [was] obtained by exploitation of an illegal arrest."[5]

The Court did not discount the significance of

---

[1] According to petitioner, his girlfriend became upset upon hearing the officer advise petitioner to cooperate. Contrary to the allegations in the dissent, at no point did the officer contradict petitioner's version of his girlfriend's emotional state or petitioner's statement that his girlfriend was present at the time the officer advised him to cooperate. In fact, the testimony from both petitioner and the officer with respect to this visit are consistent. The officer testified only that he advised petitioner to cooperate between the time petitioner signed a rights form at the commencement of this interrogation period and the time that petitioner signed the statement of confession. He also testified that during this same interval, he allowed the short visit between petitioner and his girlfriend. The District Court made no findings of fact with respect to these incidents. In any event, even assuming the accuracy of the dissent's version of the facts, the dissent offers no explanation for its conclusion that this 5- to 10-minute visit should be viewed as an intervening event that purges the taint of the illegal arrest.

[a] Of course, this case was decided before *Leon*.

[5] The holding in *Brown* was derived from this Court's seminal decision in *Wong Sun*, in which we rejected a "but for" test for determining whether to suppress evidence gathered following a Fourth Amendment violation.

other factors, however, noting that "*Miranda* warnings, *alone* and *per se*, cannot always make the act sufficiently a product of free will to break, for Fourth Amendment purposes, the causal connection between the illegality and the confession." *Brown* holds, therefore, that not only *Miranda* warnings, but also "[t]he temporal of intervening circumstances, and, particularly, the purpose and flagrancy of the official misconduct are all relevant."

In light of those factors, the *Brown* Court reviewed the record and found that "*Brown's* first statement was separated from his illegal arrest by less than two hours, and [that] there was no intervening event of significance whatsoever." Moreover, the police conduct in arresting *Brown* was particularly egregious. The "impropriety of the arrest was obvious," and the "manner in which Brown's arrest was effected gives the appearance of having been calculated to cause surprise, fright, and confusion." The Court held that as a consequence the confession should have been suppressed.

Four Terms later, in *Dunaway*, this Court reaffirmed the *Brown* rule that in order to use at trial statements obtained following an arrest on less than probable cause

> "the prosecution must show not only that the statements meet the Fifth Amendment voluntariness standard, but also that the causal connection between the statements and the illegal arrest is broken sufficiently to purge the primary taint of the illegal arrest."

Finding the facts in *Dunaway* to be "virtually a replica of the situation in *Brown*," the Court held that the petitioner's confession should have been suppressed. Critical to the Court's holding was its observation that the petitioner "confessed without any intervening event of significance."

### III

Our task is to apply the law as articulated in *Brown* and *Dunaway* to the facts of this case.

The first significant consideration is that following his unlawful arrest, Taylor was warned on three separate occasions that he

> "had a right to remain silent, [and] anything he said could be used against him in a court of law[;] he had the right to have an attorney present, [and] if he could not afford one, the State would appoint one for him [;] he could answer questions but he could stop answering at any time."

Under *Brown* and *Dunaway*, these warnings must

be counted as "an important factor . . . in determining whether the confession [was] obtained by exploitation of an illegal arrest," though they are, standing alone, insufficient to prove that the primary taint of an illegal arrest had been purged.

Second, in contrast to the facts in *Brown*, the facts in the present case show that the petitioner was not subjected to intimidating police misconduct. In *Brown*, police had broken into the petitioner's house and searched it. When the petitioner later came home, two officers pointed their guns at him and arrested him, leading the Court to conclude that "[t]he manner in which [the petitioner's] arrest was effected gives the appearance of having been calculated to cause surprise, fright, and confusion." By contrast, nothing in the record before us indicates that the petitioner's arrest was violent, or designed to "cause surprise, fright, and confusion." Instead, Montgomery officers approached Taylor, asked him his name, and told him that he was under arrest for the Moseley robbery. They then searched him, advised him of his rights, and took him to the police station.

Third, while in both *Brown* and *Dunaway* there was "no intervening event of significance whatsoever," in the present case Taylor's girlfriend and neighbor came to the police station and asked to speak with him. Before meeting with his two friends, the petitioner steadfastly had denied involvement in the Moseley robbery. Immediately following the meeting, the petitioner gave a complete and detailed confession of his participation in the armed robbery. This meeting between the petitioner and his two friends, as described by the police in their testimony at the suppression hearing, plainly constituted an intervening circumstance.

Finally, the record reveals that the petitioner spent most of the time between his arrest and confession by himself. In *Dunaway* and *Brown*, by contrast, the defendants were interrogated continuously before they made incriminating statements.

In sum, when these four factors are considered together,[7] it is obvious that there is not sufficient basis on which to overturn the trial court's finding that "there were enough intervening factors" to overcome the taint of the illegal arrest. In fact, I believe it is clear that the State carried its burden of

---

[7] The Court has taken each circumstance out of context and examined it to see whether it alone would be enough to purge the taint of the illegal arrest. The Court's failure to consider the circumstances of this case as a whole may have contributed to its erroneous conclusion.

proof. The petitioner was warned of his rights to remain silent and to have a lawyer present, and there is no dispute that he understood those rights or that he waived them voluntarily and without coercion. After receiving three sets of such warnings, he met with his girlfriend and neighbor, *at his request.* Following that meeting, at which no police officers were present, the petitioner decided to confess to this participation in the robbery. The petitioner's confession was not proximately caused by his illegal arrest, but was the product of a decision based both on knowledge of his constitutional rights and on the discussion with his friends. Accordingly, I respectfully dissent.

## QUESTIONS AND NOTES

**1.** Given that the very purpose of *Miranda* warnings is to dissipate the inherent coercion of the police station, why aren't they per se sufficient to dissipate the taint of an unlawful arrest in cases like *Brown, Dunaway*, and *Taylor*?

**2.** The *Taylor* confession came six hours after the unlawful arrest whereas the *Brown* and *Dunaway* confessions came only two hours after the unlawful arrest. Which way should that distinction cut? Why? Suppose the defendant had been held without interrogation for three days following his unlawful arrest. What result? Why?

**3.** Had you been on the Court would you have concurred with Marshall? O'Connor? Neither? Explain.

**4.** In *Harris*, the Court found that a *Payton* violation has very little taint to dissipate. As you read the opinion, assess the persuasiveness of that perspective.

### New York v. Harris
495 U.S. 14 (1990)

JUSTICE WHITE delivered the opinion of the Court.

On January 11, 1984, New York City police found the body of Ms. Thelma Staton murdered in her apartment. Various facts gave the officers probable cause to believe that the respondent in this case, Bernard Harris, had killed Ms. Staton. As a result, on January 16, 1984, three police officers went to Harris' apartment to take him into custody. They did not first obtain an arrest warrant.

When the police arrived, they knocked on the door, displaying their guns and badges. Harris let them enter. Once inside, the officers read Harris his rights under *Miranda*. Harris acknowledged that he understood the warnings, and agreed to answer the officers' questions. At that point, he reportedly admitted that he had killed Ms. Staton.

Harris was arrested, taken to the station house, and again informed of his *Miranda* rights. He then signed a written inculpatory statement. The police subsequently read Harris the *Miranda* warnings a third time and videotaped an incriminating interview between Harris and a district attorney, even though Harris had indicated that he wanted to end the interrogation.

The trial court suppressed Harris' first and third statements; the State does not challenge those rulings. The sole issue in this case is whether Harris' second statement—the written statement made at the station house—should have been suppressed because the police, by entering Harris' home without warrant and without his consent, violated *Payton v. New York*, which held that the Fourth Amendment prohibits the police from effecting a warrantless and nonconsensual entry into a suspect's home in order to make a routine felony arrest.

For present purposes, we accept the finding below that Harris did not consent to the police officer's entry into his home and the conclusion that the police had probable cause to arrest him. It is also evident, in light of *Payton*, that arresting Harris in his home without an arrest warrant violated the Fourth Amendment. [I]n this context, we have stated that "[t]he penalties visited upon the Government, and in turn upon the public, because its officers have violated the law must bear some relation to the purposes which the law is to serve." In light of these principles, we decline to apply the exclusionary rule in this context because the rule in Payton was designed to protect the physical integrity of the home; it was not intended to grant criminal suspects, like Harris, protection for statements made outside their premises where the police have probable cause to arrest the suspect for committing a crime.

*Payton* itself emphasized that our holding in that case stemmed from the "overriding respect for the sanctity of the home that has been embedded in our traditions since the origins of the Republic." Although it had long been settled that a warrantless arrest in a public place was permissible as long as the arresting officer had probable cause, *Payton* nevertheless drew a line at the entrance to the home. This special solicitude was necessary because " 'physical entry of the home is the chief evil against which the wording of the Fourth Amendment is directed.' " The arrest warrant was required to "interpose the magistrate's determination of probable cause" to arrest before the officers could enter a house to effect an arrest.

Nothing in the reasoning of that case suggests that an arrest in a home without a warrant but with probable cause somehow renders unlawful continued custody of the suspect once he is removed from the house. There could be no valid claim here that Harris was immune from prosecution because his person was the fruit of an illegal arrest. Nor is there any claim that the warrantless arrest required the police to release Harris or that Harris could not be immediately rearrested if momentarily released. Because the officers had probable cause to arrest Harris for a crime, Harris was not unlawfully in custody when he was removed to the station house, given *Miranda* warnings, and allowed to talk. For Fourth Amendment purposes, the legal issue is the same as it would be had the police arrested Harris on his doorstep, illegally entered his home to search for evidence, and later interrogated Harris at the station house. Similarly, if the police had made a warrantless entry into Harris' home, not found him there, but arrested him on the street when he returned, a later statement made by him after proper warnings would no doubt be admissible.

This case is therefore different from *Brown, Dunaway*, and *Taylor*. In each of those cases, evidence obtained from a criminal defendant following arrest was suppressed because the police lacked probable cause. The three cases stand for the familiar proposition that the indirect fruits of an illegal search or arrest should be suppressed when they bear a sufficiently close relationship to the underlying illegality. See also *Wong Sun*. We have emphasized, however, that attenuation analysis is only appropriate where, as a threshold matter, courts determine that "the challenged evidence is in some sense the product of illegal governmental activity."

Harris' statement taken at the police station was not the product of being in unlawful custody. Neither was it the fruit of having been arrested in the home rather than someplace else. Here, the police had a justification to question Harris prior to his arrest; therefore, his subsequent statement was not an exploitation of the illegal entry into Harris' home.

We do not hold, as the dissent suggests, that a statement taken by the police while a suspect is in custody is always admissible as long as the suspect is in legal custody. Statements taken during legal custody would of course be inadmissible, for example, if they were the product of coercion, if *Miranda* warnings were not given, or if there was violation of the rule of *Edwards*. We do hold that the station house statement in this case was admissible because Harris was in legal custody, as the dissent concedes, and because the statement, while the product of an arrest and being in custody, was not the fruit of the fact that the arrest was made in the house rather than someplace else.

To put the matter another way, suppressing the statement taken outside the house would not serve the purpose of the rule that made Harris' in-house arrest illegal. The warrant requirement for an arrest in the home is imposed to protect the home, and anything incriminating the police gathered from arresting Harris in his home, rather than elsewhere, has been excluded, as it should have been; the purpose of the rule has thereby been vindicated. We are not required by the Constitution to go further and suppress statements later made by Harris in order to deter police from violating *Payton*. "As cases considering the use of unlawfully obtained evidence in criminal trials themselves make clear, it does not follow from the emphasis on the exclusionary rule's deterrent value that 'anything which deters illegal searches is thereby commanded by the Fourth Amendment.' " *Leon*. Even though we decline to suppress statements made outside the home following a *Payton* violation, the principal incentive to obey *Payton* still obtains: the police know that a warrantless entry will lead to the suppression of any evidence found, or statements taken, inside the home. If we did suppress statements like Harris', moreover, the incremental deterrent value would be minimal. Given that the police have probable cause to arrest a suspect in Harris' position, they need not violate *Payton* in order to interrogate the suspect. It is doubtful therefore that the desire to secure a statement from a criminal suspect would motivate the police to violate *Payton*. As a result, suppressing a station house statement obtained after a *Payton* violation will have little effect on the officers' actions, one way or another.

We hold that, where the police have probable cause to arrest a suspect, the exclusionary rule does not bar the State's use of a statement made by the defendant outside of his home, even though the statement is taken after an arrest made in the home in violation of *Payton*. The judgment of the court below is accordingly

Reversed.

JUSTICE MARSHALL, with whom JUSTICE BRENNAN, JUSTICE BLACKMUN, and JUSTICE STEVENS join, dissenting.

Police officers entered Bernard Harris' home and arrested him there. They did not have an arrest warrant, he did not consent to their entry, and exigent circumstances did not exist. An arrest in such circumstances violates the Fourth Amendment. See *Payton*. About an hour after his arrest, Harris made an incriminating statement, which the government subsequently used at his trial. The majority concedes that the fruits of the illegal entry must be suppressed. The sole question before us is whether Harris' statement falls within that category.

The majority answers this question by adopting a broad and unprecedented principle, holding that "where the police have probable cause to arrest a suspect, the exclusionary rule does not bar the State's use of a statement made by the defendant outside of his home, even though the statement is taken after an arrest made in the home in violation of *Payton*." The majority's conclusion is wrong. Its reasoning amounts to nothing more than an analytical sleight of hand, resting on errors in logic, misreadings of our cases, and an apparent blindness to the incentives the Court's ruling creates for knowing and intentional constitutional violations by the police. I dissent.

I

In recent years, this Court has repeatedly stated that the principal purpose of the Fourth Amendment's exclusionary rule is to eliminate incentives for police officers to violate that Amendment. See *e.g., Leon*. A police officer who violates the Constitution usually does so to obtain evidence that he could not secure lawfully. The best way to deter him is to provide that any evidence so obtained will not be admitted at trial. Deterrence of constitutional violations thus requires the suppression not only of evidence seized during an unconstitutional search, but also of "derivative evidence, both tangible and testimonial, that is the product of the primary evidence, or that is otherwise acquired as an indirect result of the unlawful search." Not all evidence connected to a constitutional violation is suppressible, however. Rather, the Court has asked " 'whether, granting establishment of the primary illegality, the evidence to which instant objection is made has been come at by exploitation of that illegality or instead by means sufficiently distinguishable to be purged of the primary taint.' "

Because deterrence is a principal purpose of the exclusionary rule, our attenuation analysis must be driven by an understanding of how extensive exclusion must be to deter violations of the Fourth Amendment. We have long held that where police have obtained a statement after violating the Fourth Amendment, the interest in deterrence does not disappear simply because the statement was voluntary, as required by the Fifth Amendment. See, *e.g., Brown, Dunaway*, and *Taylor*. Police officers are well aware that simply because a statement is "voluntary" does not mean that it was entirely unaffected by the Fourth Amendment violation.

Attenuation analysis *assumes* that the statement is "voluntary" and asks whether the connection between the illegal police conduct and the statement nevertheless requires suppression to deter Fourth Amendment violations. That question cannot be answered with a set of *per se* rules. An inquiry into whether a suspect's statement is properly treated as attributable to a Fourth Amendment violation or to the suspect's independent act of will has an irreducibly psychological aspect, and irrebuttable presumptions are peculiarly unhelpful in such a context. Accordingly, we have identified several factors as relevant to the issue of attenuation: the length of time between the arrest and the statement, the presence of intervening circumstances, and the "purpose of flagrancy" of the violation. *Brown*.

We have identified the last factor as "particularly" important. When a police officer intentionally violates what he knows to be a constitutional command, exclusion is essential to conform police behavior to the law. Such a "flagrant" violation is in marked contrast to a violation that is the product of a good-faith misunderstanding of the relevant constitutional requirements. This Court has suggested that excluding evidence that is the product of the latter variety of violation may result in deterrence of legitimate law enforcement efforts. *Leon*. Whatever the truth of the theory, the concern that officers who act in good faith will be overdeterred is nonexistent when, based on a cynical calculus of the likely results of a suppression hearing, an officer intentionally decides to violate what he knows to be a constitutional command.

An application of the *Brown* factors to this case compels the conclusion that Harris' statement at the station house must be suppressed. About an hour elapsed between the illegal arrest and Harris' confession, without any intervening factor other than the warnings required by *Miranda*.

As to the flagrancy of the violation, petitioner does not dispute that the officers were aware that the Fourth Amendment prohibited them from arresting Harris in his home without a warrant. Notwithstanding the officers' knowledge that a warrant is required for a routine arrest in the home,

> "the police went to defendants apartment to arrest him and, as the police conceded, if defendant refused to talk to them there they intended to take him into custody for questioning. Nevertheless, they made no attempt to obtain a warrant although five days had elapsed between the killing and the arrest and they had developed evidence of probable cause early in their investigation. Indeed, one of the officers testified that it was departmental policy not to get warrants before making arrests in the home. From this statement a reasonable inference can be drawn . . . that the department's policy was a device used to avoid restrictions on questioning a suspect until after the police had strengthened their case with a confession. Thus, the police illegality was knowing and intentional, in the language of *Brown*, it 'had a quality of purposefulness,' and the linkage between the illegality and the confession is clearly established." 72 N.Y.2d 614, 622, 532 N.E.2d 1229, 1233-1234 (1988) (citation omitted).[2]

---

[2] The "restrictions on questioning" to which the court refers are restrictions imposed by New York law. New York law provides that an arrest warrant may not issue until an "accusatory instrument" has been filed against the suspect. N.Y. Crim. Proc. Law § 120.20 (McKinney 1981). The New York courts have held that police officers may not question a suspect in the absence of an attorney once such an accusatory instrument has been filed. People v. Samuels, 49 N.Y. 2d 218, 400 N. E. 2d 1344 (1980). These two rules operate to prohibit police from questioning a suspect after arresting him in his home unless his lawyer is present. If the police comply with Payton, the suspect's lawyer will likely tell

In short, the officers decide, apparently consistent with a "departmental policy," to violate Harris' Fourth Amendment rights so they could get evidence that they could not otherwise obtain. As the trial court held, "No more clear violation of [*Payton*], in my view, could be established." Where, as here, there is a particularly flagrant constitutional violation and little in the way of elapsed time or intervening circumstances, the statement in the police station must be suppressed.

## II

Had the Court analyzed this case as our precedents dictate that it should, I could end my discussion here—the dispute would reduce to an application of the *Brown* factors to the constitutional wrong and the inculpatory statement that followed. But the majority chooses no such unremarkable battleground. Instead, the Court redrafts our cases in the service of conclusions they straightforwardly and explicitly reject. Specifically, the Court finds suppression unwarranted on the authority of its newly fashioned per se rule. In the majority's view, when police officers make a warrantless home arrest in violation of *Payton*, their physical exit from the suspect's home *necessarily* breaks the causal chain between the illegality and any subsequent statement by the suspect, such that the statement is admissible regardless of the *Brown* factors.

The Court purports to defend its new rule on the basis of the self-evident proposition that the Fourth Amendment does not necessarily require the police to release or to forgo the prosecution of a suspect arrested in violation of *Payton*. To the Court, it follows as a matter of course from this proposition that a Payton violation cannot in any way be the "cause" of a statement obtained from his home and is being lawfully detained. Because an attenuation inquiry presupposes *some* connection between the illegality and the statement, the Court concludes that no such inquiry is necessary here. Neither logic nor precedent supports that conclusion.

### A

The majority's *per se* rule in this case fails to

---

him not to say anything, and the police will get nothing. On the other hand, if they violate Payton by refusing to obtain a warrant, the suspect's right to counsel will not have attached at the time of the arrest, and the police may be able to question him without interference by a lawyer. The lower court's inference that a departmental policy of violating the Fourth Amendment existed was thus fully justified.

take account of our repeated holdings that violations of privacy in the home are especially invasive. Rather, its rule is necessarily premised on the proposition that the effect of a *Payton* violation magically vanishes once the suspect is dragged from his home. But the concerns that make a warrantless home arrest a violation of the Fourth Amendment are nothing so evanescent. A person who is forcibly separated from his family and home in the dark of night after uniformed officers have broken down his door, handcuffed him, and forced him at gunpoint to accompany them to a police station does not suddenly breathe a sigh of relief at the moment he is dragged across his doorstep. Rather, the suspect is likely to be so frightened and rattled that he will say something incriminating. These effects, of course, extend far beyond the moment the physical occupation of the home ends. The entire focus of the *Brown* factors is to fix the point at which those effects are sufficiently dissipated that deterrence is not meaningfully advanced by suppression. The majority's assertion, as though the proposition were axiomatic, that the effects of such an intrusion *must* end when the violation ends is both undefended and indefensible. The Court's saying it may make it law, but does not make it true.

### B

The majority's reading of our cases similarly lacks foundation. In the majority's view, our attenuation cases are not concerned with the lingering taint of an illegal arrest; rather, they focus solely on whether a subsequently obtained statement is made during an illegal detention of the suspect. In the Court's view, if (and only if) the detention is illegal at the moment the statement is made will it be suppressed. Unlike an arrest without probable cause, *Payton* violation alone does not make the subsequent detention of the suspect illegal. Thus, the Court argues, no statement made after *Payton* violation has ended is suppressible by reason of the Fourth Amendment violation as long as the police have probable cause.

The majority's theory lacks any support in our cases. In each case presenting issues similar to those here, we have asked the same question: whether the invasion of privacy occasioned by the illegal *arrest* taints a statement made after the violation has ended — stated another way, whether the arrest caused the statement.

Indeed, such an approach would render irrelevant the first and second of the *Brown* factors, which focus, respectively, on the passage of time and the existence of intervening factors between the illegality and the subsequently obtained statement. If, as the majority claims, the *Brown* analysis does not even *apply* unless the illegality is ongoing at the time the evidence is secured, no time would ever pass and no circumstance would ever intervene between the illegality and that statement.

### C

Perhaps the most alarming aspect of the Court's ruling is its practical consequences for the deterrence of *Payton* violations. Imagine a police officer who has probable cause to arrest a suspect but lacks a warrant. The officer knows if he were to break into the home to make the arrest without first securing a warrant, he would violate the Fourth Amendment and any evidence he finds in the house would be suppressed. Of course, if he does not enter the house, he will not be able to use any evidence inside the house either, for the simple reason that he will never see it. The officer also knows, though, that waiting for the suspect to leave his house before arresting him could entail a lot of waiting, and the time he would spend getting a warrant would be better spent arresting criminals. The officer could leave the scene to obtain a warrant, thus avoiding some of the delay, but that would entail giving the suspect an opportunity to flee.

More important, the officer knows that if he breaks into the house without a warrant and drags the suspect outside, the suspect, shaken by the enormous invasion of privacy he has just undergone, may say something incriminating. Before today's decision, the government would only be able to use that evidence if the Court found that the taint of the arrest had been attenuated; after the decision, the evidence will be admissible regardless of whether it was the product of the unconstitutional arrest.[5] Thus, the officer envisions the following best-case scenario if he chooses to violate the Constitution: He avoids a major expenditure of time and effort, ensures that the suspect will not escape, and procures the most damaging evidence of all, a confession. His worst-case scenario is that he will avoid a major expenditure

---

[5] Indeed, if the officer, as here, works in New York State, the Court's assertion that "[i]t is doubtful therefore that the desire to secure a statement from a criminal suspect would motivate the police to violate *Payton*," takes on a singularly ironic cast. The court below found as a matter of fact that the officers in this case had intentionally violated Payton for precisely the reason the Court identifies as "doubtful." See n. 2, *supra*, and accompanying text.

of effort, ensure that the suspect will not escape, and will see evidence in the house (which would have remained unknown absent the constitutional violation) that cannot be used in the prosecution's case in chief. The Court thus creates powerful incentives for police officers to violate the Fourth Amendment. In the context of our constitutional rights and the sanctity of our homes, we cannot afford to presume that officers will be entirely impervious to those incentives.

I dissent.

## QUESTIONS AND NOTES

**1.** Is it clear that *Harris'* first and third statements were properly excluded? Why?

**2.** Is (should) this case (be) the same as one in which the police arrested Harris outside of his home, entered to make an illegal search, and subsequently obtained a confession from him? Explain.

**3.** If the police had arrested Harris in his home, taken him outside, released him, and then rearrested him outside of the home pursuant to the probable cause that they already had, would there be any merit to the dissent's position? Explain.

**4.** Do you think that *Harris* is likely to retard adherence to *Payton*? Why? Do you think that the majority (consisting of White and Rehnquist, who dissented in *Payton*, and O'Connor, Scalia, and Kennedy who were not on the Court when *Payton* was decided) really care?

**5.** We conclude this section with *Ceccolini*, a case indicating that some types of evidence can be more easily attenuated than other types of evidence.

### United States v. Ceccolini
### 435 U.S. 268 (1978)

Mr. Justice REHNQUIST delivered the opinion of the Court.

In December 1974, Ronald Biro, a uniformed police officer on assignment to patrol school crossings, entered respondent's place of business, the Sleepy Hollow Flower Shop, in North Tarrytown, N.Y. He went behind the customer counter and, in the words of Ichabod Crane, one of Tarrytown's more illustrious inhabitants of days gone past, "tarried," spending his short break engaged in conversation with his friend Lois Hennessey, an employee of the shop. During the course of the conversation he noticed an envelope with money sticking out of it lying on the drawer of the cash register behind the counter. Biro picked up the envelope and, upon examining its contents, discovered that it contained not only money but policy slips. He placed the envelope back on the register and, without telling Hennessey what he had seen, asked her to whom the envelope belonged. She replied that the envelope belonged to respondent Ceccolini, and that he had instructed her to give it to someone.

The next day, Officer Biro mentioned his discovery to North Tarrytown detectives who in turn told Lance Emory, an FBI agent. This very ordinary incident in the lives of Biro and Hennessey requires us, over three years later, to decide whether Hennessey's testimony against respondent Ceccolini should have been suppressed in his trial for perjury. Respondent was charged with that offense because he denied that he knew anything of, or was in any way involved with, gambling operations.

I

During the latter part of 1973, the Federal Bureau of Investigation was exploring suspected gambling operations in North Tarrytown. Among the establishments under surveillance was respondent's place of business, which was a frequent and regular stop of one Francis Millow, himself a suspect in the investigation. While the investigation continued on a reduced scale after December 1973, surveillance of the flower shop was curtailed at that time. It was thus a full year after this discontinuance of FBI surveillance that Biro spent his patrol break behind the counter with Hennessey. When Biro's discovery of the policy slips was reported the following day to Emory, Emory was not fully informed of the manner in which Biro had obtained the information. Four months later, Emory interviewed Hennessey at her home for about half an hour in the presence of her mother and two sisters. He identified himself, indicated that he had learned through the local police department that she worked for respondent, and told her that the Government would appreciate any information regarding respondent's activities that she had acquired in the shop. Emory did not specifically refer to the incident involving Officer Biro. Hennessey told Emory that she was studying police science in college and would be willing to help. She then related the events which had occurred during her visit with Officer Biro.

In May 1975, respondent was summoned before a federal grand jury where he testified that he had never taken policy bets for Francis Millow at the flower shop. The next week Hennessey testified to the contrary, and shortly thereafter respondent was indicted for perjury. Respondent waived a jury, and with the consent of all parties the District Court considered simultaneously with the trial on the merits respondent's motion to suppress both the policy slips and the testimony of Hennessey. At the conclusion of the evidence, the District Court excluded from its consideration "the envelope and the contents of the envelope," but nonetheless found respondent guilty of the offense charged. The court then, granted respondent's motion to suppress the testimony of Hennessey, because she "first came directly to the attention of the government as a result of an illegal search" and the Government had not "sustained its burden of showing that Lois Hennessey's testimony definitely would have been obtained without the illegal search."

The Court of Appeals affirmed this ruling on the Government's appeal, reasoning that "the road to Miss Henness[e]y's testimony from Officer Biro's concededly unconstitutional search is both straight and uninterrupted." 542 F.2d, at 142. Because we decide that the Court of Appeals was wrong in concluding that there was insufficient attenuation between Officer Biro's search and Hennessey's testimony at the trial, we also do not reach the Government's contention that the exclusionary rule should not be applied when the evidence derived from the search is being used to prove a subsequent crime such as perjury.

## II

The "road" to which the Court of Appeals analogized the train of events from Biro's discovery of the policy slips to Hennessey's testimony at respondent's trial for perjury is one of literally thousands of such roads traveled periodically between an original investigative discovery and the ultimate trial of the accused. The constitutional question under the Fourth Amendment was phrased in *Wong Sun* as whether "the connection between the lawless conduct of the police and the discovery of the challenged evidence has 'become so attenuated as to dissipate the taint.'" The question was in turn derived from the Court's earlier decision in *Nardone v. United States*, 308 U.S. 338, 341 (1939), where Mr. Justice Frankfurter stated for the Court:

"Here, as in the *Silverthorne* case [*Silverthorne Lumber Co. v. United States*], the facts improperly obtained do not 'become sacred and inaccessible. If knowledge of them is gained from an independent source they may be proved like any others, but the knowledge gained by the Government's own wrong cannot be used by it' simply because it is used derivatively. 251 U.S. 385, 392, 40 S.Ct. 182, 64 L.Ed. 319.

"In practice this generalized statement may conceal concrete complexities. Sophisticated argument may prove a causal connection between information obtained through illicit wire-tapping and the Government's proof. As a matter of good sense, however, such connection may have become so attenuated as to dissipate the taint."

This, of course, makes it perfectly clear, if indeed ever there was any doubt about the matter, that the question of causal connection in this setting, as in so many other questions with which the law concerns itself, is not to be determined solely through the sort of analysis which would be applicable in the physical sciences. The issue cannot be decided on the basis of causation in the logical sense alone, but necessarily includes other elements as well. And our cases subsequent to *Nardone*, have laid out the fundamental tenets of the exclusionary rule, from which the elements that are relevant to the causal inquiry can be divined.

An examination of these cases leads us to reject the Government's suggestion that we adopt what would in practice amount to a per se rule that the testimony of a live witness should not be excluded at trial no matter how close and proximate the connection between it and a violation of the Fourth Amendment. We also reaffirm the holding of *Wong Sun*, that "verbal evidence which derives so immediately from an unlawful entry and an unauthorized arrest as the officers' action in the present case is no less the 'fruit' of official illegality than the more common tangible fruits of the unwarranted intrusion." We are of the view, however, that cases decided since *Wong Sun* significantly qualify its further observation that "the policies underlying the exclusionary rule [do not] invite any logical distinction between physical and verbal evidence." Rather, at least in a case such as this, where not only was the alleged "fruit of the poisonous tree" the testimony of a live witness, but unlike *Wong Sun* the witness was not a putative defendant, an examination of our cases persuades us that the Court of Appeals was simply wrong in concluding that if the road were uninterrupted, its length was immaterial. Its length, we hold, is material, as are certain other factors enumerated below to which the court gave insufficient weight.

Even in situations where the exclusionary rule is plainly applicable, we have declined to adopt a "per se or 'but for' rule" that would make inadmissible any evidence, whether tangible or live-witness testimony, which somehow came to light through a chain of causation that began with an illegal arrest. *Brown v. Illinois*.

Evaluating the standards for application of the exclusionary rule to live-witness testimony in light of this balance, we are first impelled to conclude that the degree of free will exercised by the witness is not irrelevant in determining the extent to which the basic purpose of the exclusionary rule will be advanced by its application. This is certainly true when the challenged statements are made by a putative defendant after arrest, *Wong Sun, Brown v. Illinois,* and *a fortiori* is true of testimony given by nondefendants.

The greater the willingness of the witness to freely testify, the greater the likelihood that he or she will be discovered by legal means and, concomitantly, the smaller the incentive to conduct an illegal search to discover the witness.[4] Witnesses are not like guns or documents which remain hidden from view until one turns over a sofa or opens a filing cabinet. Witnesses can, and often do, come forward and offer evidence entirely of their own volition. And evaluated properly, the degree of free will necessary to dissipate the taint will very likely be found more often in the case of live-witness testimony than other kinds of evidence. The time, place and manner of the initial questioning of the witness may be such that any statements are truly the product of detached reflection and a desire to be cooperative on the part of the witness. And the illegality which led to the discovery of the witness very often will not play any meaningful part in the witness' willingness to testify.

"The proffer of a living witness is not to be mechanically equated with the proffer of inanimate evidentiary objects illegally seized. The fact that the name of a potential witness is disclosed to police is of no evidentiary significance, per se, since the living witness is an individual human personality whose attributes of will, perception, memory and volition interact to determine what testimony he will give. The uniqueness of this human process distinguishes the evidentiary character of a witness from the relative immutability of inanimate evidence." *Smith v. United States*, 117 U.S.App.D.C. 1, 3-4, 324 F.2d 879, 881-882 (1963) (Burger, J.).

Another factor which not only is relevant in determining the usefulness of the exclusionary rule in a particular context, but also seems to us to differentiate the testimony of all live witnesses — even putative defendants — from the exclusion of the typical documentary evidence, is that such exclusion would perpetually disable a witness from testifying about relevant and material facts, regardless of how unrelated such testimony might be to the purpose of the originally illegal search or the evidence discovered thereby. Rules which disqualify knowledgeable witnesses from testifying at trial are, in the words of Professor McCormick, "serious obstructions to the ascertainment of truth"; accordingly, "[f]or a century the course of legal evolution has been in the direction of sweeping away these obstructions." C. McCormick, Law of Evidence § 71 (1954). Alluding to the enormous cost engendered by such a permanent disability in an analogous context, we have specifically refused to hold that "making a confession under circumstances which preclude its use, perpetually disables the confessor from making a usable one after those conditions have been removed." *United States v. Bayer*, 331 U.S. 532, 541 (1947). For many of these same reasons, the Court has also held admissible at trial testimony of a witness whose identity was disclosed by the defendant's statement given after inadequate *Miranda* warnings. *Michigan v. Tucker*, 417 U.S. 433, 450-451 (1974).

"For, when balancing the interests involved, we must weight the strong interest under any system of justice of making available to the trier of fact all concededly relevant and trustworthy evidence which either party

---

[4] Of course, the analysis might be different where the search was conducted by the police for the specific purpose of discovering potential witnesses.

seeks to adduce. . . . Here respondent's own statement, which might have helped the prosecution show respondent's guilty conscience at trial, had already been excised from the prosecution's case. To extend the excision further under the circumstances of this case and exclude relevant testimony of a third-party witness would require far more persuasive arguments than those advanced by respondent."

In short, since the cost of excluding live-witness testimony often will be greater, a closer, more direct link between the illegality and that kind of testimony is required.

This is not to say, of course, that live-witness testimony is always or even usually more reliable or dependable than inanimate evidence. Indeed, just the opposite may be true. But a determination that the discovery of certain evidence is sufficiently unrelated to or independent of the constitutional violation to permit its introduction at trial is not a determination which rests on the comparative reliability of that evidence. Attenuation analysis, appropriately concerned with the differences between live-witness testimony and inanimate evidence, can consistently focus on the factors enumerated above with respect to the former, but on different factors with respect to the latter.

In holding that considerations relating to the exclusionary rule and the constitutional principles which it is designed to protect must play a factor in the attenuation analysis, we do no more than reaffirm an observation made by this Court half a century ago:

"A criminal prosecution is more than a game in which the Government may be checkmated and the game lost merely because its officers have not played according to rule." *McGuire v. United States*, 273 U.S. 95, 99 (1927).

The penalties visited upon the Government, and in turn upon the public, because its officers have violated the law must bear some relation to the purposes which the law is to serve.

### III

Viewing this case in the light of the principles just discussed, we hold that the Court of Appeals erred in holding that the degree of attenuation was not sufficient to dissipate the connection between the illegality and the testimony. The evidence indicates overwhelmingly that the testimony given by the witness was an act of her own free will in no way coerced or even induced by official authority as a result of Biro's discovery of the policy slips. Nor

were the slips themselves used in questioning Hennessey. Substantial periods of time elapsed between the time of the illegal search and the initial contact with the witness, on the one hand, and between the latter and the testimony at trial on the other. While the particular knowledge to which Hennessey testified at trial can be logically traced back to Biro's discovery of the policy slips, both the identity of Hennessey and her relationship with the respondent were well known to those investigating the case. There is, in addition, not the slightest evidence to suggest that Biro entered the shop or picked up the envelope with the intent of finding tangible evidence bearing on an illicit gambling operation, much less any suggestion that he entered the shop and searched with the intent of finding a willing and knowledgeable witness to testify against respondent. Application of the exclusionary rule in this situation could not have the slightest deterrent effect on the behavior of an officer such as Biro. The cost of permanently silencing Hennessey is too great for an evenhanded system of law enforcement to bear in order to secure such a speculative and very likely negligible deterrent effect.

Obviously no mathematical weight can be assigned to any of the factors which we have discussed, but just as obviously they all point to the conclusion that the exclusionary rule should be invoked with much greater reluctance where the claim is based on a causal relationship between a constitutional violation and the discovery of a live witness than when a similar claim is advanced to support suppression of an inanimate object. The judgment of the Court of Appeals is accordingly

Reversed.

Mr. JUSTICE BLACKMUN took no part in the consideration or decision of this case.

Mr. CHIEF JUSTICE BURGER, concurring in the judgment.

I agree with the Court's ultimate conclusion that there is a fundamental difference, for purposes of the exclusionary rule, between live-witness testimony and other types of evidence. I perceive this distinction to be so fundamental, however, that I would not prevent a factfinder from hearing and considering the relevant statements of any witness, except perhaps under the most remarkable of circumstances—although none such have ever been postulated that would lead me to exclude the testimony of a live witness.

To appreciate this position, it is essential to bear in mind the purported justification for employing the exclusionary rule in a Fourth Amendment context:

deterrence of official misconduct. As an abstract intellectual proposition this can be buttressed by a plausible rationale since there is at least some comprehensible connection – albeit largely and dubiously speculative – between the exclusion of evidence and the deterrence of intentional illegality on the part of a police officer. But if that is the purpose of the rule, it seems to me that the appropriate inquiry in every case in which a defendant seeks the exclusion of otherwise admissible and reliable evidence is whether official conduct in reality will be measurably altered by taking such a course.

On the facts of this case the Court is, of course, correct in holding that the "[a]pplication of the exclusionary rule in this situation could not have the slightest deterrent effect on the behavior of an officer such as Biro." Reaching this result, however, requires no judicial excursion into an area about which "philosophers have been able to argue endlessly," namely, the degree of "free will" exercised by a person when engaging in an act such as speaking.

It can, of course, be argued, that the prospect of finding a helpful witness may play some role in a policeman's decision to be indifferent about Fourth Amendment procedures. The answer to this point, however, is that we have never insisted on employing the exclusionary rule whenever there is some possibility, no matter how remote, of deterring police misconduct. Rather, we balance the cost to society of losing perfectly competent evidence against the prospect of incrementally enhancing Fourth Amendment values. See, *e.g., Calandra.*

Using this approach it strikes me as evident that the permanent silencing of a witness – who, after all, is appearing under oath – is not worth the high price the exclusionary rule exacts. Any rule of law which operates to keep an eyewitness to a crime – a murder, for example – from telling the jury what that person saw has a rational basis roughly comparable to the primitive rituals of human sacrifice.

I would, therefore, resolve the case of a living witness on a per se basis, holding that such testimony is always admissible, provided it meets all other traditional evidentiary requirements. At very least this solution would alleviate the burden – now squarely thrust upon courts – of determining in each instance whether the witness possessed that elusive quality characterized by the term "free will."[4]

---

[4] Perhaps a case might arise in which the police conducted a search only for the purposes of obtaining the name of witnesses. In such a circumstance it is possibly arguable that the exclusion of any testimony gained as a result of the search would have an effect on official behavior. This clearly did not occur here,

MR. JUSTICE MARSHALL, with whom MR. JUSTICE BRENNAN joins, dissenting.

While "reaffirm[ing]" the holding of *Wong Sun* that verbal evidence, like physical evidence, may be "fruit of the poisonous tree," the Court today "significantly qualif[ies]" *Wong Sun's* further conclusion, that no " 'logical distinction' " can be drawn between verbal and physical evidence for purposes of the exclusionary rule. In my view, the distinction that the Court attempts to draw cannot withstand close analysis. To extend "a time-worn metaphor," I do not believe that the same tree, having its roots in an unconstitutional search or seizure, can bear two different kinds of fruit, with one kind less susceptible than the other of exclusion on Fourth Amendment grounds. I therefore dissent.

The Court correctly states the question before us: whether the connection between the police officer's concededly unconstitutional search and Hennessey's disputed testimony was "so attenuated as to dissipate the taint." In resolving questions of attenuation, courts typically scrutinize the facts of the individual case, with particular attention to such matters as the "temporal proximity" of the official illegality and the discovery of the evidence, "the presence of intervening circumstances," and "the purpose and flagrancy of the official misconduct." *Brown.* The Court retains this general framework, but states that "[a]ttenuation analysis" should be "concerned with the differences between live-witness testimony and inanimate evidence." The differences noted by the Court, however, have to a large extent already been accommodated by current doctrine. Where they have not been so accommodated, it is because the differences asserted are either illusory or of no relevance to the issue of attenuation.

One difference mentioned by the Court is that witnesses, unlike inanimate objects, "can, and often do, come forward and offer evidence entirely of their own volition." Recognition of this obvious fact does nothing to advance the attenuation inquiry. We long ago held that, if knowledge of evidence is gained from a source independent of police illegality, the evidence should be admitted. This "independent source" rule would plainly apply to a witness whose

---

nor can I conceive of many instances in which it would. In any event, the decision to exclude such testimony should depend on the officers' motivation and not on the "free will" of the witnesses. I would not want to speculate, however, as to whether such an unlikely case would justify modifying a per se approach to this general problem. **(Footnote repositioned ed.)**

identity is discovered in an illegal search but who later comes to the police for reasons unrelated to the official misconduct. In the instant case, however, as the Court recognizes there is a "'straight and uninterrupted'" road between the illegal search and the disputed testimony.

Even where the road is uninterrupted, in some cases the Government may be able to show that the illegally discovered evidence would inevitably have come to light in the normal course of a legal police investigation. Assuming such evidence is admissible – a proposition that has been questioned, *Fitzpatrick v. New York*, 414 U.S. 1050 (1973) (White, J., dissenting from denial of certiorari) – this "inevitable discovery" rule would apply to admit the testimony of a witness who, in the absence of police misconduct, would have come forward "entirely of [his or her] own volition." Again, however, no such situation is presented by this case, since the Court accepts the findings of the two lower courts that Hennessey's testimony would not inevitably have been discovered.

Both the independent source and inevitable discovery rules, moreover, can apply to physical evidence as well as to verbal evidence. The police may show, for example, that they learned from an independent source, or would inevitably have discovered through legal means, the location of an object that they also knew about as a result of illegal police activity. It may be that verbal evidence is more likely to have an independent source, because live witnesses can indeed come forward of their own volition, but this simply underscores the degree to which the Court's approach involves a form of judicial "double counting." The Court would apparently first determine whether the evidence stemmed from an independent source or would inevitably have been discovered; if neither of these rules was found to apply, as here, the Court would still somehow take into account the fact that, as a general proposition (but not in the particular case), witnesses sometimes do come forward of their own volition.

The Court makes a related point that "[t]he greater the willingness of the witness to freely testify, . . . the smaller the incentive to conduct an illegal search to discover the witness." The somewhat incredible premise of this statement is that the police in fact refrain from illegal behavior in which they would otherwise engage because they know in advance both that a witness will be willing to testify and that he or she "will be discovered by legal means." This reasoning surely reverses the normal sequence of events; the instances must be very few in which a witness' willingness to testify is known

before he or she is discovered. In this case, for example, the police did not even know that Hennessey was a potentially valuable witness, much less whether she would be willing to testify, prior to conducting the illegal search. When the police are certain that a witness "will be discovered by legal means," if they ever can be certain about such a fact – they of course have no incentive to find him or her by illegal means, but the same can be said about physical objects that the police know will be discovered legally.

The only other point made by the Court is that exclusion of testimony "perpetually disable[s] a witness from testifying about relevant and material facts." The "perpetual . . . disable[ment]" of which the Court speaks, however, applies as much to physical as to verbal evidence. When excluded, both types of evidence are lost for the duration of the particular trial, despite their being "relevant and material . . . [and] unrelated . . . to the purpose of the originally illegal search." Moreover, while it is true that "often" the exclusion of testimony will be very costly to society, least as often the exclusion of physical evidence – such as heroin in a narcotics possession case or business records in a tax case – will be as costly to the same societal interests. But other, more important societal interests, have led to the rule, which the Court today reaffirms, that "fruits of the poisonous tree" must be excluded despite their probative value, unless the facts of the case justify a finding of sufficient attenuation.

The facts of this case do not justify such a finding. Although, as the Court notes, four months elapsed between the illegal search and the FBI's first contact with Hennessey, the critical evidence was provided at the time and place of the search, when the police officer questioned Hennessey and she identified respondent. The time that elapsed thereafter is of no more relevance than would be a similar time period between the discovery of an object during an illegal search and its later introduction into evidence at trial. In this case, moreover, there were no intervening circumstances between Hennessey's statement at the time of the search and her later testimony. She did not come to the authorities and ask to testify, despite being a student of police science; an FBI agent had to go to her home and interrogate her.

Finally, whatever the police officer's purpose in the flower shop on the day of the search, the search itself was not even of arguable legality, as was conceded by the Government below. It is also undisputed that the shop had been under surveillance as part of an ongoing gambling investigation in which the local police force had actively participated; its participation included interception of at least one of respondent's telephone conversations in the very month of the search. Under all of the circumstances, the connection here between the official illegality and the disputed testimony cannot be deemed "so attenuated as to dissipate the taint." The District Court therefore properly excluded the testimony.

I would affirm the judgment of the Court of Appeals.

## QUESTIONS AND NOTES

**1.** With which, if any, of the three opinions (Rehnquist, Burger, Marshall) did you agree? Why?

**2.** Considering the *Brown* factors (temporal proximity, intervening circumstances, and purpose and flagrancy of the illegality) is there anything about a live witness that makes it more likely that the taint will be dissipated as contrasted to (a). tangible evidence, or (b). the defendant's own statements?

**3.** As between Hennessey's statement in this case and *Wong Sun's* statement three days after his arrest in *Wong Sun*, which was the stronger case for finding the taint dissipated? If you said Hennessey's statement, was Justice Marshall's dissent necessarily wrong?

## B.  Miranda

In *New York v. Quarles*, chapter 16, Sec. G, supra, a majority of the Court found no violation of *Miranda* because of the "emergency." Consequently, it was unnecessary for the Court to assess the impact of the attenuation doctrine on the admissibility of the gun. For Justice O'Connor, who found a Miranda violation, such an assessment was necessary. We begin this section by examining that aspect of *Quarles*. If you have forgotten the basic fact pattern or the holding, you should, of course, refresh your recollection by rereading the case.

### New York v. Quarles
#### 467 U.S. 649 (1984)

Justice O'CONNOR, concurring in part in the judgment and dissenting in part.

#### II

The court below assumed, without discussion, that the privilege against self-incrimination required that the gun derived from respondent's statement also be suppressed, whether or not the State could independently link it to him. That conclusion was, in my view, incorrect.

#### A

The distinction between testimonial and nontestimonial evidence was explored in some detail in *Schmerber v. California*, a decision this Court handed down within a week of deciding *Miranda*.

The defendant in *Schmerber* had argued that the privilege against self-incrimination barred the state from compelling him to submit to a blood test, the results of which would be used to prove his guilt at trial. This Court favored an approach that protected the "accused only from being compelled to testify against himself, or otherwise provide the State with evidence of a testimonial or communicative nature." The blood tests were admissible because they were neither testimonial nor communicative in nature.

In subsequent decisions, the Court relied on *Schmerber* in holding the privilege inapplicable to situations where the accused was compelled to stand in a lineup and utter words that allegedly had been spoken by the robber, see *Wade,* to provide handwriting samples, see *Gilbert v. California*, 388 U.S. 263, 265-266,

(1967), and to supply voice exemplars. See *United States v. Dionisio*, 410 U.S. 1, 5-7, (1973). "The distinction which . . . emerged [in these cases], often expressed in different ways, [was] that the privilege is a bar against compelling 'communications' or 'testimony,' but that compulsion which makes a suspect or accused the source of 'real or physical evidence' does not violate it." *Schmerber*.

### B

The gun respondent was compelled to supply is clearly evidence of the "real or physical" sort. What makes the question of its admissibility difficult is the fact that, in asking respondent to produce the gun, the police also "compelled" him, in the *Miranda* sense, to create an incriminating testimonial response. In other words, the case is problematic because police compelled respondent not only to provide the gun but also to admit that he knew where it was and that it was his.

It is settled that *Miranda* did not itself determine whether physical evidence obtained in this manner would be admissible. See *Michigan v. Tucker*, 417 U.S., at 445-446, 447, 452, and n. 26. But the Court in *Schmerber*, with *Miranda* fresh on its mind, did address the issue. In concluding that the privilege did not require suppression of compelled blood tests, the Court noted:

> "This conclusion would not necessarily govern had the State tried to show that the accused had incriminated himself when told that he would have to be tested. Such incriminating evidence may be an unavoidable byproduct of the compulsion to take the test, especially for an individual who fears the extraction or opposes it on religious grounds. If it wishes to compel persons to submit to such attempts to discover evidence, the State may have to forgo the advantage of any testimonial products of administering the test—products which would fall within the privilege."

Thus, *Schmerber* resolved the dilemma by allowing admission of the nontestimonial, but not the testimonial, products of the State's compulsion.

[B]ased on the distinction first articulated in *Schmerber*, "a strong analytical argument can be made for an intermediate rule whereby[,] although [the police] cannot require the suspect to speak by punishment or force, the nontestimonial [evidence derived from] speech that is [itself] excludable for failure to comply with the *Miranda* code could still be used." H. Friendly, Benchmarks, 280 (1967).

To be sure, admission of nontestimonial evidence secured through informal custodial interrogation will reduce the incentives to enforce the *Miranda* code. But that fact simply begs the question of how much enforcement is appropriate. There are some situations, as the Court's struggle to accommodate a "public safety" exception demonstrates, in which the societal cost of administering the *Miranda* warnings is very high indeed.[3] The *Miranda* decision quite practically does not express any societal interest in having those warnings administered for their own sake. Rather, the warnings and waiver are only required to ensure that "testimony" used against the accused at trial is voluntarily given. Therefore, if the testimonial aspects of the accused's custodial communications are suppressed, the failure to administer the *Miranda* warnings should cease to be of concern. Cf. *Weatherford v. Bursey*, 429 U.S. 545 (1977) (where interference with assistance of counsel has no effect on trial, no Sixth Amendment violation lies). The harm caused by failure to administer *Miranda* warnings relates only to admission of testimonial self-incriminations, and the suppression of such incriminations should by itself produce the optimal enforcement of the *Miranda* rule.

### C

There are, of course, decisions of this Court which suggest that the privilege against self-incrimination requires suppression of not only compelled statements but also of all evidence derived therefrom. See, e.g., *Maness v. Meyers*, 419 U.S. 449 (1975); *Kastigar v. United States*, 406 U.S. 441 (1972); *McCarthy v. Arndstein*, 266 U.S. 34 (1924); *Counselman v. Hitchcock*, 142 U.S. 547 (1892). In each of these cases, however, the Court was responding to the dilemma that confronts persons asserting their Fifth Amendment privilege to a court or other tribunal vested with the contempt power. In each instance, the tribunal can require witnesses to appear without any showing of probable cause to believe they have committed an offense or that they have relevant information to convey, and require the witnesses to testify even if they have formally and expressly asserted a privilege of silence. Individuals in this situation are faced with what Justice Goldberg once described as "the cruel trilemma of self-accusation, perjury, or contempt." *Murphy v. Waterfront Comm'n*, 378 U.S. 52, 55 (1964). If the

---

[3] The most obvious example, first suggested by Judge Henry Friendly, involves interrogation directed to the discovery and termination of an on-going criminal activity such as kidnapping or extortion. See Friendly, The Bill of Rights as a Code of Criminal Procedure, 53 Calif.L.Rev. 929, 949 (1965).

witness' invocation of the privilege at trial is not to be defeated by the State's refusal to let him remain silent at an earlier proceeding, the witness has to be protected "against the use of his compelled answers and evidence derived therefrom in any subsequent criminal case. . . ." *Lefkowitz v. Turley*, 414 U.S. 70, 78 (1973).

By contrast, suspects subject to informal custodial police interrogation of the type involved in this case are not in the same position as witnesses required to appear before a court, grand jury, or other such formal tribunal. Where independent evidence leads police to a suspect, and probable cause justifies his arrest, the suspect cannot seriously urge that the police have somehow unfairly infringed on his right "to a private enclave where he may lead a private life." Moreover, when a suspect interjects not the privilege itself but a post hoc complaint that the police failed to administer *Miranda* warnings, he invokes only an irrebuttable presumption that the interrogation was coercive. He does not show that a privilege was raised and that the police actually or overtly coerced him to provide testimony and other evidence to be used against him at trial. See *Johnson v. New Jersey*, 384 U.S. 719, 730 (1966). He could have remained silent and the interrogator could not have punished him for refusing to speak. Indeed, the accused is in the unique position of seeking the protection of the privilege without having timely asserted it. The person in police custody surely may sense that he is in "trouble," but he is in no position to protest that he faced the Hobson's choice of self-accusation, perjury, or contempt. He therefore has a much less sympathetic case for obtaining the benefit of a broad suppression ruling.

Indeed, whatever case can be made for suppression evaporates when the statements themselves are not admitted, given the rationale of the *Schmerber* line of cases. Certainly interrogation which provides leads to other evidence does not offend the values underlying the Fifth Amendment privilege any more than the compulsory taking of blood samples, fingerprints, or voice exemplars, all of which may be compelled in an "attempt to discover evidence that might be used to prosecute [a defendant] for a criminal offense." Use of a suspect's answers "merely to find other evidence establishing his connection with the crime [simply] differs only by a shade from the permitted use for that purpose of his body or his blood." H. Friendly, Benchmarks 280 (1967). The values underlying the privilege may justify exclusion of an unwarned person's out-of-court statements, as perhaps they may justify exclusion of statements and

derivative evidence compelled under the threat of contempt. But when the only evidence to be admitted is derivative evidence such as a gun–derived not from actual compulsion but from a statement taken in the absence of *Miranda* warnings–those values simply cannot require suppression, at least no more so than they would for other such nontestimonial evidence.[4]

On the other hand, if a suspect is subject to abusive police practices and actually or overtly compelled to speak, it is reasonable to infer both an unwillingness to speak and a perceptible assertion of the privilege. See *Mincey v. Arizona*, 437 U.S. 385, 396-402 (1978). Thus, when the *Miranda* violation consists of a deliberate and flagrant abuse of the accused's constitutional rights, amounting to a denial of due process, application of a broader exclusionary rule is warranted. Of course, "a defendant raising [such] a coerced confession claim . . . must first prevail in a voluntariness hearing before his confession and evidence derived from it [will] become inadmissible." *Kastigar v. United States*, 406 U.S., at 462. By contrast, where the accused proves only that the police failed to administer the *Miranda* warnings, exclusion of the statement itself is all that will and should be required.[5] Limitation of the *Miranda* prohibition to testimonial use of the statements themselves adequately serves the purposes of the privilege against self-incrimination.

---

[4] In suggesting that *Wong Sun v. United States*, 371 U.S. 471 (1963), requires exclusion of the gun, JUSTICE MARSHALL fails to acknowledge this Court's holding in *Michigan v. Tucker*, 417 U.S. 433, 445-446 (1974). In *Tucker*, the Court very clearly held that *Wong Sun* is inapplicable in cases involving mere departures from *Miranda*. *Wong Sun* and its "fruit of the poisonous tree" analysis lead to exclusion of derivative evidence only where the underlying police misconduct infringes a "core" constitutional right. Failure to administer *Miranda* warnings violates only a nonconstitutional prophylactic.

[5] Respondent has not previously contended that his confession was so blatantly coerced as to constitute a violation of due process. He has argued only that police failed to administer *Miranda* warnings. He has proved, therefore, only that his statement was presumptively compelled. In any event, that is a question for the trial court on remand to decide in the first instance, not for this Court to decide on certiorari review.

## QUESTIONS AND NOTES

**1.** Why did Justice O'Connor think that *Schmerber* had any relevance to the admissibility of the gun? Do you agree? Explain.

**2.** Apart from *Schmerber*, what is the theory behind Justice O'Connor's opinion? Does it make sense?

**3.** The influence of Justice O'Connor's concurrence in *Quarles's* can be seen in her opinion for the Court in *Elstad*.

### Oregon v. Elstad
### 470 U.S. 298 (1985)

Justice O'CONNOR delivered the opinion of the Court.

This case requires us to decide whether an initial failure of law enforcement officers to administer the warnings required by *Miranda v. Arizona*, 384 U.S. 436, 86 S.Ct. 1602, 16 L.Ed.2d 694 (1966), without more, "taints" subsequent admissions made after a suspect has been fully advised of and has waived his *Miranda* rights. Respondent, Michael James Elstad, was convicted of burglary by an Oregon trial court. The Oregon Court of Appeals reversed, holding that respondent's signed confession, although voluntary, was rendered inadmissible by a prior remark made in response to questioning without benefit of *Miranda* warnings. We granted certiorari, 465 U.S. 1078, 104 S.Ct. 1437, 79 L.Ed.2d 759 (1984), and we now reverse.

I

In December 1981, the home of Mr. and Mrs. Gilbert Gross, in the town of Salem, Ore., was burglarized. Missing were art objects and furnishings valued at $150,000. A witness to the burglary contacted the Polk County Sheriff's office, implicating respondent Michael Elstad, an 18-year-old neighbor and friend of the Grosses' teenage son. Thereupon, Officers Burke and McAllister went to the home of respondent Elstad, with a warrant for his arrest. Elstad's mother answered the door. She led the officers to her son's room where he lay on his bed, clad in shorts and listening to his stereo. The officers asked him to get dressed and to accompany them into the living room. Officer McAllister asked respondent's mother to step into the kitchen, where he explained that they had a warrant for her son's arrest for the burglary of a neighbor's residence. Officer Burke remained with Elstad in the living room. He later testified:

"I sat down with Mr. Elstad and I asked him if he was aware of why Detective McAllister and myself were there to talk with him. He stated no, he had no idea why we were there. I then asked him if he knew a person by the name of Gross, and he said yes, he did, and also added that he heard that there was a robbery at the Gross house. And at that point I told Mr. Elstad that I felt he was involved in that, and he looked at me and stated, 'Yes, I was there.'"

The officers then escorted Elstad to the back of the patrol car. As they were about to leave for the Polk County Sheriff's office, Elstad's father arrived home and came to the rear of the patrol car. The officers advised him that his son was a suspect in the burglary. Officer Burke testified that Mr. Elstad became quite agitated, opened the rear door of the car and admonished his son: "I told you that you were going to get into trouble. You wouldn't listen to me. You never learn."

Elstad was transported to the Sheriff's headquarters and approximately one hour later, Officers Burke and McAllister joined him in McAllister's office. McAllister then advised respondent for the first time of his *Miranda* rights, reading from a standard card. Respondent indicated he understood his rights, and, having these rights in mind, wished to speak with the officers. Elstad gave a full statement, explaining that he had known that the Gross family was out of town and had been paid to lead several acquaintances to the Gross residence and show them how to gain entry through a defective sliding glass door. The statement was typed, reviewed by respondent, read back to him for correction, initialed and signed by Elstad and both officers. As an afterthought, Elstad added and initialed the sentence, "After leaving the house Robby & I went back to [the] van & Robby handed me a small bag of grass." Respondent concedes that the officers made no threats or promise either at his residence or at the Sheriff's office.

## II

The arguments advanced in favor of suppression of respondent's written confession rely heavily on metaphor. One metaphor, familiar from the Fourth Amendment context, would require that respondent's confession, regardless of its integrity, voluntariness, and probative value, be suppressed as the "tainted fruit of the poisonous tree" of the *Miranda* violation. A second metaphor questions whether a confession can be truly voluntary once the "cat is out of the bag." Taken out of context, each of these metaphors can be misleading. They should not be used to obscure fundamental differences between the role of the Fourth Amendment exclusionary rule and the function of *Miranda* in guarding against the prosecutorial use of compelled statements as prohibited by the Fifth Amendment. The Oregon court assumed and respondent here contends that a failure to administer *Miranda* warnings necessarily breeds the same consequences as police infringement of a constitutional right, so that evidence uncovered following an unwarned statement must be suppressed as "fruit of the poisonous tree." We believe this view misconstrues the nature of the protections afforded by *Miranda* warnings and therefore misreads the consequences of police failure to supply them.

### A

Prior to *Miranda*, the admissibility of an accused's in-custody statements was judged solely by whether they were "voluntary" within the meaning of the Due Process Clause. The Court in *Miranda* required suppression of many statements that would have been admissible under traditional due process analysis by presuming that statements made while in custody and without adequate warnings were protected by the Fifth Amendment. The Fifth Amendment, of course, is not concerned with nontestimonial evidence. See *Schmerber*. Nor is it concerned with moral and psychological pressures to confess emanating from sources other than official coercion. See *Innis*. Voluntary statements "remain a proper element in law enforcement." See *Miranda*. "Indeed, far from being prohibited by the Constitution, admissions of guilt by wrongdoers, if not coerced, are inherently desirable. . . . Absent some officially coerced self-accusation, the Fifth Amendment privilege is not violated by even the most damning admissions." *United States v. Washington*, 431 U.S. 181, 187 (1977).

Respondent's contention that his confession was tainted by the earlier failure of the police to provide *Miranda* warnings and must be excluded as "fruit of the poisonous tree" assumes the existence of a constitutional violation. This figure of speech is drawn from *Wong Sun* in which the Court held that evidence and witnesses discovered as a result of a search in violation of the Fourth Amendment must be excluded from evidence. The *Wong Sun* doctrine applies as well when the fruit of the Fourth Amendment violation is a confession. It is settled law that "a confession obtained through custodial interrogation after an illegal arrest should be excluded unless intervening events break the causal connection between the illegal arrest and the confession so that the confession is 'sufficiently an act of free will to purge the primary taint.'" *Taylor*.

But as we explained in *Quarles* and *Tucker*, a procedural *Miranda* violation differs in significant respects from violations of the Fourth Amendment, which have traditionally mandated a broad application of the "fruits" doctrine. The purpose of the Fourth Amendment exclusionary rule is to deter unreasonable searches, no matter how probative their fruits. "The exclusionary rule, . . . when utilized to effectuate the Fourth Amendment, serves interests and policies that are distinct from those it serves under the Fifth." Where a Fourth Amendment violation "taints" the confession, a finding of voluntariness for the purposes of the Fifth Amendment is merely a threshold requirement in determining whether the confession may be admitted in evidence. *Taylor*. Beyond this, the prosecution must show a sufficient break in events to undermine the inference that the confession was caused by the Fourth Amendment violation.

The *Miranda* exclusionary rule, however, serves the Fifth Amendment and sweeps more broadly than the Fifth Amendment itself. It may be triggered even in the absence of a Fifth Amendment violation.[1] The Fifth Amendment prohibits use by the prosecution in its case in chief only of *compelled* testimony. Failure to administer *Miranda* warnings creates a presumption of compulsion. Consequently, unwarned statements that are otherwise voluntary

---

[1] JUSTICE STEVENS expresses puzzlement at our statement that a simple failure to administer *Miranda* warnings is not in itself a violation of the Fifth Amendment. Yet the Court so held in *New York v. Quarles*, 467 U.S. 649, 654 (1983), and *Michigan v. Tucker*, 417 U.S. 433, 444 (1974). The *Miranda* Court itself recognized this point when it disclaimed any intent to create a "constitutional straitjacket" and invited Congress and the States to suggest "potential alternatives for protecting the privilege" A *Miranda* violation does not *constitute* coercion but rather affords a bright-line, legal presumption of coercion, requiring suppression of all unwarned statements. It has never been remotely suggested that any statement taken from Mr. Elstad without benefit of *Miranda* warnings would be admissible.

within the meaning of the Fifth Amendment must nevertheless be excluded from evidence under *Miranda*. Thus, in the individual case, *Miranda*'s preventive medicine provides a remedy even to the defendant who has suffered no identifiable constitutional harm.

In *Michigan v. Tucker*, the Court was asked to extend the *Wong Sun* fruits doctrine to suppress the testimony of a witness for the prosecution whose identity was discovered as the result of a statement taken from the accused without benefit of full *Miranda* warnings. As in respondent's case, the breach of the *Miranda* procedures in *Tucker* involved no actual compulsion. The Court concluded that the unwarned questioning "did not abridge respondent's constitutional privilege . . . but departed only from the prophylactic standards later laid down by this Court in *Miranda* to safeguard that privilege." Since there was no actual infringement of the suspect's constitutional rights, the case was not controlled by the doctrine expressed in *Wong Sun* that fruits of a constitutional violation must be suppressed. In deciding "how sweeping the judicially imposed consequences" of a failure to administer *Miranda* warnings should be, the *Tucker* Court noted that neither the general goal of deterring improper police conduct nor the Fifth Amendment goal of assuring trustworthy evidence would be served by suppression of the witness' testimony. The unwarned confession must, of course, be suppressed, but the Court ruled that introduction of the third-party witness' testimony did not violate Tucker's Fifth Amendment rights.

We believe that this reasoning applies with equal force when the alleged "fruit" of a noncoercive *Miranda* violation is neither a witness nor an article of evidence but the accused's own voluntary testimony. As in *Tucker*, the absence of any coercion or improper tactics undercuts the twin rationales—trustworthiness and deterrence—for a broader rule. Once warned, the suspect is free to exercise his own volition in deciding whether or not to make a statement to the authorities. The Court has often noted: "'[A] living witness is not to be mechanically equated with the proffer of inanimate evidentiary objects illegally seized. . . . [T]he living witness is an individual human personality whose attributes of will, perception, memory and volition interact to determine what testimony he will give.'" *Ceccolini*.

Because *Miranda* warnings may inhibit persons from giving information, this Court has determined that they need be administered only after the person is taken into "custody" or his freedom has otherwise been significantly restrained. Unfortunately, the task of defining "custody" is a slippery one, and "policemen investigating serious crimes [cannot realistically be expected to] make no errors whatsoever."

If errors are made by law enforcement officers in administering the prophylactic *Miranda* procedures, they should not breed the same irremediable consequences as police infringement of the Fifth Amendment itself. It is an unwarranted extension of *Miranda* to hold that a simple failure to administer the warnings, unaccompanied by any actual coercion or other circumstances calculated to undermine the suspect's ability to exercise his free will, so taints the investigatory process that a subsequent voluntary and informed waiver is ineffective for some indeterminate period. Though *Miranda* requires that the unwarned admission must be suppressed, the admissibility of any subsequent statement should turn in these circumstances solely on whether it is knowingly and voluntarily made.

B

The Oregon court, however, believed that the unwarned remark compromised the voluntariness of respondent's later confession. It was the court's view that the prior answer and not the unwarned questioning impaired respondent's ability to give a valid waiver and that only lapse of time and change of place could dissipate what it termed the "coercive impact" of the inadmissible statement. When a prior statement is actually coerced, the time that passes between confessions, the change in place of interrogations, and the change in identity of the interrogators all bear on whether that coercion has carried over into the second confession. See *Westover v. United States*, decided together with *Miranda*. The failure of police to administer *Miranda* warnings does not mean that the statements received have actually been coerced, but only that courts will presume the privilege against compulsory self-incrimination has not been intelligently exercised. Of the courts that have considered whether a properly warned confession must be suppressed because it was preceded by an unwarned but clearly voluntary admission, the majority have explicitly or implicitly recognized that *Westover's* requirement of a break in the stream of events is inapposite. In these circumstances, a careful and thorough administration of *Miranda* warnings serves to cure the condition that rendered the unwarned statement inadmissible. The warning conveys the relevant information and thereafter the suspect's choice whether to exercise his privilege to remain silent should ordinarily be viewed as an "act of free will."

The Oregon court nevertheless identified a subtle form of lingering compulsion, the psychological impact of the suspect's conviction that he has let the cat out of the bag and, in so doing, has sealed his own fate. But endowing the psychological effects of *voluntary* unwarned admissions with constitutional implications would, practically speaking, disable the police from obtaining the suspect's informed cooperation even when the official coercion proscribed by the Fifth Amendment played no part in either his warned or unwarned confessions. As the Court remarked in *Bayer*:

"[A]fter an accused has once let the cat out of the bag by confessing, no matter what the inducement, he is never thereafter free of the psychological and practical disadvantages of having confessed. He can never get the cat back in the bag. The secret is out for good. In such a sense, a later confession may always be looked upon as fruit of the first. But this Court has never gone so far as to hold that making a confession under circumstances which preclude its use, perpetually disables the confessor from making a usable one after those conditions have been removed."

Even in such extreme cases as *Lyons v. Oklahoma*, 322 U.S. 596 (1944), in which police forced a full confession from the accused through unconscionable methods of interrogation, the Court has assumed that the coercive effect of the confession could, with time, be dissipated.

This Court has never held that the psychological impact of voluntary disclosure of a guilty secret qualifies as state compulsion or compromises the voluntariness of a subsequent informed waiver. The Oregon court, by adopting this expansive view of Fifth Amendment compulsion, effectively immunizes a suspect who responds to pre-*Miranda* warning questions from the consequences of his subsequent informed waiver of the privilege of remaining silent. This immunity comes at a high cost to legitimate law enforcement activity, while adding little desirable protection to the individual's interest in not being *compelled* to testify against himself.

There is a vast difference between the direct consequences flowing from coercion of a confession by physical violence or other deliberate means calculated to break the suspect's will and the uncertain consequences of disclosure of a "guilty secret" freely given in response to an unwarned but noncoercive question, as in this case. Justice BRENNAN's contention that it is impossible to perceive any causal distinction between this case and one involving a confession that is coerced by torture is wholly unpersuasive. Certainly, in respondent's case, the causal connection between any psychological disadvantage created by his admission and his ultimate decision to cooperate is speculative and attenuated at best. It is difficult to tell with certainty what motivates a suspect to speak. A suspect's confession may be traced to factors as disparate as "a prearrest event such as a visit with a minister," *Dunaway v. New York*, 442 U.S. at 220, (STEVENS, J., concurring),

or an intervening event such as the exchange of words respondent had with his father. We must conclude that, absent deliberately coercive or improper tactics in obtaining the initial statement, the mere fact that a suspect has made an unwarned admission does not warrant a presumption of compulsion. A subsequent administration of *Miranda* warnings to a suspect who has given a voluntary but unwarned statement ordinarily should suffice to remove the conditions that precluded admission of the earlier statement. In such circumstances, the finder of fact may reasonably conclude that the suspect made a rational and intelligent choice whether to waive or invoke his rights.

### III

There is no question that respondent knowingly and voluntarily waived his right to remain silent before he described his participation in the burglary. It is also beyond dispute that respondent's earlier remark was voluntary, within the meaning of the Fifth Amendment. Neither the environment nor the manner of either "interrogation" was coercive. The initial conversation took place at midday, in the living room area of respondent's own home, with his mother in the kitchen area, a few steps away. Although in retrospect the officers testified that respondent was then in custody, at the time he made his statement he had not been informed that he was under arrest. The arresting officers' testimony indicates that the brief stop in the living room before proceeding to the station house was not to interrogate the suspect but to notify his mother of the reason for his arrest.

The State has conceded the issue of custody and thus we must assume that Burke breached *Miranda* procedures in failing to administer *Miranda* warnings before initiating the discussion in the living room. This breach may have been the result of confusion as to whether the brief exchange qualified as "custodial interrogation" or it may simply have reflected Burke's reluctance to initiate an alarming police procedure before McAllister had spoken with respondent's mother. Whatever the reason for Burke's oversight, the incident had none of the earmarks of coercion. Nor did the officers exploit the unwarned admission to pressure respondent into waiving his right to remain silent.

Respondent, however, has argued that he was unable to give a fully *informed* waiver of his rights because he was unaware that his prior statement could not be used against him. Respondent suggests that Officer McAllister, to cure this deficiency, should have added an additional warning to those given him at the Sheriff's office. Such a requirement is neither practicable nor constitutionally necessary. In many cases, a breach of *Miranda* procedures may not be identified as such until long after full *Miranda* warnings are administered and a valid confession obtained. The standard *Miranda* warnings explicitly inform the suspect of his right to consult a lawyer before speaking. Police officers are ill-equipped to pinch-hit for counsel, construing the murky and difficult questions of when "custody" begins or whether a given unwarned statement will ultimately be held admissible.

This Court has never embraced the theory that a defendant's ignorance of the full consequences of his decisions vitiates their voluntariness. If the prosecution has actually violated the defendant's Fifth Amendment rights by introducing an inadmissible confession at trial, compelling the defendant to testify in rebuttal, the rule announced in *Harrison v. United States* 392 U.S. 219 (1968), precludes use of that testimony on retrial. "Having 'released the spring' by using the petitioner's unlawfully obtained confessions against him, the Government must show that its illegal action did not induce his testimony." But the Court has refused to find that a defendant who confesses, after being falsely told that his codefendant has turned State's evidence, does so involuntarily. *Frazier v. Cupp*, 394 U.S. 731, 739, 89 S.Ct. 1420, 1424, 22 L.Ed.2d 684 (1969). The Court has also rejected the argument that a defendant's ignorance that a prior coerced confession could not be admitted in evidence compromised the voluntariness of his guilty plea. Likewise, in *California v. Beheler*, 463 U.S. 1121 (1983) the Court declined to accept defendant's contention that, because he was unaware of the potential adverse consequences of statements he made to the police, his participation in the interview was involuntary. Thus we have not held that the sine qua non for a knowing and voluntary waiver of the right to remain silent is a full and complete appreciation of all of the consequences flowing from the nature and the quality of the evidence in the case.

## IV

When police ask questions of a suspect in custody without administering the required warnings, *Miranda* dictates that the answers received be presumed compelled and that they be excluded from evidence at trial in the State's case in chief. The Court has carefully adhered to this principle, permitting a narrow exception only where pressing public safety concerns demanded. *Quarles*. The Court today in no way retreats from the bright-line rule of *Miranda*. We do not imply that good faith excuses a failure to administer *Miranda* warnings; nor do we condone inherently coercive police tactics or methods offensive to due process that render the initial admission involuntary and undermine the suspect's will to invoke his rights once they are read to him. A handful

of courts have, however, applied our precedents relating to confessions obtained under coercive circumstances to situations involving wholly voluntary admissions, requiring a passage of time or break in events before a second, fully warned statement can be deemed voluntary. Far from establishing a rigid rule, we direct courts to avoid one; there is no warrant for presuming coercive effect where the suspect's initial inculpatory statement, though technically in violation of *Miranda*, was voluntary.[5] The relevant inquiry is whether, in fact, the second statement was also voluntarily made. As in any such inquiry, the finder of fact must examine the surrounding circumstances and the entire course of police conduct with respect to the suspect in evaluating the voluntariness of his statements. The fact that a suspect chooses to speak after being informed of his rights is, of course, highly probative. We find that the dictates of *Miranda* and the goals of the Fifth Amendment proscription against use of compelled testimony are fully satisfied in the circumstances of this case by barring use of the unwarned statement in the case in chief. No further purpose is served by imputing "taint" to subsequent statements obtained pursuant to a voluntary and knowing waiver. We hold today that a suspect who has once responded to unwarned yet uncoercive questioning is not thereby disabled from waiving his rights and confessing after he has been given the requisite *Miranda* warnings.

The judgment of the Court of Appeals of Oregon is reversed, and the case is remanded for further proceedings not inconsistent with this opinion.

Justice BRENNAN, with whom Justice MARSHALL joins, dissenting.

The Self-Incrimination Clause of the Fifth Amendment guarantees every individual that, if taken into official custody, he shall be informed of important constitutional rights and be given the opportunity knowingly and voluntarily to waive those rights before being interrogated about suspected wrongdoing. *Miranda*. This guarantee embodies our society's conviction that "no system of criminal justice can, or should, survive if it comes to depend for its continued effectiveness on the citizens' abdication through unawareness of their constitutional rights." *Escobedo*.

Even while purporting to reaffirm these constitutional guarantees, the Court has engaged of late in

---

[5] JUSTICE BRENNAN, with an apocalyptic tone, heralds this opinion as dealing a "crippling blow to *Miranda*." JUSTICE BRENNAN not only distorts the reasoning and holding of our decision, but, worse, invites trial courts and prosecutors to do the same.

a studied campaign to strip the *Miranda* decision piecemeal and to undermine the rights *Miranda* sought to secure. Today's decision not only extends this effort a further step, but delivers a potentially crippling blow to *Miranda* and the ability of courts to safeguard the rights of persons accused of crime. For at least with respect to successive confessions, the Court today appears to strip remedies for *Miranda* violations of the "fruit of the poisonous tree" doctrine prohibiting the use of evidence presumptively derived from official illegality.

Two major premises undergird the Court's decision. The Court rejects as nothing more than "speculative" the long-recognized presumption that an illegally extracted confession causes the accused to confess again out of the mistaken belief that he already has sealed his fate, and it condemns as " 'extravagant' " the requirement that the prosecution affirmatively rebut the presumption before the subsequent confession may be admitted. The Court instead adopts a new rule that, so long as the accused is given the usual *Miranda* warnings before further interrogation, the taint of a previous confession obtained in violation of *Miranda* "ordinarily" must be viewed as *automatically* dissipated.

The Court's decision says much about the way the Court currently goes about implementing its agenda. In imposing its new rule, for example, the Court mischaracterizes our precedents, obfuscates the central issues, and altogether ignores the practical realities of custodial interrogation that have led nearly every lower court to reject its simplistic reasoning. Moreover, the Court adopts startling and unprecedented methods of construing constitutional guarantees. Finally the Court reaches out once again to address issues not before us. For example, although the State of Oregon has conceded that the arresting officers broke the law in this case, the Court goes out of its way to suggest that they may have been objectively justified in doing so.

Today's decision, in short, threatens disastrous consequences far beyond the outcome in this case. As the Court has not seen fit to provide a full explanation for this result, I believe it essential to consider in detail the premises, reasoning, and implications of the Court's opinion.

## I

The threshold question is this: What effect should an admission or confession of guilt obtained in violation of an accused's *Miranda* rights be presumed to have upon the voluntariness of subsequent confessions that are preceded by *Miranda* warnings? Relying on the "cat out of the bag" analysis of *United States v. Bayer*, the Oregon Court of Appeals held that the first confession presumptively taints subsequent confessions in such circumstances. On the specific facts of this case, the court below found that

the prosecution had not rebutted this presumption. Rather, given the temporal proximity of Elstad's second confession to his first and the absence of any significant intervening circumstances, the court correctly concluded that there had not been "a sufficient break in the stream of events between [the] inadmissible statement and the written confession to insulate the latter statement from the effect of what went before."

The Court today sweeps aside this common-sense approach as "speculative" reasoning, adopting instead a rule that "the psychological impact of *voluntary* disclosure of a guilty secret" neither "qualifies as state compulsion" nor "compromises the voluntariness" of subsequent confession. (emphasis added). So long as suspect received the usual *Miranda* warnings before further interrogation, the Court reasons, the fact that he "is free to exercise his own volition in deciding whether or not to make" further confessions "ordinarily" is a sufficient "cure" and serves to break any causal connection between the illegal confession and subsequent statements.

The Court's marble-palace psychoanalysis is tidy, but it flies in the fact of our own precedents, demonstrates a starling unawareness of the realities of police interrogation, and is completely out of tune with the experience of state and federal courts over the last 20 years. Perhaps the Court has grasped some psychological truth that has eluded persons far more experienced in these matters; if so, the Court owes an explanation of how so many could have been so wrong for so many years.

### A

#### (1)

This Court has had long experience with the problem of confessions obtained after an earlier confession has been illegally secured. Subsequent confessions in these circumstances are not per se inadmissible, but the prosecution must demonstrate facts "sufficient to insulate the [subsequent] statement from the effect of all that went before." *Clewis v. Texas,* 386 U.S. 707, 710 (1967).

One of the factors that can vitiate the voluntariness of a subsequent confession is the hopeless feeling of an accused that he has nothing to lose by repeating his confession, even where the circumstances that rendered his first confession illegal have been removed. As the Court observed in *United States v. Bayer*, 331 U.S., at 540, 67 S.Ct., at 1394:

"[A]fter an accused has once let the cat out of the bag by confessing, no matter what the inducement, he is never thereafter free of the psychological and practical disadvantages of having confessed. He can never get the cat back in the bag. The secret is out for good. In such a sense, a later confession always may be looked upon as a fruit of the first."

The Court today decries the "irremediable consequences" of this reasoning, but it has always been clear that even after "let[ting] the cat out of the bag" the accused is not "perpetually disable[d]" from giving an admissible subsequent confession. *Bayer.* Rather, we have held that subsequent confessions in such circumstances may be admitted if the prosecution demonstrates that, "[c]onsidering the 'totality of the circumstances,'" there was a "'break in the stream of events . . . sufficient to insulate'" the subsequent confession from the damning impact of the first. *Darwin v. Connecticut,* 391 U.S. 346, 349 (1968).

(2)

Our precedents did not develop in a vacuum. They reflect an understanding of the realities of police interrogation and the everyday experience of lower courts. Expert interrogators, far from dismissing a first admission or confession as creating merely a "speculative and attenuated" disadvantage for a suspect, understand that such revelations frequently lead directly to a full confession. Standard interrogation manuals advise that "[t]he securing of the first admission is the biggest stumbling block. . . ." A. Aubry & R. Caputo, Criminal Interrogation 290 (3d ed 1980). If this first admission can be obtained, "there is every reason to expect that the first admission will lead to others, and eventually to the full confession." Ibid.

The practical experience of state and federal courts confirms the experts' understanding. From this experience, lower courts have concluded that a first confession obtained without proper *Miranda* warnings, far from creating merely some "speculative and attenuated" disadvantage for the accused, frequently enables the authorities to obtain subsequent confessions on a "silver platter."

One police practice that courts have frequently encountered involves the withholding of *Miranda* warnings until the end of an interrogation session. Specifically, the police escort a suspect into a room, sit him down and, without explaining his Fifth Amendment rights or obtaining a knowing and voluntary waiver of those rights, interrogate him about his suspected criminal activity. If the police obtain a confession, it is then typed up, the police hand the suspect a pen for his signature, and—just before he signs—the police advise him of his *Miranda* rights and ask him to proceed. Alternatively, the police may call a stenographer in after they have obtained the confession, advise the suspect for the first time of his *Miranda* rights, and ask him to repeat what he has just told them. In such circumstances, the process of giving *Miranda* warnings and obtaining the final confession is "'merely a formalizing, a setting down almost as a scrivener does, [of] what ha[s] already taken [place].'" *People v. Raddatz,* 91 Ill.App.2d 425, 430, 235 N.E.2d 353, 356 (1968) (quoting trial court). In such situations, where "it was all over except for reading aloud and explaining the written waiver of the *Miranda* safeguards," courts have time and again concluded that "[t]he giving of the *Miranda* warnings before reducing the product of the day's work to written form could not undo what had been done or make legal what was illegal." *People v. Bodner,* 75 App.Div.2d 440, 448, 430 N.Y.S.2d 433, 438 (1980).

There are numerous variations on this theme. [T]he suspect might be questioned by arresting officers "in the field" and without *Miranda* warnings, as was young Elstad in the instant case. After making incriminating admissions or a confession, the suspect is then brought into the station house and either questioned by the same officers again or asked to repeat his earlier statements to another officer.

For all practical purposes, the prewarning and post-warning questioning are often but stages of one overall interrogation. Whether or not the authorities explicitly confront the suspect with his earlier illegal admissions makes no significant difference, of course, because the suspect knows that the authorities know of his earlier statements and most frequently will believe that those statements already have sealed his fate. Thus a suspect in such circumstances is likely to conclude that "he might as well answer the questions put to him, since the [authorities are] already aware of the earlier answers."

I would have thought that the Court, instead of dismissing the "cat out of the bag" presumption out of hand, would have accounted for these practical realities. Compare *Nardone v. United States,* 308 U.S., at 342 (derivative-evidence rules should be grounded on the "learning, good sense, fairness and courage" of lower-court judges). Expert interrogators and experienced lower-court judges will be startled, to say the least, to learn that the connection between multiple confessions is "speculative" and that a subsequent rendition of *Miranda* warnings "ordinarily" enables the accused in these circumstances to exercise his "free will" and to make "a rational and intelligent choice whether to waive or invoke his rights."

B

The Court's new approach is therefore completely at odds with established dissipation analysis. A comparison of the Court's analysis with the factors most frequently relied on by lower courts in considering the admissibility of subsequent confessions demonstrates the practical and legal flaws of the new rule.

*Advice that earlier confession may be inadmissible.* The most effective means to ensure the voluntariness of an accused's subsequent confession is to advise the accused that his earlier admissions may not be admissible and therefore that he need not speak solely out of a belief that "the cat is out of the bag." Many courts have required such warnings in the absence of other dissipating factors, and this Court has not uncovered anything to suggest that this approach has not succeeded in the real world. The Court, however, believes that law enforcement authorities could never possibly understand "the murky and difficult questio[n]" of when *Miranda* warnings must be given, and therefore that they are "ill-equipped" to make the decision whether supplementary warnings might be required.

This reasoning is unpersuasive for two reasons. First, the whole point of *Miranda* and its progeny has been to prescribe "bright line" rules for the authorities to follow. Although borderline cases will of course occasionally arise, thus militating against a per se rule requiring supplementary warnings, the experience of the lower courts demonstrates that the vast majority of confrontations implicating this question involve obvious *Miranda* violations. The occasional "murky and difficult" case should not preclude consideration of supplementary warnings in situations where the authorities could not possibly have acted in an objectively reasonable manner in their earlier interrogation of the accused. Second, even where the authorities are not certain that an earlier confession has been illegally obtained, courts and commentators have recognized that a supplementary warning merely advising the accused that his earlier confession *may* be inadmissible can dispel his belief that he has nothing to lose by repetition.

*Proximity in time and place.* Courts have frequently concluded that a subsequent confession was so removed in time and place from the first that the accused most likely was able fully to exercise his independent judgment in deciding whether to speak again. As in the instant case, however, a second confession frequently follows immediately on the heels of the first and is obtained by the same officials in the same or similar coercive surroundings. In such situations, it is wholly unreasonable to assume that the mere rendition of *Miranda* warnings will safeguard the accused's freedom of action.

*Intervening factors.* Some lower courts have found that because of intervening factors—such as consultation with a lawyer or family members, or an independent decision to speak—an accused's subsequent confession could not fairly be attributed to the earlier statement taken in violation of *Miranda.* On the other hand, where as here an accused has continuously been in custody and there is no legitimate suggestion of an intervening event sufficient to break the impact of the first confession, subsequent confessions are inadmissible. The Court reasons, however, that because "[a] suspect's confession may be traced to . . . an intervening event," it "*must* [be] conclude[d]" that subsequent *Miranda* warnings presumptively enable the suspect to make "a rational and intelligent choice" whether to repeat his confession. (emphasis added). In applying the intervening-events inquiry, however, "courts must use a surgeon's scalpel and not a meat axe." Cf. 3 W. La-Fave, Search and Seizure, § 11.4, p. 624 (1978). The only proper inquiry is whether a meaningful intervening event actually occurred, not whether a court simply chooses to shut its eyes to human nature and the realities of custodial interrogation.

## II

Not content merely to ignore the practical realities of police interrogation and the likely effects of its abolition of the derivative-evidence presumption, the Court goes on to assert that nothing in the Fifth Amendment or the general judicial policy of deterring illegal police conduct "ordinarily" requires the suppression of evidence derived proximately from a confession obtained in violation of *Miranda.* The Court does not limit its analysis to successive confessions, but recurrently refers generally to the "fruits" of the illegal confession. Thus the potential impact of the Court's reasoning might extend far beyond the "cat out of the bag" context to include the discovery of physical evidence and other derivative fruits of *Miranda* violations as well.[29]

### A

Twice in the last 10 years, however, the Court has suggested that the *Miranda* safeguards are not themselves rights guaranteed by the Fifth Amendment. In *Tucker,* the Court stated that *Miranda* had only prescribed "recommended" procedural safeguards "to provide practical reinforcement for the right against compulsory self-incrimination," the violation of which may not necessarily violate the Fifth Amendment itself. And in *Quarles,* the Court last

---

[29] Notwithstanding the sweep of the Court's language, today's opinion surely ought not be read as also foreclosing application of the traditional derivative-evidence presumption to physical evidence obtained as a proximate result of a *Miranda* violation. The Court relies heavily on individual "volition" as an insulating factor in successive-confession cases. Although the Court's reliance on this factor is clearly misplaced the factor is altogether missing in the context of inanimate evidence.

Term disturbingly rejected the argument that a confession "must be *presumed* compelled because of . . . failure to read [the accused] his *Miranda* warnings." (emphasis in original).

These assertions are erroneous. *Miranda's* requirement of warnings and an effective waiver was not merely an exercise of supervisory authority over interrogation practices. As Justice Douglas noted in his *Tucker* dissent:

> "*Miranda's* purpose was not promulgation of judicially preferred standards for police interrogation, a function we are quite powerless to perform; the decision enunciated '*constitutional* standards for protection of the privilege' against self-incrimination. (emphasis in original).

*Miranda* clearly emphasized that warnings and an informed waiver are essential to the Fifth Amendment privilege itself. As noted in *Tucker*, *Miranda* did state that the Constitution does not require "'adherence to any particular solution'" for providing the required knowledge and obtaining an informed waiver. But to rely solely on this language in concluding that the *Miranda* warnings are not constitutional rights, as did the Court in *Tucker*, ignores the central issue. The Court in *Tucker* omitted to mention that in *Miranda*, after concluding that no "particular solution" is required, we went on to emphasize that "unless we are shown other procedures which are at least as effective in apprising accused persons of their right of silence and in assuring a continuous opportunity to exercise it, the [prescribed] safeguards must be observed." Thus "the use of [any] admissions obtained in the absence of the required warnings [is] a flat violation of the Self-Incrimination Clause of the Fifth Amendment. . . ."

The Court today finally recognizes these flaws in the logic of *Tucker* and *Quarles*. Although disastrous in so many other respects, today's opinion at least has the virtue of rejecting the inaccurate assertion in *Quarles* that confessions extracted in violation of *Miranda* are not presumptively coerced for Fifth Amendment purposes. Instead, the Court holds squarely that there is an "irrebuttable" presumption that such confessions are indeed coerced and are therefore inadmissible under the Fifth Amendment except in narrow circumstances. [31]

## B

Unfortunately, the Court takes away with one hand far more than what it has given with the other. Although the Court concedes, as it must, that a confession obtained in violation of *Miranda* is irrebuttably presumed to be coerced and that the Self-Incrimination Clause therefore prevents its use in the prosecution's case in chief, the Court goes on to hold that nothing in the Fifth Amendment prevents the introduction at trial of evidence proximately derived from the illegal confession. It contends, for example, that the Fifth Amendment prohibits introduction "only" of the "compelled testimony," and that this constitutional guarantee "is not concerned with nontestimonial evidence."

This narrow compass of the protection against compelled self-incrimination does not accord with our historic understanding of the Fifth Amendment. Although the Self-Incrimination Clause "protects an accused only from being compelled to testify against himself, or otherwise provide the State with evidence of a testimonial or communicative nature," *Schmerber*, it prohibits the use of such communications "against" the accused in any way. The Fifth Amendment therefore contains a self-executing rule commanding the exclusion of evidence derived from such communications. [32]

## D

Not content with its handiwork discussed above, the Court goes on and devotes considerable effort to suggesting that, "[u]nfortunately," *Miranda* is such an inherently "slippery," "murky," and "difficult" concept that the authorities in general, and the police officer conducting the interrogation in this case in particular, cannot be faulted for failing to advise a suspect of his rights and to obtain an informed waiver. *Miranda* will become "murky," however, only because the Court's opinion today threatens to become a self-fulfilling prophecy. Although borderline cases occasionally have arisen respecting the concepts of "custody" and "interrogation," until today there has been nothing "slippery," "murky," or "difficult" about *Miranda* in the overwhelming majority of cases. The whole point of the Court's work in this area has been to prescribe "bright line" rules to give clear guidance to the authorities.

---

[31] The exceptions are where a confession is used to impeach the defendant's trial testimony, *Harris v. New York*, 401 U.S. 222 (1971), and where *Miranda* warnings were not given because of "pressing public safety concerns," *Quarles*.

[32] The Court's reliance on *Schmereber* in support of its constricted view of the Fifth Amendment, is wholly inappropriate. *Schmerber* had nothing to do with the derivative-evidence rule, but held only that the evidence compelled in the first instance in that case – blood samples – was nontestimonial in nature.

Rather than acknowledge that the police in this case clearly broke the law, the Court bends over backwards to suggest why the officers may have been justified in failing to obey *Miranda*.

*First.* The Court asserts that "[n]either the environment nor the manner of either 'interrogation' was coercive," noting that the initial interrogation took place in Elstad's "own home." The Court also believes that, "[a]lthough in retrospect the officers testified that respondent was then in custody, at the time he made his statement he had not been informed that he was under arrest." There is no question, however, that Michael Elstad was in custody and "deprived of his freedom of action in [a] significant way" at the time he was interrogated. Two police officers had entered his bedroom, ordered him to get out of bed and come with them, stood over him while he dressed, taken him downstairs, and separated him from his mother. The officers themselves acknowledged that Elstad was then under arrest. Moreover, we have made clear that police interrogation of an accused in custody triggers the *Miranda* safeguard even if he is in the "familiar surroundings" of his own home, precisely because he is no less "'deprived of his freedom of action'" there than if he were at a police station. *Orozco.*

Thus because Elstad was in custody, the circumstances of his interrogation were inherently coercive, and the Court once again flouts settled law in suggesting otherwise.

*Second.* Without anything in the record to support its speculation, the Court suggests that Officer Burke's violation of *Miranda* "may have been the result of confusion as to whether the brief exchange qualified as 'custodial interrogation'. . . ." There was no confusion on this point until today. Burke made Elstad sit down and, standing over him, said "[y]ou know why we're here," asked if he knew the Gross family, and "asked what he knew about the burglary." This questioning obviously constituted interrogation because it was "reasonably likely to evoke an incriminating response" from Elstad, as it did. *Innis.*

*Third.* The Court contends that the interrogation might be excusable because "the brief stop in the living room before proceeding to the station house was not to interrogate the suspect but to notify his mother of the reason for his arrest." Officer Burke's partner did take Elstad's mother into the kitchen to inform her of the charges, but Burke took Elstad into another room, sat him down, and interrogated him concerning "what he knew about the burglary."

How can the Court possibly describe this interrogation as merely informing Elstad's mother of his arrest?

*Finally.* The Court suggests that Burke's violation of Elstad's Fifth Amendment rights "may simply have reflected Burke's reluctance to initiate an alarming police procedure before McAllister had spoken with respondent's mother." As the officers themselves acknowledged, however, the fact that they "[took] the young fellow out of bed" had "[o]bviously" already created "tension and stress" for the mother, which surely was not lessened when she learned that her son was under arrest. And if Elstad's mother was in earshot, as the Court assumes, it is difficult to perceive how listening to the *Miranda* warnings would be any more "alarming" to her than what she actually heard—actual interrogation of her son, including Burke's direct accusation that the boy had committed a felony. Most importantly, an individual's constitutional rights should not turn on whether his relatives might be upset. Surely there is no "tender feelings" exception to the Fifth Amendment privilege against self-incrimination.

### III

The Court's decision today vividly reflects its impatience with the constitutional rights that the authorities attack as standing in the way of combating crime. But the States that adopted the Bill of Rights struck that balance and it is not for this Court to balance the Bill of Rights away on a cost/benefit scale "where the 'costs' of excluding illegally obtained evidence loom to exaggerated heights and where the 'benefits' of such exclusion are made to disappear with a mere wave of the hand." *Leon*, (BRENNAN, J., dissenting).

The lesson of today's decision is that, at least for now, what the Court decrees are "legitimate" violations by authorities of the rights embodied in *Miranda* shall "ordinarily" go undeterred. It is but the latest of the escalating number of decisions that are making this tribunal increasingly irrelevant in the protection of individual rights, and that are requiring other tribunals to shoulder the burden. "There is hope, however, that in time this or some later Court will restore these precious freedoms to their rightful place as a primary protection for our citizens against overreaching officialdom."

I dissent.

Justice STEVENS, dissenting.

The Court concludes its opinion with a carefully phrased statement of its holding:

> "We hold today that a suspect who has once responded to unwarned yet uncoercive questioning is not thereby disabled from waiving his rights and confessing after he has been

given the requisite *Miranda* warnings."

I find nothing objectionable in such a holding. Moreover, because the Court expressly endorses the "bright-line rule of *Miranda*," which conclusively presumes that incriminating statements obtained from a suspect in custody without administering the required warnings are the product of compulsion, and because the Court places so much emphasis on the special facts of this case, I am persuaded that the Court intends its holding to apply only to a narrow category of cases in which the initial questioning of the suspect was made in a totally uncoercive setting and in which the first confession obviously had no influence on the second. I nevertheless dissent because even such a narrowly confined exception is inconsistent with the Court's prior cases, because the attempt to identify its boundaries in future cases will breed confusion and uncertainty in the administration of criminal justice, and because it denigrates the importance of one of the core constitutional rights that protects every American citizen from the kind of tyranny that has flourished in other societies.

I

The desire to achieve a just result in this particular case has produced an opinion that is somewhat opaque and internally inconsistent. If I read it correctly, its conclusion rests on two untenable premises: (1) that the respondent's first confession was not the product of coercion; and (2) that no constitutional right was violated when respondent was questioned in a tranquil, domestic setting.

Even before *Miranda* it had been recognized that police interrogation of a suspect who has been taken into custody is presumptively coercive. That presumption had its greatest force when the questioning occurred in a police station, when it was prolonged, and when there was evidence that the prisoner had suffered physical injury. To rebut the presumption, the prosecutor had the burden of proving the absence of any actual coercion. Because police officers are generally more credible witnesses than prisoners and because it is always difficult for triers of fact to disregard evidence of guilt when addressing a procedural question, more often than not the presumption of coercion afforded only slight protection to the accused.

*Miranda* clarified the law in three important respects. First, it provided the prosecutor with a simple method of overcoming the presumption of coercion. If the police interrogation is preceded by the warning specified in that opinion, the usual presumption does not attach. Second, it provided an important protection to the accused by making the presumption of coercion irrebuttable if the prescribed warnings are not given. Third, the decision made it clear that a self-incriminatory statement made in response to custodial interrogation was always to be considered "compelled" within the meaning of the Fifth Amendment to the Federal Constitution if the interrogation had not been preceded by appropriate warnings. Thus the irrebuttable presumption of coercion that applies to such a self-incriminatory statement, like a finding of actual coercion, renders the resulting confession inadmissible as a matter of federal constitutional law.

In my opinion, the Court's attempt to fashion a distinction between actual coercion "by physical violence or other deliberate means calculated to break the suspect's will," and irrebuttably presumed coercion cannot succeed. The presumption is only legitimate if it is assumed that there is always a coercive aspect to custodial interrogation that is not preceded by adequate advice of the constitutional right to remain silent. Although I would not support it, I could understand a rule that refused to apply the presumption unless the interrogation took place in an especially coercive setting—perhaps only in the police station itself—but if the presumption arises whenever the accused has been taken into custody or his freedom has been restrained in any significant way, it will surely be futile to try to develop subcategories of custodial interrogation.[10] Indeed, a major purpose of treating the presumption of coercion as irrebuttable is to avoid the kind of fact-bound inquiry that today's decision will surely engender.

As I read the Court's opinion, it expressly accepts the proposition that routine *Miranda* warnings will not be sufficient to overcome the presumption of coercion and thereby make a second confession admissible when an earlier confession is tainted by coercion "by physical violence or other deliberate means calculated to break the suspect's will." Even in such a case, however, it is not necessary to assume that the earlier confession will always "effectively immunize" a later voluntary confession. But surely the fact that an earlier confession was obtained by

---

[10] Of course, in *Orozco* this Court rejected the contention that *Miranda* warnings were inapplicable because a defendant "was interrogated on his own bed, in familiar surrounds"

unlawful methods should add force to the presumption of coercion that attaches to subsequent custodial interrogation and should require the prosecutor to shoulder a heavier burden of rebuttal than in a routine case. Simple logic, as well as the interest in not providing an affirmative incentive to police misconduct, requires that result. I see no reason why the violation of a rule that is as well recognized and easily administered as the duty to give *Miranda* warnings should not also impose an additional burden on the prosecutor.[13] If we are faithful to the holding in *Miranda* itself, when we are considering the admissibility of evidence in the prosecutor's case in chief, we should not try to fashion a distinction between police misconduct that warrants a finding of actual coercion and police misconduct that establishes an irrebuttable presumption of coercion.

## II

For me, the most disturbing aspect of the Court's opinion is its somewhat opaque characterization of the police misconduct in this case. The Court appears ambivalent on the question whether there was any constitutional violation.[14] This ambivalence is either disingenuous or completely lawless. This Court's power to require state courts to exclude probative self-incriminatory statements rests entirely on the premise that the use of such evidence violates the Federal Constitution. The same constitutional analysis applies whether the custodial interrogation is actually coercive or irrebuttably presumed to be coercive. If the Court does not accept that premise, it must regard the holding in the *Miranda* case itself, as well as all of the federal jurisprudence that has evolved from that decision, as nothing more than an illegitimate exercise of raw judicial power. If the Court accepts the proposition that respondent's self-incriminatory statement was inadmissible, it must also acknowledge that the Federal Constitution protected him from custodial police interrogation without first being advised of his right to remain silent.

Indeed, the Court's holding rests on its view that there were no "improper tactics in obtaining the initial statement."

The source of respondent's constitutional protection is the Fifth Amendment's privilege against compelled self-incrimination that is secured against state invasion by the Due Process Clause of the Fourteenth Amendment. Like many other provisions of the Bill of Rights, that provision is merely a procedural safeguard. It is, however, the specific provision that protects all citizens from the kind of custodial interrogation that was once employed by the Star Chamber, by "the Germans of the 1930's and early 1940's," and by some of our own police departments only a few decades ago. Custodial interrogation that violates that provision of the Bill of Rights is a classic example of a violation of a constitutional right.

I respectfully dissent.

---

[13] I am not persuaded that the *Miranda* rule is so "murky," that the law enforcement profession would be unable to identify the cases in which a supplementary warning would be appropriate. *Miranda* was written, in part, "to give concrete constitutional guidelines for law enforcement agencies and courts to follow." Nearly two decades after the disposition, it is undisputed that the *Miranda* rule – now so deeply embedded in our culture that most school children know not only the warnings, but also when they are required – has given that clarity.

---

[14] Indeed, the Court's holding rests on its view that there were no "improper tactics in obtaining the initial statement."

## QUESTIONS AND NOTES

**1.** Do you believe that Elstad was in custody at the time of his initial confession?

**2.** If the answer to question 1 is even arguably "no," might that have influenced the Court's decision?

**3.** Is *Elstad* an unfortunate decision because it blurs *Miranda*'s bright lines?

**4.** Would (should) *Elstad* have been different if the police had referred to his earlier confession to overcome his reluctance to give a post-*Miranda*-warning confession?

**5.** Do Stevens and Brennan differ in their respective readings of the Court's opinion? To the extent that they do, whose reading is more accurate? Why?

**6.** Given the opening two sentences of Justice Stevens' opinion, why did he dissent?

**7.** According to the dissents, what more should the police have done to render Elstad's second confession admissible? Why wasn't this required by the majority?

**8.** Is *Elstad* likely to encourage police to ignore *Miranda*? If so, is that an unmitigated evil?

# 22.

# INEVITABLE DISCOVERY

In the preceding chapter, we focused on the attenuation doctrine. The clearest illustration of attenuation occurs when the source of the evidence is actually and demonstrably independent of the illegality. For example in *Brewer v. Williams*, Chapter 17, supra, suppose that when Williams told Detective Leaming where the child's body was buried, Leaming responded: "I know, we found it four hours ago." Under that hypothetical circumstance, the body would, of course, be admissible. In the real world, its admissibility was dependent on whether it would have inevitably been discovered without Williams' post-Christian burial speech statement. In *Nix v. Williams*, the Court resolved that issue.

## Nix v. Williams
### 467 U.S. 431 (1984)

Chief Justice BURGER delivered the opinion of the Court.

We granted certiorari to consider whether, at respondent Williams' second murder trial in state court, evidence pertaining to the discovery and condition of the victim's body was properly admitted on the ground that it would ultimately or inevitably have been discovered even if no violation of any constitutional or statutory provision had taken place.

### I

#### Second Trial

At Williams' second trial in 1977 in the Iowa court, the prosecution did not offer Williams' statements into evidence, nor did it seek to show that Williams had directed the police to the child's body. However, evidence of the condition of her body as it was found, articles and photographs of her clothing, and the results of post mortem medical and chemical tests on the body were admitted. The trial court concluded that the State had proved by a preponderance of the evidence that, if the search had not been suspended and Williams had not led the police to the victim, her body would have been discovered "*within a short time*" in essentially the same condition as it was actually found. The trial court also ruled that if the police had not located the body, "the search would clearly have been taken up again where it left off, given the extreme circumstances of this case and the body would [have] been found *in short order*." (emphasis added).

In finding that the body would have been discovered in essentially the same condition as it was actually found, the court noted that freezing temperatures had prevailed and tissue deterioration would have been suspended. The challenged evidence was admitted and the jury again found Williams guilty of first-degree murder; he was sentenced to life in prison.

## II

### A

The Iowa Supreme Court correctly stated that the "vast majority" of all courts, both state and federal, recognize an inevitable discovery exception to the Exclusionary Rule. We are now urged to adopt and apply the so-called ultimate or inevitable discovery exception to the Exclusionary Rule.

Williams contends that evidence of the body's location and condition is "fruit of the poisonous tree," i.e., the "fruit" or product of Detective Leaming's plea to help the child's parents give her "a Christian burial," which this Court had already held equated to interrogation. He contends that admitting the challenged evidence violated the Sixth Amendment whether it would have been inevitably discovered or not. Williams also contends that, if the inevitable discovery doctrine is constitutionally permissible, it must include a threshold showing of police good faith.

### B

The doctrine requiring courts to suppress evidence as the tainted "fruit" of unlawful governmental conduct had its genesis in *Silverthorne Lumber Co. v. United States*, 251 U.S. 385, 40 S.Ct. 182, 64 L.Ed. 319 (1920); there, the Court held that the Exclusionary Rule applies not only to the illegally obtained evidence itself, but also to other incriminating evidence derived from the primary evidence. The holding of *Silverthorne* was carefully limited, however, for the Court emphasized that such information does not automatically become "sacred and inaccessible."

> "If knowledge of [such facts] is gained from an *independent source*, they may be proved like any others. . . ." (emphasis added).

*Wong Sun* extended the Exclusionary Rule to evidence that was the indirect product or "fruit" of unlawful police conduct, but there again the Court emphasized that evidence that has been illegally obtained need not always be suppressed, stating:

> "We need not hold that all evidence is 'fruit of the poisonous tree' simply because it would

not have come to light but for the illegal actions of the police. Rather, the more apt question in such a case is 'whether, granting establishment of the primary illegality, the evidence to which instant objection is made has been come at by exploitation of that illegality or instead by means sufficiently distinguishable to be purged of the primary taint.'"

The Court thus pointedly negated the kind of good-faith requirement advanced by the Court of Appeals in reversing the District Court.

Although *Silverthorne* and *Wong Sun* involved violations of the Fourth Amendment, the "fruit of the poisonous tree" doctrine has not been limited to cases in which there has been a Fourth Amendment violation. The Court has applied the doctrine where the violations were of the Sixth Amendment, see *United States v. Wade*, 388 U.S. 218 (1967), as well as of the Fifth Amendment.

The core rationale consistently advanced by this Court for extending the Exclusionary Rule to evidence that is the fruit of unlawful police conduct has been that this admittedly drastic and socially costly course is needed to deter police from violations of constitutional and statutory protections. This Court has accepted the argument that the way to ensure such protections is to exclude evidence seized as a result of such violations notwithstanding the high social cost of letting persons obviously guilty go unpunished for their crimes. On this rationale, the prosecution is not to be put in a better position than it would have been in if no illegality had transpired.

By contrast, the derivative evidence analysis ensures that the prosecution is not put in a *worse* position simply because of some earlier police error or misconduct. The independent source doctrine allows admission of evidence that has been discovered by means wholly independent of any constitutional violation. That doctrine, although closely related to the inevitable discovery doctrine, does not apply here; Williams' statements to Leaming indeed led police to the child's body, but that is not the whole story. The independent source doctrine teaches us that the interest of society in deterring unlawful police conduct and the public interest in having juries receive all probative evidence of a crime are properly balanced by putting the police in the same, not a *worse*, position than they would have been in if no police error or misconduct had occurred. When the challenged evidence has an independent source, exclusion of such evidence would put the police in a worse position than they would have been in absent any error or violation. There is a functional similarity between these two doctrines in that exclusion of evidence that would inevitably have been discovered would also put the government in a worse position, because the police would have obtained that evidence if no misconduct had taken place. Thus, while the independent source exception would not justify admission of evidence in this case, its rationale is wholly consistent with and justifies our adoption of the ultimate or inevitable discovery exception to the Exclusionary Rule.

It is clear that the cases implementing the Exclusionary Rule "begin with the premise that the challenged evidence is *in some sense* the product of illegal governmental activity." *United States v. Crews*, 445 U.S. 463, 471 (1980) (emphasis added). Of course, this does not end the inquiry. If the prosecution can establish by a preponderance of the evidence that the information ultimately or inevitably would have been discovered by lawful means – here the volunteers' search – then the deterrence rationale has so little basis that the evidence should be received. Anything less would reject logic, experience, and common sense.[5]

---

[5] As to the quantum of proof, we have already established some relevant guidelines. In *United States v. Matlock*, 415 U.S. 164, 178, n. 14, 94 S.Ct. 988, 996, n. 14, 39 L.Ed.2d 242 (1974) (emphasis added), we stated that "the controlling burden of proof at suppression hearings should impose *no greater burden* than proof by a preponderance of the evidence." In *Lego v. Twomey*, 404 U.S. 477, 488, 92 S.Ct. 619, 626, 30 L.Ed.2d 618 (1972), we observed "from our experience [that] no substantial evidence has accumulated that federal rights have suffered from determining admissibility by a preponderance of the evidence" and held that the prosecution must prove by a preponderance of the evidence that a confession sought to be used at trial was voluntary. We are unwilling to impose added burdens on the already difficult task of proving guilt in criminal cases by enlarging the barrier to placing evidence of unquestioned truth before juries. Williams argues that the preponderance of the evidence standard used by the Iowa courts is inconsistent with *United States v. Wade*. In requiring clear and convincing evidence of an independent source for an in-court identification, the Court gave weight to the effect an uncounseled pre-trial identification has in "crystalliz[ing] the witnesses' identification of the defendant for the future reference." The Court noted as well that possible unfairness at the lineup "may be the sole means of attack upon the unequivocal courtroom identification," *ibid.*, and recognized the difficulty of de-

The requirement that the prosecution must prove the absence of bad faith, imposed here by the Court of Appeals, would place courts in the position of withholding from juries relevant and undoubted truth that would have been available to police absent any unlawful police activity. Of course, that view would put the police in a *worse* position than they would have been in if no unlawful conduct had transpired. And, of equal importance, it wholly fails to take into account the enormous societal cost of excluding truth in the search for truth in the administration of justice. Nothing in this Court's prior holdings supports any such formalistic, pointless, and punitive approach.

The Court of Appeals concluded, without analysis, that if an absence of bad faith requirement were not imposed, "the temptation to risk deliberate violations of the Sixth Amendment would be too great, and the deterrent effect of the Exclusionary Rule reduced too far." We reject that view. A police officer who is faced with the opportunity to obtain evidence illegally will rarely, if ever, be in a position to calculate whether the evidence sought would inevitably be discovered. Cf. *Ceccolini*: "[T]he concept of effective deterrence assumes that the police officer consciously realizes the probable consequences of a presumably impermissible course of conduct." (Opinion concurring in judgment.) On the other hand, when an officer is aware that the evidence will inevitably be discovered, he will try to avoid engaging in any questionable practice. In that situation, there will be little to gain from taking any dubious "shortcuts" to obtain the evidence. Significant disincentives to obtaining evidence illegally – including the possibility of departmental discipline and civil liability – also lessen the likelihood that the ultimate or inevitable discovery exception will promote police misconduct. In these circumstances, the societal costs of the Exclusionary Rule far outweigh any possible benefits to deterrence that a good-faith requirement might produce.

Williams contends that because he did not waive his right to the assistance of counsel, the Court may not balance competing values in deciding whether

---

termining whether an in-court identification was based on independent recollection unaided by the lineup identification, id., at 240-241, 87 S.Ct., at 1939-1940. By contrast, inevitable discovery involves no speculative elements but focuses on demonstrated historical facts capable of ready verification or impeachment and does not require a departure from the usual burden of proof at suppression hearings.

the challenged evidence was properly admitted. He argues that, unlike the Exclusionary Rule in the Fourth Amendment context, the essential purpose of which is to deter police misconduct, the Sixth Amendment Exclusionary Rule is designed to protect the right to a fair trial and the integrity of the fact-finding process. Williams contends that, when those interests are at stake, the societal costs of excluding evidence obtained from responses presumed involuntary are irrelevant in determining whether such evidence should be excluded. We disagree.

Exclusion of physical evidence that would inevitably have been discovered adds nothing to either the integrity or fairness of a criminal trial. The Sixth Amendment right to counsel protects against unfairness by preserving the adversary process in which the reliability of proffered evidence may be tested in cross-examination. Here, however, Detective Leaming's conduct did nothing to impugn the reliability of the evidence in question—the body of the child and its condition as it was found, articles of clothing found on the body, and the autopsy. No one would seriously contend that the presence of counsel in the police car when Leaming appealed to Williams' decent human instincts would have had any bearing on the reliability of the body as evidence. Suppression, in these circumstances, would do nothing whatever to promote the integrity of the trial process, but would inflict a wholly unacceptable burden on the administration of criminal justice.

More than a half century ago, Judge, later Justice, Cardozo made his seminal observation that under the Exclusionary Rule "[t]he criminal is to go free because the constable has blundered." *People v. Defore*, 242 N.Y. 13, 21, 150 N.E. 585, 587 (1926). Prophetically, he went on to consider "how far-reaching in its effect upon society" the Exclusionary Rule would be when "[t]he pettiest peace officer would have it in his power through overzeal or indiscretion to confer immunity upon an offender for crimes the most flagitious." Some day, Cardozo speculated, some court might press the Exclusionary Rule to the outer limits of its logic—or beyond— and suppress evidence relating to the "body of a murdered" victim because of the means by which it was found. Cardozo's prophecy was fulfilled in *Killough v. United States*, 114 U.S.App.D.C. 305, 309, 315 F.2d 241, 245 (1962) (en banc). But when, as here, the evidence in question would inevitably have been discovered without reference to the police error or misconduct, there is no nexus sufficient to provide a taint and the evidence is admissible.

### C

The Court of Appeals did not find it necessary to consider whether the record fairly supported the finding that the volunteer search party would ultimately or inevitably have discovered the victim's body. However, three courts independently reviewing the evidence have found that the body of the child inevitably would have been found by the searchers. Williams challenges these findings, asserting that the record contains only the "*post hoc* rationalization" that the search efforts would have proceeded two and one-half miles into Polk County where Williams had led police to the body.

When that challenge was made at the suppression hearing preceding Williams' second trial, the prosecution offered the testimony of Agent Ruxlow of the Iowa Bureau of Criminal Investigation. Ruxlow had organized and directed some 200 volunteers who were searching for the child's body. The searchers were instructed "to check all the roads, the ditches, any culverts. . . . If they came upon any abandoned farm buildings, they were instructed to go onto the property and search those abandoned farm buildings or any other places where a small child could be secreted." Ruxlow testified that he marked off highway maps of Poweshiek and Jasper Counties in grid fashion, divided the volunteers into teams of four to six persons, and assigned each team to search specific grid areas. Ruxlow also testified that, if the search had not been suspended because of Williams' promised cooperation, it would have continued into Polk County, using the same grid system. Although he had previously marked off into grids only the highway maps of Poweshiek and Jasper Counties, Ruxlow had obtained a map of Polk County, which he said he would have marked off in the same manner had it been necessary for the search to continue.

The search had commenced at approximately 10 a.m. and moved westward through Poweshiek County into Jasper County. At approximately 3 p.m., after Williams had volunteered to cooperate with the police, Officer Leaming, who was in the police car with Williams, sent word to Ruxlow and the other Special Agent directing the search to meet him at the Grinnell truck stop and the search was suspended at that time. Ruxlow also stated that he was "under the impression that there was a possibility" that Williams would lead them to the child's body at that time. The search was not resumed once it was learned that Williams had led the police to the body, id., which was found two and one-half miles from where the search had stopped in what would have been the eastern most grid to be searched in Polk County. There was testimony that it would have taken an additional three to five hours to discover the body if the search had continued, the body was found near a culvert, one of the kinds of places the teams had been specifically directed to search.

On this record it is clear that the search parties were approaching the actual location of the body and we are satisfied, along with three courts earlier, that the volunteer search teams would have resumed the search had Williams not earlier led the police to the body and the body inevitably would have been found.

The judgment of the Court of Appeals is reversed, and the case is remanded for further proceedings consistent with this opinion.

Justice WHITE, concurring.

I join fully in the opinion of the Court. I write separately only to point out that many of Justice Stevens' remarks are beside the point when it is recalled that *Brewer v. Williams* was a 5-4 decision and that four members of the Court, including myself, were of the view that Officer Leaming had done nothing wrong at all, let alone anything unconstitutional. Three of us observed that: "To anyone not lost in the intricacies of the prophylactic rules of *Miranda*, the result in this case seems utterly senseless. . . ." It is thus an unjustified reflection on Officer Leaming to say that he "decide[d] to dispense with the requirements of the law," or that he decided "to take procedural shortcuts instead of complying with the law." He was no doubt acting as many competent police officers would have acted under similar circumstances and in light of the then-existing law. That five Justices later thought he was mistaken does not call for making him out to be a villain or for a lecture on deliberate police misconduct and its resulting costs to society.

Justice STEVENS, concurring in the judgment.

This litigation is exceptional for at least three reasons. The facts are unusually tragic; it involves an unusually clear violation of constitutional rights; and it graphically illustrates the societal costs that may be incurred when police officers decide to dispense with the requirements of law. Because the Court does not adequately discuss any of these aspects of the case, I am unable to join its opinion.

## I

There can be no denying that the character of the crime may have an impact on the decisional process. As the Court was required to hold, however, that does not permit any court to condone a violation of constitutional rights.[1] Today's decision is no more

an ad hoc response to the pressures engendered by the special facts of the case than was *Williams I*. It was the majority in *Williams I* that recognized that "evidence of where the body was found and of its condition might well be admissible on the theory that the body would have been discovered in any event, even had incriminating statements not been elicited from Williams." It was the author of today's opinion of the Court who characterized this rule of law as a "remarkable" and "unlikely theory." (BURGER, C.J., dissenting). The rule of law that the Court adopts today has an integrity of its own and is not merely the product of the hydraulic pressures associated with hard cases or strong words.

## II

The constitutional violation that gave rise to the decision in *Williams I* is neither acknowledged nor fairly explained in the Court's opinion. Yet the propriety of admitting evidence relating to the victims' body can only be evaluated if that constitutional violation is properly identified.

*Williams I* held that Detective Leaming had violated "the clear rule of *Massiah*" by deliberately eliciting incriminating statements from respondent during the pendency of the adversarial process and outside of that process. See 430 U.S., at 399-401, 97 S.Ct., at 1239-1241. The violation was aggravated by the fact that Detective Leaming had breached a promise to counsel, an act which can only undermine the role of counsel in the adversarial process. The "Christian burial speech" was nothing less than an attempt to substitute an ex parte, inquisitorial process for the clash of adversaries commanded by the Constitution.[5] Thus the now-familiar

---

state mental institution. The emotional aspects of the case make it difficult to decide dispassionately, but do not qualify our obligation to apply the law with an eye to the future as well as with concern for the result in the particular case before us." (concurring opinion).

[5] "The whole point of *Massiah* is the prevention of the state from taking advantage of an uncounseled defendant once sixth amendment rights attach. The Christian burial speech was an attempt to take advantage of Williams. The attempt itself *is* what *Massiah* prohibits. The attempt violates the constitutional mandate that the system proceed, after some point, only in an accusatorial manner." Grano, *Rhode Island v. Innis*: A Need to Reconsider the Constitutional Premises Underlying the Law of Confessions, 17 Am.Crim.L.Rev. 1, 35 (1979) (emphasis in original).

---

[1] As I wrote at the time:

"Nothing we write, no matter how well reasoned or forcefully expressed, can bring back the victim of this tragedy or undo the consequences of the official neglect which led to the respondent's escape from a

plaint that "[t]he criminal is to go free because the constable has blundered," is entirely beside the point. More pertinent is what The Chief Justice wrote for the Court on another occasion: "This is not a case where, in Justice Cardozo's words, 'the constable . . . blundered,' rather, it is one where the 'constable' planned an impermissible interference with the right to the assistance of counsel." *United States v. Henry*, 447 U.S. 264, 274-275 (1980) (footnote and citation omitted).

### III

Once the constitutional violation is properly identified, the answers to the questions presented in this case follow readily. Admission of the victim's body, if it would have been discovered anyway, means that the trial in this case was not the product of an inquisitorial process; that process was untainted by illegality. The good or bad faith of Detective Leaming is therefore simply irrelevant. If the trial process was not tainted as a result of his conduct, this defendant received the type of trial that the Sixth Amendment envisions. See *Weatherford v. Bursey*; *United States v. Wade*. Generalizations about the Exclusionary Rule employed by the majority, simply do not address the primary question in the case.

The majority is correct to insist that any rule of exclusion not provide the authorities with an incentive to commit violations of the Constitution. If the inevitable discovery rule provided such an incentive by permitting the prosecution to avoid the uncertainties inherent in its search for evidence, it would undermine the constitutional guarantee itself, and therefore be inconsistent with the deterrent purposes of the Exclusionary Rule. But when the burden of proof on the inevitable discovery question is placed on the prosecution, it must bear the risk of error in the determination made necessary by its constitutional violation. The uncertainty as to whether the body would have been discovered can be resolved in its favor here only because, as the Court explains, petitioner adduced evidence demonstrating that at the time of the constitutional violation an investigation was already under way which, in the natural and probable course of events, would have soon discovered the body. This is not a case in which the prosecution can escape responsibility for a constitutional violation through speculation; to the extent uncertainty was created by the constitutional violation the prosecution was required to resolve that uncertainty through proof.[8] Even if Detective Leaming acted in

bad faith in the sense that he deliberately violated the Constitution in order to avoid the possibility that the body would not be discovered, the prosecution ultimately does not avoid that risk; its burden of proof forces it to assume the risk. The need to adduce proof sufficient to discharge its burden, and the difficulty in predicting whether such proof will be available or sufficient, means that the inevitable discovery rule does not permit state officials to avoid the uncertainty they would have faced but for the constitutional violation.

The majority refers to the "societal cost" of excluding probative evidence. In my view, the more relevant cost is that imposed on society by police officers who decide to take procedural shortcuts instead of complying with the law. What is the consequence of the shortcut that Detective Leaming took when he decided to question Williams in this case and not to wait an hour or so until he arrived in Des Moines?[9] The answer is years and years of unnecessary but costly litigation. Instead of having a 1969 conviction affirmed in routine fashion, the case is still alive 15 years later. Thanks to Detective Leaming, the State of Iowa has expended vast sums of money and countless hours of professional labor in his defense. That expenditure surely provides an adequate deterrent to similar violations; the responsibility for that expenditure lies not with the Constitution, but rather with the constable.

Accordingly, I concur in the Court's judgment.

Justice BRENNAN, with whom Justice MARSHALL joins, dissenting.

To the extent that today's decision adopts [the] "inevitable discovery" exception to the exclusionary rule, it simply acknowledges a doctrine that is

the evidence rather than by clear and convincing evidence. An inevitable discovery finding is based on objective evidence concerning the scope of the ongoing investigation which can be objectively verified or impeached. Hence an extraordinary burden of proof is not needed in order to preserve the defendant's ability to subject the prosecution's case to the meaningful adversarial testing required by the Sixth Amendment.

[9] In this connection, it is worth noting, as Justice MARSHALL did in *Williams I*, that in light of the assistance that respondent's attorney had provided to the Des Moines police, it seems apparent that the lawyer intended to learn the location of the body from his client and then reveal it to the police. Thus, the need for a shortcut was practically nonexistent.

---

[8] I agree with the majority's holding that the prosecution must prove that the evidence would have been inevitably discovered by a preponderance of

akin to the "independent source" exception first recognized by the Court in *Silverthorne Lumber Co.* In particular, the Court concludes that unconstitutionally obtained evidence may be admitted at trial if it inevitably would have been discovered in the same condition by an independent line of investigation that was already being pursued when the constitutional violation occurred. As has every federal Court of Appeals previously addressing this issue, I agree that in these circumstances the "inevitable discovery" exception to the exclusionary rule is consistent with the requirements of the Constitution.

In its zealous efforts to emasculate the exclusionary rule, however, the Court loses sight of the crucial difference between the "inevitable discovery" doctrine and the "independent source" exception from which it is derived. When properly applied, the "independent source" exception allows the prosecution to use evidence only if it was, in fact, obtained by fully lawful means. It therefore does no violence to the constitutional protections that the exclusionary rule is meant to enforce. The "inevitable discovery" exception is likewise compatible with the Constitution, though it differs in one key respect from its next of kin: specifically, the evidence sought to be introduced at trial has not actually been obtained from an independent source, but rather would have been discovered as a matter of course if independent investigations were allowed to proceed.

In my view, this distinction should require that the government satisfy a heightened burden of proof before it is allowed to use such evidence. The inevitable discovery exception necessarily implicates a hypothetical finding that differs in kind from the factual finding that precedes application of the independent source rule. To ensure that this hypothetical finding is narrowly confined to circumstances that are functionally equivalent to an independent source, and to protect fully the fundamental rights served by the exclusionary rule, I would require clear and convincing evidence before concluding that the government had met its burden of proof on this issue. See *Wade*. Increasing the burden of proof serves to impress the fact finder with the importance of the decision and thereby reduces the risk that illegally obtained evidence will be admitted. Cf. *Addington v. Texas*, 441 U.S. 418, 427, 99 S.Ct. 1804, 1810, 60 L.Ed.2d 323 (1979); *Santosky v. Kramer*, 455 U.S. 745, 764, 102 S.Ct. 1388, 1399, 71 L.Ed.2d 599 (1982) ("Raising the standard of proof would have both practical and symbolic consequences"). Because the lower courts did not impose such a requirement, I would remand this case for application of this heightened burden of proof by the lower courts in the first instance. I am therefore unable to join either the Court's opinion or its judgment.

## QUESTIONS AND NOTES

**1.** The entire Court accepts the inevitable discovery exception to the exclusionary rule. Do you agree? Why? Why not?

**2.** The entire Court also seems to agree that "good faith" is irrelevant. Do you agree? Why? Why not?

**3.** If it mattered, would you assess Leaming's behavior as "good faith," "bad faith," or neither? Explain.

**4.** Did the Court adopt an appropriate burden of proof? Did Justice Brennan?

**5.** Linguistically speaking, how can something be "inevitable," if it is only more likely than not?

**6.** Assess the following observation of Professor Phillip Johnson, made before the Supreme Court's decision in *Nix v. Williams*:

> The fact that constitutional law is complex and technical suggests to me that it should be enforced with a sense of proportion. Granting that Captain Leaming crossed a certain line that the Supreme Court has drawn, and even granting that he ought to have known better, his misdeed was what we criminal lawyers call *malum prohibitum*, rather than *malum in se*. Legalisms aside, what he did was to appeal to the conscience of a suspected murderer to do the only decent and honorable thing: to reveal where he had hidden the body, so the police could recover it and return it to the grieving

family for burial. Perhaps the police ought not to be allowed to make such an appeal to a suspect in their custody, but in my opinion somebody ought to do it.

We have stringent rules governing police interrogation of suspects for good reason. Not so long ago, the "third degree" was a standard and acknowledged police investigative tool. Suspects were arrested and rearrested on flimsy grounds, kept awake while relays of questioners wore them down, stripped naked and threatened with beatings, pressured, cajoled, and tricked into confessing. The characteristic vice of dedicated policemen is that they tend to see themselves as fighting a war against the criminal elements of society. From this it is only a short step to the conclusion that the end justifies the means. The courts are entirely right to take strong measures to keep this mentality in check.

But we lawyers, a class which includes judges, also have our characteristic faults. One of these is a tendency to make a fetish of procedure, so that the merits of a dispute become obscured in an endless tangle of arguments about how the dispute ought to have been resolved. Another is a tendency to become captured by our own abstractions, so that we push every principle to the limits of its logic and sometimes beyond. Society has police to protect it from thieves and murderers, and it has lawyers to protect it from the police. No one has yet discovered how to protect society from the lawyers.

Johnson, The Return of the Christian Burial Speech, 32 Emory L.J. 349, 381 (1983).

**7.** The separate issue of inevitable discovery, or independent source, as applied to a search warrant obtained after a warrantless search was explored in *Murray*.

## Murray v. United States
### 487 U.S. 533 (1988)

Justice SCALIA delivered the opinion of the Court.

In *Segura v. United States*, 468 U.S. 796 (1984), we held that police officers' illegal entry upon private premises did not require suppression of evidence subsequently discovered at those premises when executing a search warrant obtained on the basis of information wholly unconnected with the initial entry. In these consolidated cases we are faced with the question whether, again assuming evidence obtained pursuant to an independently obtained search warrant, the portion of such evidence that had been observed in plain view at the time of a prior illegal entry must be suppressed.

### I

Both cases arise out of the conviction of petitioner Michael F. Murray, petitioner James D. Carter, and others for conspiracy to possess and distribute illegal drugs. Insofar as relevant for our purposes, the facts are as follows: Based on information received from informants, federal law enforcement agents had been surveilling petitioner Murray and several of his co-conspirators. At about 1:45 p.m. on April 6, 1983, they observed Murray drive a truck and Carter drive a green camper, into a warehouse in South Boston. When the petitioners drove the vehicles out about 20 minutes later, the surveilling agents saw within the warehouse two individuals and a tractor-trailer rig bearing a long, dark container. Murray and Carter later turned over the truck and camper to other drivers, who were in turn followed and ultimately arrested, and the vehicles lawfully seized. Both vehicles were found to contain marijuana.

After receiving this information, several of the agents converged on the South Boston warehouse and forced entry. They found the warehouse unoccupied, but observed in plain view numerous burlap-wrapped bales that were later found to contain marijuana. They left without disturbing the bales, kept the warehouse under surveillance, and did not reenter it until they had a search warrant. In applying for the warrant, the agents did not mention the prior entry, and did not rely on any observations made during that entry. When the warrant was issued—at 10:40 p.m., approximately eight hours after the initial entry—the agents immediately reentered the warehouse and seized 270 bales of marijuana and notebooks listing customers for whom the bales were destined.

## II

The exclusionary rule prohibits introduction into evidence of tangible materials seized during an unlawful search, and of testimony concerning knowledge acquired during an unlawful search, *Silverman v. United States*, 365 U.S. 505, 81 S.Ct. 679, 5 L.Ed.2d 734 (1961). Beyond that, the exclusionary rule also prohibits the introduction of derivative evidence, both tangible and testimonial, that is the product of the primary evidence, or that is otherwise acquired as an indirect result of the unlawful search, up to the point at which the connection with the unlawful search becomes "so attenuated as to dissipate the taint," *Nardone*. See *Wong Sun*.

Almost simultaneously with our development of the exclusionary rule, in the first quarter of this century, we also announced what has come to be known as the "independent source" doctrine. See *Silverthorne Lumber Co.* That doctrine, which has been applied to evidence acquired not only through Fourth Amendment violations but also through Fifth and Sixth Amendment violations, has recently been described as follows:

> "[T]he interest of society in deterring unlawful police conduct and the public interest in having juries receive all probative evidence of a crime are properly balanced by putting the police in the same, not a worse, position that they would have been in if no police error or misconduct had occurred. . . . When the challenged evidence has an independent source, exclusion of such evidence would put the police in a worse position than they would have been in absent any error or violation."

The dispute here is over the scope of this doctrine. Petitioners contend that it applies only to evidence obtained for the first time during an independent lawful search. The Government argues that it applies also to evidence initially discovered during, or as a consequence of, an unlawful search, but later obtained independently from activities untainted by the initial illegality. We think the Government's view has better support in both precedent and policy.

Our cases have used the concept of "independent source" in a more general and a more specific sense.

The more general sense identifies *all* evidence acquired in a fashion untainted by the illegal evidence-gathering activity. Thus, where an unlawful entry has given investigators knowledge of facts x and y, but fact z has been learned by other means, fact z can be said to be admissible because derived from an "independent source." This is how we used the term in *Segura v. United States*. In that case, agents unlawfully entered the defendant's apartment and remained there until a search warrant was obtained. The admissibility of what they discovered while waiting in the apartment was not before us, but we held that the evidence found for the first time during the execution of the valid and untainted search warrant was admissible because it was discovered pursuant to an "independent source."

The original use of the term, however, and its more important use for purposes of these cases, was more specific. It was originally applied in the exclusionary rule context, by Justice Holmes, with reference to that particular category of evidence acquired by an untainted search *which is identical to the evidence unlawfully acquired*—that is, in the example just given, to knowledge of facts x and y derived from an independent source:

> "The essence of a provision forbidding the acquisition of evidence in a certain way is that not merely evidence so acquired shall not be used before the Court but that it shall not be used at all. Of course this does not mean that the facts thus obtained become sacred and inaccessible. If knowledge of them is gained from an independent source they may be proved like any others."

We recently assumed this application of the independent source doctrine (in the Sixth Amendment context) in *Nix v. Williams*.

Petitioners' asserted policy basis for excluding evidence which is initially discovered during an illegal search, but is subsequently acquired through an independent and lawful source, is that a contrary rule will remove all deterrence to, and indeed positively encourage, unlawful police searches. As petitioners see the incentives, law enforcement officers will routinely enter without a warrant to make sure that what they expect to be on the premises is in fact there. If it is not, they will have spared themselves the time and trouble of getting a warrant; if it is, they can get the warrant and use the evidence despite the unlawful entry. Brief for Petitioners 42. We see the incentives differently. An officer with probable cause sufficient to obtain a search warrant would be foolish to enter the premises first in an unlawful manner. By doing so, he would risk suppression of all evidence on the premises, both seen and unseen, since his action would add to the normal burden of convincing a magistrate that there is probable cause the much more onerous burden of convincing a trial court that no information gained from the illegal entry affected either the law enforcement officers' decision to seek a warrant or the magistrate's decision to grant it. See Part III, infra. Nor would the officer without sufficient probable cause to obtain a search warrant have any added incentive to conduct an unlawful entry, since whatever he finds cannot be used to establish probable cause before a magistrate.[2]

## III

To apply what we have said to the present cases: Knowledge that the marijuana was in the warehouse was assuredly acquired at the time of the unlawful entry. But it was also acquired at the time of entry pursuant to the warrant, and if that later acquisition was not the result of the earlier entry there is no reason why the independent source doctrine should not apply. Invoking the exclusionary rule would put the police (and society) not in the same position they would have occupied if no violation occurred, but in a *worse* one. See *Nix v. Williams*.

---

[2] JUSTICE MARSHALL argues, in effect, that where the police cannot point to some historically verifiable fact demonstrating that the subsequent search pursuant to a warrant was wholly unaffected by the prior illegal search—*e.g.*, that they had already sought the warrant before entering the premises—we should adopt a per se rule of inadmissibility. We do not believe that such a prophylactic exception to the independent source rule is necessary. To say that a district court must be satisfied that a warrant would have been sought without the illegal entry is not to give dispositive effect to police officer's assurances on the point. Where the facts render those assurances implausible, the independent source doctrine will not apply.

We might note that there is no basis for pointing to the present cases as an example of a "search first, warrant later" mentality. The District Court found that the agents entered the warehouse "in an effort to apprehend any participants who might have remained inside and to guard against the destruction of possibly critical evidence." While they may have misjudged the existence of sufficient exigent circumstances to justify the warrantless entry (the Court of Appeals did not reach that issue and neither do we), there is nothing to suggest that they went in merely to see if there was anything worth getting a warrant for.

The ultimate question, therefore, is whether the search pursuant to warrant was in fact a genuinely independent source of the information and tangible evidence at issue here. This would not have been the case if the agents' decision to seek the warrant was prompted by what they had seen during the initial entry,[3] or if information obtained during that entry was presented to the Magistrate and affected his decision to issue the warrant. On this point the Court of Appeals said the following:

> "[W]e can be absolutely certain that the warrantless entry in no way contributed in the slightest either to the issuance of a warrant or to the discovery of the evidence during the lawful search that occurred pursuant to the warrant.

> "This is as clear a case as can be imagined where the discovery of the contraband in plain view was totally irrelevant to the later securing of a warrant and the successful search that ensued. As there was no causal link whatever between the illegal entry and the discovery of the challenged evidence, we find no error in the court's refusal to suppress." *United States v. Moscatiello*, 771 F.2d, at 603, 604.

Although these statements can be read to provide emphatic support for the Government's position, it is the function of the District Court rather than the Court of Appeals to determine the facts, and we do not think the Court of Appeals' conclusions are supported by adequate findings. The District Court found that the agents did not reveal their warrantless entry to the Magistrate, and that they did not include in their application for a warrant any recitation of

---

[3] JUSTICE MARSHALL argues that "the relevant question [is] whether, even if the initial entry uncovered no evidence, the officers would return immediately with a warrant to conduct a second search." We do not see how this is "relevant" at all. To determine whether the warrant was independent of the illegal entry, one must ask whether it would have been sought even if what actually happened had not occurred—not whether it would have been sought if something else had happened. That is to say, what counts is whether the actual illegal search had any effect in producing the warrant, not whether some hypothetical illegal search would have aborted the warrant. Only that much is needed to assure that what comes before the court is not the product of illegality; to go further than that would be to expand our existing exclusionary rule.

their observations in the warehouse. It did not, however, explicitly find that the agents would have sought a warrant if they had not earlier entered the warehouse. The Government concedes this in its brief. To be sure, the District Court did determine that the purpose of the warrantless entry was in part "to guard against the destruction of possibly critical evidence," and one could perhaps infer from this that the agents who made the entry already planned to obtain that "critical evidence" through a warrant-authorized search. That inference is not, however, clear enough to justify the conclusion that the District Court's findings amounted to a determination of independent source.

Accordingly, we vacate the judgment and remand these cases to the Court of Appeals with instructions that it remand to the District Court for determination whether the warrant-authorized search of the warehouse was an independent source of the challenged evidence in the sense we have described.

Justice BRENNAN and Justice KENNEDY took no part in the consideration or decision of these cases.

Justice MARSHALL, with whom Justice STEVENS and Justice O'CONNOR join, dissenting.

The Court today holds that the "independent source" exception to the exclusionary rule may justify admitting evidence discovered during an illegal warrantless search that is later "rediscovered" by the same team of investigators during a search pursuant to a warrant obtained immediately after the illegal search. I believe the Court's decision, by failing to provide sufficient guarantees that the subsequent search was, in fact, independent of the illegal search, emasculates the Warrant Clause and undermines the deterrence function of the exclusionary rule. I therefore dissent.

This Court has stated frequently that the exclusionary rule is principally designed to deter violations of the Fourth Amendment. By excluding evidence discovered in violation of the Fourth Amendment, the rule "compel[s] respect for the constitutional guaranty in the only effectively available way, by removing the incentive to disregard it." The Court has crafted exceptions to the exclusionary rule when the purposes of the rule are not furthered by the exclusion. As the Court today recognizes, the independent source exception to the exclusionary rule "allows admission of evidence that has been discovered by means wholly independent of any constitutional violation." The independent source exception, like the inevitable discovery exception, is primarily based on a practical view that under certain circumstances the beneficial deterrent effect that exclusion will have on future constitutional violations is too slight to justify the social cost of excluding probative evidence from a criminal trial. When the seizure of the evidence at issue is "wholly independent of" the constitutional violation, then exclusion arguably will have no effect on a law enforcement officer's incentive to commit an unlawful search.[1]

Given the underlying justification for the independent source exception, any inquiry into the exception's application must keep sight of the practical effect admission will have on the incentives facing law enforcement officers to engage in unlawful conduct. The proper scope of the independent source exception, and guidelines for its application, cannot be divined in a factual vacuum; instead, they must be informed by the nature of the constitutional violation and the deterrent effect of exclusion in particular circumstances. In holding that the independent source exception may apply to the facts of these cases, I believe the Court loses sight of the practical moorings of the independent source exception and creates an affirmative incentive for unconstitutional searches. This holding can find no justification in the purposes underlying both the exclusionary rule and the independent source exception.

The factual setting of the instant case is straightforward. Federal Bureau of Investigation (FBI) and Drug Enforcement Agency (DEA) agents stopped two vehicles after they left a warehouse and discovered bales of marijuana. DEA Supervisor Garibotto and an assistant United States attorney then returned to the warehouse, which had been under surveillance for several hours. After demands that the warehouse door be opened went unanswered, Supervisor Garibotto forced open the door with a tire iron. A number of agents entered the warehouse. No persons were found inside, but the agents saw numerous bales of marijuana in plain view. Supervisor Garibotto then ordered everyone out of the warehouse. Agents did not reenter the warehouse until a warrant was obtained some eight hours later. The warehouse was kept under surveillance during the interim.

---

[1] The clearest case for the application of the independent course exception is when a wholly separate line of investigation, shielded from information gathered in an illegal search, turns up the same evidence through a separate, lawful search. Under these circumstance, there is little doubt that the lawful search was not connected to the constitutional violation. The exclusion of such evidence would not significantly add to the deterrence facing the law enforcement officers conducting the illegal search, because they would have little reason to anticipate the separate investigation leading to the same evidence.

It is undisputed that the agents made no effort to obtain a warrant prior to the initial entry. The agents had not begun to prepare a warrant affidavit, and according to FBI Agent Cleary, who supervised the FBI's involvement, they had not even engaged in any discussions of obtaining a warrant. The affidavit in support of the warrant obtained after the initial search was prepared by DEA Agent Keaney, who had tactical control over the DEA agents, and who had participated in the initial search of the warehouse. The affidavit did not mention the warrantless search of the warehouse, nor did it cite information obtained from that search. In determining that the challenged evidence was admissible, the Court of Appeals assumed that the initial warrantless entry was not justified by exigent circumstances and that the search therefore violated the Warrant Clause of the Fourth Amendment.

Under the circumstances of these cases, the admission of the evidence "reseized" during the second search severely undermines the deterrence function of the exclusionary rule. Indeed, admission in these cases affirmatively encourages illegal searches. The incentives for such illegal conduct are clear. Obtaining a warrant is inconvenient and time consuming. Even when officers have probable cause to support a warrant application, therefore, they have an incentive first to determine whether it is worthwhile to obtain a warrant. Probable cause is much less than certainty, and many "confirmatory" searches will result in the discovery that no evidence is present, thus saving the police the time and trouble of getting a warrant. If contraband is discovered, however, the officers may later seek a warrant to shield the evidence from the taint of the illegal search. The police thus know in advance that they have little to lose and much to gain by forgoing the bother of obtaining a warrant and undertaking an illegal search.

The Court, however, "see[s] the incentives differently." Under the Court's view, today's decision does not provide an incentive for unlawful searches, because the officer undertaking the search would know that "his action would add to the normal burden of convincing a magistrate that there is probable cause the much more onerous burden of convincing a trial court that no information gained from the illegal entry affected either the law enforcement officers' decision to seek a warrant or the magistrate's decision to grant it." The Court, however, provides no hint of why this risk would actually seem significant to the officers. Under the circumstances of these cases, the officers committing the illegal search have both knowledge and control of the factors central to

the trial court's determination. First, it is a simple matter, as was done in these cases, to exclude from the warrant application any information gained from the initial entry so that the magistrate's determination of probable cause is not influenced by the prior illegal search. Second, today's decision makes the application of the independent source exception turn entirely on an evaluation of the officers' intent. It normally will be difficult for the trial court to verify, or the defendant to rebut, an assertion by officers that they always intended to obtain a warrant, regardless of the results of the illegal search.[2] The testimony of the officers conducting the illegal search is the only direct evidence of intent, and the defendant will be relegated simply to arguing that the officers should not be believed. Under these circumstances, the litigation risk described by the Court seems hardly a risk at all; it does not significantly dampen the incentive to conduct the initial illegal search.[3]

---

[2] Such an intent-based rule is of dubious value for other reasons as well. First, the intent of the officers prior to the illegal entry often will be of little significance to the relevant question: whether, even if the initial entry uncovered no evidence, the officers would return immediately with a warrant to conduct a second search. Officers who have probable cause to believe contraband is present genuinely might intend later to obtain a warrant, but after the illegal search uncovers no such contraband, those same offices might decide their time is better spend than to return with a warrant. In addition, such an intent rule will be difficult to apply. The Court fails to describe how a trial court will properly evaluate whether the law enforcement officers fully intended to obtain a warrant regardless of what they discovered the illegal search. The obvious question is whose intent is relevant? Intentions clearly may differ both among supervisory officers and among officers who initiate the illegal search.

[3] The litigation risk facing these law enforcement officers may be contrasted with the risk faced by the officer in *Nix v. Williams. Nix* involved an application of the inevitable discovery exception to the exclusionary rule. In that case, the Court stressed that an officer "who is faced with the opportunity to obtain evidence illegally will rarely, if ever, be in a position to calculate whether the evidence sought would inevitably be discovered." Unlike the officer in *Nix*, who had no way of knowing about the progress of a wholly separate line of investigation that already had begun at the time of his unconstitutional

The strong Fourth Amendment interest in eliminating these incentives for illegal entry should cause this Court to scrutinize closely the application of the independent source exception to evidence obtained under the circumstances of the instant cases; respect for the constitutional guaranty requires a rule that does not undermine the deterrence function of the exclusionary rule. When, as here, the same team of investigators is involved in both the first and second search, there is a significant danger that the "independence" of the source will in fact be illusory, and that the initial search will have affected the decision to obtain a warrant notwithstanding the officers' subsequent assertions to the contrary. It is therefore crucial that the factual premise of the exception — complete independence — be clearly established before the exception can justify admission of the evidence. I believe the Court's reliance on the intent of the law enforcement officers who conducted the warrantless search provides insufficient guarantees that the subsequent legal search was unaffected by the prior illegal search.

In the instant cases, there are no "demonstrated historical facts" capable of supporting a finding that the subsequent warrant search was wholly unaffected by the prior illegal search. The same team of investigators was involved in both searches. The warrant was obtained immediately after the illegal search, and no effort was made to obtain a warrant prior to the discovery of the marijuana during the illegal search. The only evidence available that the warrant search was wholly independent is the testimony of the agents who conducted the illegal search. Under these circumstances, the threat that the subsequent search was tainted by the illegal search is too great to allow for the application of the independent source exception[4]. The Court's contrary holding lends itself

to easy abuse, and offers an incentive to bypass the constitutional requirement that probable cause be assessed by a neutral and detached magistrate before the police invade an individual's privacy.[5]

The decision in *Segura* is not to the contrary. In *Segura*, the Court expressly distinguished between evidence discovered during an initial warrantless entry and evidence that was not discovered until a subsequent legal search. The Court held that under those circumstances, when no information from an illegal search was used in a subsequent warrant application, the warrant provided an independent source for the evidence first uncovered in the second, lawful search.

*Segura* is readily distinguished from the present cases. The admission of evidence first discovered during a legal search does not significantly lessen the deterrence facing the law enforcement officers contemplating an illegal entry so long as the evidence that is seen is excluded. This was clearly the view of Chief Justice BURGER, joined by Justice O'CONNOR, when he stated that the Court's ruling would not significantly detract from the deterrent effects of the exclusionary rule because "officers who enter illegally will recognize that whatever evidence they discover as a direct result of the entry may be suppressed, as it was by the Court of Appeals in this case." As I argue above, extending *Segura* to cover evidence discovered during an initial illegal search will eradicate this remaining deterrence to illegal entry. Moreover, there is less reason to believe that an initial illegal entry was prompted by a desire to determine whether to bother to get a warrant in the first place, and thus was not wholly independent of the second search, if officers understand that evidence they discover during the illegal search will be excluded even if they subsequently return with a warrant.

---

conduct, the officers in the instant cases, at least under the Court's analysis, have complete knowledge and control over the factors relevant to the determination of "independence."

[4] To conclude that the initial search had no effect on the decision to obtain a warrant, and thus that the warrant search was an "independent source" of the challenged evidence, one would have to assume that even if the officers entered the premises and discovered no contraband, they nonetheless would have gone to the Magistrate, sworn that they had probable cause to believe that contraband was in the building, and then returned to conduct another search. Although such a scenario is possible, I believe it is more plausible to believe that the officers

---

would not have chosen to return immediately to the premises with a warrant to search for evidence had they not discovered evidence during the initial search.

[5] Given that the law enforcement officers in these cases made no movement to obtain a warrant prior to the illegal search, these cases do not present the more difficult issue whether, in light of the strong interest in deterring illegal warrantless searches, the evidence discovered during an illegal search ever may be admitted under the independent source exception when the second legal search is conducted by the same investigative team pursuing the same line of investigation.

In sum, under circumstances as are presented in these cases, when the very law enforcement officers who participate in an illegal search immediately thereafter obtain a warrant to search the same premises, I believe the evidence discovered during the initial illegal entry must be suppressed. Any other result emasculates the Warrant Clause and provides an intolerable incentive for warrantless searches. I respectfully dissent.

Justice STEVENS, dissenting.

While I join Justice MARSHALL's opinion explaining why the majority's extension of the Court's holding in *Segura* "emasculates the Warrant Clause and provides an intolerable incentive for warrantless searches," I remain convinced that the *Segura* decision itself was unacceptable because, even then, it was obvious that it would "provide government agents with an affirmative incentive to engage in unconstitutional violations of the privacy of the home,". . . . I fear that the Court has taken another unfortunate step down the path to a system of "law enforcement unfettered by process concerns." In due course, I trust it will pause long enough to remember that "the efforts of the courts and their officials to bring the guilty to punishment, praiseworthy as they are, are not to be aided by the sacrifice of those great principles established by years of endeavor and suffering which have resulted in their embodiment in the fundamental law of the land." *Weeks v. United States*, 232 U.S. 383 (1914).

## QUESTIONS AND NOTES

**1.** Does *Murray* create an incentive for the police to enter a home without a warrant?

**2.** If your answer to question 1 was "yes." was the decision necessarily incorrect?

**3.** Does the Court's requirement that the police establish that they would have obtained a warrant regardless of their discovery eliminate the concern expressed in question 1? Does it reduce it?

**4.** If you disagree with the Court in *Murray*, do you also support Justice Stevens' rejection of *Segura*? Explain.

**5.** Is it relevant that the purpose of the warrant requirement is to prevent the intrusion in the first place wrong?

# 23.

# ENTRAPMENT

We close volume one of this book by looking at entrapment, a classic hybrid between substantive criminal law and criminal procedure (police practices). Whether this subject belongs in criminal law or criminal procedure depends in significant part on one's theory of entrapment. To the extent that an entrapped defendant is less culpable than a similarly-situated non-entrapped defendant, the subject is a species of substantive criminal law. On the other hand, if entrapment is designed to control police excesses in ferreting out crime, one can view it as a relative (however distant) of unreasonable searches and seizures, coerced confessions, and due process violations.

For the most part, Supreme Court doctrine focuses on the predisposition of the defendant, thereby rendering the doctrine a species of substantive criminal law. However, that perspective of entrapment has not been historically shared by all of the Supreme Court Justices, and has been clearly rejected by some state courts (*See e.g. State v. Powell*, 726 P.2d 266 (Haw. 1986)), and condemned by some thoughtful commentators [*See e.g.* Webster, *Building a Better Mousetrap: Reconstructing Federal Entrapment Theory from Sorrells to Mathews*, 32 Ariz. L. Rev. 605 (1990)). Because entrapment doctrine, for the most part, does not emanate from the Constitution, states are free to develop their own law on the subject.

In part A of this chapter, we focus on the Supreme Court's debate on and treatment of the concept of predisposition. In part B our focus is on the emerging due process defense against government overreaching.

## A.  The Relevance of Predisposition

### Sherman v. United States
356 U.S. 369 (1958)

MR. CHIEF JUSTICE WARREN delivered the opinion of the Court.

The issue before us is whether petitioner's conviction should be set aside on the ground that as a matter of law the defense of entrapment was established. Petitioner was convicted under an indictment charging three sales of narcotics in violation of 21 U. S. C. § 174.

In late August 1951, Kalchinian, a government

informer, first met petitioner at a doctor's office where apparently both were being treated to be cured of narcotics addiction. Several accidental meetings followed, either at the doctor's office or at the pharmacy where both filled their prescriptions from the doctor. From mere greetings, conversation progressed to a discussion of mutual experiences and problems, including their attempts to overcome addiction to narcotics. Finally Kalchinian asked petitioner if he knew of a good source of narcotics. He asked petitioner to supply him with a source because he was not responding to treatment. From the first, petitioner tried to avoid the issue. Not until after a number of repetitions of the request, predicated on Kalchinian's presumed suffering, did petitioner finally acquiesce. Several times thereafter he obtained a quantity of narcotics which he shared with Kalchinian. Each time petitioner told Kalchinian that the total cost of narcotics he obtained was twenty-five dollars and that Kalchinian owed him fifteen dollars. The informer thus bore the cost of his share of the narcotics plus the taxi and other expenses necessary to obtain the drug. After several such sales Kalchinian informed agents of the Bureau of Narcotics that he had another seller for them. On three occasions during November 1951, government agents observed petitioner give narcotics to Kalchinian in return for money supplied by the Government.

At the trial the factual issue was whether the informer had convinced an otherwise unwilling person to commit a criminal act or whether petitioner was already predisposed to commit the act and exhibited only the natural hesitancy of one acquainted with the narcotics trade. The issue of entrapment went to the jury, and a conviction resulted. Petitioner was sentenced to imprisonment for ten years.

In *Sorrells v. United States*, 287 U.S. 435 (1932), this Court firmly recognized the defense of entrapment in the federal courts. The intervening years have in no way detracted from the principles underlying that decision. The function of law enforcement is the prevention of crime and the apprehension of criminals. Manifestly, that function does not include the manufacturing of crime. Criminal activity is such that stealth and strategy are necessary weapons in the arsenal of the police officer. However, "a different question is presented when the criminal design originates with the officials of the Government, and they implant in the mind of an innocent person the disposition to commit the alleged offense and induce its commission in order that they may prosecute." Then stealth and strategy become as objectionable police methods as the coerced confession and the unlawful search. Congress could not have intended that its statutes were to be enforced by tempting innocent persons into violations.

However, the fact that government agents "merely afford opportunities or facilities for the commission of the offense does not" constitute entrapment. Entrapment occurs only when the criminal conduct was "the product of the *creative* activity" of law-enforcement officials. (Emphasis supplied.) To determine whether entrapment has been established, a line must be drawn between the trap for the unwary innocent and the trap for the unwary criminal. The principles by which the courts are to make this determination were outlined in *Sorrells*. On the one hand, at trial the accused may examine the conduct of the government agent; and on the other hand, the accused will be subjected to an "appropriate and searching inquiry into his own conduct and predisposition" as bearing on his claim of innocence.

We conclude from the evidence that entrapment was established as a matter of law. In so holding, we are not choosing between conflicting witnesses, nor judging credibility. Aside from recalling Kalchinian, who was the Government's witness, the defense called no witnesses. We reach our conclusion from the undisputed testimony of the prosecution's witnesses.

It is patently clear that petitioner was induced by Kalchinian. The informer himself testified that, believing petitioner to be undergoing a cure for narcotics addiction, he nonetheless sought to persuade petitioner to obtain for him a source of narcotics. In Kalchinian's own words we are told of the accidental, yet recurring, meetings, the ensuing conversations concerning mutual experiences in regard to narcotics addiction, and then of Kalchinian's resort to sympathy. One request was not enough, for Kalchinian tells us that additional ones were necessary to overcome, first, petitioner's refusal, then his evasiveness, and then his hesitancy in order to achieve capitulation. Kalchinian not only procured a source of narcotics but apparently also induced petitioner to return to the habit. Finally, assured of a catch, Kalchinian informed the authorities so that they could close the net. The Government cannot disown Kalchinian and insist it is not responsible for his actions. Although he was not being paid, Kalchinian was an active government informer who had but recently been the instigator of at least two other prosecutions. Undoubtedly the impetus for such achievements was the fact that in 1951 Kalchinian was himself under criminal charges for illegally selling narcotics and had not yet been sentenced.[3] It makes no difference that the sales for which petitioner was convicted occurred after a series of sales. They were not independent acts subsequent to the inducement but part of a course of conduct which was the product of the inducement. In his testimony the federal agent in charge of the case admitted that he never bothered to question Kalchinian about the way he had made contact with petitioner. The Government cannot make such use of an informer and then claim disassociation through ignorance.

The Government sought to overcome the defense of entrapment by claiming that petitioner evinced a ''ready complaisance'' to accede to Kalchinian's request. Aside from a record of past convictions, which we discuss in the following paragraph, the Government's case is unsupported. There is no evidence that petitioner himself was in the trade. When his apartment was searched after arrest, no narcotics were found. There is no significant evidence that petitioner even made a profit on any sale to Kalchinian. The Government's characterization of petitioner's hesitancy to Kalchinian's request as the natural wariness of the criminal cannot fill the evidentiary void.

The Government's additional evidence in the second trial to show that petitioner was ready and willing to sell narcotics should the opportunity present itself was petitioner's record of two past narcotics convictions. In 1942 petitioner was convicted of illegally selling narcotics; in 1946 he was convicted of illegally possessing them. However, a nine-year-old sales conviction and a five-year-old possession conviction are insufficient to prove petitioner had a readiness to sell narcotics at the time Kalchinian approached him, particularly when we must assume from the record he was trying to overcome the narcotics habit at the time.

The case at bar illustrates an evil which the defense of entrapment is designed to overcome. The government informer entices someone attempting to avoid narcotics not only into carrying out an illegal sale but also into returning to the habit of use. Selecting the proper time, the informer then tells the government agent. The set-up is accepted by the agent without even a question as to the manner in which

the informer encountered the seller. Thus the Government plays on the weaknesses of an innocent party and beguiles him into committing crimes which he otherwise would not have attempted. Law enforcement does not require methods such as this.

It has been suggested that in overturning this conviction we should reassess the doctrine of entrapment according to principles announced in the separate opinion of Mr. Justice Roberts in *Sorrells* 435, 453. To do so would be to decide the case on grounds rejected by the majority in *Sorrells* and, so far as the record shows, not raised here or below by the parties before us.

At least two important issues of law enforcement and trial procedure would have to be decided without the benefit of argument by the parties, one party being the Government. Mr. Justice Roberts asserted that although the defendant could claim that the Government had induced him to commit the crime, the Government could not reply by showing that the defendant's criminal conduct was due to his own readiness and not to the persuasion of government agents. The handicap thus placed on the prosecution is obvious. Furthermore, it was the position of Mr. Justice Roberts that the factual issue of entrapment—now limited to the question of what the government agents did—should be decided by the judge, not the jury. Not only was this rejected by the Court in *Sorrells,* but where the issue has been presented to them, the Courts of Appeals have since *Sorrells* unanimously concluded that unless it can be decided as a matter of law, the issue of whether a defendant has been entrapped is for the jury as part of its function of determining the guilt or innocence of the accused.

To dispose of this case on the ground suggested would entail both overruling a leading decision of this Court and brushing aside the possibility that we would be creating more problems than we would supposedly be solving.

The judgment of the Court of Appeals is reversed and the case is remanded to the District Court with instructions to dismiss the indictment.

MR. JUSTICE FRANKFURTER, whom MR. JUSTICE DOUGLAS, MR. JUSTICE HARLAN, and MR. JUSTICE BRENNAN join, concurring in the result.

Although agreeing with the Court that the undisputed facts show entrapment as a matter of law, I reach this result by a route different from the Court's.

It is surely sheer fiction to suggest that a conviction cannot be had when a defendant has been entrapped by government officers or informers because

---

[3] Kalchinian received a suspended sentence in 1952 after a statement by the United States Attorney to the Judge that he had been cooperative with the Government.

"Congress could not have intended that its statutes were to be enforced by tempting innocent persons into violations." In these cases raising claims of entrapment, the only legislative intention that can with any show of reason be extracted from the statute is the intention to make criminal precisely the conduct in which the defendant has engaged. That conduct includes all the elements necessary to constitute criminality. Without compulsion and "knowingly," where that is requisite, the defendant has violated the statutory command. If he is to be relieved from the usual punitive consequences, it is on no account because he is innocent of the offense described. In these circumstances, conduct is not less criminal because the result of temptation, whether the tempter is a private person or a government agent or informer.

The courts refuse to convict an entrapped defendant, not because his conduct falls outside the proscription of the statute, but because, even if his guilt be admitted, the methods employed on behalf of the Government to bring about conviction cannot be countenanced. As Mr. Justice Holmes said in *Olmstead v. United States*, 277 U.S. 438, 470 (dissenting), in another connection, "It is desirable that criminals should be detected, and to that end that all available evidence should be used. It also is desirable that the Government should not itself foster and pay for other crimes, when they are the means by which the evidence is to be obtained. . . . [F]or my part I think it a less evil that some criminals should escape than that the Government should play an ignoble part." Insofar as they are used as instrumentalities in the administration of criminal justice, the federal courts have an obligation to set their face against enforcement of the law by lawless means or means that violate rationally vindicated standards of justice, and to refuse to sustain such methods by effectuating them. They do this in the exercise of a recognized jurisdiction to formulate and apply "proper standards for the enforcement of the federal criminal law in the federal courts," *McNabb v. United States*, 318 U.S. 332, 341, an obligation that goes beyond the conviction of the particular defendant before the court. Public confidence in the fair and honorable administration of justice, upon which ultimately depends the rule of law, is the transcending value at stake.

The formulation of these standards does not in any way conflict with the statute the defendant has violated, or involve the initiation of a judicial policy disregarding or qualifying that framed by Congress. A false choice is put when it is said that either the defendant's conduct does not fall within the statute or he must be convicted. The statute is wholly directed to defining and prohibiting the substantive offense concerned and expresses no purpose, either permissive or prohibitory, regarding the police conduct that will be tolerated in the detection of crime. A statute prohibiting the sale of narcotics is as silent on the question of entrapment as it is on the admissibility of illegally obtained evidence. It is enacted, however, on the basis of certain presuppositions concerning the established legal order and the role of the courts within that system in formulating standards for the administration of criminal justice when Congress itself has not specifically legislated to that end. Specific statutes are to be fitted into an antecedent legal system.

It might be thought that it is largely an academic question whether the court's finding a bar to conviction derives from the statute or from a supervisory jurisdiction over the administration of criminal justice; under either theory substantially the same considerations will determine whether the defense of entrapment is sustained. But to look to a statute for guidance in the application of a policy not remotely within the contemplation of Congress at the time of its enactment is to distort analysis. It is to run the risk, furthermore, that the court will shirk the responsibility that is necessarily in its keeping, if Congress is truly silent, to accommodate the dangers of overzealous law enforcement and civilized methods adequate to counter the ingenuity of modern criminals. The reasons that actually underlie the defense of entrapment can too easily be lost sight of in the pursuit of a wholly fictitious congressional intent.

The crucial question, not easy of answer, to which the court must direct itself is whether the police conduct revealed in the particular case falls below standards, to which common feelings respond, for the proper use of governmental power. For answer it is wholly irrelevant to ask if the "intention" to commit the crime originated with the defendant or government officers, or if the criminal conduct was the product of "the creative activity" of law-enforcement officials. Yet in the present case the Court repeats and purports to apply these unrevealing tests. Of course in every case of this kind the intention that the particular crime be committed originates with the police, and without their inducement the crime would not have occurred. But it is perfectly clear from such decisions as the decoy letter cases in this Court, e.g., *Grimm v. United States*, 156 U.S. 604, where the police in effect simply furnished the opportunity for the commission of the crime, that this is not enough to enable the defendant to escape conviction.

The intention referred to, therefore, must be a general intention or predisposition to commit, whenever the opportunity should arise, crimes of the kind solicited, and in proof of such a predisposition evidence has often been admitted to show the defendant's reputation, criminal activities, and prior disposition. The danger of prejudice in such a situation, particularly if the issue of entrapment must be submitted to the jury and disposed of by a general verdict of guilty or innocent, is evident. The defendant must either forego the claim of entrapment or run the substantial risk that, in spite of instructions, the jury will allow a criminal record or bad reputation to weigh in its determination of guilt of the specific offense of which he stands charged. Furthermore, a test that looks to the character and predisposition of the defendant rather than the conduct of the police loses sight of the underlying reason for the defense of entrapment. No matter what the defendant's past record and present inclinations to criminality, or the depths to which he has sunk in the estimation of society, certain police conduct to ensnare him into further crime is not to be tolerated by an advanced society. And in the present case it is clear that the Court in fact reverses the conviction because of the conduct of the informer Kalchinian, and not because the Government has failed to draw a convincing picture of petitioner's past criminal conduct. Permissible police activity does not vary according to the particular defendant concerned; surely if two suspects have been solicited at the same time in the same manner, one should not go to jail simply because he has been convicted before and is said to have a criminal disposition. No more does it vary according to the suspicions, reasonable or unreasonable, of the police concerning the defendant's activities. Appeals to sympathy, friendship, the possibility of exorbitant gain, and so forth, can no more be tolerated when directed against a past offender than against an ordinary law-abiding citizen. A contrary view runs afoul of fundamental principles of equality under law, and would espouse the notion that when dealing with the criminal classes anything goes. The possibility that no matter what his past crimes and general disposition the defendant might not have committed the particular crime unless confronted with inordinate inducements, must not be ignored. Past crimes do not forever outlaw the criminal and open him to police practices, aimed at securing his repeated conviction, from which the ordinary citizen is protected. The whole ameliorative hopes of modern penology and prison administration strongly counsel against such a view.

This does not mean that the police may not act so as to detect those engaged in criminal conduct and ready and willing to commit further crimes should the occasion arise. Such indeed is their obligation. It does mean that in holding out inducements they should act in such a manner as is likely to induce to the commission of crime only these persons and not others who would normally avoid crime and through self-struggle resist ordinary temptations. This test shifts attention from the record and predisposition of the particular defendant to the conduct of the police and the likelihood, objectively considered, that it would entrap only those ready and willing to commit crime. It is as objective a test as the subject matter permits, and will give guidance in regulating police conduct that is lacking when the reasonableness of police suspicions must be judged or the criminal disposition of the defendant retrospectively appraised. It draws directly on the fundamental intuition that led in the first instance to the outlawing of ''entrapment'' as a prosecutorial instrument. The power of government is abused and directed to an end for which it was not constituted when employed to promote rather than detect crime and to bring about the downfall of those who, left to themselves, might well have obeyed the law. Human nature is weak enough and sufficiently beset by temptations without government adding to them and generating crime.

What police conduct is to be condemned, because likely to induce those not otherwise ready and willing to commit crime, must be picked out from case to case as new situations arise involving different crimes and new methods of detection. The *Sorrells* case involved persistent solicitation in the face of obvious reluctance, and appeals to sentiments aroused by reminiscences of experiences as companions in arms in the World War. Particularly reprehensible in the present case was the use of repeated requests to overcome petitioner's hesitancy, coupled with appeals to sympathy based on mutual experiences with narcotics addiction. Evidence of the setting in which the inducement took place is of course highly relevant in judging its likely effect, and the court should also consider the nature of the crime involved, its secrecy and difficulty of detection, and the manner in which the particular criminal business is usually carried on.

As Mr. Justice Roberts convincingly urged in the *Sorrells* case, such a judgment, aimed at blocking off areas of impermissible police conduct, is appropriate for the court and not the jury. ''The protection of its own functions and the preservation of the purity of its own temple belongs only to the court. It is the province of the court and of the court alone to protect itself and the government from such prostitution of the criminal law. The violation of the principles of justice by the entrapment of the unwary into crime should be dealt with by the court no matter by whom or at what stage of the proceedings the facts are brought to its attention." 287 U.S., at 457 (separate opinion). Equally important is the consideration that a jury verdict, although it may settle the issue of entrapment in the particular case, cannot give significant guidance for official conduct for the future. Only the court, through the gradual evolution of explicit standards in accumulated precedents, can do this with the degree of certainty that the wise administration of criminal justice demands.

## QUESTIONS AND NOTES

**1.** Do you think that the Supreme Court reversed Sherman's conviction because he was basically innocent or because it disapproved of the police practices in this case? Explain.

**2.** Do you think Sherman was less culpable than the average drug dealer? If so, should he have been released even if Kalchinian did not work for the government?

**3.** Do you disapprove of the police practices employed in *Sherman*? Why? Why not?

**4.** In an ideal system of jurisprudence, would the entrapment issue be resolved by a judge or a jury? Why?

**5.** In *Sherman*, the Court noted that the issue was not Sherman's predisposition when he made the *last* sale to Kalchinian, but his predisposition when he made the *first* sale? In *Jacobson*, the Court considered the extent to which the government could create a predisposition to criminality by non-criminal entreaties designed to play on the susceptibilities of the ultimate defendant.

### Jacobson v. United States
### 503 U.S. 540 (1993)

JUSTICE WHITE delivered the opinion of the Court.

On September 24, 1987, petitioner Keith Jacobson was indicted for violating a provision of the Child Protection Act of 1984, which criminalizes the knowing receipt through the mails of a "visual depiction [that] involves the use of a minor engaging in sexually explicit conduct. . . ." Petitioner defended on the ground that the Government entrapped him into committing the crime through a series of communications from undercover agents that spanned the 26 months preceding his arrest. Petitioner was found guilty after a jury trial. The Court of Appeals affirmed his conviction, holding that the Government had carried its burden of proving beyond reasonable doubt that petitioner was predisposed to break the law and hence was not entrapped. Because the Government overstepped the line between setting a trap for the "unwary innocent" and the "unwary criminal," *Sherman*, and as a matter of law failed to establish that petitioner was independently predisposed to commit the crime for which he was arrested, we reverse the Court of Appeals' judgment affirming his conviction.

I

In February 1984, petitioner, a 56-year-old veteran-turned-farmer who supported his elderly father in Nebraska, ordered two magazines and a brochure from a California adult bookstore. The magazines, entitled Bare Boys I and Bare Boys II, contained photographs of nude preteen and teenage boys. The contents of the magazines startled petitioner, who testified that he had expected to receive photographs of "young men 18 years or older." On cross-examination, he explained his response to the magazines:

"PROSECUTOR: You were shocked and surprised that there were pictures of very young boys without clothes on, is that correct?

"JACOBSON: Yes, I was.

"PROSECUTOR: Were you offended?

. . . . .

"JACOBSON: I was not offended because I thought these were a nudist type publication. Many of the pictures were out in a rural or outdoor setting. There was—I didn't draw any sexual connotation or connection with that."

The young men depicted in the magazines were not engaged in sexual activity, and petitioner's receipt of the magazines was legal under both federal and Nebraska law. Within three months, the law with respect to child pornography changed; Congress passed the Act illegalizing the receipt through the mails of sexually explicit depictions of children. In the very month that the new provision became law, postal inspectors found petitioner's name on the mailing list of the California bookstore that had mailed him Bare Boys I and II. There followed over the next 2½ years, repeated efforts by two Government agencies, through five fictitious organizations and a bogus pen pal, to explore petitioner's willingness to break the new law by ordering sexually explicit photographs of children through the mail.

The Government began its efforts in January 1985 when a postal inspector sent petitioner a letter supposedly from the American Hedonist Society, which in fact was a fictitious organization. The letter included a membership application and stated the Society's doctrine: that members had the right to read what we desire, the right to discuss similar interests with those who share our philosophy, and finally that we have the "right to seek pleasure without restrictions being placed on us by outdated puritan morality." Petitioner enrolled in the organization and returned a sexual attitude questionnaire that asked him to rank on a scale of one to four his enjoyment of various sexual materials, with one being "really enjoy," two being "enjoy," three being "somewhat enjoy," and four being "do not enjoy." Petitioner ranked the entry "pre-teen sex" as a two, but indicated that he was opposed to pedophilia.

For a time, the Government left petitioner alone. But then a new "prohibited mail specialist" in the Postal Service found petitioner's name in a file, and in May 1986, petitioner received a solicitation from a second fictitious consumer research company, "Midlands Data Research," seeking a response from those who "believe in the joys of sex and the complete awareness of those lusty and youthful lads and lasses of the neophite [sic] age." The letter never explained whether "neophite" referred to minors or young adults. Petitioner responded: "Please feel free to send me more information, I am interested in teenage sexuality. Please keep my name confidential."

Petitioner then heard from yet another Government creation, "Heartland Institute for a New Tomorrow" (HINT), which proclaimed that it was "an organization founded to protect and promote sexual freedom and freedom of choice. We believe that arbitrarily imposed legislative sanctions restricting your sexual freedom should be rescinded through the legislative process." The letter also enclosed a second survey. Petitioner indicated that his interest in "preteen sex-homosexual" material was above average, but not high. In response to another question, petitioner wrote: "Not only sexual expression but freedom of the press is under attack. We must be ever vigilant to counter attack right wing fundamentalists who are determined to curtail our freedoms."

"HINT" replied, portraying itself as a lobbying organization seeking to repeal "all statutes which regulate sexual activities, except those laws which deal with violent behavior, such as rape. HINT is also lobbying to eliminate any legal definition of the age of consent." These lobbying efforts were to be funded by sales from a catalog to be published in the future "offering the sale of various items which we believe you will find to be both interesting and stimulating." HINT also provided computer matching of group members with similar survey responses; and, although petitioner was supplied with a list of potential "pen pals," he did not initiate any correspondence.

Nevertheless, the Government's "prohibited mail specialist" began writing to petitioner, using the pseudonym "Carl Long." The letters employed a tactic known as "mirroring," which the inspector described as "reflecting whatever the interests are of the person we are writing to." Petitioner responded at first, indicating that his interest was primarily in "male-male items." Inspector "Long" wrote back:

> "My interests too are primarily male-male items. Are you satisfied with the type of VCR tapes available? Personally, I like the amateur stuff better if its [sic] well produced as it can get more kinky and also seems more real. I think the actors enjoy it more."

Petitioner responded:

> "As far as my likes are concerned, I like good looking young guys (in their late teens and early 20's) doing their thing together."

Petitioner's letters to "Long" made no reference to child pornography. After writing two letters, petitioner discontinued the correspondence.

By March 1987, 34 months had passed since the Government obtained petitioner's name from the mailing list of the California bookstore, and 26 months had passed since the Postal Service had commenced its mailings to petitioner. Although petitioner had responded to surveys and letters, the Government had no evidence that petitioner had ever intentionally possessed or been exposed to child pornography. The Postal Service had not checked petitioner's mail to determine whether he was receiving questionable mailings from persons – other than the Government – involved in the child pornography industry.

At this point, a second Government agency, the Customs Service, included petitioner in its own child pornography sting, "Operation Borderline," after receiving his name on lists submitted by the Postal Service. Using the name of a fictitious Canadian company called "Produit Outaouais," the Customs Service mailed petitioner a brochure advertising photographs of young boys engaging in sex. Petitioner placed an order that was never filled.

The Postal Service also continued its efforts in the *Jacobson* case, writing to petitioner as the "Far Eastern Trading Company Ltd." The letter began:

> "As many of you know, much hysterical nonsense has appeared in the American media concerning pornography and what must be done to stop it from coming across your borders. This brief letter does not allow us to give much comments; however, why is your government spending millions of dollars to exercise international censorship while tons of drugs, which makes yours the world's most crime ridden country are passed through easily."

The letter went on to say:

> "We have devised a method of getting these to you without prying eyes of U.S. Customs seizing your mail. . . . After consultations with American solicitors, we have been advised that once we have posted our material through your system, it cannot be opened for any inspection without authorization of a judge."

The letter invited petitioner to send for more information. It also asked petitioner to sign an affirmation that he was "not a law enforcement officer or agent of the U.S. Government acting in an undercover capacity for the purpose of entrapping Far Eastern Trading Company, its agents or customers." Petitioner responded. A catalogue was sent, and petitioner ordered Boys Who Love Boys, a pornographic magazine depicting young boys engaged in various sexual activities. Petitioner was arrested after a controlled delivery of a photocopy of the magazine.

When petitioner was asked at trial why he placed such an order, he explained that the Government had succeeded in piquing his curiosity:

> "Well, the statement was made of all the trouble and the hysteria over pornography and I wanted to see what the material was. It didn't describe the – I didn't know for sure what kind of sexual action they were referring to in the Canadian letter. . . ."

In petitioner's home, the Government found the Bare Boys magazines and materials that the Government had sent to him in the course of its protracted investigation, but no other materials that would indicate that petitioner collected or was actively interested in child pornography.

The trial court instructed the jury on the petitioner's entrapment defense,[1] petitioner was convicted.

II

There can be no dispute about the evils of child pornography or the difficulties that laws and law enforcement have encountered in eliminating it. Likewise, there can be no dispute that the Government may use undercover agents to enforce the law. "It is well settled that the fact that officers or employees of the Government merely afford opportunities or facilities for the commission of the offense does not defeat the prosecution. Artifice and stratagem may be employed to catch those engaged in criminal enterprises."

In their zeal to enforce the law, however, Government agents may not originate a criminal design,

---

[1] The jury was instructed:

"As mentioned, one of the issues in this case is whether the defendant was entrapped. If the defendant was entrapped he must be found not guilty. The government has the burden of proving beyond a reasonable doubt that the defendant was not entrapped.

"If the defendant before contact with law-enforcement officers or their agents did not have any intent or disposition to commit the crime charged and was induced or persuaded by law-enforcement officers or their agents to commit that crime, then he was entrapped. On the other hand, if the defendant before contact with law-enforcement officers or their agents did have an intent or disposition to commit the crime charged, then he was not entrapped even though law-enforcement officers or their agents provided a favorable opportunity to commit the crime or made committing the crime easier or even participated in acts essential to the crime."

implant in an innocent person's mind the disposition to commit a criminal act, and then induce commission of the crime so that the Government may prosecute. *Sherman*. Where the Government has induced an individual to break the law and the defense of entrapment is at issue, as it was in this case, the prosecution must prove beyond reasonable doubt that the defendant was disposed to commit the criminal act prior to first being approached by Government agents.[2]

Thus, an agent deployed to stop the traffic in

---

[2] Inducement is not at issue in this case. The Government does not dispute that it induced petitioner to commit the crime. The sole issue is whether the Government carried its burden of proving that petitioner was predisposed to violate the law before the Government intervened. The dissent is mistaken in claiming that this is an innovation in entrapment law and in suggesting that the Government's conduct prior to the moment of solicitation is irrelevant. The Court rejected these arguments five decades ago in *Sorrells*, when the Court wrote that the Government may not punish an individual "for an alleged offense which is the product of the creative activity of its own officials" and that in such a case the Government "is in no position to object to evidence of the activities of its representatives in relation to the accused. . . ." Indeed, the proposition that the accused must be predisposed prior to contact with law enforcement officers is so firmly established that the Government conceded the point at oral argument, submitting that the evidence it developed during the course of its investigation was probative because it indicated petitioner's state of mind prior to the commencement of the Government's investigation.

This long-established standard in no way encroaches upon Government investigatory activities. Indeed, the Government's internal guidelines for undercover operations provide that an inducement to commit a crime should not be offered unless:

"(a) there is a reasonable indication, based on information developed through informants or other means, that the subject is engaging, has engaged, or is likely to engage in illegal activity of a similar type; or (b) the opportunity for illegal activity has been structured so that there is reason for believing that persons drawn to the opportunity, or brought to it, are predisposed to engage in the contemplated illegal activity." Attorney General's Guidelines on FBI Undercover Operations (Dec. 31, 1980)

illegal drugs may offer the opportunity to buy or sell drugs, and, if the offer is accepted, make an arrest on the spot or later. In such a typical case, or in a more elaborate "sting" operation involving government-sponsored fencing where the defendant is simply provided with the opportunity to commit a crime, the entrapment defense is of little use because the ready commission of the criminal act amply demonstrates the defendant's predisposition. Had the agents in this case simply offered petitioner the opportunity to order child pornography through the mails, and petitioner—who must be presumed to know the law—had promptly availed himself of this criminal opportunity, it is unlikely that his entrapment defense would have warranted a jury instruction.

But that is not what happened here. By the time petitioner finally placed his order, he had already been the target of 26 months of repeated mailings and communications from Government agents and fictitious organizations. Therefore, although he had become predisposed to break the law by May 1987, it is our view that the Government did not prove that this predisposition was independent and not the product of the attention that the Government had directed at petitioner since January 1985. *Sorrells, Sherman*.

The prosecution's evidence of predisposition falls into two categories: evidence developed prior to the Postal Service's mail campaign, and that developed during the course of the investigation. The sole piece of preinvestigation evidence is petitioner's 1984 order and receipt of the Bare Boys magazines. But this is scant if any proof of petitioner's predisposition to commit an illegal act, the criminal character of which a defendant is presumed to know. It may indicate a predisposition to view sexually-oriented photographs that are responsive to his sexual tastes; but evidence that merely indicates a generic inclination to act within a broad range, not all of which is criminal, is of little probative value in establishing predisposition.

Furthermore, petitioner was acting within the law at the time he received these magazines. Receipt through the mails of sexually explicit depictions of children for noncommercial use did not become illegal under federal law until May 1984, and Nebraska had no law that forbade petitioner's possession of such material until 1988. Evidence of predisposition to do what once was lawful is not, by itself, sufficient to show predisposition to do what is now illegal, for there is a common understanding that most people obey the law even when they disapprove of it. This obedience may reflect a generalized respect for legality or the fear of prosecution, but for whatever reason, the law's prohibitions are matters of consequence. Hence, the fact that petitioner legally ordered and received the Bare Boys magazines does little to further the Government's burden of proving that petitioner was predisposed to commit a criminal act. This is particularly true given petitioner's unchallenged testimony was that he did not know until they arrived that the magazines would depict minors.

The prosecution's evidence gathered during the investigation also fails to carry the Government's burden. Petitioner's responses to the many communications prior to the ultimate criminal act were at most indicative of certain personal inclinations, including a predisposition to view photographs of pre-teen sex and a willingness to promote a given agenda by supporting lobbying organizations. Even so, petitioner's responses hardly support an inference that he would commit the crime of receiving child pornography through the mails.[3] Furthermore, a person's inclinations and "fantasies . . . are his own and beyond the reach of government . . ."

On the other hand, the strong arguable inference is that, by waving the banner of individual rights and disparaging the legitimacy and constitutionality of efforts to restrict the availability of sexually explicit materials, the Government not only excited petitioner's interest in sexually explicit materials banned by law but also exerted substantial pressure on petitioner to obtain and read such material as part of a fight against censorship and the infringement of individual rights. For instance, HINT described itself as "an organization founded to protect and promote sexual freedom and freedom of choice" and stated that "the most appropriate means to accomplish [its] objectives is to promote honest dialogue among concerned individuals and to continue its lobbying efforts with State Legislators." These lobbying efforts were to be financed through catalogue sales. Mailings from the equally fictitious American Hedonist Society, and the correspondence from the non-existent Carl Long, endorsed these themes.

Similarly, the two solicitations in the spring of

---

[3] We do not hold, as the dissent suggests, that the Government was required to prove that petitioner knowingly violated the law. We simply conclude that proof that petitioner engaged in legal conduct and possessed certain generalized personal inclinations is not sufficient evidence to prove beyond a reasonable doubt that he would have been predisposed to commit the crime charged independent of the Government's coaxing.

1987 raised the spectre of censorship while suggesting that petitioner ought to be allowed to do what he had been solicited to do. The mailing from the Customs Service referred to "the worldwide ban and intense enforcement on this type of material," observed that "what was legal and commonplace is now an underground and secretive service," and emphasized that "this environment forces us to take extreme measures" to insure delivery. The Postal Service solicitation described the concern about child pornography as "hysterical nonsense," decried "international censorship," and assured petitioner, based on consultation with "American solicitors" that an order that had been posted could not be opened for inspection without authorization of a judge. It further asked petitioner to affirm that he was not a government agent attempting to entrap the mail order company or its customers. In these particulars, both government solicitations suggested that receiving this material was something that petitioner ought to be allowed to do.

Petitioner's ready response to these solicitations cannot be enough to establish beyond reasonable doubt that he was predisposed, prior to the Government acts intended to create predisposition, to commit the crime of receiving child pornography through the mails. The evidence that petitioner was ready and willing to commit the offense came only after the Government had devoted 2 1/2 years to convincing him that he had or should have the right to engage in the very behavior proscribed by law. Rational jurors could not say beyond a reasonable doubt that petitioner possessed the requisite predisposition prior to the Government's investigation and that it existed independent of the Government's many and varied approaches to petitioner. As was explained in *Sherman*, where entrapment was found as a matter of law, "the Government [may not] play on the weaknesses of an innocent party and beguile him into committing crimes which he otherwise would not have attempted."

Law enforcement officials go too far when they "implant in the mind of an innocent person the disposition to commit the alleged offense and induce its commission in order that they may prosecute." Like the *Sorrells* court, we are "unable to conclude that it was the intention of the Congress in enacting this statute that its processes of detection and enforcement should be abused by the instigation by government officials of an act on the part of persons otherwise innocent in order to lure them to its commission and to punish them." When the Government's quest for convictions leads to the apprehension of an otherwise law-abiding citizen who, if left to his own devices, likely would have never run afoul of the law, the courts should intervene.

Because we conclude that this is such a case and that the prosecution failed, as a matter of law, to adduce evidence to support the jury verdict that petitioner was predisposed, independent of the Government's acts and beyond a reasonable doubt, to violate the law by receiving child pornography through the mails, we reverse the Court of Appeals' judgment affirming the conviction of Keith Jacobson.

DISSENT: JUSTICE O'CONNOR, with whom THE CHIEF JUSTICE and JUSTICE KENNEDY join, and with whom JUSTICE SCALIA joins except as to Part II, dissenting.

Keith Jacobson was offered only two opportunities to buy child pornography through the mail. Both times, he ordered. Both times, he asked for opportunities to buy more. He needed no Government agent to coax, threaten, or persuade him; no one played on his sympathies, friendship, or suggested that his committing the crime would further a greater good. In fact, no Government agent even contacted him face-to-face. The Government contends that from the enthusiasm with which Mr. Jacobson responded to the chance to commit a crime, a reasonable jury could permissibly infer beyond a reasonable doubt that he was predisposed to commit the crime. I agree.

The first time the Government sent Mr. Jacobson a catalog of illegal materials, he ordered a set of photographs advertised as picturing "young boys in sex action fun." He enclosed the following note with his order: "I received your brochure and decided to place an order. If I like your product, I will order more later." For reasons undisclosed in the record, Mr. Jacobson's order was never delivered.

The second time the Government sent a catalog of illegal materials, Mr. Jacobson ordered a magazine called "Boys Who Love Boys," described as: "11 year old and 14 year old boys get it on in every way possible. Oral, anal sex and heavy masturbation. If you love boys, you will be delighted with this." Along with his order, Mr. Jacobson sent the following note: "Will order other items later. I want to be discreet in order to protect you and me."

Government agents admittedly did not offer Mr. Jacobson the chance to buy child pornography right away. Instead, they first sent questionnaires in order to make sure that he was generally interested in the subject matter. Indeed, a "cold call" in such a business would not only risk rebuff and suspicion, but might also shock and offend the uninitiated, or expose minors to suggestive materials. Mr. Jacobson's responses to the questionnaires gave the investigators reason to think he would be interested in photographs depicting preteen sex.

The Court, however, concludes that a reasonable jury could not have found Mr. Jacobson to be predisposed beyond a reasonable doubt on the basis of his responses to the Government's catalogs, even though it admits that, by that time, he was predisposed to commit the crime. The Government, the Court holds, failed to provide evidence that Mr. Jacobson's obvious predisposition at the time of the crime "was independent and not the product of the attention that the Government had directed at petitioner." In so holding, I believe the Court fails to acknowledge the reasonableness of the jury's inference from the evidence, redefines "predisposition," and introduces a new requirement that Government sting operations have a reasonable suspicion of illegal activity before contacting a suspect.

I

This Court has held previously that a defendant's predisposition is to be assessed as of the time the Government agent first suggested the crime, not when the Government agent first became involved. *Sherman.* Until the Government actually makes a suggestion of criminal conduct, it could not be said to have "implanted in the mind of an innocent person the disposition to commit the alleged offense and induce its commission. . . ." *Sorrells.* Even in *Sherman,* in which the Court held that the defendant had been entrapped as a matter of law, the Government agent had repeatedly and unsuccessfully coaxed the defendant to buy drugs, ultimately succeeding only by playing on the defendant's sympathy. The Court found lack of predisposition based on the Government's numerous unsuccessful attempts to induce the crime, not on the basis of preliminary contacts with the defendant.

Today, the Court holds that Government conduct may be considered to create a predisposition to commit a crime, even before any Government action to induce the commission of the crime. In my view, this holding changes entrapment doctrine. Generally, the inquiry is whether a suspect is predisposed before the Government induces the commission of the crime, not before the Government makes initial contact with him. There is no dispute here that the Government's questionnaires and letters were not sufficient to establish inducement; they did not even suggest that Mr. Jacobson should engage in any illegal activity. If all the Government had done was to send these materials, Mr. Jacobson's entrapment defense would fail. Yet the Court holds that the Government must prove not only that a suspect was predisposed to commit the crime before the opportunity to commit it arose, but also before the Government came on the scene.

The rule that preliminary Government contact can create a predisposition has the potential to be misread by lower courts as well as criminal investigators as requiring that the Government must have sufficient evidence of a defendant's predisposition before it ever seeks to contact him. Surely the Court cannot intend to impose such a requirement, for it would mean that the Government must have a reasonable suspicion of criminal activity before it begins an investigation, a condition that we have never before imposed. The Court denies that its new rule will affect run-of-the-mill sting operations, and one hopes that it means what it says. Nonetheless, after this case, every defendant will claim that something the Government agent did before soliciting the crime "created" a predisposition that was not there before. For example, a bribe taker will claim that the description of the amount of money available was so enticing that it implanted a disposition to accept the bribe later offered. A drug buyer will claim that the description of the drug's purity and effects was so tempting that it created the urge to try it for the first time. In short, the Court's opinion could be read to prohibit the Government from advertising the seductions of criminal activity as part of its sting operation, for fear of creating a predisposition in its suspects. That limitation would be especially likely to hamper sting operations such as this one, which mimic the advertising done by genuine purveyors of pornography. No doubt the Court would protest that its opinion does not stand for so broad a proposition, but the apparent lack of a principled basis for distinguishing these scenarios exposes a flaw in the more limited rule the Court today adopts.

The Court's rule is all the more troubling because it does not distinguish between Government conduct that merely highlights the temptation of the crime itself, and Government conduct that threatens, coerces, or leads a suspect to commit a crime in order to fulfill some other obligation. For example, in *Sorrells*, the Government agent repeatedly asked for illegal liquor, coaxing the defendant to accede on the ground that "one former war buddy would get liquor for another." In *Sherman*, the Government agent played on the defendant's sympathies, pretending to be going through drug withdrawal and begging the defendant to relieve his distress by helping him buy drugs.

The Government conduct in this case is not comparable. While the Court states that the Government "exerted substantial pressure on petitioner to obtain and read such material as part of a fight against censorship and the infringement of individual rights," one looks at the record in vain for evidence of such "substantial pressure." The most one finds is letters advocating legislative action to liberalize obscenity laws, letters which could easily be ignored or thrown away. Much later, the Government sent separate mailings of catalogs of illegal materials. Nowhere did the Government suggest that the proceeds of the sale of the illegal materials would be used to support legislative reforms. While one of the HINT letters suggested that lobbying efforts would be funded by sales from a catalog, the catalogs actually sent, nearly a year later, were from different fictitious entities (Produit Outaouais and Far Eastern Trading Company), and gave no suggestion that money would be used for any political purposes. Nor did the Government claim to be organizing a civil disobedience movement, which would protest the pornography laws by breaking them. Contrary to the gloss given the evidence by the Court, the Government's suggestions of illegality may also have made buyers beware, and increased the mystique of the materials offered: "[f]or those of you who have enjoyed youthful material . . . we have devised a method of getting these to you without prying eyes of U.S. Customs seizing your mail." Mr. Jacobson's curiosity to see what "all the trouble and the hysteria" was about, is certainly susceptible of more than one interpretation. And it is the jury that is charged with the obligation of interpreting it. In sum, the Court fails to construe the evidence in the light most favorable to the Government, and fails to draw all reasonable inferences in the Government's favor. It was surely reasonable for the jury to infer that Mr. Jacobson was predisposed beyond a reasonable doubt, even if other inferences from the evidence were also possible.

## II

The second puzzling thing about the Court's opinion is its redefinition of predisposition. The Court acknowledges that "petitioner's responses to the many communications prior to the ultimate criminal act were . . . indicative of certain personal inclinations, including a predisposition to view photographs of preteen sex. . . ." If true, this should have settled the matter; Mr. Jacobson was predisposed to engage in the illegal conduct. Yet, the Court concludes, "petitioner's responses hardly support an inference that he would commit the crime of receiving child pornography through the mails."

The Court seems to add something new to the burden of proving predisposition. Not only must the Government show that a defendant was predisposed to engage in the illegal conduct, here, receiving photographs of minors engaged in sex, but also that the defendant was predisposed to break the law knowingly in order to do so. The statute violated here, however, does not require proof of specific intent to break the law; it requires only knowing receipt of visual depictions produced by using minors engaged in sexually explicit conduct. Under the Court's analysis, however, the Government must prove more to show predisposition than it need prove in order to convict.

The Court ignores the judgment of Congress that specific intent is not an element of the crime of receiving sexually explicit photographs of minors. The elements of predisposition should track the elements of the crime. The predisposition requirement is meant to eliminate the entrapment defense for those defendants who would have committed the crime anyway, even absent Government inducement. Because a defendant might very well be convicted of the crime here absent Government inducement even though he did not know his conduct was illegal, a specific intent requirement does little to distinguish between those who would commit the crime without the inducement and those who would not. In sum, although the fact that Mr. Jacobson's purchases of Bare Boys I and Bare Boys II were legal at the time may have some relevance to the question of predisposition, it is not, as the Court suggests, dispositive.

The crux of the Court's concern in this case is that the Government went too far and "abused" the "processes of detection and enforcement" by luring an innocent person to violate the law. Consequently, the Court holds that the Government failed to prove beyond a reasonable doubt that Mr. Jacobson was predisposed to commit the crime. It was, however, the jury's task, as the conscience of the community, to decide whether or not Mr. Jacobson was a willing participant in the criminal activity here or an innocent dupe. The jury is the traditional "defense against arbitrary law enforcement." *Duncan v. Louisiana*, 391 U.S. 145 (1968). Indeed, in *Sorrells*, in which the Court was also concerned about overzealous law enforcement, the Court did not decide itself that the Government conduct constituted entrapment, but left the issue to the jury. There is no dispute that the jury in this case was fully and accurately instructed on the law of entrapment, and nonetheless found Mr. Jacobson guilty. Because I believe there was sufficient evidence to uphold the jury's verdict, I respectfully dissent.

## QUESTIONS AND NOTES

**1.** Unlike in *Sherman*, both the majority and the dissent in *Jacobson* appear content with the "predisposition" prerequisite required by the majority in *Sherman* and *Sorrells*. On what point do the majority and dissent differ? Who, in your judgment, got it right?

**2.** Does the majority require some form of reasonable suspicion prior to targeting a potential criminal (such as a purchaser of child pornography)? Should reasonable suspicion be required? Why? Why not?

**3.** If reasonable suspicion were required, would (should) predisposition be irreleveant?

**4.** Did the government do anything in *Jacobson* to render it likely that a nonpredisposed person would commit the crime?

**5.** Was the essential wrong in *Jacobson* the inefficient use of government resources? Should that be the concern of the entrapment defense? *See* Posner, *An Economic Theory of The Criminal Law* 85 Colum. L. Rev. 1193, 1220 (1985).

## B. The Due Process Defense

### United States v. Gamble
### 737 F.2d 853 (10th. Cir. 1984)

LOGAN, Circuit Judge

Defendant, John Gamble, a physician practicing in Kansas City, Kansas, was convicted on four counts of mail fraud. The charges against defendant resulted from an elaborate undercover investigation by United States postal inspectors.

United States postal inspectors concocted two schemes that ultimately involved defendant. In each scheme United States postal inspectors used fictitious names to obtain Missouri driver's licenses. The inspectors then registered automobiles they did not own and obtained insurance for the automobiles under those names. In cooperation with the Kansas City, Missouri, Police Department, the postal inspectors obtained accident reports for collisions that never occurred. The police officer who filled out the fictitious accident reports testified at trial that normally he would face severe sanctions for filling out false reports.

In each of the schemes the police issued a ticket to one of the inspectors and described the accidents in such a way that the inspector cited would be liable for any damages. After receiving the citations, the inspectors appeared in Municipal Court in Kansas City, Missouri, and pleaded guilty before prosecutors and judges who were unaware that the tickets were shams.

The first fictitious accident report, which was filed on May 6, 1980, described a one-car accident in which the driver of the vehicle, in an attempt to miss a stopped vehicle, swerved and struck a post. Postal Inspectors Armstrong and Gillis posed as passengers in the vehicle. Following this fictitious accident the inspectors visited defendant's office, asking him to help them perpetrate a fraud on the insurance company.

Posing as husband and wife, Armstrong and Gillis visited defendant's office seven times. On their first visit the inspectors' temperatures, weights, and blood pressures were checked. They filled out medical information forms, writing "traffic accident" in the blank for type of injury. When Inspector Armstrong met defendant, he told defendant that he had broken his glasses but had suffered no injuries and that he wanted to obtain some funds from the insurance company. Defendant described the procedure for filing claims with the insurance company and then conducted a routine physical examination of each inspector. On each subsequent visit the inspectors' weights, blood pressures, and temperatures apparently were checked. During the second visit defendant asked if he needed to do anything. Inspector Armstrong said no and stated that he had not yet contacted the insurance company. Subsequently, Inspector Armstrong told Jim Amen, an adjuster for State Farm Insurance Company, about injuries in his back and neck.

On the fourth visit the inspectors informed defendant that they had contacted State Farm Insurance Company. Later, Inspector Armstrong spoke with defendant's assistant, who prepared an insurance form and asked several questions. Armstrong told the assistant to write down that he had been unable to work for almost two months. When Inspectors Armstrong and Gillis visited defendant for the last time, they brought a draft from State Farm Insurance Company for $180, the total medical expense reported to the insurer. Defendant calculated that since they had already paid him $104, they owed him $66. (Correctly subtracted the figure was $76. Defendant had previously made the inspectors pay $10 or $12 apiece at each office visit when they saw defendant.) The inspectors gave defendant a $66 money order and kept the draft.

The second undercover operation began with a false accident report filed on July 9, 1980, which described a rear-end collision. Postal Inspectors Robert Bush and Donjette Gilmore posed as husband and wife and claimed to have been in the car that was hit. They visited defendant's office five times. Apparently at each visit the inspectors were given routine tests. When the inspectors first saw defendant, he asked what was wrong. Bush indicated that nothing was wrong but that the person who was responsible was insured and that there was a chance to make some money. Bush affirmed the doctor's stated assumption that they wanted to take advantage of the situation. Defendant then said, "You'll just have to play it up. You can't go out there tell that man ah, I wasn't hurt." Defendant also said, "You gotta have a back injury and you gotta have a neck injury or something. . . . We have to write it up to that effect and you'll make some money out of the deal." Defendant suggested neck and back injuries would be best because they are hard to prove and told them to come back in a few weeks to fill out the insurance papers.

Several weeks later the inspectors informed defendant that they had contacted the insurance company, and they discussed with defendant the insurer's method of handling claims. At a later visit defendant filled out a handwritten bill and put it in an envelope provided by the inspectors that was addressed to Farmers Insurance Group. Defendant handed the envelope back to Inspector Bush and asked him to take care of it. On December 11, 1980, the inspectors brought a draft for $160 from Farmers Insurance Group to defendant's office. A secretary reimbursed them for the $50 they had paid during previous office visits, and the inspectors signed the draft over to defendant.

## II

Defendant contends that the government's conduct in formulating, carrying out, and enmeshing defendant in the mail fraud scheme was so outrageous that defendant's conviction should be overturned as a violation of due process of law. The Supreme Court recognized this defense in *United States v. Russell*, 411 U.S. 423 (1973), when it stated, "[W]e may some day be presented with a situation in which the conduct of law enforcement agents is so outrageous that due process principles would absolutely bar the government from invoking judicial processes to obtain a conviction, cf. *Rochin*."

When the Supreme Court considered the due process defense three years later in *Hampton v. United States*, 425 U.S. 484 (1976), the eight Justices who participated divided into three groups. The plurality opinion, written by Justice Rehnquist, stated that absent a violation of some protected right of the defendant, the Due Process Clause cannot be invoked to overturn a conviction because of governmental misconduct. Justice Rehnquist wrote, "The remedy of the criminal defendant with respect to the acts of Government agents . . . lies solely in the defense of entrapment." The due process defense survives, however, because a majority of the Justices, two who concurred in the result of the case and three who dissented, rejected the position "that the concept of fundamental fairness inherent in the guarantee of due process would never prevent the conviction of a predisposed defendant, regardless of the outrageousness of police behavior in light of the surrounding circumstances." (Powell, J., concurring). (Brennan, J., dissenting). Justice Powell added, "I emphasize that the cases, if any, in which proof of predisposition is not dispositive will be rare. Police overinvolvement in crime would have to reach a demonstrable level of outrageousness before it could bar conviction."

The defense that the government's conduct was so outrageous as to require reversal on due process grounds is often raised but is almost never successful. No Supreme Court case and only two circuit court opinions have set aside convictions on that basis. In *United States v. Twigg*, 588 F.2d 373 (3d Cir. 1978), a Drug Enforcement Agency (DEA) informant, as part of a plea bargain, involved defendant Neville in establishing a laboratory for the production of a controlled substance, methamphetamine hydrochloride (speed). The government gratuitously supplied about twenty percent of the glassware and an indispensable ingredient, phenyl-2-propanone. The DEA made arrangements with chemical supply houses to facilitate the purchase of the rest of the materials, and the DEA informant, operating under a business name supplied by the DEA, purchased all of the equipment and chemicals with the exception of a separatory funnel. When the participants encountered problems in locating an adequate production site, the government solved the problem by providing an isolated farmhouse. The DEA informant provided the expertise to run the laboratory. Neither Twigg nor Neville knew how to manufacture speed, and each provided only minimal assistance at the specific direction of the informant. The Third Circuit stated, "[W]e are not only concerned with the supply by government agents of necessary ingredients for manufacture, but we also have before us a crime . . . conceived and contrived by government agents." It reversed both convictions. In discussing the government's conduct the court noted in regard to Neville,

> "They [the government] set him up, encouraged him, provided the essential supplies and technical expertise, and when he and Kubica encountered difficulties in consummating the crime, they assisted in finding solutions. This egregious conduct on the part of government agents generated new crimes by the defendant merely for the sake of pressing criminal charges against him when, as far as the record reveals, he was lawfully and peacefully minding his own affairs. Fundamental fairness does not permit us to countenance such actions by law enforcement officials and prosecution for a crime so fomented by them will be barred."

It is important to note that the entrapment defense, which requires an absence of predisposition to commit the crime, is not involved in the instant case. Nevertheless, in a sense, entrapment and the due process defense are on a continuum, because both are based on the principle "that courts must be closed to the trial of a crime instigated by the government's own agents. No other issue, no comparison of equities as between the guilty official and the guilty defendant, has any place in the enforcement of this overruling principle of public policy." In stating that until the government provided the means to manufacture speed the *Twigg* defendant Neville was "minding his own affairs," the court notes precisely the point on the entrapment-due process continuum that the two concepts begin to merge. Although the due process defense purportedly ignores the defendant's predisposition to commit the crime charged, the defense nevertheless is concerned with the extent of government involvement in crime and the type of opportunity to become involved with crime that this conduct provides to the unwitting defendant. "[W]hen the government permits itself to become enmeshed in criminal activity, from beginning to end . . . the same underlying objections which render entrapment repugnant to American criminal justice are operative."

In the case at bar the government conceived and directed a crime in which defendant participated. The government used fictitious names to obtain driver's licenses, obtained insurance under those names for automobiles they did not own, orchestrated the production of false accident reports, appeared in court and pleaded guilty to traffic violations, and solicited defendant's aid in making false claims against insurance companies. Of the government agencies involved only the Kansas City, Missouri, Police Department knew of the operation. Involved without their knowledge were judges, prosecutors, state licensing authorities, and insurance companies. The government agents submitted the false claims to the insurance companies and lied to the companies about their injuries.

The government agents in the case before us displayed shocking disregard for the legal system. But these actions did not directly induce defendant to participate in the fraudulent scheme. Perhaps the false statements to state agents and the courts helped the inspectors obtain the medical forms defendant filled out and ultimately secure the settlement check. But defendant did not rely on any display of fictitious credentials or falsified documents; apparently he relied entirely upon what his "patients" told him. Therefore, we must ignore these acts of the government agents in evaluating defendant's due process claim.

Some of the artifices that the government inspectors used in the scheme, however, did directly contribute to defendant's decision to participate. The postal inspectors, with their elaborate machinations, sowed the seeds of criminality and brought defendant into their scheme. This brings the case closer to government manufacture of crime than the sting, Abscam, and other operations in which undercover agents set themselves up as amenable to lawbreaking schemes brought to them by others. But did the action of the government agents cross the due process line? We recognize that "because the difficulties in detecting covert crime often warrant secretive investigations, involvement of Government agents must be of the tenor to shock the conscience before a violation of the due process clause will be found." In common with other courts we have struggled to draw the line that defines and identifies what is governmental involvement so outrageous as to warrant finding a due process violation.

The government here enmeshed in criminal schemes fabricated entirely by government agents a black doctor who had no criminal record and with respect to whom the agents had no apparent hint of a predisposition to criminal activity. The government sent agents apparently posing as poor people to a doctor serving a ghetto community to seek to have the doctor help them out financially in appealing circumstances, circumstances in which the doctor might appear callous if he did not cooperate. The record implies that the inspectors pretended to be economically disadvantaged people typical of defendant's patient population. Sympathy based upon economic disadvantage or race may have been played upon as a factor in inducing defendant to join what he informed the inspectors was "the white boys' game." Defendant sought very little profit from his participation, apparently charging only normal office rates for the time he spent with the inspectors.

We must conclude, however, that the government's conduct was insufficient to violate defendant's right to due process. Insurance fraud on a small scale no doubt is very widespread in this country. Many professional or business people may not regard it a serious infraction of society's rules to assist customers or patients in the small scale cheating of insurance companies. Yet, like the Second Circuit in *Myers*, which said it could not accept an "inducement" argument that a proferred bribe was so large a congressman could not be expected to resist, we cannot accept the notion that insurance cheating is so commonplace that it is improper for the government to try to catch and convict citizens who engage in it. We have held that the government need not have a reasonable suspicion of wrongdoing in order to conduct an undercover investigation of a particular person. No issue of impermissible selective prosecution was raised in the instant case. See

*Yick Wo v. Hopkins*, 118 U.S. 356 (1886).

### III

We have also considered defendant's conviction and the government agents' conduct in light of our supervisory power over the administration of criminal justice. But the breadth of the Supreme Court's language in *United States v. Payner*, requires us to conclude, despite the differences between *Payner* and the case at bar, that we may not fashion a "subconstitutional" rule to permit dismissal of this case because of the government agents' conduct. In *Payner* government agents sought to examine materials in a third party's briefcase that they thought might incriminate defendant. To gain access to the briefcase a government agent introduced the owner of the briefcase, Michael Wolstencroft, to Sybol Kennedy, a female private investigator who worked for the agent. Wolstencroft and Kennedy spent time together in Kennedy's apartment, where Wolstencroft left his locked briefcase while the two went out to eat at a restaurant. While one government agent acted as a "lookout" at the restaurant, other agents entered the apartment with a key furnished by Kennedy, took the briefcase to a locksmith who made a key for it, opened the briefcase and photographed documents in it that led to evidence used to convict Payner. Payner, of course, did not have standing to object to the search. The district court found that the United States "knowingly and willfully participated" in the illegal search. Nonetheless, the Supreme Court refused to affirm the use of the courts' supervisory power to suppress the evidence. It agreed with a government argument that even though the evidence was tainted with gross illegalities, "such an extension of the supervisory power would enable federal courts to exercise a standardless discretion."

AFFIRMED.

## QUESTIONS AND NOTES

**1.** Do you think that the government did anything wrong in *Gamble*? If so what was it? If not, why not?

**2.** Do you think that the government did anything wrong in *Twigg*? If so what? If not, why not?

**3.** Should the government be required to have reasonable suspicion (or probable cause) (or a warrant) before it engages in practices such as those described in *Gamble* or *Twigg*?

**4.** When the government is excessively involved, predisposition is irrelevant. Does this comport with your notion of sound jurisprudence? Explain.

**5.** Arguably, it is not even necessary that the inducement be of the type likely to tempt a hypothetically nonpredisposed person (for example, in *Twigg*, it is doubtful that a totally nonpredisposed person would go into the drug business simply because it was there). Is there a good reason for not even requiring at least that much?

# LAW REVIEW BIBLIOGRAPHY

**Chapter 1    The Protections of and Rationale for The Fourth Amendment**

**Chapter 2    Probable Cause**

LaFave, Wayne. *Probable Cause From Informants: The Effects of Murphy's Law on Fourth Amendment Adjudication.* 1977 U. ILL. L. F. 1.

LaFave, Wayne. *The Fourth Amendment Today: A Bicentennial Appraisal.* 32 VILL. L. REV. 1061 (1987).

Loewy, Arnold. *Protecting Citizens From Cops and Crooks: An Assessment of the Supreme Court's Interpretation of the Fourth Amendment During the 1982 Term.* 62 N.C. L. REV. 329 (1984).

Slobogin, Christopher. *The World Without a Fourth Amendment.* 39 UCLA L. REV. 1 (1991).

**Chapter 3    The Need for a Warrant**

Amar, Akhil Reed. *Fourth Amendment First Principles.* 107 HARV. L. REV. 757 (1994).

LaFave, Wayne. *"Seizures" Typology: Classifying Detentions of the Person to Resolve Warrant, Grounds, and Search Issues.* 17 U. MICH. J.L. REF. 417 (1984).

Maclin, Tracey. *When The Cure For The Fourth Amendment Is Worse Than The Disease.* 68 S. CAL. L. REV. 1 (1994).

Stuntz, William. *Warrants and Fourth Amendment Remedies.* 77 VA. L. REV. 881 (1991).

Sundby, Scott E. *"Everyman"'s Fourth Amendment: Privacy Or Mutual Trust Between Government And Citizen?* 94 COLUM. L. REV. 1751 (1994).

**Chapter 4    Arrests**

Groot, Roger D. *Arrests in Private Dwellings.* 67 VA. L. REV. 275 (1981).

Karsch, Mitchell. *Excessive Force and the Fourth Amendment: When Does Seizure End?* 58 FORDHAM L. REVIEW 823 (1990).

Schroeder, William. *Factoring the Seriousness of the Offense into Fourth Amendment Equations – Warrantless Entries into Premises: The Legacy of* Welsh v. Wisconsin. 38 U. KAN. L. REV. 439 (1990).

### Chapter 5     Plain View

Butterfoss, Edwin. *Solving the Pretext Puzzle: The Importance of Ulterior Motives and Fabrications in the Supreme Court's Fourth Amendment Pretext Doctrine.* 79 KY. L. J. 1 (1991).

Haddad, James B. *Pretextual Fourth Amendment Activity: Another Viewpoint.* 18 U. MICH. J. L. REF. 639 (1985).

Wallin, Howard. *The Uncertain Scope of the Plain View Doctrine.* 16 U. BALT. L. REV. 266 (1987).

### Chapter 6     Automobiles

Gardner, Martin R. *Searches and Seizures of Automobiles and Their Contents: Fourth Amendment Considerations in a Post-*Ross World. 62 NEB. L. REV. 1 (1983).

Grano, Joseph. *Rethinking the Fourth Amendment Warrant Requirement.* 19 AM. CRIM. L. REV. 603 (1982).

Rudstein, David S. *The Search of an Automobile Incident to an Arrest: An Analysis of* New York v. Belton. 67 MARQ. L. REV. 205 (1984).

Wilson, Vivian D. *The Warrantless Automobile Search: Exception Without Justification.* 32 HASTINGS L.J. 127 (1980).

### Chapter 7     Limited Searches on Less Than Probable Cause

Amar, Akhil Reed. *Fourth Amendment First Principles.* 107 HARV. L. REV. 757 (1994).

Dix, George. *Non-Arrest Investigatory Detentions in Search and Seizure Law.* 1985 DUKE L.J. 849 (1985).

LaFave, Wayne. *"Street Encounters" and the Constitution: Terry, Sibron, Peters, and Beyond.* 67 MICH. L. REV. 39 (1968).

LaFave, Wayne. *Controlling Discretion by Administrative Regulations: The Use, Misuse, and Nonuse of Police Rules and Policies in Fourth Amendment Adjudication.* 89 MICH. L. REV. 442 (1990).

Maclin, Tracey. *The Decline of the Right of Locomotion: The Fourth Amendment on the Streets.* 75 CORNELL L. REV. 1258 (1990).

Sundby, Scott E. *A Return to Fourth Amendment Basics: Undoing the Mischief of Camara and Terry.* 72 MINN. L. REV. 383 (1988).

Williamson, Richard. *The Dimensions of Seizure: The Concepts of "Stop" and "Arrest."* 43 OHIO ST. L. J. 771 (1982).

### Chapter 8     Unusual Situations

Green, Bruce A. *"Power, Not Reason": Justice Marshall's Valedictory and the Fourth Amendment in the Supreme Court's 1990 Term.* 70 N.C. L. REV. 373 (1992).

Greenberg, Peter S. *The Balance of Interests Theory and the Fourth Amendment: A Selective Analysis of Supreme Court Action Since Camara and See.* 61 CAL. L. REV. 1011 (1973).

McManis, Charles R. and Barbara M. McManis. *Structuring Administrative Inspections: Is There Any Warrant for a Search Warrant?* 26 AM. U. L. REV. 942 (1977).

Stuntz, William. *Warrants and Fourth Amendment Remedies.* 77 VA. L. REV. 881 (1991).

**Chapter 9     Seizures**

Butterfoss, Edwin. *Bright Line Seizures: The Need for Clarity in Determining When Fourth Amendment Activity Begins.* 79 J. CRIM. L. & C. 437 (1988).

LaFave, Wayne. *Pinguitudinous Police, Pachydermatous Prey: Whence Fourth Amendment "Seizures"?* 1991 U. ILL. L. REV. 729 (1991).

Misner, Robert L. *The New Attempt Law: Unsuspected Threat to the Fourth Amendment.* 33 STAN. L. REV. 201 (1981).

Williamson, Richard. *The Dimensions of Seizure: The Concepts of "Stop" and "Arrest."* 43 OHIO ST. L. J. (1982).

**Chapter 10     Searches**

Amar, Akhil Reed. *Fourth Amendment First Principles.* 107 HARV. L. REV. 757 (1994).

Burkoff, John M. *When Is a Search Not a "Search"?: Fourth Amendment Doublethink.* 15 U. TOL. L. REV. 515 (1984).

Gutterman, Melvin. *A Formulation of the Value and Means Models of the Fourth Amendment in the Age of Technologically Enhanced Surveillance.* 39 SYRACUSE L. REV. 647 (1988).

Junker, John. *The Structure of the Fourth Amendment: The Scope of the Protection.* 79 J. CRIM. L. & CRIMINOLOGY 1105 (1989).

Katz, Lewis. *In Search of a Fourth Amendment for the Twenty-First Century.* 65 IND. L. REV. 549 (1990).

Loewy, Arnold H. *A Modest Proposal for Fighting Organized Crime: Stop Taking the Fourth Amendment So Seriously.* 16 RUTGERS L.J. 831 (1985).

Loewy, Arnold H. *The Fourth Amendment as a Device for Protecting the Innocent.* 81 MICH. L. REV. 1229 (1983).

Maclin, Tracey. *When the Cure for the Fourth Amendment Is Worse Than the Disease.* 68 S. CAL. L. REV. 1 (1994).

Power, Robert. *Technology and the Fourth Amendment:  A Proposed Formulation for Visual Searches.* 80 J. CRIM. L. & CRIMINOLOGY 1 (1989).

Serr, Brian J. *Great Expectations of Privacy: A New Model for Fourth Amendment Protection.* 73 MINN. L. REV. 583 (1989).

Seidman, Louis Michael. *The Problems with Privacy's Problem.* 93 MICH. L. REV. 1079 (1995).

Slobogin, Christopher and Joseph E. Schumacher. *Reasonable Expectations of Privacy and Autonomy in Fourth Amendment Cases: An Empirical Look at Understandings Recognized and Permitted by Society.* 42 DUKE L.J. 727 (1993).

Stuntz, William J. *Privacy's Problem and the Law of Criminal Procedure.* 93 MICH. L. REV. 1016 (1995).

Sundby, Scott E. *"Everyman"'s Fourth Amendment: Privacy or Mutual Trust Between Government and Citizen?* 94 COLUM. L. REV. 1751 (1994).

### Chapter 11    What Items May Be Seized?

Amar, Akhil Reed. *Fourth Amendment First Principles.* 107 HARV. L. REV. 757 (1994).

Loewy, Arnold H. *The Fourth Amendment as a Device for Protecting the Innocent.* 87 MICH. L. REV. 1229 (1983).

White, James B. *Forgotten Points in the "Exclusionary Rule" Debate.* 81 MICH. L. REV. (1983).

### Chapter 12    Consent

Coombs, Mary. *Shared Privacy and the Fourth Amendment, or the Rights of Relationships.* 75 CAL. L. REV. 1593 (1987).

Deschene, Robert. *The Problem of Third-Party Consent in Fourth Amendment Searches: Toward a "Conservative" Reading of the* Matlock *Decision.* 42 ME. L. REV. 159 (1990).

Gardner, Martin. *Consent as a Bar to Fourth Amendment Scope: A Critique of a Common Theory.* 71 J. CRIM. L. & CRIMINOLOGY 443 (1980).

Goldberger, Peter. *Consent, Expectations of Privacy, and the Meaning of "Search" in the Fourth Amendment.* 75 J. CRIM. L. & CRIMINOLOGY 319 (1984).

Loewy, Arnold H. *The Fourth Amendment as a Device for Protecting the Innocent.* 81 MICH. L. REV. 1229 (1983).

### Chapter 13    The Exclusionary Rule

Amar, Akhil Reed. *Fourth Amendment First Principles.* 107 HARV. L. REV. 757 (1994).

Dripps, Donald. *Living with Leon.* 95 YALE L.J. 906 (1986).

Forbes, Jessica. *The Inevitable Discovery Doctrine, Primary Evidence, and the Emasculation of the Fourth Amendment.* 55 FORDHAM L. REVIEW 1221 (1987).

Heffernan, William C. and Richard W. Lovely. *Evaluating the Fourth Amendment Exclusionary Rule: The Problem of Police Compliance with the Law.* 24 U. MICH. J.L. REF. 311 (1991).

LaFave, Wayne. *Controlling Discretion by Administrative Regulations: The Use, Misuse, and Nonuse of Police Rules and Policies in Fourth Amendment Adjudication.* 89 MICH. L. REV. 442 (1990).

Loewy, Arnold H. *Police-Obtained Evidence and the Constitution: Distinguishing Unconstitutionally Obtained Evidence From Unconstitutionally Used Evidence.* 87 MICH. L. REV. 907 (1989).

Loewy, Arnold H. *A Modest Proposal for Fighting Organized Crime: Stop Taking the Fourth Amendment So Seriously.* 16 RUTGERS L.J. 831 (1985).

Loewy, Arnold H. *The Fourth Amendment as a Device for Protecting the Innocent.* 81 MICH. L. REV. 1229 (1983).

Maclin, Tracey. *When the Cure for the Fourth Amendment Is Worse Than the Disease.* 68 S. CAL. L. REV. 1 (1994).

Seidman, Louis Michael. *The Problems with Privacy's Problem.* 93 MICH. L. REV. 1079 (1995).

Stewart, Potter. *The Road to* Mapp v. Ohio *and Beyond: The Origins, Development and Future of the Exclusionary Rule in Search-and-Seizure Cases.* 83 COLUM. L. REV. 1365 (1983).

Stuntz, William J. *Privacy's Problem and the Law of Criminal Procedure.* 93 MICH. L. REV. 1016 (1995).

**Chapter 14    Confessions, Voluntariness**

Grano, Joseph. *Selling the Idea to Tell the Truth: The Professional Interrogator and Modern Confessions Law.* 84 MICH. L. REV. 662 (1986).

Loewy, Arnold H. *Police-Obtained Evidence and the Constitution: Distinguishing Unconstitutionally Obtained Evidence From Unconstitutionally Used Evidence.* 87 MICH. L. REV. 907 (1989).

Rosenberg, Irene and Yale Rosenberg. *A Modest Proposal for the Abolition of Custodial Interrogation.* 68 N.C. L. REV. 69 (1989).

Stuntz, William. *Waiving Rights in Criminal Procedure.* 75 VA. L. REV. 761 (1989).

**Chapter 15    Right To Counsel**

Berger, Vivian O. *The Supreme Court and Defense Counsel: Old Roads, New Paths — A Dead End?* 86 COLUM. L. REV. 9 (1986).

Tomkovicz, James. *An Adversary System Defense of the Right to Counsel Against Informants: Truth, Fair Play, and the Massiah Doctrine.* 22 U.C. DAVIS L. REV. 1 (1988).

Tomkovicz, James. *The Truth About Massiah.* 23 U. MICH. J.L. REF. 641 (1990).

**Chapter 16    Miranda**

Ainsworth, Janet E. *In a Different Registrar: The Pragmatics of Powerlessness in Police Interrogation.* 103 YALE 259 (1993).

Amar, Akhil Reed and Renee B. Lettow. *Fifth Amendment First Principles: The Self-Incrimination Clause.* 93 MICH. L. REV. 857 (1995).

Berger, Mark. *Compromise and Continuity: Miranda Waivers, Confession Admissibility, and the Retention of Interrogation Protections.* 49 U. PITT. L. REV. 1007 (1988).

Caplan, Gerald. *Questioning Miranda.* 38 VAND. L. REV. 1417 (1985)

Gardner, Martin R. *The Emerging Good Faith Exception to the Miranda Rule — A Critique.* 35 HASTINGS L.J. 429 (1984).

Grano, Joseph. *Miranda's Constitutional Difficulties: A Reply to Professor Schulhofer.* 55 U. CHI. L. REV. 174 (1988).

Kamisar, Yale. *On The "Fruits" Of Miranda Violations, Coerced Confessions, and Compelled Testimony.* 93 MICH. L. REV. 929 (1995).

Loewy, Arnold H. *Police-Obtained Evidence and the Constitution: Distinguishing Unconstitutionally Obtained Evidence From Unconstitutionally Used Evidence.* 87 MICH. L. REV. 907 (1989).

Ogletree, Charles J. *Are Confessions Really Good for the Soul?: A Proposal to Mirandize Miranda.* 100 HARV. L. REV. 1826 (1987).

Schulhofer, Stephen. *Reconsidering Miranda.* 54 U. CHI. L. REV. 435 (1987).

White, Welsh. *Defending Miranda: A Reply to Professor Caplan.* 39 VAND. L. REV. 581 (1986).

White, Welsh. *Police Trickery in Inducing Confessions.* 127 U. PA. L. REV. 581 (1979).

Yeager, Daniel. *Rethinking Custodial Interrogation.* 28 AM. CRIM. L. REV. 1 (1990).

## Chapter 17    The Right To Counsel and Confessions

Kamisar, Yale. *Brewer v. Williams, Massiah and Miranda: What Is "Interrogation"? When Does It Matter?* 67 GEO. L.J. 1 (1978).

Loewy, Arnold H. *Police-Obtained Evidence and the Constitution: Distinguishing Unconstitutionally Obtained Evidence from Unconstitutionally Used Evidence.* 87 MICH. L. REV. 907 (1989).

Tomkovicz, James. *The Truth About Massiah.* 23 U. MICH. J.L. REF. 641 (1990).

Uviller, H. Richard. *Evidence from the Mind of the Criminal Suspect.* 87 COLUM. L. REV. 1137 (1987).

## Chapter 18    Voluntariness Revisited

Grano, Joseph. *Voluntariness, Free Will and the Law of Confessions.* 65 VA. L. REV. 1 (1979).

Ogletree, Charles J. Arizona v. Fulminante: *The Harm of Applying Harmless Error to Coerced Confessions.* 105 HARV. L. REV. 152 (1991).

## Chapter 19    Due Process Outside Of The Confession Context

Grano, Joseph. Kirby, Biggers, and Ash: *Do Any Constitutional Safeguards Remain Against the Danger of Convicting the Innocent?* 72 MICH. L. REV. 717 (1974).

Levine, Felice J. and June L. Tapp. *The Psychology of Criminal Identification: The Gap from Wade to Kirby.* 121 U. PA. L. REV. 1079 (1973).

Loewy, Arnold H. *Police-Obtained Evidence and the Constitution: Distinguishing Unconstitutionally Obtained Evidence From Unconstitutionally Used Evidence.* 87 MICH. L. REV. 907 (1989).

Pulaski, Charles A. Neil v. Biggers: The Supreme Court Dismantles the Wade Trilogy's Due Process Protection. 26 STAN. L. REV. 1097 (1974).

Rosenberg, Benjamin. *Rethinking the Right to Due Process in Connection With Pretrial Identification Procedures: An Analysis and a Proposal.* 79 KY. L.J. 259 (1991).

## Chapter 20    Identification Procedures

## Chapter 21    Attenuation

Comment. *Fruit of the Poisonous Tree—A Plea for Relevant Criteria.* 115 U. PA. L. REV. 1136 (1967).

Note. *The Attenuation Exception to the Exclusionary Rule: A Study in Attenuated Principle and Dissipated Logic.* 75 J. CRIM. L. & CRIMINOLOGY 139 (1984).

**Chapter 22      Inevitable Discovery**

Forbes, Jessica. *The Inevitable Discovery Doctrine, Primary Evidence, and the Emasculation of the Fourth Amendment.* 55 FORDHAM L. REVIEW 1221 (1987).

Johnson, Phillip E. *The Return of the Christian Burial Speech.* 32 EMORY L.J. 349 (1983).

**Chapter 23      Entrapment**

Carlson, Jonathan. *The Act Requirement and the Foundations of the Entrapment Defense.* 73 VA. L. REV. 1011 (1987).

Gershman, Bennett L. *Abscam, the Judiciary, and the Ethics of Entrapment.* 91 YALE L.J. 1565 (1982).

Webster, Laura Gardner. *Building a Better Mousetrap: Reconstructing Federal Entrapment Theory from* Sorrells *to* Mathews. 32 ARIZ. L. REV. 605 (1990).

Whelan, Maura F.J. *Lead Us Not Into (Unwarranted) Temptation: A Proposal to Replace the Entrapment Defense with a Reasonable Suspicion Requirement.* 133 U. PA. L. REV. 1193 (1985).